D1105744

Praise for the Reformation Commentary on Scripture

"Protestant reformers were fundamentally exegetes as much as theologians, yet (except for figures like Luther and Calvin) their commentaries and sermons have been neglected because these writings are not available in modern editions or languages. That makes this new series of Reformation Commentary on Scripture most welcome as a way to provide access to some of the wealth of biblical exposition of the sixteenth and seventeenth centuries. The editor's introduction explains the nature of the sources and the selection process; the intended audience of modern pastors and students of the Bible has led to a focus on theological and practical comments. Although it will be of use to students of the Reformation, this series is far from being an esoteric study of largely forgotten voices; this collection of reforming comments, comprehending every verse and provided with topical headings, will serve contemporary pastors and preachers very well."

Elsie Anne McKee, *Archibald Alexander Professor of Reformation Studies and the History of Worship, Princeton Theological Seminary*

"This series provides an excellent introduction to the history of biblical exegesis in the Reformation period. The introductions are accurate, clear and informative, and the passages intelligently chosen to give the reader a good idea of methods deployed and issues at stake. It puts precritical exegesis in its context and so presents it in its correct light. Highly recommended as reference book, course book and general reading for students and all interested lay and clerical readers."

Irena Backus, *Professeure Ordinaire, Institut d'histoire de la Réformation, Université de Genève*

"The Reformation Commentary on Scripture is a major publishing event—for those with historical interest in the founding convictions of Protestantism, but even more for those who care about understanding the Bible. As with IVP Academic's earlier Ancient Christian Commentary on Scripture, this effort brings flesh and blood to 'the communion of saints' by letting believers of our day look over the shoulders of giants from the past. By connecting the past with the present, and by doing so with the Bible at the center, the editors of this series perform a great service for the church. The series deserves the widest possible support."

Mark A. Noll, *Francis A. McAnaney Professor of History, University of Notre Dame*

"For those who preach and teach Scripture in the church, the Reformation Commentary on Scripture is a significant publishing event. Pastors and other church leaders will find delightful surprises, challenging enigmas and edifying insights in this series, as many Reformational voices are newly translated into English. The lively conversation in these pages can ignite today's pastoral imagination for fresh and faithful expositions of Scripture."

J. Todd Billings, *Gordon H. Girod Research Professor of Reformed Theology, Western Theological Seminary*

"The reformers discerned rightly what the church desperately needed in the sixteenth century—the bold proclamation of the Word based on careful study of the sacred Scriptures. We need not only to hear that same call again for our own day but also to learn from the Reformation how to do it. This commentary series is a godsend!"

Richard J. Mouw, *President Emeritus, Fuller Theological Seminary*

"Like the Ancient Christian Commentary on Scripture, the Reformation Commentary on Scripture does a masterful job of offering excellent selections from well-known and not-so-well-known exegetes. The editor's introductory survey is, by itself, worth the price of the book. It is easy to forget that there were more hands, hearts and minds involved in the Reformation than Luther and Calvin. Furthermore, encounters even with these figures are often limited to familiar quotes on familiar topics. However, the Reformation Commentary helps us to recognize the breadth and depth of exegetical interests and skill that fueled and continue to fuel faithful meditation on God's Word. I heartily recommend this series as a tremendous resource not only for ministry but for personal edification."

Michael S. Horton, *J. G. Machen Professor of Systematic Theology and Apologetics,*
Westminster Seminary, California

"The Reformation was ignited by a fresh reading of Scripture. In this series of commentaries, we contemporary interpreters are allowed to feel some of the excitement, surprise and wonder of our spiritual forebears. Luther, Calvin and their fellow revolutionaries were masterful interpreters of the Word. Now, in this remarkable series, some of our very best Reformation scholars open up the riches of the Reformation's reading of the Scripture."

William H. Willimon, *Professor of the Practice of Christian Ministry, Duke Divinity School*

"The Reformation Scripture principle set the entirety of Christian life and thought under the governance of the divine Word, and pressed the church to renew its exegetical labors. This series promises to place before the contemporary church the fruit of those labors, and so to exemplify life under the Word."

John Webster, *Professor of Divinity, University of St. Andrews*[†]

"Since Gerhard Ebeling's pioneering work on Luther's exegesis seventy years ago, the history of biblical interpretation has occupied many Reformation scholars and become a vital part of study of the period. The Reformation Commentary on Scripture provides fresh materials for students of Reformation-era biblical interpretation and for twenty-first-century preachers to mine the rich stores of insights from leading reformers of the sixteenth century into both the text of Scripture itself and its application in sixteenth-century contexts. This series will strengthen our understanding of the period of the Reformation and enable us to apply its insights to our own days and its challenges to the church."

Robert Kolb, *Professor Emeritus, Concordia Theological Seminary*

"The multivolume Ancient Christian Commentary on Scripture is a valuable resource for those who wish to know how the Fathers interpreted a passage of Scripture but who lack the time or the opportunity to search through the many individual works. This new Reformation Commentary on Scripture will do the same for the reformers and is to be warmly welcomed. It will provide much easier access to the exegetical treasures of the Reformation and will hopefully encourage readers to go back to some of the original works themselves."

Anthony N. S. Lane, *Professor of Historical Theology and Director of Research, London School of Theology*

"This volume of the RCS project is an invaluable source for pastors and the historically/biblically interested that provides unparalleled access not only to commentaries of the leading Protestant reformers but also to a host of nowadays unknown commentaters on Galatians and Ephesians. The RCS is sure to enhance and enliven contemporary exegesis. With its wide scope, the collection will enrich our understanding of the variety of Reformation thought and biblical exegesis."

Sigrun Haude, *Associate Professor of Reformation and Early Modern European History,*
University of Cincinnati

"This grand project sets before scholars, pastors, teachers, students and growing Christians an experience that can only be likened to stumbling into a group Bible study only to discover that your fellow participants include some of the most significant Christians of the Reformation and post-Reformation (for that matter, of any) era. Here the Word of God is explained in a variety of accents: German, Swiss, French, Dutch, English, Scottish and more. Each one vibrates with a thrilling sense of the living nature of God's Word and its power to transform individuals, churches and even whole communities. Here is a series to anticipate, enjoy and treasure."

Sinclair Ferguson, *Senior Minister, First Presbyterian Church, Columbia, South Carolina*

"I strongly endorse the Reformation Commentary on Scripture. Introducing how the Bible was interpreted during the age of the Reformation, these volumes will not only renew contemporary preaching, but they will also help us understand more fully how reading and meditating on Scripture can, in fact, change our lives!"

Lois Malcolm, *Associate Professor of Systematic Theology, Luther Seminary*

"Discerning the true significance of movements in theology requires acquaintance with their biblical exegesis. This is supremely so with the Reformation, which was essentially a biblical revival. The Reformation Commentary on Scripture will fill a yawning gap, just as the Ancient Christian Commentary did before it, and the first volume gets the series off to a fine start, whetting the appetite for more. Most heartily do I welcome and commend this long overdue project."

J. I. Packer, *Retired Board of Governors Professor of Theology, Regent College*

"There is no telling the benefits to emerge from the publication of this magnificent Reformation Commentary on Scripture series! Now exegetical and theological treasures from Reformation era commentators will be at our fingertips, providing new insights from old sources to give light for the present and future. This series is a gift to scholars and to the church; a wonderful resource to enhance our study of the written Word of God for generations to come!"

Donald K. McKim, *Executive Editor of Theology and Reference, Westminster John Knox Press*

"Why was this not done before? The publication of the Reformation Commentary on Scripture should be greeted with enthusiasm by every believing Christian—but especially by those who will preach and teach the Word of God. This commentary series brings the very best of the Reformation heritage to the task of exegesis and exposition, and each volume in this series represents a veritable feast that takes us back to the sixteenth century to enrich the preaching and teaching of God's Word in our own time."

R. Albert Mohler Jr., *President, The Southern Baptist Theological Seminary*

"Today more than ever, the Christian past is the church's future. InterVarsity Press has already brought the voice of the ancients to our ears. Now, in the Reformation Commentary on Scripture, we hear a timely word from the first Protestants as well."

Bryan Litfin, *Professor of Theology, Moody Bible Institute*

"I am delighted to see the Reformation Commentary on Scripture. The editors of this series have done us all a service by gleaning from these rich fields of biblical reflection. May God use this new life for these old words to give him glory and to build his church."

Mark Dever, *Senior Pastor, Capitol Hill Baptist Church, and President of 9Marks.org Ministries*

"Monumental and magisterial, the Reformation Commentary on Scripture, edited by Timothy George, is a remarkably bold and visionary undertaking. Bringing together a wealth of resources, these volumes will provide historians, theologians, biblical scholars, pastors and students with a fresh look at the exegetical insights of those who shaped and influenced the sixteenth-century Reformation. With this marvelous publication, InterVarsity Press has reached yet another plateau of excellence. We pray that this superb series will be used of God to strengthen both church and academy."

David S. Dockery, *President, Trinity International University*

"Detached from her roots, the church cannot reach the world as God intends. While every generation must steward the scriptural insights God grants it, only arrogance or ignorance causes leaders to ignore the contributions of those faithful leaders before us. The Reformation Commentary on Scripture roots our thought in great insights of faithful leaders of the Reformation to further biblical preaching and teaching in this generation."

Bryan Chapell, *Chancellor and Professor of Practical Theology, Covenant Theological Seminary*

"After reading several volumes of the Reformation Commentary on Scripture, I exclaimed, 'Hey, this is just what the doctor ordered—I mean Doctor Martinus Lutherus!' The church of today bearing his name needs a strong dose of the medicine this doctor prescribed for the ailing church of the sixteenth century. The reforming fire of Christ-centered preaching that Luther ignited is the only hope to reclaim the impact of the gospel to keep the Reformation going, not for its own sake but to further the renewal of the worldwide church of Christ today. This series of commentaries will equip preachers to step into their pulpits with confidence in the same living Word that inspired the witness of Luther and Calvin and many other lesser-known Reformers."

Carl E. Braaten, *Cofounder of the Center for Catholic and Evangelical Theology*

"As a pastor, how does one cultivate a knowledge of the history of interpretation? That's where IVP's Reformation Commentary on Scripture and its forerunner, the Ancient Christian Commentary on Scripture, come in. They do an excellent job in helping pastors become more aware of the history of exegesis for the benefit of their congregations. Every pastor should have access to a set of each."

Carl R. Trueman, *Paul Woolley Chair of Church History, Westminster Theological Seminary*

REFORMATION COMMENTARY ON SCRIPTURE

OLD TESTAMENT
XI

JEREMIAH, LAMENTATIONS

EDITED BY
J. JEFFERY TYLER

GENERAL EDITOR
TIMOTHY GEORGE

ASSOCIATE GENERAL EDITOR
SCOTT M. MANETSCH

An imprint of InterVarsity Press
Downers Grove, Illinois

To my parents and grandparents,
and to their devotion to the Bible
and the God who speaks within

Marcia and John Tyler†
Rev. Lawrence and Marjory Doorn
Irene† and Pearl Tyler†

InterVarsity Press
P.O. Box 1400, Downers Grove, IL 60515-1426
www.ivpress.com
email@ivpress.com

InterVarsity Press® is the book-publishing division of InterVarsity Christian Fellowship/USA®, a movement of students and faculty active on campus at hundreds of universities, colleges and schools of nursing in the United States of America, and a member movement of the International Fellowship of Evangelical Students. For information about local and regional activities, visit intervarsity.org.

This publication contains The Holy Bible, English Standard Version®, copyright © 2001 by Crossway, a publishing ministry of Good News Publishers. The ESV® text appearing in this publication is reproduced and published by cooperation between Good News Publishers and InterVarsity Press and by permission of Good News Publishers. Unauthorized reproduction of this publication is prohibited.

The Holy Bible, English Standard Version (ESV) is adapted from the Revised Standard Version of the Bible, copyright Division of Christian Education of the National Council of the Churches of Christ in the U.S.A. All rights reserved.

English Standard Version®, ESV® and ESV® logo are trademarks of Good News Publishers located in Wheaton, Illinois. Used by permission.

Excerpts from The Complete Writings of Menno Simons, c. 1496-1561 are copyright © 1956, 1984 by Herald Press, Scottdale, PA 15683. Used by permission.

Excerpts from The Essential Carlstadt: Fifteen Tracts are copyright © 1995 by Herald Press, Waterloo, Ontario. Used by permission.

Excerpts from Luther's Works vols. 2, 9, 16, 17, 18, 19, 20, 27, 75, and 76, are copyright © 1960, 1968, 1968, 1973, 1973, 1974, 1973, 1964, 2013, 2013 by Concordia Publishing House, cph.org. Used by permission. All rights reserved.

Excerpts from Luther's Works vols. 31, 35, 36, 39, 41, 45, 46, 47, and 52 are copyright ©1957, 1960, 1959, 1970, 1966, 1962, 1967, 1971, 1974 by Fortress Press. Used by permission.

Excerpts from The Collected Works of Thomas Müntzer are copyright © 1988 by T&T Clark, an imprint of Bloomsbury Publishing Plc. Used by permission.

Excerpts from Commentary on the Lamentations of the Prophet Jeremiah by Peter Martyr Vermigli are copyright ©2002 Truman State University Press. Used by permission.

Design: Cindy Kiple
Images: Wooden cross: iStockphoto
　　The Protestant Church in Lyon: The Protestant Church in Lyon, called "The Paradise" at Bibliotheque Publique et Universitaire, Geneva, Switzerland. Erich Lessing/Art Resource, NY.

ISBN 978-0-8308-2961-3 (print)
ISBN 978-0-8308-8730-9 (digital)

Printed in the United States of America ♾

InterVarsity Press is committed to ecological stewardship and to the conservation of natural resources in all our operations. This book was printed using sustainably sourced paper.

Library of Congress Cataloging-in-Publication Data

A catalog record for this book is available from the Library of Congress.

| P | 26 | 25 | 24 | 23 | 22 | 21 | 20 | 19 | 18 | 17 | 16 | 15 | 14 | 13 | 12 | 11 | 10 | 9 | 8 | 7 | 6 | 5 | 4 | 3 | 2 | 1 |
| Y | 41 | 40 | 39 | 38 | 37 | 36 | 35 | 34 | 33 | 32 | 31 | 30 | 29 | 28 | 27 | 26 | 25 | 24 | 23 | 22 | 21 | 20 | 19 | 18 |

Reformation Commentary on Scripture
Project Staff

Project Editor
David W. McNutt

---

*Senior Production Manager
and Managing Editor*
Benjamin M. McCoy

Associate Managing Editor
Elissa Schauer

Copyeditor
Jeffrey A. Reimer

Assistant Project Editors
Andre A. Gazal
Todd R. Hains

Editorial and Research Assistants
David J. Hooper
Ashley Davila

Assistants to the General Editors
Le-Ann Little
Jason Odom

Design
Cindy Kiple

Design Assistant
Beth McGill

Content Production
Richard M. Chung
Maureen G. Tobey
Daniel van Loon
Jeanna L. Wiggins

Proofreader
Travis Ables

Print Coordinator
Jim Erhart

InterVarsity Press

Publisher
Jeff Crosby

Associate Publisher, Director of Editorial
Cindy Bunch

Editorial Director, IVP Academic
Jon Boyd

CONTENTS

ACKNOWLEDGMENTS

Jeremiah had his Baruch, so I am grateful to those who have spurred, guided, and assisted me in bringing this commentary to life. Initial inklings I owe to Michael Omartian's *White Horse* album and especially to Abraham Heschel's two-volume work that sparked my curiosity about Jeremiah.[1] First and foremost I want to thank Scott Manetsch, who cajoled me with the idea of this volume some years ago and has given me invaluable advice and encouragement along the way. I am grateful to the many InterVarsity Press editors and staff who make this kind of book come to be, including Brannon Ellis and Todd Hains, who assisted in the early stages. Particular and hearty thanks go to David McNutt for his exceptional direction and guidance in the final years of editing this volume.

Several Hope College colleagues have been especially helpful. Early on research librarian and art historian Jessica Hronchek put me in touch with key resources. Brad Richmond, professor of music, suggested sixteenth-century music on Lamentations, especially Thomas Tallis. Dean of the Chapel Trygve Johnson has listened to my musings on Jeremiah and put up with the provocative quotations I have shared with him from Reformation preachers. In my own department, Jared Ortiz, professor of Catholic theology and history, shared his expertise on patristic sources, and Barry Bandstra, professor of Old Testament, helped me sort through issues and verses and was an invaluable resource for this foray into his neck of the woods.

Taking a step beyond Hope College, I am deeply grateful to another member of the extraordinary Bandstra family: Daniel Bandstra crosschecked, corrected, and vastly improved my Latin translations and helped me sort out some puzzling passages linguistically and historically. Random conversations can make all the difference in a project. My thanks to John Frymire, who met with me in Fort Worth, Texas, and pointed me to Johannnes Wild. Dean Wenthe, editor of the Jeremiah-Lamentations volume in the Ancient Christian Commentary on Scripture, gave me an old-fashioned phone call one day and got me thinking about other sources I might consult.

I completed a substantial portion of the translation work for this volume, first supported by the Simon den Uyl Summer Fellowship in 2015 and then a sabbatical the following fall, both funded by Hope College.

Nothing like this ever comes to completion for me without the support, encouragement, and patience of my remarkable and lovely wife, Beth. She put up with Jeremiah haunting our holidays

---

[1]Abraham J. Heschel, *The Prophets*, 2 vols. (New York: Harper and Row, 1962).

and shadowing our vacations for years. Our boys, Sam and Robbie, kept me sane and solvent by interrupting my work on a regular basis to tell me about their teenaged lives.

Books are born of communities. I was fortunate to grow up in Bethel Reformed Church, a small congregation in Kalamazoo, Michigan, that loved to study the Bible; Will DeYoung stirred me with his curiosity about biblical prophecy; Jim Decker was the finest lay scholar of Scripture I have ever known and my cherished friend and mentor; and Rev. Harold Cupery taught me biblical interpretation in his fine expository sermons, every Sunday and year after year.

Most of all I am grateful to grandparents and parents who modeled for me a life devoted to Scripture. To my grandmother Irene, who first awakened my interest in Scripture, and to my grandfather Pearl, who overcame illiteracy to read the Bible with benefit. To my in-laws: Marjory, whose life and service in the church has mirrored the Word, and to Rev. Larry Doorn, whose discipline in preaching the lectionary has meant that Scripture reads us first; it shapes and speaks to our experiences and lives. Finally, to my father, John, who I can still see in my mind's eye, in his recliner, laboring and sounding out the words of the Bible; reading never came easy to him, but he did it anyway. And to my mother, Marcia, whose quiet and daily rhythm of Bible reading and prayer has never ceased to inspire me. To them this commentary is dedicated.

J. Jeffery Tyler

ABBREVIATIONS

ACCS	Ancient Christian Commentary on Scripture. 29 vols. Edited by Thomas C. Oden. Downers Grove, IL: InterVarsity Press, 1998–2009.
ACT	Ancient Christian Texts.
ARG	*Archiv für Reformationsgeschichte*
BoC	*The Book of Concord: The Confessions of the Evangelical Lutheran Church.* Translated and edited by Theodore G. Tappert et al. Philadelphia: Fortress: 1959.
CCSL	Corpus Christianorum: Series Latina.
CO	*Ioannis Calvini Opera quae supersunt omnia.* 59 vols. Corpus Reformatorum 29–88. Edited by G. Baum, E. Cunitz, and E. Reuss. Brunswick and Berlin: C. A. Schwetschke, 1863–1900. Digital copy online at archive-ouverte.unige.ch/Calvin.
CRR	Classics of the Radical Reformation. 12 vols. Waterloo, ON, and Scottdale, PA: Herald Press, 1973–2010.
CTS	Calvin Translation Society edition of Calvin's commentaries. 46 vols. Edinburgh, 1843–1855. Several reprints, but variously bound; volume numbers (when cited) are relative to specific commentaries and not to the entire set.
HBOT	*Hebrew Bible/Old Testament: The History of Its Interpretation.* Edited by Magne Saebø. 3 vols. Göttingen: Vandenhoeck and Ruprecht, 1996–2015.
LCC	Library of Christian Classics.
LW	*Luther's Works [American Edition].* 82 vols. planned. St. Louis: Concordia; Philadelphia: Fortress, 1955–1986; 2009–.
PL	Patrologia cursus completus. Series Latina. 221 vols. Edited by J.-P. Migne. Paris: Migne, 1844–1864.
SCES	Sixteenth Century Essays and Studies.
SMRT	Studies in Medieval and Reformation Traditions.
SupCalv	*Supplementa Calviniana.* 11+ vols. Neukirchen: Neukirchener, 1961–.
WA	*D. Martin Luthers Werke, Kritische Gesamtausgabe: [Schriften].* 73 vols. Weimar: Hermann Böhlaus Nachfolger, 1883–2009. Digital copy online at archive.org.

BIBLE TRANSLATIONS

CEB	Common English Bible
ESV	English Standard Version
KJV	King James Version
LXX	Septuagint
NASB	New American Standard Bible
NIV	New International Version
NKJV	New King James Version
NRSV	New Revised Standard Version
Vg	Vulgate

A GUIDE TO USING THIS COMMENTARY

Several features have been incorporated into the design of this commentary. The following comments are intended to assist readers in making full use of this volume.

Pericopes of Scripture

The scriptural text has been divided into pericopes, or passages, usually several verses in length. Each of these pericopes is given a heading, which appears at the beginning of the pericope. For example, the first pericope in this commentary is Jeremiah 1:1-3, "The Prophet's Times and Call." This heading is followed by the Scripture passage quoted in the English Standard Version (ESV). The Scripture passage is provided for the convenience of readers, but it is also in keeping with Reformation-era commentaries, which often followed the patristic and medieval commentary tradition, in which the citations of the reformers were arranged according to the text of Scripture.

Overviews

Following each pericope of text is an overview of the Reformation authors' comments on that pericope. The format of this overview varies among the volumes of this series, depending on the requirements of the specific book(s) of Scripture. The function of the overview is to identify succinctly the key exegetical, theological, and pastoral concerns of the Reformation writers arising from the pericope, providing the reader with an orientation to Reformation-era approaches and emphases. It tracks a reasonably cohesive thread of argument among reformers' comments, even though they are derived from diverse sources and generations. Thus, the summaries do not proceed chronologically or by verse sequence. Rather, they seek to rehearse the overall course of the reformers' comments on that pericope.

We do not assume that the commentators themselves anticipated or expressed a formally received cohesive argument but rather that the various arguments tend to flow in a plausible, recognizable pattern. Modern readers can thus glimpse aspects of continuity in the flow of diverse exegetical traditions representing various generations and geographical locations.

Topical Headings

An abundance of varied Reformation-era comment is available for each pericope. For this reason we have broken the pericopes into two levels. First is the verse with its topical heading. The reformers' comments are then focused on aspects of each verse, with topical headings summarizing the essence of the individual comment by evoking a key phrase, metaphor, or idea. This feature provides a bridge by which modern readers can enter into the heart of the Reformation-era comment.

Identifying the Reformation Authors, Texts, and Events

Following the topical heading of each section of comment, the name of the Reformation commentator is given. An English translation (where needed) of the reformer's comment is then provided. This is immediately followed by the title of the original work rendered in English.

Readers who wish to pursue a deeper investigation of the reformers' works cited in this commentary will find full bibliographic detail for each Reformation title provided in the bibliography at the back of the volume. Information on English translations (where available) and standard original-language editions and critical editions of the works cited is found in the bibliography. The Biographical Sketches section provides brief overviews of the life and work of each commentator, and each confession or collaborative work, appearing in the present volume (as well as in any previous volumes). Finally, a Timeline of the Reformation offers broader context for people, places, and events relevant to the commentators and their works.

Footnotes and Back Matter

To aid the reader in exploring the background and texts in further detail, this commentary utilizes footnotes. The use and content of footnotes may vary among the volumes in this series. Where footnotes appear, a footnote number directs the reader to a note at the bottom of the page, where one will find annotations (clarifications or biblical cross references), information on English translations (where available) or standard original-language editions of the work cited.

Where original-language texts have remained untranslated into English, we provide new translations. Where there is any serious ambiguity or textual problem in the selection, we have tried to reflect the best available textual tradition. Wherever current English translations are already well rendered, they are utilized, but where necessary they are stylistically updated. A single asterisk (*) indicates that a previous English translation has been updated to modern English or amended for easier reading. We have standardized spellings and made grammatical variables uniform so that our English references will not reflect the linguistic oddities of the older English translations. For ease of reading we have in some cases removed superfluous conjunctions.

GENERAL INTRODUCTION

The Reformation Commentary on Scripture (RCS) is a twenty-eight-volume series of exegetical comment covering the entire Bible and gathered from the writings of sixteenth-century preachers, scholars and reformers. The RCS is intended as a sequel to the highly acclaimed Ancient Christian Commentary on Scripture (ACCS), and as such its overall concept, method, format, and audience are similar to the earlier series. Both series are committed to the renewal of the church through careful study and meditative reflection on the Old and New Testaments, the charter documents of Christianity, read in the context of the worshiping, believing community of faith across the centuries. However, the patristic and Reformation eras are separated by nearly a millennium, and the challenges of reading Scripture with the reformers require special attention to their context, resources and assumptions. The purpose of this general introduction is to present an overview of the context and process of biblical interpretation in the age of the Reformation.

Goals

The Reformation Commentary on Scripture seeks to introduce its readers to the depth and richness of exegetical ferment that defined the Reformation era. The RCS has four goals: the enrichment of contemporary biblical interpretation through exposure to Reformation-era biblical exegesis; the renewal of contemporary preaching through exposure to the biblical insights of the Reformation writers; a deeper understanding of the Reformation itself and the breadth of perspectives represented within it; and a recovery of the profound integration of the life of faith and the life of the mind that should characterize Christian scholarship. Each of these goals requires a brief comment.

Renewing contemporary biblical interpretation. During the past half-century, biblical hermeneutics has become a major growth industry in the academic world. One of the consequences of the historical-critical hegemony of biblical studies has been the privileging of contemporary philosophies and ideologies at the expense of a commitment to the Christian church as the primary reading community within which and for which biblical exegesis is done. Reading Scripture with the church fathers and the reformers is a corrective to all such imperialism of the present. One of the greatest skills required for a fruitful interpretation of the Bible is the ability to listen. We rightly emphasize the importance of listening to the voices of contextual theologies today, but in doing so we often marginalize or ignore another crucial context—the community of believing Christians through the centuries. The serious study of Scripture requires more than the latest

Bible translation in one hand and the latest commentary (or niche study Bible) in the other. John L. Thompson has called on Christians today to practice the art of "reading the Bible with the dead."[1] The RCS presents carefully selected comments from the extant commentaries of the Reformation as an encouragement to more in-depth study of this important epoch in the history of biblical interpretation.

Strengthening contemporary preaching. The Protestant reformers identified the public preaching of the Word of God as an indispensible means of grace and a sure sign of the true church. Through the words of the preacher, the living voice of the gospel (*viva vox evangelii*) is heard. Luther famously said that the church is not a "pen house" but a "mouth house."[2] The Reformation in Switzerland began when Huldrych Zwingli entered the pulpit of the Grossmünster in Zurich on January 1, 1519, and began to preach a series of expositional sermons chapter by chapter from the Gospel of Matthew. In the following years he extended this homiletical approach to other books of the Old and New Testaments. Calvin followed a similar pattern in Geneva. Many of the commentaries represented in this series were either originally presented as sermons or were written to support the regular preaching ministry of local church pastors. Luther said that the preacher should be a *bonus textualis*—a good one with a text—well-versed in the Scriptures. Preachers in the Reformation traditions preached not only about the Bible but also from it, and this required more than a passing acquaintance with its contents. Those who have been charged with the office of preaching in the church today can find wisdom and insight—and fresh perspectives—in the sermons of the Reformation and the biblical commentaries read and studied by preachers of the sixteenth century.

Deepening understanding of the Reformation. Some scholars of the sixteenth century prefer to speak of the period they study in the plural, the European Reformations, to indicate that many diverse impulses for reform were at work in this turbulent age of transition from medieval to modern times.[3] While this point is well taken, the RCS follows the time-honored tradition of using *Reformation* in the singular form to indicate not only a major moment in the history of Christianity in the West but also, as Hans J. Hillerbrand has put it, "an essential cohesiveness in the heterogeneous pursuits of religious reform in the sixteenth century."[4] At the same time, in developing guidelines to assist the volume editors in making judicious selections from the vast amount of commentary material available in this period, we have stressed the multifaceted character of the Reformation across many confessions, theological orientations, and political settings.

Advancing Christian scholarship. By assembling and disseminating numerous voices from such a signal period as the Reformation, the RCS aims to make a significant contribution to the ever-growing stream of Christian scholarship. The post-Enlightenment split between the study of the Bible as an academic discipline and the reading of the Bible as spiritual nurture was foreign

---

[1]John L. Thompson, *Reading the Bible with the Dead* (Grand Rapids: Eerdmans, 2007).
[2]WA 10,2:48.
[3]See Carter Lindberg, *The European Reformations*, 2nd ed. (Malden, MA: Wiley-Blackwell, 2010).
[4]Hans J. Hillerbrand, *The Division of Christendom* (Louisville, KY: Westminster John Knox, 2007), x. Hillerbrand has also edited the standard reference work in Reformation studies, *OER*. See also Diarmaid MacCulloch, *The Reformation* (New York: Viking, 2003), and Patrick Collinson, *The Reformation: A History* (New York: Random House, 2004).

to the reformers. For them the study of the Bible was transformative at the most basic level of the human person: *coram deo*.

The reformers all repudiated the idea that the Bible could be studied and understood with dispassionate objectivity, as a cold artifact from antiquity. Luther's famous Reformation break-through triggered by his laborious study of the Psalms and Paul's letter to the Romans is well known, but the experience of Cambridge scholar Thomas Bilney was perhaps more typical. When Erasmus's critical edition of the Greek New Testament was published in 1516, it was accompanied by a new translation in elegant Latin. Attracted by the classical beauty of Erasmus's Latin, Bilney came across this statement in 1 Timothy 1:15: "Christ Jesus came into the world to save sinners." In the Greek this sentence is described as *pistos ho logos*, which the Vulgate had rendered *fidelis sermo*, "a faithful saying." Erasmus chose a different word for the Greek *pistos*—*certus*, "sure, certain." When Bilney grasped the meaning of this word applied to the announcement of salvation in Christ, he tells us that "immediately, I felt a marvellous comfort and quietness, insomuch as 'my bruised bones leaped for joy.'"[5]

Luther described the way the Bible was meant to function in the minds and hearts of believers when he reproached himself and others for studying the nativity narrative with such cool unconcern:

> I hate myself because when I see Christ laid in the manger or in the lap of his mother and hear the angels sing, my heart does not leap into flame. With what good reason should we all despise our-selves that we remain so cold when this word is spoken to us, over which everyone should dance and leap and burn for joy! We act as though it were a frigid historical fact that does not smite our hearts, as if someone were merely relating that the sultan has a crown of gold.[6]

It was a core conviction of the Reformation that the careful study and meditative listening to the Scriptures, what the monks called *lectio divina*, could yield transformative results for *all* of life. The value of such a rich commentary, therefore, lies not only in the impressive volume of Reformation-era voices that are presented throughout the course of the series but in the many particular fields for which their respective lives and ministries are relevant. The Reformation is consequential for historical studies, both church as well as secular history. Biblical and theological studies, to say nothing of pastoral and spiritual studies, also stand to benefit and progress immensely from re-newed engagement today, as mediated through the RCS, with the reformers of yesteryear.

Perspectives

In setting forth the perspectives and parameters of the RCS, the following considerations have proved helpful.

Chronology. When did the Reformation begin, and how long did it last? In some traditional accounts, the answer was clear: the Reformation began with the posting of Luther's Ninety-five

---

[5]John Foxe, *The Acts and Monuments of John Foxe: A New and Complete Edition*, 8 vols., ed. Stephen Reed Cattley (London: R. B. Seeley & W. Burnside, 1837), 4:635; quoting Ps 51:8; cited in A. G. Dickens, *The English Reformation*, 2nd ed. (University Park, PA: The Pennsylvannia State University Press, 1991), 102.
[6]WA 49:176-77, quoted in Roland Bainton, "The Bible in the Reformation," in *CHB*, 3:23.

Theses at Wittenberg in 1517 and ended with the death of Calvin in Geneva in 1564. Apart from reducing the Reformation to a largely German event with a side trip to Switzerland, this perspective fails to do justice to the important events that led up to Luther's break with Rome and its many reverberations throughout Europe and beyond. In choosing commentary selections for the RCS, we have adopted the concept of the long sixteenth century, say, from the late 1400s to the mid-seventeenth century. Thus we have included commentary selections from early or pre-Reformation writers such as John Colet and Jacques Lefèvre d'Étaples to seventeenth-century figures such as Henry Ainsworth and Johann Gerhard.

Confession. The RCS concentrates primarily, though not exclusively, on the exegetical writings of the Protestant reformers. While the ACCS provided a compendium of key consensual exegetes of the early Christian centuries, the Catholic/Protestant confessional divide in the sixteenth century tested the very idea of consensus, especially with reference to ecclesiology and soteriology. While many able and worthy exegetes faithful to the Roman Catholic Church were active during this period, this project has chosen to include primarily those figures that represent perspectives within the Protestant Reformation. For this reason we have not included comments on the apocryphal or deuterocanonical writings.

We recognize that "Protestant" and "Catholic" as contradistinctive labels are anachronistic terms for the early decades of the sixteenth century before the hardening of confessional identities surrounding the Council of Trent (1545–1563). Protestant figures such as Philipp Melanchthon, Johannes Oecolampadius and John Calvin were all products of the revival of sacred letters known as biblical humanism. They shared an approach to biblical interpretation that owed much to Desiderius Erasmus and other scholars who remained loyal to the Church of Rome. Careful comparative studies of Protestant and Catholic exegesis in the sixteenth century have shown surprising areas of agreement when the focus was the study of a particular biblical text rather than the standard confessional debates.

At the same time, exegetical differences among the various Protestant groups could become strident and church-dividing. The most famous example of this is the interpretive impasse between Luther and Zwingli over the meaning of "This is my body" (Mt 26:26) in the words of institution. Their disagreement at the Colloquy of Marburg in 1529 had important christological and pastoral implications, as well as social and political consequences. Luther refused fellowship with Zwingli and his party at the end of the colloquy; in no small measure this bitter division led to the separate trajectories pursued by Lutheran and Reformed Protestantism to this day. In Elizabethan England, Puritans and Anglicans agreed that "Holy Scripture containeth all things necessary to salvation: so that whatsoever is not read therein, nor may be proved thereby, is not to be required of any man" (article 6 of the Thirty-Nine Articles of Religion), yet on the basis of their differing interpretations of the Bible they fought bitterly over the structures of the church, the clothing of the clergy and the ways of worship. On the matter of infant baptism, Catholics and Protestants alike agreed on its propriety, though there were various theories as to how a practice not mentioned in the Bible could be justified biblically. The Anabaptists were outliers on this subject. They rejected infant baptism altogether. They appealed to the example of the baptism of Jesus and to his final words as recorded in the Gospel of Matthew (Mt 28:19-20): "Go therefore, and make disciples of all nations, baptizing them in the name of the Father, and of the Son, and of the Holy Spirit, teaching them to observe all that I have commanded you." New Testament Christians, they argued, are to follow not only the commands of Jesus in the Great Commission, but also the exact order in which they were given: evangelize, baptize, catechize.

These and many other differences of interpretation among the various Protestant groups are reflected in their many sermons, commentaries and public disputations. In the RCS, the volume editors' introduction to each volume is intended to help the reader understand the nature and significance of doctrinal conversations and disputes that resulted in particular, and frequently clashing, interpretations. Footnotes throughout the text will be provided to explain obscure references, unusual expressions and other matters that require special comment. Volume editors have chosen comments on the Bible across a wide range of sixteenth-century confessions and schools of interpretation: biblical humanists, Lutheran, Reformed, Anglican, Puritan, and Anabaptist. We have not pursued passages from post-Tridentine Catholic authors or from radical spiritualists and antitrinitarian writers, though sufficient material is available from these sources to justify another series.

Format. The design of the RCS is intended to offer reader-friendly access to these classic texts. The availability of digital resources has given access to a huge residual database of sixteenth-century exegetical comment hitherto available only in major research universities and rare book collections. The RCS has benefited greatly from online databases such as Alexander Street Press's Digital Library of Classical Protestant Texts (DLCPT) and Early English Books Online as well as freely accessible databases like the Post-Reformation Digital Library (prdl.org). Through the help of RCS editorial advisor Herman Selderhuis, we have also had access to the special Reformation collections of the Johannes a Lasco Bibliothek in Emden, Germany. In addition, modern critical editions and translations of Reformation sources have been published over the past generation. Original translations of Reformation sources are given unless an acceptable translation already exists.

Each volume in the RCS will include an introduction by the volume editor placing that portion of the canon within the historical context of the Protestant Reformation and presenting a summary of the theological themes, interpretive issues and reception of the particular book(s). The commentary itself consists of particular pericopes identified by a pericope heading; the biblical text in the English Standard Version (ESV), with significant textual variants registered in the footnotes; an overview of the pericope in which principal exegetical and theological concerns of the Reformation writers are succinctly noted; and excerpts from the Reformation writers identified by name according to the conventions of the *Oxford Encyclopedia of the Reformation.* Each volume will also include a bibliography of sources cited, as well as an appendix of authors and source works.

The Reformation era was a time of verbal as well as physical violence, and this fact has presented a challenge for this project. Without unduly sanitizing the texts, where they contain anti-Semitic, sexist or inordinately polemical rhetoric, we have not felt obliged to parade such comments either. We have noted the abridgement of texts with ellipses and an explanatory footnote.

While this procedure would not be valid in the critical edition of such a text, we have deemed it appropriate in a series whose primary purpose is pastoral and devotional. When translating *homo* or similar terms that refer to the human race as a whole or to individual persons without reference to gender, we have used alternative English expressions to the word *man* (or derivative constructions that formerly were used generically to signify humanity at large), whenever such substitutions can be made without producing an awkward or artificial construction.

As is true in the ACCS, we have made a special effort where possible to include the voices of women, though we acknowledge the difficulty of doing so for the early modern period when for a variety of social and cultural reasons few theological and biblical works were published by women. However, recent scholarship has focused on a number of female leaders whose literary remains show us how they understood and interpreted the Bible. Women who made significant contributions to the Reformation include Marguerite d'Angoulême, sister of King Francis I, who supported French reformist evangelicals including Calvin and who published a religious poem influenced by Luther's theology, *The Mirror of the Sinful Soul*; Argula von Grumbach, a Bavarian noblewoman who defended the teachings of Luther and Melanchthon before the theologians of the University of Ingolstadt; Katharina Schütz Zell, the wife of a former priest, Matthias Zell, and a remarkable reformer in her own right—she conducted funerals, compiled hymnbooks, defended the downtrodden, and published a defense of clerical marriage as well as composing works of consolation on divine comfort and pleas for the toleration of Anabaptists and Catholics alike; and Anne Askew, a Protestant martyr put to death in 1546 after demonstrating remarkable biblical prowess in her examinations by church officials. Other echoes of faithful women in the age of the Reformation are found in their letters, translations, poems, hymns, court depositions, and martyr records.

Lay culture, learned culture. In recent decades, much attention has been given to what is called "reforming from below," that is, the expressions of religious beliefs and churchly life that characterized the popular culture of the majority of the population in the era of the Reformation. Social historians have taught us to examine the diverse pieties of townspeople and city folk, of rural religion and village life, the emergence of lay theologies, and the experiences of women in the religious tumults of Reformation Europe.[7] Formal commentaries by their nature are artifacts of learned culture. Almost all of them were written in Latin, the lingua franca of learned discourse well past the age of the Reformation. Biblical commentaries were certainly not the primary means by which the Protestant Reformation spread so rapidly across wide sectors of sixteenth-century society. Small pamphlets and broadsheets, later called *Flugschriften* ("flying writings"), with their graphic woodcuts and cartoon-like depictions of Reformation personalities and events, became the means of choice for mass communication in the early age of printing. Sermons and works of devotion were also printed with appealing visual aids. Luther's early writings were often accompanied by drawings and sketches from Lucas Cranach and other artists. This was done "above all for the sake of children and simple folk," as Luther

---

[7]See Peter Matheson, ed., *Reformation Christianity* (Minneapolis: Fortress, 2007).

put it, "who are more easily moved by pictures and images to recall divine history than through mere words or doctrines."[8]

We should be cautious, however, in drawing too sharp a distinction between learned and lay culture in this period. The phenomenon of preaching was a kind of verbal bridge between scholars at their desks and the thousands of illiterate or semiliterate listeners whose views were shaped by the results of Reformation exegesis. According to contemporary witness, more than one thousand people were crowding into Geneva to hear Calvin expound the Scriptures every day.[9] An example of how learned theological works by Reformation scholars were received across divisions of class and social status comes from Lazare Drilhon, an apothecary of Toulon. He was accused of heresy in May 1545 when a cache of prohibited books was found hidden in his garden shed. In addition to devotional works, the French New Testament and a copy of Calvin's Genevan liturgy, there was found a series of biblical commentaries, translated from the Latin into French: Martin Bucer's on Matthew, François Lambert's on the Apocalypse and one by Oecolampadius on 1 John.[10] Biblical exegesis in the sixteenth century was not limited to the kind of full-length commentaries found in Drilhon's shed. Citations from the Bible and expositions of its meaning permeate the extant literature of sermons, letters, court depositions, doctrinal treatises, records of public disputations and even last wills and testaments. While most of the selections in the RCS will be drawn from formal commentary literature, other sources of biblical reflection will also be considered.

Historical Context

The medieval legacy. On October 18, 1512, the degree *Doctor in Biblia* was conferred on Martin Luther, and he began his career as a professor in the University of Wittenberg. As is well known, Luther was also a monk who had taken solemn vows in the Augustinian Order of Hermits at Erfurt. These two settings—the university and the monastery—both deeply rooted in the Middle Ages, form the background not only for Luther's personal vocation as a reformer but also for the history of the biblical commentary in the age of the Reformation. Since the time of the Venerable Bede (d. 735), sometimes called "the last of the Fathers," serious study of the Bible had taken place primarily in the context of cloistered monasteries. The Rule of St. Benedict brought together *lectio* and *meditatio*, the knowledge of letters and the life of prayer. The liturgy was the medium through which the daily reading of the Bible, especially the Psalms, and the sayings of the church fathers came together in the spiritual formation of the monks.[11] Essential to this understanding was a belief in the unity of the people of God throughout time as well as space, and an awareness that life in this world was a preparation for the beatific vision in the next.

---

[8]Martin Luther, "Personal Prayer Book," LW 43:42-43* (WA 10,2:458); quoted in R. W. Scribner, *For the Sake of Simple Folk: Popular Propaganda for the German Reformation* (Cambridge: Cambridge University Press, 1981), xi.

[9]Letter of De Beaulieu to Guillaume Farel (1561) in *Theodor Beza nach handschriftlichen und anderen gleichzeitigen Quellen*, ed. J. W. Baum (Leipzig: Weidmann, 1851), 2:92.

[10]Francis Higman, "A Heretic's Library: The Drilhon Inventory" (1545), in Francis Higman, *Lire et Découvire: la circulation des idées au temps de la Réforme* (Geneva: Droz, 1998), 65-85.

[11]See the classic study by Jean Leclercq, *The Love of Learning and the Desire for God* (New York: Fordham University Press, 1961).

The source of theology was the study of the sacred page (*sacra pagina*); its object was the accumulation of knowledge not for its own sake but for the obtaining of eternal life. For these monks, the Bible had God for its author, salvation for its end and unadulterated truth for its matter, though they would not have expressed it in such an Aristotelian way. The medieval method of interpreting the Bible owed much to Augustine's *On Christian Doctrine*. In addition to setting forth a series of rules (drawn from an earlier work by Tyconius), Augustine stressed the importance of distinguishing the literal and spiritual or allegorical senses of Scripture. While the literal sense was not disparaged, the allegorical was valued because it enabled the believer to obtain spiritual benefit from the obscure places in the Bible, especially in the Old Testament. For Augustine, as for the monks who followed him, the goal of scriptural exegesis was freighted with eschatological meaning; its purpose was to induce faith, hope, and love and so to advance in one's pilgrimage toward that city with foundations (see Heb 11:10).

Building on the work of Augustine and other church fathers going back to Origen, medieval exegetes came to understand Scripture as possessed of four possible meanings, the famous *quadriga*. The literal meaning was retained, of course, but the spiritual meaning was now subdivided into three senses: the allegorical, the moral, and the anagogical. Medieval exegetes often referred to the four meanings of Scripture in a popular rhyme:

> The letter shows us what God and our fathers did;
> The allegory shows us where our faith is hid;
> The moral meaning gives us rules of daily life;
> The anagogy shows us where we end our strife.[12]

In this schema, the three spiritual meanings of the text correspond to the three theological virtues: faith (allegory), hope (anagogy), and love (the moral meaning). It should be noted that this way of approaching the Bible assumed a high doctrine of scriptural inspiration: the multiple meanings inherent in the text had been placed there by the Holy Spirit for the benefit of the people of God. The biblical justification for this method went back to the apostle Paul, who had used the words *allegory* and *type* when applying Old Testament events to believers in Christ (Gal 4:21-31; 1 Cor 10:1-11). The problem with this approach was knowing how to relate each of the four senses to one another and how to prevent Scripture from becoming a nose of wax turned this way and that by various interpreters. As G. R. Evans explains, "Any interpretation which could be put upon the text and was in keeping with the faith and edifying, had the warrant of God himself, for no human reader had the ingenuity to find more than God had put there."[13]

With the rise of the universities in the eleventh century, theology and the study of Scripture moved from the cloister into the classroom. Scripture and the Fathers were still important, but they came to function more as footnotes to the theological questions debated in the schools and brought together in an impressive systematic way in works such as Peter Lombard's *Books of Sentences* (the standard theology textbook of the Middle Ages) and the great scholastic *summae* of the thirteenth

---

[12]Robert M. Grant, *A Short History of the Interpretation of the Bible* (New York: Macmillan, 1963), 119. A translation of the well-known Latin quatrain: *Littera gesta docet/Quid credas allegoria/Moralis quid agas/Quo tendas anagogia.*

[13]G. R. Evans, *The Language and Logic of the Bible: The Road to Reformation* (Cambridge: Cambridge University Press, 1985), 42.

century. Indispensible to the study of the Bible in the later Middle Ages was the *Glossa ordinaria*, a collection of exegetical opinions by the church fathers and other commentators. Heiko Oberman summarized the transition from devotion to dialectic this way: "When, due to the scientific revolution of the twelfth century, Scripture became the *object* of study rather than the *subject* through which God speaks to the student, the difference between the two modes of speaking was investigated in terms of the texts themselves rather than in their relation to the recipients."[14] It was possible, of course, to be both a scholastic theologian and a master of the spiritual life. Meister Eckhart, for example, wrote commentaries on the Old Testament in Latin and works of mystical theology in German, reflecting what had come to be seen as a division of labor between the two.

An increasing focus on the text of Scripture led to a revival of interest in its literal sense. The two key figures in this development were Thomas Aquinas (d. 1274) and Nicholas of Lyra (d. 1340). Thomas is best remembered for his *Summa Theologiae*, but he was also a prolific commentator on the Bible. Thomas did not abandon the multiple senses of Scripture but declared that all the senses were founded on one—the literal—and this sense eclipsed allegory as the basis of sacred doctrine. Nicholas of Lyra was a Franciscan scholar who made use of the Hebrew text of the Old Testament and quoted liberally from works of Jewish scholars, especially the learned French rabbi Salomon Rashi (d. 1105). After Aquinas, Lyra was the strongest defender of the literal, historical meaning of Scripture as the primary basis of theological disputation. His *Postilla*, as his notes were called—the abbreviated form of *post illa verba textus*, meaning "after these words from Scripture"—were widely circulated in the late Middle Ages and became the first biblical commentary to be printed in the fifteenth century. More than any other commentator from the period of high scholasticism, Lyra and his work were greatly valued by the early reformers. According to an old Latin pun, *Nisi Lyra lyrasset, Lutherus non saltasset*, "If Lyra had not played his lyre, Luther would not have danced."[15] While Luther was never an uncritical disciple of any teacher, he did praise Lyra as a good Hebraist and quoted him more than one hundred times in his lectures on Genesis, where he declared, "I prefer him to almost all other interpreters of Scripture."[16]

Sacred philology. The sixteenth century has been called a golden age of biblical interpretation, and it is a fact that the age of the Reformation witnessed an explosion of commentary writing unparalleled in the history of the Christian church. Kenneth Hagen has cataloged forty-five commentaries on Hebrews between 1516 (Erasmus) and 1598 (Beza).[17] During the sixteenth century, more than seventy new commentaries on Romans were published, five of them by Melanchthon alone, and nearly one hundred commentaries on the Bible's prayer book, the Psalms.[18] There were two developments in the fifteenth century that presaged this development and without which it

---

[14]Heiko Oberman, *Forerunners of the Reformation* (Philadelphia: Fortress, 1966), 284.

[15]Nicholas of Lyra, *The Postilla of Nicolas of Lyra on the Song of Songs*, trans. and ed. James George Kiecker (Milwaukee: Marquette University Press, 1998), 19.

[16]LW 2:164 (WA 42:377).

[17]Kenneth Hagen, *Hebrews Commenting from Erasmus to Bèze, 1516–1598* (Tübingen: Mohr, 1981).

[18]R. Gerald Hobbs, "Biblical Commentaries," *OER* 1:167-71. See in general David C. Steinmetz, ed., *The Bible in the Sixteenth Century* (Durham: Duke University Press, 1990).

could not have taken place: the invention of printing and the rediscovery of a vast store of ancient learning hitherto unknown or unavailable to scholars in the West.

It is now commonplace to say that what the computer has become in our generation, the printing press was to the world of Erasmus, Luther, and other leaders of the Reformation. Johannes Gutenberg, a goldsmith by trade, developed a metal alloy suitable for type and a machine that would allow printed characters to be cast with relative ease, placed in even lines of composition and then manipulated again and again, making possible the mass production of an unbelievable number of texts. In 1455, the Gutenberg Bible, the masterpiece of the typographical revolution, was published at Mainz in double columns in gothic type. Forty-seven copies of the beautiful Gutenberg Bible are still extant, each consisting of more than one thousand colorfully illuminated and impeccably printed pages. What began at Gutenberg's print shop in Mainz on the Rhine River soon spread, like McDonald's or Starbucks in our day, into every nook and cranny of the known world. Printing presses sprang up in Rome (1464), Venice (1469), Paris (1470), the Netherlands (1471), Switzerland (1472), Spain (1474), England (1476), Sweden (1483), and Constantinople (1490). By 1500, these and other presses across Europe had published some twenty-seven thousand titles, most of them in Latin. Erasmus once compared himself with an obscure preacher whose sermons were heard by only a few people in one or two churches while his books were read in every country in the world. Erasmus was not known for his humility, but in this case he was simply telling the truth.[19]

The Italian humanist Lorenzo Valla (d. 1457) died in the early dawn of the age of printing, but his critical and philological studies would be taken up by others who believed that genuine reform in church and society could come about only by returning to the wellsprings of ancient learning and wisdom—*ad fontes*, "back to the sources!" Valla is best remembered for undermining a major claim made by defenders of the papacy when he proved by philological research that the so-called Donation of Constantine, which had bolstered papal assertions of temporal sovereignty, was a forgery. But it was Valla's *Collatio Novi Testamenti* of 1444 that would have such a great effect on the renewal of biblical studies in the next century. Erasmus discovered the manuscript of this work while rummaging through an old library in Belgium and published it at Paris in 1505. In the preface to his edition of Valla, Erasmus gave the rationale that would guide his own labors in textual criticism. Just as Jerome had translated the Latin Vulgate from older versions and copies of the Scriptures in his day, so now Jerome's own text must be subjected to careful scrutiny and correction. Erasmus would be *Hieronymus redivivus*, a new Jerome come back to life to advance the cause of sacred philology. The restoration of the Scriptures and the writings of the church fathers would usher in what Erasmus believed would be a golden age of peace and learning. In 1516, the Basel publisher Froben brought out Erasmus's *Novum Instrumentum*, the first published edition of the Greek New Testament. Erasmus's Greek New Testament would go through five editions in his lifetime, each one with new emendations to the text and a growing section of annotations that expanded to include not only technical notes about the text but also theological comment. The influence of Erasmus's Greek New

---

[19]E. Harris Harbison, *The Christian Scholar in the Age of the Reformation* (New York: Charles Scribner's Sons, 1956), 80.

Testament was enormous. It formed the basis for Robert Estienne's *Novum Testamentum Graece* of 1550, which in turn was used to establish the Greek *Textus Receptus* for a number of late Reformation translations including the King James Version of 1611.

For all his expertise in Greek, Erasmus was a poor student of Hebrew and only published commentaries on several of the psalms. However, the renaissance of Hebrew letters was part of the wider program of biblical humanism as reflected in the establishment of trilingual colleges devoted to the study of Hebrew, Greek and Latin (the three languages written on the *titulus* of Jesus' cross [Jn 19:20]) at Alcalá in Spain, Wittenberg in Germany, Louvain in Belgium, and Paris in France. While it is true that some medieval commentators, especially Nicholas of Lyra, had been informed by the study of Hebrew and rabbinics in their biblical work, it was the publication of Johannes Reuchlin's *De rudimentis hebraicis* (1506), a combined grammar and dictionary, that led to the recovery of *veritas Hebraica*, as Jerome had referred to the true voice of the Hebrew Scriptures. The pursuit of Hebrew studies was carried forward in the Reformation by two great scholars, Konrad Pellikan and Sebastian Münster. Pellikan was a former Franciscan friar who embraced the Protestant cause and played a major role in the Zurich reformation. He had published a Hebrew grammar even prior to Reuchlin and produced a commentary on nearly the entire Bible that appeared in seven volumes between 1532 and 1539. Münster was Pellikan's student and taught Hebrew at the University of Heidelberg before taking up a similar position in Basel. Like his mentor, Münster was a great collector of Hebraica and published a series of excellent grammars, dictionaries and rabbinic texts. Münster did for the Hebrew Old Testament what Erasmus had done for the Greek New Testament. His *Hebraica Biblia* offered a fresh Latin translation of the Old Testament with annotations from medieval rabbinic exegesis.

Luther first learned Hebrew with Reuchlin's grammar in hand but took advantage of other published resources, such as the four-volume Hebrew Bible published at Venice by Daniel Bomberg in 1516 to 1517. He also gathered his own circle of Hebrew experts, his *sanhedrin* he called it, who helped him with his German translation of the Old Testament. We do not know where William Tyndale learned Hebrew, though perhaps it was in Worms, where there was a thriving rabbinical school during his stay there. In any event, he had sufficiently mastered the language to bring out a freshly translated Pentateuch that was published at Antwerp in 1530. By the time the English separatist scholar Henry Ainsworth published his prolix commentaries on the Pentateuch in 1616, the knowledge of Hebrew, as well as Greek, was taken for granted by every serious scholar of the Bible. In the preface to his commentary on Genesis, Ainsworth explained that "the literal sense of Moses's Hebrew (which is the tongue wherein he wrote the law), is the ground of all interpretation, and that language hath figures and properties of speech, different from ours: These therefore in the first place are to be opened that the natural meaning of the Scripture, being known, the mysteries of godliness therein implied, may be better discerned."[20]

The restoration of the biblical text in the original languages made possible the revival of scriptural exposition reflected in the floodtide of sermon literature and commentary work. Of even

---

[20]Henry Ainsworth, *Annotations upon the First Book of Moses Called Genesis* (Amsterdam, 1616), preface (unpaginated).

more far-reaching import was the steady stream of vernacular Bibles in the sixteenth century. In the introduction to his 1516 edition of the New Testament, Erasmus had expressed his desire that the Scriptures be translated into all languages so that "the lowliest women" could read the Gospels and the Pauline epistles and "the farmer sing some portion of them at the plow, the weaver hum some parts of them to the movement of his shuttle, the traveler lighten the weariness of the journey with stories of this kind."[21] Like Erasmus, Tyndale wanted the Bible to be available in the language of the common people. He once said to a learned divine that if God spared his life he would cause the boy who drives the plow to know more of the Scriptures than he did![22] The project of allowing the Bible to speak in the language of the mother in the house, the children in the street and the cheesemonger in the marketplace was met with stiff opposition by certain Catholic polemicists such as Johann Eck, Luther's antagonist at the Leipzig Debate of 1519. In his *Enchiridion* (1525), Eck derided the "inky theologians" whose translations paraded the Bible before "the untutored crowd" and subjected it to the judgment of "laymen and crazy old women."[23] In fact, some fourteen German Bibles had already been published prior to Luther's September Testament of 1522, which he translated from Erasmus's Greek New Testament in less than three months' time while sequestered in the Wartburg. Luther's German New Testament became the first best-seller in the world, appearing in forty-three distinct editions between 1522 and 1525 with upward of one hundred thousand copies issued in these three years. It is estimated that 5 percent of the German population may have been literate at this time, but this rate increased as the century wore on due in no small part to the unmitigated success of vernacular Bibles.[24]

Luther's German Bible (inclusive of the Old Testament from 1534) was the most successful venture of its kind, but it was not alone in the field. Hans Denck and Ludwig Hätzer, leaders in the early Anabaptist movement, translated the prophetic books of the Old Testament from Hebrew into German in 1527. This work influenced the Swiss-German Bible of 1531 published by Leo Jud and other pastors in Zurich. Tyndale's influence on the English language rivaled that of Luther on German. At a time when English was regarded as "that obscure and remote dialect of German spoken in an off-shore island," Tyndale, with his remarkable linguistic ability (he was fluent in eight languages), "made a language for England," as his modern editor David Daniell has put it.[25] Tyndale was imprisoned and executed near Brussels in 1536, but the influence of his biblical work among the common people of England was already being felt. There is no reason to doubt the authenticity of John Foxe's recollection of how Tyndale's New Testament was received in England during the 1520s and 1530s:

---

[21]John C. Olin, *Christian Humanism and the Reformation* (New York: Fordham University Press, 1987), 101.

[22]This famous statement of Tyndale was quoted by John Foxe in his *Acts and Monuments of Matters Happening in the Church* (London, 1563). See Henry Wansbrough, "Tyndale," in *The Bible in the Renaissance*, ed. Richard Griffith (Aldershot, UK: Ashgate, 2001), 124.

[23]John Eck, *Enchiridion of Commonplaces*, trans. Ford Lewis Battles (Grand Rapids: Baker, 1979), 47-49.

[24]The effect of printing on the spread of the Reformation has been much debated. See the classic study by Elizabeth L. Eisenstein, *The Printing Press as an Agent of Change* (Cambridge: Cambridge University Press, 1979). More recent studies include Mark U. Edwards Jr., *Printing, Propaganda and Martin Luther* (Minneapolis: Fortress, 1994), and Andrew Pettegree and Matthew Hall, "The Reformation and the Book: A Reconsideration," *Historical Journal* 47 (2004): 1-24.

[25]David Daniell, *William Tyndale: A Biography* (New Haven: Yale University Press, 1994), 3.

The fervent zeal of those Christian days seemed much superior to these our days and times; as manifestly may appear by their sitting up all night in reading and hearing; also by their expenses and charges in buying of books in English, of whom some gave five marks, some more, some less, for a book: some gave a load of hay for a few chapters of St. James, or of St. Paul in English.[26]

Calvin helped to revise and contributed three prefaces to the French Bible translated by his cousin Pierre Robert Olivétan and originally published at Neuchâtel in 1535. Clément Marot and Beza provided a fresh translation of the Psalms with each psalm rendered in poetic form and accompanied by monophonic musical settings for congregational singing. The Bay Psalter, the first book printed in America, was an English adaptation of this work. Geneva also provided the provenance of the most influential Italian Bible published by Giovanni Diodati in 1607. The flowering of biblical humanism in vernacular Bibles resulted in new translations in all of the major language groups of Europe: Spanish (1569), Portuguese (1681), Dutch (New Testament, 1523; Old Testament, 1527), Danish (1550), Czech (1579–1593/94), Hungarian (New Testament, 1541; complete Bible, 1590), Polish (1563), Swedish (1541), and even Arabic (1591).[27]

Patterns of Reformation

Once the text of the Bible had been placed in the hands of the people, in cheap and easily available editions, what further need was there of published expositions such as commentaries? Given the Protestant doctrine of the priesthood of all believers, was there any longer a need for learned clergy and their bookish religion? Some radical reformers thought not. Sebastian Franck searched for the true church of the Spirit "scattered among the heathen and the weeds" but could not find it in any of the institutional structures of his time. *Veritas non potest scribi, aut exprimi*, he said, "truth can neither be spoken nor written."[28] Kaspar von Schwenckfeld so emphasized religious inwardness that he suspended external observance of the Lord's Supper and downplayed the readable, audible Scriptures in favor of the Word within. This trajectory would lead to the rise of the Quakers in the next century, but it was pursued neither by the mainline reformers nor by most of the Anabaptists. Article 7 of the Augsburg Confession (1530) declared the one holy Christian church to be "the assembly of all believers among whom the Gospel is purely preached and the holy sacraments are administered according to the Gospel."[29]

Historians of the nineteenth century referred to the material and formal principles of the Reformation. In this construal, the matter at stake was the meaning of the Christian gospel: the liberating insight that helpless sinners are graciously justified by the gift of faith alone, apart from any works or merits of their own, entirely on the basis of Christ's atoning work on the cross. For Luther especially, justification by faith alone became the criterion by which all other doctrines and

---

[26]Foxe, *Acts and Monuments*, 4:218.
[27]On vernacular translations of the Bible, see *CHB* 3:94-140 and Jaroslav Pelikan, *The Reformation of the Bible/The Bible of the Reformation* (New Haven: Yale University Press, 1996), 41-62.
[28]Sebastian Franck, *280 Paradoxes or Wondrous Sayings*, trans. E. J. Furcha (Lewiston, NY: Edwin Mellen Press, 1986), 10, 212.
[29]BoC 42 (BSLK 61).

practices of the church were to be judged. The cross proves everything, he said at the Heidelberg disputation in 1518. The distinction between law and gospel thus became the primary hermeneutical key that unlocked the true meaning of Scripture.

The formal principle of the Reformation, *sola Scriptura*, was closely bound up with proper distinctions between Scripture and tradition. "Scripture alone," said Luther, "is the true lord and master of all writings and doctrine on earth. If that is not granted, what is Scripture good for? The more we reject it, the more we become satisfied with human books and human teachers."[30] On the basis of this principle, the reformers challenged the structures and institutions of the medieval Catholic Church. Even a simple layperson, they asserted, armed with Scripture should be believed above a pope or a council without it. But, however boldly asserted, the doctrine of the primacy of Scripture did not absolve the reformers from dealing with a host of hermeneutical issues that became matters of contention both between Rome and the Reformation and within each of these two communities: the extent of the biblical canon, the validity of critical study of the Bible, the perspicuity of Scripture and its relation to preaching, and the retention of devotional and liturgical practices such as holy days, incense, the burning of candles, the sprinkling of holy water, church art, and musical instruments. Zwingli, the Puritans, and the radicals dismissed such things as a rubbish heap of ceremonials that amounted to nothing but tomfoolery, while Lutherans and Anglicans retained most of them as consonant with Scripture and valuable aids to worship.

It is important to note that while the mainline reformers differed among themselves on many matters, overwhelmingly they saw themselves as part of the ongoing Catholic tradition, indeed as the legitimate bearers of it. This was seen in numerous ways including their sense of continuity with the church of the preceding centuries; their embrace of the ecumenical orthodoxy of the early church; and their desire to read the Bible in dialogue with the exegetical tradition of the church.

In their biblical commentaries, the reformers of the sixteenth century revealed a close familiarity with the preceding exegetical tradition, and they used it respectfully as well as critically in their own expositions of the sacred text. For them, *sola Scriptura* was not *nuda Scriptura*. Rather, the Scriptures were seen as the book given to the church, gathered and guided by the Holy Spirit. In his restatement of the Vincentian canon, Calvin defined the church as "a society of all the saints, a society which, spread over the whole world, and existing in all ages, and bound together by the one doctrine and the one spirit of Christ, cultivates and observes unity of faith and brotherly concord. With this church we deny that we have any disagreement. Nay, rather, as we revere her as our mother, so we desire to remain in her bosom." Defined thus, the church has a real, albeit relative and circumscribed, authority since, as Calvin admits, "We cannot fly without wings."[31] While the reformers could not agree with the Council of Trent (though some recent Catholic theologians have challenged this interpretation) that Scripture and tradition were two separate and equal sources of divine revelation,

---

[30]LW 32:11-12* (WA 7:317).
[31]John C. Olin, ed., *John Calvin and Jacopo Sadoleto: A Reformation Debate* (New York: Harper Torchbooks, 1966), 61-62, 77.

they did believe in the coinherence of Scripture and tradition. This conviction shaped the way they read and interpreted the Bible.[32]

Schools of Exegesis

The reformers were passionate about biblical exegesis, but they showed little concern for hermeneutics as a separate field of inquiry. Niels Hemmingsen, a Lutheran theologian in Denmark, did write a treatise, *De methodis* (1555), in which he offered a philosophical and theological framework for the interpretation of Scripture. This was followed by the *Clavis Scripturae Sacrae* (1567) of Matthias Flacius Illyricus, which contains some fifty rules for studying the Bible drawn from Scripture itself.[33] However, hermeneutics as we know it came of age only in the Enlightenment and should not be backloaded into the Reformation. It is also true that the word *commentary* did not mean in the sixteenth century what it means for us today. Erasmus provided both annotations and paraphrases on the New Testament, the former a series of critical notes on the text but also containing points of doctrinal substance, the latter a theological overview and brief exposition. Most of Calvin's commentaries began as sermons or lectures presented in the course of his pastoral ministry. In the dedication to his 1519 study of Galatians, Luther declared that his work was "not so much a commentary as a testimony of my faith in Christ."[34] The exegetical work of the reformers was embodied in a wide variety of forms and genres, and the RCS has worked with this broader concept in setting the guidelines for this compendium.

The Protestant reformers shared in common a number of key interpretive principles such as the priority of the grammatical-historical sense of Scripture and the christological centeredness of the entire Bible, but they also developed a number of distinct approaches and schools of exegesis.[35] For the purposes of the RCS, we note the following key figures and families of interpretation in this period.

Biblical humanism. The key figure is Erasmus, whose importance is hard to exaggerate for Catholic and Protestant exegetes alike. His annotated Greek New Testament and fresh Latin translation challenged the hegemony of the Vulgate tradition and was doubtless a factor in the decision of the Council of Trent to establish the Vulgate edition as authentic and normative. Erasmus believed that the wide distribution of the Scriptures would contribute to personal spiritual renewal and the reform of society. In 1547, the English translation of Erasmus's *Paraphrases* was ordered to be placed in every parish church in England. John Colet first encouraged Erasmus

---

[32]See Timothy George, "An Evangelical Reflection on Scripture and Tradition," *Pro Ecclesia* 9 (2000): 184-207.

[33]See Kenneth G. Hagen, "'*De Exegetica Methodo*': Niels Hemmingsen's *De Methodis* (1555)," in *The Bible in the Sixteenth Century*, ed. David C. Steinmetz (Durham: Duke University Press, 1990), 181-96.

[34]LW 27:159 (WA 2:449). See Kenneth Hagen, "What Did the Term *Commentarius* Mean to Sixteenth-Century Theologians?" in *Théorie et pratique de l'exégèse*, eds. Irena Backus and Francis M. Higman (Geneva: Droz, 1990), 13-38.

[35]I follow here the sketch of Irena Backus, "Biblical Hermeneutics and Exegesis," *OER* 1:152-58. In this work, Backus confines herself to Continental developments, whereas we have noted the exegetical contribution of the English Reformation as well. For more comprehensive listings of sixteenth-century commentators, see Gerald Bray, *Biblical Interpretation* (Downers Grove, IL: InterVarsity Press, 1996), 165-212; and Richard A. Muller, "Biblical Interpretation in the Sixteenth and Seventeenth Centuries," *DMBI* 22-44.

to learn Greek, though he never took up the language himself. Colet's lectures on Paul's epistles at Oxford are reflected in his commentaries on Romans and 1 Corinthians.

Jacques Lefèvre d'Étaples has been called the "French Erasmus" because of his great learning and support for early reform movements in his native land. He published a major edition of the Psalter, as well as commentaries on the Pauline Epistles (1512), the Gospels (1522), and the General Epistles (1527). Guillaume Farel, the early reformer of Geneva, was a disciple of Lefèvre, and the young Calvin also came within his sphere of influence.

Among pre-Tridentine Catholic reformers, special attention should be given to Thomas de Vio, better known as Cajetan. He is best remembered for confronting Martin Luther on behalf of the pope in 1518, but his biblical commentaries (on nearly every book of the Bible) are virtually free of polemic. Like Erasmus, he dared to criticize the Vulgate on linguistic grounds. His commentary on Romans supported the doctrine of justification by grace applied by faith based on the "alien righteousness" of God in Christ. Jared Wicks sums up Cajetan's significance in this way: "Cajetan's combination of passion for pristine biblical meaning with his fully developed theological horizon of understanding indicates, in an intriguing manner, something of the breadth of possibilities open to Roman Catholics before a more restrictive settlement came to exercise its hold on many Catholic interpreters in the wake of the Council of Trent."[36] Girolamo Seripando, like Cajetan, was a cardinal in the Catholic Church, though he belonged to the Augustinian rather than the Dominican order. He was an outstanding classical scholar and published commentaries on Romans and Galatians. Also important is Jacopo Sadoleto, another cardinal, best known for his 1539 letter to the people of Geneva beseeching them to return to the Church of Rome, to which Calvin replied with a manifesto of his own. Sadoleto published a commentary on Romans in 1535. Bucer once commended Sadoleto's teaching on justification as approximating that of the reformers, while others saw him tilting away from the Augustinian tradition toward Pelagianism.[37]

Luther and the Wittenberg School. It was in the name of the Word of God, and specifically as a doctor of Scripture, that Luther challenged the church of his day and inaugurated the Reformation. Though Luther renounced his monastic vows, he never lost that sense of intimacy with *sacra pagina* he first acquired as a young monk. Luther provided three rules for reading the Bible: prayer, meditation, and struggle (*tentatio*). His exegetical output was enormous. In the American edition of Luther's works, thirty out of the fifty-five volumes are devoted to his biblical studies, and additional translations are planned. Many of his commentaries originated as sermons or lecture notes presented to his students at the university and to his parishioners at Wittenberg's parish church of St. Mary. Luther referred to Galatians as his bride: "The Epistle to the Galatians is my dear epistle. I have betrothed myself to it. It is my Käthe von Bora."[38] He considered his 1535 commentary on Galatians his greatest exegetical work, although his massive commentary on Genesis

---

[36]Jared Wicks, "Tommaso de Vio Cajetan (1469-1534)," *DMBI* 283-87, here 286.

[37]See the discussion by Bernard Roussel, "Martin Bucer et Jacques Sadolet: la concorde possible," *Bulletin de la Société de l'histoire de protestantisme français* (1976): 525-50, and T. H. L. Parker, *Commentaries on the Epistle to the Romans, 1532–1542* (Edinburgh: T&T Clark, 1986), 25-34.

[38]WATR 1:69 no. 146; cf. LW 54:20 no. 146. I have followed Rörer's variant on Dietrich's notes.

(eight volumes in LW), which he worked on for ten years (1535–1545), must be considered his crowning work. Luther's principles of biblical interpretation are found in his *Open Letter on Translating* and in the prefaces he wrote to all the books of the Bible.

Philipp Melanchthon was brought to Wittenberg to teach Greek in 1518 and proved to be an able associate to Luther in the reform of the church. A set of his lecture notes on Romans was published without his knowledge in 1522. This was revised and expanded many times until his large commentary of 1556. Melanchthon also commented on other New Testament books including Matthew, John, Galatians, and the Petrine epistles, as well as Proverbs, Daniel, and Ecclesiastes. Though he was well trained in the humanist disciplines, Melanchthon devoted little attention to critical and textual matters in his commentaries. Rather, he followed the primary argument of the biblical writer and gathered from this exposition a series of doctrinal topics for special consideration. This method lay behind Melanchthon's *Loci communes* (1521), the first Protestant theology textbook to be published. Another Wittenberger was Johannes Bugenhagen of Pomerania, a prolific commentator on both the Old and New Testaments. His commentary on the Psalms (1524), translated into German by Bucer, applied Luther's teaching on justification to the Psalter. He also wrote a commentary on Job and annotations on many of the books in the Bible. The Lutheran exegetical tradition was shaped by many other scholar-reformers including Andreas Osiander, Johannes Brenz, Caspar Cruciger, Erasmus Sarcerius, Georg Maior, Jacob Andreae, Nikolaus Selnecker, and Johann Gerhard.

The Strasbourg-Basel tradition. Bucer, the son of a shoemaker in Alsace, became the leader of the Reformation in Strasbourg. A former Dominican, he was early on influenced by Erasmus and continued to share his passion for Christian unity. Bucer was the most ecumenical of the Protestant reformers seeking rapprochement with Catholics on justification and an armistice between Luther and Zwingli in their strife over the Lord's Supper. Bucer also had a decisive influence on Calvin, though the latter characterized his biblical commentaries as longwinded and repetitious.[39] In his exegetical work, Bucer made ample use of patristic and medieval sources, though he criticized the abuse and overuse of allegory as "the most blatant insult to the Holy Spirit."[40] He declared that the purpose of his commentaries was "to help inexperienced brethren [perhaps like the apothecary Drilhon, who owned a French translation of Bucer's *Commentary on Matthew*] to understand each of the words and actions of Christ, and in their proper order as far as possible, and to retain an explanation of them in their natural meaning, so that they will not distort God's Word through age-old aberrations or by inept interpretation, but rather with a faithful comprehension of everything as written by the Spirit of God, they may expound to all the churches in their firm upbuilding in faith and love."[41] In addition to writing commentaries on all four Gospels, Bucer published commentaries on Judges, the Psalms, Zephaniah, Romans, and Ephesians. In the early years of the Reformation, there was a great deal of back and forth between Strasbourg and Basel, and both

---

[39]CNTC 8:3 (CO 10:404).

[40]*DMBI* 249; P. Scherding and F. Wendel, eds., "Un Traité d'exégèse pratique de Bucer," *Revue d'histoire et de philosophie religieuses* 26 (1946): 32-75, here 56.

[41]Martin Bucer, *Enarrationes perpetuae in sacra quatuor evangelia*, 2nd ed. (Strasbourg: Georg Ulrich Andlanus, 1530), 10r; quoted in D. F. Wright, "Martin Bucer," *DMBI* 290.

were centers of a lively publishing trade. Wolfgang Capito, Bucer's associate at Strasbourg, was a notable Hebraist and composed commentaries on Hosea (1529) and Habakkuk (1527).

At Basel, the great Sebastian Münster defended the use of Jewish sources in the Christian study of the Old Testament and published, in addition to his famous Hebrew grammar, an annotated version of the Gospel of Matthew translated from Greek into Hebrew. Oecolampadius, Basel's chief reformer, had been a proofreader in Froben's publishing house and worked with Erasmus on his Greek New Testament and his critical edition of Jerome. From 1523 he was both a preacher and professor of Holy Scripture at Basel. He defended Zwingli's eucharistic theology at the Colloquy of Marburg and published commentaries on 1 John (1524), Romans (1525), and Haggai–Malachi (1525). Oecolampadius was succeeded by Simon Grynaeus, a classical scholar who taught Greek and supported Bucer's efforts to bring Lutherans and Zwinglians together. More in line with Erasmus was Sebastian Castellio, who came to Basel after his expulsion from Geneva in 1545. He is best remembered for questioning the canonicity of the Song of Songs and for his annotations and French translation of the Bible.

The Zurich group. Biblical exegesis in Zurich was centered on the distinctive institution of the *Prophezei*, which began on June 19, 1525. On five days a week, at seven o'clock in the morning, all of the ministers and theological students in Zurich gathered into the choir of the Grossmünster to engage in a period of intense exegesis and interpretation of Scripture. After Zwingli had opened the meeting with prayer, the text of the day was read in Latin, Greek, and Hebrew, followed by appropriate textual or exegetical comments. One of the ministers then delivered a sermon on the passage in German that was heard by many of Zurich's citizens who stopped by the cathedral on their way to work. This institute for advanced biblical studies had an enormous influence as a model for Reformed academies and seminaries throughout Europe. It was also the seedbed for sermon series in Zurich's churches and the extensive exegetical publications of Zwingli, Leo Jud, Konrad Pellikan, Heinrich Bullinger, Oswald Myconius, and Rudolf Gwalther. Zwingli had memorized in Greek all of the Pauline epistles, and this bore fruit in his powerful expository preaching and biblical exegesis. He took seriously the role of grammar, rhetoric, and historical research in explaining the biblical text. For example, he disagreed with Bucer on the value of the Septuagint, regarding it as a trustworthy witness to a proto-Hebrew version earlier than the Masoretic text.

Zwingli's work was carried forward by his successor Bullinger, one of the most formidable scholars and networkers among the reformers. He composed commentaries on Daniel (1565), the Gospels (1542–1546), the Epistles (1537), Acts (1533), and Revelation (1557). He collaborated with Calvin to produce the *Consensus Tigurinus* (1549), a Reformed accord on the nature of the Lord's Supper, and produced a series of fifty sermons on Christian doctrine, known as *Decades*, which became required reading in Elizabethan England. As the *Antistes* ("overseer") of the Zurich church for forty-four years, Bullinger faced opposition from nascent Anabaptism on the one hand and resurgent Catholicism on the other. The need for a well-trained clergy and scholarly resources, including Scripture commentaries, arose from the fact that the Bible was "difficult or obscure to the unlearned, unskillful, unexercised, and malicious or corrupted wills." While forswearing papal claims to infallibility, Bullinger and other leaders of the magisterial Reformation saw the need for a kind of Protestant magisterium as a check against the tendency to read the Bible in "such sense as everyone shall be persuaded in himself to be most convenient."[42]

Two other commentators can be treated in connection with the Zurich group, though each of them had a wide-ranging ministry across the Reformation fronts. A former Benedictine monk, Wolfgang Musculus, embraced the Reformation in the 1520s and served briefly as the secretary to Bucer in Strasbourg. He shared Bucer's desire for Protestant unity and served for seventeen years (1531–1548) as a pastor and reformer in Augsburg. After a brief time in Zurich, where he came under the influence of Bullinger, Musculus was called to Bern, where he taught the Scriptures and published commentaries on the Psalms, the Decalogue, Genesis, Romans, Isaiah, 1 and 2 Corinthians, Galatians and Ephesians, Philippians, Colossians, 1 and 2 Thessalonians, and 1 Timothy. Drawing on his exegetical writings, Musculus also produced a compendium of Protestant theology that was translated into English in 1563 as *Commonplaces of Christian Religion*.

Peter Martyr Vermigli was a Florentine-born scholar and Augustinian friar who embraced the Reformation and fled to Switzerland in 1542. Over the next twenty years, he would gain an international reputation as a prolific scholar and leading theologian within the Reformed community. He lectured on the Old Testament at Strasbourg, was made regius professor at Oxford, corresponded with the Italian refugee church in Geneva and spent the last years of his life as professor of Hebrew at Zurich. Vermigli published commentaries on 1 Corinthians, Romans, and Judges during his lifetime. His biblical lectures on Genesis, Lamentations, 1 and 2 Samuel, and 1 and 2 Kings were published posthumously. The most influential of his writings was the *Loci communes* (*Commonplaces*), a theological compendium drawn from his exegetical writings.

The Genevan reformers. What Zwingli and Bullinger were to Zurich, Calvin and Beza were to Geneva. Calvin has been called "the father of modern biblical scholarship," and his exegetical work is without parallel in the Reformation. Because of the success of his *Institutes of the Christian Religion* Calvin has sometimes been thought of as a man of one book, but he always intended the *Institutes*, which went through eight editions in Latin and five in French during his lifetime, to serve as a guide to the study of the Bible, to show the reader "what he ought especially to seek in Scripture and to what end he ought to relate its contents." Jacob Arminius, who modified several principles of Calvin's theology, recommended his commentaries next to the Bible, for, as he said, Calvin "is incomparable in the interpretation of Scripture."[43] Drawing on his superb knowledge of Greek and Hebrew and his thorough training in humanist rhetoric, Calvin produced commentaries on all of the New Testament books except 2 and 3 John and Revelation. Calvin's Old Testament commentaries originated as sermon and lecture series and include Genesis, Psalms, Hosea, Isaiah, minor prophets, Daniel, Jeremiah and Lamentations, a harmony of the last four books of Moses,

---

[42]Euan Cameron, *The European Reformation* (Oxford: Oxford University Press, 1991), 120.

[43]Letter to Sebastian Egbert (May 3, 1607), in *Praestantium ac eruditorum virorum epistolae ecclesiasticae et theologicae varii argumenti*, ed. Christiaan Hartsoeker (Amsterdam: Henricus Dendrinus, 1660), 236-37. Quoted in A. M. Hunter, *The Teaching of Calvin* (London: James Clarke, 1950), 20.

Ezekiel 1–20, and Joshua. Calvin sought for brevity and clarity in all of his exegetical work. He emphasized the illumination of the Holy Spirit as essential to a proper understanding of the text. Calvin underscored the continuity between the two Testaments (one covenant in two dispensations) and sought to apply the plain or natural sense of the text to the church of his day. In the preface to his own influential commentary on Romans, Karl Barth described how Calvin worked to recover the mind of Paul and make the apostle's message relevant to his day:

> How energetically Calvin goes to work, first scientifically establishing the text ("what stands there?"), then following along the footsteps of its thought; that is to say, he conducts a discussion with it until the wall between the first and the sixteenth centuries becomes transparent, and until there in the first century Paul speaks and here the man of the sixteenth century hears, until indeed the conversation between document and reader becomes concentrated upon the substance (which must be the same now as then).[44]

Beza was elected moderator of Geneva's Company of Pastors after Calvin's death in 1564 and guided the Genevan Reformation over the next four decades. His annotated Latin translation of the Greek New Testament (1556) and his further revisions of the Greek text established his reputation as the leading textual critic of the sixteenth century after Erasmus. Beza completed the translation of Marot's metrical Psalter, which became a centerpiece of Huguenot piety and Reformed church life. Though known for his polemical writings on grace, free will, and predestination, Beza's work is marked by a strong pastoral orientation and concern for a Scripture-based spirituality.

Robert Estienne (Stephanus) was a printer-scholar who had served the royal household in Paris. After his conversion to Protestantism, in 1550 he moved to Geneva, where he published a series of notable editions and translations of the Bible. He also produced sermons and commentaries on Job, Ecclesiastes, the Song of Songs, Romans and Hebrews, as well as dictionaries, concordances, and a thesaurus of biblical terms. He also published the first editions of the Bible with chapters divided into verses, an innovation that quickly became universally accepted.

The British Reformation. Commentary writing in England and Scotland lagged behind the continental Reformation for several reasons. In 1500, there were only three publishing houses in England compared with more than two hundred on the Continent. A 1408 statute against publishing or reading the Bible in English, stemming from the days of Lollardy, stifled the free flow of ideas, as was seen in the fate of Tyndale. Moreover, the nature of the English Reformation from Henry through Elizabeth provided little stability for the flourishing of biblical scholarship. In the sixteenth century, many "hot-gospel" Protestants in England were edified by the English translations of commentaries and theological writings by the Continental reformers. The influence of Calvin and Beza was felt especially in the Geneva Bible with its "Protestant glosses" of theological notes and references.

During the later Elizabethan and Stuart church, however, the indigenous English commentary came into its own. Both Anglicans and Puritans contributed to this outpouring of biblical studies.

---

[44]Karl Barth, *Die Römerbrief* (Zurich: TVZ, 1940), II, translated by T. H. L. Parker as the epigraph to *Calvin's New Testament Commentaries*, 2nd ed. (Louisville, KY: Westminster John Knox, 1993).

The sermons of Lancelot Andrewes and John Donne are replete with exegetical insights based on a close study of the Greek and Hebrew texts. Among the Reformed authors in England, none was more influential than William Perkins, the greatest of the early Puritan theologians, who published commentaries on Galatians, Jude, Revelation, and the Sermon on the Mount (Mt 5–7). John Cotton, one of his students, wrote commentaries on the Song of Songs, Ecclesiastes, and Revelation before departing for New England in 1633. The separatist pastor Henry Ainsworth was an outstanding scholar of Hebrew and wrote major commentaries on the Pentateuch, the Psalms, and the Song of Songs. In Scotland, Robert Rollock, the first principal of Edinburgh University (1585), wrote numerous commentaries including those on the Psalms, Ephesians, Daniel, Romans, 1 and 2 Thessalonians, John, Colossians, and Hebrews. Joseph Mede and Thomas Brightman were leading authorities on Revelation and contributed to the apocalyptic thought of the seventeenth century. Mention should also be made of Archbishop James Ussher, whose *Annals of the Old Testament* was published in 1650. Ussher developed a keen interest in biblical chronology and calculated that the creation of the world had taken place on October 26, 4004 B.C. As late as 1945, the Scofield Reference Bible still retained this date next to Genesis 1:1, but later editions omitted it because of the lack of evidence on which to fix such dates.[45]

Anabaptism. Irena Backus has noted that there was no school of "dissident" exegesis during the Reformation, and the reasons are not hard to find. The radical Reformation was an ill-defined movement that existed on the margins of official church life in the sixteenth century. The denial of infant baptism and the refusal to swear an oath marked radicals as a seditious element in society, and they were persecuted by Protestants and Catholics alike. However, in the RCS we have made an attempt to include some voices of the radical Reformation, especially among the Anabaptists. While the Anabaptists published few commentaries in the sixteenth century, they were avid readers and quoters of the Bible. Numerous exegetical gems can be found in their letters, treatises, martyr acts (especially *The Martyrs' Mirror*), hymns, and histories. They placed a strong emphasis on the memorizing of Scripture and quoted liberally from vernacular translations of the Bible. George H. Williams has noted that "many an Anabaptist theological tract was really a beautiful mosaic of Scripture texts."[46] In general, most Anabaptists accepted the apocryphal books as canonical, contrasted outer word and inner spirit with relative degrees of strictness and saw the New Testament as normative for church life and social ethics (witness their pacifism, nonswearing, emphasis on believers' baptism and congregational discipline).

We have noted the Old Testament translation of Ludwig Hätzer, who became an antitrinitarian, and Hans Denck that they published at Worms in 1527. Denck also wrote a notable commentary on Micah. Conrad Grebel belonged to a Greek reading circle in Zurich and came to his Anabaptist convictions while poring over the text of Erasmus's New Testament. The only Anabaptist leader with university credentials was Balthasar Hubmaier, who was made a doctor of theology (Ingolstadt, 1512) in the same year as Luther. His reflections on the Bible are found in his numerous

---

[45]*The New Scofield Reference Bible* (New York: Oxford University Press, 1967), vi.
[46]George H. Williams, *The Radical Reformation*, 3rd ed. (Kirksville, MO: Sixteenth Century Journal Publishers, 1992), 1247.

writings, which include the first catechism of the Reformation (1526), a two-part treatise on the freedom of the will and a major work (*On the Sword*) setting forth positive attitudes toward the role of government and the Christian's place in society. Melchior Hoffman was an apocalyptic seer who wrote commentaries on Romans, Revelation, and Daniel 12. He predicted that Christ would return in 1533. More temperate was Pilgram Marpeck, a mining engineer who embraced Anabaptism and traveled widely throughout Switzerland and south Germany, from Strasbourg to Augsburg. His "Admonition of 1542" is the longest published defense of Anabaptist views on baptism and the Lord's Supper. He also wrote many letters that functioned as theological tracts for the congregations he had founded dealing with topics such as the fruits of repentance, the lowliness of Christ, and the unity of the church. Menno Simons, a former Catholic priest, became the most outstanding leader of the Dutch Anabaptist movement. His masterpiece was the *Foundation of Christian Doctrine* published in 1540. His other writings include *Meditation on the Twenty-fifth Psalm* (1537); *A Personal Exegesis of Psalm Twenty-five* modeled on the style of Augustine's *Confessions*; *Confession of the Triune God* (1550), directed against Adam Pastor, a former disciple of Menno who came to doubt the divinity of Christ; *Meditations and Prayers for Mealtime* (1557); and the *Cross of the Saints* (1554), an exhortation to faithfulness in the face of persecution. Like many other Anabaptists, Menno emphasized the centrality of discipleship (*Nachfolge*) as a deliberate repudiation of the old life and a radical commitment to follow Jesus as Lord.

Reading Scripture with the Reformers

In 1947, Gerhard Ebeling set forth his thesis that the history of the Christian church is the history of the interpretation of Scripture. Since that time, the place of the Bible in the story of the church has been investigated from many angles. A better understanding of the history of exegesis has been aided by new critical editions and scholarly discussions of the primary sources. The *Cambridge History of the Bible*, published in three volumes (1963–1970), remains a standard reference work in the field. The ACCS built on, and itself contributed to, the recovery of patristic biblical wisdom of both East and West. Beryl Smalley's *The Study of the Bible in the Middle Ages* (1940) and Henri de Lubac's *Medieval Exegesis: The Four Senses of Scripture* (1959) are essential reading for understanding the monastic and scholastic settings of commentary work between Augustine and Luther. The Reformation took place during what has been called "le grand siècle de la Bible."[47] Aided by the tools of Renaissance humanism and the dynamic impetus of Reformation theology (including permutations and reactions against it), the sixteenth century produced an unprecedented number of commentaries on every book in the Bible. Drawing from this vast storehouse of exegetical treasures, the RCS allows us to read Scripture along with the reformers. In doing so, it serves as a practical homiletic and devotional guide to some of the greatest masters of biblical interpretation in the history of the church.

The RCS gladly acknowledges its affinity with and dependence on recent scholarly investigations of Reformation-era exegesis. Between 1976 and 1990, three international colloquia on the

---

[47]J.-R. Aarmogathe, ed., *Bible de tous les temps*, 8 vols.; vol. 6, *Le grand siècle de la Bible* (Paris: Beauchesne, 1989).

history of biblical exegesis in the sixteenth century took place in Geneva and in Durham, North Carolina.[48] Among those participating in these three gatherings were a number of scholars who have produced groundbreaking works in the study of biblical interpretation in the Reformation. These include Elsie McKee, Irena Backus, Kenneth Hagen, Scott H. Hendrix, Richard A. Muller, Guy Bedouelle, Gerald Hobbs, John B. Payne, Bernard Roussel, Pierre Fraenkel, and David C. Steinmetz (1936–2015). Among other scholars whose works are indispensible for the study of this field are Heinrich Bornkamm, Jaroslav Pelikan, Heiko A. Oberman, James S. Preus, T. H. L. Parker, David F. Wright, Tony Lane, John L. Thompson, Frank A. James, and Timothy J. Wengert.[49] Among these scholars no one has had a greater influence on the study of Reformation exegesis than David C. Steinmetz. A student of Oberman, he emphasized the importance of understanding the Reformation in medieval perspective. In addition to important studies on Luther and Staupitz, he pioneered the method of comparative exegesis showing both continuity and discontinuity between major Reformation figures and the preceding exegetical traditions (see his *Luther in Context* and *Calvin in Context*). From his base at Duke University, he spawned what might be called a Steinmetz school, a cadre of students and scholars whose work on the Bible in the Reformation era continues to shape the field. Steinmetz served on the RCS Board of Editorial Advisors, and a number of our volume editors pursued doctoral studies under his supervision.

In 1980, Steinmetz published "The Superiority of Pre-critical Exegesis," a seminal essay that not only placed Reformation exegesis in the context of the preceding fifteen centuries of the church's study of the Bible but also challenged certain assumptions underlying the hegemony of historical-critical exegesis of the post-Enlightenment academy.[50] Steinmetz helps us to approach the reformers and other precritical interpreters of the Bible on their own terms as faithful witnesses to the church's apostolic tradition. For them, a specific book or pericope had to be understood within the scope of the consensus of the canon. Thus the reformers, no less than the Fathers and the schoolmen, interpreted the hymn of the Johannine prologue about the preexistent Christ in consonance with the creation narrative of Genesis 1. In the same way, Psalm 22, Isaiah 53, and Daniel 7 are seen as part of an overarching storyline that finds ultimate fulfillment in Jesus Christ. Reading the Bible with the resources of the new learning, the reformers challenged the exegetical conclusions of their medieval predecessors at many points. However, unlike Alexander Campbell in the nineteenth century, their aim was not to "open the New Testament as if mortal man had never seen

---

[48]Olivier Fatio and Pierre Fraenkel, eds., *Histoire de l'exégèse au XVIe siècle: texts du colloque international tenu à Genève en 1976* (Geneva: Droz, 1978); David C. Steinmetz, ed., *The Bible in the Sixteenth Century* [Second International Colloquy on the History of Biblical Exegesis in the Sixteenth Century] (Durham: Duke University Press, 1990); Irena Backus and Francis M. Higman, eds., *Théorie et pratique de l'exégèse. Actes du troisième colloque international sur l'histoire de l'exégèse biblique au XVIe siècle, Genève, 31 août–2 septembre 1988* (Geneva: Droz, 1990); see also Guy Bedouelle and Bernard Roussel, eds., *Bible de tous les temps*, 8 vols.; vol. 5, *Le temps des Réformes et la Bible* (Paris: Beauchesne, 1989).

[49]For bibliographical references and evaluation of these and other contributors to the scholarly study of Reformation-era exegesis, see Richard A. Muller, "Biblical Interpretation in the Era of the Reformation: The View From the Middle Ages," in *Biblical Interpretation in the Era of the Reformation: Essays Presented to David C. Steinmetz in Honor of His Sixtieth Birthday*, ed. Richard A. Muller and John L. Thompson (Grand Rapids: Eerdmans, 1996), 3-22.

[50]David C. Steinmetz, "The Superiority of Pre-Critical Exegesis," *Theology Today* 37 (1980): 27-38.

it before."[51] Rather, they wanted to do their biblical work as part of an interpretive conversation within the family of the people of God. In the reformers' emphatic turn to the literal sense, which prompted their many blasts against the unrestrained use of allegory, their work was an extension of a similar impulse made by Thomas Aquinas and Nicholas of Lyra.

This is not to discount the radically new insights gained by the reformers in their dynamic engagement with the text of Scripture; nor should we dismiss in a reactionary way the light shed on the meaning of the Bible by the scholarly accomplishments of the past two centuries. However, it is to acknowledge that the church's exegetical tradition is an indispensable aid for the proper interpretation of Scripture. And this means, as Richard Muller has said, that "while it is often appropriate to recognize that traditionary readings of the text are erroneous on the grounds offered by the historical-critical method, we ought also to recognize that the conclusions offered by historical-critical exegesis may themselves be quite erroneous on the grounds provided by the exegesis of the patristic, medieval, and reformation periods."[52] The RCS wishes to commend the exegetical work of the Reformation era as a program of retrieval for the sake of renewal—spiritual réssourcement for believers committed to the life of faith today.

George Herbert was an English pastor and poet who reaped the benefits of the renewal of biblical studies in the age of the Reformation. He referred to the Scriptures as a book of infinite sweetness, "a mass of strange delights," a book with secrets to make the life of anyone good. In describing the various means pastors require to be fully furnished in the work of their calling, Herbert provided a rationale for the history of exegesis and for the Reformation Commentary on Scripture:

> The fourth means are commenters and Fathers, who have handled the places controverted, which the parson by no means refuseth. As he doth not so study others as to neglect the grace of God in himself and what the Holy Spirit teacheth him, so doth he assure himself that God in all ages hath had his servants to whom he hath revealed his Truth, as well as to him; and that as one country doth not bear all things that there may be a commerce, so neither hath God opened or will open all to one, that there may be a traffic in knowledge between the servants of God for the planting both of love and humility. Wherefore he hath one comment[ary] at least upon every book of Scripture, and ploughing with this, and his own meditations, he enters into the secrets of God treasured in the holy Scripture.[53]

Timothy George
General Editor

---

[51]Alexander Campbell, *Memoirs of Alexander Campbell*, ed. Robert Richardson (Cincinnati: Standard Publishing Company, 1872), 97.

[52]Richard A. Muller and John L. Thompson, "The Significance of Precritical Exegesis: Retrospect and Prospect," in *Biblical Interpretation in the Era of the Reformation: Essays Presented to David C. Steinmetz in Honor of His Sixtieth Birthday*, ed. Richard A. Muller and John L. Thompson (Grand Rapids: Eerdmans, 1996), 342.

[53]George Herbert, *The Complete English Poems* (London: Penguin, 1991), 205.

INTRODUCTION TO
JEREMIAH AND LAMENTATIONS

We can see him still, this Jeremiah the prophet. He first appeared to the public in October 1512, five years before Martin Luther posted his Ninety-Five Theses—the traditional date marking the Reformation's beginning. Up near the northwest corner he sits, on the ceiling of the Sistine Chapel in Rome. Despite his aged visage, his head of untamed hair and beard, Jeremiah's bodily presence is broad, even powerful. Yet he seems spent with exhaustion. He is hunched over—perhaps taxed with grief, weary of fruitless labor, or mired in shadowy thought. Jeremiah's torso tilts to the right, straining with weighted head and balancing on the elbow pressing his right, cloaked thigh. His right index finger and thumb cradle his cheek bones just below the nose and above the mouth, as if he silences breath, as if Jeremiah has no more to say or perhaps too much—more than he would like, more than he can bear. His lifeless left arm rests on his thigh; he idly fingers the fabric in his lap.

On the floor to his right a scroll rests, fallen and rumpled from his hand; we can see the *aleph*, the first letter of the Hebrew alphabet. This is Jeremiah's book of Lamentations, completed while grieving; or perhaps his book only begun; a first chapter scrawled just before his inertia and sorrow descend. At this moment he might be pondering another staggering prophecy or swallowing back mournful verse that simply must soon burst forth. Meanwhile, above Jeremiah's bowed, oblivious head—on the ceilinged canvas of the chapel—the Almighty creates; and separates light from darkness.

Renaissance artists would recognize the prophet's seated pose: Jeremiah in the grip of melancholy—the condition of paralysis and possibility, immobilized by sadness and uncertainty, falling into temptation or despair; but maybe—just maybe—on the edge of illumination, revelation, or creative ecstasy. Melancholy is to be desired; she is the mother of genius.[1] Artists might recognize this Sistine Jeremiah as the man himself—Michelangelo (1475–1564)—the prophet as self-portrait of the artist. Jeremiah's boots belong to a sculptor. Michelangelo himself was prone to melancholy. In his *School of Athens*, Raphael (1483–1520) painted a younger Michelangelo settled in Jeremiah's Sistine pose—front and slightly off center—lost in his thoughts and aloof from the conversing of gathered philosophers around him.[2]

---

[1]See Reuben Sánchez, *Typology and Iconography in Donne, Herbert, and Milton: Fashioning the Self After Jeremiah* (New York: Palgrave MacMillan, 2014), 1-14, 137-46, 217-19; Maria Ruvoldt, *The Italian Renaissance: Metaphors of Sex, Sleep, and Dreams* (Cambridge: Cambridge University Press, 2004), 54-60, 141-56.
[2]Rona Goffen, *Renaissance Rivals: Michelangelo, Leonardo, Raphael, Titian* (New Haven, CT: Yale University Press, 2002), 215-25.

For most of the sixteenth and seventeenth centuries, however, Jeremiah would be known and envisioned through text. Commentaries, lectures, sermons, treatises, and letters would unfold Jeremiah's prophecies, actions, and laments, often chapter by chapter and verse by verse. The melancholic prophet would invigorate radicals, consume biblical scholars, inspire preachers, and console the mourning. Through Jeremiah and his interpreters, the interplay of two reform movements opens before us—the tragic aftermath of King Josiah's reformation (2 Kings 23; 2 Chron 34–35) and the unfolding of Europe's Reformation over two thousand years later.

Although Michelangelo may have brushed his self-portrait in the guise of *the* melancholic prophet, for the most part Jeremiah did not attract extensive attention in the first few years of the early modern Reformation—especially among biblical scholars. To be sure, a particular passage might inform and buttress an argument. For example, in September of 1520 Martin Luther cited the fifty-first chapter of Jeremiah in personal support for Pope Leo X (1475–1521, r. 1513–1521), while claiming at the same time that the Roman curia was worse off than any Babylon or Sodom.[3] Not surprisingly the New Testament Gospels and Epistles of Paul were of ultimate concern for early Protestants, and books such as the Psalms in the Old Testament received primary attention. Nearly fourteen years would pass after 1517 before Protestants produced their first scholarly works on Jeremiah. In the meantime, the prophet did not disappear. Jeremiah would have an immediate impact on church and society even in the early 1520s.

Today the landscape of research on Jeremiah—his prophecies and lamentations in the Reformation era—is at best vaguely mapped terrain.[4] Yet an inquisitive traveler can plot a preliminary course through the sixteenth and early seventeenth centuries using key events and documents. Many general narratives of the Reformation tend to follow a relatively tidy path, beginning first with the Lutheran and Reformed traditions and then turning to a selected progression of Anabaptists, Anglicans, and Roman Catholic Reformers. But surveying the impact of Jeremiah—and the sixteenth-century literature expounding and applying his life, prophecies, and laments—suggests a dramatically different starting point.[5]

Jeremiah in the Reformation Era

Jeremiah in the Radical Reformation and Anabaptist traditions. The prophet Jeremiah does come into view quite early and vividly among a few authors and leaders grouped together in the unwieldly category of "radical reformers." Because Jeremiah's prophecies rained down condemnation on the ancient Judean priesthood and monarchy—and because he ministered in an era of catastrophic siege, destruction, and defeat—it made sense to the first Protestants attentive to

---

[3]LW 31:336-37 (WA 7:44); citing Jer 51:9.

[4]There is no broad survey on the interpretation of Jeremiah in Christian history comparable to Brevard S. Childs's *The Struggle to Understand Isaiah as Christian Scripture* (Grand Rapids: Eerdmans, 2004).

[5]This introduction takes on the voice of sixteenth- and seventeenth-century authors, who assumed Jeremiah's authorship of both Jeremiah and Lamentations and the historicity of accounts found in both books; for modern explorations of the historical accuracy of Jeremiah, see Jack R. Lundbom, *The Early Career of the Prophet Jeremiah* (Eugene, OR: Wipf and Stock, 2012), and John Brian Job, *Jeremiah's Kings: A Study of the Monarchy in Jeremiah* (Aldershot: Ashgate, 2006), esp. 1-14, 171-201.

Jeremiah that his prophecies also portended cataclysmic change and complete transformation in their time. With a few exceptions, this wing of the Reformation—a wing Lutheran, Reformed, and Roman Catholic believers came to despise—found in Jeremiah's proclamations both telling signs of the last days and evidence of the sort of genuine and unbending faith required when facing fierce resistance from a depraved church and corrupt kingdom. Thomas Müntzer (c. 1489–1525) was among the earliest and short-lived of the so-called radical reformers. In sharp contrast to a Roman Catholic priesthood Müntzer deemed corrupt and a "bookish" Christianity he came to despise in Luther's Wittenberg, Müntzer discovered in Jeremiah's prophecies what he believed to be firm evidence that the true believer could hear the living voice of God and sense acutely the Spirit of Christ within. Readiness to face suffering and persecution, as Jeremiah had done, was further proof of authentic faith.[6] A true preacher would display what Müntzer called "a consuming and truly earnest zeal to root out, tear down and scatter the counterfeit Christians and destroy every scrap of wicked faith."[7]

A decade after Müntzer's capture and beheading, and after the wider German Peasants' Revolt (1524–1525) to which he contributed, another dramatic development unfolded within a different sect of radical reformers. In northwest Germany, Anabaptists seized control of the city of Münster, demanded that all residents be rebaptized, and crowned John of Leiden as their Davidic king. The Old Testament prophets provided ample inspiration to this short-lived kingdom in 1534–1535.[8] Anticipating an imminent last judgment and eager to join this new Jerusalem in Münster, three thousand Dutch Anabaptists—men, women, and children—departed their homes in March of 1534. They looked to the prophet Jeremiah, who they believed would appear to guide them to the new Zion that he had anticipated in Jeremiah 51:6.[9]

Before and after Müntzer and Münster, however, the vast majority of radical reformers, and Anabaptists in particular, rejected reform promoted at the point of a sword.[10] Yet the writings of Jeremiah still attracted their sustained attention. In fact, the earliest recorded Anabaptist sermon (c. 1527), traditionally attributed to Eitelhans Langenmantel (d. 1528), expounds on Jeremiah 7:3-4. Among the earliest radical reformers, Andreas Bodenstein von Karlstadt (1486–1541) turned to Jeremiah as a true and tested guide to Christian ministry and spirituality. Some of his most striking citations of Jeremiah occur in writings he penned and published during his first years after departing Wittenberg following his falling out with Luther in 1522. Free of his academic standing and his official status as an ordained cleric, Karlstadt found sustenance and guidance

---

[6]*The Collected Works of Thomas Müntzer*, ed. and trans. Peter Matheson (Edinburgh: T&T Clark, 1988), 44, 235-36, 357-58, 366, 374.

[7]Ibid., 218; citing Jer 1:6, 9-10. Müntzer was particularly indebted to the late medieval commentary of Pseudo-Joachim on Jeremiah; see below lvii-lviii, and see George Hunston Williams, *The Radical Reformation*, 3rd ed., SCES 15 (Kirksville, MO: Sixteenth Century Journal, 1992), 129n32.

[8]Henning Graf von Reventlow, *History of Biblical Interpretation*, vol. 3, *Renaissance, Reformation, Humanism*, trans. James O'Duke (Atlanta: Society of Biblical Literature, 2010), 176-86, esp. 183-84.

[9]Cornelius Krahn, *Dutch Anabaptism: Origin, Spread, Life and Thought (1450–1600)* (The Hague: Martinus Nijhoff, 1968), 145-47.

[10]See, e.g., "The Schleitheim Articles," in *The Radical Reformation*, ed. Michael G. Baylor (New York: Cambridge University Press, 1991), 176-77; Balthasar Hubmaier, "On the Sword," CRR 5:492-523; and James M. Stayer, *Anabaptism and the Sword* (Lawrence, KS: Coronado Press, 1972).

in Jeremiah as he initially pastored a country church, wrote to and sought contact with other like-minded radical reformers, and embraced life as a layman among the people. In response to Jeremiah's initial hesitation when confronted with God's calling (Jer 1:6) and thereafter Jeremiah's subsequent and strident voice in prophecy, Karlstadt likewise justified his period of quietude and then his sudden appearance in print in 1523.[11] Moreover, he pondered his former life as scholar of Scripture—reminiscing about his academic and pastoral work, including his lectures on Jeremiah given at Wittenberg in 1522.[12] Karlstadt relates in his treatise "The Meaning of the Term *Gelassen* and Where in Scripture It Is Found":

> I fancied myself a Christian when I picked profound and beautiful sayings out of Jeremiah's writings, for a disputation, lecture, or sermon, or for other speeches and writings, and I thought that this ought to please God extremely well. But when I began to think and reflect properly, I discovered that I had neither come to know God nor to love the highest good as a good. I saw that the created letter was what I had come to know and love; in that I rested.[13]

In contrast, Karlstadt now sought a life in imitation of Jeremiah's submission to God: a life shorn of creaturely attractions, blessed with circumcised ears to hear the divine voice, and a heart bound to God alone.[14]

One additional example must suffice here to draw the connections between Jeremiah and the Radical Reformation. Fourteen years after Karlstadt's departure from Wittenberg and a year after the Anabaptist community in Münster was besieged and obliterated, Menno Simons (c. 1496–1561)—a Frisian pastor in his thirties—came forward to lead these surviving Anabaptists. After his baptism Simons found himself a wanted man; he spent the rest of his life moving among Anabaptist communities in the Netherlands and northern Germany, while providing guidance in his many letters, confessions, and treatises.[15] In Jeremiah's prophecies Menno found perceptive warnings about the world and its false remedies, the deceptive words of false prophets, and the emptiness of outward ceremony.[16] In the life, suffering, and faithful ministry of Jeremiah, Menno discovered a welcome affirmation of his own sacrifices and vivid confirmation of his calling to rebuke the unfaithful.

> These his predictions, faithful warnings, visions, and rebukes out of the mouth of the Lord became to [Jeremiah] as sharp piercing thorns. Men cast aside his word and his admonitions and would have nothing of them. The pious prophet and true servant of God they made out to be a faithless traitor, a rebel, and a heretic. The Word of the Lord was the occasion of daily mockery. He was often apprehended and beaten and thrown into vile and evil-smelling pits. They plotted his death.

---

[11]See "Reasons Why Andreas Carlstadt Remained Silent for a Time," CRR 8:169-284, esp. 175.

[12]These lectures were delivered just prior to his departure from the university; Volker Gummelt, "Bugenhagens Handschrift von Karlstadts Jeremiavorlesung aus dem Jahre 1522," *ARG* 86 (1995): 56-66.

[13]Karlstadt, CRR 8:140. See p. 18 in this volume.

[14]Ibid., 144-47.

[15]See G. Waite, "Menno Simons," in *OER* 3:55-56.

[16]*The Complete Writings of Menno Simons, c. 1496–1561*, trans. Leonard Verduin, ed. John C. Wegner (Scottdale, PA: Herald Press, 1956), 157, 161, 237, 370.

He was so pressed and weighed down with the cross that he at one time resolved in his heart to preach no more in the name of the Lord. Yes, he cursed the day of his birth and the man who brought the message to his father that a man-child was born to him. In this way the worthy man of God had to bear the heavy bag of sand for many years for the sake of the Word and the truth of the Lord. He had to give his ear to all who reproach, and his back to all who strike, until the waters of affliction rose in the mouths of the haughty, rebellious, and unbelieving people, and they saw, alas too late, that Jeremiah was God's true messenger and a true prophet.[17]

For the most part sixteenth-century Anabaptists, like Menno Simons, emphasized the Gospels and Epistles of the New Testament. The life and teachings of Jesus and the apostles trumped the commands and rituals of the Old Testament when discerning Christian belief and practice.[18] Yet the example of the ancient prophets proved likewise compelling for the Radical Reformation, as Brad Gregory points out:

If God had revealed himself through his prophets in ancient Israel, why could he not do so also in contemporary Germany? Those versed in scripture knew that God, speaking through the prophet Joel, had said: "I will pour out my spirit on all flesh; your sons and daughters shall prophesy, your old men shall dream dreams and your young men shall see visions" (Joel 2:28), a verse that Peter had repeated among those gathered in Jerusalem at Pentecost (Acts 2:17). This, Peter said, would happen "in the last days," the era in which so many Christians of the early Reformation thought they were living.[19]

Indeed, Anabaptist leaders such as Hans Denck, Conrad Grebel, David Joris, Dirk Philips, Pilgram Marpeck, and Peter Riedemann cite Jeremiah's prophecy of the "new covenant"—that great hinge of Christian Scripture—anchored in the Old Testament by Jeremiah 31:31-34 and in the New Testament by Hebrews 8. Additionally, the experience of such sixteenth-century Anabaptists—ancestors of the modern Mennonites and Amish—mirrored the life of Jeremiah in his isolation, suffering, and imprisonment. His faithfulness to a message scorned equally by temple priests and unrepentant rulers seemed all too familiar. Meanwhile, they believed that Jeremiah's proclamation of a new age—when God would "write his law upon the very hearts of believers" (Jer 31:33)—was being fulfilled in scattered Anabaptist communities across Europe.

There is a great deal more we would like to know about those we categorize as "radical reformers" and their interpretations of Jeremiah. But few of their leaders were trained academics apt or able to produce biblical commentaries, theological treatises, and sermon collections;[20] and many

---

[17]Ibid., 591; citing Jer 38:1-13; 20:9, 14-15. See pp. 4-5 in this volume.

[18]See Stuart Murray, "Biblical Interpretation Among the Anabaptists Reformers," in *A History of Biblical Interpretation*, vol. 2, *The Medieval Through the Reformation Periods*, ed. Alan J. Hauser and Duane F. Watson (Grand Rapids: Eerdmans, 2009), 412-14.

[19]Brad S. Gregory, "The Radical Reformation," in *The Oxford Illustrated History of the Reformation*, ed. Peter Marshall (Oxford: Oxford University Press, 2015), 132-33.

[20]Karlstadt is an obvious exception as a professor early in his life at the University of Wittenberg and later at the University of Basel. Balthasar Hubmaier held a doctorate in theology from the University of Ingolstadt; Hans Denck, along with Ludwig Hetzer, produced a German translation of the Hebrew Prophets in 1527; see Timothy George, *Reading Scripture with the Reformers* (Downers Grove, IL: IVP Academic, 2011), 205-6. Though not a formal scholar, Menno Simons produced numerous writings, which survive to this day; the English translation of his work, *The Complete Writings of Menno Simons*, runs to over one thousand pages.

of them—even if they aspired to do so—were battered by persecution, harried in flight, and silenced by drowning, burning, or beheading.[21] Preserving handwritten copies of their works and finding a publisher must have been daunting tasks. Even as the Radical Reformation may lay claim to the earliest appropriation of the example and spirit of Jeremiah, the labor of interpreting his book, chapter by chapter and verse by verse, fell to others—the Lutherans, Reformed, and Roman Catholics, who dominate this Reformation commentary on Scripture. These scholars often lectured, wrote, and published long tomes in the employ of universities and academies. City-states, territories, and kingdoms sheltered the pulpits in which they preached. Their "official Christianity" allowed the study of Jeremiah to flourish, though the Anabaptists came to know the contours of the prophet's life in distinctive ways as well.

Jeremiah in the Lutheran tradition. Although Martin Luther (1483–1546) translated the Bible into German and lectured on the Scriptures throughout his university career, his contributions to the study of Jeremiah would be of surprisingly limited importance. To be sure, Luther published a preface to the prophet Jeremiah, but did so along with similar prefaces to other books of the Bible and even the books of the Apocrypha.[22] Though Luther lectured on the Old Testament from 1513 to 1515, 1517 to 1530, and 1535 to 1545—and focused, in particular, on the Minor Prophets and Isaiah from 1524 to 1530—he never once offered a course on Jeremiah or penned a major work devoted to the prophet. Perhaps by 1530 Luther had grown weary of the Hebrew prophets in general. Several years before he would finally publish a German edition of all the prophetic books in 1532, Luther and his translation team seemed spent with the effort.

> We are sweating over the work of putting the Prophets into German. God, how much of it there is, and how hard it is to make these Hebrew writers talk German! They resist us, and do not want to leave their Hebrew and imitate our German barbarisms. It is like making a nightingale leave her own sweet song and imitate the monotonous voice of a cuckoo.[23]

Indeed, in his brief preface to Jeremiah, Luther began: "Few comments are needed for an understanding of Jeremiah, if one will only pay attention to the events that took place under the kings in whose time he preached."[24] Likewise, Luther seldom seemed to make Jeremiah the focus of his preaching. His two sermons on Jeremiah 23:5-8 are the exception, which he delivered on the 18th and 25th of November 1526 and subsequently published to wide distribution.[25]

---

[21]Brad Gregory estimates that five hundred German-speaking Anabaptists alone were executed between 1527 and 1530, constituting 60 percent of the German-speaking Anabaptists killed between 1525 and 1618; see "The Radical Reformation," 131. Accounts of Anabaptist martyrdom may be found amid a great narrative of Christian martyrdom in history in Thieleman J. van Braght, ed., *The Bloody Theater, or Martyrs' Mirror of the Defenseless Christians*, trans. Joseph F. Sohm (1886; repr., Scottdale, PA: Herald Press, 1938).

[22]Luther completed his translation of the Old Testament Prophets in 1532; his "Preface to the Prophet Jeremiah" appeared in 1532 and 1545; LW 35:279-83 (WA DB 11.1:190-95).

[23]Cited in E. Theodore Bachmann's introduction to Luther's Prefaces in LW 35:229.

[24]LW 35:279 (WA DB 11.1:190, 191).

[25]WA 20:547-80; Luther's sermons were first printed in Wittenberg under the title *Ein Epistel auß dem Propheten Jeremia, von Christus reych, und christlicher freyheit gepredigt* (Wittenberg: Hans Weiß, 1527). An English translation was printed in London with the title *A fruteful and godly exposition and delcaracion of the kyngdom of Christ and of the christen lybertye, made upon the words of the prophete Jeremye . . .* (London: Gwalter Lynne, 1548).

Yet, despite Luther's seeming oversight, a fresh look at his lectures on the Hebrew Prophets might yield a different conclusion. Luther cites Jeremiah and Lamentations fifty-three times in his lectures on Isaiah and ninety-two times in his lectures on the Minor Prophets. And Luther occasionally adds significant commentary to some of the Jeremiah passages to which he refers. In other words, Jeremiah was a vital part of Luther's work on the Old Testament in the latter half of the 1520s, not only as an essential part of the translation project Luther completed and the sequence of prefaces he wrote, but also in the lectures he delivered on prophetic Scripture.

What did Philipp Melanchthon (1497–1560), Luther's esteemed younger colleague, contribute on Jeremiah? Melanchthon came to the University of Wittenberg to teach Greek and thereby produced commentaries and annotations on the Gospels and the Pauline Epistles. But the Old Testament also received his scholarly attention. In addition to works on Genesis, Exodus, Psalms, Ecclesiastes, and Daniel, Melanchthon was particularly consumed with Proverbs and penned three commentaries on this book of wisdom.[26] But in the end, like Luther, his one dedicated contribution to the study of Jeremiah would be a concise treatise for readers in their study of the prophet and his writings.[27] Melanchthon's introductory treatise connects the message and times of Jeremiah to the difficult circumstances facing the German church in the late 1540s after Martin Luther's death and allows for comparison with Luther's earlier "Preface to the Prophet Jeremiah," first published in 1532.[28]

Given the fact that the theological curriculum at Wittenberg stipulated a regular cycle of lectures on Romans, John, the Psalms, Genesis, and Isaiah, one might excuse Luther and Melanchthon's relative neglect of Jeremiah.[29] But ten years after Karlstadt's 1522 lectures on the prophet, Johannes Bugenhagen (1485–1558) stepped forward to teach on Jeremiah from 1532 to 1534. Bugenhagen had come to Wittenberg in 1521 after an early career as an administrator, ordained priest, and monastic lecturer. Over the next decade Bugenhagen would take on pastoral and preaching duties in Wittenberg while earning his doctorate there in 1533. Twelve years after completing his lectures, he would continue on to publish what would be his magnum opus as a biblical scholar— his massive commentary on Jeremiah.[30]

Why did it take Bugenhagen so long to be the first Lutheran to produce a complete exegetical volume on this Old Testament prophet? In addition to his many duties in Wittenberg and beyond in other Lutheran territories and churches, Bugenhagen may well have labored slowly under the daunting task of interpreting in print the entirety of Jeremiah. Even twenty-first-century scholar Jack R. Lundbom, author of the most ambitious current commentary series on Jeremiah, wrote in the preface to his first volume:

---

[26]Timothy Wengert, "Biblical Interpretation in the Works of Philip Melanchthon," in Hauser and Watson, *A History of Biblical Interpretation*, 2:330-32.

[27]"The Lessons of Jeremiah's Prophecy, 1548," trans. Scott Hendrix, in *Early Protestant Spirituality*, Classics of Western Spirituality (Mahwah, NJ: Paulist, 2009), 62-68; the original was titled *Argumentum in Ieremiam Prophetam* (Frankfurt: Peter Brubach, 1548).

[28]Scott Hendrix, introduction to "Lessons of Jeremiah's Prophecy, 1548," 62.

[29]Wengert, "Biblical Interpretation," 329.

[30]Johannes Bugenhagen, *In Ieremiam Prophetam Commentarium Iohannis Bugenhagij Pomerani, Doctoris & Pastoris Ecclesiae Wittembergensis* (Wittenberg: Seitz, 1546).

I know now myself from personal experience that writing a commentary on this, the largest and arguably most complex book of the Hebrew Bible/Old Testament, is enough to make one despair—not once, but many times—of ever finishing, and so completing the first of two projected volumes is cause for celebration. I hope, with God's help, to see the completion of Volume II.[31]

Bugenhagen's work on Jeremiah, composed in Latin, comes in at nearly 1,200 pages, almost 950 of which are devoted to the books of Jeremiah and Lamentations. Bugenhagen supplemented his commentary with an index, introductory prefaces—including reprints of Luther's prefaces to Jeremiah and the Old Testament Prophets—and inserted his own treatise on blasphemy against the Holy Spirit. In addition to offering summaries of each chapter of Jeremiah and Lamentations, Bugenhagen delves into specific phrases in individual verses and ponders at length questions related to the biblical text. He not only pauses in his narrative to ponder the sweep of Scripture on a given issue but also offers a periodic excursus on topics such as repentance, excommunication, free will, and the Sabbath. In many ways, this commentary serves as a general introduction to theology and the Bible as a whole.[32]

Lutherans would continue to build on the work of the Wittenberg school of biblical studies in the sixteenth century. Eighteen years after the appearance of Bugenhagen's remarkable tome, Nikolaus Selnecker (1530–1592) turned to Jeremiah. Selnecker taught at the Universities of Jena and Leipzig in Germany while pastoring churches and attempting to guide Lutherans through the rough and tumble of church politics in the 1560s.[33] The title of Selnecker's commentary is revealing: *The Whole Prophet Jeremiah, Interpreted for the Instruction and Consolation of Pious Christians in Dangerous Times.*[34] This first Reformation commentary on Jeremiah in the German language aimed at a wider audience of theologians, pastors, and learned laypeople. Therein Selnecker offered exegetical analysis and homiletic exposition on sections and phrases of each chapter of Jeremiah. Throughout the work he wove his reflections on the personal, societal, and ecclesiastical challenges facing not only the clergy but also the "common folk" in mid-sixteenth-century Germany.[35] Like Bugenhagen before him he also oriented readers to the Lutheran tradition by including an edition of Martin Luther's "Preface to the Prophet Jeremiah"—though this time in German.[36]

A Lutheran pastor preparing a sermon on Jeremiah at the end of the century might supplement the commentaries of Bugenhagen and Selnecker with two additional resources. For a Lutheran voice from southern Germany one might turn to Johannes Brenz (1499–1570), Lutheran reformer of the south

---

[31]Jack Lundbom, preface to *Jeremiah 1–20: A New Translation with Introduction and Commentary*, Anchor Bible 21A (New Haven, CT: Yale University Press, 1999), xv.

[32]See Ferdinand Ahuis on Bugenhagen's scholarly development, especially between his lectures and commentary, including his use of Hebrew with the assistance of professor of Hebrew Matthäus Aurogallus; "*De litera et spiritu*': Johannes Bugenhagens *Jeremiakommentar von 1546 als Krönung seiner exegetischen Arbeit,*" *Lutherjahrbuch* 77 (2010): 155-82.

[33]Selnecker was among the team of theologians who drafted the Formula of Concord (1577) and promoted its acceptance in Lutheran churches; Robert Kolb, "Selnecker, Nikolaus," in *OER* 4:43.

[34]Nikolaus Selnecker, *Der gantze Prophet Jeremias / Zu diesen schweren vnnd gefehrlichen zeiten, frommen Christen zum vnterricht vnd Trost* (Leipzig: Jakob Bärwald, 1566).

[35]Ibid., B1r.

[36]Ibid., D2v-D4r.

German duchy of Württemberg.[37] Brenz had preached on Jeremiah in 1525 in the city of Schwäbisch-Hall. His *Brief and Vigorous Annotations on the Prophet Jeremiah* appeared in print in 1580, a decade after his death.[38] Finally, for a succinct and substantive Lutheran study of Jeremiah at the close of the sixteenth century, one might choose to consult another south German—Johann Pappus (1549–1610) and his commentary *On All the Prophets*.[39] As a theologian, professor of Hebrew, and esteemed preacher in the cathedral in Strasbourg, Pappus had the singular ability to give clear and informative overviews of the essential interpretive issues and doctrinal relevance of each chapter of Jeremiah.[40]

Jeremiah in the Reformed tradition. The life and books of Jeremiah emboldened religious radicals, affirmed the Anabaptists, and spurred Lutheran scholarship from Wittenberg to Württemberg to Strasbourg. Yet above all others, the Swiss cantons of Basel and Zürich might be deemed the most fertile nursery of Jeremiah studies in the early Protestant Reformation. Basel was a vibrant center for Renaissance humanists devoted to the study of the Bible and early Christian texts. The prince of humanists and lifelong Roman Catholic Desiderius Erasmus of Rotterdam (1466–1536) published his critical edition of the Greek New Testament here in 1516—the *Novum Instrumentum*—and his nine-volume edition of the early church biblical scholar Jerome.[41] Among the scholars assisting Erasmus in Basel was Johannes Oecolampadius (1482–1531), a gifted linguist, especially in Hebrew. In 1525 he published his landmark *Commentary on Isaiah*.[42] Two years after his death in 1531, Oecolampadius's *Commentary on the Prophet Jeremiah* appeared.[43] This first Protestant commentary on Jeremiah had predated the work of the Lutheran Johannes Bugenhagen by fifteen years. In over 550 pages Oecolampadius interprets Jeremiah chapter by chapter and verse by verse. Even as he attends to the intricacies of the Hebrew text, Oecolampadius likewise explores the relationship of Jeremiah to the wider narrative, history, and theology of the Old and New Testaments. Likewise, advice for the church and individual believer is close at hand throughout the commentary.[44]

---

[37]James Estes describes Brenz as "arguably the most important Lutheran theologian of his time after Melanchthon." James Estes, "Brenz, Johannes," in *OER* 1:214.

[38]Johannes Brenz, "Breves, sed nervosae Annotationes in Ieremiam," in *Operum reverendi et clarissimi theologi, D. Ioannis Brentii, praepositi Stutgardiani* (Tübingen: Georg Gruppenbach, 1580), 4:870-948. On Brenz's considerable contribution to biblical studies in the sixteenth century, see Robert Kolb, *Martin Luther and the Enduring Word of God: The Wittenberg School and Its Scripture-Centered Proclamation* (Grand Rapids: Baker Academic, 2016), 267-68.

[39]Johann Pappus, *In Omnes Prophetas, tam Maiores quatuor, 1. Jesaiam, 2. Jeremiam, 3. Jezechielem, 4. Danielem, quam Minores duodecim* (Frankfurt am Main: Spiessius, 1593).

[40]A different approach can be found in Phillip Heilbrunner's *Jeremiae prophetae monumenta quae extant; omnia in locos communes theologicos digesta et quaestionibus methodi illustrata* (Lauingen: Reinmichelius, 1586); he samples the content of Jeremiah by topics such as the Word of God, God, the Trinity, the Messiah, creation, providence, sin, free will, the ministry, and magistrates.

[41]On Erasmus and Basel see George, *Reading Scripture with the Reformers*, 77, 222.

[42]On the singular accomplishment of his Isaiah commentary, see Peter Opitz, "The Exegetical and Hermeneutical Work of John Oecolampadius, Huldrych Zwingli, and John Calvin," in *HBOT* 2:409-10.

[43]Johannes Oecolampadius, *In Hieremiam prophetam commentariorum libri tres. Ejusdem in threnos Hieremiae enarrationes* (Strasbourg: Matthias Apiarius, 1533).

[44]One can make the case that Strasbourg should be included here, along with Basel and Zürich, as settings for Jeremiah studies. In fact, scholars have debated the degree of impact of Wolfgang Capito—a former Basel colleague of Oecolampadius—on the text and theology of Oecolampadius's commentary. Capito saw to its publication in Strasbourg after the death of Oecolampadius. See R. Gerald Hobbs, "Pluriformity of Early Reformation Scriptural Interpretation," in *HBOT* 2:457; and Jeff Fisher, *A Christoscopic Reading of Scripture: Johannes Oecolampadius on Hebrews* (Göttingen: Vandenhoeck and Ruprecht, 2016), 198-207.

In his work on the Old Testament, Oecolampadius likely benefited from the expertise of two colleagues in Basel. Sebastian Münster (1488–1553) would arrive in the city in 1528 and thus toward the end of the life of Oecolampadius. He brought extraordinary mastery of Hebrew to Basel and would go on to publish over sixty works on Hebrew grammar, Jewish scholarship, and rabbinic sources.[45] Münster's *Temple of the Lord* would make available his revised Hebrew text of the Old Testament along with illuminating annotations on each book therein, including Jeremiah.[46] If Münster connected to the last years of Oecolampadius, then another colleague's friendship stretched across his Basel years. Konrad Pellikan (1478–1556), a Hebrew scholar, had been associated with Erasmus and Oecolampadius in Basel, promoted the publication of Luther's works in the city, and joined the university faculty along with Oecolampadius in 1523. Years before—in 1509—Pellikan had taught Hebrew to a linguistic prodigy—Sebastian Münster. However, Pellikan's future lay not in Basel but in Zürich, to which Huldrych Zwingli had invited him to become professor of Old Testament in 1526. Pellikan would remain in Zürich the rest of his life and while there would produce a seven-volume commentary on the Old and New Testaments as well as the Apocrypha, thus providing succinct and informative analysis of the text of Jeremiah and Lamentations.[47]

When Pellikan settled in Zürich, he joined in Zwingli's ongoing reform of the churches in the city and came to participate in a new institution called "the Prophecy." A year before Pellikan's arrival, clergy and theology students had begun to gather regularly on weekday mornings to study the Old Testament text in Hebrew and Greek.[48] Pellikan took up the role of expounding the Hebrew text of the day as part of a larger program devoted to examination of Scripture book by book. In this way, the very study and preaching of the Bible in Zürich came to be thought of as prophecy itself—a calling that Isaiah, Jeremiah, and Amos had previously fulfilled.[49]

Appropriately, the study of Jeremiah benefited from this "prophetic" endeavor in Zürich. Huldrych Zwingli (1484–1531)—founder of Reformed Protestantism in Zürich—turned to Jeremiah in both sermons and commentary. An astute listener recorded and preserved notes as Zwingli, in the last years of his life, preached on Jeremiah. Zwingli's sermons reveal how the prophet's life and prophecies applied to faith, doctrine, and daily life in Zürich.[50] Zwingli himself saw to the publication of his *Explanations on the Prophet Jeremiah*, which appeared in 1531.[51] Therein Zwingli examines specific phrases in each chapter of Jeremiah and Lamentations; often his annotations are short, perhaps echoing the kind of brief explanations one might have heard among students and colleagues during morning sessions of the Prophecy. But on occasion Zwingli indulges in

---

[45]J. Friedman, "Münster, Sebastian," in *OER* 3:98-99.

[46]*Miqdaš YHWH: 'esrim wĕ'arba' sifre hammikhtav haqqadosh 'im 'āthiqatho kol.* (Basel: Michael Isinginius and Henricus Petrus, 1546), annotations therein on Jeremiah: 3C2v-3M1r.

[47]Konrad Pellikan, *Commentaria Bibliorum Et Illa Brevia Quidem Ac Catholica / 3: In Hoc Continentur Prophetae Posteriores Omnes, Videlicet Sermones Prophetarum maiorum, Isaiae, Jeremiae, Ezechielis, Danielis, & minorum Duodecim* (Zürich: Froschouer, 1540). See Christoph Zürcher, *Konrad Pellikan's Wirken in Zürich 1526–1556* (Zürich: Theologischer Verlag, 1975), esp. 111-17.

[48]For more details on "the Prophecy," see Timothy George, "General Introduction" to this volume, pp. xxxiv-xxxv.

[49]Peter Opitz, "John Oecolampadius, Huldrych Zwingli, and John Calvin," in *HBOT* 2:421.

[50]Huldrych Zwingli, *Aus Zwinglis Predigten zu Jesaja und Jeremia. Unbekannte Nachschriften, ausgewählt und sprachlich bearbeitet von Oskar Farner* (Zürich: Berichtaus, 1957).

[51]Huldrych Zwingli, *Complanationis Ieremiae prophetae foetura prima cum apologia quur quidque sic versum sit* (Zürich: Froschouer, 1531).

spirited elaborations that swell to paragraphs and sometimes a page. It is certainly possible that Zwingli died on the battlefield at Kappel in October of 1531 with Jeremiah on his mind.

Fortunately, Zwingli's successor, Heinrich Bullinger (1504–1575), took up the reform work and Protestant scholarship for which Zürich had become well-known alongside Basel, Strasbourg, and Wittenberg. In the last year of his life (1575) a complete edition of Bullinger's preaching on the whole of Jeremiah and Lamentations appeared in print.[52] These 170 sermons, composed in Latin, attend to the basic meaning of the text, the doctrines found therein, and the implications for church, Reformation, and Christian soul. Printed marginal comments direct the reader to the content of virtually every paragraph. The entire collection of sermons runs to well over 600 pages, thus making it a worthy parallel to the earlier works of Bugenhagen, Oecolampadius, and Selnecker. Meanwhile, a contemporary of Bullinger had already put forth what would become the most well-known of all Reformation works on Jeremiah; that man wrote, lectured, and sermonized on the western edge of Switzerland and in the republic of Geneva.[53]

The professors, preachers, and pastors we have met thus far were tireless students of the Bible; John Calvin (1509–1564) is surely worthy to stand among them. Scholars estimate that Calvin delivered about two thousand sermons on the Old Testament; he did so by preaching five days a week—every other week—and this in addition to Sunday sermons on the New Testament and the Psalms.[54] His preaching on Jeremiah occurred in the late 1540s and stretched to about 1550. Of the several hundred sermons he may well have delivered on the prophet, twenty-five survive.[55] Calvin the preacher, who brought the lessons of Jeremiah into the streets and souls of Geneva, complements Calvin the lecturer, who wove practical Christianity and theological subtlety into his analysis of the biblical text. Just over four years before his death—April 15, 1560—Calvin commenced his lectures on Jeremiah.[56] After 194 lectures he completed Jeremiah, turned to Lamentations, and wrapped up the series in late 1562. One year later still the Latin edition of his lectures appeared, to be followed by the French edition in 1565.[57] Calvin's "commentary" is the longest of all Reformation works on Jeremiah and Lamentations; the latest English edition is divided into five volumes and numbers a combined 2,556 pages. Like Zwingli over three decades before, the last years of Calvin's life might be deemed "prophetic," since he turned to Ezekiel in January of 1563 and reached the Ezekiel 20:44 prior to his death in May of 1564.[58]

---

[52]Heinrich Bullinger, *Jeremias fidelissimus et laboriosissimus Dei Propheta: concionibus CLXX expositus* (Zürich: Froschauer, 1575). An earlier edition of twenty-six sermons, covering the first six chapters of Jeremiah, had appeared nearly twenty years before: *In Ieremiae prophetae sermonem vel orationem primam, sex primis capitibus comprehensam* (Zürich: Froschauer, 1557).

[53]Though Geneva had intimate ties with Protestant cantons in the sixteenth century, the city did not join the Swiss Confederacy until 1815.

[54]Opitz, "John Oecolampadius, Huldrych Zwingli, and John Calvin," 2:439.

[55]John Calvin, *Sermons on Jeremiah*, trans. Blair Reynolds, Texts and Studies in Religion 46 (Lewiston, NY: Edwin Mellen, 1990), iii.

[56]We refer to his presentations on Jeremiah as his "commentary," but the texture of Calvin's lectures are clearly present in the nineteenth-century text still used today by English readers. Throughout the commentary Calvin often closes a session by commenting that he is out of time and thereby offers a prayer.

[57]T. H. L. Parker, *Calvin's Old Testament Commentaries* (Philadelphia: Westminster John Knox, 1986), 17, 29; Wulfert de Greef, *The Writings of John Calvin: An Introductory Guide*, trans Lyle D. Bierma (Grand Rapids: Baker, 1993), 109.

[58]For a later work from the German Reformed tradition see Johannes Piscator, *Commentarius in Prophetam Jeremiam, et eiusdem Lamentationes* (Herborn: Corvinus, 1614).

Jeremiah in the Roman Catholic tradition. Roman Catholic publications on Jeremiah appeared much later than the earliest Lutheran and Reformed works in the Reformation era. But the Society of Jesus took up the task in earnest and produced significant volumes in the early seventeenth century. Juan de Maldonado, SJ (c. 1533–1583), was the first of such scholars. He was trained in Salamanca, taught in Paris and Bourges, and served the Jesuit General Congregation in Rome. Maldonado composed his work on Jeremiah and the prophets in Bourges in the 1570s, which in turn was published in 1611, after his death.[59] Maldonado's commentary demonstrates his faithfulness to the Latin Vulgate, displays his command of Hebrew and rabbinic sources, and reflects his polemical engagement with Reformed theologians and communities in France.[60]

Cornelius À Lapide, SJ (1567–1637), succeeded Maldonado in the study of Jeremiah, while providing commentary on most of the Old Testament. If Maldonado's work tended to focus directly on the biblical text, À Lapide's verse-by-verse commentary on Jeremiah, Lamentations, and Baruch branched out frequently to buttress his arguments with lengthy citations from patristic and medieval sources.[61] In addition, Pierre Gibert notes À Lapide's role as an advisor to the philosopher René Descartes and thereby his attention to rationality and science in his approach to the Old Testament.[62]

A dramatically different approach to Jeremiah appears in the mystical writings of St. John of the Cross (1542–1591). He was educated in Salamanca, received ordination, and, inspired by Teresa of Ávila, devoted the latter half of his life to reforming the Carmelite order.[63] In works such as "The Ascent of Mt. Carmel," "The Dark Night," and "The Living Flame of Love," he describes a kind of spirituality that shares a striking kinship with the interpretations of some Protestants of the Radical Reformation and their reading of Jeremiah. A determination to sever creaturely attachments, a desire to see the world with divine perception, and a deep awareness that intimacy with God produces tribulation and suffering—such yearnings link the Spanish mystic to the prophets of ancient Israel and Judea and some of his sixteenth-century counterparts. Indeed, it is Jeremiah who appears to understand profoundly the "dark night" St. John of the Cross desired, described, and endured.

Jeremiah and the Reformation in England and Scotland. Writings distinctive to England and Scotland on Jeremiah, for the most part, came much later than their counterparts on the European continent. Scholarship on the role of Scripture in the English Reformation has focused on the progression of specific editions—the English Bibles of William Tyndale and Miles Coverdale, the "Great Bible," the Geneva Bible, the Bishops' Bible, the Douai-Rheims Bible, and the

---

[59]Juan de Maldonado, SJ, *Commentarii in Prophetas IIII Ieremiam, Baruch, Ezechielem & Danielem*, ed. Johann Kinckius (Cologne: Johann Kinckius, 1611), 1-246.

[60]See Jared Wicks, "Catholic Old Testament Interpretation in the Reformation and Early Confessional Eras," in *HBOT* 2:643-44; Reventlow, *Renaissance, Reformation, Humanism*, 201-9.

[61]Cornelius À Lapide, *Commentaria in Ieremiam Prophetam, Threnos, et Baruch* (Antwerp: Martin Nutium et al., 1621). Shortly before À Lapide's commentary appeared, Christophorus de Castro, SJ, published his *Commentariorum in Ieremiae Prophetias, Lamentationes, et Baruch* (Mainz: Schönwetter, 1616).

[62]Pierre Gibert, "The Catholic Counterpart to the Protestant Orthodoxy," in *HBOT* 2:764-67.

[63]J. Blinkhoff, "John of the Cross," in *OER* 2:351.

King James Version. Meanwhile, few biblical commentaries were produced in England during the Reformation era.[64] In fact, the sermons on Jonah of John Hooper (c. 1500–1555), delivered and published in 1550, constitute the first commentary on the Old Testament "made in England" and disseminated in English.[65]

John Knox (1513–1572) does, however, allow us to tie together the prophet Jeremiah with Reformation developments in England, Scotland, and the European continent. Between the late 1540s and 1554, Knox preached reform in St. Andrews, Scotland, was imprisoned and sent to the galleys for his Protestant faith, preached again—this time in Berwick and Newcastle—and served as a royal chaplain in England. With the ascension of Mary Tudor, a Roman Catholic monarch in England, Knox chose exile in Europe. During his time on the Continent Knox might have been found pastoring a church in Frankfurt and conferring with Calvin in Geneva and Bullinger in Zürich. In 1559 he returned across the English Channel to help guide the Scottish Reformation.[66] During his exile on the Continent, Knox wrote two treatises that embody Jeremiah's prophetic voice and delve deeply into biblical history. In *A Godly Letter of Warning and Admonition* and *A Faithful Admonition*, written in 1554, Knox directed true believers to hear Jeremiah speak yet again; to renounce idolatry and ponder the plight of England under Queen Mary in light of the ancient Judean kingdom and its catastrophic defeat at the hands of the Babylonians.[67] Such would be the fate of England if she did not repent of her unfaithfulness. The voice of Jeremiah is crucial for Knox. As Rudolph Almasy puts it:

> As Jeremiah was commanded to write, so too is Knox commanded. The use of Jeremiah is more than merely sounding like a Jeremiah. It is a rehearsal of a call by God to minister, Knox finding a scriptural model which reflects his life as well as one of his voices, a scriptural model he can be absorbed into, Jeremiah as the prophetic text into which he disappears and into which his readers are also invited to be absorbed. As Knox appropriates the Jeremian voice, his exile becomes irrelevant, for the voice enables him to stand apart, separated as Jeremiah from the wicked nation, an absent presence so to speak.[68]

The treatises of Knox illustrate how the life, prophecies, and history of Jeremiah might be used to inform, imagine, and decipher religion and politics in the mid-sixteenth century.

A century after Knox's pleas from exile, John Mayer (1583–1664) published *A Commentary upon All the Prophets Both Great and Small*.[69] Mayer's close reading of Scripture was both a milestone in English literature on Jeremiah and an exemplar of scholarship throughout the Reformation era.

---

[64] Lee W. Gibbs, "Biblical Interpretation in England," in Hauser and Watson, *A History of Biblical Interpretation*, 2:387-95; Henry Wansbrough, "History and Impact of English Bible Translations," in *HBOT* 2:536-52.

[65] Richard Rex, "Humanism and Reformation in England and Scotland," in *HBOT* 2:529-35.

[66] See Jane Dawson, *John Knox* (New Haven, CT: Yale University Press, 2015), 82-182; J. Wormald, "Knox, John," in *OER* 2:380-81.

[67] David Laing, ed., *The Works of John Knox* (1846; repr., Carlisle, PA: Banner of Truth Trust, 2014), 159-216, 255-330; on Jeremiah's decisive impact on Knox, see Richard G. Kyle and Dale W. Johnson, *John Knox: An Introduction to His Life and Works* (Eugene, OR: Wipf and Stock, 2009), 70-72, 81-83.

[68] Rudolph P. Almasy, "John Knox and *A Godly Letter*: Fashioning and Refashioning the Exilic I," in *Literature and the Scottish Reformation*, ed. Crawford Gribben and David George Mullan (London: Ashgate, 2009), 103.

[69] John Mayer, *A Commentary upon All the Prophets Both Great and Small* (London: A. Miller and E. Cotes, 1652); on Jeremiah, 327-479.

Mayer was a Separatist and pastor, who had been educated in the 1590s at St. John's College, Cambridge. He pursued a distinctive scholarly agenda: to bring the breadth and depth of biblical exposition—ancient and "modern"—to a broad English-speaking audience.[70] Mayer not only leaned heavily on John Calvin's commentary but also consulted, compared, and cited authorities from the early church, Middle Ages, and Reformation to determine his reading of a phrase or passage. With his inclusion of Calvin and others Mayer updated the long history of Christian exegesis in order to encompass and include the riches of sixteenth-century scholarship on the Bible.

Mayer's interpretation of Jeremiah might be compared to the renowned preaching of Anglican clergyman John Donne (1572–1631). Though the books of Jeremiah rarely provided his primary sermon text, Donne turned in his preaching to the prophet fairly frequently in order to ponder the interplay of sin, suffering, and divine grace. The searing lyricism of Jeremiah may mingle as well with Donne's poetry, as in Sonnet 14, "Batter my heart, Three-person'd God":

> Take me to you, imprison me, for I
> Except you enthrall me, never shall be free,
> Nor ever chaste, except you ravish me.[71]

Indeed, Donne's struggle with illness and melancholy may have made Jeremiah, and Lamentations in particular, distinctly appealing to him as a resource for personal reflection and as content for his sermons.[72] Other prominent English churchmen who preached on Jeremiah include the theologian and priest Richard Hooker (1554–1600), the establishment bishop Lancelot Andrewes (1555–1626), and the Puritan John Trapp (1601–1669). Hooker's influential *Lawes of Ecclesiastical Polity* responded to Puritan thought and shaped Anglican church governance, Andrewes's exegesis on Jeremiah occurs throughout his numerous sermons on passages from the lectionary, and Trapp published an extensive commentary on Jeremiah as part of a multivolume commentary on the whole Bible.

Additionally noteworthy are the many women across theological traditions who offered significant spiritual insight in their written reflections on various passages of Jeremiah. In keeping with the goal of the RCS, several female commentators are represented in this volume, including Katharina Schütz Zell (1497/1498–1562), Argula von Grumbach (c. 1490–c. 1564), Marguerite of Navarre (1492–1549), and Lady Jane Grey (1537–1554).

Lamentations in the Reformation Era

Scholars in the sixteenth and seventeenth centuries assumed Jeremiah's authorship both of his prophecies, contained in the book of Jeremiah, and the songs of mourning that followed thereafter in the Old Testament.[73] As a result, many commentators—Á Lapide, Bugenhagen, Bullinger,

---

[70]See Philip Withington, *Society in Early Modern England: The Vernacular Origins of Some Powerful Ideas* (Cambridge: Polity Press, 2010), 86; Carl L. Beckwith, ed., *Ezekiel, Daniel*, RCS OT 12 (Downers Grove, IL: IVP Academic, 2012), xliii.

[71]A likely echo of Jer 20:7; suggested in C. J. Sharp, "Jeremiah," in *The Oxford Encyclopedia of the Books of the Bible*, ed. Michael D. Coogan (Oxford: Oxford University Press, 2011), 1:429.

[72]See Sánchez, *Typology and Iconography*, 38-68.

[73]On the historical impact of Lamentations, see Paul M. Joyce and Diana Lipton, *Lamentations Through the Centuries* (Chichester, UK: Wiley-Blackwell, 2013).

Calvin, Oecolampadius, Selnecker, and Zwingli—composed combined works on Jeremiah-Lamentations or published companion volumes on Lamentations.[74] Yet others wrote exclusively on Lamentations in their textual encounter with Jeremiah.

When passing from the book of Jeremiah to Lamentations in the sixteenth century, we not only encounter varied readings of the text but also navigate a range of soundscapes and settings for worship. Long before the Reformation Jeremiah had come to play a central role in the liturgies of Maundy Thursday, Good Friday, and Holy Saturday. In such settings the Lamentations of Jeremiah served to depict the anguish of the Jews after the destruction of Jerusalem in 587 BC, give voice to the suffering of Christ on the way to the cross, and provide words and phrases to clergy and worshipers mourning their sins during the drama of Holy Week. In Roman Catholic churches of the sixteenth century, liturgical elaboration and innovation included the chanting of Lamentations.[75] For example, Thomas Tallis (c. 1505–1585) composed musical settings for Lamentations in Elizabethan England, as did Giovanni Pierluigi da Palestrina (c. 1525–1594) for the papal palace in Rome.[76] However, if Martin Luther is at all indicative, then his rejection of the many hours of Holy Week services and rites meant that Jeremiah's place in the passion was likewise diminished in most Protestant services.[77]

Given the liturgical importance of Jeremiah in the Holy Week liturgy, it is not surprising that Roman Catholics turned a homiletic, scholarly, and creative eye to Lamentations. Noteworthy homilies survive from the esteemed Franciscan preacher Johannes Wild (c. 1495–1554). Wild became a preacher in the Franciscan church in Mainz in 1528 and ascended to the prestigious cathedral pulpit in 1539.[78] His sermons on Lamentations appeared in a collection published about eight years after his death and join the nearly two hundred editions of his works printed for Catholic clergymen.[79] In his preaching on the first three chapters of Lamentations, Wild draws vivid comparisons between the devastation of Jerusalem in the sixth century BC and the crises of the church—both societal and spiritual—in his own day. Along with Wild's homiletic literature, printers saw to the publication of the exegetical works of Hector Pinto (1528–1584), a brother of the order of St. Jerome and professor of theology at the University of Coimbra in Portugal. In addition to commentaries on Isaiah and Ezekiel, Pinto's *Commentary on Daniel, Nahum, and the Lamentations of Jeremiah* appeared in 1595;

---

[74]See Á Lapide, *Commentarium in Jeremiam*, 283-356; Bugenhagen, *In Ieremiam . . . Threni*, C1r-H2v; Bullinger, *Conciones*, 287r-315v; Calvin, CTS 21:299-528 (CO 39:505-645); Oecolampadius, *In Hieremiam . . . In Threnos*, 2P2v-2Y4v, Selnecker, *Threni*; Zwingli, *Complanationis*, R1r-S1v.

[75]See Robert L. Kendrick, *Singing Jeremiah: Music and Meaning in Holy Week* (Bloomington: Indiana University Press, 2014); note the appendix in which the verse patterns of Lamentations for a number of liturgies across Europe are charted.

[76]On background to their compositions, see Joyce and Lipton, *Lamentations*, 33-34, 41-43. In addition, note settings of Lamentations composed by Cristóbal de Morales, Tomás Luis de Victoria, Carpentras (Elzéar Genet), and Orlande de Lassus; see Sánchez, *Typology and Iconography*, 8-9.

[77]See Susan Karant-Nunn, *The Reformation of Feeling: Shaping the Religious Emotions in Early Modern Germany* (Oxford: Oxford University Press, 2010), 78-82.

[78]See John M. Frymire, *The Primacy of the Postils: Catholics, Protestants, and the Dissemination of Ideas in Early Modern Germany*, SMRT 147 (Leiden: Brill, 2010), 514 n. 7; and K. B. Brown, "Wild, Johann," in *OER* 4:273-74.

[79]Johannes Wild, In *Threnos Hieremiae Prophetae Conciones. In Epitome sermonum reuerendi D. Ioan. Feri dominicalium* (Lyon: Iacobi Iuntae et al.,1562), 441-566.

the final section devotes nearly 150 pages to the five chapters of Lamentations.[80] A third Roman Catholic scholar, Guillaume Du Vair (1556–1621) offered a completely different approach to the mournful songs of Jeremiah. Du Vair—a French churchman, statesman, and Stoic philosopher—approached Lamentations with a meditative strategy and drafted what might be termed "paraphrases" today. Particularly intriguing is Du Vair's practice of rewriting the verses of Lamentations in terms of human emotion and life experience near the end of the sixteenth century. In this way, he chooses imagination and re-creation over linguistic analysis of the Hebrew or Latin text of Lamentations.[81]

Along with the volumes of Bugenhagen, Bullinger, Calvin, Oecolampadius, Selnecker, and Zwingli on Lamentations, two Protestant works bear singular mention. First, Daniel Toussain (1541–1602)—a Swiss Reformed clergyman and theologian—composed a book that bears certain similarities to the meditations of Guillaume Du Vair. Although Toussain describes literary and theological features of Jeremiah's songs of grief, his paraphrase of the text and his pastoral observations on issues of heart, mind, and soul draw the reader into the emotional, spiritual, and doctrinal issues Toussain's parishioners must have encountered.[82] Second, a Protestant Italian refugee took up lecturing on Lamentations in Strasbourg in 1542. The resulting commentary of Peter Martyr Vermigli (1499–1562) would appear after his death in Zürich.[83] Vermigli's career and itinerant life stretched from Roman Catholic Italy to Protestant England to Reformed Switzerland; trained as a Roman Catholic in Thomistic method and Augustinian theology, he would come to excel in Old Testament, Hebrew and Jewish scholarship, and Reformed doctrine. Vermigli's commentary on Lamentations displays his ability to disseminate intimate knowledge of Hebrew, share his formidable command of Jewish learning, and extend these insights to the message of the New Testament.[84] Wild, Pinto, Du Vair, Toussain, and Vermigli embody the range of preaching, scholarship, and meditation on the book of Lamentations in the sixteenth and early seventeenth centuries.

Sources for the Study of Jeremiah and Lamentations in the Reformation Era

Patristic sources. Although the slogan "Scripture alone" has long been associated with the Protestant Reformation, in reality the veritable explosion of biblical scholarship among Protestants and Roman Catholics was dependent on the flourishing of the print industry and the many books

---

[80]Hector Pinto, *Commentaria in Danielem, Nahum, & Threnos Ieremiae* (Antwerp: Martin Nutij, 1595).

[81]Guillaume Du Vair, *Meditations upon the Lamentations of Ieremy, translated out of French into English by A. I.* (London: W. Hall, 1609). French Edition: *Meditations sur les lamentations de Jeremie* (Lyon: Jacques Faure, 1593).

[82]Daniel Toussain, *The Lamentations and the Holy Mournings of the Prophet Jeremiah* (London: John Windet, 1587); German edition: *Lamentationes Jeremiae prophetae . . . : adjuncta paraphrasi, annotationibus etiam . . . illustratae* (Frankfurt am Main: Wechel, 1580).

[83]Peter Martyr Vermigli, *In Lamentationes Sanctissimi Ieremiae Prophetae Commentarium* (Zürich: Jacob Bodmer, 1629). English edition: *Commentary on the Lamentations of the Prophet Jeremiah*, trans. and ed. Dan Shute, Peter Martyr Library 6, SCES 55 (Kirksville, MO: Truman State University Press, 2002). For the approach of a fellow Italian Roman Catholic turned Reformed scholar on Jeremiah and Lamentations, see Giovanni Diodati's *Pious Annotations upon the Holy Bible* (London: Nicolas Fussell, 1651); see also the work of Heidelberg professor David Pareus, *Lamentationes Ieremiae Prophetae . . .* (Frankfurt am Main: Wechel, 1581).

[84]See M. W. Anderson, "Vermigli, Peter Martyr," in *OER* 4:228-30; and Dan Shute's introduction to Vermigli's *Commentary on the Lamentations*, xv-lxviii.

that came off the presses to aid in the study of the Bible. The church fathers of early Christianity became available in new and corrected editions. Protestants and Roman Catholics consulted the works of Origen (c. 185–c. 254) and Theodoret of Cyr (c. 393–c. 460) on Jeremiah.[85] But no ancient Christian scholar drew more consistent attention from Reformation commentators than Jerome (c. 345–420)—the great biblical expositor and architect of the Vulgate Bible. Jerome's influence soared afresh in part due to his *Commentary on Jeremiah* and in part due to the nine-volume edition of Jerome's works produced by Erasmus in Basel in 1516.[86] The legacy of early Christian writing on Jeremiah can be more fully explored in the *Jeremiah, Lamentations* volume of the Ancient Christian Commentary on Scripture.[87]

Medieval sources. Renaissance and Reformation—for some time these joined terms have conjured great epochs of history, twin ages of refreshment and revitalization after the moldy and murky Middle Ages. Did not the Reformers leap over this shadowy epoch in order to explore golden-aged Greece and Rome, Scripture and Early Christianity? In reality, sixteenth- and seventeenth-century biblical scholars were indebted to their medieval predecessors. Depending on one's own library, scholarly networks, and nearby collections the knowledge and insight of many centuries might lie close at hand.

A number of medieval scholars wrote on Jeremiah and had the good fortune of having their writings preserved, hand-copied, distributed, and later printed. Among the earliest works are the commentaries on Jeremiah and Lamentations of the abbot of Fulda Rabanus Maurus (c. 776–856) and the Benedictine monk Paschasius Radbertus (790–865).[88] The thirteenth century saw not only a flourishing of scholastic theology but also impressive contributions to the study of Jeremiah from the Dominicans Hugh of St. Cher (c. 1190–1263),[89] Albert the Great (c. 1200–1280),[90] and Thomas Aquinas (c. 1225–1274).[91] This century likewise witnessed the appearance of a text of uncertain authorship—the *Commentary on Jeremiah* attributed to the monk, mystic, and hermit Joachim of Fiore (c. 1130–c. 1202).[92] Today this mystical interpretation of Jeremiah has been attributed to an unknown disciple or posthumous follower of Joachim—given the name Pseudo-Joachim—who presents himself in the commentary as a second or new Jeremiah

---

[85]See the modern editions: Theodoret of Cyrus, *Commentaries on the Prophets*, vol. 1, trans. Robert C. Hill (Brookline, MA: Holy Cross Orthodox Press, 2006); and Origen, *Homilies on Jeremiah, Homily on 1 Kings 28*, trans. John Clark Smith, Fathers of the Church 97 (Washington, DC: Catholic University of America Press, 1998).

[86]Jerome, *Commentary on Jeremiah*, trans. Michael Graves, ed. Christopher A. Hall, Ancient Christian Texts (Downers Grove, IL: IVP Academic, 2011).

[87]Dean O. Wenthe, ed., *Jeremiah, Lamentations*, ACCS OT 12 (Downers Grove, IL: InterVarsity Press, 2009); therein Jerome is the most frequently cited patristic source.

[88]Maurus, *Expositionis super Jeremiam prophetam*, PL 111:793-1272; Radbertus, *In Threnos sive Lamentationes Jeremiae*, PL 120:1059-1256.

[89]For Hugh of St. Cher's Postils on the Bible, see *Biblia latina cum postillis Hugonis de Sancto Caro* (Basel Amerbach, 1498) and the seventeenth-century edition: *Hugonis de Sancto Charo S. Romanae Ecclesiae Tituli S. Sabinae Cardinalis primi Ordinis Praedicatorum Tomus quartus in Libros prophetarum Isaiae, Ieremiae [et] eiusdem Threnorum, Baruch* (Lyon: Hugetan, Barbier, 1669), on Jeremiah see 2F3r-3E6r.

[90]Albert the Great's commentary on Lamentations and the Minor Prophets is available in an early modern edition: *Beati Alberti Magni . . . Commentarii in Threnos Ieremiae, in Baruch, in Danielem, in 12 Proph. Minors* (Lyon: Hugetan et al., 1651).

[91]See his *In Jeremiam Prophetam Expositio*, in Sancti Thomae Aquinatis, Opera Omnia 14 (Parma: Fiaccadori, 1863).

[92]Joachim of Fiore, *Eximij profundissimique sacrorum eloquiorum perscrutatoris ac futurorum prenunciatoris abbatis Ioachi[mi] Florensis Scriptum super Hieremiam prophetam* (Venice: Soardi, 1516).

and the commentary as the "equivalent" of the ancient book of Jeremiah freshly applied to events in the thirteenth century.[93]

Two medieval scholarly projects, however, tower above all others in terms of scope and impact. The noted Franciscan biblical scholar Nicholas of Lyra (c. 1270–1349) composed the first complete single-author commentary on the whole Bible—his multivolume *Postilla litteralis super totum Bibliam*. Lyra's work came to be revered not only because of his distinctive literal and historical approach to Scripture but especially because of his command of Hebrew and his use of Jewish scholarship in interpreting the Bible. Lyra's influence on Martin Luther's Old Testament expositions was so well-known that it even led to the exaggerated, though memorable maxim: "If Lyra had not played his lyre, Luther would not have danced."[94]

Interpretation of Scripture took a different form in the *Glossa ordinaria*—the revered study Bible of the Middle Ages. The title gives away the actual format of the work: each passage of Scripture appeared in the center of a page, which in turn was amplified and explained by glosses—the commentary of various patristic and medieval authorities framed the biblical passage in the wide margins to the left and right, the top and bottom of the page. This format facilitated deep reading of Scripture, but it also meant that the *Glossa ordinaria* was an expensive and lengthy work—requiring nineteen to twenty-three hand-copied volumes to cover the whole Bible. The printing press revolutionized the production the Glossed Bible in Strasbourg in 1480–1481, covering the whole of Scripture in just four volumes. It was reprinted in Venice, this time with the addition of the *Postilla* of Nicholas of Lyra. Today scholars continue to study the impact of the *Glossa ordinaria* on biblical studies in the Reformation era.[95]

Jewish sources. One final and dramatic development transformed the study of Scripture and made scholars even more eager to examine closely the text of the Old Testament. With the exception of a few patristic scholars like Origen and Jerome, and medieval commentators like Nicholas of Lyra, few Christian interpreters were capable of using Hebrew extensively in their study of Scripture. Yet by the middle of the sixteenth century, chairs in Hebrew at European universities and the use of Hebrew in commentaries and lectures on the Old Testament had become commonplace.[96] Moreover, Christian scholars were studying ancient Jewish and medieval rabbinic

[93]Printed editions of the *Super Hieremiam* of Pseudo-Joachim appeared in Venice in 1516 and 1525, and Cologne in 1577; Robert Moynihan, "The Development of the 'Pseudo-Joachim' Commentary 'Super Hieremiam'; New Manuscript Evidence," *Mélanges de l'Ecole française de Rome, Moyen-Age, Temps modernes* 98 (1986): 110-19.

[94]See the later print version of Lyra's commentary on Jeremiah in volume 2 of his *Postilla literalis super totum Bibliam* (Strasbourg: Henricus Ariminensis, 1477), 720r-761v. On Lyra's influence on Luther, see Erik Herrmann, "Luther's Absorbtion of Medieval Biblical Interpretation and His Use of the Church Fathers," in *The Oxford Handbook of Martin Luther's Theology*, ed. Robert Kolb, Irene Dingel, and L'ubomír Batka (Oxford: Oxford University Press, 2014), 75-76.

[95]A modern critical edition of the *Glossa ordinaria* on Lamentations 1—with text in Latin and English—is *Gilbertus Universalis: Glossa Ordinaria in Lamentationes Ieremie Prophete Prothemata et Liber I*, ed. A. Andrée (Stockholm: Almqvist and Wiksell, 2005); an edition of a very early version of the *Glossa ordinaria* on Jeremiah can be found in PL 114:11-62. On reception in the Reformation era, see Karlfried Froehlich, "The Fate of the *Glossa Ordinaria* in the Sixteenth Century," in *Die Patristik in der Bibelexegese des 16. Jahrhunderts*, ed. David Steinmetz, Wolfenbüttler Forschungen 85 (Wiesbaden: Harrassowitz, 1999), 19-47; and Froehlich, "Martin Luther and the Glossa Ordinaria," *Lutheran Quarterly* 23 (2009): 29-48.

[96]See Stephen G. Burnett, *Christian Hebraism in the Reformation Era (1500–1660): Authors, Books, and the Transmission of Jewish Learning* (Leiden: Brill, 2012), esp. 49-64.

works as aids in deciphering Hebrew Scripture and in establishing accurate interpretations. For the books of Jeremiah and Lamentations three Jewish authorities were often consulted among others: the commentators Rashi (Rabbi Solomon ben Isaac, 1040–1105), Rabbi David Kimhi (c. 1160–1235), and especially the ancient Targum Jonathan—the Aramaic targumim devoted to the Hebrew Prophets and traditionally attributed to Jonathan ben Uzziel (c. first century AD).[97]

In one sense, the Reformation can be envisioned as a great harvest of ancient and medieval exegesis—Christian and Jewish. This bountiful learning—amplified and advanced by the recovery and elaboration of Greek, Latin, and Hebrew sources and resources—fueled the great age of biblical scholarship in early modern Europe. In this way, *sola Scriptura* was not so much the denial of past masters of Scripture and theology, but the application of scholarly resources—theological, historical, and linguistic—in order to lift up the biblical text itself. Thus John Calvin comments on Jeremiah 22:6: "Interpreters differ as to the meaning of the words. I will not repeat their views, nor is it necessary: I will only state what seems to me to be the real meaning."[98] In this way he alerts the reader that he will not clutter his commentary with all the authorities and views he has consulted or considered. Rather, he will deliver the interpretation he believes best fits the biblical text—*sola Scriptura*.

In fact, what strikes one in the corpus of writings and sermons on Jeremiah is not so much the absence of citations from past masters, but how often scholars and preachers cross-referenced Jeremiah with other books of the Bible. Such frequent citation brings Jeremiah into intimate connection first with the Old Testament Prophets, second with the historical books, third the Torah, and finally culminates with the intertwined passages of Jeremiah and the New Testament. Therefore, the phrase "Scripture alone" captures the tireless attempt to find the fulsome, kaleidoscopic, and yet single message of the Bible embedded in Jeremiah's life and times, prophecies and laments. Even so, Reformation scholarship would not have been possible without patristic, medieval, and Jewish learning.[99]

Jeremiah and Lamentations Reformation Issues and Debates

Passages in Jeremiah and Lamentations rarely come to mind quickly when recalling signature debates of the Reformation; there are no hotly contested verses on justification by faith, the real presence in the Lord's Supper, or the authority of the papacy. However, the richness and range of issues addressed in the books attributed to Jeremiah prompted commentators, pastors, and preachers to deliberate on many burning issues and questions of the Reformation. Indeed, the

---

[97]On Jewish sources and Peter Martyr Vermigli's *Commentary on Lamentations*, see the introduction of Daniel Shute therein, xx-xxxii; on the targum and Christian study of the Old Testament, see Stephen G. Burnett, "The Targum in Christian Scholarship to 1800," in *A Jewish Targum in a Christian World*, ed. Alberdina Houtman, Eveline van Staalduine-Sulman, and Hans-Martin Kirn (Leiden: Brill, 2014), 250-65.

[98]Calvin, CTS 19:84* (CO 38:376).

[99]Throughout his 1652 commentary on the Prophets, John Mayer comments primarily on the biblical text before him and brings in related passages from Scripture. Yet Mayer also connects to the broader exegetical sweep of Christianity: not only to Calvin first and foremost but also to other authorities such as Theodoret of Cyrus, Jerome, Rabanus Maurus, Hugh of St. Cher, Thomas Aquinas, and Nicholas of Lyra; see, e.g., Mayer on Jer 6, *A Commentary upon the Prophets*, 355.

prophecies, narratives, and laments of Jeremiah and the events and crises of his own time sparked comparisons and highlighted parallels with the unfolding of history in the sixteenth and seventeenth centuries. A series of categories may best serve to organize and illustrate the convergence between Jeremiah and the Reformation era: a sort of "call" and "hoped-for response" characteristic of prophetic literature.

The call to prophesy. The book of Jeremiah begins with a call to prophesy, a summons woven into the very birth and being of a boy (Jer 1:4-8). Jeremiah would be destined to proclaim in the towns of Judea and streets of Jerusalem (Jer 11:6), in the gates of the temple and the court of the king (e.g., Jer 7:2; 17:19; 22:1; 34:2); in letters sent, books written, and scrolls dictated—dictated, burned, and dictated again (Jer 29; 30; 36). Many of the preachers, pastors, and theologians of the Reformation era—from itinerant Anabaptist communities to Lutheran Wittenberg to Reformed Zürich and Geneva—would recognize and emulate this call to prophesy in word, text, and deed.[100] Jeremiah's calling and prophetic ministry offered an intriguing scriptural template to Protestants, who were redefining or, in their view, restoring the rightful identity of the clergy in terms of sacramental identity, marital status, and pastoral role. Above all else, Jeremiah proclaimed the Word of God. Though only the son of a priest (Jer 1:1) Jeremiah's prophecies and predictions would trump the temple, its priests, and ceremonies; they perished in the sack of Jerusalem, yet the Word of God and its prophet endured. The elevation and mastery of preaching was central to the Protestant Reformation and the purpose for which scholars wrote lengthy commentaries; for many Protestants, especially Reformed and low church traditions, the proclamation of the Word—and not the Eucharist—would be the central event of worship and the paramount task of the pastor. The prophetic ministry of Jeremiah confirmed and embodied these changes.

The book of Jeremiah, however, could be both helpful and complicated when used to reform the clergy. Protestants championed the "priesthood of all believers" (1 Pet 2:4-10). Jeremiah lived out this doctrine. Though not an ordained priest in the strict sense, he preached the Word, interceded in prayer, and experienced unmediated intimacy with God. Still, most Protestants came to recognize the need for divinely called and thoroughly trained ordained ministers. Fortunately the book of Jeremiah could prove useful—even among the pastors and lay preachers of the Radical Reformation—in discerning, exposing, and deposing corrupt clergy and "false prophets."[101] Still certain passages in Jeremiah were problematic for Protestants and needed explanation. What of God's command that Jeremiah forgo marriage and fatherhood (Jer 16:2)? Does this passage not affirm clerical celibacy? Moreover, Jeremiah might be used to point out limits to the doctrine of the priesthood of all believers and to provide examples of those truly set apart by God in sacramental calling or singular vocation. For example, the obscure and nomadic people known as the Rechabites appeared before Jeremiah during the siege of Jerusalem (Jer 35). Roman Catholics

---

[100]Zürich's school of theological training called "the Prophecy" is the most obvious example. On Luther as prophet, see Robert Kolb, *Martin Luther as Prophet, Teacher, and Hero: Images of the Reformer, 1520–1620* (Grand Rapids: Baker, 1999); on Calvin see Jan Balserak, *John Calvin as Sixteenth-Century Prophet* (Oxford: Oxford University Press, 2014).

[101]See Jer 2:8; 5:30-31; 10:21; 14:13-16; 23:1-2, 11-40; 26:7-11; 27:9-10, 14-22; 28:1-17; 29:15-32; Lam 2:14; 4:13-14.

would argue that their ascetic lifestyle and stated convictions prefigure the holy vows of monks and nuns; Protestants thought otherwise. Likewise, there is the singular status of the Virgin Mary, perhaps prophesied by Jeremiah himself (Jer 31:22). But Protestants also alerted readers to Jeremiah's suggestive words about the idolatrous worship of "the Queen of Heaven" (Jer 7:18-19; 44:16-19); such passages served as a warning about exaggerating Mary's status. Jeremiah's call to prophesy, his prophetic career, and the prophecies he delivered raised fresh questions about the nature of ministry, and a set-apart ministry in particular.

Finally, Jeremiah's biographical chapters provided scriptural case studies on a prophet's decidedly political role. Indeed, all too often Jeremiah found himself tasked with giving bad news to the king, his courtiers, and princes—messages that seemed to offer rather stern consolation: "surrender to the officials of the king of Babylon, then your life shall be spared" (Jer 38:17); "seek the welfare of the city where I have sent you into exile, and pray to the Lord on its behalf" (Jer 29:4-7); "if you will remain in this land, then I will build you up and not pull you down; I will plant you, and not pluck you up" (Jer 42:10-12). Clergy in the sixteenth and seventeenth centuries had not yet experienced what we would today describe as "the separation of church and state." Pastors and theologians might be called on to advise their rulers and give an accounting of their reforms and sermons. Such encounters required a blend of boldness, eloquence, and deference, especially if a ruler or governing council was unlikely to approve of clerical counsel or appreciate unsolicited pastoral admonishment. As Jeremiah and other prophets knew all too well, an audience with a sovereign could end in reprimand, prison, or death. Still this difficult work as well belonged to the prophet's vocation.

The call to repentance. Declarations of divine judgment roll from the lips of Jeremiah in wave upon wave, and each tide lifts up judgment in searing, staggering, and terrifying detail. Of the fifty-two chapters of Jeremiah and the five chapters of Lamentations not a single one escapes the litany of wrath.[102] Indeed, it is striking how commentators of the Reformation era describe and dissect without flinching war, famine, drought, disease, and destruction—the human trauma, environmental degradation, and cultural annihilation—verse by verse, and chapter after chapter. Their steady interpretive gaze reminds us that the biblical world was vividly similar to the early modern Europe they themselves inhabited.[103] In addition, across all the Christian traditions there is an acceptance of God's decisive hand in the destruction of humanity, society, and nature. Peace and prosperity were rare and miraculous gifts. Thus there was at the time of the Reformation something of an established science to the study of God's wrathful ways, especially when interpreting Jeremiah.

Equally striking throughout Jeremiah is the steady call to repent, avert disaster, and embrace God's gracious forgiveness and sure blessing.[104] The nature of repentance was a contested issue in the Reformation. Protestants had done away with the precise rhythm and practice of medieval penance—

---

[102]One can make the case for Jer 40–41 as "nonjudgment chapters," but the conditions therein described are the result of divine punishment. Jer 31 is the most hopeful by far, though Jer 31:28-30 dips back into the usual themes.

[103]See Andrew Cunningham and Ole Peter Grell, *The Four Horsemen of the Apocalypse: Religion, War, Famine and Death in Reformation Europe* (Cambridge: Cambridge University Press, 2000).

[104]See Jer 3:12-14; 4:1-4, 8, 14; 5:1-5; 6:26; 7:5-7, 25; 9:20; 13:15-16; 14:20-21; 17:14; 18:7-8; 21:8; 22:21; 25:4-6; 26:1-3, 13; 31:18-20; 35:14-15; Lam 1:18, 22; 2:18-19; 3:39-42.

contrition or remorse for sin, confession to a priest, and works of satisfaction. To be sure, Roman Catholics continued the practice of penance and found confirmation in the mournful verses of Lamentations: a text known to them in the liturgical chants of Holy Week. However, for Protestants the book of Jeremiah brought evidence of a sort of repentance they had come to recognize. Indeed, the prophet's summons to repentance required remorse, confession of sin, and a turning to God in faith. Meanwhile, priestly ministrations would only serve to produce greater offense:

> What use to me is frankincense that comes from Sheba,
> or sweet cane from a distant land?
> Your burnt offerings are not acceptable,
> nor your sacrifices pleasing to me. (Jer 6:20)

And the holiest of sanctuaries would not suffice: "Do not trust in these deceptive words: 'This is the temple of the LORD, the temple of the LORD, the temple of the LORD'" (Jer 7:4). True repentance required not a trust in rituals and ceremonies, but raw honesty about the human condition:

> The heart is deceitful above all things,
> and desperately sick;
> who can understand it? (Jer 17:9)

Time and again, Jeremiah calls his listeners to turn to the Word of God and so turn back to God. To be sure Protestants expected their pastors to assist parishioners individually in their struggle with sin. But as with Jeremiah's prophecies, a good deal of pastoral care and direction would come through preaching, hearing, and obeying the Word of God.

The call to renounce idolatry. A substantial portion of Jeremiah's prophecy addresses the intricacies of human sinfulness—both individual and corporate. To read the commentaries and sermons of the reformers is to contemplate the sort of unfaithfulness, disobedience, indifference, and open contempt for the Word of God they observed every day in their churches and communities. But of all sins, idolatry was the rotting center of Judea's corruption and the sin at the heart of God's unrelenting wrath. Such idolatry might be construed in various ways: the worship of other gods, the adoration of the Lord and other gods simultaneously, or expressing devotion to a distorted image of the true God. Child sacrifice was among the most offensive practices censured by Jeremiah; divine punishment would be returned in kind— with idolaters reduced to cannibalism and their corpses consumed by predators (Jer 19:4-9; 32:34-5). Idolatrous ceremonies performed within the temple would only be remedied by the utter destruction of the temple itself. Likewise, the holy sanctuary was defiled and required demolition because the hands submitting sacrifices to God in the temple had also extended offerings to other gods elsewhere and had committed murder, indulged adultery, and oppressed the poor (7:5-15; 32:34). Thus the temple had become a "den of robbers," a charge Jesus himself would repeat later (Jer 7:11; Mt 21:13). Indeed, the final and last chance to avert disaster was not participation in a vigil of prayer or fervent celebration in the temple, but rather obedience to God's demand that slaves be set free (34:8-22).

Idolatry was likewise an urgent issue for Protestants. Working from the inside out: they feared false ideas of God and salvation, godless ceremonies practiced in human worship, and the physical images of lesser "gods" or "saints" worshiped at altars within churches and sought after in pilgrimage to distant shrines. They found in Jeremiah clear evidence that idolatry indicated the utter demise of true and godly religion. The effort to eradicate idolatrous ideas, practices, and places was a hallmark of Protestant reforms. Even as God had employed the Babylonians to ravage Judea, and thereby cleanse the landscape of godless shrines and spaces—including the temple in Jerusalem—so reformers revised worship services, stripped church sanctuaries of images, and closed monasteries.

To put it another way, in elevating Christ alone, grace alone, and faith alone Protestants sought to strip away many medieval practices and beliefs that they believed encouraged idolatry and served to undermine the good news of the gospel. Public debates, printed pamphlets, and sermons challenging pilgrimages, indulgences, transubstantiation, monastic vows, and intercession of the saints were meant to unmask false worship and expose idols. The prophecies and history of Jeremiah were compelling precisely because Jewish religion had been simplified and reduced to its essence as the land of Judaea had been invaded, the city of Jerusalem sacked, and the very temple itself leveled. Jeremiah and the godly remnant were left with their faith in God alone and reliance on God's grace alone, even as many of them faced the allure of idols in Babylon and Egypt. Many Protestants believed that the Christian faith could only be restored to clarity and integrity by escaping the exile they now suffered in an idolatrous medieval Babylon and by undertaking singular reforms of doctrine, worship, and life; it was time to leave behind the exile in Babylon.

The call to suffering. The life of Jeremiah is a daunting narrative. He bears a stark and severe message that will leave him unwedded and without children, despised by his small-town neighbors, and persecuted by the powerful in Jerusalem. Beyond the physical abuse and filthy incarceration he receives, Jeremiah attests to an even deeper and more profound form of suffering. He speaks of "pain unending" and "incurable wounds" (Jer 15:18); the divine Word he carries sears his heart and smolders in his bones until it bursts forth (Jer 20:9); he is a drunken man, overcome by the message he bears (Jer 23:9); he grieves day and night for his people (Jer 9:1). Like Job, he curses the day of his birth (Jer 15:10; 20:14-18; Job 3:1-26).

Reformation interpreters recognize the contours of Jeremiah's life. Suffering is part and parcel of the fallen world in which we live, and hardship is a fact of the Christian life. The call to prophetic ministry demands a distinctive spiritual stamina and willingness to endure difficulty and face fierce opposition to biblical proclamation. In fact, the trials and tribulations of Jeremiah prompted writers of the Reformation era to ponder the nature of human distress and the role of suffering in forming Christian faith. Through commentaries, sermons, and writings we can understand how they articulated and measured emotion, grief, and despair and how they made sense of tragedy and suffering. We can measure the degree to which there was what Susan Karant-Nunn calls "a Reformation of feeling."[105] Indeed, it is striking that not all of the interpreters of Jeremiah

---

[105]Karant-Nunn, *Reformation of Feeling.*

and Lamentations were enamored of Jeremiah's most desperate responses to suffering. While some hold up Jeremiah's behavior and laments as laudable and acceptable—or at least tolerable and understandable under the circumstances—others find him inappropriate, intemperate, or even blasphemous. Is Jeremiah ever the sterling paragon of faith or is he on occasion a pathetic reminder of human finitude and an example to be avoided at all costs?

The call to bear witness. In most basic terms, the writings of Jeremiah suggest a call to pay careful attention and to bear witness to what one encounters. Jeremiah himself must attend to the oracles he is inspired to deliver, the God who places a Word in Jeremiah's mouth and heart (Jer 1:9; 20:9), the people who despise this Word and behave contrariwise, and the future God intends—both grim and gracious. The book of Lamentations bears witness to the acute suffering of the Jewish people—their humiliation, degradation, and starvation. Therein Jeremiah chronicles the crushing sense of divine disapproval and abandonment. There is a distinctive summons here to describe every sordid street scene, recall every disconsolate conversation, and measure the anguish of every internal tremor. To do less would be to disregard the hard lessons learned and delay the lamentations that spur deep and lasting repentance. These graphic, detailed, and anguished Scriptures moved interpreters of Reformation Europe to tell us of their own lives, losses, and urgent longings.

The call to bear witness is likewise a summons to attend to the patterns of God's moving in history. The narrative of Jeremiah's time prompted commentators, writers, and preachers to triangulate anew the unfolding events of their own time. In the summer of 1520 Martin Luther published *The Babylonian Captivity of the Church*. The title of this work recalled not only the ancient exile of Israel to Babylon but also the more recent Avignon papacy (1309–1377), when the papal office resided in Avignon, a period that the Italian humanist Petrarch (1304–1374) reportedly termed "the Babylonian captivity" of the church. Although the papal office returned to Rome, the circumstances led to the Great Western Schism, during which three different clergy claimed to be the rightful pope, which was only resolved by the Council of Constance (1417). Drawing on that recent history, Luther challenged the church's sacramental system and detailed how the body of Christ had been imprisoned behind three captivities constructed by the medieval church and the papacy: (1) withholding the cup from the laity, (2) the doctrine of transubstantiation, and (3) the sacrifice of the Mass.[106] These and other reforms Luther advocated promised to deliver the church from this long and tormented exile. There was, however, a second model of judgment and exile present when commentators and preachers turned to Jeremiah. In this narrative the threat of exile for early modern Europeans loomed in the future. The renewal of church and society under Luther and the Protestants echoed the reforms of the ancient Jewish king Josiah, which were in turn undone by his wicked sons—the kings whom Jeremiah condemned and suffered throughout his prophetic work. By the mid-sixteenth century it was becoming increasingly clear that much of Europe would remain Roman Catholic and that

---

[106]LW 36:3-126.

some Protestant cities and lands would return to the Catholic fold. Would the judgment of God rain down on these unfaithful Christians who clung to their idolatrous ways?

Meanwhile, the Ottoman Empire and Islam seemed poised to reprise the role of ancient Babylon. In fact, the Muslim Turks had conquered Constantinople in 1453 and were at the gates of Vienna in 1529. The Battle of Mohács (1526) had already proved disastrous for Christians in eastern Europe; in 1541 the Ottomans would annex part of Hungary. Stories of slaughter, rapine, and slavery were drifting across western Europe. What would Jeremiah prophesy to these nations? Was a Babylonian exile behind them or still to come? The call to bear witness to history lay heavily on interpreters of Jeremiah.

The call to covenant with God. The books of Jeremiah offer a number of prophecies that Christians have claimed portend the coming of Christ. There is the promise of the righteous branch of David (Jer 23:5-6), the "woman [who] encircles a man" (Jer 31:22), and "Rachel . . . weeping for her children" (31:15; Mt 2:18). Lamentations seems to anticipate the passion of Christ. But no chapter in Jeremiah is likely more beloved and decisive for Christians than Jeremiah 31 and the promise of a new covenant with God.

> Behold, the days are coming, declares the Lord, when I will make a new covenant with the house of Israel and the house of Judah, not like the covenant that I made with their fathers on the day when I took them by the hand to bring them out of the land of Egypt, my covenant that they broke, though I was their husband, declares the Lord. For this is the covenant that I will make with the house of Israel after those days, declares the Lord: I will put my law within them, and I will write it on their hearts. And I will be their God, and they shall be my people. And no longer shall each one teach his neighbor and each his brother, saying, "Know the Lord," for they shall all know me, from the least of them to the greatest, declares the Lord. For I will forgive their iniquity, and I will remember their sin no more. (Jer 31:31-34)

The covenant lingers in the background of most prophecies of Jeremiah. It takes lucid form in the unfaithfulness of Jeremiah's contemporaries to their covenant promises (Jer 2:1-25; 11:1-8; 34:14-18) and in God's faithfulness to his people despite human betrayal (Jer 23:1-8; 33:14-26).

In the prophecy of the old and new covenants Christians have found vivid promises of the newer testament to come and of life in Christ. For Protestants, many beliefs and practices of the medieval church smacked of the old covenant of external rites and works, while justification by faith brought one to the heart of the new covenant. Still Reformation commentators and theologians came to wrestle with a series of related questions. Are there two different covenants—one old and one new? If so, what do they share in common and what distinguishes them? Or is there one covenant, expressed in old and new forms, and to which God is ever faithful? And what of the covenant people of God? What is the fate of the Jews—the contemporaries of Jeremiah and those of Reformation Europe? Has their covenant come to an end? If God so judged and rejected the people of the old covenant, what would this portend for the church, especially a church that spurns true reform? And how do the other nations fit into the covenant—the Gentiles, who are judged so harshly in the latter chapters of Jeremiah?

Questions regarding God's covenant faithfulness similarly prompted discussion among interpreters of Jeremiah about election and free will. Should the Jewish remnant, which survived the Babylonian invasion and exile, be credited with their survival? Or given the total depravity of humanity, is this evidence of God's necessary and unconditional election? Jeremiah's visit to the Potter's house and the message he received there (Jer 18) likewise underscores God's sovereign and decisive power over the very substance of the people of Israel and their history. Similarly, there are God's commands to Jeremiah: "Do not pray for them; I will not hear your prayer."[107] Do these passages confirm election? The call to covenant penetrates to the depth of God's relationship with sinful and redeemed humanity.

The call to hope in God. In the turbulent sea of judgment and tribulation in Jeremiah's books, there are verdant islands of hope and assurance; a hope and assurance always rooted in God's nature and faithfulness.

> But this I call to mind,
>   and therefore I have hope:
> The steadfast love of the LORD never ceases;
>   his mercies never come to an end;
>   they are new every morning;
>   great is your faithfulness.
> "The LORD is my portion," says my soul,
>   "therefore I will hope in him."
> The LORD is good to those who wait for him,
>   to the soul who seeks him.
> It is good that one should wait quietly
>   for the salvation of the LORD. (Lam 3:22-26)

Similar to the rhythmic calls for repentance in Jeremiah, there are periodic declarations of God's sovereign, righteous, and gracious nature;[108] and there are visions of blessed life beyond judgment, destruction, and exile.[109] In the midst of his suffering Jeremiah can also say,

> Your words were found, and I ate them,
>   and your words became to me a joy
>   and the delight of my heart,
> for I am called by your name,
>   O LORD, God of hosts. (Jer 15:16)

Like Jeremiah, those who hope in God "ask for the ancient paths" (Jer 6:16), seek "the way life" and not "the way of death" (Jer 21:8), and trust in the Lord alone (Jer 17:7). Those who hope in the true God extend hope to others: they rescue the victim from the oppressor, never harm

---

[107]See Jer 7:16; 11:14; 14:11-12; 15:1.

[108]See Jer 5:22; 9:23-24; 10:6-7, 12-13, 16; 16:19-21; 20:11-13; 23:23-24; 27:5; 31:35-36; 32:16-24; 33:1-3; Lam 3:21-23, 31-33, 37-38.

[109]See Jer 3:15-18; 12:16; 16:14-15; 23:3-8; 24:4-7; 29:1-14; 30:1-3, 8-11, 16-22; 31:1-14, 16-40; 32:1-23, 27, 37-44; 33:6-26; 35:18-19; 38:20; 39:15-18; 42:7-12; 46:27-28; 48:47; 49:6, 39; Lam 3:25-27; 5:19-21.

the alien, the orphan, or the widow (Jer 22:2-3). Those who love and rely on God alone reflect the divine nature:

> Let not the wise man boast in his wisdom, let not the mighty man boast in his might, let not the rich man boast in his riches, but let him who boasts boast in this, that he understands and knows me, that I am the Lord who practices steadfast love, justice, and righteousness in the earth. For in these things I delight, declares the Lord. (Jer 9:23-24)

Throughout the books of Jeremiah, Christian interpreters discovered time and again echoes and indicators that pointed to the new covenant made manifest in Jesus Christ. They believed that the rugged and enduring hope embodied in the prophecies and laments of Jeremiah found their fulfillment in the New Testament and were renewed once more in the churches of Reformation Europe. To this good news Christian authors turned when reading Jeremiah and Lamentations. Thus it is not surprising that Johannes Oecolampadius, biblical scholar and reformer in Basel, Switzerland, deemed Jeremiah to have the very character of Jesus himself:

> For forty-one years Jeremiah foretold with tears, weeping, and lament the miserable destruction of the city and in vain he called the people to turn back from their madness. In doing so he is doubtless a type of our Christ. . . . And let no one think, "therefore, nothing of this pertains to us." Indeed, those things which he wrote hold good, as much in our times as in his own, for we too are led away into captivity. This is the aim of this prophet: that he might warn us, lest we are driven into captivity, or so that, for those held in captivity, succeeding generations might return to freedom through divine mercy.[110]

J. Jeffery Tyler

---

[110]Oecolampadius, *In Hieremiam*, bk. 1: A1v. See pp. 3-4 in this volume.

COMMENTARY ON JEREMIAH

JEREMIAH 1:1-3
THE PROPHET'S TIMES AND CALL

¹*The words of Jeremiah, the son of Hilkiah, one of the priests who were in Anathoth in the land of Benjamin,* ²*to whom the word of the LORD came in the days of Josiah the son of Amon, king of Judah, in the thirteenth year of his reign.* ³*It came also in the days*

of Jehoiakim the son of Josiah, king of Judah, and until the end of the eleventh year of Zedekiah, the son of Josiah, king of Judah, until the captivity of Jerusalem in the fifth month.

OVERVIEW: The first three verses of Jeremiah offer a remarkably concise and detailed introduction to the prophet and his world. Reformation commentators identified Jeremiah's place in Jewish society and variously mapped out his relationship to Jewish history in the late seventh and sixth centuries before Christ. Moreover, they elaborated on these verses in order to provide an introduction to Jeremiah's character, message, mission, and suffering. They pondered the meaning and relevance of Jeremiah's prophecies to his own time and to developments in sixteenth-century Europe.

The reforms of King Josiah, the idolatrous resistance of the Jewish people, and the resulting message of Jeremiah seemed to mirror in uncanny ways the birth of the Protestant Reformation and the fierce resistance it came to encounter. As commentators wrote about Jeremiah, they were likewise writing the history of their own time. Would the Reformation continue to expand or wither in the face of human wickedness and divine wrath? Would their commentaries and sermons find a fruitful hearing among the faithful or echo Jeremiah's unheeded prophecies and his "failed"

mission to spur repentance and conversion? Regardless of the outcome, the prophet of God must stand forth unashamed, though grief and suffering may be one's lot in life.

1:1-3 The Word of the Lord Comes to Jeremiah

THE TIMES AND MINISTRY OF JEREMIAH. SEBASTIAN MÜNSTER: Jeremiah was the son of Hilkiah, a priest, who under Josiah king of Judah discovered in the house of the Lord the book of the law in the eighteenth year of his reign. In fact, Jeremiah began to prophesy in the thirteenth year of the reign of Josiah, when the king, priests, and people were living in a most disgusting way—until the book of divine law was discovered. Then the pious king, making up his mind, restored the worship of God and wiped out idolatry, as was recorded before in the book of the Kings. . . . Jeremiah prophesied from the thirteenth year of Josiah until the Babylonian captivity—nearly forty-one years. And finally, writing in a book, he shows that he himself had preached the Word of

God for a long time, but he accomplished nothing among the people in so much time. And then how long he lived in Egypt. THE TEMPLE OF THE LORD, JEREMIAH 1:1-3.[1]

AN ORDINARY TEACHER, AN EXTRAORDINARY CALL. THE ENGLISH ANNOTATIONS: The prophet Jeremiah was a priest, and so an ordinary teacher (which some other prophets were not) before his entrance upon this extraordinary employment. This he began (being in his younger years thereunto called) under a good king, Josiah. In times, though bad enough (the main body of the people, notwithstanding all the care and endeavor of that godly governor, continued their former idolatry and other evil courses), yet not so bad as they later proved, when that pious prince was taken away by premature death, who, up until then, kept them within some compass of external conformity, and restrained them from the public profession and open practice of such abominations while he lived. But the kings who succeeded him were themselves also addicted to like impieties and excesses. And, [since the kings were] complying with the people therein, all things in short time grew to such a height of corruption, both in church and state, that the prophet, as one striving and struggling against the stiff streams of a strong torrent, for a long time labored in vain to reclaim them. And having endured much opposition by the false prophets, and sustained much hard measure from the priests, princes, and people, for the faithful performance and due execution of his office (under which some expressions of human frailty, sometimes, broke from him), he was at length constrained to denounce from God the utter ruin and destruction of that whole state, which, by the Chaldeans, God accordingly made good. Nevertheless, for the comfort and support of the faithful, he foretells their return after seventy years of captivity, and the enlargement of the church by that blessed branch, the Messiah, and furthermore adjoins diverse prophecies against those several nations that had

been either the destroyers or the oppressors of God's people.

Upon the conquest of the city by the Chaldeans, he was set at liberty by special appointment of the king of Babylon. . . . But he was shortly afterward carried away by force to Egypt among the rest of the people, by Prince Johanan and his accomplices, after they had murdered Gedaliah, whom the Chaldean king had made governor of the land, for fear of the Chaldeans, against God's express charge. There he continued prophesying, how long it is not certain. Nevertheless, being called into that office in the thirteenth year of Josiah, it could not have been less than between forty and fifty years that he spent in that employment. In Egypt it is not unlikely that he ended his days, though how, in what manner, or by what means is as uncertain as the time of his abode in those parts. ANNOTATIONS ON JEREMIAH.[2]

JEREMIAH IN THE PAST, PRESENT, AND FUTURE. KONRAD PELLIKAN: By the command of God the faithful and godly prophet, the determined and doggedly persistent Jeremiah, preached these sermons concerning his times to the kings, princes, priests, and peoples. And he wrote them down not only for the people of his own generation but also for those to come in every age, since divine piety provides similar medicines for similar illnesses, and the Spirit is the rector of the church. In fact, in his own time both the people and the kings were impious, except for Josiah alone, in whose time Jeremiah prophesied for eighteen years. Very soon the people would be forced into exile. They did not accept the admonitions of God, but persecuted and imprisoned the preachers of the Word of God, even to death and prison. At that time the entire state was corrupt. So it is now as well: while the world is in a wicked state—as it nearly always is—the provident works of God are revealed through the mouths of the prophets, so that the people might attend to their prophecies. It is already so that prophecies in some ages have not

---

[1] Münster, *Miqdaš YHWH*, 857; citing 2 Kings 22.

[2] Downame, ed., *Annotations*, 9B1r*; citing Jer 43:1-7.

been sincerely understood, so that it may not be useful to prophesy. It is a sure sign of the coming destruction of those who scorn the improvement of their lives or refuse to listen to the word of the Lord through the prophets. COMMENTARY ON JEREMIAH 1:1.[3]

JEREMIAH AMONG THE PROPHETS. PHILIPP MELANCHTHON: Forty years Jeremiah wanders like a deserter; he is ridiculed as a fool, put in jail, released, and imprisoned again. Unlike Isaiah, Elijah, or Elisha he performs no glorious unexpected miracles; rather, he appears weak because through him God will do great things and save the elect. THE LESSONS OF JEREMIAH'S PROPHECY.[4]

CLAIM YOUR NAME. NIKOLAUS SELNECKER: Jeremiah established his origins and family background at the same time that he preached according to the will of God, which hereafter would be said in the twenty-fifth chapter. Here is something that would be especially good to teach in the church of God: Jeremiah was not ashamed of his name and was not a corner gossip. He did not avoid the light, which is unfortunately the practice today. THE WHOLE PROPHET JEREMIAH 1:1.[5]

WHY THE PROPHET'S NAME MATTERS. JOHANNES BUGENHAGEN: Jeremiah begins his book with a title and inscription in the custom of the other prophets so that you might take heed. These words of Jeremiah are similar to the way Matthew begins his book: "The book of the generations," etc. Jeremiah adds the name of his father, tribe, and place or country, lest another Jeremiah be assumed. For there is no doubt that there were many named Jeremiah, as among us there are many named John, Peter, etc. Jeremiah is interpreted as "the loftiness of the Lord" or as "exalting the Lord," which was not an empty name for this prophet. Since indeed he in his own preaching exalted and praised God, and condemned errors, idolatry, and ungodly worship.

In the past certain people among us have not added their names to their own books, either due to some fear or in the vain superstition that they would seem to be seeking their own glory. So it happens that afterward we (since we have no way of judging) force on such books the names of Augustine, Ambrose, or others. Therefore, those to whom God gives authority in the church, and those who are among the saints—that is the Christian faithful, who have given a good testimony in their vocation—those who are mighty in the Word of God and sincere in discussing the Scriptures, ought to ascribe their own names to their books, so that posterity might see what we have taught and how through our doctrine God preserved his church. Through our teaching he might judge other writings, which are perchance put forward under our name, so that we are not said to teach that which we condemn. This is not to seek our own glory. Indeed, we do not preach, except that we preach God, but to preach is a gift and a ministry that God gave and commended to us for the glory of his name. COMMENTARY ON JEREMIAH 1:1.[6]

A PROPHET AND TYPE OF CHRIST. JOHANNES OECOLAMPADIUS: Jerusalem was to be overthrown by the Chaldeans, and the people were to be led into a crushing captivity. At this moment God chose a most holy prophet—Jeremiah—whose prophecy we now undertake to explain. We would note that Christ did the same thing as well. For forty-one years Jeremiah foretold with tears, weeping, and lament the miserable destruction of the city, and in vain he called the people to turn back from their madness. In doing so he is doubtless a type of our Christ, who himself preached a much more serious wrath of God to the Jews, who did not believe it was near at hand. Indeed, when he is able by no remedies to recall the people from madness, God usually does this, so that they might see that he inflicted these punishments justly. Thus, anyone who reads the most faithful rebukes of Jeremiah will be unable to deny

[3]Pellikan, *Commentaria Bibliorum*, 3:2O3v.
[4]Melanchthon, "Lessons," 65.
[5]Selnecker, *Der gantze Prophet Jeremias*, A1v.
[6]Bugenhagen, *In Ieremiam*, E3r-v; citing Mt 1:1.

that God did nothing more justly than when he rebuked the pride of the people with the harshness of captivity. And let no one think, "therefore, nothing of this pertains to us." Indeed, those things he wrote hold good, as much in our times as in his own, for we too are led away into captivity. This is the aim of this prophet: that he might warn us, lest we are driven into captivity, or so that, for those held in captivity, succeeding generations might return to freedom through divine mercy. This itself let us be taught, lest we be led into the captivity of sin and the devil, who is our spiritual Nebuchadnezzar, and king of Babylon, that is the prince of this world. COMMENTARY ON JEREMIAH 1:1.[7]

CHARGE, COMMISSION, OR CONTENT? THE ENGLISH ANNOTATIONS: Now, by the "word of the Lord" here, some understand a *charge* or *commission*, made out by God to Jeremiah, for the exercise and execution of his prophetic employment and the publishing of these his prophecies.... Others conceive it to design the subject matter of his prophecy, or that which was revealed to him, and was enjoined to publish.... "The word of the Lord" here and the "words of Jeremiah" are in effect and substance one and the same and are called "the word of the Lord" because they proceed from him and are delivered in his name. They are the words of Jeremiah because he delivered them as God's mouth and messenger . . . to his people. And I incline toward this latter understanding, though the word may well contain both, since the former also, together with the revelation, did constantly concur. ANNOTATIONS ON JEREMIAH 1:2.[8]

JEREMIAH AND THE KINGS OF JUDAH. HULDRYCH ZWINGLI: Jeremiah has a list of the periods of King Josiah and the sons that succeeded him. Josiah reigned thirty-one years. Therefore Jeremiah commenced his prophecy in the thirteenth year of Josiah's reign and under him he completed eighteen

years as a prophet. The sons of Josiah were Jehoahaz, Jehoiakim, and Zedekiah. Jehoahaz, who is passed over here in silence on account of the brevity of his reign, ruled only three months. When Jehoahaz was captured and deported to Egypt, his brother Jehoiakim succeeded to the throne, who after eleven years of affairs was led away to Babylon instead. Then he accepted his son Jehoiachin as his successor; after three months and ten days his reign was taken away and they deported him suddenly to Babylon, where his father was. Zedekiah was left, to whom the kingdom returned in the restoration. He governed miserably for eleven years and departed from his kingdom wretchedly; already the third one captured from the bloodline of Josiah and dragged to hostile Babylon.

Therefore, all the years that Jeremiah prophesied, until the captivity, were forty-one years, six months, and ten days. . . . No admonition or rebuke of the faithful Jeremiah was able to turn those sprung from Josiah from idolatry, impudence, tyranny, and dissipation, while four kings in succession—I consider if I should withdraw this example (how much of such things should you remember?)—were captured and dragged off into servitude and prison. So with certain ones of us, who despite grief do not cease to draw innocent blood, deny or transgress the law, and reward the warnings of the prophets with bloodshed; not just to diminish their own people with collections [i.e., tax or debts], but destroy them, to do everything with audacity, to resist profession of the truth; to traffic, to lust, to mock, to associate with prostitutes; cheat, swear falsely, fight, defraud, swindle: all this they do not stop doing until that evil whirlwind comes from the north and scatters misery equally everywhere, and the unhappy offspring of the most holy king Josiah is taken away. EXPLANATIONS OF THE PROPHET JEREMIAH 1:3.[9]

THE LIFE, WORK, AND SUFFERING OF JEREMIAH. MENNO SIMONS: Jeremiah the son of Hilkiah, a priest of the priests of Anathoth, a man

---

[7]Oecolampadius, *In Hieremiam*, 1:A1v.
[8]Downame, ed., *Annotations*, 9B1v*; citing Hos 1:1; Lk 3:2; Jn 10:35; 1 Kings 12:24; Esther 1:12; 3:15; Jer 26:1; Is 2:1; Gen 15:1; Jer 15:19; 26:12, 15; Mic 1:1; Zeph 1:1.

[9]Zwingli, *Complanationes*, 73-74.

sanctified from his mother's womb, who was chosen of God to be a prophet and a seer from his youth—this man rebuked Judah and Benjamin most sternly for their disobedience, their stubbornness, all manner of transgressions, false worship, idolatry, and bloodshed, out of the mouth of God and his law. He preached repentance and reform and prophesied the promised Messiah, whom he called the righteous Branch and Root of David. He preached the coming judgment and wrath of God, namely, the captivity and downfall of the king, the destruction of the city and temple, and the captivity of the people for seventy years, etc.

And these his predictions, faithful warnings, visions, and rebukes out of the mouth of the Lord became to him as sharp piercing thorns. Men cast aside his word and his admonitions and would have nothing of them. The pious prophet and true servant of God they made out to be a faithless traitor, a rebel, and a heretic. The word of the Lord was the occasion of daily mockery. He was often apprehended and beaten and thrown into vile and evil-smelling pits. They plotted his death. He was so pressed and weighed down with the cross that he at one time resolved in his heart to preach no more in the name of the Lord. Yes, he cursed the day of his birth and the man who brought the message to his father that a man-child was born to him. In this way the worthy man of God had to bear the heavy bag of sand for many years for the sake of the Word and the truth of the Lord. He had to give his ear to all who reproach, and his back to all who strike, until the waters of affliction rose in the mouths of the haughty, rebellious, and unbelieving people, and they saw, alas too late, that Jeremiah was God's true messenger and a true prophet. And on top of all of this he had to bring his life to a close in Egypt under the stones with which he had been stoned to death as a sign of appreciation for his great love and his difficult, bitter work. CROSS OF THE SAINTS.[10]

JEREMIAH THE PRIEST. JOHN CALVIN: With regard to Jeremiah's father, it is nothing strange that the rabbis have regarded him as the high priest; for we know that they are always prone to vain boastings. Ambition possessed them, and hence they have said that Jeremiah was the son of the high priest, in order to add to the splendor of his character. But what does the prophet himself say? He declares indeed that he was the son of Hilkiah, but does not say that this was the high priest; on the contrary he adds that he was from "the priests that were at Anathoth in the land of Benjamin." Now we know that this was an insignificant village, not far from Jerusalem. . . . Since then Jeremiah only says that he came from Anathoth, why should we suppose him to be the son of the high priest? . . .

Jeremiah says further that he was of the priestly order. Hence the prophetic office was more suitable to him than many of the other prophets, such as Amos and Isaiah. God took Isaiah from the court, as he was of the royal family, and made him a prophet. Amos was in a different situation; he was taken from the shepherds, for he was a shepherd. Since God appointed such prophets over his church, he no doubt thus intended to cast a reflection on the idleness and sloth of the priests. For, though all the priests were not prophets, yet they ought to have been taken from that order; for the priestly order was as it were the nursery of the prophets. COMMENTARY ON JEREMIAH 1:1.[11]

JEREMIAH'S TIME AND OUR TIME. HEINRICH BULLINGER: Indeed, just as the Babylonian captivity follows the prophecy of Jeremiah, so certainly and soon the Lord will judge the world. To be sure, in the same manner the remarkable reformation of the church through King Josiah preceded the Babylonian captivity, since the reformation had been instituted and advanced up to a certain point according to the Word of God. Nevertheless, not everyone accommodated themselves to this reformation, but they were secretly worshiping idols, as they certainly thought

---

[10]Simons, *Complete Writings*, 591; citing Jer 23:5; 33:15; 38:1-13; 20:9, 14-15.

[11]CTS 17:32-33* (CO 37:473).

they were living in better times; they were, I say, expecting the restitution of idolatry or treacherously resisting the efforts of the holy Josiah or at least detracting from them. In the same way, the pious reformation of the churches holds fast to the clear preaching of the gospel in our age, in many places, against which meanwhile the most wicked folk—both hypocrites and open idolaters—are threatening and hoping that soon all those things will either be condemned by a general council or cut down by the sword of Catholic kings, that is, by the papists. Idolaters, when King Josiah was taken away, were thinking that their own things were in a safe haven.

But, in fact, we do not read of any other time in which the Jewish state was more weakened. Four kings in a row, and in a short time indeed, were captured and mostly unhappily taken away—Jehoahaz, Jehoiakim, Jehoiachin, and Zedekiah. I do not know if I could come up with [an example of] so great a calamity in any time or kingdom, where we read that all happiness has been destroyed as in this kingdom. In the same way, many good men have been lost, sincere learning has been practically suppressed, and the papists seem to themselves at the moment to reign secure and to triumph. But an extraordinary evil will suddenly crush them. And since it is necessary for the judgment of God to be preached to the ungodly, and for the godly to be retained in office through learning, exhortation, and consolation, therefore our clement and merciful God desires fully that humanity be wholly saved and freed from destruction. So God sends Jeremiah as his public crier, so that the ungodly might be terrified through him and the godly might be truly revived, rather than God destroying the people with most exquisite evils. In the same way, God now awakens preachers of the gospel; yes indeed he awakens this teaching of Jeremiah, so that it will be preached again in the church before the great judgment, so that there will be no one who perishes through ignorance, or has a just excuse for his evil works. From all these things your love understands how very useful the exposition of this book will be and how necessary. Sermon on Jeremiah 1:1-4.[12]

---

[12]Bullinger, *Conciones*, 1r-v.

JEREMIAH 1:4-19
THE CALLING OF JEREMIAH

⁴*Now the word of the L*ORD *came to me, saying,*

⁵*"Before I formed you in the womb I knew you,*
and before you were born I consecrated you;
I appointed you a prophet to the nations."

⁶*Then I said, "Ah, L*ORD *G*OD*! Behold, I do not*
know how to speak, for I am only a youth." ⁷But the
Lord said to me,

"Do not say, 'I am only a youth';
for to all to whom I send you, you shall go,
and whatever I command you, you shall speak.
⁸*Do not be afraid of them,*
for I am with you to deliver you,
*declares the L*ORD*."*

⁹*Then the L*ORD *put out his hand and touched my*
*mouth. And the L*ORD *said to me,*

"Behold, I have put my words in your mouth.
¹⁰*See, I have set you this day over nations and*
over kingdoms,
to pluck up and to break down,
to destroy and to overthrow,
to build and to plant."

¹¹*And the word of the L*ORD *came to me, saying,*
"Jeremiah, what do you see?" And I said, "I see an
almond*ᵃ branch." ¹²Then the L*ORD *said to me, "You*
have seen well, for I am watching over my word to
perform it."

¹³*The word of the L*ORD *came to me a second time,*
saying, "What do you see?" And I said, "I see a
boiling pot, facing away from the north." ¹⁴Then the
*L*ORD *said to me, "Out of the north disaster*ᵇ *shall be*
let loose upon all the inhabitants of the land. ¹⁵For
behold, I am calling all the tribes of the kingdoms of
*the north, declares the L*ORD*, and they shall come,*
and every one shall set his throne at the entrance of
the gates of Jerusalem, against all its walls all around
and against all the cities of Judah. ¹⁶And I will declare
my judgments against them, for all their evil in
forsaking me. They have made offerings to other gods
and worshiped the works of their own hands. ¹⁷But
*you, dress yourself for work;*ᶜ *arise, and say to them*
everything that I command you. Do not be dismayed
by them, lest I dismay you before them. ¹⁸And I,
behold, I make you this day a fortified city, an iron
pillar, and bronze walls, against the whole land,
against the kings of Judah, its officials, its priests, and
the people of the land. ¹⁹They will fight against you,
but they shall not prevail against you, for I am with
*you, declares the L*ORD*, to deliver you."*

a *Almond* sounds like the Hebrew for *watching* (compare verse 12)   **b** The Hebrew word can mean *evil, harm,* or *disaster,* depending on the context; so throughout Jeremiah   **c** Hebrew *gird up your loins*

OVERVIEW: Jeremiah's calling is among the most vivid and compelling in all of Scripture. Surely it stands alongside the calling of Abraham (Gen 12:1-3; Gen 15:1-21), Moses (Ex 3), Isaiah (Is 6), and Paul (Acts 9). Exploring a call to proclaim and prophesy was an urgent matter in the Reformation era. In less than a decade Protestants had attracted and created a new generation of clergy, most of whom would be married and all of whom would serve beyond the episcopal oversight of the Roman Catholic Church. What did it mean to receive a call to ministry? How did one discern such a call? What was the role of the church in recognizing and confirming this vocation? What sort of skill, education, training, and knowledge did ministry require? And most of all, what did it mean to be God's faithful preacher and prophet? God's claim on the life of Jeremiah offered crucial guidance and opened further lines of inquiry.

Reformation commentators were particularly concerned with Jeremiah's formation and consecration in the womb (Jer 1:5). Some believed that this divine action marks Jeremiah for divine service after he is born; his prophetic calling is foreknown and his path is set. Others point to an actual prenatal sanctification, which has positive implications for the sacrament of infant baptism and divine grace among children.

The latter verses of chapter 1 (Jer 1:7-19) prompt reflection on Jeremiah's calling to preach judgment to the nations. The nature of divine punishment, the accountability of idolaters, and the relationship of judgment to grace: these themes appear often among sixteenth- and seventeenth-century preachers and scholars as they comment on the whole of Jeremiah and Lamentations. Of particular concern is the right and power to proclaim and execute divine chastisement against the hypocritical and ungodly. In the name of reform, violent and radical movements emerged in the 1520s and 1530s, typified here by the firebrand preacher Thomas Müntzer and the Anabaptist kingdom of Münster. It was one thing to claim a call to ministry like Jeremiah's, but quite another to claim to be *the* Jeremiah of the sixteenth century and unleash divine punishment with one's own hands.

1:4-8 Jeremiah Called Before Birth

JEREMIAH'S VOCATION—CALL AND RESPONSE. HEINRICH BULLINGER: Here the calling, sanctification, and mission of Jeremiah is described in the words of the Lord; for here God explains and announces to Jeremiah the task for which he had chosen him, and the task he wanted [Jeremiah] to do. "I chose and I intended for you, that you would be a prophet. Therefore, take up the office which has been offered, and preach my word to the people." From the beginning, God indeed says, "I knew you before I formed you in the womb"; for to God everything is always present, even the past and the future; for he is governor of all things and preserves all things—all-powerful and all-knowing. Then he says, "I sanctified you before you were born from your mother's womb. . . ." And he says, "I destined and provided you as a prophet to the nations." For the providence of God has sanctified and set apart Jeremiah for the office of prophesying. For that reason, when he had been born and when he was approaching his twentieth year, God called him and sent him into that service into which he had decided to send him when he was not yet born. Therefore God now follows his own plan and leads into an actual act, which is usually [only] spoken, as he revealed to the prophet his plan and indicated what he was to do. But we should observe that the Lord clearly said that he had destined Jeremiah to be a prophet to the nations, obviously not only for the good of the Jews but also for the other nations to whom he prophesied, even for our own salvation and our posterity—even to the end of the age. So let us not reject this blessing offered to us by the Lord.

But from these brief words of the Lord many quite beneficial dogmas are supplied to us. Indeed, we learn from these words that there will always be a need for ministers of the church, who need to be ordained by a calling and a legitimate mission. So indeed, even in the Gospel, our Lord instituted the apostles and the seventy disciples. . . .

There follows the manner in which Jeremiah conducted himself, once he was called by God to the office of preaching. He turns this down modestly, with a [contrary] prayer of supplication and by confessing that he is not equal to such a great duty. "Ah, Ah," he says; that is the word of one grieving and shouting out and begging off, as we say in German "Ey, Ey, Ey." He adds the cause of this exclamation: "I don't know how to talk." Of course, Jeremiah was able to speak; indeed, he was not mute. He pled that he was not instructed in as much eloquence as was suitable for an orator, especially one who would be destined to execute such great causes, and to carry them out, so to speak, in the theater of the whole world before kings, princes, priests, the learned and the common people. . . .

But let us listen to how the Lord refutes the arguments of Jeremiah, how he orders Jeremiah to receive his condition, and again how he consoles the worried person, and confirms and instructs them in their office. This must certainly be extended to all who are called by God and burdened by dangerous and difficult tasks. Indeed, these things are all written for our instruction and confirmation. Therefore, we will think that they were written for each of us as individuals. Simply, God refutes [Jeremiah's] excuse and says, "Do not say, 'I am a boy.'" The reason: "Because I send you." "Lo," he says, "I send you, I say, God: clement, good, true, and powerful. I am not so unfaithful that I would not instruct you in the necessary faculties; nor am I so slow that I would neglect you, nor am I a weak one who is incapable. And indeed, when I myself send you, I will instruct you in those things, which I know you will need." SERMON ON JEREMIAH 1:4-10.[1]

A FOREBODING CALLING AND AN UNUSUAL CONCEPTION. NIKOLAUS SELNECKER: God here calls the prophet Jeremiah to the office of preaching. But Jeremiah knew fully that the danger was very great, that he would have to be a severe preacher, who would uprightly and explicitly point out sins and punishment and thereby fiercely and forcefully threaten people due to the command of God. At the same time he would have to proclaim certain future punishments regarding when the king of Babylon would destroy the land and temple, and capture the people and lead them away. Moreover, Jeremiah knew that the people did not want to be punished whether in person or life and that they were not willing to suffer the truth. They also held it to be a great lie and a shameful presumption when Jeremiah would prophesy and proclaim a particular punishment for them. In addition, Jeremiah named all of them that he warned: blasphemers, rabble-rousers, restless and brawlers. And as the twenty-ninth chapter of Jeremiah shows, he named the insane and the enraged. Therefore, Jeremiah resisted God's calling and held himself as too weak, too little, and too incapable for such a high, difficult, and utterly dangerous office. But God comforted, strengthened, and drove him; and God gave him the grace,

courage, heart, blessing, and a rightful peace, a fearless spirit, and a mouth to open and say what there was to say according to the Word of God. . . .

So God establishes order in his church and the beloved office of preaching and sends out true teachers, prophets, apostles, and pastors and other servants of his Word and at all times arouses them to go forth to plant his Word with preaching and teaching.

The papists think that Jeremiah was born without sin, because the text here states, "I have sanctified you," that is, "I have chosen you and so ordered you before you were born from your mother so that you shall be my prophet." But such an understanding is false and also absurd. Even little boys in school know that. THE WHOLE PROPHET JEREMIAH 1:4-10.[2]

A TRUE AND FALSE CALLING FROM GOD. JOHANNES BUGENHAGEN: The calling of the prophet is described throughout this chapter. He receives a command from God regarding what he ought to prophesy or preach. Granted, you are so learned and you accepted from God the grace to teach and examine the Word of God and the Holy Scriptures. Nevertheless, two things are required that you might be a public doctor or that you might teach people in public. First, you must have a vocation; that is, you must have been called by God, or by men in the name of God, to preaching and teaching. Second, having been called, you must sincerely teach the Word of God, and nothing else, lest in the ordinary power of teaching you abuse what you have received, and you boast that you alone have been called. But also recognize to what you have been called. They [the verses] concern this point also, lest you neglect your duty or having been called to speak the truth, you do so for your own honor; or lest you think of what is convenient for peace, in the same way that impious preachers are called blind watchmen, and mute dogs who do not have the power to bark. Each thing is here commanded of Jeremiah; he is called for preaching,

---

[1]Bullinger, *Conciones*, 3r-v, 4r; citing Lk 10:1-24.

[2]Selnecker, *Der gantze Prophet Jeremias*, A1r-v.

for the Lord said, "Whatever I will entrust to you, you will say to them," just as it says, "you are to speak nothing else, nor may you be silent."

In your calling you will endure many adversities, because "truth gives birth to hate," as Terence says.† But trust this, the Lord is with you. You will see the fruit of your labors at some time. As the Lord says here to Jeremiah, "Be not afraid, I myself am with you," etc. Certainly now God has preserved the church through the misery and affliction of Jeremiah, lest they might have fallen away from God or despaired on account of the evils they were about to suffer, or despaired of God's promises as sinners who provoked God's anger against themselves. Without a calling, pseudo-prophets were running about, that is, teaching the people in various places, as Jeremiah says in chapter 23: "I did not send them," etc. Therefore the Lord was not with them, but they seduced their hearers with their own doctrine and with a perversion of the Scriptures. If, in fact, they did not want to seem like anything other than doctors of the Word of God, still the Lord says, "You have perverted the words of the living God, the Lord of Hosts, our God." So the fanatical spirits teach their errors under the name of the Word of God and Holy Scripture. COMMENTARY ON JEREMIAH 1:4.³

CALLED FROM THE WOMB. JOHANNES BRENZ: Concerning the calling to preach the Word of God: the Lord chooses one from the womb. "How will they preach," Paul says, "unless they have been sent?" No one seizes this honor for himself, but only the one who is called by God. Thus Jeremiah was bound to this duty from the womb so that he might preach the word of the Lord, lest he mix in his own imaginings in place of the Word of God—as if in not being sent he would be haranguing others. So we read concerning Paul in Galatians 1: "God who set me apart from my mother's womb and called me through his grace." Similarly John the Baptist in Luke 1: "He was already filled

with the Holy Spirit in his mother's womb." He, therefore, commends in this passage the diligent providence of God, his care for us, and he confirms our faith in adversity. These passages were not written for Jeremiah, John, and Paul, but for us, whom we know are a matter of concern to our Lord and who are called before his eyes.... Ephesians 1: "He chose us in him, before he had laid down the foundations of the world." He chooses us, however, and calls us to his grace from the womb. But he does not initially reveal election or vocation, as you see in Jeremiah or Paul, who were both called from the womb. But this calling was revealed to the one in his youth, and the other then in his old age. ANNOTATIONS ON JEREMIAH 1:5.⁴

SANCTIFIED IN THE WOMB AND INFANT BAPTISM. HANS NADLER: Therefore no one can legitimately reject infant baptism.... We have Scripture and examples by which it is shown that children well may and can believe even if they have neither speech nor understanding. In Psalm 106 this is written concerning the Jews: "They sacrificed their sons and daughters to devils and shed innocent blood." If it was innocent blood (as the text says) then they were obviously pure and holy children, which they could not have been without the Spirit and faith. The innocent children whom Herod killed were also children but still were holy and blessed. In Matthew 19 Christ says that the kingdom of heaven belongs to the children. Also we read concerning Jeremiah that he was sanctified in his mother's womb. Similarly we read in Luke 1 about Saint John the Baptist that he was filled with the Holy Spirit even in his mother's womb. Since the children are capable of and participate in such lofty things as the Word, the Spirit, and the kingdom of God, how can one truthfully say that they are unable to believe and that they are not to be baptized? A DECLARATION OF THE NEEDLE MERCHANT.⁵

³Bugenhagen, *In Ieremiam*, F1r–F2r; citing Is 56:10; Jer 23:21.
†Terence, *Andria*, line 68.
⁴Brenz, *Annotationes in Jeremiam*, 870; citing Rom 10:15; Gal 1:15; Lk 1:41; Eph 1:4.
⁵CRR 10:150; citing Ps 106:37; Mt 19:14; Jer 1:5; Lk 1:41.

GOD'S FOREKNOWLEDGE AND JEREMIAH'S CALLING.

JOHN CALVIN: Jeremiah then was not actually sanctified in the womb, but set apart according to God's predestination and hidden purpose; that is, God chose him then to be a prophet. It may be asked, whether he was not chosen before the creation of the world? To this it may readily be answered—that he was indeed foreknown by God before the world was made; but Scripture accommodates itself to the measure of our capacities, when it speaks of the generation of anyone: it is then the same as though God had said of Jeremiah—that he was formed a human being for this end—that in due time he might come forth as a prophet. COMMENTARY ON JEREMIAH 1:4-5.[6]

I FORMED, KNEW, AND SANCTIFIED YOU AS AN INFANT.

JOHANNES OECOLAMPADIUS: God says [several things] in order. . . . First, "Before I formed you. . . ." "Formation" means much "excellence of constitution"; for God so strengthens nature that it may endure injury, as in patience of the spirit, and lest any melancholy exists. Notwithstanding that, not all may be fit for prophecy. Indeed, I confess that nothing holds up against the Spirit, who chooses the kind of people in whom his own gift would not be disgraced, but rather recognized. Lest anyone [suppose] I am speaking of melancholy, attributing it to a fault, here there is an investigation of profound mysteries.

Second, "I knew you." So also in Isaiah 49: "The Lord," as he says, "called me from the womb." From the organs of my mother, he remembered my name. Just as in the verse "For Esau he holds in hate, Jacob he loves." The word connotes knowledge, the word connotes love. To the virgins who have been shut out, he says, "I do not know you." . . . "Depart from me you workers of iniquity, I do not know you."

Third, "I have sanctified you." That is, I have set you apart for this ministry, to such an extent that parents in some manner acknowledge the gifts of vocation, and there was no work on account of it,

so that we establish the imparted habits, qualities, and so forth, of faith. It is enough that the child was found in the grace of election, for the Holy Spirit at an opportune time was able to work his own will. For that ought to be without doubt for you, even concerning the children of Christians, if the parents offer them for baptism. I say it is enough, because they considered the Holy Spirit to be present, likewise even Paul in the womb was sanctified, who nevertheless for a long time lived without the law and the Spirit. So there are certain ones who are sanctified in the womb, just as even the Evangelists say the same thing of John the Baptist. In the womb, therefore, there is an infant capable of grace. Why therefore would you deny this? It is clear that grace works deeply even for infants. COMMENTARY ON JEREMIAH 1:5.[7]

JEREMIAH'S UNIQUE CONCEPTION.

DIRK PHILIPS: Some throw before us that Jeremiah was sanctified in his mother's womb, Jeremiah 1; and that John in his mother's womb rejoiced in Christ his Lord and Savior, Luke 1.

. . . This is with Jeremiah and John an exceptional and marvelous work of God and not a general rule, just as Isaac was supernaturally conceived of Sarah through faith, Genesis 17. That took place because he in godly works and as a figure bore the image of Jesus Christ. Thus it also took place with Jeremiah and John, namely, since God wanted to accomplish something exalted and marvelous with the two of them, therefore, they were also filled with the Holy Spirit from the mother's womb. But not all children are as a Jeremiah and John. THE ENCHIRIDION.[8]

TWO WAYS OF INTERPRETING THIS VERSE.

THE ENGLISH ANNOTATIONS: The words may be taken in two ways: either as spoken by way of injunction, as if it were said, "Make no such excuses, nor use any such pretenses, but do as I bid you, go

---

[6]CTS 17:37* (CO 37:475).

[7]Oecolampadius, *In Hieremiam*, 1:A2v; citing Is 49:1; Mal 1:2-3; Rom 9:13; Mt 25:12; 7:23; Gal 1:15; Lk 1:41.
[8]CRR 6:88-89; citing Lk 1:41; Gen 17:16-17; Rom 4:19; Heb 11:11.

wherever I send you, speak whatever I give you in charge," ... or as delivered by way of predication and promise, as if God had said, "Talk not of your years, or your inability to speak, you will be furnished with sufficiency of ability, both to go wheresoever I shall see good to send you, and to speak whatsoever I shall give you in charge." ANNOTATIONS ON JEREMIAH 1:7.[9]

1:9-19 A Prophet to the Nations

DESTROY THE FALSE CHRISTIANS. THOMAS MÜNTZER: When the preacher who has been under God's judgment has the words of God put in his mouth they are not accompanied by honey-sweet words and hypocrisy, but with a consuming and truly earnest zeal to root out, tear down, and scatter the counterfeit Christians and destroy every scrap of the wicked faith, which, like artful thieves, they have stolen from others by eavesdropping on them or reading their books. ON COUNTERFEIT FAITH.[10]

AWAIT THE POWER OF GOD WITHIN. ANDREAS BODENSTEIN VON KARLSTADT: "No one ought to consider himself a pastor, church leader, or bishop unless he was chosen by God to be responsible for those people. . . ."

The work of laborers and shepherds reminds me to hold back, for true shepherds and harvesters among the people have authority over those to whom God sends them (not that they are to rule people for wicked gain). Rather, they have been placed over the people that they might carry out God's word mightily and with great joy, to pluck up and destroy and scatter and grind down every heart with God's word, as with a sharp sword and heavy hammer for which it has been sent. Then again, true shepherds are to gather in what has been scattered, make whole what has been broken, and return what is fugitive and gone astray. They are to heal what is diseased and straighten out everything through God's word. . . .

Since I do not find such fruit within me, it is better for me not to try to be tree or root, but rather to wait until I am wonderfully kindled and uplifted by the Spirit that works within unto such public proclamation—the Spirit, which holds all hearts in hand and moves every shepherd to speak or be silent as he wills. Scripture indicates that no one must think himself a shepherd or a pastor unless he discerns such power of the Word of God within himself. REASONS WHY ANDREAS KARLSTADT REMAINED SILENT.[11]

TEARING DOWN AND BUILDING UP. JOHANNES BUGENHAGEN: These things are said in general what the prophet will do through his own preaching. Indeed, all holy preachers do these things; in the preaching of repentance they weed out the errors of humanity through the law; they demolish, ruin, and scatter untrue doctrines, false worship of God, idolatry, contempt of God, blasphemy, disobedience, and other evils. Likewise, they threaten the ungodly that unless they repent they will be rooted up, weeded out, ruined, and scattered in eternity. In truly preaching the forgiveness of sin through the gospel they build up and plant; that is, to the repentant they promise with certainty eternal life. These are the commands given to preachers, as in the last chapter of the Gospel of Luke. It is necessary for penance and the remission of sins to be preached in the name of Christ among all the nations.

Furthermore, Jeremiah tears down and builds up in a remarkable and singular way in his prophecy and preaching. He roots out, tears down, ruins, and scatters, when he preaches the exile in Babylon, the destruction about to happen to the kingdom of Judah, the temple, and all holy places through the wrath of God and on account of the sins of the kings, priests, nobility, and people. In contrast, Jeremiah builds up and plants them, so that they might remain with fixed roots in their land when he preached the return from captivity after seventy years, and so that having come back they might possesses their land until God would complete in that place all of his promises concerning Christ, etc. Thus in a great spirit

---

[9]Downame, ed., *Annotations*, 9B2r*; citing Num 22:30, 35; 26:2; Mt 10:27; Ex 20:3, 7, 15, 17; Mt 19:8; Mk 10:19; Ex 3:12; 4:11, 12; Judg 6:14, 16; Mt 10:19, 20; Mk 13:11; Lk 21:14, 15.
[10]Müntzer, *Collected Works*, 218; citing Jer 23:30.

[11]CRR 8:175.

and fortitude or power (which at that time no king or military force was equal to, or able to resist) God enlivens and encourages Jeremiah and miraculously preserves his church at that time. . . .

The seditious peasants and the Münster Anabaptists shouted from these and similar Scriptures: "As Jeremiah spoke, 'so that you root up' etc., therefore, we will kill with the sword and will destroy whatever appears to us." But you see that those folk were fanatics, and so I will not speak of the fact that no one from among them was a Jeremiah. Thomas Müntzer shouted, "The Sword of God and Gideon." But he was no Gideon, much less God. This was a falsehood of the devil, who "was a murderer from the beginning." See not only what is said in the Word of God but also whether it is said to you in particular. Some passages are speaking of princes, some of preachers, others of parents etc., lest indeed you cry out immediately, "this is spoken in Scripture, therefore I will do it." COMMENTARY ON JEREMIAH 1:10-16.[12]

HOW GOD USES IMAGES. ST. JOHN OF THE CROSS: It is noteworthy that as the five exterior senses send the images and species of their objects to these interior senses, so God and the devil can supernaturally represent to these faculties—without exterior senses—the same images and species; indeed, much more beautiful and perfect ones. God often represents many things to individuals through these images, and teaches them great wisdom, as is obvious through Scripture. For example . . . Jeremiah saw the rod keeping watch. THE ASCENT OF MOUNT CARMEL.[13]

JUDGMENT AND HOPE. MARTIN LUTHER: Jeremiah also foretold the punishment that was at hand, namely, the destruction of Jerusalem and of the whole land, and the Babylonian captivity, indeed the punishment of all nations as well. Yet, along with this, he gives comfort and promises that at a definite time, after the punishment is over, they shall be released and shall return to their land and to Jerusalem, etc. And this is the most important thing in Jeremiah. It was for this very thing that Jeremiah was raised up, as is indicated in the first chapter by the vision of the rod and the boiling pots coming from the north.

And this was highly necessary; for since this cruel hardship was to come upon the people, and they were to be uprooted and carried away out of their land, many pious souls—such as Daniel and others—would have been driven to despair of God and his promises. For they would not have been able to think otherwise than that it was all over with them, that they were utterly cast off by God, and that no Christ would ever come, but that God, in great anger, had taken back his promises because of the people's sin. PREFACE TO THE PROPHET JEREMIAH.[14]

WHY AN ALMOND TREE? JOHN TRAPP: It has its name in Hebrew from "watching," because it watches, as it were, to bud and bear before other trees, even in the deep of winter, and when it is coldest. Hereby the prophet is animated, though young, and assured that he shall have the fruit of his so early labors. God cares not for those *arbores autumnales* [autumn trees], trees that do not bud until the latter end of the harvest. The truth of all his predictions is designed, though little believed by most: the speediness also of their performance, as verse 12 and Ezekiel 7:10-11, a good comment on this text, [indicate]. The sins of God's people, says one, are sooner ripe than those of other heathens, because they have the constant light and heart of his Word to hasten their maturity. This was typified by the basket of summer fruits, and by the almond tree in this text. As the almond tree, says another, has a bitter rind but a sweet kernel, so has sanctified affliction; and again, as the almond tree is made more fruitful by driving nails into it, letting out a noxious gum that hinders the fruitfulness thereof, so is a good person made better by afflictions. COMMENTARY ON JEREMIAH 1:11.[15]

---

[12]Bugenhagen, *In Ieremiam*, G2v-G3r; citing Lk 24:44-49; Jn 8:44.
[13]St. John of the Cross, *Collected Works*, 220.

[14]LW 35:279-280 (WA, DB 11.1:191); citing Dan 9:2.
[15]Trapp, *A Commentary or Exposition*, 222-23*; citing Jude 13.

A BOILING POT. JOHANNES OECOLAMPADIUS: Jeremiah is not sent to the people right at the beginning, rather he is first prepared and strengthened, lest he perhaps fear that the Lord on account of his mercy might call off his sentence [of judgment] just as he did with Ninevites. Therefore, Jeremiah hears that the Lord will keep watch, and he says the same thing a second time and also that the prophecy had not been suspended, but he confirms it. He sees a pot come to boil. Jerusalem is compared to a pot or cauldron, a boiling pot in which carnal people are brought to a boil with fire, so that they are boiled up like foam through the heat. So the great testing will be in the church, so that they may depart from us who are not of us: "I will lead the third part through fire and I will refine them, as silver is refined, and as gold is tested," Zechariah 13. Indeed, they will all be led into the captivity of sinners, and they will lament in their consciences. On account of this affliction it is rightly called a narrow [necked] cauldron. COMMENTARY ON JEREMIAH 1:11-13.[16]

PRIMARY OBEDIENCE IS OWED TO THE WORD OF GOD. ARGULA VON GRUMBACH: One knows very well the importance of one's duty to obey the authorities. But where the Word of God is concerned neither pope, emperor, nor princes … have any jurisdiction. For my part, I have to confess in the name of God and by my soul's salvation, that if I were to deny Luther and Melanchthon's writing I would be denying God and his word, which may God forbid forever. Amen.

Haven't you read the first chapter of Jeremiah, where the Lord says to him: "What do you see?" He says: "I see a vigilant rod." Says the Lord: "You see correctly, for I am ceaselessly vigilant in order to bring my words to pass." He asks him again: "What else do you see?" "I see a burning pot, and the face of God from midnight." Says the Lord: "You have seen correctly; for from midnight, every evil will be revealed to every inhabitant of the earth." The pot burns; and truly you and your university will never

extinguish it. And neither the pope with his decretals nor Aristotle, who has never been a Christian, nor you yourselves can manage it. You may imagine that you can defy God, cast down his prophets and apostles from heaven, and banish them from the world. This shall not happen. I beseech you my masters, let [Christ] stay, have no doubt about it: God will surely preserve his holy and blessed word. As he has hitherto declared, has done in the Old and New Testament, still does, and will continue to do. TO THE UNIVERSITY OF INGOLSTADT.[17]

A CITY SCORCHING UNDER SIEGE. THE ENGLISH ANNOTATIONS: Now this pot, thus seething, or boiling, with fire under it, resembles Jerusalem, and the grievous conditions of its inhabitants during the siege of the city. Though some would have the analogy consist in the liquor boiling over out of the pot, and the inhabitants by violence cast out of the city, I suppose rather the miseries contained within are intended here.… And thus the people themselves seem to have understood the passage, when in derision, as pointing this at Jeremiah they say, "The city is the cauldron and we are the flesh." Nor is it the flesh, but the liquor, wherein it is sod that is wont in boiling to run over. Nevertheless, by the pot, some here understand, not the city of Jerusalem, but the Chaldean army, that should come in like a seething pot full of scalding water upon them, and not upon the city of Jerusalem only, but upon the whole country of Judea, not unlike those vials and vessels that are said to be poured out upon several persons and places. Moreover, one proceeds further, and would have it be a deep hearth of fire that the Assyrian, Chaldean, and other Asian kings, with whom fire was esteemed as a deity and worshiped as a god, were wont to have carried it before them and their armies when they went forth upon any expedition.… But I conceive it much safer to interpret Scripture by Scripture, and one prophet by another, living especially together around the same

[16]Oecolampadius, *In Hieremiam*, 1:Biv; citing Jon 3:10-4:2; Zech 13:9.

[17]Argula, *A Woman's Voice*, 76-77*; citing Acts 5:19; 5:29; Mt 21:39; Mic 3:3; Rev 16:9, 11.

time, and having reference, in likelihood, to one another. ANNOTATIONS ON JEREMIAH 1:13.[18]

KINGS, IDOLATRY, AND UNFAITHFULNESS.

JOHANNES OECOLAMPADIUS: As the punishment is just, he adds the sin: "They have such kings by law who have abandoned their God and true King. They do not attend to my judgment. Therefore, others will give judgment on my behalf." Behold how God explains himself from the beginning. "How would I defend those who do not know me as God, because they worship foreign gods?" They are destitute of faith. This prophecy was spoken under the most religious king Josiah, when many people had the appearance of holiness and everyone would testify that God is one. But meanwhile they were yoking themselves to foreign gods, by which they were declaring themselves actually to have left behind the only true God. They followed these idols with great devotion, and before them they burned incense.

This can be understood similarly today. As true religion is abandoned, the whole world comes to falsehood. The person is more to be punished who does not adore some saint, that is, some effigy of a person, than the one who blasphemes Christ, the image of the Father's substance. Faithlessness is true idolatry and apostasy, on account of which the enemy will lead you into Babylon, as in 1 Thessalonians 2. Because they did not receive a love of the truth, so that they might be saved, therefore God sent to them an error as religious practice, so that they might believe a lie and all might be judged who did not believe the truth, but agreed to iniquity. As in Romans 1: God gave over to a false perception those who worshiped that known thing, not that it is equal certainly in spirit and faith, hence they turned to the cult of idols. For the various kinds of sin, while they reign in us, deliver us up to many tyrants, who boldly rule among us, so that it is impossible that we might come to believe or abandon our sins. COMMENTARY ON JEREMIAH 1:16.[19]

AS A PREACHER, JEREMIAH IS AN IRON PILLAR.

LANCELOT ANDREWES: For sure, the Christian duty of bearing wrong, where it is well persuaded, does mainly strengthen the civil [obligation] of doing no wrong, and the Christian [obligation] of departing with our own charitably does strengthen the civil [duty] of not taking other people's injury; and so, of the rest. That he called it not amiss that called divinity the backbone of the prince's law, and consequently, religion [as the backbone] of the commonwealth. So that, not only Moses, and Paul, by calling on the name of God, but Elijah and Jeremiah, by teaching the will of God—not by prayer but by preaching—[these] are one, an "iron pillar," the other, "the chariot and horsemen of Israel," in his time. SERMON ON PSALM 75:3.[20]

---

[18]Downame, ed., *Annotations*, 9B2v-9B3r*; citing Ezek 11:3, 7; 24:3, 5; 11:3; Rev 15:7; 16:1, 4, 8, 12, 17.

[19]Oecolampadius, *In Heremiam*, 1:B2r; citing Rom 1:18-32.
[20]Andrewes, *Works*, 2:8.

JEREMIAH 2:1-37
ISRAEL FORSAKES THE LORD

¹The word of the Lord came to me, saying, ²"Go and proclaim in the hearing of Jerusalem, Thus says the Lord,

"I remember the devotion of your youth,
    your love as a bride,
how you followed me in the wilderness,
    in a land not sown.
³Israel was holy to the Lord,
    the firstfruits of his harvest.
All who ate of it incurred guilt;
    disaster came upon them,
declares the Lord."

⁴Hear the word of the Lord, O house of Jacob, and all the clans of the house of Israel. ⁵Thus says the Lord:

"What wrong did your fathers find in me
    that they went far from me,
and went after worthlessness, and became
    worthless?
⁶They did not say, 'Where is the Lord
    who brought us up from the land of Egypt,
who led us in the wilderness,
    in a land of deserts and pits,
in a land of drought and deep darkness,
    in a land that none passes through,
    where no man dwells?'
⁷And I brought you into a plentiful land
    to enjoy its fruits and its good things.
But when you came in, you defiled my land
    and made my heritage an abomination.
⁸The priests did not say, 'Where is the Lord?'
    Those who handle the law did not know me;
the shepherds[a] transgressed against me;
    the prophets prophesied by Baal
    and went after things that do not profit.

⁹"Therefore I still contend with you,
    declares the Lord,
    and with your children's children I will
        contend.

¹⁰For cross to the coasts of Cyprus and see,
    or send to Kedar and examine with care;
    see if there has been such a thing.
¹¹Has a nation changed its gods,
    even though they are no gods?
But my people have changed their glory
    for that which does not profit.
¹²Be appalled, O heavens, at this;
    be shocked, be utterly desolate,
declares the Lord,
¹³for my people have committed two evils:
they have forsaken me,
    the fountain of living waters,
and hewed out cisterns for themselves,
    broken cisterns that can hold no water.

¹⁴"Is Israel a slave? Is he a homeborn servant?
    Why then has he become a prey?
¹⁵The lions have roared against him;
    they have roared loudly.
They have made his land a waste;
    his cities are in ruins, without inhabitant.
¹⁶Moreover, the men of Memphis and
        Tahpanhes
have shaved[b] the crown of your head.
¹⁷Have you not brought this upon yourself
    by forsaking the Lord your God,
    when he led you in the way?
¹⁸And now what do you gain by going to Egypt
    to drink the waters of the Nile?
Or what do you gain by going to Assyria
    to drink the waters of the Euphrates?[c]
¹⁹Your evil will chastise you,
    and your apostasy will reprove you.
Know and see that it is evil and bitter
    for you to forsake the Lord your God;
    the fear of me is not in you,
declares the Lord GOD of hosts.

²⁰"For long ago I broke your yoke
    and burst your bonds;

but you said, 'I will not serve.'
Yes, on every high hill
 and under every green tree
 you bowed down like a whore.
²¹Yet I planted you a choice vine,
 wholly of pure seed.
How then have you turned degenerate
 and become a wild vine?
²²Though you wash yourself with lye
 and use much soap,
 the stain of your guilt is still before me,
declares the Lord GOD.
²³How can you say, 'I am not unclean,
 I have not gone after the Baals'?
Look at your way in the valley;
 know what you have done—
a restless young camel running here and there,
 ²⁴a wild donkey used to the wilderness,
in her heat sniffing the wind!
 Who can restrain her lust?
None who seek her need weary themselves;
 in her month they will find her.
²⁵Keep your feet from going unshod
 and your throat from thirst.
But you said, 'It is hopeless,
 for I have loved foreigners,
 and after them I will go.'

²⁶"As a thief is shamed when caught,
 so the house of Israel shall be shamed:
they, their kings, their officials,
 their priests, and their prophets,
²⁷who say to a tree, 'You are my father,'
 and to a stone, 'You gave me birth.'
For they have turned their back to me,
 and not their face.
But in the time of their trouble they say,
 'Arise and save us!'
²⁸But where are your gods
 that you made for yourself?
Let them arise, if they can save you,
 in your time of trouble;

for as many as your cities
 are your gods, O Judah.

²⁹"Why do you contend with me?
 You have all transgressed against me,
declares the Lord.
³⁰In vain have I struck your children;
 they took no correction;
your own sword devoured your prophets
 like a ravening lion.
³¹And you, O generation, behold the word of
  the Lord.
Have I been a wilderness to Israel,
 or a land of thick darkness?
Why then do my people say, 'We are free,
 we will come no more to you'?
³²Can a virgin forget her ornaments,
 or a bride her attire?
Yet my people have forgotten me
 days without number.

³³"How well you direct your course
 to seek love!
So that even to wicked women
 you have taught your ways.
³⁴Also on your skirts is found
 the lifeblood of the guiltless poor;
you did not find them breaking in.
 Yet in spite of all these things
³⁵you say, 'I am innocent;
 surely his anger has turned from me.'
Behold, I will bring you to judgment
 for saying, 'I have not sinned.'
³⁶How much you go about,
 changing your way!
You shall be put to shame by Egypt
 as you were put to shame by Assyria.
³⁷From it too you will come away
 with your hands on your head,
for the Lord has rejected those in whom you
  trust,
 and you will not prosper by them.

a Or *rulers* b Hebrew *grazed* c Hebrew *the River*

OVERVIEW: This long chapter of Jeremiah describes Israel's adultery and idolatry in a graphic and searing set of roles and symbols: the unfaithful bride, the ungrateful recipient, the broken cistern, the broken yoke, the wild vine, the uncleansed stain, the wild camel, the donkey in heat, and the bloodied oppressor of the poor. Reformation-era commentators not only sought to describe with care the sin of Israel but also found ample opportunity to discuss the many forms of idolatry in their own day and to issue a call to full and singular faith in God. Much of the symbolic language not only details Israel's outward sins but also captures the inner landscape of a soul tormented by temptation and unholy desire. Thus interpreters diagnose sin in great detail, point out resistance to preaching of repentance and gospel in their own time, and remind readers that an adulterous and complacent church might face a judgment similar to ancient Israel.

Moreover, it is clear that most commentary on Jeremiah occurred from the 1530s onward, when hope that the Reformation would sweep across the whole of Europe gradually dimmed. The spread of Protestant movements continued in some regions, but had slowed dramatically in others. Spain and Italy remained solidly Roman Catholic. Protestant commentators warn readers of the continuation and promotion of idolatrous ceremonies and of saints and their pilgrimage sites—the empty cisterns and shrines to Baal of their sixteenth century.

2:1-12 You Have Abandoned Me for Foreign Gods

KNOWING THE LETTER AND KNOWING GOD.
ANDREAS BODENSTEIN VON KARLSTADT: I fancied myself a Christian when I picked profound and beautiful sayings out of Jeremiah's writings for a disputation, lecture, or sermon, or for other speeches and writings, and I thought that this ought to please God extremely well. But when I began to think and reflect properly, I discovered that I had neither come to know God nor to love the highest good as a good. I saw that the created letter was what I had come to know and love; in

that I rested; it had become my God, and I did not notice that God said through Jeremiah, "Those who kept my commandments knew me and did not ask for me." Note this, how can one handle and keep God's law when one does not know God or ask for him? THE MEANING OF THE TERM *GELASSEN*.[1]

REPENTANCE FOR AN UNFAITHFUL SPOUSE.
JOHANNES BUGENHAGEN: In this next chapter we see the calling of the prophet and the command concerning what he ought to prophesy. Truly this prophet Jeremiah, according to the vocation that he received from the Lord, begins to prophesy or to preach repentance. He disputes with the people concerning their ingratitude and their forgetfulness regarding the favors of God, whom they ought to acknowledge as God their Father. Jeremiah harshly reproaches their grave idolatry and contempt for the Word of God, whence he says it will happen that they may perish. If an exceptional bridegroom falls in love with an unworthy bride, and makes her a partner in all the good things he has, would you not say the worst sort of thing, if afterward, forgetful of these things, she showed contempt for her husband? If only we would not be guilty of the same ingratitude, we who by the blood of Christ have been freed, not from Egypt, but from sin and hell. See truly how much he loves, he who calls back even the adulteress and ungrateful one and threatens her with evil things to this end: that she not perish. COMMENTARY ON JEREMIAH 2:1-2.[2]

ALLEGORY OF MARRIAGE. HULDRYCH ZWINGLI: It seems that two things are to be examined, two things on account of which God does not casually forget him, that is, Israel. Certainly there is that goodness and intact love from his youth with which he followed after God. Moreover, the prophet puts forward an allegory of a wife, who when she is young is indeed yielding and loving with her husband; she promptly obeys his every command and follows after him everywhere and

---

[1] CRR 8:140.
[2] Bugenhagen, *In Ieremiam*, O2v.

back. Thus a youthful or childlike Israel embodied in Abraham, Isaac, and Jacob minds and loves God, and follows him from Chaldea into Canaan, from Canaan to Mesopotamia and Egypt, and out of Egypt through the desert, an uninhabitable place, destitute of necessary things. EXPLANATIONS OF THE PROPHET JEREMIAH 2:2.[3]

GOD'S LOVE AND THE FOURTH STEP OF LOVE. ST. JOHN OF THE CROSS: This [fourth] degree of love is a very elevated step. For as the soul at this stage through so genuine a love pursues God in the spirit of suffering for his sake. His Majesty frequently gives it joy by paying it visits of spiritual delight. For this immense love that Christ, the Word, has cannot long endure the sufferings of his beloved without responding. God affirms this through Jeremiah: "I have remembered you, pitying your youth and tenderness when you followed me in the desert." Spiritually speaking, the desert is an interior detachment from every creature in which the soul neither pauses nor rests in anything. THE DARK NIGHT.[4]

THE FIRST FRUITS OF GOD'S HARVEST. JUAN DE MALDONADO: "Israel is holy to the Lord." This is not a profane people, as others are, but Israel is consecrated to God. Therefore, when Israel betrays the Lord, or falls into servitude, Israel is guilty of sacrilege. "His firstfruits:" this metaphor signifies in two ways. First, Israel was the first people to be chosen by God, so they were the firstfruits consecrated to God. . . . Moreover, 2 Thessalonians 2:13 says: "We ought always to give thanks for you, brothers, because God chose you as the firstfruits of salvation." As David also says in Psalm 74:2: "Remember your congregation, which you have possessed from the beginning." The second metaphor is that no one except God is allowed to afflict or consume the Jewish people without committing the sin of sacrilege. Likewise no one except the priests are allowed to eat the firstfruits. Therefore, as indicated above, after the Chaldeans afflict God's people with a

harsh servitude, they receive punishment. COMMENTARY ON THE PROPHETS, JEREMIAH 2:3.[5]

REPENTANCE AND KNOWLEDGE OF BIBLICAL HISTORY. JOHANNES BUGENHAGEN: This is a grievous complaint; Jeremiah upbraids the people, in this preaching of the law on repentance, sin, ingratitude, idolatry, and contempt of God, who had brought the people forth from Egypt through the Red Sea and through the desert, into the best land—as a groom leads his graceful bride forth from every evil and danger of body and soul into all his good things both corporeal and spiritual. Indeed, God gave to them a physical kingdom and a priesthood that is his word and his worship. Read about the blessings of God furnished to the people in the law in Exodus and Joshua. Read about the contempt of the people, princes, priests, and prophets, and their idolatry in the book of Judges, in 1 and 2 Kings, and 2 Chronicles, etc. In vain do they read the prophets, and in vain do we write to those who do not know the histories. COMMENTARY ON JEREMIAH 2:5.[6]

IDOLATROUS VANITIES IN OUR TIME. JOHANNES OECOLAMPADIUS: "They have gone far from me." "They have abandoned my law, which I gave to them, and they do not hear my voice, and do not walk in it. But they go after the thoughts of their own hearts." Then they call on the Baals, which is a vanity in this way: the idols that remain today are no fewer than they were long ago. Thus, let me remain silent concerning those Baals who were worshiped in temples. But if you consider current doctrines, you will see how at once a most foolish person can degenerate from faith into idolatrous works, how a defection is made at once from God to the saints, from truth to a lie, from true religion to hypocrisy. Who has kept in mind how many evils have abounded from free will, the Mass, and the doctrine of purgatory? All of these things had their beginnings from the most ancient ones, and all those

---

[3]Zwingli, *Complanationes*, 76.
[4]St. John of the Cross, *Collected Works*, 443.

[5]Maldonado, *Commentarii in Prophetas*, 8; citing Num 5:9.
[6]Bugenhagen, *In Ieremiam*, P1r-v.

things were held in a certain approved and received version of holiness. Whoever withdraws from faith is far away from God. Vain are those deeds, because idols do not give aid, as in Romans 1: "They died away in their thoughts and are so in their foolish deeds, and their foolish hearts are left in darkness."

. . . Ingratitude grows to this extent: that they do not consider what and how great are the benefits they recently received, and just so with us. How the glory of that One is transferred into the likeness of a young bull. Scripture has to inculcate the exodus from Egypt more often, because the miracles were done among greater things. See if they do not fall silent before these blessings—those who seek salvation in the works of the law. So it is said to them, "Has Christ died in vain for you?" For to them it said that Christ was crucified before their very eyes. Similarly with the Corinthians: "The one is of Paul, the other of Apollos"; they do not grasp how the Lord frees them through the cross from the Egypt of the devil. So they hear: "Is Paul crucified for us so that in that man he might help you to glory?" Neither Francis nor Benedict led you from the Egypt of sin, nor did they drown Pharaoh—but Christ did![†] Those who hide the light of the gospel with a multitude of ceremonies not only have forgotten God but also return to Egypt. COMMENTARY ON JEREMIAH 2:5-6.[7]

THE LIFE-GIVING LAND OF FAITH. JOHANNES OECOLAMPADIUS: "And he led you into a fertile land." The faith of the church is to us as a place on the earth, when we indeed believe in Christ and truly eat all the good things of the earth. If you hear me, you will consume the good things of the earth; we will be participants even here through the taste of faith and through the foretaste of the Spirit. How great are the joys of the faithful, which neither the eye has seen nor the ear has heard. Christ himself is our land and vine because we are planted in him. We will consume his fruit, in which we continue through faith, which leads to

the highest knowledge of Christ. The land is contaminated if the unworthy inhabit it and unbelievers throw away the name of faith, through which the name of God is blasphemed among the nations; for indeed the land is made sterile through human sin. COMMENTARY ON JEREMIAH 2:7.[8]

THE GIFT OF TRUE AND GODLY TEACHERS. NIKOLAUS SELNECKER: The prophet takes up the priests, particularly the learned shepherds, teachers, and prophets. It is terrible that those who are to show others the right way and with good examples, those who should illumine the way ahead with a light, are the ones who first deviate from the Word of God. They soil themselves with false teaching and indecent living. What good can come of that? How shall the poor little sheep be grazed? That means, as Christ says, "It would have been better for anyone who causes these little ones who believe in me to stumble that a millstone be hung on his neck and he be thrown into the depths of the sea," Matthew 18.

"I must always reprimand you and will plead with your children."

How very hard these words are and how great and severe a complaint against our disobedient folk. We warn and threaten those who do not want to follow God and his word. So they have also in themselves a pure trust that God first looks upon those who deliberately sin and God still does not withdraw from us. But God initially goes forth with his word and reprimands us through his law and shows us our sins and misdeeds. And he wants to reprimand and punish us through his word so that he might again bring us to right and to gain us. Therefore, he needs true preachers to lead us urgently to his word and through it chastises our evil being. This is truly a great grace of God, who does not for even an hour withdraw his hand from us, but always seeks after us with warnings, with bitter, earnest, and honorable punishments and threats as long as it is permissible with us. But we truly do not want to hear or follow. So that means, "The people no longer want

---

[7]Oecolampadius, *In Hieremiam*, 1:B4v; citing Rom 1:21; Gal 2:21; 1 Cor 3:4; 1:13. †St. Francis of Assisi (d. 1226) and St. Benedict of Nursia (d. 547).

[8]Oecolampadius, *In Hieremiam*, 1:C1r; citing Is 1:19.

to allow my Spirit to correct them," Genesis 6. And again, "So shall you come to be as it is when I withdraw my hand from you."

If true and pious teachers bring before us God's word and honor, the salvation of Christ, and the blessing of a true and earnest sense of our sins, vices, and offenses, what should we do? Should we grumble and thereby appear angry? Should we get agitated as most do—the princes, lords, honorable people, citizens, farmers, teachers, and unlearned? When we understand and still have a fragment of a fitting fear of God in our hearts, and do not despise the testimony of our own knowledge, so we should heartily thank God that he has given us such teachers who without timidity show us the Word of God, what is deficient in us, and how we behave against God, and that we at that time should return to God. THE WHOLE PROPHET JEREMIAH 2:8-10.[9]

THE DEVOTION OF IDOLATERS AND THE GLORY OF GOD. NIKOLAUS SELNECKER: Scholars debate about what Kethim and Kedar are. Jeremiah does not name these lands to praise and approve of their heathen idolatry, but that he might make the Jews thereby blush and be ashamed, as he wants to say. The island of Kethim is from Macedonia and Greece, and also the Italian lands. And Kedar is from Arabia. All of these idols, which are truly no gods, they honor and do not allow themselves to turn away. "But my people—who know me as their own true, eternal God, and have my word, and promises—abandon me, are disobedient to me, and lose the true glory. That is me—the true God—I alone am your honor, fame, and glory."

Note here where God's word is purely and publicly taught, that is the glory of God. We have no better glory than if we have the Word of God. Other worldly forms of glory cannot be compared to it. Thereby speaks David, "When I have you, Lord, I ask nothing of heaven and earth." Similarly, he says, "How beautiful is your dwelling place."

But how fiercely God burns when one deviates from the word he himself has revealed to us and one turns himself to a human law and serves false gods that have been erected. THE WHOLE PROPHET JEREMIAH 2:10-12.[10]

2:13 You Have Me, the Fountain of Living Waters

A HUNGER AND THIRST FOR CREATURES. ST. JOHN OF THE CROSS: For the sake of a clearer and fuller understanding of our assertions, it will be beneficial to explain here and now how these appetites can cause harm in two principal ways within those in whom they dwell: They deprive them of God's Spirit; and they weary, torment, darken, defile, and weaken them. Jeremiah mentions this in chapter 2. . . . Their appetite and joy are already so extended and dispersed among creatures—and with such anxiety—that they cannot be satisfied. Rather, their appetite and thirst increase more as they regress further from God, the fount that alone can satisfy them. To these individuals God refers through Jeremiah. . . . The reason for this dissatisfaction is that creatures do not slake the thirst of the avaricious, but rather intensify it. THE ASCENT OF MOUNT CARMEL.[11]

THE ONLY REMEDY FOR SIN. MENNO SIMONS: O worthy reader, we testify the truth in Christ. Take it to heart. You may believe, seek, carry on, hope where and what you please; but we are sure of this, that you will find in the Word of God no other remedy for your sins that is satisfactory to God than the one we have pointed out to you, which is Christ Jesus—if the Scriptures are not spurious and false. . . .

All those then who seek other remedies for their sins, however glorious and holy they may seem, other than this God-provided remedy, these forsake the Lord's death, which he died for us,

---

[9]Selnecker, *Der gantze Prophet Jeremias*, B2v-B3v; citing Mt 18:6; Gen 6:3; Num 14:27.

[10]Selnecker, *Der gantze Prophet Jeremias*, B3v-B4r; citing Ps 73:25; 84:1.

[11]St. John of the Cross, *Collected Works*, 130, 300.

and his innocent blood, which he shed for us. They are those of whom the Lord complains through his prophet Jeremiah: My people have committed two evils; they have forsaken me, the fountain of living waters, and have hewn them out cisterns that can hold no water. FOUNDATION OF CHRISTIAN DOCTRINE.[12]

DIVINE CISTERNS AND CHRIST THE UNICORN. PAUL GLOCK: For just as all the animals in the forest know that they must follow the unicorn and wait on him as on their prince—for through him the water must be purified—even so all the devout are to go to no well except the one to which their unicorn Christ first went and from which he drank himself. Then we will not be punished along with Israel through the prophet Jeremiah. . . . "Whoever follows me," says Christ, "does not walk in darkness, but will have the light of life." For he leads his sheep to the right pasture and to the living well, which never runs dry. May the Lord give us all a great thirst for this well, like the thirst of a stag for a water brook. LETTER TO HIS WIFE, ELSE.[13]

GOD, OUR FONT OF LIVING WATER. JOHANNES BUGENHAGEN: By this most elegant allegory or erudite simile he describes the sin of the Jews, on account of which they were going to perish unless they repented and returned to the Lord, whom they had abandoned. . . .

God says that he himself is the font and spring of living waters, that is, the water, which suggests further a perpetual flowing forth and flowing to us, without our reckoning or work, a water born of a fountain of goodness and abundance. Having the Word of God, which means believing, we then have a favorable God and Father toward us; he grants every mercy, that is, he pours his favor over us, whom he makes his sons through faith, just as it says in John 1: "He gives them the power to become children of God." To those who believe in his name, who are not of blood etc., he brings to mind to us in

perpetuity a pure fountain of living water with his goodness and grace without our works. Not in our own merit: for indeed we are sinners, and on our own we are condemned; that is, he suggests and pours forth all things to those of us who believe in Christ; those things that are eternal and temporal (this is living water), the word of eternal life, given to the pious by preachers and doctors, he gives his sacraments; he gives his righteousness or the forgiveness of sins, encouragement, consolation, his Holy Spirit in various gifts, with which the church is built up and adorned. He is present to us in all of our temptation and the necessities of body and soul, he offers daily bread; he helps us with all things, which tend to victory, according to the promise. All these things are added to us; Christ preserves us, lest we perish through the devil, the world, and our own flesh. COMMENTARY ON JEREMIAH 2:13.[14]

2:14-37 Faithful God and Adulterous Israel

OVERCONFIDENT BELIEVERS AND PUNISHING PREDATORS. HEINRICH BULLINGER: After the remembrance of their sins, Jeremiah now turns to punishment, recalling how much evil they were suffering and the greater suffering they were about to undergo. Not indeed because of any moroseness in God, who in fact presently desires to heal them right after that, but because of their own particular guilt, I say, on account of their sins and because they reject all the remedies of God. Therefore, he everywhere recalls and censures their sins. Such things are to be applied to us and to our own time, in which the same sins are to be found in the church of God. Therefore, since God is the same and does not change, he necessarily manages us with the same punishments or even worse ones. Today wars are begotten from wars and no rest can be hoped for. Italy burns with factions and wars; they are fighting in France; Germany mounts expeditions; great is the fear of the Turk. Meanwhile miserable humans are familiar with diseases and a lack of goods. What shall I say? We zealously serve a true God, but when

---

[12]Simons, *Complete Writings*, 157.
[13]CRR 10:306; citing John 8:11-13; Ps 42:1.

[14]Bugenhagen, *In Ieremiam*, R1r-v; citing Jn 1:12.

he already calls us into the way of salvation through the gospel, we turn our backs on God, nay rather having turned, we attack the ministers of God and tear them to pieces because of the truth they preach.

Now the Jews indeed, because they believed and boasted that they were the children of God—just as in John 8 they were boasting against the Lord—they did not suppose that those evils would come upon them, nor were they rightly thinking even about their current calamities in which they were already entangled and afflicted. So also today we boast rashly and in vain in the name "Christian," assuming that God will never abandon the church nor give her into the hands of the Turks or other infidel tyrants. . . .

Moreover, God explains more fully how they were exposed to all as prey for the hunt. "Over him", he says, "the Lions are roaring." In the Hebrew language they are young lions, for they are more ferocious. Also in the Proverbs of Solomon, the most savage tyrants are signified by lions. The "roar" or "growl" of the lion expresses its savagery, and that which follows: "they have made their land a wilderness." With fire and iron they have destroyed those regions, so that when the farmers had been slaughtered, and the towns and villages had been burned up, no one inhabited the land; it is infested with wild animals; it is no longer farmed and [is now] bristling with thorns and thickets. SERMON ON JEREMIAH 2:14-19.[15]

A SLAVE OR A SON? THE ENGLISH ANNOTATIONS: Some take this to be spoken as if God should demand of them whether he had used Israel as a slave and not as a son, so it should be, as afterward. Others, rather referring to it as his evil entreaty and base usage by others; is he a slave, that he is so slavishly used? And the Jewish doctors here fitly add, how it comes to pass that he who was in so great respect and reckoning with God . . . so that he related to him as his "firstborn son" should now be left unto such a deplorable condition, so that everyone should at pleasure wrong him and

dominer over him as if he were a common slave. Though herein they seem to be out of the way in that they make this the demand not of God or the prophet but of Israel itself, or of the people, by which God, by the prophet, should return answer unto. ANNOTATIONS ON JEREMIAH 2:14.[16]

IDOLATRY MAKES WORSE ALL THAT IT TOUCHES. RICHARD HOOKER: Paul and Barnabas, when infidels admiring their virtues went about to sacrifice to them, rent their garments in token of horror, and as frightened persons ran crying through the press of the people, "O people, why do you do these things?" They knew the force of that dreadful curse whereunto idolatry makes subject. Nor is there cause why the guilty, sustaining the same, should grudge or complain of injustice. For whatsoever evil befalls, in that respect, they have made themselves worthy to suffer it. As for those things either *whereon* or else *wherewith* superstition works, polluted they are by such abuse and deprived of that dignity which their nature delights in. For there is nothing that grieves and, as it were, even loath itself whenever iniquity causes it to serve vile purposes. Idolatry, therefore, makes whatever it touches worse. LAWES OF ECCLESIASTICAL POLITY.[17]

GOD DOES NOT FORSAKE US, BUT WE HIM. LANCELOT ANDREWES: It is we who forsake him, not he us. It is the ship that moves, though they that be in it think the land goes from them, not they from it. Seems there any variation, as that of night? It is *umbra terrae* [shadow of the earth] that makes it, the light makes it not. Is there anything resembling a shadow? A vapor rises from us, makes the cloud, which is a penthouse between, and takes him from our sight. That vapor is our lust, there is the *apud quem* [with whom]. Is any tempted? It is our own lust that does it, that entices us to sin, that brings us to the shadow of death. It is not God. No more than he can be tempted; no more can he tempt any. If we

---

[15]Bullinger, *Conciones*, 14r-v; citing Prov 28:15.

[16]Downame, ed., *Annotations*, 9B4v*; citing Deut 8:5; 32:6, Jer 49:1; Ex 4:22.
[17]Hooker, *Lawes of Ecclesiastical Polity* 5.17; citing Acts 14:14.

find any change, the *apud* [by] is with us, not him; we change; he is unchanged. Surely, a person goes about as a shadow. His ways are the truth. He cannot deny himself. SERMON ON JAMES 1:16-17.[18]

SIN IS BITTERSWEET. JOHN TRAPP: So all sin will prove in the issue, and when the bottom of the bag is turned upward. There will be bitterness in the end, as Abner said to Joab. Laban will show himself at parting, howsoever. Tamar will be more hated than ever she was loved. Drunkenness is sweet, but wormwood is bitter. These inhabitants of Jerusalem were made drunk, but with wormwood. They found that sin was a *dulcacidum*, "a bitter sweet." Sweet in the mouth, but bitter in the stomach, as that passage in Revelation; like in Adam's apple or Esau's pottage, or Jonathan's honey, or Judas's thirty pieces, whereof he would gladly have been rid but could not. They burnt like a spark of hellfire in his hand, but especially in his conscience. The devil, with the panther, hides his deformed head till his sweet scent has drawn other beasts into his danger, and then he devours them. Did we consider what sin will cost us at last, when we are naive? COMMENTARY ON JEREMIAH 2:19.[19]

REJECTING THE YOKE AND INDULGING IN SIN. NIKOLAUS SELNECKER: For of old you have broken your yoke and torn apart your bands; and said, "I will not submit." This is a serious complaint. You act unjustly and are idolatrous, evil and impenitent, and yet you want to go unpunished. First, Jeremiah scolds the Jewish people because of idolatry, that they honor other gods, which cannot even help them. Second, they themselves lean on foreign help and wisdom with the heathen, at the same time that they want to protect themselves against all misfortune and future punishment. Third, they hold all such things as pious and righteous; the longer the idolatry and other shameful things go, the greater they become. So it is now with both of our adversaries—what the papists do and the

errors that they themselves confess. Since they do not want to have their errors reprimanded and also their unrepentant life among us to be exaggerated, so this is their misery upon misery. One wants to be pious in short order, when one at the same time does something terrible. One even boasts of public offenses— prostitution, usury, gluttony, fraud, and the like. And such an unrepentant life can be so torn apart that one hardly ever observes what one wants to recognize as a sin. As they often allow themselves to say: they know that in ten years they have not committed a sin. But at the same time they are blasphemers, criminals, greedy misers, robbers, sorcerers, drunkards, usurers, and rebels. When now true teachers according to their office see and reprimand such terrible confidence and lack of repentance, so they say, "What? They want the pastors to correct us? We will in no way put ourselves under them." That is, "We neither want to know nor allow ourselves to be corrected. We want to live just as the others do. Let us tear up these bands and let us throw your yoke off us. . . ."

These are the godless things people are saying in today's times at court, in the presence of great lords, princes, and noble people, but also among citizens, city councilors, and others. And such talk is established here and there in their work, as these are an example before their eyes.

The prophet names all idolatry and unrepentant life as "prostitution" because one abandons God and is unfaithful, a perjurer on his word, runs off to other horrible places, and allows himself to become involved among nasty foreigners. That is, to be involved with idolaters and falsely ordered worship, and pursue a fully unrepentant life in many sins and against one's conscience. THE WHOLE PROPHET JEREMIAH 2:20.[20]

THE LUSCIOUS GRAPES OF CHRIST. PAUL GLOCK: A noble bunch of grapes is shown to us. . . . It is the true plant of righteousness, carried by two men. The one goes ahead and is aware of its weight. But he does not fully see the grape. The other walks behind. He also knows the weight but has

---

[18]Andrewes, *Works*, 3:74*; citing Ps. 39:11.
[19]Trapp, *A Commentary or Exposition*, 227*; citing 2 Sam 3:15; Lam 3:15.

[20]Selnecker, *Der gantze Prophet Jeremias*, C2v-C4v.

the advantage in that he sees it. These are the two Testaments, it seems to me, which both bring us to Christ, who cools our thirsty mouths with the luscious grapes. He has also let us into a land from where they came, and has planted us in it as a seedling, that we might also bear such fruit that might be food for the hungry. It is written, "I planted you a noble vine, a true seed, how have you then become a wild vine, wrong and degenerate?" LETTER TO HIS WIFE, ELSE.[21]

WORSHIPING THE TRUE GOD AND BEING TRULY CLEANSED OF SIN. HEINRICH BULLINGER:

The Jews had their own expiations, ablutions, sacrifices, fasts, prayers, and laments, with which they strove to cleanse themselves of their sins. For all that, they were meanwhile destitute of true faith and clung to idolatry, which was worthless in atoning for their sins. So Isaiah also testifies in chapter 1 and Jeremiah asserts the same thing here, saying, "If you have washed yourself with niter and multiplied borates for yourself," or "You have used such herbs in abundance for cleansing," nevertheless the stain of your iniquities will remain no less before God; that is, it will not be blotted out. I say it will stay fresh on you like some stain on a garment, indeed a great number of stains, washed in vain. Indeed, you are deceived as long as you suppose that sins are cleansed by any external cleansings, and that sins are forgiven based on sacrifices and expiations. In fact, we are cleansed by the blood of Christ through faith, and then the repentant life follows the expiation, a life in which with all foreign gods cast aside, we call on the one true God, and we depend on this God alone for all things while zealously crucifying the old self and making all our plans, words, and deeds according to the new self.

"How, therefore, can you say, 'I am not polluted, nor have I followed Baalim, or any foreign gods or idols?'" Indeed, much idol worship was directed to the true God: and the Jews were also worshiping other gods in such a way that they no less also worshiped the true God, or they certainly wanted

to seem to worship God no less. But since God commanded that he be worshiped alone, and forbade them to have other gods and forbade them to make any image or adore any image, everyone who did not simply obey the divine law was gravely sinning against God and his will. And so likewise also today they gravely sin who worship other gods along with the one God, and prostrate themselves while praying before idols; and then refer all things to the cult of eternal divinity. . . .

If you truly believe that God is present everywhere, that the singular and only God is sufficient for all necessary things, even for the giving of salvation in the first place; if you worship this God alone with your whole heart, soul, and strength; and if you only pray to that one alone through Jesus Christ, if you adore this one and only God: why do you seek to make supplications among Mary of Loreto, the Marian Queen of Bergamo, or Mary of Aquitaine? Why do you visit the thresholds of Peter and Paul? Why do you make pilgrimages to visit Saint James of Compostella in Spain, Saint Michael or Saint Jodocus in France?[†] Finally, why do you sacrifice[‡] and consecrate your sons and daughters to those I do not know: Benedict, Dominic, Rupert, Francis, Claire, and other obscure gods whom I do not know.[§] Your children were already consecrated to God at baptism. Or is this devotion not able to satisfy you, though it satisfied the apostles? SERMON ON JEREMIAH 2:22-23.[22]

THE WILD CAMEL AND ASS, THE MONK AND ISRAEL. HEINRICH BULLINGER: Once Jeremiah has sought two examples of particularly fast and

---

[21]CRR 10:303.

[22]Bullinger, *Conciones*, 16v, 17r-v; citing Is 1:16-18. [†]Bullinger has in mind here a series of pilgrimage sites and shrines, including the tombs of Saints Peter and Paul in Rome; shrines dedicated to Saint Mary of Loreto in Italy; possibly the Sanctuary of the Virgin near Bergamo, Italy; possibly the Black Madonna of Rocamadour in France; Saint James in Compostella, Spain; Mont Saint-Michel on the coast of Normandy; and Saint Jodocus in Brittany, France. [‡]Bullinger uses the verb *immolare*—to burn or kill in a sacrifice— in order to suggest a connection between worship of Baalim and child sacrifice in ancient Canaan and children consecrated to Christian saints. [§]Saint Benedict of Nursia (d. 547), Saint Dominic (d. 1221), St. Rupert of Salzburg (d. 710), Saint Francis of Assisi (d. 1226), and Saint Claire of Assisi (d. 1253).

fierce animals, he shows by enlarging on this theme how freely and madly they were carried into the worship of foreign gods and into the preservation of those cults to which they were accustomed. . . . "First," he says, "you are similar to the female camel, an extremely fast dromedary. Just as the camel with utmost freedom runs on its routes, so you are very prepared to move quickly to follow your idols and foreign cults. . . . Just as the wild ass is accustomed to the desert and cannot be tamed, so you are accustomed to the sacred groves and high places and foreign cults. But you cannot be led to the legitimate worship of God." So they were found to be, and so those asses are found still, the monks, who, as they seclude themselves from people, are not able to be tamed by humans so that they might be useful to the church and society. Just as the wild ass in her time, because of the violent desire of her soul, breathes out in a pant, in German "she sniffs and purrs," so even you Israel amuse yourself like one who is raving after the loves of a foreign cult, and you lean with the greatest zeal on idolatry. SERMON ON JEREMIAH 2:23-24.[23]

SINFUL CRAVINGS. ST. JOHN OF THE CROSS: People seeking the satisfaction of their desires grow tired, because they are like the famished who open their mouths to satisfy themselves with air. But they find that instead of being filled the mouth dries up more since air is not one's proper food. With this in mind Jeremiah says: "In the appetite of his will he drew in the air of his attachment." To comment on the dryness in which the soul is left, he immediately adds the advice: . . . Hold back your foot (that is, your mind) from nakedness and your throat from thirst (that is your will from satisfying its desire, which only causes greater thirst). THE ASCENT OF MOUNT CARMEL.[24]

IMPOTENT IDOLS, THEN AND NOW. KONRAD PELLIKAN: A fault is more disagreeable when one pretends to be confused, which is not an effective way to hide. The thief can only be confused when apprehended in theft. So Israel is openly confounded in its filthy idolatry, in which it surpasses all the other nations and which suits her least of all of them. Israel has always had as favorable to herself the all-powerful God of gods, whom it has despised in order to embrace vain, deaf, and base idols. Certainly, not only the common people want to be stupid in this way, but also their kings, princes, priests, and prophets. Who does not marvel that they were all so excited with such a great madness? Of course, these folk are prudent according to their generation. They are not afraid to say to a tree, "you are my father" and to a stone, "you gave birth to me." As they turned toward their idols, they turned their back and not their face to the Lord. These folk are completely foolish and ungodly. Very soon they will experience calamity and misfortune, from which their false gods will not be able to save them. At that time they will call on me in vain for their salvation. I will answer them: let those gods who are listening hear them, whom, after I was abandoned, preferred to worship with so much superstition that they had as many idols as towns. Not much different, even if it is not greater, is the error of Christians, whose cities are distinguished by their particular patron deities [i.e., saints], so that not a few cities worship and invoke these gods, if ever they fall on hard times, so with more confidence than if they were calling on God himself. This passage and others like it ought to be discussed more widely; so that with other passages also, the faithful people must be taught with more solid doctrine about various errors, by which they will know what is true and holy. COMMENTARY ON JEREMIAH 2:25-27.[25]

OF NOT WORSHIPING THE MOTHER OF GOD AND THE SAINTS. THOMAS MÜNTZER: First, dear Christians, let us give ourselves a jolt, and see if we too are like the heathen. The heathen worship Lady Venus, Juno, etc. so as to assure

---

[23]Bullinger, *Conciones*, 17v.
[24]St. John of the Cross, *Collected Works*, 132; citing Jer 2:24, 25.
[25]Pellikan, *Commentaria Bibliorum*, 3:206r.

themselves of fine children and avoid the pains of childbirth, and they have other gods as well. In the very same way we call on the mother of God, honoring her conception, and then go on to call on St. Margaret, contrary to the explicit text of the Bible: "You shall give birth to your children in pain." PROTESTATION OR PROPOSITION.[26]

GOD CONVERSES FIERCELY WITH HIS PEOPLE.

HEINRICH BULLINGER: God refutes them with yet another tenacious argument concerning their rebellion and develops it. "I indeed have been a father to you and to your sons up to this point; I wanted to lead those disobedient and prodigal sons with scourges into a better result. You all, however, have been stubborn in your sins; you have refused to reform yourselves, neither have you accepted any correction, nor will you. . . . You are sons and so you are rebels, and you have been discovered and convicted of open rebellion. . . ."

To these words he adds that the good Lord faithfully sends prophets to you, as he once did to your fathers. But what is this? You have unsheathed the sword against the prophets of God. They have perished by hanging; they buried the prophets by stoning, or drove them from their cities, and condemned them to exile; they pressed them with the most serious animosities and hurled every insult at them. The prophet represents this cruelty with an added similitude: You are like a lion—ravaging, mutilating, enraged, and ruinous. . . .

Accordingly and with good reason, Jeremiah shouts, "What a generation! What an age! Oh what pathetic people, and what a wretched time." This exclamation ignites his oration and excites their sleepy lethargy. . . . God says, "Am I a desert to Israel? Or a gloomy, foggy land?" Has God ever shown himself to be barren or difficult to Israel? Indeed, God is to his people a paradise and a sea or cornucopia of all good things. . . . For there is no darkness in God. . . . So Jeremiah attacks them with inner fire and says, "Why, therefore do my people say? 'we have forsaken you and withdrawn from you,

and will come to you no more.'" So above they have said, . . . "because I love strange [gods] and I will go after them." SERMON ON JEREMIAH 2:29-31.[27]

ORNAMENTS OF MARRIAGE. HEINRICH

BULLINGER: Jeremiah amplifies on their wicked defection from God with a comparison, so that it might shine forth all the more. A virgin with much effort may make her ornaments . . . and they are kept as precious valuables. . . . A bride may make her own ornaments or she may receive them as gifts from the bridegroom. . . . She esteems them highly and certainly would never forget them. After the marriage the bride delights in thinking about the ornaments. If she loses them, she seeks diligently and has no peace until they are found. God should have been like the ornaments of Israel the virgin. Faith in God ought to have been like the noble gift of the bride, as if received in the Jewish manner from the bridegroom, the Messiah of God, a gift in which they could delight in perpetuity and contemplate with the thought of this union in their hearts, while pondering the one true God alone, loving him alone and worshiping him alone. "But my foolish and ungrateful people have forgotten me for many ages now. They have other jewels in which they delight, namely, their horrible idols and foreign gods; they forget me and make supplication to their foreign cults and sacraments." SERMON ON JEREMIAH 2:32-33.[28]

THE BLOODIED WINGS OF EAGLES. HEINRICH

BULLINGER: "In your wings," he says, "the blood of souls is discovered"; that is, the souls of poor and innocent people (thus "flesh" is written to mean whole human being, likewise "soul"); these qualities [i.e., poverty and innocence] greatly increase the crime. Moreover, Jeremiah seems to allude to eagles, who, while snatching and tearing apart small birds, spatter their wings with their gore; so that the predation of the eagles themselves is immediately apparent. Therefore, this verse signifies that the

---

[26]Müntzer, *Collected Works*, 198; citing Jer 2:20-21, 28; Gen 3:16.

[27]Bullinger, *Conciones*, 19v-20r.
[28]Bullinger, *Conciones*, 20r-v.

cruelty of the Jews is manifest and out in the open. . . .
Indeed, they were spilling the blood of the prophets
in the temple and synagogues. They were spilling the
blood of oppressed orphans, widows, and tormented
folk in the gates, marketplace, law courts, cities, and
fields. Sermon on Jeremiah 2:34.[29]

Appearing Innocent and Being Guilty.
John Calvin: Let it in the first place be observed
that nothing is so displeasing to God as this
headstrong presumption, that is, when we seek to
appear innocent, while our own conscience condemns us. Then in the second place observe that all
who thus perversely rebel and strive dishonestly and
shamelessly to defend their own vices contend at the
same time with God: for false excuses have ever this
tendency—to charge God with unjust severity. But
we see what such people gain for themselves; for
God shows that he will be at length their judge, and
that he will openly discover the vices of those who
thought they could excuse themselves by evasions
and by false charges against God. They then who
thus obstinately resist God must at length, according
to what the prophet declares, come to this end—
that they will be constrained to acknowledge that
God has not been too violently angry with them, but

has only executed a just punishment. Commentary
on Jeremiah 2:35.[30]

**Looking for Aid Among Other Nations
Like a Harlot.** John Calvin: When any
danger was close, the Jews sought aid, now in
Egypt, then in Assyria. Yet they knew that this was
forbidden them; not that it was in itself evil or a
bad thing to seek help from neighbors, but because
it was God's will that the safety and security of that
people should be dependent on him only. For he
had taken them under his safeguard. When they
wandered here and there, it was an evidence of
unbelief; and what they attributed to the Egyptians
or to the Assyrians, they took away from their own
God, who had promised that their safety would be
the object of his care. Hence he compares these
movements to wanton levity; they were like those
promiscuous women who wander in all directions.
Now such a woman must be wholly shameless,
when she thus seeks the gratification of her lust; for
harlots often wait for the coming of lovers; but
when they wander everywhere, they are altogether
abominable. This then is what the prophet means,
that is, that "the Jews ran here and there." Commentary on Jeremiah 2:36.[31]

---

[29]Bullinger, *Conciones*, 20v.

[30]CTS 17:145-46* (CO 37:473).
[31]CTS 17:147* (CO 37:542).

JEREMIAH 3:1-25
THE FAITHFUL GOD AND UNFAITHFUL ISRAEL

[1]"If[a] a man divorces his wife
   and she goes from him
and becomes another man's wife,
   will he return to her?
Would not that land be greatly polluted?
You have played the whore with many lovers;
   and would you return to me?
declares the LORD.
[2]Lift up your eyes to the bare heights, and see!
   Where have you not been ravished?
By the waysides you have sat awaiting lovers
   like an Arab in the wilderness.
You have polluted the land
   with your vile whoredom.
[3]Therefore the showers have been withheld,
   and the spring rain has not come;
yet you have the forehead of a whore;
   you refuse to be ashamed.
[4]Have you not just now called to me,
   'My father, you are the friend of my youth—
[5]will he be angry forever,
   will he be indignant to the end?'
Behold, you have spoken,
   but you have done all the evil that you could."

[6]The Lord said to me in the days of King Josiah: "Have you seen what she did, that faithless one, Israel, how she went up on every high hill and under every green tree, and there played the whore? [7]And I thought, 'After she has done all this she will return to me,' but she did not return, and her treacherous sister Judah saw it. [8]She saw that for all the adulteries of that faithless one, Israel, I had sent her away with a decree of divorce. Yet her treacherous sister Judah did not fear, but she too went and played the whore. [9]Because she took her whoredom lightly, she polluted the land, committing adultery with stone and tree. [10]Yet for all this her treacherous sister Judah did not return to me with her whole heart, but in pretense, declares the Lord."

[11]And the Lord said to me, "Faithless Israel has shown herself more righteous than treacherous Judah. [12]Go, and proclaim these words toward the north, and say,

"'Return, faithless Israel,
   declares the LORD.
I will not look on you in anger,
   for I am merciful,
declares the LORD;
I will not be angry forever.
[13]Only acknowledge your guilt,
   that you rebelled against the LORD your God
and scattered your favors among foreigners
     under every green tree,
   and that you have not obeyed my voice,
declares the LORD.
[14]Return, O faithless children,
declares the LORD;
   for I am your master;
I will take you, one from a city and two from a
     family,
   and I will bring you to Zion.

[15]"'And I will give you shepherds after my own heart, who will feed you with knowledge and understanding. [16]And when you have multiplied and been fruitful in the land, in those days, declares the Lord, they shall no more say, "The ark of the covenant of the Lord." It shall not come to mind or be remembered or missed; it shall not be made again. [17]At that time Jerusalem shall be called the throne of the Lord, and all nations shall gather to it, to the presence of the Lord in Jerusalem, and they shall no more stubbornly follow their own evil heart. [18]In those days the house of Judah shall join the house of Israel, and together they shall come from the land of the north to the land that I gave your fathers for a heritage.

[19]"'I said,

   How I would set you among my sons,
and give you a pleasant land,

a heritage most beautiful of all nations.
And I thought you would call me, My Father,
and would not turn from following me.
²⁰Surely, as a treacherous wife leaves her husband,
so have you been treacherous to me, O
house of Israel,
declares the Lord.'"

²¹A voice on the bare heights is heard,
the weeping and pleading of Israel's sons
because they have perverted their way;
they have forgotten the Lord their God.
²²"Return, O faithless sons;
I will heal your faithlessness."

"Behold, we come to you,
for you are the Lord our God.
²³Truly the hills are a delusion,
the orgiesᵇ on the mountains.
Truly in the Lord our God
is the salvation of Israel.

²⁴"But from our youth the shameful thing has
devoured all for which our fathers labored, their flocks
and their herds, their sons and their daughters. ²⁵Let
us lie down in our shame, and let our dishonor cover
us. For we have sinned against the Lord our God, we
and our fathers, from our youth even to this day, and
we have not obeyed the voice of the Lord our God."

a Septuagint, Syriac; Hebrew *Saying, "If*   b Hebrew *commotion*

Overview: It may seem that Reformation-era preachers and scholars were unduly fascinated by the intricate details of Jeremiah's prophecies, Old Testament law, and Jewish culture. But it must be remembered that Protestants faced the task of reshaping congregations and drafting regulations to guide pastors as they dealt with issues of doctrine, morality, and marriage. Jeremiah provided a valuable gateway to the meaning of the entire Old Testament since his prophecies laid bare secret sins, trumpeted the heart of true worship, and exemplified profound devotion to God.

Even more striking, in response to chapter 3 commentators describe not only a searing call to repentance but also a full-blown proclamation of the gospel. Although Judah did not take seriously the judgment and the fate of her sister, Israel, sixteenth-century Christians might avoid this mistake of their biblical predecessors as Protestant churches grew and new pastors emerged attuned to God's "own heart" (Jer 3:15). In fact, the prophecies of Jeremiah not only detail in telling fashion the judgment of God but also point to the hope and promise of Jesus Christ for the Jews and for all the nations. Yet in all times and places Christ must still be approached through true repentance, conversion, and faith.

3:1-5 Unfaithful Israel and a Polluted Promised Land

God Bids the Unfaithful to Return to Him. Marguerite of Navarre:

You called out to me in a loud voice,
saying: My daughter, listen and look,
turn your attention toward me.
Forget your people among whom you have
taken refuge
and the grand house of your first father
which you have made your sojourn.
The king, moved by deep loyalty, will soon
desire your beauty.

But when this so sweet and grace-inspired
prayer
was of no avail, it was you who sought me out:
come to me all you who are weary
and heavy-laden with grief;
it is I who will comfort
and restore you with my bread.

Alas, I did not heed these words;
worse still, hearing them, I questioned
whether they were yours.
Perhaps it was meaningless Scripture,
for up to that point, I was so silly

that I read without feeling.
I came to understand that the vines
bearing poison
and wiles grapes instead of good fruit
were intended for me who had acted in this
    fashion.
I rather believed that the wife's cried and
    pleadings,
saying: return, return Shunammite,
were so that, at the worst of my sinning,
I might seek to escape from that place
where you in your compassion saw me
    thrashing about.
In the midst of it all, I pretended indifference.
But when I fell upon the passage in Jeremiah,
I confess I had
fear in my heart, was shamefaced,
and indeed, let it be said,
even had tears in my eyes,
in your honor, lowering my pride.
Through your holy prophet you said:
If a wife forsakes her husband
and gives herself to another,
it is unheard of that the husband
should seek to take her back,
to look upon or ever speak with her again.
Is she not polluted,
evil, and of no worth?
The law gives her up to justice
and permanently banishes her.
But you who left
my sweet embrace and wickedly committed
    fornication with others,
and in my stead put false lovers,
you may nevertheless come back to me.
I do not wish to hold a grudge against you.
Lift your eyes and look with care
and you will see what state
your sins have finally brought you, and
    where at this moment,
you lie prostrate.

THE MIRROR OF THE SINFUL SOUL.[1]

---

[1]Marguerite of Navarre, "The Mirror of a Sinful Soul," lines 711-66 in *Selected Writings*, 112-15; citing Ps 44; Mt 11; Deut 32; Is 5; Song 6.

MARRIAGE LAW AND DIVINE GRACE. HEINRICH BULLINGER: After the divine prophet has convicted the Jews of many and grave sins, he immediately calls them to repentance. Jeremiah shows that God is clement, well-disposed, and favorable to all who truly revere him. Now he proposes a legal example, offered in Deuteronomy 24. This example was sought, and adapted to the trustworthy and inestimable facility and grace of God the Father, and instituted by law, that if a man rejects his wife, and has given to her a bill of divorce, and she goes away from her husband, and marries another man, the law is that the first husband may not drag her away from her second husband. In addition, if the later husband dies, by no means is the first husband allowed to take her back in marriage. The reason attached to the law is this: "lest the land be polluted." Now Jeremiah too repeats this law in his own time....

Scripture conveys that the pact and covenant between God and humanity is a marriage. Idolatry—the worship and invocation of foreign gods—violates the integrity of this marriage. Moreover, the Jews have polluted themselves with idols and foreign cults; therefore they are considered answerable to the charge of fornication and adultery. Therefore, God was able to reject them and has rejected them. Here, however, a singular example of God's grace, mercy, and benevolence reveals itself. Indeed, no husband takes back a wife he has rejected—still less an adulteress or dirty prostitute. Rather, he abhors her forever. Nevertheless, God calls back not only a spouse he has rejected, but even the most shameless adulteress; he calls her back to the former relationship and the dignity of marriage. "You," he says, "have not only married another and been rejected; you are also a prostitute ... with quite a few lovers and paramours—not just with one or another. You have prostituted yourself shamelessly with anyone who showed up. Nevertheless, I will pardon this foulness and take it from you and urge you to return to me. 'Return,' I say, 'to me.'" What does it mean to return to the Lord? It means leaving behind the gods, cults, and reliance on everything except God and then to embrace God alone; adore, invoke, and worship God alone; depend on the Word of him alone; and serve him in righteousness. Believe and live in an upright manner. This is true piety: repentance and conversion to God. SERMON ON JEREMIAH 3:1-5.[2]

RAIN, BARRENNESS, AND POLLUTION. CORNELIUS À LAPIDE: Reader, learn here that public sin, when it is not punished, pollutes the whole earth and commonwealth, and therefore God punishes it with a public disaster. . . .

Note: In Scripture they refer to the rain as "late" that in Palestine falls in the time of spring (in March), by which the crops become ripe, just as they call that rain "early" that falls in October immediately after the sowing and waters the sown seeds, and makes them sprout, obviously through the drops, as it says here, falling constantly and slowly, from which it is called here "drops of rain." It is especially necessary to have rain for the crops in these two times of the year. COMMENTARY ON THE PROPHET JEREMIAH 3:3.[3]

SPIRITUAL ADULTERY AND UNBELIEF. JOHANNES BUGENHAGEN: "Forehead of a prostitute." The adulteress denies her turpitude and thus wants to seem to be a lady. The prostitute, however, as a contemptible harlot, is shameless. Thus there come at last from among the hypocrites those who think in that way when they are contending with the Word of God; they are atheists, Lucianists, Epicureans, or Sadducees. We are then convinced by the Word of God that our own worship, religious practices, and observances are nothing and that they are impiety and idolatry; and therefore even those things that are preached from the Word of God may be nothing among us. We want to believe neither this nor that. "Let us eat and drink, tomorrow we die"; nothing remains after this life. This belief was already common long ago in Italy, especially in Rome in the most holy palaces. Now it also appears

among the holy fathers, our papists, who are among us: "Do you think that the dead will rise again?"

Christ says, "Beware of the yeast of the Pharisees and the Sadducees or the yeast of the Herodians"; and the yeast of the old bread, 1 Corinthians 5. In contrast, this is the true Word of God and the gospel of the glory of Christ—Deuteronomy 8, "man does not live by bread alone," etc. The yeast of the Pharisees is justification by the doctrine of works, false worship, and empty religious practices. The yeast of the Sadducees or the yeast of the Herodians (who were circumcised and observed legal sacrifices, but did not believe) is this: do you think that what is preached is true? "Good Christian," some Italian man says, "Do you really," so to speak, "hope that the last judgment and resurrection of the dead will happen? Since our fathers until now it has changed; all things thus stay the same as they were from the beginning," etc., 2 Peter 3. One must be profoundly cautious with this yeast because we are inclined to be unfaithful and "perverse companions corrupt good morals," 1 Corinthians 15. Here plainly the Epicureans become shameless even in conscience before God; as Paul in Ephesians 4 says: after they come so far as to give up pain (that is, to have a conscience), "they have given themselves up to licentiousness, greedy for the practice of every kind of uncleanness." We see that cardinals have come to this point, and bishops, anti-Christians, monks, and canons, who are ashamed of no wickedness; thereafter they have resolved to blaspheme and persecute the gospel of Christ and preserve their impious rites, so that, for instance, the common folk are controlled by their perverse opinions.

When the impious and vainly religious are condemned by the Word of God for their hypocrisy and lies, they become imposters, like the Herodians and the Sadducees, about whom the first Psalm says, "Blessed is the man who does not sit in the seat of imposters." COMMENTARY ON JEREMIAH 3:3.[4]

---

[2]Bullinger, *Conciones*, 21v-22r; citing Deut 24:1-4.
[3]À Lapide, *Commentarium in Jeremiam*, 23-24.

[4]Bugenhagen, *In Ieremiam*, V1r-V2r; citing Is 22:13; 1 Cor 15:32; Acts 26:8; Mt 16:6; Mk 8:15; Lk 12:1; 1 Cor 5:6-7; Deut 8:3; Mt 4:4; 2 Pet 3:4; 1 Cor 15:33; Eph 4:19; Ps 1:1. Lucianists: Bugenhagen may have in mind either disciples of the Gnostic teacher Lucian (d. 180) or

3:6-25 God's Gracious Call to Repentance

THE CONSEQUENCES OF IDOLATRY. HEINRICH BULLINGER: Now Jeremiah introduces a document from his times, lest we are not aware that this sermon was spoken in the times of Josiah, when a holy prince mediated and undertook a reformation. However, the wretched people preferred to stick in the mire of ungodliness, though they certainly pretended to approve this reformation. Then he amplifies the sins of the Judeans with a comparison, since not even the miserable destruction of the ten tribes, or Israelites, was able to move them.

First, Jeremiah remembers how the people of Israel behaved and then what God in turn did with them. He calls the Israelites and Jews "sisters." Indeed, before the kingdom was cut in two, they were one people, descendants of the same father, Jacob, or Israel. He speaks of both sisters as apostates, harlots, and rebels by name, for with stubborn hearts they rejected the Word of God and followed the desires of their hearts. Furthermore, they treacherously violated their covenant, marriage, pacts, friendship, and association with God. Thus Israel broke the covenant, forsook the Word of God, neglected the temple of the Lord, and trampled on all the holy things of God; they piled up and built temples, high places, and shrines both sacred and profane everywhere. . . .

Further, Jeremiah adds Judah to this example. He says, Israel's sinning sister, namely Judah, sees this. Therefore, she does not sin through ignorance. . . . Finally he adds what Judah has seen, namely, that God gave to Israel a libel of divorce or adultery because of those spiritual fornications; that is, he cut down the ten tribes and saw that they were led into captivity by Shalmaneser.[†] This cruel, wretched, and calamitous example did nothing to move Judah. Judah feared not, cared not, and thought not that the annihilation of his brothers pertained to her. Judah did not think to herself: if these people perished because of their idolatry, then you will perish too. Indeed, she too had also lost her way; the miserable sister was also devoted to idols. . . .

Moreover, she had offered herself to all sorts of adulterers, to the point that she was hopelessly in love with stones and wooden things, and she also worshiped these, because they were the paramours she loved. Indeed, idolaters say that they do not worship wood and stone, but rather those who the wood and stones symbolize. But meanwhile they manifestly declare that they are also greatly charmed by the idols themselves; they fall in love with them, and their nobles make them. By that fact it happens that the land is polluted by an inexpiable expiation and everything is made unfortunate and calamitous. As often as this has happened, likewise the people have often sinned. To this sacred history testifies.

Our own age testifies that the church never goes unpunished when it rejects or neglects salvation in Christ and his holy gospel. We are not ignorant of what Asia and Africa, and not least of all parts of Europe—Greece, Illyricum, and Pannonia—have suffered from the Saracens and Turks. But how few in Poland, Germany, Denmark, England, France, and Italy are moved by these miserable examples! So what do we think is going to happen? Eventually these kingdoms will perish because of impenitence and rebellion. SERMON ON JEREMIAH 3:6-10.[5]

THE ENGLISH JOSIAH. JOHN TRAPP: This is the beginning of a new sermon, as most hold. Josiah was a religious prince, and a zealous reformer, and hypocrisy reigned exceedingly in his days, as we see here, and as holy Bradford in his letters complains, that it did likewise in King Edward VI's days (who was our English Josiah), among the great ones especially, who were very corrupt. COMMENTARY ON JEREMIAH 3:6.[6]

---

followers of the martyr Lucian of Antioch (d. 312), who is sometimes viewed as a source for Arianism, which denied the divinity of Christ.

[5]Bullinger, *Conciones*, 23r-v. [†]Shalmaneser V, King of Assyria (727–722 BC).
[6]Trapp, *A Commentary or Exposition*, 231*. John Bradford (1510–1555) was an English reformer and chaplain to Edward VI (r. 1547–1553).

Faithlessness and the Elect. Johannes Oecolampadius: "Apostate," "hypocrite": for Judah had many chances to live in a more holy way, such as the priesthood and worship in the temple and frequent prophecies. But she always looked in her heart to her heathen fickleness: even stubbornness and surrender to a false idea—or a lapse into sin—did not suffice to correct them. We learn here that God frightfully permits sin to fall among the elect, so that they might repent of their former lives. "Those people honor me with their lips, but their hearts are far from me," and in Malachi in which we say, "the table of the Lord is despised." Commentary on Jeremiah 3:10.[7]

I Am Your Man. Johann Arndt: The union of God with humanity occurs by healing repentance or conversion to God as true regret and sorrow for sins and by faith. "Return, faithless Israel, says the Lord, I will not look on you in anger, for I am merciful. . . ." With these gracious and loving words God our heavenly Father promises and will bring it about that humankind will return to him again and be united with him. Adultery breaks up this marital union and splits apart the two that should be one flesh. Sin and misdeeds bring about such a spiritual divorce between God and humanity. Healing repentance, however, brings about spiritual remarriage and union. Therefore, our merciful God and Father, who does not wish to be eternally angry with us, speaks to us in these words: Be converted to me for I am your man; I will be faithful to you; you have gone about with many harlots but have come back again, says the Lord. True Christianity.[8]

True Confession. Johannes Oecolampadius: "Know your iniquity." Behold confession alone is required, so that we acknowledge ourselves as sinners and give to the Lord glory, as John says: "If we confess our sins, he is faithful and just and will forgive us our sins and cleanse us of all iniquity." He shows that their sin is that they followed idols, that is, everything that sets itself up against the knowledge of God, and [and against] following the pure and only Word of God. Commentary on Jeremiah 3:13.[9]

Our Gentle Lord's Call to Repent. Desiderius Erasmus: I include not only the books of the New Testament, which is the law of grace, but also those of the Old Testament, which is supposed to be more severe. Let us hear how gently the Lord in Jeremiah calls his people to repentance, portraying them as a bride who has deserted her husband and prostituted herself to all comers: "Turn again, you rebellious children," says the Lord, "for I am your husband." Sermon on Mercy.[10]

Shepherd of the Faithful. Johannes Oecolampadius: "Return, rebellious sons." This is two things: leave those things behind and see my kindness. The Lord receives you and will be your shepherd. "I rejected you and again I will take you back. Even if there is only one in the city who returns, I will receive him and if there are only two among all the families, I will not neglect them." This is an indication of how small will be the remnant of those to be received. Many are called, only a few are elect.

"I will give you pastors." It seems before he chose a people, an angry God gave evil shepherds as well as decidedly good ones. They may have righteous and hypocritical priests who are ignorant of the law and God. He himself will give to you doctors who will not lead you back to the elements of the world, but will lead you to knowledge of God and will give an understanding that is allowed to only a very few, and not to those disdaining to bear the cross after Christ. They are shepherds according to the heart of God, who teach according to the Spirit and the Word of God and that they might please God, leading us into spiritual things: these will be

---

[7]Oecolampadius, *In Hieremiam*, 1:E4r; citing Is 29:13; Mt 15:8; Mk 7:6; Mal 1:7, 12.

[8]Arndt, *True Christianity*, 253-54; citing Mt 19:5-6.

[9]Oecolampadius, *In Hieremiam*, 1:F1r; citing 1 Jn 1:9.

[10]Erasmus, *Collected Works*, 70:111.

apostles and those who follow them. COMMEN-
TARY ON JEREMIAH 3:14-15.[11]

THE CHURCH AS THE THRONE OF GOD.

SEBASTIAN MÜNSTER: "The ark of the covenant of
the Lord." In those days, he says, the entire form of
worship of God will be abolished, which was
existing in the ceremonies of the temple. Not the
earthly Jerusalem, but the spiritual one—namely,
the church—will be the throne of God. In
Jerusalem all the nations will be gathered, or some
from every nation, because of the name of the Lord.
In the time of the gospel there will not be physical
sacrifices, but spiritual sacrifices, namely, expressions of thanksgiving. Then the church will be the
throne of the Lord, in which Christ is seated as
head and king. Moreover, all the nations will
embrace the truth of the Word of God. They will
not walk in their own thoughts, but will attend to
the single Word of God. THE TEMPLE OF THE
LORD, JEREMIAH 3:16.[12]

SALVATION FOR THE NATIONS IN CHRIST.

JOHANNES BUGENHAGEN: So they see here that
the Jewish form of worship, as commanded in the
law, was destroyed, where it says the ark of the
Lord is to be left behind and the place of the ark
outside of which one is not allowed to make
sacrifices—after that place was revealed in Jerusalem. Moreover, in what way will Jerusalem be the
throne of the Lord, when there will be in that place
no ark and no seat of God for propitiation,
according to the promise in Exodus 36 and 1 Kings
8 and 9? Add to this, when were all the tribes
converted to the feast and gathered in Jerusalem?
In short, they may see what the prophet says
concerning the restoration, not only of Judah, but
also of Israel, and that from them there will again
be one kingdom, as there was one under David and
Solomon. But only the restoration of Judah was
promised after seventy years, not the kingdom of
Israel. The tribe of Judah with the tribe of Benja-

min were restored, and they returned to their
homes and fields, as in the laws of Ezra. But
concerning the restoration of Israel, I will say other
things in this prophet. Likewise to those returned
here also the inheritance of the nations is promised.
Now I will pass over in silence the grace of God,
which is here described, which neither the Jews nor
any other righteous were able to understand. The
Jews show to us that all these things were completed in their own earthly kingdom after captivity.
And when they were not able to show it, we
showed that these things were completed in Christ
in such a way that not an iota from these things
might perish, with ourselves attesting and the other
prophets and passages of Scripture.

First it says, "Return, O children who deserted
me," in which grace alone is proclaimed, lest we lay
claim to our own merit. Indeed, he does not just
call us sinners. . . .

Second, "for I will betroth myself to you": So
the amazing grace of Christ our spouse is signified
to us in this image of marriage. . . .

Third, he says, "I will take you, as one man leads
a whole city and two a whole region or land." Or
thus: "I will take you, one with a city and two with
a nation. . . ." This was done when he began to
proclaim the gospel. One brought along many, that
is, converted to Christ, a few preachers brought
along many nations. . . .

Fourth, he says, "I will bring you into Zion";
below he says, "into Jerusalem"; here the church of
Christ in Scripture is called Zion and Jerusalem. . . .

Fifth, he says, "I will give you pastors after my
own heart, who feed you with doctrine and
wisdom"; these are the preachers promised against
the pseudo-prophets and the traditions of the
Pharisees. . . .

Sixth, he says, "And when you shall be multiplied and increase in the land in those days, says
the Lord"; they will not speak any more of the ark
of the covenant of the Lord. There will be no
memory of it, nor will anyone preach about it
anymore; they will not seek it, nor will any such
thing come to be; that is, they will not sacrifice
there. But in those days they will call Jerusalem the

---

[11]Oecolampadius, *In Hieremiam*, 1:F1r.
[12]Münster, *Miqdaš YHWH*, 862.

throne of the Lord. And all the nations will be gathered to Jerusalem on account of the name of the Lord, which will be in Jerusalem. . . .

Here is made clear the abolition and abrogation of the law and the old observances that were taught to the Jews by God. . . . In fact, in that heavenly Jerusalem, that is, in the church of Christ, there is another mercy seat and another throne of the Lord, outside of which God cannot be found. . . .

Seventh, Jeremiah says, "When all the nations will be gathered in Zion" (when Jerusalem would contain these nations) "and they shall not walk after the perverse thoughts of their own perverse hearts." The Jews had the written law, and through it they were not able to be justified. The nations do not have the law and they are justified (as you see here). Therefore, justification before God is not from the law, but from the grace (as is said here) of the betrothal, when we believe the promises of grace in Christ. . . .

Eighth, he says, "In those days the house of Judah will go to the house of Israel and they will come together from the land of the north into the land that I gave to their fathers as an inheritance. . . ." In the same way, these things are said concerning a spiritual restoration, by which people, who were cast away by God on account sin and impiety, are restored by faith to Christ when the gospel has been preached. At that time many from Israel, many from every nation under heaven, are living in Jerusalem because of religion. COMMENTARY ON JEREMIAH 3:14-18.[13]

DIVINE PUNISHMENT AND TRUE REPENTANCE.

JOHANN PAPPUS: After the above promises . . . the doctrine of repentance follows. Moreover, the Lord shows not only what he requires from those who repent but also what he censures in them. At the very least, he requires this, that we call him Father and we do not withdraw from him. People who know what is to be expected from the Lord call him Father and do not recede from him; they are ashamed and repent of their wicked crimes, rely on

the promises of grace, and adhere to that grace with their whole heart. On the other hand, they do not call him Father who always have doubts about his grace, and in hard times vacillate without true faith, and who lean on their own or another's resources rather than on the Lord himself. Then God rebukes any contempt of himself, and at that time shows himself to those who despise him, when we do not call him Father, when we withdraw from him.

In fact, that sin tends to spur so much indignation toward God, that he avenges it with the most bitter punishments, that is, so that the voice of wailing and the lamentations of the children of Israel are heard even on the streets themselves. In fact, after the beginning of this part, both arguments for repentance are briefly repeated—the one based on the promises of grace, and the other based on the threat of punishments—and then there is attached a certain formula of prayer, which people may use to repent, so that they confess their unworthiness and implore divine mercy. Moreover, the reason for the prayer is added: why grace ought to be sought from God and anticipated. The first of the causes is this: because help can be found in no one else: since those idols that seem to help, help the least. Indeed, however richly idolatry flourishes, that is how richly the punishment flows—so much more severe is the vengeance that follows.

The second reason is taken from bygone evils and the example of the ancestors. Indeed, all the Judeans confess that their own ancestors, who had not turned to the Lord, endured the gravest calamities. A third reason comes from the dread of future evil. Since indeed they are compelled to acknowledge that they have persevered in their great impiety, nothing could be more certain than that upon them also that same servitude would come because of divine censure—unless they repent. But with these same arguments we too are unable to stir anyone else to repentance, though we ought to. Indeed, since the divine norm of governance is perpetual and just, no one ought to promise themselves impunity when they participate in those sins, which they know were

---

[13]Bugenhagen, *In Ieremiam*, Y2r- Z1r; citing Deut 12:1-32; Neh 8:1-18; Ezra 9:1-15; Mt 5:18.

avenged in others. ON ALL THE PROPHETS, JEREMIAH 3:19-25.[14]

RETURNING CHILDREN, A LOVING FATHER, AND A NEW WEDDING. NIKOLAUS SELNECKER: That is the other part of this chapter—a remarkably beautiful gospel sermon. With us everything is lost. We lay captured by the devil and can't help ourselves. We fall ever further and deeper into our sins, and we are by nature children of wrath. Our works do not help us. Our free will hates the justice of God, and the good is dead to us. It is a hopeless angst, doubt, anger, and death. Each one is damned who does not do all that is written and commanded in the law. There is no single person born from Adam who is an exception. Everyone is fallen and does nothing useful. Everything is useless to everyone.

But now comes the fatherly and dear voice of God. "'Return, you rebellious children.' You are rebellious and have abandoned me. But I will again help you. Only listen to me and follow me. You cannot help yourselves. 'I, I am he who will blot out your violations of my will and I will not remember your sins,' Isaiah 43. What I have planned for you is the history of all things from grace. Therefore I want to be joined with you. I want to be your bridegroom and husband. So it stands in Hosea: 'I will say to the Lord, I will betroth you to me forever. I will be engaged to you in righteousness and justice, in grace and mercy. In faithfulness I will be betrothed to you, and you shall know the Lord,'" Hosea 2. This happens through the Son of God, our own true savior and eternal bridegroom, Jesus Christ, who loves us and gave himself for us;

he has cleansed and sanctified us; he is our head and has become our bridegroom. . . .

We should hereafter clearly consider the most prominent point in this lovely sermon. First, God says, "Return, you rebellious children." Therefore, he shows that we are children of the wrath of nature. But he wants to take pity on us. Second, he says that he wants himself to be joined with us. That is, he wants to celebrate a new wedding with us and give to us his only begotten Son as a bridegroom, so that we would now be the dear children of the beloved Son. Third, he says that he wants to receive us, so that we should lead in a whole city and second an entire land and should be a true teacher and teach many things and bring many back, and lead them to Christ the Lord. THE WHOLE PROPHET JEREMIAH 3:22.[15]

THE WICKED WALLOW IN THEIR WICKEDNESS. THE ENGLISH ANNOTATIONS: As a person who is in desperate straits, or discontent and not knowing which way to help himself, is inclined to cast himself down upon his couch, or as sick people unable any longer to hold up their head are compelled to take themselves to bed, or as some sluggards who lie overhead and ears wrapped up and buried (as it were) in their bedclothes, as the apostle describes the wicked of the world, who as swine which lie wallowing in mire and dirt "lay down in wickedness," and the Latin proverb, that they all lie in leaven, as overhead and ears in it. ANNOTATIONS ON JEREMIAH 3:25.[16]

---

[14]Pappus, *In Omnes Prophetas*, 72v.

[15]Selnecker, *Der gantze Prophet Jeremias*, F11-v; citing Is 43:25; Hos 2:19.

[16]Downame, ed., *Annotations*, 9C1r*; citing 1 Kings 21:4; 2 Sam 13:5; 2 Kings 1:4; 1 Jn 5:19.

JEREMIAH 4:1-31
A CALL TO REPENT AND
JUDGMENT FROM THE NORTH

¹"If you return, O Israel,
declares the Lord,
   to me you should return.
If you remove your detestable things from my
     presence,
   and do not waver,
²and if you swear, 'As the Lord lives,'
   in truth, in justice, and in righteousness,
then nations shall bless themselves in him,
   and in him shall they glory."

³For thus says the Lord to the men of Judah and
Jerusalem:

"Break up your fallow ground,
   and sow not among thorns.
⁴Circumcise yourselves to the Lord;
   remove the foreskin of your hearts,
   O men of Judah and inhabitants of
     Jerusalem;
lest my wrath go forth like fire,
   and burn with none to quench it,
   because of the evil of your deeds."

⁵Declare in Judah, and proclaim in Jerusalem,
and say,

"Blow the trumpet through the land;
   cry aloud and say,
'Assemble, and let us go
   into the fortified cities!'
⁶Raise a standard toward Zion,
   flee for safety, stay not,
for I bring disaster from the north,
   and great destruction.
⁷A lion has gone up from his thicket,
   a destroyer of nations has set out;
   he has gone out from his place
to make your land a waste;
   your cities will be ruins
   without inhabitant.

⁸For this put on sackcloth,
   lament and wail,
for the fierce anger of the Lord
   has not turned back from us."

⁹"In that day, declares the Lord, courage shall fail
both king and officials. The priests shall be appalled
and the prophets astounded." ¹⁰Then I said, "Ah, Lord
GOD, surely you have utterly deceived this people and
Jerusalem, saying, 'It shall be well with you,' whereas
the sword has reached their very life."

¹¹At that time it will be said to this people and to
Jerusalem, "A hot wind from the bare heights in the
desert toward the daughter of my people, not to
winnow or cleanse, ¹²a wind too full for this comes for
me. Now it is I who speak in judgment upon them."

¹³ Behold, he comes up like clouds;
   his chariots like the whirlwind;
his horses are swifter than eagles—
   woe to us, for we are ruined!
¹⁴ O Jerusalem, wash your heart from evil,
   that you may be saved.
How long shall your wicked thoughts
   lodge within you?
¹⁵ For a voice declares from Dan
   and proclaims trouble from Mount Ephraim.
¹⁶ Warn the nations that he is coming;
   announce to Jerusalem,
"Besiegers come from a distant land;
   they shout against the cities of Judah.
¹⁷ Like keepers of a field are they against her all
     around,
   because she has rebelled against me,
declares the Lord.
¹⁸ Your ways and your deeds
   have brought this upon you.
This is your doom, and it is bitter;
   it has reached your very heart."

¹⁹ My anguish, my anguish! I writhe in pain!
    Oh the walls of my heart!
My heart is beating wildly;
    I cannot keep silent,
for I hear the sound of the trumpet,
    the alarm of war.
²⁰ Crash follows hard on crash;
    the whole land is laid waste.
Suddenly my tents are laid waste,
    my curtains in a moment.
²¹ How long must I see the standard
    and hear the sound of the trumpet?

²² "For my people are foolish;
    they know me not;
they are stupid children;
    they have no understanding.
They are 'wise'—in doing evil!
    But how to do good they know not."

²³ I looked on the earth, and behold, it was
        without form and void;
    and to the heavens, and they had no light.
²⁴ I looked on the mountains, and behold, they
        were quaking,
    and all the hills moved to and fro.
²⁵ I looked, and behold, there was no man,
    and all the birds of the air had fled.
²⁶ I looked, and behold, the fruitful land was a
        desert,

and all its cities were laid in ruins
    before the Lord, before his fierce anger.

²⁷ For thus says the Lord, "The whole land shall be a desolation; yet I will not make a full end.

²⁸ "For this the earth shall mourn,
    and the heavens above be dark;
for I have spoken; I have purposed;
    I have not relented, nor will I turn back."

²⁹ At the noise of horseman and archer
    every city takes to flight;
they enter thickets; they climb among rocks;
    all the cities are forsaken,
    and no man dwells in them.
³⁰ And you, O desolate one,
what do you mean that you dress in scarlet,
    that you adorn yourself with ornaments of
        gold,
    that you enlarge your eyes with paint?
In vain you beautify yourself.
    Your lovers despise you;
    they seek your life.
³¹ For I heard a cry as of a woman in labor,
    anguish as of one giving birth to her first child,
the cry of the daughter of Zion gasping for
        breath,
    stretching out her hands,
"Woe is me! I am fainting before murderers."

OVERVIEW: Reformation commentators debate the true nature of sin and its manifestation in behavior, belief, and heart. Medieval Europe had been awash in all manner of religious observance and acts of penance meant to combat sin, deepen devotion, and bring renewal. But in the minds of many seeking reform in the sixteenth century such religion had only served to multiply sin, deepen idolatry, and breed hypocrisy. Fortunately Scripture provides wisdom and direction. Indeed, interpreters discover in the prophecies of Jeremiah a profound analysis of both sinful behavior and the wayward heart, of open idolatry and internal corruption; and they explore a staggering message and threat of God's fierce response to empty worship and deceitful behavior. Much as priestly ceremony and intercession had failed the Jewish people of Jeremiah's day, so likewise Protestants argue that the ministrations of the papists had deceived and damaged the church with their false penance and empty religious practices. At the same time Protestant pastors and theologians sought to reveal the subtleties of sin and unmask false religion, to teach the nature of true repentance and preach the gospel of grace and faith in Christ.

Moreover, the prophecies of Jeremiah unveil the judgment of God in startling and stark detail—in "wars and rumors" of war and in the deceit of human hearts. Here commentators are struck by the roaring lions God unleashes—the enemies of the Jews near and far and the devil and Antichrist who hunt faithful souls in all times. In the Reformation era the Muslim Turks were ever poised on the eastern borders to ravage Christian Europe and bring a tyranny God had ordained for unbelievers and hypocrites. Meanwhile, Jeremiah mourns the devastation of his people and his land: a reminder to Protestant pastors and theologians that this too may be their lot. When Reformation fails and the people choose deception and darkness over truth and light, then Christian leaders are called to grieve, lament, and testify to God's steadfast judgment. In fact, this lingering grief extends beyond humanity. The verses of Jeremiah prompt commentators to reflect on the suffering of nature, earth, and heavens due to human sin and divine retribution. Here we find the reformers exploring themes that would someday be called "environmental" or "ecological."

4:1-4 Repent and Return to Me

AN EARNEST CALL TO REPENTANCE. NIKO-LAUS SELNECKER: This is throughout a sermon on repentance, in which Jeremiah earnestly warns the people to return to God. So God would be gracious because there would be the betterment of their lives and the recognition and confession of their sins. The punishments would either be taken away completely or at least alleviated. But this prophecy also comes to pass precisely because people do not want to better themselves. God would allow King Nebuchadnezzar of Babylon to come. Because of their sins God would will that the land be ravaged, and the people taken prisoner and led away—as indeed it would happen. We should let such things be a warning to us and an example to be spoken and stipulated, so that through a rightly active repentance we can escape the future and long-earned anger of God and be

amended by the Word of God. THE WHOLE PROPHET JEREMIAH 4:1.[1]

BEWARE OF FALSE REPENTANCE. JOHANNES BUGENHAGEN: This is an exceptional passage about repentance (if someone is able to see it); for false forms of penance are many. Hypocrites indeed—when they are pressed by hunger, epidemic, war, and other evils—are changed and they preach repentance, but they do not return to the Lord. As it says here: "if you are willing to return, Israel, then return to me"; that is, give up your errors, idolatry, empty cults, and false religious practices. "And convert or return to me, that is to my Word...." If you would have removed your abominations from before my face (which you judge to be holy worship), of course, you would not migrate into captivity in Babylon. Certain ones say, "We have given up our evil ways and return to God so that he might free us," but in what manner are they converted? They are certainly not converted to God, the gospel of the glory of God, but to abominations (as with our papists), to their satisfactions for sins; they multiply their self-administered fasting, as he who says, "I fast until the Sabbath." They increase what they call processions; they invoke the patronage of saints, seek papal indulgences in their holy places, and multiply their worship services which they call "of God." ... Indeed these things are penances and conversions, but they do not turn from error to the Word of God, from their blasphemies to God. Now they provoke God to anger even more in their vain and blasphemous cults and their unfaithfulness. COMMENTARY ON JEREMIAH 4:1.[2]

TRUE REPENTANCE IS NOT MERELY INTELLECTUAL. LANCELOT ANDREWES: Why, where should we turn from sin but to God? Yes, we may be sure that it is not for nothing that God sets this down. In Jeremiah it is more plain: "If you return, return to me, says the Lord," which would have been needless if we could turn to nothing else, were it not possible

---

[1]Selnecker, *Der gantze Prophet Jeremias*, G3r-v.
[2]Bugenhagen, *In Ieremiam*, 2A1r-v.

to find many turnings, leaving one byway to take another, from this extreme turn to that, and never to God at all. They that have been given to the flesh, if they cease to be so, they turn; but if they become as worldly now as they were fleshly before, they turn not to God. They who from the dotage of superstition run into the frenzy of profaneness, they who, although abhorring idols, fall and commit sacrilege, however they turn, they turn to God.

And this is even the *motus diurnus* [daily motion] [or] the common turning of the world, as Moses expresses it, "to add drunkenness to thirst"; from too little to too much, running from one extreme into another. Would God it were not needful for me to make this note! But the true turn is *ad Me* [to me], turning from sin to God. Otherwise in very deed we turn from this sin to that sin, but not "from sin"; or, to speak more properly, we turn to sin; we turn not from sin, if we give up one evil way to take another.

And this is also needful. For, I know not how, but by some conceive of our conversion to be a turning of the brain only, by doting too much on the word *resipiscere* [to repent] as merely a mental matter. Whereas before we thought thus and thus, and held to such and such positions, we are now of another mind than before, and this is our turning. . . . Nay, to say the truth where conversion is mentioned, [it is done so] in a manner that it takes place *in corde* [in the heart]. And so [it] requires not only an alteration of the mind, but of the will, a change not of certain notions only in the head, but of the affections of the heart too. SERMON ON JOEL 2: 12-13.[3]

SWEARING GODLY OATHS. SEBASTIAN MÜNSTER: Jeremiah says that it is permitted to swear in the name of God. But not in vain: that is, not unless necessity compels it, and not in falsehood. Even if judges compel someone to swear contrary to justice and truth, one must not obey them. Indeed, it will happen, says the prophet, that the nations, which swear on the names of their own gods, will religiously call blessings on themselves and will bless by the consecrated name of God, which is blasphemed among you. Thus Scripture allows, entrusts, and commends the swearing of oaths while adding three conditions. First, one may only swear in the Lord alone. Second, swearing should not happen casually, but when necessity demands it. Third, an oath is sworn in truth and spirit, lest someone knowingly intends to deceive. THE TEMPLE OF THE LORD, JEREMIAH 4:2.[4]

LIMITATIONS IMPOSED BY THIS OATH.
LANCELOT ANDREWES: "'You shall swear, 'The Lord lives,'" or as Moses says, by "God's name." Which clause first limits by what we are to swear, and excludes: (1) Swearing by those which are "no gods," either idols [that are] forbidden in the law (either to swear by them alone, or to join God and them together); (2) or creatures which our Savior Christ forbids.

And sure, as to swear by them is derogatory to ourselves, seeing thereby we make them our betters, for everyone who swears "swears by [something] greater than oneself"; so it is highly injurious to the majesty of God, seeing to swear by a creature is to ascribe unto it power to see and know all things, and to take vengeance on perjury, which in divinity to think or say, is manifest blasphemy. SERMON ON JEREMIAH 4:2.[5]

HARVESTING TRUE HOPE. HULDRYCH ZWINGLI: "Break in some newly plowed land and do not sow among thorns!" This is proverbial speech. Whoever sows in good soil and neither in unfruitful soil, nor among thorns, will harvest a good crop of grain. "If you are thankful and hope in me, you will be rewarded and your hope will not be disappointed. If you sow among thorns, so you will experience how thorns do not allow the grain to grow. If you seek the help of strange gods and hope in them, then your hope will be disappointed." SERMON ON JEREMIAH 4:3.[6]

---

[3]Andrewes, *Works*, 1:363-364*; citing Rom. 2:22 and Deut. 29:19.

[4]Münster, *Miqdaš YHWH*, 864.
[5]Andrewes, *Works*, 5:73*; citing Deut 6:13; Jer 5:7; Ex 23:13; Josh 23:7; Amos 8:14; Zeph 1:5; Mt 5:34-36; Heb 6:16.
[6]Zwingli, *Predigten*, 177-78.

CIRCUMCISION OF THE HEART. JOHANNES
OECOLAMPADIUS: Circumcision is twofold,
external and internal, of the body and of the heart;
in the heart and in thoughts we are circumcised to
the Lord. As it says in Deuteronomy 10, "Circumcise the foreskin of your heart, and your neck, lest
you be hardened even further." Moreover, this is
the work of the Lord. Deuteronomy 30: "The Lord
your God will circumcise your heart and the heart
of your offspring, so that you love the Lord your
God with your whole heart and whole soul, so
that you are able to live." Concerning this in
Romans the second chapter: "Not he who is
publicly a Jew is a Jew, nor is it a circumcision that
is manifest in the flesh, but he who will be a Jew in
secret is a Jew, and circumcision of the heart is
circumcision, which accords not in letter, but in
spirit, whose praise is not of men, but of God." As
in Colossians 2: "you were circumcised in a
circumcision that is not with hands," but a
circumcision of the foreskin of the heart, of evil
desire, deeds, and thoughts, which are causes of
offence before the Lord.

How great are the punishments, moreover,
because the anger of the Lord is compared to an
inextinguishable fire, and a fierce flame, ignited by
our evil works. Indeed it is the greatest of all
punishments to know that God, the creator of all
things, is angry with and opposed to you. That
threat comes frequently: indeed, God is a consuming fire; Isaiah, the last chapter: "Behold the Lord
will come in fire." Nahum 1: "His indignation will
be widespread like fire." Isaiah: "And there may not
be one who could extinguish it." There will be
freedom from captivity, when, external things being
disregarded, we take care to renew the internal
person. On the other hand captivity and dire
servitude impotently compel the man foreign to
the strength of the spirit with the thorn of the flesh,
and therefore exhort him to a circumcision of the
heart. COMMENTARY ON JEREMIAH 4:4.[7]

4:5-18 Disaster from the North

**PROCLAIM DANGER, FLEE TO ZION AND THE
CHURCH.** JOHANNES OECOLAMPADIUS: Announce this in Judah. See the attentiveness by
which the scout ought to proclaim danger and
sword to the people to whom he is responsible. For
he gives his message through other people, so that
he might be heard: the trumpet is sounded through
the whole land, since the danger is universal,
especially the captivity of consciences, and all must
be called and gathered and they must go to the
fortified cities; that is, they must make a study of
faith and charity. Indeed, "a brother who is helped
by a brother is like a walled city," Proverbs 18; and
"the name of the Lord is a tower of strength...."
This second thing must be admonished, that the
faithful flee to Zion and the church, from which
come the law of the Spirit, and the apostolic
teaching, for by gathering there we are able to be
saved. The others in clever pride ... willingly yield.
While those straggling sectarians are wandering
around, they are easily made prey to enemies.
COMMENTARY ON JEREMIAH 4:5.[8]

WHEN THE ENEMY COMES. NIKOLAUS SEL-
NECKER: This is a severe irony. When the fire begins
and you have not bettered yourself, nothing will
help, including what you have prepared and the
power you display. When today or tomorrow the
Turks come—or another enemy—and we Germans
have not improved ourselves, nothing will help;
even if all the kings, princes, and cities are mobilized
and gather together, and have a great fortress.
Thereafter they will abandon it. For against the
Lord negotiations count as if no negotiations take
place and against his wrath no power helps. THE
WHOLE PROPHET JEREMIAH 4:5.[9]

THE LION ROARS. JOHANNES OECOLAMPADIUS:
Prophecy predicts that these matters will, of course,
certainly come to pass. But the Jews' repentance was

---

[7]Oecolampadius, *In Hieremiam*, 1:F3v-F4r; citing Deut 10:16; 30:6;
Rom 2:28-29; Col 2:11; Deut 4:24; Heb 12:29; Is 66:15-16; Nahum
1:6; Is 66:24.

[8]Oecolampadius, *In Hieremiam*, 1:F4r; citing Prov 18:19; 18:10.
[9]Selnecker, *Der gantze Prophet Jeremias*, H2r-v.

false, for they were not truly repentant even when they were besieged. Another history has it in this way: Nebuchadnezzar is spoken of as the lion, just as the king of Egypt is the snake and the former thereafter from the north. Peter the apostle, however, calls the devil a lion, who goes around roaring like a lion. And the Antichrist himself maintains the service of the lion in his persecuting the good people, but in persecution there are many who seem to be faithful, but are truly wanting. Churches perish by the multitude; the shepherds perish; indeed, having got the opportunity and license, the Antichrist creeps in and so desolates the land that you can hardly find a truly faithful person who puts hope in the Lord. Indeed it is all hypocrites wandering around. And Jerusalem and Zion, where the word of the Lord reigns, had few inhabitants. Behold, Paul and Peter predicted that this evil would burden us, that those most grievous times were to come. So then it is right to repent in sackcloth and ashes, that is, we ought to make ourselves strangers to pleasure, crucify our flesh and chastise it, lest we are to become the reprobate. For sackcloth and ashes are nothing in repentance, except insofar as they comply with humility, and thereafter the heart submits to cleansing. The Lord sees hypocrisy, and so his anger flows thereby. Let us by external symbols bear witness to internal grief. The Lord is enraged as long as hypocrisy endures. COMMENTARY ON JEREMIAH 4:7.[10]

NO ESCAPE FROM DIVINE JUDGMENT. KONRAD PELLIKAN: To accommodate to the word of the Lord Jeremiah always goes back to the insolent and headstrong: "No practice or reformation of the faith has improved you." He remains firm on this: "You perceive the extreme destruction and anger of the Lord; you may bear that just judgment, which you are not able to avoid and you may grieve in sackcloth and ashes in an unfruitful penance that is too late in coming. . . ."

The false prophets were always shouting "Peace, Peace"; and the priests were always shouting, "the

temple, the temple"; the princes, who all deceived the king, were always persuaded that neighboring nations would help them. Now when the enemy overwhelms them and the full council of the king perishes, they do not want their hearts to be in the hands of the Lord. They have been abandoned by God, they fall and perish; the princes are thrown into confusion; the priests are stupefied and struck down in terror; the king's council falls, the mind of the false prophet is snatched away. Everyone is equally confounded by the anger of the Lord, which leaves no guidance. COMMENTARY ON JEREMIAH 4:8-9.[11]

DOES GOD DECEIVE US? ST. JOHN OF THE CROSS: We must not consider a prophecy from the perspective of our perception and language, for God's language is another one, according to the spirit, very different from what we understand, and difficult. This is so true that even Jeremiah, a prophet himself, observing that the ideas in God's words were so different from the meaning the people would ordinarily find in them, seems to be beguiled and defends the people: . . . "Alas, alas, alas, Lord God, have you perchance deceived this people and Jerusalem, saying: Peace will come to you, and behold the sword reaches even to the soul?" . . .

The reason for the misunderstanding was that the promised peace was to be effected between God and humans through the Messiah who was to be sent to them, whereas they took the words to mean temporal peace. THE ASCENT OF MOUNT CARMEL.[12]

BETRAYED BY THEIR OWN SELF-DECEPTION. HULDRYCH ZWINGLI: "Truly, you have deceived." . . . Jeremiah rejects the error of the people in the Lord; it is not as if God has deceived them because he had promised peace, but because we are foolish mortals who hesitantly demand the good things God has promised to us, and for which we care even less. God had promised salvation to Israel in

[10]Oecolampadius, *In Hieremiam*, 1:F4v-G1r; citing 1 Pet 5:8; 2 Thess 2:1-11; 2 Pet 3:3-7.

[11]Pellikan, *Commentaria Bibliorum*, 3:2P2v; citing Jer 6:14; 8:11; 7:4. [12]St. John of the Cross, *Collected Works*, 216.

the land, but this salvation is through the law. If they would safeguard the laws concerning these things, then they would not run away to strange gods. Therefore, they demanded perpetual salvation, even though they trampled down the laws and proclaimed themselves to the Lord. Thus, this is the sense of the prophet: the miserable people rely on the peace and salvation that you [God] have promised them; meanwhile you [God] have neglected such peace and salvation because you have threatened the transgressors with destruction. EXPLANATIONS OF THE PROPHET JEREMIAH 4:10.[13]

THE DECEPTION OF THE PROPHETS. JOHANNES OECOLAMPADIUS: The prophet repeats what is said by the people: does God seduce and allow so many thousands to err, in such a grand thing, so that they cry out? The law does not perish by the priests. Is the church able to err? Why does God permit them to be stupefied through the prophets? Concerning this complaint of the flesh he renders this reasoning; Ezekiel 13. "You ask according to iniquity, so the iniquity of the prophets will be. When the prophet has erred and deceived the people, I, the Lord, deceived him." For lately all ascribe salvation to works, as if peace would be from us, and in such great works and satisfactions the sword comes to the soul. COMMENTARY ON JEREMIAH 4:10.[14]

LIKE A FIERCE, HOT WIND. SEBASTIAN MÜNSTER: The Hebrew actually says, "a splendid wind." This wind, however, signifies an enemy army glittering with weapons, which is compared to a desert wind because just as the wind in the desert is harsher, especially in the higher places where there are no obstacles, so the host of the Chaldeans will go around any and every obstacle put up by the Judeans and devastate the land. THE TEMPLE OF THE LORD, JEREMIAH 4:11-13.[15]

CARNAL HEARTS CONTAIN MALIGNANT VAGRANTS. JOHN TRAPP: Creep they will, but why should they lodge there? Why should the devil be at inn with us? Be anyone's bedfellow, as he is the angry person's? David often communed with his own heart, and his spirit made diligent search for such vagrants. . . . Carnal hearts are stews of unclean thoughts, slaughterhouses of cruel and bloody thoughts, a very forge and mint of false politic, undermining thoughts, yea, often a little hell of confused and black imaginations. They had need therefore to be carefully cleaned, and kept with all custody. Grace begins at the center, and from thence goes to the circumference. Grace and nature begin at the heart. Art begins with the face and outward lineaments; so does hypocrisy at outward paintings and expressions; it clenches the outside of the cup and platter, when the inside is full of ravening and wickedness. COMMENTARY ON JEREMIAH 4:14.[16]

THE COMING OF WRATHFUL GUARDIANS. NIKOLAUS SELNECKER: "A cry comes from Dan and a message from the mountain of Ephraim." This is on the mountain of Lebanon that comes to an end in the land of Canaan where the sun sets and from which a part of the Jordan arises. Then there is Ephraim. These places are named because the military forces of Babylon would have their thrust and free way through these places to Jerusalem. In the same way we speak about the Turks. There is a cry from Hungary or Austria as the Turks have armed themselves with great power and soon will be underway. "The guardians come from distant lands." That means that the enemy is no longer far away. He names them "guardians" in a contradictory way—as an antiphrasis—the enraged tyrants who devastate and destroy everything. Jeremiah wants thereby to indicate the negligence of the king, princes, and priests and that they have been punished. They should be the guardians of the churches and schools, and should support the common good. But most of them are wolves and destroyers of their churches,

---

[13]Zwingli, *Complanationis*, 85.
[14]Oecolampadius, *In Hieremiam*, 1:G1v; citing Ezek 13:1-16.
[15]Münster, *Miqdaš YHWH*, 864.

[16]Trapp, *A Commentary or Exposition*, 236*; citing Ezek 4:16; Ps 77:6; Lk 11:39.

lands, and people. They inquire about nothing according to the Word of God. They are surely Epicurean paunches, who look after their own bellies; they feed, drink, and suck themselves to exhaustion, and pursue mischief. So other guardians must come, who must make a certain end of these supposed guardians . . . and wipe them out. There will again be a cry against them because of their ways, as the foreign peoples—the Turks, Muscovites, and the like—unleash the horrifying, growling dog. THE WHOLE PROPHET JEREMIAH 4:15-18.[17]

4:19-31 Anguish over Judah's Desolation

THE GRIEF OF SYMPATHY AND COMPASSION.
NIKOLAUS SELNECKER: "How this pains me in my heart; my heart pounds in my body and I have no rest." This is a lamentation and heartfelt sympathy with the people who do not understand the will of God in action and do not want to convert; therefore they must go to their doom. For it is painful when one sees that someone maliciously corrupts oneself and neither wants to listen, nor to see, nor to follow what one can yet gain from God's grace, blessing, and peace. And one can have concord and rest. Jeremiah would have extensive experience of such lamentation in his songs of Lamentation. Even Christ the Lord himself wept over Jerusalem in Luke 19. And all we God-fearing people weep today for ourselves and for poor Germany, which also does not recognize the time of its devastating judgment—neither the grace, nor the wrath and what they mean. Oh the pain! We must die. But God be praised, which means thereby: "I will absolutely not give up. I will, nevertheless, preserve those who are mine. No one shall tear my little sheep from my hands. Where I am, there my people will be also. Yea, in my anger I will think on my compassion and to all who return to me, I will show grace. My compassion is too fierce for me to act according to my furious wrath." "For I am God and not a man," Hosea 11. THE WHOLE PROPHET JEREMIAH 4:19.[18]

THE PROPHET'S ANGUISH. JOHANNES OECO-
LAMPADIUS: "My bowels!" Jeremiah sees the plundering of his homeland, Anathoth, which is on the route to the environs of Jerusalem, and sees that in pain. For he was not able to contain himself; he suffered in his guts because of too much lamentation. Such are the emotions of the prophets, that they are weakened with those who are weak, as Paul says, "Who is weak, and I am not weak?" Behold, while we are not taught by someone else's dangers, then we are afflicted by our own. For a long time I have proclaimed the ruin of our country and some do not believe it. "The ribs around my heart are shaken." That is, I grieve to the deepest, and because of that I am not able to be silent: the voice of the trumpet in plunder, when soldiers exhort themselves. Thus one sadness follows after another. COMMENTARY ON JEREMIAH 4:19.[19]

THE DESTRUCTION OF THE TABERNACLES.
JUAN DE MALDONADO: "Grief upon grief," that is, calamity upon calamity, "was summoned," that is, was prompted by God. By this word they signify that it happened not by chance, but by the divine plan, as Psalm 104:16 states: "God called down famine on the earth." Jeremiah says that it was called "grief upon grief"; for first the people were afflicted by famine, then by the sword, or first by siege, and then by captivity. "Suddenly my tents are destroyed." These "tents" seem to refer to the neighboring cities and the "hides" are the smaller towns. Or again "tents" and "hides" can be understood as repetition. Other scholars think that "tabernacle" is to be understood as "temple," because it had been covered with red and blue hides; see Exodus 26:14. But these terms seem rather to deal with military tents and regular tents. COMMENTARY ON THE PROPHETS, JEREMIAH 4:20.[20]

---

[17]Selnecker, *Der gantze Prophet Jeremias*, H3v-H4r.
[18]Selnecker, *Der gantze Prophet Jeremias*, H4r-v; citing Lk 19:41-42; Hos 11:9.

[19]Oecolampadius, *In Hieremiam*, 1:G2v-G3r; citing 2 Cor 11:29.
[20]Maldonado, *Commentarii in Prophetas*, 25; citing Ps 105:16. By "hides," Maldonado means "military leather tents."

WISDOM, WORSHIP, AND THE WORD. JO-
HANNES BUGENHAGEN: "They are wise"; we are
wise in other things, even to the doing of that
which God prohibits. We religiously support and
defend human doctrines, fictitious rites, and false
religions. But to the Word of God, which is truly
credible and the highest wisdom, we bring
stubborn resistance. We refuse to learn so that we
might know and do the will of God, which is our
true foolishness and so much madness. Of which
the Psalms sing, "The fool says in his heart, there is
no God," or "God is nothing," etc. Ephesians 2: "We
were without God in this world," because we were
without the Word of God. God is grasped in the
Word of God in this world. If you have contempt
for the Word of God, you have contempt for God
and you are utterly foolish because meanwhile you
imagine yourself to be a devoted worshiper of God
through I don't know what works. As Christ says
from Isaiah, "In vain they worship me, teaching the
doctrines and commands of humans." COMMEN-
TARY ON JEREMIAH 4:22.[21]

THE WICKED ARE WISE IN THE WORLD. JOHN
TRAPP: Wise are the wicked in their generation,
subtle and sly, but so is the serpent, or the fox. The
swine that wanders can make better shift to get
home than the sheep can to the fold. They have
received the spirit of this world; the devil also
works effectually in them as a smith in his forge.
Hence, they are wise to do evil. Elymas was a very
subtle fellow, but the devil's child, and so the more
dangerous. COMMENTARY ON JEREMIAH 4:22.[22]

**THE DESPAIR AND DARKNESS OF THE
UNGODLY.** JOHANNES BUGENHAGEN: Jeremiah
describes the future devastation in tragic terms.
He says, moreover, that there is likewise no light
in the future. This is not so much hyperbole, as
certain people suppose, as it is a simple prayer
without form; as if you might consider the

minds and consciences of the impious, when
they suddenly fall into unexpected ruin. Now I
will pass over in silence that the Hebrews
otherwise say "light" for "prosperity" and "darkness" for "unhappiness." When the impious will
suddenly fall under the judgment of God, not
even the light of the sun is light, but immediately the darkness of desperation swoops down
on them. They do not have hope in the prayers
of faith, while the pious do have hope in
temptation and in their own darkness. See what
I am saying about this passage: the Jews said
there is no brightness in heaven because they
were perishing. Meanwhile who doubts that the
victorious Babylonians had the brightness of
heaven? As Isaiah 13 says: the Babylonians are
denied the light of the sun and moon, because
when they are perishing, everything seems to
them to be darkness, because of the magnitude
of their terror and grief. Meanwhile, the victorious Medes and Persians have the light. I warn
you of this, because you will see certain interpreters who do not heed these things. Immediately in such passages, apart from all judgment,
they are confounded by absurd allegories, and
interpret them to be about the last day of the
world, when these signs proceed in the sun,
moon, and stars according to the prophecy of
Christ. COMMENTARY ON JEREMIAH 4:23.[23]

DARKNESS COMPARED TO GOD. ST. JOHN OF
THE CROSS: All creatures of heaven and earth are
nothing when compared to God, as Jeremiah
points out ... "I looked at the earth, and it was
empty and nothing. ..." By saying that he saw an
empty earth, he meant that all its creatures were
nothing and that the earth too was nothing. In
stating that he looked up to the heavens and
beheld no light, he meant that all the heavenly
luminaries were pure darkness in comparison to
God. All creatures considered in this way are
nothing, and a person's attachment to them are less
than nothing since these attachments are an

---

[21]Bugenhagen, *In Ieremiam*, 2K1r-v; citing Ps 14:1; Eph 2:1-3; Mt
15:9; Mk 7:7; Is 29:13.
[22]Trapp, *A Commentary or Exposition*, 237*; citing 1 Cor 2:12; Eph
2:2; Acts 13:10.
[23]Bugenhagen, *In Ieremiam*, 2K2r; citing Is 13:10.

impediment to and deprive the soul of transformation in God. THE ASCENT OF MOUNT CARMEL.[24]

BIRDS FALL FROM THE SKY AND PLACES LIE DESOLATE.

KONRAD PELLIKAN: A fierce solitude is threatened here; it is as if the present is depicted, so that the birds are not able to remain in the sky where people do not exist. The living birds have been dragged down to the ground. Now Mt. Carmel and the most revered places are deserted and the cities are swept away. These things are coming, not so much from cruel enemies and people, but from the vengeful judgment and hand of the Lord. He will not bear such contempt any further; his anger and days of fury the impious were not capable of fearing. But they will be more terrified by the justice of those days, which they will perceive and bewail. COMMENTARY ON JEREMIAH 4:25-26.[25]

THE ELECT IN THE MIDST OF DESTRUCTION.

JOHANNES OECOLAMPADIUS: He proceeds further and says that the earth will be destroyed in that way, and it would be now as it was when it was made in the beginning; . . . not only in the earth but also in the heavens on account of the harsh atmosphere. For the first heaven was created without light or sun. The discourse is hyperbolic here, just as it is in the following verses. In this we are warned of the final judgment, at which day heaven and earth will pass away. Nevertheless, God leaves behind a seed. There is nothing so high, broad, strong, or firm that it will not perish. The birds of the heavens and humanity will perish; that is, no one is spared—neither in the countryside nor in the cities. So they will abandon all the cities and this is so when ascending to Jerusalem. These things are eminently arranged in our own times: indeed, see what Scriptures have not been dragged into some unfamiliar reading? Which of the sacraments has not been defiled? Which rank of society has

preserved their own honor? Neither the kings, nor the bishops, nor the lay folk, nor the monks, nor the nuns do so. Everywhere there is disorder; everywhere there is devastation; the mountains are princes, and hills are our guides. And behold there is not a person there, that is, either of common of stock, or even of the forefathers. They have fled these deserted lands and migrated to cultivated lands where they might find nourishment. Whence it says, "They emigrated and the cities were destroyed"; that is, the whole of the churches were depopulated, namely, by the punishments sent by God's anger. So indeed the appearance of the Lord's anger is explained.

On this account "the earth shall mourn." But God does not make an end to the world, so that he might preserve his elect, just as Noah was saved in the ark during the flood. So also the earth will be destroyed up to a point, but God will preserve his seed. God has said nothing less through the prophets. So it will happen: the earth will greatly mourn; it will be utterly destroyed. And heaven will contain itself, so that it will not rain, as it says, "the heavens are bronze, the earth iron, for God will fulfill his word." COMMENTARY ON JEREMIAH 4:27-28.[26]

THE LAND AND THE HEAVENS MOURN.

JOHN CALVIN: The mourning of the land is to be taken for its desolation. . . . Jeremiah does not speak of the inhabitants of the land. . . . for the prophet here ascribes terror and sorrow to the very elements, which is much more striking than if he said that all people would be in sorrow and grief. The same also must be thought of the heavens. Indeed, the latter clause proves that he does not speak of the inhabitants, but of the land itself, which, though without reason, seems yet to dread God's vengeance. And thus the prophet upbraids people with their insensitivity; for when God appeared as judge from heaven, they were not touched with any fear. "Mourn then shall the land and covered shall be the heaven with darkness." That is, though people

---

[24]St. John of the Cross, *Collected Works*, 124.
[25]Pellikan, *Commentaria Bibliorum*, 3:2P3r.

[26]Oecolampadius, *In Hieremiam*, 1:G3v; citing Lev. 26:19.

remain stupid, yet both heaven and earth shall feel how dreadful God's judgment will be. Commentary on Jeremiah 4:28.[27]

Terrified Flight into the Clouds. John Calvin: By saying that at the "voice" or sound of the "horsemen and bowman" there would be a universal flight, he means that the enemies would come with such recklessness that the Jews would not dare to wait for their presence, but would flee here and there before they were attacked.... Then it follows, "They will ascend into the clouds," or into the "thicknesses": this may be applied to the enemies to show that they would be so nimble and active as to fly, as it were, to the clouds, and climb the highest rocks. But I prefer to connect this sentence with the former, intimating that to ascend to the clouds would not be too arduous for the Jews in their anxious flight. Inasmuch as the tops of mountains were often covered with thick trees in order to form a dark shade, this passage may mean that they fled to such places.... Hence, the meaning would be more evident if we retain the word "clouds."... The enemies of the Jews would in swiftness be equal to the eagles while pursuing them; or what is commonly thought, that the terror felt by the Jews would be so great that in their flight they would not seek recesses nearby, but would flee to the highest tops of mountains and hide themselves among the trees, as though they had climbed into the clouds. Commentary on Jeremiah 4:29.[28]

Israel Adorned Like Jezebel. Cornelius À Lapide: Jeremiah alludes to Jezebel, who, when Jehu entered into Samaria as an enemy, painted her eyes with stibnite and adorned her head, so that like a prostitute she might seduce Jehu into loving her. But she did so in vain. Indeed, Jehu was seeking her life and the kingdom. Therefore the sense of this passage is, "Oh Israel, once you were my people; now you so carefully adorn yourself with robes and with necklaces, rings, and stibnite—just like a prostitute for your lovers. Do you now think that you will have those lovers as friends or allies? You are mistaken; for they themselves will strip away your robes and goods and every adornment. Therefore, you will be adorned in vain—in Hebrew *titiappi*—that is, you will paint yourself; you will attain beauty for yourself with rouge, so that you would seem to be beautiful and striking." Note: these lovers are foreign nations, especially the Chaldeans, whose friendship the Judeans were winning over for themselves by worshiping their idols. Commentary on the Prophet Jeremiah 4:30.[29]

Unbearable Suffering and Divine Wrath. Konrad Pellikan: Jeremiah describes how Jerusalem was to be destroyed with such fierce cruelty, how it would fall upon godless citizens and those dying by famine, disease, and the sword, and when they would be desperate concerning the grace of God. Eventually the people would be afflicted unto death and the hellish punishments would begin, while within and without they would be afflicted without hope of avoiding torment and the wrath of God. The degree of anguish is comparable to a woman in labor, first to women giving birth, and then for someone breathing out the spirit who is bearing a most grievous sadness, while shouting and gesturing miserably: "Oh the grief comes over me because I fall among that whole multitude that is perishing and is being cut down." Whatever a woman suffers when giving birth to her children or in the brutal perishing of her children, this is said to be endured in Jerusalem among her citizens and children; for they had not returned to the Lord and were always ungrateful for his benefits. Commentary on Jeremiah 4:31.[30]

---

[27]CTS 17:242 (CO 37:600).
[28]CTS 17:244-45 (CO 37:601-2).

[29]À Lapide, *Commentarium in Jeremiam*, 34; citing 2 Kings 9:30-37.
[30]Pellikan, *Commentaria Bibliorum*, 3:2P3v.

JEREMIAH 5:1-31
A STUBBORN AND REBELLIOUS PEOPLE

¹*Run to and fro through the streets of Jerusalem,*
* look and take note!*
Search her squares to see
* if you can find a man,*
one who does justice
* and seeks truth,*
that I may pardon her.
²*Though they say, "As the Lord lives,"*
* yet they swear falsely.*
³*O Lord, do not your eyes look for truth?*
You have struck them down,
* but they felt no anguish;*
you have consumed them,
* but they refused to take correction.*
They have made their faces harder than rock;
* they have refused to repent.*

⁴*Then I said, "These are only the poor;*
* they have no sense;*
for they do not know the way of the Lord,
* the justice of their God.*
⁵*I will go to the great*
* and will speak to them,*
for they know the way of the Lord,
* the justice of their God."*
But they all alike had broken the yoke;
* they had burst the bonds.*

⁶*Therefore a lion from the forest shall strike*
*   them down;*
* a wolf from the desert shall devastate them.*
A leopard is watching their cities;
* everyone who goes out of them shall be torn*
*   in pieces,*
because their transgressions are many,
* their apostasies are great.*

⁷*"How can I pardon you?*
* Your children have forsaken me*
* and have sworn by those who are no gods.*
When I fed them to the full,

* they committed adultery*
* and trooped to the houses of whores.*
⁸*They were well-fed, lusty stallions,*
* each neighing for his neighbor's wife.*
⁹*Shall I not punish them for these things?*
declares the Lord;
* and shall I not avenge myself*
* on a nation such as this?*

¹⁰*"Go up through her vine rows and destroy,*
* but make not a full end;*
strip away her branches,
* for they are not the Lord's.*
¹¹*For the house of Israel and the house of Judah*
* have been utterly treacherous to me,*
declares the Lord.
¹²*They have spoken falsely of the Lord*
* and have said, 'He will do nothing;*
no disaster will come upon us,
* nor shall we see sword or famine.*
¹³*The prophets will become wind;*
* the word is not in them.*
Thus shall it be done to them!'"

¹⁴*Therefore thus says the Lord, the God of hosts:*
"Because you have spoken this word,
behold, I am making my words in your mouth
*   a fire,*
* and this people wood, and the fire shall*
*   consume them.*
¹⁵*Behold, I am bringing against you*
* a nation from afar, O house of Israel,*
declares the Lord.
It is an enduring nation;
* it is an ancient nation,*
a nation whose language you do not know,
* nor can you understand what they say.*
¹⁶*Their quiver is like an open tomb;*
* they are all mighty warriors.*
¹⁷*They shall eat up your harvest and your food;*

they shall eat up your sons and your
daughters;
they shall eat up your flocks and your herds;
they shall eat up your vines and your fig trees;
your fortified cities in which you trust
they shall beat down with the sword."

[18]"But even in those days, declares the Lord, I will not make a full end of you. [19]And when your people say, 'Why has the Lord our God done all these things to us?' you shall say to them, 'As you have forsaken me and served foreign gods in your land, so you shall serve foreigners in a land that is not yours.'"

[20]Declare this in the house of Jacob;
proclaim it in Judah:
[21]"Hear this, O foolish and senseless people,
who have eyes, but see not,
who have ears, but hear not.
[22]Do you not fear me? declares the Lord.
Do you not tremble before me?
I placed the sand as the boundary for the sea,
a perpetual barrier that it cannot pass;
though the waves toss, they cannot prevail;
though they roar, they cannot pass over it.
[23]But this people has a stubborn and rebellious
heart;
they have turned aside and gone away.
[24]They do not say in their hearts,
'Let us fear the Lord our God,

who gives the rain in its season,
the autumn rain and the spring rain,
and keeps for us
the weeks appointed for the harvest.'
[25]Your iniquities have turned these away,
and your sins have kept good from you.
[26]For wicked men are found among my people;
they lurk like fowlers lying in wait.[a]
They set a trap;
they catch men.
[27]Like a cage full of birds,
their houses are full of deceit;
therefore they have become great and rich;
[28]they have grown fat and sleek.
They know no bounds in deeds of evil;
they judge not with justice
the cause of the fatherless, to make it prosper,
and they do not defend the rights of the needy.
[29]Shall I not punish them for these things?
declares the Lord,
and shall I not avenge myself
on a nation such as this?"

[30]An appalling and horrible thing
has happened in the land:
[31]the prophets prophesy falsely,
and the priests rule at their direction;
my people love to have it so,
but what will you do when the end comes?

a The meaning of the Hebrew is uncertain

Overview: In this chapter commentators expound on Jeremiah's prophecies concerning a refusal to repent, continued and unabated idolatry, and the decisive divine judgment that surely would follow with the Babylonians from the north. It struck many readers that in Christian Europe and ancient Judea the people of God ought to have known better and lived out their covenant promises; instead they were ungrateful for God's lavish provision and seemed unconcerned about or even oblivious to God's staggering power and fierce wrath. Such disturbing and lax disregard for divine commands extended beyond worship to Jewish society, where open adultery and calculated exploitation of the poor ignited divine censure.

Who was responsible for the miserable state of things? Were ungodly priests, princes, and merchants primarily to blame? Were the common folk innocent and ignorant victims of the powerful, or were they equally culpable and complicit in the immorality of their teachers and rulers? The Reformation of the church was not envisioned without consideration of reforms in government and society. But what really could be accomplished if religious leaders and the ruling class remained spiritually unrepentant and rapacious in their policies? Interpreters of Jeremiah pondered to what degree the common people would be reliable as agents of real change in church and society. Moreover, while most commentators encouraged perseverance under unjust and unspiritual rulers, a few advocated for violent rebellion or withdrawal from society into earnest and sincere Christian communities. Regardless, in all circumstances the faithful were commanded to draw near to the Word of God and to Christ for salvation.

5:1-13 Jerusalem Refuses to Repent

No Godly People Remain While God Judges and Seeks Them. Nikolaus Selnecker: Up to this point we have received some difficult preaching from Jeremiah. But now it is certainly more difficult, for the true preacher of repentance does not take it easy and will not be lazy. But he will go forth much the same way once and always: so long as one improves oneself and even if no improvement follows. . . .

First, God shows that in the whole Jewish land there was no just or pious person, neither among the people nor among the authorities. The priests were discovered to be sinners too. Therefore, which did God want? Should he lengthen the punishment, strengthen it, or alleviate it? This is a severe sermon; much harder than what there is in Psalm 14: "The fools say, 'There is no God.' They are corrupt and do nothing. There is no one who does good." There God himself speaks of the sins of all people, the terrible and the damned, as they are all by nature the children of wrath. But here he speaks of his own people or he speaks only of his own church, to which he had given his Word and had revealed his will. In such churches now not one person is found that holds dearly to God's Word and command and asks about faith. They are named as they wish: prophets, priests, preachers, pastors, doctors of the soul, princes, lords, authorities, councilmen, nobles, citizens, farmers, men, women, children—large and small, tall and short.

Is that not to be pitied and a lamentable complaint? Thereby, we read also in the first book of Moses, in the eighteenth chapter, that not ten God-fearing people could be found in Sodom. Also at the time of the flood there were only eight people preserved on the surface of the earth. And at the time of the birth of the incarnate Christ the church was a tiny little dwelling: namely, Zechariah, Simeon, Anna, Elisabeth, Mary, Joseph, etc. So the Son of God himself says of his own time in Luke 18: "Nevertheless, when the son of Man comes will he find faith on the earth?"

Second, God shows the causes of his willing the Babylonians, Chaldeans, and Assyrians to destroy, lead away, and consume the Jews; for he says that their sins are too many and they remain stubborn in their disobedience. "They have forsaken me and pursue idolatry and live in sin against their own consciences. When I address and reprimand them, they don't recognize it and say, that is not the Word of God, which the prophets and true teachers say." . . .

Oh dear lords, princes, magistrates, officers, nobles, and others, who are at court, who sit in your councilmen's houses, in offices and other places. Do you really want to see that the salvation of your soul depends on this word? It is the word of the eternal, omnipotent majesty of God. . . .

Third, God also shows in a time of punishing the sins of his people that he wants to save them. The Chaldeans must come, who are among the first people known after the flood among the pagans. They must devour, destroy, and consume you. You will not understand their language, which among the other plagues is not the worst. So one is not alone, but interacts with and lives with strange and foreign people. You cannot gain anything from what they are saying and what they want to have from you. But so it goes for all who actually despise the Word of God. They would need to be punished with sword and hunger, with all sorts of plagues, with foreign nations, and other awful and disgusting things. And thereby, one should not ask, "Where did this misfortune come from?" Then it should be said, "You have despised God and you have earned it." As the saying goes, "He who despises me, must be despised. . . ."

Yet the Lord does not reject completely, but he grieves fully and again he has compassion according to his great goodness. THE WHOLE PROPHET JEREMIAH 5.[1]

SIN OF THE COMMON AND THE POWERFUL. JOHANNES BUGENHAGEN: In this chapter the just cause of the damnation of the impious is articulated, namely . . . that they show contempt for God in their own words and they defend their own idolatry as the worship of God—not only the common people do this, but also and much more the leaders and rulers of the people, with the prophets and the priests, who are the leaders of iniquity. When the rabble is accused, no one concludes that the impiety is so great among wise, powerful, honest, and holy men. "But these are blind men and leaders of the blind, so that together they all fall into the pit."

To be noted is the story of Genesis 18. God wants to spare Sodom on account of ten just men, so here God wants to spare Jerusalem and the kingdom of Judah, if some there are discovered to be just. In the same way, because of one man, Joseph, God blessed all of Egypt. So on account of the prayers of the pious in perpetuity he blesses many impious people, giving grains of the field, peace etc. With these words the prophet indicates the singular impiety among those people: that it was not possible there to discover any just person, who feared God and did justice. Indeed, what integrity would remain among deceptive teachers and false forms of worship? The teachers lead astray, the princes are led astray, and together in their tyranny they defend false doctrines. COMMENTARY ON JEREMIAH 5:1.[2]

ENGLAND LIKE JUDEA IN THE TIME OF JEREMIAH. JOHN KNOX: Their precedents I judge sufficient to prove that the entire multitude and all the estates in this our age have been and do

remain wicked, if not worse than those against whom Jeremiah prophesied. Now let us see what happened in Judah: mischief upon mischief until finally the Lord in his anger took away King Josiah because God was determined to destroy Judah as he had before destroyed Israel. After the death of the godly king the trouble was great; widespread and sudden were the changes in that commonwealth. The kings were taken prisoner one after another in a short time. What other miseries were there for that stubborn nation? O God, for your great mercy's sake, never give your small and sorely afflicted flock in the realm of England either reprieve or allow it to learn from experience! For in all their troubles no repentance has appeared. That you may learn from the prophet, so he cries, "You have struck them, O Lord, but they have not mourned; you have destroyed them, but they have not received discipline. . . ." For God commanded the prophet to stand in the entrance of the Lord's house and to speak to all the cities of Judah that come to worship in the house of the Lord; and was commanded to keep no word back, if perchance, says the Lord, they might listen and turn from their wicked way. Here it is to be noted that immediately after the death of the godly king, they entered into iniquity. A GODLY LETTER OF WARNING AND ADMONITION.[3]

ROME A HARLOT LIKE JERUSALEM. JOHN TRAPP: Where it was strange [that] there should be such a rarity of righteous ones . . . like Rome is at this day. All of Rome has become a brothel. She had a Mancinelli, a Savonarola, and some few other Jeremiahs, to tell her own, but she soon took an order with them. The primitive Christians called heathens "pagans" because country people living *in pagis*, that is, in hamlets and villages, were heathenish for the most part, even after the cities were converted, and had many good people in

---

[1]Selnecker, *Der gantze Prophet Jeremias*, J1r-J4r; citing Ps 14:1; Gen 18:22-33; 6:5-9; Lk 18:8.
[2]Bugenhagen, *In Ieremiam*, 2Lv; citing Mt 15:14; Gen 18:22-33; 41:37-57.

[3]Knox, *Works*, 3:178-79. Knox draws a comparison here between the godly Jewish King Josiah and the wickedness of people after his death, and the realm of England after the death of King Edward (r. 1547–1553) and subsequent rule of Queen Mary I (r. 1553–1558).

them; but Jerusalem here afforded hardly any one. COMMENTARY ON JEREMIAH 5:1.[4]

JEREMIAH SEARCHES IN VAIN AMONG THE PEASANTS. THOMAS MÜNTZER: Jeremiah runs around in every direction, through all the alleyways, trying to find any persons who are exerting themselves to attain divine faith and judgment. He comes to the poor peasants and asks them about faith. They direct him to the priests and the biblical scholars. Yes, the poor, wretched peasants know nothing about it, since they have put their trust in the most poisonous people. So the prophet reflects: "O God, the peasants are poor, care-worn folk. They have spent their life in a grim struggle for bread in order to fill the throats of the most godless tyrants. What chance have such poor, coarse folk of knowing anything?" Jeremiah goes on in chapter 5: "I thought, Lord, I will go to the bigwigs. Surely they will look after poor folk and deal with them like good shepherds. They will make due provision in word and deed for their faith and judgment. I will talk with them about this; they will surely know." Sure, sure, in fact they know much less than the sorriest [peasant did].

How has this come to pass? Simply because every peasant wanted a priest, to ensure them an easy time. Now they are no longer so enthusiastic, for nowhere in the world is there much concern to encourage a true priesthood. On the contrary, the world tends to knock a true priest's head off, so that it rolls at his feet. A really good ministry tastes like bitter gall to it. A MANIFEST EXPOSÉ OF FALSE FAITH.[5]

RULERS NEGLECT THEIR CALLING, COMMON FOLK SUFFER. MENNO SIMONS: You see, dear sirs and rulers, this is really the office to which you are called [to punish transgressors and protect the good]. Whether you fulfill these requirements piously and faithfully I will leave to your consideration. I think with the holy Jeremiah that you have all broken the yoke and rent the bands. For you reject and detest as an abomination and a venomous serpent the dear Word of God, which you should introduce in the pure fear of God. The false teachers and prophets who deceive the whole world, and whom according to the Word of God we should shun, are kept in high esteem by you. The poor miserable sheep who in their weakness would sincerely fear and obey the Lord, and who would not speak an evil word to anyone because they dare not do aught against his Word; who lead a pious, penitent life, and make the right use of his holy sacraments, according to the Scriptures, abhor with mortal fear all false doctrines, sects, and wickedness, these are exiled from city and country and are often sentenced to fire, water, or sword. Their goods are confiscated; their children, who according to the words of the prophet are not responsible for their transgressions of their fathers . . . these are thrust forth, divested and naked, and the labor and sweat of their parents they must leave in the hands of these avaricious, greedy, unmerciful, and bloodthirsty bandits. REPLY TO FALSE ACCUSATIONS.[6]

SINFUL JEWS, PREDATORS, AND THE MESSIAH. JOHANN PAPPUS: There are three types of sins for which the Jews are accused in this part: contempt for the word of God, zeal for idolatry, and false security. The Lord says, "Your children have forsaken me." However, to forsake the Lord is nothing other than to despise his Word, which explains his will to us, and not obey it or give ear to it. This is a sin because for the most part . . . they are injured by the simulation of piety. . . . Then the prophet accuses them of idolatry, which he compares to adultery, not only because the similarity among the two sins is great, but also because all the most terrible sins of lust are normally committed in the course of idolatry. But

---

[4]Trapp, *A Commentary or Exposition,* 238*; citing Is 1:21. Antonio Mancinelli (1452–1505) was a humanist scholar in Vallerti and Rome; Savonarola (1452–1498) was a Dominican preacher and reformer in Florence who was critical of Pope Alexander VI and was accused of and executed for false prophecies and political intrigue. [5]Müntzer, *Collected Works,* 294*. [6]Simons, *Complete Works,* 551.

the prophet puts forth an image of both adulteries, that is, both spiritual and the physical adulteries, an image taken from the energy and madness of a kind of horse, because even if it seems to keep some of the timidity of its related blood, nevertheless, it is stimulated by lustful desire . . . The third type of sin is a blameworthy sense of security, of one who lies regarding the Lord and says, "He does not exist. . . ."

Therefore, on account of these sins the prophet announces the most serious punishments to the Judeans, and first indeed he compares that enemy through whom they will be afflicted to the lion, the evening wolf, and the leopard. Various peoples are signified by different types of animals like this in Daniel 7. But in this passage the Chaldean enemy alone is spoken of as different animals: the lion because of its power, the evening wolf because it will be a cunning enemy—comparable to the wolf in its patient discipline for its evening prey—and finally the panther because of its speed and unexpected attack. Second, it is shown that the punishments, which the Lord threatens, will be most just. This is shown to the Judeans themselves, who were brought forward as if in court, and they are convicted by their own consciences. In the third place the power itself and cruelty of the enemy is described with many words to this end, that perhaps by this account the Jews might be moved to seriously repent.

Nevertheless, finally, it was just as necessary to preserve the promises concerning the Messiah, which could not have been fulfilled in the land of Chaldea and outside of Judea; lest an occasion for despair in the faith of those promises be given to anyone. Therefore, a note of consolation is added in turn. "Even in those days," says the Lord, "I will not make an end to you." In these words are tacitly promised both the return from exile and, after the return, the fulfillment of the promises concerning the Messiah. ON ALL THE PROPHETS, JEREMIAH 5:6-18.[7]

FULLNESS LEADS TO TROUBLE. JOHN TRAPP: Fullness in good people often breeds forgetfulness,

and in bad people, filthiness. Gluttony is the gallery that incontinency walks through. The Israelites ate and drank and rose up to play with their Midianite mistresses, thus provoking of God's fierce wrath. Fullness of bread made way to Sodom's sin. Lunatics, when the moon is declining and in the wane, are sober enough, but when full, more wild and exorbitant. Ceres and Bacchus are great friends to Venus and so forth. Watch, therefore, and feed with fear. COMMENTARY ON JEREMIAH 5:7.[8]

DIVINE VENGEANCE EXECUTES DIVINE JUSTICE. LANCELOT ANDREWES: In moral divinity, if we go that way, the proper work of justice is to give to each person their due. Corrective justice, [which is] to do justice, [is] to inflict correction where it is due, and to sin, it is due. The difference only is: correction, for the most part, is done upon others. In repentance, it reflects and is done upon ourselves.

If you will put more life into it, and utter it more pathetically, go by the way of the affections. Anger is the predominant affection. The proper work of anger is to be avenged. "What, shall I not visit? Shall not my soul be avenged on such an indignity?" says Indignation. As anger, then, [is] the chief passion, so [it is] the chief action. The apostle therefore leaves not off till he has asked . . . "What revenge? What punishment?" That is Paul's last question. He comes not to his period till he has shut up all with that. For till that be done all is not done. That is the very end [consummatum est] of all true repentance. SERMON ON MATTHEW 3:8.[9]

NEIGHING AFTER YOUR NEIGHBOR'S WIFE. MENNO SIMONS: I do not mean to say that a person who has in days gone by ignorantly done this thing [deflower a virgin] must leave the wife whom he afterward married and take in her stead the violated one. Not at all, for I doubt not but that the merciful Father will graciously overlook the errors of those who have ignorantly committed them and who will now fear and gladly do what is

[7]Pappus, In Omnes Prophetas, 74v-75r.

[8]Trapp, A Commentary or Exposition, 239*.
[9]Andrewes, Works 1:441*; citing 2 Cor 7:11.

right. But I write this that everyone should guard themselves against such disgrace, and reflect more profoundly upon the command of the Lord and on love, and observe how Christ is so wholly despised by the world. For alas, they are altogether driven by their accursed lusts, whether they are lords, princes, monks, noble or ignoble, burghers or peasants, with few exceptions. They pursue the improper, devilish shame and accursed adultery with such an avidity as of a hound after a hare. "They are," says Jeremiah, "as fed horses in the morning; every one neighed after his neighbor's wife." THE TRUE CHRISTIAN FAITH.[10]

NEIGHING LIKE A STALLION SENSING A MARE IN HEAT. THE ENGLISH ANNOTATIONS: This [passage] one of the Jewish doctors fondly expounds concerning their coming abroad with jollity. When they come out in the morning from their idolatrous bed, as shamelessly glorifying in their sin and shame, like horses, he says, that, having fed well in the night, neigh in the morning. But the prophet's purpose here is not to express the disposition or carriage of these loose and lewd persons when their filthy lust is satisfied, but rather their earnestness and eagerness in seeking after those with whom they may satisfy their unbridled lust. Nor is the neighing here alluded to the neighing of a horse, out of alacrity or courage . . . , but [rather] his neighing upon the sight or scent of the mare, while he proceeds from unquietness, until he can come at her. ANNOTATIONS ON JEREMIAH 5:8.[11]

DENYING GOD AT HIS WORD. JOHANNES BUGENHAGEN: "They deny the Lord." You have here a clear text: that the Lord is denied when his Word is denied, because . . . in this world we possess God in his Word. You are without God, when you do not have the Word of God. Of course, they say that that which Jeremiah and the other prophets proclaim is not the Lord himself, but the devil, as impious Germans today say, "This is not

the gospel; what is now preached is not Christ, but it is the devil. . . . The prophets or preachers speak vain things and heresies. They do not have the oracles of God." Thus the impious blaspheme. This truly is to deny God and his Christ. COMMENTARY ON JEREMIAH 5:12.[12]

5:14-31 The Lord Proclaims Judgment

DIVINE BLESSING AND HUMAN INGRATITUDE. HEINRICH BULLINGER: Again and as if starting afresh, the Lord instructs the prophet and orders him to preach to the people of Judah, to reprimand their abundant sins; for by chance they might repent, fear God, and avoid perishing. Therefore let us observe at the beginning the mandate of God, ordering Jeremiah to announce and preach this: certainly the part that came before concerning the supplication that the wicked and impenitent ought to undertake, but especially this which soon follows: "Hear this, I beg you, O foolish and senseless people, etc. . . ." God orders the prophet to rebuke the people for their blindness, deafness, foolishness, hardness or impenetrable stubbornness, disobedience, rebellion, and certainly their shameful ingratitude. It is not a crime if a father, magistrate, prophet, or sincere friend calls a fool someone who is in fact a fool. If someone out of hatred or malice calls another person insipid or foolish with intent to inflict injury, they sin against the law of the Lord.

Further, Jeremiah more significantly declares in what way they are foolish, blind, and deaf, giving the rationale for calling them that and explaining how they are disobedient, ungrateful, and stubborn. Indeed, he demonstrates two great blessings of God, which he presented before their eyes, and which he kindly bestows on them. But they do not observe these things, nor do they consider them important, nor do they show that they are grateful to God. At the same time as he explains these blessings, he all the more clearly shows their sins and malice. Moses in the first chapter of the first book of the Bible shows that the nature of the waters was poured

---

[10]Simons, *Complete Works*, 379.
[11]Downame, ed., *Annotations*, 9F2r*; citing Job 39:19, 25.

[12]Bugenhagen, *In Ieremiam*, 2L2v-2L3r.

around and covered the earth, but God with one singular blessing commanded that the waters recede into the deep so that the land might stand out. God named the mass of waters "the sea" and that which was dry or made dry by the departure of the waters he called "the land." He also set a limit or boundary for the sea that it would never cross, so that the land would always stand free of the water, suitable for human habitation, and suitable to sustain and nourish humanity.... Jeremiah certainly in the same mode says most elegantly that God placed the sandy shore as a boundary or limit for the sea, and did this by perpetual decree.... Indeed, it is true that sometimes the sea, bursting the levees, pours itself out and has poured itself out across a continent and has destroyed fields, regions, and cities. Truly these things are the judgments of God....

Jeremiah, however, applies this extraordinary work of God to his own design through an interrogation. He says: will you not have something to fear from this God? Will you not tremble, having seen and heard such things about the power of God? Or will you not blush, when you hear that the waves of the sea do not cross the boundary established by God, but of their own free will they obey God?... In this way the sin of the Jews is amplified....

Jeremiah proceeds to remember another extraordinary benefit of God and at the same time rebukes the sin of ingratitude, stubbornness, blindness, and deafness among his people. This extraordinary benefit and great power of God is that he gives to us the late and early rainy seasons.... Truly already this characteristic in the people was to be greatly cursed, that, ungrateful to such a generous God, they neither feared nor loved their benefactor. Jeremiah expresses it when he says: "They did not say in their hearts, 'At any rate, we will fear the Lord our God.'" SERMON ON JEREMIAH 5:19-25.[13]

BEWARE APOSTATES! JOHN TRAPP: Gone are they, and return they will not. Apostates are dangerous creatures, and mischievous above others.

Witness Julian,[†] once a forward professor; Lucian[‡] [was] once a preacher at Antioch; Staphylus and Latomus§ [were] once great Lutherans, [but] afterward [became] eager popelings. Harding[◊] was the target of popery in England (says Pierre du Moulin,[△] against which he had once been a thundering preacher in this land, wishing he could cry out against it "as loud as the bells of Olseney"). The lady Jane Grey, whose chaplain he had sometimes been, gave him excellent counsel in a letter, but he was revolted and gone past call. COMMENTARY ON JEREMIAH 5:23.[14]

THE RICH AS A REFUGE—NOT A TRAP—FOR THE POOR. HEINRICH BULLINGER: The prophet proceeds then to explain to the people what he had been commanded by God to say, and to explain the cause of their evils, namely, that they did not derive these from any peevishness of God, but from the people's own guilt and corruption. Therefore, Jeremiah accuses the Jewish people of an extreme corporate wickedness. He shows that no one is sincere or honest among all the levels and orders of the people. In fact, Jeremiah enumerates the crimes

---

[13]Bullinger, *Conciones*, 39r, 39v, 40r-v; citing Mt 5: 21-26; Gen 1:9-10.

[14]Trapp, *A Commentary or Exposition*, 241*. †Julian the Apostate, Roman emperor who, though raised a Christian, subscribed very strongly to pagan philosophy, especially Neoplatonism, and tried to return the Roman Empire to paganism. ‡Lucian of Antioch (d. 312) was a priest and martyr believed by many at the time to have been the chief source of Arius's heretical theology. §Friedrich Staphylus (1512–1564) was a Lutheran theologian who converted to Roman Catholicism; Jacobus Latomus (Jacques Masson) (1475–1544) was a Flemish theologian who served on the faculty of the University of Louvain. He was a theological advisor to the Inquisition, and he distinguished himself with his many treatises against Luther and Tyndale. ◊Thomas Harding (1516–1572) was an English Catholic controversialist, previously a Protestant and chaplain to Lady Jane Grey (1536–1553), who converted to Catholicism shortly after Mary Tudor (1516–1558); Harding is best known for his protracted literary war with Protestant apologist John Jewel (1522–1571). △Pierre du Moulin (1568–1659) was a Huguenot minister from France who also lived in England mainly during the reign of James I (r. 1603–1625). He writes about Harding's defection to Catholicism in his work *Tirannie que les papes ont exercé depuis quelque siècles sur les roys d'Angleterre*. An English translation of this work was published posthumously in 1574 as *Tyranny that the Popes exercised for some centuries over the kings of England*. See also *Acts and Monuments*, fol. 1291.

of the wealthy merchants, the crooked judges, prophets, and priests, and, finally, the people themselves. Moreover, all these things point to the same end: that they acknowledge these vices and outrages, repent and live, and not perish.

First, Jeremiah censures the wealthy merchants among the people. Their sin is not that they are rich. Indeed, there were many holy people who were wealthy in both Testaments of Scripture, without vice, living according the apostolic rule, handed down in 1 Timothy 6. Thus it is not a sin to do business, only do to the other person what you would have them do to you. It is most significant that as soon as Jeremiah accuses them, he calls them impious. In fact, impiety stains their wealth and corrupts their dealings. An impious man does not care about God; on the contrary he despises God and having heard his law—"do not steal, avoid the love of riches . . ."—he thinks in his heart, nay he even often says out loud, "he obtains wealth too late, who wishes to live according to the precept of divine law." Truly, the impious act insincerely with people, but they corrupt everything with their depraved arts, lies, deception, fraud, theft, usury, plundering, and their many deceits. Therefore, Jeremiah compares people who are greedy to bird catchers and hunters. The rich ought to be a refuge for the poor, but their avarice already makes them the torturers, hunters, and bird catchers of the poor. SERMON ON JEREMIAH 5:26-29.[15]

DEVILISH HONEY IN THE BEAKS OF LITTLE BIRDS. JÖRG HAUG: Proper discernment or understanding born out of fear and wisdom of God holds still and awaits the imprint . . . of the divine will, lest deception enter along with truth and the wisdom of God, for the angel of darkness and error often disguises himself as an angel of light and intrudes proper discernment and subverts it. These are the wolves or deceivers who disguise their true nature and evil intentions under sheepskins, that is, under good appearance, in order to destroy mercilessly the sheepfold and sheep stall of Christ. . . . When they

wish to deceive, they speak in a high, sweet, flattering voice. They polish their act and scatter their seed like a fowler who throws something out to the unsuspecting little birds, puts honey into their beaks but means to poison them. When they eat this food, it tastes sweet but is bitter in their belly. At present the whole world eats of it and it tastes very sweet in their mouth, but oh, how very bitter it will become in their bellies! Therefore it is necessary to examine oneself and to permit Christ the crucified one to open one's discernment within, that is, the Christ who wells up from within. A CHRISTIAN ORDER.[16]

PREFERRING FALSE PROPHECIES. JOHANNES OECOLAMPADIUS: "Foolishness and Disgrace." These things are foolish and more disgraceful than what it is right to say, for with lies and flattery preachers and teachers affirm all those things, and they say these things are good, which the crowd takes hold of even among us. The priesthood is for the forgiveness of sins, which they simply have put forward; therefrom the priests began to dominate, and that was agreeable to the people, lest they might renew their lives through repentance. Indeed, they paid for indulgences with a few coins and they went astray, falsely secure with a curse and the sentence of death reigning in their hearts. They said that the pope is the rock on which the church is built. From that, the pope strengthened tyranny and an astonishing foolishness, which is how the people so permitted themselves to become insane in their own great wickedness. They were prophesying so that when parents ought to be supported, sons would say that in part that the use of the money was to be yielded to the priests. So gold is given with a supposedly good heart, and from this the priests were receiving gifts.

They were prophesying that for those who were buried in Franciscan cowls, a third part of their sins was thereby remitted. Likewise they set them free through the Masses of St. Gregory, and again through the designated stations of the cross. All those things were deemed more worthy than the

---

[15]Bullinger, *Conciones*, 41r-v; citing 1 Tim 6:1-10.

[16]CRR 10:10-11; citing 2 Cor 11:14.

actual renewal of a life. About that renewal there was at most silence. How finally did filth and foolishness rush in? Will you not grow wholly dull and most foul? Now it is pleasing and acceptable to say that good is evil: at one time you knew the nature of evil and it made you ashamed of yourselves. COMMENTARY ON JEREMIAH 5:30-31.[17]

THE DAY OF GOD'S WRATH. LANCELOT ANDREWES: When that day comes, how then? The prophet's ordinary question [is], "What will you do at the last?" How will you be saved in *Die illo*, "in that day?"

We speak sometime of great days here—alas! Small in respect of this. Great it is, and notable as much for the fear, as for anything else in it. This [is] a terrible one indeed, *et quis potest sustinere*, "Who can abide it?" says Joel in the second chapter. Look to it then on whom he pours not his Spirit here, [but] on them he will pour something else there, the vials of his wrath. SERMON ON ACTS 2:16-21.[18]

THE TEACHERS THE PEOPLE PREFER. DIRK PHILIPS: Since the people are so minded that they hold good teaching in contempt, as Paul says, and have such weak ears that they desire more to hear what is pleasing than fruitful teaching, therefore they choose such teachers for themselves, after whom their ears itch. And it then happens just as the Lord said through the prophet: "It is horrible and dangerous in the land: the prophets teach lies and the priests rule in their office. . . ." Therefore, Christ also said to his disciples, "Woe to you, when all speak well of you. . . ." Contrary to this you are blessed "when people revile you and persecute you. . . ."

Therefore it is certain that the true teachers must be tested with the cross. And this comes because they desire and speak other than the world: therefore the world hates them. THE ENCHIRIDION.[19]

---

[17]Oecolampadius, *In Hieremiam*, 1:Iiv.
[18]Andrewes, *Works*, 3:316-17*; citing Joel 2:11.

[19]CRR 6:213; citing 2 Tim 4:3; Lk 6:26; Mt 5:11-12.

JEREMIAH 6:1-30
DISASTER IS COMING

¹Flee for safety, O people of Benjamin,
    from the midst of Jerusalem!
Blow the trumpet in Tekoa,
    and raise a signal on Beth-haccherem,
for disaster looms out of the north,
    and great destruction.
²The lovely and delicately bred I will destroy,
    the daughter of Zion.ᵃ
³Shepherds with their flocks shall come against
      her;
    they shall pitch their tents around her;
    they shall pasture, each in his place.
⁴"Prepare war against her;
    arise, and let us attack at noon!
Woe to us, for the day declines,
    for the shadows of evening lengthen!
⁵Arise, and let us attack by night
    and destroy her palaces!"

⁶For thus says the Lord of hosts:
"Cut down her trees;
    cast up a siege mound against Jerusalem.
This is the city that must be punished;
    there is nothing but oppression within her.
⁷As a well keeps its water fresh,
    so she keeps fresh her evil;
violence and destruction are heard within her;
    sickness and wounds are ever before me.
⁸Be warned, O Jerusalem,
    lest I turn from you in disgust,
lest I make you a desolation,
    an uninhabited land."

⁹Thus says the Lord of hosts:
"They shall glean thoroughly as a vine
    the remnant of Israel;
like a grape gatherer pass your hand again
    over its branches."
¹⁰To whom shall I speak and give warning,
    that they may hear?
Behold, their ears are uncircumcised,

    they cannot listen;
behold, the word of the Lord is to them an
      object of scorn;
    they take no pleasure in it.
¹¹Therefore I am full of the wrath of the Lord;
    I am weary of holding it in.
"Pour it out upon the children in the street,
    and upon the gatherings of young men, also;
both husband and wife shall be taken,
    the elderly and the very aged.
¹²Their houses shall be turned over to others,
    their fields and wives together,
for I will stretch out my hand
    against the inhabitants of the land,"
declares the Lord.
¹³"For from the least to the greatest of them,
    everyone is greedy for unjust gain;
and from prophet to priest,
    everyone deals falsely.
¹⁴They have healed the wound of my people
      lightly,
    saying, 'Peace, peace,'
    when there is no peace.
¹⁵Were they ashamed when they committed
      abomination?
    No, they were not at all ashamed;
    they did not know how to blush.
Therefore they shall fall among those who fall;
    at the time that I punish them, they shall be
      overthrown,"
says the Lord.

¹⁶Thus says the Lord:
"Stand by the roads, and look,
    and ask for the ancient paths,
where the good way is; and walk in it,
    and find rest for your souls.
But they said, 'We will not walk in it.'
¹⁷I set watchmen over you, saying,
    'Pay attention to the sound of the trumpet!'

But they said, 'We will not pay attention.'
¹⁸Therefore hear, O nations,
　and know, O congregation, what will
　　happen to them.
¹⁹Hear, O earth; behold, I am bringing disaster
　　upon this people,
　the fruit of their devices,
because they have not paid attention to my words;
　and as for my law, they have rejected it.
²⁰What use to me is frankincense that comes
　　from Sheba,
　or sweet cane from a distant land?
Your burnt offerings are not acceptable,
　nor your sacrifices pleasing to me.
²¹Therefore thus says the Lord:
'Behold, I will lay before this people
　stumbling blocks against which they shall
　　stumble;
fathers and sons together,
　neighbor and friend shall perish.'"

²²Thus says the Lord:
"Behold, a people is coming from the north
　　country,
　a great nation is stirring from the farthest
　　parts of the earth.
²³They lay hold on bow and javelin;
　they are cruel and have no mercy;
　the sound of them is like the roaring sea;
they ride on horses,

set in array as a man for battle,
　against you, O daughter of Zion!"
²⁴We have heard the report of it;
　our hands fall helpless;
anguish has taken hold of us,
　pain as of a woman in labor.
²⁵Go not out into the field,
　nor walk on the road,
for the enemy has a sword;
　terror is on every side.
²⁶O daughter of my people, put on sackcloth,
　and roll in ashes;
make mourning as for an only son,
　most bitter lamentation,
for suddenly the destroyer
　will come upon us.

²⁷"I have made you a tester of metals among
　　my people,
　that you may know and test their ways.
²⁸They are all stubbornly rebellious,
　going about with slanders;
they are bronze and iron;
　all of them act corruptly.
²⁹The bellows blow fiercely;
　the lead is consumed by the fire;
in vain the refining goes on,
　for the wicked are not removed.
³⁰Rejected silver they are called,
　for the Lord has rejected them."

a Or I have likened the daughter of Zion to the loveliest pasture

---

OVERVIEW: Warfare was a fact of life in the centuries of the Reformation. From the German Peasants' War (1524–1525) to the end of the Thirty Years' War (1618–1648) and the English Civil Wars (1642–1651), the peoples and powers of Europe endured a steady diet of violence and military confrontation often fed by religious conviction and confession. Meanwhile, to the east the Ottoman Turks sought to expand their kingdom and spread Islam deeper into the heart of Europe. Besieged cites and fleeing refugees, marauding armies and ravaged rural landscapes, peoples of the eastern borderlands—slaughtered, enslaved, raped—the world of Jeremiah was painfully familiar to early modern Europeans. Sometimes it seemed like the end of the world was close at hand. Even so sixteenth-century expositors expounded on Jeremiah without flinching; they combed the biblical text for details of battle and destruction as well as larger patterns of change and causality. Unrestrained sin and shameless immorality, empty ritual and exploitive religion, divine wrath and providence—all could dissolve the bonds of society and move kingdoms to violence.

Still, in the gathering darkness, God's fatherly affection yet reached out for the repentant and the remnant of true believers. This gospel alone was the one true and sure hope for people caught up in the unremitting threat of war and destruction. Like Jeremiah, the true church remains as a witness and refuge, a watchman and refiner of faith. God calls the faithful to the one true way and tests them in the purifying flames of suffering. It is no accident that Reformation comes in violent and tumultuous times, when war is an ever-present threat and naysayers and false prophets command the masses.

6:1-13 Impending Invasion and Disaster for Jerusalem

NO DEFENSE APART FROM GOD. JOHANNES BUGENHAGEN: Jerusalem was located by lot in the tribe of Benjamin, as in Joshua 18. Tekoa is called after the wise woman in 2 Samuel 14 and at Beth-haccherem fortifications were placed, in which the Jews hoped that their stationed garrisons would impede Babylonian forces and keep them from Jerusalem. As it happened the blasphemers were making a show of such things against the prediction of Jeremiah. Therefore, he ridicules them, preaching that every effort of the impious was ineffectual, because the Lord, who cannot lie, spoke against them. When the help of God has been lost, there is no help. COMMENTARY ON JEREMIAH 6:1.[1]

JERUSALEM COVETED AND CAPTURED. KONRAD PELLIKAN: To the extent that Jerusalem was much more splendid and glorious than other illustrious cities and accustomed to greater delights, the shepherds of the people and kings of every place ardently coveted her, all of them standing crowded on each other in this desire: the Egyptians, of course, and the Idumeans, Syrians, Assyrians, Greeks, and Ethiopians. Just as shepherds tend not

to pass up the most beautiful pastures, but arrange their flocks there, each in their own place, in the same way will those once glorious peoples invade the daughter of Zion—that royal city—and each prince with his own company of soldiers will surround her with camps in a circle . . . so that no one will escape, and so that they would attack her from every direction, with no one helping, and so that each enemy from his own place would invade the wall. Just as the prophet preached the history of this accomplishment—which he would see—so Christ preached that it would be repeated a second time. COMMENTARY ON JEREMIAH 6:2-3.[2]

THE SHADOWS OF WAR DESCEND. JOHANNES OECOLAMPADIUS: "Consecrate war against her." So they urge each other on. A mutual war is sanctified, from which one may not give up, just as something is holy because one may not violate it, and walls are holy, which one may not go over. The voice of the enemy is this: "let us arise at midday and at night"; that is, "let us take no break from war. Even if the sun burns, even if the icy night descends, the work of attacking will need to be urged on until their palaces are destroyed." Here the prophet inserts a parenthesis, "Woe to you," because the day wanes; that is, the time of rest will not be long; the day of peace wanes; now already the shadows are scattered: evening is nigh, for the shadows are getting long. So great is the rage of the enemy that they think there is no time too short for conquering us completely. Soon they will rush in with hostility. COMMENTARY ON JEREMIAH 6:4.[3]

FACING THE REALITY OF WAR AND SIEGE PAST, PRESENT, AND FUTURE. JOHANN PAPPUS: One finds an enemy more fearful who governs their soldiers with determined regularity, than an enemy who denies nothing to the inclination of the soldiers. Today wars are not wars, but just highway robberies, where neither wealthy people nor soldiers recognize their duty. In the Babylonian

---

[1]Bugenhagen, *In Ieremiam*, 2M2v; citing 2 Sam 14:1-20.

[2]Pellikan, *Commentaria Bibliorum*, 3:2P5r.
[3]Oecolampadius, *In Hieremiam*, 1:I2v.

host there was going to be the greatest zeal, and excitement of spirit, and determination, so much so that they would rest neither at midday, nor at night while crushing the unsuspecting Jews. "Hew her wood." Already with these words Jeremiah describes the siege of Jerusalem and the siege works being put up around the city. Moreover, the prophets tend to use such dramatic assertions in predicting future calamities that [in a way] they seem not to be predicting future events, nor even to be pointing a finger at present events, but to be narrating events that had already happened. In the same way, concerning the last siege, the Lord says, "The day will come to you, when your enemies will surround your wall with ramparts and confine you on every side and throw you to the ground." ON ALL THE PROPHETS, JEREMIAH 6:4-6.[4]

A FOUNTAIN OF VICE. JOHN CALVIN: [Jeremiah says] ... that violence, oppression, devastation, grief, and smiting streamed forth like waters from a fountain. It is possible for many vices to break out from a place, but repentance afterward follows; but when men cease not, and heap vices on vices, it then appears that they swell with wickedness, and even burst with it, as they cannot repress it: they are like a fountain, which ever bubbles up, and cannot contain its own waters. ... What the prophet means is that the Jews had so given themselves to their vices that they were ever contriving some new ways of doing evil, as waters never cease to stream forth from a fountain. COMMENTARY ON JEREMIAH 6:7.[5]

DID GOD REPENT? JOHN CALVIN: God is not indeed subject to grief or to repentance; but his ineffable goodness cannot otherwise be expressed to us but by such a mode of speaking. So also, in this passage, we see that God as it were restrains himself; for he had previously commanded the enemies to ascend the walls quickly, overturn the towers, and destroy the whole city, but now as though he has

repented, he says, "Be instructed, Jerusalem"; that is, "Can we not yet be reconciled?" It is like the conduct of an offended father who intends to punish his son, and yet desires to moderate his displeasure, and to blend some indulgence with rigor. "Be then instructed"; that is, "There is yet room for reconciliation, if you wish. If you show yourself willing to give up the perversity that has provoked me, I will in return prove myself to be your father." COMMENTARY ON JEREMIAH 6:8.[6]

A TIME FOR TURNING TO GOD'S FATHERLY GRACE. NIKOLAUS SELNECKER: "Reform yourself, Jerusalem. ..." Your offenses and violence cry out over you. You are stuffed full with malice, and your sins stink. You do no good and you do not intend to. Rather, you only laugh about it whenever one directs you to repentance. I say to you, God speaks and admonishes you himself: "Reform yourself. In this way you can have a gracious God and Father in Me." If not, God says, "So will I turn my heart and love from you and turn all of my fatherly care away from you. I will become an enemy, who will devastate you and ruin everything."

Here we see how gracious God is in his handling of us, that God in the midst of his wrath is always pondering grace and calls us to repentance. Whoever now turns himself to God and follows God, to him God will be gracious. Oh what a time it is now for us Germans to take such a word earnestly to heart and begin to pray: Oh, you dear Father God of our Lord Jesus Christ. Oh, be gracious to us, have mercy on us, and forgive us our great and numerous sins. THE WHOLE PROPHET JEREMIAH 6:8.[7]

THEY WILL LEAVE NOTHING BEHIND. JUAN DE MALDONADO: "They shall gather all the way to the cluster of grapes." Some interpret this so that the sense would be that the Chaldeans will not destroy Jerusalem completely, but they will leave some remnant, just as grape gatherers leave behind

---

[4]Pappus, *In Omnes Prophetas*, 76r; citing Lk 19:43-44.
[5]CTS 17:322* (CO 37:647-48).
[6]CTS 17:323-4* (CO 37:648-49).
[7]Selnecker, *Der gantze Prophet Jeremais*, K3r.

immature clusters of grapes but collect the mature ones. But to me the sense seems to be entirely opposite, that the Chaldeans will leave nothing behind that they did not tear to pieces. They will lead into captivity not only the male princes but also everyone from the least to the greatest. This is indicated by what follows, "turn back your hand." That indicates a comparison: "like a grape gatherer to his basket." That is, after they have gathered grapes, they return, and glean; that is, they collect the clusters if they have left any behind. Thus, when the Chaldeans have led away the first citizens of the city, they also will take away all of the lowest citizens. COMMENTARY ON THE PROPHETS, JEREMIAH 6:9.[8]

UNCIRCUMCISED HEARTS AND EARS. ANDREAS BODENSTEIN VON KARLSTADT: Note what Jeremiah says, "Uncircumcised ears cannot hear what God teaches." This is the same as when Christ says, "Whoever does not forsake everything cannot be my disciple." I note clearly then that an unyielded ear is an uncircumcised ear. And it cannot hear for the reason that it is preoccupied with desire and trusts in other teachings and creatures. This is what God says through Jeremiah. "I said, hear my voice, then I will be your God and you my people. But they did not hear. . . . " It is now clear that an uncircumcised heart or ear is a heart or ear that delights in other teachings that were not given by God, or one that otherwise delights in, loves, finds comfort in, or fears and worries about other things. Not all of its love or pain is in God or for God's sake. THE MEANING OF THE TERM *GELASSEN*.[9]

DOES JEREMIAH GO TOO FAR? MARTIN LUTHER: In Jeremiah 6 we read, further, "Their ears are uncircumcised, they cannot listen." Well, well, my dear Jeremiah, you are surely dealing roughly and inconsiderately with the noble, chosen, holy, circumcised people of God. Do you mean to say that such a holy nation has uncircumcised ears?

And, what is far worse, that they are unable to hear? Is that not tantamount to saying they are not God's people? For he who cannot hear or bear to hear God's Word is not of God's people. And if they are not God's people, then they are the devil's people; and then neither circumcising, nor skinning nor scraping will avail. For God's sake, Jeremiah, stop talking like that! How can you despise and condemn holy circumcision so horribly that you separate the chosen, circumcised, holy people from God and consign them to the devil as banished and damned? Do they not praise God for having set them apart through circumcision both from the devil and from all the other nations and for making them a holy and peculiar people? Yea, "He has spoken blasphemy! Crucify him, crucify him!" ON THE JEWS AND THEIR LIES.[10]

WHEN THE ENEMY COMES AND OUR COURAGE FAILS. NIKOLAUS SELNECKER: "A man and a woman, the old and full of days will be taken. . . . " We are able to find this passage useful because of the Turks. And we know what sort of lamentation this is: godly parents can understand it and take it to heart. Their children have often experienced this in Hungary, in many places in Austria, and elsewhere. The enemies (he will from now on say) arrive here as quickly as an arrow and they roar like a turbulent sea. When we hear of them our fists fall to our sides. We are terrified and fall in on ourselves, lose all courage, and have no hope. We fear the roaring horn. None are sure of themselves with a sword. What we have, we must give over to the enemy. The children are cut in two or otherwise captured and led away. The women and young girls are defiled. We become a poor people and concern ourselves with death, which now appears among us. And the barrel has been poured out on the ground. What is the source of such horrible misfortune?

Jeremiah answers and says, "The least and the greatest covet, the prophets and the priests teach a false worship." Hence comes all the misfortune, says Jeremiah, that is present in every level of society;

---

[8]Maldonado, *Commentarii in Prophetas*, 31-32.
[9]CRR 8:146; citing Lk 14:33; Jer 7:23

[10]LW 47:154 (WA 53:431); citing Lk 23:21.

from the lowest to the highest there is a disorder, overconfidence, and malice, which could not be greater, except that the priests themselves are the servants of their bellies. When they have enough goods for the day and have their fill, they contend that there is nothing urgent. "Their god is their belly." The Whole Prophet Jeremiah 6:11-13.[11]

Pastors Don't Enjoy Preaching Judgment. John Trapp: As I hitherto have done, and could still [do] in compassion, but out of necessity I must obey God's will, and be the messenger of his wrath. It is a folly to think that God's ministers delight in flinging daggers at others' breasts, or handfuls of hellfire at their faces. Commentary on Jeremiah 6:11.[12]

The Executioner and His Sword. Martin Luther: This is directed against those who make people happy by saying: "There is still a great deal of time." These things are said since this is also why sudden destruction will come to you. "They say: Peace, peace. . . ." But I am not predicting for times far in the future; but the judgment has been determined now, and the resolution has been concluded. He stands to execute judgment like an executioner brandishing a sword in his hand to cut off a criminal's head forthwith, as the psalm says: "He has stretched his bow." Lecture on Isaiah 3:13.[13]

England Will Suffer Like Judea. John Knox: The only comfort and joy of the soul is God by his Word expelling ignorance, sin, and death, and in the place of these planting true knowledge of himself and with the same justice and life that is Christ Jesus, his Son. If either profit of body or soul moves us, then it is necessary that we avoid idolatry. For it is plain that the soul has neither life nor comfort except by God alone, with whom idolaters have no other fellowship or participation except with the devils. And even if abominable idolatries triumph for a moment, yet the hour approaches when God's vengeance shall strike not only at their souls, but even their vile carcasses shall be plagued, as God has before threatened. Their cities shall be burned, their land laid waste, their enemies shall dwell in their strongholds, their wives, children, and daughters shall be defiled, their children shall die by the sword; they shall find no mercy because they have refused the God of all mercies, though he lovingly and long called upon them. You would know the time and what certainty I have of this. To God I will appoint no time, but . . . plagues shall fall upon the realm of England (and it will happen or it will long be prevented by repentance). I am as sure of this as I say that my God lives. A Godly Letter of Warning and Admonition.[14]

6:14-30 Why God Hardens the People

Why God Hardens the People. Martin Luther: We learn from Jeremiah among others that, as usual, the nearer the punishment, the worse people become; and that the more one preaches to them, the more they despise his preaching. Thus we understand that when it is God's will to inflict punishment, he makes the people to become hardened so they may be destroyed without any mercy and not appease God's wrath with any repentance. . . .

So it goes everywhere even now. Now that the end of the world is approaching, the people rage and rave most horribly against God. They blaspheme and damn God's Word, though they well know that it is God's Word and truth. Besides so many fearful signs and wonders are appearing, both in the heavens and among all creatures which threaten them terribly. It is indeed a wicked and miserable time, even worse than that of Jeremiah.

But so it will be and must be. The people begin to feel secure and sing, "Peace; all is well." They simply persecute everything that accords with the will of God and disregard all the threatening signs, until, as St. Paul says, "Destruction suddenly

---

[11]Selnecker, *Der gantze Prophet Jeremias* (1566), L2r-v; citing Phil 3:19.
[12]Trapp, *A Commentary or Exposition*, 243*.
[13]LW 16:46 (WA 31.2:33); citing Is 3:13; Ps 7:12.

[14]Knox, *Works*, 3:166-67*; citing Lev 26.

surprises them and destroys them before they know it." PREFACE TO THE PROPHET JEREMIAH.[15]

A MOST BITTER BITTERNESS AND A PEACE WITHOUT PEACE.

MARTIN BUCER: Once it was predicted and now the time of fulfillment has come: "Behold in peace my most bitter bitterness." Bitter first in the slaughter of martyrs, more bitter later in the conflicts with heretics, most bitter now in the characters of the church's servants. One cannot flee them or rout them: so strong have they become and multiplied beyond numbering. Intestinal and incurable is the plague of the church and therefore peace its most bitter bitterness. But in what peace? It is both "peace and not peace." Peace from the pagans, and peace from the heretics; but not, surely, from the children. There is a voice wailing at this time: "I have nourished and raised children, but they have despised me." They have despised and dirtied me by a shameful life, shameful gain, shameful commerce, a business walking in darkness. What is left but the noonday devil to rise from the middle of things, to seduce, if there are any left in Christ. CONCERNING THE KINGDOM OF CHRIST.[16]

TRUE PEACE PREVAILS ONLY THROUGH GOD'S RIGHTEOUSNESS.

LANCELOT ANDREWES: Now because there is *vana salus*, "a vain salvation," as David says, and a peace falsely so called, "a peace which is no peace," as Jeremiah says, to the end therefore that our salvation that might be substantial, and our peace genuine, it behooves us to lay a sure groundwork for them both, and to set a true root of this branch, which is the name Jehovah. For such as the root of this branch is, then salvation and peace will be the fruit. If it be human righteousness which is vain, it will be also *vana salus hominis* [vain safety of humanity], vain and soon at an end; and the peace, like the world's peace, is vain and of no certainty. But if "Jehovah" be "our righteousness," [then] look how he is so we [also]

will be, everlasting salvation, "a peace which passes all understanding." SERMON ON JEREMIAH 23:6.[17]

REMAIN ON THE OLD PATHS.

JOHN TRAPP: Chalked out by the word, and walked in by the patriarchs. Think not, as some do nowadays, by running through all religions to find out the right, for this is . . . as Junius phrases it, to seek a way where none is to be found. How many religions are there now among us? So many people, so many minds. . . . As one complained of old, one is nobody who cannot invent a new way; but as old wine is better, so is the old way. Hold to it, therefore. COMMENTARY ON JEREMIAH 6:14.[18]

AN APPETITE FOR DECEPTION AND WICKEDNESS.

KONRAD PELLIKAN: The false prophets, deceptively advancing their own complaint, promised the kings and the people that everything was safe and whole, in order to free them from the fear of grief, while extreme ruin was imminent—as ruin fell upon them the false prophets discerned good things, though not without ignominy. But among those who were like themselves, they did not blush about their wicked deeds and their treachery. Rather, they multiplied their sin in contempt and squandered the simplicity of the common people in lament and fasting. The false prophets were about to be destroyed along with the people they deceived—not that they were completely unwilling. They could have resisted these evils if they had loved the pursuit of truth, and had not preferred to hear things more pleasing than true. COMMENTARY ON JEREMIAH 6:15.[19]

FAITH OF OUR FATHERS.

JOHANNES BUGENHAGEN: "Stand on the way." The clement and merciful Lord does not want sinners to perish, but that they might be converted. Therefore here he engages with the seductive hypocrites and with those who

---

[17]Andrewes, *Works*, 5:110*; citing Phil 4:7.
[18]Trapp, *A Commentary or Exposition*, 243*. Franciscus Junius (1545–1602) was a French Reformed theologian and biblical scholar.
[19]Pellikan, *Commentaria Bibliorum*, 3:2P5v.

---

[15]LW 35:281-2 (WA, DB 11.1:193-94); citing Jer 8:11; 1 Thess 5:3.
[16]Bucer, *De Regno Christi*, 210-11; citing Is 38:17; Is 1:2; Ps 91:6.

have been seduced, who (as in our day) glory in their fathers and their ancient faith. He suggests that they look to the fathers of the faith—Abraham, Isaac, Jacob, David, and others—who were justified by faith and teach that one is to be justified by faith. This, Jeremiah says, is the true way and ancient faith. Just as the angel in Luke 1 is interpreted from Malachi saying, " . . . that he might turn the hearts of the fathers to the sons" and the unbelievers to the prudence of the just. These are the fathers of faith who believed the Word of God or had trust in God and this very thing they sincerely taught others, just as the holy prophets and apostles of God, who have this mandate from God so to teach. Those past fathers, however, who withdrew from faith and dared to teach something other than what the Word of God ordains, are those concerning whom the psalm says: "lest they become as their fathers, a depraved and exasperating generation," a generation that neither set its heart straight, nor did its spirit trust in God. As in Jeremiah 16: "Truly our fathers have possessed lies" etc., as also above at the end of chapter 3. COMMENTARY ON JEREMIAH 6:16.[20]

DO NOT BLINDLY TRUST LEADERS. THE ENGLISH ANNOTATIONS: God proceeds here by the prophet to convince this people of their obstinacy, and turns his speech now from the false prophets that seduced them to those who were seduced by them, and relates to both the advice he had from time to time given them and how they still refused to hear it. And in this verse, he seems to anticipate an objection that the people might make, alleging for themselves that they want the way in which their priests and prophets directed and led them. To which the Lord answers that he had from time to time admonished them to do as travelers are inclined to do when they are at a loss or doubt their way, seeing diverse ways or paths before them, and not knowing which of them leads to the place for which they are bound. They are careful to inquire of those who are able to inform them which is the way that leads to such a place, and so should they do, if they doubted the way they were in or of those diverse ways to which they were invited by those prophets who spoke to them in the name of the Lord as did both the prophets of God and the false prophets. They should make a stand and enter into due consideration concerning which of them were the way that might conduce to their good and welfare. And to help themselves further in this inquiry, they should have recourse to God's oracles and the sacred records of the former ages and times therein registered, and to consider what way it was that is therein commended to them and has ever proved successful and advantageous to those who walked in it. Betaking themselves of that [way] and walking in it, whatsoever anyone might suggest to the contrary, they should be sure to do well as those before them had done. ANNOTATIONS ON JEREMIAH 6:16.[21]

RETURN TO THE OLD CUSTOMS. LANCELOT ANDREWES: And do not the prophets say the same: "Stand upon the ways"—it is Jeremiah, "and there look for the good old way, and take that way; it is the only way to find rest for your souls."

All which I have said up to this point agrees with that which all the fathers in the first Nicene Council took up, and which ever since has been the church's cry, "Let old customs prevail," let them carry it. SERMON ON MATTHEW 12:39-40.[22]

THE ANCIENT PATHS OF THE ANCIENT OF DAYS. JOHN DONNE: "Stand in the way," God says in Jeremiah, "and ask for the old way, which is the good way." We must put off the old man, but not the Ancient One. We may put off that religion which we think old, because it is a little older than ourselves, and not rely upon that. . . . But the "Ancient of Days," him whose name is "He that is, and was, and is forever," and so involves, and

---

[20]Bugenhagen, *In Ieremiam*, 2M3v; citing Lk 1:16; Mal 4:6; Ps 78:8; Jer 16:19; 3:24-25.

[21]Downame, ed., *Annotations*, 9G1r-v*; citing Deut 32:7; Is 8:20; Mal 4:4; Lk 16:29; 1 Thess 5:21; 1 Jn 4:1.
[22]Andrewes, *Works*, 2:411*.

enwraps in himself all the Fathers—him we must put on. SERMON ON PSALM 38:4.[23]

THE TRUE WAY AND THE FALSE WAY. JOHANNES OECOLAMPADIUS: [God] gives the reason for which he permitted the Jews to be seduced through the false prophets: because they did not believe in those who were truly calling them to examine their spirits. Learn in what manner God here raises the cause of their excuse. Indeed, there stands before their eyes good and evil, just as in chapter 21: "Behold I myself put before you the way of life and death." And in Ecclesiasticus 15: "He put before you water and fire, to whatever you wish extend your hand, before a man is life and death, good, and evil; whatever pleases him will be given to him." So it is in this passage, for we are at a crossroads; let us see therefore which is to be chosen, whether that which the false prophets say, or that which the true prophets say. Indeed, you will not be absolved, if through shamelessness, you have not looked to your own well-being.

Accordingly, the Lord ordered too that we guard against false prophets: so in this verse we have the precept concerning the testing of the spirit and the fact that free will does not vote against grace. As in 1 Kings 18: Elijah proclaims, "How long will you go limping between this and that way? If the Lord is God, follow him; if Baal, follow him." So there are two ways. The true prophets say, "Be taught and return from your evil ways, and then you will not fall into the hands of your enemies." And lying prophets say: "Good is the path on which you are going, so don't depart from it; in vain the prophets frighten you, that you will fall into the hand of your enemies; don't be afraid, there is peace." Therefore, examine closely and test inwardly the calculations of your mind: which is the good way? Seek the way that is the ancient one, as John says: "It is neither a new way nor a new law." The ancient way is this: that good people ought to suffer persecution in the service of love. So it always was: those who sought the truth were aided

by God. Those who sought false prophets strayed from the truth and were deserted by God. Walk in the way, that is, undertake it, and go in the better way. Matthew 11: there "you will find rest for your souls." Christ, therefore, and the glory of Christ: that is the way. Let them boast who have discovered that way in their consciences through faith. COMMENTARY ON JEREMIAH 6:16.[24]

THE MERCY OF GOD AND THE RELIGION OF UNREPENTANT SINNERS. HEINRICH BULLINGER: Although they were impiously rebellious in this way, nevertheless, because of his ineffable mercy in this place, God did not yet reject those who deserved abandonment and renunciation; rather, he continued to send the prophets. Here as in Ezekiel 3 and 33, he calls them watchers or sentinels: "I have appointed watchmen over you. . . ." In fact, God establishes in his church prophets or preachers, just like sentinels and watchmen, naturally so that they announce beforehand the coming anger of the Lord through disease, sword, and famine, and so that the people, terrified by this serious denunciation, might change their habits and behavior. Elsewhere and also here the people show that they are rebellious and stubborn, after God tried everything with them. Indeed, by way of an answer, they say, "We will not pay attention." In the same way today those bold people decline to hear the serious threats coming from the Word of the Lord, and those impious and impenitent people rush forward into any kind of sin, while shouting: "To Cynosarges with those clamorous and their menacing preachers.[†] We will proceed in the manner we have received and not even do a little bit of the things suggested in those sullen and quarrelsome sermons." And so at the moment there stand opposed to each other on one hand the ineffable mercy of God, who is busy enough curing sinners and the wicked with his Word, and on the other hand the hopeless, incurable malice and stubbornness of the rebels

---

[23]Donne, *Sermons*, 2:103*; citing Dan 7:22; Rev 1:4.

[24]Oecolampadius, *In Hieremiam*, 1:I3v-K1r; citing Jer 21:8; Sir 15:16; 1 Kings 18:21; 1 Jn 2:7; Mt 11:29.

who so far spurn and spit on all of the clemency and paternal care of God. . . .

God said, "Behold I myself will bring evil etc." "I, I say, am all-powerful, severe, and just." However the evil he names is war, and a sea of evil things flowing over them. He adds "the fruit of their own thoughts," or "retribution for their thoughts"—of course, a well-deserved prize for their sins and something they have earned. The fruit of malice and rebellion is evil but at the same time just, an owed treatment, so that those who lived in a bad way perish in a bad way. So the apostle proclaims in Romans 6: "The wages of sin is death." The undoubted dogma of our religion is this: that God is a just avenger of wickedness. . . .

Nevertheless, in these matters the miserable consoled themselves with sacrifices, in which they trusted, believing that they were purified by them; and not just that they were purified, but that they deserved good things from God, who would love them because of the sacrifices themselves. Therefore, they believed that the threats of Jeremiah were empty. In fact, we are accustomed now, I would say even in our age, to be consoled completely, of course, that it will happen that God will be favorable to us due to our offerings; on account of our singing and reading, our Masses and liturgical worship, and our Gregorian supplications, and because the ceremonies of this type that I hardly even know about. Truly, God is not moved at all by those ceremonies through which the Judeans also wished to deserve well from him, since God himself established them. SERMON ON JEREMIAH 6:17-20.[25]

REPENT BEFORE THE FEROCIOUS ENEMY ARRIVES. HEINRICH BULLINGER: In these portraits of the enemy, Jeremiah first shows who would come and from where—"a strike from the north"—indicating here, as before, the Babylonians or Chaldeans. He says that they are to be roused,

namely, by a just God, from the sides of the earth. Or as the Old Latin Bible interprets it: "From the ends of the earth," namely, from the side and the borders or almost the ends of the land of Judah. . . . Then he adds, "a great nation," signifying by their abundance and strength, or by their multitude and power, that they will be formidable. Again he describes the same people regarding their arsenal: "They will lay hold of bow and lance"; others translate this as "arrow and shield. . . ." He adds that they will be a brutal, cruel, barbarous, and savage people, who will show no mercy to anyone. In fact, sometimes among enemies you might find those who are clement, kind, and merciful; they spare people on the basis of age and sex. But these enemies are not like that. . . .

Now he adds a metaphor by which he amplifies and expresses the horrible arrival and progress of the enemy: "Their voice roars and storms like a raging sea. . . ." Many descriptions like this can be found in Homer and Virgil. Moreover, to these things he adds that the Babylonian forces would have not only foot soldiers but also horsemen—swift and very powerful—who are far more terrifying than infantry. . . . Finally, "all these things," Jeremiah says, "come through divine power and are procured most diligently and intended against you, O daughter of Zion, so that you may be punished." He warns them therefore to repent in time. Jeremiah warns those of old age and indeed constant dignity to think and look upon their own dignity while God still calls them "daughter of Zion," at any rate "daughter of God," adopted by God out of grace. If only she would remember that she is a daughter of God and not act shamefully in the eyes of God. But since God is able to rouse and draw up against any nation the unconquered armies of Tartars, Turks, Persians, or other nations, then let us repent in time. SERMON ON JEREMIAH 6:21-26.[26]

EXCESSIVE EMOTION NEED NOT ACCOMPANY TRUE REPENTANCE. RICHARD HOOKER: "Now there are . . . [some] who, doubting not of God's

---

[25]Bullinger, *Conciones,* 47r, 47v; citing Ezek 3:16-27; 33:1-20; Rom 6:23. †Bullinger refers to a city known for its gymnasium and philosophers, such as Antisthenes, who shaped the Cynic branch of Greek philosophy.

[26]Bullinger, *Conciones,* 48r-v.

mercy toward all who perfectly repent, remain notwithstanding scrupulous, and troubled with continual fear, lest defects in their own repentance be a bar against them. These cast themselves first into very great and perhaps needless agonies, through misconstruction of things spoken, about proportioning our griefs to our sins for which they never think they have wept and mourned enough. Yea, if they have not always a stream of tears at commandment they take it for a sign of a heart congealed and hardened in sin. When to keep the wound of contrition bleeding, they unfold the circumstances of their transgressions, and endeavor to leave out nothing which may be heavy against themselves. Yet do what they can, they are still fearful, lest herein also they do not that which they ought. [When they] come to prayer, their coldness takes all heart and courage from them. With fasting albeit their flesh should be withered, and their blood clean dried up, would they ever the less object, "What is this to David's humiliation," wherein notwithstanding there was anything more than necessary. LAWES OF ECCLESIASTICAL POLITY[27]

JEREMIAH THE REFINER AND THE IMPURE PEOPLE.

JOHANNES BUGENHAGEN: "A Tester." God says to the prophet as in Ezekiel 3: "I have given to you a watchman for the house of Israel," etc. The Old Latin interpreter rightly said "Examiner," if you understand rightly. As in "to prove" or "to examine by fire," as you often read in the Psalms and Prophets. . . . The Refiner or Prover, that is, the smith who tests metals in fire, is Jeremiah or the preaching of the law, which is tough on the tough, as a hammer wears down stones and forms iron. These are bronze and iron; that is, they are hard. Against them the prophet wastes oil and effort, as is commonly said. That which he says in this way is a similitude or allegory of smelting. They are all defiant apostates; that is, they are hard who desert the faith or a covenant or vow of first command; they resist smelting. Those folk walk in insidious ways; that is, certain people who to a high extent

give the appearance of smelting themselves, nevertheless are not purified in the fire of testing or smelting; evil slag or dross and whatever foreign thing there is is not separated from them. But they continue to act fraudulently before God in their hypocrisy and before others by deceit and fraud. Therefore, after smelting, that is the preaching of the law or repentance and the threat of God, they are discovered to be bronze, rejected iron, and useless silver; that is, they are not what they want to seem to be. "It was consumed" signifies that everything tried on them, by which they might be purified, has been in vain. COMMENTARY ON JEREMIAH 6:27-29.[28]

BRASS AND IRON ARE NOT GOLD AND SILVER.

JOHN TRAPP: Just as base and drossy, false and feculent metals would appear to be silver and gold, so a sincere and holy people which in reality are a degenerate and hypocritical generation. As Theodoret has it here: naught, and good for naught. Not unlike those stones brought home in great quantity by Captain Forbisher in the reign of Queen Elizabeth. He thought them to be minerals of good worth, but when there could be drawn from them neither gold nor silver, they were cast forth to mend the highways. COMMENTARY ON JEREMIAH 6:28.[29]

ONLY GOD'S BREATH CAN BLOW AWAY SIN.

LANCELOT ANDREWES: The soil of sin is so baked on people; they [are] so hard frozen in the dregs of it, our wind cannot dissolve it. Hear the prophet, after he had been long blowing at the sins of the people. "The bellows," says he, "are burnt, the iron of them consumed, the founder melts in vain; for all

---

[27]Hooker, Lawes of Ecclesiastical Polity, 6:6*.

[28]Bugenhagen, In Ieremiam, 2N1r-v; citing Ezek 3:17.
[29]Trapp, A Commentary or Exposition, 245*. Theodoret of Cyr (393–460) was an early Christian theologian, exegete, and apologist. "Captain Forbisher" refers to Sir Martin Frobisher (1535–1594), who was an English seaman and privateer who made three voyages to the New World to look for the Northwest Passage. On his second voyage he found what he thought was gold ore and carried two hundred tons of it on three ships. Eventually, it was discovered that the ore was really iron pyrite. See James McDermott, Martin Frobisher: Elizabethan Privateer (New Haven: Yale University Press, 2001).

his blowing, the dross will not blow away." But . . . says God, let me take it in hand, let me but blow with my wind, and "I [will] scatter your transgressions as a mist, and make your sins like a morning cloud to vanish away." We then turn to him whose divine power, whose immortal breath can do it, [and] do it by himself, and if by himself, by also him into whom he will inspire it. SERMON ON JOHN 20:22.[30]

---

[30]Andrewes, *Works*, 3:269*; citing Is.44:22.

JEREMIAH 7:1-29
EVIL IN THE LAND

¹*The word that came to Jeremiah from the Lord:* ²*"Stand in the gate of the Lord's house, and proclaim there this word, and say, Hear the word of the Lord, all you men of Judah who enter these gates to worship the Lord. ³Thus says the Lord of hosts, the God of Israel: Amend your ways and your deeds, and I will let you dwell in this place. ⁴Do not trust in these deceptive words: 'This is the temple of the Lord, the temple of the Lord, the temple of the Lord.'*

⁵*"For if you truly amend your ways and your deeds, if you truly execute justice one with another, ⁶if you do not oppress the sojourner, the fatherless, or the widow, or shed innocent blood in this place, and if you do not go after other gods to your own harm, ⁷then I will let you dwell in this place, in the land that I gave of old to your fathers forever.*

⁸*"Behold, you trust in deceptive words to no avail. ⁹Will you steal, murder, commit adultery, swear falsely, make offerings to Baal, and go after other gods that you have not known, ¹⁰and then come and stand before me in this house, which is called by my name, and say, 'We are delivered!'—only to go on doing all these abominations? ¹¹Has this house, which is called by my name, become a den of robbers in your eyes? Behold, I myself have seen it, declares the Lord. ¹²Go now to my place that was in Shiloh, where I made my name dwell at first, and see what I did to it because of the evil of my people Israel. ¹³And now, because you have done all these things, declares the Lord, and when I spoke to you persistently you did not listen, and when I called you, you did not answer, ¹⁴therefore I will do to the house that is called by my name, and in which you trust, and to the place that I gave to you and to your fathers, as I did to Shiloh. ¹⁵And I will cast you out of my sight, as I cast out all your kinsmen, all the offspring of Ephraim.*

¹⁶*"As for you, do not pray for this people, or lift up a cry or prayer for them, and do not intercede with me, for I will not hear you. ¹⁷Do you not see what they are doing in the cities of Judah and in the streets of Jerusalem? ¹⁸The children gather wood, the fathers kindle fire, and the women knead dough, to make cakes for the queen of heaven. And they pour out drink offerings to other gods, to provoke me to anger. ¹⁹Is it I whom they provoke? declares the Lord. Is it not themselves, to their own shame? ²⁰Therefore thus says the Lord God: Behold, my anger and my wrath will be poured out on this place, upon man and beast, upon the trees of the field and the fruit of the ground; it will burn and not be quenched."*

²¹*Thus says the Lord of hosts, the God of Israel: "Add your burnt offerings to your sacrifices, and eat the flesh. ²²For in the day that I brought them out of the land of Egypt, I did not speak to your fathers or command them concerning burnt offerings and sacrifices. ²³But this command I gave them: 'Obey my voice, and I will be your God, and you shall be my people. And walk in all the way that I command you, that it may be well with you.' ²⁴But they did not obey or incline their ear, but walked in their own counsels and the stubbornness of their evil hearts, and went backward and not forward. ²⁵From the day that your fathers came out of the land of Egypt to this day, I have persistently sent all my servants the prophets to them, day after day. ²⁶Yet they did not listen to me or incline their ear, but stiffened their neck. They did worse than their fathers.*

²⁷*"So you shall speak all these words to them, but they will not listen to you. You shall call to them, but they will not answer you. ²⁸And you shall say to them, 'This is the nation that did not obey the voice of the Lord their God, and did not accept discipline; truth has perished; it is cut off from their lips.*

²⁹*"'Cut off your hair and cast it away;*
raise a lamentation on the bare heights,
for the Lord has rejected and forsaken
the generation of his wrath.'

OVERVIEW: The Protestant Reformation sought to alter radically the sacred geography of Europe. The landscape of belief and practice comes to mind first. Protestants called for repentance and faith in Christ while condemning the intercession of saints, monastic vows, and the celebration of idolatrous, unscriptural ceremonies. Jeremiah himself proclaimed such an essential Jewish faith—not only shorn of insincere sacrifices and empty temple observance, but also renewed by authentic confession of sin and heartfelt devotion to God. Likewise Protestants proclaimed an essential Christianity, captured in the slogans "Scripture alone," "grace alone," "faith alone," and "Christ alone."

Yet actual physical geography was at stake as well. A network of Christian holy sites—monasteries and cathedrals, shrines of saints and sanctuaries of relics—had developed over a thousand years across Europe. These institutions promised to inspire, heal, and comfort the faithful. Such locations were essential to local economies reliant on pilgrims and their need for food, shelter, and objects of devotion.

For our Reformation commentators, the seventh chapter of Jeremiah revealed that sacred landscapes were malleable. After all, God had seen fit to dwell or be manifest in sacred places throughout the Holy Land. Mount Sinai, the sanctuary at Shiloh, and the temple in Jerusalem were such sites. Ultimately a place was made sacred by God's singular presence—by the very Word of God—and was made permanent by true worship and devotion. When idolatry spread and evil infected ancient Judea, God abandoned those holy spaces and brought such a fearsome judgment that the entire sacred landscape would be swept away by the invading Babylonians. Protestant commentators on Jeremiah were keen to press for a new geography of souls and churches where Scripture, preaching, and the true sacraments embodied the very presence of God. Such change not only dismembered the very arteries of the old Western church but also challenged human lords and monarchs whose kingdoms and sovereignty were nourished by these ancient bloodlines.

Jeremiah and the Reformers would be cast as rebels and traitors to such sacred bodies.

7:1-15 Jeremiah Declares God's Judgment

JUDGMENT PROCLAIMED IN PUBLIC. JOHANNES OECOLAMPADIUS: Here there is not only a new prophecy, but a new section of Jeremiah begins, though we hear nothing strange to our ears. For in the whole book the same argument is considered from beginning to end, namely, that the Jewish people, because of their stubborn wickedness and contempt for the Word of God, would rightly be led into a grave captivity. Here we see Jeremiah doing the same things as before, but there is now a greater zeal and freedom of speaking. For these things are being spoken of "in the gate"; he stands there or nearby and excommunicates all of the people as if with a terrible sword. . . . For God does not want his Word taught in corners, but in the most populated places. So Christ testified before Annas that he said nothing in secret. Meanwhile observe the obedience of the prophet. COMMENTARY ON JEREMIAH 7:1-2.[1]

BUILD A TEMPLE FOR GOD IN YOUR SOUL. EITELHANS LANGENMANTEL: O dearly beloved brothers and sisters in this Christian gathering: Let us note well the first plank of this house, as Christ teaches us: "Refrain from sin." For sin has no place in this house. If we build with sin we are not building the house of God, but rather the house of darkness. But when we refrain from sin, we will not dishonor the name of God, but praise, extol and honor it, and begin to love him with our whole hearts, for he first loved us. . . .

Forget all monasteries, priests, and churches, together with all that is inside them and takes place in them, that we may become a temple of God, since God does not dwell in temples made with hands . . . but in temples which come from heaven, the souls and spirits of people who live in

---

[1]Oecolampadius, *In Hieremiam*, 1:K2r-v; citing Jn 18:20.

faith and do his will. God speaks further. "I will dwell in you and walk in you." . . . If God is to dwell and walk in us, he cannot dwell in this temple until all that is opposed to God is removed. Where we find many pictures and a lot of foreign merchandise, there God cannot dwell. A SERMON ON SIN, REPENTANCE, AND SALVATION.[2]

THE EXTERNAL WORSHIP GOD REJECTS. JOHANNES OECOLAMPADIUS: These are the false prophets: or the people who are, rather, against Jeremiah, the prophet of the Lord. On this matter by reason of vehemence and certainty they say three times "the temple of the Lord, the temple of the Lord, the temple of the Lord." These are human teachings, because everyone is a liar and the words of all people are lies. No one is able to promise anything to us, except God. Thus do not believe anyone who promises anything other than the Word of God.

"The temple of the Lord": mark these words; they did not say an offering of the Lord, nor a priest, nor a vestibule, but in one word they encompass the entire outer worship of the Lord, and that is not just at any one moment. Therefore, the temple was demolished under the Babylonians and restored through Ezra. Roman soldiers destroyed it a second time, and it ceased to exist, just as Christ prophesied: "not one stone will remain on top of another." What do you say, Jeremiah? Would so many Masses perish? So many offerings, musical instruments, glittering vestments, most precious tables, and bells: how would God despise those things? Why does God, which they adorn, not rightly defend them? Should not the kingdom of heaven be promised in exchange for those things, and given for an indulgence? In one word, although these are celebrated magnificently, they are nevertheless the words of a lie; and indeed they had once been established by God, but afterward God did not

order them rebuilt. Why then is it surprising if the ceremonies fall together with the temple? COMMENTARY ON JEREMIAH 7:4.[3]

THE TEMPLE IS NOT IMPORTANT IN ITSELF. JOHN TRAPP: These buildings, or these three parts of the temple, [are] the most holy place, the sanctuary, and the outer court. To these are made the promises of God's perpetual residence; therefore, we are safe from all danger while we here take sanctuary. The Romish crew, in like manner, have nothing in their mouths so much as, "the Church, the Church, the Catholic Church," and therein, like oyster wives, they out-cry us. Many also among ourselves cry, "The temple of the Lord, the temple of the Lord," who yet do nothing to care for the Lord of the temple. They glory in external privileges and secure themselves therein, as the Jews fable that Og, king of Bashan, escaped the flood by riding astride upon the ark without. COMMENTARY ON JEREMIAH 7:4.[4]

WHEN GOD REMOVES PROMISES. MARTIN LUTHER: In the Word of God there are twofold promises; some are simple, without any addition, and these properly refer to Christ. They are utterly without our endeavor but suit Christ alone, and they refer to Christ's kingdom against sin and death. . . . Other promises are legal and conditional, not absolute, as when God says, "If you do this, if you do that." The Jews, however, did not understand them as being conditional in this way. Thus God threatens that the temple will be destroyed and that Jerusalem will be laid waste by the king of Babylon. When they hear this, the Jews object, "But God promised this temple," not understanding that this promise is conditional. So our papists, who hold the office of the church, exclaim loudly, confident that the Spirit is with them, trusting in the promise. Thus he rejects the plea "the temple of the Lord. . . ." God takes the promise away. "If you

---

[2]CRR 10:113, 115; citing Jn 8:11; Mt 3:2; 1 Jn 4:19; Acts 7:48; 17:24; 1 Pet 2:1-9; 2 Cor 6:14-17; Ex 1:20-21. The authorship of Langenmantel is disputed among scholars, though his name is traditionally associated with this early Anabaptist sermon of the Reformation.

[3]Oecolampadius, *In Hieremiam*, 1:K3v; citing Mt 24:2; Mk 13:2; Lk 21:6.

[4]Trapp, *A Commentary or Exposition*, 246*; citing Ps 132:14; Mic 3:11.

are unwilling, I will not keep the promises." When the condition no longer obtains, the promise comes to an end. It is true, the temple was holy and the city was holy, because God had established them by means of the Word that went before. The things that were done were holy. When the Word ceases, all covenants come to an end. If the Jews had accepted Christ's kingdom and Christ himself, the promises would have stood, and the temple would have remained. But when they refused, the Romans came and destroyed it. Therefore this passage is in opposition to a legal and conditional promise, since they did not keep the Word of God. LECTURES ON ISAIAH 66:1.[5]

OBEDIENCE IN CEREMONIES. MENNO SIMONS: Brethren, it was not allowed to change one single word of the Mosaic ceremonies from what they were contained in the law, for the Almighty God does not want us to follow our own inclinations with regard to ceremonies that he has not commanded us, but desires us to observe his goodwill and pleasure. For that purpose he has commanded them. In the outward ceremonies as such God takes no pleasure; but he has commanded them because he ever requires of us faithful obedience. His wrath has often come upon those who changed the ceremonies, as in the case of Nadab and Abihu . . . and many others. For he demands, yes, demands, us not to follow our own opinion, but to hear, believe, and obey his voice. CHRISTIAN BAPTISM.[6]

A FALSE REPENTANCE. JOHANNES BRENZ: "Behold, you put confidence in yourselves. . . ." This is hypocritical repentance. It does not "purge the old yeast," but preserves it. Moreover, this repentance hides itself and draws over itself showy works undertaken without the authorization of the Word; these are specious acts by which this repentance thinks it is justified. And thus hypocrisy does not recognize its sins, but covering them with its own precepts, it is secure in mind, and it

does not fear the judgment of the Lord and ascribes salvation to its own abominable works. As below in Jeremiah 44: "We will make sacrifice to the queen of heaven; we will offer libations to her, for we have been satisfied with bread. It was well with us and we did not see evil."

"We have been set free. . . ." This confidence in the flesh is condemned in the Scriptures in every place. As below in Jeremiah 5: "He will do nothing, nor will evil come upon us. We will see neither sword, nor famine." And in Isaiah 28, "We have entered into a covenant with death and we have an understanding with the realm of the dead. When the scourge goes by, it will not come upon us because we have established a lie as our refuge."

"Is this a den of robbers? . . ." First Kings 8: "Give ear to the prayer of your servants, who are making petition in this place." Solomon dedicated the temple there so that whoever prayed in that place would be heard there. But in the beginning, when the Israelites occupied Canaan, they established a tabernacle of the covenant at Shiloh, as in Joshua 18 and Judges 20. That place functioned as a temple for them the whole time that Solomon was building the temple in Jerusalem. But because of the godlessness of the people of Israel, Shiloh was cast off, as Psalm 78 testifies. God rejected his tabernacle at Shiloh, where he had dwelt with people. This indicates a most severe wrath of the Lord: that on account of the people he did not appear in that place, and in the same sanctuary. Moreover, there is this sentence: "do not boast about the temple: indeed because of your ungodliness it has been made a den of robbers." ANNOTATIONS ON JEREMIAH 7:8-12.[7]

DON'T PRETEND GOD IS COMPLICIT IN YOUR EVILDOING. THE ENGLISH ANNOTATIONS: Do you hold my house, my palace, to be a hole, or a hold, for thieves and robbers to shroud and shelter themselves in? And that by performance of some

---

[5]LW 17:395-96 (WA 31.2:568).
[6]Simons, *Complete Works*, 237; citing Lev 10:1-3.

[7]Brenz, *Annotationes in Jeremiam*, 882v-883r; citing 1 Cor 5:7; Jer 44:16-19; Jer 5:12; Is 28:15; 2 Kings 8:28; Josh 18:1; Judg 20:27; Ps 78:60; Mt 21:13.

formalities there, you are not only discharged of the guilt of your former sins but also have liberty to sin afresh? And so make me both a patron of your base and abominable courses, and a panderer also thereunto. I abhor and abominate both your wicked ways and these your thoughts, and all your sacrifices and services the rather for them. ANNOTATIONS ON JEREMIAH 7:11.[8]

WHY HOLY PLACES ARE HOLY. JOHANNES BUGENHAGEN: "Go to my place in Shiloh." The first tabernacle of the Lord was in Shiloh with the ark, and the worship of God was there: Joshua 18. This place was thrown down because of the sins of the people and of the priestly sons of Eli . . . as the psalm sings. So God rejected the tabernacle at Shiloh, his tabernacle wherein he had dwelt among the people. From bygone times, therefore, they knew that it was not necessary to trust in a place that for one reason or another was formerly holy at one time. For a place is holy because of the Word of God, which is heard in the place and by which it is sanctified; when the Word goes away from there, the place is no longer holy of itself. It is far from being the case that it would bring holiness to others. Thus the land is holy where God spoke to Moses from the burning bush. Thereafter, because God did not speak there, there was no holiness there. So the place Bethel is holy; it is the house of God and a gate of heaven because God spoke to Jacob there and promised the gospel and a blessing of all the nations through Christ: Genesis 28. Indeed, the church of Christ and the kingdom of heaven is present where the Word of God and the gospel of the kingdom are genuinely preached. Afterward at Bethel the devil reigned, a king being established there through Jeroboam with a golden calf. Thus Jerusalem is a holy city and the temple is holy because of the Word and worship of God. So now truly God is present with the holy angels, where the gospel is genuinely preached and the sacraments are received as Christ instituted. Indeed, people are sanctified through the Word, so that God dwells in them. According to that quotation of Paul, "the temple of God is holy; you are that temple." And Christ says, "Let us come to him and let us make a mansion with him." COMMENTARY ON JEREMIAH 7:12.[9]

JEREMIAH THE HERETIC, TRAITOR, AND SEDUCER OF THE PEOPLE. JOHN KNOX: Now let us consider the prophet's part. Jeremiah had spoken against the temple, saying, it would be destroyed and made like Shiloh (which the Lord had also destroyed), and the ark of his covenant especially, principally because of the iniquity of the priests. And was this not a judgment on heresy? Do you not think so? No less have I warned you about how it is said to be in England; that all the doctrine that Winchester and tonsured clergy now maintain is the doctrine of the devil;[†] and therefore it will shortly provoke God's vengeance to strike all that adheres thereto. Jeremiah said that Jerusalem would be set on fire and laid waist unless Zedekiah should surrender himself to the hands of Nebuchadnezzar. And was this not as great a treason as to say that the city of London should be made a desert if Jezebel be maintained in her authority?[‡] Jeremiah commanded openly that all who wanted to avoid God's vengeance should leave the city of Jerusalem and seek the favors of their enemies. And was not this as great a form of treason as now to say that England shall be given into the hands of strange nations? Jeremiah did openly preach that the religion that was used was devilish, albeit their forefathers had followed the same. And what is this but to affirm that general councils and what is called the universal church is the malignant church and the congregation of the Antichrist? In short, if people's judgments may have a place, Jeremiah was a heretic; he was a seditious fellow and a seducer of the people. He discouraged the hearts of strong men of war and was unfriendly to that faith which Pashhur and his companions taught the people. And therefore Jeremiah is condemned to prison

---

[8]Downame, ed., *Annotations*, 9G3r*; citing Mt 21:13; Mk 11:17; Lk 19:46; Prov 15:8-9, 26; 21:27; Is 61:8.

[9]Bugenhagen, *In Ieremiam*, 2O3r; citing Josh 18:1; 1 Sam 4:12-22; Ps 78:60; Ex 3; Gen 28:11-22; 1 Kings 12:25-33; 1 Cor 3:17; Jn 14:2-3.

and judged worthy of death. For the king could deny nothing to his princes. Among whom, I think, Pashhur had been, as it were, chief chancellor (he was an old enemy of Jeremiah) through whom not only the king but also the whole multitude of people was so blind that they boldly cried, "Nothing bad will happen to us." A GODLY LETTER OF WARNING AND ADMONITION.[10]

THE PRAYERS OF THE RIGHTEOUS FOR THE WICKED. RICHARD HOOKER: "Touching Martyrs," Cyprian answers "that it ought not in this case to seem offensive though they were denied, seeing God himself did refuse to yield to the piety of his own righteous saints making suit for obdurate Jews." As for the parties, in whose behalf such shifts were used, to have their desire, was in very truth a way of making them more guilty. Such peace granted contrary to the vigor of the gospel, contrary to the law of our Lord and God, does but under the color of merciful relaxation deceive sinners, and by soft handling destroy them, a grace dangerous for the giver, and to him who receives it, nothing at all is available. LAWES OF ECCLESIASTICAL POLITY.[11]

PRAYER, DIVINE WRATH, AND THE FRAGILE REFORMATION. NIKOLAUS SELNECKER: "I have let my sermons go forth always, but you have not wanted to listen. I call you, but you do not want to answer." Matthew 11: the Son of God speaks of the same thing, "To whom shall I compare this genera-tion? We played the pipe for you, and you would not dance. We have lamented and you did not weep. . . ." In this lamentable and dangerous time we should take this word fully to heart. You should listen to us, as we are now in the fiftieth year that God's voice, word, and gospel have been heard loud and clear. And God be praised, it can still be heard with the reform of our lives. That we know, see, and experience daily. How should this actually play out for us? That would mean, "Alas, Alas, I will do to you as I did to Shiloh, Jerusalem, and other lands and peoples. I will cast you out from my presence."

This is a hard and difficult sermon that not every person can endure. How then can the pious Jeremiah and this sermon be grasped and understood? See Jeremiah 26. Thus one grumbles as one wishes. So clearly things proceed as always, when one does not turn to God and ask about God's grace and forgiveness of sins, and stands apart from one's own sins. Moreover, hear further and see now the weather and thunder of God's wrath, which one is allowed to see and hear.

For so says God, "You shall not pray for this people. I will not hear you." That is so awful and terrifying that the hair would stand up on top of your head—if you listen to this word. Therefore, it is still a greater consolation when one is sure that there are yet God-fearing people that go with their prayers to God and fall into his arms and nurture and so hold off his wrath and fury. So Moses prays for the people, that God would not destroy them in his righteous wrath and fury: Exodus 32. This we also had with such a hero as Dr. Luther, who could write and speak with certainty. While he lived, peace and unity would remain. But as he has died, so now one should watch and hold on to prayer. . . . It is certain that Germany at this time has long lain in the ashes and has God's word no longer, since the prayers of God-fearing, pious hearts do not turn away God's punishments. THE WHOLE PROPHET JEREMIAH 7:13-16.[12]

---

[10]Knox, *Works*, 3:185-6*; citing Jer 7:12-14, 38:17, Jer 20. †A reference to Stephen Gardiner (1483–1555), who was bishop of Winchester from 1531 until he was deposed under King Edward VI in 1551. He was restored to his see by Queen Mary Tudor in 1553. Gardiner also served as lord chancellor under Queen Mary. Gardiner, moreover, was a chief theological opponent of Archbishop Thomas Cranmer, who was burned at the stake in 1556. See Glyn Redworth, *In Defence of the Church Catholic: The Life of Stephen Gardiner* (Oxford: Blackwell, 1990). †A reference to Queen Mary Tudor (r. 1553–1558) of England as Jezebel. Mary married King Philip II of Spain in Winchester in 1554.
[11]Hooker, *Lawes of Ecclesiastical Polity*, 5:5*. Hooker cites Cyprian's *Liber de lapsis* 16-19. Here Cyprian was addressing the fact that those who suffered during the persecution under the emperor Decius (249–251) took it upon themselves to absolve other Christians who, out of fear, sacrificed to the official Roman gods.

[12]Selnecker, *Der gantze Prophet Jeremias*, P1r-v; citing Mt 11:17; Ex 32:11-14.

7:16-29 External Ceremonies Versus True Piety

How Idols Come to Be Worshiped. Martin Luther: This is another stumbling block against which the prophet Jeremiah frequently rails with many words, inasmuch as he often mentions the queen of heaven. [The Jews] used to worship the moon and the stars of heaven, which Moses forbade with a clear law. . . . Therefore that religious practice and wicked worship was an old thing. They had taken it over from their ancestors who had lived under Moses. In addition, to this wickedness they used to add the veneer of this splendor of piety, that they were worshiping in the presence of God, which nowhere declared itself more clearly than in the sun, moon, and stars. Then that foolish mob began to worship God not only under or in the sun but even worshiped the very sun and moon themselves. No doubt many of our people do the same thing today. They were very much interested in idolatry and even worshipped the actual wooden statues of the saints. Lectures on Zephaniah 1:5.[13]

God's Judgment on the Queen of Heaven and the Saintly Idols. Nikolaus Selnecker: "The children gather wood and the father ignites the fire." This is the reason why God is so enraged over his people, namely, because of all the idolatry, contempt for God's word, hypocrisy, or lack of devotion. . . .

Melecheth is understood as the queen of heaven, that is, the star, which one calls Venus, as the learned explain. This is how one understands bad things such as the effect of powerful weather or a thunderstorm in heaven; also rain, dew, snow, frost, ice, cold, heat, light, and blinding light and the like. So the Jews worshiped because they wanted good weather, so that they could have enough wine, grain, bread, and other essential nourishment that grows richly through good weather. They also wanted to avoid the fruit of thunder, hail, lightning, mildew, and other violent storms; just as in the proper time

all would be received, as in baptism. St. Urban gives good weather for wine. St. Alexis is against thunder and lightning. St. Nicholas is against violent storms at sea. St. George is against every kind of war, rebellion, and the like.

How fiercely God burns against idolatry is shown here with all of these awful words. "My wrath," God says, "and my fury is spread over this place, over people, cattle, trees, and all crops. My wrath will so burn that no one would be able to put it out." The Whole Prophet Jeremiah 7:18-21.[14]

External Sacrifices and Internal Purity. Johannes Oecolampadius: The impious excuse themselves and say they will escape punishment, "for will not the sacrifices and offerings which we offer protect us?" God responds, "in no way," as the previous chapter rejects this: "lest you think that anything comes favorably to me from your sordidness." Because God said, "They did not follow me, nor will they yield anything to me. Though you do not bring a sacrifice, only be such a one who lives purely." . . . He says, "consume the flesh": "uninjured faith and obedience are sufficient for me, which is proved in patience." Still today God does not require such things from the use of the sacraments and prayers, but from the love which is to be protected. Even if the sacraments pertain to the external economy of the church, prayers also sharpen faith like a touchstone. Commentary on Jeremiah 7:21.[15]

Following Our Own Commandments. Martin Luther: God speaks to them: "Add your burnt offerings to your sacrifices. . . ." There we hear again that God does not want all these things that he commanded himself. And there are many more passages like these in both the Old Testament and the New.

But why all this? Because . . . all of our own self-chosen works and commandments, which have torment and grief in them, please us better than

---

[13]LW 18:323 (WA 13:482-83); citing Jer 44:17-19; Deut 17:3; Zeph 1:5.

[14]Selnecker, *Der gantze Prophet Jeremias*, P3v-P4r.
[15]Oecolampadius, *In Hieremiam*, I:L2v.

what God has commanded. We also heed them more and apply much more diligence to them than to God's commandments. And that properly vexes God to the highest degree, so that he in turn despises and rejects our own works and commandments, even as we have despised his commandments and works. LECTURES ON ZECHARIAH 7:4-6.[16]

REJECT THE PROPHETS AND RECEIVE THE GENERATION OF GOD'S WRATH. JOHN DONNE: God acts in the same way in Jeremiah as in Isaiah and in Ezekiel. "I have sent to you my servants, the prophets." God has no other servants for this purpose but his prophets. If the dangers before you have been preached to you by God's appointment, then God has acted. You must not do as the rich man did on behalf of his brethren and look for messengers among the dead. You must neither wait for instruction, nor amendment, until you are, as the apostle says, as good as dead and ready to die. You must not wait until a judgment befalls you and then presume understanding from that vexation or repentance because of that affliction; for this is to hearken after messengers from the realm of the dead, to think of nothing until we are ready to join them. But as Abraham says to the rich man, "Your brothers have the Law and the Prophets," and that is enough; that is all. So God says here, "I have sent them all my servants, the prophets." That is enough and that is all: especially when "he has risen early and sent his prophets"; that is, he has given us sufficiently early warning before calamity comes near to our own gates. But when they rejected and despised all of his prophesies and denounced his future judgments, then the sentence follows—the final, fearful sentence, "The Lord has forsaken and rejected them." Who has he rejected? "The Lord has forsaken and rejected the generation of his wrath."

The generation of his wrath? There is more horror, more consternation in that manner of expressing rejection than in rejection itself. There is an insupportable weight in that word, "his wrath."

But even that word is multiplied in the other phrase; "the generation of his wrath." God has forgotten that "Israel is his son and his firstborn." So he avowed him to be in Moses' commission to Pharaoh. God has forgotten that "he rebuked kings for his sake"; this God testifies that he has done so on Israel's behalf in the Psalms. God has forgotten that "they were heirs according to the promise"; that is their designation in the apostle Paul. God has forgotten that they were "the apple of his own eye"; that they were "as the signet upon his own hand." God has forgotten that "Ephraim is his dear son," that he is "a pleasing child, a child for whom his bowels were troubled." God has forgotten all of these fatherly inclinations and familial relations, all of these incorporations and gatherings of Israel, into his very own bosom.

So Israel has become "the generation of his wrath" and not just the subject of his wrath. It is not just that God exercises one act of indignation alone, such as adding poverty or sickness to their captivity. Nor is it even adding spiritual calamities to temporal ones or sadness of heart and dejection of spirit to the oppressions of the body. Rather, God threatens that for their grievous sins he will multiply lives upon them and make them immortal for immortal torments. They shall be "a generation of his wrath"; for they shall die in this world in his displeasure and receive a new birth, a new generation in the world to come with a new capacity for new miseries; they shall die in the next world every minute, deprived of the sight of God and every minute receive a new generation, a new birth, a new ability to experience real and sensible torments.

When God has sent his servants the prophets, and so done all that is necessary for his people in advance, and risen early to send those prophets, and warned them with ample time to avoid danger—and they are not affected by those predictions—so God will make them, including ourselves and any state or church—the generation of his wrath. SERMON ON ISAIAH 53:1.[17]

---

[16]LW 20:261 (WA 23:591).

[17]Donne, *Sermons*, 8:300-301*; citing 1 Cor 15:29; Lk 16:19-31; Ex 4:22; Ps 105:14; Gal 3:29; Deut 32:10; Hag 2:23; Jer 31:20.

DID GOD DEMAND SACRIFICES AND BURNT OFFERINGS? JOHANN PAPPUS: Jeremiah reprimands Jewish sacrifices, which, of course, are according to the command of Moses that pertains to the ceremonies themselves. But they were carried out without true repentance. Indeed on that account, to this reprimand of the sacrifices are joined censure, contempt for the Word, and the warnings and prophecies. But how is it that God "commanded nothing concerning sacrifices"? This has been explained variously by interpreters. Jerome says that the first Decalogue had been given to them written on stone tablets by the finger of God, and after the body and head of the calf of idolatry had been struck, he commanded that these sacrifices be made to himself rather than to demons. Still, the Lord did not order the same sacrifices to be offered to himself, which before had been offered to demons. Others say that this is absurd: sacrificial victims were certainly required, like the Passover lamb in the exodus. Nevertheless, since victims can be offered without any sacrifice at all [i.e., in the paschal ceremony], the Lord says that he did not demand sacrifices. Still, the simplest response is this: the Lord did not demand the sort of sacrifices that the many hearers of Jeremiah were offering apart from true piety. It is not ultimately the sacrifice itself that is demanded, but before the sacrifice there must be fear of God and true obedience. As Hosea says in chapter 6, "I want mercy and not sacrifice, and acknowledgment of God rather than burnt offerings." ON ALL THE PROPHETS, JEREMIAH 7:21-28.[18]

CREATURELY ATTACHMENTS IN THE SOUL. ANDREAS BODENSTEIN VON KARLSTADT: When we discover that we are unable to divest ourselves of all creatures—be they holy or unholy, spiritual or corporeal, heavenly or earthly—we should not dream of becoming an apprentice of Christ. Let no one think that God enters, as long as creatures fill, comfort, and please the soul. . . . "They departed from me in the desires and the wickedness of their hearts and refused to hear me." If we turn our backs on such a Lord and repudiate him, should he then turn his face toward us and be well-disposed? No, these two-timers (several of those cheese hunters) have turned his forgiveness into a lottery. They mean by *renunciare* to have nothing in public, but to be laden with riches inside the monastery. They do nothing good externally, but inside they are full of blood (i.e., envy and hatred). They renounce and resist the world, but at the same time they are ensnared by the devil and the world. THE MEANING OF THE TERM GELASSENHEIT.[19]

SHORN HAIR WILL NOT SAVE YOU. JOHN MAYER: In bidding Jerusalem then to cut her hair, Jeremiah means that her Nazirites[†] now might as well cut off their hair as maintain it, for they will be neither more acceptable because of their hair, nor because of their sacrifices. . . . God's wrath would come upon them, as indeed it did. The prophet, therefore, does not exhort them to repent again, as he had done many times before, but he speaks against desperate and impenitent people who denounce a judgment that ought to make them howl and cry. But when they are on their high places and see the irresistible forces of their enemies coming against them and camping around them on every side, they should not pretend that any outward holiness or worship would help them. This cutting off the hair displays an extreme sorrow. . . . The same was done to servants, and this thereby shows the lowest ebb of misery and servitude to enemies. . . . The daughters of Jerusalem were so proud they were threatened with baldness. . . . Among the heathen it was common in extreme sorrow to pull off the hair, and to shave servants and slaves. COMMENTARY ON JEREMIAH 7:29.[20]

---

[18]Pappus, *In Omnes Prophetas*, 78v; citing Hos 6:6. Jerome, *Commentary on Jeremiah*, 52.

[19]CRR 8:144-145; citing Jer 7:24. By "cheese hunters," Karlstadt refers to monks and friars who were accused of hunting good food and stuffing themselves with cheese rather than God. See Thomas M. Lindsay, *A History of the Reformation*, 2nd ed. (New York: Scribner's, 1910), 143, 302.

[20]Mayer, *A Commentary*, 357*; citing Job 1:10; Is 15:2; Ezek 27:31; Is 3:17; Jer 7:20; Mic 1:16; Hab 3:13. †See Numbers 6 on the vow of the Nazirites.

IDOLATROUS VOWS MERIT DEATH. ANDREAS BODENSTEIN VON KARLSTADT: Scripture says that anyone who makes vows and renders sacrifices unto the gods and not to God alone ought to be killed. At one time the Jews made their vows to alien gods. And now Christians render vows and sacrifices unto the saints. Both of which are wrong. Therefore God has established a law by which anyone who renders vows or sacrifices unto gods and not unto God alone is to be slain. REGARDING VOWS.[21]

---

[21]CRR 8:54.

JEREMIAH 7:30–8:3
THE VALLEY OF SLAUGHTER

[30]"For the sons of Judah have done evil in my sight, declares the Lord. They have set their detestable things in the house that is called by my name, to defile it. [31]And they have built the high places of Topheth, which is in the Valley of the Son of Hinnom, to burn their sons and their daughters in the fire, which I did not command, nor did it come into my mind. [32]Therefore, behold, the days are coming, declares the Lord, when it will no more be called Topheth, or the Valley of the Son of Hinnom, but the Valley of Slaughter; for they will bury in Topheth, because there is no room elsewhere. [33]And the dead bodies of this people will be food for the birds of the air, and for the beasts of the earth, and none will frighten them away. [34]And I will silence in the cities of Judah and in the streets of Jerusalem the voice of mirth and the voice of gladness, the voice of the bridegroom and the voice of the bride, for the land shall become a waste.

8 [1]"At that time, declares the Lord, the bones of the kings of Judah, the bones of its officials, the bones of the priests, the bones of the prophets, and the bones of the inhabitants of Jerusalem shall be brought out of their tombs. [2]And they shall be spread before the sun and the moon and all the host of heaven, which they have loved and served, which they have gone after, and which they have sought and worshiped. And they shall not be gathered or buried. They shall be as dung on the surface of the ground. [3]Death shall be preferred to life by all the remnant that remains of this evil family in all the places where I have driven them, declares the Lord of hosts.

OVERVIEW: The biblical text drew Reformation commentators and preachers to expound on the consequences of sin and false religion without flinching. Rituals in the Valley of the Son of Hinnom revealed the grotesque perversion of true sacrificial offerings to God and the perennial desire to earn salvation by works and ceremonies. Divine judgment of such outer action and inner disposition would be swift and severe; it would even fit the crime as the unfaithful people of God would in turn be slaughtered and defiled in a way that mirrored their own sins. Such were the outcomes of a religion twisted by idolatry, undone by a warped theology, and laid bare by fierce wrath. For these reasons, the Reformation was a matter of life and death.

7:30–8:3 They Have Done Evil in My Sight

CHILD SACRIFICES. JOHANNES BUGENHAGEN: "And they built the high altars at Topheth." This place is called in Hebrew gē ben-hinnôm, gē, "valley," ben, "of the sons," "of Hinnom" in Joshua 15; in the valley of the portion of the tribe of Judah. There impious Jews burned their sons and daughters to the idol Molech. You have this account in the history of King Josiah. That horrendous sin was against the law of Deuteronomy 18, even as King Ahaz did in 2 Kings 16 and King Manasseh in 2 Kings 21; so it says in the psalm, "They sacrificed their sons and daughters to demons. And they poured out innocent blood, the blood of their sons and daughters, which they sacrificed to the graven images of Canaan." Meanwhile they wanted this impiety to seem as if it was done in the example of Abraham offering his son etc. COMMENTARY ON JEREMIAH 7:31.[1]

DEVOURING AND FLAYING THE PEOPLE. MARTIN LUTHER: Jeremiah calls this valley Gehinnam, and from this Christ has taken the

---

[1]Bugenhagen, *In Ieremiam*, 2P4r-v; citing Josh 15:8; 2 Kings 23:10; Deut 18:9-12; 2 Kings 16:10-16; 21:1-9; Ps 106:37-38.

name Gehenna. . . . I think that [the word *Hinnam*] may come from the word Jhana, which means to devour and flay, as the mighty lords and usurers devour the people, flay them, and suck them dry. So Gehinnam means a valley of flayers, who, when they should be feeding the people with the living Word of God as shepherd and preachers, instead devour, destroy, and flay the poor people in body, soul, and property with their poisonous, ungodly doctrine. Such are the shepherds that the universities, the synagogues of destruction, give to us. THE MISUSE OF THE MASS.[2]

CRUEL SACRIFICES MADE WITHOUT FAITH.
PHILIPP MELANCHTHON: This wicked idea about works has always clung to the world. The Gentiles had sacrifices that they took over from the patriarchs. They imitated their works, but did not keep their faith, believing that these works were a propitiation and price that reconciled God to them. The people of the Old Testament imitated these sacrifices with the notion that on account of them they had a gracious God, so to say, *ex opere operato*.[†] Here we see how vehemently the prophets rebuke people. . . . "I did not command concerning burnt offerings." Such passages do not condemn sacrifices that God surely commanded as outward observances in the state, but they do condemn the wicked belief of those who did away with faith in the notion that through these works they placated the wrath of God. Because no works can put the conscience at rest, they kept thinking up new works beyond God's commandment. The people of Israel had seen the prophets' sacrifice on the high places. The examples of the saints call forth imitation in those who hope that by similar actions they can obtain grace. Therefore the people began zealously to copy this action in order thereby to merit grace, righteousness, and the forgiveness of sins. But the prophets did not sacrifice on the high places to merit grace and forgiveness of sins by this deed, but because they were teaching in these places and thus gave evidence of their faith.

The people heard that Abraham had offered up his son. And so they put their sons to death in order by this cruel and painful deed to placate the wrath of God. But Abraham did not offer up his son with the idea that this work was a price or a propitiation for which he would be accounted righteous. Thus the Lord's Supper was instituted in the church so that this sign reminds us of the promises of Christ, the remembrance might strengthen our faith and we might publicly confess our faith and announce the blessings of Christ, as Paul says, "As often as you do this, you proclaim the Lord's death." APOLOGY OF THE AUGSBURG CONFESSION.[3]

THOSE WHO SACRIFICE TO IDOLS WILL BE SLAUGHTERED. KONRAD PELLIKAN: A vengeance worthy of so great a crime is predicted here. Those who sacrifice to idols were so cruel to their own that they would in turn take the place of their sacrifices as abominable food for the birds and the beasts of the fields. In that location they went against the precept of God, and to his injury; they were not ashamed to admit such cruel practices. Indeed it will hereafter be called "the valley of slaughter," that is, of the slaughtered people; because in that place the number to be buried will be huge—the number of Judeans—and the Babylonians will have to bury them there, because there will not be another place more suitable when such a great multitude has to be buried. COMMENTARY ON JEREMIAH 7:32-33.[4]

THE VOICE OF THE BRIDEGROOM. HULDRYCH ZWINGLI: [In this verse] God threatens to suspend what he would usually give. Therefore, it is permitted also to those who are acceptable to God that they rejoice with the bridegroom. For even Christ

---

[2]LW 36:225 (WA 8:559-560).

[3]BoC 135-36; citing Jer 7:22; 1 Sam 9:12-13; 1 Kings 18:20-40; Gen 22:1-24; Lev 20:1-9; 2 Kings 23:10; Jer 19:5; 32:35; 1 Cor 11:26. [†]The Latin phrase *ex opere operato*, "by the work performed," affirmed the medieval Catholic view that the correct and priestly performance of the sacrament conveyed grace to the recipient unless the recipient placed an obstacle to grace. By comparison, *ex opere operantis*, "by the work of the worker," affirmed that the moral condition of the priest or the proper attitude of the recipient in the celebration of the sacrament would determine its efficacy. [4]Pellikan, *Commentaria Bibliorum*, 3:2Qiv.

converted water into wine at a wedding, as a first means of great joy. And so all the less is Anabaptist hypocrisy able to mock such decent and moderate things.[†] We condemn overabundance and every type of excess. But there are things that should be tolerated, and certainly not be abolished; such are public and honorable unions and feasts, as long as they are rare. . . . Christ himself instituted a meal among others for a specific reason: so that we might be joined together in one body and bread. EXPLANATIONS OF THE PROPHET JEREMIAH 7:34.[5]

THE BONES OF IDOLATERS DEFILED AND SCATTERED. KONRAD PELLIKAN: Jeremiah continues by predicting disaster for the Jews because of their idolatry. He says that when Jerusalem is captured the cruel Babylonian and the greedy soldier will engage in every form of cruelty. He will consider as nothing the crime of digging up graves. In a little while he will not spare the bones of the dead; he will seek treasure in the most hidden places of the ungodly kings and princes, priests, and false prophets, who had always promised peace. The Babylonians will expose their bones, drag them out in the open as a mockery, an abomination, and to a most cruel fate. For those who had been so often warned in their own life, defied the Word of God and had offered their prohibited worship to the sun, the moon, the stars, and the rest of those monstrous idols. Those people were now in turn exposed to hate, scattered by the feet of those trampling on them, and compelled to serve, after death, those whom while alive they loved more than the Creator. Those were the gods to whom with all their longing they offered that worship that was in truth owed to God alone. They made offerings to those gods whom they invoked as their supporters while neglecting the Lord. Now their bones would lie scattered about after being dragged from their graves as a mark of their impiety. And from this time forward they would be turned into an example for all, to the shame of the idolaters themselves, because they worshiped those things that were not able to save them from such great evil. COMMENTARY ON JEREMIAH 8:1-2.[6]

BETTER OFF DEAD THAN ALIVE. JOHN CALVIN: Jeremiah intimates in this verse that all survivors would be doubly miserable, as it would be better for them to die at once than to pine away in unceasing evils. The meaning of the passage is this: however dreadful God's judgment would be—when slaughter everywhere prevailed, and dead bodies were dragged out that had previously been buried—yet all this would be a slight punishment in comparison with what God would inflict on the rest that remained alive. He also intimates that their life would be more miserable than death itself—yes, than even ten deaths. . . . They would not be allowed to live in their own country, but would become aliens—and they would find in their exile God's hand against them, and as if it were following them everywhere. COMMENTARY ON JEREMIAH 8:3.[7]

---

[5]Zwingli, *Complanationis*, 95. [†]Zwingli may be referring here to the view that Anabaptists exclude all practices not found in the Bible. In this sense, Zwingli may claim that Anabaptists become as impoverished as a Jerusalem that no longer heard the sound of nuptial celebrations. [6]Pellikan, *Commentaria Bibliorum*, 3:2Q1v-2Q2r. [7]CTS 17:421-22* (CO 38:3-4).

JEREMIAH 8:4-17
SIN AND TREACHERY

⁴"You shall say to them, Thus says the Lord:
When men fall, do they not rise again?
   If one turns away, does he not return?
⁵Why then has this people turned away
   in perpetual backsliding?
They hold fast to deceit;
   they refuse to return.
⁶I have paid attention and listened,
   but they have not spoken rightly;
no man relents of his evil,
   saying, 'What have I done?'
Everyone turns to his own course,
   like a horse plunging headlong into battle.
⁷Even the stork in the heavens
   knows her times,
and the turtledove, swallow, and crane[a]
   keep the time of their coming,
but my people know not
   the rules[b] of the Lord.

⁸"How can you say, 'We are wise,
   and the law of the Lord is with us'?
But behold, the lying pen of the scribes
   has made it into a lie.
⁹The wise men shall be put to shame;
   they shall be dismayed and taken;
behold, they have rejected the word of the Lord,
   so what wisdom is in them?
¹⁰Therefore I will give their wives to others
   and their fields to conquerors,
because from the least to the greatest
   everyone is greedy for unjust gain;
from prophet to priest,
   everyone deals falsely.
¹¹They have healed the wound of my people
   lightly,

saying, 'Peace, peace,'
   when there is no peace.
¹²Were they ashamed when they committed
   abomination?
No, they were not at all ashamed;
   they did not know how to blush.
Therefore they shall fall among the fallen;
   when I punish them, they shall be overthrown,
says the Lord.
¹³When I would gather them, declares the Lord,
   there are no grapes on the vine,
   nor figs on the fig tree;
even the leaves are withered,
   and what I gave them has passed away
      from them."[c]

¹⁴Why do we sit still?
Gather together; let us go into the fortified cities
   and perish there,
for the Lord our God has doomed us to perish
   and has given us poisoned water to drink,
   because we have sinned against the Lord.
¹⁵We looked for peace, but no good came;
   for a time of healing, but behold, terror.

¹⁶"The snorting of their horses is heard from
   Dan;
   at the sound of the neighing of their stallions
   the whole land quakes.
They come and devour the land and all that
   fills it,
   the city and those who dwell in it.
¹⁷For behold, I am sending among you serpents,
   adders that cannot be charmed,
   and they shall bite you,"
declares the Lord.

a The meaning of the Hebrew word is uncertain   b Or *just decrees*   c The meaning of the Hebrew is uncertain

OVERVIEW: Justification by faith alone was a byword of the Protestant Reformation. But what sort of faith justified? What is true faith? What counterfeit forms masquerade as faith? In this portion of Jeremiah commentators found hallmarks of true faith: a willingness to repent and turn to God alone for assistance, attentiveness to the Word of God in devotion and worship, acute discernment of the seasons of God's grace and judgment, and preference for a lived faith in the Holy Spirit over the dead letter of texts about faith.

Moreover, true faith has implications for society. Instead of a true faith that seeks equity and justice, false faith ignores suffering and justifies greed. Even spiritual leaders and religious institutions may participate in the oppression of the poor. Such a perversion of faith and justice brings the sort of divine judgment that destroys kingdoms and societies.

8:4-9 The Blindness of the Nation

HELP FOR THE LOST AND THE FALLEN. THE ENGLISH ANNOTATIONS: Is there anyone so absurd and witless that when they have fallen by accident will choose to lie still and not try to get up again or will refuse help from anyone who offers them assistance? Here is the folly of this people: they have fallen for their sin, yet they refuse to rise or be raised up again by those who have taken pains to help them for that purpose. Some render these words, "Are they so fallen that they are incapable of rising again?" as "Do they deem their case so desperate?"

". . . And will not someone who has gone astray want to return again?" Will not someone who has gone off the path against their will desire to return to it or be willing to accept help from those who can direct them back on the path? For those of the Jewish people and our own so render it thus: "if one did return, then would not God also return?" As if to say, undoubtedly God would do so. ANNOTATIONS ON JEREMIAH 8:4.[1]

GOD'S MESSAGE TO THE GODLY AND UNGODLY. JOHN CALVIN: Though God had reminded his prophet of this [judgment], yet he still invites the Jews to repentance; not that there was any hope of restoring them to a right mind (for he had said that they were wholly irreclaimable), but that their perverseness might be less excusable; and it was also his object to afford some relief to the small number of the godly who still remained; for they had not all fallen away into impiety, though the great body of the people had become corrupt. God then partly to aggravate the sin of the ungodly, and partly to provide for his faithful people, exhorts those to repentance who were yet wholly intractable. And here we ought to consider that God's goodness, when abused, brings a much heavier judgment. God does here in a manner contend with the wickedness of his people by setting before them the hope of pardon, if they repented. COMMENTARY ON JEREMIAH 8:4-5.[2]

WITHOUT THE WORD WE ARE LIKE RUSHING HORSES. JOHANNES BUGENHAGEN: "I myself see and hear." So also in Malachi 3: "I will draw near to you for judgment and I will be a swift witness," etc. And in the psalm: "The Lord looked down from heaven on the sons of humanity, so that he might see if there is anyone who understands or seeks the Lord," etc.

The hypocrite does not believe that God sees and hears everything; that is, they do not fear God, although they conceive of a conscientious worship of God. Therefore, even given admonitions from the Word the hypocrite does not repent of error and idolatry or consider, "what am I doing?" or "From whence will I know what sort of things are pleasing to God?" Instead they go forward like a rushing horse, not permitting themselves to be held back by the Word of God. So it is among us: no one is able to give a reason from the Word of God for their own devotion and worship; no one has been doing anything on the basis of faith; no one is certain that the things they were doing

---

[1]Downame, ed., *Annotations*, 9G4v*; citing Eccles 4:10; Hos 14:1; Jer 2:25; 3:1; Zech 1:3.

[2]CTS 17:423* (CO 38:4).

would please God. Nevertheless, we are going forward like the blind and leaders of the blind, as a horse running fiercely against weapons in battle. If no one speaks or teaches the good, that is the genuine Word of God, how will anyone know? Thus false doctrine is the source of all iniquity and idolatry. COMMENTARY ON JEREMIAH 8:6.[3]

FAILURE TO OBSERVE GOD'S SEASONS OF GRACE AND JUDGMENT. THE ENGLISH ANNOTATIONS: These words confirm not only the obstinacy and willfulness but also the stupidity and dullness of the people, wherein they fall short even of unreasonable creatures. Therefore, even the diverse sorts of creatures here mentioned duly observe the times of their coming and going from place to place, from one region to another according to the season of the year. But the sort of people described here do not have the discernment to take notice of and observe God's plans and dealings with them—the seasons of grace and the mercies he offers to them or the time of wrath wherein he shows himself to be displeased with them. ANNOTATIONS ON JEREMIAH 8:7.[4]

REFUSAL TO REPENT IS WORSE THAN INITIAL SIN. LANCELOT ANDREWES: Sin [is] a fall, an error, a rebellion: we see [that] "sin abounds"; will you see, how "grace over-abounds"? Yet not such a fall but we may be raised, not such a departure but there is place left to return; no, nor such a rebellion, but if it stops may hope for a pardon. For behold! He, even he, God, from whom we thus fall, depart, and revolt, reaches his hand to them that fall, turns not away from them that turn to him, is ready to receive them to grace, even them that rebelled against him. It is so: for he speaks to them, treats with them, asks of them, why they will not rise, return, [and] submit themselves.

Which is more yet. If you mark, he does not complain and challenge them for any of all those

three, for falling, straying, or for rebelling; the point he presses is not our falling, but our lying still; not our departing, but our not returning; nor our breaking off, but our holding out. Why fail, or stray, or revolt? But why rise you not, return you not and submit you not yourselves? Thus might he have framed his questions. Shall they fall and not stand? He does not, but thus. Shall they fall and not rise? Shall they turn from the right and not keep it? No. But shall they turn from it, and not turn to it? As much to say as, "Though you have fallen, yet lie not still; erred, yet go not on; sinned, yet continue not in sin; and neither your fall, error, nor sin, shall be your destruction or do you hurt."

Nay, which is farther and beyond all, it is not these either, though this be wrong enough, yet upon the point this is not the very matter. Neither our lying still, nor our going on, nor standing out, so they have an end: [that] they all and every one of them may have hope. "Perpetual" is the word, and perpetual is the thing. Not why these, any of these, or all of these; but why these perpetually? To do thus, to do it and never leave doing it; to make no end of sin, but our own end; to make a perpetuity of sin; never to rise, return, repent—for repentance is opposite not to sin, but to the continuance of it—that is the point. SERMON ON JEREMIAH 8:4-7.[5]

LOOK INTO THE MIRROR OF ANIMALS. DAVID JORIS: Follow my advice and teaching in the Lord that I counsel you, if you do not wish to err. . . .

Delight more and more in your work, not tiring on the path, but be strengthened in the battle. For the lust of the Spirit will illuminate and sweeten for you all things that previously were bitter or sour. Things that were heavy or a burden for you will become light. What was unbelievable or invisible to you, you will see face-to-face with truth in the Spirit. Indeed you will taste and feel when you previously were too weak. You will become strong from this, for where you were once dead, you will become living.

---

[3]Bugenhagen, *In Ieremiam*, 2Q2v; citing Mal 3:5; Ps 14:2; Mt 5:4.
[4]Downame, ed., *Annotations*, 9G4v*; citing Job 39:26.

[5]Andrewes, *Works*, 1:333-34*; citing Rom. 5:20.

See, this you will meet with, and so you will be changed and quickened through the clarity of Christ. All of you who are sustaining struggle, suffering, and defeat will, according to your wish, defeat the evil with the good, which you love or take pride in, and possess the kingdom of God. Therefore, hasten, hasten, to come to the rest in the Garden of Eden, into the life. O all of you, the children of truth, sons and daughters of Abraham, of the almighty Father, who desire to escape the wrath and the great anger of God, know your visitation and behold your valuable time. Look in the mirror of the animals, O Israel, and do not be blind or disobedient. See, the owl knows its time, the swallow knows its time, the cuckoo knows its time, the finch and herring know their time. But if the fisherman or seaman do not perceive or observe these times, then they will catch nothing. If the finch catcher does not closely observe the finch, it will fly away. It is the same for you. If you do not seek the Lord while he is to be found, then you will lose him. If you do not call out to him while he is nearby, then he will leave your sight. A BLESSED INSTRUCTION.[6]

THOSE WHO OPPOSE THE LIVING WORD.

THOMAS MÜNTZER: When their faith comes under scrutiny there is no people on earth that opposes the Holy Spirit and the living Word more strenuously than these useless Christian priests. In his eighth chapter, Jeremiah certainly turns these points most cogently against those who cannot understand that all Scripture must be complemented by the experience of faith and that this is altogether infallible.

In short, these men have a lying pen, for they reject the living Word (which no created being can understand unless it is ready to suffer), and they usurp words that they will never ever hear themselves. THE PRAGUE MANIFESTO.[7]

TRUE BELIEVERS SUFFER. THOMAS MÜNTZER: There are, by my soul, others, apart from students

and priests and monks, who welcome bookish truth and warm flattery and pomp. But when God wants to write something in their hearts there is no people under the sun that is more opposed to the living Word of God than they are. Nor do they suffer any trials of faith in the spirit of the fear of God: for they are dispatched into the lake where the false prophets will be tormented with Antichrist from generation to generation, amen. Nor do they want the spirit of the fear of God to alarm them. That is why they never stop deriding the trials of faith, for they are the people of whom Jeremiah speaks. . . . For they have no experience of their own that they could employ in the explanation of holy Scripture. Their only way to write is a hypocritical one that throws away the authentic words, and even though they use them they will never pay heed to them from eternity to eternity. For God only speaks through the readiness of the creatures to suffer, which is what the hearts of unbelievers lack. . . . Unbelievers absolutely refuse to become conformed with Christ by their suffering; they want to achieve it all by honey-sweet thoughts. THE PRAGUE MANIFESTO.[8]

8:10-17 No Healing, Only Terror

THE PRICE OF GREED. NIKOLAUS SELNECKER: "Therefore I will give your wives to strangers, and your fields to your pursuers." . . . The unrepentant Jews must come into the hands of their enemies and observe their wives, children, and goods taken by foreign owners. So we Christians must fear likewise before the Turk (so you must prepare yourselves, as good Christians desire to be, and treat those nearby in a Turkish way) because he leads our wives and children away from us, defiles and harms them, and takes and ruins everything we have; he hunts us, takes us captive, martyrs and strangles us. The cause, then, is the avarice of all in general, both small and great, teacher and listener. THE WHOLE PROPHET JEREMIAH 8:10.[9]

[6]CRR 7:251-52.
[7]Müntzer, *Collected Works*, 374.
[8]Müntzer, *Collected Works*, 366.
[9]Selnecker, *Der gantze Prophet Jeremias*, R3r.

WHEN AVARICE AND INJUSTICE DEPRIVES US OF ALL THINGS. JOHN CALVIN: God here threatens punishment because he found that his efforts had resulted in no change and that he was dealing with obstinate people; for he had tested them to see if they might be redeemable. But having seen that exhortations were of no avail, he now comes to extreme severity: "I will give," he says, "their wives to strangers." God sets forth, by a particular instance, the evils that usually accompany wars: and nothing is more distressing than when a wife is snatched away from her husband; for if husbands had their option, they would prefer instant death than to bear such a disgrace. Jeremiah then shows that the most atrocious thing that happens to conquered nations was coming to the Jews—that their men would be deprived of their wives.

He afterward says the same thing of their fields; God declares that he will give "the fields to their possessors." By this mode of speaking he intimates that they would be deprived of their fields, not for a short time, but perpetually. There is, indeed, a contrast here implied: for it sometimes happens that enemies prevail and plunder everything; but yet they do not take possession of fields for any length of time. . . . But when God calls enemies "possessors," he means that there would be such a calamity that the Jews would for a long time, even all their lives, be banished from their country, and would lose their possessions. They thought that the land was so given to them, that it could never be taken from them: and doubtless the Lord would have never expelled them had they not defiled it with their pollutions; but as they had polluted [the land] by their sins, they deserved to be banished from it. . . .

He afterward mentions the reason why God had resolved to deal so severely with them: "For they were," he says, "from the least to the greatest given up to avarice." He means that no equity prevailed among the people; for under one kind of sin he includes all fraud, exploitation, and every kind of injustice. God then says that everyone was addicted to his own gain, so that they practiced mutual wrongs without any regard to what was right and just. He then enlarges on the subject

and says, "All, from the prophet to the priest, acted deceitfully. . . ." Jeremiah in various ways sets forth the wrongs by which people harassed one another. Nor does he exclude violence when he speaks of fraud; but it is the same as though he said that they, being forgetful of what was right, practiced fraud of every kind. It was, indeed, a dreadful thing that there remained no rectitude or justice in the prophets and priests that God had constituted to be leaders; they ought to have carried light for others and to have displayed the right way for the people. Since then even these people acted deceitfully, there must have been among the common people the most disgraceful injustice. Hence the prophet shows by these words that God could not be charged with too much rigor, as though he treated the people cruelly; for there was such a mass of wickedness, that it could no longer be endured. COMMENTARY ON JEREMIAH 8:10.[10]

CORRUPTION IN COURT, MARKET, AND CHURCH. MENNO SIMONS: I do not know where to find the mighty and the rich, in what courts to find judges, lawyers, and advocates, in what city and country to find merchants and retailers, or in what cloister and church to find preachers, priests, and monks, who believe and follow Christ, who out of a new and penitent heart spurn all improper practices, fraud, crafty theft, shady business, and wicked gain, and say with Zacchaeus, "Those whom we have defrauded we will repay fourfold." The prophet complains that everyone from the least even to the greatest is given to covetousness. THE TRUE CHRISTIAN FAITH.[11]

THE DANGERS OF HUMAN ALLIANCE AND RELIANCE. NIKOLAUS SELNECKER: "Assemble yourselves, and let us move to fortified cities. . . ." Irony! No authority, power or assembly will be of help; as Solomon says, "There is neither wisdom, nor understanding, nor counsel against the Lord."

---

[10]CTS 17:435-436* (CO 38:12).
[11]Simons, *Complete Writings*, 370; citing Lk 19:8.

When one forgets God and entrusts oneself to human assistance, one will have neither fortune nor salvation. . . . The whole kingdom of the Jews would certainly be destroyed with human aid. Moreover, we praise ourselves as good Christians; we see and know such things, but follow these unfortunate examples. For what alliance does one seek when the princes and cities are not hopeful and they want to be more certain? We do not believe that God is strong enough to take on our concerns and so do not hold to God thereby. Otherwise we would leave ourselves to his goodness and power and not so readily look around for fleshly protection. Many, though, have the opinion that such occurrences are without sin; such proposals belong to the temporal authority and they should not be corrected by preachers, who have a different calling. That would be fine to say, I confess, if while the authorities are not being prompted, they would all flee to God. . . . But the authorities are unfortunate when they are alone, that is, without faith in God. Yes, it is blasphemous to trust in one or another power. In fact, such blasphemous trust in all alliances the prophets condemn anyway. . . .

The "bitter drink" means all of the misery and misfortune, our sins, cries, and struggles, wretchedness, war, persecution, threats, and even more that give pain and anxiety to body and soul. For such a drink God gives to the wicked and terrifies them. . . . God is the judge, and the Lord has a goblet in his hand, filled with strong wine, and he gives the same to others. But the godless must drink all of it and suck down the dregs. THE WHOLE PROPHET JEREMIAH 8:14-15.[12]

THE CALLING TO REBUKE AND CORRECT.

MENNO SIMONS: To rebuke or reprove in true Christian zeal and unfeigned love their false doctrine, deceiving, unscriptural sacraments, and their willful and carnal life, with the Spirit, Word, and life of Christ, and to point them to the glorious example of the prophets, of the apostles of Christ, and of all the true servants of God—this he [Gellius Faber] calls slandering. So that our work of love is verily given the worst possible meaning. This is, alas, the way it goes. If we write and speak mournfully, it is called sighing and groaning; if we reprove sharply, it is called invective slander. "If we pipe, they do not dance. If we mourn, they do not lament," as Christ said. It is wrongfully spoken, no matter what we say to the perverse. "Although they commit abomination, yet they are not ashamed, neither do they blush." REPLY TO GELLIUS FABER.[13]

POISONOUS POETRY, LOST IN TRANSLATION.

THE ENGLISH ANNOTATIONS: There is an elegant consonance in the original, between the word that signifies serpent and this of biting, differing but in a letter, and that also a similarity of sound, the one from the other, which our English cannot express. Hereby it appears that the kind of serpents here alluded to are not those that have their sting in the tail, as the scorpion, but have venom in or around their teeth, as asps and vipers as well as our adders and snakes. ANNOTATIONS ON JEREMIAH 8:17.[14]

---

[12]Selnecker, *Der gantze Prophet Jeremias*, R3v-r4v; citing Prov 21:30.

[13]Simons, *Complete Writings*, 638-39; citing Mt 11:17; Lk 7:32. Simons responds to Gellius Faber (1498–1564), a Lutheran pastor in Emden, East Friesland, who attacked the Anabaptists in writing in 1552; Simons, *Complete Writings*, 624.

[14]Downame, ed., *Annotations*, 9H2r*; citing Rev 9:10.

JEREMIAH 8:18–9:26
JEREMIAH GRIEVES FOR HIS PEOPLE

[18]My joy is gone; grief is upon me;[a]
　my heart is sick within me.
[19]Behold, the cry of the daughter of my people
　from the length and breadth of the land:
"Is the Lord not in Zion?
　Is her King not in her?"
"Why have they provoked me to anger with
　　their carved images
　and with their foreign idols?"
[20]"The harvest is past, the summer is ended,
　and we are not saved."
[21]For the wound of the daughter of my people is
　my heart wounded;
　I mourn, and dismay has taken hold on me.

[22]Is there no balm in Gilead?
　Is there no physician there?
Why then has the health of the daughter of
　my people
　not been restored?

9 [b]Oh that my head were waters,
　　and my eyes a fountain of tears,
that I might weep day and night
　for the slain of the daughter of my people!
[2c]Oh that I had in the desert
　a travelers' lodging place,
that I might leave my people
　and go away from them!
For they are all adulterers,
　a company of treacherous men.
[3]They bend their tongue like a bow;
　falsehood and not truth has grown strong[d]
　　in the land;
for they proceed from evil to evil,
　and they do not know me, declares the Lord.
[4]Let everyone beware of his neighbor,
　and put no trust in any brother,
for every brother is a deceiver,
　and every neighbor goes about as a slanderer.

[5]Everyone deceives his neighbor,
　and no one speaks the truth;
they have taught their tongue to speak lies;
　they weary themselves committing iniquity.
[6]Heaping oppression upon oppression, and
　　deceit upon deceit,
　they refuse to know me, declares the Lord.

[7]Therefore thus says the Lord of hosts:
"Behold, I will refine them and test them,
　for what else can I do, because of my people?
[8]Their tongue is a deadly arrow;
　it speaks deceitfully;
with his mouth each speaks peace to his neighbor,
　but in his heart he plans an ambush for him.
[9]Shall I not punish them for these things?
　　declares the Lord,
　and shall I not avenge myself
　on a nation such as this?

[10]"I will take up weeping and wailing for the
　　mountains,
　and a lamentation for the pastures of the
　　wilderness,
because they are laid waste so that no one
　　passes through,
　and the lowing of cattle is not heard;
both the birds of the air and the beasts
　have fled and are gone.
[11]I will make Jerusalem a heap of ruins,
　a lair of jackals,
and I will make the cities of Judah a desolation,
　without inhabitant."

[12]Who is the man so wise that he can understand this? To whom has the mouth of the Lord spoken, that he may declare it? Why is the land ruined and laid waste like a wilderness, so that no one passes through? [13]And the Lord says: "Because they have forsaken my law that I set before them, and have not obeyed my voice or walked in accord with it,

¹⁴*but have stubbornly followed their own hearts and have gone after the Baals, as their fathers taught them.* ¹⁵*Therefore thus says the Lord of hosts, the God of Israel: Behold, I will feed this people with bitter food, and give them poisonous water to drink.* ¹⁶*I will scatter them among the nations whom neither they nor their fathers have known, and I will send the sword after them, until I have consumed them."*

¹⁷*Thus says the Lord of hosts:*
"Consider, and call for the mourning women to
come;
send for the skillful women to come;
¹⁸*let them make haste and raise a wailing over us,*
that our eyes may run down with tears
and our eyelids flow with water.
¹⁹*For a sound of wailing is heard from Zion:*
'How we are ruined!
We are utterly shamed,
because we have left the land,
because they have cast down our dwellings.'"

²⁰*Hear, O women, the word of the Lord,*
and let your ear receive the word of his mouth;
teach to your daughters a lament,

and each to her neighbor a dirge.
²¹*For death has come up into our windows;*
it has entered our palaces,
cutting off the children from the streets
and the young men from the squares.
²²*Speak: "Thus declares the Lord,*
'The dead bodies of men shall fall
like dung upon the open field,
like sheaves after the reaper,
and none shall gather them.'"

²³*Thus says the Lord: "Let not the wise man boast in his wisdom, let not the mighty man boast in his might, let not the rich man boast in his riches,* ²⁴*but let him who boasts boast in this, that he understands and knows me, that I am the Lord who practices steadfast love, justice, and righteousness in the earth. For in these things I delight, declares the Lord."*

²⁵*"Behold, the days are coming, declares the Lord, when I will punish all those who are circumcised merely in the flesh—* ²⁶*Egypt, Judah, Edom, the sons of Ammon, Moab, and all who dwell in the desert who cut the corners of their hair, for all these nations are uncircumcised, and all the house of Israel are uncircumcised in heart."*

a Compare Septuagint; the meaning of the Hebrew is uncertain   b Ch 8:23 in Hebrew   c Ch 9:1 in Hebrew   d Septuagint; Hebrew *and not for truth they have grown strong*

OVERVIEW: The grief and lamentations expressed in the prophecies of Jeremiah presented challenges to sixteenth-century interpreters. Who is represented as speaking? Is it Jeremiah or the Jewish people or God? Who is expressing anguish and for what reason? And is such emotion legitimate or indicative of hostility or indifference to God's providence? Such debates about voice in the biblical text give us access to perceptions of the human passions and emotions that nearly five centuries ago Christians deemed godly or ungodly, appropriate or inappropriate. In particular, such expressions—often articulated in metaphors or illustrated in life circumstances—might conceal hypocrisy and contempt for God's judgment or

mercy; or they might reveal true despair, expose a deep desire to repent, or lay bare rampant injustice and oppression in society. The crosscurrents of such emotions and expressions played out in Jeremiah's prophecies in lavish detail.

Moreover, such expressions were manifest in specific behaviors, beliefs, and life circumstances. In fact, God would surely test and measure true faith and devotion and bring severe judgment where idolatry and unbelief reigned. Jeremiah's prophecies on such matters and particularly on true knowledge of God provided Protestant commentators with the opportunity to lay out and interconnect essentials of true Christian theology, worship, and life.

8:18–9:11 Anguish for God's Wayward People

Jeremiah's Sorrow. The English Annotations: After God's menacing speech in verse 17 the words of the prophet prophesy his exceeding, great, and continual sorrow for the woeful condition of his people. Jeremiah was by no means able to ease this sorrow himself, though he sometimes tried to do so. Annotations on Jeremiah 8:18.[1]

Strength in Sorrow Against God. John Calvin: The prophet . . . means that he sought "strength in his sorrow," but that his "heart was weak." He no doubt, I think, sets forth in this verse the perverse character of the people, that they sought through their obstinacy to drive away every punishment. This could not indeed be referred to himself, or to those who were like him, as we know how fearful are God's servants with regard to his wrath; for as the fear of God prevails in their hearts, so they are easily terrified by his judgment; but hypocrites and wicked people ever harden themselves as far as they can. They then strengthened themselves against God, and thought in this way to be conquerors. Since they thus perversely contended with God, the prophet sets forth here the great hardness of the people: "I would," he says, "strengthen myself in my sorrow; but my heart is within me weak"; that is, "in vain are these remedies tried; in vain have you hitherto endeavored to strengthen yourselves, and have sought fortresses and strongholds against God; for sorrow will at length prevail, as the Lord will add troubles to troubles, so that you must at length succumb to them."

He means the same when he says, "His heart was within him weak": "I have," he says, "been oppressed with sorrow, when I thought I had strength enough to resist." For thus the ungodly think manfully to act when they madly resist God; but at length they find in that moment that they seek in vain so to strengthen themselves; for our heart, he says, will become weak within us, and our inability will at last oppress and overwhelm us. Commentary on Jeremiah 8:18.[2]

God's Fatherly Heart. Nikolaus Selnecker: What follows in this chapter is the threat that God will allow the king of Babylon to destroy his people in every way. The enemy is no longer far off, as he preached about above in the fourth chapter. It is amazing, though, to recognize God's great mercy and fatherly heart, that he has compassion on us and a heartfelt sympathy for us, when we must be punished for our sins. Then he also says, "I mourn in my heart, that my people are destroyed. I sorrow deeply and have pain within." For God does not want the death of a sinner, but that a sinner would himself return and live. The Whole Prophet Jeremiah 8:18-19.[3]

A Plea from Exile. Konrad Pellikan: I seem myself to hear the voice of the anxious shout of the children of Israel in the most remote provinces of their exile as they lament in this way. "Has he completely abandoned Jerusalem, the city chosen by God? Has the presence of her grace completely abandoned her? Has she spurned the habitation of her glory so that in her there is no king whatsoever who would be able to defend, avenge, and restore her?" I moreover hear the Lord responding in this way to this grievance: "Why did these men of Judah and residents of Jerusalem not change, why did they continue to agitate me with such great blasphemies and irritate me with their graven images? They certainly knew that those things especially displease me. How often I have forbidden these images from being made, kept, and worshiped. I have warned them constantly that they should beware of the vanity of foreign pollutions. But I have done so in vain. Commentary on Jeremiah 8:19.[4]

A Lament About Summer Passed and Egyptian Absence. Cornelius À Lapide: "The harvest is passed." This is the voice of the

---

[1] Downame, ed., *Annotations*, 9H1v*.

[2] CTS 17:447* (CO 38:19).
[3] Selnecker, *Der gantze Prophet Jeremias*, R4v; citing 2 Pet 3:9.
[4] Pellikan, *Commentaria Bibliorum*, 3:2Qv.

Jewish people lamenting their long misfortune, especially the siege they had endured for a whole summer in that year; for the Egyptians' support, which they had promised and which might free the Jews, had not endured. Moreover, they were thinking that the Egyptians would not come until after the coming months of May and June, when people were less occupied in raising crops. Then they thought that the Egyptians would come after the summer and in grape-gathering season, but they had still not come. COMMENTARY ON THE PROPHET JEREMIAH 8:20.[5]

THE SEASON OF OUR DELIVERANCE HAS PASSED. JOHN CALVIN: The prophet now shows the hindrance found in the name of the people. At the time Jeremiah spoke, the Jews confidently boasted that God was their defender; and they did not think that the Chaldeans were preparing for an expedition. But as they were inflated with false confidence, the prophet here recites what they would presently say, "The harvest has passed, the summer has ended, and we have not been saved"; that is, "We thought that the associates with whom we have made alliances would at length come to our aid; and we have in this respect been deceived." In saying that "the harvest had passed," some think that they expected help from the Egyptians after they had gathered their corn into barns; for there is then more leisure, and then also there are provisions for the army. But the prophet seems to include the whole time suitable for carrying on war; as though he had said, "What will become of us in the end? For if the Egyptians intended to bring help, they would have done so at the suitable time of the year; but the harvest has past and the summer has ended: will they come now, when the severity of winter constrains them to stay home?" COMMENTARY ON JEREMIAH 8:20.[6]

SORROW FOR THOSE WHO DESIRE NONE. JOHN CALVIN: The hardness of the people was so great that the threats we have observed did not

touch them. So the prophet now ascribes to himself what he had before attributed to them. We then see how the prophet varies his mode of speaking; it was necessary, for he was at a loss as to finding a way to address them with sufficient strength to penetrate their stony and even iron hearts. We need not wonder, then, that the prophet uses so many figurative terms; for it was necessary to set before them God's judgment in various ways, so that the people might be awakened from their sluggish state.

Jeremiah then says that he was "bruised for the bruising of his people." Most of them no doubt ridiculed him, saying, "Oh! You are grieving for your own evil; it is well and prosperous with us: who has asked you for this pity? Do not think that you can gain our favor, for we are contented with our lot. Weep rather for your own calamities, if you have any at home; but allow us at the same time to enjoy our pleasures, since God is propitious and indulgent to us"; so was the prophet derided. Yet he warns the obstinate people that they might have less excuse: he says that he was "rendered black"; for sorrow brings blackness with it and makes the human face dark; it is a metaphorical expression. He says at last that he was "astonished." The astonishment with which he was seized he no doubt sets down as being the opposite of the people's torpor and insensibility, for they had no fear for themselves. COMMENTARY ON JEREMIAH 8:21.[7]

REJECTING THE PLACE AND PHYSICIANS OF HEALING. JOHANNES BUGENHAGEN: "Gilead," or "Galaad," is a most fertile mountain as you see in Numbers 32, to the rear of the Phoenicians and Arabia, adjoining the hills of Lebanon, and extending through the desert, all the way to that place across the Jordan, where once Sihon king of the Ammonites dwelt. There Reuben, Gad, and the half of the tribe of Manasseh received their portion, as it says in Joshua 13 and Deuteronomy 3. Whence the land of half of the tribes of Israel were beyond the Jordan, which the Jews first occupied, that land is called Gilead in Joshua 22, Numbers 32, and

---

[5]À Lapide, *Commentarium in Jeremiam*, 59.
[6]CTS 17:453* (CO 38:22-23).

[7]CTS 17:454-55* (CO 38:23-24).

elsewhere. Here Jeremiah alludes, however, to the fecundity of the place, where many herbs of medicinal value grew. By taking up an analogy from medicine, he rebukes the people: they were perishing of their own free will because they despised the medicine, which is present in their land, that is, the Word of God and the Physician, that is, from the prophets and the holy preachers, who administer the ointments and bandages of health through the Word. COMMENTARY ON JEREMIAH 8:22.[8]

TEARS FOR THE LOST. JOHANNES OECOLAMPA-DIUS: [The prophet] suffers so greatly that he even longs to be changed completely into a fountain, so that he might flow forth and produce perpetual and continual waters. It is typically Hebrew to say, "who will give, for . . . if only . . ." so that by this one might show the magnitude of the calamity. It is as if he says that the waters do not suffice for my weeping. The preachers and those prelates use this voice to bemoan the souls of their subjects, because they are killed through spiritual enemies. Doubtless if one could see and consider how many thousands of souls perish daily, seduced by the charms of this world, it would hardly be surprising if one spoke in the same way. COMMENTARY ON JEREMIAH 9:1.[9]

THE WEEPING OF GOD. JOHN DONNE: God had an aversion and was late in making places of torment; it was displeasing for him to speak of judgments or of those who extort judgments from him. How plentifully, how abundantly is the word "blessed" multiplied in the book of Psalms? "Blessed" and "blessed" in every psalm, and in every verse; the book seems to be made out of that word "blessed." . . . In all the book there is not one "Woe" so proclaimed, not one "woe" upon any soul in that book.

When this "woe" is pronounced in one of the prophets, it is the woe of lament and not the woe of rebuke. That "woe" is a voice of compassion in him that speaks it and not of destruction to them to whom it is spoken. God in the person of Jeremiah weeps in contemplation of the calamities threatened, "Oh that my head were waters. . . ." It is God that was their Father, and it is God, their God, that slew them; but yet, that God, their Father, weeps over the slaughter. So in the person of Isaiah, God weeps again, "I will bewail you with weeping and I will water you with tears." SERMON ON PSALM 64:10.[10]

GODLY ANGUISH IN A SINFUL WORLD. NIKOLAUS SELNECKER: This sermon of Jeremiah originates in response to contempt for the Word of God, which God will not tolerate. The prophet places before us a complaint and the silent suffering of all God-fearing people. When they see the great confidence of the world and its common and public vice, deceit, gluttony, divorce, lies, and betrayal, so the God-fearing are deeply grieved; they sigh and moan. They want to see things improve, but they cannot make changes. The world is too wicked. The godly complain about it. So they must be ridiculed, as they alone want to be pious and holy. They scold others about these things when they fulfill their office, so they are hated and come often thereby into danger to both body and life. They silence themselves about such things, but they torment themselves in their conscience and have a nagging worm, which eats at them because of their silence. They have the urging of the Holy Spirit, who either compels their mouths to open and censure error, sin, and vice, or the Spirit preaches to them in their hearts, when they do not speak and reprimand. So God truly will set them to speaking about it and hold them accountable. . . . So pious and true teachers and other God-fearing Christians do, when they live and dwell near godless people, who want no reprimand, help, or correction, but who go forth in all confidence and malice, and say nothing according to God's Word and preaching, or as senseless heads at court or

---

[8]Bugenhagen, *In Ieremiam*, 2Q3r; citing Josh 13:8-32; Deut 3:13.
[9]Oecolampadius, *In Hieremiam*, 1:N2r.

[10]Donne, *Sermons*, 7:243*; citing Is 16:9.

common rabble in the cities or villages. They ask nothing of the pastors. Such things we draw from these words, as here stands: "Oh that I had enough water to weep," etc. So the Son of God also weeps over Jerusalem.

What follows from such revolting behavior and untruth Jeremiah shows further on because God cannot tolerate such sin any longer, but must punish the people. As Micah also says in chapter 7, godly people are gone from the land, and the upright are no longer among the people. They lie in wait for blood; one hunts the other that he might harm him; they plan it out before they do evil. THE WHOLE PROPHET JEREMIAH 9:1-6.[11]

MOURNING OVER SIN. LANCELOT ANDREWES: If weep we cannot, mourn we can, and mourn we must. *Et vos non luxistis* says the apostle; he says not, *et vos flevistis,* "and you have not wept," but "and you have not mourned"; as if he should say, "That you should have done [this] at the least." Mourning they call the sorrow which reason itself can yield. In schools they term it, *Dolorem appretiativum,* "valuing what should be," rating what the sins deserve though we have it not to lay down; yet, what they deserve we should, and that we can. These and these sins I have committed, so many, so heinous, so often repeat, so long lain in; these deserve to be bewailed even with tears of blood.

This we can do; and this too [we] wish with the prophet, and so let wish, "O that my head were full of water, and my eyes fountains of tears," do it as it should be done! This we can. And we can complain and bemoan ourselves as does the prophet, with very little variation from him. "My leanness, my leanness, says he, Woe is me! My dryness, my dryness, may each of us say, woe is me!" The transgressors have offended; the transgressors have grievously offended. Grievously offend we can, grievously lament we cannot, "my dryness, my dryness, woe is me!" Nay, we need not vary, we may even let his own word, "leanness," alone. For dry

and lean both is our sorrow; God knows: God help us, this mourn we can.

And last, this we can [do], even humbly beseech our merciful God and Father, in default of ours to accept the strong crying of bitter tears which in the days of his flesh, his blessed Son in great agony shed for us; for us I say that we should, but we are not able to do the like for ourselves, that which is wanting in ours [and] may be supplied from thence. These, by the grace of God, we may do in discharge of this point. These let us do, and it will be accepted. SERMON ON JOEL 2:12-13.[12]

THE FRUIT OF IDOLATRY. JOHANNES OECOLAMPADIUS: "Adulterers and idolaters." "If only I were in some deserted forest in a little hut, in which travelers hide themselves from the rain, so I might not see such evil things." With similar feeling David says, "Who will give me wings and I will fly away. . . ." Again Jeremiah returns to their sin, because they are all adulterers, that is, idolaters, and they break the faith, which they owe to God. In this way they come together so they may cheat. Indeed, truth always has disciples; it censures in the first place the inner evil of those things, which are present in thoughts and then in words. This shows that faith, truth, and charity have disappeared through adultery. Since they do not preserve faith in God, what will prevent them from failing to preserve their neighbor? Indeed, because they do not know God—on account of their infidelity—impiety bears this fruit, so that they move from evil to evil, just as good people move from virtue to virtue. This is what the prophet Joel says, "Blood smeared blood." COMMENTARY ON JEREMIAH 9:2.[13]

A DESIRE TO LIVE IN THE WILDERNESS. JOHN CALVIN: Here the prophet entertains another wish. He had before wished that his head were waters, that he might shed tears. And he had wished his eyes to be fountains of tears. But now, after having duly considered the wickedness of the people, he

---

[11]Selnecker, *Der gantze Prophet Jeremias,* S1r-v; S3r; citing Lk 19:41-44; Mic 7:2.

[12]Andrewes, *Works,* 1:370-71*; citing 1 Cor 5:2; Ps 114:8; Heb 5:7.
[13]Oecolampadius, *In Hieremiam,* 1:N2v; citing Ps 55:7; Hos 4:2.

puts off every feeling of humanity, and as one incensed, he desires to move elsewhere and wholly to leave the people; for their impiety had so prevailed that he could no longer live among them. It is indeed certain that the prophet had no common grief, when he perceived that God's dreadful vengeance was not far distant: it is also certain that he was moved and constrained by their detestable conduct to desire to be removed to some other place. But he speaks not only for his own sake; for he regards his own nation and expresses his feelings that he might more effectually touch their hearts. We must then understand that so great was the sympathy of the prophet that he was not satisfied with shedding tears, but that he wished that his whole head would flow into tears. It appears, also, that he was so moved with indignation that he wished wholly to leave his own people. But, as I have said, his object was to try, if he could, to restore them to the right way.

He then shows, in this verse, that the Jews had become so detestable, that all the true servants of God wished to be removed far away from them: who then will set me in the desert? He does not seek another country for himself. Does he desire to dwell in a pleasant situation or that some comfortable asylum should be offered to him? Rather, he desires to be placed in the desert or in the lodging of travelers. He speaks not of those lodgings or inns, which were in villages and towns, but of a lodging in the desert. Typically, when a long and tedious journey is made through forests some sheds are formed, so that when a traveler is overtaken by the darkness of night, he might be protected by some covering and so not have to lie down in the open air. The prophet speaks of this kind of lodging: then he no doubt means a shed; but as to the word, we may retain, as I have said, its proper meaning. This means that it is better to dwell in the desert among wild beasts than to be among that abominable people. By expressing this wish he no doubt inflamed the fury of the whole people or at least of most of them. But it was necessary to address them so forcefully since they refused to submit to any sort of wholesome warning and counsel. Thus they were forcibly

irritated and urged by such reproofs as these.

"I will leave my people." This sentence is dramatic in tone; for one's native soil is delightful to everyone, and it is also delightful to dwell among one's own people. So then the prophet wished to move into the desert and leave his own people, to depart from all his relatives and the nation from which he sprang. COMMENTARY ON JEREMIAH 9:2.[14]

GOD'S REFINING FIRE. JOHN CALVIN: "I will try" or "melt them," he says, "and I will prove them." Since they had put on a false color, the prophet says that a test was needed. When anyone presents copper or any other metal as if it is gold, they are disproved by a test. Any imposter might otherwise sell dross for silver: the spurious metal that is passed as gold, or silver, must be proved; it must be cast into the fire and melted. Because the Jews thought that they had honest deceptions to cover their base character, God gives the answer that he had yet a way to discover their deceitfulness, and so tells them, "When anyone brings in dross for silver or copper for gold, the goldsmith has a furnace and tests it. So will I try and melt you; for you think that you can dazzle my eyes by false pretenses: this will do nothing for you." In short, God intimates that he had means ready at hand to discover their deceitfulness, and that thus their hypocrisy would be of no advantage to them, as his judgments would be like a furnace. As then stubble or wood cast into the furnace is immediately burned, so hypocrites cannot endure God's judgment. COMMENTARY ON JEREMIAH 9:7.[15]

ARROWS OF DECEIT. JOHN CALVIN: The prophet again complains of the deceitfulness of their tongues; he compares them to deadly or drawn out arrows. Gold is said to be drawn out when refined by repeated melting; so arrows when sharpened are more piercing. The prophet then says that their tongues were like deadly or sharpened arrows. How so? Because they ever spoke deceitfully by either

---

[14]CTS 17:458-59* (CO 38:25-26).
[15]CTS 17:470* (CO 38:33).

slandering or ensnaring others. But the expression is general; and the prophet no doubt meant to include all modes of deceiving; for afterward it follows, "With the mouth they speak peace"; that is, everyone professed friendship, and their words were honey; and yet within . . . they concealed their plans. COMMENTARY ON JEREMIAH 9:8.[16]

THE WASTELAND OF FORMER HABITATIONS.

JOHANNES BUGENHAGEN: Jeremiah signifies that "in the mountains," as in the vineyards, pastures, villages, and everywhere, there will be misery when the Babylonian forces approach. Note that these dwellings of the desert or wilderness are not called places of empty wilderness, where no one lives, since then they could not be called dwelling places. Rather, they are called villages and the tents of shepherds, where there is not a multitude of people and businesses, as in the cities. But here there is only the cultivation of the fields and the shepherding of cattle. . . .

"The dwelling place of dragons":[†] so Scripture is used to describing the devastation and loss of the state, as we Germans speak concerning changes in a good state. Formerly all things were rightly governed there; now there is nothing living there except the demons. Or perhaps the lairs of dragons were in the land of Israel after the people having been carried off. The Samaritans filled the void when there was neither prophecy in that place nor the teaching of the Word of God, nor a king; that is, neither spiritual nor secular government, as in previous times. COMMENTARY ON JEREMIAH 9:10-11.[17]

9:12-26 Turn to the Lord

LIFE, DESTRUCTION, AND FOLLOWING THE LAW. HEINRICH BULLINGER: Truly, there is no subject that requires more explanation than causality, as a rule it comes back ever anew to this: explaining why the Holy City had to be razed to its

foundation, and why the land of Judah with its people and all of its animals had to be laid waste. The prophet uses a dialogue in which he poses questions and God then responds. Indeed, in this way everything becomes not only evident, but also even more clear. So the prophet poses a question, so that at the same time he might gravely censure the folly of those who both wish to seem wise, and those who have been admonished so many times by the Word of God. Yet nevertheless they did not know the causes of their own destruction. The prophet says, "If anyone among you is wise, and indeed truly wise, he would understand this. If anyone had diligently attended to the things that the voice of God himself had announced, no doubt he would already be able to announce it himself." What is the issue? The reason why that people perishes, and why their cities are reduced to a wasteland. But there is no one who wants to be wise, or to receive a sermon from God, so that he might be able or willing to report the true cause of destruction. But I would desire that God himself explain the cause to us anew. . . .

God says, "The reason for the people perishing is that they forsake my law," etc. This is the first thing that seems important to God: he gave or dispensed his law and his will to us, which has been comprehended in writing and set forth magnificently not only through angels, patriarchs, and prophets but also through God's very own self: with his own mouth with great glory and majesty on Mt. Sinai; and then through the inspiration of the Holy Spirit. God proclaimed this law through the wisest people, through people highly celebrated throughout the whole world, made illustrious by the authority of miracles: Moses, Samuel, Elijah, Isaiah, Daniel, and many others; and even through the most praiseworthy and glorious kings in the world: David, Solomon, Jehoshaphat, Hezekiah, and Josiah. In addition, God sent his only-begotten Son, his wisdom, into the world, who handed down the same law to us with us own mouth. Finally, he undertook to convey his will to us in letters through his apostles and disciples, but also for the whole world. He laid out his doctrine that

---

[16]CTS 17:471-72* (CO 38:34).
[17]Bugenhagen, *In Ieremiam*, 2R2v-2R3r, 2R4v. [†]"A lair of jackals" in the ESV.

is translated into the languages of every nation. And this is the instrument of his Holy Spirit, this holy book here: inviolable, heavenly, and divine. . . .

The prophet continues: "They did not walk in it." Indeed, the Lord requires, as St. James says, "that we become not only hearers, but also doers of the Word of God." Now some of the people did some of the good things, which could happen without great effort. They got rid of the idols, pulled down the altars, and no longer called on their deities. Meanwhile, they did not curse the idols of their hearts. . . . But, you say, if they did not hear the Word of God, nor direct and accommodate their lives, words, and deeds to the commands of God—that is, to walk in the words or law of God—what therefore did they do? Did they live without any religion like insensible things? The Word of God continues: "But they went after the thoughts of their hearts." That is, some turned and went after arrogance, others went for depravity, stubbornness, and the delusions of their heart. . . . Thus Jeremiah was not able to make progress with these Jews, just as today we are not able to make progress with those infected by the papists' leaven. So it is that our papists stray after their deities, just as the Israelites walked after the Baalim. SERMON ON JEREMIAH 9:12-14.[18]

GOD PURSUES THE WICKED WITH WORD AND SWORD. HEINRICH BULLINGER: After he shows why they had to be destroyed, Jeremiah returns quickly to pursue their destruction itself, and diligently recites the calamities with which they would be buried. God seems, in the punishment borne by the wicked, to measure out a retribution equal to the crime. God recalls three points. First, that the Word of God was extremely bitter to the people, and prophetic preaching, which is elsewhere called the heavenly bread and the drink of life, was like wormwood to them. Therefore they deserved to be robbed of life-giving food, and to be nourished by wormwood and bile, that is, the most bitter of things. . . . Second, God did not scatter his

people, but he gathered them again into a unity and he commanded that with their whole heart they might worship the one God and completely and securely depend on him alone. But they preferred to run up and down, to seek many gods for themselves, and indeed to seek new gods every day, gods that their ancestors did not know. Hence, they completely deserved to be scattered and, indeed, to be led captive to nations whose names their fathers and even they themselves did not know, so that even there they could serve new and exotic deities. Third, they tyrannically misused the sword especially against the priests and prophets of God, and against the sincere confessors and worshipers of God. For that reason the Lord says, "I will send the sword against them," so that even if they flee desperately, nevertheless, the sword will overtake them and destroy them. SERMON ON JEREMIAH 9:15-16.[19]

MOURNING WOMEN, JUDGMENT, AND DEATH. JOHN MAYER: Seeing that the Jews were not easily moved to lament their own coming destruction, the prophet bids them to call mourning women. These mournful women can represent the case of the dead, and their loose living thereby; and the sad condition of all people, who cannot live long, but must die also, and be plucked from wives, children, and all that they have within a short time. Such folk are carried into the land of darkness, to become worms' meat, are robbed of their understanding, wit, reason and utterance, strength and beauty; for in a short time their anatomy turns to something horrid. The prophet might be able to move them, but he could not do so with his most pathetic representation of God's destructive judgments on them. So the prophet spoke this way to make them ashamed; as if he had said, "If after this much speaking, no sorrow can be stirred up in your hard and unbelieving hearts, then go to such theatrical women, and see if by them you can be brought to sorrow." For by showing extreme grief and acting out the part of mourners with skill, such women got tears and tears

---

[18]Bullinger, *Conciones*, 71r-72r; citing Jas 1:22.

[19]Bullinger, *Conciones*, 72v.

of abundance from the eyes of all watching. Thus, in the most pathetic way that he could find, Jeremiah performed the part of an entire kingdom of people perishing together and represented the same in the most horrid manner and as if before their very eyes. But they did not lament, even though the case was not about someone else, but about them. His request that they call for such women is not serious, but ironic; he mocks their vanity, in that they were moved by something of little importance, and were not grieved at all, but rather laughed at all his efforts to elicit sorrow, as if no such thing should ever happen to them. . . .

"Hear the word of the Lord, you women. . . ." Jeremiah had asked them before to call and hire mourning women to help them feign grief, and he wanted the women to do so in a convincing fashion, so that spectators might be moved to shed tears. Now the prophet enlarges on this point, calling on all women to mourn and not the few hired women mentioned before; for he was speaking to women all over the land. He speaks to women rather than men here, because by nature they were more apt to weep at their calamities, and he had begun to speak of them and the men had not been left untouched. . . .

But what does it mean that "death comes to their windows"? The Jews think if their walls are strong and their gates and doors are shut fast and barred that no enemy can come to hurt them, but they shall be utterly deceived. Death shall be sent in by the highest windows. God can bring destruction in any way, and they are but fools that think otherwise. Therefore, mourn all tenderhearted women for those things that will surely come and teach your daughters to mourn, for the judgment shall extend to you all, young and old; and the strong palaces of the great ones shall defend them no better than the cottages of the poor. COMMENTARY ON JEREMIAH 9:17-21.[20]

LEFT TO ROT IN THE FIELD. JOHN CALVIN: I rather think that [this verse] refers to those ears of corn that are not gathered while the reapers collect their handfuls. They do not, indeed, leave complete handfuls, nor cast them away; but it happens through carelessness that a few ears escape them. Then the prophet says that the Jews would be like those ears of corn that the reapers pass by and leave behind; and there is no one afterward to gather them; and those ears of corn that thus remain in the field either rot by themselves or are devoured by wild beasts. He then means that there would be no residue of the people, for all from the least to the greatest would be given up to destruction. COMMENTARY ON JEREMIAH 9:22.[21]

TRUST IN THE LORD ALONE, BUT USE WISDOM, MIGHT, AND RICHES. JOHANNES BUGENHAGEN: "Let the wise man not boast." Here is the epilogue, and the argument to this point and height of all the pious preaching, in which, as by an exclamation, he confounds and condemns all human confidence, not only of the Gentiles, but also of the Jews, that is, those who claim that they themselves are the people of God. If someone does not have trust in God, but has contempt for God, he is damned. . . . Do not trust that you are strong and powerful or glory in your own power; do not trust in weapons, the abundant armies of neighbors, fortified cities, the multitude of your army, or your own powers and works; for they will not do you any good and you will lose as much as you trust in such things. No one will be safe, except one whose help and strength is God, his refuge and protection, as is sung in the psalm. As David says, "I will not hope in my bow and my sword will not save me," etc.

Salvation from people is useless. In God we will perform strong deeds, and he will in no way lead us into tribulations. Nevertheless, David uses his bow and his sword, just as one ought to use wisdom and council. But to trust in such things is impiety. To not wish to use such things, which God gives, would be to tempt God against the command: "You shall not test the Lord your God." Furthermore, "You rich people should not glory and trust in your riches," which will do no good on the day of

---

[20]Mayer, *A Commentary*, 362-63*.

[21]CTS 17:495* (CO 38:48-49).

the wrath of the Lord. You read of this concerning the rich man in the Gospel, which says, "My soul, you have many good things stored up for many years" etc. Riches often provided the destruction for their masters: is it therefore not right to have them? This is not said. Rather, riches are gifts of God and they are to be used well if you have them. But it is prohibited to trust in them, lest you serve mammon and make from them a god for yourself—certainly the most shameful sort of idolatry. COMMENTARY ON JEREMIAH 9:23-24.[22]

GIVE GLORY TO GOD ALONE. JOHANNES OECOLAMPADIUS: Wisdom frees some people from certain dangers, through which they can escape; strength saves others, by which they prepare the way; riches, however, save not a few, by which they ransom themselves. Otherwise when the Lord begins to judge, all those above things will be in vain, just as is clear at the hour of death. There will be no way of freedom other than through faith, which works through love, just as it says here: glory in the knowledge of God, which gives faith and, of course, is through faith. So do works after the example of God the merciful and just judge; we ourselves should practice mercy, justice, and judgment. Indeed, the Lord requires this of us and not hollow ceremonies, and worship according to the traditions of people, in which we follow the wickedness of our own hearts and the Baals of our fathers.

There are those who undermine free will with this verse, but this is not discussed here; neither is presumption to be taken away from these verses. For concerning the knowledge of God we are not allowed to glory in ourselves, as if this knowledge comes from us. In fact, no one has this "except the Father reveals it to him." As Paul says to the Corinthians, "He that boasts, let him boast in the Lord"; that is, if someone recognizes anything of excellence in themselves, let them give glory to the Lord, from whom they received it. We are never

allowed to boast, but if we are allowed to give glory, above all we glory in the cross of Christ. But that glorying ought to be different from the desire to boast. Otherwise this glorying would be more serious; it would be boasting in any external thing. Indeed, one becomes hateful to God, when one is pleasing to oneself. Therefore, Paul does well to add "giving glory in the Lord." Moreover, a mode of evading the wrath of God is shown here; for those who are like that, even if they are punished by evil people, nevertheless they go in glory with the good, just as it was with Daniel and the others who were led into Babylon. They were wonderfully exalted through the Lord, so that for a long time they were happier among their enemies than when they were living at home. Among mercy, judgment, and righteousness, they wanted this to be the distinction.

Mercy has no regard for merits; so we pray to be preserved regardless of merit, through the mercy of God alone, knowing that in his sight we are not able to endure with our own works. Therefrom we learn the example of our heavenly father, who made his sun to rise over the good and the evil, so that we might be prepared to benefit in every way regardless of any consideration. Judgment frees the burdened from the lies of others, punishing the impious and the guilty. As it says in the Psalm, "O Lord, give judgment to the king, that he might free the poor man from the mighty." This power is divine, and it is not entrusted to all, but to prelates and princes, for whom it is right to aid the poor and the oppressed regardless of personal status.... Thus knowledge of God would be in place of wisdom, strength, and riches. In this way we may be wise, strong, and wealthy. COMMENTARY ON JEREMIAH 9:23-24.[23]

GLORY AND BOAST ONLY IN THE LORD. KATHARINA SCHÜTZ ZELL: They say pride makes me so set on remaining in my own ideas and understanding and unwilling to be taught by someone else. God knows that this is a blind and

---

[22]Bugenhagen, *In Ieremiam*, 2S1r, 2S2r; citing Ps 46:1; 44:6; Deut 6:16; Mt 4:7; Lk 12:19.

[23]Oecolampadius, *In Hieremiam*, 1:O1r- O2r; citing Mt 6:17; 2 Cor 10:17; Mt 5:45; Ps 72:1-2.

presumptuous judgment! My pride, glory, and boast is in only in my Lord Jesus Christ, as the prophet says, "The one who wants to glory, let him glory in the Lord." I have always listened in my heart to the saying of God: "Hear, O Israel; in yourself is destruction, but in me is your salvation." And again, "The one who wants to be taught must be taught by God (not by himself)"; and St. Paul says, "No one is wise of himself"; and the dear James says, "The one who wants wisdom, let him ask it of God." That I have done from my youth on.

From my youth on I have zealously sought and prayed for God's wisdom, which he has also given to me. From a child in my dear father's house onward he laid the foundation stone in my heart to despise the world and exercise myself in his religion. That I did under the papacy with great earnestness. In that time of ignorance I very zealously, with great pain of body and anxiety of heart, sought out so many clergy and God-fearing people to experience the way to heaven; about that I will say no more. How very wonderfully the Lord led me then! And afterward he did not leave me in my distress. He sent to me, and to many poor and afflicted consciences, the dear and (I hope) now blessed Martin Luther, who showed me my error and pointed me to Christ, in whom I would find rest. Then God opened my understanding to comprehend the holy Scriptures, which I had previously read as a closed book and had not understood; then the Lamb opened the book of the seven seals and took away my lack of understanding and gave comfort in my heart. So it happened to me as to one lost and benighted in a wild forest where many murderers lived: God sent that person an angel who led him out of the forest and showed him the right path. So I have not (as these relate) chosen my own ideas, but I have let the will of God be more pleasing to me than my own. God has sent his Holy Spirit in my heart and allowed the messengers he has sent to teach me with outward writings and words so that the longer the time the more I have come to the knowledge of Christ. I have not been passive and lazy in that but have sought out, loved, and listened

to you and others of God's learned ones and never closed my heart to anyone's teaching or exhortation. TO CASPAR SCHWENCKFELD.[24]

IN WHAT SHALL WE BOAST? MARTIN LUTHER: "For then I will remove from your midst your proudly exultant ones." It as if he were saying, "Up to now you have always been charged with having had false teachers with impure speech, officials with itching ears. The prophets always blamed you because of 'your proudly exultant ones,' that is, those who kept boasting of the righteousness of the flesh and of their works. But these I will remove from your midst. You see, I teach something different—that people must despair completely of their strength, their wisdom, and the righteousness of the flesh; that all people are guilty of damnation; that there is nothing in which the flesh can boast of itself, as the apostle says in Romans 3, 'Then what becomes of our boasting? It is excluded,' etc. Also, 'That every mouth be shut and the whole world become accountable to God,' so that 'whoever glories, let him glory in the Lord.'" LECTURE ON ZEPHANIAH 3:11.[25]

THE SOURCE OF OUR RIGHTEOUSNESS. MARTIN LUTHER: It is said in Jeremiah 9, "Let him who glories, glory in this, that he understands and knows me." Therefore this knowledge is the formal and substantial righteousness of Christians, that is, faith in Christ, which I obtain through the Word. The Word I receive through the intellect, but to assent to that Word is the work of the Holy Spirit. It is not the work of reason, which always seeks its own kind of righteousness. The Word, however, sets forth another righteousness through the consideration and the promises of Scripture, which cause this faith to be accounted for as righteousness. This is our glory to know for certain that our righteousness is divine in God and does not impute our sins. Therefore our righteousness is nothing else

---

[24]Zell, *Church Mother*, 206-7*; citing 1 Cor 1:31; Deut 6:4; Hos 13:9; Is 54:13; Rom 12:16; Jas 1:5; 1 Pet 2:6; Mt 11:29; Rev 5:1, 8-9.
[25]LW 18:357-58 (WA 13:505); citing Zeph 3:11; Rom 3:27; 3:19; 1 Cor 1:31.

than knowing God. Let the Christian who has been persuaded by these words cling firmly to them, and let them not be deceived by any pretense of works or by their own suffering, but rather let them say, "It is written that the knowledge of God is our righteousness, and therefore no monk, no celibate, etc., is justified." LECTURE ON ISAIAH 53:11.[26]

GLORY IN GOD'S MERCY, JUSTICE, AND JUDGMENT. JOHN CALVIN: With experience as our teacher we find God just as he declares himself in his Word. In Jeremiah, where God declares in what character he would have us know him, he puts forward a less full description but one plainly amounting to the same thing. "Let him who glories, glory in this," he says, "that he knows that I am the Lord who exercise mercy, judgment, and justice in the earth." Certainly these three things are especially necessary for us to know: mercy on which alone the salvation of us all rests; judgment, which is daily exercised against wrongdoers, and in even greater severity awaits them their everlasting ruin; justice, whereby believers are preserved, and most tenderly nourished. When these are understood, the prophecy witnesses that you have abundant reason to glory in God. Yet neither his truth, nor power, nor holiness, nor goodness is thus overlooked. For how could we have the requisite knowledge of his justice, mercy, and judgment unless that knowledge rested on his unbending truth? And without understanding his power, how could we believe that he rules the earth in judgment and justice? But whence comes his mercy save from his goodness? . . .

Indeed, the knowledge of God set forth for us in Scripture is destined for the very same goal as the knowledge whose imprint shines in his creatures, in that it invites us first to fear God, then to trust in him. By this we can learn to worship him both with perfect innocence of life and with unfeigned obedience, then to depend wholly on his goodness. INSTITUTES OF THE CHRISTIAN RELIGION.[27]

CIRCUMCISED IN THE FLESH ALONE. KONRAD PELLIKAN: "Before long I will visit and punish everyone circumcised in the flesh, whether Jew, Egyptian, Edomite, or a Saracen, Ammonite, or Moabite." It is likely true that all the descendants, both of Abraham and of Lot, wanted to be pleasing to the Lord in circumcision, however much they lived in sin and did not abhor idols. I will punish them all along with the rest of the uncircumcised and those who have a foreskin throughout the whole world. Indeed, before me they are considered equal to the uncircumcised, because it is not so much the foreskin of the flesh as the hardness of the heart and eagerness of the heart and soul to do shameful things that I pursue with hatred and shall avenge. Moreover, the houses of Israel, however much they are free to pursue their pleasure after the foreskin is cut off, lean on and are attached to an idolatry that is most hateful to me. I wanted them to be chaste, godly, fair, and fully righteous in the worship of the one true God. COMMENTARY ON JEREMIAH 9:25-26.[28]

---

[26]LW 17: 230 (WA 31.2: 439-440); citing Jer 9:24.

[27]Calvin, *Institutes* 1.10.2; citing 1 Cor 1:31.
[28]Pellikan, *Commentaria Bibliorum*, 3:2Q5v.

JEREMIAH 10:1-25
IDOLS AND THE LIVING GOD

¹Hear the word that the LORD speaks to you, O house of Israel. ²Thus says the LORD:

"Learn not the way of the nations,
  nor be dismayed at the signs of the heavens
  because the nations are dismayed at them,
³for the customs of the peoples are vanity.[a]
A tree from the forest is cut down
  and worked with an axe by the hands of a
    craftsman.
⁴They decorate it with silver and gold;
  they fasten it with hammer and nails
  so that it cannot move.
⁵Their idols[b] are like scarecrows in a
    cucumber field,
  and they cannot speak;
they have to be carried,
  for they cannot walk.
Do not be afraid of them,
  for they cannot do evil,
  neither is it in them to do good."

⁶There is none like you, O LORD;
  you are great, and your name is great in might.
⁷Who would not fear you, O King of the nations?
  For this is your due;
for among all the wise ones of the nations
  and in all their kingdoms
  there is none like you.
⁸They are both stupid and foolish;
  the instruction of idols is but wood!
⁹Beaten silver is brought from Tarshish,
  and gold from Uphaz.
They are the work of the craftsman and of the
    hands of the goldsmith;
  their clothing is violet and purple;
  they are all the work of skilled men.
¹⁰But the LORD is the true God;
  he is the living God and the everlasting King.
At his wrath the earth quakes,
  and the nations cannot endure his indignation.

¹¹Thus shall you say to them: "The gods who did not make the heavens and the earth shall perish from the earth and from under the heavens."[c]

¹²It is he who made the earth by his power,
  who established the world by his wisdom,
  and by his understanding stretched out the
    heavens.
¹³When he utters his voice, there is a tumult of
    waters in the heavens,
  and he makes the mist rise from the ends of
    the earth.
He makes lightning for the rain,
  and he brings forth the wind from his
    storehouses.
¹⁴Every man is stupid and without knowledge;
  every goldsmith is put to shame by his idols,
for his images are false,
  and there is no breath in them.
¹⁵They are worthless, a work of delusion;
  at the time of their punishment they shall
    perish.
¹⁶Not like these is he who is the portion of
    Jacob,
  for he is the one who formed all things,
and Israel is the tribe of his inheritance;
  the LORD of hosts is his name.

¹⁷Gather up your bundle from the ground,
  O you who dwell under siege!
¹⁸For thus says the LORD:
"Behold, I am slinging out the inhabitants of
    the land
  at this time,
and I will bring distress on them,
  that they may feel it."
¹⁹Woe is me because of my hurt!
  My wound is grievous.
But I said, "Truly this is an affliction,
  and I must bear it."
²⁰My tent is destroyed,

and all my cords are broken;
my children have gone from me,
    and they are not;
there is no one to spread my tent again
    and to set up my curtains.
²¹For the shepherds are stupid
    and do not inquire of the LORD;
therefore they have not prospered,
    and all their flock is scattered.

²²A voice, a rumor! Behold, it comes!—
    a great commotion out of the north country
to make the cities of Judah a desolation,
    a lair of jackals.

²³I know, O LORD, that the way of man is not
        in himself,
    that it is not in man who walks to direct
        his steps.
²⁴Correct me, O LORD, but in justice;
    not in your anger, lest you bring me to nothing.

²⁵Pour out your wrath on the nations that
        know you not,
    and on the peoples that call not on your name,
for they have devoured Jacob;
    they have devoured him and consumed him,
    and have laid waste his habitation.

a Or *vapor*, or *mist*   b Hebrew *They*   c This verse is in Aramaic

---

OVERVIEW: Rooting out idolatry, both overt and hidden, was a central concern of the Reformation. In response to Jeremiah 10 commentators consider the sort of idolatry encountered in devotion to images of foreign gods, the power of nature, the stars of heaven, the wielding of political power, and excessive trust in human knowledge. The allure of Babylonian pomp and prowess had tempted the ancient exiled Jews to adopt new deities and practices, just as unfaithful rulers would mislead their subjects in sixteenth-century Europe. Most troublesome of all, idolatry was on open display when veneration of the saints or superstitious devotion to the elements of the Mass replaced a true reverence fitting for God alone. Indeed, every believer—even Jeremiah himself—had to be on guard against false worship and humbly seek divine correction.

10:1-10 The Foolishness of Idolatry

THE GOD BEHIND ALL THINGS. JOHANNES BUGENHAGEN: Beginning in this chapter there now follows some new sermons, in which the prophet faithfully teaches the people concerning the commands of the first table of the Ten Commandments. In this way he might deliver

some from the wiles of the devil, so that they might learn to understand about God, either in their own land, or afterward when they had been taken off into captivity—as happened with illustrious men who were abducted such as Hananiah, Azariah, Mishael,[†] Daniel, and Ezekiel, etc. In the meantime while Jeremiah does these things, he does not fail to remember the principal cause for which God himself had summoned him. Thus, he would be the prophet of the captivity in Babylon, as you will see. COMMENTARY ON JEREMIAH 10.[1]

FEAR GOD, NOT THE STARS. JOHN CALVIN: The prophet forbids God's children "to fear the stars and signs of heaven," as unbelievers commonly do. Surely he does not condemn every sort of fear. But when unbelievers transfer the government of the universe from God to the stars, they fancy that their bliss or their misery depends upon the decrees and indications of the stars, not upon God's will; so it comes about that their fear is transferred from him, toward whom alone they ought to direct it, to stars and comets. Let him, therefore, who would beware of this infidelity ever remember that there is no erratic power, or

---

[1]Bugenhagen, *In Ieremiam*, 2T iv. †The Jewish names of Shadrach, Meshach, and Abednego (Dan 1:6-7).

action, or motion in creatures, but that they are governed by God's secret plan in such a way that nothing happens except what is knowingly and willingly decreed by him. INSTITUTES OF THE CHRISTIAN RELIGION.[2]

CHRISTIANS ARE NOT BOUND TO THE RULE OF HEAVEN. JOHANNES BUGENHAGEN: "Signs in heaven." There are truly signs, and they portend something without a doubt; particularly those that appear contrary to custom, as Christ predicts: "There will be signs in the sun and moon and stars," etc. But the pious who are under the care and hand of God the Father do not need to fear; for God, as the Psalms sing, "feeds them in famine, preserves them in war, frees them in death, saves them in sin, glorifies them in disgrace." These signs of heaven may signify wicked things and divine threats. They will not destroy me because God the Creator of signs is my Father, and he preserves me even in the infernal regions. He alone I ought to fear, not the signs of heaven.

Meanwhile I will ask for the clemency of the high Father, so that he might turn evil things away from us, which justly threaten us in signs. For God is free and not tied to signs, and he is able to bring things about even to this extent: that even the sun, the greatest of signs, might stand still, as in the time of Joshua, or go backward, as in the time of Ezekiel, contrary to its nature and the force of its own path. This prophet Jeremiah forbids heathen and superstitious observances of signs. When a Christian ignores and neglects such things, he gives honor to God according to his Word, no matter what will come in hand on account of his vocation. Though the Christian does not expect better times, nevertheless they pray meanwhile that their sacrifice might be accepted by the Lord. The Christian is not bound to the rule of heaven, and yet foolish people today suppose it is the highest piety to be bound to the rules of monks. COMMENTARY ON JEREMIAH 10:2.[3]

ORDINARY AND EXTRAORDINARY SIGNS. THE ENGLISH ANNOTATIONS: As if the event of things or the issue of your affairs depended upon those fond stargazers who bear people in hand and take upon themselves thereby to determine and foretell what good or bad successes people's designs should have. Nevertheless, there are two sorts of signs. First, natural and ordinary [signs], [which are] the stars themselves being set in the sky to distinguish the times and seasons of the year, to which may be added the conjunctions of them with one another, or oppositions of them one to another, where the eclipses of some of them at some time do proceed. These are those signs, which, coming in a constant course and continued tenor (in regard whereof people skillful therein are able either going backward, to tell how it has been with them for thousands of years past, or looking forward, how it will be for as many, if the world itself should so long continue). God would not have his people be affected or affrighted with, as if in regard of them, or from them, any evil in the success of their affairs could betide them. Other signs are extraordinary, in dreadful apparitions, beside the ordinary course of this creature, by which the Lord does sometimes give notice to his people, of his displeasure and warning of ensuing wrath, and these God does not inhibit his people to be affected with, and taking of them to heart. ANNOTATIONS ON JEREMIAH 10:2.[4]

THE HEAVENS, TRUE AND FALSE WORSHIP. NIKOLAUS SELNECKER: This is a sermon in which Jeremiah will exhort the Jews to true worship, in which they should avoid all idolatry and not engage in heathen worship. But if they do such a thing, they will be wiped out and the land will be destroyed. . . . The first teaching in the chapter is the difference between the right and true church—the people or congregation of God—and the other heathens or sects, which are full of superstition. The latter honor foreign gods, who can neither see nor hear; they pray to stones

---

[2]Calvin, *Institutes* 1.16.3.
[3]Bugenhagen, *In Ieremiam*, 2T3r; citing Lk 21:25, 12:5; Josh 10:12-14; Is 38:8.

[4]Downame, ed., *Annotations*, 9H4v*; citing Is 47:12-13; Joel 2:30-31; Lk 21:11, 25.

and wooden images, call on dead saints or other dead people, and create their own gods. They depend more on creatures than on God, who created everything. They tremble before signs in heaven—if they are truly signs and have meaning—whenever they do not appear according to their natural movements or natural order, as are the great conjunctions of the planets and the eclipses of the sun and moon. Christ preached about this in Luke 21: "There will be signs in the sun and the moon and the stars"; these will signify and point to the assurance of God's wrath and future punishment. But as we have had and seen so many signs in the heavens this year, they certainly seem to have become common. There are people who were nearly damaged and devastated who do not want to observe anymore. Yet what a great misfortune the hard weather has been for us; but it will come when it wills. If one so speaks, I say that they are signs that should not terrify the God-fearing person or cause one to fear as in heathen wisdom. Now it should proceed as it is in the church of God. Otherwise, it would be as if God is no longer our true Father, to whom we are to return. Also he can preserve, provide, protect, and defend in relation to all natural means. Then when we fear God, we should not regard the signs of heaven, but should regard the godless and unrepentant and their punishment and the rod proclaimed to them so that they do not return to God in time. THE WHOLE PROPHET JEREMIAH 10:1-5.[5]

THE ONE GOD WHO STANDS ALONE. HEINRICH BULLINGER: To those on the opposite side, Jeremiah objects that the majesty of God is very great. This objection has another part, even several parts. In general he says (1) "There is no one like you, Lord." That is, there is no one and no thing in the whole universe that can be compared to you. You are greater than all things that have been made. (2) You are great. Indeed, he is immense, eternal, and omnipotent. (3) The name of God is great in power; truly he reveals this with his great deeds and immense strength. (4) He is King of the nations. Surely, he is the Lord of all peoples. Who therefore does not fear you? These things are completely different from the vanity of the idols. (5) Authority is yours: and all creatures should obey you and be subject to you. (6) And he adds another one: There is no one like you among all the wise people of every nation, and in every nation under the sun. Therefore who would not adore this One alone, worship him alone, and inwardly depend on him alone? To God alone be the glory! SERMON ON JEREMIAH 10:6-7.[6]

GREATER THAN GREAT. JOHN TRAPP: God is Great, Greater, Greatest. [He is] Greatness itself. He is a degree above the superlative. Think the same of his other names and attributes, many of which we have mentioned in this and the following verses, which are therefore highly to be prized and often to be perused. Leonardus Lessius, a little before his death, finished his book concerning the fifty names of Almighty God, often affirming in that little book that he had found more light and spiritual support under those grievous fits of the stone that he suffered than in all his voluminous commentaries on Aquinas and his *Summa*, which he had well-nigh fitted for the press. COMMENTARY ON JEREMIAH 10:6.[7]

MAKING UP A RELIGION. KONRAD PELLIKAN: Kings learn their lack of self-restraint with this effect: they are not embarrassed to labor at so great a folly, and they are not afraid to worship those things that are obviously extremely vacuous, such as the wooden idols themselves. Wherever kings drive out wisdom in the most important and divine matters, in that place the greatest fools are found by the way they honor wood itself, fear it, and address it. They desire to adorn it with silver, thin and finely worked by craftsmen, delivered by

---

[5]Selnecker, *Der gantze Prophet Jeremias*, T4r- V1r; citing Lk 21:25.

[6]Bullinger, *Conciones*, 78v.
[7]Trapp, *A Commentary or Exposition*, 256*; citing Ps 77:13; Job 33:12; Ps 95:3; 145:3. Leonardus Lessius (1554–1623) was a Flemish Jesuit theologian.

dangerous labors and at great expense from remote islands of the sea. Then, with the significant skill of artisans, they cover the wood with the most precious thing of all—gold—likewise delivered from abroad. Not content with these things, they clothe this piece of wood with robes of purple and hyacinth. And this all the wisest people of the nations do, contrary to their reason and true erudition. Yet through reason and erudition they are not ignorant that there is one, greatest, and best Creator of all things. Still they foolishly impose this idolatry on the people and make up a religion, which they themselves pursue even to the point of offending the true God, which was their highest folly. COMMENTARY ON JEREMIAH 10:8-9.[8]

10:11-25 False Gods and the True God

THE ONLY GOD OF HEAVEN AND EARTH.
JOHANNES OECOLAMPADIUS: These idols are emptiness and falsehood, while God is truth. These idols are dead; God is the source of life. Christ said, "I am the way, the truth, and the life." They are weakness; God is strength and the strength of all things, and this strength is so great that the whole world is not able to withstand it. God shakes the earth, admonishing through the prophets, and often they affect the movements of the earth. What philosophers attribute to enclosed air is simply attributed to God in Scripture, who likewise in this way uses the ministry of angels, as we read in Acts, concerning the freeing of Paul and Barnabas. The movement of the earth occurred when the law was given and when Christ was crucified. . . .

This is written in Chaldean so that it might be announced to the Jews, who were carrying on among the Chaldeans in the mixing of the nations. Thereby it teaches that the confusion of idols is hardly to be passed over in silence. And confession is necessary for salvation. Whoever sells themselves before a god, let them perish and be utterly blotted out: since those who lift themselves up over all things, will end up below all things. . . .

Here you have true philosophy and the origin of all things. What is it that a philosopher says, that earth naturally descends to a middle point? This indeed is not to pose a cause. However, Jeremiah clearly says, "He who makes the earth in power," because the earth does not have its foundation except through the will of God on whom it rests rather than on a middle point. In his wisdom God made the world into a habitation that he might gird it with seas, and water it with rivers and springs, so that humans would be able to inhabit it conveniently. He stretched out the heavens, which seems to us like a tabernacle, so that we might live under it. Although it is above and wants to run in its perpetual course from east to west, we do not sufficiently grasp it. There are those of the stars that remain immovably fixed above; there are those that pass by in a uniform way and those that wander as if in an uncertain course. Winds also come to be from vapors lifted from the earth, as with rain. This is what we read in Genesis: "And a mist ascended over the earth and watered all the face of the ground." The wind is said to be in the treasure house of God, because it is not known whence it comes, and where it goes away to; the wind is born when the mists ascend from dryness, and however the rain is made from wetness. Great is this miracle of God, when rain descends with fiery hail and the fire cannot be extinguished. COMMENTARY ON JEREMIAH 10:10-12.[9]

AN ANSWER TO BABYLONIAN IDOLATRY.
SEBASTIAN MÜNSTER: This verse is written in Chaldean, and the Jews who are already living in Babylon are instructed to answer with this verse to the Babylonians who are recommending the worship of idols. They are not to answer in Hebrew, which the Babylonians did not understand, but in Chaldean, their national language. So Jonathan the Chaldean† translates this verse in this way: "This is a transcript of the letter which Jeremiah the Prophet sent to the rest of the Elders,

---

[8]Pellikan, Commentaria Bibliorum, 3:2Q4v.

[9]Oecolampadius, In Hieremiam, 1:O4r-v; citing Jn 14:6; Acts 16:25-40; Gen 2:6.

who were in the captivity in Babylon. 'If those people among whom you are living say to you, 'worship idols, O house of Israel,' you will respond to them in this manner: 'The idols which you worship are without divinity, they are not able to send rain from the heavens, nor are they able to make the earth produce fruit. Therefore, those who worship them will perish and will be destroyed under these very heavens.'" THE TEMPLE OF THE LORD, JEREMIAH 10:11.[10]

STAND FIRM AGAINST THE IDOLATROUS MASS. JOHN KNOX: The question and debate stands as yet neither decided nor resolved: is the Mass God's true service or is it idolatry? In this question and otherwise we, to whom God has revealed his truth, are called as witnesses. When we crouch and kneel, when we beckon and when we bow, and finally when we give and put our presence before that idol, what kind of witness are we? Assuredly we are false witnesses against God and against our neighbor: against God in that we honor an idol with our bodily presence, which is no small insult to his glory in this time of battle. Against our neighbor, for we confirm ignorance in error to the condemnation of both of us. But when we abstain from all fellowship with idolatry, whatever happens then, we bear witness truly and do our duty to God's glory.... Let no one judge that I am more rigorous and severe in requiring that we absent ourselves from all idolatry. . . . No, brethren, I have learned always to be content and keep my affirmation within the bounds of God's Scriptures. And to that shall Jeremiah the prophet witness, when he was writing to those who were either prisoners in Babylon or else that shortly would be prisoners for their offenses. The prophet gives his counsel

and exhortation; he had forbidden them from following the vain religion of that people; for their idols were no gods. At last he says, "You shall say to them, 'the gods that made neither heaven nor earth shall perish from the earth and from under heaven.'" A GODLY LETTER OF WARNING AND ADMONITION.[11]

NATURE ATTESTS TO GOD'S POWER AND BLESSING. KONRAD PELLIKAN: Whatever in heaven and earth is found to be admirable, dreadful, magnificent, and useful is a work of God. Naturally, the sound of thunder and the flow and motion of the waters are stimulated by the command of God. By his command the vapors are lifted in different places from the land and sea, and they collect in the air. He himself directs the lightning strikes in rain showers and leads the winds from their storehouses. The nature, strength, and origin of these things is told by philosophical authors, though not without a great deal of ignorance. Nevertheless, the faithful know that these are the works of their God; for these works they admire, worship, and praise him. They credit to him all the things they have received, which they use and need. They adore his power, goodness, wisdom, and grace. COMMENTARY ON JEREMIAH 10:13.[12]

THE FOLLY OF HUMAN WISDOM. DESIDERIUS ERASMUS: The author of Ecclesiastes wrote in chapter 1: "The number of fools is infinite."[†] When he announces the number to be infinite he does not seem to embrace all mortals; except for the very few people, whom I doubt anyone has happened to see. But the noble Jeremiah confesses this even more fully in chapter 10: "All people," he says, "are made fools by their own wisdom." To God alone he attributed wisdom, leaving folly for all of humanity. And above Jeremiah says, "Let one not glory in one's own wisdom." Why, our excellent Jeremiah, should a person not glory in

---

[10]Münster, *Miqdaš YHWH*, 877. [†]Münster cites the Targum Jonathan, or Targumim to the Prophets, a fourth-century-AD Jewish work of translation and commentary attributed by tradition to Jonathan ben Uzziel, the disciple of the Elder Hillel (first century AD); see Bruce Chilton, "Targum," in *Dictionary of Biblical Interpretation*, ed. John H. Hayes (Nashville: Abingdon, 1999), 2:531-34.

[11]Knox, *Works*, 3:200-201*. [12]Pellikan, *Commentaria Bibliorum*, 3:2Q5r.

their wisdom? Without doubt, he says that a person has no wisdom. But I return to Ecclesiastes. There the author exclaims, "Vanity, vanity, all is vanity." What else do you believe he means . . . except that life is nothing other than a game of folly? THE PRAISE OF FOLLY.[13]

GOD WORKS IN THOSE WHO DESPISE THEIR WILL.

LANCELOT ANDREWES: That God's will may be done in us, we must be possessed with a base conceit of our own will, and have a high and reverent opinion of God's will; we must be persuaded that our own will is blind and childish and perverse, and therefore [as] Solomon says, . . . "Do not lean to your own wisdom." "Everyone is a beast by their knowledge." And to express the fault of humanity's will, Job says that humanity is *tanquam pullus asini*, "like a wild donkey's colt," which of all other beasts is most foolish. But be he never so wise naturally, yet he is but a fool in heavenly things, as St. Paul witnesses. SERMON 11 ON THE LORD'S PRAYER.[14]

THE RULE ABOUT EXCESSIVE KNOWLEDGE.

JOHN DONNE: A person may have too much of a thing: "a full soul will tread honey under its feet." One may take in knowledge until one is ignorant. Let the prophet Jeremiah state the rule: "Every person becomes a fool through knowledge," by being arrogant and excessively valuing one's knowledge. Let Adam be the example of this rule: his eyes were opened by eating the fruit, and he knew so much he was ashamed of it. Let the apostle be the physician, the moderator: let us be wise in self-restraint and not dive into secrets and unrevealed mysteries. There is enough of this doctrine in the fable of Actaeon, who saw more than he should have and thus perished.[†] This is also abundantly expressed in the Oracle of Truth: Uzzah was overly zealous in fulfilling an office that

was not assigned to him and in assisting the ark of the covenant he thereby suffered. SERMON ON PSALM 62:9.[15]

THE INHERITANCE OF ISRAEL.

CORNELIUS À LAPIDE: "The portion of Jacob is not similar to these." That is, God is not similar to idols; God, who is the hereditary portion of Israel. "My portion," says David, "is God in eternity," because, of course, Israel was holding on to God: the worship of God, his friendship, law, and all good things. Again, Israel is the "rod of inheritance," that is the inheritance of God; because God was holding on to this people as they descended from their fathers, like an inheritance of his own through hereditary succession. For indeed, they used to measure and divide their inheritances with rods and cords; thus "rod" and "cord" signify a hereditary portion. . . . That is, the rod or the scepter of the inheritance of God, for God established his kingdom in Israel. COMMENTARY ON PROPHET JEREMIAH 10:16.[16]

COMPELLED TO FACE THE TRUTH.

KONRAD PELLIKAN: "I will hurl those ungodly inhabitants of my land like a sling, and by casting them down I will fling them into a faraway people and into places thus far unknown to them, both so that the words of the prophets will be found to be true and so that the people themselves will not be found in their own land." Some of the Jews, to the extent that they do find it, add these two phrases to the following line, namely, that the rejected Jews discover the tribulations that will compel them to cry out and to say, "Woe is me because of my destruction and because of the grave anguish of my affliction." Now they are compelled to confess their sins: that they refused to hear the admonitions of the prophets and Word of the Lord, that they

---

[13]Erasmus, *Moriae encomium*, 284-85; citing Eccles 1:15; Jer 9:23; Eccles 12:8. [†]Erasmus cites the Vulgate, which varies from modern translations, though this may well summarize the whole first chapter of Ecclesiastes.
[14]Andrewes, *Works*, 5:401*; citing Prov 3:5; Job 11:12; 1 Cor 2:14.

[15]Donne, *Sermons*, 6:307*; citing Prov 27:7; Gen 3:7; Rom 12:3; 2 Sam 6:6-8. [†]Donne refers to the Greek myth of the hunter Actaeon, who accidently came across the goddess Artemis naked. This forbidden view resulted in his death.
[16]À Lapide, *Commentarium Jeremiam*, 71; citing Ps 73:26; 16:5; Num 18:20; Deut 32:8; Ps 74:2; 105:11.

stubbornly believed themselves when they promised that everything was safe. Now indeed, willingly or unwillingly, they experience the severity of the punishment and confess that it turned out justly for them according to their sin, and that they hope that they might be able to endure the wrath of God more patiently. COMMENTARY ON JEREMIAH 10:17-19.[17]

LAMENTATION FOR A DESPERATE, UNFAITHFUL LAND. NIKOLAUS SELNECKER: The other part of this chapter is a lament—heartfelt and painful: "Oh my sorrow and heart's anguish; my people will neither listen nor follow." They remain in their old ways and in their idolatry. They attend to the momentary and not the eternal. They maintain their idolatrous masses and against their conscience they behave unjustly. Oh the misery! What should be done about it? What good is it to hope? What sort of victory can we have against the Turks? What should we do among ourselves for rest, peace, unity, common good, and blessing? Everything is gone. This is my trouble; I must endure it. "I will bear the wrath of the Lord, for I have sinned against him." Pious princes and teachers are for the most part deceased. The shepherds, who are still at hand, have become fools and do not ask about the Lord. Godless authorities and false teachers are not so attentive to the Word, honor of God, or their office when they have enough and things appear great. So it goes over and over, so that we can be described as the leaves that wilt as our sins drive us forward like the wind. "We pine away in our sins." A person will say, see how things are going in Germany today? What is happening? Where are the lords? Where are the teachers? Where is the government? "There lay a great heap of battered corpses without number and one has to fall over their corpses. All about us is this great whoredom that the beautiful and beloved whores have willed; they go about with witchcraft and with their whoring, violence, and idolatry. They have acquired

land and people." God be gracious to us and help us. THE WHOLE PROPHET JEREMIAH 10:19-21.[18]

CHALLENGING THE RULERS WITH JEREMIAH. ARGULA VON GRUMBACH: Do not let what is said about me scandalize you; as far as my own person is concerned, I pay no heed to their persecution. It is a joy to me to be reviled for the sake of the holy gospel. God forgive them, they know not what they do. I pray with all my heart that my God may enlighten them [the princes] and beg you also to pray for them and for all whose hearts are hardened. . . . "The shepherds acted foolishly; they did not seek the Lord, so they understood nothing, and all their flock is destroyed." And Jeremiah: "You have perverted the word of the living God and imposed burdens; and I will give you over to an eternal disgrace that will never be taken away." TO THE HONORABLE, WISE COUNCIL OF THE TOWN INGOLSTADT.[19]

DIVINE AND HUMAN WILLING. BALTHASAR HUBMAIER: Beloved in God: I know and must confess with the prophet Jeremiah that "the way of human beings does not lie in their own power; nor does it lie in the power of humankind to govern their own steps." The human heart undertakes also to do something for itself, but God directs and controls according to his pleasure. For I had always intended to remain alone in my barrel and cave and not at all to creep out into the light, not that I feared the light, but in order that I might remain in peace. But God ordained it differently and has pulled me out against my will to give account to anybody who requests it concerning my faith as it is in me, namely, in the matter of infant baptism and the true baptism in Christ. ON THE CHRISTIAN BAPTISM OF BELIEVERS.[20]

A CHRISTLIKE PROPHET WHO KNOWS HIS SIN. PHILIPP MELANCHTHON: Through their trials true prophets taste the sufferings of Christ,

---

[17]Pellikan, *Commentaria Bibliorum*, 3:2Q5r.

[18]Selnecker, *Der gantze Prophet Jeremias*, V3v-V4r; citing Mic 7:9; Is 64:7; Nahum 3:1-4.
[19]Argula, *A Woman's Voice*, 121; citing Mt 10:32; Lk 23:34; Jer 23:36, 40.
[20]CRR 5:97.

which the attacks on Jeremiah also signify. They know well the wrath of God against sin, how God is provoked to horrible anger by the idolatry of the people and the audacity of hypocrites, who were teaching lies and boasting that they were divinely sent prophets. They see the world's contempt for God on all sides, but they also know their own uncleanness and fear they may be rejected together with the people. Indeed, they are afraid that God's wrath might swallow the entire church without any remnant being saved. So it happened in the flood, in the fiery obliteration of Sodom, the destruction of Egypt, and later in the defeat of the Canaanites. The prophets keep these examples before their eyes, mourning and pleading that the church not be utterly destroyed and themselves with it. Hence the cry in chapter 10: "Correct me, O Lord, but in just measure. . . ."

The prophet's prayer teaches something else that deserves consideration. It is necessary for the church to be chastised, as he says here: "Correct me." He also says, "You chastised me, O Lord, and I took the discipline; I was like a calf untrained." These are not light chastisements but indicate that we are thoroughly rejected and damned by God.

In this trial the church receives consolation and teaches that discipline is imposed so that we may be called back to repentance. It is not the will of God that we perish. For that reason the prophet asks to be corrected in judgment, not in anger, lest he perish utterly. . . .

We ought to keep in mind, therefore, the prophet praying and his prayers, which are filled with teachings about sin, the wrath of God, punishment, and that faith that accepts the remission of sins based on the unwavering promise of a coming savior. THE LESSONS OF JEREMIAH'S PROPHECY.[21]

THE BLESSED CHASTISEMENT OF GOD. JOHN CALVIN: Wherever punishment is for vengeance, here the curse and wrath of God manifest themselves, and these he always withholds from believers. On the other hand, chastisement is a blessing of God and also bears witness to his love, as Scripture teaches.

The Lord chastens his servants sorely, but he does not give them over to death. Therefore, they confess that to be beaten with his rod has been good for them and has furthered their true instruction. Just as we read everywhere that the saints took such punishments with a calm mind, so they have always prayed fervently to escape scourgings of the first sort. "Correct me, O Lord," says Jeremiah, "but in judgment, not in your anger, lest perchance you bring me to nothing. . . ." Moreover, David says, "O Lord Rebuke me not in your anger, nor chasten me in your wrath." INSTITUTES OF THE CHRISTIAN RELIGION.[22]

---

[21]Melanchthon, "Lessons," 65-66; citing Jer 31:18.
[22]Calvin, *Institutes* 3.4.32; citing Job 5:17; Prov 3:11-12; Heb 12:5-6; Ps 118:18; 119:71; Ps 6:1; 38:2.

JEREMIAH 11:1-23
THE BROKEN COVENANT

¹The word that came to Jeremiah from the Lord: ²"Hear the words of this covenant, and speak to the men of Judah and the inhabitants of Jerusalem. ³You shall say to them, Thus says the Lord, the God of Israel: Cursed be the man who does not hear the words of this covenant ⁴that I commanded your fathers when I brought them out of the land of Egypt, from the iron furnace, saying, Listen to my voice, and do all that I command you. So shall you be my people, and I will be your God, ⁵that I may confirm the oath that I swore to your fathers, to give them a land flowing with milk and honey, as at this day." Then I answered, "So be it, Lord."

⁶And the Lord said to me, "Proclaim all these words in the cities of Judah and in the streets of Jerusalem: Hear the words of this covenant and do them. ⁷For I solemnly warned your fathers when I brought them up out of the land of Egypt, warning them persistently, even to this day, saying, Obey my voice. ⁸Yet they did not obey or incline their ear, but everyone walked in the stubbornness of his evil heart. Therefore I brought upon them all the words of this covenant, which I commanded them to do, but they did not."

⁹Again the Lord said to me, "A conspiracy exists among the men of Judah and the inhabitants of Jerusalem. ¹⁰They have turned back to the iniquities of their forefathers, who refused to hear my words. They have gone after other gods to serve them. The house of Israel and the house of Judah have broken my covenant that I made with their fathers. ¹¹Therefore, thus says the Lord, Behold, I am bringing disaster upon them that they cannot escape. Though they cry to me, I will not listen to them. ¹²Then the cities of Judah and the inhabitants of Jerusalem will go and cry to the gods to whom they make offerings, but they cannot save them in the time of their trouble. ¹³For your gods have become as many as your cities, O Judah, and as many as the streets of Jerusalem are the altars you have set up to shame, altars to make offerings to Baal.

¹⁴"Therefore do not pray for this people, or lift up a cry or prayer on their behalf, for I will not listen when they call to me in the time of their trouble. ¹⁵What right has my beloved in my house, when she has done many vile deeds? Can even sacrificial flesh avert your doom? Can you then exult? ¹⁶The Lord once called you 'a green olive tree, beautiful with good fruit.' But with the roar of a great tempest he will set fire to it, and its branches will be consumed. ¹⁷The Lord of hosts, who planted you, has decreed disaster against you, because of the evil that the house of Israel and the house of Judah have done, provoking me to anger by making offerings to Baal."

¹⁸The Lord made it known to me and I knew;
　　then you showed me their deeds.
¹⁹But I was like a gentle lamb
　　led to the slaughter.
I did not know it was against me
　　they devised schemes, saying,
"Let us destroy the tree with its fruit,
　　let us cut him off from the land of the living,
　　that his name be remembered no more."
²⁰But, O Lord of hosts, who judges righteously,
　　who tests the heart and the mind,
let me see your vengeance upon them,
　　for to you have I committed my cause.

²¹Therefore thus says the Lord concerning the men of Anathoth, who seek your life, and say, "Do not prophesy in the name of the Lord, or you will die by our hand"— ²²therefore thus says the Lord of hosts: "Behold, I will punish them. The young men shall die by the sword, their sons and their daughters shall die by famine, ²³and none of them shall be left. For I will bring disaster upon the men of Anathoth, the year of their punishment."

OVERVIEW: The nature of idolatry was an urgent issue for sixteenth- and seventeenth-century commentators and preachers. This sin decisively violated God's covenant relationship with the faithful as laid out in the Old and New Testaments. Idolatry might be variously described as worship of other gods, as the worship of God and other gods together, or as a perversion of the true worship of the one true God. Protestants identified particular religious practices of their time as obviously and sometimes subtly idolatrous. Moreover, the example of Jeremiah underscored that faithful prophets and preachers of every age, who confront the covenant people of God with their false worship and devotion, must be ready to face hostility and persecution. Such difficulty is part and parcel of a calling to the ministry of Reformation prophecy and preaching.

11:1-17 The Dangers of Unfaithfulness

COVENANT—OLD AND NEW TESTAMENT. HULDRYCH ZWINGLI: Whoever wants to be in the covenant of God should so behave according to this covenant. As God in the Old Testament concluded a covenant with his people and meant offerings to be a sign of the covenant, so has God concluded a covenant with us in the New Testament in the blood of Christ, our head, that we might change according to the law of God. This means that we should be renewed daily in right and true innocence and piety. SERMON ON JEREMIAH 11.[1]

A COVENANT GOD AND PEOPLE. JOHANNES BUGENHAGEN: On the basis of the first commandment Jeremiah warns them of the covenant of God, that God agreed on with their fathers, when he led them out of the land of Egypt, namely, that he promised that he himself would be their God and they through this promise or this covenant would be the special people of God. Moses went up on the mountain to God; "The Lord called him from the

mountain and said, 'This you will say to the house of Jacob and you will announce to the sons of Israel; you yourselves have seen what I did to the Egyptians and how I carried you on the wings of eagles and brought you to myself. Therefore, if you will hear my voice and keep my covenant, you will be my own people out of all the peoples. . . .'" God entered into this covenant with them, before he gave to them the Ten Commandments, that they would be a holy people of God through faith in this promise and in the covenant of God and through faith in the mercy of God they would have God. Indeed, what would the commandments of God accomplish among people who do not have God, except damnation? And certainly no people follow the commandments of God and become obedient to God except the people of God, that is, those who believe. COMMENTARY ON JEREMIAH 11:1.[2]

COVENANT AND GOSPEL TOGETHER. NIKOLAUS SELNECKER: Here we see how God brings together the law and the teaching of the holy gospel and wants to have both taught to his people. In that way he would be recognized as the true God, who exercises his right and justice over grace and mercy, and over all those who fear and love him. Concerning this Moses spoke in Exodus 19: "So shall you say to the house of Jacob and to the children of Israel. 'You have seen what I did in Egypt. . . . So you shall be my own possession among all the nations. For the whole earth is mine. You will be a kingdom of priests and a holy nation.'" This is the covenant, in which you should be obedient and true to God through faith in Christ. The same Peter says in 1 Peter: "You are a chosen lineage, a royal priesthood, a holy people of his possession, that you should proclaim the praise of the one who called you from darkness into his wonderful light. . . ."

Jeremiah also recounts the great deeds of God, especially that God led his people from Egypt and also that the ingratitude of the people would be recognized and how much they would be spurred

---

[1]Zwingli, *Predigten*, 200-201.   [2]Bugenhagen, *In Ieremiam*, 3B1r-v; citing 19:3-4; Ex 20:1-26.

to repentance and conversion. The slavery in Egypt he names an iron oven; that is, they were plagued not only in body but also in the conscience religiously; they had little consolation or hope. Because they were rescued from there, they should be even more grateful to God. . . .

Why is the exodus from Egypt considered so often in the Prophets and the Psalms? This is the main reason: we are headed for true eternity. The omnipotent God does such wonderful works in all of our desperate situations. We trust and know that God desires and can help and save us when every human help is at an end. So is the exodus a true type of the redemption accomplished through Jesus Christ, who led us from the house of the enslaved and from prison, and saved us from death, sin, hell, and devil. He has called us and chosen us as his possession. THE WHOLE PROPHET JEREMIAH 11:1-8.[3]

DO NOT ADD TO GOD'S COMMANDS. MENNO SIMONS: All things that they instituted and practiced as holy worship without the command- ment of God, or against it (even though it was said to be done in honor of the living God who had so gloriously led their fathers and them from the land of Egypt), were nothing less than open idolatry, spiritual adultery, infidelity, apostasy, blasphemy, and a lamentable abomination, as we have briefly shown here from the prophetic Scriptures. God is a God who does not need our labors and sacrifices, because he has made all things. Mine, he says, are the cattle on a thousand hills. What then can I offer? He will take no other sacrifices than those alone which are commanded in his holy Word, as Samuel spoke unto Saul, "Behold, to obey is better than sacrifice." The Lord God of Israel spoke through Jeremiah saying, "Obey my voice and do according to all that I have commanded you, so shall you be my people, and I will be your God." WHY I DO NOT CEASE TEACHING AND WRITING.[4]

IDOLATRY AS WORSHIPING GOD IN OUR OWN WAY. MARTIN LUTHER: Since the prophets cry out against idolatry, it is necessary to know the form this idolatry took. In our time, under the papacy, many people are flattering themselves pleasantly, imagining that they themselves are not idolaters, like the children of Israel. This is also why they think disparagingly of the prophets—especially of this part of their message in which they rebuke idola- try—as not being applicable to them. These people are far too pure and holy to commit idolatry, and it would be ridiculous for them to be afraid or terrified because of threats and denunciations against idolatry. But that is the very same thing the people of Israel did. They simply would not believe that they were idolatrous; the threatenings of the prophets therefore had to appear as lies, and the prophets themselves had to be condemned as heretics.

The children of Israel were not such mad saints as to worship mere wood or stone. This was especially true of the kings, princes, priests, and prophets, and yet they were the most idolatrous of all. Their idolatry, however, consisted in letting go of the worship that had been instituted and ordered at Jerusalem—and wherever else God would have it—and of trying to do it better somewhere else. They instituted and established it elsewhere, out of their own notions and opinions, and without God's command. They concocted new forms and persons and times for worship, even though Moses had always forbidden this. . . . This false thinking was their idolatry. Yet they regarded it as a fine and precious thing and relied on it as if they had done it well, though it was outright disobedience and apostasy from God and his commands. PREFACE TO THE PROPHETS.[5]

A CONSPIRACY DURING THE REIGN OF JEHOIAKIM. THE ENGLISH ANNOTATIONS: Because it might be said, what does all of this have to do with those living now if their forefathers in former ages broke covenant with God, and smarted them for the same? God therefore tells the prophet

---

[3]Selnecker, *Der gantze Prophet Jeremias*, X2v-X3r; citing Ex 19:4-6; 1 Peter 2:9; Deut 4:20.
[4]Simons, *Complete Writings*, 296; citing Ps 50:10; 1 Sam 15:22; 2 Cor 6:17.

[5]LW 35:268-69 (WA DB 11.1:7-8).

that the main body of the Jewish people, and those of Jerusalem among the rest, had made a general revolt from him and taken themselves to those idolatrous courses that their forefathers took before them. And hence the Jewish commenters, not without some good probability, gather that this prophecy was delivered in the reign of Jehoiakim, during which time they fell back from God's service and worship which were restored, established, and settled in the days of good Josiah. Annotations on Jeremiah 11:9.[6]

The Prayers God Truly Hears. Johannes Brenz: What does it mean when he says in this passage that he will bring evil upon the people, when nevertheless at other times he calls himself a helper in times of need? And what does it mean when he says he will not hear their prayers, even though he says, "Ask and you shall receive" and "It will happen that before they call out, I will hear them"? I answer: notice that all the promises were made for the faithful or the believers. God will free people from their difficulties, but only the pious. God hears prayers, but only those of the godly, that is, those who believe. The ungodly do not know the God who can free them from their difficulties, but they tremble in his presence as at the sight of the executioner. They cry out, not in faith, but in anguish: just like Esau, who was regretful to the point of tears and sought to repent, but did not achieve it. Annotations on Jeremiah 11:11.[7]

The Wicked Will Not Be Heard. Richard Hooker: Virtue and godliness of life are required at the hands of the minister of God, not only in that he is to teach and instruct the people, who, for the most part, are either led away by the ill example, then directed aright by the wholesome instruction of them, whose life swerves from the rule of their own doctrine, but also much more in regard of this other part of their function, whether we respect

the weakness of the people apt to loath and abhor the sanctuary, when they that perform the service thereof are such as the sons of Eli were; or else consider the inclination of God himself, who requires the lifting up of pure hands in prayer, and has given the world plainly to understand that the wicked, although they cry, shall not be heard. They are no fit supplicants to seek his mercy in behalf of others, whose unrepented sins provoke his just indignation. Lawes of Ecclesiastical Polity.[8]

Everyone Creates Their Own Idol and Their Own God. John Calvin: "Then shall the cities of Judah and inhabitants of Jerusalem, go and cry unto gods. . . ." The prophet . . . shows in these words that they were not touched by a true and sincere feeling of repentance who cried thus indiscriminately to God and to idols.

But another question may be raised: how could they flee to God and to foreign gods too? The ready answer is this, that the unbelieving, in a turbulent state of mind, turn here and there, so that they lay hold of nothing certain or sure and fixed. This we see in the papists—they cry to God and at the same time to a great number of gods. . . . People naturally are led to God when any distress holds them bound; hence they call on God: but afterward, being not satisfied with him alone, they turn to their own devices, and heap together . . . a vast multitude of gods.

"For according to the number of cities were your gods. . . ." There seems, however, to be some inconsistency in the words; for if they all worshiped Baal, where could be found the multitude of gods that the prophet condemns? It then follows that the same form of superstition was present everywhere or that they did not burn incense to Baal in every place. But from this place and others we may gather that this [Baal] was a common name; for though all idols had their distinctive names, yet this name was applied indiscriminately, and all idols had it in common. For what does Baal mean but a patron, or an inferior god, who procured the favor of the supreme God? The

---

[6]Downame, ed., *Annotations*, 9I3v*.

[7]Brenz, *Annotationes in Jeremiam*, 889; citing Mt 7:7; Is 65:24; Gen 27:1-46; Heb 12:16-17.

[8]Hooker, *Lawes of Ecclesiastical Polity*, 5:25*; citing 1 Sam 2:12-15.

prophets often use the word in the plural number, and called the lesser or inferior gods Baalim, who were regarded as mediators or angels. . . .

But what the prophet condemned in the people was, as we see, daily practiced. For there is no end, when people once depart ever so little from the pure worship of the only true God: for when anything is blended with [true worship], one error immediately produces another; so various errors will accumulate until people fall into a labyrinth from which there is no exit. This is clearly seen under the papacy. At first Satan by spurious pretenses led people away from the simple worship of God and his pure doctrine: and as there is in all an inbred curiosity, everyone had a desire to add something of his own. So it has happened that a very great mass of errors and superstitions has prevailed. . . . We hence also learn that all the superstitions among the whole people had the same root; for though they differed in particulars, they all yet proceeded from the same principle; for everyone wished to have their own god. Thus it happened that every city had its patron, and every family devised a god for itself. COMMENTARY ON JEREMIAH 11:12-13.[9]

WHEN GOD DOES NOT HEAR OUR PRAYERS.
JOHN DONNE: Shall any be able to cry to God and not be heard? Yes, to cry, and to cry for their trouble; for all this may be done and yet neither a true prayer be made, nor a right foundation laid when only impatience about affliction extorts, presses, and vents out a cry. God will not hear them. No, nor when people are so unable to pray for themselves, God will not hear any other person pray for them. Three times God reproves the prophet Jeremiah because of his charitable disposition of praying for that people. "Do not lift up a cry or a prayer for them." "Not a cry, by way of reminding me of their pressures and afflictions, as though that should move me. Not a prayer that reminds me of my covenant of mercy toward them, as though that should bind me. . . ." O how contagious and pestilent are the sins of humanity, that thus (if we may so speak) they infect God himself! How violent, how impetuous, how tempestuous are the sins of humanity that can thus (if we may so speak) transport God himself and carry him beyond himself! For he himself is mercy, and yet there is no room for our own prayers, no room for the prayers of others to open any door, any pore of mercy to flow out, or to breathe out upon us.

Truly, beloved, it is hard to conceive how any height of sin in humanity should work in this way upon God, so that God throws humanity away without any intention of taking humanity up again or any possibility of returning to God. But to impute distemper to God, that God would peremptorily hate humanity, thus irreparably destroy humanity, before he considered humanity as a sinner—a manifold sinner and as an obdurate sinner—before he considered humanity as a creature, that first God should mean to damn humanity or mean to make humanity in order to damn humanity: this is to impute to God a more bitter and worse affected nature than falls into any person. Does anyone desire that his enemy would have a son so that he might kill that son? Does anyone give life to a son so that he might disinherit him? Does God hate anyone simply because he will hate them? Deliver me, O Lord from my sins, pardon them, and then return to your first purposes for me; for I am sure they were good, until I was ill. And my illness did not come from you, but I multiplied it all by myself. Thus, you might restrain and bridle me so that I cannot come near to you through any of those ways which you have opened in your church: prayer, preaching, sacraments, absolution; all would be unavailable to me and have no effect on me.

Therefore, as God would have us conserve the dignity of our nature in his image, we should not descend to . . . those two sins, which are the womb and mother of every other—pride and lust (the greatest spiritual and the greatest bodily sin)—because thereby we lose all understanding, which is the matter upon which grace works. SERMON ON PSALM 32:9.[10]

---

[9]CTS 18:91-94* (CO 38:111-13).

[10]Donne, *Sermons*, 9:389-90*; citing Jer 7:16.

PRAYER PROHIBITED. JOHN CALVIN: God prohibits Jeremiah to pray, this was not done for his sake only, but he had a regard also to the whole people, that they might know that a sentence was pronounced on them, and that there was no hope left. We hence see that God positively declares that it was his purpose to destroy the people, and that therefore there was no room for prayer.

But it may be asked, whether the prophet, by going on in praying, offended God? For we shall see that he was still so anxious for the welfare of the people that he ceased not to pray. . . . But we must observe that God, when he thus issues a simple prohibition, often stimulates the prayers of his people . . . as God did not speak for the sake of Jeremiah, but for the people, the prophet is not to be charged with rashness or presumption, or foolish stubbornness or inconsiderate zeal, for having afterward prayed, he knew that this was not so much for his sake as on account of the people.

. . . There is another thing to be observed—that Jeremiah was not forbidden to pray for the remnant, that is, for the elect, and for the seed from which the church was afterward to arise; but he was forbidden to pray for the whole body of the people: and no doubt he felt assured from that time that no remedy could be applied, and that the people would be driven into exile. . . . Jeremiah might still pray for the elect, and also for the new church, that is, for the renewal of the church. COMMENTARY ON JEREMIAH 11:14.[11]

SACRIFICE AND IDOLATRY IN THE TEMPLE. SEBASTIAN MÜNSTER: These words of the prophet are spoken for God. The "house" means the temple of the Lord, in which God was certainly not being worshiped. But the whole of Judea, because so very few feared God, worshiped the idol Baal. And so it follows: "the benefits of the fleshly sacrifices of the sanctuary are passed on to you, but the sense is that the sacrifices and offerings of the temple have been transferred into the cult of idols. And when you did this evil thing, you rejoiced

when rather you ought to be disturbed." Others explain the flesh in terms of humanity, according to which all flesh corrupts their way and now the sense will be that "all holy people must be moved away from you, lest they be contaminated by your evil." THE TEMPLE OF THE LORD, JEREMIAH 11:15.[12]

THE OLIVE TREE—FERTILE AND SEVERED. JOHN MAYER: "The Lord called your name a green Olive Tree." To make their misery more apparent, Jeremiah recounts that the Jews were a green and flourishing olive tree, as in Romans 11. They are set forth as branches of the best olive. In Revelation 11 we read of two witnesses of God called olive trees, which shows that this is a name of those that are most famous and excellent, such as Enoch and Elijah, whom Tertullian calls "the white robbed witnesses of eternity"; they are glorious for their eternity, even in their bodies.[†] Of the olive tree there are many rare properties by which the church is displayed. First, the wood of the tree does not rot over time, either by moisture or worms, which is the emblem of eternity. Second, it is very fruitful; so the just are compared to trees that in their time bear more fruit. Third, the tree produces more oil than any other; Isaiah 5 refers to a fertile soil where the vine was planted and is said to be the child of an olive. Fourth, the leaves of the olive tree never wither, but are always green. . . . Fifth, an olive branch is an emblem of peace; Noah sent out the dove that returned with an olive branch in her mouth. . . . Sixth, the olive tree is a sign of mercy; for that reason Solomon made two cherubim of olive wood and placed them as a cover for the mercy seat. Seventh, the olive tree though very fruitful, has very small and green leaves. . . . So those who are fruitful make no outward show, but are full of mercy and peace, and are green through joy in tribulation and have oil in their lamps until the end. . . .

But in comparison to the beginning of the verse, "The Lord called your name an olive . . . ," the verse further relates that the branches of this olive tree are cut off when the Chaldeans burn the city and

---

[11]CTS 18:96-97* (CO 38:113-14).

[12]Münster, *Miqdaš YHWH*, 879.

the temple with fire, and all the palaces and stately buildings—as if they were branches of the this olive tree. . . . This voice may be understood either as the voice of God calling the Chaldeans to complete this execution . . . or the raucous voice of the Chaldeans, when they destroyed the Jews. COMMENTARY ON JEREMIAH 11:16-17.[13]

11:18-23 The Prophet's Life Threatened

THE PERSECUTION OF PREACHERS. JOHANNES BUGENHAGEN: From this passage all the way to the words of the following chapter, "the Lord says these things against all my worst neighbors, etc." Jeremiah describes his cross and terrors, and certainly the uncommon cost of such a great proclamation for such a great man, so that you may see here that Christ is speaking. "In this way those people who came before you acted toward the prophets." Read also Matthew 10 concerning the cross and the persecution of preachers: "The servant is not greater than his Lord." For even Christ, the lord of all, who prophesied, suffered such things. "But blessed is God, and the father of all consolation," because in such terrors and dangers, even if the devil oppresses us with the temptation of despair, his mercies preserve us in his Word and office so that we are not confident in ourselves, but in God who raises the dead. . . .

In our office through God we learn of the malice of people and of country folk against the preachers of the gospel. . . . How much envy and wickedness is there among the sects and false teachers? We are often compelled to say with the psalm against false brothers, "You truly are of one heart with me, my guide and my familiar one, who together with me used to enjoy sweet foods; we walked together with the throng into the house of God. . . ." Likewise, "He who eats my bread now raises his heel against me." Such is the world. We were ignorant of such things. . . . Against no evil folk is one allowed to exercise malice, as against the professors of the gospel. Thanks be to God, who has not deserted us, but exposes to us the envy and malice of Satan, and preserves us in our office and our confession. COMMENTARY ON JEREMIAH 11:18.[14]

A LIVING SACRIFICE. JOHANNES OECOLAMPADIUS: "I am like a lamb led to slaughter." On no occasion is this fulfilled in the book of Jeremiah; even by the men of Anathoth. However much they meditated on his death, in the end he was killed in Egypt. He who is able to have such patience in other things also has it in persecutions. The prophet knew that he had to live, and for that reason he compared himself to a lamb or ox for sacrifice. For the figure is fulfilled enough in this part, but in truth the thing itself stands in this way: Christ is the lamb, silent like a lamb before the shearer. Jeremiah is not ignorant of what the paschal lamb signifies. As in the Gospel of John, "Behold the Lamb of God, who takes away the sins of the world." Finally, Christ was the last offering and sacrifice for the sins of the world, as in the letter to the Hebrews. COMMENTARY ON JEREMIAH 11:19.[15]

THE DANGERS AND OPPORTUNITIES OF BEING A PROPHET. JOHANN PAPPUS: The latter part of this chapter narrates the danger to the prophet that his own people of Anathoth created. Indeed, since the sermons of our prophet were all laid out in this common argument—that the greatest misfortune menaced Judea—his people secretly deliberated to stop him from spreading this kind of bad news by taking him from their midst. The prophet could neither ignore this situation, nor immediately flee from danger, unless the Lord suggested something in a peculiar revelation.

Instead, the Lord taught him with this example: those who admirably keep a diligent faith in their divinely mandated office will be exposed to a great deal of danger; they are

---

[13]Mayer, *A Commentary*, 370*; citing Rom 11:24; Zech 4:14; Rev 11:4; Ps 92:12-14; Is 5:1-2; Hos 14:6; Gen 8:11; 1 Kings 6:23-28; Mt 25:1-13. †Tertullian, *De anima* 50.

[14]Bugenhagen, *In Ieremiam*, 3D1r-v, 3D2r-v; citing Mt 5:11-12, 10:16-25, 10:24; 2 Cor 1:3-7; Ps. 55:13-14, 41:9.

[15]Oecolampadius, *In Hieremiam*, 1:Q1r; citing Is 53:7; Jn 1:29; Heb 10:1-18.

themselves warned not to despair on account of the whim of the ear of the people, if indeed they are trying to please not humans, but the Lord. Moreover, God teaches this example: the concern the Lord has for pious ministers; for ministers will be marvelously freed from many dangers, which they themselves by their own diligence would not be able to foresee or avoid.

Therefore, we are taught that we must commend our every conflict and situation, in oneness with Jeremiah, to the Lord who, just as he tests our hearts and inner convictions, nevertheless is the righteous vindicator of every injustice. . . . The venerable scholars did not observe this verse according to the proper signification of the Hebrew language, but twist this passage variously. Some apply it to the crucifixion of Christ; so the true bread of life was crucified. Others connect this verse to the Lord's Supper, so that the tree of life is shown to us in that bread of the Eucharist. But these things are all outside the intention of this passage, in which nothing else is signified than the cruel and bloodthirsty spirit of the people of Anathoth, who wanted to destroy the prophet completely. ON ALL THE PROPHETS, JEREMIAH 11:18-23.[16]

PERSECUTED, BUT NOT PERSECUTORS. DIRK PHILIPS: The entire holy Scripture testifies that the righteous must suffer and possess their soul with patience. And that does not miss it, for where a pious Abel is, there is an evil Cain against him. Where a chosen David is, there is a rejected Saul who persecuted him. Where was Christ born, there is a Herod who seeks his life. . . .

Thus the true Christian must be persecuted here for the sake of truth and righteousness, but they persecute no one because of their faith. For Christ sent his disciples as lambs among wolves. But the lamb does not strangle the wolf but the wolf the lamb. Therefore, they can never more exist or be considered a congregation of the Lord who persecute others on account of their faith. . . .

Therefore, it is nothing more than fig leaves woven together to cover their shame that some want to adorn their tyranny with the Scripture, and object that they kill no Christians but heretics, and that God has commanded such through Moses. Yes, the world certainly holds the most pious Christians as the worst of all heretics, just as all good prophets are always considered liars by the world. THE ENCHIRIDION.[17]

---

[16]Pappus, *In Omnes Prophetas*, 83r-v.

[17]CRR 6:374-75; citing Lk 21:17; Gen 4:1-2; 1 Sam 18:1-30; Mt 2:16; 10:16.

JEREMIAH 12:1-17
JEREMIAH'S COMPLAINT
AND THE LORD'S ANSWER

¹Righteous are you, O Lord,
  when I complain to you;
  yet I would plead my case before you.
Why does the way of the wicked prosper?
  Why do all who are treacherous thrive?
²You plant them, and they take root;
  they grow and produce fruit;
you are near in their mouth
  and far from their heart.
³But you, O Lord, know me;
  you see me, and test my heart toward you.
Pull them out like sheep for the slaughter,
  and set them apart for the day of slaughter.
⁴How long will the land mourn
  and the grass of every field wither?
For the evil of those who dwell in it
  the beasts and the birds are swept away,
  because they said, "He will not see our
    latter end."

⁵"If you have raced with men on foot, and they
    have wearied you,
  how will you compete with horses?
And if in a safe land you are so trusting,
  what will you do in the thicket of the Jordan?
⁶For even your brothers and the house of your
    father,
  even they have dealt treacherously with you;
  they are in full cry after you;
do not believe them,
  though they speak friendly words to you."

⁷"I have forsaken my house;
  I have abandoned my heritage;
I have given the beloved of my soul
  into the hands of her enemies.
⁸My heritage has become to me
  like a lion in the forest;

she has lifted up her voice against me;
  therefore I hate her.
⁹Is my heritage to me like a hyena's lair?
  Are the birds of prey against her all around?
Go, assemble all the wild beasts;
  bring them to devour.
¹⁰Many shepherds have destroyed my vineyard;
  they have trampled down my portion;
they have made my pleasant portion
  a desolate wilderness.
¹¹They have made it a desolation;
  desolate, it mourns to me.
The whole land is made desolate,
  but no man lays it to heart.
¹²Upon all the bare heights in the desert
  destroyers have come,
for the sword of the Lord devours
  from one end of the land to the other;
  no flesh has peace.
¹³They have sown wheat and have reaped thorns;
  they have tired themselves out but profit
    nothing.
They shall be ashamed of their[a] harvests
  because of the fierce anger of the Lord."

¹⁴Thus says the Lord concerning all my evil neighbors who touch the heritage that I have given my people Israel to inherit: "Behold, I will pluck them up from their land, and I will pluck up the house of Judah from among them. ¹⁵And after I have plucked them up, I will again have compassion on them, and I will bring them again each to his heritage and each to his land. ¹⁶And it shall come to pass, if they will diligently learn the ways of my people, to swear by my name, 'As the Lord lives,' even as they taught my people to swear by Baal, then they shall be built up in the midst of my people. ¹⁷But if any nation will not listen, then I will utterly pluck it up and destroy it, declares the Lord."

a Hebrew *your*

OVERVIEW: Jeremiah's frustrations, experiences, and prophecies would serve to guide the pastors and preachers of the sixteenth and seventeenth centuries. Like Jeremiah, those who took up the proclamation of the Word of God would not be able to assume prosperity and praise in return. Rather, preachers would be more likely to persevere in their calling when they understood why the wicked continue to resist the Word and to flourish even as the Word goes forth.

Moreover, reformers should anticipate opposition at home from family and friends even as they might be called on to testify in the courts of the powerful. Faithfulness to the truth would require suffering. Yet pastors and preachers would also need to guard their own hearts and monitor their temporal goods: to be diligent and humble stewards of the resources given to them, lest they be accused of fleecing the flock of their tithes. Under these conditions a reformed clergy would face considerable challenges: to be wise readers of the harsh and hostile world in which they ministered, humble servants who carefully avoided the worldly temptations of ministry, and stalwart preachers of divine judgment for the wicked and glorious hope for the faithful. Jeremiah would be their model of steadfast ministry and rugged confidence in God's enduring and sustaining grace.

12:1-4 Jeremiah Complains

THE SCANDAL OF THE WICKED WHO FLOURISH. JOHANNES BUGENHAGEN: First . . . Jeremiah describes that scandal, by which even the godly meet with temptation; because the ungodly do well, while they have contempt for and hate the truth; for the impious are boastful as in chapter 7 above: "Nothing evil happened to us even after we did these abominations." And from Malachi: "Whoever does evil pleases the Lord and the Lord delights in such things, or to be sure where is the God who avenges?" Habakkuk suffers this scandal in chapter 1: "Why do you watch those who despise you and you are silent, when the wicked man devours one who is more just than himself?" These things are also much discussed in Job. COMMENTARY ON JEREMIAH 12:1.[1]

THE LIVING DEAD. JOHANNES OECOLAMPADIUS: Why does the way of the wicked prosper? He does not say "life," but "way." Indeed, these people are the living dead. How well, he says, do the wicked succeed who are unworthy of this life? He is not, however, speaking of the nations, but concerning the wicked people of Anathoth, and of hypocrites and antichrists, who walk among us but are not of us. Those folk have an abundance of riches, honors, luxuries, friends, strength upon strength, beauty, and every blessing of this life; meanwhile good and just people are oppressed. The prophets and apostles understand this. All sinners do well, who fawn upon princes, who favor the very same superstition. But if one would want to proclaim the truth rightly, they will certainly find themselves many adversaries. COMMENTARY ON JEREMIAH 12:1.[2]

WHERE IS GOD'S PROVIDENCE WHEN THE WICKED PROSPER? KONRAD PELLIKAN: Your providence seems to have planted those who are ungodly in the most fertile fields, where everything grows and advances more favorably. Moreover, their roots seem to have extended and hold fast in a state of prosperity, so that they cannot be pulled up easily. Their fruit also seems to increase in a multitude of offshoots, which grow among familiar things and continually reproduce themselves among the proud and ungodly. Meanwhile, they seek whatever immediately succeeds, even if their vows are displeasing to you. They undertake nothing for you, and dwell in the evil councils of their hearts. An account of your providence is nothing among them. COMMENTARY ON JEREMIAH 12:2.[3]

TEMPORAL HONORS AND ETERNAL JUDGMENT. HULDRYCH ZWINGLI: "But you, O Lord, know me." Whenever the godless are not punished here and brought to disgrace, then we are not allowed to see

---

[1]Bugenhagen, *In Ieremiam*, 3D4v; citing Jer 7:10; Mal 2:17; Hab 1:13.
[2]Oecolampadius, *In Hieremiam*, 1:Q2v.
[3]Pellikan, *Commentaria Bibliorum*, 3:2R1r.

it happen here on earth. There is certainly a judgment that God reaches here on earth, but it is a small one over against eternal judgment. It is a small judgment and disgrace when this only happens for awhile here before the world and likewise a small honor when one is honored here. Far more fearsome is the judgment when someone is disgraced before the angels and the whole world. And what an honor it is to come before the world to be honored. Should not a person here below gladly suffer all concerning God's will and justice, so that one comes to honor in eternity and becomes a friend of all the angels and citizens of the kingdom of heaven? Sermon on Jeremiah 12:3.[4]

God Is a Great Cook. Martin Luther: How it vexed the prophet to see the ungodly Chaldeans have such good fortune and rejoice over it, while all other countries and nations weep and mourn! They are happy and suppose that they had done the right thing. Lo, how this victory and good fortune tickles them! They are jubilant, but they do not know that God is thereby fattening them for the slaughter. All of this is written also for our sake. Such and similar examples should comfort us when we, too, behold the wicked faring so well and when they boast and rejoice over us in our misery. Then our one thought must be that they are cattle fattened for the slaughter. For fattened cattle are not raised for anyone's amusement nor to serve any other purpose than to be slaughtered for the kitchen. But the animals that are raised for human amusement or for other purposes are kept lean and slender. God is a great cook. He also maintains a large kitchen: therefore he fattens them well, giving them a greater abundance of goods, honor, pleasure, and power than he does all others. He lets them exult and dance even on the necks and bodies of his children. That is how Herod's daughter danced for St. John, and that is the way the world exulted when the apostles sorrowed, as Christ says. . . . Thus this tickled the king of Babylon and his people uncommonly, especially when he defeated the Jews, who

were reputed to be invincible because of their God. Lectures on Habakkuk 1:15.[5]

The Unfaithful Mock God's Prophet. Nikolaus Selnecker: This is a lament about how everything is flattened, withered, ruined, exhausted, and deserted. . . . It is miserable, when a poor growing season, a rise in prices, and a great hunger sets in; the poor people are desperate for food and drink, and they die because of hunger. Jeremiah speaks: this is a punishment of God, which comes to people who pursue malice, despise the Word of God, and do not want to follow their true preachers, but spurn them. When they are warned, they ridicule Jeremiah and say, "Yes, he knows well how it is going for us. How does this one know what God has for us—if he will punish or not? Who ordered him to tell us? Away with such a prophet! He is nothing to us." The Whole Prophet Jeremiah 12:4.[6]

12:5-17 The Lord Replies

Running with Horses. Johannes Oecolampadius: "If you run with footmen," God responds to the prophet: why are you even more eager to learn secret things, when you are not able to comprehend human and earthly things? Behold, you were not able through yourself to inquire into the knowledge and counsel of people—people who are like you. How, therefore, are you able to search carefully through divine things? You were not aware that your citizens were planning to mix lethal drinks for you: by what means will you investigate the method for governing this world, my universe?

Therefore let not the secrets of these works of God worry you, such as why for the most part the impious do well and the pious poorly. Consider weak people. You were not able to compete in the race with runners, how will you join in with running horses? This sentiment is hardly absurd, if you continue from first things. At the same time it

---

[4]Zwingli, Predigten, 204.

[5]LW 19:185 (WA 19:383); citing Mt 14:6; Jn 16:20.
[6]Selnecker, Der gantze Prophet Jeremias, Z1v-Z2r.

incites you in so many words toward acting simply in the Lord. For nothing is safe, if you apply the following things that the prophet was about to discover: when he discovered that his most grave enemies were among his household and close neighbors, who were equal in custom and condition. For a long time the urbane insolence both of the king and of the princes will grievously bear upon you; for this reason you will look to me alone.

There are those interpreters who think that these words condemn the confidence of the prophet. "When living with the people of Anathoth, you seemed to have a weak and despairing soul, as the footmen judged it. How, therefore, will you run in Jerusalem with the powerful, who are like horses? And those who do not resist flesh and blood, how will they withstand enemy princes? Indeed, another parable says this very thing. You were hoping that you would find peace in Anathoth, where you ought not to have expected hate among honest people and friends. What therefore will it be like in Jerusalem, where there are people so arrogant and those who are inflated like the Jordan River? COMMENTARY ON JEREMIAH 12:5.[7]

COMMON AND POWERFUL ENEMIES OF THE WORD. JOHANNES BUGENHAGEN: "If with footmen." This expression is allegorical. God calls the people of Anathoth "footmen," as humble folk or inferiors. He calls the people of Jerusalem, however, "the horsemen," as the more powerful. So he repeats this again, when he calls Anathoth the land of peace, that is, friendly, which ought to love Jeremiah as its citizen, because it is customary for a homeland to be a refuge and asylum for its own. Jerusalem, however, he calls the pride of the Jordan, for the Jordan is a river in the land of the Jews, which nevertheless does not extend to Jerusalem, as . . . at the end of Deuteronomy, whence the whole land of the Jews is called here "of Jordan." The pride of this Jordan or Jewish homeland is Jerusalem, because it is the greatest, most formidable, powerful, and beautiful city in which both the royal seat and the temple exist,

whence it is also called the Holy City, sanctified by preaching, holy things, and the worship of God. Even Virgil on account of power, fortifications, and beauty said, "Proud Troy has fallen."[†]

Therefore, God here responds to the prophet who is suffering a trial. "If you are afraid among your fellow rustic citizens, who seem to be friends in your homeland, you will be much more afraid among the rulers and priests of Jerusalem, who will have less patience with your preaching. Thus do not fear. I am with you. Only do not believe them— even your brothers—even when they say good things to you. In these present dangers it is profitable to know the enemy. Matthew 10: I send you as sheep among wolves. . . . Beware of those people," etc. As Micah 7 says, "No one believes their neighbor. No one trusts their leaders. Guard the opening of your mouth from the one who sleeps in your bosom. Indeed, the son despises the father; the daughter rejects the mother; the daughter-in-law resists the father-in-law. The enemies of a person are those of his own house." If you adhere to the Word of God, the world will consider you with hatred, even those most intimately joined to you, who hate the word. COMMENTARY ON JEREMIAH 12:5.[8]

HOW WILL YOU WITHSTAND PERSECUTION? JOHN TRAPP: These are proverbial speeches, both of which serve one purpose: Can you bear the small things in order to bear the serious ones? How would you endure wounds for Christ, if you cannot endure words? Says one, "And how will you fry a faggot that startles at a reproach for the truth?" While William Cobberly, [a] martyr [who] was under duress, along with his wife, called Alice, being apprehended, was detained in the keeper's house. Meanwhile the keeper's wife had secretly heated a key fire-hot and laid it in the grass on the back side, so when speaking to Alice Cobberly to fetch her the key in all haste, she went with speed to bring the key, and taking it up in haste, did piteously burn her

[7]Oecolampadius, *In Hieremiam*, 1:Q3r-v.

[8]Bugenhagen, *In Ieremiam*, 3E1v -3E2r; citing Deut 27:1-13; Mt 10:16-17; Mic 7:5-6. [†]Virgil, *Aeneid* 2.3.1-8.

hand, whereupon she cried out . . . , to which the other replied, if you cannot abide the burning of your hand, how will you be able to abide the burning of your whole body? And so she afterward revoked. COMMENTARY ON JEREMIAH 12:5.[9]

COMMON AND UNCOMMON TRIALS. ST. JOHN OF THE CROSS: There are many who desire to advance and persistently beseech God to bring them to this state of perfection. Yet when God wills to conduct them through the initial trials and mortifications, as is necessary, they are unwilling to suffer them and they shun them, flee from the narrow road of life and seek the broad road of their own consolation, which is that of their own perdition. . . . They hardly even begin to walk along this road by submitting . . . to ordinary sufferings.

We can answer them with Jeremiah's words: "If you have grown weary running with footmen. . . ." This is like saying: If by the common trials (on foot) that form part of human life, it seemed to you that you were running because there were so many, and you took such short steps, how will you keep up with the horse's stride, which signifies more than ordinary trials for which human strength and speed is not enough? THE LIVING FLAME OF LOVE.[10]

THE RAGE OF FRIENDS AND RELATIVES. JOHN CALVIN: The prophet no doubt was commanded to preach and write in God's name; and yet he had regard to the people, who would have hardened themselves against his preaching, had he not more fully set forth the dreadful judgment of God. Hence he says, "Surely even your brethren and the house of your father. . . ." [This is] an amplification, when he says that not only the citizens of Jerusalem and the whole people had conspired against the prophet but also his own relations and friends. . . . We see how emphatically God speaks; and there is an implied comparison between the citizens of Anathoth and the rest of the Jews, for they did not

deal with a brother and one of themselves with any more courtesy than those not related to them. . . . "And these [folk] have cried after you." . . . To cry after one is an evidence of settled hatred; for when an enemy stands his ground and offers resistance, it is no wonder that we assail him; but when he turns his back and allows that he is conquered, and declines to fight, it seems that we are burning with a furious hatred, when we follow him and draw him to fight against his will. . . . To show this blind fury God said that they "cried after Jeremiah." COMMENTARY ON JEREMIAH 12:6.[11]

BELOVED PEOPLE, SAVAGE LAND. SEBASTIAN MÜNSTER: "Beloved of my soul." This is a Hebraism for "My people, whom I have loved from my soul." Because of their iniquities I have given them into the hands of their enemies. I have even abandoned my temple and have dread for the whole land of my inheritance. It is as when someone is walking through a forest and hears a roaring lion, so one avoids that place. Thus, because of the bellowing of the poor, who suffer the violence and treachery of the powerful, I have deserted my land. Moreover, because of my abandonment it will happen that the ruin of my people will be so great that even the greedy birds will soak themselves in the blood of those slaughtered and the beasts of the field will tear apart their bodies. THE TEMPLE OF THE LORD, JEREMIAH 12:7-9.[12]

THE BIRDS SURROUNDING JUDAH. THE ENGLISH ANNOTATIONS: By another similitude, God seems here to set out the cause of his disaffection toward his people: because they became like ramping lions, so like ravenous fowls, for which cause also the Lord was resolved to beset them with enemies, [so] that as birds of prey should in like manner prey upon them, as they had done upon others, and call those in upon them who as wild beasts should devour them. Some read the words as an interrogation, joined

---

[9]Trapp, *A Commentary or Exposition*, 260*. A faggot is a meatball made of offcuts and offal.
[10]St. John of the Cross, *Collected Works*, 668; citing Mt 7:14, 13; Jer 12:5.

[11]CTS 18:134* (CO 38:137).
[12]Münster, *Miqdaš YHWH*, 880.

with admiration, "Is my heritage become thus to me? Are the birds roundabout against her?" Others consider it an enunciation, as our version exhibits. The Jewish critics and the use of the particle carry it in the former way, to which therefore I am also inclined, yet so, as that I conceive a defect of the negative in the text, which in such interrogations is not unusual . . . , and so I suppose the words may well be rendered, "Is not my heritage such a bird to me?" "Are not the birds," or, "Shall not the birds," be "roundabout against her?" as thus our more ancient English exhibited it, in which effect also, comes home to the present version. ANNOTATIONS ON JEREMIAH 12:9.[13]

RULING PASSIONS AND SUBJECTS. HULDRYCH

ZWINGLI: "Many shepherds have destroyed my vineyard" etc. As long as the shepherds (that means the authorities and the princes) break the law, so it will go with the people. So long as they look after the law, the people cannot fully go to ruin. Therefore, the authorities should not allow themselves to lead from their passions. The passions are like hornets; they become furious and they sting; they set the ruling people against their subjects. SERMON ON JEREMIAH 12:10.[14]

SHEPHERDS OF THE CHURCH, NEITHER RICH

NOR POOR. JOHN DONNE: God complains that they have "trod his portion underfoot." That is, the shepherds first neglected his people (for God's people are "his portion"). Then, whatever pious people had given to the church, is his "portion" too, and that portion they had trodden under foot; not neglected it, nor despised it; for they collected it and audited it carefully enough, but they trod it underfoot, when that which was given for the sustenance of the priest they turned to their own splendor, glory, and indulgence. But as Christ will be fed in the poor that are hungry, and he will be clothed in the poor that are naked, so he would be enriched in those

poor ministers who serve at his altar. When Christ would be so fed, he desires not feasts and banquets; when he would be clothed, he desires not the comfortable raiment fit for king's houses, nor embroideries, nor perfumes. When he would be enriched in the poor churchman, he desires not that he should be a sponge to soak up the sweat of others and live idly. But yet, as he would not be starved in the hungry, nor submitted to cold and unwelcome air in the naked, so neither would he be made contemptible, nor destitute in a minister of his church. . . . I speak of the clergy in the most proper sense, that is, that they minister and officiate; that they personally and ardently do the service of the church. SERMON ON EZEKIEL 34:19.[15]

SEWING DEFIANCE AND REAPING WRATH.

KONRAD PELLIKAN: The destroyers come not only to one part of this land, but to every part. In every place the attacking sword of the Lord is seen— even to the ends of the earth—and there is no escape or salvation. Before the people were always making promises over against the predictions of the prophets; but they are nowhere proved. They believed all things opposite to the prophets; they knew better. So it is to sew wheat and to harvest thorns. The legacy of their crops will be nothing. Though they promised themselves that their storehouses would be full, they would be confounded by their expectations because of the wrath of the Lord toward their transgressions of the law. Such will be the experience all the ungodly, who were found to be safe and happy for a while without a fear of God. So the Lord wills unexpectedly, when they store up treasures for themselves on the day of vindication and righteous judgment, which is their worthy inheritance. COMMENTARY ON JEREMIAH 12:12-13.[16]

THE NATIONS REDEEMED. JOHANNES BUGENHA-

GEN: "The Lord speaks against" all my wicked neighbors: This is a singular prophecy. He prophecies

---

[13]Downame, ed., *Annotations*, 9Kɪv*; citing 1 Sam 2:27-28; Job 20:4; Jer 31:20.
[14]Zwingli, *Predigten*, 204.
[15]Donne, *Sermons*, 10:142-43*; citing Mt 25:35-36; 11:8.
[16]Pellikan, *Commentaria Bibliorum*, 3:2Rɪv.

that not only Judea but also the whole of Syria and Egypt are to be devastated by the Babylonians. Read Judith 2 and 3. Likewise the Babylonians would perish through the Medes and Persians, which he also said above in Jeremiah 9 and that you will see clearly below in chapters 46 to 51.

Truly the prophet adds a great consolation to his Jews, lest they think that the promise of God has perished, when they were discarded on account of their sins. Indeed, "God is true, although every person is a liar." For he predicts and promises that the Jews will be returned to their own land, of course, after seventy years of captivity, as is said elsewhere, because of the promise of God. And the neighboring nations will be restored to their lands solely by the mercy of God; as it says in the Psalm: "You, Lord, will save people and beasts." Then, he says, they will come from the nations in the greatest glory through God to my people, as those who now either hate Judah on account of the law of God, and say in the psalm "Raze it, raze, down to the foundations," or lead it astray to their own idolatry and eternal ruin. Then they will approach and glorify my people, and become their disciples while receiving from them the Word of God. Then among my Jews there will be teachers and instructors of the nations. And such nations will be built up; that is, they will do well and be rich in the midst of my people, namely, . . . through the teaching of my people. I do not care that such nations are not of the flesh of Abraham, when meanwhile they are my people and my children through the faith of Abraham. COMMENTARY ON JEREMIAH 12:14-17.[17]

PUNISHING AND SAVING THE JEWS AND THE NATIONS. HEINRICH BULLINGER: With elegant words the Lord indicates that he will now pronounce his sentence against the evil neighbors of the Jews. He speaks of the people of Sidon, Tyre, Ammon, Moab, Edom, and Philistia. Indeed these nations truly hated the Jewish people and fully exulted in their misfortunes; they added

misfortune to their misfortune by almost always joining themselves with enemies and rejoicing whenever the Jewish religion seemed threatened with ruin. He calls them his neighbors. To be sure, dominion over the whole world belongs to the Lord our God, who chose for himself as his personal property the Jewish people; for that reason here he calls the nations that are near and bordering the Jews "his own neighbors" (and indeed bad neighbors). Indeed there follows the reason why God called them evil: those who "touch the inheritance etc." But the proper interpretation of this passage is twofold. Either, "who touch the inheritance that I possess—namely, my people of Israel" or, "who touch (the land), which I made for my people Israel to inherit." In either case the sense ends up the same and is clear. "I will pronounce my judgment also against those who afflict my church."

Finally Jeremiah . . . now begins in a prophetic manner to announce better and clearly gospel-themed things. For in the beginning Jeremiah teaches the captive and afflicted people of God that they would be returned to their land, and then that the nations likewise would be joined to the people of God. I say that they would be called and so would be received into the society and communion of all the good things of the people of God. And indeed he says this clearly, distinctly, and elegantly. Indeed at first he says, "It will happen that when I have uprooted them, I will again turn to them." That is, "It will happen that just as I was turned away from them and in my anger and ruined them, so again I shall turn to them and I shall restore them with my grace." Accordingly, the Lord does not afflict for all time, but sets a limit, and at some time he makes an end of evil. Thus, this is a remarkable passage about the grace and clemency of God, who receives the afflicted into grace, nor does he oppress sinners and miserable people with his anger for all time. Furthermore, after the restitution of the people of Israel, the prophet goes on to mention the vocation of the nations. But this entire promise is conditional, having this sense: if

---

17 Bugenhagen *In Ieremiam*, 3E2v; citing Rom 3:4; Ps 36:6; 137:7.

the nations would hear the preaching of the truth and believe, they will join with the people of God and will be participants in all the good things that a benevolent God promises to his people. But if they do not believe, they will perish. SERMON ON JEREMIAH 12:14-17.[18]

---

[18]Bullinger, *Conciones*, 94v, 95r-v.

JEREMIAH 13:1-27
SIGNS OF JUDGMENT

¹Thus says the LORD to me, "Go and buy a linen loincloth and put it around your waist, and do not dip it in water." ²So I bought a loincloth according to the word of the LORD, and put it around my waist. ³And the word of the LORD came to me a second time, ⁴"Take the loincloth that you have bought, which is around your waist, and arise, go to the Euphrates and hide it there in a cleft of the rock." ⁵So I went and hid it by the Euphrates, as the LORD commanded me. ⁶And after many days the LORD said to me, "Arise, go to the Euphrates, and take from there the loincloth that I commanded you to hide there." ⁷Then I went to the Euphrates, and dug, and I took the loincloth from the place where I had hidden it. And behold, the loincloth was spoiled; it was good for nothing.

⁸Then the word of the LORD came to me: ⁹"Thus says the LORD: Even so will I spoil the pride of Judah and the great pride of Jerusalem. ¹⁰This evil people, who refuse to hear my words, who stubbornly follow their own heart and have gone after other gods to serve them and worship them, shall be like this loincloth, which is good for nothing. ¹¹For as the loincloth clings to the waist of a man, so I made the whole house of Israel and the whole house of Judah cling to me, declares the LORD, that they might be for me a people, a name, a praise, and a glory, but they would not listen.

¹²"You shall speak to them this word: 'Thus says the LORD, the God of Israel, "Every jar shall be filled with wine."' And they will say to you, 'Do we not indeed know that every jar will be filled with wine?' ¹³Then you shall say to them, 'Thus says the Lord: Behold, I will fill with drunkenness all the inhabitants of this land: the kings who sit on David's throne, the priests, the prophets, and all the inhabitants of Jerusalem. ¹⁴And I will dash them one against another, fathers and sons together, declares the LORD. I will not pity or spare or have compassion, that I should not destroy them.'"

¹⁵Hear and give ear; be not proud,
for the LORD has spoken.

¹⁶Give glory to the LORD your God
before he brings darkness,
before your feet stumble
on the twilight mountains,
and while you look for light
he turns it into gloom
and makes it deep darkness.
¹⁷But if you will not listen,
my soul will weep in secret for your pride;
my eyes will weep bitterly and run down
with tears,
because the LORD's flock has been taken
captive.

¹⁸Say to the king and the queen mother:
"Take a lowly seat,
for your beautiful crown
has come down from your head."
¹⁹The cities of the Negeb are shut up,
with none to open them;
all Judah is taken into exile,
wholly taken into exile.

²⁰"Lift up your eyes and see
those who come from the north.
Where is the flock that was given you,
your beautiful flock?
²¹What will you say when they set as head
over you
those whom you yourself have taught to be
friends to you?
Will not pangs take hold of you
like those of a woman in labor?
²²And if you say in your heart,
'Why have these things come upon me?'
it is for the greatness of your iniquity
that your skirts are lifted up
and you suffer violence.
²³Can the Ethiopian change his skin
or the leopard his spots?
Then also you can do good

who are accustomed to do evil.
²⁴I will scatter you[a] like chaff
    driven by the wind from the desert.
²⁵This is your lot,
    the portion I have measured out to you,
        declares the LORD,
because you have forgotten me
    and trusted in lies.

²⁶I myself will lift up your skirts over your face,
    and your shame will be seen.
²⁷I have seen your abominations,
    your adulteries and neighings, your lewd
        whorings,
    on the hills in the field.
Woe to you, O Jerusalem!
    How long will it be before you are made clean?"

a Hebrew *them*

OVERVIEW: The prophecies of Jeremiah are rich in imagery and visually graphic: the ruined loincloth and the broken jar, the dark mountain and the woman in labor; the human body exposed, the Ethiopian's skin, and the leopard's spots. Such language could make the divine message vivid and the threat of judgment unforgettable. The very nature of idolatry was also embodied in visual objects and graven images that displaced the one, holy God. Reformation interpreters were keen to help readers decipher the signs of Jeremiah and to approach symbolic language in appropriate ways. Such decoding was all the more pressing in an age when Christians were divided about the meaning of sacramental signs, the actual number of sacraments, and the threat of idolatry in forms old and new. Such idolatry might appear yet again in the things that some deemed efficacious and preferred to God's aid and providence—including relics of the human body and shrines of the saints. In addition, the sustained unfaithfulness of God's people would lead to fierce and sure judgment and destruction.

13:1-11 The Ruined Loincloth

SIGNS ADDED TO THE WORD. MARTIN LUTHER: This, you see, is a custom of all the prophets and everywhere in Scripture—to add some sign that confirms the Word. For instance, Isaiah, in chapter 20, is commanded to loosen the sackcloth from his loins, take the sandals off his feet, and go about naked and barefoot. With this sign he was confirming his preaching of the devastation and stripping of Egypt (which he had prophesied) by the king of the Assyrians. There are many other signs of this type in Jeremiah as well—in chapter 13—for instance, where he speaks about the loincloth rotted when Jeremiah had hidden it. With this sign the Lord wanted to confirm his humbling of the Jews, who had gone away from true worship and the correct Word in their wickedness. Jeremiah also has this kind of sign when the cup of the Lord's fury is given to him so that he may give it to the heathen to drink; and again when he wore a wooden yoke about his neck to signify thereby that all nations were going to be subject to the power of the Chaldeans, that they all would come under the power of that king. Thus, through all time signs are added to the Word. Noah had the rainbow, and we have baptism and the Eucharist. LECTURE ON ZECHARIAH 6:10.[1]

PROPHETIC DREAMS. JOHANNES OECOLAMPADIUS: "Thus, the Lord said to me." Behold again there is a new argument here, for he discusses the same things as above, and they are discussed in the whole book. You know, however, this argument does not seem to be something he did, but is a prophetic vision. Indeed they used to suppose that they acted in a vision just as happens in dreams. And so many visions happen among the prophets, as in the nude walk of Isaiah, the marriage of

---

[1]LW 20:67-68* (WA 13:606-7); citing Jer 25:15-38; 27:2; Gen 9:13-17.

Hosea, the sleep of Ezekiel for 390 days, and the like. COMMENTARY ON JEREMIAH 13:1.[2]

THE LOOSENED BELT. JOHANNES BUGENHAGEN: When signs are added to words in more powerful ways they move the soul and aid the memory. Here the Lord orders the prophet to declare with a sign the coming downfall of the unfaithful people. A linen belt is applied to the prophet; that is, the people are drawn to the Word of God or to God, because God gives to them the law, the promises, and the good prophets. The belt, however, was not dipped in the water, because the prophet or the Word of God did not command the people, as is said at the end of this chapter. Afterward, the belt was loosened, taken outside of Judea, and concealed in the Assyrian or Babylonian Euphrates River. Over time the belt rotted. This signifies that the prophet and the Word of God have released the unbelieving people from the Holy Land and the Babylonians have carried them away. After the people were truly cut loose and cast away, they would perish in the land of the Babylonians and would be dispersed into many places for seventy years. COMMENTARY ON JEREMIAH 13:1-7.[3]

THE GIRDLE AS INTIMATE CONNECTION TO GOD. JOHN MAYER: The Lord commanded Jeremiah to take a linen girdle and, having worn it awhile, to go hide it by the Euphrates River in Babylon and after a time to go and take it up out of the ground again. When he did this, he found it so corrupted that it was good for nothing. Then the Lord said that Israel was to him like a girdle, which he had put near to his loins, the seat of his affections, to show his great love for that people. But whereas he expected to receive praise and glory from them, they in contrast were so corrupted by their wickedness that now the Lord rejected them....

The Lord would not have this girdle washed, but taken as it was to show that the Jewish nation, when the Lord first chose it, was black with sin, and nothing pleasant. But the Lord took the girdle and wore it so that by the dear affection he gave to it, Israel might in this election be sanctified and made white and glorious before all the nations nearby; Israel would be "a glory and praise," which the church is, when she lives in obedience to God's laws.... The Jewish priests must wear a linen girdle in their ministrations to make them mindful of continence. Here the girdle is an emblem of chaste love, which is how God loved Israel. God espoused himself to that state alone and required that Israel should likewise be knit in chaste love to him. But Israel in contrast committed adultery by worshiping strange gods, and so God bids Jeremiah to take the girdle to the Euphrates ... to show the captivity that would shortly come into the country around the Euphrates, that is, in Babylon. There they would lie rotting in baseness, servility, and sin for many years....

Moreover, (1) a girdle is an ensign of honor, being beautifully crafted with gold and precious stones.... (2) Christ appears glorious encircled with a golden girdle.... (3) A girdle is a military implement for which it is said, "Fasten your loins with the girdle of truth," which is when we are firm and steadfast in the truth ... as the loins fastened with a girdle are strengthened to travel. As with Israel, so every faithful person, without being worthy on their own, is dear to God, and is near to him, not as leather or a woolen girdle above our clothes, but a linen worn next to the skin. COMMENTARY ON JEREMIAH 13:1-11.[4]

13:12-14 The Jars Filled with Wine

BROKEN BY THE SPIRIT OF ERROR. JOHN MAYER: After the girdle was put forward as a similitude for the baseness of the Jews, now God shows their destruction by a similitude of bottles. People use earthen bottles to carry wine from place to place; if they are broken against one another, then they are worthless. Then much good wine is

---

[2]Oecolampadius, *In Hieremiam*, 1:R1v-R2r; citing Is 20:1-6; Hos 1:2-3; Ezek 4:4-5.
[3]Bugenhagen, *In Ieremiam*, 3F1r.

[4]Mayer, *A Commentary*, 375-76*; citing Rev. 1:13; Eph 6:14.

spilled by this means and so they are even worse off. In a like manner, God shows that the chief people of the Jews—kings, priests, and prophets—should be filled with drunkenness and broken against one another, not by the drunkenness of wine, but by the spirit of error. . . . For in the time while they were drunk, the Chaldeans would come and destroy them all. Moreover, the strength they relied on proved no better than earthen bottles being broken with a knock one against the other. COMMENTARY ON JEREMIAH 13:12-13.[5]

THE MEANING OF BOTTLES AND INEBRIA-TION. JOHN CALVIN:

This general statement might have appeared to be of no weight; for what instruction does this contain? "Every bottle shall be filled with wine"? It is like saying that a tankard is made to carry wine and that bowls are made for drinking; this is well known, even to children. And then it might have been said that this was unworthy of a prophet [to say]. "What? What did you say? Did you say that bottles are receptacles of wine, even as a hat is made to cover the head, or clothes to keep off the cold? Are you mocking us with childish things?"

But it was God's particular object thus to rouse the people who were asleep in their delusions, and who were also by no means attentive to spiritual instruction. It was then his purpose to show by the most trifling and as it were frivolous things that they were not possessed with much clear-sightedness so as to perceive even the most obvious things. They indeed all knew that bottles were made for wine, but they did not understand that they [themselves] were the bottles or were like bottles. We have indeed said that they were inflated with so much arrogance that they seemed like hard rocks. So their contempt for all threats [of judgment] was the result because they did not consider what they [truly] were. The prophet then says that they were like bottles; though God had indeed chosen them for an excellent use, yet, forgetful of their frailty, they had marred their own excellency, so that they were no longer of any use, except that God would inebriate them with giddiness and also with calamities. . . .

It may now be asked, what was this drunkenness that the prophet announces? It may be understood in two ways—either that God would give them up to a reprobate mind or that he would make them drunk with evils and calamities; for when God deprives people of a right mind, it is to prepare them for extreme vengeance. But the prophet seems to have something further in view—that this people would be given up to the most grievous evils, which would wholly fill them with amazement. Yet it appears that the first evil is intended here. . . . Thus they were all to be broken, as it were, to pieces. God then not only points out that calamity was close at hand for the Jews, but also the manner of it; that is, that every one of them would draw their own brethren to ruin as though they inflicted wounds on one another. COMMENTARY ON JEREMIAH 13:12-14.[6]

ADDICTED TO THE WINE OF WRATH. THE ENGLISH ANNOTATIONS:

Since you are so addicted to wine and excess, you shall have wine until you are full. I will fill all sorts of people among you—from the highest to the lowest—with another sort of wine that you desire and delight in—until you are completely drunk with it. From the cup of my wrath I will pour out the terror of anguish, perplexity, and astonishment upon you so that you shall be at your wits end and shall no longer know what to do or which way to turn. ANNOTATIONS ON JEREMIAH 13:13.[7]

THE WINE OF BABYLON. KONRAD PELLIKAN:

The Lord alludes to those who are inebriated, who thrust themselves forward, who grow hostile, made mad with wine, and are set in motion, not able to stand still, whom the Lord will make to drink and make drunk with wine from the cup of Babylon. Not only the fathers who accomplished this

---

[5]Mayer, A Commentary, 377*.

[6]CTS 18:170-71* (CO 38:159-60).
[7]Downame, ed., Annotations, 9K3r*; citing Is 5:11-12, 22, 22:13.

impiety and knowingly rejected the word of the Lord, but also their more innocent children, who nevertheless have not fallen off from their hereditary employment, having been established in depravity by their parents. "I will hardly pity them, nor will I spare them by burying them all any less in captivity." COMMENTARY ON JEREMIAH 13:14.[8]

13:15-27 Exile Threatened

THE PROPER BEARING OF A PROPHET. KONRAD PELLIKAN: Whenever Jeremiah himself proclaimed a fierce revelation from the Lord, still he did not despair of the goodness of God, and in fact he desired it. Meanwhile, so that the Jews might be converted in their hearts and even as their stubbornness grew, and so that the justice of God might shine more clearly, he did not cease to exhort them and did not refuse to give his message to the ungodly, whom he wanted not to die, but to live. Jeremiah omitted nothing that pertained to calling them back. But they were continuously more proud, and they despised the riches of God's goodness. COMMENTARY ON JEREMIAH 13:15.[9]

RELYING ON OTHERS AND RELYING ON GOD. NIKOLAUS SELNECKER: "Now listen and pay attention and do not resist, for the Lord has spoken." This is a heartfelt request and admonition to repentance and conversion to God, that one should not despise God's word and warning. For God will not allow himself to be ridiculed and despised. One should turn oneself in time and heart to God, before it becomes dark, that is, before misfortune comes and before God completely withdraws his hand. For Jeremiah the dark mountains refer to the assistance of the Egyptians, the power and support on which the Jews rely. With their help the Jews think that they can mount a resistance against the Babylonians. But God speaks a "no" to this. "You will be," he says, "allowed to be trapped in darkness and misfortune;

you will be overwhelmed and defeated"—as it then did happen.

Therefore, next to the admonition to repentance, there is also a secret sermon against the Jews, that they are relying on an alliance with the king of Egypt, when they should in every way rely on their refuge and hope in God. They should be like a good child who in an urgent situation seeks no other than his own father. God also reprimands this trust in alliances and human help in Isaiah 30 and presents this beautiful saying: "When you remain quiet, so will you be helped. In rest and hope will be your strength." Through rest and hope you would be strong, that is, when you fear God, obey him, call on him, and remain patient, turn to him, and be humble. Then there is no hardship. But this will not be so, when we can rely on human power and do not want to rely on God. Therefore, it happens also that it goes better than one thinks, or can see overall, especially when some war and great hardship occurs. Such things deeply hurt the pious teachers and Christians, that they also weep and lament about them, because someone does not trust and follow God, and does not hear his voice or want to call on him. THE WHOLE PROPHET JEREMIAH 13:15-17.[10]

GOSPEL LIGHT IN THE DARKNESS. MENNO SIMONS: Praise the Most High, all you who fear the Lord, that he has manifested his immeasurably great love and grace toward us poor sinners in this dreadful time of unbelief, that he has permitted the clear light of his holy gospel, and the true knowledge of his Son Jesus Christ, to shine forth out of the darkness, the light that was concealed for so many centuries in this dark Egypt under the thick clouds of the abominations of the Antichrist. Therefore, let us guard it carefully and walk in it diligently, lest it turn into thick, deathly darkness again, as the prophet Jeremiah has it. FOUNDATION OF CHRISTIAN DOCTRINE.[11]

---

[8]Pellikan, *Commentaria Bibliorum*, 3:2R2v.
[9]Pellikan, *Commentaria Bibliorum*, 3:2R2v

[10]Selnecker, *Der gantze Prophet Jeremias*, Z3v-Z4r-v; citing Is 30:15.
[11]Simons, *Complete Writings*, 158.

THE PROPHET'S LAST OPTION. THE ENGLISH ANNOTATIONS: All the prophet can do when he is not able to prevail upon the people and bring them to serious consideration of God's message that he delivered to them—a message inviting them into a severe humiliation and abasement of their haughty minds—is this: In his tender affection for them he shall go away alone and there mourn their foolish pride and the miseries and deportation that will befall God's people. ANNOTATIONS ON JEREMIAH 13:17.[12]

TEARS DEMONSTRATE COMPASSION. JOHN TRAPP: Good men are apt to weep; and simple emotions are apprehended in a noble mind. Good ministers should be full of compassionate tears, weeping in secret over their people's unprofitableness and their danger thereby. The breast and right shoulder of the sacrifice belonged to the priest to show that he should be a breast to love and a shoulder to support the people in their troubles and burdens. COMMENTARY ON JEREMIAH 13:17.[13]

THE PASSING GREATNESS OF EARTHLY KINGDOMS. LANCELOT ANDREWES: Jezebel had a glorious kingdom, but within a few years it was said of her, *Ubi est illa Jezabel?* "Where is that Jezebel?" When it was fulfilled which the prophet Jeremiah foretold, "Tell the king and queen, 'Humble yourselves, for your dignity shall be taken away, and the crown of your glory shall fall down,' and the like is the greatness of all earthly kingdoms; and therefore Christ teaches us to direct our petitions to him, 'whose kingdom is everlasting,' whose power endures forever and ever," not to a mortal king, but to God *Qui solus habet* etc., "who alone has immortality," who being himself an everlasting and incorruptible king who fades not. This is our hope and perfection of our desires, and therefore as the creed has his period in life everlasting, so last of all we are taught to pray for glory everlasting. SERMON 14 ON THE LORD'S PRAYER.[14]

CONFRONTING AN UNJUST KING. NIKOLAUS SELNECKER: "Say to the king and the queen, sit down." This is a difficult sermon; for therein he attacks the head and addresses King Jehoiachin. Because of his sins the king along with his people must be captured and led away. These are the reasons. First, he and the queen have the crown of glory on their heads, but the crisis is so great and misfortune is at the door. That is, they are confident and proud; they have had good times, anticipate their pleasures, and have had good weather. Things go as they expect. Second, they pay little attention to the hot stove. . . . That is, they do not take their office seriously. They rarely ask about their subjects: how they are living, what they are seeking, how their fear of God is; how piety, fear of God, morality, and mercy can be maintained among them; and how they can restore truth. The king and queen rarely ask if the poor are protected and supported, the widows and orphans defended, and how to strengthen them by offering a hand. Third, they pay attention to their officials, that is, those that are near to them, their faithful assistants and servants—those that want to be princes and heads. So they see through the finger and allow the poor to be oppressed and plagued by their servants. No one can speak to the officials; they do what they want, take and rip things away for themselves when they please; they suck the poor dry. . . . Therefore God says, "I must see what is to be done. Anxiety has arrived, like a woman in childbirth, so your enemy draws near and will bring you under his yoke and so your lords and princes will be as well." THE WHOLE PROPHET JEREMIAH 13:18-21.[15]

PERPETUAL SIN SYMBOLIZED IN CLOTHING. JOHN CALVIN: He described that multitude of iniquity as a perverse wickedness that prevailed

---

[12]Downame, ed., *Annotations*, 9K2v*.
[13]Trapp, *A Commentary or Exposition*, 264*.

[14]Andrewes, *Works*, 5:466*. Citing 2 Kings 9:37; Ps. 145:13; 1 Tim 6:16; 1 Pet. 5:4; 1:4.
[15]Selnecker, *Der gantze Prophet Jeremias*, Z4r-v.

among the Jews; for a long time they had not ceased to provoke the wrath of God. Had they only once sinned, or had they been guilty of one kind of sin, there would have been some hope of pardon. At least God would not have executed a punishment so severe. But as there had been an uninterrupted course of sinning, the prophet shows that it would not be right to spare them any longer.

As to the simile, it is a form of speaking often used by the prophets, that is, to denude the soles of the feet, and to discover the skirts. We know that people clothe themselves, not only to preserve them from cold, but that they also cover the body for the sake of modesty: there is, therefore, a twofold use of garments, the one occasioned by necessity and the other by decency. As then clothes are partly made for this end—to cover what could not be decently shown or left bare without shame, the prophets use this mode of speaking when they have in view to show that one is exposed to public reprimand. COMMENTARY ON JEREMIAH 13:22.[16]

CHANGING ONE'S SKIN AND LIFE. HULDRYCH ZWINGLI: "Can the Moor change his skin or the panther his spots?" The panther is a terrifying, ravenous animal with many spots. He wants to say: as an Ethiopian and a panther under no conditions can change the colors that nature attached to them, so your immoral life can in no way be changed until it perishes. You are always and so often immersed in wickedness that your color will never, ever fade. SERMON ON JEREMIAH 13:23.[17]

HABITUAL SINS ARE DANGEROUS ROUTINES. JOHN TRAPP: Custom in sin takes away the sense of it, and becomes a second nature, which though expelled with a fork, as it were, will yet return again. It looks for continual entertainment where it has once gotten a haunt, as humors fall toward their old issue. Says Lucian, "an evil custom is not easily left." COMMENTARY ON JEREMIAH 13:23.[18]

THE VOICE OF STRANGERS, THE VOICE OF GOD. JOHANNES BUGENHAGEN: "You have trusted in falsehood." He calls the doctrines and commands of people a lie, a religious and specious worship. This the impious priests and pseudo-prophets were teaching, once they had left behind the Word of God, which they had received. So he says, "you have forgotten me"; that is, "my words and the faith towards me. You prostitute, you have cast me away and have taken up foreign gods, adulterers, the voice of strangers, and other cults, concerning which I did not command you and from which I had prohibited you. You knew the prostitute and the shameless harlot, but you ought to have preserved the faith you promised to me and kept inviolate the covenant of marriage. You ought not to hear and follow the adulterers, that is, foreign gods, and teaching foreign to me—other cults, other religions. Nevertheless, forgetting our holy covenant, you have defected from faith to the teaching of demons found in the hypocritical speech of liars." Against this, Christ says in John 10, "My sheep hear my voice and they follow me and they do not follow the stranger"; they flee from him; because they do not know the voice of strangers. COMMENTARY ON JEREMIAH 13:25.[19]

EXPOSING THE BODY OF SIN. JOHN CALVIN: This mode of speaking occurs often in the prophets. . . . It is as though a vile woman was condemned to bear the disgrace of being stripped of her garments and exposed to the public, that all might abhor a spectacle so base and disgraceful. God . . . assumed the character of a husband to his people: as then he had been so shamefully despised, he now says, that he had in readiness the punishment of casting the skirts of his people over their faces, that their reproach or baseness might appear by exposing their unattractive parts. COMMENTARY ON JEREMIAH 13:26.[20]

---

[16]CTS 18:190* (CO 38:171).
[17]Zwingli, *Predigten*, 207.
[18]Trapp, *A Commentary or Exposition*, 265*.

[19]Bugenhagen, *In Ieremiam*, 3F4v; citing Jn 10:27.
[20]CTS 18:197-198* (CO 38:175).

THE GEOGRAPHY OF IDOLATRY—PLACE AND BEHAVIOR. JUAN DE MALDONADO: Jeremiah calls idolatry "adultery, whinnying, and the wickedness of fornication." "Upon the hills" appears next. Here there should be a distinction. He says, "upon the hills," for this reason: because it was "in the hills" where they were accustomed to making burnt offerings to idols. It is as if he says, "There is no hill on which the traces of your impiety are not imprinted." "In the field," that is, in a sacred grove, where there were shrines of the idols. "You will not be made clean after me": that is, by following me. But you will not repent; as he said above: the Ethiopian would sooner change his skin. COMMENTARY ON THE PROPHETS, JEREMIAH 13:27.[21]

JEREMIAH PERSISTS, DESPITE A LACK OF VISIBLE FRUIT. JOHN TRAPP: He closes with this emphatic and most affectionate contestation, pressing them to hearty and speedy repentance, as he had done before, with little good success. The cock crowed, though Peter still denied his master. Peter knocked still, though Rhoda did not open to him. He launched out into the deep, though he had labored all night for nothing. So did good Jeremiah here, in obedience to God, and goodwill to his unworthy countrymen. COMMENTARY ON JEREMIAH 13:27.[22]

---

[21]Maldonado, *Commentarii in Prophetas*, 65.

[22]Trapp, *A Commentary or Exposition*, 265*; citing Lk 22:54-62; Acts 12:13.

JEREMIAH 14:1-22
CATASTROPHIC JUDGMENT
AND FALSE PROPHETS

¹The word of the LORD that came to Jeremiah concerning the drought:

²"Judah mourns,
    and her gates languish;
her people lament on the ground,
    and the cry of Jerusalem goes up.
³Her nobles send their servants for water;
    they come to the cisterns;
they find no water;
    they return with their vessels empty;
they are ashamed and confounded
    and cover their heads.
⁴Because of the ground that is dismayed,
    since there is no rain on the land,
the farmers are ashamed;
    they cover their heads.
⁵Even the doe in the field forsakes her newborn
        fawn
    because there is no grass.
⁶The wild donkeys stand on the bare heights;
    they pant for air like jackals;
their eyes fail
    because there is no vegetation.

⁷"Though our iniquities testify against us,
    act, O LORD, for your name's sake;
for our backslidings are many;
    we have sinned against you.
⁸O you hope of Israel,
    its savior in time of trouble,
why should you be like a stranger in the land,
    like a traveler who turns aside to tarry for
        a night?
⁹Why should you be like a man confused,
    like a mighty warrior who cannot save?
Yet you, O LORD, are in the midst of us,
    and we are called by your name;
    do not leave us."

¹⁰Thus says the Lord concerning this people:
"They have loved to wander thus;
    they have not restrained their feet;
therefore the Lord does not accept them;
    now he will remember their iniquity
    and punish their sins."

¹¹The LORD said to me: "Do not pray for the welfare of this people. ¹²Though they fast, I will not hear their cry, and though they offer burnt offering and grain offering, I will not accept them. But I will consume them by the sword, by famine, and by pestilence." ¹³Then I said: "Ah, Lord GOD, behold, the prophets say to them, 'You shall not see the sword, nor shall you have famine, but I will give you assured peace in this place.'" ¹⁴And the LORD said to me: "The prophets are prophesying lies in my name. I did not send them, nor did I command them or speak to them. They are prophesying to you a lying vision, worthless divination, and the deceit of their own minds. ¹⁵Therefore thus says the LORD concerning the prophets who prophesy in my name although I did not send them, and who say, 'Sword and famine shall not come upon this land': By sword and famine those prophets shall be consumed. ¹⁶And the people to whom they prophesy shall be cast out in the streets of Jerusalem, victims of famine and sword, with none to bury them—them, their wives, their sons, and their daughters. For I will pour out their evil upon them.

¹⁷"You shall say to them this word:
'Let my eyes run down with tears night and day,
    and let them not cease,
for the virgin daughter of my people is
        shattered with a great wound,
    with a very grievous blow.
¹⁸If I go out into the field,
    behold, those pierced by the sword!
And if I enter the city,
    behold, the diseases of famine!

*For both prophet and priest ply their trade
    through the land
    and have no knowledge.'"*

*¹⁹Have you utterly rejected Judah?
    Does your soul loathe Zion?
Why have you struck us down
    so that there is no healing for us?
We looked for peace, but no good came;
    for a time of healing, but behold, terror.
²⁰We acknowledge our wickedness, O LORD,
    and the iniquity of our fathers,*

*for we have sinned against you.
²¹Do not spurn us, for your name's sake;
    do not dishonor your glorious throne;
    remember and do not break your covenant
        with us.
²²Are there any among the false gods of the
        nations that can bring rain?
    Or can the heavens give showers?
Are you not he, O LORD our God?
    We set our hope on you,
    for you do all these things.*

OVERVIEW: Biblical commentators of the Reformation era assumed a direct and discernable connection between divine purpose and earthly disasters—natural and human-made. Jeremiah attests to this: famine, war, and disease are a clear sign of divine judgment and both a symptom and vivid reflection of rampant sin and spiritual destitution. Nature and society mirror and illustrate the state of religious malaise among God's people. Idolatry and unfaithfulness have dire and deadly societal and environmental consequences. The threat of false prophecy was an urgent matter in the sixteenth and seventeenth centuries, given that Roman Catholics and Protestants labeled one another as false prophets who seduced the people with heresy and thereby brought disaster crashing down on Europe. Distinguishing true and false prophets was a matter of life and death for this world and the next.

Moreover, given Jeremiah's dire descriptions of drought, starvation, and despair, given his proclamation of unremitting divine judgment and unanswered prayer, what hope could the people of God find in this prophecy? Our commentators and preachers find in the closing verses of this chapter a model of repentance and hope in God. They are keen to lift up and amplify the echoes of the gospel wherever Jeremiah portends, especially among his prophecies of savage destruction and acute suffering.

14:1-12 Famine, Sword, and Pestilence

A FAMINE OF THE WORD OF GOD. JOHANNES OECOLAMPADIUS: Jeremiah prophesies the most severe famine. It would be like a war laying waste to everything that was then present; for there is no other evil more severe than famine. Indeed, nothing is more miserable than for everyone to die in common, publicly from hunger. Through that particular evil of hunger he prophesies the horror of captivity. These words describe a voice taken away in a barren time, when robust rains are denied to the grazing animals of the earth. So it is even in the Lord's field, unless the clouds of the prophets rain down the righteousness of God, which God by his own incarnate Word grants even to us. By this we learn even in today's captivity of souls that nothing is graver than the privation of the Word of God, by which souls are fed. About such famine Amos the prophet provides a word: "I will send famine upon the earth; neither a famine of bread, nor a thirst for water, but a famine and thirst for hearing the word of the Lord. And they will wander from sea to sea, and from the north to the east they will go about seeking the word and not finding it." In this way are our evil things to be considered. COMMENTARY ON JEREMIAH 14:1.[1]

LAMENTATION IN A TIME OF FAMINE. JOHN CALVIN: The prophet intimates in these words that

---

[1]Oecolampadius, *In Hieremiam*, 1:S1v; citing Amos 8:11-12.

so great would be the scarcity as to appear to be a manifest and remarkable evidence of God's vengeance; for when God punishes us in a common way, we for the most part refer the event to some fortuitous circumstances, and the devil ever retains our minds in the consideration of secondary causes. Hence, the prophet declares here that an event so unusual could not be ascribed to natural causes, even that the earth should be so sterile, but it was the extraordinary judgment of God. . . .

"His gates have been weakened" or scattered. In mentioning gates he takes a part for the whole, for he means the cities: but as judgments were usually administered at the gates, and as people often assembled there, he says that the gates would be reduced to solitude, so that hardly anyone would appear there. He . . . adds, "They have become darkened to the ground," or, in plainer words, they became overwhelmed with grief; but the proper meaning of the word is to become darkened. And he says, "to the ground," as though he said that they would be so cast down so as to lie in the dust, and would not dare to raise up their heads, nor would they be able to do so, being so worn down by want and famine. . . .

He afterward adds, "the cry of Jerusalem has ascended." Here he sets forth their despair: for in doubtful matters we are used to deliberating and devising remedies; but when we are destitute of any counsel or advice, and when no hope appears, we then break out into crying. We hence see that it was an evidence of despair when "the cry of Jerusalem ascended"; for they would not be able to complain and to unburden their cares and grief by pouring them into the bosoms of one another, but all of them would cry and howl. COMMENTARY ON JEREMIAH 14:2.[2]

A Famine of Word and Spirit. JOHANNES OECOLAMPADIUS: Jeremiah continues in explaining famine. The cisterns were dry, which ought to have caught rain water because they were made by digging in places with more of an incline. In vain will the magistrate send people away from every place with empty vessels, for out of false hope they will return to those cisterns. Where contempt of the truth occurs once, afterward it tends to hide itself, even when it is manifested in the mouth of preachers. So the Lord orders us "to walk in the light, while we have the light . . ." before the sun grows dark. The apostles are sent, but somehow the fountains are plugged and there may be such a drought that those who come after find nothing; even Scripture is veiled. It may be allowed that they have the letter of Scripture without the spirit, which is empty and without fruit. "We have our treasure in earthen vessels" and "You examine the Scriptures because you think in them you have eternal life." As Isaiah says, "Draw water from the wells of the savior." Therefore, while we refuse to comply with the precept of those people, we will listen with merit: for they did not discover the water. They were an empty vessel, until Christ himself became a teacher to us. So it is that our consciences are not given joy, but in attempting by human ability to discover salvation they are confounded, whether they may attempt this in nature or in Scripture. And just like the hemophiliac woman we apply all of our faculties in vain among the doctors, until we will be healed by the efficacious Word of life. COMMENTARY ON JEREMIAH 14:3.[3]

No Water and No Repentance. KONRAD PELLIKAN: Those who had greater wealth or power were sending those who had less to get drinking water. But nothing was found in the wells, since the Lord was exacting punishment from the impious as he had already and often promised through the prophet. Therefore they were confused among themselves and yet they did not improve themselves. Indeed by the working of the head repentance was avoided; anxiety endured for a long time, but nevertheless they did not turn to the Lord in faith and humility. COMMENTARY ON JEREMIAH 14:3-4.[4]

---

[2]CTS 18:204-205* (CO 38:179-180).

[3]Oecolampadius, *In Hieremiam*, 1:S1v-S2r; citing Jn 12:35; 2 Cor 4:7; Jn 5:39; Is 12:3; Lk 8:43-48.
[4]Pellikan, *Commentaria Bibliorum*, 3:2R3v.

EVEN HEARTY ANIMALS SUFFER THE FAMINE.
JOHN CALVIN: Jeremiah now comes to animals: he said before that people would be visited with thirst, and then that the ground would become dry, so that the farmer would be ashamed. He now says that the wild asses and does would become partakers of this scarcity. "The doe," he says, "has brought forth in the field," which was not usual; but he says that such would be the drought that the hinds would come forth in the plains. The female deer, we know, wander in solitary places and there seek their food, and do not thus expose themselves; for they have a natural timidity that keeps them from encountering danger. But he says that does, pregnant with young, shall be constrained by famine to come to the fields and bring forth there and then flee away: and yet they prefer their young to their own life. But the prophet here shows that there would be something extraordinary in that vengeance of God, which was nigh the Jews, in order that they might know that God had armed the heavens and the earth and all the elements against them; for this they had so deserved.

The same thing is said of the wild asses . . . and yet this animal, we know, can endure for a long time. But the prophet . . . intended to show that there would be in this scarcity some remarkable evidence of God's vengeance. . . . For great is the heat of serpents; on account of inward burning they are constrained to draw in wind to allay the heat within. The prophet says that wild asses were like serpents, for they were burning with a long famine, so that they were seeking food in the wind itself, or by respiration. COMMENTARY ON JEREMIAH 14:5-6.[5]

HOW TO CONFESS SIN. NIKOLAUS SELNECKER: "Oh Lord, our misdeeds have testified, but help us because of the willing of your name." This is a pleasant prayer; therein Jeremiah first confesses the sins of the people. For when one wants to pray correctly and have a gracious God, one must first recognize their sins and then from there they can be fully confessed. When that does not happen,

there will be evil and only great pain and disturbance in one's conscience. As David says in Psalm 32: "When I kept silence my bones wasted away through my daily groaning." Therefore, I say that I will confess my transgression to the Lord that he may forgive the misdeeds of my sins. That is also the reason why Jeremiah, Daniel, David, and all the saints first confess their sins humbly before God; they admit their guilt and call upon God alone. "Lord, go not before the court with your servant. Lord, do not deal with us according to our sins and do not repay us according to our misdeeds." THE WHOLE PROPHET JEREMIAH 14:7.[6]

A STRANGER IN THE LAND? NIKOLAUS SELNECKER: "So declares the Lord, they like to run here and there and not remain at home." Jeremiah, you are certainly not allowed so to pray, God says, and not allowed to call me a guest or wandering stranger. For I protect my people as a true father should protect his children. But you yourselves behave as strangers and guests who do not want to remain with me and do not recognize me as your father. But you run here and there seeking another savior, pursue idolatry, and lean on human assistance, your fortress, and on the king of Egypt. But you do not want to be engaged with me, nor lean on me, and wait and hope on my help. So I will likewise not listen to you, for you do not believe in me. Sword, hunger, and disease shall be your reward. THE WHOLE PROPHET JEREMIAH 14:8-11.[7]

BLIND TO THE AID OF GOD. JOHANNES BRENZ: The natural person does not perceive things that are of the Spirit. Therefore, it is impossible for a human being to hope for help from God, unless the help were present, placed before their eyes and unless they sense it. God alone and the Word alone give no confidence to the flesh. Nevertheless, we should be lacking in every kind of help, spiritual or carnal, if we want to perceive the liberation of the

---

[5] CTS 17:208-9* (CO 38:181-82).

[6] Selnecker, *Der gantze Prophet Jeremias*, A3v-A4r; citing Ps 32:3; 103:10.
[7] Selnecker, *Der gantze Prophet Jeremias*, A4r-v.

Lord; because as long as we can sense any kind of help, we attribute it to earthly causes and not to the Lord. ANNOTATIONS ON JEREMIAH 14:9-10.[8]

WHEN THE LORD DOES NOT HEAR OUR PRAYER. JOHANNES OECOLAMPADIUS: As the prophet persists in prayer, the Lord keeps him from his intention. By that itself those people commit a more serious sin than one which would deserve pardon. And he adds, "It is lawful now that they fast, offer sacrifices and make offerings, but I will not hear them because this particular prayer is more pleasing to God, and more effective, than a foreign prayer. Nevertheless, I will destroy them by sword, famine, and plague": some perish by the strength of sword and persecution, others by want of food and apart from another evil, others through an internal and contagious disease. The people will fall by this threefold type of death. And all of those, because they are not led by the Spirit of God: on that account they will perish. COMMENTARY ON JEREMIAH 14:11.[9]

14:13-18 Lying Prophets

THE SEDUCTION OF FALSE PROPHETS. JOHANNES BUGENHAGEN: Here the prophet is anxious for the impious and ungrateful people; they refuse to accept blame before God because of the false prophets. But the Lord responds: "If the blind lead the blind, both will fall into a ditch." The people want to be seduced and blaspheme the Word of God. Meanwhile, they receive the false prophets, concerning which we have a command: "Beware of the false prophets, who come to you in sheep's clothing, inwardly, however, they are rapacious wolves." "By their fruits, that is, by their false teaching, you Christians, who have learned of Christ, you will know them."

"I have not sent them." So even today it is a great and diabolical sin that the popes and other heretics teach what God did not command. In their lies

there is a certain diabolical audacity, whether they attribute the teachings of demons to the revelation of the Holy Spirit or not. Christ will not bear this blasphemy further; Christ now kills the Antichrist with "the breath of his mouth," that is, the preaching of the gospel; as in Paul, Christ will obliterate the Antichrist "in the brightness of his coming." COMMENTARY ON JEREMIAH 14:13-14.[10]

THE GUILT OF FALSE PROPHETS AND TEACHERS. NIKOLAUS SELNECKER: God answers Jeremiah with such hard words and says that the guilt does not belong primarily to the people, but to the prophets and teachers, who do not speak the truth to the people. They neither warn nor admonish them to repentance. They do not readily open their mouths when the worst crisis obviously requires it. They are mute dogs who do not bark when the wolf comes. They make people comfortable in their sins and say, "there is no crisis." THE WHOLE PROPHET JEREMIAH 14:13-14.[11]

THE AWFUL LEGACY OF FALSE PROPHECY. KONRAD PELLIKAN: Let those false prophets beware, lest any of them nurse the people of God with deception, perish with those they have deceived, lie unburied, shamefully paraded before people, hateful to God, and convicted of falsehood with their father. The word of the Lord shouts everywhere that those with a zest for godlessness and those who do not fear the Lord will finally be punished with sword, famine, disease, and wild beasts—even in this life. Therefore, those who prophesy safety for sinners like this, including the seducers of the people and the false prophets, are clearly gathered to be judged along with the people themselves who willingly give ear to them. . . .

Often people are the cause of false doctrine. While they only want to hear pleasing things, they are eager with their ears to listen to those preaching things that are easy and that they willingly embrace,

---

[8]Brenz, *Annotationes in Jeremiam*, 894.
[9]Oecolampadius, *In Hieremiam*, 1:S3v.

[10]Bugenhagen, *In Ieremiam*, 3G3v-3G4r; citing Mt 15:14; Lk 6:39; Mt 7:15-16; 2 Thess 2:8.
[11]Selnecker, *Der gantze Prophet Jeremias*, A4v; citing Is 56:10.

so that they are not compelled to change their customs and bear discipline. They will be thrown onto the streets of Jerusalem and openly displayed with wicked disgrace. They will be excommunicated—both the prophets and the disciples who believe in them—from the fellowship of the saints. So also in the Babylonian destruction it befell the false prophets, that they were destroyed along with the people they had deceived. . . .

Such impending evil could not possibly be wept over sufficiently even if, day and night, their eyes made tears. Naturally Jeremiah depicts the contrition of the city and the people so that everything is practically before your eyes: plague, famine, discord, treachery, anger, and hate within the walls; bodies of the dead were scattered everywhere in the fields for the birds first, and then the beasts to consume. But all this was done without respect for the status of persons. At first the prophet is mentioned, then the priest; if any of them survived, they would be sent as exiles and captives into remote and unknown regions. COMMENTARY ON JEREMIAH 14:15-18.[12]

THE DECEIVED PEOPLE ARE PUNISHED TWICE.

JOHN TRAPP: They shall be no more excused for their having been deluded than he that, in his intoxication, commits adultery or murder is excused by his drunkenness. A drunkard, says Aristotle, deserves double punishment, first for his drunkenness, and then for the sin committed in and by his drunkenness. COMMENTARY ON JEREMIAH 14:16.[13]

14:19-22 A Cry of Despair, Repentance, and Hope in God

A LAMENT FOR THE PEOPLE, THE TEMPLE, AND SALVATION. KONRAD PELLIKAN: Jeremiah tries to offer a prayer, but he is not allowed to finish, since he will not be heard: it is more like a lament than a prayer. "Did you so undeservedly reject the Jewish people? Did you feel disgust at the temple and the worship that was offered to you there? Why have you smitten us so incurably? We expected salvation and peace, but received no good thing. The blow becomes ever more desperate and ruinous; the fear and dread grow greater." COMMENTARY ON JEREMIAH 14:19.[14]

PRAYER AND THE WILL OF GOD. JOHN CALVIN: After the prophet proclaimed God's judgment, he prays for a way to render God merciful. Not only does he pray for himself, but he also encourages the faithful to do the same. . . .

God revealed to him that this prayer will not be answered as matters stand. It is not that God does not hear the prayers of his people, for he always accepts them, but most often he does not fulfill them in the way they have requested. Their prayers are answered, but not according to their desires. . . . For our benefit, listen to what the prophet says: "Lord, have you rejected Judah? Is Zion an abomination to you?" as if he were saying "True it is you may reject us for our demerits, but consider what Jerusalem is: it is the place where your temple is built. You have wished your name to be invoked in this place and wished people to come from afar to invoke it, and you have said that you will fulfill those who pray in this place. What will happen now? People will say that you have defaulted on your promise. . . ."

Furthermore, it is not only a question of God's grace but also of his majesty. He has said that he wishes to be honored in this place. When it is razed, where then will God reign? That would detract not only from us and our salvation but also from God. . . . We must not presume to counsel God in any matters whatsoever. Our prayers are not made with this intention. There is no need for this audacious wish to make God wiser by our promptings. . . . God has promised to dwell in the midst of us, who are the congregation in his name. . . .

Thus we see that the complaints we make against God serve us and not him. . . . When such reveries float through our heads, we must reject

---

[12]Pellikan, *Commentaria Bibliorum*, 3:2R4r.
[13]Trapp, *A Commentary or Exposition*, 267*. Aristotle, *Ethics* l.3 C.5.
[14]Pellikan, *Commentaria Bibliorum*, 3:2R4r.

them; we must take all the deficiencies and afflictions that torment us and cast them upon him, that they be remedied. . . .

We are certain, then, that having recourse to God's promise, it is impossible for us to be confused. When all the people are moved by rage against the church, God will step in and put them down. The reason is that he has promised to do so. He does this purely by his own bounty. . . . Let us not, then, dream up methods to preserve the church; let us be certain that he will protect it. SERMON ON JEREMIAH 14:19-21.[15]

THE RAIN AND REIGN OF GRACE. JOHANNES BUGENHAGEN: Jeremiah understands this as the ark of propitiation[†] over which God was seated and heard the invocations of the people, according to his promise; lest the temple with its propitiation be profaned by the Gentiles. . . . Through allegory or rather through the signification of the Holy Spirit, the throne of the glory of God is this: the people in which God reigns, as now the Christians are. Truly, moreover, "Christ is our propitiation," as in Romans 3. Therefore, it is permitted to use these prayers against heretics, tyrants, Turks, etc. But it is even more splendid that one remember the covenant of God, through which we are accepted by God. Indeed, when we let go of the covenant, then the throne of glory, the sacraments, and all the holy things of God are worth nothing to us. And the teaching of the demons, the voices of foreigners—the foreign gods, in which faith is aban-

doned—do not give us rain. We act with evil consciences even in good times. Yet all creatures of God were created good and with the ability to perceive with thanksgiving the faithful one. . . . The prophet remembers the singularity of rain, because from the drought and sterility of the land there is a word, which signifies that in this deprivation of charity the year's crop is nothing, nor is it able to provide aid apart from God. COMMENTARY ON JEREMIAH 14:20-22.[16]

DO NOT CUT GOD TO PIECES. JOHN CALVIN: When [Jeremiah] refers to the power of God, he speaks of rain, which means that God is all-powerful. He means that everything comes from God. . . . As we are predisposed to attribute the power of God to creatures, so we must attend to this teaching all the more.

Why does each wish to have their own patron and to have recourse to the saints? Because we imagine God to be decapitated and cut in pieces, as if God said, "My power to whoever can have it!" One saint heals fevers; another cataracts; another inflammations; another, persons plagued by gravel; another, tooth problems; and others heal all sorts of ailments. It is as if they carved up God and the pieces of his power among themselves. . . . [It is] as if he resigned his office to others because he was no longer pleased to carry it out. SERMON ON JEREMIAH 14:20-22.[17]

---

[15]Calvin, *Sermons*, 1-4 (SupCalv 6:1-3).

[16]Bugenhagen, *In Ieremiam*, 3G4r-v; citing Rom 3:24-25. [†]That is, the mercy seat.
[17]Calvin, *Sermons*, 14-15 (SupCalv 6:8-9).

JEREMIAH 15:1-21
GOD'S JUDGMENT AND JEREMIAH'S ANGUISH

¹Then the Lord said to me, "Though Moses and Samuel stood before me, yet my heart would not turn toward this people. Send them out of my sight, and let them go! ²And when they ask you, 'Where shall we go?' you shall say to them, 'Thus says the Lord:

"'Those who are for pestilence, to pestilence,
    and those who are for the sword, to the sword;
    those who are for famine, to famine,
    and those who are for captivity, to captivity.'

³I will appoint over them four kinds of destroyers, declares the Lord: the sword to kill, the dogs to tear, and the birds of the air and the beasts of the earth to devour and destroy. ⁴And I will make them a horror to all the kingdoms of the earth because of what Manasseh the son of Hezekiah, king of Judah, did in Jerusalem.

⁵"Who will have pity on you, O Jerusalem,
    or who will grieve for you?
Who will turn aside
    to ask about your welfare?
⁶You have rejected me, declares the Lord;
    you keep going backward,
so I have stretched out my hand against you
    and destroyed you—
    I am weary of relenting.
⁷I have winnowed them with a winnowing fork
    in the gates of the land;
I have bereaved them; I have destroyed my people;
    they did not turn from their ways.
⁸I have made their widows more in number
    than the sand of the seas;
I have brought against the mothers of young men
    a destroyer at noonday;
I have made anguish and terror
    fall upon them suddenly.
⁹She who bore seven has grown feeble;
    she has fainted away;
her sun went down while it was yet day;
    she has been shamed and disgraced.

And the rest of them I will give to the sword
    before their enemies,
declares the Lord."

¹⁰Woe is me, my mother, that you bore me, a man of strife and contention to the whole land! I have not lent, nor have I borrowed, yet all of them curse me. ¹¹The Lord said, "Have I not[a] set you free for their good? Have I not pleaded for you before the enemy in the time of trouble and in the time of distress? ¹²Can one break iron, iron from the north, and bronze?

¹³"Your wealth and your treasures I will give as spoil, without price, for all your sins, throughout all your territory. ¹⁴I will make you serve your enemies in a land that you do not know, for in my anger a fire is kindled that shall burn forever."

¹⁵O Lord, you know;
    remember me and visit me,
    and take vengeance for me on my persecutors.
In your forbearance take me not away;
    know that for your sake I bear reproach.
¹⁶Your words were found, and I ate them,
    and your words became to me a joy
    and the delight of my heart,
for I am called by your name,
    O Lord, God of hosts.
¹⁷I did not sit in the company of revelers,
    nor did I rejoice;
I sat alone, because your hand was upon me,
    for you had filled me with indignation.
¹⁸Why is my pain unceasing,
    my wound incurable,
    refusing to be healed?
Will you be to me like a deceitful brook,
    like waters that fail?

¹⁹Therefore thus says the Lord:
"If you return, I will restore you,
    and you shall stand before me.
If you utter what is precious, and not what is

worthless,
　you shall be as my mouth.
They shall turn to you,
　but you shall not turn to them.
²⁰And I will make you to this people
　a fortified wall of bronze;
they will fight against you,

but they shall not prevail over you,
　for I am with you
　　to save you and deliver you,
declares the LORD.
²¹I will deliver you out of the hand of the
　　wicked,
　and redeem you from the grasp of the ruthless."

a The meaning of the Hebrew is uncertain

OVERVIEW: This chapter presented Reformation commentators and preachers with a range of urgent theological and pastoral issues: a judgment of God so severe and certain that prayers would not be heard; the raw and anguished cries of Jeremiah that seemed potentially blasphemous; the brokenness and apparent failure of God's prophet; and the burden of ministry in service to a demanding and faithful God.

In an age when the very concept of "saint" was under scrutiny, interpreters ponder to what degree Jeremiah appears as the worst of sinners or as a paragon of rugged faith. Moreover, in Jeremiah's suffering the true demands and toll of preaching and ministry are laid bare. To be called to the pastorate and the pulpit means donning the mantle of the prophet. In fact, Jeremiah's vulnerability and fragility provide expositors with a singular opportunity to explore spiritual suffering and to offer pastoral advice to all believers facing exhaustion and despair.

15:1-9 The Lord Will Not Relent

A PROPHET'S PRAYER AND GOD'S RESPONSE.
THE ENGLISH ANNOTATIONS: This chapter depends on the former one. . . . The prophet had complained to God about his grievous judgment in the current drought, and this moved Jeremiah to intercede on behalf of the people for the removal of the drought. In this verse God tells the prophet that he was very far from what the prophet had requested for them. Because the people had left

God, God would leave them and expel them from the land. Instead of removing the present judgment, God would consume them with other additional judgments. ANNOTATIONS ON JEREMIAH 15:1[1]

GOD ACCEPTS PRAYERS MADE PER HIS GENERAL WILL. RICHARD HOOKER: Concerning those who crave God's mercy and do not receive it, let us not think that our Savior incorrectly instructed his disciples when he willed them to pray for a peace that seemed like too great a blessing. Or that the prayers of the prophet Jeremiah offended God because God resolutely denied any favor for those whom [Jeremiah] made supplication. And if anyone doubts that God would accept prayers when they are opposite to his will or not grant them when they are according to what God wills, our answer is that in such cases God accepts [such prayers] in that they are comfortable to his general inclination that all people might be saved. Yet God always grants [such prayers], even as God sometimes has a more privately occasioned will that determines a contrary [answer]. So this other way should be the rule of our actions: even our requests for things opposed to the will of God are no less gracious in his sight. LAWES OF ECCLESIASTICAL POLITY.[2]

THE JEWS OF JEREMIAH'S TIME. MARTIN LUTHER: Since neither our diligent prayer to God nor our sincere warning to [all good Christians]

---

[1]Downame, ed., *Annotations*, 9L2v*.
[2]Hooker, *Lawes of Ecclesiastical Polity*, 5.49*.

availed, one can readily infer what this means: namely, that God considers them to be hardened and blinded; they are guilty of so much innocent blood, blasphemy, and shameful, impenitent living that he does not consider that they are worthy to receive a single good thought or emotion or that they will pay any attention to a word of wholesome and peaceful admonition. Their condition is like that of the Jews at the time of Jeremiah, when God said to them: "Though Moses and Samuel stood before me, yet my heart would not turn to this people. . . ." And in Jeremiah 7, he said, "As for you, do not pray for this people, or lift up a cry or prayer for them, and do not intercede with me, for I do not hear you." DR. MARTIN LUTHER'S WARNING TO HIS DEAR GERMAN PEOPLE.[3]

JUDGMENT AND UNANSWERED PRAYER. JOHANNES BUGENHAGEN: Here the Lord responds to the prophet as he prays, as we read above in chapter 7, lest Jeremiah pray for blasphemers and those stubborn folk who have contempt for the Word of God. Indeed, one is not able to use ignorance as a pretext for such contempt. Of course, after Moses there were so many eminent prophets and the extraordinary benefits and mercies of God that should be known. Indeed, read this in Jeremiah 7. God names two of the greatest prophets, Moses and Samuel, whom he would not wish to hear even if they could be present and speak on behalf of those who loved and increased the sins of Manasseh, king of Judah. With Moses and Samuel in mind Jeremiah would suffer less if he too were not heard. In this way God might make Jeremiah more certain concerning his judgment, which he established among his despisers, and among those who blaspheme God but do so not out of ignorance. Horrendous is blasphemy in the Holy Spirit, an attack on recognized truth. . . .

"You, Prophet: proclaim their expulsion from my face, that is, from the land I had chosen, so that I might live with them." Note that here are four plagues of God: plague, war, famine, and captivity. It is more tolerable to perish of plague than of war, and

to perish in war or with the sword than in famine; and to perish in famine is more tolerable than in captivity, which is a long-lasting evil, especially under the Babylonians, as it is for us under the Turks. So it says in the Psalm: "By the rivers of Babylon we sat and wept." COMMENTARY ON JEREMIAH 15:1-4.[4]

GENERATIONAL SIN, MULTIPLE CALAMITIES, AND THE GOSPEL. NIKOLAUS SELNECKER: God threatens four types of plague, among which one is always worse than the others—disease, war, hunger, and captivity. It is dreadful that God threatens these people so that they must pay for the sins and guilt of King Manasseh many years before. So says the first commandment, that God will pursue the sins of the father to the third and fourth generation, namely, those who hate him, who soil themselves with idolatry and other heinous sins and do not return. But when one repents and believes the gospel, that means—as it is written in Ezekiel 18—that the son shall not carry the offenses of his father, because he does what is right and good. Thus, whatever soul sins will perish. Therefore, we should guard ourselves from sinning, want to follow God's word, and not walk in the footsteps of our elders, who either erred in their teaching or were wicked in their living. . . .

No plague comes alone, but it brings along many others and has a great association and connection among the many forms of ruin and misfortune. How seldom a sickness comes alone, but it has many evil causes with it. And one devil has many others under him. Thus, one tends to say, "there is no single calamity." When misfortune comes, it makes a huge pile of misfortune. When God extends punishment for a long time, and no improvement follows, he allows the punishment to come with violence—either one after the other, or all at the same time and in a high pile. And God does not show pity easily until one again clings to God. THE WHOLE PROPHET JEREMIAH 15:2-5.[5]

---

[3]LW 47:11 (WA 30.3:276); citing Jer 7:16.

[4]Bugenhagen, *In Ieremiam*, 3H2r-v; citing Jer 7:16, 5-7; Ps 137:1.
[5]Selnecker, *Der gantze Prophet Jeremias*, B2r-v; citing 2 Kings 21:1-18; Ezek 18:20.

JUDGMENT IN THE GATES. JOHN MAYER: "I will fan them . . .": This is a metaphor taken from something like loose grains in a windy door blown in with the chaff. This shows that the Jews would be like chaff. . . . Some interpreters understand the word "gates" to mean "cities," as if he had said, "I will turn your cities into fields, the walls and buildings will be broken down"; for there were threshing floors and places to winnow corn. Or the gates were understood as places of judgment. The Lord means that he would sentence them so that they would be used like chaff, that is, scattered everywhere. Some think of "gates" as the uttermost parts of the land, because the gates are at the edges of cities. Some think it means that "I will make you poor, so that you shall beg at the gates of cities and at the gates of the rich." Still, the first interpretation above is the best. COMMENTARY ON JEREMIAH 15:7.[6]

THE PLIGHT OF MOTHERS. JOHN MAYER: This passage signifies "a young man," but with this clarification, "a chosen young man," but the singular is put forward for the plural, wasters or spoilers, chosen for their extraordinary valor in accomplishing this destruction. And by "the mother" may be understood either mothers likewise, the singular being put forward for the plural; as if he had said that not only innumerable widows shall be made, as their husbands were destroyed, but all mothers together, as if one of them will be made childless; the Chaldean youth will come upon them and will waste and destroy their children. Or it could be "the mother city," as the Greeks give the name metropolis to a chief city. "At noonday" means that the Chaldeans do not come upon them secretly or treacherously, but openly by an irresistible force. . . . "She who has given birth to seven languishes." That is, the mother of many children pines away with sorrow after seeing all of them destroyed. COMMENTARY ON JEREMIAH 15:8-9.[7]

15:10-21 Jeremiah's Complaint and God's Answer

THE PRICE OF PROPHESYING. JOHANNES BUGENHAGEN: "Woe is me." The phrase belongs to the prophet in temptation under the cross and persecution of his work . . . as in chapter 20, where Jeremiah says, "Cursed is the day on which I was born, and the day on which my mother gave birth to me; let it not be blessed." "If only I had not been born to such calamity. What shall I do on the earth? All hate me, not because I am to blame, but because of the truth and Word of God. God compels me to a duty which is detestable to all." This is the price of prophesying, even among those who seem not to manifest hatred toward preaching the Word of God. They spit out utterances in preaching with venomous words; they slander in silence; they pretend. And meanwhile there are good people who do not want to seem to hate the Word. But they are full of envy and malevolence. Here the preachers sin with impatience; they would rather stay away from their duty than to endure such things. But God knows by what necessity and obedience in duty they may come through. Therefore, freely, as a Father, he bears their infirmities, and saves those who despise the work in their own judgments. As it is written concerning Christ in Isaiah 40: "He will carry those who are offspring." And as Paul said in 2 Corinthians 1: "Blessed is the God and father of our Lord Jesus Christ, the Father of mercies, and the God of all comfort". COMMENTARY ON JEREMIAH 15:10.[8]

A MAN OF STRIFE AND HIS MOTHER. JOHN CALVIN: When he saw that his labor availed nothing or was not as fruitful as he had wished, the prophet no doubt felt somewhat human and showed his own weakness. It must, however, be observed that he was so restrained by the secret power of the Holy Spirit that he did not break forth intemperately. . . .

---

[6]Mayer, *Commentary*, 382*.
[7]Mayer, *Commentary*, 382*.

[8]Bugenhagen, *In Ieremiam*, 3H3r-v; citing Jer 20:14; Is 40:11; 2 Cor 1:3.

But he addresses his mother as though he counted his life as a curse; what does this mean? . . . We learn from these words that the prophet was not so composed and calm in his mind, but that he felt angry when he saw that he had less of an impact on others than he had wished. Yet it is evident from the context that all of this was expressed for the benefit of the public, even that the Jews might know that their hardness of heart in despising God's devoted servant and maliciously opposing him would not turn out to their benefit.

He calls himself "a man of strife," not only because he was constrained to contend with the people, for this he had in common with all the prophets. God does not send them to flatter or please the world; they must therefore contend with the world for no one is brought to a right state so as to understand the yoke of God willingly and submissively, until they are proven guilty. . . . But Jeremiah calls himself "a man of strife and contention," because he was slanderously spoken of throughout Judea, as one who through his irritability drove the whole people to contention and strife. This then is to be referred to the false judgments formed by the people; for there was hardly anyone who did not say that he was a turbulent man, and that if he was removed, there would have been tranquility in the city and throughout the whole land. . . .

But as to the exclamation regarding his mother . . . it was evidence of an intemperate feeling; for if he had spoken in a composed state of mind, what did he have to do with his mother so as to make her an associate of the evil of which he complains? He indeed seems to ascribe a part of the blame to his mother, because she had given him birth. Now this appears unreasonable. But it may at the same time be easily gathered that the prophet was not led away by so great a vehemence, except for the sake of promoting the public good, and that it was for this end that he uttered his complaint; for it was not his purpose to condemn his mother, though at the first view it appears so; but though she was innocent, he still shows that he was unjustly loaded with such slander that he was a man of strife and contention; as though Jeremiah had said: "Inquire of my mother, who gave birth to me, as to whether I was contentious from the womb." COMMENTARY ON JEREMIAH 15:10.[9]

SEEING THINGS AS THEY REALLY ARE. MARTIN LUTHER: The worst sin is not to accept the Word. For such there is no help. There is neither hearing nor speaking in a situation where the more we cry, the more they rage. It is therefore safer to keep silent than to speak. Contempt for God and blasphemy against him are dominant in the world. I would not have believed it if I had not experienced it myself. Those who see things as they really are could wish that they had died at birth. So Jonah cries, "Take my life from me, I beseech thee, for it is better for me to die than to live," and Jeremiah says that the Word has become the source of confusion for him the whole day. LECTURES ON ISAIAH 65:12.[10]

A DESPONDENT PROPHET AND FALSE CHARGES. HEINRICH BULLINGER: Since the Jewish people were perpetually unchanged and were continuing in their usual sins without any repentance, the prophet could do nothing other than thunder away against them and preach every unfortunate thing against them. Given the disposition of the ungodly, they were only able to hate the prophet, whom they also buried in wagons of abuse. Otherwise, although the man is a prophet, he digresses a bit in this passage into his circumstances, and grieving; he complains impatiently enough, and deplores his miserable luck. The Lord himself responds to him. But this digression is not completely alien to the topic he discusses. It also has its own use and result. For we learn from this grievance that even holy people, who are called to the most splendid duties, still remain humans subject to human passions. And we learn that the Stoics are wrong, who think that that no disturbances befall strong people.

---

[9]CTS 18: 267-69* (CO 38:217-19).
[10]LW 17:383 (WA 31.2:559); citing Jn 4:3; 20:14.

Likewise the example of Jeremiah shows what any prophet can anticipate. He experienced the animosity of the world and the heights of ingratitude. Therefore you should expect equal results, if the Lord gives something a little better, that is, something for which everyone should give thanks. But the fact that Jeremiah complained, and all but found fault with the Lord, is hardly something we should imitate. Indeed, he sins against the Lord, and not lightly. Therefore, let us learn to recognize not only our own weakness but also that of the saints; let us learn to attribute nothing to our human strength and to always fear, lest we are cast down by our passions. But we should be watchful and prayerful, so that the Lord keeps us in his hands. Here the Lord graciously takes back the reverent Jeremiah. In this way, God shows that with kindness he truly takes back to himself all sinners who are truly reverent through repentance.

Jeremiah certainly poured out the fire of his soul before the Lord. He exclaimed that he was miserable, he whom his mother gave birth to, as if he felt that he would have been happier if he had never been born. He adds the reason why he considers himself miserable. "Throughout the kingdom I am considered a litigious man and a man of controversy and disagreements. I whom everyone attacks as one who disturbs the public peace, or whom they call a reviler on account of my ministry and the freedom and necessity of my speech." Likewise, today many people call the heralds of the gospel quarrelers, seditious people, and bringers of discord. Jeremiah adds that he is unfairly and hostilely attacked by everyone, since he himself has given no occasion for such hate. "Those who conduct banking business and put forth their money in usury, expose themselves to the hatred of many. Truly, I have never involved myself in any banking transactions, so I have less hatred and more kindness. Nevertheless, they persecute me and everyone attacks me with accusations as if I am the most sordid usurer; everyone curses me." This certainly is the lot of faithful haranguers who in fact act according to the apostolic mandate and ought to involve themselves minimally in worldly affairs. They aim for this alone: that they subject themselves wholly to the business of heaven, and carry that out in a most unencumbered way. SERMON ON JEREMIAH 15:10.[11]

THE INFIRMITY OF STRONG PEOPLE. JOHN DONNE: Jonah was angry because his prophecy was not executed, because God would not follow Jonah's prophecy with the destruction of Nineveh. Jeremiah was angry because his prophecy would be executed. Jeremiah preached this severe teaching and his audience hated him: "Woe is me, my mother. . . ." "I preach only the messages of God (and woe unto to me if I do not preach them). I preach only the sense of God's indignation on my own soul and conscious of my own sins. I impute nothing to anyone else that I do not first confess of myself before God. I do not search another person's memory—what someone did last year, last week, or even last night. I only gather into my memory and power in the presence of my God and his church, the history of my own youth." Yet I am a "contentious man," says Jeremiah, "a worm and a burden to every tender conscience." As he says, "I strive with the whole earth"; "I am a bitter and satirical preacher. This is what wearies me," he says. "I have neither lent with usury, nor have men lent to me with usury." "Yet, it as though I were an oppressive lender or a fraudulent borrower"; "every one of them curses me.'"

This is a natural infirmity, which the strongest of people, since they are human, cannot let go. If their purposes do not prosper, they are weary of their work and weary of their lives. There can be no greater ingratitude to God than to desire to be nothing at all, rather than to be what God desired you to be: to desire to leave the world rather than to glorify God through your patience in the world. But when this infirmity overtakes God's children: "They suffer as humans, but are sustained as friends of God."† They are under calamities, as they are human, but yet they come to recollect themselves and to bear those calamities, as valiant soldiers, as

---

[11]Bullinger, *Conciones*, 109v; citing 2 Tim 2:4.

faithful servants, as bosom friends of Almighty God. SERMON ON PSALM 38:2.[12]

JEREMIAH AMONG THE GREAT AND SAINTED MEN OF STRIFE.

CORNELIUS À LAPIDE: This is an exclamation, in which the prophet laments from a natural sense of suffering that he was begotten by some unknown fate, to be a man of hatred and reproach to everyone, because of his prophetic threats. He calls himself "a man of strife and contention." That is, he is exposed to the injuries, hate, and abuse of all, he with whom everyone quarrels and disputes. . . . Thus Christ was a man of strife, and was placed into our ruin and for the resurrection of many. . . . Thus those who want to reform deformed and fallen governments and religion are men of strife to immoral folk. . . . Such a man of strife was St. Paul. . . . Such a man of strife was the truly immortal St. Athanasius, who nearly alone provoked a war with the whole world of Arians and subdued them. Such a man of strife was St. Benedict, who at the beginning of his conversion incurred the hate of certain elder monks because he wanted to dissuade them from a licentious life to one of discipline. . . . Such men of strife were St. Jerome, St. John Chrysostom, St. Gregory of Nazianzus, St. Thomas of Canterbury, and St. Thomas More, and in this time our blessed father Ignatius, whose presence everywhere aroused a tempest of the ungodly and demons. For this reason Ignatius himself, having learned from long experience, grieved and feared that prosperity might sometime be taken away on all sides from the progress of the Society of Jesus. COMMENTARY ON THE PROPHET JEREMIAH 15:10.[13]

THE CONSOLATION OF WEAK SAINTS.

NIKOLAUS SELNECKER: "Woe to my mother, that you gave birth to me; one against whom everyone contends and fights." Here Jeremiah laments his misery, difficult office, and the danger that comes with it. He goes into this later in the twentieth chapter; he is impatient like Job and curses his day of birth. When we learn to recognize weaknesses in the saints and great people, we are assured they also have their whining moments and sinning. Dr. Luther, the God-blessed one, tended to say that he would rather read about the great saints in history that experienced weakness and pitfalls; because of this he himself was consoled by them. So it is to encounter such remarkable people. When we experience and feel our weakness, fear, cowardice, and pitfalls, should we fall back and lose heart? We learn here that we should be sympathetic with each other and help alleviate the weakness of others, shelter each other with consolation and not condemn each other hour after hour and so reject each other and give ourselves to the devil. So it is for someone who has stumbled over weakness.

But God does not reject Jeremiah or other weak saints, but he consoles them. God helps Jeremiah get back on his feet, strengthens and instructs him, and promises him his grace and mercy, that he wants to protect him and preserve him, that he does not want his poor little house and church to perish among enemies. What consolation we should have and hold in our difficulties, and in our calling, so that we forge ahead truly and diligently, and order our matters and lives to God. He will not leave us as orphans. We learn too and see how it is goes for true preachers and teachers in their office and what kind of misery, temptation, pain, anxiety, and difficulty they carry and suffer—more and greater than many hundreds of people. All honest and true-hearted preachers in their office fully experience and can attest to difficulty and can be run down by it. So the rest of the world sleeps, snores, and lives in all their pleasures, goes into the spring and enjoys the good weather. But preachers quake with sadness and have much anxious sweat, few good days, and great care and work all the time.

---

[12]Donne, *Sermons*, 2:52-53*; citing Jer 15:10. †A quotation attributed to John Chrysostom.

[13]À Lapide, *Commentarium in Jeremiam*, 100. À Lapide cites saints who like Jeremiah suffered for their faith, some of whom were martyred at the hands of the political powers: Jerome (c. 347–419/420), John Chrysostom (349–407), Gregory Nazianzus (329–389), Thomas (Becket) of Canterbury (1118–1170), Thomas More (1478–1535), and Ignatius of Loyola (1491–1556).

Jeremiah experiences fully that he is practiced in the cross and learns what his own weak nature can do, namely, nothing in such temptations. He learns what an enemy the devil is for the pious, what the world is, and how God is truly with him, calls him, holds him, consoles and strengthens him. THE WHOLE PROPHET JEREMIAH 15:10.[14]

I HAVE INJURED NO ONE. JUAN DE MALDONADO: This is an exclamation of Jeremiah, in which he laments that he was born by some fate to be a reproach to all, because he announced the truth. "A man of strife": that is, exposed to quarrels and abuse from everyone. "I have not lent on interest": that is, I have done injury to no one. Jeremiah has one kind of injury stand for them all. Moreover, he seems to argue that it is not only a sin to give money in usury, but also to receive it, which is contrary to the determinations of the theologians. But he does understand, I think, that no one ever bothered to loan himself money at interest.[†] COMMENTARY ON THE PROPHETS, JEREMIAH 15:10.[15]

BLIND TO THE AID OF GOD. JOHANNES BRENZ: The human being does not perceive things that are of the Spirit. Therefore, it is impossible for a human being to hope for help from God, unless God is placed directly before their eyes and unless they sense God. God alone and the Word alone give no confidence to the flesh. It may be wholly necessary that we forsake every form of assistance, whether physical or spiritual, if in tribulation and anguish we want to recognize the freedom of the Lord. How long is carnal help sensed, but the flesh ascribes it to the flesh, and not to God? ANNOTATIONS ON JEREMIAH 15:10.[16]

GOD WILL EXALT HIS PROPHETS AND MINISTERS. HEINRICH BULLINGER: We must admire the goodness of a most merciful God, who does not reject the murmuring prophet, but consoles him fully. But in order that his promise might find more faith, he confirms it with an oath. For this is a formula for swearing an oath: "if there is no remnant to your good." Indeed, we have to understand in addition, "then let me perish," or, "I am not God, unless I make it happen that you have some good remnant." By "remnant" he means either the outcome of actual events, or the end of this tragedy, or the leftover or remaining days of the prophet's life. We say in German, "There will still be a good ending." Then the same formula of swearing adds, "If I do not make this happen for you in the time of tribulation of the enemy." It is as if God says, "I will certainly cause this so that your enemy will become as a suppliant to you." God will take up your case like a patron and work for you, and if necessary intercede for you.

History certainly testifies that King Zedekiah himself called Jeremiah to himself in the most difficult time of the siege of Jerusalem and practically begged him as a suppliant for his counsel. Moreover, we read that Nabuzaradan, a prince of the army of Babylon, took up the cause of Jeremiah to defend him in the final crisis of the city and the citizens. Read chapters 38 and 39 of this prophet's book. The proverb that follows pertains to this: "Can iron sharpen iron, or steel sharpen steel?" Others read this as bronze. In fact iron is hardly sharpened, or "consumed," by iron, but rather it is refined by being struck. Jeremiah is compared to iron, and the iron of the north is the Babylonians. Therefore the sense is: even if the Babylonians will be extremely harsh as they besiege and destroy the city, nevertheless they will not destroy you. All these developments serve to illustrate the glory of God and the honor of Jeremiah. This promise, which pertains to Jeremiah in a peculiar and particular way, nevertheless extends no less to all the ministers of God, whom the Lord will never fail. "I am with you," he says, "even to the end of the age." Therefore, even if misfortune and difficulties

---

[14]Selnecker, *Der gantze Prophet Jeremias*, B3r-v; citing Job 3:1-11; see LW 6:177 (WA 44:132), in RCS OT 5:362.

[15]Maldonado, *Commentarii in Prophetas*, 72. †Usury, the practice of charging interest on money lent to others, is forbidden in the Old Testament (Ex 22:25; Lev 25:36). The rejection of usury continued well into the Reformation, though new practices were challenging the prohibition on charging interest.

[16]Brenz, *Annotationes in Jeremiam*, 894.

in our time overwhelm us too and we are similarly swept away by a violent storm, nevertheless God has his means and measures, by which he is able to save us. . . . Let us trust in the Lord our God. Let us do our duty, and let us entrust every outcome to God, secure in the fact that he sees us and cares for all that is ours. SERMON ON JEREMIAH 15:11-14.[17]

THE HARD METAL OF THE NORTH. GIOVANNI DIODATI: It is possible to break iron, the iron and brass of the north; that is to say, "is it in my power, Jeremiah, to break my decrees or to keep back, or take power away from my words?" Or does the verse mean, "Oh you Jewish Nation, I will send against you the northern Chaldeans, which are a warlike and invincible nation." The northern part of the world was most fully endowed with hard metals for the making of weapons. ANNOTATIONS ON JEREMIAH 15:12.[18]

GET USED TO TAKING SOME HARD KNOCKS. THOMAS MÜNTZER: In view of the wretched, ruinous condition of the poor Christian church, it should be realized that no advice or help can be given until we have industrious, unflagging servants of God who are ready, day in, day out, to promote the knowledge of the biblical books through singing, reading, and preaching. This will mean, however, that either the heads of our delicate priests get used to taking some hard knocks, or else they will have to abandon their trade. What alternative is there, while ravaging wolves are so grievously devastating the Christian people. . . . For our situation today is the same as that of the good prophets, Isaiah, Jeremiah, Ezekiel, and the others, when the whole congregation of God's elect had become completely caught up in idolatrous ways. As a result, not even God could help them, but had to let them be captured and transported and tormented under the heathen until they learned to recognize his holy name again, as Isaiah 29,

Jeremiah 15, Ezekiel 36, and Psalm 88 testify. SERMON TO THE PRINCES.[19]

BEARING ALL THINGS BRAVELY FOR GOD. KONRAD PELLIKAN: The prophet prays to the Lord: "You, O Lord, are our one and only Lord. I pray in the midst of so much danger and persecution, in such a difficult function, by which I am pressed in your name. Remember me, grant to me courage and grace that I may be defended by perseverance and not fail in tribulation. Do not permit me to be overwhelmed in wickedness while following your righteousness; do not patiently bear the impious enemies of your word. But quickly take me away from such great dangers and disgraces, which I bear for you." Indeed, the servant of God ought to be always prepared to bear all things bravely for God. Nevertheless, he often can pray that the Lord will humble and overwhelm the impious and offer a place of peace and salvation to the faithful. COMMENTARY ON JEREMIAH 15:15.[20]

WHEN WE CONSUME THE WORD OF GOD. DIRK PHILIPS: We are called heretics and Anabaptists by the world, corrupters of the sacraments, new Pharisees, too strict observers of excommunication, merciless judges, and separators of marriage. Despite this we commend all our concerns to Almighty God who knows that in this we are unjustly defamed and detracted. . . .

Now, however, we are seated under the shadow of the Almighty, and protected under his wings, saying with Jeremiah: "O Lord, you know that I have suffered reproach for you. Your words have been found and I have eaten them." EVANGELICAL EXCOMMUNICATION.[21]

FEASTING ON THE WORD. JOHN MAYER: [Jeremiah says] I did not take on this prophetic office [of my own accord], for which I am so hated for my efforts. But when I thought about it, your

---

[17]Bullinger, *Conciones*, 109v-110r; citing Mt 28:20; Prov 27:17; Mt 28:20.
[18]Diodati, *Pious Annotations*, 65*.
[19]Müntzer, *Collected Works*, 230; citing Is 29:17-24; Ezek 36:20-23; Ps 89:30-45.
[20]Pellikan, *Commentaria Bibliorum*, 3:2R5r.
[21]CRR 6:609.

words came to me. And whether I wanted to or not, I was forced into it. . . . I ate them, that is, I received them into my heart, and not my mouth only, as many do. But I applied myself with a true heart to obey them as you commanded, believing them to be your word; for whoever does this, God's words become a food that is eaten and nourishes to eternal life, and so Christ is his substantial Word. "And it was sweet to me." Here Jeremiah is similar to Ezekiel; for they both had unspeakable inward joy through this spiritual eating, and so shall all others have that eat in a similar way. COMMENTARY ON JEREMIAH 15:16.[22]

DIGESTING THE SWEET WORD OF GOD. JOHN CALVIN: "I did eat" [your words]. Jeremiah here testifies that he submitted to God's command from the heart and with a sincere feeling. We indeed know that many chatter about heavenly mysteries and have the words of God on their tongues; but the prophet says that he had "eaten the words" of God; that is, he brought forth nothing from the tip of his tongue, as the proverb is, but spoke from the bottom of his heart, while engaged in the work of his calling. This metaphor of eating is well known and sufficiently common in Scripture. When we are said to eat Christ the reference is no doubt to the union we have with him, because we are one body and one spirit. So also we are said to eat the Word of God—not when we only taste it and immediately spit it out again as disgusted people do—but also when we receive it inwardly and digest what the Lord sets before us. For celestial truth is compared to food, and we know by the experience of faith how fit the comparison is. Since, then, celestial truth is good to feed spiritually to our souls, we are justly said to eat it when we do not reject it, but greedily receive it, and so really chew and digest it so that it becomes nourishment. This then is what the prophet meant: for he did not act a fable on the stage when teaching the people, but performed with real earnestness the office committed to him,

not like an actor, as the case is with many who boast themselves to be ministers of the Word, but he was a faithful and true minister of God. . . .

It may however be asked, how could the Word of God be so sweet and pleasant to the prophet when yet it was so full of bitterness? For we have seen elsewhere that many tears were shed by the holy man, and he had expressed a wish that his eyes would flow as though they were fountains of water. How then could these things agree—the grief and sorrow the holy man felt for God's judgments and the joy and gladness he mentions? . . . These two feelings, though apparently opposite, were connected together in the prophets; they as human beings deplored and mourned the ruin of the people, and yet, through the power of the Spirit, they performed their office and approved of the just vengeance of God. Thus then the Word of God became a joy to the prophet, not that he was untouched by a deep feeling for the destruction of his people, but that he rose above all human feelings, so as fully to approve of God's judgments. COMMENTARY ON JEREMIAH 15:16.[23]

PREACHING FAITHFULLY RESULTS IN LONELINESS. THE ENGLISH ANNOTATIONS: Alone or solitary refers either to withdrawing oneself from company, as persons full of grief and heaviness are inclined to do, or to being deserted and forsaken by all. But this seems rather to imply a voluntary and affected privacy, "because of your hand," that is, as some, because I am at hand with you, and yield constant obedience to you in the faithful discharge of my ministerial employment, in regard whereof, they refuse to have any society with me. So "hand" should mean ministry, but "because of thine hand" seems here rather to import, in regard of your injunction and those messages which you sent by me, full of menaces and dreadful denunciations of calamities and destruction to befall my people. ANNOTATIONS ON JEREMIAH 5:17.[24]

---

[22]Mayer, *Commentary*, 384*; citing Ezek 2:8.

[23]CTS 18:283-85* (CO 38:226-27); citing Mt 26:26; Jer 9:1.
[24]Downame, ed., *Annotations*, 9L4v*; citing Ps 102:7; Jer 13:17; Lam 3:18; Ps 88:8, 18; Mal 1:1; Ezek 3:14.

JEREMIAH DISTURBED IN THE FLESH, FAITHFUL IN DOCTRINE. JOHN CALVIN: Jeremiah has before shown that he possessed a heroic courage in despising all the splendor of the world, and in regarding as nothing those proud men who boasted that they were the rulers of the church: but he now confesses his infirmity; and there is no doubt but that he was often agitated by different thoughts and feelings; and this necessarily happens to us, because the flesh always fights against the spirit. For though the prophet announced nothing human when he declared the truth of God, yet he was not wholly exempt from sorrow and fear and other feelings of the flesh. For we must always distinguish, when we speak of the prophets and the apostles, between the truth, which was pure, free from every imperfection, and their own persons, as they commonly say of themselves. Nor were they so perfectly renewed but that some remnant of the flesh still continued in them. So then Jeremiah was in himself disturbed with anxiety and fear, and affected with weariness, and wished to shake off the burden he felt so heavy on his shoulders. He was then subject to these feelings, that is, as to himself; yet his doctrine was free of every defect, for the Holy Spirit guided his mind, his thoughts, and his tongue, so that there was in it nothing human. COMMENTARY ON JEREMIAH 15:18.[25]

THE SIN OF JEREMIAH. SEBASTIAN MÜNSTER: "Why is my grief perpetual?" "Grief" is what he calls that perpetual contention and persecution, which his people were pursuing against him. Further, the "unfaithful waters" are in Hebrew "the waters that act unfaithfully." Moreover, this is the sense as Jonathan translates it: "Do not let your word be a lie to me, and like the bubbling up of waters of a spring, whose waters have failed. . . ."† Since the prophet sinned through these words, showing the disturbance of his soul, the Lord refutes him in the words that follow: "if you will return," that is, "if you would repent from your unbelief, in which you revile my Word, then as befitting your manliness

you will attempt to bring this rebellious people back to you and to make the ungodly just." "[Then] you shall be as my mouth" etc. "You will not be afraid of them, since I have made you 'into a brass wall'" etc. We must note that this fall of Jeremiah is for our benefit. The Lord placed his hand under the falling Jeremiah, so he would not be shattered. "If you will acknowledge your sin," the Lord says, "and will pursue repentance, I will take you back into the dignity of your previous function." THE TEMPLE OF THE LORD, JEREMIAH 15:18-20.[26]

CLING TO AND MINISTER BEFORE THE LORD. JOHANNES BUGENHAGEN: "If you cling to me." "If Christ remains in me and I in him, then I bear much fruit." We cling to God when we hold to faith in his Word, and "we do not depart from faith and towards the teachings of the demons, who in hypocrisy speak lies, whose consciences have been seared. . . ." Now God clings to us, as Christ says, "If he loves me, he will keep my word, and my father will love him and we will come to him and we will make our mansion with him. You will remain my preacher. You will stand before me, even before my face, as a priest sacrificing is said to stand before the Lord," as in Luke 1, when you read of Zechariah. "You will stand before me, that is, truly you will be my minister, prophet, and preacher. I will be present to your ministry, and I will make your office fortunate. And if you will teach the just so that they separate themselves from perversity, if you will separate the precious from the vile, you will be my mouth, that is my teacher. Now you are truly proven in order to sincerely teach the Word of God and I will encourage you." COMMENTARY ON JEREMIAH 15:19.[27]

---

[26]Münster, *Miqdaš YHWH* (1546), 886; citing Jer 1:18. †Münster cites the Targum Jonathan, or Targumim to the Prophets, a fourth-century-AD Jewish work of translation and commentary attributed by tradition to Jonathan ben Uzziel, the disciple of the Elder Hillel (first century AD); see Bruce Chilton, "Targum," in *Dictionary of Biblical Interpretation*, ed. John H. Hayes (Nashville: Abingdon, 1999), 2:531-34.
[27]Bugenhagen, *In Ieremiam*, 31r-v; citing Jn 15:5; 1 Tim 4:1; Jn 14:1-2; Lk 1:8.

---

[25]CTS 18:290* (CO 38:231).

THE GODLY AND THE WICKED NEED TO HEAR DIFFERENT MESSAGES. THE ENGLISH ANNOTATIONS: This some think refers to doctrine only; if you are careful to teach nothing but the pure truth of God without mixture of other base or vile stuff, such as the false prophets are inclined to mingle. Others think that this refers rather to people; that which the latter term does necessarily carry it to, being used of people only; if you shall draw out the precious from the vile by converting those that are vile, that is, wicked ones, from their wickedness and making precious ones of them, which God's ministers are ministerially said to do, or (which seems the genuine sense of the text, and is by the most and best approved), if in your teaching you put a difference between the godly and the wicked, by confirming and comforting the one and by sharply reproving, convincing, and menacing the other, contrary to the practice of the false prophets described. ANNOTATIONS ON JEREMIAH 15:19.[28]

HOW CHRISTIANS SHOULD SEPARATE THE PRECIOUS FROM THE VILE. LANCELOT ANDREWES: Well then, what shall we do, "to sever the precious from the vile"; "Jesus Christ from others; determine the *hic est Ille* ["This is he"]. This, according to Saint John, is done in these two ways: (1) It is that Jesus Christ who comes in "water and blood" together, and not in either one alone, *hic est Ille.* If he is only in one of those, he is another Jesus. (2) "That Jesus" who has "the Spirit to bear witness concerning him" is the true [Jesus]. If he lacks this witness, *hic non est Ille* [He is not the true Jesus]. Under the first we shall learn of Christ aright. For as many learn of a false Christ, so it is possible for others to learn about the true Christ falsely. "You have not so learned Christ," says the apostle, that is, not amiss you have not, meaning some others have. And just as you learn Christ aright, so learn to acknowledge the Spirit rightly, and not shoot him off, but know he is to have a chief holy day among our fasts, as he has a part, and a principal part in the test of whosoever shall be saved. SERMON ON 1 JOHN 5:6.[29]

---

[28]Downame, ed., *Annotations*, 9L4v*; citing 1 Pet 2:2; Jer 23:26, 28; Dan 12:3; Jer 23:33; Mal 4:6; Lk 1:16; Ezek 13:19, 22; 22:26.

[29]Andrewes, *Works*, 3:345-56*; citing 1 Jn 5:6; Eph. 4:20.

JEREMIAH 16:1-21
DIVINE JUDGMENT AND RESTORATION

¹The word of the LORD came to me: ²"You shall not take a wife, nor shall you have sons or daughters in this place. ³For thus says the LORD concerning the sons and daughters who are born in this place, and concerning the mothers who bore them and the fathers who fathered them in this land: ⁴They shall die of deadly diseases. They shall not be lamented, nor shall they be buried. They shall be as dung on the surface of the ground. They shall perish by the sword and by famine, and their dead bodies shall be food for the birds of the air and for the beasts of the earth.

⁵"For thus says the LORD: Do not enter the house of mourning, or go to lament or grieve for them, for I have taken away my peace from this people, my steadfast love and mercy, declares the LORD. ⁶Both great and small shall die in this land. They shall not be buried, and no one shall lament for them or cut himself or make himself bald for them. ⁷No one shall break bread for the mourner, to comfort him for the dead, nor shall anyone give him the cup of consolation to drink for his father or his mother. ⁸You shall not go into the house of feasting to sit with them, to eat and drink. ⁹For thus says the LORD of hosts, the God of Israel: Behold, I will silence in this place, before your eyes and in your days, the voice of mirth and the voice of gladness, the voice of the bridegroom and the voice of the bride.

¹⁰"And when you tell this people all these words, and they say to you, 'Why has the Lord pronounced all this great evil against us? What is our iniquity? What is the sin that we have committed against the LORD our God?' ¹¹then you shall say to them: 'Because your fathers have forsaken me, declares the Lord, and have gone after other gods and have served and worshiped them, and have forsaken me and have not kept my law, ¹²and because you have done worse than your fathers, for behold, every one of you follows his stubborn, evil will, refusing to listen to me. ¹³Therefore I will hurl you out of this land into a land that neither you nor your fathers have known, and there you shall serve other gods day and night, for I will show you no favor.'

¹⁴"Therefore, behold, the days are coming, declares the LORD, when it shall no longer be said, 'As the LORD lives who brought up the people of Israel out of the land of Egypt,' ¹⁵but 'As the LORD lives who brought up the people of Israel out of the north country and out of all the countries where he had driven them.' For I will bring them back to their own land that I gave to their fathers.

¹⁶"Behold, I am sending for many fishers, declares the LORD, and they shall catch them. And afterward I will send for many hunters, and they shall hunt them from every mountain and every hill, and out of the clefts of the rocks. ¹⁷For my eyes are on all their ways. They are not hidden from me, nor is their iniquity concealed from my eyes. ¹⁸But first I will doubly repay their iniquity and their sin, because they have polluted my land with the carcasses of their detestable idols, and have filled my inheritance with their abominations."

¹⁹O LORD, my strength and my stronghold,
   my refuge in the day of trouble,
to you shall the nations come
   from the ends of the earth and say:
"Our fathers have inherited nothing but lies,
   worthless things in which there is no profit.
²⁰Can man make for himself gods?
   Such are not gods!"

²¹"Therefore, behold, I will make them know, this once I will make them know my power and my might, and they shall know that my name is the LORD."

OVERVIEW: In some passages the prophecies of Jeremiah seem to overturn and contradict common teachings found throughout Scripture: do not get married; do not comfort the grieving or celebrate with the joyful; fishers of men will come to snare and drag the Jews into exile. Such instructions and themes in Jeremiah could prove volatile and confusing in the Reformation era, when the nature of marriage generally, clergy marriage in particular, and the superiority of celibacy were hotly contested and those of every confessional identity were seeking to reform church, society, and cultural practices. Were Jeremiah's sermons gripping illustrations of divine judgment for a peculiar time or perpetual commands for the godly that dwell among unbelievers? And were sixteenth- and seventeenth-century Europeans living in a world akin to Jeremiah's or a world of imminent hope and renewal to which some verses of Jeremiah 16 did not apply? Despite the persistent emphasis on divine judgment in Jeremiah, interpreters also found in the promises of Jewish restoration and the salvation of the nations the very message of the gospel and the resonance of a covenant that linked the Old and New Testament peoples of God.

16:1-13 Famine, Sword, and Death

DO NOT MARRY OR OFFER CONSOLATION.
JOHANNES BUGENHAGEN: The verses in this chapter again are full with violent menace, in addition to the few in which he speaks concerning a restoration of the people. God says, "Oh Jeremiah, do not take a wife and do not bear children here, for I am going to destroy everything," says the Lord, "lest you become twice as miserable in the time of captivity"; as Christ says in Luke 23, the Jewish women in the Roman captivity would say, "Blessed are the sterile women, those whose wombs have not given birth, and the breasts that have not given milk." And God continues this further, saying, "Do not enter a house of mourning," etc., "because they are all unworthy of every consolation, those whom I am about to destroy." Jeremiah was not keeping this command of God to himself in secret, but

God commanded him to announce this to the people, so that they might know why Jeremiah was so acting; so that the people might be moved to repentance not only by the words but also by signs of the prophet.

"Do not take a wife." Unworthy are those filthy pigs—papists, harlots, adulterers, sodomites, murders, and blasphemers—who from this passage and through the holy Scriptures are refuted by us. Inasmuch as anti-Christians prohibit marriage, as Paul proclaimed concerning them through the Spirit; the prohibition of marriage, he says, is stupid. Like an ass playing the lyre, they cite these words from Jeremiah for their own impure celibacy and not otherwise is the quote from that impious man in the gospel, "I took a wife; therefore I am not able to come." In addition to these passages they disgrace women and virgins with many filthy things, as asses themselves would be able to produce. A woman defecates; therefore she is not to be taken as a bride, lest we most holy priests be made impure through a woman, through the marriage God created, instituted, and blessed. COMMENTARY ON JEREMIAH 16.[1]

MARRIAGE IN A TIME OF JUDGMENT.
JOHANNES OECOLAMPADIUS: Ingenious is the spirit of our prophet, to discuss the same thing through various arguments and with these distinctive signs—all effective at rousing people; for the whole of precepts and doctrine is held together with a few themes. Therefore, all things are given so that they might persuade us unto obedience and respect of doctrine. And so the same argument that had been made thus far is found in this passage, where taking a wife is prohibited. This parable must be seen according to the common rule of parables; a likeness of the part is assumed, from which there is a likeness of the whole. Indeed, marriages are not simply prohibited, as if shameful to the prophet or the man of God. . . . Marriages are prohibited in this particular designated place,

---

[1]Bugenhagen, *In Ieremiam*, 314r-v; citing Lk 23:29; 1 Tim 4:3; Lk 14:20.

on account of the disaster that is to be inferred by this sign as if by a visual sign. Marriage is therefore free and in its proper place necessary. Indeed, it is a common rule that those who are not continent take a wife; it pertains to both sexes and every order and condition of life. For the rest, as I have said, through abstinence from marriage, as is prescribed here, God shows that the time is very dangerous and that there is not much future in that place. But for the sake of future generations God most importantly established marriage. COMMENTARY ON JEREMIAH 16:1.[2]

WAS JEREMIAH MARRIED? JOHN MAYER: The prophet is prompted by another sign to declare what he had prophesied about the evil death to befall the land of Judea, namely, he did neither take a wife nor beget children because the people of that land should die miserably, and their bodies should be as dung upon the earth. It may seem ill-mannered to question whether Jeremiah was married already, or if it is here intimated that a celibate life is commended to prophets. But it is most probable that Jeremiah was not married; for if he had been, this prohibition would not have been needed; he would not take another wife, if one was alive. Although polygamy was practiced by other men in those days, even by Abraham and Jacob occasionally and for a mystical signification, yet it was not practiced by any other prophet and was in fact condemned. COMMENTARY ON JEREMIAH 16:1-4.[3]

THREE REASONS FOR CELIBACY. MARTIN LUTHER: The first category [of people who have a valid reason for a vow of celibacy], Christ calls "eunuchs who have been so from birth"; these are the ones whom people call impotent, who are by nature not equipped to produce seed and multiply because they are physically frigid or weak or have some other bodily deficiency that makes them unfit for the estate of marriage. Such cases occur among both men and women. . . .

The second category, those who Christ says "have been made eunuchs by men": the castrated are an unhappy lot, for though they are unequipped for marriage, they are nevertheless not free from evil desire. . . .

The third category consist of those spiritually rich and exalted persons, bridled by the grace of God, who are equipped for marriage by nature and physical capacity, and nevertheless voluntarily remain celibate. These put it this way, "I could marry if I wish; I am capable of it. But it does not attract me. I would rather work for the kingdom of heaven, i.e., the gospel and beget spiritual children." Such persons are rare, not one in a thousand, for they are a special miracle of God. No one should venture on such a life unless he is especially called by God, like Jeremiah, or unless he finds God's grace to be so powerful within him that the divine injunction, "Be fruitful and multiply," has no place in him. THE ESTATE OF MARRIAGE.[4]

WHY WE BURY THE DEAD. JOHN CALVIN: When the prophet says that they will have no tomb but will be meat for the birds and beasts of the earth, he is admonishing us that whatsoever happens in the world is the judgment of God. . . . Now if one asks whether burial profits the dead, since they cannot feel hot or cold, it would seem that the prophet has omitted any mention of this in his recitation of God's threats. . . . Yet the tomb is a sign of our resurrection. Our bodies, though they rot away, sleep in the tomb; death is merely night; the day will come when God will awaken us. This is how the tomb is a memorial to the resurrection. The fact that we rot in the earth does not mean we will not be resurrected someday. That is why the tomb was so honored among the patriarchs. Both Joseph and Jacob refer to the kingdom of God in their requests that their bones be taken from Egypt and buried in the Promised Land. . . . Now the prophet tells the Jews they will be denied burial, as if he were saying, "You are so wicked that you deserve punishment in life and in death; you

---

[2]Oecolampadius, *In Hieremiam*, 1:U2r-v.
[3]Mayer, *Commentary*, 385-86*; citing Mal 2:15.

[4]LW 45:19, 21* (WA 10.2:278, 279); citing Mt 19:12; Gen 1:28.

have known his judgment against your sins; and after you die, you will face an even more severe judgment." That is why the prophet says that "they will be thrown on the ground. . . ."

Our Lord ordained burial in order that we recognize that we are not like a beast or dog, but go on to a better life than this one. SERMON ON JEREMIAH 16:4.[5]

THE DEAD ARE NOT MOURNED. THE ENGLISH ANNOTATIONS: No solemn lamentation shall be made for the dead, either because those who are gone and have been taken away from present evils are considered happier than those who have survived or because everyone is so taken up with their own particular and personal fears, cares, and calamities that they shall have no energy or leisure to look after their deceased or to express any solemnity about them. ANNOTATIONS ON THE BOOK OF JEREMIAH 16:4.[6]

DO NOT MOURN WITH THOSE WHO MOURN. JOHANNES BUGENHAGEN: Paul says, "Rejoice with those who rejoice, mourn with those who mourn," which is love among Christians themselves. Here, however, God forbids the prophet in both ways, lest he mourn with those mourning, and lest he rejoice with the joyful. Besides which, he should remove himself from those mourning and rejoicing on account of their insolence before destruction. He says, "I have taken away my peace"; that is, "I have taken away all of my goods from this people—my grace or favor, and mercy. So only my anger may remain over this contemptuous people." As John the Baptist says, "He who does not believe in the Son, the wrath of God remains over him." Likewise, "I will take away from this place the voice of the bridegroom and the bride," the rejoicing of weddings, which though they may not be common among friends are still very much so among the bridegroom and bride; that is, the joys of marriage,

which, since they are not common among friends, are greatest between bride and bridegroom.

In summary, through the Babylonian captivity it would happen that in this place people would no longer gather together, neither for mourning nor rejoicing. "When the people have been cast away, in this optimal and holy land, where my kingdom and priesthood is, there will be left a most shameful appearance of all things." The legitimate commonwealth will be destroyed, the temple torn apart, the kingdom of God, that is, the Word of God and all the holy things of God, will be taken away from you. As Christ himself said to the Jews, "Your abandoned house will be left behind." "The kingdom of God will be taken from you and will be given to a Gentile nation as the fruit of his actions." These judgments of God have been proposed, so that we might fear and not continue to despise the Word of God, but that we repent, lest we perish as we see that they have perished. "Do you not know that the patience of God anticipates your repentance?" Christ says in Luke 13, "Unless you repent, you all will likewise perish." COMMENTARY ON JEREMIAH 16:5-8.[7]

WHY PEOPLE LIE UNBURIED. GIOVANNI DIODATI: See Deuteronomy 16:14 concerning these banquets. Now by forbidding this God would set before the eyes of his people the horror of the approaching desolation. Because of the great number of the dead and the terror of the living, there would be neither time nor means to observe the ceremonies for burials. Besides, both the cruelty of people and fear of the enemy would cause people to forgo and leave undone these honorable duties. ANNOTATIONS ON JEREMIAH 16:6.[8]

COMMUNAL COMFORT FOR THE GRIEVING. GIOVANNI DIODATI: It was the ancient practice among the Jews that when anyone died in a house, the neighbors, friends, and kinfolk would come

---

[5]Calvin, *Sermons*, 96-97 (SupCalv 6:60).

[6]Downame, ed., *Annotations*, 9M1r*, citing Job 27:15; Ps 78:64; Jer 8:3; 22:10; Rev 14:13; Ezek 24:16, 23; Amos 6:10.

[7]Bugenhagen, *In Ieremiam*, 3K1r-v; citing Rom 12:15; Jn 3:36; Mt 23:38; Lk 13:35; Rom 2:4; Lk 13:3.

[8]Diodati, *Pious Annotations*, 66*; citing Job 27:15; Ps 78:64; Ezek 24:17, 22; Amos 6:10.

there and bring bread, wine, and meat to prepare. They did so because people in the house could not make such things because of their fresh grief. So they invited their friends to eat, comfort themselves, and overcome their grief. ANNOTATIONS ON JEREMIAH 16:7.[9]

NO TIME FOR MERRYMAKING. JOHN CALVIN: The prophet must not go to the banquet, in order to signify that each must reflect on himself and on the punishment at hand. When God threatens us, does he intend to bring an end to the daily order of our lives so that we no longer live in the world? No, he intends only that we be terrified enough to repent. It is sufficient that we examine our faults, ask for pardon, and have a strong desire to return to the path of righteousness. When all this is accomplished in us, God will be content and the preaching of his Word efficacious. Thus, if he calls us to sackcloth and ashes and we do not forsake rejoicing, would this not be out of spite for him? When we persist in our vices, does not this not mean that we pay no attention to him, to his goodness, or to anything that is good? . . .

It is not, then, merely a matter of merrymaking, but of contempt for the Word of God, which is so much the more common today because it is forbidden. . . . But God says that he is a living God and will not pardon their sins. We cannot afford to be cheerful. There is no question about it. One cannot be attacked more readily than when they are merrymaking. . . .

This is especially said to the prophet in order that the levity of ministers does not become an occasion to mock God's teaching. What would happen if, after a minister preaches, he goes out to have some fun? Would this not be taken as an example that each should abandon himself to vice? . . . The prophet was no companion of those who preach and afterward go out for an evening of debauchery. Now some fine pastors of the church hear of the lechers in the whorehouses and taverns; they reprimand them severely and most ungra-

ciously; then, like shameless whores, they go to them to vomit forth their blasphemies. . . . When we reprimand vices, let each think on himself, that God have occasion to treat us in all mercy and bounty. SERMON ON JEREMIAH 16:8-10.[10]

A LACK OF CONSCIENCE AND WISE CONCERN. JOHANN PAPPUS: The next part of chapter 16 explains the causes of the threats in the verses above. But nevertheless, as we have said, Jeremiah has consolations and prayers mixed in with judgment. . . . At the beginning of this part the stubborn lack of concern among the Jews is refuted—the Jews who dared to argue with the Lord. Therefore the Lord is about to punish them as if their consciences themselves do not testify against them.

Furthermore, we see this today . . . also in the impious and untroubled in the world. People, as if they have perpetrated no evil, when difficult circumstances assail them, even dare to find fault with the Lord. Next, we will observe that in this passage the Jews are to be accused of abandoning the Lord and of idolatry, which is always linked with contempt of God and an impious lack of concern. It should be noted that the descendants are accused of being worse than their ancestors. Of course, impiety always gets worse over time, and parents ought to refrain from idolatry by name and other sins of that type, lest they harm their children and descendants by their example. ON ALL THE PROPHETS, JEREMIAH 16:10-13.[11]

16:14-21 The Lord Will Restore Israel

CAPTIVITY IN EGYPT AND IN BABYLON. HULDRYCH ZWINGLI: One reads here of the captivity in Egypt. But this was a minor captivity— child's play—in comparison with what the Jews would yet experience and suffer. In Egypt they were imprisoned without guilt and were horribly burdened, tormented, and brutalized. But that was the most unpleasant thing one might say. Such a

---

[9]Diodati, *Pious Annotations*, 66*.

[10]Calvin, *Sermons*, 105-8 (SupCalv 6:65-67).
[11]Pappus, *In Omnes Prophetas*, 88v.

holy people that God had rescued from an earlier captivity and through his grace had led them to the Holy Land: see how they had become unfaithful people and fallen after God's great deeds. Now they were so burdened with their own vices that God had to scatter them in a foreign land, into captivity in Babylon. Remember your earlier captivity, return, and reform yourself! If this does not happen, you will yet suffer far more difficult things. SERMON ON JEREMIAH 16:14.[12]

WHY TEMPORAL PUNISHMENTS LINGER.

NIKOLAUS SELNECKER: "See the time is coming, says the Lord, when one will no longer say, 'The Lord lives, who led the children of Israel out of Egypt. . . .'" Prior to this the prophet had preached the law to the people. Here he consoles them again and preaches the beloved gospel and promises them that God will release them from captivity and bring them home when they repent of their sins that have been punished in this world. Then just as God at the same time dismisses the eternal punishment for all of those who believe in his Son and return to him, so he often lets the temporal punishment continue so that sins can be recognized more clearly and the people will have more cause to call on God and return to him. He does alleviate the punishment and often takes it away completely. THE WHOLE PROPHET JEREMIAH 16:14-15.[13]

AWFUL CAPTIVITY AND UNPARALLELED DELIVERANCE.

THE ENGLISH ANNOTATIONS: The captivity in Babylon would be so grievous and tedious and the deliverance of the Jews from captivity by the ministry of Cyrus would be so strange and great that it would seem to erase their memory of the deliverance from Egypt. But even more than this it means for them that spiritual deliverance and liberty from servitude to sin and Satan which Christ purchased for them. ANNOTATIONS ON JEREMIAH 16:15.[14]

FISHERS AND HUNTERS OF PEOPLE.

JOHANNES BUGENHAGEN: First, God sends against Judah many fishers, of course, the Chaldeans, who have taken away many fish from Judah, that is, the treasure, the warriors, the best artisans, the king, etc. Nevertheless, they left in that sea, that is, in Judah, many fish, that is, the commonwealth, the kingdom, and priesthood, as you read in 2 Kings 24. Afterward he sent hunters against those beasts who despise God, who "hunted them on every mountain," etc.; that is, they have taken away everything and everything holy, and they have destroyed everything not sacred, as you read in 2 Kings 25. Because, he says, "for my eyes," etc., that is, the hypocrites are not able to hide when God apprehends them in his judgment: "It is horrible to fall into the hands of the living God." Thus with these words the prophet, after inserting the promise of the restoration, returns again to the threat, by which he threatens them with captivity. As he says, "He will indeed be the salvation of this people, but not now." It is necessary that the impious first be pressed into captivity and the elect be purged by the same as if by fire, so that they "will not be condemned with this world": 1 Corinthians 11. Before God said, "I will send many fisherman and then many hunters." But it is necessary to see that these are evil fishers and hunters, as God says, because through them he wants to punish the iniquity of the people. They achieve nothing here, those who imagine that these things are said concerning the apostles, to whom Christ says, "I will make you fishers of men," which is certainly for the salvation of people and not their perishing. COMMENTARY ON JEREMIAH 16:16-17.[15]

THE CROSS FOR THE ISRAELITES.

JOHANNES BRENZ: The Spirit in this passage explains the nature of the New Testament and its benefit. Indeed, the Spirit shows that God is favorable to us, who cares for all our paths and cleanses us of our iniquity. But what are these to the Israelites who

---

[12]Zwingli, *Predigten*, 212-13.
[13]Selnecker, *Der gantze Prophet Jeremiah*, C3r-v.
[14]Downame, ed., *Annotations*, 9M1v*; citing Is 43:18.
[15]Bugenhagen, *In Ieremiam*, 3K3r-v; citing Heb 10:31; 1 Cor 11:32; Mk 1:17; Mt 4:19.

were to be destroyed in the imminent captivity? Were these New Testament promises for their consolation? Absolutely! For the remission of sins is obtained in the cross through Christ. Moreover, this is distributed through the Word to all believers, so that in this passage the Spirit, by means of promises, distributed the remission of sins to the Israelites. This was done in the cross once and for all, so that, having been cleansed of their sins, they could either flee captivity, or not fall into it. ANNOTATIONS ON JEREMIAH 16:17.[16]

DOUBLE THE INIQUITIES. JUAN DE MALDONADO: "And I will repay first." That is, before I will bring them back from exile, I will make them pay the penalties that they owe. "Double iniquities," that is, "many"—a concrete number in place of an indefinite one. It as if he says, "I will punish every type of their iniquity." Or as Jonathan interprets this passage: "I will punish double sin; I have punished the sin of their fathers and now I will punish their own sin."[†] Or, "Just as I have punished the sin of their fathers, so I shall now punish their own sin." "With the carcasses of their idols," that is, with the corpses of beasts, which they used to sacrifice to their idols. Or the corpses of their sons. "Indeed they sacrificed their own sons and their own daughters to demons." COMMENTARY ON THE PROPHETS, JEREMIAH 16:18.[17]

SOMETIMES THE SAINTS ACT AS THE WICKED. JOHN TRAPP: Here the prophet excessively protests against God, as [being] less faithful, or less mindful with regard to promised preservation. [The prophet said] this in a fit of diffidence and discontent, as the best [saints] have their outbursts, and the greatest lamps have needed snuffers. The Milesians, says the philosopher, are not fools, yet they do the things

that fools used to do, so that saints often do as wicked ones, but not in the same manner and degree. COMMENTARY ON JEREMIAH 16:18.[18]

THE JEWS, THE GENTILES, AND THE COVENANT. JOHN CALVIN: What the prophet had says here might appear contrary to the promises of God, and wholly subversive to the covenant he had made with Abraham. God had chosen for himself one people from the whole world. Now when this people has been trodden underfoot, what could the most perfect of the faithful suppose but that the covenant was rendered void, since God had resolved to destroy the Jews and to obliterate their name? This was then a most grievous trial, and sufficient to shake the strongest minds. The prophet, therefore, now returns to the subject and anticipates this temptation; and seeing people in despair he turns to God and speaks of the calling of the Gentiles, which was completely sufficient to remove that stumbling block. . . .

When any one reads the whole chapter, one might think that Jeremiah abruptly turns to address God; but . . . his purpose was to fortify himself and the faithful against [despair], which otherwise would have shaken all the faithful. And Jeremiah shows what is best to do in a troubled and dark state of things, for Satan hunts for nothing more than to involve us in various and intricate disputes, and he is an acute disputant, yes, and a sophist; we are also very ready to receive what he may suggest, and thus it happens that the thoughts which we either attain ourselves or too readily receive when offered by the artifice of Satan often overwhelm us. There is then no better remedy than to break off such disputes and to turn our eyes and all our thoughts to God. This the prophet did. . . .

We now see that Jeremiah sets the conversion of the Gentiles in opposition to the destruction he had before announced; for the truth of God and his mercy were so connected with the salvation of

---

[16]Brenz, *Annotationes in Jeremiam*, 899.

[17]Maldonado, *Commentarii in Prophetas*, 77; citing Ps 106:37.
[†]Maldonado cites the Targum Jonathan, or Targumim to the Prophets, a fourth-century-AD Jewish work of translation and commentary attributed by tradition to Jonathan ben Uzziel, the disciple of the Elder Hillel (first century AD); see Bruce Chilton, "Targum," in *Dictionary of Biblical Interpretation*, ed. John H. Hayes (Nashville: Abingdon, 1999), 2:531-34.

[18]Trapp, *A Commentary or Exposition*, 270*. "The Philosopher" was the name by which many medieval and early modern authors referred to Aristotle. See Aristotle, *Nicomachean Ethics* 8.

the chosen people that their destruction seemed to obliterate them. Therefore, the prophet sets forth in opposition to this the conversion of the Gentiles, as though he said, "Though the race of Abraham perishes, yet God's covenant fails not, nor is there any reduction of his grace, for he will convert all the Gentiles to himself." Someone may object and say that though the Gentiles will be converted, yet the covenant of God could not have been valid and perpetual, except the posterity of Abraham were heirs of the grace that God had promised to them. To this there is a ready answer: for when God turned the Gentiles to himself he was mindful of his promise, so as to gather a church to himself both from the Jews and the Gentiles, as we know that Christ came to proclaim peace to those far off and those who are near. COMMENTARY ON JEREMIAH 16:19.[19]

KNOW THE HEAVY HAND OF JUDGMENT. THE ENGLISH ANNOTATIONS: The heaviness of my hand, and what I am able to do by the sight and sense of those dreadful judgments [which are] now pronounced, but not believed, when they are executed. For [the people of Judah] seem to go out of the way here, both those who understand the place of God's power manifested to me in the deliverance and restitution of the Jewish people, and also those interpret it as referring to God's might and majesty to be made known for conversion of the Gentiles together with the Jews, as if the "them" here mentioned were not the same as the "them" in the foregoing branch. ANNOTATIONS ON JEREMIAH 16:21.[20]

SALVATION FOR HUMANITY. NIKOLAUS SELNECKER: At the end of the chapter there is a beautiful prophecy concerning the calling of the pagans to the kingdom of Jesus Christ. This is an expression of thanksgiving, that God is so gracious and does not want humanity to be lost. But he wills that everyone hear his Son, Jesus Christ, and through him be joyful. To this point are the beautiful words: "God so loved the world. . . ." For through Christ we have recognized, seen, grasped, and remember God, who is the only eternal, true, omnipotent and all-powerful Jehovah. THE WHOLE PROPHET JEREMIAH 16:19-21.[21]

ANCHOR YOUR FAITH AND CHURCH IN GOD AND HIS WORD. JOHN CALVIN: We cannot attain faith by things in this world, but must look beyond this world to the sole power of God. Our faith must be like an anchor, which is small and unseen when thrown in the water but that nevertheless holds the ship and all that is within it. We must ground our faith, not by looking down, but by looking on high, where it has its immutable foundation; our Lord has promised that when the sun and the moon will be in the sky that we will not doubt that there is a church on earth. . . . It seems that this small church of God is about to perish because of our sins. Let us return to God. Although this church seems almost nothing, let us have faith that God will see to it that there will always be people to serve him. Let us conclude, then, that as long as God is in the heavens, there will be a church on earth. As long as he reigns from above, he will have his body down here. . . . [Jeremiah] is not speaking according to his own belief on these matters. Nor does he have the foolish presumptuousness to dictate the law to God. Where, then, does his faith come from? He speaks according to the word and will of God. God does not reign according to our thoughts, but according to what he has judged and proclaimed by his word. The prophet finds his assurance in the word because God has spoken it. SERMON ON JEREMIAH 16:19-21.[22]

---

[19]CTS 18:329-30* (CO 38:255-56).
[20]Downame, ed., *Annotations*, 9M2v*; citing Ps 90:11.
[21]Selnecker, *Der gantze Prophet Jeremiah*, C3v-C4r; citing Jn 3:16.
[22]Calvin, *Sermons*, 142-44 (SupCalv 6:88-89).

JEREMIAH 17:1-27
SIN, JUDGMENT, AND SABBATH

¹"The sin of Judah is written with a pen of iron; with a point of diamond it is engraved on the tablet of their heart, and on the horns of their altars, ²while their children remember their altars and their Asherim, beside every green tree and on the high hills, ³on the mountains in the open country. Your wealth and all your treasures I will give for spoil as the price of your high places for sin throughout all your territory. ⁴You shall loosen your hand from your heritage that I gave to you, and I will make you serve your enemies in a land that you do not know, for in my anger a fire is kindled that shall burn forever."

⁵Thus says the LORD:
"Cursed is the man who trusts in man
    and makes flesh his strength,ᵃ
    whose heart turns away from the LORD.
⁶He is like a shrub in the desert,
    and shall not see any good come.
He shall dwell in the parched places of the
        wilderness,
    in an uninhabited salt land.

⁷"Blessed is the man who trusts in the LORD,
    whose trust is the LORD.
⁸He is like a tree planted by water,
    that sends out its roots by the stream,
and does not fear when heat comes,
    for its leaves remain green,
and is not anxious in the year of drought,
    for it does not cease to bear fruit."

⁹The heart is deceitful above all things,
    and desperately sick;
    who can understand it?
¹⁰"I the LORD search the heart
    and test the mind,ᵇ
to give every man according to his ways,
    according to the fruit of his deeds."
¹¹Like the partridge that gathers a brood that
        she did not hatch,

so is he who gets riches but not by justice;
in the midst of his days they will leave him,
    and at his end he will be a fool.

¹²A glorious throne set on high from the
        beginning
    is the place of our sanctuary.
¹³O LORD, the hope of Israel,
    all who forsake you shall be put to shame;
those who turn away from youᶜ shall be written
        in the earth,
    for they have forsaken the LORD, the
        fountain of living water.
¹⁴Heal me, O LORD, and I shall be healed;
    save me, and I shall be saved,
    for you are my praise.
¹⁵Behold, they say to me,
    "Where is the word of the LORD?
    Let it come!"
¹⁶I have not run away from being your
        shepherd,
    nor have I desired the day of sickness.
You know what came out of my lips;
    it was before your face.
¹⁷Be not a terror to me;
    you are my refuge in the day of disaster.
¹⁸Let those be put to shame who persecute me,
    but let me not be put to shame;
let them be dismayed,
    but let me not be dismayed;
bring upon them the day of disaster;
    destroy them with double destruction!

¹⁹Thus said the LORD to me: "Go and stand in the People's Gate, by which the kings of Judah enter and by which they go out, and in all the gates of Jerusalem, ²⁰and say: 'Hear the word of the LORD, you kings of Judah, and all Judah, and all the inhabitants of Jerusalem, who enter by these gates. ²¹Thus says the LORD: Take care for the sake of your lives, and do not bear a burden on the Sabbath day or bring it in by the

gates of Jerusalem. [22]And do not carry a burden out of your houses on the Sabbath or do any work, but keep the Sabbath day holy, as I commanded your fathers. [23]Yet they did not listen or incline their ear, but stiffened their neck, that they might not hear and receive instruction.

[24]"But if you listen to me, declares the LORD, and bring in no burden by the gates of this city on the Sabbath day, but keep the Sabbath day holy and do no work on it, [25]then there shall enter by the gates of this city kings and princes who sit on the throne of David, riding in chariots and on horses, they and their officials, the men of Judah and the inhabitants of

Jerusalem. And this city shall be inhabited forever. [26]And people shall come from the cities of Judah and the places around Jerusalem, from the land of Benjamin, from the Shephelah, from the hill country, and from the Negeb, bringing burnt offerings and sacrifices, grain offerings and frankincense, and bringing thank offerings to the house of the LORD. [27]But if you do not listen to me, to keep the Sabbath day holy, and not to bear a burden and enter by the gates of Jerusalem on the Sabbath day, then I will kindle a fire in its gates, and it shall devour the palaces of Jerusalem and shall not be quenched.'"

a Hebrew *arm*   b Hebrew *kidneys*   c Hebrew *me*

OVERVIEW: Efforts to reform the church centered not only on right doctrine but also on true and holy worship of God. As Jeremiah challenged the idolatry, hypocrisy, and disobedience of his kin, so commentators found similar behaviors and inclinations to confront and challenge in the sixteenth and seventeenth centuries. Confession of sin was a particularly thorny issue: both in terms of identifying sincere repentance and the implications of sin confessed without private and meticulous confession to a priest. Sabbath observance was likewise a matter of urgent concern. As Protestants replaced the medieval Mass and eliminated related ceremonies, they risked losing the loyalty and presence of parishioners. The urgency and centrality of worship for right faith and Christian integrity had to be made clear. Finally, as often occurs in Jeremiah, particular passages illustrate the sort of devotion and theological clarity required of those engaged in ministry and struggling with resistance to the Word of God.

17:1-13 The Sin of Judah

THE TWO CHURCHES. JOHANNES BUGENHAGEN: "The sin of Judah is written with a pen of iron and with the point of a diamond"; or with a sharp instrument made of unbreakable adamantine stone; a sin was written and engraved deeply on the

stone tables of their hearts, so that the sin written with a hard and sharp pen on hard stones would not be effaced easily. This sin speaks to the foreign teaching and worship of God or idolatry, which they accepted through the preaching of the false prophets and in contempt of the Word of God. They so accepted it that they were persuaded that it was the true worship of the God of Israel, and they were persuaded on the other hand that the teaching and worship practices of the holy prophets since Moses, which were the Word of God, were heresy, blasphemy, and seduction. On that account they thought the holy prophets, along with all who embraced the teaching and religion of the holy prophets, were rightly killed as if according to law, since the law of God condemned them in Deuteronomy 13. They themselves, as if in accordance with the law, condemned the martyrs of the law and of the worship of God.

So today the gospel condemns those who do not believe to eternal death and saves those who believe. As it says, "The one who believes and is baptized will be saved; but the one who does not believe will be condemned." On the other hand, to be sure, those who do not believe praise unbelievers and condemn the gospel and those who believe the gospel. These are the two churches, so to speak, of Abel and Cain—of believers and unbelievers—the church of the sons of God and the church of hypocrites; they always remain in the world and the latter persecutes the former. COMMENTARY ON JEREMIAH 17:1.[1]

THE UNFORGIVEABLE SIN. JOHANNES BRENZ: At the end of the last chapter Jeremiah prophesied that the sins of the nations would be absolved through the Lord. In this chapter, however, the Spirit teaches that the sin of the Jews and all the impious is unforgivable, because it is a sin in the Holy Spirit. Acts 7: "You always resisted the Holy Spirit; you are just like your fathers." Matthew 12: "Whoever has spoken a word against the Spirit, it will not be forgiven for him." Unbelief or stubborn contempt for the word is a sin against the Holy Spirit; for the Word of the Spirit is truth, and the Holy Spirit is the Spirit of truth. Therefore, the one who resists the Spirit resists the acknowledged truth. ANNOTATIONS ON JEREMIAH 17:1.[2]

AN INDELIBLE STAIN. JOHN TRAPP: The first four verses of this chapter are left out by the Septuagint. Jerome says the translators omitted them . . . in favor and for the honor of their countrymen the Jews, but that was no just reason. "Forever, O Lord, your word is settled in heaven," though there were not a Bible left on earth. These sinners against their own souls had their adultery so deeply engraved on their hearts that they could not remove the stamp, and the guilt thereof stuck so fast to their consciences that they could hardly get off either the sting or the stain thereof. COMMENTARY ON JEREMIAH 17:1.[3]

DENYING OUR HIDDEN SINS AND LOVING IDOLS. JOHN CALVIN: We wish to erase the memory of our sins, but we do not have the means. God has told us that if we wish to be absolved of his judgment, we must condemn ourselves. If we wish him to forget our faults, we must remember them. . . .

That is why the prophet says that "their sins will be written with an iron pen," for the Jews, sinful as they were, wished to persuade themselves that God is content with them and the prophets did not have to cry out after them. . . . [Jeremiah] says that they are written on "the horns of their altars," to show their works make manifest the evil in their hearts. The prophet, of course, is speaking according to ancient custom. Whereas we write with a pen, they used stilettos to cut into wax. He says that their sins are written with a diamond to reveal that they cannot be erased as one can erase something written in wax. . . . It seems strange that God says their sins are irremissible; for in all of Scripture, he promises that if we are only touched by repentance, he is ready to receive us in mercy. It seems contradictory, then, when he says that sin will not be erased from Judah, that is, from all the people. The solution is that the prophet condemns them without remission because they are so hardened; for if they had any true repentance in themselves, they would have remission. . . . The prophet, as we have seen, is speaking to those who do not wish to obey God. . . .

Here, then, is our trial; God will produce what was hidden in our hearts, and our works will be brought forth. By this we are admonished stronger than ever not to ensnarl ourselves in our hypocrisy by trying to hide our faults to the extent that we believe we have none; for in the end our faults will be made known further than we thought. . . . Whatever cunning spirit we have, we employ to justify ourselves. Nevertheless, our conscience is like an executioner who declares that we cannot escape the hand of God. Now if our conscience can bring forth all that is hidden, what will it be like when Jesus Christ will sit in judgment and not in a human fashion? Our consciences will be manifest and laid bare before him, and all that has been hidden away will be brought to light. This day is called the Great Day, for all will come into play. . . .

When the prophet speaks of "the horns of the altars," that signifies the idolatry committed by the Jews under the guise of good intentions. It was not their intention to offend God when they employed their goods to build chapels and other things at the temple. They thought they were serving God. . . . Let

---

[1]Bugenhagen, *In Ieremiam*, 3Nir-v; citing Mk 16:16.
[2]Brenz, *Annotationes in Jeremiam*, 900; citing Acts 7:51; Mt 12:32.
[3]Trapp, *A Commentary or Exposition*, 272*; citing Ps 119:89.

us not deceive ourselves by our good intentions. Let us follow the Word of God and know that however the Jews intended to please God, this was no excuse. The same holds for all the services we invent. He adds that "their sons will remember their altars. . . ." That means that they are as carried away with their foolish superstitions as is the adulterer with his adultery. They are incessantly driven by a foolish love. Scripture sometimes calls idolatry adultery; for just as an adulterer is consumed by his foolish love, so are the idolaters consumed by their superstitions. Once Satan has baited a person into idolatry, they are carried away by foolish love. Let us look to how it was when we were yet among the papists. Without being pushed, we ran about here and there. The poor papists employ their goods in baptizing chapels, paying for the ornaments, and in making beautiful glass and other things. They are certainly not lacking in ambition. One must give to a temple and then to a foundation. After hearing one Mass, one must return to hear another. After dinner one must return to Vespers and Compline. After supper, one must return for the benediction. In short, one is never finished. That is how it goes with idolaters. . . .

The prophet adds, "And you will serve your enemies in a land which you know not.". . . If we do not wish to serve God in peace, he will send us to an unknown land where we will not have the leisure to serve him in peace. Why is it that he maintains us in a certain place, save for us to serve him in all holiness? SERMON ON JEREMIAH 17:1-4.[4]

TRUSTING IN PEOPLE IS LIKE PLAYING WITH FIRE. HULDRYCH ZWINGLI: "Cursed is the one who trusts in people." Trust is not when we believe a person who speaks to us or does something with us; for here trust is lacking in some way. But trust is this: to sacrifice for another, to offer oneself for the welfare and good of another. To this extent only God can support human beings. Should we "trust" people, or should we trust God alone? Should we lean on people, or trust no creature or

created thing, and instead hope in God for our welfare and seek it with a firm faith?

Therefore, God alone is sufficient, strong, powerful, and well-disposed to give us everything; a creature is much too weak. For example: There is a person on the one side and fire on the other; and that person is like a child who plays with fire: a spark falls into materials so that the fire easily lights and comes to burn. Likewise, when a person is like a reckless child with fire, then they are not directed by the Spirit of God and held in discipline, so that they fear God in all things, come to him for help in their temptations, and are careful to attend worship. When temptations set in, then we come easily to burn and run after our desires: honor, riches, and lust. Those who come to God are disgusted with their sins, so that they keep them at a distance. SERMON ON JEREMIAH 17:5.[5]

BEWARE OF COVENANTS WITH OTHERS.
THOMAS MÜNTZER: The most important thing of all, one that requires the most scrupulous attention, is that no one should put their trust in the covenant,[†] for the one who puts their hopes in humanity is accursed of God. It should only be a deterrent to the godless, to make them cease their raging until the elect have been able to search the depths of God's knowledge and wisdom with all the testimony pertaining to them. When the pious make a covenant, even though there be evildoers in it too, the latter will not succeed in pushing through their evil aims; the bluff honesty of the good folk will prevent them. THOMAS MÜNTZER TO JOHN ZEISS.[6]

BAPTISM AS TRUST IN GOD ALONE. ARGULA VON GRUMBACH: If I have acted wrongly I will, of course, gladly endure the punishment. But do not think you should be criticizing me, for no one should criticize us for doing what God has commanded us to do. And indeed in this case, too, I am not under constraint to obey anyone at all; for I vowed at baptism to believe in God, to confess

---

[4]Calvin, *Sermons*, 153-56, 158-59, 163 (SupCalv 6:94-95, 95-96, 97-98, 99).

[5]Zwingli, *Predigten*, 214-215.
[6]Müntzer, *Collected Works*, 102. [†]That is, feudal duties.

him, and to renounce the devil and all his illusions. I can never hope to fulfill such a lofty vow, until I am born anew through death. For while we live in the flesh we are sinners. As it says in the book of Proverbs, chapter 20: "Who can say, 'my heart is pure and I am without sin'?" And in Jeremiah 17: "Cursed is the one who trusts in mortals, but blessed is the one who trusts in God." To THE NOBLE AND HONORABLE ADAM VON THERING.[7]

LIKE A TREE PLANTED BY WATER. NIKOLAUS SELNECKER: This part is a marvelous consolation that everyone should know, that the one who clings to God and his Word is the one who is able to remain secure and whole; for God wants to help everyone who leans on him. But when one relies on others, rather than on God, that one will be disgraced. This section of Jeremiah belongs to the First and Ninety-Second Psalms of David, from which Jeremiah has taken these words: "that one who relies on the Lord is like a tree planted by water"; for David says, a God-fearing and righteous person who "delights in the word of the Lord . . . is like a tree planted on a pool of water; he brings his fruit in season, his leaves do not wither, and what he does prospers." Therefore, "the righteous will flourish as a palm tree and will grow like a cedar in Lebanon. They will be planted in the house of the Lord and will flourish in the courts of God. When they grow old, then they will still bloom—fruitful and fresh—and proclaim that the Lord who is upright is my refuge; there is no unrighteousness in him"; for a palm tree is green in summer and winter and produces its sap daily because it grows nowhere other than in sandy places with abundant water. So the God-fearing person, who trusts in God and is filled with the Holy Spirit, has grace and blessings; and in every situation this person already belongs to what honors God; nothing hinders this person—neither hail, nor lightening, neither rain nor snow. He is free in every case— through severe storms—because he has vigor and sap in his roots. Therefore, when a cross or

persecution comes, he poses no questions about it; for he has the sap and he always moves forward. No one is able to fight against him, nor dampen his abilities, nor press out his sap, because he lives. He is oriented toward what God wants. THE WHOLE PROPHET JEREMIAH 17:7-8.[8]

PERVERTED AND HOSTILE TO GOD. THE FORMULA OF CONCORD: The Word of God testifies that in divine matters the intellect, heart, and will of a natural, unregenerated person is not only totally turned away from God but is also turned and perverted against God and toward all evil. Again, that person is not only weak, impotent, incapable, and dead to good but also by original sin is so miserably perverted, poisoned, and corrupted that by disposition and nature is thoroughly wicked, opposed and hostile to God, and all too mighty, alive, and active for everything that is displeasing to God and contrary to his will. "The imagination of the human heart is evil from youth." "The human heart is deceitful and desperately wicked. . . ." St. Paul explains this text: "The mind that is set on the flesh is hostile to God," and again "The desires of the flesh are against the Spirit, and these are opposed to each other." SOLID DECLARATION, ARTICLE 2, FREE WILL.[9]

THE HEART IS A TROJAN HORSE. JOHN TRAPP: [The heart is] desperately bent upon deadly mischief. So that he gave no evil counsel who said to his friend . . . "so see to yourself, that you beware of your own heart." Another prayed not amiss, "Lord, keep me from that naughty man, myself." "Take heed of the devil and the world" (said a certain martyr in a letter to his wife), "but especially your own heart." Our enemies do not search far for us; we surround them with walls on every side. We have a Trojan horse full of armed enemies in the citadel of our hearts. We have enough Jebusites within us to undo us; we can neither put them to flight nor burn them. It is therefore characteristic of

---

[7]Argula, *A Woman's Voice*, 142; citing Prov 20:9.

[8]Selnecker, *Der gantze Prophet Jeremias*, C3v-C4r; citing Ps 1:3; 92:12-15.

[9]BoC 523-24; citing Gen 8:21; Rom 8:7; Gal 5:17.

a good person, as Epictetus, the heathen, says, that "he carefully watch himself as his own deadly enemy." COMMENTARY ON JEREMIAH 17:9.[10]

ONLY GOD KNOWS. JOHN CALVIN: We may gather from this passage a general truth—that the recesses of the heart are so hidden that no judgment can be formed of humankind by any human being. We indeed know that there are appearances of virtue in many, but it belongs to God alone to search human hearts and to try the reins. Rashly then do many form an estimate of someone's character according to their own apprehensions or the measure of their own knowledge; for the human heart is ever false and deceitful. . . . Described here is the character of all humankind, until God regenerates his elect. As then there is no purity except from the Spirit of God, as long as people continue in their own nature, their hearts are full of deceit and fraud. So the fairest splendor is nothing but hypocrisy, which is abominable in the sight of God. COMMENTARY ON JEREMIAH 17:9-10.[11]

FAITH OF THE HEART. JOHANNES BUGENHAGEN: "Deceitful." So great is the blindness and in addition to this the malice of the human heart that when it hears that it is needful to believe in God, the heart immediately responds. If it is only to be believed, then religion is truly easy: who would not believe? We are not Turks or foreign people, but the people of God. Nevertheless, the impious heart despairs here in adversity and does not consider God blameless through faith. In prosperous times truly the impious heart can be restrained by neither fear of God nor rebuke from the Word of God; and the heart contrives for itself such a pretense against the Word of God that it does not wish to be considered impious. Truly, as it says in Galatians 6, "God, who knows all things, is not mocked." Indeed, God examines two hearts, that is, the deliberations and

innermost parts, that is, the human passions, and God judges not according to outward appearance. . . . If indeed a tree is known by its fruit, we are not able to behold a person in his heart, so that one might see the faithfulness or unfaithfulness of another person. God, however, observes with his own eyes a person's faith, as Jeremiah says in chapter 5 above. Good tree, you are so on account of faith, that is, because you are faithful and a son of God. COMMENTARY ON JEREMIAH 17:8-10.[12]

NO ONE CAN RECOUNT EVERY SIN. AUGSBURG CONFESSION: Concerning confession we teach that no one should be compelled to recount sins in detail, for this is impossible. As the psalmist says, "Who can discern his errors?" Jeremiah also says, "The heart is desperately corrupt, who can understand it?" Our wretched human nature is so deeply submerged in sins that it is unable to perceive or know them all, and if we were to be so absolved only from those that we can enumerate we would be helped but little. On this account there is no need to compel people to give a detailed account of their sins. . . . Yet the preachers on our side diligently teach that confession is to be retained for the sake of absolution (which is its chief and most important part), for the consolation of terrified consciences, and also for other reasons. ARTICLE 25.[13]

THE SPIRIT WORKS AND THE HEART DECEIVES. LANCELOT ANDREWES: As for what is in the heart, *quis cognoscit illud*, "who knows it?" Not we ourselves; our own hearts often deceive us. And there is a *verbis confitentur*, "a confession with the mouth," [with those] *factis negant*, "who deny with their deeds"; and that deceives too. But there is *opus fidei*, "the work of faith," *fides quae operator*, a "faith that works"—that is St. Paul's faith; that can show itself by its working—that is St. James's faith; and there may well be the Spirit. But without works, it may not be there. For without works, St. James's faith is flat, it is "a dead faith"; it is the carcass of

---

[10]Trapp, *A Commentary or Exposition*, 274*; citing Epictetus, *Enchiridion* 72. Epictetus (AD 55–135) was a Stoic philosopher.
[11]CTS 18:356* (CO 38:271).

[12]Bugenhagen, *In Ieremiam*, 3N4v; citing Gal. 6:7; Jer 5:3, 23.
[13]BoC 62-63; citing Ps 19:12.

faith, and there is no Spirit in it. If there is no Spirit, there is no work. For *usque adeo proprium est operari Spiritui, ut nisi operetur nec sit;* "it is so kind for the Spirit to be working, as if he is not if he does not work." If no one works, *spectrum est, non Spiritus,* "it is a flying shadow, but not Spirit," if it does not work. SERMON ON ACTS 19:1-3.[14]

THE INNER TEMPLE. PILGRAM MARPECK: If we received it by grace and prayer, such knowledge in Christ is also life eternal. Hence our joy toward one another is complete in God, and thus we rejoice in you and hope that you are also rejoicing with us in the truth. Because the Jerusalem that is above is only built by Jesus Christ in the Spirit, the heart is the inner and only temple. This Jerusalem is the place of worship, namely, in spirit and in truth. Human hearts, the hearts of the true believers, are the inner sanctuary, the holy of holies into which no one can enter except our high priest. To him alone the sanctuary and holy of holies have been dedicated by God the Father, who is able to search the heart, thoughts, and soul. ON THE INNER CHURCH.[15]

THE PARTRIDGE AND UNJUST WEALTH. GIOVANNI DIODATI: The partridge written about here gathers other partridges and the eggs of other birds and hatches them as her own. But once the young ones hatch, they fly away to the right mother as soon as they hear her voice. Others expound it as this partridge gathers many eggs but does not hatch them because the cock partridge discovers them and breaks the eggs. So wealth acquired by evil means either returns to its rightful owner or ends up lost. This shows one's . . . false confidence, namely, in riches. ANNOTATIONS ON JEREMIAH 17:11.[16]

WHERE GOD DWELLS. JOHANNES BUGENHAGEN: "The place of our sanctuary." Just as in the Babylonian captivity, where the Jews did not have a king in the kingdom from the lineage of David and had governors instead, so likewise in the reconstructed temple they did not have those highest holy things, the ark of the covenant, the mercy seat, the cherubim, the tables of the law, which all perished through the fire as the temple was burned; nor were those things restored after the captivity. But only the holy of holies, an obscure place without light, was made in the temple as it had been before. But now the holy of holies was empty, except that God dwelt and was adored there, according to his promise, and once a year on the Day of Atonement the high priest entered, etc., as you read in Moses, until at length, the Son of God took on flesh and adorned that last and final temple, as Malachi prophesied.

From this history I understand Jeremiah here to speak against the confidence the Jews had in being justified through the temple, the ark and propitiation, as mentioned above in Jeremiah 7. Without a doubt those things were for believers the surest signs of the presence of God according to the promise of God; for that reason they sought God and found him in that place. "For even heaven cannot contain him; for God is beyond containing," as Solomon says in his prayer about the temple. Nevertheless, he is most certainly there, where in his word and promise he says that he would be present. For indeed God cannot be a liar. . . . In fact at that time those signs existed of themselves, as that very thing that the Word of God proclaimed that they were: the temple was the house of God, where God truly dwelt among humanity, the altar was truly the altar of God, where God received the sacrifices offered according to the law. . . . But the impious neglected the word and promise of God, and faith in God, and only looked on external things, and in those, which is most impious, they had faith, and therefore they multiplied temples and altars and sacrifices elsewhere. COMMENTARY ON JEREMIAH 17:12.[17]

---

[14]Andrewes, *Works*, 3:193-94*; citing Tit 1:16; 1 Thess 1:3; Gal 5:6; Jas 2:17-18.

[15]CRR 12:622; citing Jn 16:24; Gal 4:26; 1 Kings 6:16; Heb 9:7; Jer 9:10.

[16]Diodati, *Pious Annotations* 67*.

[17]Bugenhagen, *In Ieremiam*, 3O1v-3O2r; citing Lev 16:8-34; Lev 23:27-32; Mal 3:1; 1 Kings 8:27.

WHERE IS GOD'S THRONE? JUAN DE MALDO-
NADO: "A glorious throne." This is an exclamation
of the prophet. He says, "We do not trust in
humanity, nor do we like someone else's offspring
follow an unrelated partridge, nor let us like a
partridge brood over someone else's eggs. But we
must trust in the Lord alone. Glorious and lofty is
his throne, which has been from all eternity, and it
is our refuge, and the place whence we are sanctified, or which we sanctify by adoring God alone."
Others interpret the verse in this way: "just as the
throne of glory was on high from the beginning,"
that is, just as God has lived from the beginning in
heaven, so also he has lived in our temple, which is
the place of our sanctification. Thus some say that
he does not see, or does not care, what people do.
But this interpretation is rather forced. COMMEN-
TARY ON THE PROPHETS, JEREMIAH 17:11-12.[18]

TRUST IN THE LORD ALONE. ARGULA VON
GRUMBACH:

> In chapter 2 of Jeremiah
> I hear the Lord complain and sigh
> Alas, they have forsaken me, the well
> From which the living water spills.
> Elsewhere Jeremiah speaks again
> From God's own mouth he tells me plain
> It's found in chapter 17
> He speaks again, on the same theme
> Lord, all are shamed who you forsake
> Seek their thirst elsewhere to slake
> For their arteries are torn
> From where the living water runs
> From God's mouth he speaks yet more
> If you heal me, I'm healed for sure
> That all this was spoken by God above
> Jeremiah tells me in his words
> Who trusts in mortals is accursed
> Build on God and you are blessed

AN ANSWER IN VERSE TO A MEMBER OF THE
UNIVERSITY OF INGOLSTADT.[19]

17:14-18 Jeremiah Prays for Deliverance

YOU ALONE CAN HEAL ME, EVEN IF I FAIL.
KONRAD PELLIKAN: Jeremiah says, "You, Lord
God and no other is able to heal me and these, your
people. If you deem it worthy to save them, then
they will be saved; if you deem it worthy to
condemn them, they will be damned. Indeed, in
none of their works will he find anything other
than sin and ungodliness, thus we will be able to
glory in you alone and your grace. For all that I too
may be rejected by that ungodly people; nevertheless, I will be able to openly boast in your clemency
because I have diligently and faithfully carried out
the work of prophesying that was commanded,
even if I accomplish nothing good." COMMENTARY
ON JEREMIAH 17:14.[20]

FAITHFUL TO HIS CALLING. JOHANNES OECO-
LAMPADIUS: "And I am not troubled." Behold, you
know, Lord, that I do not have recourse to myself.
First, I refused [my calling] and testified that I am
only a boy. But at your command I entered service
and I explained your commands to the people.
Neither have I been made a shepherd or lord of the
flock. But I have followed you, as you called, as a
servant; and I have not preceded you. For I have
concluded enough, how much trouble that amount
of duty would bring me, and I was not eager to
approach the hatred of people, which one rushes
into—whoever reproves villainous people. Therefore the true prophet is called, while Pharisees and
others in the age of Christ thrust themselves on
the people as pernicious liars. Whence Christ said,
"Everyone who came before me was a thief or
robber." COMMENTARY ON JEREMIAH 17:16.[21]

PASTORING IS DIFFICULT! JOHN TRAPP: I have
neither rashly taken up the work of the ministry . . .
where I have been your under-shepherd, but [I] was
rightly called by you to it, and [I] have obeyed the
call. Neither have I been over-hasty to rid my hands

---

[18]Maldonado, *Commentarii in Prophetas*, 81; citing 1 Cor 6:19.
[19]Argula, *A Woman's Voice*, 188; citing Jer 2:13.
[20]Pellikan, *Commentaria Bibliorum*, 3:2S1r-v.
[21]Oecolampadius, *In Hieremiam*, 1:Y2r-v, 94r-v; citing Jer 1:6; Jn 10:8.

of this so troublesome and thankless employment. [Hugh] Latimer, in one of his sermons, speaking of a minister who gave this answer [as to] why he left preaching, [answered] because he saw he did no good but got the hatred of many. This, he said, was a naughty, a very naughty, answer. COMMENTARY ON JEREMIAH 17:16.[22]

BE A TERROR TO MY ENEMIES AND A FRIEND TO ME. KONRAD PELLIKAN: "Be not a terror to me, my hope in time of affliction." Grant abundant grace, O God, that I might attend to my duty, so that neither infidelity nor negligence makes it necessary for me to fear the severity of your righteous judgment. Rather, may I be able to be hopeful because of my sincerity of conscience and your goodness, if ever I am attacked by adversity or some examination of my works and obedience.

"Let them be confounded who persecute me. . . ." Rather, let the ungodly be confounded, who say, "Let his word come, we do not know the Lord; the Lord did not send you." They persecute me even until prison and death. I, however, rely on the testimony of my good conscience. Let me have you as a friend and I would fear no person. Grant to them that they might recognize their iniquities and dread your judgment. Indeed, I know your grace and I depend completely on your will and grace, so that I am not afraid to take refuge in you. But if, as they have done so far, they refuse to repent, and continue to act maliciously and show contempt for you, I ask that you violently attack them and so grind them down so that they are instructed by the punishments to confess the truth of your words and the justice of your works, and so that they understand your judgment, because they rejected your grace. COMMENTARY ON JEREMIAH 17:17-18.[23]

RELIGIOUS WORKS GIVE NO INWARD PEACE. MARTIN LUTHER: The papists, having abandoned faith, have venerated sects, works designed to gain righteousness, vigils, cowls, and even their own lice, invoking the aid of unknown saints, and have fallen not only away from God but in opposition to God. This is what it means to "fall backward," not forward. Therefore we must be admonished to pray to God in a most watchful manner. "And be broken." Jeremiah states that they are afflicted with a twofold grief: (1) of the heart, where the heart, wearied and disquieted by all works, has no inward peace, and the more it labors, the more it is disturbed; (2) the body, namely, they cheat themselves and nature by vigils and food the body needs, as Paul says in Colossians 2. Although they live in riches without sweat, they cannot use their riches freely and pleasantly so that the body may have enough. Thus the Jews and the papists have no inward peace, and they cannot freely make use of any creatures outwardly. LECTURES ON ISAIAH 28:13.[24]

17:19-27 Keep the Sabbath Holy

HONOR THE SABBATH IN DEED AND MIND. JOHANNES OECOLAMPADIUS: The devastation of the city of Jerusalem was to me a remarkable work of divine justice and, to be sure, horrible to hear. Many prophets predicted this, who in the texts they rendered have been read through subsequent ages and through which they were devoted to reforming all posterity. Here one precept alone is commanded that on the face of it seems very easy, which indeed, when it has been held in contempt, exposes the people as all the more impious because it was so easy to observe. Of course, it orders nothing besides rest from labor. But soon concerning these matters there was more certainty. It is told to the prophet that in the gate of the kings, that is, of the king and his sons, he is to rebuke the people for violating the Sabbath.

For some of the people living in that place went on the Sabbath day through the gate and out of the city, contrary to the law, which forbids one to go from his own place on the Sabbath day. Thereafter, Jeremiah strongly attests to this in all the remaining

---

[22]Trapp, *A Commentary or Exposition*, 275*. Hugh Latimer (1487–1555) was an English bishop, reformer, preacher, and martyr.
[23]Pellikan, *Commentaria Bibliorum*, 3:2S1v.
[24]LW 16:227 (WA 31.2:162); citing Is 28:13; Col 2:23.

gates and shouts at the whole people because all of them were transgressing the law. As to the rest, he reproaches in the first place the kings, because from their laziness or their example the desire to transgress against the Lord, having been taught to the people, was quite prominent. They should not carry a burden on the Sabbath, nor take anything from their house in public, as the prophet orders according to Moses. This is a type of law even we observe: when we clear and sanctify the Sabbath day to the Lord, we let go of the burdens of our harmful desires, by which we are at leisure and free for the Lord; we do not go out; neither do we enter into our activities. But with a free mind, since we have closed our gates and shuttered the doors of our senses, we celebrate days of rest for the Lord. . . . For to sanctify this last day of the week to the Lord is among the first things required of us, to whom the end times have come. In fact, we have a perpetual and most complete Sabbath, if we meditate continually on the law of the Lord. . . . Indeed, it is a figure of Christ dying and resting; for he blesses and sanctifies the fearlessness of creatures; they will perish so that thereby they might be glorified and sanctified. So our fearlessness and Sabbath is blessed, because the blessed Sabbath of Christ is the beginning of our resurrection and life. COMMENTARY ON JEREMIAH 17:19-22.[25]

THE SABBATH AND CREATION. SEBASTIAN MÜNSTER: "You shall sanctify the Sabbath day." From "sanctification of the Sabbath" understand that he refers to the true and sincere worship of God. Indeed, the Sabbath is a symbol of the creation of the world, which leads us to recognize the magnificence of our Creator. Nevertheless, the ceremonial Sabbath, for which the Jews strive steadfastly even to this day, was taken away. Furthermore, Christ declared that the leisure of the Sabbath would be turned into employment for this reason: since "the Sabbath is for man and not man for the Sabbath." Therefore, he encourages the Jews

toward the observation of divine mandates. THE TEMPLE OF THE LORD, JEREMIAH 17:24.[26]

THE SABBATH—EXTERNAL OBSERVANCE AND INTERNAL TRANSFORMATION. JOHANNES BRENZ: Why does Jeremiah take time to urge the day of Sabbath so strongly, as if there were not many more necessary commands than observing the Sabbath? For the same reason that Moses emphasized this command in the law, and in the Gospel bitter contentions arose among the Pharisees and Christ because of the Sabbath. My response is that observation of the whole law hangs from correct observation of the Sabbath, just as the violation of the whole law follows from the violation of the Sabbath. Those who think that observation of the Sabbath is only an external matter completely diverge from heaven. For indeed, though external observation was commanded "until the time of reformation," this was not completely true; for that external observation was a sign that God would purify us. How? The flesh possessed our whole nature—the will of the flesh, desire, lust, love of self, and contempt for others. Therefore, if we want to follow the rules of either faith or love, first it will be necessary to annul our own works, so that God may do his works in us—the works of the Spirit. Moreover, this will come to be if we believe the word we have heard. Then we are given this by faith in the Spirit of Christ. His works are the mortification, and then the restoration of the flesh, cleansing the flesh, and then accomplishing his works. E.g.: the Word of God: Christ forgives our sins. If I will believe in this, I am given the Spirit, who is revealed in me too, showing me first the gravity of my sin, either excess or envy, and thereafter he vivifies, consoles, and finally produces modesty and love of neighbor. ANNOTATIONS ON JEREMIAH 17:24.[27]

COMMANDS REGARDING THE SABBATH APPLY TO PLACES OF WORSHIP. RICHARD HOOKER: The argument our Savior uses against the profaners

---

[25]Oecolampadius, *In Hieremiam.* 1:Y2v-Y3r, Y3v; citing Ex 16:29-30; 20:10; Num 15:32-36.

[26]Münster, *Miqdaš YHWH*, 890; citing Mk 2:27.
[27]Brenz, *Annotationes in Jeremiam*, 901-2; citing Heb 9:10.

of the temple he takes from the use whereunto it was with solemnity consecrated. And as the prophet Jeremiah forbids the carrying of burdens on the Sabbath because that was a sanctified day, so because the temple was a place sanctified, our Lord would not permit, no, not the carriage of a vessel through the temple. The two commandments there in the law [are] conjoined: "You shall keep my Sabbaths, and reverence my sanctuary." Out of those the apostle's words, "Have you not houses to eat and drink," albeit temples such as now were not then erected for the exercise of Christian religion, it has been nevertheless not absurdly conceived that he teaches what difference should be made between house and house: he shows [the difference between] that which is fit for the dwelling place of God and what [is meant] for human habitation. He requires that Christians in their homes take common food, [but] in the house of the Lord none but that food which is heavenly. He instructs them that as in the one place they use to refresh their bodies so they may in the other learn to seek the nourishment of their souls, and as [in their house] they sustain temporal life, so here [in the church] they would learn to make provision for eternal [life]. Christ could not suffer that the temple should serve as a place of market, nor the apostle of Christ that the church should be made an inn. When therefore we sanctify or hallow churches that which we do is only to testify that we make them places of public use, that we invest God himself with them, that we sever them from common uses. LAWES OF ECCLE-SIASTICAL POLITY.[28]

GODLY MAGISTRATES AND GODLY WORSHIP. JOHN CALVIN: We have seen why our Lord so strongly commanded the day of rest.... The Jews, then, were separated from others in order to be God's own.... [Likewise] it was necessary for us to be sanctified and that we must not be governed by our own spirit but subjugate ourselves to God in order that he govern us throughout our life.

Therefore, we see that this ceremony of rest was a great sign of the time of the law. That is why God complains bitterly when it is profaned and violated; for this is a sign that we do not wish to live in obedience to him. We have shown that if we are contemptuous toward the sacraments, which bear spiritual significance, we have not taken God seriously, who ordained them. If we hold baptism in contempt, we have not taken into account the blood of Jesus Christ and therefore do not know what it is to be a Christian. If we do not take Communion as we should, we are culpable of the death of Jesus Christ as if we have murdered him, although his body and blood are not within our grasp, and we are also culpable of having dishonored him....

Furthermore, although we do not have to observe the Sabbath, we are commanded to observe a day of rest. True, we must cease and desist from our own works every day, but this is especially true on the day of rest. Nevertheless, there are so many nonchalant ones that will not come to the temple unless they are coerced. Therefore, God wished there to be a day upon which all Christians would rest from their labors to devote themselves to his service. It is not that God is served by our laziness but that he wished there to be a day upon which we would have the leisure to devote ourselves to prayers and orisons and to come together to confess our faith. God, then, ordained the day of rest in order that, not being preoccupied with our tasks, we could come to temple. Now, if we do not observe this practice, we show well that we do not take God seriously. When Sunday rolls around, those who were unable to leave the city all week because of their businesses wish to have a festival to show off their wares. Others, who did not have a chance to play all week, devote Sundays to pleasurable outings. They seem to think that the day of rest was ordained expressly for them to take up their favorite pastimes....

If people stop to contemplate the works of God, they come to love him so much the more. Now, if we do not do this, if instead of contemplating all the good things he has given us, we go off on the day of rest to take up our pastimes, our frolics and vices, it is certain that he will not tolerate this

---

[28]Hooker, *Lawes of Ecclesiastical Polity* 5.12*; citing Mark 11:16; Lev 26:2; 1 Cor 11:22.

without avenging himself. . . . If we observe the day of rest, our Lord will multiply his grace in us. But, if we disobey his ordinance, he will consume us all in an inextinguishable fire. . . . Sermon on Jeremiah 17:24-27.[29]

Temporal and Spiritual Order. John Calvin: When our Lord says that "the kings will be seated on the throne of David" and adds that "people will come from the cities of Judah . . . ," he had two things in mind, which are the basic principles of all mortal life. First, we must have magistrates according to his will. Second, we must have an ecclesiastical order over us, so that we are ready to obey him in all matters. These are the two principal blessings that we should desire. . . .

There are two things we must understand from this passage [about magistrates]. The first is that we will never have good magistrates unless God has elected them, as he has elected the house of David to reign over the Jews. The reason why kings, princes, and magistrates perpetuate so much evil is that they were not elected by God. Insofar as our Lord did not elect them, this means that they came to power by themselves. For this reason, they have not come to govern but to destroy. . . . The second is that God does us no small favor when he gives us good magistrates. People are often destitute. Why? The magistrate is not worthy of their office. Whereas we would be at peace if we had good magistrates, we have only tyrants who take pleasure in tormenting all and wish only to destroy everything . . .

Now we come to the point where [the prophet] says that "people will come from all the lands to offer sacrifices at the temple." By this, as I have said, the prophet shows that it is not enough that we have terrestrial police to maintain order. We must have spiritual ones to ensure that God is honored and that communal prayers are offered. . . . Gathering at the temple was intended to bring the people together, to symbolize Jesus Christ, and to lead the people to him. Today, now that we have the Truth, the kind of sacrifice that God demands is that we come to praise and honor him. It is a singular blessing that God wishes to be served by us. How is this to be accomplished? Through our use of his sacraments; for from them flow prayer and all the rest, namely, a Christian life, in which we strive for nothing save that God be praised throughout the world. That is why I say that if we are so ungrateful as to hold the civil police in contempt, so much the more contemptuous are we of the Christian life. Sermon on Jeremiah 17:24-27.[30]

---

[29]Calvin, *Sermons*, 224-27 (SupCalv 6:133-35). [30]Calvin, *Sermons*, 227-31 (SupCalv 6:135-36).

JEREMIAH 18:1-23
THE POTTER AND THE CLAY

¹The word that came to Jeremiah from the Lord: ²"Arise, and go down to the potter's house, and there I will let you hear[a] my words." ³So I went down to the potter's house, and there he was working at his wheel. ⁴And the vessel he was making of clay was spoiled in the potter's hand, and he reworked it into another vessel, as it seemed good to the potter to do.

⁵Then the word of the Lord came to me: ⁶"O house of Israel, can I not do with you as this potter has done? declares the Lord. Behold, like the clay in the potter's hand, so are you in my hand, O house of Israel. ⁷If at any time I declare concerning a nation or a kingdom, that I will pluck up and break down and destroy it, ⁸and if that nation, concerning which I have spoken, turns from its evil, I will relent of the disaster that I intended to do to it. ⁹And if at any time I declare concerning a nation or a kingdom that I will build and plant it, ¹⁰and if it does evil in my sight, not listening to my voice, then I will relent of the good that I had intended to do to it. ¹¹Now, therefore, say to the men of Judah and the inhabitants of Jerusalem: 'Thus says the Lord, Behold, I am shaping disaster against you and devising a plan against you. Return, every one from his evil way, and amend your ways and your deeds.'

¹²"But they say, 'That is in vain! We will follow our own plans, and will every one act according to the stubbornness of his evil heart.'

¹³"Therefore thus says the Lord:
Ask among the nations,
   Who has heard the like of this?
The virgin Israel
   has done a very horrible thing.
¹⁴Does the snow of Lebanon leave
   the crags of Sirion?[b]
Do the mountain waters run dry,[c]
   the cold flowing streams?
¹⁵But my people have forgotten me;
   they make offerings to false gods;
they made them stumble in their ways,
   in the ancient roads,
and to walk into side roads,
   not the highway,
¹⁶making their land a horror,
   a thing to be hissed at forever.
Everyone who passes by it is horrified
   and shakes his head.
¹⁷Like the east wind I will scatter them
   before the enemy.
I will show them my back, not my face,
   in the day of their calamity."

¹⁸Then they said, "Come, let us make plots against Jeremiah, for the law shall not perish from the priest, nor counsel from the wise, nor the word from the prophet. Come, let us strike him with the tongue, and let us not pay attention to any of his words."

¹⁹Hear me, O Lord,
   and listen to the voice of my adversaries.
²⁰Should good be repaid with evil?
   Yet they have dug a pit for my life.
Remember how I stood before you
   to speak good for them,
   to turn away your wrath from them.
²¹Therefore deliver up their children to famine;
   give them over to the power of the sword;
let their wives become childless and widowed.
   May their men meet death by pestilence,
   their youths be struck down by the sword
     in battle.
²²May a cry be heard from their houses,
   when you bring the plunderer suddenly
     upon them!
For they have dug a pit to take me
   and laid snares for my feet.
²³Yet you, O Lord, know
   all their plotting to kill me.
Forgive not their iniquity,
   nor blot out their sin from your sight.
Let them be overthrown before you;
   deal with them in the time of your anger.

a Or will cause you to hear   b Hebrew of the field   c Hebrew Are foreign waters plucked up

OVERVIEW: This prophecy of Jeremiah raised profound theological and pastoral issues for commentators. The account of the potter and the clay led to discussions of the relationship of human free will to divine sovereignty—a perennial topic in the Reformation era. The matter of God's possible repentance prompted similar questions about the impact of human action on God's decrees. Moreover, as Jeremiah knew, such high theological matters had serious real-world implications for prophets, preachers, and pastors who sought to confront sin and provide comfort to their hearers even as such a prophecy or sermon might elicit fierce resistance and put faithful messengers in grave danger. The response of Jeremiah to such threats was all too familiar for these interpreters of Scripture.

18:1-11 The Lord Is a Potter

GOD TEACHES THROUGH EVERYDAY THINGS AND CREATURES. JOHANNES BRENZ: All the works of God were like this in the beginning, in that they seemed foolish to reason. But under this foolishness God is glorified and the faith of the saints is cultivated. Thus, in this passage the Spirit will say that the prophet, nay rather, the world, and all people are in the hand and power of the Lord; God is able to bend and shape them according to his will. He leads the prophet to the house of the potter—first so that we may know that it is the glory of the Lord that a wise person should seem subject to folly, and then so that the faith of the prophet might be cultivated. For an unfaithful person, considering the work that was commanded, and not him that commands, either would not have gone or would have thought it was not a command of the Lord. Indeed, why send the prophet to the potter? Is the house of the potter a school, or a book of the Bible, from which the way of the Lord and his word might be learned? In fact, creatures are dissertations on the word of the Lord: Romans 1, Hebrews 11, and Job 12: "Examine the beasts of burden, and they will speak to you; speak to the

earth and it will respond to you, and the fish of the sea will give account." ANNOTATIONS ON JEREMIAH 8:1-4.[1]

EXTERNAL SIGNS FOR FAITH. JOHANNES OECOLAMPADIUS: "Rise up and go down to the house of the potter." The prophet could have understood these things in a vision of a quiet home. But God wanted not only to speak to him but also to show him; for external signs, which are subject to the eyes, do they not move the soul of a passionate person? Such is the rationale of the sacraments. They are visible words, and bring the same Christ to a believer's senses, just as words normally do when they are heard. COMMENTARY ON JEREMIAH 18:2.[2]

BECOMING GOD'S PERFECT CLAY. JOHN DONNE: "Arise and go down into the house of the potter," says the prophet Jeremiah. As the expositors say, this is said in consideration of your mortality. It is "arise and go down": a descent with an ascension. Our grave is upward, and our heart is upon Jacob's ladder and in a way nearer to heaven. Our daily funerals are symbols of that: for though we are laid down in the earth at the end of the funeral, we are lifted up on men's shoulders before that. We rise in the descent to death, and so we do in the descent to the contemplation of death. In the entire potter's house, is there one vessel made of better stuff than clay? This is the potter's material. And of all forms, the circle is most perfect. So do you resent being made into that circle when you return to earth again? SERMON ON 1 CORINTHIANS 15:26.[3]

THE POTTER, THE CLAY, AND FREE WILL. JOHANNES BUGENHAGEN: In this similitude of the potter and the clay and in his exposition, as here the Lord explains, you have a certain and singular interpretation of all the passages of Scripture, in which the Lord warns that he is about to destroy the

---

[1]Brenz, *Annotationes in Jeremiam*, 902; citing 1 Cor 1:18–2:5; Rom 1:20; Heb 11:1-40; Job 12:7-8.
[2]Oecolampadius, *In Hieremiam*, 1:Z2v.
[3]Donne, *Sermons*, 4:51-52*.

impious. But of course, it is understood that all such things will come to be unless the people repent. . . .

Moreover, who does not see here the divine patience and blessing toward those who are mistaken and are sinners? He says that whatever humans are doing wrong now will be counted as nothing. "Only let them return to my word." Read Ezekiel 18 and other passages. . . . On the basis of this text the defenders of free will labor; those who extol our free will over against the grace of God are truly laboring here. We, however, without offense, commend here the grace of God in Christ, according to the word of Christ: "without me you can do nothing." "May your will be done, as in heaven, so on the earth." COMMENTARY ON JEREMIAH 18:1-5.[4]

WE ARE THE CLAY OF THE POTTER. MARTIN LUTHER: "We are the clay and you are the potter. . . ." "As you promised: if we sinned, you would change us. You would throw us into the lump and make us new again." There is a similar passage in Jeremiah 18, where the prophet pressed the shape of a vessel into the lump and fashioned another vessel. So we are in the hand of God, and even though we are evil he thrusts us into the lump, into the Babylonian captivity, until the clay has been worked through better so that it becomes more pleasing. Then it will become a new lump. It is as if he were saying: "The fact that you have trampled the clay will not harm us who are broken, if only you remain the potter and will reshape us." This is the task of a potter. Summary: "You are our Father, as well as our artisan and potter, and you will restore us who are broken." In this way the clay will be turned into a fine little jug again. Summary: Our breaking is done in hope that we shall be shaped anew. Thus in all temptations let us firmly believe that we are not mire of the streets but clay of the potter, God, who will reshape us. We are clay of the potter, not the mire of the streets. LECTURE ON ISAIAH 64:8.[5]

GOD THE POTTER, SOVEREIGN OVER CREATION. NIKOLAUS SELNECKER: This is a striking sermon and admonition to repentance, in which God gladly wants to show mercy on his people and to spare them so they improve themselves. . . .

So now God wants us to better ourselves, abstain from our sins, and to bring ourselves back to God. Thereby God desires to spare us, and hold back all misfortune, that he might repent of what he had conceived against us. But where we obstinately continue in our sins and deliberately resisted the Word of God and the Holy Spirit, God as a potter wants to break us and throw us down as unrepentant and ill-behaved children; and give his word to another nation. So related to that point is the allegory of the potter and the clay, and it speaks of the punishment that belongs to unrepentant and ill-behaved children. Elsewhere humanity is also compared to clay in holy Scripture. As in Isaiah 64, "You, Lord, are the potter and we are the clay; we are all the work of your hand." That is, you have created us and made us in your image. We are your people and your creation. Therefore, be gracious to us and think not eternally on our sins. Moreover, Paul in Romans 9 says, "A work does not say to its master, why did you make me?" The potter makes something from the lump of clay, an object for honorable use and an object for regular use. That is, God has pity on us out of grace because of his love for his Son. He condemns and rejects all who do not believe in his Son and does so in righteous anger, which no one can hinder or dispute.

Furthermore, we must adjust to the mode of speaking in Scripture, when we read that God repents of misfortune or good. As in Genesis 6, "I repent," God says, "that I have made humanity." What terrible things there are in this Word; for God wants to show his great and righteous anger against sin when thereby no warning or reprimand is able to help. Still no one thinks to refrain from sin, but the longer that goes the greater God is agitated. THE WHOLE PROPHET JEREMIAH 18:1-10.[6]

---

[4]Bugenhagen, *In Ieremiam*, 3R1r; citing Ezek 18:21-32; Jn 15:5; Mt 6:10.
[5]LW 17:371-72* (WA 31.2:549).

[6] Selnecker. *Der gantze Prophet Jeremias*, F2v, F2v-F3r; citing Is 64:8, Rom 9:20, Gen 6:6.

THE POTTER AND THE CLAY TEACH DIVINE ELECTION. JOHN CALVIN: The Lord says to the prophet, "You see that the potter has the power to make of earth that which he wishes. At the very least, I have as much power over these people. Although I promised their fathers to be their God and to sustain their descendants, I am well able to destroy them. On the contrary, if they return to me, though it seems they must perish, I will completely restore them. You will say this to them in order that when I warn them, they do not harden themselves but come to me." That is the crux of the matter. . . .

The prophet says, "Cursed be those who rise up against their Creator, for humanity is like a clay pot. God can do with him what he wishes, just as the potter can do what he wants with the clay." The prophet wishes to reprimand this pride, but St. Paul goes further yet in the ninth chapter of Romans, where he says that the Lord will pity whom he would pity and be merciful to those whom he would be merciful, and to those destined for eternal death he says, "You will perish." Before the creation of the world, our Lord elected those he wished to save and this without regard to their merits. He did this rather than abandoning them, although he hardened those he wished to perish. This astonishes us and we say, "How can this be? Is it the office of God to play with people as if they were a ball? If we do evil, why does he accuse us? Is he just? This is how people rise up against God. St. Paul knew well how to combat this pride. He focused especially upon the infirmity of our understanding. He rebukes them saying, "How, poor wretch, can you talk back to God? You are less than a clay pot. You see that the pot allows the potter to make what it wishes. Yet you wish to challenge God." Here St. Paul shears off our horns. True, God can satisfy our idle curiosity, but we are not high-minded enough to comprehend his works. We must humble ourselves, for all true wisdom consists of the fact that we humble ourselves and do not exceed our limitations. Furthermore, it would be overly presumptuous to assume that God is obligated to answer to us at our beck and call. Let us close the door on all curiosity and be content with what he has told us. SERMON ON JEREMIAH 18:1-10.[7]

GOD HAS THE CLAY IN HIS POWER. JOHANNES OECOLAMPADIUS: "Behold, just as clay in the hand." Now he explains what he has shown in the particular visible sign of the potter. He says, "The Lord showed me what this signifies, namely, that a creature is in the hand of God, just as clay is in the hand of the potter. From the same clay he makes one vessel for honor, and another for disgrace. We do not have that by which we may boast—even if we have something of holiness—neither are we able to boast concerning the liberty of free will. The clay is without effect through itself; it is pliable to the hand of the potter. But if anything less fitting is rejected, then those of us who are not capable of the Word of God are rejected." If someone asks why Jacob is chosen and Esau rejected, the response is that God is the Lord and has the clay in his power. COMMENTARY ON JEREMIAH 18:6.[8]

NOT A PASSAGE ABOUT FREE WILL. JUAN DE MALDONADO: Heretics abuse such passages when they lift up free will for discussion. We have amply refuted them in the books against the errors of the Lutherans and Calvinists. To this passage it will be enough to say that here the soul is not dealt with, but it concerns the body, death, and life, bad and good fortune, captivity and freedom. As if he says, I am able to kill and bring to life, to lead someone to hell and back. COMMENTARY ON THE PROPHETS, JEREMIAH 18:6.[9]

PROPHETIC WARNING IS AN ACT OF DIVINE MERCY. THE ENGLISH ANNOTATIONS: The Lord in these words shows the reason why he had enjoined Jeremiah to meet him at the potter's work house so that there, by a vivid demonstration, [he

---

[7]Calvin, *Sermons*, 238-40 (SupCalv 6:141-42); citing Rom 9:18; Eph 1:4-5; Rom 9:20-21.
[8]Oecolampadius, *In Hieremiam*, 1:Z2v-Z3r; 98v-99r; citing Mal 1:2-3; Rom 9:13.
[9]Maldonado, *Commentarii in Prophetas*, 83; citing 1 Kings 2:6; Is 45:9; Rom 9:20.

would] show him how he was able, without further ado, to deal with this people. He was able to destroy them, and might well do so without further warning. It was his mere mercy, if he gave them any warning, since they deserved ill of him before he did so, and that as he had framed them, and made them a people, a nation, a church, a state formerly, so he could again mar them, especially since that they had first so corrupted and marred themselves by their sins so to unmake them either [as a] people, [a] nation, [a] church, or [a] state, and either remake or frame them again such as they were before, or make others [to be] such in their room. They [thus] had no just cause to complain, if ever they do so. ANNOTATIONS ON JEREMIAH 18:6.[10]

SALVATION IN OUR ANGUISH. HANS DENCK: Eternal salvation begins before we are even aware of it when the Lord places us in the remotest part of hell, so that we become poor in spirit, thinking that we are going to die within ourselves. Unspeakable moaning and crying sets in, for it appears God has utterly forgotten us and has turned his back on us, as if unwilling either to accept or to hear our crying and imploring. DIVINE ORDER.[11]

GOD'S PUNISHMENT UPON THE NATIONS. KONRAD PELLIKAN: However it might be that the works of God are ordained by his providence, according to a logic unknown to us, who neither ought nor are able to know all things, nevertheless, God does want us to know this: that if ever a foreign people is threatened with destruction or any kind of punishment because of their present or past sins, this destruction and punishment will not be undertaken against them, as if they could find no grace at all: if they turn to good, amend their lives, receive the predictions of the prophets with reverence and fear, and, having been corrected, beg for divine grace. Likewise the divine promises appear under the condition of keeping the law and

piety in God; when these are transgressed, the promise ceases. So also the threats of God against the people of God cease, if they emend their lives for the better. That is, the Lord repents of the evil he has threatened, and spares those who have converted, by the one infallible will that works all things. COMMENTARY ON JEREMIAH 18:7-10.[12]

HOW THE WICKED AND FAITHFUL RESPOND TO JUDGMENT. MARTIN LUTHER: "If that nation . . . turns from its evil, I shall repent of the evil I intended. . . ." This repentance is often attributed to God, namely, when he changes his mind about an evil he had intended to inflict. The sense is as if you would say: "He is easily moved to forgive." These are promises that are very beautiful, very rich, and very broad. They are held forth by the Holy Spirit for this purpose, that in a time of the wrath and anger of the Lord the feeble heart and conscience which is looking for consolation should run to them and remember them. After all, it is wonderful to see here the plan of the Holy Spirit, who up to now has been heaping up and enlarging the threat in order to send them back to the goodness and mercy of God, indicating by this that the wrath and anger of God work toward salvation, so that sinners who have thus been terrified by the threats and judgment of God come to their senses and accept and recognize God as their merciful Father. In this way, you see, he terrifies sinners in such a way that they lift up their hearts and hope in the mercy of God. This is the custom of all the prophets—they first terrify with very violent and bitter threats, but they immediately add very great and very sweet promises about the mercy and goodness of God. The effect of each word (that is, of threats and promises), however, is different in the righteous from what is among the wicked. You see, the wicked use neither threats nor promises correctly. When they hear threats, they do not think the threats apply to them. This is the way they support their own hypocrisy. Thus they remain obdurate in their wickedness, which they

---

[10]Downame, ed., *Annotations*, 9N2v*; citing Is 43:1; 44:2; 64:8; Deut 32:5-6; Is 1:4, 25-26; Jer 33:7; Rom 11:23-24; Num 14:12; Mt 3:9; Rom 11:11, 17; Is 45:9; Rom 9:20. [11]Denck, *Selected Writings*, 83*; citing Mt 5:3; Ps 22:1-2. [12]Pellikan, *Commentaria Bibliorum*, 3:2S2r-v.

nevertheless think is the epitome of righteousness. Therefore such broad promises, which require nothing but broken and contrite hearts, are also not effective in them. And because this does not happen in the wicked through threats, neither are promises effective in them. The righteous, on the other hand, use them correctly, for they are bruised and cast down by the angry threats of God; they bear divine judgment; they recognize their sin and their damnation. So, when they hear these promises, they turn to the mercy of God. In this way their consciences again are lifted up and become peaceful. LECTURE ON JOEL 2:13.[13]

WHAT GOD DOES AND WHAT THE BELIEVER DOES. BALTHASAR HUBMAIER: "I know, Lord, that it is not the way of a human being, nor of man, that he walks and directs his footsteps."... The prophet speaks here of those things that concern the salvation of the soul in which the human being, outside of the divine Word and leading, is completely helpless and wholly ignorant. How then could he will the good or walk uprightly? Therefore without ceasing he calls to God with the prophet: "Lord, my God, direct my ways before your face."... If now God sends his word, then the human being is able to know, desire, and walk the way of the divine footsteps, as the counter Scriptures show clearly. It is up to the human being to prepare the heart, but up to God to govern the tongue. Jeremiah says also: "Let every person turn away from his evil way and direct your ways and thoughts." It follows that it now lies in our power to prepare the heart, to turn, to lead our ways and deeds according to the sent Word of God, to guide and direct ourselves according to these Scriptures, which you, dear friend, also must accept besides your own in a whole judgment. FREEDOM OF THE WILL.[14]

REPENTANCE—THE WEAPON OF A CHRISTIAN. MARTIN LUTHER: Since the Turk is the wrath of the Lord our God and the servant of the raging

devil, the first thing to be done is to smite the devil, his lord, and take the rod out of God's hand, so that the Turk may be found only, in his own strength, all by himself, without the devil's help and without God's hand. This should be done by Sir Christian, that is, by the pious, holy, precious body of Christians. They are the people who have arms for this war and they know how to use them. If the Turk's god, the devil, is not beaten first, there is reason to fear that the Turk will not be so easy to beat. Now the devil is a spirit and cannot be beaten with armor, muskets, horses, and soldiers, and God's wrath cannot be allayed by them, as it is written in Psalm 33, "His delight is not in the strength of the horse, nor his pleasure in the legs of a human being; but the Lord takes pleasure in those who fear him, in those who hope in his steadfast love." Christian weapons and power must do it.

Here you ask, "Who are the Christians and where does one find them?" Answer: There are not many of them, but they are everywhere, though they are spread thin and live far apart, under good and bad princes. Christendom must continue to the end, as the article of the creed says, "I believe in the holy Christian church." So it must be possible to find them. Every pastor ought diligently to drive people to repentance by showing our great and numberless sins and our ingratitude, by which we have earned God's wrath and disfavor, so that he justly gives us into the hands of the devil and the Turk....

This fight must be begun with repentance, and we must reform our lives, or we shall fight in vain; as the prophet Jeremiah says in chapter 18, "If at anytime I declare concerning a nation or kingdom that I will pluck and break down and destroy it, and if that nation concerning which I have spoken turns from its evil, I will repent of the evil that I intended to do to it." And again, "And if at any time I declare concerning a nation or a kingdom that I will build and plant it, and it does evil in my sight, not listening to my voice, then I will repent of the good which I had intended to do to it.... Return, every one of you and amend your ways and your doings." We may apply these words to ourselves, for God is devising evil against us because of our

---

[13]LW 18:97-98 (WA 13:100-101).
[14]CRR 5:484-85; citing Jer 10:23; Ps 5:8; 106:4-5; Prov 16:9.

wickedness and is certainly preparing the Turk against us. ON WAR AGAINST THE TURK.[15]

18:12-23 A Forgetful People

HOW WE RESPOND TO GOD'S WORD AND JUDGMENT. JOHN CALVIN: We have seen how God turns the wheel to mold us as seems good to him. We have seen that whatever form he gives us, he can change in an instant, so that we are consequently changed. We have said that this is not a wheel of fortune, but that God governs fairly. If he sustains us in equity, that is the work of his grace. On the contrary, when we are so evil that we abandon him, he still turns the wheel, but he regrets the good he has done for us. . . .

After God has spoken generally, he does speak specifically because each is inclined to let his teaching pass him by. . . . When God's judgment is mentioned, people will say, "Oh! His judgment upon those people was well spoken, but he does not seem to have anything to say to us." To preach the Word of God, I must make an examination of my life, and my mirror is the Word of God. It also serves as a mirror for all of us. Before looking into this mirror, we think that we are beautiful and clean. He puts the Word before our eyes in order that we come to know our faults and humble ourselves. . . . The prophet says, "You [of] Judah," because they were the ones to whom he had been sent as a prophet. It is as if I were to say now, "You of Geneva," for we have the gospel. When he admonishes them, each must look to himself and know the prophet is speaking to us and not to people far away from here. . . .

When he says, "Make good your ways," it seems as if there is a capacity in a person to change himself without the grace of God. Indeed, the papists use this passage to support their notion of free will, although they are forced to admit that God has the greater share of this power. Nevertheless, they give human beings a share of God's power. . . . [But] the prophet does not say, "You can go to God of your own free will." Instead he says, "Look to your calling and not to your power." After God has shown us what we must do, we cannot say, "I cannot do that," for God has said it will be so. After he has admonished us, he then gives us the power to do what he commanded. Therefore, after having heard his teaching, we must go to him and pray that it please him to make us profit in his teaching. That is how we will receive nothing in vain. That is how Scripture must be received! . . .

They reply, "All is lost." Look to ourselves. See that we do no less. How do these warnings benefit us? How have we profited from the fact that if we are touched by his bounty to return and convert to him in total obedience, he will receive us in all mercy, notwithstanding our evil lives? SERMON ON JEREMIAH 18:11-14.[16]

THE GODLESS CONDEMN US. JOHN CALVIN: "Go among the pagans. . . ." Here the prophet is following up the remarks he made in the second chapter: "Visit the pagans. They are loyal to their gods. Although they are merely idols, they are loyal to them. But my people are not loyal to me. Is this not a monstrous thing?" Now he says as much in [this] later passage: "Look to the pagans, if they have seen such things. Have they abandoned their religion? No." . . . [The prophet] says, "When a man will have water in his fields, he will go fetch the snows of Lebanon." This is foreign water because it comes from snow, yet the man is content with it and does not search elsewhere. Now, when God is present to us, not only does his grace flow to us but we are led to the very source. Jesus Christ is the fountain that is present to us. We will never need the cold waters of snow, for he gives himself to us. We will share in the grace of Christ. Are we not, then, accountable? . . . If we do not serve God, the pagans alone will be sufficient to condemn us. This is also true . . . of the stubbornness of papists. They do not have true religion, but they will not abandon what they have. . . . We seek the Turks,

---

[15]LW 46:170-71 (WA 30.2:116-17); citing Ps 147:10.

[16]Calvin, *Sermons*, 250-51, 254-55, 256-57 (SupCalv 6:147-48, 149-50, 151).

who are hardheaded about this law of Muhammad as they can be. We see the Jews, who did not know what God they worshiped, yet they went about their religious affairs with an inexpressible mania. When we see such obstinacy everywhere, do we think that what we are doing is pleasing to God? SERMON ON JEREMIAH 18:13-15.[17]

GOD'S BACK AND COUNTENANCE. NIKOLAUS SELNECKER: One sin comes after the other. The people neither want to listen nor to follow. They forget God and all of his benefits quicker than the snow melts away. They no longer pay attention to what is happening—be it good or bad, blessing or reprimand—and they are ungrateful and overconfident. . . . "They travel on unseemly streets and do not know the right way to me, but the longer they go, the further they are from me." Therefore, the Lord says, "I will allow an east wind to blow," that is, "a strong, burning wind" that gives them pain and consumes them. That will be the king of Babylon. "I will turn my back and not turn my countenance." That is, you shall no longer have a church, pulpit, or gathering in a synagogue. . . . God shows us his countenance when we hear the Word of God in church and school, and can be lead and have the right use of the most worthy sacrament. He shows us his back, when we are robbed of the Word and cannot hear it, like the poor captive Christians in Turkey or wherever God's Word cannot be heard in a church. There is none of that because of heathen idolatry, the Muhammadan Qur'an, and other horrible blasphemy and errors. THE WHOLE PROPHET JEREMIAH 18:14-17.[18]

PERPETUAL STUMBLING BLOCKS. JOHANNES BUGENHAGEN: Truly, he speaks of the stumbling blocks of teaching, false religion, and morals. Indeed, those things seduce some, so that their impious cult would continue even to future generations. . . . Where there are stumbling blocks of doctrine and false religion, there too are

stumbling blocks of morals; even if at first they do not appear so, but seem to be the religion of angels. So this is among our papists, among whom morals are utterly corrupted; as Isaiah rightly says to them, "Princes of Sodom and the people of Gomorrah, Hear the word of the Lord," etc. These stumbling blocks, Jeremiah says, are placed in the people's way continually; that is, people never cease to imagine new forms of worship, new religions, new kinds of merit, new works, and new sacrifices, as our popes have done. As Moses says in the canticle, "New gods had recently appeared, which their fathers did not worship." Each is a false religion because it does not have the sure Word of God and is not able to consist of just one error: repeatedly, the teachings of demons, by which the false religion hands itself over to the contempt of the Word of God, drags it into other errors, all of which it represents as the worship of God, righteousness, and salvation. COMMENTARY ON JEREMIAH 18:15.[19]

THE WORDS OF JEREMIAH, THE WORDS OF CHRIST. HULDRYCH ZWINGLI: "Let us forge plans against Jeremiah." "To forge" means to deliberate on and shape up some schemes, to go into consultation, just as their plans came out when they conspired together. This is how you draw in another person: with certain feelings and with good and sweet words, with benefits and gifts, bribery and slander against our enemy. The prophet gives a substantial description about this, as the same also happens to Christ; thus self-aware and educated people would say that these are the words of Christ. The situation laid out here is similar: as Jeremiah explains his angry words and considers them, so Christ also did (especially when the Jews argued with him, "you are children of Abraham," he said, "you will die in your sins"). So these people use their fathers, the law, and the prophets as an excuse and boast of themselves. SERMON ON JEREMIAH 18:18.[20]

---

[17]Calvin, *Sermons*, 260-61 (SupCalv 6:153); citing Jer 2:10-13.
[18]Selnecker, *Der gantze Prophet Jeremias*, F4v.
[19]Bugenhagen, *In Ieremiam*, 3Rlv-4Rr; citing Col 2:18; Is 1:10; Deut 32:17.
[20]Zwingli, *Predigten*, 177-78; citing Jn 8:31-46.

UNPUNISHED AND UNFORGIVEN SINS ARE NOT FORGOTTEN. JOHN TRAPP: A heavy curse. Woe to such as [have] whole debts stand uncanceled in God's book. Their sins may sleep a long time, like a sleeping debt, not called for many years, as Saul's sinning slaying the Gibeonites was not punished until forty years after, [or] as Joab's killing of Abner slept all David's days. People's consciences may also sleep (in such a case) for a season, but their damnation sleeps not, nor can their condition be safe until God has wiped out their sins for his own sake. Until he has crossed out the black lines of our iniquities with the red lines of his Son's blood, and taken out of his coffers so much as may fully satisfy. COMMENTARY ON JEREMIAH 18:23.[21]

HOW TO DEAL WITH THE GODLESS. NIKOLAUS SELNECKER: Jeremiah speaks of such sins and idolatry, so that the people pursue him with anger, violence, and tyranny and want the pious Jeremiah to be dead. They plot against him and say, "Dear people, we should not have to put up with that. We must have some earnest insight, and we must discover a right and proper approach. What would that be? The prophet Jeremiah addresses us; he reprimands us and gives us to the devil, so we cannot reform ourselves, and he threatens us with the wrath of God and future punishments. He does so not in secret, but publicly to every person. Is Jeremiah the only one who arrives at such nonsense? Who is he, anyway? There are other prophets and preachers who speak the truth no less, but who are absolutely better and greater than he is, and are also in the same office that he holds. They have their souls and consciences to protect, as fully as Jeremiah. They teach righteously and make it pleasing to us. They do not err in the law and never fail to give advice. Therefore, let's put Jeremiah behind us, or he will cause an immediate rebellion. We could have all out chaos and then our churches

would have no impact and they would perish. We have plenty of teachers. There are no such villagers, who want to tell us that we are failing. We want to remain well without Jeremiah; let him stay where he is. Our priests, who are with us, cannot err in the law; they teach righteously and lack no advice." As the papists say, "The church, the church cannot err. Are we the Lutherans? There is very little against us. We are the church and have the power and cannot fail. We never give up or speak in error. With our tongues we want to beat them to death, that is, the slanderers, and all the heretics we condemn, exile, and hunt them right out of our land; we flog, burn, martyr, and kill them."

. . . So Jeremiah prayed to God. Jeremiah sincerely wanted and was entrusted to threaten the evil folk, to beat and tear them out by the roots and above all to eradicate and destroy them along with their tribe and relations, children and friends. . . .

This is a such a severe command, a prophecy issued regarding how it should go with the godless, when they persist in their stubbornness. . . . We see this in the Psalms that David often wishes evil on the godless. . . . But we should also speak of this command from where we are today. This command actually took effect among the Jews and was fulfilled. And we should orient ourselves to the command of our Lord Christ in Matthew 5: "Bless those who curse you; do good to those who hate you. Pray for those who insult and persecute you, that is, do not be vengeful, but gladly forgive each other's failings, and pray for your enemy that he would be enlightened, turned and converted, and the same for others." And that we would do so from the heart. When that does not help and the godless pursue their tyranny with false teaching and persecution, then it is time to pray that God not only resist them but also show them an example of his wrath. THE WHOLE PROPHET JEREMIAH 18:18-23.[22]

---

[21]Trapp, *A Commentary or Exposition*, 279*; citing 2 Sam 21:1-14; 3:27-29.

[22]Selnecker, *Der gantze Prophet Jeremias*, F4v-G1v; citing Jer 1:10; Mt 5:11, 38-45.

JEREMIAH 19:1-15
THE BROKEN FLASK

[1]*Thus says the Lord, "Go, buy a potter's earthenware flask, and take some of the elders of the people and some of the elders of the priests,* [2]*and go out to the Valley of the Son of Hinnom at the entry of the Potsherd Gate, and proclaim there the words that I tell you.* [3]*You shall say, 'Hear the word of the Lord, O kings of Judah and inhabitants of Jerusalem. Thus says the Lord of hosts, the God of Israel: Behold, I am bringing such disaster upon this place that the ears of everyone who hears of it will tingle.* [4]*Because the people have forsaken me and have profaned this place by making offerings in it to other gods whom neither they nor their fathers nor the kings of Judah have known; and because they have filled this place with the blood of innocents,* [5]*and have built the high places of Baal to burn their sons in the fire as burnt offerings to Baal, which I did not command or decree, nor did it come into my mind—* [6]*therefore, behold, days are coming, declares the Lord, when this place shall no more be called Topheth, or the Valley of the Son of Hinnom, but the Valley of Slaughter.* [7]*And in this place I will make void the plans of Judah and Jerusalem, and will cause their people to fall by the sword before their enemies, and by the hand of those who seek their life. I will give their dead bodies for food to the birds of the air and to the beasts of the earth.* [8]*And I will make this city a horror, a thing to be hissed at. Everyone who passes by it will be horrified and will hiss because of all its wounds.* [9]*And I will make them eat the flesh of their sons and their daughters, and everyone shall eat the flesh of his neighbor in the siege and in the distress, with which their enemies and those who seek their life afflict them.'*

[10]*"Then you shall break the flask in the sight of the men who go with you,* [11]*and shall say to them, 'Thus says the Lord of hosts: So will I break this people and this city, as one breaks a potter's vessel, so that it can never be mended. Men shall bury in Topheth because there will be no place else to bury.* [12]*Thus will I do to this place, declares the Lord, and to its inhabitants, making this city like Topheth.* [13]*The houses of Jerusalem and the houses of the kings of Judah—all the houses on whose roofs offerings have been offered to all the host of heaven, and drink offerings have been poured out to other gods—shall be defiled like the place of Topheth.'"*

[14]*Then Jeremiah came from Topheth, where the Lord had sent him to prophesy, and he stood in the court of the Lord's house and said to all the people:* [15]*"Thus says the Lord of hosts, the God of Israel, behold, I am bringing upon this city and upon all its towns all the disaster that I have pronounced against it, because they have stiffened their neck, refusing to hear my words."*

Overview: Commentators continue to describe and decipher another prophecy on divine judgment even as they face a series of related challenges. First and foremost, unlike the potter and the clay of Jeremiah 18—which promises possible though painful redemption—the broken flask of Jeremiah 19 proclaims certain and final destruction. Therein interpreters sought to look at divine judgment with an unflinching gaze while distinguishing how it applied to the godless and yet might discipline and encourage the faithful. Idolatrous worship spurred this latest prophetic pronouncement of wrath. Here in Jeremiah, however, the variant and devious forms of adoration and supplication had drifted into an even more sinister imitation of Canaanite cults—the sacrifice of children. Such a warping and perversion of worship raised fresh concerns for Reformation-era expositors, who ponder the shape of Sunday services and the sort of veneration of saints and their shrines that might in some way embody exactly what Jeremiah so fiercely condemned. Divine wrath was sure to come to body and soul as manifest in images of corpses unburied and graves defiled.

19:1-9 *The Valley of Slaughter*

GOD IS LIKE A PATIENT EXECUTIONER.
NIKOLAUS SELNECKER: This chapter can be understood on the basis of the seventh chapter. God gives to the prophet a new sign, by which he should proclaim the coming wrath. Namely, he should take an earthen vessel and break it in the presence of the priests and elders as an image, showing that God will break and punish them because of their idolatry, government, city, temple, and valley, in which they sacrificed their children to Moloch. God had the prophets proclaim the future punishment so often and in so many ways; all of it is a sign that God always wants and demands repentance—that one should return to him. Wherever this did not happen, God determined and allowed the punishment to take its course. God does have a long view and gives room and time for repentance. . . . An active executioner does not flee, threaten with blows, or hurry due to anger. Eventually he takes the life, but does it without rushing, waits always for improvement, threatens with his sword, gives many signs of his wrath until at long last all the signs for the unrepentant are exhausted—all the threats, admonitions, and shouting. So he is entrusted to unleash his anger . . . with hunger, disease, war, and other horrible punishments. As Jeremiah says at the end: God, therefore, punishes them so fiercely because they are so stiff-necked and will not listen to his Word. THE WHOLE PROPHET JEREMIAH, CHAPTER 19.[1]

GOD'S WORD IN THE PROPHET. JOHANNES BUGENHAGEN: In another sign Jeremiah condemns the idolatry, which they called the worship of God in Gehinnom, in the valley of Topheth, and concerning which very similar words were spoken above in chapter 7. Indeed, with the same sign he prophesies and preaches against them of the evil of slaughter and captivity. When this is done he goes out from the valley of Hinnom or Topheth and prophesies the same thing in the atrium of the temple in Jerusalem. The prophet subjects himself to great danger in obeying God. Therefore, he is thrown into prison, as you read in a later chapter. God left nothing out in Jeremiah that pertained to the threatening, so that the obstinate would be more severely condemned and the elect would return from impiety, which we mentioned elsewhere. . . . For there are such a series of sermons and admonitions through words and signs that they could not have been in vain, as God testifies concerning his word in Isaiah 55: "As the rain and snow come down from heaven and do not return above, but water the earth and fill it and make it sprout seed, so that it gives seed to the sower and bread to the eater. So will my word be that goes forth from my mouth. It shall not return to me empty, but it shall do that which I purpose and prosper in those things for which I send it." COMMENTARY ON JEREMIAH 19.[2]

A BURIAL PLACE FOR MANY—FAITHFUL AND UNFAITHFUL. CORNELIUS À LAPIDE: "And go to the valley of the Son of Hinnom." For "valley" the Septuagint translates this as *polyandrion*, as if to say, "a multitude of bodies of men." So it is also in the Basilica of St. Peter's here in Rome, in a certain crypt near the crypt of St. Peter and the inscription on it reads "Polyandrion," for in it the bodies of many faithful are buried, who, granted, were not canonized, but nevertheless they died piously in the hope of the blessed resurrection. Such polyandria are the ossuaries in cemeteries, which are heaps of the skulls and bones of Christians. Jeremiah led them there, so that they considered their own tombs in this valley . . . and that their bodies are like clay, which shortly would be crushed, and thrown out like excrement in Topheth and their souls would be in Gehenna,

---

[1]Selnecker, *Der gantze Prophet Jeremias*, G2v; citing Jer 7:30-34.

[2]Bugenhagen, *In Ieremiam*, 3R4r-v; citing Jer 7:31-33, 37:1-21; Is 55:10-11.

because of the Chaldeans, that is, through the demons. Thus as they considered these things the Jews might repent and worship and fear the true God. Indeed Jeremiah saw that the hard and stubborn Jews were not persuaded by words, and so he gave them an object lesson, namely, a living representation, indeed a view of their own deaths and tombs. COMMENTARY ON THE PROPHET JEREMIAH 19:2.[3]

BREAKING POTS TO SHOW GOD'S IMMINENT JUDGMENT. JOHN MAYER: After teaching by one sign of a potter making and breaking his pots at his pleasure, now the Lord diverts Jeremiah to teach by another sign: a pot taken to the valley of the son of Hinnom to be broken there in the sight of some priests and elders called there by Jeremiah. By the former sign God showed that they were in his hands, as the pots in the hands of the potter, so that whenever he was displeased he could break them by his judgments. Thus being broken, they could be reconciled to him by their repentance and God would make them an even more prosperous and flourishing nation than they were before. Now he shows by the second sign that he could not only break them, so as they could not be repaired again, but that he would certainly do it because of their obstinate sinning. God spoke this concerning the wicked Jews then alive, and at the same time he excluded the faithful remnant whom he promised to replant and build again. . . . The prophet is ordered to show this in the valley of the son of Hinnom, otherwise called Topheth. Concerning this see chapter 7, where the same threat is made about this; that where such abominable sins were committed such dreadful judgments should be executed as they had sinned therein unnaturally. They had burned their sons and daughters in sacrifices to Moloch, so in Jerusalem, which was nearby, they should eat the flesh of their sons and daughters from extreme hunger in the time of siege. COMMENTARY ON JEREMIAH 19:1-3.[4]

THE SOUND OF JUDGMENT. JOHANNES BRENZ: "His ears shall ring." Ringing happens to the ears from a very loud sound. Just as eyes typically become impaired before a very bright light, which the faculties of the eyes are not able to bear, so there is a ringing of the ears when they have been exposed to a very loud sound. But still there is no louder sound than the law and judgment of the Lord: one can hear about it even to his death. Exodus 20: "The whole people perceived the voices and the torches, the sounding of the trumpet, and they were terrified and said to Moses: 'You speak to us, do not let the Lord speak to us, lest we die.'" Isaiah 11: "The breath of his lips destroys the wicked." Moreover, Peter demonstrated this very deed in the case of Ananias in Acts 5: "'You are not a liar to humans, but to God.' Hearing these words Ananias collapsed on the ground and died." ANNOTATIONS ON JEREMIAH 19:3.[5]

OUR SAINTLY FATHERS, FALSE GODS, AND THE SAINTS. JOHN MAYER: "And they have burned incense to strange gods, which neither their fathers nor they have known." Jerome says that their fathers were godly, for those who had lived in the time when idolatry took place among them were not worthy to be called "fathers," but only the most ancient Abraham, Isaac, and Jacob, Moses, Samuel, and David, whose understanding and acknowledgment were regulated by the law of God.[†] Therefore, similar objections may be raised against the papists now. They offer and pray to saints departed and their images, which neither your fathers nor you have known, that is, Peter and Paul and the other apostles, and the first preachers of the gospel did not know these saints or gods. COMMENTARY ON JEREMIAH 19:4.[6]

---

[3]À Lapide, *Commentarium in Jeremiam*, 125; citing Jer 7:31-33.
[4]Mayer, *A Commentary*, 397*; citing Jer 7:31-33.

[5]Brenz, *Annotationes in Jeremiam*, 903; citing Ex 20:18-19; Is 11:4; Acts 5:3, 5.
[6]Mayer, *A Commentary*, 398*. [†]The early church father Jerome (d. 420) references how heretics tend to ignore their spiritual fathers, like "the apostles and apostolic men," and choose instead to sacrifice to foreign gods; Jerome, *Commentary on Jeremiah*, 118. Mayer extends this mantle of heresy to his own time.

DO ONLY WHAT GOD COMMANDS. MARTIN LUTHER: Jeremiah 19 says regarding the great Baal worship that they even sacrificed and burned their children, thinking they thereby did a great service to God. But God said, "I have not commanded it, and it never entered my heart," etc. From this it also becomes clear that nothing should be preached or presented to the people that God has neither commanded nor desired. Now we are certain that the pope with his papists has no commandment from God to propagate his own teaching in Christendom. It is nothing but a trick of the devil to hinder God and his commandment and the salvation of humankind. ANSWER TO THE HYPERCHRISTIAN BOOK.[7]

PATRON IDOLS AND THE BLOOD OF INFANTS. JOHN CALVIN: [The Jews] had "burned incense" to Baal. They pretended, no doubt, [to burn it for] the name of God; but yet it was a most preposterous superstition, when they worshiped inferior gods, as the papists do this very day. The word "Baal" is sometimes used in the singular number by the prophets, and sometimes in the plural: but what is "Baal"? A patron. They were not content with one patron, but everyone desired a patron for themselves: hence under the words "Baal" and "Baalim" the prophets characterized all fictitious modes of worship: when they worshiped God's name, they blended in the worship of patrons....

The Jews might have raised such an objection as the papists do this very day—that their modes of worship were not devised in their time, but that they had derived them from their ancestors. But God regarded as nothing those kings and fathers that had long before degenerated from the true and genuine religion. It must be here observed that true knowledge is connected with truthfulness: for they who had first contrived new forms of worship doubtless followed their own foolish imaginations....

He last adds that this place was "filled with the blood of innocents"; for there they killed their children. And by this circumstance Jeremiah again amplifies the wickedness of the people; for they had not only despised God and his law, but also cruelly destroyed their innocent infants; and thus he proved them guilty not only of impiety and profaneness in vitiating the worship of God, but also of brutal and barbarous savageness in not sparing innocent blood. COMMENTARY ON JEREMIAH 19:4-5.[8]

THE VALLEY OF TOPHETH—JOY, HELL, AND ROTTING CORPSES. JOHN CALVIN: The prophet was sent by God's bidding to the house of the potter that he might there take an earthen bottle, carry it to Topheth, and there explain the judgment of God.... This seemed incredible to the Jews; for they had chosen that place for themselves to perform their superstitions: they thought therefore that a great part of their safety depended on their false worship....

And it is certain that this name, Topheth, was given to the valley of Hinnom, because of the hilarity and joy that thence arose among the people; for they thought that God was favorable to them, when they so diligently offered there their sacrifices, and yet they provoked his wrath. Then Topheth is to be taken in a good sense, when we regard the origin of the word. It is indeed true that in Isaiah 30 Topheth is to be taken for Gehenna; but it may be that the prophets had now begun so to curse the place just as one calls hell indiscriminately Gehenna and Topheth.... Now, the reason why the prophets and other faithful people called the place hell was plainly this—because the devil reigned in that place, when God's worship became vitiated, and the whole of true religion was subverted....

He then adds, "I will give your carcass to be meat to the birds of heaven...." [This] is deemed a punishment inflicted by heaven when the carcasses of the dead remain unburied; for it is the last office of humanity to bury the dead. And this is a distinction that God would have between humanity and animals, for animals have not the honor of a burial. It has also been ever granted as a singular privilege

---

[7]LW 39:195-96 (WA 7:665).

[8]CTS 18:439-40* (CO 38:324-25).

to humanity to be buried, in order to set forth the hope of the resurrection. When, therefore, a burial is denied, it is a proof of extreme dishonor. COMMENTARY ON JEREMIAH 19:6-7.[9]

WHAT BURIALS SAY ABOUT US. HULDRYCH ZWINGLI: "Your corpses will be given to the animals of the field to eat." "Your offenses will be so dreadful, that you cannot lament for yourselves when you are buried like robbers, thieves, and murderers. Your bodies must be defiled and be left lying about for beasts of prey to eat—so great and noble are you. Yet, why do we place so much worth on a burial for our corpses, that they not be dug up, or that they are buried or not, that they are consumed by wild animals or if they rot in the earth?" Diogenes had fun with this issue. He had asked that if one liked him, then when he died, put a stick in his hand. When someone asked him what he wanted to say thereby, Diogenes replied, "Then I can drive away the dogs and chase off the birds so they don't eat me." SERMON ON JEREMIAH 19:7.[10]

A CITY THAT ABANDONED ITS GOD. KONRAD PELLIKAN: Who would believe that the capital of the Israelite nation, whose God was the Lord, where he was uniquely worshiped—and where the glorious temple and ark of the Lord were—would all be destroyed? Nevertheless, as this was predicted, so it came to be because of the malice and disobedience of the people. In order that it would be seen that nothing was accepted by God as much as obedience or faith, which they were lacking, neither is there nor was there a destruction more famous than the destruction of that city, where the worship owed to God, and justice, and holy religion had not been preserved. Thus that city was destroyed and laid low so many times, because it had abandoned its God so many times, so that it

found no sympathy from passersby. COMMENTARY ON JEREMIAH 19:8.[11]

THE WORST OF EARTHLY CALAMITIES. JOHN CALVIN: Here the prophet goes further; so atrocious would be the calamity that even fathers and mothers would not abstain from their children, but would devour their flesh. This was indeed monstrous. It has sometimes happened that husbands, in a state of extreme despondency, have killed their wives and children (anxious to exempt them from the lust of enemies) or have kindled a fire in the midst of the forum in order to cast their children and wives on the pile, and afterward die themselves; but it was more barbarous and brutal for a father to eat the flesh of his son. The prophet then describes an unusual vengeance of God, which could not be classed among the calamities that usually happen to humankind.

We know that this was also done in the last siege of Jerusalem; for Josephus shows at large that mothers in a brutal manner slew their children, and that they so lay in wait for one another that they snatched at anything to eat. This was also an evidence of God's dreadful vengeance. COMMENTARY ON JEREMIAH 19:9.[12]

A MISERY BEYOND ALL TEARS. MARTIN LUTHER: It should not be considered important that our possessions and rights are torn away, since it is settled in heaven that in this life Christians suffer oppression, Nimrods, and mighty hunters. Nor will the church be freed from this condition except by death. . . . But it is a misery beyond all tears that these things are done by brothers and fathers to brothers and sons (as the Lord says in the prophet that the children are devoured by their parents), something that would scarcely be done by a Turk; or if it were done, at least the holy name of Christ would not be used as a cloak for such foul abominations, which is the most intolerable affront

---

[9]CTS 18:441-44* (CO 38:325-26); citing Is 30:33.
[10]Zwingli, *Predigten*, 222-23. Zwingli quotes the ancient Cynic philosopher Diogenes (d. c. 323 BC). The Cynics aimed for simplicity and elimination of unnecessary demands and anxieties in one's life. Zwingli here seems to poke fun at excessive concern about our burial arrangements.

[11]Pellikan, *Commentaria Bibliorum*, 3:2S3v.
[12]CTS 18:446* (CO 38:328-29). Calvin cites a well-known account from the Jewish historian Flavius Josephus (d. AD 100), in *The Jewish War* 6.3.

of all to Christ and the church. By all means let property and life go to ruin. 1519 LECTURES ON GALATIANS.[13]

19:10-15 The Lord Will Break Judah

GOD IS RESPONSIBLE. JOHN DONNE: "I will break them as a potter's vessel. . . ." Do not honor the malice of your enemy so much as to say that your misery comes from him. Do not dishonor the complexion of the times so much as to say that your misery comes from them. Do not justify the deity of Fortune so much as to say that misery comes from her. Find God pleased with you and you have a hook in the nostrils of every Leviathan; power cannot shake you. When you have a piece of wood to cast into the waters of Marah, the bitterness of the times cannot hurt you. When you have a rock to dwell upon, then the dream of Fortune's wheel cannot overturn you. But if the Lord is angry, he needs no trumpets to call in armies. If he but whispers for the fly and the bee, then even with such a little thing in his hand he can discomfort, fluster, dissolve, weaken, impair, and annihilate the very marrow of your soul. Everything is his. . . . Your sickness is his sword, and therefore it is he who strikes you with it. Turn upon that consideration: The Lord is angry. SERMON ON PSALM 38:3.[14]

WHEN WE IGNORE GOD AS SOURCE OF OUR SUFFERING. JOHN DONNE: [When we so respond] God can work no cure in us, do no good upon us by breaking us; not by breaking us in our health—for we attribute that to weakness of stomach, overindulgence; not by breaking us in our standing in society—for we impute that to falsehood in servants, oppression in adversaries, and iniquity in judges; not by breaking us in our honor—for we will find cause for that in factions, conspiracies, and corrupt dealings in court. God cannot break us with his corrections whenever we

attribute them to some natural or some accidental cause and never think of God's judgments, which are the true cause of these afflictions. God cannot break us by breaking our backs, by placing heavy loads of calamity upon us, nor by breaking our hearts, by putting us into a sad, heavy, and fruitless sorrow and melancholy over worldly losses.

[When those judgments fail] then God comes to break us by breaking our necks, by casting us into the bottomless pit, and falling upon us there in wrath and indignation. "I will beat them as small as dust in the wind" and tread them as flat as clay in the streets. Such breaking will be like the breaking of the potter's vessel, which is broken without pity (no pity from God, no mercy, neither shall anyone pity them—no compassion, no sorrow). And in this breaking, the prophet says, there is found neither a piece to take to the fire at the hearth, nor a piece with which to bring water from the well. That is, they themselves shall be incapable of receiving any beam of grace from heaven, or any spark of zeal in themselves (not a piece of broken pottery to hold fire from the hearth), and incapable of holding any drop of Christ's blood from heaven, or of any tear of contrition in themselves—not a piece with which to fetch water from the well. "I will break them as a potter's vessel," says God in Jeremiah. Here there shall be no possible means (of those means which God has ordained for his church) to put them back together again: no voice of God's word to draw them in, no threats of God's judgment to drive them, no censure of God's church to hold them, no sacrament to cement and glue them together as Christ's body. SERMON ON MATTHEW 21:44.[15]

A GENERATION BROKEN, A NEW GENERATION RESTORED. CORNELIUS À LAPIDE: "Thus I will break the people, just as the potter's vessel is broken, so that it cannot be made whole again." Granted, after seventy years of captivity, the Jews would reestablish their nation. Nevertheless, this would be like a different and new race, another and new

---

[13]LW 27:158-59* (WA 2:448); citing Gen 10:8-9.
[14]Donne, Sermons, 2:86*; citing Job 41:1-2; Ex 15:22-25.

[15]Donne, Sermons, 2:193-94*; citing Ps 18:42; Is 30:14.

generation. Second and even better, "Thus I will break them," that is, "Thus the rod of destruction, with which I have threatened you, I will fully complete, so that those in the present time will be broken, such that of themselves they could not be renewed. But after seventy years, as if in another age or another time, they will be reestablished by me alone." By human power the Jews were not able to be restored, but by divine power it will be done. Thus Christ says, what is impossible for humanity is possible for God. See Maldonado and Castro. COMMENTARY ON THE PROPHET JEREMIAH 19:11.[16]

THE DESIRE FOR RELIGIOUS VARIETY AND THE FIRMNESS OF THE TRUE GOD. HULDRYCH ZWINGLI: Here we come to the immoderate desire for the insanity of new things, so that when people hold foreign rites in public, their empty souls are not able to be satisfied with God. This is true for Christians and their myriad of sacred things that are not able to fulfill the superstitions of the foolish, unless their innermost yearnings bubble forth to

idols, which stand forth for worshipful admiration and on very familiar terms. But when by duty these things come into use among the ungodly, where truly there is no true recognition of the true God, what remains that is firm and solid? Or what kind of religion does not hold fast to the true God? EXPLANATIONS OF THE PROPHET JEREMIAH 19:13.[17]

WHEN DIVINE THREAT BECOMES ACTION. JOHANNES BRENZ: "Behold I will bring upon this city." This is the confirmation of the evil things that the Lord has spoken over Judah and Jerusalem. As if he says, "Before I have threatened you horribly, so that I might invite you to repent. Now, since I see greater ungodliness just after I threatened etc., there will not only be words of threat, but also their effect." Indeed, all the judgments of God and the curses of the law are threats that invite us to repent. But if these things are unfaithfully despised, they will no longer be threats, but our very own perception of horrible judgment as they happen. ANNOTATIONS ON JEREMIAH 19:15.[18]

---

[16]À Lapide, *Commentarium in Jeremiam*, 126; citing Matt 19:26. À Lapide cites Juan de Maldonado and Cristoforus de Castro—fellow Jesuit biblical scholars and commentators on Jeremiah.

[17]Zwingli, *Complanationis*, 116.
[18]Brenz, *Annotationes in Jeremiam*, 903.

JEREMIAH 20:1-18
JEREMIAH SUFFERS PERSECUTION
AND INNER TURMOIL

¹Now Pashhur the priest, the son of Immer, who was chief officer in the house of the LORD, heard Jeremiah prophesying these things. ²Then Pashhur beat Jeremiah the prophet, and put him in the stocks that were in the upper Benjamin Gate of the house of the LORD. ³The next day, when Pashhur released Jeremiah from the stocks, Jeremiah said to him, "The LORD does not call your name Pashhur, but Terror on Every Side. ⁴For thus says the LORD: Behold, I will make you a terror to yourself and to all your friends. They shall fall by the sword of their enemies while you look on. And I will give all Judah into the hand of the king of Babylon. He shall carry them captive to Babylon, and shall strike them down with the sword. ⁵Moreover, I will give all the wealth of the city, all its gains, all its prized belongings, and all the treasures of the kings of Judah into the hand of their enemies, who shall plunder them and seize them and carry them to Babylon. ⁶And you, Pashhur, and all who dwell in your house, shall go into captivity. To Babylon you shall go, and there you shall die, and there you shall be buried, you and all your friends, to whom you have prophesied falsely."

⁷O LORD, you have deceived me,
    and I was deceived;
you are stronger than I,
    and you have prevailed.
I have become a laughingstock all the day;
    everyone mocks me.
⁸For whenever I speak, I cry out,
    I shout, "Violence and destruction!"
For the word of the LORD has become for me
    a reproach and derision all day long.
⁹If I say, "I will not mention him,
    or speak any more in his name,"
there is in my heart as it were a burning fire
    shut up in my bones,

and I am weary with holding it in,
    and I cannot.
¹⁰For I hear many whispering.
    Terror is on every side!
"Denounce him! Let us denounce him!"
    say all my close friends,
    watching for my fall.
"Perhaps he will be deceived;
    then we can overcome him
    and take our revenge on him."
¹¹But the LORD is with me as a dread warrior;
    therefore my persecutors will stumble;
    they will not overcome me.
They will be greatly shamed,
    for they will not succeed.
Their eternal dishonor
    will never be forgotten.
¹²O LORD of hosts, who tests the righteous,
    who sees the heart and the mind,ᵃ
let me see your vengeance upon them,
    for to you have I committed my cause.

¹³Sing to the LORD;
    praise the LORD!
For he has delivered the life of the needy
    from the hand of evildoers.

¹⁴Cursed be the day
    on which I was born!
The day when my mother bore me,
    let it not be blessed!
¹⁵Cursed be the man who brought the news to
        my father,
"A son is born to you,"
    making him very glad.
¹⁶Let that man be like the cities
    that the LORD overthrew without pity;
let him hear a cry in the morning
    and an alarm at noon,

[17]*because he did not kill me in the womb;*
so my mother would have been my grave,
and her womb forever great.

[18]*Why did I come out from the womb*
to see toil and sorrow,
and spend my days in shame?

a Hebrew *kidneys*

OVERVIEW: Religious confrontation was a commonplace of the Reformation era. Many pastors, priests, and theologians witnessed or participated in religious debates, state-sponsored tribunals, public protests, and disruptions of worship. In this narrative from the life of Jeremiah they found a prophet who knew firsthand the apprehensions of official scrutiny, public humiliation, and physical harm and yet seemed to find the courage to confront accusers and proclaim the Word of God in reply. Even so, Jeremiah's inner dialogue echoed with the anguish of his isolation and abuse and the staggering price of carrying the divine message. As with Jeremiah 15 commentators wrestled with the prophet's responses: were his doubts and frustrations typical of someone in a demanding ministry or had Jeremiah descended into blasphemy and despair?

20:1-6 Jeremiah Persecuted by Pashhur

THE COMPOSURE OF THE PROPHET AND THE OUTBURSTS OF THE WICKED. HULDRYCH ZWINGLI: When the priest Pashhur heard that Jeremiah was preaching without pause, he allowed Jeremiah to be struck and put him in stocks. Likewise, Jesus would be struck before Caiaphas, because he refused to give proof of the truth. So also Paul was struck before Ananias. Those who are teachers of the law ought to protect the people through the law of God from violence and tyranny. But they violated the law and struck the confessors of the truth in an unjust way. . . .

"You [to Pashhur and the like] are not the only ones who will be afraid, but you will be made afraid of others you should console. Whenever someone rushes about and does something in an emotional way—and when other people stand there as if they are a rock or a mountain—those rushing about will see urgent times soon enough; for them there is no strength or persistence, but rather fear and terror. In fact, there is no valor or courage without wisdom and virtue. Where passion reigns and one does not strive for the right, there one will not endure; that person will be ignorant in hard times, and act in violent outbursts and without consideration. Fear is a cruel advisor. When there is impudence without fear, then that is truly evil." SERMON ON JEREMIAH 20:1-4.[1]

STRUCK BY THE HIGH PRIEST. JOHANNES BUGENHAGEN: Until now no king, prince, or crowd has dared to touch Jeremiah; the impious high priest is the first to lay hands on Jeremiah, the holy prophet; he with his priests had done less than others to sustain the Word of God. On his own authority Pashhur seems to do this, as the prophet is judged to be seditious because he preaches apart from the authority of the high priests. So also later it would happen for Christ and the apostles in that place. So it is likewise today for preachers of the gospel. Thus, rulers would not become brutal against us, except by instigation of the priestly papists. Truly with the notion of greater righteousness the Jewish priests raved against the prophets and also so do our condemned priests, when they seemed to have the law on their side; the latter, however, have no notion of guidance from the Word of God. Therefore, Jeremiah prophesies against the high priest, his friends, and the whole people. COMMENTARY ON JEREMIAH 20:1-2.[2]

---

[1]Zwingli, *Predigten*, 223-24; citing Jn 18:19-23; Acts 23:2-3.
[2]Bugenhagen, *In Ieremiam* 3S2v-3S3r.

HOW KINGS AND RELIGIOUS LEADERS ABUSE THE TRUE PROPHETS. NIKOLAUS SELNECKER: This chapter shows how it goes for true preachers. They are hated, beaten, imprisoned, and ridiculed. Despite this abuse they should be able to wait in their office in silence. Of course, it has to be their own friends and acquaintances that hate and strike them, and engage them in an unfriendly manner. So it was for the court preacher of King Ahab, who struck the prophet Micaiah on the cheek in 1 Kings 22. Thereafter more injustice occurred, and the king had Micaiah thrown into a dungeon. Such is the reward for extolling God's word. The same servant of the godless and the world challenges God's word. Thus the punishment must happen. Ahab and his queen, Jezebel, must be killed in a gruesome way; her blood must be licked up by dogs. Zedekiah, the false court preacher and minister to Baal, had to leave; he crept away and died. So also the high priest Pashhur is threatened, that he would be captured, imprisoned, and die wretchedly, because he struck poor Jeremiah who had been ordered to bring the Word of God. So we see how it generally goes for pious and true preachers. . . .

Jeremiah changes the name of the high priest and says he should not be called Pashhur, but Magor. But in German Pashhur means something like "an extravagant nobleman, an onlooker, a superficial and fearless man who boasts about himself and changes day to day." Therefore, he is proud and cocky . . . but Magor means "fear, terror, and angst." . . . That is, one does not know what to do or where to begin. Certainly with these words Jeremiah sees the future journey or peregrination, on which the king of Babylon will take all away the Jews to Babylon. THE WHOLE PROPHET JEREMIAH 20:1-6.[3]

RECEIVE THE PROPHET'S MEDICINE. HULDRYCH ZWINGLI: "There you shall die and be buried." Here one sees that dying in bed is not always the best death. Everyone has earned a hard death. Some who die by the sword might just be blessed in this way. But this one who dies in bed is damned.

The prophet is like a physician, who from time to time is responsible for someone he does not want to help or put up with, especially when the sick person is impatient. So the prophet must do for us; for we are sick and we struggle to change our minds and try not to push the medicine away (when we do not want to be destroyed). So it may be bitter, yet it brings healing, even when the flesh is difficult and against it. We can expect no healing, unless we grasp the Word of God. SERMON ON JEREMIAH 20:6.[4]

RIDICULING THOSE WHO RECEIVE DIVINE MESSAGES. THOMAS MÜNTZER: With very few exceptions they teach that God no longer reveals his divine mysteries to his dear friends through genuine visions or direct words etc. So they adhere to their bookish ways and make a laughingstock of those who have experience of the revelation of God, as the godless once did with Jeremiah: "Say, friend, have you had a message from God recently? Or have you been questioning or consulting him recently? Is the spirit of Christ in you?" They go on like this, pouring out contempt and scorn. What happened in Jeremiah's time was no small matter, was it? Jeremiah warned the poor blind people how painful their imprisonment in Babylon would be. . . . But it all seemed absurd to them. They said to the good prophets: "Yes, yes, how nice of God to issue these fatherly warnings." But what happened to this crowd of smart alecks during their imprisonment in Babylon? Just this: they were put to shame by the pagan king Nebuchadnezzar! SERMON TO THE PRINCES.[5]

20:7-18 The Anguish of Jeremiah

A COMPLAINT BEFORE GOD. JOHANNES OECOLAMPADIUS: "You have deceived me, Lord." In the customary usage Jeremiah makes his case complaining before the Lord. The judgment: "If there is anything misleading in my words, so that

---

[3]Selnecker, *Der gantze Prophet Jeremias*, G3r-G4v; citing 1 Kings 22:13-28, 37; 2 Kings 9:36.

[4]Zwingli, *Predigten*, 224.
[5]Müntzer, *Collected Works*, 235-36; citing Sir 34:10.

they shout against me, which I don't believe, then truly you deceived me; indeed, I did not act of my own accord, but you called me. I declined, but you compelled me as I ran away. You ordered me to say everything. Those people, however, ridiculed me and demanded my death. Your word was despised; perhaps it would have been enough for me thereafter to be silent and to say nothing more to them, and to shake the dust from my feet, as I shout 'devastation' and 'plundering.' For they want to destroy me: murder, murder!" Indeed, the grief of prophets is the greatest, because they teach in vain. COMMENTARY ON JEREMIAH 20:7.[6]

HATING GOD AND ADORING THE DEVIL.
JOHANNES BUGENHAGEN: From this passage to the end of the chapter the prophet is described as miserably vexed by himself, and with a variety of emotions, so that you might see what becomes of us when left to ourselves. Now he accuses God. Then he gives thanks and trusts in his goodness. Then again he curses his own birth and seems nearly to blaspheme. These things are not done together, but appear in this confused ordering and description. Indeed, they cannot cohere together, since giving thanks and trusting in God are the greatest and only piety, but the rest are nothing other than horrible and damnable sins, except that God does not impute them to his elect while left to their temptation. That which you read all mixed up at the same time will not then be mixed up for you, when you understand that these things were said by Jeremiah not all at once or at the same time, but in various times or hours. When he sees that God is with him in his mandated office, however much his adversaries persecute him from time to time, he says, "The Lord is with me," etc. But when he is lost in himself in persecution and the horror of death, he says, "Lord, you have persuaded me," etc. and "Cursed is the day." etc. . . .

But you may ask, what is most important in his description of such temptation? I respond: there can be some occasions—although this is an extreme one, if not singular—when we turn away

our consideration from the Word and will of God, that is, from our vocation. We begin to argue with God and to demand, "Why did this or that happen?" This is a grave and dangerous temptation. Here Jeremiah sees that those who condemn the Word flourish among the Jews; he sees himself not only despised among his own people but also endangered in his life. Moreover, all the kingdoms of the Gentiles are in their greatest glory, but the people of God, both perish and are about to perish with all their holy things of God. Here a thought creeps up: does God abandon people of all other religions and accept only a few of us? Here we begin to hate God and give adoration to the devil, saying, "God, you persuaded me" etc. These are horrible sins, which we do not understand until we look back on them afterward; then we seem to have been in death and hell in the midst of all the devils. Then we give thanks to God for our freedom. As the psalm says, "You led my soul out of hell and saved me from those going down into the pit." COMMENTARY ON JEREMIAH 20:7-18.[7]

GROWTH IN FAITH LEADS TO THE CROSS.
JOHANNES BRENZ: It is an exclamation of the prophet. The Hebrew text says, "You have seduced me and I have been seduced." These are the basics of faith and the apostolate. Indeed, in the beginning God does not cast down the faithful person or the apostle into great dangers, but seduces with promises and benefits, and feeds us with milk, until we grow so that we can be nourished by more solid food, namely, the cross. We can see this in the case of the apostles, who at the beginning heard the promises, "You are blessed, since your reward will be abundant in heaven." ANNOTATIONS ON JEREMIAH 20:7.[8]

WORLDLY WISDOM AND CONVICTIONS OF THE HEART. NIKOLAUS SELNECKER: Here we have a clarification and example of the sayings of Paul in 2 Corinthians 7—outer struggle and inner fear. For

---

[6]Oecolampadius, *In Hieremiam*, 2:B1r.

[7]Bugenhagen, *In Ieremiam*, 3S3v, 3T1v; citing Ps 30:3.
[8]Brenz, *Annotationes in Jeremiam*, 905.

example, "We do not want you to be uninformed, dear brothers, about our troubles. . . ." Jeremiah is in even greater danger of limb and life and waits patiently in a dungeon. He can easily overcome and bear the bodily misfortune. But within his heart and conscience he feels miserable and fears what he thinks, "See, whence I come to this point, that I must bear this alone, while others do not? Everyone else has good days, gracious lords, and favorable advice, and they have all good things; they act as if everyone is fully satisfied with them. I alone must be despised and tormented. So I also could have good days and enjoy the people's grace and favor. Must I then ever be the one whose jaw opens too wide and speaks the truth? What difficulty comes upon me? I would rather that not everything be made right and be reformed; I would rather not threaten to hammer them. The stone is too heavy for me. I cannot raise it. Who knows if I'm doing the right thing, especially because I am alone and others want very little understanding; yet such folk have nothing to do. I always want to be silent and keep my mouth shut. I can preach, but at the same time I do not want to speak and they do not want to hear it." . . .

With such thoughts and the like Jeremiah moves and acts as a rational man, who is worldly wise; no one can condemn him or reprimand him for that. He has to say and confess all his reasoning, which he rightly does; so when he can go around and avoid some misfortune, he does it. It is a robust madness and impulsive move to put oneself in danger, to reject dear friendships in favor of enemies and disfavor, to refuse to learn how to move, achieve, and orient oneself to the world. Worldly-wise folk know and practice all of this; thus no water is muddied and neither the fox nor the wolf bites. . . . But when they are in danger, they would rather plan, do, manage, and speak of something against their conscience; they would rather avoid the least and smallest danger and let a black cloud simply pass over them.

"But there is in my heart," says Jeremiah, "a burning fire in my bones that I could not ignore. I could not bear it. . . ." I find here an entirely different meaning than that which comes from my reason

and what my thoughts speak to me. I notice that I am not oriented toward others or allowed to look at worldly wisdom. My conscience will have no rest. I speak. God is no longer patient with me. I would thereby be sick, sad, melancholic, and lack strength. My heart and body would be burdened as if a millstone lay on them and burned me, as if my heart and body lay in the middle of a fire—until I thought otherwise. Then I looked to the office that God had once commanded me to take up and take it for myself. I would wait, for it appears like danger— what and how great it would seem to be. Then I think, what kind of office do I have, whom do I serve, who tests my heart, who hears my tongue and my words, to whom do I have to give an account today or tomorrow? What do I have to show for myself if I remain speechless and refuse to speak what I have to say to the godless? So again I take up my courage, call on God and the Holy Spirit, and consider how I do this for God and could be responsible for the God-fearing and be accountable. . . .

In these words Jeremiah gives stunning expression—as he does in further chapters to follow—to the heavy burden of the preaching office and how a true teacher has enough to do and must endure so much angst, exhaustion, and work, and thereby will be little honored. Just as the world is ungrateful, so true teachers are even less appreciated. We see also how God allows his saints to experience many misfortunes in the world, and thereby they gain practice and through difficulty they are shaped. While they are gifted at times, they are also impatient, often complain and are unwilling—as with Jeremiah, Job, Habakkuk, and others. But as God again helps up Jeremiah, so also he will do for us; we will be overcome by some of the same thoughts and impatience, but also trust God to comfort, strengthen, and help us to know that we are yet not alone in this life and that we should be thankful eternally. Therefore, help us, our true and beloved Immanuel, Jesus Christ. Amen. THE WHOLE PROPHET JEREMIAH 20:7-10.[9]

---

[9]Selnecker, *Der gantze Prophet Jeremias*, G4r-v, H1v-H3v; citing 2 Cor 7:5; 1:8-11.

SHOULD THE PREACHER KEEP SILENT?

MARTIN LUTHER: Isaiah might have said, "I was not a bit interested in them. I am not going to preach to them anymore." So Jeremiah said, "The word of the Lord has become for me a reproach." So Jeremiah complains, since these many reproaches offend us. So it was with me, Martin Luther, that I would often determine not to preach anymore. Every magistrate and every noble does nothing; in fact, they despise the words. No village can support one minister, or pastor. No school can support one coworker, so that the ministers of the church die of starvation, while at the same time the people with extreme greed amass everything for themselves. This excessive contempt for the gospel and this blasphemy among the people causes our preachers to become altogether weary. So the prophet was mocked by excessive contempt and derision, and felt like saying, "I would just as soon keep silent altogether and let them sweat it out themselves. Yet it is not for their sakes that I have assumed this office. There are others who will receive my words and for their sakes I will preach." Meanwhile our people cry, "I have enough to eat and drink, I do not need a pastor. Faith! Faith! He who does not have food and clothing is sinning against himself. . . ." In short, because of the ungodly I would keep silent, just as our people care nothing if no word would be preached. Yet among them there are certain remnants, and for their sakes, for those good people, I will speak, even though a number of reasons should dictate silence. So Jeremiah said, "I will keep silent. But there is a burning in my bones." He could not keep silent because his conscience was driving him. LECTURE ON ISAIAH 62:1.[10]

KEEP PREACHING!

MARTIN LUTHER: We are exhorted to preach the word, because the Word of God will not go out and return empty. So it is here. When your word has been in the earth, then the inhabitants learn righteousness. Then by the gleam of the gospel they learn true righteousness, because they learn hypocrisy and ungodliness when the gospel is lacking. For since such fruit of the Word is to learn righteousness from it, therefore we must earnestly see to it that the word is heard everywhere for the progress of righteousness and for a warning against presumptuousness and self-glorification. So this has hitherto been our experience: since the word was lacking, we fell into every ungodliness and hit upon different ways. There was no instruction in sure righteousness and therefore we must with extreme diligence watch for the word by which we get so great a treasure. Therefore Paul admonishes Timothy: "Be urgent in season and out of season." This advice must be given to those who at any time become delinquent, as also the prophets complain: "The word of the Lord has become for me a reproach and derision all day long." So it seems and happens to our preachers that by their earnest preaching they apparently accomplish nothing among the people. This text comforts those preachers and assures them that they are not preaching into a void, even though barely two were listening to it. LECTURE ON ISAIAH 26:10.[11]

PROPHECY AS A TRIAL.

ST. JOHN OF THE CROSS: Believe me, people cannot completely grasp the meaning of God's locutions and deeds; nor, without much error and confusion, can they determine this meaning by what appears to be so.

The prophets, entrusted with the Word of God, were well aware of this. Prophecy for them was a severe trial because, as we affirmed, the people observed that a good portion of prophecy did not come about in accord with the letter of what was said to them. As a result the people laughed at the prophets and made much fun of them. It reached such a point that Jeremiah exclaimed: "They mock me all day long." THE ASCENT OF MOUNT CARMEL.[12]

WHEN A PROPHET OR TEACHER WANTS TO GIVE UP.

JOHN CALVIN: I rather think that the prophet had another kind of trial—he brought down a greater vengeance of God by his cries, as

---

[10]LW 17:343-44 (WA 31.2:526-27); citing Jer 4:19.

[11]LW 16:204 (WA 31.2:144), citing Is 55:11; 2 Tim 4:2.
[12]St. John of the Cross, *Collected Works*, 222.

though he had said, "To what purpose should I furnish God with weapons by my preaching? since I do nothing but increase his wrath. . . ." The meaning is that the prophet saw no other fruit to his labor, but that people were rendered more insolent, and from being thieves became robbers, and from being disdainful became ruffians, so that they increasingly kindled God's wrath, and more fully abandoned themselves. . . .

Now this passage is especially worthy of being observed; for not only teachers are influenced by this feeling, but all the godly without exception. For when we see that people are, as it were, made worse through God's Word, we begin to doubt whether it be expedient to bury every remembrance of God and to extinguish his word, rather than to increase the licentiousness of people, they being already inclined enough to commit sin. . . .

But the way is shown by which God aided his servant. The Word of God became "as a burning fire in his heart," and it was also "closed up in his bones," so that he was led by an ardent zeal and could not be himself without going onward in the course of his office. COMMENTARY ON JEREMIAH 20:8-9.[13]

JEREMIAH REASSURES HIMSELF. THE ENGLISH ANNOTATIONS: After the former storm of discontent and doubt arising from the apprehension and consideration of the general conspiracy and banding together of persons maliciously and mischievously disposed against him, which seemed shrewdly to have staggered him, the prophet in the next passage here begins to recover himself and to strengthen his faith against all oppositions; [he was] assured of God's constant presence with him and powerful protection of him according to his promise, one of infinite might, able to terrify the most terrible among them that thus plot together and set themselves against me, thinking thereby to frighten and daunt me. ANNOTATIONS ON JEREMIAH 20:11.[14]

THE DISTRESS OF THE PROPHETS AND SAINTS. PHILIPP MELANCHTHON: Jeremiah keeps the faith that has been entrusted to the prophet, but not without great conflict: "If I say, 'I will not mention him or speak any more in his name,' then within me there is something like a burning fire shut up in my bones. . . ." At this point he almost succumbs to his distress, but soon he is raised up again, saying, "But the Lord is with me like a dread warrior; therefore my persecutors will stumble, and they will not prevail." Then a powerful impatience wells up in him again so that he appears to lose hope and to rage against the will of God.

These struggles are peculiar to the saints and through them they discern the magnitude of sin in human nature. They match what Paul describes in Romans 7 and agree with what he says elsewhere about torments or thorns being given to him in the flesh, that is, extreme fear and trepidation. In the midst of these torments, however, the Spirit yearns for help "with sighs too deep for words," and it prevails. THE LESSONS OF JEREMIAH'S PROPHECY.[15]

JEREMIAH IS LIKE MOSES IN HIS ZEAL. MENNO SIMONS: Such a faithful shepherd the faithful Moses was, for when the Lord informed him that Israel had made a molten calf he hastened from the mountain, and when he heard the tumult and saw the multitude playing and dancing, he burned internally in zealous wrath. . . .

So also was the worthy prophet Jeremiah, although burdened with suffering and cares, because of much distress and cross-bearing (with which his faithful service was not a little burdened). He had determined in his heart to prophesy no more in the name of the Lord, yet when he saw that the people were ungodly, and neither acted nor spoke aright, he said, "God's word was in my heart as a burning fire shut up in my bones, so that I all but perished and could hardly bear it." FOUNDATION OF CHRISTIAN DOCTRINE.[16]

---

[13]CTS 19:28-29* (CO 38:344-45).
[14]Downame, ed., *Annotations*, 9O2v*; citing Jer 1:19; 15:20, 21; 35:14; Ps 46:7; Rom 8:31; Jer 11:21.

[15]Melanchthon, "Lessons," 67; citing 2 Cor 12:7; Rom 8:26.
[16]Simons, *Complete Writings*, 160-61*; citing Ex 32:7-10.

WHAT THE FAITHFUL HEART NEEDS AND DESIRES. KONRAD PELLIKAN: "You, Lord of hosts, prove the just." The Lord alone knows how to prove the just, as God alone sees the secret things of the heart and the faith which justifies. Although he is the champion of human fragility against all the ungodliness, nevertheless, he allows the just to be tested, so that they might be exercised unto a greater faithfulness and humbled, so that they pray more ardently for growth in righteousness and more diligently commend themselves to divine goodness, on which they rely completely and by which they are not deceived. Moreover, they wish for the vengeance of God, but not out of hate or impatience, but rather to the glory of God, whose righteousness and power have been unjustly despised by the impious. COMMENTARY ON JEREMIAH 20:12.[17]

FREE FROM TEMPTATION. JOHANNES BUGENHAGEN: "Sing to the Lord." Free from temptation and anguish we arouse heaven and earth, and all creatures to praise God with us. Everything seems to rejoice with us. This is sung in the Psalms: "Praise the Lord from the heavens." Or as Christ says, "Angels rejoice over one sinner who repents." But truly if it were up to us we would be forsaken in temptation. . . . The degree of this hell or infernal temptation cannot be adequately described by any words. For in that place God is not God, light is not light. . . . But death and devil reign. Just as among the liberated nothing else is heard than "Sing, praise, bless! Blessed is God! We praise you God!" That is, nothing other than giving thanks. So among the vexed there is nothing other than cursing and "Let the mountains fall on us." But the elect pronounce such things in error. Truly it is far different, when God, who is not deceived, pronounces so, "Better for that person if they had not been born." COMMENTARY ON JEREMIAH 20:13.[18]

THE MOST DIFFICULT TRIAL. MARTIN LUTHER: We have described three attacks. The first is that of the flesh, against which God consoles us with his righteousness; the second is that of the world, against which he promises that we shall be conquerors and threshers; the third is that of Satan. He wearies us in our private life, he attacks individuals with various dangers, with hatred, envy, and lust. So it was with Job and Jeremiah, who in their trials wished they had not been born. This is the worst and most difficult trial, of which Christ said concerning Judas: "It would have been better for that person if they had not been born." These are peculiarly the temptations employed by Satan. He completely wearies us needy and poor little people who are parched with thirst. St. Paul aptly speaks of "sighs too deep for words." LECTURE ON ISAIAH 4:17.[19]

CELEBRATE ONLY ONE BIRTH. JOHN DONNE: None of the saints of God, nor those who were noted to be good examples in their religion, and sanctified people, ever celebrate with any festive solemnity their own birthday. Pharaoh celebrated his own nativity, but who would make Pharaoh an example? Herod celebrated his nativity, but who would think it an honor to be like Herod? Besides, he polluted that celebration with the blood of John the Baptist. But the just contemplation of the miseries and calamities of this life, into which our birthday is the door, and the entrance, is so far from giving any just occasion for a celebration. This has often moved the best disposed saints and servants of God to become upset, to utter maledictions and curses against their birthdays. "Cursed is the day on which I was born, and let that day on which my mother bore me not be blessed." "Let that day perish on which I was born; let that day be dark and let not God regard it from above."

How much misery is predicted for us, when we usually come weeping into the world. In the whole sweep of history we read of only one child—Zoroaster—who laughed at his birth.† What miserable

---

[17]Pellikan, *Commentaria Bibliorum*, 3:2S4v.

[18]Bugenhagen, *In Ieremiam*, 3T3v-3T4r; citing Ps 148:1; Lk 15:7; Hos 10:8; Mt 26:24; Mk 14:21; Lk 23:30.

[19]LW 17:47* (WA 31.2:297); citing Job 3:3; Mt 26:24; Rom 8:26.

revolutions and changes, what downfalls, what broken necks and collapses, may we be ordained to, when we consider that in our coming into this world and out of our mother's womb things only go well if a child comes out head first and then still falls straight into the calamities which we all must suffer? Though the days of the martyrs, which are celebrated in the Christian church, are ordinarily called *natalitia martyrum*—the birthday of the martyrs—yet that is not intended to refer to their birth into the world, but to their birth into the next world, when by death their souls were newly delivered from their prisons here and newly born into the kingdom of heaven. For that reason the day of their death is called their birthday and celebrated in the church under that name. Only Jesus Christ was in "the fullness of time" at his birth. This is not because he avoided a painful life as he passed through, but because the work of redemption was his entire work, and all that Christ said, did, or suffered converged upon our salvation. Thus his mother's swaddling him in small clothing and Joseph's shrouding him in a funeral sheet; thus Christ cold lying in his manger and Christ cold and dying upon the cross: the birth of this boy is the consummation of all things. His birth and death occurred "in the fullness of time." SERMON ON GALATIANS 4:4-5.[20]

THE TRIAL OF THE QUESTION, WHY? MARTIN

LUTHER: See Job and Jeremiah, who cursed God with this "Why" concerning their birth. The trial of the saints is extremely violent: "Why should God act thus?" So here the Jews have their own "Why," as if to say, "The king of Babylon is a murderer and a wicked tyrant, he is condemned.

But we are godly people, and we are cast down as doing injury." The children of God have all the afflictions. The ungodly children of Satan enjoy the highest state of well-being. Everything seems the opposite of what it should be. The godly are maltreated; the ungodly receive gifts. In this vein the flesh blasphemes the work of God. So today we see our word and God's word to be futile, everything seems exactly the opposite of what it should be, and then we see God's work to be unjust. So God and Satan weary us with masks and external spirits so that we are led to believe that what is of God is Satan, and what is Satan is of God, and then we say in our heart, "I wish I had never been born." All of us must experience this mood. All the godly have felt this mood together with Christ, who cried out on the cross, "My God, my God, why have you forsaken me?" Or with Jeremiah who said "Cursed be the day on which I was born!" . . . Just so it has often happened to me, Martin Luther, that I was sorry that I ever treated a passage of the gospel. These are powerful blasts. Then Satan comes and says, "Do you think so many holy fathers and bishops were unlearned and our ten so learned?" When such trials of "Why" come, beware that you do not answer and allow these attacks to get control. Rather, close your eyes and kill reason and take refuge with the Word. Do not let the "Why" get into your heart. The devil is too powerful; you cannot cope with the situation. LECTURE ON ISAIAH 45:9.[21]

WHAT WE LEARN FROM THE BLASPHEMOUS THOUGHTS OF JEREMIAH. JOHN CALVIN: We

may say that [Jeremiah] was tried by a new temptation, yet this seems by no means satisfactory, though it is in this way that interpreters commonly untie the knot. But it seems to me a feeling unworthy of the holy man to pass suddenly from thanksgiving to God into imprecations as though he had forgotten himself. I, therefore, doubt not but that the prophet here relates how grievously he had been harassed by his own thoughts. . . .

---

[20]Donne, *Sermons*, 6:332-33*; citing Gen 40:20; Mt 14:6; Job 3:3-4; Gal 4:4. In the early church *natalitia martyrum* were celebrations at the grave of a martyr on the date of a martyr's death, commemorating when a martyr was born into eternal life. At such celebrations, the faith of the martyr would be proclaimed along with the narrative of suffering and death. †Zoroaster (c. 628–c. 551 BC) was a priest and religious reformer who founded Zoroastrianism. Pliny the Elder (AD 23–79) reports that Zoroaster laughed at his own birth and pulsated with wisdom as an infant: Pliny, *The Natural History* 15.

[21]LW 17:128-29* (WA 31.2:360-61); citing Job 3:3; Mt 27:46.

In short, the prophet teaches us here that he was not only opposed by enemies but also distressed inwardly in his mind, so that he was carried away contrary to reason and judgment, by turbulent emotions that even led him to give utterance to vile blasphemies. For what is here said cannot be easily excused; but the prophet most grievously sinned when he became calumnious toward God; for a man must be in a state of despair when he curses the day on which he was born. People, indeed, like to celebrate their birthday; and it was a custom that formerly prevailed to acknowledge yearly that they owed it to God's invaluable goodness that they were brought forth into vital light. As then it is a reason for thanksgiving. It is evident when we turn to a curse what ought to rouse us to praise God, we are no longer in a right mind, nor possessed of reason, but that we are seized as it were with a sacrilegious madness; and yet into this state the prophet had fallen.

We may then learn in this passage with what care every one of us ought to watch ourselves, lest we be carried away by a violent feeling, so as to become intemperate and unruly.

At the same time I allow, and it is what we ought to carefully notice, that the origin of his zeal was right. For though the prophet indirectly blamed God, we ought yet to consider the source of his complaint; he did not curse his birthday because he was afflicted with diseases or because he could not endure poverty and want, or because he suffered some private evils;† no, nothing of this kind was the case with the prophet; but the reason was that because he saw that all his labor was lost, which he spent for the purpose of securing the wellbeing of the people. . . .

But we are here reminded how much vigilance we ought to exercise over ourselves; for in most instances, when we become weary of life and desire death, and hate the world, with the light and all the blessings of God, how is it that we are thus influenced, except that disdain reigns within us, or that we cannot with resignation bear insults, or that poverty is too grievous to us, or that some troubles press on us too heavily? It is not then that we are influenced by a zeal for God. . . . Seized with

so violent a feeling, we ought surely to exercise the more care to restrain our feelings; and though many things may daily happen to us that may produce weariness, or overwhelm us with so much disdain as to render all things hateful to us, we ought yet to contend against such feelings; and if we cannot, at the first effort, repress and subdue them, we ought, at least, according to the example of the prophet, to learn to correct them by degrees, until God cheers and comforts us, so that we may rejoice and sing a song of thanksgiving. COMMENTARY ON JEREMIAH 20:14-16.[22]

DID JEREMIAH COMMIT A MORTAL SIN?
CORNELIUS À LAPIDE: Like Job 3, Jeremiah curses the day of his birth. Some think these words were spoken by Jeremiah as he was disturbed in his spirit. Indeed they seem to be the words of a desperate, impatient, and vengeful soul. Whence Calvin said that these are the cries of a desperate man, that they are a sacrilegious furor against the Jews, and that they are blasphemies and affronts to the God of nature and author of his origin. But really this blasphemy doesn't hold up. . . . A little before this passage, Jeremiah praised God with great affection. And who believes that here Jeremiah sins with a mortal sin, nay rather with this most severe curse? Who says this of him, I say, who was "sanctified from the womb?" . . .

I answer . . . that this is a mode of speech of the Hebrews, who would understand through so great a curse the interjection of one who wishes, as if saying today, "If only that would not have happened!" Thus in chapter 3 of Job, "He cursed," that is, as he spoke, he wished, saying: "Let the day on which I was born perish." Indeed just as it is a good thing for a day to exist, so for the same day it is an evil thing not to exist. Therefore, Jeremiah curses the day of his birth; that is, it is as if he wishes evil for it, namely, the evil of nonexistence. Because that day was for him the cause and portal of so many evils, both public evils—as he prophesied and saw the destruction of

---

[22]CTS 19:44-47* (CO 38:352-53). †Calvin may be alluding here to Job 3.

his very own city and people—and personal evils—since because of this he was odious to all, as if he were a false prophet, an enemy of his homeland, and as if he was a disgrace to all. It is as if he says, "Would that that day had never been, would that I had never been born!" Indeed it is better not to exist than to feel badly and be so miserable all the time. Jeremiah uses this phrase for his pathos, so that he might show what great straits and what grievous evils he suffered, and how unwillingly he points towards and preaches the destruction of Jerusalem, so that the Jews might see that he preached this very message not of his own will, but compelled by God. . . .

Here Jeremiah changes the topic away from the conditions of grace, merit, and sin, away from the ordination of God, away from the future condition of glory, and he only looks at natural goods and evils. Indeed, these are the exclamations of simple nature, and the wishes of simple nature, or rather, mere wishes or hopes concerning a bygone and impossible thing: hopes that he expresses with the vehemence of grief, as if naturally, and that reason allows though clouded and almost overwhelmed with pain. COMMENTARY ON THE PROPHET JEREMIAH 20:14.[23]

THE HUMAN WEAKNESS OF JEREMIAH. HULD-RYCH ZWINGLI: Here we see what manifold challenges and temptations there were, which were chosen by God. This curse and impatience is not an example for us that we should imitate, but more so an open confession of the prophet in light of his human weakness, which he here suffers. As if he wanted to say: I am weak and a complete lack of strength and a state of frustration has come so far upon me, that I say, "Curse this day."

"May the day that my mother gave birth to me not be blessed." That means, "Why did I not die as soon as I came into my mother's womb?" Job says the same thing in chapter 3: "It would be better not to be born or to die in childhood, if one was born." We see here that on earth everything is trouble and work. This has been determined for us by God that

we might be tested constantly and at all times and that we spend our lives on honorable things (in our work, not in idleness). The soul is a dynamic power; when we are always doing the work God has placed upon us, then that is a good and honorable thing. SERMON ON JEREMIAH 20:14-18.[24]

ETERNAL LIFE AND DEATH IN THE WOMB. JOHANNES OECOLAMPADIUS: Jeremiah addresses God as Job does, when he says, "Why did you not close the door of the womb on me?" Infants who die inside the womb before birth, where an embryo is to be born, have a mother's uterus as their tomb. The course of life is not long, when death happens to someone being born even before life begins. But is this happier, to the extent that fewer of the troubles of life come to pass? I ask you, what is this life of humankind? How loathsome is this theater of hardships? Jeremiah calls conception "eternal." If one has died before the day of birth, then their mother's womb would be his tomb. For that short space of life would be eternity to that one for whom, alive, no other time would come to light. For they would taste nothing of this life besides the nourishment of pregnancy within the closed womb of their mother. Therefore, conception is called "eternal" not simply because it exists within the briefest space of time, but also in comparison if one dies before this life. But if in desolation a person of God wishes they hadn't been born, how would this be compared to an impending external judgment with the impious? Or would it not be better for them if they had never been begotten into this light? The pious deplore such feelings, if in these verses human beings and their judgment are conflicted. The highest tranquility and calm arises, where one begins to taste the sweetness of the Sunday cross amid the bitter poisons of calamities. So Paul himself accepted such an apostolic sentence of death, by which, nevertheless without doubt, through self-denial he was directly set free. COMMENTARY ON JEREMIAH 20:17.[25]

---

[23]À Lapide, *Commentarium in Jeremiam*, 130-32; citing Jer 1:5; Job 3:1.

[24]Zwingli, *Predigten*, 226-27; citing Job 3:1.
[25]Oecolampadius, *In Hieremiam*, 2:B2v-B3r; citing Job 3:10; Phil 1:21-26.

JEREMIAH 21:1-10
JERUSALEM WILL FALL TO NEBUCHADNEZZAR

¹*This is the word that came to Jeremiah from the Lord, when King Zedekiah sent to him Pashhur the son of Malchiah and Zephaniah the priest, the son of Maaseiah, saying,* ²*"Inquire of the* L*ORD for us, for Nebuchadnezzar*ᵃ *king of Babylon is making war against us. Perhaps the* L*ORD will deal with us according to all his wonderful deeds and will make him withdraw from us."*

³*Then Jeremiah said to them: "Thus you shall say to Zedekiah,* ⁴*Thus says the* L*ORD, the God of Israel: Behold, I will turn back the weapons of war that are in your hands and with which you are fighting against the king of Babylon and against the Chaldeans who are besieging you outside the walls. And I will bring them together into the midst of this city.* ⁵*I myself will fight against you with outstretched hand and strong arm, in anger and in fury and in great wrath.* ⁶*And I will strike down the inhabitants of this city, both man and beast. They shall die of a great*

pestilence. ⁷*Afterward, declares the* L*ORD, I will give Zedekiah king of Judah and his servants and the people in this city who survive the pestilence, sword, and famine into the hand of Nebuchadnezzar king of Babylon and into the hand of their enemies, into the hand of those who seek their lives. He shall strike them down with the edge of the sword. He shall not pity them or spare them or have compassion.'*

⁸*"And to this people you shall say: 'Thus says the* L*ORD: Behold, I set before you the way of life and the way of death.* ⁹*He who stays in this city shall die by the sword, by famine, and by pestilence, but he who goes out and surrenders to the Chaldeans who are besieging you shall live and shall have his life as a prize of war.* ¹⁰*For I have set my face against this city for harm and not for good, declares the* L*ORD: it shall be given into the hand of the king of Babylon, and he shall burn it with fire.'"*

a Hebrew *Nebuchadrezzar*, an alternate spelling of *Nebuchadnezzar* (king of Babylon) occurring frequently from Jeremiah 21–52; this latter spelling is used throughout Jeremiah for consistency

---

OVERVIEW: This chapter marks a crucial shift in the message of Jeremiah. Henceforth, most of Jeremiah's prophecies and related narratives deal directly with the invasion of the Babylonians, the siege and destruction of Jerusalem, and the fate of the Jews and neighboring nations. When considering these dire circumstances, Reformation commentators reflect on the true role of godly rulers, the prophetic approach to authority, and the hard choices faced by the faithful in times of war and violence. Under such conditions true repentance and submission to divine lordship are put to the test.

21:1-7 The City Will Fall

THE ORDER OF JEREMIAH. JUAN DE MALDONADO: We have noted in our commentaries on

Isaiah that almost every one of the chapters of the prophets is a single prophecy, and to a certain extent they are like individual books published at various times and having various titles. They preserve neither a continuous narrative nor a temporal sequence. But thereafter they were collected from some number of books into one volume. This is worth remembering with reference to this passage, since the prophecy of this chapter was published many years after all the preceding ones. The previous chapters were written long before the arrival of the Chaldeans; this one was written when they were just arriving. Nor is the order of time preserved; indeed in the following chapters some things are spoken of which happened before the time when Zedekiah reigned.[†] The Pashhur here is not the one from the preceding chapter, who struck

Jeremiah, as Jerome observes.† This man is called Emmer, the son of Malchiah. COMMENTARY ON THE PROPHETS, JEREMIAH 21:1.[1]

THE ORDER OF THE BOOK OF JEREMIAH.

HEINRICH BULLINGER: This historical account is added to what has been covered previously and is written concerning the siege of the city of Jerusalem through Nebuchadnezzar and the calamitous outcome through him. This account alters the natural flow of the book of Jeremiah, and is skillfully inserted here. Indeed, before the orations of Jeremiah that follow, which are here related, Jeremiah spoke of the times of Jehoiakim and Jehoiachin. Apparently the siege begun by the Babylonian prince occurs not long after Jeremiah breaks the pots in Topheth and after he was struck and bound by the priest Pashhur. SERMON ON JEREMIAH 21:1.[2]

ZEDEKIAH RECOGNIZES HE NEEDS THE PROPHET.

JOHN TRAPP: The history is here set down out of course, for Jerusalem was not besieged until chapter 32, and Jehoiakim reigned in chapter 25. It was the ninth year of Zedekiah that this present prophecy was uttered. This Zedekiah was one of those half-finished virtuous men (as Philo calls some professors), cakes half-baked. No flat atheist, nor yet a pious prince. Of Galba the emperor, as also of Richard III, it is recorded that they were bad men but good princes. We cannot say so much of Zedekiah. He is chiefly accused of two things: (1) He broke his oath and faith pledged to the king of Babylon. (2) He humbled not himself before Jeremiah the prophet, who spoke from the mouth of the Lord. Up until this point, he had not, but now in his distress he seeks the prophet, and thus sends an embassy. Kings care not for soldiers (said a great commander) "till their crowns hang on the one side of their heads." Sure it is that some of them slight God's ministers, till they cannot tell what to do without them, as here. Kingdoms have their cares, and thrones their thorns. Antigonus cried out of his diadem ... "O base rag," not worth taking up at a man's feet. Julian complained of his own unhappiness at being made emperor. Diocletian laid down the empire as weary of it. Thirty of the ancient kings of this our land, says Capgrave, resigned their crowns, such were their cares, crosses, and emulations. Zedekiah now could gladly have done as much. But since that could not be, he sent to Jeremiah, whom in his prosperity he had slighted, and (to gratify his wicked counselors) wrongfully imprisoned. COMMENTARY ON JEREMIAH 21:1.[3]

SEEKING A MUTE GOD.

JOHANNES BUGENHAGEN: As is reported at the end of 2 Kings, the king of Judah in Jerusalem was beset by Babylonian forces. In order to consult with the Lord he sent an honorable legation to Jeremiah—as Pharaoh had said to Moses and Aaron during the plague: "Pray for me to the Lord, who is used to speaking to others. I do not know the Lord." He was like Esau, who wept and wailed profoundly before his father—not because he had sinned in his contempt for the gift of the firstborn of God—but on account of his condemnation and the punishment of sin, which is the penance of the impious and condemned or at the very least of hypocrites for a time. Esau in one meal exchanged his right as the firstborn. You know that afterward when he wanted at the very least to procure a blessing by the law of inheritances, he was refused. He did not find a place of repentance; nevertheless he tried to gain it with tears; that is, in his weeping and sorrow he did not receive the right of primogeniture that he had

---

[1]Maldonado, *Commentarii in Prophetas*, 92-93. †To address the complex sequence of Jeremiah, Cornelius À Lapide, provides a *chronotaxis oraculorum*—a chronology of the events and prophecies in the chapters of Jeremiah at the beginning of his commentary—from the birth of Jeremiah and reign of King Josiah through Kings Jehoiakim and Zedekiah to Jeremiah's time in Egypt: *Commentarium in Jeremiam*, 5-7. ‡Jerome, *Commentary on Jeremiah*, 125. [2]Bullinger, *Conciones*, 134v.

[3]Trapp, *A Commentary or Exposition*, 284*; citing 2 Kings 25:1-2; Hos 7:8; Ezek 17:16; 2 Chron 36:12-13. Philo of Alexandria (20 BC–AD 40) was a Jewish scholar of Judaism and Hellenistic philosophy; on half-finished men, see Philo's *On Rewards and Punishments* 2.9. Trapp refers to Roman emperor Galba (3 BC–AD 69, r. 68–69); King Richard III of England (1452–1485, r. 1483–1485); Roman emperor Julian (c. 331–363, r. 363–365), known as "the Apostate"; and Roman emperor Diocletian (245–316, r. 284–305).

sold before. Indeed, likewise Zedekiah did not want to turn to the Lord to become someone better, but only to be free of present danger. . . . In this trial, the impious worship of God, which the people had taken up for themselves in contempt of the Word of God, does no good. Now they want as a protector he whom they did not want to have as God. They want a mute god, that is, one who does not speak and one they do not want through the Word of God. COMMENTARY ON JEREMIAH 21:1-2.[4]

DOING BATTLE WITH GOD AS WARRIOR, DYING AN UNMANLY DEATH. HULDRYCH
ZWINGLI: "I will turn back the weapons of war in your hand." This comes from a competition in the ring, where one must first lay down his weapons and then each must grab his own for the competition. God says, "I will fight with you; you have fought against me long enough. Let us see, who is stronger! Your spit, which you aim at your enemy, will come back against you. You cannot stab your enemy to death; for another fights and battles with you. I fight with you; for you have enraged me. But if you were one with me, then the enemy could be overcome."

"You shall die through a great plague." The soldier and the hero: he stands there with his weapons and armor; he imagines that he will conquer death. But God will not allow it to come to that. The warrior will not enjoy much honor, so that he would be allowed to struggle bravely and to die bravely and honorably. But he must die a shameful death—from disease or starvation. SERMON ON JEREMIAH 21:3-6.[5]

I WILL DEFEND YOUR ENEMIES. THE ENGLISH
ANNOTATIONS: I will be so far from relieving you and succoring you that I will turn the weapons that you fight with away from your enemies and turn them back upon and against you. I will do this by setting you by the ears among yourselves. Or I will cause your enemies to recoil and turn back without [you] doing any damage to them. All of your fighting against them shall be in vain and to no purpose. ANNOTATIONS ON JEREMIAH 21:4.[6]

THE KING'S INQUIRY AND THE LORD'S RE-
SPONSE. HEINRICH BULLINGER: At the beginning of the chapter a brief title is placed as short authentication of the history, which is the occasion of the response of Jeremiah. Before all else, God is indicated as the author, so that they are less likely to despise everything that tends to come in the narratives and speeches. The occasion is the inquiry of King Zedekiah. Indeed, the king of Babylon has besieged Jerusalem, so King Zedekiah sends an honorary delegation to Jeremiah, requesting that Jeremiah ask or consult with the Lord, if perchance a miracle might occur for the miserable city and free her from this severe siege. The time in which these things are covered is the ninth year of Zedekiah. The beginning of the siege also occurs in the ninth year of Zedekiah. Therefore, the prophet labored for nine years under this king, but not without being harassed. Meanwhile, the astonishing goodness of God had shone forth for the longest time—very unlike the wicked deeds of the people— and there was the expectation of repentance. . . .

Some who sent this delegation to him, and even an honorable one, had up to this point despised Jeremiah and had thrown him in prison. Now the things of the ungodly were coming back on them, as before; thus they were arranging certain matters before God, which they had mocked previously; for now they had become suppliants. . . .

Look at the inquiry they propose to Jeremiah. There is certainly no word concerning repentance or the amending of their lives. They simply beg for liberation from their present danger; for it was necessary so that they might continue to lead their pleasant lives. "Consult," they say, and "put our case to the Lord; see if he will not free us again from the Babylonians, and through a miracle, as he had freed

---

[4]Bugenhagen, *In Ieremiam*, 3Viv; citing 2 Kings 24:1–25:30; 2 Chron 36:11; Ex 8:8; 9:27-28; Gen 27:34; Heb 12:15-17; Gen 25:29-34.
[5]Zwingli, *Predigten*, 228-29. Zwingli's experience as a battlefield chaplain for cantons of the Swiss Confederacy likely informs the martial tone and code of bravery described here. It was in this capacity that Zwingli was killed in the Second Battle of Kappel in 1531.

[6]Downame, ed., *Annotations*, 9O3r*; citing Jer 13:13; Ps 89:41.

King Hezekiah from Sennacherib, King of the Assyrians through an angel." This is the inclination of humanity: to direct what miracles God should do and to demand signs, by which we are rescued from the evil around us. But the Lord commands others: "Do not put the Lord your God to the test"; but take care always to do what God commands of you.

Now, therefore, we must consider the nature of the response of Jeremiah to the inquiry proposed by the delegation. There are various things to examine; nevertheless certain things can be gathered in this chapter. (1) Jeremiah brings into view the unfortunate events of war. Indeed, all their defenses and weapons will be turned against them, their city and towns will be captured; they will be destroyed by disease and famine; "you will be slain by the sword"; accordingly, there will be no miraculous liberation from God. (2) He exposes in particular what will happen to the king and his people because of wretched superstitions; when they are captured, he says, they will be cut down without mercy. (3) Meanwhile, this council is beneficial for the people, if they follow it. (4) Moreover, he prescribes what should be done in the court of the king. (5) Finally, he confounds their vain hope and shows that they are not able to be freed from the walls of that place because of the impending wrath of God. . . . Above all Jeremiah diligently points out that the Lord himself is the author of all things. Indeed, one is not to respond to God by inquiring out of one's own will, but one is to consult the Lord out of the very mouth of the Lord. From the beginning Jeremiah shows the unfortunate events of war. The Lord would not free them through a miracle, but instead would hand them over to the power of the enemy. SERMON ON JEREMIAH 21:1-7.[7]

BOUND BY OATH, EVEN TO PAGAN KINGS.

MARTIN LUTHER: These people are disloyal and guilty of perjury to their rulers, to whom they have taken oaths and done homage. In God's sight this is a great sin that does not go unpunished. The good

king Zedekiah perished miserably because of such perjury; he did not keep the oath he gave to the heathen emperor at Babylon. Such people may think or persuade themselves that it is within their own power and choice to go from one lord to another, as though they are free to do or not do whatever they pleased, forgetting God's commandment and not remembering their oath by which they are bound to be obedient until they are compelled by force to abandon that loyalty or are put to death because of it. This is what the peasants wanted to do in the recent rebellion, and this is why they were beaten.[†] For just as a man may not slay himself, but must submit to being slain by the violence of others, so no one should evade their obedience or their oath unless they are released from it by others, either by force or by favor and permission. ON WAR AGAINST THE TURK.[8]

21:8-10 Life and Death

A CHOICE BETWEEN TWO PUNISHMENTS.

JOHANNES OECOLAMPADIUS: God imparts some mercy to the people, which is this: If they want to, they are able to be freed of a greater evil; God gives them the way of life and the way of death. He says, however, that death means the ruin of the people when they fend off the Babylonian host from themselves, who in fact were carrying out the Lord's business. But what God calls life is to be given over to the enemy in servitude through surrender. This exile they tried to escape, and they were prevented from escaping by a more severe punishment. For in being rescued from exile they were tormented in a cruel way. But the deserters (the people who went willingly to the enemy), united with the calamity of others, likewise seemed to live. However, to live is to act suitably, not just to be given life. Therefore this passage is to be understood through the comparison. . . . Free will does not add anything in the matters of captive

---

[7]Bullinger, *Conciones*, 134v-135v; citing 2 Kings 19:1-37; Deut 6:16; Mt 4:7; Lk 4:12.

[8]LW 46:193-94 (WA 30.2:138). [†]Luther refers to the German Peasants' Revolt (1524–1525), which had occurred about four years before Luther wrote this treatise.

people, as certain people want to seem to think here, but it brings a choice among two punishments; both choices are inclined to serve the will and favor of God, or through his indignation to fall with varying disaster on those present. . . . He who preferred to surrender to the Chaldeans and to enemies would have a profitable life and live pleasantly. For the perishing of the city has been decreed. It is preferable to bear however much tribulation of the flesh, than to be handed over in one's soul to the assembly of the impious, whether in flattery, or cooperation, or error at the same time, when in fact, the Lord destroys the impious. COMMENTARY ON JEREMIAH 21:8-9.[9]

A TREASONOUS COMMAND? HULDRYCH ZWINGLI: For "those about to fall to the enemy" the Hebrews have the word for "passing over"; as in German, "to fall out." That is, taken as "to fall out" in Latin, "to pass over" or "defect" to the enemy. In this passage it is clear what a dangerous thing the prophecy is. Indeed, what could the recommendation that they go over to the enemy look like to everyone, except betrayal and high treason? But

Jeremiah is commanded to submit to this danger. Thus the one who orders this is also consoling him. EXPLANATIONS OF THE PROPHET JEREMIAH 21: 9.[10]

THE HARD PROMISES OF GOD WILL BE FULFILLED. JOHANN PAPPUS: Jeremiah advised that a surrender to the enemy should be made. A vindication of the city should not be expected. . . . Our prophet was persistent in this matter, for contrary to the custom of all the other prophets, he was commanded to persuade his listeners to surrender themselves to the dominion of the enemy, while many of the prophets before him assured the people of divine promises in which God would preserve them. And he was ordered to persuade them that it would not be as it was long before in the time of Isaiah, when there were two illustrious liberations of the Jewish kingdom from their neighboring enemy. But our prophet teaches that the promises will be fulfilled in a different way, namely, that the people would first be led into captivity and then led back from it, and then finally the promises about the Messiah would be fulfilled. ON ALL THE PROPHETS, JEREMIAH 21:8-10.[11]

---

[9]Oecolampadius, *In Hieremiam*, 2:C1r-v.

[10]Zwingli, *Complanationis*, 118.
[11]Pappus, *In Omnes Prophetas*, 92r; citing 2 Kings 18:1–20:21.

JEREMIAH 21:11–22:30
PROPHECIES TO THE KINGS OF JUDAH

[11] "And to the house of the king of Judah say, 'Hear the word of the LORD, [12] O house of David! Thus says the LORD:

"'Execute justice in the morning,
  and deliver from the hand of the oppressor
  him who has been robbed,
lest my wrath go forth like fire,
  and burn with none to quench it,
  because of your evil deeds.'"

[13] "Behold, I am against you, O inhabitant of
    the valley,
  O rock of the plain,
declares the LORD;
you who say, 'Who shall come down against us,
  or who shall enter our habitations?'
[14] I will punish you according to the fruit of
    your deeds,
declares the LORD;
  I will kindle a fire in her forest,
  and it shall devour all that is around her."

22 Thus says the LORD: "Go down to the house of the king of Judah and speak there this word, [2] and say, 'Hear the word of the LORD, O king of Judah, who sits on the throne of David, you, and your servants, and your people who enter these gates. [3] Thus says the LORD: Do justice and righteousness, and deliver from the hand of the oppressor him who has been robbed. And do no wrong or violence to the resident alien, the fatherless, and the widow, nor shed innocent blood in this place. [4] For if you will indeed obey this word, then there shall enter the gates of this house kings who sit on the throne of David, riding in chariots and on horses, they and their servants and their people. [5] But if you will not obey these words, I swear by myself, declares the LORD, that this house shall become a desolation. [6] For thus says the LORD concerning the house of the king of Judah:

"'You are like Gilead to me,
  like the summit of Lebanon,
yet surely I will make you a desert,
  an uninhabited city.[a]
[7] I will prepare destroyers against you,
  each with his weapons,
and they shall cut down your choicest cedars
  and cast them into the fire.

[8] "'And many nations will pass by this city, and every man will say to his neighbor, "Why has the LORD dealt thus with this great city?" [9] And they will answer, "Because they have forsaken the covenant of the Lord their God and worshiped other gods and served them."'"

[10] Weep not for him who is dead,
  nor grieve for him,
but weep bitterly for him who goes away,
  for he shall return no more
  to see his native land.

[11] For thus says the LORD concerning Shallum the son of Josiah, king of Judah, who reigned instead of Josiah his father, and who went away from this place: "He shall return here no more, [12] but in the place where they have carried him captive, there shall he die, and he shall never see this land again."

[13] "Woe to him who builds his house by
    unrighteousness,
  and his upper rooms by injustice,
who makes his neighbor serve him for nothing
  and does not give him his wages,
[14] who says, 'I will build myself a great house
    with spacious upper rooms,'
who cuts out windows for it,
  paneling it with cedar
  and painting it with vermilion.
[15] Do you think you are a king
  because you compete in cedar?
Did not your father eat and drink

207

and do justice and righteousness?
　Then it was well with him.
¹⁶He judged the cause of the poor and needy;
　then it was well.
Is not this to know me?
　declares the LORD.
¹⁷But you have eyes and heart
　only for your dishonest gain,
for shedding innocent blood,
　and for practicing oppression and violence."

¹⁸Therefore thus says the LORD concerning Jehoiakim the son of Josiah, king of Judah:

"They shall not lament for him, saying,
　'Ah, my brother!' or 'Ah, sister!'
They shall not lament for him, saying,
　'Ah, lord!' or 'Ah, his majesty!'
¹⁹With the burial of a donkey he shall be buried,
　dragged and dumped beyond the gates of
　　Jerusalem."

²⁰"Go up to Lebanon, and cry out,
　and lift up your voice in Bashan;
cry out from Abarim,
　for all your lovers are destroyed.
²¹I spoke to you in your prosperity,
　but you said, 'I will not listen.'
This has been your way from your youth,
　that you have not obeyed my voice.
²²The wind shall shepherd all your shepherds,
　and your lovers shall go into captivity;

a Hebrew *cities*

then you will be ashamed and confounded
　because of all your evil.
²³O inhabitant of Lebanon,
　nested among the cedars,
how you will be pitied when pangs come
　upon you,
　pain as of a woman in labor!"

²⁴"As I live, declares the LORD, though Coniah the son of Jehoiakim, king of Judah, were the signet ring on my right hand, yet I would tear you off ²⁵and give you into the hand of those who seek your life, into the hand of those of whom you are afraid, even into the hand of Nebuchadnezzar king of Babylon and into the hand of the Chaldeans. ²⁶I will hurl you and the mother who bore you into another country, where you were not born, and there you shall die. ²⁷But to the land to which they will long to return, there they shall not return."

²⁸Is this man Coniah a despised, broken pot,
　a vessel no one cares for?
Why are he and his children hurled and cast
　into a land that they do not know?
²⁹O land, land, land,
　hear the word of the LORD!
³⁰Thus says the LORD:
"Write this man down as childless,
　a man who shall not succeed in his days,
for none of his offspring shall succeed
　in sitting on the throne of David
　and ruling again in Judah."

OVERVIEW: In these prophecies of Jeremiah to the kings of Judah, Reformation commentators found ample opportunity to decry wicked rulers and praise the godly King Josiah. Therein expectations of effective and just political rule in Reformation Europe are revealed. Unfortunately the sons of Josiah did not emulate their father, leading to the destruction of the Jewish kingdom. Unlike many of the prophecies emphasizing idolatry as the fatal sin of the people, these verses underscore the connec-tion between divine wrath and the exploitation of the vulnerable and the poor. In the Reformation era rights and privileges were carefully defined and limited by one's place on the social ladder. How then could justice be enforced and the suffering of the poor overcome in line with Jeremiah's teaching?

Moreover, the demise of the royal houses of David and Josiah attest to the failure of leaders who choose human allies over the God who alone saves. For our interpreters the ultimate destiny of

David's line lies not among the captives in Babylon, but in the Messiah to come in the New Testament.

21:11–22:10 Message to the House of David

TRUSTING IN WALLS AND HUMAN AID.
JOHANN PAPPUS: The third part of chapter 21 initially addresses the house, that is, the household of the king. But in the course of his speech Jeremiah directs his message to the entire city of Jerusalem. This city is called "the inhabitant of the valley and the rock of the plain" because it is situated in a steep and uneven place among the valleys and mountains, which themselves once spread out at the highest point into a plain. In short, they should have confidence neither in the walls of cities, nor in other defenses, but they should either repent or expect certain destruction. Indeed, they are most foully deceived who while they provoke the Lord daily to a just punishment with their sins and stubborn shamelessness nevertheless hope that they will be safe through human assistance. ON ALL THE PROPHETS, JEREMIAH 21:11-14.[1]

THEY CONSUME THE POOR.
JOHANNES BUGEN-HAGEN: The poor and powerless were plundered; that is, their possessions and goods of the field, home, and vineyard were taken away from them through the powerful who perverted the law. That is, through deceitful lies and with an appearance of law they demanded those things from the judges as if they rightfully belonged to themselves and the impious judges gave the verdict to the powerful, and so the wretches were despoiled. "Listen, I beg you, you heads of the houses of Jacob and princes in the house of Israel. Was it not for you to know justice? But you hold good to be hateful, and you love evil. You tear off the flesh of my people, and as you tear, you break their bones just as if you were putting them in a pot and putting their flesh in a cauldron." COMMENTARY ON JEREMIAH 21:12.[2]

NO DEFENSE AGAINST THE LORD.
THE ENGLISH ANNOTATIONS: At the end of this answer returned to the messengers of Zedekiah, God through the prophet meets [them] head on with their presumptuous conceit. They regarded their city in terms of its situation and fortifications, to be an impregnable place and thereby able to withstand the greatest armies or force that could be raised or made against the city. The Lord tells them that he himself will come against them at the head of those who invade and assault them. This is what they fondly and vainly suppose is not feasible. ANNOTATIONS ON JEREMIAH 21:13.[3]

A FIERCE JUDGMENT ON UNJUST RULERS.
NIKOLAUS SELNECKER: To such contempt for God's Word and his true warning there tends to follow what we see here. The enemy is nearly here. God's wrath burns now and is at its most intense. Through the prophet Jeremiah he speaks and proclaims to the king and people: "He will himself fight with the king of Babylon against the city of Jerusalem and the Jews and let fly disease and famine. He will consume through the sword, because there is utterly no reform found there." God especially threatens the king and the authorities because those in the government have been lazy and careless; they have not punished evil nor given assistance to the poor. So God will not allow such sins to go forth unpunished. Thus God wills that princes, lords, and other authorities take up their offices with true effort and an upright fear of God and apply the pure and wholesome teaching of the law and gospel: protect, nurture, love, and honor true teachers; receive their subjects justly and defend them and protect them from themselves; spur subjects to earnest prayer. Do not burden them except for an emergency; do not suck them dry and make them poor. As Micah says in chapter 3: "Hear, you heads and princes; you should be fair and know what is right. But you hate the good and love the wretched. You tear the skin from the people and the flesh from their bones, and eat the flesh of my people. And when you have torn

---
[1]Pappus, *In Omnes Prophetas*, 92r.
[2]Bugenhagen, *In Ieremiam*, 3V3r; citing Mic 3:1-3.

[3]Downame, ed., *Annotations*, 9O3v*.

209

the skin from them, you break their bones and cut them up like meat in a pot and like meat in a kettle." That is, "You leave nothing for them, and consume their sweat, blood, and hard work. Therefore, when you cry out to the Lord, he will not listen to you, but will hide his face from you. . . ."

Such a harsh warning and the like should really enliven and move the hearts of the authorities to remember their office, observe God's grace and blessing, and flee from such wretched punishment. Whoever the princes, lords, and authorities are who do this, God will watch over them, protect them, rule them, and bring to them justice and honor. But those who despise God's Word, and do not want to be moral, God will leave them to know, be reprimanded, warned, and punished. To those who take up their offices earnestly and eagerly, who nurture their own passions and do not apply a just law or care for the poor, God will send forth his severe response. Like a fire God will allow it to burn so that no one can put it out. And when you call out, he will not listen to you. THE WHOLE PROPHET JEREMIAH 21:3-14.[4]

HOPE AND ADMONISHMENT. JOHANNES OECO-LAMPADIUS: Jeremiah has this order of history, so that it might be understood from the sequencing of the words. In chapter 21 King Zedekiah appealed to the prophet through an honorable delegation so that Jeremiah might pour out prayers for Zedekiah and the kingdom before the Lord. To those consulting the oracle of the prophet he soon answered unpropitious and ominous things, which came to pass against the king and his friends. The prophet explained these things to the ambassadors with an example. But certainly this response goes to the end of verse 12 in chapter 21. He later produces a hope of kindness, by exhorting them with the prophecy that a king would arise like a shoot from the just David, so that in the early morning daily he would give fair judgment for the people. Indeed, the whole chapter that precedes chapter 22 seems to be a continuous sermon, and God's disposition toward the legates

acting openly seems to be beyond the need to answer the prayer of the prophet. Finally, because the Lord is exceedingly merciful and invites everyone to repent, by his command he directs the prophet to go with rather soothing commands to the palace, so that the king might be moved by his authority to repent. When, in a series of acts, he admonishes us, the course of words is such that at first he terrifies us and afterward he warns us to turn back to the way of salvation. Therefore, one might hear the same oracle twice, once as he delivers it to the ambassadors of the king, once as with his own words he explains it before the king. With his own ears the king received the will of God from the mouth of the prophet, but nevertheless he did not return to the duty that had been demanded of him. It is so true that most people hear the word of salvation, and in this way it leads to their own condemnation. COMMENTARY ON JEREMIAH 22:1.[5]

WHY GOD ADDRESSES RULERS FIRST. JOHN CALVIN: The prophet is again bidden to reprove the king and his counselors; but the exhortation is at the same time extended to the whole people. It was necessary to begin with the head, that the common people might know that it was not a matter to be trifled with, as God would not spare—no—not even the king himself and his courtiers; for a greater terror seized the lower orders when they saw the highest laid prostrate. . . .

We must at the same time observe . . . that they could not escape the calamity that was at hand; but the exile would have been much milder, and also their return would have been more certain, and they would have found in various ways that they had not been rejected by God, though for a time chastised. . . .

[The prophet] speaks of the king as "sitting on the throne of David"; but not . . . for the sake of honor, but for the purpose of enhancing his guilt; for he occupied a sacred throne, of which he was wholly unworthy. . . . The throne of David was more eminent than any other; for it was a priestly

---

[4]Selnecker, *Der gantze Prophet Jeremias*, H4v4-I2r; citing Mic 3:1-3.

[5]Oecolampadius, *In Hieremiam*, 2:C2v-C3r; citing Jer 23:5-7.

kingdom and a type of that celestial kingdom that was afterward fully revealed in Christ. Because the kings of Judah, the descendants of David, were types of Christ, their impiety was less tolerable, when, unmindful of their vocation, they departed from the piety of their father David and became wholly degenerate. COMMENTARY ON JEREMIAH 22:1-2.[6]

THE SOCIETY OF POOR PEOPLE—GOD'S SERVANTS. HULDRYCH ZWINGLI: "Do not afflict the stranger, orphan, and widow." "The earth is the Lord's and everything in it": The reciprocity of all things, including humanity, the whole world and whatever lives in it, corresponds to a divine order. God himself allows people to change residences from one place to another, so that citizens, residents, immigrants, and strangers are made. Likewise, the holy fathers—Abraham, Isaac, and Jacob . . . —become pilgrims and strangers by divine order. The Lord also requires—as the prophets and the whole of Scripture warn—that we should take the foreigner into consideration. Moreover, in the law of Moses it is commanded that the people of Israel treat kindly and do well by the foreigner; as they were also foreigners in the land of Egypt. The same goes for the orphan: the sheep should not be with the wolf, so they should not be handed over to unfaithful and predatory foster parents. Foreigners, orphans, widows, and day laborers are often trapped in debt and unfairly oppressed. The society of poor people are also the servants of God; when you do not attend to them, then these sins cry out to heaven. When one deals unfairly with them, this becomes like the testimony to the Lord of those sorely burdened children of Israel in Egypt. Their cries rise up to God on high. These are the gifts and good deeds of princes: to practice the law and justice and with their power to free the oppressed, as is said here. This sort of authority should be carried out above any other.

The judge should protect the orphan and the widow, when they suffer injustice, especially when they are unable to take action for themselves. There are so many who cannot risk legal action, or are simply incapable of doing it. Likely they conceal a related injustice done to them, or in these matters they have made complaint to one authority after another. The powerful need no defense; they can defend themselves. For the defenseless and the truly destitute the judge and the authorities are set up as the first line of defense. When the authorities fail to do this, then God hears when the poor cry to him. God is concerned for them above all. So the prophet orders here: the kings and authorities should be warned that the orphans and widows shall be treated justly. SERMON ON JEREMIAH 22:3.[7]

EQUITY FOR STRANGERS, ORPHANS, AND WIDOWS. JOHN CALVIN: [The prophet] says, first, "Do judgment and justice." This belonged especially to the king and his judges and governors; for private individuals, we know, had no power to protect property; for though everyone ought to resist wrongs and evil deeds, yet this was the special duty of the judges whom God had armed with the sword for this purpose. To "do judgment" means to render to everyone according to their right; but when the two words, *judgment* and *justice*, are connected together by justice, we are to understand equity, so that every one has their own right; and by judgment is to be understood the execution of due punishment. . . .

The prophet now adds other things that he had not mentioned in the preceding chapter; "defraud not," he says, "the stranger and the orphan and the widow." It is what is often said in Scripture, that it is not right to defraud any one; for God would exempt all from being wronged, and not only strangers, orphans, and widows. But as orphans have no knowledge or wisdom, they are exposed, as it were, to plunder; and also widows because they are in themselves helpless; and strangers, because they have no friends to undertake their cause. Hence God, in a special manner, requires a regard to be held for strangers, orphans, and widows. There is another reason; for when their right is

---

[6]CTS 19:74-76* (CO 38:371-72).

[7]Zwingli, *Predigten*, 230-32; citing Ps 24:1; Ex 3:7.

rendered to strangers, orphans, and widows, equity no doubt shines forth more conspicuously. When anyone brings friends with them, and employs them in the defense of their cause, the judge is thereby influenced; and the one who is a native will have their relations and neighbors to support their cause; and the one who is rich and possessing power will also influence the judge, so that they dare not do anything notoriously wrong; but when the stranger, or the orphan, or the widow comes before the judge, the judge can with impunity oppress them all. Hence, if the judge judges rightly, it is no doubt a conspicuous proof of the judge's integrity and uprightness. COMMENTARY ON JEREMIAH 22:3.[8]

GOD IS NO RESPECTER OF PERSONS. JO-HANNES OECOLAMPADIUS: God wants everyone to carry out earnest acts of mercy, so that he can more generously grant every kind of happiness. Certainly if there was true judgment according to the Word of God in the church, today we would not deplore its great calamity. But there is in the church an utmost respect of persons; powerful evil people are pardoned; poor good people are condemned; and the effusion of blood certainly provokes the wrath of God. God swears by himself that he does not consider anyone more important than anyone else. See, therefore, that an oath is not evil through itself; only let it be for the glory of God and the welfare of one's neighbor. COMMENTARY ON JEREMIAH 22:4.[9]

THE HOUSE OF DAVID—TEMPORAL AND ETERNAL. KONRAD PELLIKAN: The Lord solemnly vows to uphold an irrevocable judgment that was sanctioned for use for all of the sons of Josiah; who because in these matters they deserted the narrow path of their holy father, all as one ended badly and destroyed the kingdom along with the royal city and the entire house—nay, even the house of David. Thus the kingdom promised to

him would not continue in temporal glory, but would collapse in a repulsive way until it would be restored and perpetuated by Christ, the son of David. COMMENTARY ON JEREMIAH 22:5.[10]

GILEAD AS A SYMBOL OF COVENANT AND DEVASTATION. JOHN MAYER: "You are to me Gilead. . . ." Gilead was on the other side of the Jordan; in former times it was a fruitful country, especially of Balaam, but then belonged to the ten tribes that were carried away as captives. Gilead was a spectacle of desolation, as Shiloh had been called before, which had flourished because the ark was there; when the ark was gone, a desert place grew up in Shiloh. So the king's palace, the head of the house of Jerusalem, was called Lebanon for the frequency of houses therein. . . . And Gilead is called the head of Lebanon, because the forest begins there and extends far south. . . . Gilead first got its name from a heap of stones, because Jacob and Laban had made a covenant there; and for a witness they made a great heap of stones; because Gilead in Hebrew means "heap." It was a kind of mountain and therefore appropriately spoken of as a way of setting forth Mount Zion, where the king dwelt, and in Zion, where a covenant was made with God by sacrifice as in Gilead. . . . As the covenant had been notoriously broken in Jerusalem, therefore it was more worthy to be made a desert than Gilead. COMMENTARY ON JEREMIAH 22:6.[11]

NOWHERE IS SAFE FROM GOD'S JUDGMENT. THE ENGLISH ANNOTATIONS: Because the judgment threatened might seem to them very unlikely to take place, trusting partly in their wealth and partly in their strength, arising as well from the natural situation of the place, as from their works and fortifications around it. God further tells them that though their land were as wealthy as Gilead, and their structures as strong

---

[8]CTS 19:77-78* (CO 38:372-73).
[9]Oecolampadius, *In Hieremiam*, 2:C3v.

[10]Pellikan, *Commentaria Bibliorum*, 3:2S6r.
[11]Mayer, *A Commentary*, 404*; citing Num 22:1–24:25; Jer 7:12-14; Gen 31:45-50.

and impregnable, as if they were situated on the highest part of Mount Lebanon, yet he would reduce their whole land and head city to a wild wilderness, and make the other cities about it like a vast desert. ANNOTATIONS ON JEREMIAH 22:6.[12]

SANCTIFIED FOR DESTRUCTION. JOHANNES OECOLAMPADIUS: "And I will sanctify. . . ." That is, I will ordain destroyers thus to this matter, so that no one may impede them, nor will they do anything else in particular, those who are prepared for this one thing, so that they might lead you back to destruction. As it is not allowed to violate holy things and to convert them to a profane use, so the destroyers will do nothing else. Isaiah says, "There is none that shall faint or labor among them. . . . Their belt will not be loosened." So the Lord has sanctified their weapons, hammers, saws, and all such things, so that they might be suitable for demolishing the temple. Just as once they had cut down the trees used for building in Lebanon, so now they will gather the beams and paneled ceilings from the temple building and cast them into the fire. So those whom God once allowed to grow in their errors, so that they would finally come into the ministry of Christ, he gave up in those times. Indeed, we are wild olive trees planted among the native olive trees; when God will again see what trees are useless, he will tear them out and throw them in the fire. COMMENTARY ON JEREMIAH 22:7.[13]

TRAVELERS PONDER THE RUINS OF JERUSALEM. HEINRICH BULLINGER: Jeremiah shows the cause of this destruction yet again and does so by taking on the voice of another person; for he most elegantly imagines and puts forward travelers like those looking about the plains and asking where Troy was, or in this case where the city of Jerusalem had stood. Then they confer among themselves and they ask what caused the destruction of this celebrated city and they respond to one another, "Because they abandoned the covenant . . ." etc. Moreover, he shows the consequences of deserting and violating the covenant of the Lord. "They adored strange gods and served them." We have this today in the worship of God, in which many foolishly think they can earn much merit before God. The Lord grants everything to us already so that we can continue steadfastly in the covenant of God. Amen. SERMON ON JEREMIAH 22:8-9.[14]

22:11-30 Message to the Sons of Josiah

LAMENT THE GOOD RULER LOST AND THE RULER NOW IN POWER. NIKOLAUS SELNECKER: "Do not weep for the dead," that is, for the godly King Josiah, who has died and received a deadly wound at Megiddo. The whole of Judah and Jerusalem bore his mourning in 2 Kings 23. These things about him have occurred. "You have declared that he was a godly prince," says Jeremiah. "You have a virtuous reason to weep. How do you reckon your current Lord in comparison to Josiah? This one goes to extremes to work you to death and scrape you up; he torments you and treats you like dogs. He is proud and lavish, troublesome and arrogant. Therefore, he also must be dragged into captivity, so that he never returns. Cry and lament that the present is not as it was before. Josiah was a godly king, who maintained justice and righteousness, loved my Word, and looked after his subjects so that they were in good standing and did well. At the same time he suffered his loss and affliction in the last war, in which he was wounded, died, and was able to be buried. Moreover, God forgives such a one as Josiah; he is a prized and blessed hero and died well. He suffered the misfortune, in which we now live and he was not allowed to see or experience. But how are things now for us? What sort of overlord do we have? His eyes and heart are neither accustomed to God, nor do they fear the knowledge and summons of God. But they are turned to cruelty, exploitation, and scratching his itch with

---

[12]Downame, ed., *Annotations*, 9O4r*; citing Jer 17:3.

[13]Oecolampadius, *In Hieremiam*, 2:C3v; citing Is 5:27; Mt 7:19; Lk 13:6.

[14]Bullinger, *Conciones*, 139r.

splendid things, pride in his power, and heinous crimes." We can truly say that these days we have such rulers in many places in our Germany and we lament to God.

Against the king, Jehoiakim or Eliakim, Jeremiah prophesies that he will be buried like a donkey and thrown out before the gate of Jerusalem. The Whole Prophet Jeremiah 22:10-19.[15]

Worldly Sins and Worldly Goods.

Johannes Bugenhagen: "Woe to the one who builds." There are other remarkable prophecies against Jehoiakim, king of Judah—impious and proud. Jehoiakim did not to any extent find fault with the expanded kingdom and lavish food, for these are not forbidden to kings. But he prepared these things with injury to his subjects, whom he oppressed and to whom he did not restore wages. He was a man without fear of God, who wanted to perish. He was not different from certain rulers now who waste everything and want to seem famous and generous. They harm and oppress their subjects; neither are they troubled with the impious because these rulers perish with their subjects, which is the height of foolishness. They do not permit themselves to be troubled, lest they suffer admonishment. Here the building and food of the king are not criticized because it adds: "Did your father also eat and drink?" His father was most holy Josiah. It was not because he ate and drank that he was holy and his kingdom was remarkable in its majesty. It was because he feared God. The glory and splendor of his kingdom he regarded as a gift from God. He was the father of his subjects, not only in attending to peace and a fit kingdom, but also in religion, etc. It is necessary to record this because of the Anabaptists, who are beginning to teach a new monasticism. . . . They want to forbid rulers the use of the things and the glories of the world, thus creating sins where there are none. Meanwhile they do not see their own horrendous sins.

They believe themselves to be just, not on account of Christ, but because of their poverty and contempt for parents, wives, etc. Commentary on Jeremiah 22:13.[16]

Godly Rulers, Unjust Tyrants, and the Oppressed.

Heinrich Bullinger: Here Jeremiah inserts a summary of his argument. He commends the example of the fathers, their righteousness and godliness. He does so through an exclamation, through questioning an imagined person; he says, "Was this not because he knew me, says the Lord?" This example was here before and is even here today: you shall imitate the examples of your parents: David, Jehoshaphat, Hezekiah, and Josiah. In German we say, "I think that I know God, so I honor him." Moreover, the apostle Paul maintains that if we know God truly and from the heart, then let us bring forth our knowledge in holy works. Indeed, Paul says, "They say they know God, but by their actions they deny him."

Jeremiah puts forward others who are opposite and unlike King Jehoiakim with his supporters; Jehoiakim stinks and gushes forth with so much wickedness. Further, "before your eyes," Jeremiah says, "you have regard for nothing except profit and avarice. In contrast, your fathers looked around widely for others"; Jeremiah says that they were just and righteous; free people were added under them, "but you are greedy, unjust, and sordid. Your fathers refrained from shedding blood and took care lest they shed the blood of the innocent. But you spill the blood of your innocent people who disapprove of superstition, ungodliness, and your cruelty. Your fathers lifted up the oppressed and conferred many and great benefits upon people. You oppress the miserable people; you do not free the oppressed; you miserably and fiercely plunder those you ought to have helped." Thus, in this prince we have a singular image of tyrants. Save us and free us from them, O Lord. Sermon on Jeremiah 22:15-17.[17]

---

[15]Selnecker, *Der gantze Prophet Jeremias*, L4r-v; citing 2 Kings 23:29-30.

[16]Bugenhagen, *In Ieremiam*, 3X3r-v.
[17]Bullinger, *Conciones*, 140v; citing Tit 1:16.

A King Dishonored in Death. Konrad Pellikan: Jeremiah prophesies by name against Jehoiakim, the second son of Josiah, that he would not be buried in the grave of the kings because he would not die in Jerusalem or in the kingdom. The prophet explains this in his own way through exaggeration. Indeed, a dignified funeral procession was not celebrated for the dead man, so that his death was mourned by public lament. But like one hated by both friends and enemies, the ungodly man perished without the sadness of his people. He is said to be unburied because we do not read that he was buried, but rather struck down by the pillaging Babylonians, bound, and led in chains to Babylon. Commentary on Jeremiah 22:18-19.[18]

Can Any Aid Be Found? Nikolaus Selnecker: Bashan and Abarim, which are here mentioned, show that the Jews cried out to and hoped in foreign help that would give them no aid. Lebanon is a very high mountain, which separates and divides the Holy Land from Phoenicia. Bashan is the good and fertile land that Moses takes up in Numbers 21. The Abarim are the mountains in the land of Moab, the last camp they had without toll, through which they traveled to from the land of Egypt. "Go there now," Jeremiah says, "to these places and onto these high mountains, to see if there might be foreign aid, those who want to free or save them. But there is no one. There is no help or guidance." "The wind blows away the shepherds"; that is, God drives your kings and priests like cows, like chaff and dust, and scatters them toward Babylon. The same happens with your lovers on whom you relied. The Whole Prophet Jeremiah 22:20-22.[19]

A Bitter Grief for All You Have Lost. Konrad Pellikan: You have already seen and you will see all the kings and shepherds of the neighboring nations, whom you always desired to have as friends despite my admonitions, led away as captives or killed by the Chaldean Empire, so that you too are confounded, giving up hope that you will be able to escape, and you will not escape. However much you built palaces for yourself into pleasing and extensive habitations, they will be destroyed with you. Not only are you confounded, but you will grieve—not with common weariness, but with the most bitter pain of childbirth—so that you are unable to do anything greater; then you will desist from your illustrious deeds and seeming glory. Commentary on Jeremiah 22:22-23.[20]

The Nature of Divine Election. Johannes Brenz: "As I live, says the Lord." The topic here pertains to the fear of the Lord. Indeed, the just person is saved with difficulty and even the elect are cast away. Surely election is a gift. Now all gifts are in the power of the one who gives, and not in our own power. Therefore they are distributed according to the will of the Lord: "You are established in faith, do not become puffed up in your spirits, but fear." Saul was chosen. Judas was chosen, but afterward they were cast away. But so it is, as Romans 11 says, "The gifts and calling of God are of this sort, that he cannot change his mind about them." This has to be understood with reference to the gifts and this calling of the whole of the people, not just one person. For God on account of some evil folk does not, therefore, cast aside a whole people, even if he would punish a whole city and region for the transgression of one man. Annotations on Jeremiah 22:24.[21]

The King Who Followed Prophecy. Nikolaus Selnecker: Concerning the third king, Jehoiachin or Jeconiah, Jeremiah prophesied that he would be captured and led away, as it happened. So Jeconiah followed the advice of Jeremiah and gave himself over to the king of Babylon, according to the word and command of the Lord. For he was at the end the best advised and flourished thereafter as it stands in Jeremiah 52: Evil-merodach

---

[18]Pellikan, *Commentaria Bibliorum*, 3:2S6r-v; citing 2 Chron 36:5-8.
[19]Selnecker, *Der gantze Prophet Jeremias*, 4L4v-Mir; citing Num 21:33-35.

[20]Pellikan, *Commentaria Bibliorum*, 3:2S6v.
[21]Brenz, *Annotationes in Jeremiam*, 908; citing Rom 11:20, 29; Num 25:1-18; Josh 7:1-26.

released him from prison, spoke in a kindly way with him, and gave him a seat superior to that of other kings who were next to him. So his situation in prison was described as pathetic, which happened because of the great misery and sorrow of the Jews. Thereby Jeremiah also cries out bitterly, sighs, and laments: "O land, O land, O land," that someone from the seed of David should sit on the throne and further rule Judea. We should understand this as the earthly monarchy, for Jeconiah lay in prison in Babylon for thirty-six years. If he truly had sons, like Shealtiel, who is mentioned by Matthew in relation to the birth of Christ, there is yet nothing more known after the captivity of the Jewish people in Babylon—or if Jeconiah freely reigned beyond servitude. But they must have been subservient to all the foreign rulers—to the Medes, then the Greeks, and on to the Maccabees. THE WHOLE PROPHET JEREMIAH 22:24-30.[22]

---

[22]Selnecker, *Der gantze Prophet Jeremias*, M1r; citing Jer 52:32-34; Mt 1:12.

JEREMIAH 23:1-40
FALSE PROPHETS AND NEW HOPE
FROM THE LINE OF DAVID

[1]*"Woe to the shepherds who destroy and scatter the sheep of my pasture!" declares the* Lord. [2]*Therefore thus says the* Lord, *the God of Israel, concerning the shepherds who care for my people: "You have scattered my flock and have driven them away, and you have not attended to them. Behold, I will attend to you for your evil deeds, declares the* Lord. [3]*Then I will gather the remnant of my flock out of all the countries where I have driven them, and I will bring them back to their fold, and they shall be fruitful and multiply.* [4]*I will set shepherds over them who will care for them, and they shall fear no more, nor be dismayed, neither shall any be missing, declares the* Lord.

[5]*"Behold, the days are coming, declares the Lord, when I will raise up for David a righteous Branch, and he shall reign as king and deal wisely, and shall execute justice and righteousness in the land.* [6]*In his days Judah will be saved, and Israel will dwell securely. And this is the name by which he will be called: 'The* Lord *is our righteousness.'*

[7]*"Therefore, behold, the days are coming, declares the Lord, when they shall no longer say, 'As the* Lord *lives who brought up the people of Israel out of the land of Egypt,'* [8]*but 'As the Lord lives who brought up and led the offspring of the house of Israel out of the north country and out of all the countries where he[a] had driven them.' Then they shall dwell in their own land."*

[9]*Concerning the prophets:*

My heart is broken within me;
    all my bones shake;
I am like a drunken man,
    like a man overcome by wine,
because of the Lord
    and because of his holy words.
[10]For the land is full of adulterers;
    because of the curse the land mourns,
    and the pastures of the wilderness are dried up.
Their course is evil,

and their might is not right.
[11]"Both prophet and priest are ungodly;
    even in my house I have found their evil,
declares the Lord.
[12]Therefore their way shall be to them
    like slippery paths in the darkness,
    into which they shall be driven and fall,
for I will bring disaster upon them
    in the year of their punishment,
declares the Lord.
[13]In the prophets of Samaria
    I saw an unsavory thing:
they prophesied by Baal
    and led my people Israel astray.
[14]But in the prophets of Jerusalem
    I have seen a horrible thing:
they commit adultery and walk in lies;
    they strengthen the hands of evildoers,
    so that no one turns from his evil;
all of them have become like Sodom to me,
    and its inhabitants like Gomorrah."
[15]Therefore thus says the Lord of hosts
    concerning the prophets:
"Behold, I will feed them with bitter food
    and give them poisoned water to drink,
for from the prophets of Jerusalem
    ungodliness has gone out into all the land."

[16]*Thus says the* Lord *of hosts: "Do not listen to the words of the prophets who prophesy to you, filling you with vain hopes. They speak visions of their own minds, not from the mouth of the* Lord. [17]*They say continually to those who despise the word of the* Lord, *'It shall be well with you'; and to everyone who stubbornly follows his own heart, they say, 'No disaster shall come upon you.'"*

[18]*For who among them has stood in the council
    of the* Lord

to see and to hear his word,
　or who has paid attention to his word
　　and listened?
[19]Behold, the storm of the LORD!
　Wrath has gone forth,
a whirling tempest;
　it will burst upon the head of the wicked.
[20]The anger of the LORD will not turn back
　until he has executed and accomplished
　the intents of his heart.
In the latter days you will understand it clearly.

[21]"I did not send the prophets,
　yet they ran;
I did not speak to them,
　yet they prophesied.
[22]But if they had stood in my council,
　then they would have proclaimed my words
　　to my people,
　and they would have turned them from their
　　evil way,
　and from the evil of their deeds.

[23]"Am I a God at hand, declares the LORD, and not a God far away? [24]Can a man hide himself in secret places so that I cannot see him? declares the LORD. Do I not fill heaven and earth? declares the LORD. [25]I have heard what the prophets have said who prophesy lies in my name, saying, 'I have dreamed, I have dreamed!' [26]How long shall there be lies in the heart of the prophets who prophesy lies, and who prophesy the deceit of their own heart, [27]who think to make my people forget my name by their dreams that they tell one another, even as their fathers forgot my name for Baal? [28]Let the prophet who has a dream tell the dream, but let him who has my word speak my word faithfully.

What has straw in common with wheat? declares the LORD. [29]Is not my word like fire, declares the LORD, and like a hammer that breaks the rock in pieces? [30]Therefore, behold, I am against the prophets, declares the Lord, who steal my words from one another. [31]Behold, I am against the prophets, declares the LORD, who use their tongues and declare, 'declares the LORD.' [32]Behold, I am against those who prophesy lying dreams, declares the LORD, and who tell them and lead my people astray by their lies and their recklessness, when I did not send them or charge them. So they do not profit this people at all, declares the LORD.

[33]"When one of this people, or a prophet or a priest asks you, 'What is the burden of the LORD?' you shall say to them, 'You are the burden,[b] and I will cast you off, declares the LORD.' [34]And as for the prophet, priest, or one of the people who says, 'The burden of the LORD,' I will punish that man and his household. [35]Thus shall you say, every one to his neighbor and every one to his brother, 'What has the LORD answered?' or 'What has the LORD spoken?' [36]But 'the burden of the LORD' you shall mention no more, for the burden is every man's own word, and you pervert the words of the living God, the LORD of hosts, our God. [37]Thus you shall say to the prophet, 'What has the LORD answered you?' or 'What has the LORD spoken?' [38]But if you say, 'The burden of the LORD,' thus says the LORD, 'Because you have said these words, "The burden of the LORD," when I sent to you, saying, "You shall not say, 'The burden of the LORD,'" [39]therefore, behold, I will surely lift you up[c] and cast you away from my presence, you and the city that I gave to you and your fathers. [40]And I will bring upon you everlasting reproach and perpetual shame, which shall not be forgotten.'"

a Septuagint; Hebrew I　b Septuagint, Vulgate; Hebrew *What burden?*　c Or *surely forget you*

OVERVIEW: This chapter of Jeremiah was among the most compelling and magnetic for Reformation interpreters from across the religious spectrum. While the initial verses prompted commentators to consider prophecies of Christ and expound on basic Christian theology, most of this chapter raised penetrating questions about identifying true and false prophets, authenticating a divine calling, and discerning God's voice in Scripture and the human heart. Some found in Jeremiah's isolated stand against religious and political powers an echo of and parallel to their own struggle. They encountered an educated clergy that seemed to lack spiritual inspiration and appeared to collude with corrupt rulers in the oppression of simple Christians and their devotion to true and prophetic Christianity.

23:1-8 The Shepherds of the Flock and the Righteous Branch

FALSE PROPHETS. JOHANNES BUGENHAGEN: When Jeremiah prophesies against the princes and the people, he prophesies also against the ecclesial shepherds, that is, the priests and prophets, who are the source and head of this condemnation of the kings and the people—if indeed the people were seduced by them. He not only condemns them but also graphically depicts throughout the chapter who they are. For there has always been disagreement in the church of God, not only concerning the fact that evil prophets and heretics are condemned and to be avoided, but also who those evil prophets and heretics might be. Indeed some, like our papists, who always condemn and besmirch the truly pious with those bad names, are truly of such a nature that they would not even spare the Son of God. But the Holy Spirit here and elsewhere portrays them with his own colors and says that they are false prophets or false preachers, who have contempt for the clear Word of God. COMMENTARY ON JEREMIAH 23:1.[1]

THE FOOD OF TRUE AND FALSE SHEPHERDS.

JOHANNES BUGENHAGEN: "Feed his sheep," says the Lord, as he said to Peter: "Feed not your sheep, but my sheep," so also below he calls to his sheep. But evil priests and false prophets do not consider themselves of the great shepherd (whence they themselves are called "pastors," and they would be, if they did their duty). They do not, I say, consider themselves to be his shepherds, ministers, and stewards, but rather to be the lords of the sheep, as if they didn't have to feed them on the Word of God, but they could do whatever they like to sheep for ambition and profit. . . .

With these words God promises he would give the people shepherds, that is, his prophets and preachers, with whom this passage deals, to feed them, that is, to teach the people with the message of repentance and the forgiveness of sins, so that like sheep from that pasture or doctrine they might have peace in eternity before God, which is fulfilled in Christ alone. . . .

Therefore, this is a prominent passage concerning Christ and the salvation of all people, or concerning the church of Christ, gathered from the Jews and the Gentiles into one kingdom of heaven. This is the kingdom of Christ over the earth until the consummation of the age, in which the church through the preachers of the gospel is security and peace eternal. As Isaiah 52 says concerning these preachers or shepherds, "How beautiful upon the mountains are the feet of those bringing good news, and announcing peace," etc. Concerning this restoration and spiritual gathering through Christ, we sing to the Holy Spirit, "You who through the diversity of all languages have gathered the nations into a unity of faith." COMMENTARY ON JEREMIAH 23:2-4.[2]

ONE WITH GOD, FREE OF CREATURELINESS.

HANS DENCK: You say: "No one is able to fulfill the law." Answer: Indeed, no ordinary person can do it. Believers, however, can do all things, not as human beings, but as those who are one with God and are free of all creatureliness, even partially free of themselves. It is impossible for good people who walk according to the flesh to do any good. Such people should know that they are living in lies and not in the truth. In actual fact all understanding, will, and the power of every creature is God's and one with him. Whoever desires to have a special or another understanding, will, or power against God's will may well imagine they have something that in reality they do not have and may think they lack that of which all creation is full. Because of this one lie alone, it is true that the Holy Spirit testifies through his own that there is something in

---

[1]Bugenhagen, *In Ieremiam*, 3Y4r-v.

[2]Bugenhagen, *In Ieremiam*, 3Z1r; 3Z4r; 3Z4v; citing Jn 21:15-17; Is 52:7.

human beings (be it understanding, will, or power, or whatever) that is against God. Let the one who has understanding take care that they are in truth not against God. THE LAW OF GOD.[3]

THE PREDESTINED REMNANT. JOHANNES OECOLAMPADIUS: "And I will gather a remnant." In every time there is a certain remnant, which no one may take from the hand of Christ—those whom he has furnished to the remnant—from them he does not lose anyone. These, moreover, are the predestined, and they are so through the blood of Christ. They are the elect friends of God, wherever they are in the world. They are encouraged in this divine illustration, so that when Christ is recognized as the true shepherd, right away they do not fear for themselves. John 10 says, "My sheep hear my voice, and I know them and they follow me, and I give them eternal life, neither will they perish in eternity, nor will anyone snatch them from my hand. My Father, who gives them to me, is greater than all, and no one is able to snatch them from the hand of my Father." COMMENTARY ON JEREMIAH 23:3.[4]

THE KINGDOM OF CHRIST AND THE REFORMATION. JOHN DONNE: [Ezekiel states,] "I will set up one shepherd, my servant David." "And I will raise up for them a plant of renown," which is what Isaiah called "a rod out of the stem of Jesse," and Jeremiah called "a righteous branch, a King that shall reign and prosper." This prophecy then comprehends the kingdom of Christ; it comprehends the whole kingdom of Christ, not only the oppression and deliverance of our forefathers from heathen and heretics in the early church, but that which also touches us more nearly, the oppression and deliverance of our fathers in the Reformation of religion, and the shaking off of the yoke of Rome, that Italian Babylon, as heavy as that of the Babylonian. SERMON ON EZEKIEL 34:19.[5]

A PROPHECY OF CHRIST THE ONLY TRUE KING AND HIS KINGDOM. MARTIN BUCER: There are no churches, or even private individuals, who, if they give themselves over completely to the kingdom of Christ, will not perceive all the happiness that the prophets foretold, even in this life, in its fashion of the moment, in such a way that they cannot thank God enough, in joy and gladness. For the Lord really repays us a hundredfold, even with persecutions, for whatever temporal thing or comfort we have sacrificed for his name or for whatever discomfort we have sustained.

From Jeremiah, the twenty-third chapter: "I shall gather the remnant of my flock. . . ." The prophet here teaches that the church of Christ must be gathered from all nations throughout the world, and that this is a work proper to our King himself. But since this is the proper and supreme work of Christ, as so many times the holy prophets tell us, it is necessary that whoever are his own should serve him in his purpose, every individual person doing their share.

There follows: "And I shall set shepherds over them to feed them. . . ." Here we are taught that after people have been gathered to the church, it ought to be the first concern of everyone who seeks the kingdom of Christ that one should serve Christ our King in this according to his own portion, so that suitable shepherds may be placed in charge of individual churches, to feed them in good faith, i.e., with deep concern to preserve them in the faith and obedience to Christ the King, and to live up to all the functions and roles of the sacred ministry, namely, by a sincere dispensation of the doctrine and sacraments of Christ and by a faithful administration of his discipline. As a result, after faith in Christ has increased among them, all will act confidently in the Lord, free from any fear or disturbance of spirit from all enemies both spiritual and temporal, and no one will abandon the grace of the kingdom of Christ that they have received.

There follows in the prophecy of Jeremiah: "Behold, the days are coming, says the Lord, when I will raise up for David a righteous branch, and he shall reign as king and administer his charge. . . ."

---

[3]Denck, *Selected Writings*, 50-51*; citing Mk 9:23.
[4]Oecolampadius, *In Hieremiam*, 2:E2r; citing Jn 10:27-29.
[5]Donne, *Sermons*, 10:141-42*; citing Ezek 34:29; Is 11:1.

The prophet testifies, first, that only Christ the Lord is truly righteous and justifies those who believe in him; second, that he alone is the only true King, and administers a true kingdom among his own subjects, and brings it about that among them all things are inaugurated and pursued prudently and happily and therefore rightly and in good order, i.e., righteously.

There follows: "In his days Judah will be saved and Israel will dwell confidently; and this is the name by which he will be called: the Lord is our righteousness." Here the prophet testifies that a sure and saving way of life can be found only in the kingdom of Christ. And those will certainly obtain it who can dare to call him by this glorious name: "The Lord is our righteousness"; i.e., Christ the King, true God and true man (for here is applied as a title the sacred name Jehovah), has reconciled us, freed from sins, to the Father and has obtained the spirit of righteousness, and so, in order that our sins may not be imputed to us in the judgment of God, he reigns and governs us effectively unto eternal life. CONCERNING THE KINGDOM OF CHRIST.[6]

CHRIST THE MESSIAH. JOHANNES BUGENHAGEN: "Behold the days are coming." The Jews are not able to deny that this passage promises Christ or the Messiah, that the King is coming, and he will reign after the Babylonian captivity from the seed of David. But they themselves being ignorant of their own Scriptures do not believe the Messiah would truly be God. Albeit they adduce as a proof that he who is the seed of Abraham and the seed of David could not be God. Christ confounds them in Matthew 22, saying: "If the Messiah is the son of David, how does David so call him in the spirit his Lord, where he says, 'The Lord said to my Lord, sit at my right hand....'" COMMENTARY ON JEREMIAH 23:5.[7]

GOD'S RIGHTEOUS RULE THROUGH CHRIST THE DAVIDIC KING. MARTIN LUTHER: These words are certainly proclaimed concerning Christ;

they assert just as the prophecy says, that he shall come from the bloodline and branch of David; from this bloodline the Savior was expected. Concerning this St. Paul spoke rightly, that he would be born according to the flesh from the seed of David. Moreover, the prophet Jeremiah wanted to make the Savior fully known—who he was and whence he would come—so that those at that time ought to believe and thereafter would believe and so that they would not grope around, looking here and there. Therefore, he tied him to the bloodline and branch of David so that he would be awaited with certainty. Through these words Jeremiah comforted the people and proclaimed to them that they should watch this lineage and that they should hold it as certain that he would not come from anywhere else than the branch of David....

Since that time the Word resounds outward and shows that there was no righteousness on the earth; not only, I say, the righteousness that is valid before God, but also the temporal and external righteousness that is more transparent than a beggar's cloak. For the world is truly the devil's school for boys. Therefore, God has established the sword and ordained the executioner that there might be some righteousness on the earth and so that the righteousness that is valid before God does not disappear....

Now this child born of David that shall be king shall be just and godly and without sin. He shall stand forth and reign in eternity. Since he is from a line and branch of David's tree, he must be mortal; he is born in the flesh in temporal life and thus he must die. Therefore, since he must always remain and reign eternally, so he must be immortal....

Now it follows further that the king does not keep everything for himself, but shall submit and sacrifice himself for other people. The prophet means that the king will proceed wisely, that is, he will reign with lucid wisdom. The prophet wants to say that he will lay aside armor, sword, club, bow, and saddle. He will find a particular way to make the people godly—not with the wheel or the gallows—but with or through the gospel. He will embrace the people so they are drawn in by the

---

[6]Bucer, *De Regno Christi*, 213-15; citing Mk 10:30.
[7]Bugenhagen, *In Ieremiam*, 4A3r-v; citing Mat 22:42-44; Ps 110:1.

best way possible—by the heart, not by the neck—in a way that they would want to submit and gladly follow. . . .

Thereafter, the prophet says that this king shall "enforce justice and righteousness upon the earth. . . ." The Jews say this with two words, and yet they do not mean anything other than what we say with "righteousness." There are two parts that belong to righteousness, so that Scripture uses these two words: *judgment* and *righteousness*. Through the court or law God punishes, and in that way he shows what is evil. Through righteousness he makes the people godly, and he saves and protects the innocent. Sermon on Jeremiah 23:5.[8]

Even Jewish Commentators Recognize the Messianic Prophesy. The English Annotations: The party here described . . . cannot be any other than our Lord and Savior Jesus Christ. Yea, the Jewish doctors themselves, both on this place and elsewhere, acknowledge that by the "bud" or "branch" or "sprout" here spoken of is meant "the Messiah." Though they add with some vain devices of their own, to confirm the same, to wit, because, say they, the letters of the word *menachem*, that signifies a comforter, and is the name of the Messiah, and the letters of the word *tsemach*, here used, so both make up the same number, to wit, 138. But this is but a frivolous fancy of theirs. Nor does the truth of God need such sandy supports. That he is styled, as here, so also Zechariah 3:8, because he was to spring up, as a bud, branch, or sprout from the root of Jesse, and of David. In regard of his meanness and weakness to outward appearance, like some young bud or tender shoot at its first sprouting, yet that should in process of time bud, sprout, and branch out like some such plant that retains its verdure perpetually, flowering and flourishing unto all eternity. Annotations on Jeremiah 23:5.[9]

David and Christ. Johannes Oecolampadius: "Behold, the days are coming." Certainly this clear passage of Hebrew is acknowledged to gaze at Christ, which you may observe well. "At that time," he says, "when I will gather my sheep, those days will be such that the number of the righteous will be multiplied, who are called a just seed, even a just shoot, as the grass is multiplied in the fields." Moreover, "David" here is Christ, by which name he is often called in the Scriptures; because he is from the seed of David. . . . Furthermore, for us he has conquered the devil, hell, and death; he abolished sin, wickedness, and the bond of sin. He reigns in prosperity from the east to the west, and he holds his ministers even to the consummation of the age. And he will be our Savior: for this reason "he is called Jesus, because he saves us from our sins," and restores and secures our consciences and justifies us through faith. "We have peace with God the Father through Christ Jesus"; he has pacified all things; "he is our peace, who has made from two people one." So they will call him "The Lord, our just one." Commentary on Jeremiah 23:5-6.[10]

The New Kingdom of Our Righteous and Just God. Martin Luther: This passage applies to the very time of the lineage of David, when this king would reign. Then shall the Jews rightly form their hope. There will be full and swift help at hand, as we say in German. On any day and in every kind of distress I will help you. This is the sort of help and resource for every misfortune and danger.

These two sentences show also that this royal kingdom is no earthly kingdom; for you know that the Jewish royal kingdom was divided into two kingdoms—the royal kingdoms of Judah and Israel. . . . This is not to be understood physically, that Judah and Israel would both again come physically into the land together, but it occurs spiritually in faith under Christ, when he would preach the gospel. Thus Christ would preach in Jerusalem and many Jews would repent and believe in Christ,

---

[8]WA 20:551-52, 555, 556-58; citing Rom 1:3.
[9]Downame, ed., *Annotations*, 9P3r*; citing Lam 1:16; Is 11:1, 10; Rev 5:5; 22:16; Is 53:3; Ps 132:17-18.

[10]Oecolampadius, *In Hieremiam*, 2:E2v; 118v; citing Mt 1:21; Rom 5:1; Eph 2:14.

both from the branch of Judah and Israel. For on Pentecost those from Judah and Israel were in Jerusalem, those from Assyria, Cilicia, Persia, Media, and from many other lands. On that day three thousand converted; they came from the lineage to Christ. Therefore, this text cannot be understood as a physical kingdom, but as Christ's spiritual kingdom, to which the Jews and Israelites should come again and become one kingdom and under no worldly king. . . .

Why does Jeremiah say that the Jews shall be helped and Israel shall dwell securely? What he wants to say is that, as long as this kingdom stands, it will be contested and finally will be destroyed. The royal family will be taken away. But they shall have assistance. So it is that the Jews have sorrow now. They were led away into a foreign land, and there they must submit to and serve others, but "I shall someday raise up a remedy so that my people will reside above forever and the whole world will be dumb and clueless." But the Jews do not understand this. For we have been shown that the kingdom of Christ submits to the cross of Christ and is never missing anymore where the kingdom of Christ is preached through the gospel. There the cross and persecution certainly follow. . . .

"And one will call him, the Lord our just one." The author has described thereby the office and the fruit of the office, namely, that he shall establish judgment and righteousness, and the people will receive help and live securely. Yet this shall happen under the cross and persecution.

Therefore, now the Holy Bible and the Jews themselves and all the holy fathers and writers are in agreement that to this name alone and essentially belongs the divine majesty and being. So we have here in the prophet Jeremiah a powerful and strong blow against the Jews and a splendid assurance; for we Christians this completely and powerfully establishes this article of our faith—that Christ is true God and of divine nature. I myself have spoken with the Jews about this. SERMON ON JEREMIAH 23:6.[11]

---

[11]WA 20:562-64, 568-69; citing Acts 2:5-11.

JEREMIAH SPEAKS OF IMPUTED RIGHTEOUSNESS.
LANCELOT ANDREWES: For a clearer understanding of this point we are to see that true righteousness, as says St. Paul, is not of human device, but takes his proof from the "Law and Prophets," [out of] which he proceeds to show first the example of Abraham and afterward of David. In the Scripture, then, there is a double righteousness set down, both in the Old and in the New Testament. In the Old, and in the very place that righteousness is named in the Bible, [it says]: "Abraham believed and it was accounted to him for righteousness." A righteousness accounted. And again, in the very next line it is mentioned, "Abraham will teach his house to do righteousness." A righteousness [that is] done. In the New likewise. The former, the fourth chapter [of] Romans [says] no fewer than eleven times, *Reputatum est illi ad justitiam*. A reputed righteousness. The latter in St. John's [first epistle]: "My beloved, let no one deceive you, he that does righteousness is righteous." A righteousness done, which [here] is nothing else but just our dealing, upright conversation, honest conversation.

Of these the latter philosophers themselves conceived and acknowledged; the other is proper to Christians only, and altogether unknown philosophy. This one is a quality of the party. The other an [act] of the judge, declaring or pronouncing [one] righteous. The one [is] ours by influence or infusion, the other by account of imputation. There is no question regarding both of these meanings. The question is, which of these meanings does the prophet intend? Of this we shall best inform ourselves by looking back to the verse before, and without so looking back we shall never understand the purpose of the passage. There the prophet speaks of one who is a king exercising his royal judicial power, and also of a king sitting down to execute judgment, and this he tells us, before he thinks proper to tell his name. Before this king thus sits down [on] his throne, to do judgment, the righteousness that will stand against the law, our conscience, Satan, sin, the gates of hell, and the power of darkness, and [thus] so stand that we may be delivered by it from death, despair, and damnation; and [therefore] entitled by it to life, salvation, and eternal happiness. That is righteousness indeed; this is the righteousness we seek for, if we may find it. And that is not the latter, but the former only, and therefore that is the true interpretation of *Jehovah our righteousness*. SERMON ON JEREMIAH 23:6.[12]

THE NEW TESTAMENT REPLACES THE OLD.
MARTIN LUTHER: The prophet will absolutely not forget, but wants to teach thoroughly, completely, and honestly what will be preached in the New Testament. Therefore, he wants to say, it is not enough when one only wants to preach what he has already heard, what one likes, or what is weakly known, and which must depend on the Old Testament. For in response the prophet speaks of Christian freedom and puts aside the Old Testament, because he wants to teach something new. So one cannot teach the New until the Old is put aside, as the epistle to Hebrews says in chapter 8. A new proclamation will ascend. Moses and the Old Testament will no longer be valid in the New, but will end. . . .

Therefore, now the prophet says here: in that time, when this righteous and godly King will rule, the law of Moses will no longer be valid. With these words he expresses and says that one will no longer say, "So truly as the Lord lives, who led the children of Israel out of the land of Egypt." This was the oath or the pledge that the Jews would say: "by the living God, who has led us out of Egypt." That is also the way to swear an oath in Scripture, and so we see it throughout the prophets. Thereby the people wanted to make certain and sure that as they would speak under the name of God and teach and preach under his command, then it would be the truth of God's Word from the living God or as "God the Lord lives. . . ."

So now this is the prophet's understanding: one will no longer preach the Old Testament; it should be left behind, unless one takes it as an example of faith, that through it we will know how God keeps his promises. But we should take from it in

preaching that the Old Testament has been put aside and that no one will be made godly or holy through the law—as the Jews believe—but through Christ alone is one made godly and justified through his righteousness.

And this message will not be preached in Judea or in one or two lands, but throughout the whole world. SERMON ON JEREMIAH 23:7-8.[13]

23:9-40 Lying Prophets Condemned

LIVING WITH FALSE PROPHETS AND REMAINING A TRUE PROPHET. NIKOLAUS SELNECKER: [This is] a difficult sermon against false teachers, who do not point to their salvation in Jesus Christ, but lead the people elsewhere: to their own dreams, human laws, and idolatry, to their own works and fabricated and false worship. "This gives me deep pain," says Jeremiah, "because my heart will break and grieve in sorrow." So it is with a heartfelt pain, when one is forced to see false teaching before his eyes. The great lords and the poor people are blinded, seduced, unnerved, and commit errors. Yet thereby they want to be right, so that all their teaching is dark and slippery. That is, it is not the Word of God; there is no light or consolation therein. One can find no rest in it. There is no substance to it; it is uncertain and corrupts body and soul. It is hypocritical and insincere, as if they are keeping up a great appearance for the world and are observed as holy people. So Jeremiah warns us, "One should protect oneself and beware, for the false prophets and hypocrites are swift ranging wolves within, and with others they betray land and people, and lead souls to the chasm of hell. They distort God's Word, and yet they say that what they speak 'is God's Word.' At the outset they console the people and make them confident, saying, 'What does that Jeremiah know? What can this poor prophet do? How does he know more than we do?' The Holy Spirit will enter Jeremiah; he has direction from the Lord. He is God's prophet. Jeremiah says that Jerusalem must be destroyed,

---

[12]Andrewes, *Works*, 5:114-15*; citing Gen 15:6; 18:19; Rom 4:3, 5-6, 8-11, 16, 22-24.

[13]WA 20:575-76, 578-79; citing Jer 31:31-34.

and he says that God will soon bring punishment. Who told him this? How can he know this? He is a fool. There is no crisis among us and we are doing fine; but he wants us to do something? We are also prophets and teachers; we know as well as he does what is happening. He sees things through what he sees around him; that's not too hard for him. Soon he will instigate a rebellion etc."

Such conversation goes on today in many places. The world does not care about what others do. One can admonish and threaten with God's wrath as fiercely as one wants, but people always think, "It won't be so bad." Finally, faith does come into play, and they must experience that it is true, and what the true preacher had long predicted in his proclamation. THE WHOLE PROPHET JEREMIAH 23:9-12.[14]

TEACHING CURSING AND ADULTERY. JOHN MAYER: Here Jeremiah mentions the foul sins in particular that reigned among the Jews. Two are named and the rest understood. The word rendered oaths . . . signifies "to swear"; but because swearing is never expressed or understood without cursing, some render it cursing, or for swearing take both of these ways, and so we shall best attain the true and full meaning: with such horrible sins did that land abound, for which it is said the land mourned by personification: to make the Jews ashamed, and especially the false prophets, to whom he chiefly speaks. . . . But shall dumb and dead creatures be affected by sorrow? Human beings, and particularly teachers, provoke such a great judgment because they are without any sense of sorrow. . . . They studied and bent all their forces to act wickedly and to encourage others both by doctrine and life to do likewise. COMMENTARY ON JEREMIAH 23:10.[15]

THE SLIPPERY WAY. JOHANNES OECOLAMPA-DIUS: Just as with the people, so also the priest: he who ought to reform others instead corrupted others with evil examples. Such a one is shown to be a syncretist, as in chapter 5 above. "Foolishness

and iniquity have been produced in the land; the prophets have prophesied lies and the priests applauded with their own hands and my people loved such things. . . ." Therefore there appears to be no purity of erudition and religion. Even "in my house," that is, in the midst of the temple, iniquity is found among the high priests. You see also in this passage of Scripture every iniquity melded together under the category of sin, not only idols, but also impiety of the heart, because their hearts had long been absent.

"Therefore the way of them will be slippery." This slippery way is a way of great danger, on which they had already trampled wearily. Or at midday shadows drew near, by which they were less able to discern where they should go and on what thing they should lean. So finally the false prophets bravely urged the exposed from behind and toward their downfall. Who, therefore, would survive? For the cause of their ruin is threefold: the slippery way, the dizzying darkness, and the instigator. Therefore, they will be tested in the most rigorous way: wherever they will go, whatever they will attempt, it will turn out badly, and every slippery thing will be in darkness. Indeed, they had lost the lamp of the Word of God, and were compelled by depraved and demonic thinking. COMMENTARY ON JEREMIAH 23:11-12.[16]

WORSHIPING IDOLS AS IF THEY ARE THE LORD. JOHANNES BUGENHAGEN: "Among the prophets in Samaria." By an example the Lord either deters or gravely condemns them. The prophets of Samaria, that is, of the kingdom of Israel, seduced the kings and people until together they altogether perished after the Assyrians abducted them. Now, however, the prophets of Jerusalem, the holy city where the Word of God should have been taught and God should have been worshiped according to the law of God, seduced with false doctrines whatever people remained throughout the whole of Judea. . . . They prophesied the worship of God under the name of

[14]Selnecker, *Der gantze Prophet Jeremias*, N2r-N3r.
[15]Mayer, *A Commentary*, 410-11*.
[16]Oecolampadius, *In Hieremiam*, 2:E4v-F1r; citing Jer 5:31.

Baal in places outside of Jerusalem and against the command of the Lord. But they prophesied the same rites of Baal under the name of God, who had brought them from Egypt into Jerusalem, as if according to the law. And they taught the people to trust in these ceremonies against the first commandment. So idolatry and hypocrisy grew, which spread from Jerusalem into the whole land of the Jews. COMMENTARY ON JEREMIAH 23:13.[17]

THE SINS OF THE PROPHETS OF JUDAH. JOHN MAYER: Here to aggravate the sins of their prophets, Jeremiah says in verse 13, "I have seen folly in the prophets of Samaria," but then speaks of the prophets of Jerusalem. Samaria was the chief city of the ten tribes of Israel, where they constantly worshiped Baal in the time of one king after another, or at the least the golden calves that Jeroboam had set up; and after many judgments brought upon them for this and their other sins, they were delivered into the hands of Shalmaneser, king of Assyria. Jerusalem was the chief city of the kingdom of Judah, where the temple stood, and the true God had sacrifices offered unto him, where also the high priest and other priests lived continually to guide the people rightly. Yet even here the prophets and priests acted abominably; neither took warning from the sufferings of Israel, for which they might justly fear greater judgments to come upon them, just as they were threatened. Then to show how they acted even more abominably, he said, "They committed adultery. . . ." For this in God's account is to be as "Sodom and Gomorrah"; these cities are a similitude for those who commit adultery.

The Hebrew also signifies "a horrible thing," . . . which shows that the prophets of Jerusalem were not only like those in Samaria, but much worse, for which Jeremiah uses a word that sets forth a hair-raising, horrid form wherein devils sometimes appeared; hereby he implies that they were devils in shape of human beings, transformed into angels of light. COMMENTARY ON JEREMIAH 23:13-14.[18]

POISON AND GALL. JOHN CALVIN: God declares that they would have poison for meat and gall for drink; as though he had said, "I will pursue them with every kind of punishment. . . ." The ungodly, indeed, always think that they can by their arts escape. . . . For as to God's children and faithful servants, evils are turned to their benefit; so as to the ungodly and their wicked despisers, all things must necessarily turn out for their ruin, even meat and drink, and their course of life, and in a word, everything. COMMENTARY ON JEREMIAH 23:15.[19]

THE INSPIRATION AND MESSAGE OF THE FALSE PROPHETS. HEINRICH BULLINGER: In the midst of his discourse against the false prophets, Jeremiah gives counsel to the all the faithful of every time about what to do when false prophets rule by the patronage and favor of kings, or they deceive and seduce everyone while going unpunished. But before everything Jeremiah shows that God is the author of his counsel, lest someone disdain this advice. He simply says, "Do not listen to them"; that is, do not heed them, do not obey the false prophets. To listen to lying teachers is to suffer harm, just as Eve was seduced. But it is much more noxious if you not only listen to liars but also believe them and obey them. But he gives the reason why the false prophets should not be heard. Indeed, they teach you vanity. Others read this as "They make you vain and foolish," "They make us into fools." The Old Latin translation interprets this verse as "they deceive you." And so therefore the false prophets should not be heard, because they are deceivers, they who preach human vanity and stupidity, not divine wisdom.

Jeremiah explains and illustrates this more fully with the two illustrations from parts of the body. First, they give voice to the vanity or vision of the heart. Second, they do not speak from the mouth of the Lord; therefore however many things they say, not from the mouth of the Lord, but from their own hearts, they should not be heard. That thing is a vision of the human heart, which was devised in

---

[17]Bugenhagen, *In Ieremiam*, 4C3v-4C4r; citing Deut 12:1-7.
[18]Mayer, *A Commentary*, 411*; citing 1 Kings 12:26-33; 2 Kings 17:1-41.

[19]CTS 19:165* (CO 38:424).

the human heart, which is offered for human pleasure, apart from the authority of and origination in the Word of God, namely, when a person says and asserts that which seems good to himself. Everything pleasing to humans and every human disposition announced concerning religion is understood here. For the mouth of the Lord is itself the revelation of the divine will through the Law and the Prophets and through the holy Scriptures. Therefore, reject every present doctrine that is not drawn from the Word or font of truth. . . .

Actually, the false prophets agitate and provoke God . . . those who reject the Word of God in following their own dreams. That is, those who do not in that correct manner trust in God, and do not worship him in the way that God himself required in his Word. But they make idols, pray to creatures, and think highly of their own inventions for worship. In doing these things they blaspheme God. But to them the false prophets were saying, "The Lord has said, 'You will have peace.'" That is, what you are following has been instituted by God. These kinds of worship of yours do not displease him. You will find grace and peace through these things, and you will be happy through all of these things. But don't these things remind some of you of papist teachings, which in and of themselves also offer promises through their preferred cults and human inventions—the forgiveness of sins, and every kind of grace and happiness? SERMON ON JEREMIAH 23:16-17.[20]

BEWARE THOSE WHO SAY WHAT YOU WANT TO HEAR. JOHN TRAPP: They promise security to the impertinent, and flatter people in their sinful and sensual practices. Socinians[†] set up a person's reason, Arminians[‡] their free will, Libertines[§] their unruly lusts, and papists gratify their senses with their forms and pomp. COMMENTARY ON JEREMIAH 23:17.[21]

WHO KNOWS THE COUNSEL OF THE LORD?

HEINRICH BULLINGER: For through an imitation Jeremiah calls to mind what the false prophets with their patrons had said against the true prophets and their teaching. Taking on the voice of a false prophet, Jeremiah says that that in truth whatever extreme things Jeremiah, Baruch, Uriah, Zephaniah, and the other prophets had forewarned as from the Lord, those things were actually made up and false. Who indeed has stood in the secret and mysterious counsel of God, who has seen and heard his word? In the voice of the false prophet he says, "Absolutely no one." He adds, "Or who has moved his own ears closer to attend to God's Word and heard it?" Thus indeed you may hear in our time many growling at the preachers, and saying, "These who preach about God, concerning the will of God, concerning rewards and punishments, and eternal life and death—they all chatter just as if they had once been in heaven and had seen those things that they explain. Anyway they are armed with shamelessness and temerity, such that they dare to chatter so. For it is certain that God never spoke to them, and that they never saw the heavens or the lower regions. It is also certain that no one at any time has returned from the dead and explained to mortals the situation in future ages. Uncertain and fabricated are all the things that are put forward by them with such confidence. (Who wants to hear what those crazy pastors have said?) Who indeed has explained to them those heavenly things?"

Indeed we preachers would not be able to explain, by our own authority, those divine and heavenly things that we offer. Indeed no human either knows those things or has seen them. Christ, however, the Son of God, who is eternally from the Father and is "in the bosom of the Father," as John says, "he has shown these things to us." Angels,

---

[20]Bullinger, *Conciones*, 147v-148r.

[21]Trapp, *A Commentary or Exposition*, 292*. †Socinians were anti-trinitarians or unitarians that originated in Poland and Lithuania in the seventeenth century. ‡Following the theology of Jacobus Arminius, Arminians rejected a Calvinist view of predestination on the basis of God's will alone, affirming instead that God predestines according to divine foreknowledge of humanity's actions and choices by their free will. §Libertines are generally labeled as those who reject all moral restraint and seek to indulge pleasures. John Calvin labeled some of his opponents libertines and charged them with denying the reality of evil, the need for repentance, or the necessity of moral restraint, among other accusations.

patriarchs, prophets, and apostles—through the grace and revelation of God—have understood these things with the greatest certainty and have even seen some of these things and revealed them to us. Finally, Christ, who rose from the dead, revealed to us the situation of the coming age. Therefore, since these witnesses are sure and worthy of faith, we announce those things we speak concerning God and divine things; we are not able to be in error or to offer uncertainties. SERMON ON JEREMIAH 23:18-20.[22]

WHEN WE REFUSE THE WORD OF GOD. JOHN KNOX: When I remember the fearful threats of God, pronounced against realms and nations, to whom the light of God's Word has been offered, and contemplate that they have refused it, my heart sincerely mourns for your present estate. Dearly beloved in our Savior Jesus Christ, with all the powers of my body and soul I tremble and shake for the plagues that are to come. But that God's true Word has been offered to the realm of England none can deny, except for those held by the devil in bondage (so God punishes their proud disobedience); they have neither eyes to see nor understanding to discern good from bad, or darkness from light. Against those in our time I will contend in no other way. So did the prophet Jeremiah against the stiff-necked and stubborn people of Judea, saying, "The wrath of God will not be turned away, until he has fulfilled the thoughts of his heart." Thus I leave those people . . . to God's hands; he shall not forget their horrible blasphemies spoken to dispute the truth of Christ and his true messengers. A GODLY LETTER OF WARNING AND ADMONITION.[23]

THOSE WHO PROCLAIM WITHOUT A CALLING. JOHN DONNE: "They were not sent. . . ." This note God lays upon those to whom he gives this vocation of his internal Spirit. Though others who come without any calling may gather people on corners and in conventicles and work upon the affections and passions—leading them to schism and sedition; and though others who come with an outward and ordinary calling alone may advance their own fortunes and increase their reputation, and draw their audience to an outward reverence of their person—to a delight in hearing them rather than others—yet, only those who have a true inward calling from the Spirit "shall turn the people from their evil ways, and from their wicked inventions." To the planning and watering of such people God gives an increase. When others come to speak with rhetorical flourish, but not to preach—to vent their own gifts or the purposes of great people for their own gifts, they will receive a proportionate reward: wind for wind, acclamation for declamation, popular praise for popular eloquence. But if they do not truly believe themselves, why should they look to others to believe in them? SERMON ON JOHN 1:8.[24]

A CALLING OF OFFICE AND WORD. MARTIN LUTHER: It is utterly wrong and futile for one to undertake a project of one's own choosing and will without God's command and Word. . . . Thus, both the office and the Word employed in the office must be comprehended in the divine command. If that is done, the work will prosper and bear fruit. But when people run without God's command or proclaim other messages than God's Word, they work nothing but harm. Jeremiah, too, drives both these facts home, saying "I did not send the prophets, yet they ran; I did not speak to them, yet they prophesied." You who are to preach, impress these two points on your minds! Note them well! They are directed to you and the people; they enable you to instruct souls. LECTURE ON JONAH 3:32.[25]

BEWARE THOSE WHO PREACH OUTSIDE THE ESTABLISHED ORDER. JOHN TRAPP: This is a notable place against lay preachers. And, as if he

---

[22]Bullinger, *Conciones*, 148r-v; citing Jn 1:18, Rev 22:8.
[23]Knox, *Works*, 3:165*.
[24]Donne, *Sermons*, 8:156*; citing 2 Chron 7:14.
[25]LW 19:83 (WA 19:233).

had lived in these loose times of ours, he thus goes on: In the fourteenth and sixteenth chapters of 1 Corinthians, order is commanded to be kept, but there are now such that as abide not in their own churches but run into others, where they teach without a calling. These do not promote, but rather hinder the cause of Christ. COMMENTARY ON JEREMIAH 23:21.[26]

SILENCING THE DEMONS AND SPEAKING IN THE SPIRIT.

MARTIN LUTHER: "I did not send the prophets. . . ." One must beware of this evil most of all. For it was on this account that Christ did not allow the demons to speak, even though they were telling the truth, lest under the guise of truth a death-dealing lie find entrance, since he who speaks of his own accord cannot speak without lying, as Christ says in John 8. Accordingly, in order that the apostles might not speak on their own authority, he gave them his Spirit, of whom he says: "For it is not you who speak, but the Spirit of your Father speaking through you." And again: "I will give you a mouth and wisdom." LECTURE ON GALATIANS (1519) 1:2.[27]

A WORD FROM THE MOUTH OF GOD AND NOT FROM BOOKS.

THOMAS MÜNTZER: Humankind does not live by bread alone but by every word that proceeds from the mouth of God; note that it proceeds from the mouth of God and not from books. It is the testimony to the true word that is found in volumes. For unless it arises from the heart it is the word of human beings, condemning the turncoat scribes, who rob the holy oracles, Jeremiah 23. The Lord has never spoken to them, yet they usurp his words. O most beloved, see to it that you prophesy, otherwise our theology will not be worth a cent. Think of your God as at hand and not distant; believe that God is more willing to speak than you are prepared to listen. LETTER TO PHILIPP MELANCHTHON.[28]

AVOID THE PREACHERS OF DREAMS.

MARTIN LUTHER: The godless preachers of dreams should be censured; in their sermons they hide these words of Christ from the hearts of the people and turn faith away from them, who want to make people godly by terrifying them, and who afterward prepare people for this day with their own good words and satisfaction for their sins. Here despair, fear, and terror must remain and grow— and with it, hatred, aversion, and abhorrence for the coming of the Lord—and enmity against God must be established in the heart. Meanwhile, they teach people to picture Christ as nothing but a stern judge whom they are to appease and expiate by their works, and never regard him as the Redeemer, as he calls and offers himself, of whom we are to expect in firm faith that out of pure grace he will redeem us from sin and all evil. SERMON FOR ADVENT, LUKE 21:25-33.[29]

THE IMPERFECT PASSION OF SOME PROPHETS.

ST. JOHN OF THE CROSS: Those who were gifted were moved to perform their works at an inopportune time by some imperfect passion that was clothed in joy and esteem for these works. When this imperfection is not present, such persons decide to perform these works when and in the manner that God moves them to do so; until then they should not work them. For this reason God complained of certain prophets through Jeremiah: "I did not send the prophets and they ran; I did not speak and they prophesied." Further on he says, "They deceived my people with their lying. . . ." He also says of them that "they behold the visions of their own heart and publish them about." This would not have happened had they overcome their abominable attachment to these works. THE ASCENT OF MOUNT CARMEL.[30]

GOD CANNOT WITHDRAW HIS PRESENCE.

RICHARD HOOKER: It is impossible that God should withdraw his presence from anything

---

[26]Trapp, *A Commentary or Exposition*, 293*.
[27]LW 27:166 (WA 2:144); citing Jn 8:44; Mt 10:20; Lk 21:15.
[28]Müntzer, *Collected Works*, 44; citing Deut 8:3; Mt 4:4.
[29]LW 75:105-6 (WA 10.1.2:112).
[30]St. John of the Cross, *Collected Works*, 325.

because the very substance of God is infinite. He fills heaven and earth although he takes up no room in either, because his substance is material, pure, and of us in this world so incomprehensible that albeit no part of us is very absent from him who is wholly present to every particular thing; yet we do not discern his presence with us any further than the simple fact that God is present, which partly by reason and more perfectly by faith we know to be firm and certain. LAWES OF ECCLESIASTICAL POLITY.[31]

GLORY OF THE SELF OVER THE GLORY OF THE LORD. KONRAD PELLIKAN: The false prophets in this passage are those who strive so that the faithful adhere to their predictions without hesitation and believe everything that they put forth even without the word of the Lord. They not only want this, but seek that their sanctity and hypocrisy is believed instead of the word of the Lord. In this way the glory of the Lord is decreased, while they, by means of their own deceits, claim for their impious selves that it is impossible that they are lying and in error, though every person is a liar, while the word of the Lord alone stands in eternity. At one time the fathers of the Jews strayed from the way while neglecting the law of God. They prostituted themselves to their own human traditions and to their errors and the worship of their own gods, whence they fell into abominable idolatry so that they worshiped Baalim instead of the true God. COMMENTARY ON JEREMIAH 23:27.[32]

HOW GOD BLOWS AWAY FALSE REVELATIONS. JOHN MAYER: "What is the chaff to the wheat?" This means that whatever a person may bring, although they pretend it to be a revelation in a dream from God, it is but as chaff, light and without substance or worth, since any blast of wind from God would make it appear as such; as when contrary to such dreams of peace and prosperity, misery and destruction actually comes;

or when Christ comes with his fan in his hand, and by his divine doctrine blows away all such vanities, and burns all those teachers and embraces them with unquenchable fire. COMMENTARY ON JEREMIAH 23:28.[33]

HOW GOD SHATTERS OUR PRESUMPTION. SCHMALKALD ARTICLES: This [the law], then, is the thunderbolt by means of which God with one blow destroys both open sinners and false saints. He allows no one to justify himself. He drives all together into terror and despair. This is the hammer of which Jeremiah speaks, "Is not my word like a hammer, which breaks the rock in pieces?" This is not *activa contritio* (artificial remorse), but *passiva contritio* (true sorrow of the heart, suffering, and pain of death).

This is what the beginning of true repentance is like. Here humankind must hear such a judgment as this: "You are of no account. Whether you are manifest sinners or saints, you must all become other than you now are and do otherwise than you now do, no matter who you are and no matter how great, wise, mighty, and holy you may think yourselves. Here no one is godly." PART 3, ARTICLE 3 PENITENCE.[34]

GOD'S FIERY WORD. MARTIN LUTHER: If every word is properly grasped, it is as fire that sets the heart aglow, as God says, "My words are like fire." And as we see, the divine Word is such that it teaches us to know God and his work, and to see that this life is nothing. For as he does not live according to this life and does not have goods, honor, and temporal power, he does not regard these things or speak of them, but teaches only the opposite. He works in a contradictory way, looks with favor on

---

[31]Hooker, *Lawes of Ecclesiastical Polity* 5.55*.
[32]Pellikan, *Commentaria Bibliorum*, 3:2T2r.

[33]Mayer, *A Commentary*, 412*.
[34]BoC 304. *Contritio activa*, or "active contrition," is the human act of turning toward God and doing acts of repentance. This form of contrition assumes an ability to earn righteousness. Protestants emphasized *contritio passiva*, or "passive contrition," which indicates a heart that God opens by grace, that in turn suffers terrors of the conscience, and is thereby able to receive the gospel; see "Contritio," in Muller, *Dictionary of Latin and Greek Theological Terms*, 82.

what the world turns away from, teaches that from which it flees, and takes up that which it leaves behind. POSTIL: CHRISTMAS DAY, LUKE 2:1-14.[35]

THREE KINDS OF FALSE PROPHETS. JOHANNES OECOLAMPADIUS: Jeremiah puts forward three different kinds of false prophets. The first are those who eavesdrop on what the true prophets convey from the Lord. They twist that which they have taken in part into their own agenda. Hananiah, son of Azzur, is an example of this.... The second kind were erudite and eloquent, who prepared their speeches with skill to procure some favor among people. They announced peace to the people, with a composed sermon and face, and they in fact accepted things as so favorable from the Lord.... The third kind are those who thrust their own false dreams on the rabble as the true oracles of God, with abundant affirmation that the prophecy was offered in a dream, so that it will be believed just like the Word of God. Indeed they do this seriously and earnestly, adding "in the name of the Lord . . ." So unto us are born so many miracles of the saints, so many apparitions of souls, so many recommendations of masses, vigils, indulgences, and made up religious things, so that almost no place is left for Christ. COMMENTARY ON JEREMIAH 23:30-31.[36]

KNOWING THE TRUTH AND STEALING THE TRUTH. HANS DENCK: The one who has received God's new covenant, i.e., in whose heart through the Holy Spirit the Law was written, is truly just.... He who does not have the Spirit and presumes to find it in Scripture looks for light and finds darkness, seeks life and finds utter death, not only in the Old Testament, but also in the New: for this reason the most learned people are most highly offended by the truth for they think that their understanding (which they have so tenderly and with great wisdom culled from holy Scripture), will not fail them. If now—to top it all—a carpenter's son comes along who has never gone to school and proves them to be liars,

where will he have learned it from? Therefore they assumed he rejected the law because he would not accept their literalistic understanding. My brethren, such happens to this very day. Blessed is the one who is not offended by Christ. The one who truly possesses truth can determine it without Scripture. The scribes could never attain to this because they did not receive their truth from the truth but they keep stealing it from the witnesses of truth.... The one who does not learn to know God through God himself has never known him. The one who diligently seeks God and is not made aware by God, how he has been with him ere he even sought him, has not yet found him and is far from him. THE LAW OF GOD.[37]

STEALING FROM THE BIBLE. THOMAS MÜNTZER: At no time in my life (God knows I am not lying) did I learn anything about the true exercise of the faith from any monk or priest, or about the edifying time of trial that clarifies faith in the spirit of the fear of God, showing the need for an elect person to have the sevenfold gift of the Holy Spirit. I have not heard from a single scholar about the order of God implanted in all creatures, not the tiniest word about it, while as to understanding the unity of all the parts those who claim to be Christians have not caught the least whiff of it—least of all the accursed priests. I have heard from them about mere Scripture, which they have stolen from the Bible like murderers and thieves. Jeremiah describes this theft as stealing the Word of God from the mouth of your neighbor; for they themselves have never heard it from God, from his very mouth. In my opinion these really are fine preachers, consecrated for just this purpose by the devil. PRAGUE MANIFESTO.[38]

PROPHETS WHO STEAL WORDS FROM ANOTHER. LEONHARD SCHIEMER: The whole world is chattering about and mouthing back and forth

---

[35]LW 75:214 (WA 10.1.1:70).

[36]Oecolampadius, *In Heremiam*, 2:G2r-v; citing Jer 28:1-17.

[37]Denck, *Selected Writings*, 59-60, 64*; citing Eph 1:1-23; Col 1:1-29; Jn 7:15.

[38]Müntzer, *Collected Works*, 357-58.

the word grace, especially our Scripture experts. They notice that there is something in Scripture called grace. Since, however, they do not possess it inwardly, they cannot say anything about it except to regard the word *grace* as the scholastics do. . . . Thus in the end we are left with nothing, and those who can chatter most about this "nothing" are called masters and doctors. . . .

They do not have the skill from God, nor are they taught by God. They have all their knowledge from other Christians and have stolen it out of their books. About them Jeremiah says: "I am against the prophets who each steal my word one from another." They have not been sent by the God of heaven but by the god of their belly, and that is why they cannot preach. LETTER TO THE CHURCH OF GOD.[39]

THE BURDEN OF GOD'S ABSENCE. JOHN DONNE: "What is the burden of the Lord?" "What burden do you have to preach to us and to talk of now?" Say to them, says God to the prophet, "This is the burden of the Lord; I will even forsake you." And as it is elegantly, emphatically, and vehemently added, "Every person's word will be their burden." That which he "says" shall be that thing that is laid to his charge. His scorning, his idle questioning of the prophet, "What burden now, what plague, what famine? . . ." "Every person's burden shall be their burden": the deriding of God's ordinance and the denouncing of his judgments in that ordinance shall be their burden; that is, these words will aggravate God's judgments upon them. Still, there is a heavier weight added: "You shall no longer say," says God to the prophet, "the burden of the Lord." That is, you shall not bestow so much care upon this people as to tell them that the Lord threatens them. God's presence in anger, and in all punishments, is weighty; but God's absence and abandonment is a much heavier burden. As (if extremes will allow for comparison) the everlasting loss of sight of God in hell is a greater torment than any lake of inextinguishable

brimstone, than any gnawing of the incessant worm, than any gnashing of teeth can present to us. SERMON ON PSALM 38:4.[40]

BEWARE OF THE BURDEN OF THE LORD. HEINRICH BULLINGER: "What burden do you announce to us, Jeremiah?" God proposes that you will respond with these words. "What burden, you ask? I will certainly throw you as a burden away," says the Lord. That response shows great indignation, and at the same time extreme brevity, as typically happens in such caustic responses. Indeed, the sense is, "What are you asking of me, what burden am I announcing? And indeed if you want to know the burden I am announcing, I say that you are utterly the burden, namely, you who have become an unbearable weight for the Lord your God. Further, he cannot bear or carry you further, but will hurl you from himself and smash you against the earth, as people do when with great indignation they throw down an unbearable and hateful burden from their shoulders and onto the ground." Moreover, he signifies to them that they would be cast out by God and ground down with many and great calamities. From this we learn that in this case we should not surrender to or keep silence before mockers or profane and impious jesters of the Word of God, but we must steadfastly announce the wrath and vindication of God to them.

Indeed, he explains further and more clearly what he had said: that God will certainly notice all such mockers and jesters, or despisers of the word of the Lord. He says that whoever speaks insolently or through mockery—whether from among the learned or the common people—is "the burden of the Lord." "I will indeed make a visitation on such a person." The word *visitation* comprises every evil, and the prophet indicates that God will most certainly and severely take vengeance on such a mocker and on their very house. But you say, what does the innocent house deserve? Know, therefore, that God does not threaten the innocent, but because the house is completely accustomed to a head of household who is an insolent, petulant, and

---

[39]CRR 10:67. [40]Donne, *Sermons*, 2:128-29*.

derisive person, it follows in insolence, petulance, and derision. Indeed, as long as the house sees and hears nothing other than ungodliness, ill humor, mockery, and abuse, the house itself gets used to that mockery. But at the end the punishment of mockers will be discussed a little more fully.

Then he teaches us what we should beware of when the Word of God is proclaimed, namely, that we not say "the burden of the Lord," that is, so that we beware lest we insolently ridicule in any way the preaching of the Word of God and that we not speak jestingly concerning the words of the Lord. Jeremiah adds this reason for this command and says that, indeed, every person's word will be their own burden. That is, because everyone says "the burden of the Lord" in a petulant, offensive, and derisive way, for every person the burden will be fully heavy enough. SERMON ON JEREMIAH 23:33-40.[41]

---

[41]Bullinger, *Conciones*, 151v-152r.

JEREMIAH 24:1-10
THE GOOD AND THE BAD FIGS

¹*After Nebuchadnezzar king of Babylon had taken into exile from Jerusalem Jeconiah the son of Jehoiakim, king of Judah, together with the officials of Judah, the craftsmen, and the metal workers, and had brought them to Babylon, the* LORD *showed me this vision: behold, two baskets of figs placed before the temple of the* LORD. ²*One basket had very good figs, like first-ripe figs, but the other basket had very bad figs, so bad that they could not be eaten.* ³*And the Lord said to me, "What do you see, Jeremiah?" I said, "Figs, the good figs very good, and the bad figs very bad, so bad that they cannot be eaten."*

⁴*Then the word of the* LORD *came to me:* ⁵*"Thus says the* LORD, *the God of Israel: Like these good figs, so I will regard as good the exiles from Judah, whom I have sent away from this place to the land of the Chaldeans.* ⁶*I will set my eyes on them for good, and I will bring them back to this land. I will build them up, and not tear them down; I will plant them, and not pluck them up.* ⁷*I will give them a heart to know that I am the* LORD, *and they shall be my people and I will be their God, for they shall return to me with their whole heart.*

⁸*"But thus says the* LORD: *Like the bad figs that are so bad they cannot be eaten, so will I treat Zedekiah the king of Judah, his officials, the remnant of Jerusalem who remain in this land, and those who dwell in the land of Egypt.* ⁹*I will make them a horror*ᵃ *to all the kingdoms of the earth, to be a reproach, a byword, a taunt, and a curse in all the places where I shall drive them.* ¹⁰*And I will send sword, famine, and pestilence upon them, until they shall be utterly destroyed from the land that I gave to them and their fathers."*

a Compare Septuagint; Hebrew *horror for evil*

OVERVIEW: This brief chapter prompted commentators to ponder and describe some perennial themes in the history of Christianity. The good and bad figs, representing one segment of the Jewish people—obedient and somewhat repentant—and the other segment—defiant and unrepentant—echo debates about true and false believers among the people of God, or to put it another way, the people of God as the visible and invisible church. In order to ponder the identity of "God's chosen," one must pose deeper questions about the origin of sustained repentance and the source of changed hearts. Is such repentance a human or divine work? Or is it a mix of the two? Does the promise of God's good future beyond all the destruction and exile and the vision of God's people redeemed and transformed rest with human initiative or with God alone?

24:1-7 Two Baskets of Figs, Two Kinds of People

A DIVIDED JEWISH PEOPLE. JOHANNES BUGENHAGEN: This vision appeared to the prophet, wherein the people had been carried away along with King Jehoiachin. Left behind in the kingdom of Judah were the poor of the land, over whom King Zedekiah was put in charge, as you read in 2 Kings 24. Jehoiachin with his mother and the princes, wise men, craftsmen, and ten thousand warriors gave themselves over to the Babylonians so that they would not destroy themselves along with the people; this he seems to have done under duress, having been persuaded by Jeremiah, as you read in chapter 21 above; for in that way it would be better for himself and the people in captivity—better than his own malice and contempt of God merited.

Here an awful testing and sorrow arose for those who were led away, when they saw that their kingdom and temple and all their sacred things had thus far been keep intact, and that they had left behind their goods, and their land, and—as it seemed—their God. They thought they had been deceived by Jeremiah and the other prophets, and now for that reason they would justly bear captivity. Meanwhile those who remained in Jerusalem were happy with their possessions and in the presence of God. It came to the point that the false prophets and King Zedekiah with his people accused the exiles of treachery, as impious and as deserters, who had been deceived by Jeremiah and other worthless folk. They boasted that they were truly strong and pious, but such people who relied on the help of God were able to remain in their own land even if the Babylonian army forbade it. Now at last the lies of the prophets were apparent, of course—of Jeremiah and the others.

So the prophet consoled the exiles with this vision and its interpretation, and he prophesied a severe destruction for the others. On this matter there is much in the prophet Ezekiel, when he was with the others in captivity. Now the Lord had two baskets full of figs standing before the temple; since one was to be cast away from the temple and the other was to be restored to the temple; the first were those who had remained in Jerusalem, and the others were those who had been taken off to Babylon. There were two baskets, when already the people of Judah had been divided into two peoples. The first people was in Babylon under the staff of the Father; the other people were in Jerusalem, who were adding more serious contempt to the sins they had already committed before that time. COMMENTARY ON JEREMIAH 24:1-4.[1]

GOD'S VISION AND TRIBUNAL. JOHN CALVIN: We now see the design of this vision. Jeremiah says that God presented the vision to him. It was necessary to say this so that his doctrine might have more weight with the people. God, indeed, often spoke without a vision. . . . [This is] the design of the vision: it was a sort of seal to what was delivered; for in order that the prophets might possess greater authority, they not only spoke but as it were sealed their doctrine, as though God had graven on it a certain mark, as it were, by his finger. . . .

"Behold," he says, "two baskets of figs set before the temple." The place ought to be noticed. It may have been that the prophet was not allowed to move a step from his own house and the vision may have been presented to him in the night, during thick darkness. But the temple is mentioned, and this shows that a part of the people had not been taken away without cause, and the other part remained in the city; for this had proceeded from God himself. For in the temple God manifested himself; and therefore the prophets, when they wished to storm the hearts of the ungodly, often said, "God shall go forth from his temple." The temple then is to be taken here for the tribunal of God. Hence he says that these two baskets were set in the temple; as though he said that the whole people stood at God's tribunal, and that those who had been already cast into exile had not been carried away at the will of their enemies, but because God planned to punish them. COMMENTARY ON JEREMIAH 24:1.[2]

A GOODNESS NOT THEIR OWN. JOHANNES BUGENHAGEN: "So I will recognize them as good through grace." He seems in this similitude to require that one say, "Thus they are good—those who have migrated." Thus this goodness would not be understood to be among the people themselves, nor the good merit of those who merited captivity by their impiety. But God establishes this benefit in his own love or grace and says that he through his own grace would recognize them, etc. That is, through the acceptance and the imputation of God they are the good figs, that is, not because of themselves, but because of the good pleasure and mercy of God toward them. Here you see how diligently the Holy Spirit speaks, lest we dream

---

[1]Bugenhagen, *In Ieremiam*, 4D4v-4E1r; citing 2 Kings 24:8-17; Jer 21:8-10.

[2]CTS 19:221* (CO 38:457-58); citing Is 26:21; Mic 1:3.

that we have human justification in the sight of God. Commentary on Jeremiah 24:5.[3]

The Good Figs and the Good News.

Nikolaus Selnecker: The good figs signify the poor Jews, King Jeconiah [Jehoiakin] and his servants and citizens, who willingly surrendered to the king of Babylon on the basis of God's order and grace. These folk call to mind God's grace, blessing, deliverance, and reconciliation through Christ. For it is deeply comforting that God says, "I will look upon them favorably and will bring them again into the land, and I will build them up, and not tear them down. I will plant them and not pluck them out. And I will give them a heart (that is other than from nature, or from their free will or their own power).... They shall return to me with their whole heart." This is such a truly living and evangelical word, which points to Christ alone, concerning the will of God the Father for his people and for us all whom he sees with gracious eyes. He does not turn his back on us, but redeems us from the prison of sin, devil, death, and hell, and builds us through his Word on the solid ground and cornerstone, which is Jesus Christ. He plants us as a true vintner, who seals us in his Son, who is the living Vine. We are the vine, and he grows us from a good seed that falls on good ground, so that we bring much fruit and he gives us a new heart through his Word and the Holy Spirit so that we recognize, honor, call on, fear, and praise him as our Father and gracious God and obey him as godly children who believe he is our heavenly and eternal Father. The Whole Prophet Jeremiah 24:4-7.[4]

New Covenant and Christ, the New Testament.

Hans Schlaffer: A goodhearted person is one whom the Father draws. He wants everyone to be saved, for he teaches and witnesses to them all. If such a person had received testimonies to the truth from all creatures and the Scriptures, which declare Christ, his teaching, life, and example, such a person finds confirmation in his heart and is thus certain that this and no other is the way of salvation; to such a one the gospel of all creatures has been preached. He is taught and made into a disciple.... This is not the old covenant that he made with the Jews who were his people then. The old covenant, confirmed with the blood of a ram, is only a figure of the new that is a true covenant, as Jeremiah says. Christ himself calls it the New Testament in his blood, which is shed for the forgiveness of sins. It is impossible to say too much in words about this new testament. For it only is the work of Spirit in the human heart and is at the same time the baptism of the Spirit and fire with which Christ baptizes. What a holy and blessed covenant it is! A Brief Instruction.[5]

God Is the Author of Repentance.

John Calvin: Here is added the main benefit, that God would not only restore the captives, that they might dwell in the land of promise, but would also change them inwardly; for unless God gives us a conviction as to our own sins, and then leads us by his Spirit to repentance, whatever benefits he may bestow on us, they will only lead to our greater ruin.... Now the prophet speaks of a much more excellent favor, that God would not only mitigate punishment, but that he would also inwardly change and reform their hearts, so that they would not only return to their own country, but would also become a true church, a name about which they had vainly boasted. For though they had been chosen to be a peculiar people, yet as they had departed from true religion, they were only a church in name. But now God promises that he would bring them not only to enjoy temporal and fading blessings but also eternal salvation, for they would truly fear and serve him.

And this is what we ought carefully to observe, for the more bountiful God is toward us, the more his vengeance is kindled by our ingratitude. What, then, would it do for us if we abound in all good

---

[3] Bugenhagen, *In Ieremiam*, 4E1r.

[4] Selnecker, *Der gantze Prophet Jeremias*, S3v-S4r; citing Eph 2:20; Mt 13:23; Lk 8:15.

[5] CRR 10:90-91; citing Jer 26:1-24; 31:31-34; Heb 8:8-13.

things, unless we had evidence of God's paternal favor toward us? But when we regard this end, that God testifies to us that he is our Father by his bounty toward us, we then make a right use of all his blessings; and God's benefits cannot lead to our salvation unless we regard them in this light. . . .

Now God says that he would "give them a heart to know him." The word heart is to be taken here for the mind or understanding, as it means often in Hebrew. It, indeed, means frequently the seat of affections, and also the soul of a person, including reason or understanding and will. . . . Yet another thing must be stated: a true knowledge of God is not, as they say, imaginary, but is ever connected with a right feeling. . . .

From the words of the prophet we learn that repentance is the peculiar gift of God. Had Jeremiah said only that they who had been previously driven by madness into ruin, would return to a sane mind, he might have appeared as one setting up free will and putting conversion in the power of humanity itself, as the papists hold. They dream that we can turn to either side, to good as well as to evil; and thus they imagine that we can, after having forsaken God, on our own return to him. But the prophet clearly shows here that it is God's peculiar gift. . . .

Since, then, God affirms that he would give them "a heart" to understand, we hence learn that humanity is by nature blind, and also that when they are blinded by the devil they cannot return to the right way, and they cannot be otherwise capable of light unless God illuminates them by his Spirit. We see then humanity from the time of the fall cannot rise again until God stretches forth his hand not only to help them (as the papists say, for they dare not claim for themselves the whole of repentance, but they split it between themselves and God), but even to do the whole work from the beginning to the end; for God is not called the helper in repentance, but the author of it. God, then, does not say, "I will help them, so that when they lift up their eyes to me, they shall immediately be assisted"; no, he does not say this. But what he says is, "I will give them a heart to understand." And as understanding or knowledge is the main thing in repentance, it follows that

humanity remains wholly under the power of the devil, and is, as it were, his slave, until God draws humanity forth from such miserable bondage. COMMENTARY ON JEREMIAH 24:7.[6]

24:8-10 Bad Figs

INDIGESTION OF THE SOUL. NIKOLAUS SELNECKER: The bad figs signify the other Jews, King Zedekiah and his people, who kept themselves in the land or thought to flee misfortune and those who did not want to willingly surrender to the king of Babylon and be led into captivity. These folk God threatens with war, hunger, and disease. From this allegory we learn to follow the Word and command of God in all things, put ourselves under the powerful hand and will of God, and receive with patience his punishment and gracious, fatherly rod. For if we do this we are pleasing to God. . . . But the rotted, evil figs . . . are capable of nothing. As the rotting figs harm the stomach and cause diarrhea, likewise the soul is harmed by everything that does not have the Word of God or goes against God's command or is undertaken by or concerns human skill and cleverness; all of this must with harm flow out—whatever is not done or completed in the fear of God. THE WHOLE PROPHET JEREMIAH 24:8.[7]

THOSE WHO WANDER FROM GOD AND REFUSE TO REPENT. JOHANNES OECOLAMPADIUS: "As a fig." Zedekiah and his own seemed before the world to be the friends of God, because they were left in the Holy Land after Jehoiachin departed. But God indicates otherwise, because he rejected Zedekiah and held him as an evil fig, which he loathed. Those who were with Zedekiah, and after his captivity, who went down to Egypt with Johanan the son of Kareah heard how much they were to be afflicted. All of them would be miserably defeated, so that they would be despised by all; just as abandoned and trembling Cain wandered over the earth—indeed, God had put a sign on him—

---

[6]CTS 19:227-29* (CO 38:461-63).
[7]Selnecker, Der gantze Prophet Jeremias, S4r-v.

when the blood of his murdered brother was heard in heaven. . . . That exile was more severe than death. But it was much more severe for those with Zedekiah, because they would not repent, even when they were bound in such evils. "And I will send the sword among them." This happened in part when Nebuchadnezzar occupied Jerusalem, and in part in Egypt, and among the paupers left in the land under Gedaliah and Johanan. Chapter 42 says, "All men who are able to set their faces to enter into Egypt so that they might live there, will die by sword, and famine, and pestilence until there is no one of them remaining." The disobedient will submit to the same punishment and repentance in bearing the cross set on them by the Lord as they refuse to take it up. Indeed, they will bear a just servitude, as they are despised among the spiritual people, and those who enjoy freedom, and perish, both in their sins, and in a famine of the word, and a contagion of evil. In short, none of them will remain in their land. God has expelled them; and they will fall into the very evils which they feared. COMMENTARY ON JEREMIAH 24:9-10.[8]

---

[8]Oecolampadius, *In Hieremiam*, 2:H1v-H2r; citing Gen 4:12-15; Jer 42:17.

JEREMIAH 25:1-38
THE EXILE AND THE CUP OF WRATH

¹*The word that came to Jeremiah concerning all the people of Judah, in the fourth year of Jehoiakim the son of Josiah, king of Judah (that was the first year of Nebuchadnezzar king of Babylon), ²which Jeremiah the prophet spoke to all the people of Judah and all the inhabitants of Jerusalem: ³"For twenty-three years, from the thirteenth year of Josiah the son of Amon, king of Judah, to this day, the word of the* Lord *has come to me, and I have spoken persistently to you, but you have not listened. ⁴You have neither listened nor inclined your ears to hear, although the* Lord *persistently sent to you all his servants the prophets, ⁵saying, 'Turn now, every one of you, from his evil way and evil deeds, and dwell upon the land that the* Lord *has given to you and your fathers from of old and forever. ⁶Do not go after other gods to serve and worship them, or provoke me to anger with the work of your hands. Then I will do you no harm.' ⁷Yet you have not listened to me, declares the* Lord, *that you might provoke me to anger with the work of your hands to your own harm.*

⁸*"Therefore thus says the* Lord *of hosts: Because you have not obeyed my words, ⁹behold, I will send for all the tribes of the north, declares the* Lord, *and for Nebuchadnezzar the king of Babylon, my servant, and I will bring them against this land and its inhabitants, and against all these surrounding nations. I will devote them to destruction, and make them a horror, a hissing, and an everlasting desolation. ¹⁰Moreover, I will banish from them the voice of mirth and the voice of gladness, the voice of the bridegroom and the voice of the bride, the grinding of the millstones and the light of the lamp. ¹¹This whole land shall become a ruin and a waste, and these nations shall serve the king of Babylon seventy years. ¹²Then after seventy years are completed, I will punish the king of Babylon and that nation, the land of the Chaldeans, for their iniquity, declares the* Lord, *making the land an everlasting waste. ¹³I will bring upon that land all the words that I have uttered against it, everything written in this book, which Jeremiah prophesied against all the nations. ¹⁴For many nations and great kings shall make slaves even of them, and I will recompense them according to their deeds and the work of their hands."*

¹⁵*Thus the* Lord, *the God of Israel, said to me: "Take from my hand this cup of the wine of wrath, and make all the nations to whom I send you drink it. ¹⁶They shall drink and stagger and be crazed because of the sword that I am sending among them."*

¹⁷*So I took the cup from the* Lord's *hand, and made all the nations to whom the* Lord *sent me drink it: ¹⁸Jerusalem and the cities of Judah, its kings and officials, to make them a desolation and a waste, a hissing and a curse, as at this day; ¹⁹Pharaoh king of Egypt, his servants, his officials, all his people, ²⁰and all the mixed tribes among them; all the kings of the land of Uz and all the kings of the land of the Philistines (Ashkelon, Gaza, Ekron, and the remnant of Ashdod); ²¹Edom, Moab, and the sons of Ammon; ²²all the kings of Tyre, all the kings of Sidon, and the kings of the coastland across the sea; ²³Dedan, Tema, Buz, and all who cut the corners of their hair; ²⁴all the kings of Arabia and all the kings of the mixed tribes who dwell in the desert; ²⁵all the kings of Zimri, all the kings of Elam, and all the kings of Media; ²⁶all the kings of the north, far and near, one after another, and all the kingdoms of the world that are on the face of the earth. And after them the king of Babylon*ᵃ *shall drink.*

²⁷*"Then you shall say to them, 'Thus says the* Lord *of hosts, the God of Israel: Drink, be drunk and vomit, fall and rise no more, because of the sword that I am sending among you.' ²⁸"And if they refuse to accept the cup from your hand to drink, then you shall say to them, 'Thus says the* Lord *of hosts: You must drink! ²⁹For behold, I begin to work disaster at the city that is called by my name, and shall you go unpunished? You shall not go unpunished, for I am summoning a sword against all the inhabitants of the earth, declares the* Lord *of hosts.'*

³⁰"You, therefore, shall prophesy against them
   all these words, and say to them:

"'The Lord will roar from on high,
   and from his holy habitation utter his voice;
he will roar mightily against his fold,
   and shout, like those who tread grapes,
   against all the inhabitants of the earth.
³¹The clamor will resound to the ends of the
      earth,
   for the Lord has an indictment against
      the nations;
he is entering into judgment with all flesh,
   and the wicked he will put to the sword,
declares the Lord.'

³²"Thus says the Lord of hosts:
Behold, disaster is going forth
   from nation to nation,
and a great tempest is stirring
   from the farthest parts of the earth!

³³"And those pierced by the Lord on that day shall
extend from one end of the earth to the other. They
shall not be lamented, or gathered, or buried; they
shall be dung on the surface of the ground.

³⁴"Wail, you shepherds, and cry out,
   and roll in ashes, you lords of the flock,
for the days of your slaughter and dispersion
      have come,
   and you shall fall like a choice vessel.
³⁵No refuge will remain for the shepherds,
   nor escape for the lords of the flock.
³⁶A voice—the cry of the shepherds,
   and the wail of the lords of the flock!
For the Lord is laying waste their pasture,
   ³⁷and the peaceful folds are devastated
      because of the fierce anger of the Lord.
³⁸Like a lion he has left his lair,
   for their land has become a waste
because of the sword of the oppressor,
   and because of his fierce anger."

a Hebrew *Sheshach*, a code name for Babylon

Overview: Reformation-era commentators were
not only focused on issues of doctrine and morality
in Jeremiah but also on the details of biblical timeline,
geography, and culture. Though suffused with
historical observations and narratives, the progression of the book of Jeremiah is not always chronological, thus compelling interpreters to piece together
the flow of events and prophecies while likewise
mapping out the places and nations named. Jeremiah
proclaimed a wrath-filled cup to both the kingdom
of Judea and the surrounding nations. In sum,
fascination with Scripture meant delving into and
identifying all aspects of the biblical text. More
importantly, the message of Jeremiah was often
embedded in and related to intricate historical details
of his time, just as application of this Scripture
would speak to the complex events and challenges of
the sixteenth and seventeenth centuries. Reformers
were keenly attentive to God's past, present, and
future work in the particulars of place and time.

25:1-14 Seventy Years of Captivity

The Dates Behind Jeremiah's Prophecies.

Nikolaus Selnecker: To understand this
history better we want to lay out this short table.

Josiah, the pious king, had begun to rule in
Judah in the year 3304 from the world's beginning
and before the birth of Christ or his incarnation in
the year 659. Josiah reigned thirty-one years. In the
same year the first Nebuchadnezzar began to reign
in Babylon or Chaldea; he reigned thirty-five years.

Jeremiah began to prophesy and preach in
Jerusalem in the thirteenth year of the reign of
Josiah. And eight years thereafter Zephaniah began
to prophesy. . . .

Josiah in the thirty-first year of his reign, due to
arrogance and recklessness, is drawn out against
Pharaoh Neco, and is shot by the guards. He dies
and with great sadness is mourned and wept over
by all of Jerusalem; he is buried by the whole

Jewish people and all the prophets. Jeremiah gives a speech for the dead Josiah. It is found in the fourth chapter of Lamentations. . . .

Joachas or Joahas or Sallum [Jehoahaz], Josiah's son, is made king in year of our Lord 3335; 628 years before Christ. He reigned three months and Neco, king of Egypt, removed him from power and took him captive. . . .

His brother, Eliakim, or Jehoiakim is installed and confirmed as king by Pharaoh Neco. . . . He reigned eleven years.

In the fourth year of the lordship of Jehoiakim Jeremiah began to prophecy that for seventy years Jerusalem would lie destroyed and the people would be led into captivity, as we see here in chapter 25.

At the beginning of the fourth year of Jehoiakim, Nebuchadnezzar II . . . begins to reign in Babylon. He reigns forty-three years. . . .

In the fifth year of the kingdom of Jehoiakim, Jehoiakim burns the book of Jeremiah. . . . At the same time . . . Nebuchadnezzar had engaged and beaten Neco, Pharaoh of Egypt, on the banks of the Euphrates. . . .

In the ninth year of his lordship in Judah, Jehoiakim is made a subject of King Nebuchadnezzar. . . .

In the eleventh year Jehoiakim breaks with Babylon, because he sees that Neco, king of Egypt, has rearmed against the Babylonians. . . .

In the same year that Nebuchadnezzar besieged the city of Tyre, he sent a great part of his army against Jerusalem. He bound King Jehoiakim with chains, strangled him, and threw him on the open field before the city, as in Jeremiah's prophecy about the unburied donkey and the wild animals and birds that consume him. . . .

Jehoiachin or Jeconiah, the son of Jehoiakim, becomes king of Judah, in the year 3346; 617 years before Christ's birth. He reigns three months and ten days. He held to the measure of the word of Jeremiah and surrendered to the king of Babylon. . . . Daniel, Ezekiel, and others go to Babylon at the same time. . . . Instead of Jehoiachin, Nebuchadnezzar makes Mathaniah king and names him Zedekiah. He reigns eleven years. . . .

In the ninth year of the kingdom of Zedekiah, Nebuchadnezzar moves with his military forces against Jerusalem. . . . Because the godless Zedekiah despised the warning and preaching of the prophet Jeremiah, Zedekiah had to be punished.

In the eleventh year of the kingdom of Zedekiah, Jerusalem is defeated and destroyed. . . . The king's eyes are put out, and he is led away with two chains to Babylon. . . . This destruction of the city of Jerusalem and the captivity lasted seventy years, until Cyrus, in the first year of his monarchy and in the twentieth year of his kingdom, gave the public decree that the Jews should go home, build their temple, and be given their freedom.

In the thirty-third year of the kingdom of Nebuchadnezzar he defeats and overwhelms the Ammonites and Moabites, and brings all of Egypt under his rule. So Jeremiah had prophesied. THE WHOLE PROPHET JEREMIAH 25:1-14.[1]

WHY A PROPHET RISES EARLY. JOHANNES BUGENHAGEN: "Rising before night" and "rising before dawn."[†] This Hebraism I have changed everywhere else in this prophet. Here, however, I have left it so that you may be accustomed to what he means. To this matter: with what a great effort we act every day, and with all our powers and effort we lean in so that all might be accomplished. We rise at night when it is still dark, nor do we sleep the whole night; we rise at dawn, and we do not wait for the rising sun, like the women who were going to anoint the body of Christ in the tomb. So it happens in Scripture that rising at night and rising at daybreak signifies taking care most diligently until it is complete. Therefore, Jeremiah says that through so many years that he most diligently preached and the Lord preached most diligently through the prophets to the stubborn people. "Nothing was neglected that pertains to your salvation and peace, yet you wish to perish in divine judgment." COMMENTARY ON JEREMIAH 25:3.[2]

---

[1]Selnecker, *Der gantze Prophet Jeremias*, T1r-T3v; citing 2 Chron 35:20-25; 2 Kings 23:31-35; Jer 36:1-32; 46:1-28; 2 Kings 24:1-7; Jer 22:19; 36:30; 2 Kings 25:1-30; Jer 39:1-18; 52:1-34; 46:1-28; 48:1-47; 49:1-39.
[2]Bugenhagen, *In Ieremiam*, 4F2r; citing Lk 24:1-6. [†]See the KJV for this phrasing.

EXILE—PHYSICAL AND SPIRITUAL. JOHANNES OECOLAMPADIUS: So every joy will be taken away and there will be joy neither in marriage, nor in harvest, nor in milling—when previously they delighted with joy in the crops that had ripened—nor in feasts for which many lamps were lit. Instead there will be devastation and deprivation for seventy years. Indeed, wherever the Word of God ends, and they are taught that it is a joke of human beings, there Jerusalem is captured and servitude of the most severe tyrant oppresses, so that the voice of God is not able to be proclaimed with joy, nor is there public or private joy of the spirit. Rather, oppressed consciences groan and a great deprivation terrifies all. Indeed the true worship of God goes silent. So where the fruits of the spirit are absent, there is deprivation and devastation of the soul. Concerning seventy years, as is said in Zechariah, there is a year of rest from sin and there is a year of fulfillment in which the Lord is merciful to his own; and in Psalm 51: the time of his mercy is coming, that is, when the Spirit will teach us within. COMMENTARY ON JEREMIAH 25:10.[3]

A SAD PROPHET IN MISERABLY EVIL DAYS. MARTIN LUTHER: Jeremiah had to be there and proclaim the punishment and the wrath, telling the people that it would not last forever, but for a fixed time, such as seventy years, and that afterward they would come into grace once again. With this promise he had also to comfort and sustain himself, or he would have had little consolation and happiness. For he was a sad and troubled prophet, and he lived in miserably evil days. Besides, he had a peculiarly difficult ministry. For over forty years down to the captivity, he had to say hard things to obstinately wicked people. Still it did little good. He had to look on while the people went from bad to worse, always wanting to kill him, and putting him to much hardship.

On top of that he had to experience and see with his own eyes how the land was destroyed and the people carried away captive, amid great misery and bloodshed. Nor does this include what he had afterward to preach and suffer in Egypt, for it is believed that he was stoned to death by the Jews in Egypt. PREFACE TO THE PROPHET JEREMIAH.[4]

GOD'S WORD AND THE BOOK OF JEREMIAH. JOHN CALVIN: God says that he had pronounced these "words"; he afterward says that Jeremiah was his minister, and as it were, his herald, and he calls him also a scribe or a writer. God then here declares that he was the author of all that Jeremiah had brought forward; and yet he leaves his own office to his minister, for it is necessary to secure authority for the prophets; otherwise, except God visibly descended from heaven, people would either indiscriminately admit what might be said, and without judgment receive falsehood and truth or they would become wholly hardened, so as to give no credit to prophetic instruction. He says, "whatsoever is written in this book." The prophet no doubt wrote down a summary of what he had delivered; for . . . it was usual with the prophets, after they had spoken at large to the people and preached diffusely, to affix a short summary to the doors of the temple. This volume then is what Jeremiah calls the book, which was composed from his public addresses. It might in common language be called a summary. COMMENTARY ON JEREMIAH 25:13.[5]

25:15-38 *The Cup of the Lord's Wrath*

THE MADNESS FROM GOD'S CUP. JOHN CALVIN: [Jeremiah] says that "a cup had been delivered" to him by God's hand; by these words [Jeremiah] intimates that he did not come forth of his own will to terrify the Jews and other nations, but that he faithfully proclaimed what had been committed to him. . . .

He calls it "the cup of the wine of fury," or of wrath. This metaphor often occurs in the Prophets, but in a different sense. For God is said sometimes

[3]Oecolampadius, *In Hieremiam*, 2:H2r; citing Zech 1:11-17.

[4]LW 35:280 (WA, DB 11.1:191-92).
[5]CTS 19:259-60* (CO 38:482-83).

to inebriate people when he stupefies them, and drives them at one time to madness, and at another time deprives them of common sense and understanding, so that they become like beasts; but he is said also to inebriate them when, by outward calamities, he fills them with astonishment. So now the prophet calls calamity the cup of wrath, even that calamity, which like fire, was to inflame the minds of all those who received no benefit from chastisements. Madness, indeed, means no other thing than the despair of those who perceive God's hand stretched out against them, and thus rage and clamor, and curse heaven and earth, themselves, and God. . . .

"And they shall drink, and be moved. . . ." Here the prophet more fully shows . . . that they were not vain terrors when he denounced God's judgments on all nations, for we call those threats childish that are not accomplished. But the prophet here declares that however obstinately the Jews and others might resist, they could not possibly escape God's vengeance. . . .

He then adds, "that they may be incensed and become distracted." These two words refer, no doubt, to the seriousness of their punishment; for he intimates that they would become, as it were, destitute of mind and reason. When God kindly chastises us, and with paternal moderation, we are then able with resignation to submit to him and flee to his mercy; but when we make a clamor and are driven almost to madness, we then show that an extreme rigor is felt and that there is no hope of pardon. The prophet, then, intended to express that so atrocious would be the calamities of the nations with whom God was angry that they would become stupefied and almost insane, and at the same time frantic, for despair would lay hold on their minds and hearts, that they would not be able to entertain any hope of deliverance, or to submit to God, but that they would, as is usual with the reprobate, rise up against God and vomit forth their blasphemies. COMMENTARY ON JEREMIAH 25:15-16.[6]

FOR THE NATIONS, NOTHING BUT THE CUP OF WRATH. NIKOLAUS SELNECKER: Jeremiah prophesied against other lands and kings and says, "The king of Babylon will overrun and destroy other surrounding lands and kingdoms; for they will drink from God's cup of wrath and God will send other troubles upon them. . . ." How much worse it will be for the godless heathens and the nations who are devastated and punished. And where they do not turn back they will be given dirty soup and wretched scum to suck. Nothing will help them: neither wisdom nor power, neither skilled arts, nor their glory. All the shepherds, that is, the princes and lords, shall be cornered and destroyed, with all their herds or with their subjects. Last, the king of Babylon and his *sesach*, that is, his power, and his joy, or his fortress city of Babylon would be surrounded, punished, and destroyed by the Persians. As hereafter Jeremiah further prophesies in chapters 50 and 51. THE WHOLE PROPHET JEREMIAH 25:17-38.[7]

THE NATIONS AND THEIR DESTINY. JOHANNES BUGENHAGEN: "To those who are in Dedan and Tema, and Buz." Dedan and Tema are cities of Idumea, as you see above in chapter 49 and in Ezekiel 25. Concerning Tema you also read in the Hebrew Obadiah 1, where the case is argued, why the prophets proclaim against the Edomites and their cities. Buz, I believe, is the royal city in Idumea or at the border of Idumea where the land Uz begins, as it is said; elsewhere the prophets call it Bozra or Bosra. There is, however, Idumea in Syria, between Arabia and Phoenicia. That region is of Esau, who is called Edom: Genesis 25, so they are Edomites or Idumeans whenever the region is called Seir, which is named after the mountain Seir.

"Ammonites and Moabites" are two peoples said to be in parts of Arabia, from the two sons of Lot: Genesis 19.

"Tyre and Zidon" or Sidon are the maritime and formerly wealthy cities in Phoenicia.

"Of the Islands across the sea": that is, those who by the interposition of the sea are separated from

---

[6]CTS 19:263-65* (CO 38:485-86).

[7]Selnecker, *Der gantze Prophet Jeremias*, T4r-v.

us or from the continent, lest you talk absurdly as if the prophet says that the islands are on the other shore of the sea, which are rather in the Mediterranean Sea, as Cyprus, Rhodes, and the Cyclades.

"Simbri": because the Persians come thereafter (says Jerome);[†] we think that Simbri is also another region of Persia. For Elam or the Elamites in sacred literature are no doubt the Persians. But the Medes here are called by their own name. These, as everyone knows, are "the Medes and Persians." . . .

But Jeremiah adds, "All the kings of the north, whose dominions either stretch to Babylon, or inhabit beyond, or are near them," but truly he also adds: "All those kings over the earth who are over the face of the earth." He is not speaking about the whole inhabited world, but about the kingdom in Asia, which is the topic of this sermon. Nevertheless, we see from this particular foray, which is horrible to put into speech, that just as all people are condemned to eternal death, unless redeemed in Christ, so all the kingdoms of the whole world are condemned to the sword, unless they repent and beg forgiveness, as Jeremiah preaches throughout his whole book. They abuse the sword; therefore they die by the sword. COMMENTARY ON JEREMIAH 25:21-26.[8]

DRINKING THE CUP AND HEARING THE WORD OF GOD. JOHANNES OECOLAMPADIUS: For a long time the flesh and the world fought against the Word of God, and they expect nothing less than that the Lord will pass judgment. So then the Lord commands, as he says, "Drink": it behooves you to drink no matter how much you spit out and become drunk; so drink until drunk. Drunkenness is certainly not tolerable. "But vomit": that is, be so filled with the wine of rage that you give back that which is above and that which was applied in excess. Those who are drunk rise up after being relieved by vomiting. "You, however, fall back from vomiting due to so much intoxication. Fall down without any hope

of rising, because of the sword of the Lord, whom you drunkards now deride in your vices. Indeed you suppose either that the sword of the Lord is nothing; or that you are able to escape it, and indeed that you will have a taste. But in truth you will be drunk on the sword and anger of God, so that thus you will immediately perish; for the vomit of intoxication will not relieve you, but you will again fall from it, nor after the fall will there be hope of rising." In this overstatement he signifies the coming of a most harsh punishment for hypocrites. O what a grave measure for sinfulness, in which all unbelievers are sinning here. Indeed, you will fall, he says, and "never rise again, that is, the punishment is perpetual, which is inflicted on you because of my wrath."

"It will be if they refuse." This repeats the verse above, so even if the people fight back and spurn the judgment of God, say to them, you will drink with drinking something that will not come to pass. That is, it will be impossible to evade this destiny, which in the prophetic manner he inculcates with an external symbol added to the words. For he offers a cup to the kings and nobles of the people, signifying the waters of adversity, which were about to overflow on account of their impiety; and it is just like a curse from the Word of God. In this manner, symbols are a reminder of the soul and of grace, if indeed they are born from the truth, so that they ought to be born entirely, if in the Holy Spirit they convict one of a made-up lie, so the use of the Word of God is received in a twofold way. One person is among those who are elect and attentively listen; the other among those who are rejected and who are lazy. The latter are united with death; the former are united with life. It is to be established in a similar way concerning symbols. The rest that were afflicted with symbols a few generations back come out of superstition and error, which in Christ ought to be believed all the less. COMMENTARY ON JEREMIAH 25:27-28.[9]

THE SHOUTING OF THE PEOPLE. THE ENGLISH ANNOTATIONS: "He shall give a shout. . . ." Some

---

[8]Bugenhagen, *In Ieremiam*, 4F3r-4F4r; citing Jer 49:7-22; Ezek 25:12-14; Obad 9-14; Deut 2:1; Gen 19:36-38. †Jerome, *Commentary on Jeremiah*, 155. [9]Oecolampadius, *In Hieremiam*, 2:I2v-I3r.

suppose that this alludes to the sort of songs workmen sang while employed in the winepress. They used to answer one another often in order to make their work go faster and more merrily away. The word signifies properly "to answer," but also sometimes means to answer one another with singing. . . . I conceive the shout here mentioned as an alarm, or shout rather, of assailants, such as they tend to make either when joining in battle or when assaulting some fort or city. This can also be compared to the shout that country people tend to make when bringing in their vintage and harvest and even more when they have their feet in the winepress and new liquor in their heads. ANNOTATIONS ON JEREMIAH 25:30.[10]

JEREMIAH PREDICTS THE FINAL JUDGMENT.

KONRAD PELLIKAN: Jeremiah is ordered to prophesy against everyone, even to those to whom he would not ever come into contact. Indeed, by the providence of God and in his fuller season they will hear the word of the Lord and understand the true things that the Lord has predicted about them. And they will believe in the Lord when they have been instructed by calamity. The Jewish people will be compelled to believe the prophets, even if they are unwilling. Someday the spirit of truth of the prophets will be commended to and known by the whole world, so that by this covenant the infallible truth of the holy Scriptures will shine forth and be affirmed. So it has happened today and from the time of Christ the whole world with harmonious faith confesses it. When the Lord roars like a lion, who will not fear? He will come with his severe judgment, to terrify all who hear, and not even spare his chosen temple and the throne of his own glory. Indeed he will summon their most cruel enemies, who will call out like coxswains' shouts, and they will encourage each other with a chorus of shouting, like those trampling out the grapes in the harvest, to lay waste to the earth along with its inhabitants.

The sound and roar of those laying waste will fill the whole earth, when the Lord will visit the iniquities of the people with his harsh judgment and he will humble every race of humanity, and prepare them to recognize himself, and to recognize the folly of idolatry, and he will adapt them to the worship of the true God, by no path easier than extreme poverty and distress. Indeed, those impious people whom he will call to faith, he will nevertheless afflict with a fitting punishment. COMMENTARY ON JEREMIAH 25:30-31.[11]

BEAUTIFUL BUT FRAGILE. THE ENGLISH

ANNOTATIONS: Some such curious utensils, such as Venice glasses and China dishes, by reason of their fragility, are with the least fall, or casualty, soon dashed to pieces, and being once broken cannot be cemented or put together again; thus there are some who are of much esteem while they are whole, but of no worth once they are broken. ANNOTATIONS ON JEREMIAH 25:34.[12]

THE PLIGHT OF THE SHEPHERDS AND THE

DEPARTED LION. JOHN MAYER: "Howl, you shepherds." Here all expositors agree that Jeremiah returns in the conclusion of this terrible prophecy against Jerusalem, and all other nations before mentioned, to the king, princes, priests, and prophets of Judea, according to the word "pastors." Seeing such great calamities to come, he said, "Howl and cry." And he gives four reasons for this: (1) Because they should be broken, as a precious vessel or a pleasant vessel; for such the Jews had been through God's peculiar favor to them—more than any other nations—as people grieve more for the breaking of china than a plain earthen pot. (2) Because they shall have no place to flee to, they or the principal of the flock, that is, the rich, who formerly had many strongholds. (3) Because their pasture would be spoiled, and their habitations cut down; wherein he continues the metaphor of shepherds and sheep, by their pasture, meaning

---

[10]Downame, ed., *Annotations*, 9R1r*; citing Ex 15:21; 1 Sam 18:7; 21:11; 29:5; Josh 6:16, 20; Jer 51:14; Is 16:9-10; Jer 48:32-33.

[11]Pellikan, *Commentaria Bibliorum*, 3:2T4r-v. [12]Downame, ed., *Annotations*, 9R1v*; citing Ps 31:12; Jer 22:28.

their fruitful country, full of corn, wine, and oil, now made desolate and destitute as a wilderness and their houses cut down; because being burnt down, they were as trees in a forest that in times past was a shelter now cut down. (3) "He leaves his den as a lion." That is, the Lord has left his temple and city, as being formerly to him like a lion's den, into which no beast dared to enter while he was there; but now being gone, any dared come and enter and take whatever they found and devoured it without fear. The next words show that the king of Babylon did exactly that. COMMENTARY ON JEREMIAH 25:34-38.[13]

GOD PRESERVES AND DESTROYS THE NATIONS. JOHANNES BUGENHAGEN: The Lord would not only preserve the Jews as before, but also those nations in their kingdoms and principalities—not through their wisdom and fortitude—but through God, who preserves all that he has made: as it says above, the God "who dwells with people" as in a tabernacle and blesses them and they are well. Where he has truly deserted the nations, they perish. . . . all those nations—from Adam and the patriarchs and from Noah and his sons—once had knowledge of God from his Word, so that you still read of remnants of this piety among the nations in Genesis and otherwise in Jonah, etc., until at length they separated away from the Word of God into human doctrines and made-up cults, that is, into idolatry, and there was a forgetting of true piety etc. So it says, ". . . their land is laid waste." As if he says, God watched over and preserved the kingdoms, so that they were not destroyed. When, however, he forsook them they could not avoid destruction. So he adds the similitude "as a young lion." The elder lion does not easily change his habitation, as he is already accustomed to it and fond of rest. But a young lion, provoked by some trifling cause, destroys everything out of anger and seeks a new dwelling. COMMENTARY ON JEREMIAH 25:38.[14]

---

[13]Mayer, *A Commentary*, 419*; citing Jer 23:1.

[14]Bugenhagen, *In Ieremiam*, 4G1v; citing Jer 31:33; Jon 1:1-2.

JEREMIAH 26:1-24
THE DANGEROUS CALLING
OF THE PROPHET

[1]In the beginning of the reign of Jehoiakim the son of Josiah, king of Judah, this word came from the Lord: [2]"Thus says the Lord: Stand in the court of the Lord's house, and speak to all the cities of Judah that come to worship in the house of the Lord all the words that I command you to speak to them; do not hold back a word. [3]It may be they will listen, and every one turn from his evil way, that I may relent of the disaster that I intend to do to them because of their evil deeds. [4]You shall say to them, 'Thus says the Lord: If you will not listen to me, to walk in my law that I have set before you, [5]and to listen to the words of my servants the prophets whom I send to you urgently, though you have not listened, [6]then I will make this house like Shiloh, and I will make this city a curse for all the nations of the earth.'"

[7]The priests and the prophets and all the people heard Jeremiah speaking these words in the house of the Lord. [8]And when Jeremiah had finished speaking all that the Lord had commanded him to speak to all the people, then the priests and the prophets and all the people laid hold of him, saying, "You shall die! [9]Why have you prophesied in the name of the Lord, saying, 'This house shall be like Shiloh, and this city shall be desolate, without inhabitant'?" And all the people gathered around Jeremiah in the house of the Lord.

[10]When the officials of Judah heard these things, they came up from the king's house to the house of the Lord and took their seat in the entry of the New Gate of the house of the Lord. [11]Then the priests and the prophets said to the officials and to all the people, "This man deserves the sentence of death, because he has prophesied against this city, as you have heard with your own ears."

[12]Then Jeremiah spoke to all the officials and all the people, saying, "The Lord sent me to prophesy against this house and this city all the words you have heard. [13]Now therefore mend your ways and your deeds, and obey the voice of the Lord your God, and the Lord will relent of the disaster that he has pronounced against you. [14]But as for me, behold, I am in your hands. Do with me as seems good and right to you. [15]Only know for certain that if you put me to death, you will bring innocent blood upon yourselves and upon this city and its inhabitants, for in truth the Lord sent me to you to speak all these words in your ears."

[16]Then the officials and all the people said to the priests and the prophets, "This man does not deserve the sentence of death, for he has spoken to us in the name of the Lord our God." [17]And certain of the elders of the land arose and spoke to all the assembled people, saying, [18]"Micah of Moresheth prophesied in the days of Hezekiah king of Judah, and said to all the people of Judah: 'Thus says the Lord of hosts,

"'Zion shall be plowed as a field;
    Jerusalem shall become a heap of ruins,
      and the mountain of the house a wooded
        height.'

[19]Did Hezekiah king of Judah and all Judah put him to death? Did he not fear the Lord and entreat the favor of the Lord, and did not the Lord relent of the disaster that he had pronounced against them? But we are about to bring great disaster upon ourselves."

[20]There was another man who prophesied in the name of the Lord, Uriah the son of Shemaiah from Kiriath-jearim. He prophesied against this city and against this land in words like those of Jeremiah. [21]And when King Jehoiakim, with all his warriors and all the officials, heard his words, the king sought to put him to death. But when Uriah heard of it, he was afraid and fled and escaped to Egypt. [22]Then King Jehoiakim sent to Egypt certain men, Elnathan the son of Achbor and others with him, [23]and they

took Uriah from Egypt and brought him to King Jehoiakim, who struck him down with the sword and dumped his dead body into the burial place of the common people.

²⁴But the hand of Ahikam the son of Shaphan was with Jeremiah so that he was not given over to the people to be put to death.

OVERVIEW: Ministry was a dangerous occupation and calling in the sixteenth and seventeenth centuries. Although most of the well-known reformers died of natural causes, they often faced suspicion, hostility, and danger. Martin Luther was a wanted man in a good part of Germany and most of Europe; John Calvin was a religious refugee from his native France and pursued his work as a foreigner and outsider to his church and community. Then there are the dramatic cases: Huldrych Zwingli's battlefield death, the executions of the Marian martyrs in England, and the countless Anabaptist women and men who were banished, tortured, and put to death.[1] In short, Jeremiah's life provided a profoundly relevant and timely example to the reformers. In this chapter, he illustrates the grave risk of faithful and public proclamation, the demeanor required of preachers facing persecution, the difficulties of ministry in the crosshairs of religious and political authorities, and the complexity of divine providence operating behind all things.

26:1-15 Jeremiah Is Threatened with Death

JEREMIAH'S DIFFICULT WORK. PHILIPP MELANCHTHON: It was even more difficult to persuade the people to accept surrender since, after the capitulation and exile of King Jehoiachin, eleven years passed before Jerusalem was besieged. Meanwhile, those who remained behind were cursing the prophet, claiming that he had misled them and that he was an imposter and a false prophet. Jeremiah nevertheless stood by his words in the face of everyone's judgment and the apparent course of events. Grave matters of this kind, when a serious crisis envelops kingdom, homeland, the people of God, the temple, and its worship, ought to be deliberated by wise counselors as best they can, but they cannot be easily put in plain words.

Jeremiah was under pressure because of the promises that seemed to contradict him; for example, "The scepter shall not depart from Judah . . . until Shiloh comes," and likewise [others that indicate] the temple and its cult will endure until the Messiah appears. In this case Jeremiah needed spiritual wisdom to interpret the promises. God fulfills them, but not in the way human reason thinks. He gives posterity to Abraham, but not in the manner he expected. Likewise, in this case, God does preserve this people and their worship, but not in the way their human reason anticipated. First, he scatters the entire people, then he thoroughly destroys the temple and abolishes its cult, but in spite of everything God fulfills his promise when the people return from exile.

We ought to learn from these things that we should give preference to the Word of God over everything else: what we experience as well as our opinions and deliberations. The apostles were promised that the church would be preserved, but they and all who listened to them were killed. In the meantime, however, the church consistently grew and flourished. Throughout our life, therefore, let us remember that divine promises are fulfilled in wondrous ways. THE LESSONS OF JEREMIAH'S PROPHECY.[2]

PROPHETS WHO LIVE AND DIE. JOHANNES BUGENHAGEN: In the twentieth chapter above it was said that the high priest did not tolerate

---

[1] Such an interest in persecution and death during the Reformation era led to several great martyrologies of the Reformation: *The Acts and Monuments of the Christian Church* (also known as *Foxe's Book of Martyrs*), *The Martyrs Mirror*, and Jean Crespin's *Histoire des Martyrs*.

[2] Melanchthon, "Lessons," 63; citing Gen 49:10; 2 Kings 24:12, 15-16; 25:2.

Jeremiah as he prophesied in the atrium of the house of the Lord, but threw him in prison. Now again as he was doing this by the command of the Lord himself, the evil priests, false prophets, and people grabbed Jeremiah so that he might be stoned—as if according to the law of the Lord—as a blasphemer and as one who speaks against the holy place. This is also how Stephen was accused in Acts.

So the impious always want to destroy the confessors of Christ, in this case it is as if they were heretics, blasphemers, and seducers; as Christ said in Matthew 5. They thus made Jeremiah free through the persuasion of the prince and counsel of Ahikam—meanwhile, God was using them as intermediaries—so that Jeremiah was preserved longer in safety. However, Uriah beforehand was killed and not saved. But God cares for his own by granting salvation either way—whether they live or die. So it happens that by this variation the wicked world is blinded; it judges that the plan of God is luck and that the pious are of no concern to God. So Herod dispatched James with the sword, as in Acts of the Apostles, but Peter escaped prison and was saved for greater things. Read Hebrews 11 concerning saints who were saved in this life, and concerning saints who were not saved in this life.

This history of Jeremiah is also the story of Martin Luther through God, if anyone understands it properly. COMMENTARY ON JEREMIAH 26.[3]

PREACHING IN THE TEMPLE COURT. JOHANNES OECOLAMPADIUS: Jeremiah had said above that judgment from the house of the Lord was about to begin, which seemed shameful to most people. Therefore, he repeats the prophecy with the same sentiment that he had formerly said. It says, "in the beginning of the reign of Jehoiakim," so that you may see that immediately after the robust reign of Josiah how great a filth of manners crept in at once. Indeed Jehoiakim's brother had reigned only three months before; and for that they decided to kill Jeremiah the prophet on the pretext that he had

disputed against the temple and the Holy City, based on the fact that he testified that hypocritical worship would not be able to save the evil people. . . .

"Thus the Lord said, 'Stand in the court.'" With great confidence he spoke this prophecy in that place where they came from all the cities to worship in the temple. Indeed, this is the place where they took part in sacrifices. So it seemed to them as if Jeremiah was keeping them away from the entrance to the temple. He, however, was encouraged and moved so that he spoke all of the words that had been commanded to him, so that indeed he did not subtract one word, and so that he was careful not to add or subtract, especially from the Word of God. . . . Truly God wanted to confront their sins in public. We detract from the Word of God . . . when we approve of the wicked and shameful actions of people, on which we ought to impress the wrath of God. COMMENTARY ON JEREMIAH 26:1-2.[4]

SPEAK BOLDLY. HULDRYCH ZWINGLI: "Leave not one word out." The prophet is now instructed that God has entrusted him to preach the Word clearly and simply and to leave nothing out. "Be genuine, bold, and speak out; do not abbreviate what you say. . . . Therefore, they will understand what I am planning insofar as they want to turn from their malice and toward me and if from now on they do not seek to make excuses." When an adversary is not present, then one is brave; but when he is present, then one is either very fearful and remains very quiet or one plays the hypocrite and wastes the opportunity, so that one takes all the power from the words. When one neither brings the matter forward nor speaks out loudly, then one allows everyone to have an excuse for his vices. Therefore, the prophet must speak out concerning these vices in an unvarnished, clear, and direct way. SERMON ON JEREMIAH 26:2.[5]

GODLY AUTHORITIES AND THE PROPHETIC OFFICE. NIKOLAUS SELNECKER: Jeremiah's colleagues and fellow clergy could not endure such

---

[3]Bugenhagen, *In Ieremiam*, 4G3v-4G4r; citing Lev 24:14-16, 23; Deut 13:1-5; Acts 6:8-15; 7:54-60; Mt 5:12; Acts 12:1-10.

[4]Oecolampadius, *In Hieremiam*, 2:I4v-KIr.
[5]Zwingli, *Predigten*, 241-42.

a sermon from the prophet. So they condemned Jeremiah to death, so that he should be turned over to the court and then stoned as a seducer, as one who curses, a blasphemer and rebel, who prophesied against the temple of God. Such actions are like what our Lord Christ himself and Stephen encountered. As Christ reports in Matthew 5 and says: "They have persecuted the prophets, who were before you."

So we also see in our times; our adversaries resist and condemn true teachers as heretics and blasphemers, who cause rebellion to and destruction of the orderly power in the church of God. Yet they know and express the commands of God with vivid words: "flee idolatry"; "we can do nothing against the word, but for it"; "you serve me in vain with human statutes"; "beware of false prophets." Christ says, "Who is not with me is against me, and who does not join me will be scattered." So Paul says, "When an angel from heaven comes and preaches another gospel," then the apostles preaches to us, "So shall it be cursed."

Upright teachers and true Christians should obey such vivid and clear commands of God and not question them. The world of pope, emperor, king, princes, pastors, and others may speak and contend with you, as they will. "Blessed are you," Christ says, "when they want to malign you for my sake and persecute you; you will be rewarded in heaven."

Though the clergy lords of the temple wanted to throttle Jeremiah, God sent some helpful means through the pious authorities; through the royal council the pious Jeremiah was saved and the above action was hindered. Then they defended the prophet Jeremiah and said, "He has spoken to us in the name of the Lord our God." With these words they showed that they held Jeremiah's message and warning to be the voice and Word of God, and they feared God's wrath more than the pastors themselves, who should have preached God's word. This is a great and glorious moment for worldly authorities, when they take on the heart of a true teacher for themselves against everyone else in the world. So it is in our time: Duke and Elector Frederick of Saxony protected and defended

Martin Luther against the pope and worldly tyranny. In this way we learn that God will not abandon his own, especially those who earnestly follow the Word, though likewise according to his will they must endure and suffer something. . . .

One may teach a long time and pursue their office a good while. Just as Jeremiah taught for forty years long—to the destruction of Jerusalem—and thereafter he also preached a while in Egypt, until he was killed by Apries, the king of Egypt. Another prophet endeavors for a short time and soon dies, or is otherwise gathered up, as with Uriah, the colleague and associate of Jeremiah. Likewise James the apostle was killed by Herod. Yet Peter came along and preached much longer. Such is God's way, and his judgments and his councils are unknown to us. THE WHOLE PROPHET JEREMIAH 25:7-24.[6]

THE TEMPLE IS TIED TO GODLINESS. JOHN CALVIN: We . . . see that the priests and prophets were not without some specious pretext for condemning Jeremiah. There is some weight in what they said, "Do you not make God contradict himself? For what you denounce in his name openly and directly conflicts with his promises; but God is ever consistent with himself; so you are a cheat and a liar, and thus one of the false prophets, whom God does not tolerate in his church." And yet what they boasted was frivolous; for God had not promised that the temple should be perpetual in order to give license to the people to indulge in all manner of wickedness. . . . For it was not right to separate two things that God had connected; he required piety and obedience from the people, and he also promised that he would be the guardian of the city, and that the temple would be safe under his protection. But the Jews had neither faith nor repentance. COMMENTARY ON JEREMIAH 26:9.[7]

---

[6]Selnecker, *Der gantze Prophet Jeremias*, V2r-v, XIV; citing Acts 6:8-15; 7:54-60; Mt 5:12; 1 Cor 10:14; 2 Cor 13:8; Mt 15:9; 12:30; Gal 1:8; Mt 5:11-12; Jer 26:16; Acts 12:1-10. Selnecker refers to Pharaoh Apries (589–570 BC); Pharaoh Amasis II (570–526) was more likely the ruler when Jeremiah lived in Egypt. [7]CTS 19:320-21* (CO 38:521).

IDOLATROUS PEOPLE OPPOSE THE PROPHET.
JOHN KNOX: It is to be noted and observed that
among those people were false prophets—not that
they were so known and esteemed by the people.
No, they were in charge of the true church of God
(so they boast themselves to be) that cannot err.
Their false prophets maintain places of idolatry (as
Winchester, Durham, London;[†] I mean that
members of the devil now hold bishoprics in
England) and yet boldly promise the people
prosperity and good luck. Thereby, the people were
so abused and blind that the words of the Jeremiah
were not regarded, as the consequences declare. All
the people apprehended Jeremiah and with one
voice cried, "he shall die, he is worthy of death."
Great was the uproar against this poor prophet. It
appears he would not have escaped if the princes of
Judah had not hastened from the king's house into
the temple and taken upon themselves the hearing
of his cause. After much debate, some defended
Jeremiah and some vehemently accused the prophet.
The text says that the hand of the son of Ahikam,
the son of Shapham, was with Jeremiah so that he
should not be given into the hands of the people to
be killed. Although the prophet very narrowly
escaped death, he did not cease from his office. A
GODLY LETTER OF WARNING AND ADMONITION.[8]

JEREMIAH DEFENDS HIS CALL. JOHN TRAPP: In
this apology of the prophet, [Jeremiah] answers for
himself with a heroic spirit, showing five noble
virtues, that are fit for a martyr, as well observed by
any expositor: (1) His prudence, in alleging his divine
mission. (2) His charity, in exhorting his enemies to
repent. (3) His humility, in saying, "Behold, I am in
your hand" etc. (4) His magnanimity and freedom of
speech, in telling them that God would revenge his
death. Last, his spiritual security and fearlessness of
death in so good a cause and with so good a conscience. COMMENTARY ON JEREMIAH 26:12-16.[9]

HOW OUR LIVES ARE IN GOD'S HANDS. JOHN
CALVIN: By saying that he was "in their hand,"
Jeremiah does not mean that he was not under the
care of God. Christ also spoke thus when he
exhorted his disciples not to fear those who could
kill the body. There is no doubt but that the hairs of
our head are numbered before God; thus it cannot
be that tyrants, however they may rage, can touch
us, no, not with their little finger, except a permission be given them. It is, then, certain that our life
can never be in the hand of human beings, for God
is its faithful keeper. But Jeremiah said this in a
human manner, that his life was in their hand; for
God's providence is hidden from us, nor can we
discover it by the eyes of faith.... We ought yet to
understand that we are by no means so exposed to
the will of the wicked that they can do what they
please with us; for God restrains them by a hidden
bridle, and rules their hands and their hearts....

We now see then in what sense Jeremiah
regarded his life as in the hand of his enemies; not
that he thought himself cast away from God, but
that he acknowledged that loosened reins were
given to the wicked to rage against him.... He
then plainly says that he did not fear death, for the
Lord would presently show himself to be an
avenger and that his blood also would be so
precious in the sight of God that the whole city,
together with the people, would be punished, were
they to deal unjustly with him. COMMENTARY ON
JEREMIAH 26:14.[10]

BE A TRUE TEACHER LIKE JEREMIAH. NIKO-
LAUS SELNECKER: "I am in your hands, do with me
as you yourselves wish; but see clearly that you not
burden yourselves with innocent blood...."
"Where you obey God and his word, and return to
him, then it will go well for you. Where you
proceed in your own ways and do not want to
place your hearts in the Word of God, things will
go badly and God will pursue and punish you; for
God cannot in the least tolerate contempt for his
word and hypocrisy."

---

[8]Knox, *Works*, 3:180-81*. [†]Knox references three prominent Marian
bishops respectively: Stephen Gardiner, bishop of Winchester
(1483–1555), Cuthbert Tunstall, bishop of Durham (1474–1559),
and Edmund Bonner, bishop of London (1500–1559).
[9]Trapp, *A Commentary or Exposition*, 301*.

[10]CTS 19:328-29* (CO 38:525); citing Mt 10:28; 10:30; Lk 12:7.

All godly preachers in our time should follow Jeremiah's example and great effort.... Even if worldly-wise people often try to possess true teachers and say, "It is preferable that you are not Jeremiah, nor a prophet; that you are not John the Baptist or an apostle, that you are not a Luther, or a person for whom we master ourselves, or to whom we should allow ourselves to submit." So true teachers should not be dismayed at such speech and at such a grip of the devil, nor thereby be terrified when they are clearly assigned to the preaching of correction and allow themselves to act on the basis of God's word, and according to the rule of law and gospel. Rather, true preachers should look straight at their office and their calling, and know this: they indeed have the office of Jeremiah, Micah, John, Paul, Ambrose, and other upright prophets, apostles, and teachers in the Old and New Testament; and they lead with the same word as led those above; they serve the same God which the others have served. Teachers today have the same people and listeners as the others once had. Yes, they still have full anger against the boastful godless and the stiff-necked people; they should preach to those who in truth rarely want to orient themselves to the gospel. THE WHOLE PROPHET JEREMIAH 26:14-15.[11]

26:16-24 Jeremiah Is Spared

JEREMIAH IS SAFE IN THE POWER OF GOD.

JOHANNES OECOLAMPADIUS: Because the Lord had promised the prophet in chapter 1 above: "They will fight against you and not prevail, for I am with you." Therefore, he arouses the placid spirits of the princes, because the heart of the king is in the hand of the Lord. Therefore, the judges consistently excuse the prophet, as Pilate excused Christ.... Jeremiah had spoken in the name of the Lord, that is, by the command and authority of God. See how the people now unite themselves with the princes and freely obey when their reasoning has been heard. But the indignation of the priests and the teachers was not satisfied; they say here of the prophet something which would be insanity: to kill the messenger of your God. COMMENTARY ON JEREMIAH 26:16.[12]

PROPHETS AND THE THREAT OF DEATH.

JOHANNES BUGENHAGEN: Whenever we may suffer for the truth and not defend ourselves even with a word, but stay mute like sheep led to slaughter, nevertheless, we ought not condemn or disapprove of what our adversaries do. So Christ did, saying, "If I have spoken well, why do you strike me?" Moreover, "Afterward you will see the Son of Man coming in the clouds of heaven." ... Indeed, no one ought to have doubted this prediction of Jeremiah: "Cease from your evil deeds and God will dwell with you in this place. If you do not cease, you will perish." What other promise and threat is repeated so often in the law of God? What other promise has been made about the temple of Solomon? How much impiety would it be to wish to shed innocent blood in the face of this indubitable truth? And the princes spoke on behalf of freeing Jeremiah on the basis of the counsel of Ahikam, who here perhaps is their chief orator. He used two stories to persuade the people. The first concerning the prophet Micah, whose book exists; the other concerning the prophet Uriah, whose story is not remembered elsewhere in Scripture. At that time, indeed, many pious prophets were killed and their names are in the Book of Life. Here certain people are astonished, because the princes introduced the story of Uriah, who died, to preserve Jeremiah. The brevity of the speech makes this obscure for them; for at that time either the necessity of the case made it brief, or the fact that the story was well known to the people to whom they were saying these things, or perhaps even the writer wrote this account with fewer words than were spoken. But in fact those things that are lacking here, the prudent reader can add to the narrative in this way: "Hezekiah did not kill Micah while he was prophesying and the Lord afterward with a great miracle freed this city from the hand of the Assyrians. But in fact Jehoiakim did kill Uriah while he was

---

[11]Selnecker, Der gantze Prophet Jeremias, V4v-X1r.

[12]Oecolampadius, In Hieremiam, 2:K3r; citing Jer 1:19; Jn 18:33-38.

prophesying similar things. And thereafter the mercenaries of Syria came against us and Jehoiachin, our king, with his queen, princes, nobility, and artisans, were led away by the king of Babylon. Therefore, the first case is to be imitated, so that it goes well for us, but one must beware the second case, lest something evil happens to us. Therefore, Jeremiah is not to be killed." COMMENTARY ON JEREMIAH 26:15-24.[13]

THE PERSECUTION OF THE PROPHETS—OLD TESTAMENT AND REFORMATION. HULDRYCH ZWINGLI: "I am in your hands." "When you rage at me—as far as concerns me and my person—I am in your power and you can surely kill me. But you will not overcome or oppress justice and truth. Nothing depends on my life. But you will awaken God's wrath against you and make it come fiercely, whenever you spill my innocent blood." So whoever proclaims God's word has to offer up their life. . . .

One of the greatest, like John the Baptist, is killed; the lesser like Peter escapes. Or just the reverse: Jeremiah—the greater one—escapes, and the lesser Uriah is killed. Here one recognizes the free choice and deliberations of God. Despite what people think and describe to themselves about their plans, things happen based on God's providence and order. Indeed, on the basis of a specific order and plan God makes things favorable for Jeremiah before the priests, so that he is saved from death. But he allows King Jehoiakim, who was enraged and hostile toward Uriah, to kill him. Yet we are mistaken if we judge these things too harshly. We see someone who is terribly enraged and berserk, so we attribute that to the person. When that person has improved and found relief, we think that the matter is resolved. But God has only chosen in one place or another to help the assailant and brute. So we attribute this to the most immediate cause, when it was actually and originally arranged by God; he guides all things—like a mason hammering a stone. Indeed, this

happens because God has decided to make clear his secret plans and intentions for people, even to many hearts, as Simeon said of Christ in Luke 2. Thus the prostitutes and rogues went to Christ; they spent time with him and did not kill him. But the Pharisees, who were viewed as godly and holy, despised, maligned, and killed him. . . .

This is the much greater destruction and form of sinning: to spill innocent blood and then want to be seen as godly. Yes, in war and the shedding of blood a desire to possess and gather riches takes hold and a kind of lust is indulged. But what a horrible vice it is when innocent Christian blood is shed. Ask yourself this: before anyone preached the gospel clearly and lucidly, who had the name of God and Jesus Christ on their lips more often than the monks, nuns, and priests? And who has resisted the gospel more now that it has come? Who persecutes it more? So it becomes clear that their godliness is really hypocrisy and deceit; for if they had the truth, they would have approved of the gospel when it came. Someone today says or proclaims: "Zurich will be destroyed"; or one might say, "Here Zurich stands, but it will become nothing but a wolf's cave" (when one thinks on their malice). When indifferent people hear such things by chance, they assume that they must be true. Say this before people and they do not weigh if these things are true; so they take this evil and twist it further. Those rascals, rogues, and heretics say, "Look! The city will be destroyed and turned into a wolf's den or a wolf's cave." "The city is neither true nor fair; yes, it is unfaithful and rebellious, and the people there care not!" There are other reasons this should trouble you; some you do not see. Yes, indeed, the shoe stomps on yet another toe: they do not look to the welfare of the city, but to their own advantage (those evil goblins!).

Thus they persecute the godly prophets and cannot tolerate the truth, but they strike against us and kill the prophets. So it happened with Christ, and so likewise with the apostles and prophets. SERMON ON JEREMIAH 26:14-24.[14]

---

[13]Bugenhagen, *In Ieremiam*, 4G4r-v; citing Jn 18:23; Mt 26:64; Mk 13:26; 14:62; Lk 21:27.

[14]Zwingli, *Predigten*, 243-45.

JEREMIAH 27:1-22
THE YOKE OF NEBUCHADNEZZAR

¹*In the beginning of the reign of Zedekiah*ᵃ *the son of Josiah, king of Judah, this word came to Jeremiah from the LORD.* ²*Thus the LORD said to me:* "*Make yourself straps and yoke-bars, and put them on your neck.* ³*Send word*ᵇ *to the king of Edom, the king of Moab, the king of the sons of Ammon, the king of Tyre, and the king of Sidon by the hand of the envoys who have come to Jerusalem to Zedekiah king of Judah.* ⁴*Give them this charge for their masters: 'Thus says the LORD of hosts, the God of Israel: This is what you shall say to your masters:* ⁵"*It is I who by my great power and my outstretched arm have made the earth, with the men and animals that are on the earth, and I give it to whomever it seems right to me.* ⁶*Now I have given all these lands into the hand of Nebuchadnezzar, the king of Babylon, my servant, and I have given him also the beasts of the field to serve him.* ⁷*All the nations shall serve him and his son and his grandson, until the time of his own land comes. Then many nations and great kings shall make him their slave.*

⁸"""*But if any nation or kingdom will not serve this Nebuchadnezzar king of Babylon, and put its neck under the yoke of the king of Babylon, I will punish that nation with the sword, with famine, and with pestilence, declares the LORD, until I have consumed it by his hand.* ⁹*So do not listen to your prophets, your diviners, your dreamers, your fortune-tellers, or your sorcerers, who are saying to you, 'You shall not serve the king of Babylon.'* ¹⁰*For it is a lie that they are prophesying to you, with the result that you will be removed far from your land, and I will drive you out, and you will perish.* ¹¹*But any nation that will bring its neck under the yoke of the king of Babylon and serve him, I will leave on its own land, to work it and dwell there, declares the LORD.*""'"

¹²*To Zedekiah king of Judah I spoke in like manner:* "*Bring your necks under the yoke of the king of Babylon, and serve him and his people and live.* ¹³*Why will you and your people die by the sword, by famine, and by pestilence, as the LORD has spoken concerning any nation that will not serve the king of Babylon?* ¹⁴*Do not listen to the words of the prophets who are saying to you, 'You shall not serve the king of Babylon,' for it is a lie that they are prophesying to you.* ¹⁵*I have not sent them, declares the LORD, but they are prophesying falsely in my name, with the result that I will drive you out and you will perish, you and the prophets who are prophesying to you.*"

¹⁶*Then I spoke to the priests and to all this people, saying,* "*Thus says the LORD: Do not listen to the words of your prophets who are prophesying to you, saying, 'Behold, the vessels of the LORD's house will now shortly be brought back from Babylon,' for it is a lie that they are prophesying to you.* ¹⁷*Do not listen to them; serve the king of Babylon and live. Why should this city become a desolation?* ¹⁸*If they are prophets, and if the word of the LORD is with them, then let them intercede with the LORD of hosts, that the vessels that are left in the house of the LORD, in the house of the king of Judah, and in Jerusalem may not go to Babylon.* ¹⁹*For thus says the LORD of hosts concerning the pillars, the sea, the stands, and the rest of the vessels that are left in this city,* ²⁰*which Nebuchadnezzar king of Babylon did not take away, when he took into exile from Jerusalem to Babylon Jeconiah the son of Jehoiakim, king of Judah, and all the nobles of Judah and Jerusalem—* ²¹*thus says the LORD of hosts, the God of Israel, concerning the vessels that are left in the house of the LORD, in the house of the king of Judah, and in Jerusalem:* ²²*They shall be carried to Babylon and remain there until the day when I visit them, declares the LORD. Then I will bring them back and restore them to this place.*"

a Or *Jehoiakim*   **b** Hebrew *Send them*

OVERVIEW: The nature of the Word of God and the Word as related to true and false prophecies shape this chapter and thereby the work of Reformation expositors. During the sixteenth century, scholars were examining not only the meaning of the text but also the text itself in order to come up with a reliable and accurate Bible in Hebrew and Greek. This text would be a basis for their own translations into Latin and vernacular languages. In fact, along with their commentary many authors often included their own translations, which they in turn elaborated and justified. Discussion of Jeremiah 27:1 is such an example that reflects both their textual and historical assumptions. Moreover, interpreters continued in the chapter to ponder the nature of signs and their relation to the Word as well as the nature of true prophecies and the counterfeit versions that convinced followers to seek alternatives. Indeed, a preference for "good news" and happy outcomes in prophecy often interfere with the ability to hear the true Word of God. If they did not listen carefully to God, false prophets might also incite rebellion against the rulers God has established.

27:1-11 The Signs of the Yoke

WHY DOES JEREMIAH REFER TO JEHOIAKIM?
JOHN CALVIN: Jeremiah prefaces this prediction by saying that it was delivered at the beginning of Jehoiakim's reign. But this beginning . . . extended to the whole of his reign while it was prosperous and entire. While, then, Jehoiakim enjoyed a quiet possession of the kingdom, Jeremiah was bidden to make known what had been committed to him, not to Jehoiakim himself, but, as we learn from the third verse, to Zedekiah. COMMENTARY ON JEREMIAH 27:1.[1]

ZEDEKIAH, NOT JEHOIAKIM. JOHANNES
BUGENHAGEN: Interpreters torment themselves at the beginning of this chapter. How is it that Jeremiah is speaking to Zedekiah as king of Judah

in verse 3 and yet doing so at the beginning of the reign of Jehoiakim in verse 1, when there are twelve years between the beginning of the reign of Jehoiakim and the reign of Zedekiah?[†]

. . . Therefore, I, while leaving that opinion to others and not being led by vain arguments, simply believe that in this verse an error has crept into the Hebrew Bible, because now Jehoiakim is read for Zedekiah. For the prophet spoke to the legates of the nations that were sent to Zedekiah, king of Judah, and he is the same Zedekiah. But in truth an error in this passage could very easily have happened to the copyists, because of the similar words at the beginning of chapter 26 and chapter 27. Indeed, both chapters begin, "In the beginning of the reign of [insert name], the son of Josiah, king of Judah, this word came. . . ." Finally, in the following chapter, Jeremiah is most clearly speaking in resonance with me: "And it came to pass in the same year, in the beginning of the reign of Zedekiah," etc. These reasons are utterly certain for me, not by my authority, but from this prophet himself and the truth of history. COMMENTARY ON JEREMIAH 27:1.[2]

CORRECTING THE TEXT. NIKOLAUS SELNECKER:
"In the beginning of the kingdom of Jehoiakim. . . ." We do not want to deviate from the order of history; for it is certain that between the beginning of the kingdom of Jehoiakim and the beginning of the lordship of Zedekiah, about which Jeremiah shall speak below, there is a span of eleven years. Therefore, there is no doubt that here an error has occurred in the copying—as can easily happen—and that Jehoiakim has replaced Zedekiah as the "son of Josiah," which is what stands at the beginning of the previous chapter. THE WHOLE PROPHET JEREMIAH 27:1.[3]

---

[1]CTS 19:348* (CO 38:540).
[2]Bugenhagen, *In Ieremiam*, 4H2v-4H3r; citing Jer 28:1. [†]The Masoretic Hebrew text and the Vulgate of Jeremiah 27:1 reads "In the beginning of the reign of Jehoiakim." Only a few Hebrew manuscripts, along with the Syriac and Arabic translations, correct "Jehoiakim" to "Zedekiah," which is demanded by context. The Old Greek Septuagint version omits Masoretic verse 1 entirely. Though the KJV and its derivatives retain Jehoiakim, most modern translations (e.g., NRSV, NIV, ESV) go with Zedekiah.
[3]Selnecker, *Der gantze Prophet Jeremias*, X3r; citing Jer 26:1.

WORD AND SIGN IN THE PROPHETS. MARTIN LUTHER: It is a custom of all the prophets to add and attach to their word a sign that is like the word. Thus Isaiah did . . . when he walked naked as a sign that the king of Assyria would pillage the land of Egypt, and Jeremiah wore thongs and yoke bars on his neck when he proclaimed the tyranny of the king of Babylon to all the Gentiles. Thus, too, the rainbow was given to Noah as a sign and circumcision to Abraham, etc. But to us Christians baptism and the sacrament were given. LECTURES ON ZECHARIAH 6:9-10.[4]

SIGNS TEACH THE WORD. MARTIN LUTHER: This is a customary procedure with the prophets. When the ungodly refuse to believe the bare Word, the prophets add an external sign. So Jeremiah, getting no results when he predicted the Babylonian captivity, wore a chain around his neck as an external sign. . . . Thus in our time the Word is read and taught by means of the tongue, the pen, songs, and paintings as a witness to the ungodly. LECTURE ON ISAIAH 30:8.[5]

TEACHING TRUE FAITH AND THE SENSES. HULDRYCH ZWINGLI: "Fit ropes and chains to your neck." What need was there for this example or odd sign? Indeed was it not enough to give a verbal warning? Unless the real reason was that these kinds of deeds would move people to accept the warnings by stirring more of the senses, and therefore working more dramatically than when only one sense is moved. If Jeremiah had only preached, the hearing alone would receive impact. But when he displays to the sight a portent similar to that which he preaches, then the two most exalted senses are excited, and arrogance is broken while lethargy is lessened. Likewise in the Lord's Supper, the mind is led more dramatically to contemplate what is done, while the symbols of seeing and tasting suggest the same thing that is preached to the ears. Nevertheless, these things are all external. Indeed only faith, which sits and rules at home, takes in the meaning of these things. If faith is lacking, then hearing the Word, seeing the gesture, and tasting the symbol inspires nothing but laughter: indeed, the gospel is foolish to the unbelieving nations. But how do these things arrive at faith, or how do they create it, or enter into it at all, and support it? Faith—that is, true faith—manifests the certainty and full assurance of grace and divine friendship. This faith is given by no one except the Father who draws us to him: therefore no external things are able to give it or make it. EXPLANATIONS OF THE PROPHET JEREMIAH 27:2.[6]

A TOLERABLE SERVITUDE. JOHANNES OECOLAMPADIUS: This prophecy is spoken against rebellious magistrates and their princes, who wanted to change the divine order apart from the divine command, forgetting covenant and servitude. For Zedekiah was bound to the king of Babylon, who had made him king and had put him in command over five neighboring kings. So Zedekiah called to himself and accepted visiting legates from the neighboring peoples, inciting many to break treaties. Thus those legates were sent from neighboring kingdoms, so that they might consult in common on defecting from Babylon. To those legates Jeremiah was ordered to speak. Therefore, God ordered him to do what ought to have been done first after eleven years. He prepared straps and a yoke and wore them on his neck as he was ordered, so that when Zedekiah had entered the kingdom Jeremiah might incite both Zedekiah and the neighboring kings with the same outrageous act, so that they would not oppose the will of the Lord. Indeed, as Jeremiah bore the yoke tied with straps to his neck, so those rebellious kings were to bear the yoke of Babylon. He seems, however, to have prepared many straps and yokes, so that he could give one to each legate to take to his lord, and at the same time to have affirmed with words that each one of them was going to undergo a Babylonian yoke on his neck for himself.

---

[4]LW 20:253* (WA 23:584); citing Is 20:2-6; Gen 9:12-16; 17:10.
[5]LW 16:255 (WA 31.2:185-86).

[6]Zwingli, *Complanationis*, 131.

You see the perpetual use of symbols; this is one which presents the grace of Christ. . . . Here we learn that the cross must be borne even under various lords and liberation through the Lord must be awaited, even if we believe that God is one. Thus the captivity of their country is announced to the legates, who were striving against the Lord to shake off a tolerable servitude. Indeed, they wanted to free themselves and yet they entangled themselves more seriously with a captivity that is signified by the chains and the yoke on their necks. They add burden to burden, just as he explained the year before. It is the custom, however, of the prophet, to fashion his prophecy with some sign and then to explain it with words. In this way he takes on the character of his people; for the neighboring peoples who remain have been captured with the Jews. Jeremiah signifies that when he sends them the yokes.

"And you shall command them." They have to work with a new command and a greater admonition. Indeed, lest they think that nothing pertains to themselves of what the Lord God of Israel speaks to the nations, he shows his omnipotence—that he created heaven and earth, that a human being is his and all things that serve human beings. And therefore his authority extends even to the Moabites and to the other peoples, whom he puts under a lord by his own decision. COMMENTARY ON JEREMIAH 27:2-4.[7]

GOD AND FOREIGN KINGDOMS. NIKOLAUS SELNECKER: This teaching is about all of the kingdoms, lands, and peoples about which Daniel speaks in chapter 2. God destroys kingdoms and sets up kings. Here God himself speaks, "I give the earth, people, and cattle to whomever I will. And now I have given all of these lands to the king of Babylon, which he shall rule over as lord." Thus, because of the sins of both lords and subjects the kingdoms and territories are destroyed and new and foreign rule overcomes them. Thus, one must be obedient according to God's order and command.

As God says to Nebuchadnezzar: "All the nations shall serve him, his son, and his son's son," until the time that the Persians overwhelm their land and it falls. And Jeremiah names Nebuchadnezzar, his son—Awil-Marduk—who was king for thirty years, and his son, Balthasar, who reigned for five years. He was executed by Cyrus when he captured the city of Babylon along with his treasurers. That is the appointed time about which God speaks here: how long the Babylonian kingdom will yet exist—about eighty years. Thereafter, the kingdom must come to the Persians, as it would happen. . . .

The next teaching is about obedience, that we are obligated to obey the authorities. As Paul preached in Romans 13, there is no power except from God alone and the current power under which we exist and live is ordained by God. Whoever resists this power resists the order of God. THE WHOLE PROPHET JEREMIAH 27:5-8.[8]

RELYING ON THE CROSS OR THE SWORD. JOHANNES OECOLAMPADIUS: "And there will be a nation and a kingdom": Whoever flees the frost against the will of God, the snow will fall on him; he who bears the cross placidly will be saved and will live tranquilly. In fact, they will find rest for their soul with Christ. But whoever rebels and takes on the sword for himself, and whoever has rebelled will perish by the sword of the Lord, either in a dismal war or in public contagion or even worse in a deadly famine; for the yoke is imposed on those who are unwilling. They now want to shake off the yoke. The Lord distributes the kingdoms of the nations and usually does so in the same manner also among his people, even if divine power deceives human intelligence with the diversity of things, and they think most things happen by chance. COMMENTARY ON JEREMIAH 27:8.[9]

GOD'S PLAN, TRUE PRAYER, AND FALSE PROPHETS. NIKOLAUS SELNECKER: The next teaching concerns false prophets and hypocritical

---

[7]Oecolampadius, *In Hieremiam*, 2:K4v-L1r.

[8]Selnecker, *Der gantze Prophet Jeremias*, X4r; citing Rom 13:1-7.
[9]Oecolampadius, *In Hieremiam*, 2:L1v.

preachers, who console the authorities and the people in the flesh. It is certain that everyone is evil and that punishment will certainly appear. But as it says in the following chapter, the false prophets preach only peace and full consolation. They are in no difficulty, yet they are certainly overconfident and godless, and do not know how to pray in a godly way. They can claim almost nothing from God. As their teaching is false, so their prayers are also false and will not be heard even if they say they are ambitious in prayer. But true teachers have God's Word; they can also pray and God will hear them. They know that God will not let their prayers be in vain, even if he waits a while to answer or it seems as if he has disappeared or closed his ears. The God-fearing know that when a punishment must come upon godless and overconfident people God still hears the prayers of the God-fearing and at the right time will help his own. So it is at the end of this passage. "They must remain in Babylon until I bring them home at the right time." As Peter says, "Humble yourselves under the mighty hand of God so that he may lift you up in his due time." God knows fully when the best times are for things. So we need not concern ourselves, but should trust in him. THE WHOLE PROPHET JEREMIAH 27:9-11.[10]

27:12-22 Do Not Listen to False Prophets

THE AUTHORITY OF PROPHETS AND KINGS. JOHN CALVIN: [Jeremiah] was set over kingdoms and nations; for the doctrine taught by the prophets is higher than all earthly rankings. Jeremiah was, indeed, one of the people, and did not exempt himself from the authority of the king. Nor did he pretend that he was released from the laws because he possessed that high dignity by which he was superior to kings, as the papal clergy do, who boast ridiculously of their immunity, which is nothing else but a license to live in wickedness. The prophet then kept himself in his own rank like others; and yet when he had to

exercise his spiritual jurisdiction in God's name, he spared neither the king nor his counselors; for he knew that his doctrine was above all kings; the prophetic office, then, is eminent above all the ranks of kings. COMMENTARY ON JEREMIAH 27:12.[11]

TRUE PROPHECY IN SCRIPTURE AND LACK OF PROPHECY TODAY. JOHN CALVIN: The object [of this prophecy] is to show the Jews that they were not to receive thoughtlessly everything presented to them under God's name, but that they were to exercise discrimination and judgment. This is a passage worthy of special notice, for the devil has ever falsely assumed God's name; and for all the errors and delusions which have ever prevailed in the world he has not obtained credit otherwise than by his false pretense. And in this day we see that many are willfully blind because they think they are excused before God, if they can pretend ignorance, and they say that they are not wickedly credulous. . . . We ought to distinguish the true from false prophets; for what purpose? So that we may receive them only, and depend on the words of those who have been sent by the Lord.

It may be here asked, how did this difference come to be? It was formerly necessary for prophets to be raised in a special manner, for it was a special gift to predict future and hidden events. Hence the prophetic office was not an ordinary office like the priestly. That promise indeed ever continued in force, "A prophet will I raise to you from the midst of your brethren." But though this was a perpetual favor conferred by God on the Israelites, yet the prophets were ever called in a special manner; no one was to take this office except endued with an extraordinary gift. Though Jeremiah was a priest, yet he was not on that account a prophet; but God as we have seen made him a prophet. But with regard to us the matter is different, for God does not in this day predict hidden events; but he would have us be satisfied with his gospel, for in it is made known to us the perfection of wisdom. We live now in "the fullness of time." God does not reveal

---

[10]Selnecker, *Der gantze Prophet Jeremias*, X4v; citing 1 Pet 5:6.

[11]CTS 19:368* (CO 38:552).

prophecies so as to point out this or that thing to us in particular. We may now obtain certainty as to the truth, if we form our judgment according the Law and the Prophets, and the Gospel. There is indeed need of the spirit of discernment. . . . So also now all doctrines ought to be examined by us; and if we follow this rule, we shall never go astray. COMMENTARY ON JEREMIAH 27:15.[12]

TRUSTING IN A HAPPY ALTERNATIVE. JOHANNES OECOLAMPADIUS: "To the priests." After the nations, king, and nobles of the people, Jeremiah was speaking jointly to the priests and all the people because there was much familiarity between the worshiping people and the Mystagogues. See the wickedness of the false prophets. It is not enough that they were instructed that the captivity of the city was threatened, but they completely preserved a contrary happiness that things in Babylon were about to fall and the vessels of the temple that were taken off with Jehoiachin, the princes, and his mother, were about to be restored at once; so quickly that at that point in time they were asserting that the vicissitudes of things were about to change. . . . They loved to claim contrary things that were fully opposed to the truth. They were lying preachers. COMMENTARY ON JEREMIAH 27:16.[13]

SUBMIT TO THE LORD AND TO BABYLON. KONRAD PELLIKAN: King Jehoiachin, his mother, and the leading citizens had already been led off to Babylon along with certain vessels that were taken from both the palace of the king and then from the temple of Solomon. But there were prophets and priests in Jerusalem, who were promising to the king and the people a return from captivity and the restoration of these kinds of vessels to their place. They should not surrender themselves up to Babylon, and instead not honor the agreement of Babylon's appointed prefects, because it was

forbidden that the holy city and temple of the Lord should come under a godless king.

Jeremiah spoke against them, contending that the prophets and priests were liars, at the same time asserting that the idea that the vessels that had been taken away would be returned was so far from being true; even those vessels that remained in the temple would soon follow as well. If they did not listen to the word of the Lord, they would be driven off to Babylon along with all the vessels and all the people. And he asserted that they were far better advised to serve the king of Babylon, than to try gratuitously for liberty, which they were never going to get. Jeremiah testified that whoever did not submit themselves to the word of the Lord and the king of Babylon would die and the city would be destroyed. COMMENTARY ON JEREMIAH 27:16-17.[14]

PROPHETS INCAPABLE OF PRAYER. JOHANNES BUGENHAGEN: "And if there are prophets, etc." These words clearly show that only those who truly have the Word of God are able to pray and intercede in times of need. Others are not able to do so: whenever hypocrites flourish and seem holy, heretics and spiritual fanatics, nevertheless, even if they boast dramatically of the Spirit, are not able to pray and are desperate in temptation. Isaiah 64: "There is no one who calls on your name, and rises up and takes hold of you." And nevertheless they all boasted in the highest worship of God and killed the prophets of true worship and condemned them. COMMENTARY ON JEREMIAH 27:18.[15]

THE FATE OF THE TEMPLE'S VESSELS AND ORNAMENTS. JOHN CALVIN: Nebuchadnezzar had in part spared the temple and the city; he had taken away chiefly the precious vessels, but had not entirely despoiled the temple of its ornaments. As then some splendor was still to be seen there, the Jews ought to have learned that God had acted kindly toward them. . . .

---

[12]CTS 19:372-73* (CO 38:554-55); citing Deut 18:18; Gal 4:4.
[13]Oecolampadius, *In Hieremiam*, 2:L3r. By "Mystagogues" Oecolampadius likely implies that the priests and prophets were initiating people into the rites of idolatrous cults.

[14]Pellikan, *Commentaria Bibliorum*, 3:2T6v.
[15]Bugenhagen, *In Ieremiam*, 4H4r; citing Is 64:7.

". . . Concerning the pillars" etc. there is no doubt but that Solomon spent much money on the pillars, as the Scripture commends his work. He adds "concerning the sea," which was a very large vessel, for from it the priests took water to wash themselves whenever they entered the temple to perform their sacred duties. And though it was made of brass, it was yet of no small value on account of its largeness. . . .

[Jeremiah] also adds "the residue of the vessels." . . . Jeremiah indirectly condemned the Jews, because they did not acknowledge that the cruelty of their enemy had been moderated by divine power. For we know how cruel the Babylonians were and how insatiable their avarice was, and that nothing would have been left in the temple had not their hands been in a manner restrained by the hidden power of God. COMMENTARY ON JEREMIAH 27:19-20.[16]

HOW THE PROPHET SPEAKS OF GOD'S JUDGMENT AND CLEMENCY. KONRAD PELLIKAN: The king of Babylon would take away and break up all the bronze that had not been removed during the first transmigration with Jehoiachin. Moreover, for as long a time as they had been in that place, that is how long the captivity of the Jews, nay even the Babylonian kingdom, would last—namely, until Cyrus after the destruction of Babylon would at the command of God grant the right of return to those who wished it—that is, after seventy years. For the returning settlers the ceremonial worship of God would be clearly promulgated, and the whole temple and priesthood would be appointed, until the lord would visit. This, as it was insupportable, was so beyond belief to the priests that they could not avoid persecuting Jeremiah, until it was all fulfilled. So it is for all enemies of the prophets, and despisers of the Word of God: they do not cease to hate the truth and godliness until they are pressed down by the weight of the divine judgment hanging over them. The prophet was not quiet about the clemency of God, neither did the Lord want his clemency to be ignored by sinners, if at any time, even rather late, they might be turned away from their faithlessness and iniquity. But here he promised them that mercy would not be denied them in the future. Indeed, he promises that they would return in their own time to their own place. Nevertheless he did not speak of that return with happiness and joy. Indeed it was a humble description. He would save the palm and the glory for a certain more famous redemption, which was to come through Christ; concerning this Isaiah beforehand had promised a great deal and about this Jeremiah was not silent. COMMENTARY ON JEREMIAH 27:21-22.[17]

---

[16]CTS 19:382-83* (CO 38:561-62).

[17]Pellikan, *Commentaria Bibliorum*, 3:2T6v-2V1r.

JEREMIAH 28:1-17
A FALSE PROPHET

¹In that same year, at the beginning of the reign of Zedekiah king of Judah, in the fifth month of the fourth year, Hananiah the son of Azzur, the prophet from Gibeon, spoke to me in the house of the LORD, in the presence of the priests and all the people, saying, ²"Thus says the LORD of hosts, the God of Israel: I have broken the yoke of the king of Babylon. ³Within two years I will bring back to this place all the vessels of the LORD's house, which Nebuchadnezzar king of Babylon took away from this place and carried to Babylon. ⁴I will also bring back to this place Jeconiah the son of Jehoiakim, king of Judah, and all the exiles from Judah who went to Babylon, declares the Lord, for I will break the yoke of the king of Babylon."

⁵Then the prophet Jeremiah spoke to Hananiah the prophet in the presence of the priests and all the people who were standing in the house of the LORD, ⁶and the prophet Jeremiah said, "Amen! May the LORD do so; may the LORD make the words that you have prophesied come true, and bring back to this place from Babylon the vessels of the house of the LORD, and all the exiles. ⁷Yet hear now this word that I speak in your hearing and in the hearing of all the people. ⁸The prophets who preceded you and me from ancient times prophesied war, famine, and pestilence against many countries and great kingdoms. ⁹As for the prophet who prophesies peace, when the word of that prophet comes to pass, then it will be known that the LORD has truly sent the prophet."

¹⁰Then the prophet Hananiah took the yoke-bars from the neck of Jeremiah the prophet and broke them. ¹¹And Hananiah spoke in the presence of all the people, saying, "Thus says the LORD: Even so will I break the yoke of Nebuchadnezzar king of Babylon from the neck of all the nations within two years." But Jeremiah the prophet went his way.

¹²Sometime after the prophet Hananiah had broken the yoke-bars from off the neck of Jeremiah the prophet, the word of the LORD came to Jeremiah: ¹³"Go, tell Hananiah, 'Thus says the LORD: You have broken wooden bars, but you have made in their place bars of iron. ¹⁴For thus says the LORD of hosts, the God of Israel: I have put upon the neck of all these nations an iron yoke to serve Nebuchadnezzar king of Babylon, and they shall serve him, for I have given to him even the beasts of the field.'" ¹⁵And Jeremiah the prophet said to the prophet Hananiah, "Listen, Hananiah, the Lord has not sent you, and you have made this people trust in a lie. ¹⁶Therefore thus says the Lord: 'Behold, I will remove you from the face of the earth. This year you shall die, because you have uttered rebellion against the Lord.'"

¹⁷In that same year, in the seventh month, the prophet Hananiah died.

OVERVIEW: Identifying the true and false messengers of God was a pressing issue for religious leaders in the Reformation era. At the very least false prophecy might generate confusion and dissent; at the worst it could foment violent rebellion and social upheaval. How then is a true prophet to be distinguished from a deceptive one? How is a false prophet to be confronted or handled? What are the signs and thematic markers of a true prophecy or a false one? The answers to these questions have grave implications for the intensity of divine judgment. Jeremiah's encounters with Hananiah provided a graphic portrayal of faithful prophecy, deceptive proclamations, and divine retribution.

28:1-11 Hananiah Opposes Jeremiah

HOW TO SPEAK TO A FALSE PROPHET. NIKO-LAUS SELNECKER: Because the false prophets and fellow pastors could neither attack the godly Jeremiah with open aggression, nor take away his honor, a false prophet steps forward and preaches against Jeremiah and reprimands him for lying. What Jeremiah had established before, the false prophet denies; he acts as a preacher of consolation who gives the people what they want to hear: "There is no difficulty ahead, and Jeremiah has not proceeded correctly when he says that God would punish the king and the people and that they would surrender to the king of Babylon. But the mirror opposite would occur. The king of Babylon would be laid low and defeated. Moreover, the people would again rise up and live in prosperity." Therefore, Hananiah took the yoke from Jeremiah's neck and broke it; we heard in the previous chapter that God had told the prophet Jeremiah to make the yoke as a sign of future captivity and servitude. Hananiah broke the yoke and held Jeremiah for a fool, liar, and rebel. Therefore, we see how God's word is always challenged. The more valuable and upright a teacher is, the more they are tormented and challenged; not only by enemies and adversaries, but also by friends, who should lead with them in this teaching and teach with them from a church pulpit. Therefore, Bernard of Clairvaux says, "There is peace from heretics and peace from pagans, but not from false brothers."[†] At the same time that we have peace from heretics and adversaries, we can have no peace with false brothers, who envy, hate, attack, and belittle us and for whom we can do nothing right—we cannot teach, speak, or preach. In the end, we do what we must.

Jeremiah answered and said, "Amen." That is, "I see willingly from the heart what you have said—that I have been lying." Still every true teacher sees some things without gladness, but that is the work they must do as a preacher of repentance and they must complete this work. You may always wish that it would not be so and that the future punishments you are to show might not happen. . . .

But Jeremiah does allow his "Amen" to be his last word (as we often say, "Oh, I only wish that what you are saying was true"). But he acts and speaks to the matters at hand. When a prophet predicts peace

and then there is always evil, so all the vices come into play. That is, one never finds that God's prophets and upright teachers have proclaimed consolation to unrepentant people, but only torment and punishment. For then one should certainly only preach the law and show the wrath of God. But false teachers always say, "There is no problem; everything is good for us. There is a good peace." They say what truly pleases the godless people. The false prophets choose not to anger or burden anyone with the ungracious or unfavorable things they find unbearable. But in the end, the truth wins out. Instead of the broken wood yoke, an iron yoke is made and Hananiah must die in the same year. THE WHOLE PROPHET JEREMIAH 28.[1]

MEN OF BLOOD AND TREACHERY. JOHANNES BUGENHAGEN: When the impious priests were hindered by the princes, so that they were not able to shed the innocent blood of Jeremiah, they turned to deception and lies, so that they might at least turn Jeremiah from his prophecy, which was intolerable to themselves. The Psalms call such defenders of perverse doctrine (like our papists) "men of blood and treachery." There is no doubt that even as Hananiah with the counsel of those men prophesied falsehood and lies, so today our papists force on us the theologizing cysts on their tongues. Here, however, Hananiah with such an appearance and authority seems to have been something extraordinary. He used that simplicity of words, so that he was able to deceive even Jeremiah. But when God revealed the truth, he was condemned and died, but not such that the wicked repented so that they might hear the Word of God. COMMENTARY ON JEREMIAH 28.[2]

DISCERNING TRUE AND FALSE PROPHETS. JOHANNES OECOLAMPADIUS: That year was the beginning of the reign, in which Zedekiah commanded five neighboring kings. Therefore it says "in

---

[1]Selnecker, *Der gantze Prophet Jeremias*, Y1r-Y2v. [†]Bernard of Clairvaux (1090–1153), *Sermon on the Song of Songs* 33, par. 16. [2]Bugenhagen, *In Ieremiam*, 4I4Iv; citing Ps 5:6; 55:23.

the beginning of the reign of Zedekiah" (you must supply, "over five other kings"). Thus, right away Zedekiah considered rebellion from the rule of the king of the Babylonians. So the prophecy above was confirmed through a testing of the prophet Jeremiah: that not only would they not shake off the yoke, but that they were going to make it heavier and remake it from wood to iron. The prophet Jeremiah was tested through a pseudo-prophet well known as to his type and place, who before all the people falsely and severely challenged the truth and through whom Jeremiah was disgraced as if he were a pseudo-prophet. Learn by these examples to discern among the true and false prophet. See in the false prophet a kind of imitation and how under a sheep's skin, the wolf hides the Word of God with a pretense. He may dare to say impudently that his own lies are a divine command, as Hananiah says what the king and others want to hear, namely, about the sorrow of the yoke of Babylon. Meanwhile they are already aspiring among themselves to defect from Babylon. Even as Jeremiah was seeing to an extent the effect on the people and his king, so he prophesied; he knew the cruel exception of Uriah, who preached as Jeremiah did the destruction of the temple. So then Hananiah announced glad things, while he rendered the prophet detested and odious to all. COMMENTARY ON JEREMIAH 28:1.[3]

FALSE AND TREACHEROUS TEACHERS, THEN AND NOW. JOHANNES BUGENHAGEN: So great is the stubbornness and contempt for God among the false teachers that they are not afraid to make light of that command of God, "You shall not take the name of your Lord in vain." In fact, there will be no impunity for one who does so. As it says in the psalm, "Men of blood and treachery will not live half of their days." So the seditious Müntzer perishes with his Zwingli. The Münsterite king perishes with his Anabaptist prophets.[†] Our papists want us to perish.... So Hananiah dares to prophesy falsely with other false prophets with great boasting of the spirit and with signs as if divine: 1 Kings 22—and

likewise all the impious teachers above in Jeremiah chapter 23. They are all condemned by the second commandment of the law: "It is a dreadful thing to fall into the hand of the living God." COMMENTARY ON JEREMIAH 28:2.[4]

DISTORTING THE MESSAGE OF THE ANCIENT PROPHETS. HULDRYCH ZWINGLI: Here perhaps it was suitable to leave bygone times behind. For in order that the impudence of the imposter might have a nose, the imposter who was just like a true prophet, said that the Lord has already determined that the power of Babylon would be broken. The pestilence of the Anabaptists acts in the same way today: if anyone has threatened anything of the old prophets that is rather steadfast or terrible, then they pollute the same word with their rash mouth, and they twist it among those who do not allow that their stupidity and malice should go away unpunished. There were those among us less than five years ago who were declaring in the marketplaces, as Jonah had done, that in forty days the Thurgau[†] would be overthrown. Moreover, they exclaimed with a savage face, in filthy garments, but with a voice so harsh that you would detect in them anger and bitterness rather than mercy. Some shouted insolently, "Woe to you, Thurgau!" Others shouted, "If they do this in the green, what will happen in the desert?" But who today remembers all of their fabrications, insolence, and audacity? EXPLANATIONS OF THE PROPHET JEREMIAH 28:2.[5]

PROPHETIC CONVICTION AND SYMPATHY FOR THE PEOPLE. JOHN CALVIN: "May God confirm

---

[4]Bugenhagen, *In Ieremiam*, 412r; citing Ex 20:7; Ps 55:23; 1 Kings 22:23; Heb 10:31. †Bugenhagen refers to the pastor and leader in the Peasants' Revolt Thomas Müntzer (d. 1525), to Huldrych Zwingli, as well as members of the radical commune in Münster, Germany (1534–1536); they were executed or died violently in wartime conditions.
[5]Zwingli, *Complanationis*, 134. †A canton in northeastern Switzerland bordering the southern shore of Lake Constance and due northeast from Zurich. The first Protestant preachers received a positive response in the Thurgau, though the account Zwingli gives here may reflect the sort of volatility there that had resulted in the sacking of a monastery in Ittingen in 1524 and remained present in anticlerical sentiments.

---

[3]Oecolampadius, *In Hieremiam*, 2:L3r-v; citing Jer 26:20-23.

your words." . . . There were two feelings in the prophets apparently contrary, and yet they were compatible with one another. Whatever God had commanded them they boldly declared, and thus they forgot their own nation when they announced anything of an adverse kind. Hence, when the prophets threatened the people and said that war or famine was near at hand, they doubtless were so endued with a heroic greatness of mind that, dismissing a regard for the people, they proceeded in the performance of their office. . . . Still they did not wholly put off every humane feeling, but they had sympathy with the miseries of the people; and though they proclaimed destruction upon them, yet they could not but receive sorrow from their own prophecies. There was, therefore, no inconsistency in Jeremiah in wishing the restoration of the vessels of the temple and the return of the exiles, while yet he ever continued in the same mind, as we hereafter shall see. COMMENTARY ON JEREMIAH 28:5-6.[6]

ONE MUST PRAY TRUTHFULLY IN MIND AND SPIRIT. LANCELOT ANDREWES: A person may desire a false thing; so did the prophet give his "Amen" to the false prophecy of Hananiah, but we must be careful that what we pray for is true; therefore, the apostle says that he will not pray "with the Spirit" only but with his "understanding" also. So our Savior tells us that we must "worship" God not in spirit only, but "in spirit and truth"; that is, we must understand that our petitions must be true and agreeable to God's will; for just as in thanksgiving it is requisite that we "sing praise with understanding," so the same must be done in prayer. They are good both to pray with the spirit and with the mind; therefore, it is better to pray with both than with one alone. Therefore, it is a marvel that any should think it enough to pray with the Spirit, though they do not know in their mind what they pray for, but pray in an unknown tongue as the church of Rome does, seeing that the apostle says he "will pray both with the spirit and with the understanding," and this understanding is not of

the words only, but also of the matter that we pray for. SERMON 19 ON THE LORD'S PRAYER.[7]

BE SURE OF YOUR PROPHECY. JOHANNES BUGENHAGEN: It is as if he is speaking up to this point to all the holy prophets who prophesy evil against us based on the threats of God and according to the law handed down through Moses. If, however, the Lord revealed something to you, because meanwhile he would want to show some favor to us, this we will see when it happens. For brief is the time of which you speak, and this has not been revealed to me. Meanwhile nevertheless, Jeremiah hints that it is a sure sign of a lie, whenever some prophet promises peace to those who have contempt for God, to whom God has threatened evils and very foul curses in the law. COMMENTARY ON JEREMIAH 28:8.[8]

TRUE PROPHETS AND TRUE SIGNS. JOHN MAYER: "The prophet that prophesied peace." . . . This is for the most part a certain rule by which to know a true prophet—whenever the event answers his prophecy—because God only sends such a prophet when he knows beforehand what will come to pass, and neither the devil nor humans know except by conjecture, by foretelling things that sometimes are true and sometimes are false. "For let them tell what shall come and we shall say they are God's." This then is the common rule by which to know a prophet, and if by this we cannot know him, then we must observe the target of his aims. If the aim is toward turning people away from God and to idols, then he is a false prophet, although his signs may be true. And this is allowed only as a way of testing the constancy of God's people in cleaving to him. Now Jeremiah proposes the first and most common form of trial: it would not be long until all would be manifest— about two years. So this was the best trial in this case, when two prophets are speaking in contrary fashion and contend for which is the true prophet. COMMENTARY ON JEREMIAH 28:9.[9]

---

[7] Andrewes, *Works*, 5:472-73*; citing 1 Cor 14:15; Jn 4:24; Ps 47:7.
[8] Bugenhagen, *In Ieremiam*, 4I2r-v.
[9] Mayer, *A Commentary*, 423*.

---

[6] CTS 19:392-93* (CO 38:568).

A New Word from the Lord? JOHANNES
OECOLAMPADIUS: When the godless see that
impiety is prospering, they swell up more; they
abuse the tenderness of God and his ministers.
Until now Jeremiah was preserving the symbol of
captivity on his neck. With this sign he was
contradicting the lie of Hananiah, that he did not
refute by mouth because he had not yet received a
new word from the Lord. Hananiah, not bearing
this, asserted the opposite in the prophetic fashion
by breaking the yoke and with an added speech.
Prior to this he usually taught through a symbol
and after that explained its significance with words.
COMMENTARY ON JEREMIAH 28:10.[10]

A Prophet Does Not Speak in Haste.
KONRAD PELLIKAN: The false prophet, who was
bold not only with words but also with deeds,
broke the shackle that he had injuriously snatched
off of Jeremiah's neck; evidently it was a shackle of
wood, for he certainly would not have been able to
break an iron one. However, Jeremiah, the prophet
of the Lord, bore this humbly, prudently, and
patiently in silence. He disguised his anguish.
Indeed, the Lord had not revealed to him what he
was to say. For the speech of saints is not hasty.
Prophets do not speak of things to come by their
own judgment, but by the divine will, whose
preconception alone is certain of the future. It is
not always a time for speaking. Jeremiah returned
home, confused not in his conscience, but in the
opinion of the crowd. He did not doubt that by
some reckoning the truth would be helped and the
lie would be suppressed. He yielded to impudence
and madness, as long as it was allowed through the
Lord, who soon called him back, not willing that a
lie should rule in perpetuity. COMMENTARY ON
JEREMIAH 28:10-11.[11]

A Time to Be Silent. JOHN CALVIN: We are
hereby reminded that we ought to consider what
occasions may require; for it is neither right nor

useful to speak always and everywhere. When,
therefore, the Lord opens our mouth, no difficulties ought to restrain us so as not to speak boldly;
but when there is no hope of doing good, it is
better sometimes to be silent than to excite a
great multitude without any profit. True indeed
is that saying of Paul that we ought to be ready
out of season; but he means that the ministers of
Christ, though they may sometimes offend and
exasperate the minds of many, should not desist,
but persevere. But Jeremiah had no hearers, and
the whole people were so incensed that he could
do nothing against that imposter even if he
exposed himself to death. He therefore was silent,
for he had already discharged the duties of his
office; he might have also withdrawn that he
might come furnished with new messages and
thus endued with new authority. COMMENTARY
ON JEREMIAH 28:11.[12]

28:12-17 The Iron Yoke

**The Iron Yoke and the Hardened
People.** JOHN MAYER: "You have broken the
yokes of wood. You have made for them yokes of
iron." That is, "Tell Hananiah the first sentence
and then you, Jeremiah, do the second sentence.
You make and wear iron yokes in token of an
even harder subjection of the nations to
Nebuchadnezzar." For whereas wooden yokes
that were assigned before were weaker and
lighter in order to show that, if they would have
yielded to God's command, then their servitude
would have been lighter. They then would have
been permitted to dwell in their own land and to
pay tribute to Nebuchadnezzar. Instead, it
would cause more grief as they were carried into
other lands. Why did these people deserve to
have their misery aggravated by the petulance of
the one man Hananiah? I answer that he was a
means to harden them all the more. COMMEN-
TARY ON JEREMIAH 28:13.[13]

[10]Oecolampadius, *In Hieremiam*, 2:M1r.
[11]Pellikan, *Commentaria Bibliorum*, 3:2V1r-v.
[12]CTS 19:403-4* (CO 38:575); citing 2 Tim 4:2.
[13]Mayer, *A Commentary*, 424*.

MAKING THE JUDGMENT OF GOD EVEN MORE SEVERE. JOHN CALVIN: It would have been a vain spectacle had Jeremiah brought only his iron band around his neck; but when he added an explanation of the symbol, he no doubt prevailed on many to believe his prophecy and rendered those inexcusable who had hardened themselves in wickedness. But it is worth observing that God replaced the wooden bands with iron bands; and he did this because the whole people had through their foolish and wicked consent approved of the madness of that imposter, who had dared to profane that symbol, by which God had testified that he did not speak in vain, but seriously by the mouth of his servant.

A profitable doctrine may be taken from this—that the ungodly by barking against God gain nothing except that they kindle more and more [God's] wrath and thus render double their own evils, like a dog, who being ensnared stubbornly strives to extricate itself from the snare and to shake it off; thus they strangle themselves. In like manner the ungodly, the more they resist God, the heavier judgment they procure for themselves. Therefore, whenever God declares to us that he is offended with our sins, we ought to take heed, lest while we seek to break the wooden bands, he prepares and forms for us bands of iron. COMMENTARY ON JEREMIAH 28:14.[14]

WHEN THE DAY OF THE LORD COMES. JOHN DONNE: The day which the lord shall bring upon secure and carnal people is darkness without light, judgments without any beams of mercy shining through them. Such judgments, whenever we consider the intensity of them, we shall find expressed to such an extraordinary degree in Jeremiah: "People shall ask one another if they are in labor—whether they are traveling with child; for I see everyone with hands on their loins like a woman in travail. Alas, because that day is great and none is like it." This is the unexpected and unconsidered strangeness of that day, if we consider the intensity and suddenness—the speed with which that day comes upon a supposedly secure person. This is intimated well in another story of the same prophet, when he had said to the prophet Hananiah that he should die within a year. When God says that his judgments will come swiftly, if we then consider this intensity or nearness of the day of the Lord—the day of his visitation—we shall be glad to say with the prophet, "As for me, you know that I did not desire that woeful day. That is, I have neither doubted that there shall be such a day, nor have I put off my repentance to that day." SERMON ON AMOS 5:18.[15]

TESTING THE PROPHET OF GOD. JOHANNES OECOLAMPADIUS: The Lord gave the prophet Jeremiah more resolve to refute the disputatious man, and it was revealed why the Lord would allow these things to happen, namely, so that after this they would learn not to oppose the divine will and ordinance; those who strive to shake off the divine will etc. implicate themselves in greater dangers; neither could they bear to listen, having been persuaded by those speaking for their own desire rather than by those speaking for the Word of God. This is an example of the justice of God. The good people were departing into captivity as commanded, so that they might be quickly free according to the Word of God. The evil folk were left behind in their residences, so that they might be consumed by a severe destruction. At the time, however, the prophet yielded to the fractured lie of Hananiah, but soon divine instruction conquered it. A bit earlier, before Jeremiah departed in sadness and grief because the words of God were ridiculed all day, he turned back happy and was strengthened by the Lord. He said to Hananiah, "You have encouraged them not to bear a light servitude, which would be most tolerable, by your fault, they will bear a harder and certainly iron servitude. So the vanity of a lie is revealed by the matter itself, and even all the nations will serve the king of Babylon and they will not be liberated until the

---

[14]CTS 19:405-6* (CO 38:576-77).   [15]Donne, *Sermons*, 2:355-56*; citing Jer 30:6-7; 17:16.

appointed time comes. You, however, showed up even as you were not sent and you have made the people trust in a lie, and you taught the lie. So within a year you will die." And so it happened. Whence this prophecy of Jeremiah was proved to be true by a new example, which ought to have encouraged others also to believe the Word of God. COMMENTARY ON JEREMIAH 28:12-17.[16]

---

[16]Oecolampadius, *In Hieremiam*, 2:M1v-M2r.

JEREMIAH 29:1-32
JEREMIAH AND THE PEOPLE IN EXILE

¹*These are the words of the letter that Jeremiah the prophet sent from Jerusalem to the surviving elders of the exiles, and to the priests, the prophets, and all the people, whom Nebuchadnezzar had taken into exile from Jerusalem to Babylon.* ²*This was after King Jeconiah and the queen mother, the eunuchs, the officials of Judah and Jerusalem, the craftsmen, and the metal workers had departed from Jerusalem.* ³*The letter was sent by the hand of Elasah the son of Shaphan and Gemariah the son of Hilkiah, whom Zedekiah king of Judah sent to Babylon to Nebuchadnezzar king of Babylon. It said:* ⁴*"Thus says the* Lord *of hosts, the God of Israel, to all the exiles whom I have sent into exile from Jerusalem to Babylon:* ⁵*Build houses and live in them; plant gardens and eat their produce.* ⁶*Take wives and have sons and daughters; take wives for your sons, and give your daughters in marriage, that they may bear sons and daughters; multiply there, and do not decrease.* ⁷*But seek the welfare of the city where I have sent you into exile, and pray to the* Lord *on its behalf, for in its welfare you will find your welfare.* ⁸*For thus says the* Lord *of hosts, the God of Israel: Do not let your prophets and your diviners who are among you deceive you, and do not listen to the dreams that they dream,ᵃ* ⁹*for it is a lie that they are prophesying to you in my name; I did not send them, declares the* Lord.

¹⁰*"For thus says the Lord: When seventy years are completed for Babylon, I will visit you, and I will fulfill to you my promise and bring you back to this place.* ¹¹*For I know the plans I have for you, declares the* Lord, *plans for welfareᵇ and not for evil, to give you a future and a hope.* ¹²*Then you will call upon me and come and pray to me, and I will hear you.* ¹³*You will seek me and find me, when you seek me with all your heart.* ¹⁴*I will be found by you, declares the* Lord, *and I will restore your fortunes and gather you from all the nations and all the places where I have driven you, declares the Lord, and I will bring you back to the place from which I sent you into exile.*

¹⁵*"Because you have said, 'The* Lord *has raised up prophets for us in Babylon,'* ¹⁶*thus says the* Lord *concerning the king who sits on the throne of David, and concerning all the people who dwell in this city, your kinsmen who did not go out with you into exile:* ¹⁷*Thus says the* Lord *of hosts, behold, I am sending on them sword, famine, and pestilence, and I will make them like vile figs that are so rotten they cannot be eaten.* ¹⁸*I will pursue them with sword, famine, and pestilence, and will make them a horror to all the kingdoms of the earth, to be a curse, a terror, a hissing, and a reproach among all the nations where I have driven them,* ¹⁹*because they did not pay attention to my words, declares the* Lord, *that I persistently sent to you by my servants the prophets, but you would not listen, declares the* Lord.' ²⁰*Hear the word of the* Lord, *all you exiles whom I sent away from Jerusalem to Babylon:* ²¹*Thus says the* Lord *of hosts, the God of Israel, concerning Ahab the son of Kolaiah and Zedekiah the son of Maaseiah, who are prophesying a lie to you in my name: Behold, I will deliver them into the hand of Nebuchadnezzar king of Babylon, and he shall strike them down before your eyes.* ²²*Because of them this curse shall be used by all the exiles from Judah in Babylon: "The Lord make you like Zedekiah and Ahab, whom the king of Babylon roasted in the fire,"* ²³*because they have done an outrageous thing in Israel, they have committed adultery with their neighbors' wives, and they have spoken in my name lying words that I did not command them. I am the one who knows, and I am witness, declares the* Lord."'

²⁴*To Shemaiah of Nehelam you shall say:* ²⁵*"Thus says the* Lord *of hosts, the God of Israel: You have sent letters in your name to all the people who are in Jerusalem, and to Zephaniah the son of Maaseiah the priest, and to all the priests, saying,* ²⁶*'The* Lord *has made you priest instead of Jehoiada the priest, to have charge in the house of the* Lord *over every madman who prophesies, to put him in the stocks and neck irons.* ²⁷*Now why have you not rebuked Jeremiah of Anathoth who is prophesying to you?* ²⁸*For he has sent*

to us in Babylon, saying, "Your exile will be long; build houses and live in them, and plant gardens and eat their produce.""

²⁹Zephaniah the priest read this letter in the hearing of Jeremiah the prophet. ³⁰Then the word of the LORD came to Jeremiah: ³¹"Send to all the exiles, saying, 'Thus says the LORD concerning Shemaiah of Nehelam:

Because Shemaiah had prophesied to you when I did not send him, and has made you trust in a lie, ³²therefore thus says the LORD: Behold, I will punish Shemaiah of Nehelam and his descendants. He shall not have anyone living among this people, and he shall not see the good that I will do to my people, declares the LORD, for he has spoken rebellion against the LORD.'"

a Hebrew *your dreams, which you cause to dream*   **b** Or *peace*

OVERVIEW: Jeremiah's correspondence with the exiled Jews in Babylon and his dealings with yet another false prophet move our commentators to ponder the nature of religious devotion and civic involvement in a hostile world. Tyrants and heathen rulers must be obeyed and endured; the rhythms of daily life must continue. Timing is everything. Counterfeit prophets guarantee swift deliverance and immediate victory. In contrast, life in exile—whether geographical or spiritual—requires steadfast and sincere faith in God's long-term promises. Therefore a vital part of ministry is unmasking and exposing these false messengers and moving believers to take the longer and deeper view of divine redemption even if decades away on earth or fulfilled in eternity.

29:1-23 Jeremiah's Letter to the Exiles

ACCEPTING A TIME OF CAPTIVITY. JOHANNES OECOLAMPADIUS: Once again our prophet endures the snares of the false prophets; just as Hananiah opposed him in person, so Shemaiah the Nehelamite, sending letters from Babylon to the priest Zephaniah, claimed that Jeremiah was a false prophet. This was done by a singular dispensation of God, so with a new opportunity the long captivity and the destruction of the city of Jerusalem might be preached more clearly. In fact, just as there were false prophets in Jerusalem announcing to citizens that the city would not be captured, and that people were about to return from a brief captivity, so also in Babylon they were prophesying false things. Therefore, since Zedekiah was sending esteemed men as legates to Babylon, namely, Elasah

and Gamariah, Jeremiah was writing through them to his own people, lest they too suffer deception; for there would be no liberation before the seventieth year. Hence they should resolve to remain, and he ordered them to build, plant, and have children; and to do everything that might support the welfare of the city of Babylon. Again it was necessary to learn this: not to try to escape the servitude of their masters against the ordinance of God; let each one remain in their vocation; one must obey various people. But when the seventy years have rolled on, that is, when the time designated by God would be fulfilled. Then the people would be effortlessly set free.

In our time God wishes indeed that we thoroughly try to be released from a spiritual Nebuchadnezzar. God always orders us to flee from a spiritual Babylon. But we escape if we mortify the deeds of the flesh on the cross of the Lord. For the rest it can be said that captivity is repentance and redemption, and a sense of grace and divine love. In that case perchance it is to be said that we ought not flee from even this kind of Babylon of ours before the time has come, but we ought to dwell through a time of penance that is seventy years in the flesh that must be mortified—until the time of liberation and the judgment of Israel would be fulfilled. Then the Lord himself will send a savior, who by his name will lead us into the freedom of the sons of God. So now is the time of the cross, and one day the time of glory will come. COMMENTARY ON JEREMIAH 29.[1]

---

[1]Oecolampadius, *In Hieremiam*, 2:M2v-M3r, 146v-146r.

How the Jews Are to Live in Exile. John Calvin: God commanded the captives to "build houses" in Chaldea, to "plant vineyards," and also to "marry wives," and to "beget children," as though they were at home. It was not, indeed, God's purpose that they should set their hearts on Chaldea; on the contrary, they were ever to think of their return. But until the end of seventy years it was God's will that they should continue quietly and not attempt this or that, but carry on the business of life as though they were in their own country. . . .

At the first view these two things seemed inconsistent—that the Jews were to live seventy years as though they were natives of that place and that their habitations were not to be changed—and yet that they were ever to look forward to a return. But these two things can well agree together; it was proof of obedience when they acknowledged that they were chastised by God's hand, and thus became willingly submissive to the end of the seventy years. But their hope . . . was to remain in suspense in order that they might not be agitated with discontent, nor be led away by some violent feeling, but that they might so pass their time as to bear their exile in such a way as to please God. . . .

We now see that Jeremiah neither encouraged the Jews to indulge in pleasures nor persuaded them to settle forever in Chaldea. It was, indeed, a fertile and pleasant land; but he did not encourage them to live there in pleasure. . . . During that time, then, he wished them to enjoy the land of Chaldea, and all its advantages, as though they were not exiles, but natives of the place. For what purpose? Not that they might give themselves up to sloth, but that they might not, by raising commotions, offend God, and in a manner close the door of his grace against themselves. Commentary on Jeremiah 29:5-6.[2]

Living with Tyrants. Johannes Oecolampadius: We are taught not only to obey tyrants who have gravely afflicted us but also to pray for them so that they may be more fortunate and prosperous, since indeed it has been provided by God that we live under them. One teaches that Gospel, "Be swift and benevolent with your accusers, when you are on the way with them, lest your adversary hand you over to a judge and the judge hands you over to the minister, and he puts you in prison." Well-being here is acceptance of a present calamity imposed through your victorious enemy. Commentary on Jeremiah 29:7.[3]

Prayer and Prosperity Under Tyrants. John Mayer: According to 1 Timothy 2 we are commanded to pray for kings that under them we may lead "a godly life in all quietness and honesty," and yet the kings were then heathen and enemies of Christians. Hereby we learn then that the vices of kings are not to triumph over our obedience to them, but we must be both subject to them in any case and must pray to God for them from the heart as the saints of God constantly did in the early church; and not rebel against them or plot their destruction as papists have impiously done many times. For "in their peace" means that we live in a kingdom that is in a prosperous estate. So we fare better, although the king is a tyrant, because all things in time of peace and fruitfulness do abound more fully. Commentary on Jeremiah 29:7.[4]

Serious Intercession for Godless Rulers. Martin Luther: Because of the abundance of horrible sins the world is now overburdened with young, impudent, and inexperienced rulers, mostly in the spiritual estate. Therefore, our age is extraordinarily perilous, and we must act very wisely and see to it that we hold government and power in the highest honor, just as Christ honored the power of Pilate, Herod, Annas, Caiaphas, and even secular princes. We must not let such grave misuse and childish governing of the prelates move us to despise authority. Otherwise we despise not only the unworthy persons who rule but their power itself. Rather, we should joyfully bear everything it

---

[2]CTS 19:418-19* (CO 38:588-90).

[3]Oecolampadius, *In Hieremiam*, 2:M3v; 147v; citing Mt 5:25.
[4]Mayer, *A Commentary*, 425*; citing 1 Tim 2:1-2.

imposes, or humble and respectfully refuse to bear it. For God neither likes nor tolerates blasphemous and wanton resistance to authority. . . .

Furthermore, there should be diligent and serious intercession for rulers before God, just as Jeremiah wrote to the children of Israel in Babylon that they should diligently pray for the king of Babylon, who had imprisoned them, destroyed them, strangled them, and done all kinds of evil things to them. A SERMON ON THE BAN.[5]

PROPHETS OF THE DEVIL AND SCHOLARS OF CHRIST.

JOHN CALVIN: Inasmuch then as from the beginning of the world Satan had never ceased to try and to attempt, as far as he could, to corrupt the truth of God or to immerse it in darkness, it has been always necessary for God's servants to be prepared to do these two things—faithfully to teach the meek and humble—and boldly to oppose the enemies of truth and break down their insolence. . . .

For while Jeremiah had many adversaries at Jerusalem, the devil was also deceiving the miserable exiles in Chaldea. He then warns them not to believe these impostors and though by way of concession he calls them prophets who were wholly unworthy of so honorable a name; he yet by way of reproach gives them afterward the name of "diviners."

. . . For we know that the devil's ministers are cherished not only through the foolish credulity of people but also through a depraved appetite. For the world is never deceived but willingly, and people, as though they were given up to their own destruction, seek for themselves falsehoods in every direction, and though unwilling to be deceived, they yet for the most part seek to be deceived. . . .

Jeremiah did not without reason reject whatever the false prophets boasted of for the purpose of gaining the approbation and applause of the people; for they were neither sent nor approved by God. So also in this day everyone who wishes to distinguish with certainty between various doctrines, by which the world is agitated, nay, shaken, can without difficulty attain this object, provided they offer

themselves as scholars to Christ, and connect the Law and the Prophets with the Gospel, and make use of this rule to prove all doctrines; and provided in the meantime they trust not their own acumen, but submit themselves to God and seek in him the spirit of judgment and discrimination. COMMENTARY ON JEREMIAH 29:8-9.[6]

THE END OF SEVENTY YEARS AS A SIGN OF GOD'S FAVOR.

JOHANNES BUGENHAGEN: "When the seventy years are completed." Of course, this happens in the beginning of the reign of the Persians, as it says at the end of Chronicles and at the beginning of Ezra. Here now is a clear passage about the seventy years before which Jeremiah adds the cause of this divine benefit, saying, "I will not do this on your merit, but because of my goodness; now it seems to you that I think of nothing else than that you perish, but I myself think of your good, so that I might give you that good end you are waiting for, that is, that which you look for from my promise. That is, so that at last you may receive all you expected and whatever promises you expected from temporal and spiritual things, concerning the Messiah in your land," etc. Here is that sentence, which the epistle to the Hebrews cites from Proverbs: "The one the father loves, he reproves, as the father in the son delights himself." And in the psalm: "His anger is for just a moment, but life is in his favor. Weeping may last the night, but joy comes in the morning." But this should not be seen with afflicted or disturbed consciences, since they have the work of the Word of God as consolation. COMMENTARY ON JEREMIAH 29:10-11.[7]

LIVING IN GOD'S TIME.

JOHN DONNE: God has said it before, and he says again to you in all your afflictions, "I know the thoughts that I think towards you. . . ." God said this when a false prophet had promised them deliverance in two years. God extends that time. God would grant

---

[5]LW 39:18-19* (WA 6:72-73); citing Bar 1:11.

[6]CTS 19:424-27* (CO 38:473).

[7]Bugenhagen, *In Ieremiam*, 4Kir-v; citing 2 Chron 36:17-21; Ezra 1:1-11; Prov 3:12; Heb 12:6; Ps 30:5.

deliverance, but he would not do it in under threescore and ten years. Do not limit God in his time, nor in his means. The mercy consists in relieving you so that the soul does not suffer. Sermon on Psalms 32:10-11.[8]

What Thoughts Does God Have Toward Us? John Calvin:

The prophet . . . says that God would restore [the Jews] to their own country; for this was the "good word," the promise of deliverance, as the word, while what the people felt was evil, and bitter, and bad when God had threatened that he would cast away the reprobate. But it is an accidental thing . . . that people find God's word to be evil for them or adverse to them; for [this fault] proceeds from their own fault and not from the nature of the word. . . .

Jeremiah confirms the same thing [in verse 11] and employs many words because it was difficult to raise up minds wholly broken down. For the world labors under two extreme evils—people sink into despair or are too much exalted by foolish pride. There is no moderation except when ruled by God's Spirit unless we rest on his word; for when people devise vain hopes for themselves, they are immediately rapt up above the clouds, fly here and there, and in short think that they can climb into heaven; this is the excess of vain and foolish confidence. But when they are dejected, then they fall down wholly frightened; they are even astonished and lifeless; they lose every feeling, receive no comfort, and cannot taste anything which God promises. And both these evils prevailed clearly among the Jews. We have seen how much the prophet labored to lay prostrate their pride and arrogance; for they laughed at all the threats and remained secure, though God, as it were, with an armed hand and a drawn sword menaced them with certain destruction. Yet nothing moved them. And when they were driven into exile, they were extremely cautious when the false prophets promised them a quick return. While in the meantime God, by his servants, showed to them

that he would be gracious to them, and after seventy years would become their deliverer. But they were deaf to all these things; they rejected with disdain all these promises and said, "What? Will God even raise the dead?"

This, then, is the reason why the prophet now speaks so largely of their future redemption; it was difficult to persuade the Jews; for as they thought that they would soon return to their own country, they could neither endure delay, nor exercise the patience which God commanded. They were at the same time . . . quite confident, inasmuch as the false prophets filled their minds with vain hopes.

[God] therefore says, "I know the thoughts which I think towards you." Some think that God claims here what peculiarly belongs to him, the foreknowledge of future things; but this is foreign to the prophet's meaning. There is here, on the contrary, an implied contrast between the certain counsel of God and the vain imaginations in which the Jews indulged themselves. The same thing is meant when Isaiah says, "As far as the heavens are from the earth, so far are my thoughts from your thoughts"; for they absurdly tended to measure God by their own ideas. When anything was promised, they reasoned about its validity and looked on all surrounding circumstances; and thus they consulted only their own brains. Hence God reproved them and showed how preposterously they acted and said that his thoughts were as remote from their thoughts as heaven is from earth. . . .

It must yet be remarked that God does not speak here of his hidden and incomprehensible counsel. What then are the thoughts of which Jeremiah now speaks? They were those respecting the people's deliverance after the time was completed, for God promised that he would be propitious to his church. We hence see here that the question is not about the hidden counsels of God, but that the reference is simply to the word that was well known to the Jews, even to the prophecy of Jeremiah, by which he had predicted that the Jews would be exiles for seventy years and would at last find that their punishment would be only a small chastisement, as it would only be for a time. . . . But still he indirectly condemns the Jews

---

[8]Donne, *Sermons*, 9:409*.

because they entertained no hope of deliverance except from what came within the reach of their senses. He then teaches us that true wisdom is to obey God and to surrender ourselves to him; and that when we do not understand his counsel, we ought with resignation to wait until the due time shall come. COMMENTARY ON JEREMIAH 29:10-11.[9]

GOD'S END FOR THE FAITHFUL. JOHANNES OECOLAMPADIUS: "For I know." It is only God's to know the future and to know what the spirit of God will decide. "I," he says, "know and no other does." But these are considerations of peace for his sons, to whom he wishes to show mercy. He does not promise peace to all. There was peace in the affliction of the Israelites in Babylon, for he also adds, "so that I may give you a good end and good expectations," that is, those things you are waiting for . . . which elsewhere signifies the end times. . . . Christ is indeed the end of the Law and Prophets, whom the people of old looked forward to as the perfect and last redeemer. Therefore, the following verses pertain to the kingdom of Christ. Indeed, to this point they have neither sought the Lord with a whole heart, nor has he yet restored the Jews from all places and nations; he only freed them from Babylon. And they are now dispersed around the globe. When an abundance of nations will have entered, then all Israel will be saved. The place from which they were expelled was not so much the land of Canaan as it was the promise of grace and the requirements of the covenant. COMMENTARY ON JEREMIAH 29:11.[10]

TRUE PRAYER—WITH SINCERITY AND INTEGRITY. JOHN CALVIN: "Then you shall call on me. . . ." Jeremiah pursues the same subject, even that the Jews after having undergone the punishment allotted to them by God would at length return to their own country and find God merciful, and hence learn that their chastisement in exile would prove useful to them. He had indeed explained this in the last verse with sufficient clarity, but he now expresses the manner: that would be calling on God. . . .

But there is an added promise: God would hear them. It may, however, appear that God promised conversion . . . and no doubt, prayer is the fruit of repentance, for it proceeds from faith and repentance is the gift of God. Further, we cannot call on God rightly and sincerely except by the guidance and teaching of the Holy Spirit; for he it is who not only dictates our words but also creates groaning in our hearts. . . .

"And you shall seek me" . . . as the Jews perversely despised all the threats of God, so it was difficult for them to receive any taste of God's goodness from his promises. This then is the reason why the prophet employs many words on this subject. By the word "seek" he means prayers and supplications. . . . Christ also, exhorting his disciples to pray says, "Seek and you shall find, knock and the door shall be opened to you." There is no doubt but that he speaks here of prayer. . . . But to seek when we feel the need of God's grace is nothing else than to pray. Hence the prophet says, "You shall seek me and you shall find me." And though he addresses the Israelites, yet this doctrine ought to be extended to the whole church; for God testifies that he will be favorable to all who flee to him.

But as hypocrites are abundantly noisy and seem to surpass the very saints in the ardor of their zeal, when the external profession is only regarded, the prophet adds, "because you seek me with your whole heart." There is no doubt but that the Jews groaned a thousand times every year when oppressed by the Chaldeans; for they had to bear all kind of reproaches and then they had nothing safe or secure. They were therefore moved due to necessity, even though they were harder than iron, to offer some prayers. But God shows that the seasonable time would not come, until their prayers proceeded from a right feeling; this he means by "the whole heart." It is indeed certain that people never turn to God with their whole heart, nor is the whole heart ever so much engaged in prayer as it ought to be; but the prophet sets the whole heart in opposition to a double heart.

---

[9]CTS 19:430-34* (CO 38:592-93); citing Ezek 37:12; Is 55:9.
[10]Oecolampadius, *In Hieremiam*, 2:M4v.

Perfection, then, is not what is to be understood here, which can never be found in humanity, but integrity and sincerity.

We now then perceive the meaning of the prophet's words—that the Jews, when they began in earnest to flee to God, would find him favorable, provided only they did this in sincerity of heart and not dishonestly. COMMENTARY ON JEREMIAH 29:12-13.[11]

WHEN GOD DOES NOT HEAR OUR PRAYERS.

HULDRYCH ZWINGLI: Only call out and he will not hear you, because your call neither comes out of your love nor your fear of God, but only from pain and fear of danger. A house is burning and the fire spreads quickly to all the neighboring houses. One of all these neighbors does not hurry out, so his house burns down in the night. So he cries out that his neighbors did not help him. And he says, "Every misfortune helps you! But you did not want to help me." A coachman does nothing when God burdens and chastises him; he does not know God until he breaks a wheel or a spoke (or when a wheel goes over a bump), then he says, "O Almighty God!" But God says to the sinner, "Why is my name in your mouth?" SERMON ON JEREMIAH 29:12.[12]

THE POWER OF SEEKING IN GOD'S NOW.

JOHN DONNE: It is a fitting time to find God—whenever your conscience tells you that God calls to you; for a rectified conscience is the Word of God. If your conscience speaks to you, now this very minute, now is the time to find God. That "now," which I just named, has past. But God gives you yet another "now." God speaks again; he speaks still and if your conscience tells you that he is speaking to you, now is that time. This Word of God, which your conscience will present to you, has one condition. Moses presented this condition to God's people; that is, "That you seek the Lord with all your heart and all your soul." There is a kind of denial of God's infinity when God is served piece by piece. . . . God is not infinite to me. I think a partial service will serve him. It is a kind of denying of the unity of God, to join other gods such as pleasure or profit to him. He is not one God to me if I join other associates and assistants to him, such as saints or angels. It is a kind of mistrust of Christ, as though I am not sure that he would stand in the favor of God, as though I am afraid that a new favorite of God might rise in heaven, to whom I might be concerned to apply myself. So it is if I make the balance so equal between serving God and mammon: if I make a formal visit to God at his house on Sunday, and then plot with the other faction—the world, the flesh, and the devil—the week after. The Lord promised a power of seeking and an infallibility of finding. But still there is this condition: "You shall seek me, and you shall find me, because you shall seek me with all your heart." This he promised for the future; this God will do. SERMON ON PSALM 32:6.[13]

GOD REGARDS REPENTANCE IN THE HEART.

RICHARD HOOKER: That which God does chiefly respect in people's penitence is their hearts. The heart is that which makes repentance sincere, sincerity [is] that which finds favor in God's sight, and the favor of God is that which supplies, by gracious acceptance, whatsoever may seem defective in the faithful heart, and [the] true offices of his servants. "Take it," says Chrysostom, "upon my credit, such is God's merciful inclination toward people, that he never refuses repentance offered with a single and sincere mind, no not even if we come to the very top of iniquity, if there is a will and desire to return, he receives, embraces, and omits nothing which may restore us to former happiness, indeed that which is yet above all the rest, albeit we cannot in the duty of satisfying him, attain what we ought, and would, but come far behind our mark, he takes nevertheless in good worth that little which we do, be it never so mean we lose not our labor therein." The least and lowest step in Chrysostom's judgment severs and sets us

---

[11]CTS 19:433-36* (CO 38:594-95); citing Mt 7:7; Lk 11:9.
[12]Zwingli, *Predigten*, 253-54.

[13]Donne, *Sermons*, 9:327*; citing Deut 4:29.

above them that perish in their sin. LAWES OF ECCLESIASTICAL POLITY.[14]

THOSE WHO SEEK TO RETURN AND THOSE WHO DO NOT. KONRAD PELLIKAN: The Lord promises to gather the Jews from every nation to which they were scattered through various kings. Indeed, Cyrus the Great, the successor to the Babylonian kingdom, granted the ability to return to the land of Judah to all who wished it. But if they made little use of that concession, it was not by the fault of the Lord, but it happened because of the impiety and arrogance of those who refused to return out of love for their sons and wives whom they had taken from foreign peoples against the law. They considered as nothing the land of their inheritance, from which they had been driven out by the neighboring tribes into the midst of the Assyrians and Chaldeans in the times of Hezekiah, Jehoiachin, and Zedekiah. To all these people the return is here promised, since it is said that they would return to the places from whence they had been forced to migrate, from every nation and every place. Indeed the degree to which they did not return happened not because of the truth and goodness of the Lord, but because of the malice of that people, who were always accustomed to resisting the Holy Spirit, as they also do today. COMMENTARY ON JEREMIAH 29:13.[15]

THE BABYLONIAN CAPTIVITY AND THE CROSS OF CHRIST. JOHANNES BRENZ: To yield to the word of the Lord is thereby to bear the cross. This you see in the transmigration to Babylon and in Christ himself. Thus in the Gospel: "Those who want to follow me must deny themselves and pick up their cross and follow me." But resurrection follows the cross. Indeed those who follow their own flesh, and live not according to the word, but for their own desires—for a time they may seem to prosper and be exalted like the cedars of Lebanon. But when they flee to the cross of Christ, instead of obtaining the resurrection they are buried by a perpetual cross. So it appears for the remnant of the Jews, who were not willing to hand themselves over freely to captivity, according to the word of the Lord. ANNOTATIONS ON JEREMIAH 29:16-17.[16]

29:24-32 Shemaiah's False Prophecy

THE VICES OF THE FALSE PROPHETS. NIKOLAUS SELNECKER: Jeremiah threatened the three false prophets with disease, hunger, and war because they had undermined those in captivity in Babylon and made them impatient. The false prophets had confirmed King Zedekiah and his people's refusal to surrender to King Nebuchadnezzar and confirmed them in their stubbornness against the Word of God. Therefore, Jeremiah says that their hope will fail and they with the king, the false prophets, and the stiff-necked people will come into the hand of the enemy, and all this misfortune will drag them down by their very own stiff necks.

But he especially points out the vices of the false prophets, how along with their false teaching they indulge in immorality. So these two things are generally together, namely, false doctrine and immorality. Jeremiah addresses Shemaiah especially, as God will severely punish him and will eradicate and destroy his entire extended family, because he wrote to Jerusalem that someone should kill Jeremiah. Such a passage is a certain witness that God will not allow the seed of the godless to rise. As David says, "You will destroy their descendants from the earth." And as Psalm 5 says, "Whoever is evil shall not remain before you, the boastful shall not stand before your eyes. You are the enemy of all who do evil and destroy those who speak lies. The Lord abhors the bloodthirsty and false." THE WHOLE PROPHET JEREMIAH 29:15-32.[17]

---

[14]Hooker, Lawes of Ecclesiastical Polity 6.5*. Hooker cites Chrysostom, Ad Theodorum Paraenesis Prior, vel de reparation lapsi 6.
[15]Pellikan, Commentaria Bibliorum, 3:2 V2r.

[16]Brenz, Annotationes in Jeremiam, 917; citing Mt 16:24; Mark 8:34; Lk 9:23.
[17]Selnecker, Der gantze Prophet Jeremias, Y4r-v; citing Ps 21:10; 5:5-6.

Jeremiah the Madman? John Mayer: "For every one that is a madman, put him in stocks." Whereby we may gather that wicked people counted the prophets of God as mad, because they were strangely moved by the Spirit of God after the manner of the "those who are seized," that are so rapt, that they act madly, as with Saul; for when the Spirit came upon him, he cast off his clothes. And likewise someone said to Jehu, referring to a prophet that came to Jehu to anoint him as king, "what did this mad fellow say to you?" Thus sometimes false prophets seemed like the true ones. Therefore, the second to the high priest had authority to judge the prophets and finding them false to put them in stocks or prison, and then to be brought forth afterward to be adjudged to death—if found false. So Pashhur, who held this office before, was threatened and dealt roughly with Jeremiah in chapter 20. Now another held that office. Commentary on Jeremiah 29:26.[18]

How Fraud, Lies, and Idolatry Are Connected. Martin Luther: God has strictly and sharply forbidden human doctrines and works in the church as being contrary to faith and leading people away from the truth; that is, they are sheer lies and fraud before God. And where the devil has got involved—that one embellishes them with God's name or the apostles' names, and sells them under these names—then they are no longer simple lies and fraud, but also horrible blasphemy, idolatry, and abomination. For then the devil makes God a liar and deceiver, as though God had spoken such lies or done such works; and the people fall for it, believe it, depend on it, as if God has said and done it, and thus they give their trust and honor, which is due to God alone, to lies and

to the devil. This is what is meant by true idolatry and blasphemy in all the prophets. Isaiah 2 says, "Their land is filled with idols; they bow down to the work of their hands to what their own fingers have made." And Jeremiah 29 says, "Because Shemaiah has prophesied to you when I did not send him, and has made you trust a lie," etc. Now you hear: he who is not sent does not have the Word of God; and by his own human doctrine he makes people trust in lies, that is, commit idolatry. Against the Roman Papacy.[19]

The Danger of Persecuting God's Holy Prophet. Konrad Pellikan: Either Zephaniah the priest was secretly accusing Jeremiah and, as an insult to him, he recited that letter which he had written to Babylon—as if thus convicting him of writing on behalf of the king of Babylon—or he may have been a good man, and favorable enough to Jeremiah, and he wanted him also to hear what Shemaiah had written against him, which seems more reasonable. . . . So therefore the Lord helped Jeremiah's trial by revealing his word, so that Jeremiah might preach about the evil that would await Shemaiah and his seed, of whom no one would ever return to Jerusalem. Indeed, either before the seventieth year he and his whole family would be dead, so that he would not be able to be among the number that returned, or he, along with his posterity, would be so formed in their treacherous hearts that they would not wish to be permitted to return. However, the case had been submitted, Shemaiah spoke of desertion from the Lord, and accused Jeremiah of falsehood, and of speaking rashly against the word of the Lord, and he attempted to persecute the holy prophet. Commentary on Jeremiah 29:29-32.[20]

---

[18]Mayer, *A Commentary*, 426*; citing 1 Sam 19:24; 2 Kings 9:11.

[19]LW 41:302-3 (WA 54:238-39); citing Is 2:8.
[20]Pellikan, *Commentaria Bibliorum*, 3:2V3r.

JEREMIAH 30:1-24
RESTORATION FOR ISRAEL AND JUDAH

¹The word that came to Jeremiah from the LORD: ²"Thus says the LORD, the God of Israel: Write in a book all the words that I have spoken to you. ³For behold, days are coming, declares the LORD, when I will restore the fortunes of my people, Israel and Judah, says the LORD, and I will bring them back to the land that I gave to their fathers, and they shall take possession of it."

⁴These are the words that the LORD spoke
concerning Israel and Judah:

⁵"Thus says the LORD:
We have heard a cry of panic,
    of terror, and no peace.
⁶Ask now, and see,
    can a man bear a child?
Why then do I see every man
    with his hands on his stomach like a woman
        in labor?
    Why has every face turned pale?
⁷Alas! That day is so great
    there is none like it;
it is a time of distress for Jacob;
    yet he shall be saved out of it.

⁸"And it shall come to pass in that day, declares the LORD of hosts, that I will break his yoke from off your neck, and I will burst your bonds, and foreigners shall no more make a servant of him.ᵃ ⁹But they shall serve the LORD their God and David their king, whom I will raise up for them.

¹⁰"Then fear not, O Jacob my servant, declares
        the LORD,
    nor be dismayed, O Israel;
for behold, I will save you from far away,
    and your offspring from the land of their
        captivity.
Jacob shall return and have quiet and ease,
    and none shall make him afraid.
¹¹For I am with you to save you,

declares the LORD;
I will make a full end of all the nations
    among whom I scattered you,
    but of you I will not make a full end.
I will discipline you in just measure,
    and I will by no means leave you unpunished.

¹²"For thus says the LORD:
Your hurt is incurable,
    and your wound is grievous.
¹³There is none to uphold your cause,
    no medicine for your wound,
    no healing for you.
¹⁴All your lovers have forgotten you;
    they care nothing for you;
for I have dealt you the blow of an enemy,
    the punishment of a merciless foe,
because your guilt is great,
    because your sins are flagrant.
¹⁵Why do you cry out over your hurt?
    Your pain is incurable.
Because your guilt is great,
    because your sins are flagrant,
    I have done these things to you.
¹⁶Therefore all who devour you shall be
        devoured,
    and all your foes, every one of them, shall go
        into captivity;
those who plunder you shall be plundered,
    and all who prey on you I will make a prey.
¹⁷For I will restore health to you,
    and your wounds I will heal,
declares the LORD,
because they have called you an outcast:
    'It is Zion, for whom no one cares!'

¹⁸"Thus says the LORD:
Behold, I will restore the fortunes of the tents of
        Jacob
    and have compassion on his dwellings;
the city shall be rebuilt on its mound,

and the palace shall stand where it used to be.
¹⁹Out of them shall come songs of thanksgiving,
and the voices of those who celebrate.
I will multiply them, and they shall not be few;
I will make them honored, and they shall
not be small.
²⁰Their children shall be as they were of old,
and their congregation shall be established
before me,
and I will punish all who oppress them.
²¹Their prince shall be one of themselves;
their ruler shall come out from their midst;
I will make him draw near, and he shall
approach me,

for who would dare of himself to approach me?
declares the LORD.
²²And you shall be my people,
and I will be your God."

²³Behold the storm of the LORD!
Wrath has gone forth,
a whirling tempest;
it will burst upon the head of the wicked.
²⁴The fierce anger of the LORD will not turn
back
until he has executed and accomplished
the intentions of his mind.
In the latter days you will understand this.

a Or *serve him*

OVERVIEW: The whole of the Bible—both the Old and New Testaments, every chapter and verse—drew the rapt attention of preachers and scholars in the sixteenth and seventeenth centuries. Beyond this focus on detail, these interpreters eagerly pursued the interrelationship of Scripture within itself, among its books, and especially across the two testaments. Commentators found a single biblical message that was intricate and yet one. This chapter of Jeremiah moved interpreters to affirm profound parallels and indeed prophecies that pertained to both the captive Jews of the Old Testament and Christian believers of the New. The promise of deliverance from Babylon mirrored salvation through Christ; law and judgment led to grace and the gospel. Meanwhile, throughout the ages humanity was still tempted to find solace in the intimates and pleasures of this life—the loves of this world—over the steadfast love and certain redemption of the God who attends both earth and heaven.

30:1-11 The Promise of Restoration

KINGDOM OF THE JEWS, KINGDOM OF THE MESSIAH. JOHANNES BUGENHAGEN: The prophet consoles the ruined people with the promises of God. That is, they have been sorely troubled by captivity and devastation, such that there could be no healing; that is, such that they were not humanly able to be redeemed. It will happen, he says, that after these your sins and after captivity in Babylon, you will be led back to your land and you will receive consolation and not by your merit: first there will be a temporal consolation and then eternal consolation in the Messiah king who was promised to you in the law and prophets. A New Testament will be published; you will no longer be under the law, but under the grace of God, of the Son of God. For this reason here as he remembered Jacob and Israel, so also he remembered Ephraim, that is, the kingdom of the ten tribes, which, before the end of the Babylonian captivity, had been under the captivity of the Assyrians for two hundred years, and which are not read to have been returned to their own lands. In fact, those people called Samaritans had come to occupy the greater part of those lands, namely, Samaria, in perpetuity, even to the more recent devastation of the Jews carried out through the Romans. It may not be doubted that some pious folk from the ten tribes joined themselves to the reverent Jews, since even in the time of Christ people lived in Jerusalem as religious Jews from every nation under the sun.

Therefore although he promises this bodily return of the Jews, nevertheless there is a longer movement to the grace of the Messiah and his kingdom, which would first come into the lands of the Jews and Samaritans, whence it would spread out into the whole world; at the same time he promises that which is the spiritual return of the whole spiritual Israel. Concerning which Paul in Romans 11 says, "And so all Israel will be saved." And as Micah has predicted in Micah: "I will gather all of you, Jacob," etc. . . . Now at that time the kingdom of Israel and the kingdom of Judah will be joined together so that they become one kingdom, which will extend from Jerusalem through the whole world. As Christ says in the last chapter of Luke: "It is necessary to preach repentance and the remission of sins in my name among all the nations, beginning from Jerusalem." As Isaiah 9 says, "His rule will be multiplied." And all will serve in the one kingdom of David, that is, in Christ who will be born of David according to the prophecies and promises of God. . . . Now the promises of God will be fulfilled in the eternal kingdom of David. COMMENTARY ON JEREMIAH 30.[1]

PROPHECIES FOR THE JEWS AND THE END TIMES. JOHANNES OECOLAMPADIUS: The Holy Spirit in Scripture after a temporal and carnal promise usually raises the minds of the prophets through spiritual and eternal promises, which are fulfilled in Christ. Accordingly Jeremiah said adequately that the people would be liberated after seventy years of captivity in Babylon, despite the contradictions of the false prophets. Then he crosses over to true freedom, about which John 8 speaks: "Unless the Son has freed you, you are not truly free." Indeed however much more calamitous it is for the soul, as opposed to the body, to be captive; the soul's freedom is that much more excellent. Meanwhile, the prophet consoles and predicts how much persecution from the anti-Christian false prophets the people of God in

Christ, the ruler of things, would bear—so much persecution that he bore his own Hananiah and Shemaiah more tolerably. And as that prophecy would occur in the end times, so it is at the end of the chapter. In the last days you will understand these things. Therefore, Jeremiah was ordered not only to speak, but to write this in a book so that it would be remembered. Indeed, prophecies are written, which pertain to the memory of posterity. Those liars [false prophets] had declared that freedom is at hand. The man of God says that after the seventieth year there will be the restoration of Judah and in the last days all Israel will be saved, as one with Judah, in a perfect salvation. COMMENTARY ON JEREMIAH 30:1-3.[2]

ON BEING ATTACHED TO GOD ALONE. ANDREAS BODENSTEIN VON KARLSTADT: In the same way in which all nations are God's, even though God attached himself in a special and unique way to his chosen nation and not to others, the heart too must bind and attach itself to God alone, even though it might have before its eyes or in its thought numerous saints, angels, and people. This is what God says, "I attached the house of Israel and Judah to myself that they might become my nation and my name's glory and praise." We must not cry or run to the saints, but to God, who attached us to himself in order that we might go after him. THE MEANING OF THE TERM GELASSENHEIT.[3]

A MESSAGE TO THE TRUE ISRAELITES AND JEWS. KONRAD PELLIKAN: Even the Jews explain this passage with reference to the times of the Messiah, since they do not suppose that Judah and Israel came back under Cyrus but, as themselves say, only the Jews came back. Since they have not yet seen either kingdom return to Jerusalem, they infer that the Messiah has not yet come. We, however, recognize the eternal Messiah and king who is from the seed of David and who reigns over

---

[1]Bugenhagen, *In Ieremiam*, 4K3r-4K4r; citing Acts 2:5-11; Rom 11:26; Mic 2:12; Lk 24:47; Is 9:2-7.

[2]Oecolampadius, *In Hieremiam*, 2:N3r; citing Jn 8:36; Jer 28:1-17; 29:24-32.
[3]CRR 8:146; citing Deut 10:15; Jer 13:11.

every person of faith in the whole world, and we know that people have not come near to the grace of God, but the grace of God has inclined itself and come down to people. It has not come to everyone, but to the elect, who are we of the blessed church and citizens of the splendid Jerusalem, in which Christ is king and presides as Emperor, which we know. But the name of Israel and Judah, I say, are truly those who in love and assurance in God have so thoroughly conquered God for themselves that he would deny nothing to those only ask for what pertains to the glory of God, that his name be sanctified; he whom they confess to be the only Lord of the universe. These are and are rightly called the children of Judah and Israel.

But those who seek what is theirs—temporal things, glory, and praise—and who do not believe in the word of the Lord, and who only chase after temporal things and live for flesh and blood like today's Jews, they are in no way able to show that they ought to be called children of Israel and Judah neither in spirit nor in truth, nor are they able to demonstrate that "according to the flesh" they are descended from any but the worst of people, who are able to offer neither a place nor a time nor persons as testimony to their salvation. Therefore, either the restoration from captivity discussed here was the Babylonian one, and it was the restoration of some of the people from all the tribes, the people to whom, if they were willing, the right of return was granted, or it is the restoration of the true Israelites into a unity of faith, in which God is truly worshiped from every part of the world. There is no doubt that the Lord rightly cares more for them than for those alone who are Israelites according to the cut-off foreskin. Such a congregation is far more illustrious than any Jewish congregation that was ever in Egypt led by Moses, or in Palestine led by Joshua, or under Samuel and David—I pass over that congregation under Zerubbabel—the Jews themselves will never amount to another congregation, even if today they all come as one to their Syria and possess it entirely, as they never did before. But the fathers of all the faithful are Abraham and Israel [Jacob], David, Hezekiah, and the like, to whom the Lord promised an inheritance

of peace and every type of sustenance. COMMENTARY ON JEREMIAH 30:4.[4]

FEAR THE BABYLONIAN INVASION. THE ENGLISH ANNOTATIONS: Some of the Jewish doctors, with whom not a few of ours concur, understand the days of the Messiah, and those of the expedition of Gog and Magog, to refer to the troubles raised in the world by way of opposition to Christian profession. But the sounder sort of ours and theirs understand these times as being those of the Babylonian invasion, when the Chaldeans, by their approach to Jerusalem and the assault thereof, filled all places thereabout much more with terror and dread as beforehand mentioned, to show how they should then be roused out of that sleep of security, wherewith the false prophets at present by preaching and promising nothing but peace to them had so deeply possessed them that God's prophets could hardly wake them out of it. Those seem to stray farthest from the scope of the place, who expound it as the Medes and Persians invading the Babylonian state, and striking a grievous terror into the Chaldeans. ANNOTATIONS ON JEREMIAH 30:5.[5]

TERROR, FEAR, AND LACK OF PEACE PORTEND CHRIST. SEBASTIAN MÜNSTER: Both Hebrews and Christians refer these words to the time of Christ. In fact, the Jews understand them as concerning the war of Gog and Magog. But Christians understand them to be concerning the persecution that Christ and the people of God have suffered from the children of this world. Just as Christ said: "I did not come to bring peace to the world, but a sword." "If they persecuted me, they will persecute you." And that which follows, "He will be saved from it," alludes to this: "Be assured; for I have overcome the world." THE TEMPLE OF THE LORD, JEREMIAH 30:5, 7.[6]

---

[4]Pellikan, *Commentaria Bibliorum*, 3:2V3r.
[5]Downame, ed., *Annotations*, 9S2v*; citing Ezek 38:1-23; Mt 10:30, 34; Lk 12:49, 51; Jer 4:9; 6:4; 14:13; Is 13:8.
[6]Münster, *Miqdaš YHWH*, 915; citing Ezek 38:1–39:29; Rev 20:8; Mt 10:34; Jn 15:20; Jn 16:33.

FAITHFUL MEN AND LABORING WOMEN.

JOHANNES OECOLAMPADIUS: See whether a man will give birth. Jeremiah sees in a vision the gestures of men as if they are in labor, which is not natural, by which he signifies that the pain of pious men is like the pain of women in strenuous labor; that is, it is bitter and fierce. When all are masculine in Christ, they will wonder how they suffered such pains, they who are sons of God, since it is characteristic of women and imperfect men to suffer in a womanish fashion like this, but not characteristic of grown men in Christ. To this the Lord alludes in John 16: "When a woman gives birth, she has pain because it is her time, but when she has given birth to a boy, she does not remember her anguish; for she rejoices that a man has been born into the world." So now you have sadness. COMMENTARY ON JEREMIAH 30:6.[7]

THE PROMISE OF AN ETERNAL KING DAVID.

NIKOLAUS SELNECKER: A certain consolation is placed before the Jews and all believers, which they can trust with their whole heart and must hold to in good times and bad. Therefore, here not only the Jews are promised a current liberation from their Babylonian captivity, but this also means the true King David is promised to them. That is, the beloved Son of God the Father, who is the Messiah, our Lord and Savior Jesus Christ, who pardons and blesses us with eternal happiness and redemption. They must hold tight to him, believe in him, and be obedient and serve him. Thus he is your prince, your principal one, your powerful and mighty commander, who comes from you, and is born from your flesh. According to the prophecy of Moses in Deuteronomy 28: "The Lord your God will raise up a prophet from among you and your brothers, to him you shall attend." THE WHOLE PROPHET JEREMIAH 30:9.[8]

THE NATURE OF CAPTIVITY AND HUMAN FREEDOM. JOHANNES BUGENHAGEN: "Certainly that day is great." That is, horrible; to which

nothing is similar. Through hyperbole in the Hebrew usage he preaches the greatest tribulation to come. What is, however, the greatest tribulation of Jacob? Not the captivity of the body, which had happened to the people, but the desperation under the law, sin, and death. It is indeed horrible to fall into the hands and judgment of God, to see eternal damnation, to see that nothing helps you to be freed, to be under the prince of darkness in perpetual desperation. He spoke such that he might signify this most severe captivity under the figure of the captivity of the body: "I will break his yoke and I have not pressed him whose yoke it is, so that they may understand that I will dissolve every captivity: not only the corporal captivity through Cyrus,[†] but also that spiritual and greatest captivity through Christ. . . ."

And so this kingdom will not be earthly, but it will be of God and will be eternal. "They will serve," he says, "the Lord their God, whom I serve in fear and in the assurance of his goodness and mercy." As to where this assurance comes from, of course, it is not through Moses or the law, but through Christ, who in this kingdom is the mediator between God and humanity. COMMENTARY ON JEREMIAH 30:7-10.[9]

GOD PRESERVES HIS PEOPLE AND PLAN.

KONRAD PELLIKAN: Whenever more people would be happily returned from the Babylonian captivity, and would suffer many inconveniences from the Samaritans and neighboring peoples, they would nevertheless always persist and succeed in the restoration of both the temple and the city. Nevertheless this passage seems far more perfectly fulfilled in the advance of the church from the time of Christ and thereafter, since those who are attached to the Lord by a firm faith are not able to be overcome by any fetters, disasters, or deaths. Indeed, those who are called from afar to himself, the Lord preserves, protects, and makes blessed, so they are not terrified by the machines of sin, death,

---

[7]Oecolampadius, *In Hieremiam*, 2:N4r; 152r; citing Jn 16:21.
[8]Selnecker, *Der gantze Prophet Jeremias*, Z2v; citing Deut 18:15.

[9]Bugenhagen, *In Ieremiam*, 4K4v-4L1r. [†]Cyrus, king of Persia (r. 559–530 BC), who conquered Babylon and freed the Jews in 539 BC.

the world, and demons. COMMENTARY ON JEREMIAH 30:10.[10]

GOD ALONE CIRCUMCISES. ANDREAS BODEN-STEIN VON KARLSTADT: Such love does not grow out of our own strength. No. God must apply the glue himself, for God says, Yes I would add him to or appropriate him for myself and he would then come to me. Why? Because how else would anyone willingly incline himself to me, to be near me?

No single heart can of its own strength empty and rid itself of creatures. God alone circumcises. For this reason children are circumcised by others. By this we indicate that no creature is able heartily and eternally to lift himself up . . . and withdraw. . . . Neither is any heart able of its own to incline itself toward or attach itself to God. Rather, God himself has to create and order all things which he wants to have in his own house or temple. THE MEANING OF THE TERM *GELASSENHEIT*.[11]

30:12-24 The Lord Will Bring Health

THE ETERNAL HEALER AND CONSOLATION. NIKOLAUS SELNECKER: We must suffer a grim punishment and the rod of God. It will come when intended. It may actually be the Turk or another servant. . . .

What should we do? Are we finished? Do we have no consolation? True, given what human advice, consolation, help, cleverness, skill, reason, power, effort, courage, power, honor, authority, commitment, and faith offers, we must fully and from here out say and confess: from now on we are lost. There is no hope for betterment. Therefore the punishment of God must certainly come, as God says, "Your harm is undoubtedly severe, and your wound cannot be healed." And for your significant misdeeds and your awful sins I will give you blows. . . . We have no one to whom we can give our guilt, because our malice is our own and our obstinate recklessness and our stubborn

senses. We must be punished soon and nothing else can be done.

But "yes, could it be? Has the Lord so willed?" There is only one for you, our Lord Jesus Christ. I know that you are my consolation; there can be no other for me. You alone are our eternal prince and ruler, who takes us up and pities us. You are the heart of the Father. Show your Father that which you have done for us is enough; then our sins will disappear. We cannot survive them; it is over for us; we cannot step into the presence of God. But you are to us a good and true human being, and you are allowed to be near to God; you are the eternal and beloved Son, in whom none can be denied. You know and see his heart, will, and thoughts. . . . In your will we know that we are God's children, the beloved among the beloved, namely, in you. You are our Mediator and our Helper in time of need. To you we flee; you are our heart's desire; in you all of our passions sigh; our souls cry out to you, our tongue and our mouth: "Help Lord! This is the moment. Stay with us, for it will soon be night." THE WHOLE PROPHET JEREMIAH 30:12-17.[12]

TRUSTING IN WORTHLESS AID. JOHANNES BUGENHAGEN: "All your lovers." There is no help for you from all those in whom you trusted before. They did not help the Jews, who were hoping in aid from Egypt and in treaties with other nations. Their religious worship of God was of no help to them, which they were trusting and which they multiplied for themselves from human doctrines. They were not assisted by any human justice, which without faith was not able to be anything other than hypocrisy, impious presumption, and idolatry. These are human lovers, which we seek for ourselves like harlots when we have abandoned the Word of God, through which God is our spouse. COMMENTARY ON JEREMIAH 30:14.[13]

DO NOT RELY ON HUMAN ALLIANCES. MARTIN LUTHER: You do not notice that you are vainly

---

[10]Pellikan, *Commentaria Bibliorum*, 3:2V3v.
[11]CRR 8:147.
[12]Selnecker, *Der gantze Prophet Jeremias*, 2A1r-2A2r.
[13]Bugenhagen, *In Ieremiam*, 4L2r-v.

trusting in the arm of the flesh. You will have crutches of reeds, and if you want to support yourself with them, you will fall. No understanding, no planning, no might will avail you. I will even make fools of your wise ones so that the very people you are so confident will stand by you will change their minds and oppose you. This is the same thing that Ezekiel 23 says: "Behold, I will rouse up against you your lovers from whom you turned in disgust, and I will bring them against you from every side . . ." etc. And we read in Jeremiah 30: "All your lovers have forgotten you." Exactly the same thing happened to the people of Constantinople when they took the Turk into alliance with them. Shortly after they became a tributary of the Turk. The same thing occurs often in our day in the case of the emperor and pope. While the emperor believes that the pope is standing by him because they have struck a treaty, when the situation becomes serious, the pope changes his mind and turns against the emperor etc. The Jews, too, have experienced the same thing. When they solicited the friendship of the Romans whom they had wanted as their auxiliaries immediately became their masters. This is also what Latin writers say with such elegance that we must seek out our peers as friends and watch out for those who are stronger. LECTURES ON OBADIAH 7.[14]

BUILDING THE SPIRITUAL CITY OF GOD.

JOHANNES OECOLAMPADIUS: Here is a taste of the redemption, about which it is written here and was granted through Zerubbabel and Ezra. For the glory was not yet steadfast, but in this way it was a prelude of the coming truth for the histories of the people of God. But these abundant goods began to be truly shown through Christ Jesus, who restored the churches, which are the tabernacles of Jacob. Indeed, they had all been forsaken, and they have been built on their own stability and the foundations of the apostles and prophets; but these are spiritually constructed. Indeed, the city is built through the Word of God, on the ruins, and the rubble of the former city will be built anew, and in

its own place it will be fortified. This is not without mystery; in the place where the flesh is mortified, the spirit of life ascends. COMMENTARY ON JEREMIAH 30:18.[15]

THE RESTORATION OF THE JEWS, WORSHIP, AND THE CHURCH.

HEINRICH BULLINGER: Now therefore the Lord explains the benefits for many people, which he intends to bestow on the afflicted, and describes abundantly the blessing of freedom from captivity and their of restoration. "Behold I will restore the captivity of the tents," etc. The Lord makes mention of the tents, to signify the ease of restoration. "I will restore your captivity as easily as people will change the location of their tents without difficulty." He adds that he will restore both the city and the temple, just as also the city walls will again be put on their ancient foundations, which are now covered with heaps of rocks and earth, which, as the books of Ezra and Nehemiah describe, was done.

To this exposition he adds what the free people and children of the church would do, or what recompense they would give to the Lord for their freedom. "The voice of exultation and praise shall rise up from among them." Indeed, the godly will offer sacrifices of praise and thanksgiving for the benefits they have received from God. And this is most acceptable to the Lord, as the Psalms testify often, but especially in Psalm 50.

Then the Lord continues in commemoration of the benefits that he promised he would grant to his people. "I will multiply them and they shall not be diminished. . . ." Briefly, just as they were multiplied from the beginning in the land of Egypt and in the land of Canaan and had lived favorably with honor and glory, so indeed it will happen for them after their liberation from Babylon. "And their assembly shall be arranged before me." That is, everywhere there will be religious and political assemblies, to which all will happily go. . . .

But these things should be explained one by one with reference to the church, in which all these

---

[14]LW 18:197-98 (WA 13:218); citing Ezek 23:22.

[15]Oecolampadius, *In Hieremiam*, 2:O3r; citing Hag 1:1.

things are most completely fulfilled; for the Lord turns the church's captivity into freedom and a happy state. The Lord builds the church that was destroyed through tyrants and he puts it on its old, that is, its only foundation: Christ. Truly, the church offers sacrifices of praise for thanksgiving, especially in the Lord's Supper, which was instituted by Christ for this purpose, and is called the Eucharist. Likewise he multiplies the church and makes it honored, whose children and assemblies adhere to one God through Christ, in whom they are directed and defended by God. To him be the glory. SERMON ON JEREMIAH 30:18-20.[16]

RETURN TO SELF-RULE. JOHN TRAPP: Foreigners shall no more domineer over them, but they shall have governors of their own nation, who shall be more tender of them and careful of their good. Some apply all this (and well they may) to Jesus Christ, who is here called *Magnificus* and *Dominator*, his "magnificent or honorable one," and his ruler, who is also one of them and proceeds from among them. COMMENTARY ON JEREMIAH 30:21.[17]

CHRIST IN THE OLD TESTAMENT AND THE LAST JUDGMENT. HEINRICH BULLINGER: Since Christ Jesus our Savior is the source and treasury of every consolation, for this reason Jeremiah now speaks concerning Christ only, and he prophesies from the mouth of God concerning his advent in the world. However, no one understands the predictions of the prophets, as if they were no good for the people of his own age, but only for the people who would come after Christ. Indeed, through Christ the ancient peoples were freed from Egypt and on account of Christ all the blessings that were gathered for them were gathered for them. Moreover, as Paul himself testifies in 1 Corinthians 10: "All of our fathers ate and drank the same spiritual food and drink with us from the rock that accompanied them; and that rock was Christ." So those things that, in the present time, are interpreted with reference to Christ are spoken to this end: that they might bring consolation to the afflicted captives and to all the afflicted faithful until the end of the age. If, moreover, the hope and consolation of the ancients was Christ, it ought to shame Christians to seek some other consolation outside of Christ, or any consolation not from Christ alone. . . .

But by way of contrast the Lord explains what punishments await unbelievers, and this through figurative speech. In fact, he compares the wrath and vengeance of God to a violent storm, which after it has heaped itself up for a long time, to the great horror of those watching, sends itself on the heads of some, whom it utterly crushes. Thus after a long delay through divine forbearance, the wrath of God is gathered, which then settles finally on the heads of the impious. This very thing Saint John the Baptist explained in the Gospel According to John in this way: "He who believes in the Son has eternal life; but truly he who does not believe in the Son, will not see life, but the wrath of God remains upon him." To these words, Jeremiah adds that the vengeance of God would be most certain, severe, and unchangeable, from which no one is able to escape and which never ceases until first it has executed all the judgments of a most righteous God against the ungodly. In vain, therefore, do many promise themselves immunity from punishment for their sins, especially disobedience to the faith. And indeed if we rightly believe and with a sincere faith embrace our Lord Jesus Christ, then the sure vengeance of God cannot not be prepared for us, since it is abolished through Christ alone. SERMON ON JEREMIAH 30:21-24.[18]

AWAITING THE FUTURE IN FAITH, CHRIST, AND EUCHARIST. HULDRYCH ZWINGLI: "In later times you will finally understand." We are compelled to confess that the advent of Christ was not commonly recognized as now it has been—now that he has come. Indeed, even if absolute faith considers predictions of the future to be no less

---

[16]Bullinger, *Conciones*, 179r-v; citing Ps 50:14-15.
[17]Trapp, *A Commentary or Exposition*, 311*; citing Deut 18:18.
[18]Bullinger, *Conciones*, 179v-180r, 180r-v; citing 1 Cor 10:3-4; Jn 3:36.

firm than those things that have already happened, nevertheless things that have already happened compel the senses to confess that they are true, but things in the future are not able to do that, namely, to compel the senses. For which reason, as in the course of things I renew this topic, in the Eucharist, and the remaining sacraments, sensible things are employed for the senses. So he promises that in future times they would very clearly understand the incarnation of Christ, which they understood feebly and generally believed. EXPLANATIONS OF THE PROPHET JEREMIAH 30:24.[19]

---

[19]Zwingli, *Complanationis*, 138.

JEREMIAH 31:1-30
THE LORD WILL TURN MOURNING INTO JOY

¹*"At that time, declares the L*ORD*, I will be the God of all the clans of Israel, and they shall be my people."*

²*Thus says the L*ORD*:*
"The people who survived the sword
found grace in the wilderness;
when Israel sought for rest,
*³the L*ORD *appeared to him^a from far away.*
I have loved you with an everlasting love;
therefore I have continued my faithfulness
to you.
⁴Again I will build you, and you shall be built,
O virgin Israel!
Again you shall adorn yourself with tambourines
and shall go forth in the dance of the
merrymakers.
⁵Again you shall plant vineyards
on the mountains of Samaria;
the planters shall plant
and shall enjoy the fruit.
⁶For there shall be a day when watchmen
will call
in the hill country of Ephraim:
'Arise, and let us go up to Zion,
*to the L*ORD *our God.'"*

⁷*For thus says the L*ORD*:*
"Sing aloud with gladness for Jacob,
and raise shouts for the chief of the nations;
proclaim, give praise, and say,
*'O L*ORD*, save your people,*
the remnant of Israel.'
⁸Behold, I will bring them from the north country
and gather them from the farthest parts of
the earth,
among them the blind and the lame,
the pregnant woman and she who is in
labor, together;
a great company, they shall return here.
⁹With weeping they shall come,
and with pleas for mercy I will lead them back,

I will make them walk by brooks of water,
in a straight path in which they shall not
stumble,
for I am a father to Israel,
and Ephraim is my firstborn.

¹⁰*"Hear the word of the L*ORD*, O nations,*
and declare it in the coastlands far away;
say, 'He who scattered Israel will gather him,
and will keep him as a shepherd keeps his
flock.'
*¹¹For the L*ORD *has ransomed Jacob*
and has redeemed him from hands too
strong for him.
¹²They shall come and sing aloud on the height
of Zion,
and they shall be radiant over the goodness
*of the L*ORD*,*
over the grain, the wine, and the oil,
and over the young of the flock and the herd;
their life shall be like a watered garden,
and they shall languish no more.
¹³Then shall the young women rejoice in the dance,
and the young men and the old shall be merry.
I will turn their mourning into joy;
I will comfort them, and give them gladness
for sorrow.
¹⁴I will feast the soul of the priests with
abundance,
and my people shall be satisfied with my
goodness,
*declares the L*ORD*."*

¹⁵*Thus says the L*ORD*:*
"A voice is heard in Ramah,
lamentation and bitter weeping.
Rachel is weeping for her children;
she refuses to be comforted for her children,
because they are no more."
*¹⁶Thus says the L*ORD*:*
"Keep your voice from weeping,

and your eyes from tears,
for there is a reward for your work,
declares the LORD,
    and they shall come back from the land of
      the enemy.
¹⁷There is hope for your future,
declares the LORD,
    and your children shall come back to their
      own country.
¹⁸I have heard Ephraim grieving,
'You have disciplined me, and I was disciplined,
    like an untrained calf;
bring me back that I may be restored,
    for you are the LORD my God.
¹⁹For after I had turned away, I relented,
    and after I was instructed, I struck my thigh;
I was ashamed, and I was confounded,
    because I bore the disgrace of my youth.'
²⁰Is Ephraim my dear son?
    Is he my darling child?
For as often as I speak against him,
    I do remember him still.
Therefore my heart^b yearns for him;
    I will surely have mercy on him,
declares the LORD.

²¹"Set up road markers for yourself;
    make yourself guideposts;
consider well the highway,
    the road by which you went.
Return, O virgin Israel,
    return to these your cities.

a Septuagint; Hebrew *me*   b Hebrew *bowels*

²²How long will you waver,
    O faithless daughter?
For the LORD has created a new thing on the
    earth:
a woman encircles a man."

²³Thus says the LORD of hosts, the God of Israel:
"Once more they shall use these words in the land of
Judah and in its cities, when I restore their fortunes:

"'The LORD bless you, O habitation of
    righteousness,
    O holy hill!'

²⁴And Judah and all its cities shall dwell there
together, and the farmers and those who wander with
their flocks. ²⁵For I will satisfy the weary soul, and
every languishing soul I will replenish."

²⁶At this I awoke and looked, and my sleep was
pleasant to me.

²⁷"Behold, the days are coming, declares the LORD,
when I will sow the house of Israel and the house of
Judah with the seed of man and the seed of beast.
²⁸And it shall come to pass that as I have watched
over them to pluck up and break down, to overthrow,
destroy, and bring harm, so I will watch over them to
build and to plant, declares the LORD. ²⁹In those days
they shall no longer say:

"'The fathers have eaten sour grapes,
    and the children's teeth are set on edge.'

³⁰But everyone shall die for his own iniquity. Each
man who eats sour grapes, his teeth shall be set on edge.

OVERVIEW: Since judgment and wrath, destruction and exile, idolatry and false prophecy dominate the preceding chapters of Jeremiah, it is not surprising that commentators seem to turn gladly to a chapter celebrating the promises of God's deliverance and salvation for society and the soul. Expositors describe not only the liberation of the people of Israel from their worldly captors but even more so the salvation of God's faithful people from sin and death; gospel themes of redemption, the church, and Christ are found embedded in this chapter. Indeed, interpreters deliberate regarding the true audience of this chapter: Does it refer to the Jews of Jeremiah's time, the Christian church to come as the "true Israel" of faith, or some combination of the two? More precisely, Jeremiah 31:15 and 22, which Christians have traditionally interpreted as prophecies of Christ, raised similar questions. To what degree do "Rachel weeping" and "a woman encircling a man" speak exclusively to the Jews in captivity, or to the Christian Messiah, or to both in some way?

31:1-14 Celebrate God's Redemption

THE GOD WHO DELIVERS AND LIBERATES.

JOHN CALVIN: We now perceive the design of the prophet . . . that there was no reason to fear that God would fail in due time to deliver his people; for it was well known that then when he became formerly the liberator of his people, his power was manifested in many and resplendent ways. It was inconceivably great since for forty years he had nourished his people in the desert, and their coming out [before that] was like the dead rising from their graves; for the Egyptians might have easily killed the whole people. So they were taken as it were from death [to life] when they were led into the land that had been promised to Abraham. There was therefore no doubt but that God would again, as he had formerly shown toward their fathers, deliver them in a wonderful way and manifest the same power in liberating them.

A profitable doctrine may be gathered from this: whenever despair presents itself to our eyes, or whenever our miseries tempt us to despair, let the benefits of God come to our minds, not only those that we ourselves have experienced, but also those that he has in all ages conferred on his church. David too speaks of this when he had this one consolation in his grief and when he was pressed down with extreme evil that almost overwhelmed him with despair, "I remember the days of old." Thus he not only called to mind the benefits of God that he himself had experienced but also what he had heard from his fathers and what he had read of in the books of Moses. In the same manner the prophet here reminds us of God's benefits, when we seem to be forsaken by him; for this one thought is capable of alleviating [our misery] and comforting us. COMMENTARY ON JEREMIAH 31:1-2.[1]

THE TRUE PEOPLE OF GOD. JOHANNES BUGEN-

HAGEN: This is the joyful dissolution of captivity after seventy years; but afterward the gospel of Christ over Jews and Gentiles was the most joyful. But just as the Israelites have not received in the flesh, after the seventy years of the Babylonian captivity, all those things that are here promised, even until today, nevertheless, I say, these very promises of God have now been fulfilled most blessedly. But you will remember what God said at the end of the preceding chapter, "On the last day," that is, "when I will cast away this people and they will no more be the people of God," just as God had horribly threatened in his curses. That final rejection and the fulfilled wrath of God were accomplished by the Romans, and after that the Jews did not have any promise of God about a return to their land. Now after fifteen hundred years they do business not laboring under some corporal captivity, as they themselves pretend, but they freely wander through the world, a people of Satan cast away from their homeland and their God, as God had warned those who were contemptuous of and who murdered both the prophets and Christ. . . .

Then, he says, I will not be the God who is apart from the people of Israel, but I will be the God of all the families of Israel and those families themselves will be my people. That is, the believing sons of God—the impious Israelites having been rejected, etc.—and those things that you now hear from the mouth of God in the words of Jeremiah, the prophet, which began to be fulfilled, albeit barely, with certain Jews after the dissolution of the Babylonian captivity—through Christ these things were completed for the first time and completely fulfilled, just as also before we have occasionally said such things based on the Scriptures, and more than once with reference to this prophet. "I will be the God of all the families of Israel." He spoke the same promise above in these words: "You will be my people; I will be your God." So you see clearly that a new testament is promised. COMMENTARY ON JEREMIAH 31.[2]

---

[1]CTS 20:55-56* (CO38:643); citing Ps 143:5.

[2]Bugenhagen, *In Ieremiam*, 4N1v, 4N2r-v; citing Jer 30:23-24; Deut 28:1-68; Lev 26:1-46; Jer 30:22.

A NEW AGE, A NEW ISRAEL. JOHANNES OECO-LAMPADIUS: "At that time." This verse is like an epilogue of the previous prophecy. The two tribes, Judah and Benjamin, were liberated from Babylon, but in Christ's reign all the families of Israel will be redeemed. But "all the families" are not all the people of Israel, who hear this, for that is Israel according to the flesh, to whom the heavenly promises are not precisely due. But in that hidden "Israel" it is widely evident through "families" that are all saved through Christ and that the carnal Israel will not be completely cast out. Indeed, when the plentitude of the nations has entered, all Israel will be saved, and the whole Israel of the spirit will be redeemed—however many among them are chosen. Meanwhile, the sons of Israel will settle without a king, without a governor, and without sacrifice. They will eventually be returned, and they will seek the Lord their God and David their king, who indeed reigns with the Father in glory and through the Holy Spirit in the hearts of the elect. COMMENTARY ON JEREMIAH 31:1.[3]

THE GIFTS OF GOD TO ALL WHO BELIEVE. JOHANN PAPPUS: The second type of benefit promised in this chapter embraces the expansion of the teaching of the gospel. In fact, so that this benefit might be so much more striking, not only is it compared to the exodus from Egypt, but it is also illustrated with other very elegant comparisons.

The exodus of the Israelites from Egypt was certainly a great benefit and work of God to be admired, as is their preservation in the desert for forty years, and their entry at last into the Promised Land. But no less admirable is the work of spreading the gospel throughout the whole world. Let us not seem to wish to squander the many proofs in a visible thing, or let it not appear from here that this benefit was related to one people alone. But indeed that act, in a fixed time, was the proof of a free and eternal love. If indeed the Jewish people were eventually cast aside after being frequently chastised, nevertheless the mercy of God, which embraces the

church, is perpetual and eternal. So in this promise we should examine all the similes to which the dissemination of the teaching itself is joined. Indeed, it is a spiritual benefit, how we are being built on the foundation of the prophets and apostles with Christ as the manifest cornerstone. It is the timbrel of joy, beating the sadness from the hearts of sinners and emerging from the curse of the law. Finally, it is a very fertile vineyard planted not only on the high places of Zion but also on the mountain of Samaria, whose fruit leads all the believers to the Lord our God. ON ALL THE PROPHETS, JEREMIAH 31:2-6.[4]

GIFTS OF PEACE. JOHANNES BUGENHAGEN: These are rightly gifts of God, which the monks and Anabaptists judge as sinful, namely, when girls go out to respectable dances, and our boys are allowed to play in the streets, which is not allowed in a time of war. This peace, therefore, ought to be recognized as a gift of God with thanksgiving. A time of peace is when people are allowed to cultivate the arts of peace, grant justice, constitute the government and order it well, educate the young, preach the gospel, take care of every honorable and household matter. We ought not to abuse this gift, so that we forget God and his precepts, but it is like those about whom the psalm sings: "whose sons are as new plants," etc., or they have said, "Blessed are the people who have these things, and blessed is the people whose God is the Lord." COMMENTARY ON JEREMIAH 31:4.[5]

WEEPING IN BABYLON, ANTICIPATING GOD'S PROMISE. NIKOLAUS SELNECKER: Jeremiah wanted these poor Jews fully to imagine the grace of God, so that they might be more patient, and at the same time know and hope that God according to his promise would again bring them home. In the future they would be happy and of good courage as they would make merry, play music, dance, plant, and go to the temple of the Lord and have a good peace. Likewise, such are God's good

---

[3]Oecolampadius, *In Hieremiam*, 2:O4v-P1r.

[4]Pappus, *In Omnes Prophetas*, 101v.
[5]Bugenhagen, *In Ieremiam*, 4N3v; citing Ps 144:12, 15.

things for all his own, who recognize, rightly need, and should be thankful to God whenever we have a current peace and can go to church to hear God's Word, which is a good thing to do together; thereby we will not forget God.

Let us pay attention to our symbol and let all Christians rhyme, so that today we might be *flentes et orantes*, weeping and praying. For this is our life. It is better that we have nothing and do not wish for something better in our own time until we depart from our own Babylon. Therefore, until we are summoned from this world, this means that "we sow with tears and will reap a harvest of joy." As Jesus says, "you will see me only a short time." That has to do with weeping and hazy air. But thereafter it will be better: "so shall the blind, lame, the pregnant woman and the woman giving birth all have all joy and a home; their trusting shall be transformed into eternal joy." THE WHOLE PROPHET JEREMIAH 31:4-8.[6]

WATCHMEN OF WORD AND WORSHIP. JOHANNES BUGENHAGEN: The cause of all the prosperity, with which God will bless the Israelites or the ten tribes, will be this: there will be watchmen present by the grace of God, that is, preachers, who will admonish the people according to the law so that they might ascend to Zion or Jerusalem to worship of the Lord and make sacrifices. The people will have the Word of God through priests, Levites, and other prophets. Therefore, the people will fear the Lord and worship according to his word and precepts, that is, according to the will of God, which is the true worship and honor of God. How can worship without the Word of God, that is, without faith, be anything other than an abomination and idolatry? COMMENTARY ON JEREMIAH 31:6.[7]

CARING FOR THE VINEYARD. THE ENGLISH ANNOTATIONS: Most say that such persons as are described are set purposefully on work by the state

to watch as sentinels on public places to decry and give warning of any enemy's approach, and the word used here seems so to be taken, which therefore most apply to ministers of the gospel. Nevertheless, I conceive rather that the allusion is to the keepers of the vineyards, whereof mention was before made, as such are designed and alluded to under this term (for of those in times of public peace and security there is not so much use), that they should be enticing and calling one to another to go worship God in the set places of his public and solemn service. Which albeit was to be in its chief and highest degree, and accomplished under the Messiah, when the faith of him should by those of that nation be embraced. Yet I believe that conceit of a great man to be a little too curious, who would have the term "Nazarenes" in the term here found alluded to, sometime given by some to the Christians. ANNOTATIONS ON JEREMIAH 31:6.[8]

SALVATION COMES THROUGH THE JEWS. KONRAD PELLIKAN: The exiles and captives with King Jehoiachin were abducted sadly and with tears, as were those who would be taken away with King Zedekiah. "But I will bring them back with consolation, and with joy I have pitied them, whom I will lead back whole and uninjured, without danger from their enemies or hindrance of waters on a straight path, as a shepherd leads his flock and a father his most loving children." Moreover Ephraim is called the firstborn of God—the people of Israel. Israel is often called Ephraim, sometimes to distinguish the kingdom of the ten tribes from the kingdom of Judah, and sometimes to refer to the great sprouting forth and multiplication of the children of God. Although a multitude of the nations shall arrive at the worship of the true God, nevertheless, salvation comes from the Jews, from whom came forth Christ, the apostles, the Evangelists, and those who planted the early churches. As is deservedly said by everyone else, as it is said by their equals, in the church of

---

[6]Selnecker, *Der gantze Prophet Jeremias*, 2A4v; citing Ps 126:5; Jn 16:16.
[7]Bugenhagen, *In Ieremiam*, 4P4r-v.

[8]Downame, ed., *Annotations*, 9T1r-v*; citing Ezek 33:2; Is 21:6; 2 Kings 17:9; 18:18; Is 52:8; 62:6; Jer 4:16-17; Jn 4:40-41; Acts 8:1, 25; 24:5; Is 11:1.

Christ the Israelite tribe will take first place for itself. COMMENTARY ON JEREMIAH 31:9.[9]

CHRIST GARDENS US. LANCELOT ANDREWES: [Christ] it is that gardens our "souls" too, and makes them, as the prophet says, "like a well-watered garden"; he weeds out of them whatsoever is noisome or unsavory, sows and plants them with true roots and seeds of righteousness, waters them with the dew of his grace, and makes them bring forth fruit to eternal life.

But it is none of all these, but besides all these, nay over and above all these, this day (if ever) most properly he was a gardener. He was one, and so after a more peculiar manner he might take this likeness on him. Christ, [after rising from the dead] was indeed a gardener, and indeed a strange one, who made such [an] herb grow out of the ground this day as the like was never seen before, a dead body to shoot forth alive out of the grave.

I ask, was he so this day alone? No, but by this profession of his, this day which he begun, he will follow to the end. For it is he, who by virtue of this morning's act, shall garden our bodies too, turn all our graves into garden plots; yea, he shall one day turn land and sea and all into a great garden, and so care for them as they shall in due time bring forth live bodies alive again. SERMON ON JOHN 20:11-17.[10]

THE PROMISES AND BOUNTY OF THE LORD. HEINRICH BULLINGER: To them he also promises: and by promising he makes credible the liberation of the Jews from Babylon; for he uses a certain new genre of speech. Indeed as long as he orders Jeremiah to announce the liberation of his people to the nations far and wide, even among the islands, those things must be quite certain. Indeed God would not order him to announce a lie to the islands and through the nations, among whom he does not want his holy name to be polluted.

Moreover, he provides words for them with which they might announce that celebrated

liberation. He says, "he who had scattered Israel," etc. These words signify that the Lord is God, who leads us to the gates of hell and back, and indeed that he who destroys is able to save. Or as Medea says in Ovid, "I was able to save, now you ask if I can destroy?"[†] Truly, it did not seem possible to the Jews that the city of Jerusalem would be destroyed. But the Lord destroyed it, and he led those he chose off to Babylon. Likewise, it seemed impossible to those very people that they would be led back and that everything would be restored. But the all-powerful God did restore everything. Another huge blessing befell them, which God wanted to be proclaimed among the nations: that the Lord not only led back and restored his people, but that he took particular care of them. Indeed, he will guard his people, he says, like a shepherd guards his flock, to whom he provides convenient and nourishing food and drink. Again he watches over them, lest they perish from disease, sickness, or attack from wild animals. But also with the words "freed," "redeemed," and "planted," he uses verbs in the past tense, speaking about a future deed, in order to signify the truth and certainty of the deed. This redemption will be so certain and accomplished that it is as if it has already been completed. The Babylonians were more powerful than the Jews, but the Almighty God surpasses them all in strength. In this we securely trust. Indeed, God is Lord of death, the world, the devil, hell, sin, and of every power. So if he wants to save us, he is able to save us in any difficulty of this age and from the desperate evils themselves. Also, the calling of the nations to the grace of the gospel of Christ is hinted at in these verses. . . .

Furthermore, he shows immediately afterward the thanks that those who have been freed will give to the Lord their liberator and benefactor in return for the vindication and blessings they have received: where the duty of Christians is pointed out, there is woven in a rather rich enumeration of the benefits to be conferred by the Lord on the people of God. For these things also the godly give thanks while praising the generosity and boundless grace of the Lord in all things. The Israelites will come to the mountain and

[9]Pellikan, *Commentaria Bibliorum*, 3:2V5r.
[10]Andrewes, *Works*, 3:16*.

to lofty Zion; they will rejoice and praise the Lord. The mount of Zion was consecrated for the temple and worship of God, and so it was a type of the church of Christ. Thus the pious celebrated God, both in the place pointed out to them by God and in the church of the saints. There follows "and they will flow"; that is, in great abundance they will gather themselves together to celebrate the goodness of the Lord, namely, to celebrate the Lord on account of his goodness and to celebrate his goodness, since from this goodness he gives to his people grain, wine, oil, and every other thing that is commemorated in this passage. He adds to these external goods another that is far more excellent—a heart that is happy and always flourishing. . . .

Therefore we learn that an abundance of all things is provided by the Lord and that the need for all things makes use of it. Clearly in all these verses God promises nothing other than that he will give an abundance of all things—to a point beyond fulfillment—to his own people. Indeed at the end he adds, "And my people shall be filled with these good things." SERMON ON JEREMIAH 31:10-14.[11]

31:15-21 Rachel's Weeping

THE PERILS OF SIEGE AND THE GRIEF OF RACHEL. JOHANNES BUGENHAGEN: "A voice is heard on high." He explains here what he has said before, "I will turn their mourning into joy." And first he speaks of the two tribes. Now, in fact, lament and shouting is heard outside Jerusalem because of the Babylonian forces—in Bethlehem and all around it in all its surrounding districts (because they were not walled places) everything is destroyed, the miserable residents perish and are carried off into captivity in Babylon, and nothing remains there except the miserable face of continuing desolation. There "Rachel is weeping for her children and does not want to receive or hear consolation from her children," that is, from the

cities and inhabitants of her land; for there was no hope of life from those who were killed, and there was no hope of return from those who were led away. Meanwhile, Jerusalem and the remaining walled cities, because they heard and saw these things, were miserably afraid, as they withstood the siege, as long as it was allowed them to do so, as is said at the end of the book of Kings.

At any rate, either a little before the siege or during the siege itself, they saw and heard the unfortified towns, among which was Bethlehem and the countryside being miserably ravaged, the people murdered and abducted, which was the beginning of the captivity of the two tribes, until Jerusalem itself was captured in the third year after she began to be besieged. Indeed, when the enemies are not able to capture fortified cities, nevertheless they miserably destroy adjacent towns which are not able to resist—as the Turk did recently in Vienna and is now doing in Hungary.[†] There is no other who fights for us except you, our God. . . .

The Gospel of Matthew says that what Jeremiah speaks of was accomplished or completed at the time when the boys of Bethlehem were being killed, as he would say. Here again what Jeremiah once predicted concerning Rachel is done; here again there is the good Rachel who weeps for her sons in Bethlehem and all its surrounding districts. In Bethlehem and its surrounding fields there arises the huge cry and lamentation of fathers and mothers because of their slaughtered sons. Why would Matthew not make this citation, when he saw an event happening again that had once occurred according to the prophet Jeremiah and when both the place and the deed agree with the words of the prophet? It is as if we ought not cite the Psalms—which usually have another history—about our own misery, temptation, and salvation. COMMENTARY ON JEREMIAH 31:15.[12]

---

[11]Bullinger, *Conciones*, 182r-182v; citing Jn 10:10. †A line from the lost tragedy *Medea* of the Roman poet Ovid (d. AD 17), which survives in the *Institutes of Oratory* (bk. 8, ch. 6) of Quintilian (d. c. AD 100).

[12]Bugenhagen, *In Ieremiam*, 4Q4r-v, 4R2v; citing 2 Kings 25; Mt 2:18. †The Ottoman Turks conquered Hungary in 1526 and ruled there until 1629. They besieged Vienna in 1529. Turkish invasion is a key influence on the Second Diet of Speyer, at which leaders of the Holy Roman Empire gathered to discuss religious policy and at which Lutheran princes "protested,"

CONSOLATION FOR RACHEL. NIKOLAUS SEL-
NECKER: This is an assurance that God wants to
restore richly the pious who grieve. This is Rachel,
the wife of the patriarch Jacob and the mother of
Joseph and Benjamin. She weeps and grieves
because of her poor children, who in her region and
the borders around Bethlehem have been brutally
murdered. Though it had not yet happened for her,
she means that the Babylonians have conquered
Jerusalem and captured the Jews, the many small
towns and cities have been plundered, robbed,
ravaged, and laid waste. As it was in such times, so
we have experienced with the Spaniards in Germany, and likewise so the poor people of Hungary
and Austria have often experienced with great
wailing and misery as the Turk has laid waste to
everything. Women and children have been
skewered and cruelly strangled. There is then a
howling and lamenting that no consolation will
help; there everything is gone, and it appears that
everything is shattered and has fallen into chaos.
There the godly Rachel weeps over her children;
that is, the whole land is in mourning, all the cities
and small towns shiver and sigh. . . . This passage
Matthew also brings and introduces from the
prophet Jeremiah, concerning the children King
Herod killed in Bethlehem and in the surrounding
area. THE WHOLE PROPHET JEREMIAH 31:15.[13]

**RACHEL'S LAMENT AND THE GOSPEL OF
MATTHEW.** JOHN CALVIN: The prophet first
describes the desolation of the land, when deprived
of its inhabitants; and second he adds a comfort—
that God would restore the captives from exile so
that the land might be again inhabited. But there is
here what they call personification, that is, an
imaginary person is introduced. The prophet lifts
up Rachel from the grave and represents her
lamenting. She had been long dead and her body

had been reduced to ashes. But the discourse has
more force when lamentation is ascribed to a dead
woman than if the prophet had said that the land
would present a sad and mournful appearance. . . .
The prophet, then, though not taught in a school of
rhetoricians, thus adorned his discourse through
the impulse of God's Spirit that he might more
effectively penetrate into the hearts of the people. . . .

This passage is quoted by Matthew, where he
gives an account of the infants under two years old
who had been slain by the command of Herod:
then he says that this prophecy was fulfilled, even
that Rachel again wept for her children. But the
explanation of this is not difficult; for Matthew
meant only that the same thing happened at the
coming of Christ as had taken place before, when
the whole country was reduced to desolation; for it
was the Evangelist's object to remove an offense
arising from novelty. As we know human minds
feel dread when anything new or unexpected
happens or has never happened before. Hence the
Evangelists often direct their attention to this point,
so that what happened in the time of Christ might
not terrify or disturb the minds of people as a new
and unexpected thing, inasmuch as the fathers
formerly had experienced the same thing. There is,
then, no reason for interpreters to torture themselves by explaining this passage allegorically; for
Matthew did not intend to lessen the authority of
ancient history, for he knew in what sense this had
been formerly said. His only object was to remind
the Jews that there was no cause for them to be
greatly astonished at that slaughter, for the region
had formerly been laid waste and bereaved of all its
inhabitants as though a mother, having had a large
family, were to lose all her children. COMMENTARY
ON JEREMIAH 31:15-16.[14]

CONSOLATION FOR ISRAEL. NIKOLAUS SEL-
NECKER: This is a very pleasant consolation and
heartfelt sermon from God. While before God had
consoled the tribe of Judah, here he consoles the
people of Israel, who long before had been led away

---

thus giving birth to the name Protestants. The ongoing threat
of Muslim Turkish invasion encouraged military collaboration
among Roman Catholics and Protestants and reminded them
of their shared Christian culture and heritage.
[13]Selnecker, *Der gantze Prophet Jeremias*, 2B1r-v; citing Gen 29:1-35;
Mt 2:18.

[14]CTS 20:88-91* (CO 38:664-66); citing Mt 2:18.

into captivity. "I have heard," says the Lord, "your repentant weeping and sadness, that you recognize and confess your misdeeds and see the reasons for my chastising you. Namely, because of your sins: you were like a lusty bullock that could not be yoked and could not be made tame; you wanted no bridle and you would not suffer or bear a yoke, nor did you allow yourself to be ruled or instructed. But now you have been chastised and in your correction you have prayed and promised to correct your lives—and you do so from the heart. You have remembered that you offended, irritated, and angered me with your sins, which is to say, it will go very badly for you when you have angered me. Therefore, I will turn the Father's heart to you; I will let my best be given for you, and I will have mercy on you. I will fulfill my promise. I will give my Son for you, who shall help you in this sinful predicament, and through my precious Son you shall be my child." THE WHOLE PROPHET JEREMIAH 31:16-18.[15]

RECOGNIZING ORIGINAL SIN. PHILIPP MELANCHTHON: So we teach nothing about original sin that is contrary to the Scripture or the church catholic, but we have cleansed and brought to light important teachings of the Scriptures and the Fathers that had been obscured by the sophistic arguments of modern theologians. . . . Recognition of original sin is a necessity, nor can we know the magnitude of the grace of Christ unless we acknowledge our faults. All the righteousness of humankind is mere hypocrisy before God unless we acknowledge that of itself the heart is lacking in love, fear, and trust in God. Thus the prophet says, "After I was instructed, I smote upon my thigh." APOLOGY OF THE AUGSBURG CONFESSION.[16]

CLEARING YOUR INNER HOUSE. HANS HUT: The farmer does not sow corn among thistles, thorns, branches, and stones. Rather, he clears them out and then does the sowing. In the same way, understand that God does not sow the Word in someone who is full of thistles and thorns, who desires only the creaturely. Worry about physical prosperity, which God forbids, must first be rooted out. The carpenter does not build a house out of uncut trees. First he cuts them down and shapes them according to his will. Only then does he build a house out of them. This is how we are to learn God's work and will in relation to us. It's like the steps people go through in getting a house ready before they move into it. We are that house, says Paul. A BEGINNING OF A TRUE CHRISTIAN LIFE.[17]

GOD MUST REVEAL OUR SIN. ANDREAS BODENSTEIN VON KARLSTADT: Through the law sin can obviously not be understood. Rather, the Spirit of God must reveal sin if one is to understand sin as sin and know evil. . . . It is written therefore: "When you showed me my transgressions, I was ashamed and beat my thighs." This is as much to say that neither law nor reason will help me to be ashamed. But when God himself reveals my sin, then shame, regret, sorrow, penance, and improvement and everything that goes with understanding evil come my way. SEVERAL MAIN POINTS OF CHRISTIAN TEACHING.[18]

DEEP REPENTANCE AND DIVINE LOVE. JOHANNES OECOLAMPADIUS: True penance is that by which one knows oneself to be nothing and a sinner and gives glory to God everywhere. Thus we say, "With you working, with me being humble, I began to grieve and to repent of my sins, to the point that I even violently shake my loins and sink down from grief, not daring to raise my eyes to heaven because of the shame of my youth." The father hears this voice of the son. He does not restrain himself from having mercy.

The days of youth, that is, the former days, are when covenant of marriage is fresh, but in the text he calls it the age of the desert. "Are you my son?" "I do not despise this voice of penitence, for it is the voice of my dearest son, whom I value highly, and I will

---

[15]Selnecker, *Der gantze Prophet Jeremias*, 2B2r-v.
[16]BoC 104.

[17]CRR 12:127; citing Mt 6:25-34; Lk 12:22-31; Heb 3:4.
[18]CRR 8:358.

permit no evil in where my beloved are. Ephraim is my people, for now, as soon as I began to speak of him, I have kept my eyes of mercy from turning away from him. But I am gazing at him without pause; I will be merciful to him. I will not turn away from his tears." Truly, God receives a contrite heart and not sacrifices. I know well enough how much misery he suffers. "For because I have adopted you into the covenant through the word of my promises, and I have declared my will in choosing, I have always loved you, even while I correct those faults by which you have transgressed against me." This is a passage for the full assurance of faith. Truly the beloved of God who fall into calamity immediately experience a paternal blessing even in the midst of the scourges themselves. It goes well for us when God begins to speak through his Son the word of salvation. In such things no evil is able to touch us. COMMENTARY ON JEREMIAH 31:19-20.[19]

THE RETURN OF A FAITHFUL, REPENTANT PEOPLE. KONRAD PELLIKAN: Another, but continuous, prophecy to the people of Israel, that even in the land of enemies the exiled people return to the Lord with their whole heart and so that even by the road on which they were carried into exile they would return with a sure returning, as if by marked paths, nor would those about to return stray from the road on which they went away. But with their righteous route preserved they would happily deserve their return to the abundant land, whenever they would be allowed by King Cyrus or Darius. Or if it pleased the Lord even more, they at least would experience elsewhere a kind and favorable master, and be able to succeed in the glory of God, which alone is the desire of the saints, not hindered from their holy endeavors by their location and with gracious divine help. Indeed, Israel was not dispersed among the nations without bearing great fruit; for there they taught the worship of one God to the nations, to whom Peter the apostle and the others apostles likewise wrote their letters and by their preaching personally

converted people of those nations to Christ. Meanwhile, God ordered that watchmen be established to pour out invocations and prayers with bitter tears for the return of the people to the Lord their Creator and to return to the way of repentance with their whole heart so that they might be permitted to return to their cities as had been promised to them in the law. COMMENTARY ON JEREMIAH 31:21.[20]

31:22 A Woman Encircles a Man

A CHRISTOLOGICAL READING. JOHANNES BUGENHAGEN: Some interpret the woman and man collectively, the singular for the plural. So the woman will encircle the man, or put on the man, or she will change into the man or will be the man; that is, those who now are afraid are like noncombatant or peaceful women, who now grieve or strike the thigh like women giving birth, who are now oppressed by a foreign yoke like a wife under a bad husband: they will be men—strong, swift, free, confident, and living well in the name of the Lord after the Babylonian captivity. So they say, "The woman will encircle or put on the man." This is a forced and violent exposition, especially on the phrase "She will encircle," so about that interpretation now I can say nothing else. . . .

Our ancestors before us understood this passage with reference to the pregnant mother of the savior, which is the true meaning of this promise. But that which is said here—"upon the earth" or "over the earth"—the interpreters have not adequately treated. Indeed they generally understand "over the earth," that is, "in the world," but nevertheless since Jeremiah here was speaking specifically about the land of Israel or the kingdom of Ephraim, as it once was, he adds this singular prophecy concerning the land where Christ would be conceived, carried in the womb of his mother, and afterward would be raised, so that in vain would the Jews ridicule our Lord Jesus Christ, calling him a Nazarene and Galilean. . . .

---

[19]Oecolampadius, *In Hieremiam*, 2:Q1v-Q2r; citing Ps 51:16-17.   [20]Pellikan, *Commentaria Bibliorum*, 3:2V6r.

The Lord will do what he has promised and will create anew a new thing that was not made or created before. A woman will encircle and carry in her womb that promised seed of a woman, not the seed of man. She will encircle and enclose within her maternal organs the greatest, most steadfast, and largest crusher of the serpent's head, that omnipotent man.... Then the Lord will create and make a new thing, so that a woman encircles in the womb the one who crushes the serpent's head, who is not the seed of a man, but the seed of a woman, that is, of the Virgin Mother. O blessed are those who will see and hear him! Would that it were permitted me to see and hear him! Nevertheless here is my hope and confidence before God. COMMENTARY ON JEREMIAH 31:22.[21]

THE WIFE'S EMBRACE AND THE DIVINE MAN. KONRAD PELLIKAN: To this point you have continually floated through the worship of various idols for long enough, nowhere finding rest or salvation, after you abandoned your Creator, and you committed adultery with the idols of the Gentiles while your legitimate husband was abandoned.

But the Lord will do an incredible and to this point unusual thing in the land: "a woman will encompass a man." The Israelite nation, after a long desertion of her husband, God, and the neglect of true piety, will return to the Lord her God, and she will embrace her husband with the arms of faith, love, and obedience and with her whole mind she will stick to her Lord with the closest bond. Yet Just as a wife holds her spouse, so Israel will hold and never desert her Lord God anymore. This is understood most fully and truly concerning those Israelites dispersed through the world who, when they were admonished by the preaching of the apostles, established the church of the Lord with the many nations in the worship of the only one and true God. Through allegory this passage is also able to be understood in relation to the Blessed Virgin and the conception of Christ, without the

seed of a man, as perfectly divine and human. COMMENTARY ON JEREMIAH 31:22.[22]

WHO IS THE WOMAN? JOHN TRAPP: Some say the Jews (who are now looked upon as weak women, and may say peaceful doe, are we anything but agitated?) shall compass about and conquer the Chaldees, those men of might. Or, as others understand it, the Christian church, though weak and inconsiderable at first, it yet shall be able, by the confession of her faith, to resist her most potent persecutors, and by faith to overcome them, as she did in the apostles, in the noble army of martyrs and confessors. The text is generally understood as speaking of Christ's wonderful conception in the womb of his Virgin Mother. COMMENTARY ON JEREMIAH 31:22.[23]

SOMETHING NEW UNDER THE SUN. JOHN DONNE: Solomon has exclaimed, "Is there anything about which one might say, 'Behold, this is new'?" He answers ... "There is nothing new under the sun." But behold here is one greater than Solomon, and he takes action by being born of a virgin. This he had said long ago in a prophecy: "The Lord has created a new thing on the earth, a woman shall encompass a man." If this had been spoken of such a woman who was not a virgin, then this would not be a new thing. But there was no prior example of this, and it occurred outside of natural reason.... If it were reasonable, it would not be a miracle. If there was a precedent for it, it would not be singular. But God intended both; it is a miracle and has happened only once.

We see in nature how trees bud out and then there is an emission and emanation of flowers and fruits without any help from humanity or any act we do to that tree. We read in Genesis that the earth produced all the plants and herbs before any rain fell upon them or anyone tilled the earth. These are helpful illustrations for us. We believe

---

[21]Bugenhagen, *In Ieremiam*, 4Viv-4V2v, 4Xir; citing Gen 3:15.

[22]Pellikan, *Commentaria Bibliorum*, 3:2V6r.

[23]Trapp, *A Commentary or Exposition*, 314*; citing 1 Jn 5:4; Acts 4:1–5:42.

that a virgin brought forth a son. But nothing from nature could be proved to someone unless one believed it beforehand. Therefore, blessed is the God who has given us the strength which the Egyptian midwives observed among the women of Israel, that they brought forth children without the help of midwives. So likewise we can humbly believe these mysteries of our religion by faith and without the hand and help of reason. SERMON ON GALATIANS 4:4-5.[24]

UNFAITHFUL ISRAEL, FAITHFUL ISRAEL, AND THE VIRGIN BIRTH. HULDRYCH ZWINGLI: "A woman will surround a man" seems to us to be a proverbial saying, referring to the greatest and closest union, namely, of the true Israel, who will be the wife, and of the man, that is, the ba'al, or husband: God. It is as if he says, "Why should I say many things about reconciliation? Just as a wife holds her husband, so Israel will hold the Lord her God."

But now it is asked right away, when will Israel hold the Lord like this? But if she says, "Truly I hold him, but he turns away from me," that can pretty much only be the reasoning of the Jews, when they say that their worship is of the one highest God and they cannot receive Christ because he cannot be God; for if he were God, God would have been Christ from eternity. But I return to their answer: "We worship the one and only God, the creator and ruler of all things, and we are his wife, they say." Why therefore, I say, is he not your husband, if you say he is? Why does he not preserve a conjugal faith with you? You stick to him; he rejects you. Therefore he is found to be faithless, since he does not repay faith with faith. If you were his faithful one, if you belonged to his house, if you were joined to him with marital bonds, if you looked up to him, and he looked down on you from on high, it would already have happened that God would not be able to wipe out the mark of faithlessness—God who, as you watched yourselves go through so many hardships, did not help you, did not embrace you, did not

make you happy. But that would be completely absurd. Who indeed believes that the divine will is so cruel and severe, that it deigns to take no account of those who most religiously worship him? Or do the holy texts and divine promises not promise something different?

Therefore Israel is the wife who embraces the Lord, but since Israel according to the flesh is not that wife, is indeed not recognized by the Lord as her husband, it is evident that this carnal wife has been divorced on account of her poisoning, and that the true Rachel or Israel, that is, the faithful scattered through the whole world, have embraced the Lord and have been made his wife. And he in turn has greeted her as wife: "I have come, my sister and my wife" etc. Indeed in this, universal refutations and rejections point as with a finger: Leah is blind; Rachel has a pleasant and intelligent face. Ishmael, Esau, and Ruben are esteemed less; Isaac, Jacob, and Judah are preferred, etc. When would I have time to call to mind all of these examples? . . .

This new thing that the Lord promised he would do over the land was done at that time, when the church, the true wife of Christ, and the true Israel embraced Christ throughout the whole world. So in this way "woman" does not so much signify the Virgin Mother of God as the fruitful church, although the bridegroom was brought into the light through the virgin, since she too surrounded him, that is, she conceived and gave birth to him, but this was predicted in other passages by other prophets, according to our reasoning, so that in this case the notion of the virgin birth need not be brought into this passage. Therefore we said that on the face of it this does not seem to be the sense: a woman, that is, a virgin, will surround, that is, will conceive and become the mother of, a man, that is, Christ, etc. For to this appearance and manner of the generation of Christ from a virgin the prophet did not look principally in this passage, but I say that in hindsight this meaning is understood. I think this is clear now. Indeed since it is established that the Israel of faith—not Israel according to the flesh—is this wife who has embraced God like a wife, and that it cannot be the

---

[24]Donne, *Sermons*, 6:337*; citing Eccles 1:9-10; Gen 1:11-12; Ex 1:19.

carnal Israel on account of the indignation, anger, and divorce in which it is even now mired; and that the Israel of faith is none other than those who have faith in Christ, and that Christ, in whom they have faith, was descended from Mary, a virgin: now, I say, from the farthest remove this too is investigated, that this embrace with which the woman, of course I mean the church, embraces Christ the bridegroom leads even the Virgin Mother of God into the theater. Indeed since Christ the husband was born of a virgin, according to the word of the apostle, now the mother herself—the mother of his "woman" [the church] and of the groom—is an attendant in the procession. She herself is not the bride, but the mother of the groom. EXPLANATIONS OF THE PROPHET JEREMIAH 31:22.[25]

THE WOMAN IS NOT THE VIRGIN MARY. JOHN CALVIN: Now follows the miracle, "A woman shall surround a man." Christians, almost with one consent, explain this of the Virgin Mary; and the "new thing" leads them to this opinion, and probably also they were anxious to lay hold on whatever might seem to refer to the mystery of our salvation. They therefore say that the "new thing" of which the prophet speaks is the Virgin carrying the infant Christ in her womb, and that he is called "man" because he was full of divine power, though he increased according to the flesh in stature, wisdom, and strength. All this is deservedly laughed at by the Jews; yet they themselves, as I think, do not rightly understand the meaning of the prophet. They apply it to the people of Israel, because they were like a woman divorced from her husband. . . . When, therefore, Jeremiah compares a woman to a man, I do not doubt that the prophet means that the Israelites, who were like women, without strength, were destitute of any means of help; but then he says that they would be superior in strength to their enemies, whose power filled the world with terror. We, indeed, know what sort of monarchy Babylon was when the Jews were led into exile. If then we consider what the Jews were

at that time, we must say that they were like weak women, while their enemies were strong and warlike: "A woman," then, "shall surround a man." COMMENTARY ON JEREMIAH 31:22.[26]

THE VIRGIN MARY AND CHRIST. JUAN DE MALDONADO: The Virgin Mary will embrace and surround Christ with her womb when he is indeed small in terms of the body, but a complete person in terms of wisdom. Indeed, this is a new and wondrous thing. Just as Isaiah says, "Behold, a virgin will conceive and bear a son." The newer interpreters of Hebrew are delirious in regard to this passage, although the older ones also interpret it with reference to Christ and the Blessed Virgin. COMMENTARY ON THE PROPHETS, JEREMIAH 31:22.[27]

31:23-30 The Lord Will Sow People, Church, and Society

JERUSALEM AS THE CITY OF THE RIGHTEOUS. JOHANNES OECOLAMPADIUS: This passage pertains to the kingdom of Christ, particularly while the Jews consent. . . . The coming happiness will be so great, he says, that those who hope God will bless the church, and who hope that it will not afterward be destroyed, will bless him for his righteousness and sanctity toward such a church, for all will desire to live there. Therefore, he will restore it to its original state, so that just as once it was the city of righteousness, so hereafter in those times the mount of Zion will be the habitation of righteousness, because all, without distinction, will be made obedient to, and will be surrendered to, the righteousness of God through faith in Jesus Christ. Isaiah 1: "Righteousness was lodged in her, but now there are murders." Again it will be changed back, so that instead of miscreants, true moderation of the heart will come to dwell. And all who belong to the land of Judah and are written in the book of life will live in that church. For that reason a great change has now been made for

---

[25]Zwingli, *Complanationis*, 140-41; citing Song 5:1; Gen 29:17.

[26]CTS 20:113-14* (CO 38:680).
[27]Maldonado, *Commentarii in Prophetas*, 141; citing Is 7:14.

believers, which is a change for the better, and has consoled the prophet who was roused by the prophecy, vision, and dream of this change; because they recognized that it was coming.

The love and the peace of the overseers, who were called farmers and shepherds, are praised. Moreover, the land was distributed in part for sewing seed and in part for grazing sheep. He says, therefore, that they all live as one on the single mountain, when often there is otherwise strife between farmers and shepherds, and they disagree with each other, just as a fatal discord broke out among the first brothers—the shepherd Abel and the farmer Cain. Therefore, a diversity of desires will not disturb the peace of the church. As Isaiah says, "The wolf and the lamb will feed together. . . ." Indeed Zion, the citadel of divine worship, will be the habitation of righteousness in the time of Christ, which it had not been before then. There-fore, because of the new and true worship, by which a new righteousness is prepared, namely, of the heart, the name of the righteousness will endure. . . . Thus the gospel will be preached to all creatures. COMMENTARY ON JEREMIAH 31:23.[28]

A COMPLETE COMMONWEALTH, A HABITATION OF RIGHTEOUSNESS. HEINRICH BULLINGER: The Lord adds that people of every kind and rank will again live there, whom he divides into city dwellers and craftsmen, farmers who cultivate the country-side—fields, I say, and vineyards—and those who follow sheep, that is, those who practice the work of grazing sheep and who live off the flock or cattle. By these types he seems to signify that the people would be restored as a whole, and that they would have everything that pertains to a complete commonwealth. There are those who relate the words "and they will live in her" to Jerusalem. But since it would be impossible for citizens, farmers, and shepherds to live in a city that does not have enough space, they infer that these words must be interpreted with reference to the church.

Now he also gives the reason why the people of Zion who will be blessed, "Since I have given drink to the weary soul, and filled every mournful heart." They were severely afflicted and exhausted in Babylon: "I have wiped away all their troubles and paid them back with joy. Moreover, I have fulfilled their longings with the most delightful abundance of every good thing." Thus every human happiness has no other source than the one God, who blesses people from his own pure grace. . . .

The prophet adds, "On that account I awoke and I looked, and my sleep was most pleasant to me." The prophet speaks in the persona of the people, who in captivity seemed to themselves to remain in the heaviest sleep, but when they were freed and led back to their homeland, it was as if they were awoken. The prophet already sees his present state as very happy, and sweet was the memory of the captivity from which he had struggled free. Indeed, the memory of evils has a certain sweetness when, after the evils have been overcome, in our happiness we think of them. Moreover, all of these things ought to be adapted to the church of Christ, for which Zion and the city of Jerusalem bore the type ahead of time. For the church, freed from captivity to sin, death, hell, and the devil, cultivates righteousness and is a participant in true holiness. And indeed the church is the particular habitation of righteousness and mount of holiness. There is no righteousness or holiness outside of the church of Christ. In the church are all kinds and all ranks of people—citi-zens, farmers, and shepherds. Indeed, faith in Christ does not reject or damn those things, which pertain to the necessities of human life; it does condemn excess and iniquity. Therefore, whether you are a citizen or a craftsman, or a farmer, your profession does not exclude you from the church of Christ and kingdom of God. For in Christ just as there is no Jew or Greek, male or female, so also there is no artisan or farmer. Finally, all these people inhabit the church in harmony, and look out for each other with sincere love.

Therefore he promises that he would multiply people, livestock, and flocks. This is to be explained

---

[28]Oecolampadius, *In Hieremiam*, 2:Q2v-Q3r; citing Is 1:21; Gen 4:1-26; Is 65:25.

with a peculiar Hebrew idiom. "I will sow the house of Israel with the seed of men and beasts"; that is, I will make it so that people and livestock joyfully produce offspring and each one is incredibly fertile, and no sterility will be found anywhere. SERMON ON JEREMIAH 31:24-28.[29]

SOUR GRAPES AND SORE TEETH. JOHANNES OECOLAMPADIUS: This was a proverb about a son being punished for his father: "Our fathers have eaten a sour grape and the teeth," etc. Therefore, with the complete restoration of things, it will not be that the sons of God are complaining and bemoaning. The blessed will feel no curse. The bitterness of the wild vine will be mellowed with the ardor and flames of divine love; therefore, their teeth will no longer be numbed. Sin is rightly compared to a sour grape, which results in numbness in the teeth, infirmity when eating the word of the Lord, and consequently a crucifying of the conscience. . . . The Hebrew word is a wild grape that has not yet matured sufficiently. COMMENTARY ON JEREMIAH 31:29.[30]

---

[29]Bullinger, *Conciones*, 186r-v; citing Gal 3:28; Col 3:11.

[30]Oecolampadius, *In Hieremiam*, 2:Q4r.

JEREMIAH 31:31-40
THE NEW COVENANT

³¹"Behold, the days are coming, declares the Lord, when I will make a new covenant with the house of Israel and the house of Judah, ³²not like the covenant that I made with their fathers on the day when I took them by the hand to bring them out of the land of Egypt, my covenant that they broke, though I was their husband, declares the Lord. ³³For this is the covenant that I will make with the house of Israel after those days, declares the Lord: I will put my law within them, and I will write it on their hearts. And I will be their God, and they shall be my people. ³⁴And no longer shall each one teach his neighbor and each his brother, saying, 'Know the Lord,' for they shall all know me, from the least of them to the greatest, declares the Lord. For I will forgive their iniquity, and I will remember their sin no more."

³⁵Thus says the Lord,
who gives the sun for light by day
     and the fixed order of the moon and the
          stars for light by night,
who stirs up the sea so that its waves roar—
     the Lord of hosts is his name:

³⁶"If this fixed order departs
     from before me, declares the Lord,
then shall the offspring of Israel cease
     from being a nation before me forever."

³⁷Thus says the Lord:
"If the heavens above can be measured,
     and the foundations of the earth below can
          be explored,
then I will cast off all the offspring of Israel
     for all that they have done,
declares the Lord."

³⁸"Behold, the days are coming, declares the Lord, when the city shall be rebuilt for the Lord from the Tower of Hananel to the Corner Gate. ³⁹And the measuring line shall go out farther, straight to the hill Gareb, and shall then turn to Goah. ⁴⁰The whole valley of the dead bodies and the ashes, and all the fields as far as the brook Kidron, to the corner of the Horse Gate toward the east, shall be sacred to the Lord. It shall not be plucked up or overthrown anymore forever."

OVERVIEW: The promise of God's new covenant, written on human hearts, is among the most decisive and magnetic passages for Christians in all of Scripture. Here connection and disconnection between Old and New Testaments, law and gospel, letter and spirit, outer religion and inner faith are spelled out in a few verses. But the relationship between the old and new covenants raised major questions for commentators of the Reformation era: Are the two covenants utterly different in form and purpose? Are there parallels between the two covenants? And what does one make of extraordinarily faithful people in the Old Testament that do appear to have God's Word etched on their hearts? To which covenant do they belong?

Moreover, such a description of God's intimate working in the human heart invites interpreters to ponder the shape of true faith and the work of the Holy Spirit in conversion and regeneration. But given such inner and individual transformation and inspiration under the new covenant, to what extent are external religious practices, the ministrations of the church, and the expertise of theologians and scholars now obsolete and unnecessary?

31:31-37 A Covenant Written on Hearts

THE LAW AND THE NEW COVENANT. JOHN CALVIN: [God] says that the covenant he will make will not be such as he "had made with their fathers."

Here he clearly distinguishes the new covenant from the law. The contrast ought to be borne in mind; for no one of the Jews thought it possible that God would add anything better to the law. . . .

It ought not to appear strange that God makes a new covenant, because [in the end] the first had been useless and was of no avail. Then he confirms this because God made the first covenant when he stretched out his hand to his ancient people, and became their liberator; and yet they "made void" that covenant. COMMENTARY ON JEREMIAH 31:31-32.[1]

A WORD NOT FROM MOSES. MARTIN LUTHER: "I will put my words in his mouth." This clearly proves that the prophet will teach something different. These are words that [God] has not yet put into the mouth of Moses or commanded; but he promises that he will do so in the future. Therefore this has to be a word other than the word of the law, which he had already most amply and perfectly given and commanded by the mouth of Moses, with such power that through its effectiveness it would drive those already terrified into death and despair. It would be vain to promise that it would be given and commanded if he had already done so by the mouth of Moses. His word must not be the word of the law, which kills and terrifies, but a word that makes alive and consoles. So we see that the prophets are instructed by this passage when they foretell another, future covenant, word, and priesthood. Thus Jeremiah: "Behold the days are coming when I make a new covenant. . . ." And Psalm 110, "You are a priest forever"; and Isaiah 2: "the Word of the Lord will go forth from Zion, etc." LECTURES ON DEUTERONOMY 18:18.[2]

THE OLD COVENANT, THE NEW COVENANT, AND CHRIST. SEBASTIAN MÜNSTER: The Lord once entered into a covenant with the Jews that was carnal and imperfect, which was tied to transitory things and destined to endure for a certain time,

and which the Jews often made void, since that law did not leave an impression on their affections as did the gospel law, which is written on the hearts of godly people. But the new covenant was confirmed by the blood of Christ; it cannot be invalidated, because it is eternal and written not on stone tablets, but on the hearts and affections of people.

Further, those laws that were established in the covenant between God and humanity were that God wants to be our God, savior, liberator, defender, and benefactor in every good thing. But our laws are that we should hear God, trust in his Word, believe that Christ is our justification and salvation, etc. Indeed a covenant does not happen without laws and conditions to be observed on both sides. This covenant, I say, which Christ has struck with us, is new, not that it was just brought in recently, since indeed the fathers of the Old Testament obtained the remission of their sins through faith in the Christ to come, and in a certain manner were under the New Testament. But because it was instituted by a new accounting through Christ, and ordained by his blood, and unfolded in the shattered shadows of the law, it flourished in hidden ways among the fathers. THE TEMPLE OF THE LORD, JEREMIAH 31:31.[3]

THE OLD COVENANT IS NOT RENEWED. MARTIN LUTHER: "Behold the days are coming, says the Lord, when I will make a new covenant. . . ." This verse really pains the Jews; for they fret and sweat remarkably in an attempt to make their first covenant eternal even though the text states clearly and lucidly that it will not be eternal, but there will be another, a new covenant. Let them carry on here as they will, saying, for example, that at the time of the Messiah their law will be renewed and will be observed by all. Jeremiah does not say that the old covenant will be renewed, but that it will not be the same covenant that they received through Moses at the time of the exodus from Egypt. It will not be the same one, but a new and different covenant. Now it is well known what kind of covenant Moses

---

[1] CTS 20:128-29* (CO 38:689).
[2] LW 9:182 (WA 14:680); citing Deut 18:18; Ps 110:4; Is 2:3.
[3] Münster, *Miqdaš YHWH*, 916.

made with them at that time. Therefore it is also clear what is meant by saying that it is not to be the old covenant; for "not to be" does not mean to renew the old, but to abolish the old and to institute something different and new. You must adhere firmly to this verse and not listen to the prattle which they dream up.... There will be a different, a new covenant, and ... God no longer wants the old one. AGAINST THE SABBATARIANS.[4]

THE OLD COVENANT IN LIGHT OF THE NEW.

JOHANNES OECOLAMPADIUS: "Behold the days are coming." In the last days, when the Messiah will reign over his gathered church, there will also be an uncommon blessedness because the covenant and friendship of God with the church will be strengthened—the church, which is called "the house of Israel" and "the house of Judah": not only will they not harm each other, but a mutual goodwill will be preserved between God and the church. Where there is a covenant, however, there are laws for both sides, and a certain certification through signs. The ancients used to enter into covenants with the blood of sheep; certain people entered into covenants by the mutual shedding of blood and barely any covenant was maintained without blood....

God brought this back as his law, namely, that what was the case would be so again: so he is their God who has chosen them in friendship. But in fact the law of the people was that they should listen to what was spoken, and trust that it would be good for them. For that reason they should be obedient and everywhere defend his glory, committing themselves to the divine rule and will, while never obeying their own will. So it says in Exodus 19, "You have seen what I did to the Egyptians, and how I carried you on the wings of eagles and took you to myself"; that is, "I alone have bestowed the duty of the mercy of God upon you and borne you." Then the people would say, "All that the Lord has spoken, we will do and hear." And in Exodus 20 wherever God sets forth, "I am the Lord your God,"

so in Exodus 24 the people add, "All the words that God has spoken we will do." Finally, all this would be confirmed through the sacred sign, namely, blood, which was sprinkled on the people with these words spoken, "This is the blood of the covenant, that the Lord established."

Thus we discover a twofold covenant—old and new, carnal and spiritual, external and internal, complete and incomplete. The old covenant, which at one time God entered into with his people—because it was carnal, imperfect, old, and led them by the hand in a shadowy fashion—did not lead them to perfection, and for that reason it would be abolished. But it was the same as the people were, and as the promises were; they were carnal. And indeed while they preserved the external rites, God preserved them in that Promised Land, while they preserved the rites by fleeing idolatry. And of such a carnal kind were the sacrifices by which they were established in possession of the land. Indeed, that covenant of Moses is considered in this section according to the conditions of covenants, which the Lord demanded from the people in addition to the covenant he entered into with their parents. Of this kind are the external circumstances and shadows of light, which in a thousand forms prefigured what was to come. Therefore, that which was bound to transitory things was temporary to the point that it need not have endured except until the time at which another, true, eternal covenant was established.

To what extent there might be something else true we will attempt to explain below. Jeremiah describes that there is something new, namely, that God's law would be written in the guts and heart, and therefore it would be eternal. They invalidated the other covenant with their sins because it was shown externally; this covenant would not be violated by a mind that has been changed for the better. The first covenant, to the extent that it was a covenant with God, was also eternal, but humanity invalidated it by its transgression of the assigned law, which tried to help by its own strengths, but was not able, since even in those external things they transgressed it to such a degree. In fact, God himself says that they made the covenant void,

---

[4]LW 16:86-87 (WA 50:329-30).

because they did not stand by the things that were agreed on, because the law that was preserved on stone tablets was not yet written on their hearts. COMMENTARY ON JEREMIAH 31:31.[5]

THE VEILED TRUTH REVEALED. JOHN MAYER: Here the prophet returns again to speak of the blessing under the gospel, and he calls this covenant or testament "new," because of its new form and the Spirit within given to the faithful to regenerate them, and the clear opening of things pertaining to the salvation that was before veiled under types and figures. For it is the same in substance with the old. But the manner of the old covenant was made by the blood of beasts, in the new this is the blood of Christ, and the signs of the old were circumcision and the Passover and of the new they are baptism and the Lord's Supper. The Spirit was not then given in a visible manner, but now it has come down upon Christ and after him upon his apostles, and upon other faithful persons—although invisibly—yet so as to be perceived by the new tongues in which they spoke and the power of working miracles until the church was planted in all the known countries of the world, as promised in Mark 16:17. The mysteries of the kingdom of heaven—now made evident—were not then so clear, but only partially seen because they were veiled under the types of temple, altar, high priest, the holy of holies, various cleansings and sacrifices. COMMENTARY ON JEREMIAH 31:31.[6]

SAME SUBSTANCE, NEW EXPRESSION. JOHN TRAPP: It is the same substance as with the former made with Adam, Noah, Abraham, Moses, as well as the Israelites in the wilderness, but it is new in respect to the form thereof, the manner of dispensing it, that is, more clearly, freely, effectually, and spiritually now under the gospel than in those days when they saw the face of God only in that dark glass of

the ceremonies, whereas now we see with open face and so forth. COMMENTARY ON JEREMIAH 31:31.[7]

THE NEW COVENANT AND THE LAW. JOHANNES BUGENHAGEN: "Behold the days are coming when I will make with my house, etc." This is a clear promise of the New Testament and the repeal of the Old. They do not understand this promise, those who imagine that the old law was only the institution of the sacrifices, the old rites and ceremonies, even as they may want to speak of the forgiveness of sins. Likewise today we see that certain people withstand the uncommon punishment of their contempt, whether papist or sectarian "Sacrament Destroyers," who have condemned our writings and doctrine. Since in hatred of us they write much, while truly they wish or ought to deal with these words of this prophet or the words in the epistle to the Hebrews, they show clearly that they are only verbose about others, but they understand nothing concerning the abolition of the law, which is through faith in Christ. What indeed would they understand here in this verse, those who do not even understand the words to know which one is the Old Testament and which one is the New Testament? . . .

"The new covenant": Teaching that the new abolishes the old, as is made clear in the epistle to the Hebrews and as is likewise the general understanding among people; this is also what Jeremiah declares with the words of God: "So this was not the covenant that I made with their fathers, when I grasped them by the hand (just as the hand of a young one is grasped so that one can be led) and I led them out of Egypt," namely, to Mt. Sinai. Therefore, this is a different covenant from that old one. Even if that covenant belonged to the old man, and it required him to be righteous before God, he did not have that righteousness nor was he able to have it. Indeed, it was impossible to justify a person through a law of commands, as Paul teaches in the Acts of the Apostles and in his epistles. And he himself was already justified through Christ, about which Paul is struggling in Romans 7, etc. There-

---

[5]Oecolampadius, *In Hieremiam*, 2:Q4v-R1r; citing Ex 19:4, 8; 20:2; 24:3, 8.
[6]Mayer, *A Commentary*, 435*.
[7]Trapp, *A Commentary or Exposition*, 315; citing 2 Cor 3:18.

fore, what do you hope for from a law that is about those who have not been justified? . . .

Christ transferred to himself this curse of the law and our damnation and abolished them for believers; he not only abolished ceremonies but also gave us the remission of sins, the imputation of righteousness, the gifts of the Holy Spirit, and life eternal, which we have through Christ alone and because of Christ alone, and in Christ alone, because we were implanted with faith in him and made sons of God. This is the New Testament, but it is for new people, who are renewed by faith and the Spirit of God, when they have cast aside the old age of the letter or of the old law. Without this Testament or new covenant all people even to the end of world—and not only unbelieving Jews—will remain under the law or the Old Testament. Indeed, they are not under grace COMMENTARY ON JEREMIAH 31:31-32.[8]

THE COVENANT OF GOD TO THE FAITHFUL.
KONRAD PELLIKAN: The same law was once given to the Jews, as regards the Decalogue, which is properly called the covenant and law of God. The law is also of the church of Christ, but it is promised that it would be impressed more firmly on the hearts of the faithful and steeped in the new oil of charity and faith, so that the faithful would not be so easily separated from God's care and so that their propensity for corporal and spiritual idolatries would be diminished. Indeed a far greater grace and glory reached the Israelites through the mystery of the kingdom of Christ than reached them as they were led out of Egypt by the ministry of Moses and made famous by the ceremonial worship of God. Indeed they broke their first covenant often, but those who take up this new covenant once will not cast it aside, even if they sin in many places and offend against it many times. Nevertheless, they will never betray their acknowledged God as the Jews did. And the Lord God will be the perpetual spouse of the church, not with the irritable face of legal difficulties with

which he subdued his servants, but with the cheerful visage of grace, with which he looks upon his children and soothes the faithful. COMMENTARY ON JEREMIAH 31:31-32.[9]

FATHERLY HELP FOR THE WEAK. THE ENGLISH
ANNOTATIONS: In this manner of speech he implies their imbecility and weakness and thus their need as younglings and weaklings to be led by the hand, and therefore speaks of his own tender affection to them and fatherly care for them, which did not drive them before him like beasts or cattle, not leave them behind him and bid them come after him, as servants, but as an affectionate father takes his young weakling and darling child by the hand, he leads him gently along with him as he is able to go. ANNOTATIONS ON JEREMIAH 31:32.[10]

SPIRITUAL AND HOLY IMPULSES. PHILIPP
MELANCHTHON: Since faith brings the Holy Spirit and produces a new life in our hearts, it must also produce spiritual impulses in our hearts. What these impulses are, the prophet shows when he says, "I will put my law upon their hearts." After we have been justified and regenerated by faith, therefore, we begin to fear and love God, pray and expect help from him, thank and praise him, and submit to him in our afflictions. Then we also begin to love our neighbor because our hearts have spiritual and holy impulses.

This cannot happen until, being justified and regenerated, we receive the Holy Spirit. APOLOGY OF THE AUGSBURG CONFESSION.[11]

WRITTEN ON OUR HEARTS. MARTIN LUTHER:
The law of the Spirit is one that is written with no letters at all, published in no words, thought of in no thoughts. On the contrary, it is the living will itself and the life of experience. Furthermore, it is the very thing that is written in the hearts only by the finger of God. Romans 5 states, "God's love has been poured into our hearts through the Holy Spirit." Jeremiah too speaks of this, as the apostle quotes

---

[8]Bugenhagen, *In Ieremiam*, 5B4r-5C1r; citing Heb 10:16-17.

[9]Pellikan, *Commentaria Bibliorum*, 3:2V6v.
[10]Downame, *Annotations*, 9v1.
[11]BoC 124.

him in Hebrews 8 and 10: "I will put my laws into their minds and write them on their hearts." This light of understanding in the mind, I say, and this flame in the heart is the law of faith, the new law of Christ, the law of the Spirit, the law of grace. It justifies, fulfills everything, and crucifies the lusts of the flesh. LECTURES ON GALATIANS (1519) 2:19.[12]

A NEW COVENANT IN THE HOLY SPIRIT AND DIVINE WORD.

JOHANNES BUGENHAGEN: "I will give my law into their hearts, etc." Clearly Paul looked back at this passage when he wrote about the letter and spirit in 2 Corinthians 3. The impiety of the lying spirits today has contempt for these words of Jeremiah and makes fully unnecessary the external word and the ministry of the Spirit or preaching of the word.

Nevertheless, Jeremiah does not say this, but that the Lord will give his law, that is, he will give the Holy Spirit, or faith, or the spirit of faith, into the hearts of people. Then it will happen that he himself will be their God, that is, their Father, according to the first commandment: "You shall have no other gods before me, or with me." And they will be his people, that is, his sons, as Galatians says: "God has sent the spirit of his Son into our hearts, crying, 'Abba, Father.' . . ." "Then it will be the case that each person will not teach his neighbor this very thing: know the Lord." And that is what he explained in this way: "For all will know me, both the greatest and the least." However, many will receive this new covenant in my kingdom, I will give to them my law, that is, the Holy Spirit in their hearts and minds. . . .

Those who are ignorant of faith need the teaching of God through the word of the gospel, because they do not yet believe or have the Spirit. Those, however, who know the faith need exhortation and consolation, and protection against heretics and fanatical spirits, so that they persist in the Word of God, grow in knowledge of Christ, and become stronger with an enduring faith. Nevertheless, who teaches, who exhorts, disputes,

consoles, and comforts, except God alone in his Spirit and through the ministry of his Word? Indeed, the Spirit is at work in us through the Word. This clearly Paul says against those fanatical spirits when he interprets this passage in 2 Corinthians 3. COMMENTARY ON JEREMIAH 31:33-34.[13]

ONE NEW COVENANT JOINED WITH THE OLD.

JOHANNES OECOLAMPADIUS: From the preceding verse of this narrative we are able to look ahead. You understand, pious reader, how this is the new covenant; and that earlier one was the Mosaic covenant—the old covenant, which was rejected, since from what has been said a careful reader could understand this just about well enough. For Jeremiah says, "The new is not as the covenant that I went into with your fathers after their liberation from Egypt, but that one came first." The pact established with Abraham, Isaac, and Jacob pertained to a people of the desert and on the strength of that agreement they obtained the land of Canaan, and whatever the Lord promised the patriarchs, the same things would pertain to all their posterity, for which reason they would joyfully win victory in the land. . . .

The prophets beheld this plan when they were going to describe the liberation from Babylon. Even beyond that they rose into that eternity that Christ was going to provide at the end of days. Therefore, Moses first preached the death of the flesh and then the forgiveness of sins—but he preached the latter in a hidden manner and the former openly, because the law was famously exhibited openly, but Christ was still hidden, wrapped in symbols because the Holy Spirit was not yet there, though it was nevertheless bearing fruit in the hearts of all the fathers. The blood of the New Testament was not yet poured out, nor was the new covenant in revelation yet; nevertheless, through that blood the consciences of the fathers were bathed. . . .

For God there is one covenant that is eternal; that covenant is distributed in various ways for a

---

[12]LW 27:234 (WA 2:419); citing Rom 5:5; Heb 8:10; 10:16.

[13]Bugenhagen, *In Ieremiam*, 5C4v-5D1r, 5D2r; citing 2 Cor 3:6; Ex 20:3; Gal 4:6.

diversity of times. Within human beings there was also always one covenant, and it will remain all the way, not only so that it is in eternal predestination. But if you will join the ministry of those people with whom the covenant was joined, it is necessary that you confess according to the substance by which I have distinguished the various covenants. For as long as you include the management of a contract in its substance, at the same time the conditions which are in the agreements are simultaneously included. So the covenant of Abraham, the covenant of Moses, and the covenant of Christ have a great diversity of natures among them, and that diversity is affirmed through Scripture. Our Lord God established with us the covenant on Horeb, "Not with our fathers did the Lord make this covenant, but with you." Here you see that Moses brought forward his covenant, a different covenant than that of his fathers. "But this covenant that I made with you is not the covenant I made with your fathers," he says. Already the covenant of Moses has been made void, because the people did not stand by what was agreed on. So clearly a new covenant through Jeremiah is promised, with a new ambassador, and nevertheless he is the same, ancient and eternal in antiquity and in eternity, even if you separate his advent from the ministry of Moses, because in Christ the covenant is called "new," because in the new form the covenant is inscribed on the heart. . . .

I recognize that when Christ is king, the Lord demands an obedience similar to that which he commended to Abraham. His, I say, is the obedience of faith, but his faith surpasses this our faith in every way, for we dwell in the clear light when Christ has already been exalted, who at that time was yet to come in humility and was awaited as through a cloud. So this covenant is new, not because it is recently delivered, but it was organized and instituted in a new pattern. For I ask you, see if Abel, Noah, and Abraham, and the other spiritual folk were not in the New Testament; because everything they say here fits them. Indeed, God had given them the law in their hearts; they were taught by the Lord, and their iniquities were forgiven. So how is the law new, when they had the same precepts of love, and the fathers preserved the same sacrifices—as John says, "Not a new command, but the old command." COMMENTARY ON JEREMIAH 33:33.[14]

REGENERATION UNDER THE LAW? JOHN CALVIN: [Jeremiah] now shows a difference between the law and the gospel, for the gospel brings with it the grace of regeneration: its doctrine, therefore, is not that of the letter, but penetrates into the heart and reforms all the inward faculties, so that the obedience is rendered to the righteousness of God.

A question may, however, be raised: was the grace of regeneration lacking for the fathers under the law? But this is quite preposterous. What, then, is meant when God denies here that the law was written on the heart before the coming of Christ? To this I answer that the fathers, who were formerly regenerated, obtained this favor through Christ, so that we may say that it was transferred to them from another source. The power then to penetrate into the heart was not inherent in the law, but it was a benefit transferred to the law from the gospel. This is one thing. Then we know that this grace of God was rare and little known under the law; but that under the gospel the gifts of the Spirit have been more abundantly poured forth and that God has dealt more bountifully with his church. . . . The law was written on stones, and was therefore a letter. But the gospel—what is it? It is spirit: that is, God not only addresses his word to human ears and sets it before their eyes, but he also inwardly teaches their hearts and minds. This is then the solution of the question: the prophet speaks of the law in itself, as apart from the gospel; for the law then is dead and destitute of the Spirit of regeneration. . . .

We may further learn from this passage how foolish the papists are in their conceit about free will. They indeed allow that without the help of God's grace we are not capable of fulfilling the law, and thus they concede something to the aid of grace and of the Spirit: but still they not only

---

[14]Oecolampadius, *In Hieremiam*, 2:R1r-v, R2r-R2v; citing Deut 5:2; 1 Jn 2:7.

imagine a form of cooperation as to free will, but ascribe it to the main work. Now the prophet here testifies that it is the peculiar work of God to write his law in our hearts. Since God then declares that this favor is justly his, and claims for himself the glory of it, how great must be human arrogance to appropriate this to themselves? . . .

[Jeremiah] adds, "And I will be their God. . . ." Here God comprehends generally the substance of his covenant; for what is the design of the law, except that the people should call upon him and that he should also exercise a care over his people? For whenever God declares that he will be our God, he offers to us his paternal favor, and declares that our salvation is the object of his care; he gives to us free access to himself, bids us to lean on his grace, and, in short, this promise contains in itself everything needed for our salvation. COMMENTARY ON JEREMIAH 31:33.[15]

THE LAW OF THE HEART IN TRADITION. JUAN DE MALDONADO: "I will give my law in their bowels." The nature of the old law used to require that it should be Scripture [or "written"], because it was of the flesh. The nature of the law of the gospel requires that it not be written, but engraved on the human heart, because it is of the spirit. Not only Jeremiah here, but also Dr. Paul teaches this: "You are a letter of Christ from our ministry, written not with ink, but with the Spirit of the living God, not on tablets of stone, but on fleshly tablets of the heart." If heretics would attend to this, they would understand that traditions are more proper to the New Testament than Scriptures, and they would stop defining faith and religion with ink. This is certainly characteristic of people who are ignorant of the very nature of the gospel, which they nevertheless so earnestly boast about. COMMENTARY ON THE PROPHETS, JEREMIAH 31:33.[16]

HAS TEACHING BEEN ABOLISHED? JOHN CALVIN: Here is mentioned another difference between the old and the new covenant, even that God, who had obscurely manifested himself under the law, would send forth a fuller light, so that the knowledge of him would be commonly enjoyed. But he extols this favor with hyperbole when he says that no one would have need of a teacher or instructor as everyone would have for themselves sufficient knowledge. We therefore consider that the object of the prophet is mainly to show that so great would be the light of the gospel, that it would be clearly evident, that God under it deals more bountifully with his people, because its truth shines forth as the sun at noonday. . . .

But we find some fanatics have ignorantly and foolishly abused this passage, seeking to put down teaching of every kind, as the Anabaptists in our day, who reject all teaching; and flattering themselves in their ignorance, they proudly boast that they are endued with the Spirit. . . . And hence it has also happened that they are inebriated with strange and horrible doctrines: for the devil, when they become swollen with so much pride, can fascinate and delude them as he pleases; and their own pride also so leads them astray that they invent dreams. COMMENTARY ON JEREMIAH 31:34.[17]

THE LAWS OF NATURE AND THE PERSEVERANCE OF THE CHURCH. JOHN CALVIN: [Jeremiah] confirms the promises we have been considering; for it was difficult to believe that the people would not only recover what they had lost but also be made much happier; for the church was then wholly in a despondent state. It was not then an easy matter to lift, as it were, from the lowest depths a miserable people and to comfort them so that they might overcome their dreadful trial; for the disorder of the church was such that it had been raised a hundred times from the dead. . . .

He says in the person of God, "I am he who created the sun, the moon, and the stars. . . ." He speaks, indeed, of their diurnal course, for we know that the prophets spoke popularly and according to the common notions. Had they philosophized, as

---

[15]CTS 20:130-33* (CO 38:690-92).
[16]Maldonado, *Commentarii in Prophetas*, 142; citing 2 Cor 3:3.

[17]CTS 134-35* (CO 38:693).

astrologers do, and spoken of the monthly course of the moon and the sun, they could not have been understood by the common people. They were, therefore, satisfied to state things which even children could comprehend, even that the sun made its circuit daily around the world, that the moon did the same, and that the stars in their turns followed; so that the moon holds the first place in the night among the stars, and that the sun rules during the day. . . .

Then in the heavens we find an order so arranged and regulated that nothing deviates from its appointed course. But in storms and tempests God seems as though he would shake the world and overturn what appears otherwise to be immovable; for even the very rocks, as it were, tremble when the sea is violently stirred up; and yet God calms the very sea. . . . He then adds, "If I removed these laws from my presence, the seed of Israel shall also fail"; that is, "As certain as is the stability of the order of nature, seen in the course of the sun and the moon, and in the turbulent sea, so certain will be the deliverance of my church, nor can it ever be destroyed. . . ." There is, therefore, no reason to fear that the safety of the church should ever fail, for the laws or decrees of nature shall never cease; that is, God, who from the beginning governed the world, will not disregard the welfare of his church, for whose sake the world has been created. Commentary on Jeremiah 31:35-36.[18]

TRUE AND FALSE ISRAELITES AND JEWS.

KONRAD PELLIKAN: "Just as one is neither able to measure the extent of the heavens, nor to investigate the foundations of the earth; so it could not happen that I would cast away all the children of Israel because of their sins." Indeed they have been numbered among the elect of God from the formation of the world and they cannot fall away from grace. Also the children of Israel, who received the word of salvation from the time of Christ, both in Judea and throughout the whole world, persevered through their generations in the church that

was gathered from Jews and Gentiles. However, the dregs of Jewish impiety, which today unhappily and insolently burden the world, are not numbered among the true Israelites, but are reckoned among the ungodly Christians and with the reprobate, bearing everywhere amazing examples of divine justice. COMMENTARY ON JEREMIAH 31:37.[19]

31:38-40 Rebuilding the City

THE CITY AND THE NEW COVENANT. JO-

HANNES BUGENHAGEN: "The city shall be rebuilt." The Tower of Hananel: 2 Esdras 3; the Gate of the Corner: 2 Kings 14; 2 Esdras 3. And he adds other places outside Jerusalem, such as the hills Gareb and Goah, and finally the valley of dead bodies and ashes, and the whole region or country of the dead, which are signified with the words "Topheth" and "Gehenna," which we discussed above in chapter 7, even to the parched Kidron, which is also mentioned as a place from the Gospel and 1 Kings 2. . . .

Therefore, he said that the city of Jerusalem will now in fact be destroyed by the Babylonians. But it will be rebuilt, as has been said, after the Babylonian captivity. Where the new covenant would have been made known, however, is through the Man encircled by the woman, through the one who crushes the serpent's head, your Messiah, and the law of God will be written on your hearts, and sin will be abolished, that is, when the kingdom of the Messiah will come, to which all nations will flow. Then there will be still yet another very different, more majestic Jerusalem, which will extend and spread out to the north and to the west, and to all parts of the world. So places that are now outside Jerusalem will be within Jerusalem; read Zechariah 2. COMMENTARY ON JEREMIAH 31:38-40.[20]

THE CHURCH, THE ETERNAL JERUSALEM. JOHN

TRAPP: This cannot be applied to the earthly Jerusalem, which was plucked up and thrown

---

[18]CTS 20:142-43* (CO 38:698-99).

[19]Pellikan, *Commentaria Bibliorum*, 3:2V6v.
[20]Bugenhagen, *In Ieremias*, 5E1v-5E2r; citing Neh 3:1; 2 Kings 14:13; Neh 3:28; Jer 7:31-32; 19:10-15; Jn 18:1, 1 Kings 2:37; Gen 3:15.

down by the Romans once and again, but especially by Aelius Adrianus, who laid the whole country to waste almost, and drove the Jews utterly out of it, and afterward set a slab of white marble over the chief gate of Jerusalem in reproach of their religion, and thus called the city by his own name, Aelia, commanding the Jews not once to look toward it from any tower or hill. It must therefore refer to the church, which cannot be ruined. COMMENTARY ON JEREMIAH 31:40.[21]

---

[21]Trapp, *A Commentary or Exposition*, 316*. Emperor Hadrian (AD 76–138) suppressed the Bar Kokhba revolt and violently persecuted the Jews.

JEREMIAH 32:1-44
JEREMIAH'S FIELD AND GOD'S DELIVERANCE

¹The word that came to Jeremiah from the LORD in the tenth year of Zedekiah king of Judah, which was the eighteenth year of Nebuchadnezzar. ²At that time the army of the king of Babylon was besieging Jerusalem, and Jeremiah the prophet was shut up in the court of the guard that was in the palace of the king of Judah. ³For Zedekiah king of Judah had imprisoned him, saying, "Why do you prophesy and say, 'Thus says the LORD: Behold, I am giving this city into the hand of the king of Babylon, and he shall capture it; ⁴Zedekiah king of Judah shall not escape out of the hand of the Chaldeans, but shall surely be given into the hand of the king of Babylon, and shall speak with him face to face and see him eye to eye. ⁵And he shall take Zedekiah to Babylon, and there he shall remain until I visit him, declares the LORD. Though you fight against the Chaldeans, you shall not succeed'?"

⁶Jeremiah said, "The word of the LORD came to me: ⁷Behold, Hanamel the son of Shallum your uncle will come to you and say, 'Buy my field that is at Anathoth, for the right of redemption by purchase is yours.' ⁸Then Hanamel my cousin came to me in the court of the guard, in accordance with the word of the LORD, and said to me, 'Buy my field that is at Anathoth in the land of Benjamin, for the right of possession and redemption is yours; buy it for yourself.' Then I knew that this was the word of the LORD.

⁹"And I bought the field at Anathoth from Hanamel my cousin, and weighed out the money to him, seventeen shekels of silver. ¹⁰I signed the deed, sealed it, got witnesses, and weighed the money on scales. ¹¹Then I took the sealed deed of purchase, containing the terms and conditions and the open copy. ¹²And I gave the deed of purchase to Baruch the son of Neriah son of Mahseiah, in the presence of Hanamel my cousin, in the presence of the witnesses who signed the deed of purchase, and in the presence of all the Judeans who were sitting in the court of the guard. ¹³I charged Baruch in their presence, saying, ¹⁴'Thus says the LORD of hosts, the God of Israel: Take these deeds, both this sealed deed of purchase and this open deed, and put them in an earthenware vessel, that they may last for a long time. ¹⁵For thus says the LORD of hosts, the God of Israel: Houses and fields and vineyards shall again be bought in this land.'

¹⁶"After I had given the deed of purchase to Baruch the son of Neriah, I prayed to the LORD, saying: ¹⁷'Ah, LORD God! It is you who have made the heavens and the earth by your great power and by your outstretched arm! Nothing is too hard for you. ¹⁸You show steadfast love to thousands, but you repay the guilt of fathers to their children after them, O great and mighty God, whose name is the LORD of hosts, ¹⁹great in counsel and mighty in deed, whose eyes are open to all the ways of the children of man, rewarding each one according to his ways and according to the fruit of his deeds. ²⁰You have shown signs and wonders in the land of Egypt, and to this day in Israel and among all mankind, and have made a name for yourself, as at this day. ²¹You brought your people Israel out of the land of Egypt with signs and wonders, with a strong hand and outstretched arm, and with great terror. ²²And you gave them this land, which you swore to their fathers to give them, a land flowing with milk and honey. ²³And they entered and took possession of it. But they did not obey your voice or walk in your law. They did nothing of all you commanded them to do. Therefore you have made all this disaster come upon them. ²⁴Behold, the siege mounds have come up to the city to take it, and because of sword and famine and pestilence the city is given into the hands of the Chaldeans who are fighting against it. What you spoke has come to pass, and behold, you see it. ²⁵Yet you, O LORD God, have said to me, "Buy the field for money and get witnesses"—though the city is given into the hands of the Chaldeans.'"

²⁶The word of the LORD came to Jeremiah: ²⁷"Behold, I am the LORD, the God of all flesh. Is anything too hard for me? ²⁸Therefore, thus says the LORD: Behold, I am giving this city into the hands of the Chaldeans and into the hand of Nebuchadnezzar

king of Babylon, and he shall capture it. ²⁹The Chaldeans who are fighting against this city shall come and set this city on fire and burn it, with the houses on whose roofs offerings have been made to Baal and drink offerings have been poured out to other gods, to provoke me to anger. ³⁰For the children of Israel and the children of Judah have done nothing but evil in my sight from their youth. The children of Israel have done nothing but provoke me to anger by the work of their hands, declares the Lord. ³¹This city has aroused my anger and wrath, from the day it was built to this day, so that I will remove it from my sight ³²because of all the evil of the children of Israel and the children of Judah that they did to provoke me to anger—their kings and their officials, their priests and their prophets, the men of Judah and the inhabitants of Jerusalem. ³³They have turned to me their back and not their face. And though I have taught them persistently, they have not listened to receive instruction. ³⁴They set up their abominations in the house that is called by my name, to defile it. ³⁵They built the high places of Baal in the Valley of the Son of Hinnom, to offer up their sons and daughters to Molech, though I did not command them, nor did it enter into my mind, that they should do this abomination, to cause Judah to sin.

³⁶"Now therefore thus says the Lord, the God of Israel, concerning this city of which you say, 'It is given into the hand of the king of Babylon by sword, by famine, and by pestilence': ³⁷Behold, I will gather them from all the countries to which I drove them in my anger and my wrath and in great indignation. I will bring them back to this place, and I will make them dwell in safety. ³⁸And they shall be my people, and I will be their God. ³⁹I will give them one heart and one way, that they may fear me forever, for their own good and the good of their children after them. ⁴⁰I will make with them an everlasting covenant, that I will not turn away from doing good to them. And I will put the fear of me in their hearts, that they may not turn from me. ⁴¹I will rejoice in doing them good, and I will plant them in this land in faithfulness, with all my heart and all my soul.

⁴²"For thus says the Lord: Just as I have brought all this great disaster upon this people, so I will bring upon them all the good that I promise them. ⁴³Fields shall be bought in this land of which you are saying, 'It is a desolation, without man or beast; it is given into the hand of the Chaldeans.' ⁴⁴Fields shall be bought for money, and deeds shall be signed and sealed and witnessed, in the land of Benjamin, in the places about Jerusalem, and in the cities of Judah, in the cities of the hill country, in the cities of the Shephelah, and in the cities of the Negeb; for I will restore their fortunes, declares the Lord."

OVERVIEW: This chapter begins with a remarkable act of hope. In the midst of siege and destruction Jeremiah buys a field. After a further summary of God's judgment on Jerusalem and Judea the chapter returns to expound on God's restoration of the land and the hearts of the people, thus amplifying the new covenant of Jeremiah 31:31-34. Reformation commentators underscore this rhythm of the Christian life. The godly must hope steadfastly and firmly in God even as judgment and suffering occur throughout the world. Indeed, God often brings renewal and salvation when least expected, a promise to which the Reformation itself attests. The assurances of God's deliverance pertain to the return of the Jews after exile, the promise of Christ and the church in the New Testament, and God's ultimate redemption in eternity.

32:1-15 Jeremiah Buys a Field

A SWEET VISION FOR THE PROPHET. JOHANNES OECOLAMPADIUS: In this chapter under the figure of a purchased field in the midst of siege Jeremiah establishes the hope of the future liberation: that the sons of Israel would return to their own land. That return itself is the type of our liberation; by this liberation through Christ the church has been given and will be given freedom.…

Moreover the figure of speech is all the greater because the prophet at that time had already been captured, when he was preaching of things to come. So in captivity he discusses the figure of the captive people, but he also receives a consolation from heaven, since he was deprived of any other consolation, and he understood that God was rather more benevolent. That vision was for Jeremiah such a sweet dream. COMMENTARY ON JEREMIAH 32:1.[1]

BUYING A FIELD, INVESTING IN THE FUTURE. JOHANNES BUGENHAGEN: Jeremiah confirms the promise concerning the return of the Jews after seventy years in an external sign. So by order of God he buys a field, while Jerusalem is already under siege and he himself is held in chains on account of the Word of God. In this sign he declares that although at that moment the Jews are being expelled from their land, nevertheless the land will certainly be restored to them. Jeremiah shows that he himself knows this with certainty. For at the height of desperation in all things he buys a field, which he knows will return to his descendants. Therefore, they should not doubt that the Word of God is utterly true concerning the promise of return. Moreover, in order to persuade them of this, he wants this purchase to be confirmed, as it is customarily done by right according to the law. He counts out silver, summons witnesses, and signs documents with the customary agreement. Finally he orders that these documents be placed in a clay vessel in the sight of all those who are present, so that they might be preserved in a confidential place, so that by this sign he might strengthen the faith of those either about to be abducted or already abducted as a sign that they would return. In this way the word and promise of God would be glorified, when after the return they would find the documents that were left behind and the field would be returned to the posterity of the prophet. COMMENTARY ON JEREMIAH 32.[2]

JEREMIAH'S PERSISTENT FAITH. NIKOLAUS SELNECKER: This is a sermon of consolation, in which God wills to bring his people out of captivity at a certain time and bring them home, even if at this time Jerusalem burns and is destroyed and the people must be led far away to live under the heathen. As Jeremiah before had often predicated and indicated, so he himself must now sit in captivity. But when seventy years have ended the people will come into their land in God's timing and they shall build again. Therefore, God wants to display this to the Jews, so he calls Jeremiah to buy a field for seven shekels and ten silver pieces. . . . So God acts even as there is great danger; Jerusalem is besieged and the king and whole people will be captured and led away. Thus God was to give the people complete assurance that they would again come into the land. . . .

We also have here an exceptional and pleasant example of the persistence of Jeremiah. He remains at all times stable in the view he has received from God. He does not dispute within himself, nor is he turned away by threats or fear, by good words or bad; nor is he led away from God's order while in a dungeon or in a prison. All upright teachers and Christians should so act, when they have God's word for themselves and recognize the truth; that they thereby must remain persistent and neither be inconsistent nor capricious, nor lose heart over all the difficulties. THE WHOLE PROPHET JEREMIAH 32.[3]

A FIELD OF TEMPORAL AND ETERNAL HOPE. JOHANNES OECOLAMPADIUS: The prophet was observing this divine decree, and hence his cousin, by divine impulse, freely complied and sold the field for seven shekels—a shekel being worth twenty obols—and ten pieces of silver. . . . Jeremiah buys the field that pertains to himself: eternal life, which is the inheritance of the pious, and by eternal predestination this field is practically delivered to good souls; so sure was Jeremiah that he parceled up everything and bought the field. He, moreover, bought from Hanamel, that is, "by the grace of God," which is from peace. For by grace alone we are saved. That field is in Anathoth and in that place humility is

---

[1]Oecolampadius, *In Hieremiam*, 2:Siv.
[2]Bugenhagen, *In Ieremiam*, 5F1r.

[3]Selnecker, *Der gantze Prophet Jeremias*, 2F1r-v, 2F2r.

exercised. The field is purchased with a coin and the seven shekels of perfect faith, and his confession is perfect—true, and not made up—that is, complete, which is what is understood by the ten pieces of silver. Finally, he will inscribe this in the book of records, sealed with the mark of the Holy Spirit, making his vocation certain through good works. Witnesses were called for this, which are also good works. Truly, however much you gain by your faith, that corresponds to the number of witnesses you will have. Moreover, the book of records is opened, if people announce those examples of the good life that are secretly contained through faith in the book of records. COMMENTARY ON JEREMIAH 32:8.[4]

PROPERTY TRANSACTIONS AND DIVINE APPROVAL. NIKOLAUS SELNECKER: We see here God's plan, order, and contract for buying and selling, the court process and the essential parts—uses and procedures, declarations, letter or means, proofs, warnings, and inheritance rights, possession, statement of character, delivery of property, witnesses, office of the notary and the like that approves, confirms and deals with the above. We should underscore such actions against the Anabaptist swarm.[†] For the above contract we must think on the twenty-fifth chapter of Leviticus. THE WHOLE PROPHET JEREMIAH 32:9-15.[5]

THE WONDROUS COUNSELS OF GOD. MARTIN LUTHER: Jeremiah had been sent to proclaim devastation; destruction had already come to the city; the Chaldeans had already taken it, and the citizens were at the point of being led away to captivity. Suddenly Jeremiah is sent to announce their salvation by the fact that he was to buy a field. All this was done for the sake of the kingdom of Judah, for the eternal promise had been attached to it. Therefore it had to be preserved until Christ came.

This is how the Lord anticipates us with his words. Although he also intended to punish this kingdom, yet he would comfort the devout. It as if he were saying, "Even if destruction is imminent, even if you will be taken prisoner and suffer for a time, yet hang on, you devout people. You will be saved. I will take you back out of captivity. I will restore your city to you again, and you are going to live safely in it. Your captivity will not last long." And so it happened, for the faithful whose hearts God had touched finally were brought back from Babylon. . . . Such are the wondrous counsels of God. He orders the prophets to declare both destruction and salvation, but the former for the wicked and the latter for the devout. It is very important to note this in all the prophets. In this way those wonderful counsels of divine majesty made fools of the wicked. In fact, even the devout were unable to understand them. We see clearly in Jeremiah how he wondered at the counsel of the Lord. LECTURE ON MICAH 4:1.[6]

HOW GOD ANSWERS PRAYER. MARTIN LUTHER: It is a rule of divine action that God does such things as no one expects. . . . In the works of God his extreme weakness appears so that the conscience despairs as if it were bereft of all help and protection. When God's help comes, it comes in such a way that no one would expect it, so that anguish and despair of heart make their presence felt. . . .

So it happened to Israel. They not only escaped from the sea unharmed, but their enemies were even submerged. There is a similar example in Jeremiah, where he was ordered to buy a field, even though Jerusalem and the land of Israel were already taken. It is as if Jeremiah were to say, "Why should I buy, since everything has been captured?" So it will happen to us: if only we could pray and seek, we would receive everything. But our heart is in such straits that it does not know what to pray for, as in Romans 8 tells us, and also Ephesians 3. He to whom we pray gives more than we, groaning, have need to pray for. So we groan and sigh and hope for little, and as we pray we confine ourselves

---

[4]Oecolampadius, *In Hieremiam*, 2:S2v-S3r.
[5]Selnecker, *Der gantze Prophet Jeremias*, 2F2v; citing Lev 25:8-54.
    [†]Selnecker refers here to the refusal of the Anabaptists to swear oaths and their emphasis on Mt 5:37 and Jas 5:12 ("Let your 'yes' be 'yes' and your 'no' be 'no'") in relation to court proceedings and legal transactions.

[6]LW 18:236-37* (WA 13:317-18); citing Ezra 1:5.

to something small. Yet God hears in such a way that he grants far more than we dare to ask for in our prayer. I, Martin Luther, had this experience. I never dared to pray for such great progress of the word and for the destruction of the pope. My heart was much too timid, because what we now experience seemed impossible, and yet it happened. LECTURE ON ISAIAH 64:3.[7]

32:16-35 Jeremiah Prays for Understanding

WITH GOD ALL THINGS ARE POSSIBLE.
NIKOLAUS SELNECKER: Jeremiah prays and consoles himself with the miracles and great deeds of God. As David says in Psalm 77: "I reflect on your miracles from long ago, and speak of your works and say what you have done." So Jeremiah tells first of the work of creation, how God has created everything and preserves all things through his divine power; how with God nothing is impossible; as the angel Gabriel said to Mary, "With God nothing is impossible." Whatever God says, and whatever he wills, so it happens as God speaks. . . . Then Jeremiah underscores how God is righteous and gracious; he punishes sin and shows mercy to all who turn to him. Therefore we should learn . . . to trust God, who from ancient times until now has done miracles and in great works beyond number he displays this to his people; and he miraculously saves them and his church from danger. Therefore, we should be confident and not doubt. Things will happen as they do. God the Lord will not pull back his hand from helping even as the Turk, the pope, or another enemy comes. But he will know to preserve his poor little ones, when we trust only in him, reform ourselves, and call on his grace and assistance. THE WHOLE PROPHET JEREMIAH 32:16-22.[8]

THE CHRISTOLOGICAL ARM OF GOD. JOHANNES OECOLAMPADIUS: "Ah!" With this single exclamation Jeremiah declares that his soul is afflicted and perplexed. "Because you have made heaven and earth, no one has any doubt but that they are allowed to hope for whatever is best, for these are all done for humanity. Moreover, you did this without being assisted by the angels, but through your absolute power—without a helper, out of nothing, and to help humanity." And this he calls his arm. It is certain, furthermore, that Christ himself is the power and wisdom of God, and therefore the arm by which God created everything. COMMENTARY ON JEREMIAH 32:17.[9]

GOD FULFILLS HIS WORD IN STRANGE WAYS.
MARTIN LUTHER: That is how reason carries on when God fulfills his words differently than it had imagined. For reason always presumes to dictate measure, time, and manner to God for keeping his promise; otherwise it refuses to believe any longer. Therefore, God cannot but fulfill his words strangely and far differently than we expect. Thus it happens that one refuses to believe God at any time. When he threatens us, our present good fortune, and the fact that we do not yet feel the coming misfortune, keep us from believing his threats. When he promises mercy, the present misfortune and the fact that we do not yet feel his future mercy keep us from believing also his promise. Then the prophets have to devote their attention first of all to the faint-hearted, unbelieving people. For how could God have initiated Christ's promised kingdom more foolishly and strangely than by having Jerusalem, where his kingdom was to be, destroyed by ungodly scorners and by his enemies while he had his own people led into exile? How could they believe that Jerusalem lying in ashes could at the same time become the most magnificent kingdom? Here reason had to sink and despair. And whoever could have sustained themselves would have had to soar above all their senses and their reason to adhere solely to God's word, beholding a new Jerusalem that was as yet not visible anywhere. They would have had to be so assured of an invisible Jerusalem

[7]LW 17:364 (WA 31.2:542-43); citing Ex 14:1-31; Rom 8:26; Eph 3:20.
[8]Selnecker, Der gantze Prophet Jeremias, 2F3r-v; citing Ps 77:11; Lk 1:37.

[9]Oecolampadius, In Hieremiam, 2:S3v; citing 1 Cor 1:30.

as though it were standing where the visible one lay in ashes before their eyes. A very fine illustration of this is found in Jeremiah 32. There the prophet is very surprised that it might be possible for God to have Jerusalem devastated and simultaneously be raised again, enabling people to buy and trade there. LECTURE ON HABAKKUK 2:1.[10]

JEREMIAH POSES A QUESTION. KONRAD PELLIKAN: After this digression, which was nevertheless necessary for the amplification of divine power, Jeremiah returns to the circumstances of his speech and his case. "Behold Lord," he says, "already the Chaldeans oppress us with the siege-works, and they attack and besiege this city, which has already been conquered by sword, famine, and disease and now will be given over to the hands of our cruel destroyers. Indeed, you have decreed it so, and it is necessary that this must happen. And how is it that you nevertheless give me an order while I am held in prison, an order that I am to buy fields in this region with money and witnesses? For we now possess nothing here of our own, but the Chaldeans are about to claim everything by right of war and have already seized everything for themselves." COMMENTARY ON JEREMIAH 32:24-25.[11]

GOD'S CLEANSING POWER IN THE VIOLENCE OF ADVERSARIES. KONRAD PELLIKAN: The Lord wants us to believe steadfastly in his omnipotence and in the truth of his words, so that however grave and unfamiliar and miraculous may be the things he decrees or preaches, he will hardly be doubted: indeed all things are both possible and good that he predicts are to come, since his works are worthy of righteousness and truth. For this city has rebelled against God. Therefore, it would be handed over to the power of ungodly people, who would destroy, when captive, a city that, when free, did not recognize its Creator. The whole city will burn with fire,

which when it was unburned offered sacrifices to foreign gods. The exalted sanctuaries and glorious palaces will be destroyed throughout the whole land, since against the law of God they have constructed high places for idols, so that, as an affront to their own God, they polluted themselves with the abominations of the Gentiles, and filled the whole region with their own idolatry. COMMENTARY ON JEREMIAH 32:26-29.[12]

THE FAITHFUL GOD AND THE UNFAITHFUL PEOPLE. JOHN CALVIN: [God] amplifies the sin of the people; for they never departed from their vices. And he mentions the ten tribes and also the tribe of Judah. The ten tribes, we know, had departed from pure worship of God, when as yet true religion continued at Jerusalem. By mentioning then the "children of Judah," he no doubt aggravated their guilt, intimating that they had fallen together with the Israelites, while yet they had for a time been preserved. . . .

And "from their youth" here is not to be understood of individuals, but is to be extended to the whole people; and so "youth" is to be taken for the time of their redemption. . . . For the church was in a manner then born and in the desert, when they had been recently brought to the light; for God had delivered them from the darkness of death. In their very childhood they began to provoke God; from that time they had always been perverse in their wickedness. . . .

Now God condemns here all ranks of people: in the first place he says that "kings" had sinned; for they not only themselves had forsaken the true worship of God but had also become the cause of defection or apostasy to others. To kings he adds "princes" or counselors, and then "priests" and "prophets." And, doubtless, the kings with their counselors ought to have been one eye, the priests and prophets the other; for two eyes in a true and legitimate government are the judges and pastors of the church. But the prophet says that the kings and their counselors had been ungodly, and then

---

[10]LW 19:190* (WA 19:387).
[11]Pellikan, *Commentaria Bibliorum*, 3:2Xiv.

[12]Pellikan, *Commentaria Bibliorum*, 3:2X2r; citing Mt 19:26.

that the priests and the prophets had been implicated in similar crimes. . . .

This passage deserves to be carefully noticed; for we see how delighted many are when the church is disturbed by discord; for they think that they are thus excused when they cast aside every care and every concern for religion; and many indulge in this kind of indifference. But if the faithful had been so careless at that time, must not religion have a thousand times vanished away, having been wholly extinguished and obliterated from their hearts? . . .

Then he amplifies their guilt by saying, "And I taught them, I rose up early. . . ." If the law had been only once promulgated, the Jews might have objected and said that they were for the most part illiterate; but no color of pretense remained for them, since the prophets were continually interpreting the law. . . .

Then he adds, that he "rose up early," that is, that he had been diligent. As a master of a family, who is mindful for his own, he early on inquires about everyone, and looks around the whole house. So also God represents himself here, speaking of his care in teaching the Israelites. COMMENTARY ON JEREMIAH 32:30-33.[13]

HOW THE CHOSEN PEOPLE HAVE BETRAYED ME. KONRAD PELLIKAN: The temple of my glory and theirs: thus only my priests ought to have entered into my full glory and majesty. But they have defiled the temple with the abominations of their idols, so that they have soiled my name; likewise, they have received a shameless adulteress into their bed and have been untrue and adulterers to me and our current marriage. Not only that: they have sacrificed my children to demons in the valley of Ben Hinnom, to their idols and their abominable rites that go against law and nature. They have casually spurned my precepts and harshly imposed their ways to provoke me to act against them in every way on the basis of my precepts. COMMENTARY ON JEREMIAH 32:34-35.[14]

LIMIT YOURSELF TO WHAT GOD HAS TAUGHT.
JOHN DONNE: Hear what God has declared; do not inquire about what he has decreed. Hear what God has said here and where he has spoken. Do not ask what he means in his unrevealed will or of things about which he has said nothing: for those who do this are often mistaken about God's mind. God protests, "It never came into my mind that they should so sin." God never did it. God never meant it that they should sin necessarily, without a willing act in themselves or that they would be damned necessarily without a connection to a sin willingly committed. . . . Does anyone put his son in school to learn what his master thinks? The Holy Spirit is sent to teach; he teaches by speaking; he speaks by his ordinance and institution in his church. All knowledge and zeal that is not kindled by the Spirit is from the beginning all smoke and all flame. Zeal without the Holy Spirit is at first cloudy ignorance—all smoke—and after that it is all crackling and crawling flame—schismatic rage and disorder. SERMON ON JOHN 14:26.[15]

32:36-44 They Shall Be My People; I Shall Be Their God.

FEAR OF GOD AND KNOWING SIN. ANDREAS BODENSTEIN VON KARLSTADT: "I shall put my fear into their inmost being and they shall not depart from me, i.e., they shall leave everything that separates or distances them from me, such as the doing of sin and they will be guided by me." Here you note that it is characteristic of the fear of God to unveil and make sin known. This fear does not come from the law, but is the righteousness from God, the ark of all God's gifts which brings about abhorrence of and flight from all that is evil and guards against falling. It is characteristic of the knowledge of sin, and adheres and is integral to the revelation of sin, to drive away from and wash off sin. Just so, it is integral to the revelation of the Son of God that we cling to him and that the heart is transformed in Christ, as it is characteristic of

[13]CTS 20:189-90, 194-97* (CO 39:25-26, 28-29).
[14]Pellikan, Commentaria Bibliorum, 3:2X2r.

[15]Donne, Sermons, 8:260-61*.

fire to warm. SEVERAL MAIN POINTS OF CHRISTIAN TEACHING.[16]

A SECURE AND ETERNAL PROMISED LAND WITH GOD. HEINRICH BULLINGER: This is the last part of this oration, in which he announces happier things. In fact, Jeremiah prophesies concerning the restoration of the captive people; the Lord wanted to bring them back into their country and bless them liberally. Therefore, this section is a true preaching or announcement of the gospel of salvation. Indeed these things were completed to some extent under Cyrus and Darius Hystaspes, and through Zerubbabel, Ezra, and Nehemiah, and truly they were completed more fully through Christ and the apostles. But they will be fulfilled most completely yet on that day of judgment, which is called by the apostles "the day of the restoration of all," and again, "the day of our redemption...."

"I myself will gather afresh those scattered into various lands due to my furor; I will lead them back into that place, into Jerusalem, I say, and into the Promised Land." The histories of Ezra and Nehemiah teach that this was done. In truth, because Jerusalem is the church of God, and the Promised Land bears the symbol of the eternal country, for that reason the Son of God came into earth from heaven and gathered again the children of God scattered throughout the whole world—just as a shepherd gathers his little sheep—into the oneness of the church. Then at the end of the age he will lead them gathered as one into their eternal homeland, just as has been copiously handed down in the holy Scriptures in John 10–11, and 1 Thessalonians 4.

"I will cause them to dwell securely." ... Certainly the tranquility of souls is promised. The apostle speaks of this, saying, "Since we are justified, we have peace from our faith" etc. But peace and tranquility or absolute security will at last be granted to all our parts in the eternal homeland. Since the blind Jews do not see this and interpret everything in a literal and temporal sense, and at the same time they see that they have never lived

safely, neither themselves nor their ancestors—their ancestors were brutally violated by the Medes, Persians, Macedonians, Greeks, and Romans, and they themselves who are alive today are miserably violated by all nations—therefore they imagine another I-don't-know-what golden age that will happen, under yet another Messiah of their own to come at some I-don't-know-when time, in which these passages might be fulfilled literally. But they are wrong, blind, and stupid; for these things have been fulfilled spiritually through the peace and security prepared for us by Christ, and these things will be fulfilled more liberally in our souls and bodies on the last day.

"They shall be my people and I will be their God." Indeed the returning Israelites did not shrink from the foreign gods and idols, but Christians adhere to the one God through Christ.... They acknowledge that they have received every abundance from God in Christ, and that God is their most beneficent father. SERMON ON JEREMIAH 32:36-38.[17]

ONE HEART AND ONE WAY. JOHANNES BUGENHAGEN: "Behold I will gather." Once again here is the promise of grace. First that they will be restored from Babylon, then the kingdom of the Messiah will come.... "And I will give to them," he says, "one heart and one way so that they fear me," that is, that they worship spiritually. The fear of the Lord in the Scriptures is the worship of God, and faith and life according to the Word of God; that is, so that all may adhere to the promise of the gospel in one faith and worship or adore the Father in Spirit, that is, in faith and truth, that is, in the Word of God.

Outside of this one faith in Christ and outside this truth of the Word of God, all forms of worship and adorations among the Turks, Jews, papists, etc, are hypocrisy, idolatry, and the lie of Satan. People do not have this one heart and this one way, but God promises here that he would grant this in the New Testament; this gift is the Holy Spirit.... Here in Jeremiah God himself responds through the New Testament, promising, "I myself will give

---

[16]CRR 8:354.

[17]Bullinger, *Conciones*, 196r-v; citing 1 Thess 4:13-17; Rom 5:1.

them one heart," and then also "one way," so that they will no longer be torn to pieces or scattered by various doctrines and forms of worship fashioned by deceptive people: Hebrews 13. In this sincere word there is unity for those who through the Spirit believe in the word. Outside of this there can be nothing other than diversity, discord, uncertainty of conscience, no peace, and no love. COMMENTARY ON JEREMIAH 32:37-39.[18]

ONE IN GOD—COMMUNITY, LIFE, COVENANT. HEINRICH BULLINGER: "I will give to them one heart and one way." The unity of hearts is accomplished in the unity of faith in one God; sincere love also joins with this one thing. In the Acts of the Apostles we read, "the faithful had one heart. . . ." Therefore, for some time after the Babylonian captivity the Jews were content with the one law of God; but thereafter they began to listen to the Tannaim and they became confused.[†] In turn, true Christians do not attend to any teachings. Indeed, they are content with the evangelical, prophetic, and apostolic doctrine, which is the only true way of salvation. Christians are not torn apart into sects and orders. Thus the monastic orders are sects foreign to Christianity. Some sects and other sects [like them] do battle with this single way. Christ is the only true way; he is the only door; the truest teaching of Christ is the path, rule, and guide of piety, life, and eternal salvation. Let all decrees, decretals, assemblies, and laws perish when they do battle against the only way of God.

"So that they may fear me all their days." Here is the result which follows from those other parts. The godly will attend to God religiously; they will love, serve, and worship him. . . . These are the truly splendid gifts we have through the grace of Christ, which is preached here in splendid ways. Moreover, the fruit of this follows, which henceforth springs forth for the godly, so that it may go well both for them, and for their children, and those after them—of course only if they enter into the holy way of their elders. "That it may be well for them,"

he said; that is, that they may be happy and blessed, especially in the coming age. . . .

"I will make an everlasting covenant with them": The nature of this covenant in the future is explained and laid out. "For I will not pull back from them, nor will I bless them any less." That is, I will cleave to them perpetually and continue to bless them. I will never abandon them in dangers, as they typically do, those who, leaving the battle line behind, or fleeing from the battle line or from the rear of the battalion, and, as it were, betray their allies to the enemy. But when he promises that he will bless us, he implies every benefit both in the present and future ages, and whatever is necessary for us for a full and eternal life. SERMON ON JEREMIAH 32:39-40.[19]

GOD'S LOVE AND JOY IN DOING GOOD. JOHANN ARNDT: The love of God, indeed, God himself, has fallen away from those people who do not find the love of neighbor in themselves. They ought therefore to be in dread and in their hearts to be repentant, to seek forgiveness from their neighbors so that God with his love might come to him once again. Everything that a person does in faith and love will then once again be good, holy, and godly. Then a person will practice God's love and mercy with joy for the sake of the indwelling love of God and it will be a joy for them to do good as God said. TRUE CHRISTIANITY.[20]

FEAR OF THE LORD, PURCHASED FIELDS, AND GOD'S FAITHFULNESS. HEINRICH BULLINGER: Now God explains more copiously what he touched on with the one word of "fear." "I will put my fear into their hearts, so that they do not abandon me." The author of this divine fear is shown to be God. This fear comes to us by the help and grace of God, not by our own merit, nor

---

[18]Bugenhagen, *In Ieremiam*, 5F1v-5F2v; citing Heb 13:7-16.

[19]Bullinger, *Conciones*, 196v-197r; citing Acts 4:32; Jn 10:9; 14:6. [†]The Tannaim were rabbis whose views are found in talmudic literature. They were Jewish teachers active in Palestine in the first two centuries AD. See Louis Jacobs, *The Jewish Religion: A Companion* (Oxford: Oxford University Press, 1995), 534-35. [20]Arndt, *True Christianity*, 127*.

by the virtues of our free will. "I myself," he says, "will give this into the heart." It will not cleave to the tongue or the upper lip, but it will cleave, fixed to the very heart, soul, and interior of a person. He will do this, moreover, "so they will not abandon me, but rather, as if bound to me by faith and love, acknowledge me, lean on me, call on me, attend to and revere me; that they might walk in my laws and not abandon me for this world, for desires and honors, but rush to me through torments, deaths, fires, and dangers." This is the true fear of God; this is the true steadfastness of Christians. . . .

And what he touched on concerning the benefits, he illustrates more clearly. "Indeed, I will rejoice over them," etc. Freely and willingly, with joy and desire, God says that he wants to bless them; and not in a coerced way, not meanly and with sadness. Then he says, "I will plant them in this land," and adds, "in truth"; for which we say in German, "with fierce loyalty"; and God says, "with my whole heart," etc. In all these is demonstrated the most excellent, singular, blessed, and faithful zeal of the Lord for all the faithful that he will plant and preserve. . . . Finally, so that he might cover all things briefly, he speaks in opposites. Just as in every way I exerted myself to roll every evil upon them, so I will strive to cover them with every good thing. With the good, I say, which in the pres-

ent he promises them. Moreover, since the destruction of the city and nation was in every way most grievous, it follows that the coming restoration of everything will be outstanding. Let us therefore rejoice in the Lord, and give eternal thanks to him, and let us try not to be deprived of so great a good through our laziness and sloth.

Finally, the Lord responds to the question Jeremiah had been asking, "While the people and city are being destroyed, why does the Lord order him to buy a field in Anathoth?" Now he answers: so that the Jewish people would understand here that "even if their city is razed to the ground, their land destroyed, and the captive people are led away, nevertheless there will be a future time when this city and this land will be inhabited and the captive people will again buy fields," etc. In this rich exposition, as by the enumeration of parts, God declares that all the promised parts of both Judea and the land will be both restored and again inhabited and cultivated. At last with one word he sums up everything: "I will lead them back" or "I will change," he says, "their captivity." . . . Therefore, let us believe the Lord our God, who promises to us sinners restoration and glory. SERMON ON JEREMIAH 32:40-44.[21]

---

[21]Bullinger, *Conciones*, 197v.

JEREMIAH 33:1-26
THE PEACE OF GOD AND
THE DAVIDIC COVENANT

¹The word of the Lord came to Jeremiah a second time, while he was still shut up in the court of the guard: ²"Thus says the Lord who made the earth,ᵃ the Lord who formed it to establish it—the Lord is his name: ³Call to me and I will answer you, and will tell you great and hidden things that you have not known. ⁴For thus says the Lord, the God of Israel, concerning the houses of this city and the houses of the kings of Judah that were torn down to make a defense against the siege mounds and against the sword: ⁵They are coming in to fight against the Chaldeans and to fill themᵇ with the dead bodies of men whom I shall strike down in my anger and my wrath, for I have hidden my face from this city because of all their evil. ⁶Behold, I will bring to it health and healing, and I will heal them and reveal to them abundance of prosperity and security. ⁷I will restore the fortunes of Judah and the fortunes of Israel, and rebuild them as they were at first. ⁸I will cleanse them from all the guilt of their sin against me, and I will forgive all the guilt of their sin and rebellion against me. ⁹And this cityᶜ shall be to me a name of joy, a praise and a glory before all the nations of the earth who shall hear of all the good that I do for them. They shall fear and tremble because of all the good and all the prosperity I provide for it.

¹⁰"Thus says the Lord: In this place of which you say, 'It is a waste without man or beast,' in the cities of Judah and the streets of Jerusalem that are desolate, without man or inhabitant or beast, there shall be heard again ¹¹the voice of mirth and the voice of gladness, the voice of the bridegroom and the voice of the bride, the voices of those who sing, as they bring thank offerings to the house of the Lord:

"'Give thanks to the Lord of hosts,
    for the Lord is good,
    for his steadfast love endures forever!'

For I will restore the fortunes of the land as at first, says the Lord.

¹²"Thus says the Lord of hosts: In this place that is waste, without man or beast, and in all of its cities, there shall again be habitations of shepherds resting their flocks. ¹³In the cities of the hill country, in the cities of the Shephelah, and in the cities of the Negeb, in the land of Benjamin, the places about Jerusalem, and in the cities of Judah, flocks shall again pass under the hands of the one who counts them, says the Lord.

¹⁴"Behold, the days are coming, declares the Lord, when I will fulfill the promise I made to the house of Israel and the house of Judah. ¹⁵In those days and at that time I will cause a righteous Branch to spring up for David, and he shall execute justice and righteousness in the land. ¹⁶In those days Judah will be saved, and Jerusalem will dwell securely. And this is the name by which it will be called: 'The Lord is our righteousness.'

¹⁷"For thus says the Lord: David shall never lack a man to sit on the throne of the house of Israel, ¹⁸and the Levitical priests shall never lack a man in my presence to offer burnt offerings, to burn grain offerings, and to make sacrifices forever."

¹⁹The word of the Lord came to Jeremiah: ²⁰"Thus says the Lord: If you can break my covenant with the day and my covenant with the night, so that day and night will not come at their appointed time, ²¹then also my covenant with David my servant may be broken, so that he shall not have a son to reign on his throne, and my covenant with the Levitical priests my ministers. ²²As the host of heaven cannot be numbered and the sands of the sea cannot be measured, so I will multiply the offspring of David my servant, and the Levitical priests who minister to me."

²³The word of the Lord came to Jeremiah: ²⁴"Have you not observed that these people are saying, 'The Lord has rejected the two clans that he chose'? Thus they have despised my people so that they are no longer a nation in their sight. ²⁵Thus says the Lord: If I have not established my covenant

*with day and night and the fixed order of heaven
and earth, ²⁶then I will reject the offspring of Jacob
and David my servant and will not choose one of his*

*offspring to rule over the offspring of Abraham, Isaac,
and Jacob. For I will restore their fortunes and will
have mercy on them."*

a Septuagint; Hebrew *it*   b That is, the torn-down houses   c Hebrew *And it*

OVERVIEW: Understanding and interpreting the relationship of the Old Testament to the New Testament has been a particular challenge for Christians. Commentators of the Reformation era unfold the promises in Jeremiah 33 that apply to the restoration of the Jews after the Babylonian exile, the promises that both pertain to the ancient Jews and to Christ and the church, and the promises that point to Christ alone. At the same time expositors ponder how Old Testament practices and offices either ended before the coming of Christ, continued in the Christian era, or were transformed in form and meaning in light of Christ.

33:1-13 The Lord Will Heal

KING AND PRIEST ON EARTH AND IN ETERNITY. JOHANNES BUGENHAGEN: Once again God promises liberation and release from captivity. And he adds that after the return although they will not especially have kings, nevertheless they will have princes and governors from the lineage of David and from Levi and Aaron: the Levites and priests, as promised and instituted, and finally from the law of God. By this God is commanding them to hope that the people would be led back not only to the land but also to God, so that there will be a holy and true government and true worship of God.

Moreover, the eternal kingdom begins later, in Christ, who is the seed of David. The Levites and priests of the law passed away and were changed— neither by the propagation of the flesh nor by mandate of the law—but by the institution of God and Christ so that they became apostles and teachers of the holy gospel. Therefore, all those are incorporated by faith into Christ, who is the king and the eternal one. They are priests—not based

on the law—but through him and on account of him: a royal priesthood and priestly kingdom— 1 Peter 2. Thus earthly things are promised first here, and then also eternal things in Christ, the eternal King and Priest. COMMENTARY ON JEREMIAH 33.[1]

JEREMIAH'S CONSISTENCY AND THE LORD'S OMNIPOTENCE. HEINRICH BULLINGER: From the beginning of this passage and onward we are reminded where this sermon was spoken by the author, when it happened, and what sort of situation the author faced at that time. As in chapter 32, Jeremiah speaks this oration while he is in prison and when the city was already about to be captured. The prophet was held captive because of his ministry and his willingness to proclaim the truth. These things remind us again about the lot of God's ministers, and what they should expect from those to whom they minister, especially if they are faithful in their office or ministry. Even so, Jeremiah changes nothing in the content of his doctrine; he says exactly the same thing while bound as when he was free and unchained. In the same way we must announce the same truth perpetually. Nothing should be taken away or changed due to adversaries or chains.

But in order that he might furnish some credibility and confirm for both the audience and the prophet those things which he was about to say to them, he puts in advance, "Thus says the Lord, who has done this." . . . God signifies that he is the author of those things that are to be said and done here, and that he himself is powerful enough, he who is able to make what he says into an absolutely certain and valid result. Finally he says that he brings about and forms every part of this work. He says, "It is the Lord

---

[1]Bugenhagen, *In Ieremiam*, 5F4r; citing 1 Pet 2:9.

who does this." It is the Lord who forms it, establishes it, preserves it, and brings it to completion. He adds to these his name—the all-powerful. . . .

Now, and also before he prophesies, the prophet is ordered to cry out or to invoke the Lord, who promises that he will reveal great and grand mysteries, mighty or hidden things (either is a valid reading), which he does not know. Therefore, he speaks concerning the scattering of the city and the people, then of the restitution of the captives, and concerning the mysteries of Christ and the church, which are too great to be comprehended in human words. Truly, Jeremiah is said not to understand these things, at least not fully. Indeed, often these same things were revealed to him and more frequently he presented them to the people. However, he did not know them on his own apart from revelation. Indeed how little there is that we understand by ourselves! Unless the Lord illuminates our souls, we have no understanding. SERMON ON JEREMIAH 33:1-3.[2]

A DOUBTING PROPHET. JOHANNES OECOLAMPADIUS: "Call to me." "Let this not be terrifying to you, that you are in prison because of the truth and that the city is besieged. Indeed, I will reveal to you consoling things, and they will be great and certain and firm, which you have not known thus far." Jeremiah seems, however, to have had his doubts when acquiring a field for the return of the people; so savage did the calamity seem. For it is difficult for human nature to hope for exaltation and life in the midst of ruin and death; nor does the natural human being sustain the hope that his body, which is about to perish, will be remade in glory. COMMENTARY ON JEREMIAH 33:3.[3]

DIVINE JUDGMENT AND REPENTANCE. JOHANN PAPPUS: The Lord briefly repeats what he had put forward at greater length in the previous chapter, namely, that his own counsel is certain and established concerning the plunder of the city at

the hand of the Babylonians, and that no one is able to withstand the strength and violence of their attack. Of course, all this because the Lord was enraged at the city contaminated by so many evils. . . . Let us strive to turn the anger of the Lord away from ourselves with sincere repentance, and let us not be the cause of our own destruction through our own evil deeds. ON ALL THE PROPHETS, JEREMIAH 33:4-5.[4]

SPIRITUAL PRAYER OVER IMAGES. ANDREAS BODENSTEIN VON KARLSTADT: No Christian can deny that spiritual prayer is a divine work which God alone effects. It is written in Jeremiah 33, "I will show them the prayer and adoration of peace and truth." That which God alone effects, no image ever can. You also must not say that an image of Christ brings you to Christ. For it is certainly true that "no one comes to me unless my Father draw him." All who come to Christ must have learned from God. ON THE REMOVAL OF IMAGES.[5]

AS IT WAS IN THE BEGINNING. JOHANNES BUGENHAGEN: "Just as from the beginning." This verse should not only be understood as, "just as from the beginning of the kingdom, when the Canaanites were expelled, and I built you up in this land," but also or especially as, "just as from the beginning," that is, "when I was first taking up your fathers—Abraham, Isaac, and Jacob—for myself as a people, who were my kingdom, my people, the just and sons of God, without an earthly kingdom, without the land of Canaan." So Abraham was already justified in his foreskin without circumcision as a son of God, as it was written concerning the uncircumcised Abraham: "Abraham believed in God and it was imputed to him as righteousness." These things do not have the flavor of the greedy and proud Jews, because they see that the Gentiles are able to reach this righteousness. Certainly when Abraham pleased God through faith, he was not a circumcised Jew, but an uncircumcised Gentile. Therefore, Abraham

---

[2]Bullinger, *Conciones*, 197v-198r.
[3]Oecolampadius, *In Hieremiam*, 2:T2v.
[4]Pappus, *In Omnes Prophetas*, 108r.
[5]CRR 8:114; citing Jn 6:44.

is also our father and the father of all—the Jews and Gentiles who believe as Abraham believed. Commentary on Jeremiah 33:7.[6]

Father Rather Than Judge. Johannes Bugenhagen: "And it will be to me." You see how much God is pleased to be our Father through the gospel rather than our Judge through the law, and that with these words he declares his love for us, by which "he has loved us and chosen us in Christ in eternity before the world was formed"; Ephesians 1. It is fair to interpret the fact that he speaks concerning flocks and shepherds with reference to the joy and abundance of life after the captivity, as Christ promised: "First, seek the kingdom of God," but, as he is here speaking about the New Testament and the kingdom of David, the shepherds are more properly teachers and sheep that are hearers and disciples in the kingdom of Christ. Commentary on Jeremiah 33:9.[7]

True Worship and the Second Temple. Konrad Pellikan: Even the Jews cannot deny that Jeremiah and Isaiah both in common preached about the happiness of those returning from Babylon and of those that would be saved through the Messiah, who they always hoped was coming, not only in these verses, but also in other passages, as too other prophets did so and even more. . . . For this reason, this passage is applied only to those returning from Babylon; indeed, already all of Judea and a great part of the land of Israel was being destroyed and Jerusalem was now under siege without hope of liberation. Nevertheless, everything that was being predicted would have to be renewed afresh at some time, so that people and animals would again inhabit this land.

And that would happen with so great a peace that people would rejoice in their marriages and nuptials would be celebrated with great joy. This would not happen without the distinguished

worship of God, which would be restored when the temple was rebuilt and the sacrifices were offered and the praises were sung to the Lord in the temple. For those who are currently captives, and who would be captives, would return, if not in their very persons, then through their descendants. Indeed, the complete restoration of the lands of Judah and Israel is promised, of such a type and completion as the sacred and everyday verses sing about. And if this happens with less majesty than there was under Solomon, it would at least be no less majestic than it was under many kings, especially under the sons of Josiah, namely before the first temple was destroyed. Indeed, sometimes under the second temple the glory of the Jews was greater than it was for many years under the first temple. But granted, there were many things missing from the second temple that had been present in the first, including, of course, the ark and the many vases. Nevertheless, the first temple was now missing many of its abominations and idols, which would not be present in the second. Commentary on Jeremiah 33:10-11.[8]

Shepherds as a Sign of Peace. John Calvin: Jeremiah speaks here of the settled happiness of the people, as though he had said that there was no reason for the Israelites to fear. . . . But in setting forth their quiet and peaceable condition, he speaks of shepherds; for we know it is a sure sign of peace, when flocks and herds are led into the fields in security. For enemies always scan for prey and experience of war proves this; for whenever incursions are made by enemies, they send spies that they may know whether there are shepherds or keepers of cattle; and then they know that there is prey for them. As then shepherds, when an invasion from enemies is dreaded, dare not go forth, and as there is then no liberty, the prophet, in order to intimate that the Jews would be in a tranquil state, says, "There shall again be a habitation of shepherds." Commentary on Jeremiah 33:12.[9]

---

[6]Bugenhagen, *In Ieremiam*, 5F4v-5G1r; citing Gen 15:6; Rom 4:3; Rom 4:1-25.
[7]Bugenhagen, *In Ieremiam*, 5G1r; citing Eph 1:4; Mt 6:33.

[8]Pellikan, *Commentaria Bibliorum*, 3:2X3r.
[9]CTS 20:245* (CO 39:61).

THE SHEPHERD KNOWS HIS SHEEP. GIOVANNI DIODATI: Jeremiah mentions the custom of shepherds, namely, that they count their sheep one by one when they come out of the covered enclosure or open pen; and then they count again as the sheep are coming in with a wand in their hand. . . . This shows the peaceable state of the country. But most of all Jeremiah means the spiritual conduct of Christ, who knows all of his sheep and calls them by name. ANNOTATIONS ON JEREMIAH 33:13.[10]

RABBINIC INTERPRETATION AND THE GOOD SHEPHERD. JUAN DE MALDONADO: "According to the hand of the counter." That is, however many [sheep] someone would be able to count. Rabbi David Kimchi and Rabi Solomon Rashi say that by "shepherd" is understood "the king" and the sheep are the citizens of Judah and Israel and that this is an allusion to the custom of shepherds, who are used to counting their sheep by hand when they return in the evening from the pasture. It is as if he says the citizens of Judah and Israel will have a king by whom they are ruled. Even better, Jonathan the Chaldean calls this shepherd "Christ." Indeed he is the good shepherd. "Counting the sheep" means recognizing them and taking care of them, lest they perish. Christ says this about himself in John 10:14; "I know my sheep." And in John 17:12 and 18:9: "I have not lost one of those that you gave to me." COMMENTARY ON THE PROPHETS, JEREMIAH 33:13.[11]

33:14-26 The Lord's Eternal Covenant with David

WORSHIP AND FAITH IN THE MESSIAH'S KINGDOM. NIKOLAUS SELNECKER: This passage repeats the marvelous promise from chapter 23,

concerning the Messiah who is, namely, Jehovah, and a branch of David; that is, the true eternal God and the true human being. Moreover, his office will be, namely, that he must be an eternal king, who reigns well and pursues justice and righteousness on the earth. Through him a great multitude will be justified as the stars in the heavens, the grass in the field, or the sand on the seashore. Because of him God the Father wills that all those who commit misdeeds, who believe in him, be forgiven. God wills this with deep gladness and does it willingly, so that his grace and mercy will thereby be recognized, his name lauded, glorified, and praised.

Furthermore, this passage shows what kind of kingdom this will be, namely, no worldly kingdom, but an eternal kingdom that never ends. Therein the priests, Levites, and offerings shall remain in eternity forever and ever; not the offerings of the law or the Levitical ceremonies of the old covenant, but the new priesthood and worship of the New Testament, the royal priesthood, in which we teach the Word of God, call on God, and achieve a royal and priestly obedience to our High King and Priest. That is, we have put on his righteousness and led a holy life, praised God, and offered a dedicated spirit and brought him a sacrifice of praise, in faith in his Son, a praise offering that recognizes his truth and gives thanks to him for all of his good works and follows him in our calling and life. Thus these are the upright offerings of the New Testament: faith, prayer, confession, gratitude, obedience, and patience in the cross. THE WHOLE PROPHET JEREMIAH 33:14-22.[12]

THE FLOURISHING OF THE BRANCH OF CHRIST. MARTIN LUTHER: Isaiah 4 says, "In that day the Branch of the Lord shall be glorious"; and Jeremiah 33 says, "At that time I will cause a righteous Branch to spring forth for David," etc. He is called a Branch, however, because without ceasing Christ is being preached in the gospel and is growing and increasing and will always gain new and more Christians out of this world.

---

[10]Diodati, *Pious Annotations*, 76*; citing Jn 10: 3, 11, 13; Lev 27:32; Ezek 20:37.

[11]Maldonado, *Commentarii in Prophetas*, 151; citing Jn 10:11, 14. Maldonado refers to the interpretations of Rabbi David Kimchi and Rabbi Solomon (Rashi), and he quotes the Targum Jonathan; he either points out that this source associates Jer 33:13 with the Jewish Messiah, or Maldonado implies that Jonathan the Chaldean was a Christian.

[12]Selnecker, *Der gantze Prophet Jeremias*, 2G2v-2G3r; citing Jer 23:5-6.

But this is a strange growing, one that looks to the world like something that is withering and perishing. For we find the cross of Christ in it and all kinds of persecution. But we also find pure growth in it; for in the midst of death there is life, in poverty riches, in disgrace honor, and so forth—amid all evil there is sheer goodness. LECTURES ON ZECHARIAH 3:8-9.[13]

CHRIST AND THE COVENANT WITH THE JEWS. JOHN CALVIN: Here the prophet shows what Paul speaks of later—that all the promises of God are in Christ, yes and amen; that is, they do not stand nor can be valid to us, except Christ interposes to sanction or confirm them. Then the efficacy of God's promises depend on Christ alone. And hence the prophets, when speaking of the grace of God, come at length to Christ, for without him all the promises would vanish away.

Let us know that the Jews had been so trained as ever to flee to God's covenant; for on the general covenant depended all particular promises. As, for instance, Jeremiah has hitherto been often prophesying God's mercy to the people after having punished them for their sins; now this promise was special. How, then, could the Jews and Israelites believe that they should return to their own country? This special promise could have been of no moment, except as it was an appendix of the covenant, even because God had adopted them as his people. And then the Jews knew that they had been chosen as a peculiar people, and that God was their Father, hence their faith in all the promises. Now, again, we must bear in mind that the covenant was founded on Christ alone; for God had not only promised to Abraham that he would be a father to his seed but had also added an earnest pledge that the redeemer would come.

We now then perceive the reason why the prophets, when they sought to strengthen the faithful in the hope of salvation, set forth Christ, because the promises had no certainty without the general covenant. And further, as the general

covenant could not stand, nor have any validity, except in Christ, this is the point to which Jeremiah now turns his attention, as we have also seen in other places, especially in the twenty-third chapter, from which he repeats this prophecy. God then promised that his people would be restored; he had also promised that he would be so propitious to them as to preserve them in safety as his people. COMMENTARY ON JEREMIAH 33:15.[14]

PRIESTHOOD AND KINGSHIP AMONG BELIEVERS. JOHANNES OECOLAMPADIUS: Our Christ is the King and Priest of a perpetual kingdom and priesthood. He will always reign and will remain "even to the consummation of the age." He reigns, moreover, in the hearts or bodily members of the elect through the Spirit. Moreover, he rules the external administration, through which the ministers and apostles announce his word, whom neither tyrants nor death can conquer. These are ministers of the Spirit, who in order to follow the Spirit act as servants by the preaching of the Word. Meanwhile the worship of God will be constant, for all believers are truly priests, who offer thoughtful sacrifices to the Lord, and who truly mortify themselves and give sacrifices. Therefore, do not believe that counterfeit priesthood, for in the church of Christ both the people and the minister are priests. Our age is bewitched by that made-up priesthood into blasphemy of the name and merits of Christ, who is our one mediator. So a secular power here is promised neither to the pope, nor to anyone else. In these offices that one pastor Christ the King reigns. COMMENTARY ON JEREMIAH 33:17.[15]

CHRIST THE PRIEST AND HIS ELECT. GIOVANNI DIODATI: "The priests," that means Christ, who was prefigured by the ancient priests. Christ shall continue forever exercising his spiritual priesthood by his perpetual intercession with God. And the lesser parts belong to this office, namely,

---

[13]LW 20:217 (WA 23:553); citing Is 4:2; 53:2.

[14]CTS 20:249-50* (CO 39:64-65); citing 2 Cor 1:20, Jer 23:5-6.
[15]Oecolampadius, *In Hieremiam*, 2:V2v; 174v; citing Mt 28:20; 1 Pet 2:9.

praises and beneficence, etc, shall be performed continually under Christ by his elect, who have been made priests by him; especially his sacred ministers in the preaching of his Word, and in all true evangelical service. ANNOTATIONS ON JEREMIAH 33:18.[16]

THE CERTAINTY OF GOD'S PROMISES. NIKO-LAUS SELNECKER: This passage is a consolation that God will certainly fulfill his promises, even if it may often appear that nothing will come of them; for God is the truth and what he promises must happen and can and shall never fail. Therefore, no one shall say, "God has rejected these two lines; he does not want Israel and Judah; he does not want Moses and Aaron; he does not want the priesthood and kingdom." No, this is not so. In fact, this view is derisive toward God and moves people toward mistrust and unbelief. When one doubts God's promise and Word, then one should hold tightly to God, his covenant, Word, and promise. As He is the eternal, omnipotent, and true God, even if God's ways and amazing deeds sometimes appear strange, he does fulfill his promise even in the midst of things that appear contrary. God's deeds are beyond human wisdom, reason, and thought. God gives us his Holy Spirit that we may hold fast to his promise and Word, in doctrine, life, cross, and death. THE WHOLE PROPHET JER-EMIAH 33:23-26.[17]

---

[16]Diodati, *Pious Annotations*, 76*.

[17]Selnecker, *Der gantze Prophet Jeremias*, 2G3r.

JEREMIAH 34:1-22
ZEDEKIAH'S DEMISE AND
THE FATE OF THE SLAVES

¹The word that came to Jeremiah from the Lord, when Nebuchadnezzar king of Babylon and all his army and all the kingdoms of the earth under his dominion and all the peoples were fighting against Jerusalem and all of its cities: ²"Thus says the Lord, the God of Israel: Go and speak to Zedekiah king of Judah and say to him, 'Thus says the Lord: Behold, I am giving this city into the hand of the king of Babylon, and he shall burn it with fire. ³You shall not escape from his hand but shall surely be captured and delivered into his hand. You shall see the king of Babylon eye to eye and speak with him face to face. And you shall go to Babylon.' ⁴Yet hear the word of the Lord, O Zedekiah king of Judah! Thus says the Lord concerning you: 'You shall not die by the sword. ⁵You shall die in peace. And as spices were burned for your fathers, the former kings who were before you, so people shall burn spices for you and lament for you, saying, "Alas, lord!"' For I have spoken the word, declares the Lord."

⁶Then Jeremiah the prophet spoke all these words to Zedekiah king of Judah, in Jerusalem, ⁷when the army of the king of Babylon was fighting against Jerusalem and against all the cities of Judah that were left, Lachish and Azekah, for these were the only fortified cities of Judah that remained.

⁸The word that came to Jeremiah from the Lord, after King Zedekiah had made a covenant with all the people in Jerusalem to make a proclamation of liberty to them, ⁹that everyone should set free his Hebrew slaves, male and female, so that no one should enslave a Jew, his brother. ¹⁰And they obeyed, all the officials and all the people who had entered into the covenant that everyone would set free his slave, male or female, so that they would not be enslaved again. They obeyed and set them free. ¹¹But afterward they turned around and took back the male and female slaves they had set free, and brought them into subjection as slaves. ¹²The word of the Lord came to Jeremiah from the Lord: ¹³"Thus says the Lord, the God of Israel: I myself made a covenant with your fathers when I brought them out of the land of Egypt, out of the house of slavery, saying, ¹⁴'At the end of seven years each of you must set free the fellow Hebrew who has been sold to you and has served you six years; you must set him free from your service.' But your fathers did not listen to me or incline their ears to me. ¹⁵You recently repented and did what was right in my eyes by proclaiming liberty, each to his neighbor, and you made a covenant before me in the house that is called by my name, ¹⁶but then you turned around and profaned my name when each of you took back his male and female slaves, whom you had set free according to their desire, and you brought them into subjection to be your slaves.

¹⁷"Therefore, thus says the Lord: You have not obeyed me by proclaiming liberty, every one to his brother and to his neighbor; behold, I proclaim to you liberty to the sword, to pestilence, and to famine, declares the Lord. I will make you a horror to all the kingdoms of the earth. ¹⁸And the men who transgressed my covenant and did not keep the terms of the covenant that they made before me, I will make them likeᵃ the calf that they cut in two and passed between its parts— ¹⁹the officials of Judah, the officials of Jerusalem, the eunuchs, the priests, and all the people of the land who passed between the parts of the calf. ²⁰And I will give them into the hand of their enemies and into the hand of those who seek their lives. Their dead bodies shall be food for the birds of the air and the beasts of the earth. ²¹And Zedekiah king of Judah and his officials I will give into the hand of their enemies and into the hand of those who seek their lives, into the hand of the army of the king of Babylon which has withdrawn from you. ²²Behold, I will command, declares

the Lord, and will bring them back to this city. And they will fight against it and take it and burn it with fire. I will make the cities of Judah a desolation without inhabitant."

a Hebrew lacks *them like*

OVERVIEW: Jeremiah's prophecy speaks to every level of society in Jerusalem—the king, the citizens of property, and their oppressed slaves. Likewise, theologians, scholars, and preachers of the sixteenth century promoted reforms of both doctrine and daily life. Thus, as this prophecy ties covenant faithfulness to the liberation of people held in unjust servitude, so commentators addressed the lingering practice of slavery on the borderlands of Europe and the true nature of sacrificial and generous care for one's neighbor. Both idolatry and social injustice break the covenant with God and show alarming ingratitude for the unmerited grace promised in Christ.

34:1-7 Zedekiah to Die in Babylon

A DECEITFUL COVENANT. JOHANNES BUGENHA-GEN: Jeremiah returns to rebuking their malice and disobedience, because of which the whole land perishes; all the way to chapter 39. The first to perish, he says, will be the city and King Zedekiah—if they do not return to the Lord; this is after the Babylonians have already destroyed the remaining cities of Judah, except the walled cities of Lachish and Azekah. After this they seem to want to obey God since in accordance with the law they dismiss those manservants and maidservants who were from the Hebrews. But soon greed and avarice dragged those servants back into servitude. They went into a covenant before God during the terrors of the siege. However, when the Babylonian army withdrew from the city they all thought themselves to be finished with danger and they violated the covenant of God. So that covenant was only a repentance of the impious. . . . Indeed, where there is no faith or Spirit of God, there the flesh cannot act otherwise. Whatever seems to be done according to the law is a sham and forced. In fact, the flesh has served desire or passion from the heart. "You are not able," Christ says, "to serve God and mammon." So they want, in fact, to avoid the present danger of siege by the sham of fearing God. COMMENTARY ON JEREMIAH 34.[1]

GOD AS A PIOUS SCHOOLMASTER. NIKOLAUS SELNECKER: Jeremiah comes again with a sermon of admonition to King Zedekiah and all the citizens of Jerusalem, who should not have forgotten the king of Babylon. Jeremiah relates how such things will happen, as is pathetically and wretchedly described later in chapter 52. Additionally God shows with concealed words not only that he now permits this unrepentant people to be captured and led away, but also thereafter how those who convert to the new covenant (about this he has spoken in chapter 31) and yet have not accepted his Son, can still come to believe in him. (One can see that they did not want to observe a few parts of the old covenant too, as they acted against the command of the year of liberation for slaves.) So God allows them to remain trapped, scattered, and in no kingdom of their own on the earth. . . .

It is a common saying: when God wants to punish a land, there must be such sins committed that one has to say, "The punishment was fully earned." This is like a pious father or schoolmaster, who has long hesitated with the rod and did not soon discipline the bad children, as they had fully earned. But he threatened them; he would surely discipline them if they did not change their behavior. But they let such threats rush by their ears and they continued together in their mischief. They continued to act beyond the limits and rush about, so that anyone must say, "The father or schoolmaster can no longer watch; now is the time

---

[1]Bugenhagen, *In Ieremiam*, 5G3v-5G4r; citing Mt 6:24; Lk 16:13.

for discipline. It was a sin, when one wanted to be nice and did not strike at once." So we see here that God had long threatened the people; he wanted them to deal with their sins. God had promised that he would punish them so that they might be pious. He wanted to show them grace and minimize the punishment. Here God also promises King Zedekiah that he will alleviate his bodily punishment; the king will not die by the sword, but will die on his bed in Babylon and be honorably buried.... But the people had wanted to know fully neither the promises nor the threats of God. THE WHOLE PROPHET JEREMIAH 34:1-5.[2]

JEWISH KINGS—CREMATED OR BURIED?

JOHANNES BUGENHAGEN: "You shall not die by the sword, but in peace," that is, without a sword. "And you shall be burned up," etc. So the translator of the Old Latin Bible has it, and generally all other translators copy this. Truly, they have the opinion that there was a royal procession in the funeral rites for certain dead kings, and that the body was burned up and bones of the burned body were preserved in a decorated tomb, as is seen in 2 Chronicles 16 concerning Asa king of Judah. But this ostentatious honor of burning seems to be denied to Joram king of Judah in 2 Chronicles 21. Interpreters seem to have accepted this idea as a history from words they did not understand, which were written about one king or another and not all the others. I do not care if certain people make up and write a history, as if it were something that was actually done and from words they did not understand. For the Jews did not burn the bodies of the dead, as certain Gentiles made a funeral pyre and put a cadaver therein. But the Hebrews not only honorably buried their people whole, but also with pomp and great expense. Abraham buried the body of his Sarah intact. And afterward Abraham was buried with her in the tomb and all the other patriarchs. Christ himself was buried with great honor and treated with

many aromatic spices. If you want to know that the history is not about burnings, but lavish burials among the Hebrews, then listen to our Evangelist John: he says, "It is customary for the Jews to bury." The Jews did not have the custom of burning the cadavers of people, but of honorable and lavish burial. This is the true history. Therefore, just as they would freshen those who were buried with perfumes, so also before the burial above the cadaver of a king or some rich person they would burn frankincense and other perfumed spices. So they would fumigate the body of the dead with great pomp and at extraordinary expense, so that a good odor would be widely sensed.... This was called then, in the common language among the Hebrews, "to burn a king," etc. So you read in the history concerning one or another king the words that were commonly known at that time, but which posterity did not understand, and which made for us, out of misunderstood words, a history that never happened....

Therefore, so that I might express the meaning of this passage in Latin, with clear words (indeed, what is the sin, if we don't count the words that are obscure to us, but we say the meaning in Latin with transparent words and remove errors) I have followed Luther, and so I made the passage read: "And just as burnings were made over your fathers, the prior kings who were before you; so the burnings will be made over you." Therefore Zedekiah seems, however he was exiled and blind, to have lived for a time among the Babylonians in peace and was with honor buried in some kingdom, in the same place along with his family, according to this prophecy. COMMENTARY ON JEREMIAH 34:4-5.[3]

A FAILED KING AND KINGDOM. KONRAD

PELLIKAN: In order that both the obedience and perseverance of the prophet and the stubbornness of the king might be apparent, here it is described how many times and in how many ways the king had been warned by the word of the Lord without

---

[2]Selnecker, *Der gantze Prophet Jeremias*, 2G3v-2G4v; citing Jer 31:1-40; Ex 21:1-36.

[3]Bugenhagen, *In Ieremiam*, 5G4r-5H1r; citing 2 Chron 16:13-14; 21:19; Gen 23:1-20; Jn 19:40.

success, so that the righteous judgment of God is made plain and so that one may fear to show contempt for the words of God and the authority of the prophets. The kingdom of Judah was so far weakened that out of so many cities only three walled ones were left subject to the king. All the other ones had been occupied or destroyed by the Babylonians. The greatest malice had led the unfortunate kings of Israel and Judah to the point that nothing of the beautiful and powerful kingdom of Solomon remained, except three cities that were themselves soon to be destroyed. COMMENTARY ON JEREMIAH 34:6-7.[4]

34:8-22 Betrayal of the Slaves and God's Covenant

ABOLISH SLAVERY AND AID THE EMANCI-PATED. ANDREAS BODENSTEIN VON KARLSTADT: "When a Hebrew servant or maid was sold to someone and had worked for six years, then the Hebrew master had to set him free in the seventh year and aid and assist him in this."

This should be done by all slave traders in Rome and elsewhere in the world. They should set the slaves free, without the latter enslaving them by force. For they anger God and besmirch the covenant and the name of God when they keep Hebrew slaves so deceitfully and cunningly, or when they recall them after their release, or when they allow them to depart without any help. For to God it is the same whether people despise and tarnish his name, glory, and commandment or whether they handle them with cunning. You find this in Jeremiah 34. Read Jeremiah's entire chapter. ON THE REMOVAL OF IMAGES.[5]

EXAMINING SLAVERY AND TRUE FREEDOM. HULDRYCH ZWINGLI: When one observes the commandment "Love your neighbor as yourself," there is no need for any other law. God gave us the highest and most perfect law; yet he knows that we

are not able to observe this. Thus the first matter is that he makes us aware of his perfection, which is a high and matchless good. God gives it without requiring return payment. Then he teaches us to know his sincerity, purity, and cleanliness. Second, we learn to see our own weakness and imperfection so that we yearn for grace. We leave ourselves to his mercy and attest to divine righteousness in our conscience, that the law is good and holy....

The most godly and upright people are those who lend to and help their neighbors without asking for anything in return and the most godly folk do so at all times. They are the friends of God. Other people are already many steps below. They help others, but they lend with a penalty registered with the authorities. In this way their love is frozen out. The gospel does not grant a slave freedom in the seventh year. The apostles grant no one freedom in the seventh year. But they teach this: when slavery has come to an end one day in the seventh year, freedom begins. This means that the true year of forgiveness through the gospel has been reached; slaves should be handled mildly and with kindness. Paul says in 1 Corinthians 7: "When one is a slave, so they are set free in Christ; when one is free, so they are now a slave in Christ." So teaches Peter as well and so rule all the apostles. They do not take the right of slave ownership from the masters, nor do they take slaves away from their masters. They do watch and prevent any rebellion from happening. Moreover, they admonish masters that they should be kind to their slaves and that slaves should be loyal and obedient....

According to divine law and natural law no single person is to be surrendered to slavery. That follows and is seen in every form of natural law; we all are born and we die. The mother of the king gives birth to the king with the same pain experienced by a poor and dying beggar. It follows that in this way every person is equal and no person is more honorable than another. Slavery was introduced by the law of the heathen. It comes first through the violence of war.... When a battle was won, those captured and spared from death were sold....

---

[4]Pellikan, *Commentaria Bibliorum*, 3:2X4r.
[5]CRR 8:125; citing Deut 15:12.

So the children of Israel insulted their freedom, because they were weak and enslaved and had given up their hopes, which is the worst sort of servitude. Thus they demanded a king. But freedom (that means freedom of the spirit that does not come from the favor of princes, through birth, or by being set free) comes from virtue, and freedom is the mother of all virtues. Freedom renews and animates all the true virtues. Of this Christ speaks in John 8: "The truth makes you free." Sermon on Jeremiah 34:10-11.[6]

You Were Once Slaves in Egypt. Heinrich Bullinger: So that the treacherous people might understand that they had seriously sinned against the Lord, Jeremiah right away introduces God himself applying his written law on this matter, especially Exodus 21. From this we learn, as if from an irrefutable example, to apply the laws of God in our sacred orations, in which we find fault with the sins of the people, seeing that it is from the laws alone that one may learn what is good and what is evil.

In the law a cited phrase is here examined: "at the end of seven years." Indeed, they say that an "end" is a boundary "from which," which is a beginning, and a boundary "to which," which is an end. They say that in the present verse one must understand the boundary "from which." Indeed there follows in clear words, "When he will have served you six years." Thus on the seventh year or at the beginning of the seventh year a slave used to be set free. We must particularly note this too: that not without reason does God mention the blessing of liberating the Jews from Egypt, from the house of slavery and bondage. Indeed, this fact ought to have forcefully stung their hearts. In fact, it is most shameful that a person who had been a slave and was then released by the kindness of the Lord as free should oppress with slavery another person of their own nation. It is much more shameful if free people are oppressed by those who were once slaves, but who have forgotten their own luck. The man in the Gospel is

gravely punished in Matthew 18, who tormented a fellow slave over a tiny debt when his own huge debt to his master had been freely forgiven. Thus we do not doubt that God in his time will subject such people to the gravest penalties and punishments. Sermon on Jeremiah 34:13-16.[7]

Should There Be Slaves Among Us? John Calvin: Though we do not read what the prophet relates here was done by God's command, yet we may easily gather that Zedekiah the king had been admonished to liberate the servants according to the law, as written in Exodus 21. It was God's will that there should be some difference between the people he had adopted and other nations. . . . It was therefore his will to establish this law among the people of Israel, that servitude should not be perpetual, except those who bound themselves willingly, of their own accord, through their whole life, according to what we read in Deuteronomy 15. . . . By these words of the prophet we learn that this command of the law had been disregarded, for at the end of the seventh year the servants were not made free. Hence, King Zedekiah, having been warned on the subject, called the people together, and by the consent of all, liberty was proclaimed according to what God had commanded. But this was done in bad faith, for soon after the servants were remanded, and thus treachery was added to cruelty. They had before unjustly oppressed their brethren, but now perjury was heaped on wickedness. We hence see that they not only wronged their own brethren, by imposing on them perpetual servitude, but they also wickedly profaned the sacred name of God, having thus violated a solemn oath. . . .

Here a question arises: is perpetual servitude so displeasing to God that it ought not to be deemed lawful? To this the answer is easy; Abraham and other fathers had servants or slaves according to the common and prevailing custom, and it was not deemed wrong in them. . . . Hence, it is without reason that any one infers that it is not lawful to exercise power over servants and maids; for on the contrary, we may reason thus: that since God

---

[6]Zwingli, *Predigten*, 268-72; citing 1 Cor 7:22; 1 Pet 2:18; 1 Sam 8:1-22; Jn 8:32.

[7]Bullinger, *Conciones*, 203r; citing Ex 21:1-10; Mt 18:21-35.

permitted the fathers to retain servants and maids, it is a lawful thing. . . . Since the Gentiles have been called to the hope of salvation, no change in this respect has been made. For the apostles did not constrain masters to liberate their servants, but only exhorted them to use kindness toward them, and to treat them humanely as their fellow servants. If, then, servitude were unlawful, the apostles never would have tolerated it. . . .

Among us servitude has been abolished, that is, that miserable condition when one had no right of their own, but when the master had power of life and death; that custom has ceased. . . . It is . . . by no means to be wished that there should be slaves among us, as there were formerly among all the nations, and as there are now among barbarians. The Spaniards know what servitude is, for they are near neighbors to the Africans and the Turks; and those they take in war they sell; and as one evil proceeds from another, so they retain miserable people as slaves throughout life. But as no necessity constrains us, our condition, as I have said, is better, that is, in having servants, and not slaves; for those called servants in this day are only hired servants. . . .

But there is no doubt that God at the same time made it known, that external enemies justly exercised cruelty toward the people, because they themselves showed no commiseration toward their own brethren. For when they ruled over their servants according to their own self-indulgence, they in vain complained of the Chaldeans or of the Assyrians; they in vain complained that the they were unjustly oppressed, or that the people of God were harassed by the violence of a tyrannical power; for they themselves were the initial source of cruelty, and not the Chaldeans or Assyrians. COMMENTARY ON JEREMIAH 34:8-17.[8]

MERCY TO SLAVES AND THE MERCY OF GOD.

JOHANNES OECOLAMPADIUS: "Astounding," he says, "is the insolence of the king, when for many years I have justly prophesied harsh things, just as

now I am wont to do, and there was yet no enemy present. Most of the cities were still intact under the king and everything was safe: at that time he did not throw me in prison. And now, in the midst of the real danger, he rouses the wrath of God against himself more and more. . . ."

And so now he urges masters to show fairness to their servants, and consider that they have a master in heaven, as in Colossians 3. He does this, moreover, through the precept of release or manumission, which the Lord gave in Exodus 21, that if anyone buys a Hebrew slave—male or female—they should release them on the seventh year. . . . In this matter, therefore, equality and humanity were recognized, because in the year of release the slaves were to be made free, so that after they experienced servitude they would enjoy freedom more moderately. But they despised this law completely, just like all the other ones. And finally Zedekiah was persuaded by the prophet that if he wanted to obtain the mercy of God, Zedekiah himself should be merciful also to his own slaves. This covenant of legally freeing slaves he stipulated to all the people. In turn, they promised as much as you like, but they didn't deliver anything except in appearance, and after that they became even more cruel, because they did everything through hypocrisy. Hence, because no mercy was found among them for their fellow slaves, they themselves were unworthy of the mercy of God. The year of release for us comes through Christ, because all our sins have been forgiven.

When indeed that Sabbath rest came to us, a true freedom for us from servitude to sin was proclaimed. But false prophets and teachers have followed, who meanwhile call us away from the freedom which is in Christ. COMMENTARY ON JEREMIAH 34:9.[9]

A COVENANT OF FORGIVENESS FOR SELF AND NEIGHBOR.

JOHANNES OECOLAMPADIUS: Before he pronounces a judgment, first he places their sin before their eyes, and upbraids it, showing that they did not transgress a human precept, but a

---

[8]CTS 20:281-84* (CO 39:85-88); citing Ex 21:2; Deut 15:16-17; Eph 6:9; Col. 4:1.

[9]Oecolampadius, *In Hieremiam*, 2:XIr; citing Col 3:22-24; Ex 21:1-11.

divine one, as is made more clear in the following chapter. For God commanded that freedom and mercy for this reason especially: because the Israelites themselves had been freed from servitude. So they were to be benevolent to their neighbor, as they had experienced the benevolence of God for themselves. Christ commanded us to forgive our neighbor their debts, as our debts were forgiven for us. Indeed since Christ freed us from a more severe servitude, he entered into such a covenant so that we might maintain mutual love. Therefore, it is absurd to disregard this covenant, which he established with us in baptism, or in repentance. COMMENTARY ON JEREMIAH 34:12.[10]

SERVANTS OF SIN OR TRUE FREEDOM? JO-HANNES OECOLAMPADIUS: Therefore, he narrates a punishment of mercilessness that is in every way just. The Hebrews did not want to set their servants free, so God wishes to send them—the free and the masters—into the filthiest servitude, where they will suffer things much more severe than what their slaves suffered, namely, to the sword, famine, disease, and the like. As servants under God they were freed from sin, but when they were made free from righteousness, they were again made slaves to sin and were handed over to death, as it says in Romans 6. If we neglect love to our neighbor, then the Lord also will show himself to be cruel toward us. COMMENTARY ON JEREMIAH 34:17.[11]

MAKING A PERMANENT COVENANT. NIKOLAUS SELNECKER: Here God speaks in a particular way.

If one wanted to establish a permanent covenant, then one is obligated to make a sacrifice with the Jews. One must divide the offering into two parts and they must make the covenant together by going between the parts as a sign that the covenant has been made permanent. Whoever would violate the covenant must be cut in two. Therefore, Abraham divided his offering down the middle and put one piece opposite the other, so that God could make a covenant with him—Genesis 15—and in the form of fire entered between the pieces to confirm the covenant. This shows without a doubt that this is a symbol and has meaning for the suffering and death of Christ, who is the righteous sacrifice for our sins; through Christ God the Father has made a permanent and eternal covenant that he is our Father and we should be his children. THE WHOLE PROPHET JEREMIAH 34:18-20.[12]

A WEAK KING, THE CAPRICE OF NATIONS, AND THE DECREE OF GOD. KONRAD PELLIKAN: The so-often-predicted captivity of the king was not able to correct the king himself, because he had no faith in the Word of God and he persevered in that contempt for the prophet to which the princes had driven him. Therefore, they all fell together into the hands of the enemy. Now granted, the Babylonians departed before the Egyptians, and the ungodly believed that they would not come back. Nevertheless, "by my command and order they will come back to destroy this city with fire and iron." COMMENTARY ON JEREMIAH 34:21-22.[13]

---

[10]Oecolampadius, *In Hieremiam*, 2:X2r; citing Mt 6:12.
[11]Oecolampadius, *In Hieremiam*, 2:X2v; citing Rom 6:20-23.

[12]Selnecker, *Der gantze Prophet Jeremias*, 2H2r.
[13]Pellikan, *Commentaria Bibliorum*, 3:2X4v.

JEREMIAH 35:1-19
THE OBEDIENCE OF THE RECHABITES

¹*The word that came to Jeremiah from the* LORD *in the days of Jehoiakim the son of Josiah, king of Judah:* ²*"Go to the house of the Rechabites and speak with them and bring them to the house of the* LORD*, into one of the chambers; then offer them wine to drink."* ³*So I took Jaazaniah the son of Jeremiah, son of Habazziniah and his brothers and all his sons and the whole house of the Rechabites.* ⁴*I brought them to the house of the* LORD *into the chamber of the sons of Hanan the son of Igdaliah, the man of God, which was near the chamber of the officials, above the chamber of Maaseiah the son of Shallum, keeper of the threshold.* ⁵*Then I set before the Rechabites pitchers full of wine, and cups, and I said to them, "Drink wine."* ⁶*But they answered, "We will drink no wine, for Jonadab the son of Rechab, our father, commanded us, 'You shall not drink wine, neither you nor your sons forever.* ⁷*You shall not build a house; you shall not sow seed; you shall not plant or have a vineyard; but you shall live in tents all your days, that you may live many days in the land where you sojourn.'* ⁸*We have obeyed the voice of Jonadab the son of Rechab, our father, in all that he commanded us, to drink no wine all our days, ourselves, our wives, our sons, or our daughters,* ⁹*and not to build houses to dwell in. We have no vineyard or field or seed,* ¹⁰*but we have lived in tents and have obeyed and done all that Jonadab our father commanded us.* ¹¹*But when Nebuchadnezzar king of Babylon came up against the land, we said, 'Come, and let us go to Jerusalem for fear of the army of the Chaldeans and the army of the Syrians.' So we are living in Jerusalem."*

¹²*Then the word of the* LORD *came to Jeremiah:* ¹³*"Thus says the* LORD *of hosts, the God of Israel: Go and say to the people of Judah and the inhabitants of Jerusalem, Will you not receive instruction and listen to my words? declares the* LORD*.* ¹⁴*The command that Jonadab the son of Rechab gave to his sons, to drink no wine, has been kept, and they drink none to this day, for they have obeyed their father's command. I have spoken to you persistently, but you have not listened to me.* ¹⁵*I have sent to you all my servants the prophets, sending them persistently, saying, 'Turn now every one of you from his evil way, and amend your deeds, and do not go after other gods to serve them, and then you shall dwell in the land that I gave to you and your fathers.' But you did not incline your ear or listen to me.* ¹⁶*The sons of Jonadab the son of Rechab have kept the command that their father gave them, but this people has not obeyed me.* ¹⁷*Therefore, thus says the* LORD*, the God of hosts, the God of Israel: Behold, I am bringing upon Judah and all the inhabitants of Jerusalem all the disaster that I have pronounced against them, because I have spoken to them and they have not listened, I have called to them and they have not answered."*

¹⁸*But to the house of the Rechabites Jeremiah said, "Thus says the* LORD *of hosts, the God of Israel: Because you have obeyed the command of Jonadab your father and kept all his precepts and done all that he commanded you,* ¹⁹*therefore thus says the* LORD *of hosts, the God of Israel: Jonadab the son of Rechab shall never lack a man to stand before me."*

OVERVIEW: In the midst of the Babylonian siege of Jerusalem a band of refugees, a people called the Rechabites, met with Jeremiah in the temple. Here God commends this people for their obedience and faithfulness to their ancestor and "father." Given their emphasis on the "priesthood of all believers" and their rejection of celibacy as a higher spiritual vocation, it is not surprising that Protestant commentators refused to identify the Rechabites as forerunners of Christian monasticism. Moreover, they were keen to describe carefully the purpose, impact, and limits of the Rechabite code. In short, this nomadic people spurred discussion on the very nature of true Christian community, honor, obedience, and holiness.

35:1-11 The Rechabites Commended

NAZIRITES AND RECHABITES AS MONKS.

ROMAN CONFUTATION OF THE AUGSBURG CONFESSION:[†] Since monastic vows have their foundation in the holy Scriptures of the Old and New Testaments, and most holy men, renowned and admirable by miracle, have lived in these religious orders with many thousand thousands, and for so many centuries their ordinances and rules of living have been received and approved throughout the entire Christian world by the Catholic Church, it is in no way to be tolerated that vows are licentiously broken without any fear of God. For, in the Old Testament, God approved the vows of the Nazirites and the vows of the Rechabites, who neither drank wine nor ate grapes; while he strictly requires that the vow once made be paid; "It is ruin to a man after vows to retract"; "The vows of the just are acceptable." God also teaches specifically through the prophet that monastic vows please him. For Isaiah 56 reads as follows: "Thus says the Lord to the eunuchs that keep my Sabbath, and choose the things that please me and take hold of my covenant, even unto them will I give in my house and within my walls a place and a name better than that of sons and of daughters. I will give them an everlasting name that shall not be cut off." But to what eunuchs does God make these promises? To those, undoubtedly, whom Christ praises, "which have made themselves eunuchs for the kingdom of heaven." CONFUTATIO PONTIFICIA.[1]

---

[1]*Confutatio Pontificia*, part 2, article 6, par. 1—On Monastic Vows, 377-78*; citing Num 6:1-21, Jer 35: 6, 19; Deut 23:21-23; Prov 20:25; Prov 15:8; Is 56:4-5; Mt 19:12. [†]The *Confutatio Pontificia*, or Roman Confutation, was published in response to the Lutherans' Augsburg Confession in 1530; this section refutes article 27 of the confession, which rejects monastic vows.

THE RECHABITES ARE NOT MONKS. PHILIPP

MELANCHTHON:[†] It is not right to compare monasticism, thought up without a Word of God as an act of worship to merit forgiveness of sins and justification, with the ritual of the Nazirites, which had a Word of God and was not meant to merit the forgiveness of sins but to be an outward exercise like the other ceremonies of the Old Testament. The same can be said about other vows described in the Old Testament.

They also cite the case of the Rechabites, who, as Jeremiah writes, neither had any possessions nor drank any wine. Yes indeed, the example of the Rechabites is a beautiful parallel to our monks, whose monasteries are fancier than kings' palaces and who live most sumptuously. Though they were poor in everything, the Rechabites were married; though our monks abound in every delight, they claim to be celibate.

Besides, examples ought to be interpreted according to this rule, that is, according to sure and clear passages of Scripture, not against the rule or the passages. It is a sure thing that our observances do not merit the forgiveness of sins or justification. When the Rechabites are praised, therefore, we must note that they did not observe their way of life out of the belief that they would merit forgiveness of sins by it, or that this work was itself an act of worship that justified, or because of it—not because of the promised Seed, through the mercy of God—they would attain eternal life. But because they had a command from their parents, they are praised for their obedience, which God commanded, "Honor your father and mother."

Then, too, the custom had an immediate purpose: since they were nomads rather than Israelites, their father apparently wanted to distinguish them by certain marks from their countrymen, lest they fall back into the wickedness of their countrymen. By these marks he wanted to remind them of the teaching of faith and immortality—surely a lawful purpose. But vastly different purposes are set forth for monasticism. They imagine that the works of monasticism are acts of worship and that they merit forgiveness of sins and justification. Thus the example of the Rechabites does not resemble monasticism. We shall not even discuss the other evils inherent in present-day monasticism. APOLOGY OF THE AUGSBURG CONFESSION.[2]

THE COMMANDS OF GOD FOR RECHABITES AND MONKS. JOHANNES BUGENHAGEN: God now confounds the disobedient and unbelieving Jews with this argument and example, saying, "Some have been discovered, namely, the Rechabites, who with their wives and children have preserved the stern law of their human father, solely on account of the mandate of the father. But my people, while summoned with such great prophecies, promises, mandates, threats, benefits, and honors of God, do not obey their spiritual Father, the God of heaven and earth. Neither do they repent after they have received blows; nor are they moved by the example of the ten tribes who were taken off to Assyria. For that reason I will preserve for myself the Rechabites and their posterity, as they are pious and lest they perish by the sword, even if they are currently besieged in Jerusalem with the others." In the same way safety is promised to the Ethiopian below in chapter 39, because he trusted the God of Israel, and safety is promised to Baruch, the scribe or notary of Jeremiah, in chapter 45. Notice here that this promise made to the Rechabites concerning the preservation of their descendants has an added condition of the law; because of the clause, "because you obey the precept of Jonadab etc.," this promise does not apply to those who after them know neither God nor Jonadab; just as it was promised to Solomon, only if his sons preserved the law, and other such promises.

It is certain that these Rechabites were pious, that is, faithful and believers in God, otherwise God would not have commended them only because of the commandment from the second table: "Honor your father and your mother that you may live long in the land." For it is right that the first table should come first and that God

should be put before people. So they were obedient to their human father without a doubt because of God and the command of God toward their father on account of the Word of God and honoring God. For that reason such observance of the law does not establish salvation, make satisfaction for sins, or achieve merit, or a single crown in heaven, which would be impious and against the first table of the law, as the "justifiers" among us do without the mandate of God—not that the Rechabites were outside the mandate of God, which commands obedience to parents. Granted, this paternal mandate was more difficult than the law requires, and therefore they could have been released from the paternal mandate. Nevertheless, they endured by their free will in that precept of the father and because of reverence for their father, in which there is meanwhile nothing against faith and nothing against the precepts of God. . . .

Such examples our "justifying" monks grab for themselves, when they do not have the mandate and Word of God that is solely required. We neither have anything without the vocation of God, nor do we, as they do, falsely call that life "spiritual" and teach it, the life that is without the Holy Spirit and is against the second commandment. Indeed, whatever is not of faith is sin, Romans 14.

So our monks on the basis of this passage in Jeremiah want freely to be Rechabites. . . . In the Rechabites there is nothing miraculous, as it seems to the monks. But only human practices appear. When the monks say here that their observances are commended by God, they are not only impious but also ridiculous. They strain to build their own presumed religion on this example of the Rechabites, without the Word of God. They are able to be Rechabites neither according to the body nor according the spirit. Relating to the body, the Rechabites did not drink wine; the monks drink wine. The Rechabites lived in tents and ordinary habitations; monks build royal palaces for themselves. The Rechabites had wives and children; the monks are celibate, even if they see something other than what they are. The Rechabites lived and sought an honest living for themselves from the work of their hands

---

[2]BoC 279-80; citing Ex 20:12. †Melanchthon writes in response to the Roman Confutation, part 2, article 6 immediately above.

along with their wives and household servants. Monks are partly mendicant and wholly mendacious as they live off the livelihood of others, etc. Pertaining to the spirit, truly the Rechabites have for themselves a mandate of God: "honor your father and mother"; monks do their own thing without the Word of God. Rechabites seek their living according to the command of God; For their living, monks fill the world with lies and false religion and therefore are excommunicated as idle and superstitious people who yet do not want to repent: 2 Thessalonians 3. COMMENTARY ON JEREMIAH 35.[3]

THE RECHABITES TEACH FAITHFULNESS AND OBEDIENCE. NIKOLAUS SELNECKER: Here God allows his people to be reprimanded by an example of human obedience—how the Rechabites followed their father in particular ways. Throughout their lives they drank no wine, as their father Jonadab had ordered. Jeremiah criticizes the people of Jerusalem because they do not follow the Word of God, as godly children ought to follow their Father.

The Rechabites are not Israelites, but are from a neighboring heathen people. It is likely though that they come from Jethro, the father-in-law of Moses; for Jonadab, which they called their father, originated from the line of Hobab or Jethro. Jonadab had lived in the time of King Jehu, one of the kings of Israel. . . . Jonadab had founded this order, named it the Rechabites, and had ordered that four rules be followed. First, they should drink no wine; second, till no piece of land or field; third plant no vineyard; and fourth, build no houses in order to live within. They should be a migratory people and pilgrims throughout their lives and live in huts, so that they remember their short and transitory lives. As the patriarch Jacob says in Genesis 47, "The time of my pilgrimage and life has been short and evil." So they would be better prepared, when a threat or misfortune came, since they could set off for other places. So they were dispersed and fearing the enemy had come to live in Jerusalem. Such a rule

they had observed for 278 years. They were praised not because they had a gracious God or forgiveness of sins (they had not observed such a rule because they wanted to be holy, righteous, or blessed), but because they had obeyed the command and order of their father and led a substantial, simple, and humble life; they were always prepared to move again as urgency required. This also showed that one would rather observe—and observe more rigorously—a human command and regulation—than God's command and word.

The chapter is held together by three points. First, it demonstrates our typically bad behavior and disobedience against God. Similar to today people pay more attention to human regulations than they do to God's commands. Thus God compares the Jews with the Rechabites. He reprimands them because the Rechabites observed the order and statutes of their ancestors and elders. But the Jews would not follow the Word of God, though he had always preached to them through his prophets. . . . Second, this chapter tells us why the Rechabites were praised, namely, that they were obedient to their father. Thus God does not look primarily at the vow—if it is legal or illegal—but he looks at the obedience of the children to their parents and ancestors and praises that. . . . Third, if this example can be used as a confirmation for vows in the cloister, as when monks and priests use this example for their fasts and vows.[†]

. . . It is certain that the Rechabites did not lead their peculiar lives so that they might earn forgiveness of sins, or at least that they might do a special worship service to benefit other people whose lives do not measure up and so that God might take notice when he is especially honored and they might be in his special graces and approval. Or that their lives would be perfect or it was urgent that they account for a mortal sin. . . . Rather, their vows are vows only for a set time and do not extend further than their ancestors, lineage, and people. THE WHOLE PROPHET JEREMIAH 35.[4]

---

[3]Bugenhagen, *In Ieremiam*, 5H3r-5I1v; citing Jer 39:15-18; 1 Kings 2:1-4; Ex 20:12; Deut 5:16; Ex 20:1-12; Rom 14:23; 2 Thess 3:6-15.

[4]Selnecker, *Der gantze Prophet* Jeremias, 2Hh2v-2I1r; citing Gen 47:9.
[†]In contrast, Cornelius À Lapide devotes much of his commentary

THE TEMPLE STAFF. GIOVANNI DIODATI: These people certainly seem to be some family of priests, or other sacred officers, whose turn it was to wait upon the service in the temple that week, according to the custom. See 2 Kings 11:5. "Man of God"—namely a prophet, or the same man, as is spoken of in 1 Chronicles 16:7. "Princes," namely, the two chief priests under the high priest; or the chief of those who were in service that week. "Keeper," that is to say, one of the porters—1 Chronicles 16:1; because porters of the temple had also to take care of the holy vessels. ANNOTATIONS ON JEREMIAH 35:4.[5]

THEY HONOR THEIR FATHER. JOHN MAYER: The prophets called the Rechabites together in the Lord's house in a chamber to offer them wine. In that chamber was a man who is said to be a man of God. This was most likely done publicly so that the city might be moved to repentance. Jeremiah seeks to make the Jews ashamed because the Rechabites obeyed their father, a mortal man, but the Jews would not obey God. The Rechabites obeyed their father in a thing harsh and unpleasant to the body; the Jews only required things of themselves that could be easily done and for a worldly good, not a spiritual one. COMMENTARY ON JEREMIAH 35:5-10.[6]

WINE FOR RECHABITES AND MONKS. KONRAD PELLIKAN: These human traditions were not against the law; they were not impossible, and they were not useless for human life, but convenient, diminishing many burdensome concerns. In their discipline they did certain things, not setting themselves out as amassing merit for themselves and sharing it with others. This was not hypocrisy, but philosophical frugality. They did not do this so that they might beg from others or be a burden or trouble for their neighbors, but neither were they for that reason idle.

We read here that this was not done as a vow to the Lord, but rather if there were some urgent necessity of nature or charity, they could drink wine without offense to God and without it being a sin. Thus, contrary to their other practice of not living in cities, where people are rarely shrewd and good, as it is in the Eclogue of Mantuanus,[†] now nevertheless the Rechabites had entered the city because of the war. But in this case they persisted in their resolution about wine, since there was no need for them to drink. And there are many people whose nature is such that they cannot drink wine, a limitation we find among few enough monks. But rather it happens that those who naturally abstained from wine since childhood learned to drink wine when they were made monks, lest it seem that this passage endorses them. Nor does an order of monks appear tolerable to them when the wine is missing. COMMENTARY ON JEREMIAH 35:6-10.[7]

THE GODLY RECHABITES. GIOVANNI DIODATI: "Jonadab": some think it the same man mentioned in 2 Kings 10:15 and so the ward "father" was to be taken for one that was born before him. Others think that it was their father indeed and that order was but newly made. "Drink no wine": this was not enjoined to establish any new or arbitrary service, or any rule of greater perfection of life, but only in imitation of the Nazirites. Thus he established his posterity in a discipline of life, free from delights and enticements of the flesh and more conformable to the pastoral life of the Midianites, who were their ancestors and more befitting those who professed to study and meditate on holy things. Now their obedience to this human command did aggravate the Jews' rebellion against the law of God. ANNOTATIONS ON JEREMIAH 35:6.[8]

ABSTAINING FROM WINE IS AN EXTERNAL FORBEARANCE. JOHN TRAPP: This they were resolved on, not because they were persuaded, as

---

on this chapter to praise of the monastic life by extensive quotation of patristic and medieval authors and examples, including Basil of Caesarea, Bernard of Clairvaux, and Francis of Assisi. See *Commentaria in Jeremiam*, 205-8.

[5]Diodati, *Pious Annotations*, 77*.
[6]Mayer, *A Commentary*, 443*.

[7]Pellikan, *Commentaria Bibliorum*, 3:2X5r. †A reference to the sixth Ecloga of the Carmelite poet Baptista Mantuanus (1448–1516); see *The Eclogues of Baptista Mantuanus* 6.90-96.
[8]Diodati, *Pious Annotations*, 77*; citing Num 6:3; 1 Cor 2:15.

Muhammad's followers are, that in every grape there dwelt a devil, but because Jonadab, the son of Rechab their progenitor had, two or three hundred years before, charged them to forebear, and not thereby to establish a new arbitrary service or any rule of greater perfection in life (as the papists misallege it in favor of monasticism and other will-worships and superstitious observances), but only as a civil ordinance, about things external, the foundation whereof is laid in the word, which commends modesty, humility, heavenly mindedness, etc. COMMENTARY ON JEREMIAH 35:6.[9]

THE CHURCH MAY PRESCRIBE FEASTS. LANCELOT ANDREWES: The synagogue of the Jews, we see, had power to prescribe fasts and did; has the church of Christ no such power? Is she in worse case than the synagogue? No indeed. If Rechab might enjoin his son, she may [enjoin] hers. She is our mother, she has the power of a mother over us, and a mother has power to give laws to her children. And so "when you fast" is, when you fast by the church's appointment also, the church's "when." This [is] sure; "No one has God for their father who does not have the church for their mother"; and that once and twice in the Proverbs ordered so as to "keep the precepts of our Father, so not to treat lightly the laws of our mother." The anger of the Father and the sorrow of the mother are together in one verse; "he that grieves her angers him." And he cannot but grieve her that little sets by her wholesome orders. SERMON ON MATTHEW 6:16.[10]

FREE SOULS, THE RECHABITES, AND THE APOSTLES. JOHANNES OECOLAMPADIUS: So this Jonadab, their father, gave four commands to his posterity. First, they should not drink wine. Second, they should not cultivate fields. Third, they should not plant vineyards. Fourth, they should not build houses to inhabit them. Those who are accustomed to the pastoral life observe such things. In fact,

Jonadab thought that this type of life would be happier, and to this he was accustomed; he did not consider it at all worthless. Indeed, drunkenness spawns many evils, from which those who do not drink wine do very well to protect themselves, if only this abstinence does not fight with their nature; for otherwise the prohibition of wine or flesh might become demonic. Similarly those who are not dedicated to the cultivations of vines and fields, and who do not have their own homes, have freer minds. But they are pilgrims on the earth, so that if ever hunger strikes, or some other adversity, they are able to depart from one region and go to another. For that reason, the Lord ordered the apostles to give up everything, so that they would be more unfettered for the preaching of the word. COMMENTARY ON JEREMIAH 35:6-7.[11]

35:12-19 Judah Will Not Listen

FATHER OF ISRAEL AND FATHER OF THE RECHABITES. JOHANNES OECOLAMPADIUS: There is a transparent delight here. In fact, the Jews are convicted here, because they are less obedient to their heavenly Father than the Rechabites are to their father in the flesh. And he only says, like Malachi, "If I am your father, where is my honor?" This is an unnatural perseverance, in that you refuse to hear the word of your God: "Am I in no way better to you than Jonadab is to the Rechabites? Truly I do not prohibit the drinking of wine, but I only demand that which is far easier, that you give up foreign gods, who are not able to help you. I do not drive you into tents, but I permit the free inhabitation of the land. Jonadab commanded this a single time, while every day I am warning and exhorting you through the prophets. He promised little things, which he was not able to give; I promise the greatest things through these commands, which I also provide to you most generously. And I don't even get you to incline your ears to me, since you both destroy the prophets and mock them." This is a more tolerable refutation than the other one in

---

[9]Trapp, *A Commentary or Exposition*, 324*; citing 2 Kings 10:15.
[10]Andrewes, *Works*, 1:391-92*; citing Prov 1:8, 17, 25; Cyprian, *De unitate ecclesiae* (CCSL 3:5-7).

[11]Oecolampadius, *In Hieremiam*, 2:X4r-v.

which God refuted them—the argument taken from the nations that do not change their own gods and from the beasts that know their time. In fact, Israel is ignoring its time of visitation. COMMENTARY ON JEREMIAH 35:12-16.[12]

HONORING PARENTS AND NOT THE PAPIST CHURCH.

JOHN CALVIN: Here the prophet, that he might move the Jews more deeply, promises a reward to the sons of Jonadab, because they obeyed their father; and he promises them a blessing from God. Nor is it to be wondered at. . . . God promises generally a reward to all who keep the law, for every command has in general connected with it the hope of reward; but this is in a special manner added to the fifth commandment; "Honor your father and mother, that you may prolong your life," etc. It is, then, nothing strange that God promised a reward to the Rechabites. . . .

But what the papists allege, that the obedience rendered to the church is on the same account pleasing to God, may . . . be easily confuted; for if the Rechabites had followed the command of their father in a thing unlawful, they would have been worthy of punishment; but as this precept . . . was not inconsistent with God's law, God approved of their obedience. But the laws that are made for the purpose of setting up fictitious modes of worship are altogether impious, for they introduce idolatry. God has prescribed how he would have us to worship him; whatever, therefore, people bring in of themselves is wholly impious, for it adulterates the pure worship of God; and further, when necessity is laid on consciences, it is . . . a tyrannical bondage. Such was not the object of Jonadab; for what he commanded his posterity was useful, and referred only to the things of this life; and it did not bind their consciences; for when it was necessary they moved to Jerusalem and dwelt as others do in houses. COMMENTARY ON JEREMIAH 18:19.[13]

REWARDED FOR HONORING THEIR PARENTS.

KONRAD PELLIKAN: Because of their obedience and in order to chastise the Jews, the Rechabites were promised long lives and the duration of their descendants, because they honored their parents with obedience, while the Jews were promised expulsion, because they stubbornly and perpetually abandoned their faith and the religion of their elders. COMMENTARY ON JEREMIAH 35:18-19.[14]

---

[12]Oecolampadius, *In Hieremiam*, 2:Y1r; citing Mal 1:6; Jer 2:11; 8:7.

[13]CTS 20:323* (CO 39:114); citing Ex 20:12.
[14]Pellikan, *Commentaria Bibliorum*, 3:2X5v.

JEREMIAH 36:1-32
JEHOIAKIM BURNS JEREMIAH'S SCROLL

[1]*In the fourth year of Jehoiakim the son of Josiah, king of Judah, this word came to Jeremiah from the* LORD: [2]*"Take a scroll and write on it all the words that I have spoken to you against Israel and Judah and all the nations, from the day I spoke to you, from the days of Josiah until today.* [3]*It may be that the house of Judah will hear all the disaster that I intend to do to them, so that every one may turn from his evil way, and that I may forgive their iniquity and their sin."*

[4]*Then Jeremiah called Baruch the son of Neriah, and Baruch wrote on a scroll at the dictation of Jeremiah all the words of the* LORD *that he had spoken to him.* [5]*And Jeremiah ordered Baruch, saying, "I am banned from going to the house of the* LORD, [6]*so you are to go, and on a day of fasting in the hearing of all the people in the* LORD's *house you shall read the words of the* LORD *from the scroll that you have written at my dictation. You shall read them also in the hearing of all the men of Judah who come out of their cities.* [7]*It may be that their plea for mercy will come before the* LORD, *and that every one will turn from his evil way, for great is the anger and wrath that the* LORD *has pronounced against this people."* [8]*And Baruch the son of Neriah did all that Jeremiah the prophet ordered him about reading from the scroll the words of the* LORD *in the* LORD's *house.*

[9]*In the fifth year of Jehoiakim the son of Josiah, king of Judah, in the ninth month, all the people in Jerusalem and all the people who came from the cities of Judah to Jerusalem proclaimed a fast before the* LORD. [10]*Then, in the hearing of all the people, Baruch read the words of Jeremiah from the scroll, in the house of the* LORD, *in the chamber of Gemariah the son of Shaphan the secretary, which was in the upper court, at the entry of the New Gate of the* LORD's *house.*

[11]*When Micaiah the son of Gemariah, son of Shaphan, heard all the words of the* LORD *from the scroll,* [12]*he went down to the king's house, into the secretary's chamber, and all the officials were sitting* there: *Elishama the secretary, Delaiah the son of Shemaiah, Elnathan the son of Achbor, Gemariah the son of Shaphan, Zedekiah the son of Hananiah, and all the officials.* [13]*And Micaiah told them all the words that he had heard, when Baruch read the scroll in the hearing of the people.* [14]*Then all the officials sent Jehudi the son of Nethaniah, son of Shelemiah, son of Cushi, to say to Baruch, "Take in your hand the scroll that you read in the hearing of the people, and come." So Baruch the son of Neriah took the scroll in his hand and came to them.* [15]*And they said to him, "Sit down and read it." So Baruch read it to them.* [16]*When they heard all the words, they turned one to another in fear. And they said to Baruch, "We must report all these words to the king."* [17]*Then they asked Baruch, "Tell us, please, how did you write all these words? Was it at his dictation?"* [18]*Baruch answered them, "He dictated all these words to me, while I wrote them with ink on the scroll."* [19]*Then the officials said to Baruch, "Go and hide, you and Jeremiah, and let no one know where you are."*

[20]*So they went into the court to the king, having put the scroll in the chamber of Elishama the secretary, and they reported all the words to the king.* [21]*Then the king sent Jehudi to get the scroll, and he took it from the chamber of Elishama the secretary. And Jehudi read it to the king and all the officials who stood beside the king.* [22]*It was the ninth month, and the king was sitting in the winter house, and there was a fire burning in the fire pot before him.* [23]*As Jehudi read three or four columns, the king would cut them off with a knife and throw them into the fire in the fire pot, until the entire scroll was consumed in the fire that was in the fire pot.* [24]*Yet neither the king nor any of his servants who heard all these words was afraid, nor did they tear their garments.* [25]*Even when Elnathan and Delaiah and Gemariah urged the king not to burn the scroll, he would not listen to them.* [26]*And the king commanded Jerahmeel the king's son and Seraiah the son of Azriel and Shelemiah the son*

of Abdeel to seize Baruch the secretary and Jeremiah the prophet, but the Lord hid them.

²⁷Now after the king had burned the scroll with the words that Baruch wrote at Jeremiah's dictation, the word of the LORD came to Jeremiah: ²⁸"Take another scroll and write on it all the former words that were in the first scroll, which Jehoiakim the king of Judah has burned. ²⁹And concerning Jehoiakim king of Judah you shall say, 'Thus says the LORD, You have burned this scroll, saying, "Why have you written in it that the king of Babylon will certainly come and destroy this land, and will cut off from it man and beast?" ³⁰Therefore thus says the LORD

concerning Jehoiakim king of Judah: He shall have none to sit on the throne of David, and his dead body shall be cast out to the heat by day and the frost by night. ³¹And I will punish him and his offspring and his servants for their iniquity. I will bring upon them and upon the inhabitants of Jerusalem and upon the people of Judah all the disaster that I have pronounced against them, but they would not hear.'"

³²Then Jeremiah took another scroll and gave it to Baruch the scribe, the son of Neriah, who wrote on it at the dictation of Jeremiah all the words of the scroll that Jehoiakim king of Judah had burned in the fire. And many similar words were added to them.

OVERVIEW: Scripture, preaching, and the printed word were essential to the Reformation. Commentators recognized the difficulties Jeremiah faced and took him as their model of courage and perseverance. In the sixteenth and seventeenth centuries, parishioners and sovereigns could prove unresponsive to biblical preaching. Resistance to the teaching of Scripture was a perennial issue. More dramatically, many books would be outlawed and burned while their authors were thereby put in grave danger. Issues of divine communication, human proclamation, and controversy over media tie the biblical age to the Reformation era.

36:1-19 The Scroll Is Read

THE MADNESS OF THE KING. JOHANNES OECOLAMPADIUS: This prophecy, which was revealed earlier, is able to be added to the above prophecy, which was revealed later, in this way: The Holy Spirit made known that the Jews had been less obedient to their Father in heaven than the Rechabites to their carnal father. For he showed how much of this kind of disobedience there had been, because the king was so insane that in his rage he tore to pieces and burned the prophecies that God had ordered to be written, and he was persecuting the prophets. This sin was punished so severely in the case of impious Jehoiakim that it ought to have

admonished others to be obedient to the Word of God. COMMENTARY ON JEREMIAH 36:1.[1]

BURNED BOOKS AND THE LIVING GOSPEL.
JOHANNES BUGENHAGEN: The whole court, as it happens, was impious along with the king. Nevertheless, God still had his own people who contradicted the king and did not consent to impiety. The book of Jeremiah was burned as heretical and treasonous writing that dishonored God. The king's people were seeking the death of Jeremiah and Baruch, his notary or scribe. But you say, why did the Lord want to send a book to the impious? I respond in this way: so they would not have an excuse and they themselves would admit of themselves how justly they perished thereafter. In the same way Christ came to the Jews and also the gospel comes to us today, so that the thoughts of many hearts might be revealed. Nevertheless he has his own elect, whom he cares for with his word in salvation.

But see the providence of God in the words of the ministers against the impious, who want the Word of God and the prophets to be extinguished. God protects and hides the prophets under his wings so that they are not found when they are sought for murder and so that the word does not perish when the books are burned. Moreover, after

---

[1]Oecolampadius, *In Hieremiam*, 2:Y1v-Y2r; citing Jer 35:1-19.

those books that were burned there will be more sermons written than before with God willing it to be so. COMMENTARY ON JEREMIAH 36.[2]

WHY WE NEED SCRIPTURE. NIKOLAUS SELNECKER: God wills that the prophet Jeremiah should compose a book of his sermons and write them down for three reasons. First, that we and all Christians to the end of the world shall learn God's Word and will do so from the Scriptures or the books of the prophets and apostles. As Paul says, "You are built on the foundation of the prophets and apostles; and Jesus Christ is the cornerstone." Thus the Son of God himself says, "Seek in the Scripture, because it testifies concerning me." And Psalm 40: "The book is written of me." Yet he also speaks as if there is no book; or as Solomon says, "There would be no end to the writing of books." But he shows here that the Holy Bible is the only true book, the source and point of origin. Apart from this book there are others that are not competent and have nothing about divine matters to offer. . . .

The second reason is that God seeks a means and way to prompt his people and to bring them to mend their ways so that they want to return to God and escape punishment. Therefore, in a certain book everything can be heard and read in one place; there people find all God wants to do in relation to them, when they do not improve. So it is for us as Christians today. Many books are written that warn us to amend ourselves, and these are simply a faithful warning, and there are sermons about repentance. These are useful for us, if we want to recognize such things and we are not completely blind. The third reason is that the people will have no excuse whenever disasters happen. They could not say that they did not have enough warning since they were instructed with sermons and books. THE WHOLE PROPHET JEREMIAH 36:1-3.[3]

BARUCH AND JEREMIAH'S BOOK. JOHANNES OECOLAMPADIUS: Some people think that the book which was taken by Baruch is Lamentations, which the Holy Spirit sang through the prophet before the destruction of Jerusalem. In contrast to this view, he was ordered to draw up all the prophecies from the days of Josiah onward. Baruch, that notary and deacon of Jeremiah, was at the same time a prophet.

Nevertheless, the book that is said to be Baruch's is counted among the Apocrypha and is not present in the Hebrew canon. But see the skillful spirit, which works through those people, through whom it wishes. To this end, Baruch is sent in the place of Jeremiah, so that by his own absence he can cry out all the more through his book and so that the people might be moved. Jeremiah says, however, "I am hindered"; not indeed by prison, because he escapes afterward, which he had not been able to do to this point. Nor do we yet find him in custody. But he was without a doubt impeded from going to the king by the Spirit of God. COMMENTARY ON JEREMIAH 36:4-6.[4]

THE WRITTEN WORD AND FASTING. JOHN CALVIN: Here the prophet declares that he dictated to Baruch, a servant of God, whatever he had previously taught. But there is no doubt but that God suggested to the prophet at the time what might have been erased from his memory; for all the things that we have some time ago said do not always occur to us. Therefore the greater part of so many words must have escaped the prophet, had not God dictated them to him. . . .

"Go you," then, he says, "and read in the volume." The prophet in this case was ready to incur any hate that might be, for he did not bid Baruch to relate from memory what he had heard from him, but ordered him to take the volume, and to read, as we shall hereafter see, "what he had written . . . read . . . to the people" in the temple, on a "fasting day." This day was chosen, first, because there was then a greater concourse of people . . . for he was to read

---

[2]Bugenhagen, *In Ieremiam*, 5K1r.
[3]Selnecker, *Der gantze Prophet Jeremias*, 2J2v-2J3r; citing Eph 2:20; Jn 5:39; Ps 40:7; Eccles 12:12.

[4]Oecolampadius, *In Hieremiam*, 2:Y2v.

these things in the ears not only of the citizens, but also of the whole people; and on fast days they were likely, as it is well-known, to come in great numbers to the city for the purpose of sacrificing. It was then God's purpose that these threats should be proclaimed, not only to the inhabitants of Jerusalem, but also to all other Jews, that their report might spread to every part of the land. In the second place, such a day was much more suitable to the message conveyed; for why was a fast enjoined, except humbly to seek God's mercy, and to abhor his wrath? As then this was the design of a fast, the Jews ought to have been then, as it were, in a submissive state of mind, prepared calmly to receive these threats, and to profit from them. COMMENTARY ON JEREMIAH 36:5-6.[5]

SHOULD SERMONS BE READ FROM A BOOK?

JOHN MAYER: Because Baruch wrote and then went and read in a public place in order to convert others, one might ask if a preacher is justified in reading another person's sermon? And if reading Scripture alone would suffice for conversion? And last, if one does not read a sermon, is one justified in delivering a sermon from memory? I answer that in the case of a sufficient preacher it is better to hear a sermon read than to hear none at all. Or to hear one read if one is too ignorant or incapable of preaching oneself. Reading the Word with God's blessing may lead to conversion. But to read and preach upon the Word is far more likely to lead to this. The same may be said regarding the reading of one's own sermon. Therefore, every preacher should be stirred up so that they can preach from memory, as Christ and the apostles did—and not from a book. The latter is more apt to move people to contempt and insult than to reverence, just as arguing is a great defect in a preacher and makes them insufficient for their office. COMMENTARY ON JEREMIAH 36:8.[6]

FEARING GOD AND FEARING POWERFUL

PEOPLE. JOHN MAYER: The part of the temple in which Baruch read was "the Chamber of Gemariah the scribe, in the upper court, in the entrance of the new gate." On the new gate, see chapter 26 of Jeremiah. On the chambers of the Lord's house, see chapter 35. Here in the door, as the word signifies, Baruch stood and read to the people who were in the court to hear Baruch. The princes were told of this and sent for Baruch so that he could read the same book to them. When they heard it, they were afraid; they said they would tell the king. Thus wicked men are sometimes afraid when they hear God's judgments, but their fear does not lead to repentance. Rather, it plunges them into yet more sin when they seek to stir up persecution for God's faithful servants. The fear of human beings works more in them than the fear of God. They thought that if these things should come to the king's ear, and they were not the first to tell him, they might come into danger as the king would be displeased. Therefore, although they believed that these threats came from God and made them fear and tremble, yet the fear of the king was greater; so the threats did not move them to work out repentance in their hearts. Thus the one who would fear God and his wrath, so as to escape it, must not fear human beings, as is expressed in Matthew 10. For these two fears cannot stand together. For example, Felix also trembled in hearing Paul, but he . . . soon shook off this fear, and kept Paul in prison to please the Jews. The princes were still sufficiently moved that they desired that both Baruch and Jeremiah be kept out of danger from the king. Therefore, they told Baruch to go hide himself and to bid Jeremiah to do the same. They knew that the king was a tyrant and upon hearing of these prophecies he would seek to slay them; for he had done so before to Uriah. So other wicked people sometimes have good affections, but they are too weak to work unto true repentance and to salvation; they shall perish anyway.

As the princes had warned Baruch, so they went and told the king. When he heard of the scroll that had been read, he cut it up with a penknife and cast it into the fire; some yet begged him not to do so. And he ordered Jeremiah and Baruch to be

---

[5]CTS 20:329-30* (CO 39:118-19).
[6]Mayer, A Commentary, 444-45*.

taken, but "the Lord hid them." That is, by God's providence, they hid themselves, so that their persecutors could not find them; just as sometimes happened when Elijah was hid from Ahab. It is also intimated here that the Lord directed them to hide, giving warrant hereby to other faithful servants to flee likewise and to hide in this time of persecution. Thereby they might be preserved and then still live to glorify God in the course of their ministry. COMMENTARY ON JEREMIAH 36:9-26.[7]

A SMUG DEMEANOR AND CONDITIONAL PROMISES. MARTIN LUTHER: Give heed to the great wrath of God, that he destroyed such a people, such holiness, and such a place of worship, lest we walk so smugly. It is like the king about whom we read in Jeremiah. The king despised the threats of the prophet who said that Jerusalem would be destroyed. He tore the book in half and said, "How can you say this in view of the great promises we have?" But they did not see that the promises were conditional where he says, "If you will continue in my Word." So Jesus says, "I am with you always, to the close of the age." He says, "with you," if you are Christians. For even Jerusalem, established on the highest promises, was rooted out; and the same thing will happen to us. God did not give his Word for us to lead wanton lives under it, but for us to lead a better life. LECTURE ON ISAIAH 64:12.[8]

36:20-32 The Scroll Is Burned

PREACHING TO THOSE WHO CANNOT HEAR. JOHN CALVIN: The prophet now relates that the princes went to the king, after having first deposited the scroll with Elishama the scribe; for as the king's ears were tender, they were unwilling to perform at once such an awful duty. And thus they who are with kings, and engage their attention, fascinate them with their flatteries; for there is in [royal] courts no independence, for the greatest

flatterer is the highest in favor. As then all courtiers seek eagerly to find out how they may please kings, so they carefully beware lest they should offend them.... We hence learn that their regard for God was small and frigid; for if they believed that Jeremiah had dictated to his scribe what he had received from the Spirit of God, the offending of the king ought not certainly to have been deemed of such importance....

In the person of Jehoiakim we see how the unbelieving shun and seek God at the same time, but with a confused mind as they know not what they seek. The king might have heedlessly despised what had been related to him; for if he wished to be free from all trouble, why did he order the roll brought to him and a part of it to be read? We hence see that the unbelieving, though they wish to go as far as possible from God, yet run to him in a sort of blind manner; but this they do not of their own accord; for God by his secret impulse draws them to himself, so as to render them more inexcusable. Hence it comes that curiosity leads many to hear the truth and some madly to ask, what is the truth to them? They are like wild beasts when they run against swords....

[Jehoiakim] cut it with a penknife, and cast it into the fire...." Here Jeremiah shows how little he had effected; for the king not only cast aside but also tore the scroll to pieces; and having torn it, he wished its memory to perish, for he cast it into the fire. This trial must have grievously affected the mind of the prophet; he had dictated that roll by God's command; he saw now that all his labor had been in vain. He might have complained to God that so much labor had been spent without fruit. For why had God bidden the scroll to be written, except for the purpose of leading the king and his counselors to repentance.... But God thus exercises his servants when he bids them to speak to the deaf or to bring light to the blind.... Let us then learn simply to obey God, though the labor he requires from us may seem useless. COMMENTARY ON JEREMIAH 36:20-23.[9]

---

[7]Mayer, *A Commentary*, 445*; citing Jer 26:10; 35:4; Mt 10:28; Acts 23:23–24:27; Jer 26:20-23.
[8]LW 17:374 (WA 31.2:551); citing Mt 28:20.

[9]CTS 20:343-45* (CO 39:127-29); citing Jn 18:38.

SELF-WILLED REASON AND RECEPTION OF TRUTH. MARTIN LUTHER: Here, then, are the three ways in which truth may be revealed: in writing, in words, and in thoughts; writing by means of books, words by means of the mouth, and thoughts by means of the heart. By no other means can one receive the teaching than through the heart, mouth, and writing.

Now all of this is of no avail in dealing with self-willed reason. It does not listen to words, nor to what is written, nor to illumination. God may try this or that with it: it suppresses and burns writing and books as did King Jehoiakim with the writings of Jeremiah. . . . [Reason] prohibits, silences, and condemns spoken words; it chases away and kills illumination together with the prophets. Oddly, no prophet was killed or chased away, or persecuted because he was chastising coarse sins, with the one exception of John the Baptist, whom Herodias put to death because he had castigated her adultery. THE GOSPEL FOR ST. STEPHEN'S DAY.[10]

GOD'S UNCONVENTIONAL PLAN. HULDRYCH ZWINGLI: See how amazing God is in his deeds! He allows the king to rage and burn the book. He allows Jeremiah to suffer a setback, as someone captured, persecuted, and oppressed him. But God did not allow everything to be destroyed. Another book would be written and the truth would come to the light of day—sharper, clearer, brighter, and more bountiful than before. . . .

Why did God not want the earlier book to survive? God willed that the prophet's work would be in his preaching, now before the king, then before the princes; another time before the Jewish people; then later before the heathen, the Babylonians and Egyptians, etc. Jeremiah would preach now with one goal, then with another, now in the court of the king, then in the outer courts of the temple, then in the temple itself, etc. But now he would need to dictate what he was preaching into a quill and that work would be burned. Such a

volume must be dictated and would require a great deal of work. And the great effort of the prophet would be visible to all. Thereby God made his own plan and his muscular and insurmountable power visible and would bring the plan of the king to ruin. SERMON ON JEREMIAH 36:27-28.[11]

BURNING BOOKS AND BURNING MARTYRS. NIKOLAUS SELNECKER: Although nothing remained of God's word in Jeremiah's scroll, the book was written anew—improved and enlarged; for God acts so that he does not allow his word to be suppressed, as we have often experienced. So a splendid teacher has burned books in great heaps; and still burns them until no book remains. Then he torments, martyrs, and burns many godly Christians and confessors of heavenly and eternal truth. But as one has said, "The blood of the martyrs is the seed of the church."[†] Through the blood of the saints who are killed the church becomes even larger and more fruitful. So we say this about godly books, "The destruction of one is the birth of another." The more one burns godly books, the more God awakens others to write and spread godly books. God gives to us grace alone, that we also keep good and godly books and through strange new books we do not want to lose the previous ones and be led into many errors. But we speak of tyrants and enemies, who do not want to tolerate good and godly books, and we do not speak of abuses and of dangerous habits. All the books without the fear of God and the desire to call on him, without godly understanding, and earnest consideration of such things: these books people write and spew forth, which unfortunately is the custom these days. THE WHOLE PROPHET JEREMIAH 36:27-28.[12]

SIN AMPLIFIES GOD'S WRATH. NIKOLAUS SELNECKER: The punishment of King Jehoiakim announced here near the end of the chapter has been discussed in Jeremiah 22. Now the plague of

---

[10]LW 52:90* (WA 10:272-73); citing Mt 14:3-12.

[11]Zwingli, *Predigten*, 279.
[12]Selnecker, *Der gantze Prophet Jeremias*, 2J4r-v. [†]Tertullian, *Apology* 50.14.

tyrants and stubborn people has only become greater. But the more they grumble and the more impatient those people become, the more wrathful God becomes and the more horribly he punishes them to the end. Examples of this throughout history and also down to our own time show this. THE WHOLE PROPHET JEREMIAH 36:29-32.[13]

A DEMONSTRATION OF GOD'S WRATH. THE ENGLISH ANNOTATIONS: That being so exposed, it may the sooner putrefy and become the more vile and loathsome; not that his body could be sensible of such usage, or himself being deceased of ought that should befall his body, but that the sight of a king's body in such a condition should be a hideous spectacle and horrid monument of God's heavy wrath and indignation against him unto all that should behold it. ANNOTATIONS ON JEREMIAH 36:30.[14]

THE TRUTH OF SCRIPTURE WILL TRIUMPH. KONRAD PELLIKAN: The truth of the Lord remains in eternity. Now that it has been seen and recognized in the world, this truth is less able to be overthrown by the princes of this world—however fierce and mighty they may be—than it was at that time when it was first heard by the most ungodly kings. Now rulers are better advised to stick to the truth than to oppose it. The faith of the godly grows with persecutions, and the strength of Scripture invincibly evades the stubbornness of heretics and unbelievers. This happened before in the times of the apostles and martyrs, by whose most constant faith, through the grace of God, the authority of Scripture was celebrated throughout the whole world. COMMENTARY ON JEREMIAH 36:32.[15]

---

[13]Selnecker, *Der gantze Prophet Jeremias*, 2J4v; Jer 22:18-23.
[14]Downame, ed., *Annotations*, 9X4r*; citing Is 66:24.

[15]Pellikan, *Commentaria Bibliorum*, 3:2Y1r.

JEREMIAH 37:1-21

JEREMIAH WARNS ZEDEKIAH AND FACES PRISON

¹*Zedekiah the son of Josiah, whom Nebuchadnezzar king of Babylon made king in the land of Judah, reigned instead of Coniah the son of Jehoiakim. ²But neither he nor his servants nor the people of the land listened to the words of the LORD that he spoke through Jeremiah the prophet.*

³*King Zedekiah sent Jehucal the son of Shelemiah, and Zephaniah the priest, the son of Maaseiah, to Jeremiah the prophet, saying, "Please pray for us to the LORD our God." ⁴Now Jeremiah was still going in and out among the people, for he had not yet been put in prison. ⁵The army of Pharaoh had come out of Egypt. And when the Chaldeans who were besieging Jerusalem heard news about them, they withdrew from Jerusalem.*

⁶*Then the word of the LORD came to Jeremiah the prophet: ⁷"Thus says the LORD, God of Israel: Thus shall you say to the king of Judah who sent you to me to inquire of me, 'Behold, Pharaoh's army that came to help you is about to return to Egypt, to its own land. ⁸And the Chaldeans shall come back and fight against this city. They shall capture it and burn it with fire. ⁹Thus says the LORD, Do not deceive yourselves, saying, "The Chaldeans will surely go away from us," for they will not go away. ¹⁰For even if you should defeat the whole army of Chaldeans who are fighting against you, and there remained of them only wounded men, every man in his tent, they would rise up and burn this city with fire.'"*

¹¹*Now when the Chaldean army had withdrawn from Jerusalem at the approach of Pharaoh's army,*

¹²*Jeremiah set out from Jerusalem to go to the land of Benjamin to receive his portion there among the people. ¹³When he was at the Benjamin Gate, a sentry there named Irijah the son of Shelemiah, son of Hananiah, seized Jeremiah the prophet, saying, "You are deserting to the Chaldeans." ¹⁴And Jeremiah said, "It is a lie; I am not deserting to the Chaldeans." But Irijah would not listen to him, and seized Jeremiah and brought him to the officials. ¹⁵And the officials were enraged at Jeremiah, and they beat him and imprisoned him in the house of Jonathan the secretary, for it had been made a prison.*

¹⁶*When Jeremiah had come to the dungeon cells and remained there many days, ¹⁷King Zedekiah sent for him and received him. The king questioned him secretly in his house and said, "Is there any word from the LORD?" Jeremiah said, "There is." Then he said, "You shall be delivered into the hand of the king of Babylon." ¹⁸Jeremiah also said to King Zedekiah, "What wrong have I done to you or your servants or this people, that you have put me in prison? ¹⁹Where are your prophets who prophesied to you, saying, 'The king of Babylon will not come against you and against this land'? ²⁰Now hear, please, O my lord the king: let my humble plea come before you and do not send me back to the house of Jonathan the secretary, lest I die there." ²¹So King Zedekiah gave orders, and they committed Jeremiah to the court of the guard. And a loaf of bread was given him daily from the bakers' street, until all the bread of the city was gone. So Jeremiah remained in the court of the guard.*

OVERVIEW: The Reformation era was an age of monarchs, magistrates, and lords. Every preacher, pastor, and theologian found themselves answering at one time or another to an emperor or king, prince or city council, bishop, inquisitor, or visitor.

Thus commentators show a keen interest in parallels between the kings of Judah and rulers of their own day and in the negotiations Jeremiah had to manage, the suffering he faced, and the demeanor he maintained while suffering in prison.

Every interpreter of Jeremiah assumed that active ministry and public preaching could lead to state scrutiny. Effective collaboration with worldly authority demanded biblical wisdom, a sophisticated political theology, and rhetorical skill. Resistance to governing powers risked interrogation, incarceration, torture, and execution.

37:1-10 Zedekiah's Vain Hope

KING ZEDEKIAH AND ENGLAND'S QUEEN. JOHN KNOX: Up to this point I have recited about the state of Judah before the destruction of Jerusalem and the subversion of that commonwealth. Now I appeal to the conscience of any impartial person: in what point do the manners, state, and government of England this day differ from the abuse and state of Judah in those days, except that they had a king, a man of his own nature (as it appears), more easy than cruel, who sometimes entreated the prophet's favor and also in some cases heard his counsel. And we have a queen, a woman of stout stomach, who in no way can abide the presence of God's prophets.† In this one thing they disagree, but in all other things they are more alike as a bean is like a nut. (1) Their king was led by pestilent priests. Who guides your queen? Do you not know? (2) Under Zedekiah and his counsel the idolatry Josiah had suppressed came to light again. But a more abominable idolatry was never present on the earth than what is now set up again by your pestilent priests among you. (3) In Jerusalem Jeremiah was persecuted and cast into prison for speaking the truth and rebuking their idolatry. What person within London torments some true prophet of God for the same cause? And O you dungeon of darkness, where that abominable idol of these days was first erected (you Tower of London, I mean), in you many Jeremiahs and others are tormented, whom God shall comfort according to his promises and shall reward their persecutions even as they half deserve. A GODLY LETTER OF WARNING AND ADMONITION.[1]

HOPING IN GOD'S ENEMIES. JOHANNES BUGENHAGEN: King Zedekiah sees that the Lord is with Jeremiah; nevertheless he is not turned away from his impiety. He only desires to avoid the present danger. He puts his trust in Pharaoh, that is, in a limb of the flesh, concerning which Isaiah speaks in chapter 30. So it is that, as the siege was relaxed for a little while, the people acted more insolently and stubbornly—as if they were done with every danger and those things that Jeremiah had prophesied in the name of the Lord were mere lies. There is no doubt here that the hypocrites made sacrifices and vows and that the certain victory of Pharaoh was boasted about (as the enemies of the Word of God are used to doing in vain hope). But these people perished when that limb of flesh was broken; while the prophet was threatening them with this evil, he himself was thrown into prison. COMMENTARY ON JEREMIAH 37.[2]

PROPHETS AND RULERS WHO PRAY. JOHANNES OECOLAMPADIUS: Here Jeremiah begins to narrate how he was thrown into prison and for what reasons. At the same time he will recount how Nebuchadnezzar besieged the city, drove back the Egyptians, overthrew the city, and freed the prophet. But first of all at one time the king held the prophet in great honor because his holiness was well-known to him, even if he revered him with a certain fox-like cunning. Indeed, he rejected the true honor that was owed to God and the prophets, because he was not listening to God's word. In fact, so far the king was letting him freely teach and he sent an honorable legation to Jeremiah so that Jeremiah might pray to God for him, as if Zedekiah were giving God his full attention. But it was mere hypocrisy. So Pharaoh falsely begged so that Moses would pray for him, and so Saul with Samuel. They were imitated by Hezekiah, who under siege sent a legation to Isaiah, Eliakim, and the secretary Shebna, and he was freed. Truly Hezekiah was humbling himself and was living piously. COMMENTARY ON JEREMIAH 37:1.[3]

---

[1]Knox, *Works*, 3:187-88*. †Knox is referring to Mary Tudor, queen of England from 1553 to 1558.

[2]Bugenhagen, *In Ieremiam*, 5K3r-v; citing Is 30:1-7.
[3]Oecolampadius, *In Hieremiam*, 2:Z1r; citing Ex 8:25-28; 9:27-28; 12:31-32; 1 Sam 15:24-31; Is 37:1-38.

JEWISH KINGS, BABYLON, AND EGYPT. JOHN CALVIN: We must bear in mind the history of that time so that we may understand the meaning of the prophet: the Jews made Jehoiachin king in the place of his father [Jehoiakim], but in the third month the army of the king of Babylon came. Then Jehoiachin surrendered himself to them of his own accord. Now the prophet had said that there would be no legitimate successor to Jehoiakim; and this was fulfilled. Though his son was set on the throne, his three months' reign was so unimportant it was deemed as nothing. And when Nebuchadnezzar saw that the people could hardly be kept in order without a king, he made Mattaniah king, whom he called Zedekiah. And Zedekiah immediately revolted [against Babylon and turned] to Egypt and made a treaty with them, in order that he might shake off the yoke of the king of Babylon. Hence the prophet says that though Zedekiah had been taught by the example of Jehoiakim and of his nephew Jehoiachin, he yet became nothing the better for it. COMMENTARY ON JEREMIAH 27:1-2.[4]

WHEN THE GODLESS SEEK THE PRAYERS OF THE GODLY. HEINRICH BULLINGER: In these difficult circumstances Zedekiah sent a legation to Jeremiah to question him concerning the outcome of the war. In fact, these were false prophets, who said that Nebuchadnezzar would never return any more, etc. But Jeremiah maintained the opposite and preached the destruction of the city and people. . . .

The king sent an honorary legation to Jeremiah for two reasons. First, so that Jeremiah might pray to the Lord for the people. Second, so that he might get a response from the Lord concerning the outcome of his affairs. Indeed, it is good and correct that intercession be sought from the faithful before the Lord in such dangerous times. In fact, such intercession does a lot of good for a lot of people. But in general, if we want to shove every great burden onto the neck and shoulders of one or another person who fears God, while we meanwhile persist in every impiety, and give no thought to emending our corrupt lives, then intercession is sought in vain. Certainly you see innumerable people today who shout to holy statues near a body, "pray for us, St. Peter, pray for us St. Andrew." They also say to saints living in this age: "I beg you, commend us to the Lord with your prayers." But from their own corrupt mores they do not stray by even a finger's width: because of this their hardness, they are not assisted by any prayers of the godly. SERMON ON JEREMIAH 37:3.[5]

JOSEPHUS THE HISTORIAN ON JEREMIAH THE PRISONER. JOHANNES OECOLAMPADIUS: Josephus the historian narrates with these words: "After Nebuchadnezzar discovered the defection of Zedekiah, who had allied himself with the king of the Egyptians, with a great army he laid waste to the countryside and neighboring cities of Judea. When Nebuchadnezzar was about to occupy Jerusalem, the Egyptians came to help the Jews, against whom the Babylonian marched, having broken the siege, and when battle had been joined, the Babylonian defeated the Egyptian. Soon the false prophets were saying that the Babylonians would not return against Jerusalem, and that their tribesmen would be departing from Babylon with the vessels. To these prophets Jeremiah objects."[†] This is covered in the thirty-fourth chapter of Jeremiah above: "Behold, I will command, the Lord says, and I will lead them back to this city and they will fight against it and will capture it." First, the priest Pashhur sent Jeremiah into prison, but he led him out the following day, as in chapter 20. Similarly in chapter 32, where it is read that he was in the court of a prison; but it was done after that with confinement, as is now read. Similarly, this can be read in chapters 33 and 36. COMMENTARY ON JEREMIAH 37:4.[6]

THE MENTALITY AND LIFE OF THOSE IN MINISTRY. HEINRICH BULLINGER: There is also

---

[4]CTS 20:361-62* (CO 39:140).

[5]Bullinger, *Conciones*, 216v, 217r-v.
[6]Oecolampadius, *In Hieremiam*, 2:Z1r-Z2v; citing Jer 34:22; 20:1-3; 32:1-2; 33:1. †Josephus, *Jewish Antiquities* 10.7.3.

added a few things about what Jeremiah's situation was like: he had not yet been hurled into jail. And so there are ups and downs in every circumstance, in the ministry and for the ministers. They do not always groan under the cross: even if they are never at leisure, nevertheless the Lord sometimes gives them some respite and better times. . . . Therefore, those who have some peace and advantage do not forget the cross, but they prepare themselves for it; and those who lament under the cross hope for better times, and in all things they entrust themselves to divine providence, which orders and governs all things rightly. What we just heard—that the king has sent a legation to the prophet—is relevant to this point; for there is occasionally a time when those who are otherwise considered more vile than dogs become valuable to others. This is often the experience of Christ's faithful and ministers of the church, as in every misfortune they look not to human beings but to the one faithful, powerful, and saving God of all who serve him. And if enemies and potentates are sometimes supplicants to them, the faithful do not indulge their passions on this occasion; they neither glory nor exult from it according to the flesh, nor do they seize this occasion to bring about their own ends, nor do they grant or bestow anything that is not proper. But in the fear of God and according to the Word of God they respond, act, and accomplish all things, while always giving thanks to God for his wise dispensation and paternal care. SERMON ON JEREMIAH 37:4.[7]

DO NOT LIFT UP YOUR HEARTS. HEINRICH BULLINGER: So Jeremiah had already prepared a few remarks in which he responded to the legates from King Zedekiah. He announced that the Chaldeans would return and resume their siege and that they would at last capture the city, and plunder and even burn it, and that therefore those who promised the people peace and security were lying and seducing them. (1) Jeremiah shows that the author of his response is the Lord God himself

of Israel. It as if he says, "It's not that you loathe my response because it appeared from my imagination. This is the response from the true, living, and eternal God." (2) He shows that the Egyptians are going to fight to no good end at all, and they will flee back to the place from which they came. Therefore, in vain the Jews have leaned upon a staff made of reeds. So again he makes it clear that no alliances will enable those people, contaminated by their ungodly lives, to escape the impending evil. (3) Moreover he shows with the most significant words that the Chaldeans would resume their siege, and indeed that they would set fire to the captured and looted city.

Thus neither walls nor any fortifications would be able to protect the unrepentant against the hand of the Lord; for the unrepentant life, incredulity, and ungodliness had reached a peak among the people. (4) Since some were promising that the Chaldeans would never return again to the city, Jeremiah is ever consistent in speaking against them. "Do not lift up your hearts," for which others translate, "Do not so lift your spirits." To lift up one's heart is a type of expression, signifying that with a great desire of the heart we long for something and that we already promise it to ourselves as if it is present and we give it to ourselves as if it has been accomplished. It is as if Jeremiah says, "I see that you practically devour this with your whole heart, but I do not wish you to put it in your mind that you will ever get this thing." (5) To these points he adds a sentence that has some hyperbole, to cut off all hope for them and show that that the Lord was going to inflict utter vengeance upon them. "It is so much the case that your city will not remain uninjured and whole, that even if you slaughtered the Babylonian host, and very few of them who are hurt and wounded remained in their tents; nevertheless those stabbed men would rise up from their tents and burn your city with fire." Such is the manner of speaking, as when it is said "the stones will cry out" and "children of Abraham will rise up from the stones." For it is necessary for the will of God to be completed altogether; it was utterly necessary for the unrepentant to be punished: the

---

[7]Bullinger, *Conciones*, 217v.

idolaters and godless people—the persecutors of the Word of God. SERMON ON JEREMIAH 37:5-10.[8]

37:11-21 Jeremiah Imprisoned

JEREMIAH'S INTENTIONS AND THE DEVIL'S DESIGNS. JOHN MAYER: Regarding Jeremiah's going to the land of Benjamin: we must understand that Anathoth was the city in which Jeremiah was a resident. Jeremiah offered to go there when he saw that he could do no good in Jerusalem through threatening and exhorting the people to repentance. Rather, he was daily in danger of being imprisoned or cut off. What Jeremiah did could be justified completely. Therefore, he took the opportunity that occurred when the siege broke off. Yet when the servants of God have only good intentions, the devil has his instruments ready to charge such servants with heinous things. Although they might purge themselves of such guilt, they suffer as evildoers most grievously. COMMENTARY ON JEREMIAH 37:11-14.[9]

JEREMIAH THE TRAITOR. JOHN CALVIN: [Jeremiah] was free to leave the city: no one before could have gone out, because the gates were closed and the city was also surrounded by enemies. It was then, he says, that he went out, that he might go to "the land of Benjamin," where . . . he was born.

But he then adds that he was intercepted by the "prefect of the ward in the gate of Benjamin." That gate had its name from its location, for a part of Jerusalem belonged to the tribe of Benjamin. . . . There then Jeremiah was intercepted by Irijah, the prefect of the ward, and not without a grievous charge: that he was escaping to the Chaldeans. The prophet attempted to clear himself, but with no effect; for an opinion prevailed that he was already in league with the enemies. He thus gained nothing by defending himself, but was taken to the princes, the king's counselors.

This passage teaches us that God's servants cannot escape without being exposed to a great deal of slander and false suspicions. . . . Faithful teachers ought indeed to remove themselves, as far as they can, from all false statements and to check the wicked and the malicious, so that they may not have the occasion to speak evil. But when the godly have done everything [they can], they will not yet exempt themselves from slander; for their words and their deeds will be misconstrued. Thus Jeremiah was loaded with false charges; for all had persuaded themselves that as much as he had praised the power of King Nebuchadnezzar, he must have been hired by the king for the purpose of discouraging the people with fear. . . . Jeremiah was apprehended as a traitor as he was leaving the city. COMMENTARY ON JEREMIAH 37:12-14.[10]

JEREMIAH THE PRISONER. JOHANNES OECOLAMPADIUS: Look, I pray, at this stupidity, how much of it there is that Jeremiah suffers. They condemn him without a hearing; they beat and lock him in an ancient prison, more horrible than any death. It is clear enough that he is there by the petition of the king, and from that it is also clear that the place was thoroughly secured. There was hardly any doubt that at that time the prison was considered very well known. The prison was quite muddy and in the home of a most avaricious scribe. For this Jonathan seems to have been very cruel and merciless. So Jeremiah begs below, that he not be sent there again. Indeed, either they had conspired in his death, or the prison was so harsh that he was plagued by the stench, the filth, and the poison of reptiles. Therefore, the patience and constancy of the prophet is clear; for he was overwhelmed by false testimony, but he was free from blame in that he did not wish to give up, and he was certainly not willing to hand himself over to the Chaldeans. COMMENTARY ON JEREMIAH 37:13-14.[11]

WHEN GOD DOES SOMETHING STRANGE. MARTIN LUTHER: "Now mark what I am going to do through the heathen. I am going to change the

---

[8]Bullinger, Conciones, 217v-218r; citing Lk 19:40; Mt 3:9; Lk 3:8.
[9]Mayer, A Commentary, 446*.
[10]CTS 20:372-73* (CO 39:147).
[11]Oecolampadius, In Hieremiam (1533), 2:Z2v.

order and perform something through the heathen, and this will seem so strange and odd to you that you will not believe it until you have experienced and felt it. In fact, all will regard my prophets Habakkuk, Jeremiah, and others like them as fools and lairs and will not believe that the words they utter are my words." In the same way King Zedekiah could not believe what Jeremiah said about this. He summoned him and asked him whether this was really God's word. What stranger thing could God do than to use his enemies, the heathen, for the destruction of his throne, his temple, his city, his people, whom he until now had glorified and preserved from all the heathen and whom he had promised that he would be their God and protector forever? LECTURES ON HABAKKUK 1:5.[12]

JEREMIAH'S PRISON. JOHN MAYER: The word for prison here signifies a sepulcher, a prison completely dark and horrible in which to be held. It can also be rendered a dungeon; therein were several cells . . . a place in which a person could not be more miserable. Such prisons they had in Athens, called *barathrum*, and at Syracuse called *latomiae*, into which people were closed up for a long period of dying. COMMENTARY ON JEREMIAH 37:16.[13]

THE STEADFAST PROPHET AND THE UNGODLY. JOHANN PAPPUS: The last part of the chapter describes the conversation between the king and the prophet, in which we ought to look upon both the impious terror of the king and the remarkable steadfastness of the prophet. Indeed it was not on that account that the king asked whether there was some word from the Lord, as if he was ignorant of God's will, which had been called to mind so many times by the prophet. But he asked as one who hoped that the prophet could be moved either by the authority of the palace or certainly by his distaste for prison to predict a more generous fate. Indeed the minds of the ungodly are arranged such that in the midst of their calamities they would

rather cheer themselves and others with a false hope than be turned from their pernicious habit of sinning. For this reason we must take pains that we not indulge the flesh too much, but rather resist temptation in the first place. . . .

Moreover, the constancy and fortitude of the prophet is most worthy of praise in this section. He not only repeats and inculcates the Word of God—even if it could come back by way of his neck (as they say)—but also with a full heart he reprimands the godless cruelty of the king, and from the outcome itself and the present calamities he argues that those false prophets are vain, however many better times they promise. But the fact that Jeremiah demanded a less severe prison was not a lack of courage. The prophet sought a modest concession, since he was to be imprisoned. Nevertheless, he was prepared to suffer every sort of extreme rather than give up as a public crier of the truth. ON ALL THE PROPHETS, JEREMIAH 37:17-21.[14]

JEREMIAH REMAINS FIRM AND SEEKS RELIEF. NIKOLAUS SELNECKER: It may seem that King Zedekiah, who has been so terrible and awful, now wants to show his work of mercy for Jeremiah and to take him in and nourish him as long as there is bread on hand in the city. Though he is a wicked tyrant, sometimes he does something good; otherwise he would be a stone-hearted and devilish sort of king if he did not want to care for innocent and desperate people. Yet it appears that the king wanted to see the truth in the prophecies and sermons of Jeremiah and so called Jeremiah to himself—not from an evil heart, but from a doubting and sad heart. He just did not know what he should do and hoped that Jeremiah would tell him something he would be glad to hear. But Jeremiah was a relentless and righteous prophet; he remained of the mind that he would and could go to his Lord, but did not change his preaching, nor make it simpler or milder. Yet he did ask about making the imprisonment, to which he would return, less severe. Thus, with a good conscience we

[12]LW 19:166* (WA 19:364); citing Jer 38:14-28.
[13]Mayer, *A Commentary*, 446*.

[14]Pappus, *In Omnes Prophetas*, 111v-112r.

are able to use and to enjoy human sustenance. We should neither scorn nor reject such things, otherwise we are seeking God and yet running our stubborn heads against a wall. THE WHOLE PROPHET JEREMIAH 37:17-21.[15]

---

[15]Selnecker, *Der gantze Prophet Jeremias*, 2K3r-v.

JEREMIAH 38:1-28
JEREMIAH, THE CISTERN,
AND KING ZEDEKIAH

¹Now Shephatiah the son of Mattan, Gedaliah the son of Pashhur, Jucal the son of Shelemiah, and Pashhur the son of Malchiah heard the words that Jeremiah was saying to all the people: ²"Thus says the LORD: He who stays in this city shall die by the sword, by famine, and by pestilence, but he who goes out to the Chaldeans shall live. He shall have his life as a prize of war, and live. ³Thus says the LORD: This city shall surely be given into the hand of the army of the king of Babylon and be taken." ⁴Then the officials said to the king, "Let this man be put to death, for he is weakening the hands of the soldiers who are left in this city, and the hands of all the people, by speaking such words to them. For this man is not seeking the welfare of this people, but their harm." ⁵King Zedekiah said, "Behold, he is in your hands, for the king can do nothing against you." ⁶So they took Jeremiah and cast him into the cistern of Malchiah, the king's son, which was in the court of the guard, letting Jeremiah down by ropes. And there was no water in the cistern, but only mud, and Jeremiah sank in the mud.

⁷When Ebed-melech the Ethiopian, a eunuch who was in the king's house, heard that they had put Jeremiah into the cistern—the king was sitting in the Benjamin Gate— ⁸Ebed-melech went from the king's house and said to the king, ⁹"My lord the king, these men have done evil in all that they did to Jeremiah the prophet by casting him into the cistern, and he will die there of hunger, for there is no bread left in the city." ¹⁰Then the king commanded Ebed-melech the Ethiopian, "Take thirty men with you from here, and lift Jeremiah the prophet out of the cistern before he dies." ¹¹So Ebed-melech took the men with him and went to the house of the king, to a wardrobe in the storehouse, and took from there old rags and worn-out clothes, which he let down to Jeremiah in the cistern by ropes. ¹²Then Ebed-melech the Ethiopian said to Jeremiah, "Put the rags and clothes between your armpits and the ropes." Jeremiah did so. ¹³Then they drew Jeremiah up with ropes and lifted him out of the cistern. And Jeremiah remained in the court of the guard.

¹⁴King Zedekiah sent for Jeremiah the prophet and received him at the third entrance of the temple of the LORD. The king said to Jeremiah, "I will ask you a question; hide nothing from me." ¹⁵Jeremiah said to Zedekiah, "If I tell you, will you not surely put me to death? And if I give you counsel, you will not listen to me." ¹⁶Then King Zedekiah swore secretly to Jeremiah, "As the LORD lives, who made our souls, I will not put you to death or deliver you into the hand of these men who seek your life."

¹⁷Then Jeremiah said to Zedekiah, "Thus says the LORD, the God of hosts, the God of Israel: If you will surrender to the officials of the king of Babylon, then your life shall be spared, and this city shall not be burned with fire, and you and your house shall live. ¹⁸But if you do not surrender to the officials of the king of Babylon, then this city shall be given into the hand of the Chaldeans, and they shall burn it with fire, and you shall not escape from their hand." ¹⁹King Zedekiah said to Jeremiah, "I am afraid of the Judeans who have deserted to the Chaldeans, lest I be handed over to them and they deal cruelly with me." ²⁰Jeremiah said, "You shall not be given to them. Obey now the voice of the LORD in what I say to you, and it shall be well with you, and your life shall be spared. ²¹But if you refuse to surrender, this is the vision which the LORD has shown to me: ²²Behold, all the women left in the house of the king of Judah were being led out to the officials of the king of Babylon and were saying,

"'Your trusted friends have deceived you
    and prevailed against you;
now that your feet are sunk in the mud,
    they turn away from you.'

²³All your wives and your sons shall be led out to the Chaldeans, and you yourself shall not escape from their hand, but shall be seized by the king of Babylon, and this city shall be burned with fire."

²⁴Then Zedekiah said to Jeremiah, "Let no one know of these words, and you shall not die. ²⁵If the officials hear that I have spoken with you and come to you and say to you, 'Tell us what you said to the king and what the king said to you; hide nothing from us

and we will not put you to death,' ²⁶then you shall say to them, 'I made a humble plea to the king that he would not send me back to the house of Jonathan to die there.'" ²⁷Then all the officials came to Jeremiah and asked him, and he answered them as the king had instructed him. So they stopped speaking with him, for the conversation had not been overheard. ²⁸And Jeremiah remained in the court of the guard until the day that Jerusalem was taken.

OVERVIEW: Christian ministry in the Reformation era was not limited to church and parish. Rulers might seek ecclesiastical advice, bring pressure to bear on the clergy, or even take their lives. Jeremiah's role as an advisor to the powerful was all too familiar. Moreover, the treacherous nature of royal courts was similarly well known, especially the courtiers and advisors seeking to sway, manipulate, and control their lords while harming others to increase their influence. Jeremiah's consultations with the king, his suffering at the hands of courtiers, and his desperate pleas are all instructive to expositors of Jeremiah. But at the center of this narrative is Ebed-melech the Ethiopian, the outsider and servant who loves mercy, defies the powerful, and saves Jeremiah's life. For our Reformation commentators, he is a shining example and an unquestioned model of faith and virtue.

38:1-6 Jeremiah Cast into the Cistern

JEREMIAH'S IMPRISONMENT. THE ENGLISH ANNOTATIONS: Poor Jeremiah has no sooner rid himself of one confinement or difficulty than he is cast into another which is as bad or even worse. From Jonathan's house, or hole rather, and at the king's command he is transferred to the prison court where he had more liberty and people had more free access to him than before. More than a few came to visit him—some, perhaps, out of kindness and goodwill. Others, like a majority of all visitors, came either with an itching affection to hear some form of novelty and strange matters or out of a deep desire to hear what

Jeremiah thought or said concerning the issue of their present troubles and difficulties. As often occurs in such cases those both good and bad are ready to inquire regarding the thoughts and speech of those who are deemed to have some spark of the prophetical spirit. But this freedom and frequency of access was a means to bring this our prophet into new troubles and painful annoyances, even to the point of endangering his very life. Jeremiah could not refuse to speak; he had to do his duty in order to acquaint those who came to him with God's mind and message: if they stayed in the city they would certainly perish, but if they yielded themselves to the Chaldeans and left the city they might save themselves. Thus some of the ill-affected princes clamored against Jeremiah to the king and thereby the king delivered Jeremiah to their designs. They put him into a worse pit or hole than the one in Jonathan's house and there Jeremiah remained struggling in the mire. ANNOTATIONS ON JEREMIAH 38.[1]

SUFFERING UNDER A WEAK KING. JOHANNES OECOLAMPADIUS: Jeremiah considered the king softer than his princely ministers and the people; for those men who at that time were adorned with the surnames of their births were clearly famous men, and they were preeminent for their significant authority, so that the king did not dare to deny anything to those pursuing iniquities. The Word of God aggravated them, because the word opposed their passions; soon they would desire to kill even

---

[1]Downame, ed., *Annotations*, 9Y1r*, citing Jer 37:21; 1 Cor 9:17; Jer 20:9.

the innocent. When they were not able to understand that Jeremiah's words exposed falsehoods, they falsely accused this soul; on that basis they said that he harangued publicly in such a way that he broke the spirits of the soldiers and the citizens.

Therefore, due to the hate of people, Jeremiah exerted himself for their destruction and not their salvation. Thus they made him out to be a disturber of the public peace. The Jews also hurled this accusation at Christ; that he stirred up the people, so Ahab regarded Elijah, and the Jews regarded Paul. Indeed, these hypocrites know that the souls of leaders are provoked by this line of reasoning, leaders to whom God has entrusted the duty of maintaining public tranquility, leaders whom we wish to have been helped more than even the ministers of God. Christ also teaches a similar message, which the world hates. In fact, he said, "The one who hates their life will save it, and the one who loves their life will lose it." All those who do not renounce their lives and this world will perish in the contagion of the world, the scarcity of the word, and in the heat of desire. However, whoever is prepared to bear the cross will be saved from the tyrants themselves. COMMENTARY ON JEREMIAH 38.[2]

PROPHESYING DEFEAT AND THE END OF LEGITIMATE RULE. JOHN CALVIN: The four princes mentioned here watched him. . . . Then . . . having insidiously watched what he said, immediately they made a commotion. They had, no doubt, contrived the ruin of the prophet before they came to the king; for the unprincipled and wicked, we know, discuss matters together when intent on mischief and their courtly arts must be taken into account. . . . Hence [Jeremiah] says the accusation was that he had not only threatened with ruin all the inhabitants of Jerusalem, but that he had also promised life to all that would go out to the Chaldeans. . . .

We have seen this elsewhere that the prophet had before said the same thing; it was not, then, a new

thing, for he had thirty years before that time clearly pronounced the same in the temple. . . . But . . . the king and his courtiers thought that he was so subdued by evil that he could hardly open his mouth. In short, they thought that the holy man had, in a manner, lost his tongue since he had been in prison. This, then, was the reason why they now accused him so gravely to the king, and declared him worthy of death. He had deserved death many years before. . . .

He then adds, "Whoever goes over to the Chaldeans shall live" . . . as though [Jeremiah] said, "He who flees to the Chaldeans shall only save their life, but must suffer the loss of all their property," as when a shipwreck is dreaded, there is no one who is not ready to save their life at the loss of all their goods; and therefore, in extreme danger the merchants are willing to cast into the sea all that they have, for they prefer to escape to the harbor empty and destitute of everything than to perish together with their riches. . . .

Then the princes accused Jeremiah on this account, that he terrified the men of war, and thus rendered them listless. It was a deceptive charge, but this slander had nothing to support it; for Jeremiah could not have been condemned as a public enemy to his country, when he earnestly exhorted them to flee and gave no hope to the people, in order that they might all, despairing of deliverance, willingly surrender themselves to their enemies.

A question may be raised here, whether it is lawful for a private individual to persuade subjects to violate their oath of allegiance to their king or prince. I now call prophets "private persons"; for I have in view civil order. Jeremiah, indeed, sustained a public character, for he was God's prophet; but as to the government of the city he was a private individual, one of the people. It seems, then, that the prophet has passed over the limits of what is right, when he persuaded the people to revolt, for that could not have been done without forfeiting allegiance to the king. To this I answer that the prophet was invested with a special command and that, therefore, he did nothing presumptuously or rashly. Though, then, the people had pledged their faith to the king to

[2]Oecolampadius, *In Hieremiam*, 2:Y1v-Y2r; citing Lk 23:5; 1 Kings 18:17-18; Acts 17:1-34; Mk 8:35; Mt 16:25; Jn 12:25.

the very end, yet as God had now delivered the city to the Chaldeans, the obligation of the oath ceased; for when governments are changed, whatever the subjects had promised is no longer binding. . . . The people, then, were not to wait until the Chaldeans broke into the city, burned its houses, and killed all they met with; but it ought to have been sufficient for them that the prediction of the prophet was the decree or sentence of God, by which they were given up to the Chaldeans. COMMENTARY ON JEREMIAH 38:1-4.[3]

THE PRINCES IGNORE THE MESSAGE, ATTACK THE MAN. JOHN TRAPP: These four princes here named to their eternal infamy were no small men, as appears in that the king was not he that could do anything against them. The grandees of the world are the greatest enemies (usually) of the truth. They had little to say against his doctrines; they quarreled with his affection, as a disturber of the public place. Ahab charged the like crime upon Elijah, the Jews upon Christ and afterward upon Paul, the heathen persecutors upon the primitive Christians, the heretics upon the orthodox, that they were seditious, antimonarchical, etc. COMMENTARY ON JEREMIAH 38:1.[4]

A TRUE REVOLUTIONARY. BALTHASAR HUBMAIER: As to the charge that I am a revolutionary, praise be to God for that! That is the same name that was also given to Christ, my Savior. He was also supposed to be an agitator who stirred up the people from Galilee to Jerusalem. . . . Jeremiah was also accused of being a divider of the soldiers in Israel, who did not desire peace but agitation. King Ahab railed at Elijah as a troubler of his country. . . . Therefore I am not at all surprised that this is happening to me, who am not worthy to loosen the thongs of their shoes. Nevertheless, this I affirm with God and with several thousand people that no preacher in the areas where I have been has gone to more trouble and labor in writing and

preaching than I in order that people should be obedient to the government. A BRIEF APOLOGIA.[5]

THE KING WHO IS NOT A KING. JOHANNES OECOLAMPADIUS: Immediately this delicate and effeminate king hands over the man of God to his enemies. He argues from necessity that no one is a suitable king who has dared to deny anything to such great men as they earnestly request it. . . . Jonathan ben Uzziel says, "He is not a king who is able to respond to you in whatever way you seek."[†] Quite unseemly is the fickleness of the king, since he is able to cast out a prophet, while he knows that he is innocent; it is no less despicable that the king lets Jeremiah be tried. It was the same with the shrewd Pilate: "Behold, he is in your hands. I give him over to your judgment; I myself wash my hands." O king of nothing, who does not oppose blood-stained men with even a little word. See his horrendous confinement: deep is the pit without waters, and muddy, and the prophet is plunged into this filth. COMMENTARY ON JEREMIAH 38:5-6.[6]

JEREMIAH, THE MAN OF SORROWS. NIKOLAUS SELNECKER: Here we see how it ends up for those who desire to throw godly and true preachers into the mire. So such people cast Jeremiah into such mire. He was truly a wretched and miserable man, full of sorrow and misery. He had fully intended and committed himself to preach to people; for in God's name one must go forth and fear no danger, disgrace, or suffering for the truth. But one must give full attention to God's command and see how God's word will triumph over those who despise and curse true preachers and consider them evil. Then try as you may, and say whatever you want: but I do not believe that I have another example of such a righteous and true teacher who was mocked,

---

[3]CTS 20:385-88* (CO 39:156-58).
[4]Trapp, A Commentary or Exposition, 332*.

[5]CRR 5:303-4; citing Lk 23:5; 1 Kings 18:17-18; Mk 1:7; Jn 1:27.
[6]Oecolampadius, In Hieremiam, 2:Y2r; citing Mt 27:24. [†]Oecolampadius cites the Targum Jonathan, or Targumim to the Prophets, a fourth-century-AD Jewish work of translation and commentary attributed by tradition to Jonathan ben Uzziel, the disciple of the Elder Hillel (first century AD); see Bruce Chilton, "Targum," in Dictionary of Biblical Interpretation, ed. John H. Hayes (Nashville: Abingdon, 1999), 2:531-34.

despised, and pursued to silence, who endured so much done to him, and withstood it all, whether long or short in duration. Then we say, "Whoever touches you touches the apple of my eye." Yet he lived and held sway and his word remained firm—the same as always—even if the world did not notice or take note of it. I want us to know fully and to share this example among others. Those of us who truly have the right teaching of the holy gospel, let us share what happened to many great people and what still happens; and let us tell of those who reached out to the true teachers and have helped them. THE WHOLE PROPHET JEREMIAH 38:6.[7]

38:7-13 Jeremiah Rescued from the Cistern

ONE AFFLICTION PREPARES FOR ANOTHER. JOHN DONNE: Previously Jeremiah had been scornfully and despitefully put in stocks by Pashhur. He had been imprisoned in the king's house before. He had been put in a dungeon and almost starved in the mire. . . . And yet he was spared for this further calamity [the destruction of Jerusalem]. Affliction is truly a part of our patrimony and our portion. If as the prodigal son did, we waste our portion (that is, make no use of our former affliction), then it is not the least part of God's bounty and liberality toward us that he gives us a new stock—a new feeling of new calamities—so that these new calamities may improve us more than the previous ones. Jeremiah's former afflictions were nothing but preparation for more. Our afflictions are no different. SERMON ON LAMENTATIONS 3:1.[8]

THE GOOD SAMARITAN OF THE OLD TESTAMENT. JOHN MAYER: This is a thing greatly to be noted, that there was not one prince or other person of the Jewish nation who was moved at the cruelty used against the prophet of God; only a stranger, a eunuch in the king's house, was affected

by it, and sought his deliverance, which tended to bring utter disgrace to the Jews. They held this view of themselves: that they were the holy seed and God's peculiar people; all others were base and vile in comparison to them. Yet now one Ethiopian had more piety in himself toward the man of God than all the Jews. And his love and piety is all the more commended by this: that he showed himself to be for Jeremiah and against the princes who held great power. So the Ethiopian spoke to the king openly—not in the privacy of the royal house—but when the king sat in the judgment seat in the gate; for in that place tribunals were commonly held among the Jews. So the Ethiopian feared neither the princes nor the envy of the people who mostly hated Jeremiah. But God stirred up the Ethiopian to this work and was with him. So he prevailed with the king, even though the king was in awe of the princes before. Now the king was also moved with compassion, and bid the Ethiopian to take with him thirty men, go, and pull Jeremiah out of the dungeon. . . .

This is a notable example that true religion stands for love and for acting on behalf of those who are in misery. So it is in the Lord's example of the Samaritan, who had compassion on the wounded man when not one Jew, priest, or Levite would show him pity. Note this encouragement for doing good. Human reason put so many difficulties before the Ethiopian, which might have seemed impossible to overcome: the power of the princes over the king, the hatred and danger that would arise when he acted, the enmity of the Jews at the gate before whom he must speak, the possibility that they would be too late and find Jeremiah dead from cold, hunger, and the noise of the place. Yet, notwithstanding all these things the Ethiopian attempted it and prevailed to his everlasting fame and great favor with the Lord. COMMENTARY ON JEREMIAH 38:7-13.[9]

THE HANDS OF A STRANGER. THE ENGLISH ANNOTATIONS: With these powerful men standing

---

[7]Selnecker, *Der gantze Prophet Jeremias*, 2Liv-2L2r; citing Is 53:3; Zech 2:8.
[8]Donne, *Sermons*, 10:200*; citing Jer 20:2; 37:15; Lk 15:13-15.

[9]Mayer, *A Commentary*, 447-48*; citing Lk 10:25-37; Jer 39:15-18.

there, who attend the king, the Ethiopian dares to speak to their very faces and in open court proclaim how they had dealt with God's prophet in secret. People should have such courage and confidence of speech in God's cause. Thus the prophet found more favor and aid at the hands of a stranger than at the hands of any of his own countrymen. ANNOTATIONS ON JEREMIAH 38:9.[10]

FAITH AS THE OBLIGATION OF DUTY. JOHN CALVIN: Let us now learn to be courageous when necessity requires, though there may not be a hope of a favorable outcome. Ebed-melech might have thought to himself that his attempt would be in vain, however strenuously he might have pleaded for Jeremiah. He might, then, have given up the purpose that he had so boldly undertaken; for those who are overly wise are often led into inactivity. What impact can you have? You are only one person and they are many. But then the [rescue] is done.

... Ebed-melech ... might have desisted. But we see that he rested in the confidence of God's favor. Let us, then, remembering his example, hope beyond hope when God requires us to do a thing, that is, when faith, the obligation of duty, demands anything from us. This thing may be done if we would only close our eyes to all obstacles and go on in our work; for events are in God's hands alone, and they will be such as he pleases. In the meantime it is simply our duty to proceed on our course though we may think that our labors will be in vain and without any fruit. Ebed-melech happily succeeded; how did he do it? He performed the part of a pious and upright person. Thus God will extend his hand to us; whatever the difficulties that may meet us, we shall overcome them all by his power and aid. COMMENTARY ON JEREMIAH 38:10.[11]

WHY THIRTY MEN? THE ENGLISH ANNOTATIONS: The hazard in which the prophet found himself required haste. And the king, now better

advised, presses for swift action and without further delay. He orders Ebed-melech, therefore, to take a competent number of people to assist him in this matter. So Ebed-melech readily takes action. But why are thirty men needed to draw up just one? To this some answer: because the pit was very deep and in all likelihood this was the upper part of the city and on a craggy hill. Yet mire was still found at the bottom of the well. Though fewer men might have sufficed for such a matter, as the Jewish doctors say, so many of them were so greatly weakened and their strength was so impaired by the famine that only a few men could not have done it. But this seems improbable. ... Rather those men came with Ebed-melech to assist him, not only in drawing up the prophet, but also in withstanding and driving off any that came to oppose them or disturb them in executing the king's command. ANNOTATIONS ON JEREMIAH 38:10-11.[12]

FRIENDS OF THE CHURCH. MARTIN LUTHER: The church never runs out of enemies and opponents; for Satan hates it and for this reason he plots against it in various ways and stirs up perils of every kind.... [But] the kingdoms of the entire world were destroyed because they harmed the church: the Babylonian, the Assyrian, the Greek, the Roman, etc.

On the other hand, there is a blessing to those who befriend the church. Thus God built houses for the midwives in Egypt because they did not hate this people. Thus the harlot Rahab with her household is preserved through the promise. The interested reader may gather more examples of the various ways in which the Lord blessed those who showed kindness either to the church or to its leading members, the teachers and prophets. Thus the woman of Zarephath, the Ethiopian in Jeremiah, and others were blessed. LECTURE ON GENESIS 12:3.[13]

---

[10]Downame, ed., *Annotations*, 9Y1v*; citing Ps 119:46.
[11]CTS 20:397* (CO 39:164-65).
[12]Downame, ed., *Annotations*, 9Y2r*.
[13]LW 2:259 (WA 42:446-47); citing Ex 1:20-21; Josh 6:25; 1 Kings 17:8-24.

38:14-28 Jeremiah Warns Zedekiah Again

LISTENING TO REASON AND FLEEING THE CROSS. JOHANNES BRENZ: It is the nature of infidelity that when necessity is evident, it indeed freely follows the word but fears the cross. In Zedekiah you have an amazing talent for rational unbelief. Whenever the cross is placed before his eyes, he expresses the opinion that he refuses the cross and he wishes to escape it. To flee to the cross, he keeps counselors from both sides; from the one side he has human reason and prudence, from the other side, the word of the Lord. Therefore, just as reason promises freedom, so too does the Word of God, but through different means. Reason considers, apart from the cross that the cross ought to be avoided, through reason's own strength and counsel, sometimes even with a pretense of the divine name. Thus, in this passage the wise counselors advise the king that, in order to flee the cross, he should resist the king of Babylon. They advised him that it would not come to pass that the Babylonians would capture the city of Jerusalem, since the temple of the Lord was in it, and the Lord would not abandon his own place. Furthermore, the Lord orders Zedekiah to flee the cross through those things that are things contrary to the cross. In fact the word urges us to flee the cross through the cross, death through death, affliction through affliction. Reason abhors such council and is scandalized by the cross. ANNOTATIONS ON JEREMIAH 38:14.[14]

FEARING THE WRONG PEOPLE AND NOT FEARING GOD. NIKOLAUS SELNECKER: As soon as Jeremiah was pulled from the mire he was called to the king, whom he had often warned and given advice as to how he could save his life and spare the whole city. But the king feared the princes more than he feared God; and he feared the Jews more than he feared the Chaldeans. He followed the false preachers more than the prophet Jeremiah, who now had no more respect either among the king's council or the people. Yet he was compelled to go to the king's court; and he went where they led him. But the godless who brought Jeremiah were afraid. Jeremiah said to the king: the king must fall into the hands of the Chaldeans and be humiliated. He heard precisely the Word of God from Jeremiah the prophet, but the king did not follow it. Instead the king's familiars, those foxtails and false prophets, had been preaching throughout the land. The king had trusted them for a long time—until he was in the middle of the flood and the current was rising and he was about to drown. Surely he had been told this was happening in many other places. From this all godly court preachers ought to learn: their office should be tended to with greatest integrity and effort and in consideration of the high souls of their lords who might speak and be like Zedekiah when he spoke. Thus God had given good warnings, and entrusted these to the king, but he was not terrified. God had shown the king his false confidence and his sins. But he would not see this, and he waited until everything was coming to pass and too much had already occurred. And the lords who were there had sunk so deep into [difficulty] they could no longer hear or allow themselves to know the truth. So they came forward and fell into one sin after the other, as so often happens when we are trapped in our sins. And then they died wretchedly and rotted away. THE WHOLE PROPHET JEREMIAH 38:14-26.[15]

ZEDEKIAH'S TRUE FEAR. JOHN TRAPP: Hypocrites will at one time or another detect themselves, as Zedekiah here plainly declares that he more fears the loss of his life, honor, wealth, etc. than of God's favor and kingdom. So do most among us: Pilate feared how Caesar would take it, should he loose Jesus. Herod laid hold of Peter, after he had killed James, that he might please the people. The Pharisees could not believe because they received glory from fellow humans. This generous king cannot endure to think that his own fugitives should flout him, but to be ruled by God and his holy prophet advising him for the best, he cannot yield. Thus still

---

[14]Brenz, *Annotationes in Jeremiam*, 932; citing 1 Cor 1:21-25.

[15]Selnecker, *Der gantze Prophet Jeremias*, 2L2v-2M1r.

vain people are niggardly of their reputation and prodigal of their souls. Do we not see them run willfully into the field, into the grave, into hell? And all, lest it should be said they have as much fear as wit. COMMENTARY ON JEREMIAH 38:19.[16]

JEREMIAH, THE LYING PROPHET. JOHANNES BUGENHAGEN:

It is disputed here and often elsewhere in the Scriptures whether the saints have sinned by lying, when often we read that they said something other than how the facts actually stood. But even as what they say may not be true, nevertheless Scripture condemns only that lie that harms and makes one sin against the Word of God, such as false doctrine and when you desire to harm someone with your words or a hypocritical fiction. Indeed a lie happens not only with words but also in the signs of both the face and the postures of a hypocrite, as Virgil says: "He feigns hope with an expression, he presses down the deep sorrow in his heart."[†] And concerning Christ who was not able to sin, Luke writes, "He acted as if he was going farther." David said something to the priest that was not true, nevertheless he did not want to harm anyone by doing this. When you wish to harm no one, but rather to do some good either for yourself or for others, that is no more against the command of God, and not against faith, than pretending something is not prohibited. The command is spoken against false doctrine. "You shall not take the Lord's name in vain"; indeed, one who does this will not go unpunished. Against other forms of lying it is said: "You shall not give false testimony," but it adds, "against your neighbor." Jeremiah here obeys the king to the good. COMMENTARY ON JEREMIAH 38:27.[17]

THE PROPHET'S DECEPTION. JOHN CALVIN:

Here, indeed, the prophet confesses that he did as the king had commanded him; but he does not commend what he had done.... Though then what Jeremiah said was in part true, that he prayed not

to be sent back to prison, yet he could not by this evasion be wholly exempted from blame.

In short, we see that even God's servants have sometimes spoken evasively when oppressed with extreme fear; and thus we are reminded to seek of God a generous mind and resolute firmness; for he alone can strengthen and sustain us when we are terrified by any fear of danger.

He says, that he "did as the king had commanded him"; but he ought rather to have harkened to God's Word, in which simplicity is enjoined. COMMENTARY ON JEREMIAH 38:27.[18]

JUDAH AND ENGLAND ON THE EVE OF DESTRUCTION. JOHN KNOX:

Consider, dear brethren, if all things are alike between England and Judah before the destruction of it. Yes, if England is perhaps worse off than Judah was, do we think that the Lord's vengeance shall sleep with many iniquities so ripe? No, dear brethren.... It may offend you that I call England worse than unthankful Judah. But if good reasons adduce and declare what make take place, then I do not fear your judgment. (1) From Jerusalem many followed the admonition of the prophet, leaving all that they had rather than abide the danger of God's plagues that were threatened. God's prophet has threatened and cried that many plagues will fall upon England, but I do not hear of many that prepare to leave. God grant that you do not repent! (2) In Jerusalem there were princes and nobles that defended Jeremiah, also that did absolve him when he was accused and unjustly condemned by pestilent priests. But the number of the nobility within England that boldly speak now in defense of God's messengers is easy to count! (3) In Jerusalem the prophet of God had liberty to speak in maintenance of his doctrine. How severe has been the trial of their doctrine and God's Word in England, and how many entreat among you now, and how many are heard in strange countries? (4) In Jerusalem was Ebed-melech, who boldly said to the king that Jeremiah was injured by the false

---

[16]Trapp, *A Commentary or Exposition*, 334*.
[17]Bugenhagen, *In Ieremiam*, 5L2r-v; citing Lk 24:28; 1 Sam 21:1-9; Ex 20:7, 16. †Virgil, *Aeneid* 1.209.

[18]CTS 20:419-20* (CO 39:179-80).

prophets and therefore obtained Jeremiah's freedom when he was condemned to death. But in England I hear of none (God stir some up!) that dare put their hands between the bloodthirsty lions and their prey; that is, between those cruel tyrants . . . and the pure holiness of God. (5) In Jerusalem, while Jeremiah was in prison, he was daily fed by the king's charges and there was a great scarcity of bread in that fair city. In London, where all plenty abounds, God's messengers are permitted to hunger . . . while a thief or murderer has seldom been handled so cruelly. A GODLY LETTER OF WARNING AND ADMONITION.[19]

[19]Knox, *Works*, 3:188-89*; citing Jer 25:1-38; 37:21.

JEREMIAH 39:1-18
THE FALL OF JERUSALEM AND JEREMIAH'S DELIVERANCE

¹*In the ninth year of Zedekiah king of Judah, in the tenth month, Nebuchadnezzar king of Babylon and all his army came against Jerusalem and besieged it. ²In the eleventh year of Zedekiah, in the fourth month, on the ninth day of the month, a breach was made in the city. ³Then all the officials of the king of Babylon came and sat in the middle gate: Nergal-sar-ezer of Samgar, Nebu-sar-sekim the Rab-saris, Nergal-sar-ezer the Rab-mag, with all the rest of the officers of the king of Babylon. ⁴When Zedekiah king of Judah and all the soldiers saw them, they fled, going out of the city at night by way of the king's garden through the gate between the two walls; and they went toward the Arabah. ⁵But the army of the Chaldeans pursued them and overtook Zedekiah in the plains of Jericho. And when they had taken him, they brought him up to Nebuchadnezzar king of Babylon, at Riblah, in the land of Hamath; and he passed sentence on him. ⁶The king of Babylon slaughtered the sons of Zedekiah at Riblah before his eyes, and the king of Babylon slaughtered all the nobles of Judah. ⁷He put out the eyes of Zedekiah and bound him in chains to take him to Babylon. ⁸The Chaldeans burned the king's house and the house of the people, and broke down the walls of Jerusalem. ⁹Then Nebuzaradan, the captain of the guard, carried into exile to Babylon the rest of the people who were left in the city, those who had deserted*

to him, and the people who remained. ¹⁰Nebuzaradan, the captain of the guard, left in the land of Judah some of the poor people who owned nothing, and gave them vineyards and fields at the same time.

¹¹Nebuchadnezzar king of Babylon gave command concerning Jeremiah through Nebuzaradan, the captain of the guard, saying, ¹²"Take him, look after him well, and do him no harm, but deal with him as he tells you." ¹³So Nebuzaradan the captain of the guard, Nebushazban the Rab-saris, Nergal-sar-ezer the Rab-mag, and all the chief officers of the king of Babylon ¹⁴sent and took Jeremiah from the court of the guard. They entrusted him to Gedaliah the son of Ahikam, son of Shaphan, that he should take him home. So he lived among the people.

¹⁵The word of the LORD came to Jeremiah while he was shut up in the court of the guard: ¹⁶"Go, and say to Ebed-melech the Ethiopian, 'Thus says the LORD of hosts, the God of Israel: Behold, I will fulfill my words against this city for harm and not for good, and they shall be accomplished before you on that day. ¹⁷But I will deliver you on that day, declares the Lord, and you shall not be given into the hand of the men of whom you are afraid. ¹⁸For I will surely save you, and you shall not fall by the sword, but you shall have your life as a prize of war, because you have put your trust in me, declares the LORD.'"

OVERVIEW: The destruction of Jerusalem, which Jeremiah had long prophesied, comes to pass suddenly with grave consequences for the people of the city, and particularly for the king, his family, and fellow princes. Commentators point out that such terrifying events lay bare the sources of support humanity tends to prefer in contrast to the nature of divine justice. While those who relied on wealth and privilege, lofty fortifications, and sacred

sanctuaries perish or are carried off into exile, Jeremiah and Ebed-melech trust in God alone and are spared in the carnage. Meanwhile the poorest of all inherit the earth and its bounty.

39:1-10 Jerusalem Destroyed

TRUSTING THE WORD OF GOD ALONE. JO-HANNES BUGENHAGEN: The impious hate and despise the Word of God until the wrath of God comes upon them. Here at last God seems to speak truthfully and he protects his own, such as Jeremiah, the Ethiopian, Baruch, and other pious folk whose names were not written down. He saves them even in the midst of the underworld and in the midst of the impious as they perish, as was said in Christ: "to rule in the midst of your enemies." Whether among friends or enemies God is concerned about us, as God was for Jeremiah. Thus Jeremiah had a better situation through the Babylonians. He was vexed and disturbed enough by his own Jewish people, as we are vexed by our papists, to whom God will give their just reward when they are done with their sins—unless meanwhile they repent and are converted to the gospel of Christ, which they now hate and persecute.

In fact, God had promised that land to believers, and he had given it after four hundred years of the promise, so that God appears truthful in his promises. Still God had threatened them that he would cast away unbelievers and despisers. Here they lose everything: the land, the kingdom, the priesthood, the holy city, the temple with all those sacred things of God, including the ark of the Lord. . . . But the place of our sanctuary, the throne of the glory of God remains always firm, because "you, Lord, are the hope of Israel," etc. So they learn not to trust in such things, as before when they shouted in Jeremiah 7, "the temple of the Lord, the temple of the Lord." The impious trusted in the gifts of God, the rites and holy things instituted by God (something I now do not say of the made-up holy cults among the papists), but they refused to have God in his very own Word, as you have seen all through Jeremiah. Therefore, they perish with their sacred things, from which they made idolatry and not the worship of God. Commentary on Jeremiah 39.[1]

Judgment Comes, for God Never Sleeps.

Heinrich Bullinger: Finally we arrive at the miserable spectacle: the destruction of that city and people that, I say, is the most ancient and celebrated in the world. Moreover, all these things did not happen by chance, but altogether in the way that Jeremiah had predicted, based on the Word of God. When again the steadfast truth of God shines forth, even if for a long time, God seems to ignore human wickedness. And even if he seems to most people to sleep with his ears closed, nevertheless, he does not sleep, neither forever nor for anyone. Indeed, he is present at the proper time, and he balances this his slowness with the severity of the punishment. Therefore, these dreadful and mournful sorts of narratives teach us to fear the Lord our God, to walk in his ways, and not provoke his wrath with insolence and rebellion. In fact, his judgments are excessively severe against the incurably sinful. The destruction of Jerusalem following the times of Christ our Lord is similar. It was predicted to happen for forty years, just as Jeremiah in his case had predicted the destruction in his time for forty years. Sermon on Jeremiah 39:1-2.[2]

The Lord's Righteous Judgment on Jerusalem and Zedekiah.

Nikolaus Selnecker: At the last the end of King Zedekiah comes and the whole people that lived in Jerusalem. . . . Here you see that Jeremiah is a righteous prophet. The city is conquered and burned. Zedekiah is caught while in flight and brought to the king of Babylon, who slaughtered the children of the king, his princes, and advisors before Zedekiah's eyes. And Zedekiah's eyes were put out and he was bound with chains and led away as a miserable, blind man to Babylon, where he would die in prison. This means that one can wait too long, until God's wrath is fulfilled. Moreover, it can also be said, "Lord, you are righteous and you are righteous in your judgments." The Whole Prophet Jeremiah 39:1-7.[3]

A Terrifying People Bring Judgment on City and King.

Heinrich Bullinger: To this point Jeremiah seems to be watching what

---

[1]Bugenhagen, In Ieremiam, 5L3v-5L4r; citing Ps 110:2; Jer 7:4.

[2]Bullinger, Conciones, 228r.
[3]Selnecker, Der gantze Prophet Jeremias, 2Miv; citing Ps 119:137.

follows as the Babylonian princes entered the city. Either thing could have happened: both that some citizens burst out of the city to the Chaldean soldiers—of them there is some mention a little later—and at the same time that the Chaldeans burst in and took possession of the city. The fact that their city was ancient, celebrated, declared holy, and finally walled to the point that it seemed to many unconquerable did no good for the impious citizens. Indeed, because God willed it to be so; they already succumbed and vanished; nor did all those things do them a whit of good, which the world otherwise used to marvel at. Thus let us not rely on any things that are destined to perish. For by God's command whatever is strongest is destroyed, and indeed unexpectedly, as if in just one moment.

The names of the princes are consecrated in writing. The names seem barbarous and harsh, and horrendous by their very sound to those listening. But when we do not want hear the sweet Word of God and rejoice in the lovable name of our heavenly Father, then we deserve what we get today also: we hear the barbarous Turkish language with a shiver, and those Turkish words that are horrendous, at least by their sound, become known to us—Abraimbassa, Bassaa, Natoliae, Beglerbeg. . . . And there are those who figure these are the personal names of Babylonian princes. Others think that some of the names are taken from their duties, which they then explain: so Serezer would be prefect of the treasury, Rabsaris, prefect of the prince's court. . . .

Already the king had escaped through that secret way along with his princes and the nobility. They did not care about the safety of the people who were left in the midst of danger. Of course, we see such things often done by other princes. There appears in this deed the miserable fate of the people and the treachery of great people. These people had previously accused Jeremiah of treachery, saying that he was preparing to flee, etc. They themselves now shamefully flee, while deserting the people, and wishing to look after their own things. Truly, the eye of the Lord, which discerns all things, saw also this their treacherous flight, and took care that every one of those on the run fell into the hands of the enemy. SERMON ON JEREMIAH 39:2-4.[4]

WHEN DIVINE PROMISES AND THREATS FAIL.

JOHANNES BUGENHAGEN: "They fled." But they were not able to escape since, indeed, the judgment of God had now caught them, which to this point they had despised. Neither the promises nor the threats of God were able to have an effect among them. So it is now with the papists, who hate and persecute the gospel of Christ and "say in their hearts, 'There is no God, God is nothing,' etc. They are corrupted and are made abominable in their pursuits. There is not one who does good things," even if they shout until they are hoarse, "Good works, good works." COMMENTARY ON JEREMIAH 39:4.[5]

PLACING HOPE IN THINGS THAT PERISH.

HEINRICH BULLINGER: He goes on briefly to remember what also happened with the city. Its venerable, even divine temple, the palace of the kings, and illustrious buildings were all destroyed. The walls of the city were razed and nearly leveled; everything was set ablaze and burned. Jeremiah had often predicted that this would happen, but they refused to believe him; they preferred to experience it for themselves. Now, therefore, within a few hours all of their wealth was burning; the temple in which they had hoped now burned. The walls and buildings, behind which they had hoped to be safe, were torn down. So perishes the hope of the ungodly. Let us not trust in such things that can be ruined, but in the living God in our time. Even in this world it is the most fortunate thing to please him. Jeremiah attended this ruin of the city with plaintive lament, so that there would be no need for our own affliction. Only let us beware, lest we are condemned by the same judgment. SERMON ON JEREMIAH 39:8.[6]

---

[4]Bullinger, *Conciones*, 228v-229r.
[5]Bugenhagen, *In Ieremiam*, 5L4v; citing Ps 14.
[6]Bullinger, *Conciones*, 230r.

GOD'S PROMISE TO THE FAITHFUL IN TIME OF JUDGMENT. JOHANNES OECOLAMPADIUS: The poor alone are saved and those who freely announce the truth; Jeremiah was like that too. For both did not conspire with the king against the command and will of God. Therefore, if we will exist as sojourners in this age, a tyrant will allow us to cultivate the fields and vineyards and for a long time will tolerate us—unless a particular duty to fight them will have been given to us. And the Lord, just as he promised his prophet, was faithfully present, cared for him honorably, set him free, and commended him to faithful Gedaliah. Meanwhile, all the others especially tried and did not flee, but rather ran into destruction in their eagerness to avoid it without God. For that reason he was sitting in the midst of the people, since God had often promised to be with him. But this was so especially when Jeremiah was freed from the reservoir of filth through Ebed-melech the Ethiopian, not for any other reason than the fact that he had trusted in God: "Behold, I will bring my words for evil, not for good." "So far I have corrected as a father corrects his sons"; "so now as a judge I will punish the accused; nor will I be appeased any more. My words will be before your eyes. That is, you will see it happen in this way, also the fact that you are set free."

Therefore, God says that the prophecy was fulfilled at that time. All the pious are able to announce it to each other. The destruction of Jerusalem bears a certain example of divine judgment. Indeed, just as the impious perished in Jerusalem, and the poor were set free and enriched with gifts, so on the day of judgment, which we await, it will come to pass, and in its own way now it is happening in the time of the revealed gospel. COMMENTARY ON JEREMIAH 39:10-11.[7]

GOD'S PROVIDENCE FOR THE POOR. THE ENGLISH ANNOTATIONS: God in his judgment most severely handled the rich and mighty that trusted fully in their own livelihood and means, while the common sort of people fared better than anyone at that moment and even better than they had in the past. By this means God in all likelihood providentially so arranged it that many poor people, who been oppressed and stripped of their possessions by the greater and wealthier people, came both to recover their own goods again and to be owners of the lands that had belonged to their oppressors in former times. ANNOTATIONS ON JEREMIAH 39:10.[8]

39:11-18 Jeremiah and Ebed-melech Spared

GOD SPARES JEREMIAH IN THE BATTLE. JOHN CALVIN: The prophet now sets forth the paternal care of God, which he had exercised in the preservation of [Jeremiah's] life and safety. The innocent, we know, are often killed in the tumult and the storming of cities is turbulent, so that many things are done without any thought; for even leaders are not able to moderate the excesses of the victorious. When therefore the Chaldeans burned the palace, Jeremiah might have perished at the same time, being suffocated by the very smoke of the fire. . . . If no one had come to Jeremiah, he might . . . have been buried under the ruins of the palace, when the king's court was burned down. . . .

It is indeed probable that the king of Babylon had heard of Jeremiah; and though he was in prison, yet the Word of God, which he boldly proclaimed, was not bound. Then the report of this might have reached the king of Babylon: and hence it was that he was disposed to preserve him; for he had given faithful counsel to Zedekiah. But Nebuchadnezzar no doubt regarded only his own advantage; and hence we ought to bear in the mind the wonderful goodness of God in preserving, as it were, by his own hand, the life of the prophet. . . .

It is not always by a voluntary act that people serve God, for many execute what God has decreed when they have no intention of doing so: and he so turns and drives them here and there that they are

---

[7]Oecolampadius, *In Hieremiam*, 3:2B1r; 193r; citing Jer 30:22; 31:33; 32:28; 39:16; Prov 3:12; Heb 12:6-7.

[8]Downame, ed., *Annotations*, 9Y3r*.

constrained, willing or unwilling, to obey his authority. Thus Nebuchadnezzar liberated Jeremiah.

And yet the prophet fully believed that he did not owe his life to King Nebuchadnezzar, but that he had been in a wonderful manner preserved by God's favor; and to show this is the design of the whole narrative. COMMENTARY ON JEREMIAH 39:11-14.[9]

GOD SUPPORTS THE FAITHFUL THROUGH FOREIGNERS. JOHANNES BRENZ:

You see how great the Lord makes those who believe in him. Granted, they seem to be abandoned before the world. Nevertheless, the Lord rouses foreign kings and the cruelest princes to care for his people: for example, Genesis 12—Pharaoh; and Genesis 20—Abimelech. These kings sought an alliance with Abraham. So in this passage Jeremiah, abandoned by his own people, was cared for by foreigners. Despised by the crowd, he was honored by a king and princes. Yet these examples are not proposing that the Lord establishes a king or a prince as a patron for every single faithful person, but only that we should learn with what attentiveness the Lord regards the faithful, even if they have been hurled into the midst of death. ANNOTATIONS ON JEREMIAH 39:11-14.[10]

THE MERCIFUL ETHIOPIAN. JOHANNES BUGENHAGEN:

Here you have two notable examples of Jeremiah and the Ethiopian and how the providence of God is moved on behalf of the pious. See the history concerning Joseph the patriarch. One must also attend diligently to the deepest thoughts of those who will be restored, as was said to the Ethiopian: "'Because you had trust in me,' says the Lord." Here trust or faith in God has such an effect that the Ethiopian because of love is not able to abandon Jeremiah as he was thrown into the reservoir, as was said in the chapter above. You see the subsequent divine effect of the promise to the Ethiopian's advantage: "Blessed are the merciful, for they will be shown mercy." Here the faithful and believing Ethiopian condemns all the Jews as unbelievers. Thus he is saved by God, while the others are perishing. COMMENTARY ON JEREMIAH 39:15-18.[11]

THE ETHIOPIAN SAVES JEREMIAH AND GOD SAVES THE ETHIOPIAN. JOHN CALVIN:

The prophet tells us here that God was not unmindful of that Ethiopian, by whom [Jeremiah] had been preserved, though he was an alien and from a barbarous nation. We have seen, however, that he alone undertook the cause of the prophet, when others, terrified by fear, did not exert themselves, or were avowedly enemies to God's servant. Ebed-melech then alone dared to go forth in a case so hopeless, and undertook the defense of the holy man. The prophet now says that this service was so acceptable that it would not be without its reward. We have said that Ebed-melech had thus manifested his concern for the prophet's life, but not without evident danger; for he knew that the princes were united against him, and that these ungodly men had drawn to their side the great part of the court and also of the common people. Then Ebed-melech roused against himself both high and low; but God aided him, so that he was not overpowered by his adversaries. In his very danger he experienced the favor of God and was protected and delivered from danger. . . .

There is then no doubt that the Spirit of God intended by the example of Ebed-melech to rouse us to the duties of humanity, even to teach us to succor the miserable, give them help as far as we can, and not avoid the hatred of people or any dangers that we may thereby incur. And as we are lazy and negligent in doing good, the reward given to the Ethiopian is set before us, so that we may know that though nothing is to be hoped from people, when we are kind and liberal, yet we shall not lose our labor, for God is rich enough, who can render to us more than can be expected from the whole world. . . .

---

[9]CTS 20:432-34* (CO 39:188-89).
[10]Brenz, *Annotationes in Jeremiam*, 933; citing Gen 12:10-20.

[11]Bugenhagen, *In Ieremiam*, 5Mır; citing Gen 37:1–47:31; Jer 38:7-13; Mt 5:7.

The word "Ethiopian" is now repeated, because God intended, in the person of an alien, indirectly to reprove the Jews; for no doubt they despised him, because he was not of the holy seed of Abraham. But God shows that he regarded him especially, while he rejected the masked and hypocritical children of Abraham. . . .

And he says, "Go and say, Behold, I am bringing my words on this city. . . ." We conclude from these words that this was spoken to Ebed-melech before the city was taken by the Chaldeans, in order that he might remain quietly at home, and not flee with the king, who, as we have seen, tried to escape. God then intended to strengthen the confidence of Ebed-melech, so that he might not fear and tremble like the others, and expose himself to death in trying to secure his safety. . . . This, then, is the reason why God declared that he was "bringing" his words for evil and not for good; for except Ebed-melech had been convinced that the city and its inhabitants were in God's hand and power he could never have been led to entertain good hope; but when he knew that the city would perish through the righteous vengeance of God, he would then be fully confident as to his own safety; for God promised to preserve him in the midst of common ruin. COMMENTARY ON JEREMIAH 39:15-18.[12]

THE GODLY ETHIOPIAN. HEINRICH BULLINGER: The oration of Jeremiah regarding the Ethiopian is very brief and contained in these headings: (1) The Lord God brings upon the city all the evils he had warned about in his word, nor did he spare it. That is signified by the phrase "for evil, and not for good." Therefore, we see again that the word of the Lord is utterly steadfast and certain. (2) The Ethiopian will see that evil with his own eyes, on that day when the Lord will impose it. Thus, not infrequently the godly are compelled to be the observers of the most severe judgments of God. (3) Moreover, this Ethiopian is removed from the communal danger. "I will deliver you," says the Lord, "so that you are not handed over to the power of the enemy you fear so terribly." Accordingly, it is not to be doubted that the Lord snatched him away from the Babylonians, or that he escaped in flight, or maybe the Lord won over to the Ethiopian the hearts of the Babylonians. (4) Meaningfully, he explains and confirms what he said: "For you should not have doubts concerning the promise of God. It is certain that you will be set free. You alone will not be killed by the sword with so many others; for you will take your life like a prize away from that dismal crowd." (5) Last, his faith is commended and, like an accounting of higher things, this is given: "I will free you because you have hoped in me." Thus this Ethiopian is established for us as an example of faith, just as many examples of this kind are put forth by the apostle in Hebrews 11. Let us also believe, therefore, in God and demonstrate our living lives with living works. Because of this our living faith, we too will be freed from evil things. SERMON ON JEREMIAH 39:16-17.[13]

---

[12]CTS 20:435-38* (CO 39:190-91); citing Jer 38:7-13. [13]Bullinger, *Conciones*, 231v.

JEREMIAH 40:1–41:18
JEREMIAH AND JUDAH
AFTER THE CONQUEST

¹The word that came to Jeremiah from the LORD after Nebuzaradan the captain of the guard had let him go from Ramah, when he took him bound in chains along with all the captives of Jerusalem and Judah who were being exiled to Babylon. ²The captain of the guard took Jeremiah and said to him, "The LORD your God pronounced this disaster against this place. ³The LORD has brought it about, and has done as he said. Because you sinned against the Lord and did not obey his voice, this thing has come upon you. ⁴Now, behold, I release you today from the chains on your hands. If it seems good to you to come with me to Babylon, come, and I will look after you well, but if it seems wrong to you to come with me to Babylon, do not come. See, the whole land is before you; go wherever you think it good and right to go. ⁵If you remain,ᵃ then return to Gedaliah the son of Ahikam, son of Shaphan, whom the king of Babylon appointed governor of the cities of Judah, and dwell with him among the people. Or go wherever you think it right to go." So the captain of the guard gave him an allowance of food and a present, and let him go. ⁶Then Jeremiah went to Gedaliah the son of Ahikam, at Mizpah, and lived with him among the people who were left in the land.

⁷When all the captains of the forces in the open country and their men heard that the king of Babylon had appointed Gedaliah the son of Ahikam governor in the land and had committed to him men, women, and children, those of the poorest of the land who had not been taken into exile to Babylon, ⁸they went to Gedaliah at Mizpah—Ishmael the son of Nethaniah, Johanan the son of Kareah, Seraiah the son of Tanhumeth, the sons of Ephai the Netophathite, Jezaniah the son of the Maacathite, they and their men. ⁹Gedaliah the son of Ahikam, son of Shaphan, swore to them and their men, saying, "Do not be afraid to serve the Chaldeans. Dwell in the land and serve the king of Babylon, and it shall be well with you. ¹⁰As for me, I will dwell at Mizpah, to represent you before the Chaldeans who will come to us. But as for you, gather wine and summer fruits and oil, and store them in your vessels, and dwell in your cities that you have taken." ¹¹Likewise, when all the Judeans who were in Moab and among the Ammonites and in Edom and in other lands heard that the king of Babylon had left a remnant in Judah and had appointed Gedaliah the son of Ahikam, son of Shaphan, as governor over them, ¹²then all the Judeans returned from all the places to which they had been driven and came to the land of Judah, to Gedaliah at Mizpah. And they gathered wine and summer fruits in great abundance.

¹³Now Johanan the son of Kareah and all the leaders of the forces in the open country came to Gedaliah at Mizpah ¹⁴and said to him, "Do you know that Baalis the king of the Ammonites has sent Ishmael the son of Nethaniah to take your life?" But Gedaliah the son of Ahikam would not believe them. ¹⁵Then Johanan the son of Kareah spoke secretly to Gedaliah at Mizpah, "Please let me go and strike down Ishmael the son of Nethaniah, and no one will know it. Why should he take your life, so that all the Judeans who are gathered about you would be scattered, and the remnant of Judah would perish?" ¹⁶But Gedaliah the son of Ahikam said to Johanan the son of Kareah, "You shall not do this thing, for you are speaking falsely of Ishmael."

41 In the seventh month, Ishmael the son of Nethaniah, son of Elishama, of the royal family, one of the chief officers of the king, came with ten men to Gedaliah the son of Ahikam, at Mizpah. As they ate bread together there at Mizpah, ²Ishmael the son of Nethaniah and the ten men with him rose up and struck down Gedaliah the son of Ahikam, son of Shaphan, with the sword, and killed him, whom the king of Babylon had appointed governor in the land. ³Ishmael also struck down all the Judeans who were with Gedaliah at Mizpah, and the Chaldean soldiers who happened to be there.

⁴On the day after the murder of Gedaliah, before anyone knew of it, ⁵eighty men arrived from Shechem and Shiloh and Samaria, with their beards shaved and their clothes torn, and their bodies gashed, bringing grain offerings and incense to present at the temple of the LORD. ⁶And Ishmael the son of Nethaniah came out from Mizpah to meet them, weeping as he came. As he met them, he said to them, "Come in to Gedaliah the son of Ahikam." ⁷When they came into the city, Ishmael the son of Nethaniah and the men with him slaughtered them and cast them into a cistern. ⁸But there were ten men among them who said to Ishmael, "Do not put us to death, for we have stores of wheat, barley, oil, and honey hidden in the fields." So he refrained and did not put them to death with their companions.

⁹Now the cistern into which Ishmael had thrown all the bodies of the men whom he had struck down along with[b] Gedaliah was the large cistern that King Asa had made for defense against Baasha king of Israel; Ishmael the son of Nethaniah filled it with the slain. ¹⁰Then Ishmael took captive all the rest of the people who were in Mizpah, the king's daughters and all the people who were left at Mizpah, whom Nebuzaradan, the captain of the guard, had commit-

ted to Gedaliah the son of Ahikam. Ishmael the son of Nethaniah took them captive and set out to cross over to the Ammonites.

¹¹But when Johanan the son of Kareah and all the leaders of the forces with him heard of all the evil that Ishmael the son of Nethaniah had done, ¹²they took all their men and went to fight against Ishmael the son of Nethaniah. They came upon him at the great pool that is in Gibeon. ¹³And when all the people who were with Ishmael saw Johanan the son of Kareah and all the leaders of the forces with him, they rejoiced. ¹⁴So all the people whom Ishmael had carried away captive from Mizpah turned around and came back, and went to Johanan the son of Kareah. ¹⁵But Ishmael the son of Nethaniah escaped from Johanan with eight men, and went to the Ammonites. ¹⁶Then Johanan the son of Kareah and all the leaders of the forces with him took from Mizpah all the rest of the people whom he had recovered from Ishmael the son of Nethaniah, after he had struck down Gedaliah the son of Ahikam— soldiers, women, children, and eunuchs, whom Johanan brought back from Gibeon. ¹⁷And they went and stayed at Geruth Chimham near Bethlehem, intending to go to Egypt ¹⁸because of the Chaldeans. For they were afraid of them, because Ishmael the son of Nethaniah had struck down Gedaliah the son of Ahikam, whom the king of Babylon had made governor over the land.

a Syriac; the meaning of the Hebrew phrase is uncertain   b Hebrew *by the hand of*

OVERVIEW: The chaos and disorder in Judea after the Babylonian invasion was painfully familiar to Reformation Europe. The threat of Ottoman invasion from the east, the cycle of violence among Europe's kingdoms, and the escalation of religious wars among Protestants and Roman Catholics posed a grave threat to the faithful and their leaders of church and state. Jeremiah the prophet and Gedaliah the governor faced the sort of treacherous circumstances that press in when civil order collapses, opportunists scheme and slaughter the innocent, and helpless refugees flee from place to place seeking

safety and consolation. Commentators ponder the hard decisions the people made, the virtues displayed, the evil unleashed, the suffering they endured, and the purposes of God throughout it all in a landscape of misery Europeans knew all too well.

THE IMPIETY OF THE REMNANT IN THE LAND. JOHANNES BUGENHAGEN: In these two chapters, namely, 40 and 41—and the three that follow— you see how openly God is acting; for the destruction of the Jews was not by chance, as it seems to the impious. Rather, this devastation was the judgment of God, with which God had threatened transgressors and those who despised his word.

While the king of Babylon left the poor in the land, over whom he placed Gedaliah in command, the princes also returned with others who had fled. Suddenly the people were no longer in danger. They were allowed again to constitute a state, cultivate fields, become very wealthy, etc., only provided that they conduct themselves under the tribute and power of the king of Babylon. But Ishmael, who was from a royal line and driven by an evil spirit, could not endure that Godalias or Gedaliah was put in command of the people, and he disturbed this security of the remaining people by killing Gedaliah, etc. Thus the remaining people endured in their impiety, even if meanwhile they feigned something else. The people ought to have perished according to the word of the Lord. Therefore, those who even before were not able to withstand the sword and hunger here do not even withstand themselves. One who openly shows contempt is not able to evade the judgment of God; for even as he is safe from others, nevertheless he cannot be safe from himself. Therefore where will the miserable one flee? So it will be for those who blaspheme God and who do not want to have God as a protector. But those who prefer him to be a Father rather than a Judge never give up their hope in him—no matter how sinful they are: this message all the prophets proclaim, and the promises of God they teach from experience. COMMENTARY ON JEREMIAH 40 AND 41.[1]

40:1-16 Jeremiah Remains in Judah

THE LIBERATED PROPHET AND THE CAPTIVE PEOPLE. JOHANNES OECOLAMPADIUS: Here . . . we will now undertake the third book of Jeremiah, which will contain the prophecies of the freed Jeremiah in which the mercy of God will again appear with a new rabble, that assembly of the poor, which was left behind and for whom God caused it to happen that the gentle and just man, Gedaliah, son of Ahikam, was appointed to command.

God had long ago freed Jeremiah from the hand of those seeking to kill him. Here the king of Babylon had appointed to rule a man of such faith and integrity. But just as the mercy of God was great, so too was the unbelief of the people great, who then were not yet chastised by so miserable a spectacle of the city captured and burned. . . . Nebuzaradan was residing with a good part of the Babylonian army in Ramah, and there he was gathering the captives who were to be taken away. Therefore Jeremiah was brought into the reproach of the nation and in his own glory he had been chained, just as he was found miserable and squalid in the court of the prison. Moreover, now he was brought before the people who were being taken away, where, with everyone watching, he would be granted a conspicuous freedom, in order to condemn those people who had hatefully afflicted such a holy man before that. When that was done, he became an assurance for them, that if they themselves had trusted in the Lord, they would likewise have been liberated. Thus the prophet was left behind with honor in the land, while those in captivity went away in shame. Nor was he bereft of the grace of prophecy in this catastrophe, but God was again speaking to him. The text does not state what God said to him, but it shows that it happened. Indeed, God wanted Jeremiah to remain with Gedaliah and with the poor of the land. COMMENTARY ON JEREMIAH 40.[2]

GOD IN BABYLONIAN KINDNESS. NIKOLAUS SELNECKER: This chapter shows how God preserved the prophet Jeremiah while at the same time the whole city and temple burned. Moreover, we see here how the enemy could be so much more pious and gentle and could behave more graciously toward the prophet Jeremiah than his friends. The Babylonians are more godly because they recognize that the city of Jerusalem and the whole people have been punished by God because of their sins. But the Jews neither want to recognize nor believe this. The Babylonians are gentler because they

---

[1]Bugenhagen, *In Ieremiam*, 5M2v-5M3r.　　[2]Oecolampadius, *In Hieremiam*, 3:2B3r-v.

honor Jeremiah and give him the choice as to whether he wants to move to Babylon so that he can converse with the king, or if he wants to stay with those who remain, or proceed to another place. Thus Jeremiah wants to remain behind with the poor people and gladly wants to help carry the common cross. So at the royal palace, with evil and heavy consciences the Babylonians enjoyed some quiet days. Then they gave Jeremiah food and gifts and let him go in the name of God. THE WHOLE PROPHET JEREMIAH 40:1-5.[3]

WHEN THE HEATHEN SPEAK GOD'S WORD. JOHN MAYER: It is remarkable here that Nebuzaradan speaks so piously.... It is a strange speech from a heathen man, but God used his tongue to say this all the more to confound the Jews and to show that they were guilty of those things with which he charged them; now at least in their misery they might be moved to repent, which they would not do in their prosperity. Just as Balaam's ass had rebuked his foolishness, so even profane people who do not know God may sometimes speak the truth of God for their own ends.... So the man possessed with a legion of demons said to Christ, "I know who you are; you are the Son of God." But God would have the heathen say these things to convince even more the wicked people in his church and to make them ashamed. COMMENTARY ON JEREMIAH 40:2-4.[4]

A PROPHET OFFERED THE WORLD CHOOSES THE POOR. JOHANNES OECOLAMPADIUS: "Now I have set you loose." "On account of your courage I have loosened you not only from fetters by which your hands were bound, but also I give you freedom so that you are a free man in all the land and kingdom and even in Babylon itself. I will put my eyes upon you; that is, I will be like a servant to you, and I will watch over you as if you were a lord, so that whatever you desire, you will obtain it by signaling your will." Certainly, this speech indicates

a singular favor and concern for Jeremiah. The Babylonian captain says, "You will be among the most distinguished for me; I will attend to you everywhere and always...." The mode of speech before the people concerning the prophet was honorable. It was as if the general spoke to the others concerning the virtues of Jeremiah. "I know that this man is so great who does not follow the delights and honors of the court. And even if still he does not have a mind to return with me to Babylon, so that he would amply experience my blessings and those of the king, meanwhile let him receive splendid provision with that most godly man, Gedaliah, and the proxy administration in the land of Judah, where he will enjoy his full freedom until he decides something else about himself." Nor was he content to have praised him in this way, but he also presented various favors and gifts, which the prophet described with two words because of the general's eagerness; thus he dismissed Jeremiah, highly honored.

"And Jeremiah went to Gedaliah." This verse declares the great mind of Jeremiah, in which he imitates Moses, who preferred to bear the shame of the Hebrews rather than reign in the court of the Egyptians. So also Jeremiah chose to remain with the poor in the land after residing in the splendors of the Babylonians. So David "I have chosen," he said, "to be humbled in the house of the Lord, rather than to live in the tabernacle of sinners." So it will be more secure for us to bear the cross and follow the crucifixion than to adhere to and perish with the Babylonians and this world, which is committed to evil. COMMENTARY ON JEREMIAH 40:4-6.[5]

SHOULD JEREMIAH ACCEPT SUCH GIFTS? JOHN CALVIN: Nebuzaradan bestowed on God's servant food and other gifts. As to food, the prophet might well have accepted it; for after the city was taken we know that he must have been in want of everything. Even before he lived very scantily and miserably, having only a piece of bread daily. And now, when Nebuzaradan

---

[3]Selnecker, *Der gantze Prophet Jeremias*, 2M2v-2M3r.
[4]Mayer, *A Commentary*, 451*; citing Num 22:1-41; Mk 5:7; Lk 8:28.

[5]Oecolampadius, *In Hieremiam*, 3:2B3v-2B4r; citing Ps 84:10.

supplied him with food, there was no reason why the holy man should not in such want receive what was given to him. But as to the "presents," Jeremiah may seem to have forgotten himself; for it was a disgrace for him to receive from an enemy of God's people a present or gifts for his teaching; for whence proceeded this benevolence and bounty to the prophet, except that Nebuzaradan knew that Jeremiah's prophecy referred to the destruction of Jeremiah's nation? It seems, then, that for this reason he wished to reward the holy man; Jeremiah ought then to have refused these presents. But it is probably that he was not enriched by a large sum of money, or costly things; Nebuzaradan only gave him some token of benevolence; and the prophet might without suspicion have received the present, not as a reward for his teaching, but rather as a confirmation of it offered by God, because the Jews had been the enemies of Jeremiah as long as he had been faithful in spending his labors among them; for when he bitterly reproved them, he had no other object but to secure their safety. But as he had been so inhumanely treated by the Jews, God intended that more humanity should be shown to him by a heathen and barbarous nation than by the children of Abraham, who boasted that they were the holy people of God. It was, then, for this reason that Jeremiah received gifts from the hands of Nebuzaradan. COMMENTARY ON JEREMIAH 40:5.[6]

CHOOSING GOD AND THE POOR OVER THE RICHES OF THIS WORLD. HEINRICH BULLINGER: Jeremiah agreed to go to Gedaliah, and chose the poor people of God in the Promised Land and fatherland over the extremely magnificent and well-furnished court of the Babylonians. In this way he seems to have imitated Moses, the most praiseworthy servant of God, about whom the apostle Paul wrote, "By faith Moses, when he had grown up, refused to be called the son of the daughter of Pharaoh. He chose to be affected by

evils together with the people of God rather than enjoying the conveniences of the sin of the moment; he judged disgrace for Christ to be of greater riches than the treasures of Egypt; indeed he had a regard for his rewards." Thus we read that the sons of Korah sang, "Because one day in your courts is better than one thousand elsewhere, I chose to sit by the door. . . ." Therefore, the uprightness of the illustrious Jeremiah is shown by this choice, and how little he thought of this world or the things which are in this world. If today the choice were offered to us, I don't know what our decision would be. Let the Lord our God direct our hearts into his glory. Amen SERMON ON JEREMIAH 40:6.[7]

JEREMIAH REJECTS A LIFE IN BABYLON. JOHN CALVIN: Here is shown to us the firmness of the prophet, that he did not hesitate to reject what Nebuzaradan kindly offered to him, and yet he might have committed a great offense in making light, as it were, of Chaldea. It was, as we know, a very pleasant country and very fertile; and tyrants cannot bear their bounty to be despised; for when they are pleased to honor any one, however little they may offer, if one refuses they regard it as a dishonor done to them. The prophet, then, might have been overcome by modesty and fear, so as to leave for Chaldea. That he dared to dwell in his own country was proof and evidence that he had more concern for religion, and more care for God's church, than for all the favors of people and all that he might have hoped from the wealth of Babylon and Chaldea.

We hence see that the prophet, in receiving presents, accepted only what he knew would be for the benefit of God's church. At the same time he made light of the offense he might have given when he chose to remain in his own country; for as we have said, it was as though he erected a flag in order to invite the Jews to return and thus to prove the truth of his prophecy regarding their example as temporary, the end of which was to be hoped for after seventy years. For this is the reason, he says,

---

[6]CTS 20:447-48* (CO 39:198).   [7]Bullinger, *Conciones*, 233v; citing Heb 11:24-6; Ps 84:10.

that he went to Gedaliah, and dwelt in the midst of the people, even among those who remained in the land. Commentary on Jeremiah 40:6.[8]

Beware of Gifts. Huldrych Zwingli: The prophet received a gift from the supreme commander. But we are not allowed to excuse a corrupt judge who receives such a gift. Then . . . one must consider the reason for such things; the reason accounts for it being good or bad. Anyone can receive some honorarium with a clean conscience, if it is given by people like the envoys of princes or cities. Why then should I not be allowed to receive a good gift from just anyone, when it is offered to me in goodwill? But then there are gifts, which one is not allowed to receive, gifts that are forbidden by imperial law; these honoraria have more to do with your borders and certain laws. For us everything has to do with corruption; you cannot give honorary gifts, if they are bribes for the judge, for justice and truth. In this case, everything is for sale; justice is for sale. If a rich person gives gifts to cover their sins, then a poor person cannot even once receive such a gift of food. But you must consider the reasons and the Word of God must discern this; otherwise this is not allowed. Gifts dazzle the eyes in certain ways and turn them away from the straight way. . . . Someone becomes a villain when they have done something unjust; they are given something and thereafter they speak and boast about it. Then the villain speaks with a godly person; he addresses them in a friendly way and offers them many good things. And the godly and good person loses their caution and then loses their good name. A godly person can certainly receive a gift from another godly citizen and with a good conscience—as long as there is no deception. Sermon on Jeremiah 40:6.[9]

The Father of the Fatherland. Huldrych Zwingli: Gedaliah is an example of love for one's country and true godliness. Gedaliah was the father of the country, though he had the same sense as any other Jew. So he thought that the Jews should be the subjects of no lord. But he also knew of God's will and vengeance. The Jews who did not want to be obedient saw only one part of the promises of God, namely, that they should have lived free in the land and under their own government. But God said this about the other part of the promises: "When you do not observe my commands, then a foreigner will rule over you. Thus you did not pay attention: you wanted to be free and to establish your own will." But the godly, as in the example of Gedaliah, saw the other part of God's promises and bent themselves patiently to the will of God. They served and were obedient to the one man God gave them to be their lord. And because the matter was settled and could not be otherwise (though he wanted it to be easier to endure), Gedaliah thought that it would be better if he were the high commander in the king's place, rather than someone more strict who would be given to them. So he drew the people to himself and held them together. Gedaliah is their father and warns them to be obedient. Sermon on Jeremiah 40:6-13.[10]

Who Can You Trust? Nikolaus Selnecker: The king of Babylon displayed to the people this grace: he did not lead everyone away, but left some remaining in the land and placed over them a distinguished and godly captain and overseer. Gedaliah the son of Ahikam, who is mentioned above in chapter 26, earnestly received the prophet Jeremiah whom the priests and other people wanted to kill. This man had believed the Word of God through Jeremiah and had surrendered himself to the Babylonians. Thus he was installed as captain over the remaining people; Jeremiah remains with him, as do the people who are received together in obedience to Gedaliah.

But the devil cannot ever remain still, and he shatters every peace, turns to this new thing, and causes a new disturbance. He accomplishes evil and trouble through this unrest. Ambitious and crude

---

[8]CTS 20:448-49* (CO 39:199).
[9]Zwingli, *Predigten*, 284-85.

[10]Zwingli, *Predigten*, 285-86.

heads tend to be active in the church and government at all times, as we experience in our own time. Because Ishmael was born from a royal line, he is determined; he does not see the great danger and does not consider the best approach. He is neither patient nor fears God, but acts straightaway and wants to kill Gedaliah. So as he sets this in motion, a new misery is served up that will fully scatter the people left behind and bring them down. Gedaliah is warned. But he is too godly and does not want to believe that Ishmael would be such an evil lad and that he would treat Gedaliah unjustly. Thus it is often good that one says, "Remember to be suspicious." And moreover, "One must be watchful, there are many who would betray us." "Trust, but don't trust too much." "Trust, but see whom it is we trust." "Ride the horse, but keep the bridle in your hand." The Whole Prophet Jeremiah 40:6-16.[11]

A Virtuous Ruler Among Vicious Adversaries. Johannes Oecolampadius: A very brief happiness: the people had not yet sufficiently boiled away their sadness, which they had received from the destruction of Jerusalem. They began to be occupied and oppressed by a new calamity, as Satan instigated through Ishmael, who was chosen as a very suitable instrument to torment the pious folk. Indeed, he noticed the well-being under the authority of a good protector, and that it depended on his success, and for that reason he prepared traps for the shepherd; once the shepherd was killed immediately the sheep would be scattered. Therefore, Ishmael, son of Nethenaiah, the most wicked man of all mortals took action: for one reason he was commended—he was born from the royal stock of David. For that reason he began to hate Gedaliah as lower born and he was hoping that he would become a tyrannical ruler once the other man was driven out. He was encouraged through Baalis, king of the Ammonites; because the plan had been communicated to other princes, so that Ishmael would have allies for his evil deed. Indeed, Ishmael is a type of Judas the betrayer, and

of those who imitate Judas. And so he had come with the first saviors, promising that he was of greater faith than the others; meanwhile he nursed so much poison of the heart. Further, Johanan and other faithful men warned Gedaliah about Ishmael, not with letters, but by exposing his affairs in person. They recognized a gift of God, which fell to the whole multitude from a good leader.

"And he did not believe." The virtue of Gedaliah was remarkable. He did not easily believe the accusers in the matter at hand, [especially Johanan] who seemed to stand out as the informer of the true crime, and was eagerly devoting himself to defending the state. Truly the magnificent Gedaliah knew of the pride and envy of Johanan and the other princes, from whence the suspicion arose that they were reporting falsehoods, especially when they accused someone who was not present but absent. If only our princes were not so credulous, then certainly the innocent might be pursued less and one might more securely act with innocence. There were many things that did not permit him to believe: first his own mind of good conscience, then the severity of the danger that threatened the waylayer from the Babylonians; in addition to these, the familiarity of Ishmael, who was not a commoner. So Gedaliah was prudently keeping in check any kind of foolish suspicion from an accusation. For when tyrants admit a suspicion just once, they can never be at rest and they are compelled to fear friends and enemies at the same time. Commentary on Jeremiah 40:13-14.[12]

Trust in God Alone. Johannes Brenz: He who rightly trusts God is also able to rightly trust people. Otherwise he either trusts more or less than is suitable. It is proper to trust in all people and yet in no one person. For we must have faith in God alone. Besides, this is love: to hope for good things about any person, and believe that they have been accepted by God. For that reason, in the faith of this matter, the Lord makes one person a helper to another, but meanwhile he sends away him who was

---

[11]Selnecker, *Der gantze Prophet Jeremias*, 2M3r-v; citing Jer 26:24.

[12]Oecolampadius, *In Hieremiam*, 3:2B4v-2C1r.

a helper so that we might learn to confide in the Lord alone. ANNOTATIONS ON JEREMIAH 40:16.[13]

41:1-18 Gedaliah Murdered

FEASTING WITH SAVAGE PEOPLE. JOHANNES OECOLAMPADIUS: In the fifth month the temple was burned, and after a brief period of time, namely, in the seventh month, Gedaliah was cut to pieces; because of these two calamities and unspeakable hunger. . . . Ishmael came, however, under the appearance of a friend, just as all false prophets and attendants of the Antichrist, who in fact participate with us in the sacraments and partake in some charity, as Judas did with Christ. In fact, our Gedaliah is a Christ; he does not refuse the betrayer at table, but the impious heart does not soften from these blessings; on the contrary it is more exasperated. Why would we prohibit from participation at the Lord's table him who has not yet with splendid arguments publicly made himself a stranger from the comfort of the kingdom? Likewise note also in this passage that Satan will take power to be savage even among good people. So the sons of Job fell as they were feasting. Johanan was cut down, and Gedaliah was killed. COMMENTARY ON JEREMIAH 41:1.[14]

GEDALIAH AS VIRTUOUS LEADER. NIKOLAUS SELNECKER: Because Gedaliah had become governor and gathered all the refugees to himself, Ishmael could not tolerate this. But at the instigation of the king of the Amorites Ishmael unleashed a new misery and slaughtered the godly Gedaliah, who did not see this deceit in Ishmael. Then this fellow Ishmael presented himself as very friendly and could conceal that he was a scoundrel and offered himself in a good word and physical signs, until he saw his opportunity to wipe everyone out with violence. So with emphatic ambition, malice, and envy as well as the pleasant appearance and

pretext of religion, he slew the head man, Gedaliah, who previously had elaborated on his virtues.

Thus Gedaliah had allowed himself to be appointed to this difficult and dangerous office during this urgent time and for the good of the people. He received the refugees. He showed that he was a true and trustworthy hero, who promised to defend and protect them. He looked out for the needs and welfare of the people, desired peace and unity, and did not believe this in a superficial way. But the others wanted to betray him and say evil things about him. Gedaliah was not suspicious or distrustful; he spoke well of his enemies and offered them true love and friendship. What other marvelous virtues could there be in a godly captain than these? He was God-fearing, godly, just, peace-loving, good-natured, and gentle. But he would have to pay for his godliness, and his loyalty would be paid back with disloyalty; this is common in the world and is neither new nor peculiar. Ishmael was an ambitious, money-grubbing, cunning, hypocritical, and evil soul, who came to Gedaliah as a friend. As his superior, Gedaliah received Ishmael in a friendly way and offered him good things. Thereafter, Ishmael slaughtered him and brought the whole people into new struggles and misery because of his poisonous actions and the devilish jealousy he should have controlled. This was the resulting crisis for the Jewish people: they had neither government, city, temple, nor king and could not remake these. THE WHOLE PROPHET JEREMIAH 41:1-3.[15]

A JOURNEY OF GRIEF AND SLAUGHTER.
JOHANNES OECOLAMPADIUS: Already Ishmael adds a more serious slaughter; for everything was considered peaceful since the enemy had withdrawn and, moreover, Gedaliah, a notably honest man, administered the kingdom in peace. But as the Lord says, when they have spoken of peace, unexpectedly destruction overwhelms them. Therefore, these simple men went out and according to the law which says, "Three times per year a

---

[13]Brenz, *Annotationes in Jeremiam*, 934.
[14]Oecolampadius, *In Hieremiam* 3:2C2r; 198r; citing Job 1:18-19.

[15]Selnecker, *Der gantze Prophet Jeremias*, 2M4r-v.

man puts himself before the Lord"; then they were to approach Jerusalem in the seventh month, on that day there was expiation and the Feast of Tabernacles. Therefore, they came mournfully, as they would mourn the city and place; and together would give their offering. Indeed, they were not ignorant of the things that had happened to the city and the temple. They had cut their beards, rent their clothes, and cut their skin, indicating that they were in mourning. To that point all the people were still bewailing the destruction of their country and religion. Therefore they wanted to make an offering in the house of the Lord, that is, in the place of the house of the Lord; perhaps some hope might appear again that the temple would be restored. There are those who think that from the remaining poor of the land they made a conjecture that the temple was still standing, but when they were made more certain of its burning, they began to take up their grief on their way.

"And Ishmael went out toward them." Look at this worst kind of genius. They mourn so they may destroy mourners. He falsely weeps, so that he arouses tears in many. As Ishmael killed Gedaliah at a feast while simulating merriment, so he deceives those poor folk who were fasting and grieving, as he grieves in appearance, and feigns an attentive spirit, as if he would lead them to Gedaliah. The murderer was afflicted about the glory of Gedaliah, even when he was dead, as his memory was becoming stronger. In the midst of the citadel—as there was a garrison there—he killed them. COMMENTARY ON JEREMIAH 41:5-6.[16]

MONSTROUS AND VIOLENT MEN, BUT MERCIFUL DEATHS. JOHN CALVIN: Here Jeremiah relates another circumstance in the nefarious conduct of Ishmael: that by flattery he enticed simple men, who feared no evil, while pretending kindness to them. The slaughter was in itself very detestable, but added to it was the most abominable deceit, for he pretended to weep with them,

and offered an act of kindness in order to bring them to Gedaliah, and then he treacherously killed them. . . . In saying that he wept, it was no doubt a sign of feigned piety. He saw these good men in torn garments and in tears on account of the temple being destroyed; he therefore pretended that he had the same feeling. This was falsely to pretend a regard for God, and his tears were those of the crocodile; for he shed tears as though he lamented the ruin of the temple and the city. He thus gained the confidence of the unwary men and then after having led them into the middle of the city, he slew them. . . .

We here see that the barbarity of Ishmael was connected with avarice. He was indeed inflamed with ferocious madness when he slew simple and innocent men; but when the hope of gain was presented to him, he spared some of them. Thus we see that he was a lion, a wolf, or a bear in savageness, but that he was also a hungry man, for as soon as he smelled the odor of prey, he spared ten out of the eighty, who probably redeemed their lives and returned home. So in one man we see there were many monsters. . . .

Here also is set before us the inscrutable purpose of God: that he suffered unhappy men to have been thus slain by robbers. They had left their houses to lament the burning of the temple. As then the ardor of their piety led them to Jerusalem; how unworthy it was that they should become prey to the barbarity of Ishmael and his associates. But . . . God has hidden ways by which he provides for the salvation of his people. He took away Gedaliah; his end indeed was sad, having been slain by Ishmael whom he had hospitably entertained. Thus God did not suffer him to be tossed about in the midst of great troubles. For Johanan the son of Kareah, who yet was a most faithful man, would have become soon troublesome to the holy man; for he became shortly thereafter the head and ringleader of an impious faction, and ferociously opposed Jeremiah. If Gedaliah had lived, he would have been assaulted on every side by his own people. It was then God's purpose to free him at once from these miserable troubles. The same thing

---

[16]Oecolampadius, *In Hieremiam*, 3:2C2v; citing Jer 6:14-15; 8:11; Ezek 7:25; Deut 16:16; Lev 16:1-34.

happened to the seventy who were slain; for the Lord removed them to their rest so that they might not be exposed to the grievous evils and calamities that soon afterward followed; for none could have been in a more miserable state than the remnant whom Nebuchadnezzar spared. We have then reason in this instance to admire the secret purpose of God, when we see that these unhappy men were killed, who yet had gone to Jerusalem for the sake of their piety. It was, in short, better for them to have been removed than to have been under the necessity of suffering many miseries yet again. Commentary on Jeremiah 41:6-8.[17]

The King's Daughters. John Mayer: It is likely that by this time many ill-affected people had resorted to Ishmael; with their help he was able to accomplish this slaughter. Concerning the king's daughters nothing is mentioned here that is contrary to the history in chapter 39. Whereas the sons of Zedekiah are said to be slain before his face, nothing is said of his daughters. It seems that they were left with Gedaliah. Now their own kinsman, who was full of every form of wickedness, carried them away with many more of his own fellow Jews into the Ammonites' country. There what humiliation they suffered only God knows. It seems that Ishmael had been in league with the king of the Ammonites to do these things, given that there was little resistance left in Judea. Commentary on Jeremiah 41:10.[18]

The Fate of Gedaliah's and Ishmael's People. Konrad Pellikan: Johanan was a better man here than Ishmael, but nevertheless he was not a good man, as can be understood from what follows. The Lord had decided to reject this nation altogether; for that reason no one amended themselves. Nevertheless, this man acted courageously for the people of God, just as before he had also faithfully instructed Gedaliah. Indeed, Johanan, hearing of so great a crime, gathered the surviving warriors as allies without delay and set out to subdue Ishmael and strip him of the spoils of his brothers, which also happened with the help of the Lord, near Gibeon, next to the fish ponds, as the people who had already been led away by Ishmael as captives willingly surrendered themselves to Johanan and rejoiced that they were conquered. And Ishmael escaped, accompanied by only eight companions, seized by godlessness, fleeing safely to some worthless people like himself. Commentary on Jeremiah 41:11-16.[19]

The Legacy of Ishmael's Violence. Johannes Oecolampadius: When Johanan repeatedly impresses on them the death of Gedaliah and the fact that he was appointed and given by the king of Babylon—it appeared that Gedaliah's death would be publicly cursed, and the fact that it was a great crime to kill the man established by the king. For such a man was killed against the ordination of God. Whence it seems that the princes did not fear harm, because it would have been far more proper to defend and obey a given prince, so that Ishmael would not have accomplished this unspeakable and criminal killing. Johanan and his men ought to have revealed it to the garrison of Chaldeans so that they might have their guards on high alert. Indeed, not without cause were they so afraid and would flee to Egypt. Indeed, what they upbraided was the sin of Ishmael. Therefore, being of bad conscience on account of the aforementioned rebellion, they reconsidered among themselves that with Gedaliah alive they had someone who would intercede for them and be acceptable to the king; now they had no one as negotiator. Thus they put their hope in humanity and not in God, which is the chief of all sins. And against the command of God they were preparing to enter Egypt. Commentary on Jeremiah 41:16.[20]

The Remnant of Gedaliah Rejects God. Konrad Pellikan: On that day, having escaped

---

[17]CTS 20:465-67* (CO 39:210-11).
[18]Mayer, *A Commentary*, 455*; citing Jer 39:6.

[19]Pellikan, *Commentaria Bibliorum*, 3:2Y5r.
[20]Oecolampadius, *In Hieremiam*, 3:2C3v-2C4r.

captivity, they settled like immigrants in that place called Chimham near Bethlehem. Long ago this place got its name from the son of Barzalli. The people settled there fearfully and anxiously, not knowing where to turn, because they did not dare to linger in the land on account of the slaughter of Gedaliah their governor and the Chaldeans. They believed that the king of Babylon would not ignore this without taking vengeance, and that before he knew the order of events, he would destroy even the innocent out of an appropriate rage. Finally, they decided to go to Egypt, given their awful fate, as the judgment of the Lord urged them on all sides toward their stubbornness, which even in these most extreme dangers they were not able to put aside. But they always continued to be rebels, who did not believe God and his prophets. Indeed, when an ungodly person has fallen into the depths of evil, he is full of contempt for God, of course, and for everything. And when he has been rejected by the Lord he cannot be corrected. An example of this still holds among today's Jews. COMMENTARY ON JEREMIAH 41:17-18.[21]

---

[21]Pellikan, *Commentaria Bibliorum*, 3:2Y5r; citing 1 Kings 2:7.

JEREMIAH 42:1–43:13
FORBIDDEN FLIGHT TO EGYPT

¹Then all the commanders of the forces, and Johanan the son of Kareah and Jezaniah the son of Hoshaiah, and all the people from the least to the greatest, came near ²and said to Jeremiah the prophet, "Let our plea for mercy come before you, and pray to the LORD your God for us, for all this remnant—because we are left with but a few, as your eyes see us— ³that the LORD your God may show us the way we should go, and the thing that we should do." ⁴Jeremiah the prophet said to them, "I have heard you. Behold, I will pray to the LORD your God according to your request, and whatever the LORD answers you I will tell you. I will keep nothing back from you." ⁵Then they said to Jeremiah, "May the LORD be a true and faithful witness against us if we do not act according to all the word with which the Lord your God sends you to us. ⁶Whether it is good or bad, we will obey the voice of the LORD our God to whom we are sending you, that it may be well with us when we obey the voice of the LORD our God."

⁷At the end of ten days the word of the LORD came to Jeremiah. ⁸Then he summoned Johanan the son of Kareah and all the commanders of the forces who were with him, and all the people from the least to the greatest, ⁹and said to them, "Thus says the LORD, the God of Israel, to whom you sent me to present your plea for mercy before him: ¹⁰If you will remain in this land, then I will build you up and not pull you down; I will plant you, and not pluck you up; for I relent of the disaster that I did to you. ¹¹Do not fear the king of Babylon, of whom you are afraid. Do not fear him, declares the LORD, for I am with you, to save you and to deliver you from his hand. ¹²I will grant you mercy, that he may have mercy on you and let you remain in your own land. ¹³But if you say, 'We will not remain in this land,' disobeying the voice of the LORD your God ¹⁴and saying, 'No, we will go to the land of Egypt, where we shall not see war or hear the sound of the trumpet or be hungry for bread, and we will dwell there,' ¹⁵then hear the word of the LORD, O remnant of Judah. Thus says the LORD of hosts, the God of Israel: If you set your faces to enter Egypt and go to live there, ¹⁶then the sword that you fear shall overtake you there in the land of Egypt, and the famine of which you are afraid shall follow close after you to Egypt, and there you shall die. ¹⁷All the men who set their faces to go to Egypt to live there shall die by the sword, by famine, and by pestilence. They shall have no remnant or survivor from the disaster that I will bring upon them.

¹⁸"For thus says the LORD of hosts, the God of Israel: As my anger and my wrath were poured out on the inhabitants of Jerusalem, so my wrath will be poured out on you when you go to Egypt. You shall become an execration, a horror, a curse, and a taunt. You shall see this place no more. ¹⁹The Lord has said to you, O remnant of Judah, 'Do not go to Egypt.' Know for a certainty that I have warned you this day ²⁰that you have gone astray at the cost of your lives. For you sent me to the LORD your God, saying, 'Pray for us to the LORD our God, and whatever the LORD our God says, declare to us and we will do it.' ²¹And I have this day declared it to you, but you have not obeyed the voice of the LORD your God in anything that he sent me to tell you. ²²Now therefore know for a certainty that you shall die by the sword, by famine, and by pestilence in the place where you desire to go to live."

43 When Jeremiah finished speaking to all the people all these words of the LORD their God, with which the Lord their God had sent him to them, ²Azariah the son of Hoshaiah and Johanan the son of Kareah and all the insolent men said to Jeremiah, "You are telling a lie. The Lord our God did not send you to say, 'Do not go to Egypt to live there,' ³but Baruch the son of Neriah has set you against us, to deliver us into the hand of the Chaldeans, that they may kill us or take us into exile in Babylon." ⁴So Johanan the son of Kareah and all the commanders of the forces and all the people did not obey the voice of the LORD, to remain in the land of

Judah. ⁵But Johanan the son of Kareah and all the commanders of the forces took all the remnant of Judah who had returned to live in the land of Judah from all the nations to which they had been driven— ⁶the men, the women, the children, the princesses, and every person whom Nebuzaradan the captain of the guard had left with Gedaliah the son of Ahikam, son of Shaphan; also Jeremiah the prophet and Baruch the son of Neriah. ⁷And they came into the land of Egypt, for they did not obey the voice of the LORD. And they arrived at Tahpanhes.

⁸Then the word of the LORD came to Jeremiah in Tahpanhes: ⁹"Take in your hands large stones and hide them in the mortar in the pavement that is at the entrance to Pharaoh's palace in Tahpanhes, in the sight of the men of Judah, ¹⁰and say to them, 'Thus says the LORD of hosts, the God of Israel: Behold, I will send and take Nebuchadnezzar the king of Babylon, my servant, and I will set his throne above these stones that I have hidden, and he will spread his royal canopy over them. ¹¹He shall come and strike the land of Egypt, giving over to the pestilence those who are doomed to the pestilence, to captivity those who are doomed to captivity, and to the sword those who are doomed to the sword. ¹²I shall kindle a fire in the temples of the gods of Egypt, and he shall burn them and carry them away captive. And he shall clean the land of Egypt as a shepherd cleans his cloak of vermin, and he shall go away from there in peace. ¹³He shall break the obelisks of Heliopolis, which is in the land of Egypt, and the temples of the gods of Egypt he shall burn with fire.'"

OVERVIEW: These chapters prompt commentators and preachers to consider the nature of godly prayer and the perseverance required in ministry. A proper orientation in prayer assumes complete submission to the will of God. The remnant of Jews under Johanan seek Jeremiah's intercession, but reject the divine answer when it fails to affirm their preferences. Yet again Jeremiah must endure still more suffering and failure: the rejection of his prayerful reply, attacks on his colleague Baruch, and his abduction and transport to Egypt—the destination that was to be avoided at all costs. With utter transparency Jeremiah illustrates the difficulties of all who minister to the people of God and the steady determination necessary to reform church and society. In addition, the faithful are directed to trust in God alone, who makes a place home and protects it for his people. To go elsewhere is to be exposed to judgment, suffering, and lethal idolatry.

42:1-22 Warning Against Going to Egypt

THE PRIESTLY JEREMIAH. PHILIPP MELANCH-THON: Let us now look at the prophet himself. Not only does he teach, foretell the exile, scare, and scold the ungodly, and then console the godly and direct them with his own counsel, but he also prays frequently for the people and thus performs all the duties of the priestly office. His prayers contain passionate complaints and manifest a keen awareness of divine wrath. THE LESSONS OF JEREMIAH'S PROPHECY.[1]

JEREMIAH'S PRAYER AND GOD'S ANSWER. JOHN MAYER: This whole chapter and the next are one continuous history, describing how Johanan and the other captains addressed Jeremiah. They desired him to pray for them and to consult with the Lord. Even as they called God to witness, so they also promised to embrace whatever answer they received. They would act on God's answer whether it pleased or displeased them, whether for good or evil. But once Jeremiah had prayed, he received an answer within ten days that the Lord promised to protect them if they should continue in their own land and not go into Egypt. God would incline Nebuchadnezzar's heart to favor them, even after the cruelty exercised against the governor Nebuchadnezzar had set up and the slain Chaldean guards that had been left

---

[1]Melanchthon, "Lessons," 65.

to guard them. But if they went to Egypt, a terrible destruction would befall the Jews. COMMENTARY ON JEREMIAH 42.[2]

EGYPT IS NOT GOD'S WILL. JOHANNES BUGENHAGEN: See the hypocrisy of the unbelieving people here and their clear impiety in the following chapter. When in need they put their trust not in God but in Egypt and thus against the first commandment. Chapter 30 of Isaiah condemns such impiety, and as chapter 31 says, "The Egyptian is a man, and not God, their horses are flesh, and not spirit." And the Lord does not want them to return to Egypt; Deuteronomy 17. Truly there was never a greater impiety than among this remnant left in the land of Judah, who do not repent even after having been compelled by God. Instead they add a more severe contempt to their prior sins. COMMENTARY ON JEREMIAH 42 AND 43.[3]

THE IDOLATRY OF FALSE PETITIONS TO GOD. JOHN KNOX: As enemies of God the chief priests and false prophets required that the king treat Jeremiah in evil ways. Sometimes he was cast into prison, sometimes he was judged and condemned to die. The most willful blindness of wicked idolaters is written and recited in the same prophet Jeremiah.

After the city of Jerusalem was burned and destroyed, the king was led away as a prisoner, his son and chief nobles were slain, and the whole vengeance of God was poured out on the disobedient. Yet a remnant was left in the land to occupy and possess it. They called upon the prophet Jeremiah to know the will and pleasure of God for them; whether they should remain still in the land of Judea, as was appointed by the Chaldeans, or if they should depart and fly away to Egypt. To give them certainty about their doubt, they desired that the prophet pray for them to God. Jeremiah agreed to grant their petition and promised to keep nothing back from them, which the Lord would open unto him. The people, in a similar manner,

took God as record keeper and witness; they made a solemn vow to obey whatever answer the Lord gave to Jeremiah.

Thus the prophet, by inspiration of the Spirit of God, and assured by revelation and knowledge of his will, commanded them "to remain in the land" in which they resided. Jeremiah also promised them that "God would plant them," and that he would repent of all the plagues that he had brought upon them, and that he would be with them to deliver them from the hands of the king of Babylon. On the contrary, if they would not obey the voice of the Lord, but would, against his command, go to Egypt thinking that there they would live in rest and abundance—without any fear of war and lack of sustenance—then the very plagues that they feared would come upon them and take them; for (the prophet says) it shall come to pass that all who stubbornly go to Egypt and remain there shall die either by sword, hunger, or pestilence. But when the prophet of God had declared this clear sentence and will of God and asked them for their answer, they gave their answer; "You are speaking a lie. . . ." Thus they refused the counsel of God, and followed their own fantasies. ADMONITION TO THE PROFESSORS OF GOD'S TRUTH IN ENGLAND.[4]

FALSELY SEEKING THE WILL OF GOD. JOHANNES OECOLAMPADIUS: It is barely possible for the ugliness of human infirmity and the deceit of hidden hypocrisy to be more clearly depicted, which they call the vanity of free will. All people are presently hanging, as it were, on the will of God, which they would obey if only they would examine it thoroughly. Nevertheless, it was not in their heart. For not only were they not able to offer such obedience, but they were also unable to wish to attempt any particular virtues.

Many people today are precisely similar to them, people who seek councils to be correctly established concerning religion from the doctors of spiritual things. Before they hear what is profitable to take place and what piety demands, they freely promise

---

[2]Mayer, *A Commentary*, 455-56*.
[3]Bugenhagen, *In Ieremiam*, 5N2v; citing Is 30:1-7; 31:3; Deut 17:16.
[4]Knox, *Works*, 3:306-7*.

everything. But when they have heard the oracle of the Spirit, they depart sadly; just as with the rich young man in the Gospels. First, such people define what they will do, and pretend some honest motive, and then they seek that they may know the will of God—if perchance they are able to hear any answer that God may give at least in part to their affected maxims. And so it is plain to see here. The Egyptian was laughing on account of the richness of his seat and the power of his kingdom, which feared nothing from the Chaldean. And the Holy Land was uneasy due to the danger of barrenness and hostile incursions, which they feared in their heart. But they knew often from the prophets and not only from Moses that they were not to go to that very place, of Egypt. Though Abraham and Jacob were allowed to go down there, nevertheless, their posterity was most terribly caught up there on account of their communion with idolatry; therefore they were prohibited by law from returning there. Thus these unbelievers feigned a respectable cause, namely, their fear of the Babylonians, who they reckoned would be implacable because of the death of Gedaliah and the Babylonian soldiers. So they turned to prayer, begging that the prophet might intercede on their behalf, so that, of course, as they went down to Egypt of their own free will they might be said to have obeyed the command of God. Who would not say that the princes and people were begging from the heart—from the greatest to the least in birth—when he considers their words? But subsequent history uncovers their foul hypocrisy. COMMENTARY ON JEREMIAH 42.[5]

DECEPTION AND TRUTH IN THE FAITH.

HULDRYCH ZWINGLI: "They said to Jeremiah, 'The Lord be a witness against us.'" This is the speech of believers, at least as the outer appearance goes. But the attitude here is godless. They are lying; what they promise they will not hold themselves to. So today the Anabaptists and all the sectarians confess with their mouths that they are enthusiastic about

keeping to things, but they do not have God in their hearts. Whoever preaches God, the saints, and whatever is godly does it more magnificently than the papists. They do not really accomplish any of this in their hypocrisy.

So it is that a lie is like a piece of defective cloth or item. On the outside it has a pleasant look, yes, a beautiful appearance. But the truth is a pleasant and fine thing—unchangeable, unbreakable, whole, and bold. You adhere to it steadfastly and firmly. Christ, the apostles, the philosophers: all of them offered it. SERMON ON JEREMIAH 42:5.[6]

THE MANY SINS OF THE REMAINING PEOPLE.

NIKOLAUS SELNECKER: Here the people together commit many sins. First, they do not trust God's help, but rely on human power; they are unbelievers and unstable. Second, they are afraid when they should not be afraid; for the king of Babylon had made promises and pledges to Jeremiah and the remaining people that they should remain securely in the land. But the godless have no peace. They are afraid of a rustling leaf. Third, they committed themselves to flee to Egypt, and they thought that they would settle there—far enough from the Babylonians. But God through Moses had prohibited any king from leading the people to Egypt again. Fourth, they act like they want to obey the word and will of God, and they do such things from sanctimonious hypocrisy when in crisis. Fifth, they make a false oath, but are unfaithful and perjurers. So after ten days the prophet Jeremiah received an answer from God the Lord and Jeremiah had revealed it to them: they should not move to Egypt, but remain in the land. But if they want to move to Egypt, they will find there what they fled from in Judea: the same sword, famine, and disease will kill them. The people did not want to hear this and were grieved; so they followed their own pigheadedness and darkness, as the next chapter shows.

Moreover, note that God waited until after ten days to answer Jeremiah; for God often delays his answer, so that we can practice our faith and

---

[5] Oecolampadius, *In Hieremiam*, 3:2C4r-v; citing Mt 19:22; Mk 10:22; Deut 17:16.

[6] Zwingli, *Predigten*, 287-88.

prayers and thereby become stronger. As David says in Psalm 40, I waited for the Lord and he inclined to me and heard my cry." THE WHOLE PROPHET JEREMIAH 42:5-22.[7]

JEREMIAH AND INTERCESSORY PRAYER. JOHANNES OECOLAMPADIUS: The prophet prayed for ten days. Because he promised that he would pray, it is certain that the man of good faith did pray. One can hardly doubt that he prayed with great fervor for the people. Indeed, it is necessary to persevere in prayer, and not stop, so that we may triumph even against wickedness. Finally, Jeremiah the intercessor for the people received the Word of God, which he offered to all the people, just as he was asked by all, so that no one might have an excuse. Meanwhile, in those days, because Jeremiah's utterance was delayed, great impatience appeared among those who were expecting an answer. COMMENTARY ON JEREMIAH 42:7.[8]

GOD PROMISES AND GOD REPENTS. JOHN CALVIN: The metaphors here used occur often in Scripture. God is said to "build up" people when he confirms them in a settled state; and in the same sense he is said to "plant" them. This . . . is especially evident in Psalm 44, where God is said to have "planted" in the land of Canaan the people he brought back from Egypt. He then promised that the condition of the people would be secure and safe and perpetual, if only they did not change their place. When he adds, I will "not pull down nor pluck up," he follows what is done commonly in Hebrew. Neither the Latins nor the Greeks speak in this manner; but negatives of this kind in Hebrew are confirmations, as though the prophet had said, "God will so plant you that your root will remain. There will be no danger of being plucked up when you have been planted by God's hand; nor will he suffer you to be subverted or pulled down when he has built you up by his own hand. . . .'"

It afterward follows, "For I repent of the evil that I have brought on you." The verb, *nuchem*, sometimes means to repent, and often to comfort; but the former sense comports better with this passage, that God repented of the evil. If, however, we prefer this rendering, "For I have received comfort," then the meaning would be, "I am satisfied with the punishment with which I have visited your sins"; for they to whom satisfaction is given are said to receive comfort. As then God was content with the punishment he had inflicted on the Jews, the words may be rendered thus: "For I have received satisfaction from the evil," or "I am satisfied with the evil," etc. The other meaning, however, is more generally taken, that God repented of the evil. . . .

We now, then, perceive what is meant by the reason here given, that the Jews were not to fear if they dwelt in the land, because God had sufficiently chastised them, and that he was so pacified that he would not further pursue them with severity. COMMENTARY ON JEREMIAH 42:10.[9]

GOD WILL BUILD UP A PEOPLE. JOHANNES OECOLAMPADIUS: "The will of the Lord is that you remain in the land of Canaan, in which he has taken care that you should be left behind, nor has he allowed you to be led from it. But if you will remain he promises excellent things; in a brief time you will be multiplied into a great people. Nor is there any reason for which you should fear the wrath either of God or of Babylon; for he himself has been appeased; and your enemy, what will he be able to do against God that he should threaten dire things? He says, however, that you must not only dwell but also build: you will inhabit by inhabiting, for he will require perfect obedience, so that you will not only inhabit the land with your body, but also assume a mind of staying."

A much greater promise and much more lavish hope is placed before us, we who persevere in our known religion, which emerges from the knowledge of Jesus Christ our Lord, and in this is our

---

[7]Selnecker, *Der gantze Prophet Jeremias*, 2O1v; citing Is 48:22; Jer 41:17; Deut 17:16; Ps 40:1-2.
[8]Oecolampadius, *In Hieremiam*, 3:2D1v.

[9]CTS 20:488-90* (CO 39:225-26); citing Ps 44:2.

spiritual worship. From there indeed we too will undoubtedly be built up and multiplied while growing in number and merit. To build up and not destroy is to advance in such complete dignity, to help the burdened joyfully—lest one be able to fall upon any repentance of works, as happens among those touched by that misfortune, where those things that were built up become displeasing and are again destroyed. Therefore, God wants to say, thus your obedience will be pleasing to me. COMMENTARY ON JEREMIAH 42:10.[10]

JEREMIAH TRIES TO PERSUADE THE PEOPLE.

KONRAD PELLIKAN: In many words Jeremiah speaks to urge them from every angle to remain in the paternal inheritance that was granted to them and not enter into Egypt. He did this by threatening the most bitter things, if they persisted in going: namely, war, and the plundering sword, famine, death, expulsion, and every form of evil. The faithful prophet omits nothing that pertains to the salvation of the nation. He also tries to move them by a fresh and horrible example, so that they would not doubt his words, and so that they would not, instructed by their own evil, despise the truth of God, and so that they may know and perceive what they had suffered for their disobedience, namely, the destruction of Jerusalem, because they refused to agree to the words of the prophet. Now let them not doubt that in Egypt they would all have abuse, horror, humiliation, and disgrace, and that they would be destroyed everywhere, and these things they would never see in their homeland. COMMENTARY ON JEREMIAH 42:15-18.[11]

IGNITING DIVINE ANGER. JOHANNES OECOLAMPADIUS:

At once they declared themselves to be disobedient: because the prophet did not respond according to their longing, so they were censured by a new and more severe oration from the prophet. But he placed before them the example of the destruction of Jerusalem. "Surely you have learned how serious it is to aggravate the Lord." He was furious at the city of Jerusalem because of their sins. His anger was molten and diffuse, just as smiths melt lead in a fire and render it malleable.... Lead that is made liquid and pourable splatters widely and burns noxiously. Thus, he says, the Lord will be even more enraged against you, if you enter Egypt. COMMENTARY ON JEREMIAH 42:18.[12]

NO ONE COULD HAVE BEEN MORE PERSUASIVE. KONRAD PELLIKAN:

One could not devise and put forward a more emphatic exhortation than Jeremiah the prophet spoke to the people. He left no stone unturned in his attempt to persuade: he testified that everything he said to the remnant of Judah was by the Lord's command: that they should not go into Egypt, and that they would be in every way guilty if they invited all of these evil things upon themselves in their disobedience, especially since they had promised before to be obedient and now would be hardly ready to obey. Indeed, even as Jeremiah was then speaking, he saw this would happen by the signs in their faces and the gestures of their bodies. He was not otherwise ignorant of their stubbornness. Therefore, he pressed them by repeating himself and insisted with every fiber of his being, but in vain. Indeed, they ought to have been an example of disobedience to the Word of God, just as their fathers were, to all times and nations. Yet at some time they were going to truly turn to the God of Israel, as this day also testifies. COMMENTARY ON JEREMIAH 42:19-22.[13]

43:1-13 Jeremiah Taken to Egypt

REPENT AND TRUST THE LORD IN DANGEROUS TIMES. JOHANN PAPPUS:

The beginning of this chapter describes the disobedience of the remaining Jewish people, who migrated to Egypt against the express command of the Lord. At the end of the chapter, moreover, the prophet threatens them with severe punishments not only in words

---

[10]Oecolampadius, *In Hieremiam*, 3:2D1v-2D2r. [11]Pellikan, *Commentaria Bibliorum*, 3:2Y6r.

[12]Oecolampadius, *In Hieremiam*, 3:2D3r. [13]Pellikan, *Commentaria Bibliorum*, 3:2Y6r.

but also in a visible symbol. And so the first part of the chapter describes a stubbornness and obstinacy of our flesh or our reason against God, which we ought especially to examine. Indeed, the leaders of this remnant were at one with the rabble itself, when they consulted the prophet, promised and even vowed that they would submit to the Word of God that they were going to hear from the prophet. Nevertheless, because the prophet advised and commanded something different from what they desired, for that reason they disregarded all fear of the Lord and broke faith in their vow and rather obeyed their own counsel.

We see, therefore, how hard it is in matters that are difficult and joined with danger to ignore the counsels of our depraved reason and to resist our corrupt passions. For this reason, without pausing, let us seek to be ruled and governed by the Lord, lest we throw ourselves into dangers that are not necessary because of the blind and foolish counsel of reason.

In the other part of the chapter we ought to consider the just judgment of the Lord: how he typically snatches away from us those very things in which we trust more than we ought to, so that we learn to put all hope and trust in him alone. The Jews migrated to Egypt for this reason, so that in that kingdom they might be more secure from the tyranny of the Babylonians. Meanwhile, they were not concerned about earnest repentance. Therefore, the Lord warned them that the Egyptians themselves would also be entangled in the same calamities and that the Egyptians were going to come under the sway of the Chaldeans. Indeed, the prophet is ordered to signify this by concealing stones in a certain place, in which the victorious Babylonian would place his imperial throne. Thus there is no sufficiently secure defense against these impending calamities, apart from true repentance. But for those impious people who wish to avoid the just punishments for their sins, it often happens as the proverb says, "He who wants to avoid Charybdis falls into the Scylla." On All the Prophets, Jeremiah 43.[14]

How Sin Multiplies. JOHANNES OECOLAMPADIUS: See how sin is increased by steps. Not only did they not keep what they had promised, but having despised the word they also accused the prophet of a lie, as if he said something to gain the favor of Baruch his disciple; and this when the prophet wanted to save them from ruin. In turn they called him a traitor and destroyer of the nation. Thus presently he shows that they did not hear the voice of God. They went away from the oracle in the same way that they had established it, and gathered the prophets and others by force so that they might as one depart. And he whom the king of Babylon had sent away free, they dragged unwilling after themselves like a slave. However, this occurred by a singular dispensation of providence, so that the prophet immediately showed that they were inexcusable, by convicting them of their sin. COMMENTARY ON JEREMIAH 43.[15]

False Accusations in God's Service. JOHN CALVIN: They afterward throw the blame on Baruch, who had been the prophet's faithful servant. As they could not find out any reason why Jeremiah should speak falsely, they turned their fury against Baruch. . . . They charged Baruch with a very great crime, that he wished to betray them to the Chaldeans, and then to expose them to slaughter, and to deliver them that they might be driven into exile. All this would have been the greatest cruelty. But then if we consider what sort of man Baruch had been, and how innocently he had conducted himself, how he had endangered his life in defending the true worship of God and prophetic doctrine, there was surely no reason for loading him with so great an accusation.

But we see that God's servants have always been exposed to extreme accusations, even when they have exhibited the greatest integrity. If then, in our time, we hear of evil reports, after having labored to act uprightly, it ought not to appear to us a hard or new thing to bear them with patience. We must,

---

[14]Pappus, *In Omnes Prophetas*, 116v.   [15]Oecolampadius, *In Hieremiam*, 3:2D3v.

indeed, do what we can to stop the mouths of the malevolent and the wicked; nor ought we to give occasion, as Paul admonishes us, to the malignant. But when we have done our duty faithfully, if yet dogs bark at us, if we be loaded with accusations and crimes, let us learn patiently to endure them. COMMENTARY ON JEREMIAH 43:3.[16]

WHY DID JEREMIAH GO TO EGYPT? JOHANNES BRENZ: If it was unjust and against the Word of God to depart for Egypt, then why does Jeremiah depart with everyone else? Should he have felt compelled? Indeed, isn't it the case that no one, even if they are compelled, ought to act against the law of God, and one should sooner give up their life than do ungodly things or assent to impiety? I answer: going to Egypt is a moderate act, not a prohibited one. For Abraham departed for Egypt, as did Jacob. Christ also fled to Egypt. But it is impious and against the Word of God to seek allies in Egypt and to trust Egypt as a place safe from the king of Babylon. In the same way, Deuteronomy 17 does not prohibit a king from having many horses where there is no need, but it does prohibit placing trust in horses. For we read that David and Solomon had many horses. Therefore, the fact that the Jews departed for Egypt was indicative of impiety and doubt in the Word of God. When this impiety is removed, the work remains free. Therefore, the prophet is compelled to depart along with everyone else, but he is not compelled to consent to their impiety and lack of faith, which he resisted even to death. Indeed, they say that he was stoned by his own people near Tahpanhes. Truly, the fact that Jeremiah allows himself to be coerced and does suffer harm in this free work is a sign of love, which suffers everything, and endures everything. In fact, faith never permits one to do evil things, but both faith and love do wish to suffer evil things for the good. ANNOTATIONS ON JEREMIAH 43:6.[17]

DIVINE MERCY AND HARD HEARTS. JOHANNES OECOLAMPADIUS: Here you see that providence is divine, because the disobedient and fugitive Jews took Jeremiah with them into Egypt, whereby it happened that Jeremiah, who openly reproached their unbelief from God, at the same time showed that the astonishing mercy of the God who did not yet desert his people who were rebellious by so many names. And so still even in Egypt he keeps offering mercy, and presents it through the prophet, to those who deserve every punishment. Otherwise he adds no consolation, no promise, but he only threatens. Indeed, they were stubborn and sinning nearly against the Holy Spirit. Certainly in quality there were those among them who fell, never to be called back, when the exiled were restored from Babylon to Judea. For which reason they are compared to something made of stone because of the hardness of their obstinacy in evil things. The act of Moses squares with this, who carried the law written on stone tablets since he had to deal with stones, that is, with human hearts. We are all stumps and stones against the Word of God granted to us. As John says, "God is able to make sons of Abraham from such stones," and fully make and grant a spirit of repentance. COMMENTARY ON JEREMIAH 43:8.[18]

SIGNS AND OBJECTS COMMUNICATE THE PROPHECY. JUAN DE MALDONADO: You are to build over them, and line them with mud, as if building a throne from them. By this you will signify that it will happen that the king of Babylon, once Egypt is occupied, will place his throne in Tahpanhes. Or this could be interpreted as, you shall hide them under the ground, as if laying the foundation for some building. Indeed at this point Jeremiah sees that he is not commanded to use just any kind of stones, but big ones, such as are customarily placed at the very bottom of a foundation. So I interpret it as suits the sense of the prophecy. For because the Jews did not believe the words of Jeremiah, God ordered him to use not

---

[16]CTS 20:506* (CO 39:237-38); citing 1 Tim 5:14.
[17]Brenz, *Annotationes in Jeremiam*, 937; citing Deut 17:16; Gen 12:10; 46:3; Mt 2:13-15; 2 Sam 8:4; 1 Kings 4:26.

[18]Oecolampadius, *In Hieremiam*, 3:2D4r; citing Mt 3:9; Lk 3:8.

only words, but also things themselves to announce to them the coming calamity. We have frequently noted above that this typically happens. Thus Jeremiah was ordered to break an earthen jar before the eyes of the Jews, to carry chains suspended from his neck, and to buy a field from Hanamel. So in this passage he is ordered to cover over large stones, or hide them under the earth, as if laying the foundation of the palace that Nebuchadnezzar was going to build in Tahpanhes. COMMENTARY ON THE PROPHETS, JEREMIAH 43:9-10.[19]

THE TRUE GOD AND THE IDOLS OF EGYPT.
HEINRICH BULLINGER: There follows an evil far more grave than these: "I will ignite," he says, "a fire in the dwellings of the gods," etc. Indeed, it seems that it would be intolerable for idolaters, if they hear that some disgrace is going to be imposed on their gods and images. Nevertheless, God says through Jeremiah that he will burn the temples of the Egyptians—inferring also their gold and silver gods—and lead them away captive to Babylon. That is, God will see to it that the Babylonians take them way. Obviously gods are not able to be either captured or burned up, but the images of the gods can be captured, led away, and burned up. Symbols take on the names of the things that are signified. And however much idolaters recognize that no evil can be inflicted on the gods, and that gods do not feel what their idols experience, nevertheless they are no less indignant if someone says that their gods are being burned or captured. In this matter they are convicted of a most grievous error. If indeed they attribute nothing to the images other than what they attribute to wood and stone, why do they lament when the same thing happens to their idols that happens to wood and stone? Or does it typically turn out differently? But they do lament: therefore they attribute more to their images than they wish to seem to attribute. Thus the Lord has willed and commanded that we not portray him with any image, certainly with the result that God

cannot be said to have been burned up or led away captive. Therefore, those who depict God with visible things have made it so that it can be said, by those infidels as they plunder our images, that our God and our deities have themselves been pillaged.

Since truly the Egyptians and Jews supposed and even boasted that Egypt was unconquerable, because it was protected by trenches and equipped with cavalry and treasures, which are the strength of war, the prophet adds that Nebuchadnezzar would conquer them without difficulty, and he would plunder the Egyptians and the whole kingdom. Jeremiah illustrated this with a parable. He says that just as a shepherd who is about to move picks up his cloak and puts it over his shoulder, and then departs—laboring, I say, under no heavy difficulty—so shall Nebuchadnezzar clothe himself with Egypt, just like a cloak. That is, he will pack up all of Egypt as his booty, and he will return unharmed to his Babylonian homeland. If he can do this unharmed, then the power of Egypt to defend its land is impotent. Thus this universal dogma can be understood: no fortifications, wealth, or military strength is able to accomplish even the smallest thing when God is angry. Therefore, people protect their homeland more effectively with the fear and observance of God than with military preparations. (Although even military preparation, if it is moderate and joined with the fear of God, hardly ought to be spurned.)

Finally, Jeremiah repeats again that both the sanctuaries of the gods and the gods alike will be burned up and to that extent the Egyptian religion would be crushed. Among others he names the dwelling of the sun god . . . or the temple of Osiris or Serapis, which was greatly celebrated by the Egyptians and that itself would be destroyed. But why should we wonder at this, when see all the gods and all the idols throughout the whole world collapse before the true preaching of the gospel? Therefore there is no doubt that Jeremiah commended true religion to the Jews, and even to all peoples, and he condemned false religion as fallen and unreal. SERMON ON JEREMIAH 43:12-13.[20]

---

[19]Maldonado, *Commentarii in Prophetas*, 181; citing Jer 19:10; 27:2; 32:6-44.

[20]Bullinger, *Conciones*, 243r-v.

JEREMIAH 44:1-30
JUDGMENT FOR IDOLATRY

¹*The word that came to Jeremiah concerning all the Judeans who lived in the land of Egypt, at Migdol, at Tahpanhes, at Memphis, and in the land of Pathros,* ²*"Thus says the* Lord *of hosts, the God of Israel: You have seen all the disaster that I brought upon Jerusalem and upon all the cities of Judah. Behold, this day they are a desolation, and no one dwells in them,* ³*because of the evil that they committed, provoking me to anger, in that they went to make offerings and serve other gods that they knew not, neither they, nor you, nor your fathers.* ⁴*Yet I persistently sent to you all my servants the prophets, saying, 'Oh, do not do this abomination that I hate!'* ⁵*But they did not listen or incline their ear, to turn from their evil and make no offerings to other gods.* ⁶*Therefore my wrath and my anger were poured out and kindled in the cities of Judah and in the streets of Jerusalem, and they became a waste and a desolation, as at this day.* ⁷*And now thus says the* Lord *God of hosts, the God of Israel: Why do you commit this great evil against yourselves, to cut off from you man and woman, infant and child, from the midst of Judah, leaving you no remnant?* ⁸*Why do you provoke me to anger with the works of your hands, making offerings to other gods in the land of Egypt where you have come to live, so that you may be cut off and become a curse and a taunt among all the nations of the earth?* ⁹*Have you forgotten the evil of your fathers, the evil of the kings of Judah, the evil of their*ᵃ *wives, your own evil, and the evil of your wives, which they committed in the land of Judah and in the streets of Jerusalem?* ¹⁰*They have not humbled themselves even to this day, nor have they feared, nor walked in my law and my statutes that I set before you and before your fathers.*

¹¹*"Therefore thus says the* Lord *of hosts, the God of Israel: Behold, I will set my face against you for harm, to cut off all Judah.* ¹²*I will take the remnant of Judah who have set their faces to come to the land of Egypt to live, and they shall all be consumed. In the land of Egypt they shall fall; by the sword and by*

famine they shall be consumed. From the least to the greatest, they shall die by the sword and by famine, and they shall become an oath, a horror, a curse, and a taunt.* ¹³*I will punish those who dwell in the land of Egypt, as I have punished Jerusalem, with the sword, with famine, and with pestilence,* ¹⁴*so that none of the remnant of Judah who have come to live in the land of Egypt shall escape or survive or return to the land of Judah, to which they desire to return to dwell there. For they shall not return, except some fugitives."*

¹⁵*Then all the men who knew that their wives had made offerings to other gods, and all the women who stood by, a great assembly, all the people who lived in Pathros in the land of Egypt, answered Jeremiah:* ¹⁶*"As for the word that you have spoken to us in the name of the* Lord, *we will not listen to you.* ¹⁷*But we will do everything that we have vowed, make offerings to the queen of heaven and pour out drink offerings to her, as we did, both we and our fathers, our kings and our officials, in the cities of Judah and in the streets of Jerusalem. For then we had plenty of food, and prospered, and saw no disaster.* ¹⁸*But since we left off making offerings to the queen of heaven and pouring out drink offerings to her, we have lacked everything and have been consumed by the sword and by famine."* ¹⁹*And the women said,*ᵇ *"When we made offerings to the queen of heaven and poured out drink offerings to her, was it without our husbands' approval that we made cakes for her bearing her image and poured out drink offerings to her?"*

²⁰*Then Jeremiah said to all the people, men and women, all the people who had given him this answer:* ²¹*"As for the offerings that you offered in the cities of Judah and in the streets of Jerusalem, you and your fathers, your kings and your officials, and the people of the land, did not the* Lord *remember them? Did it not come into his mind?* ²²*The* Lord *could no longer bear your evil deeds and the abominations that you committed. Therefore your land has become a desolation and a waste and a*

curse, without inhabitant, as it is this day. ²³It is because you made offerings and because you sinned against the LORD and did not obey the voice of the LORD or walk in his law and in his statutes and in his testimonies that this disaster has happened to you, as at this day."

²⁴Jeremiah said to all the people and all the women, "Hear the word of the LORD, all you of Judah who are in the land of Egypt. ²⁵Thus says the LORD of hosts, the God of Israel: You and your wives have declared with your mouths, and have fulfilled it with your hands, saying, 'We will surely perform our vows that we have made, to make offerings to the queen of heaven and to pour out drink offerings to her.' Then confirm your vows and perform your vows! ²⁶Therefore hear the word of the LORD, all you of Judah who dwell in the land of Egypt: Behold, I have sworn by my great name, says the LORD, that my name shall no more be invoked

by the mouth of any man of Judah in all the land of Egypt, saying, 'As the LORD God lives.' ²⁷Behold, I am watching over them for disaster and not for good. All the men of Judah who are in the land of Egypt shall be consumed by the sword and by famine, until there is an end of them. ²⁸And those who escape the sword shall return from the land of Egypt to the land of Judah, few in number; and all the remnant of Judah, who came to the land of Egypt to live, shall know whose word will stand, mine or theirs. ²⁹This shall be the sign to you, declares the LORD, that I will punish you in this place, in order that you may know that my words will surely stand against you for harm: ³⁰Thus says the LORD, Behold, I will give Pharaoh Hophra king of Egypt into the hand of his enemies and into the hand of those who seek his life, as I gave Zedekiah king of Judah into the hand of Nebuchadnezzar king of Babylon, who was his enemy and sought his life."

a Hebrew *his*   b Compare Syriac; Hebrew lacks *And the women said*

OVERVIEW: Johanan and the Jewish remnant openly and swiftly rejected God's command to remain in Judea; their departure for Egypt also marked a return to open idolatry. Protestant commentators found parallels in their own time to be telling and chilling. As the Jews in Egypt would ignore Jeremiah's prophecy and choose to worship heavenly deities, including the queen of heaven, so the European faithful might be tempted to return to the papacy, worship saints and relics, and elevate Mary to heavenly monarchy; they might be seduced to reinstate the monastic vows they had formerly abandoned. Peoples and places might forsake Protestantism and "return to Egypt."

44:1-14 Persistent Idolatry

IDOLATRY IN EGYPT. THE ENGLISH ANNOTATIONS: This is a second sermon or message that the prophet brought from God to reprove and threaten the Jewish people in Egypt, now not so much due to their disobedience in leaving their own land and

journeying to Egypt against God's command, but because of the conspicuous and abominable idolatry that they committed when they settled in various parts of Egypt. The stubborn behavior of the people shows in their refusal to give any heed to the message and their stiff resolution to persist in their idolatry. ANNOTATIONS ON JEREMIAH 44.[1]

THE DANGERS OF LIFE IN EGYPT. JOHANNES OECOLAMPADIUS: From here it is evident how much damage it brings to attempt anything against the sure Word of God. Indeed, when they had gone into Egypt, even though the Lord forbade it through the prophet, they relapsed into every impiety in which they had formerly engaged. And you see the reason why the Lord so earnestly forbade them to dwell in Egypt; lest they, of course, become companions of the sinful Egyptians. In fact, they left the true worship of God and immediately were made idolaters, and others permitted this to their wives. COMMENTARY ON JEREMIAH 44.[2]

---

[1]Downame, ed., *Annotations*, 9Z2v*.
[2]Oecolampadius, *In Hieremiam*, 3:2E2r.

Blasphemy Against the Holy Spirit.

JOHANNES BUGENHAGEN: It is horrible to see in this passage the astounding stubbornness of the impious, which is here described, against the Word of God. In fact, not even having suffered any blows and as soon as they recognized the truth of truth-speaking Jeremiah, they had wanted to return to the word of the Lord. . . . But in fact both the men and the women insolently and impudently defended their idolatry and the cult of Melecheth of heaven, which they translate as "queen of heaven." They acted as if whatever evil things happened had occurred not because of false religion, but because an impious cult had been overlooked. Amazing impiety and blasphemy! So the Romans, whenever there was something of calamity occurring, credited the misfortune they had received to Christ because of the neglect of the religion of their fathers, which was a cult of demons. Against them Augustine wrote in the books of the *City of God* and Paulus Orosius in his own complete history.[†] So also today papist impiety rejects the revelation in the Gospels. . . .

My soul trembles when I hear this; that to their prior sins and contempt for the Word of God, they add blasphemy against the Holy Spirit. I tremble even more when I hear of the dreadful and horrendous oath, judgment, and sentence of God against those who attack the truth they have acknowledged, "Behold I myself judge you through my great name," etc, and as Christ also says, "Whoever has spoken blasphemy against the Holy Spirit will not be received into eternal life, but will be guilty in the eternal judgment because they were saying that he has an unclean spirit." . . .

Therefore, Jeremiah, in the great name of God, preaches the final matter against the despising Jews who are in Egypt, and he brings forth the sentence that all those men with their wives are to perish with the Egyptians by the sword, famine, and pestilence through the king of Babylon—except for those few who might flee from Egypt into Judea, those who perhaps had blasphemed in error and ignorance, as I say concerning the blasphemy of the Spirit. COMMENTARY ON JEREMIAH 44.[3]

An Idolatrous People Immune to God's Warnings.

HEINRICH BULLINGER: In the customary fashion, the title of this sermon[†] is given beforehand, and shows that God the commander orders that Jeremiah should preach to the whole people who were then in Egypt and who had already learned to make sacrifices to foreign gods. This sermon, however, pertains to all those who are like the Jews in offering sacrifices to those who are not their gods. This seems to have been the last sermon of the prophet, since he is said to have been stoned afterward. Therefore it is severe, emphatic, and utterly impassioned. It scolds and announces certain destruction at the same time. As such, it seems to have been like the sermon of Stephen in Acts 7. The sermon is composed of three parts. First, he sadly puts forward the example of their miserable native Jerusalem, whose ashes were in reality still hot, and had not yet stopped smoking. But the people were not moved by this recent and horrible example.

Therefore, why are you amazed if likewise today you see that few are disturbed by many such examples, no matter how dreadful? However, Jeremiah assails them again with significant and obvious examples of what they have suffered and why they suffered such unspeakable things: because of their acceptance of idolatry and foreign cults. In this way they had irritated and exasperated God. But it was most foul to worship as gods those things whose true nature they did not know. Likewise today many things are worshiped whose true natures are unknown. I speak of divinities saints, relics, and other similar things of this type.

Meanwhile, Jeremiah recalls the singular goodness of God who sends prophetic men to call the people back to a better harvest by giving witness and by beseeching. Nevertheless, it is noted

---

[3]Bugenhagen, *In Ieremiam*, 5O3r-v; citing Jer 42:1-3; Mk 3:29-30.
[†]Augustine (d. 430) devotes the first nine books his *City of God* to discrediting paganism in history and the Roman Empire in particular. Around the same time Paulus Orosius (d. c. 420) wrote *The Seven Books of History Against the Pagans*.

that their impiety is unbowed and bold. Indeed, they refused to return to the way, but proceeded into their horribly corrupt desires. To these things Jeremiah suitably adds a just and deserved punishment, because, I say, the fury of God was kindled by images of metal . . . and God's fury raged against those who could would not be corrected. And this is the first part of the sermon.

Then Jeremiah scolds them severely because they were not corrected by such great evils. For they took up Egyptian rites and burned incense and they poured out libations to the sun, moon, and the host of heaven, which they also did before, when they were in their homeland—but they had stopped for a time—and now they took them up again in Egypt. God had prohibited them from going to Egypt by name, obviously so that they would not do such abominable things. But now they themselves—when they had, so to speak, shaken off the bridle—had already broken free and were impiously making sacrifices with their hands full. Now therefore, he says "Why do you commit this great evil that leads to the ruin of your souls? For because of idolatry and your false worship you will all perish." Jeremiah explains these things diligently and amply, in case they might be moved to repentance. But again with repetition he offers the examples of their elders, nor was he ashamed to add both kings and queens to his catalog of idolaters. He adds that now their children were indeed not moved in this way to transgress the law any less, but like their parents they followed the desires of their hearts, having scorned the law. No doubt the leading men were seriously angered at Jeremiah because of his freedom in preaching. But all ministers are ordered to give glory to God and to proclaim the Word of God without pause, taking no account of the ungodly, no matter how powerful and honored they may be. For we have to take our lives in our hands, and, so to speak, throw them down before the ungodly who threaten and rage on all sides. SERMON ON JEREMIAH 44.[4]

LOSING YOUR MEMORY AND LIVING WITH EVIL. JOHANNES OECOLAMPADIUS: While the ashes of your burned homeland have barely gone cold, even so your memory of how much evil you have suffered and why passes away. Where is the temple, the court of the king, where is the city, where are those magnificent walls, where is the people celebrated even by the nations, where are the venerable priests? You know what they did, nay, you know what you yourselves did. Didn't Jezebel and Manasseh and all of them act foully, whose participants you foully are?[†] Now you have not yet been shown yourselves to have truly repented. You have not been cleansed, for because you are relapsing so dangerously, you are by no means sorry. COMMENTARY ON JEREMIAH 44:8.[5]

WHEN GOD SETS HIS FACE AGAINST US. HEINRICH BULLINGER: In third and last part of this initial sermon in chapter 44, Jeremiah recites the most severe threats against the Jews, predicting certain destruction for them because of the idolatry they had taken up. Moreover, just as they had done in their sinning, so God was doing in his punishing. So they "set their face"; that is, they were utterly determined to go down to Egypt, nor would they listen to anyone suggesting sounder counsel: now, therefore, God also places and sets his face against them; I say, he will surely and severely punish them because they are incurable. Jeremiah also describes the time, manner, and reason for their punishment. They will fall, he says, by the sword; they will be destroyed by hunger, and will be taken away by diseases. And this will happen with such violence, that in the future they will become an amazement for all the nations in the world. Then again he adds to these a domestic example, from which he wants them to learn that they will not be spared, but they will certainly pay the penalty—just as surely as the Jerusalemites

---

[4]Bullinger, *Conciones*, 244r-v; citing Jer 43:11-13. [†]Bullinger's title is:

"A very severe sermon of Jeremiah accusing Jews of idolatry, which they are undertaking in Egypt." *Conciones*, 243v.
[5]Oecolampadius, *In Hieremiam*, 3:2E2v. [†]Manasseh, king of Judah (r. 687–642 BC) (2 Kings 21; 2 Chron 33) and Jezebel, wife of King Ahab of Israel (r. 869–850) (1 Kings 18–22; 2 Chron 18).

had paid it. In fact, they themselves greatly desired to return to their homeland of Judea, but the prophet denies that this will be granted to them. And so, let us know that God does not want us to adopt this custom, in which we, for our acknowledged folly, so often wish that our depraved counsels were changed. But we should sooner take care that we not admit those depraved counsels, etc. May the Lord open our minds to us. SERMON ON JEREMIAH 44:11-14.[6]

44:15-30 False Worship

BLASPHEMY AND THE PROPHET'S WORD FROM GOD. JOHANNES BUGENHAGEN: "But we will act according to every word that proceeds from our mouth," that is, "that we teach." "We do not want to receive the Word of God, but to hold fast the teaching and word of our fathers." Thus they blasphemously preferred human doctrines to the Word of God. Rather they condemned the word through human doctrines, as today with our papists, who think that God will not punish their blasphemies in the so-clear light of the gospel, when nevertheless God had proclaimed before through Moses that one is not able to lie for long. Deuteronomy 18: "He who will not hear that prophet, to him I will become an avenger." COMMENTARY ON JEREMIAH 44:17.[7]

THE TEMPTATION TO RETURN TO FORMER WICKEDNESS. MARTIN LUTHER: The masses are complaining now about various misfortunes like high prices, pestilence, wars, etc.; and it is true that these are more numerous and more frequent than they used to be. But in addition to the sins and the great ingratitude, which provoke God to inflict punishments, let the godly remember that this happens as a trial for those who believe. Let them not follow the stupid and ungodly opinion of the masses, who think that these evils can be corrected if the old wickedness of the pope is restored. If

Masses are celebrated for the dead, if indulgences are purchased, and if processions are made around the fields, as the Jews declared about the queen of heaven in Jeremiah. How much nearer to the truth is it that we are now paying the penalty for that ungodliness, especially since some still persistently advocate it while they despise the word? LECTURE ON GENESIS 12:10.[8]

FALSE APPEALS TO ANTIQUITY AND AUTHORITY. JOHN TRAPP: Antiquity is pleaded here, as well as authority, plenty, and peace. These are now the popish pleas, and the pillars of that rotten religion. It is the "old religion," they say, and has powerful princes for her patrons, and is practiced in Rome the mother church, and has plenty and peace where it is professed, and where they have nothing but Mass and Matins. These are their arguments, but very poor ones, as were easy to evince. But as women (counted the devoted sex) have always carried a great stroke with their husbands, as did Eve, Jezebel, Eudoxia, etc. So the people are indeed a weighty but unwieldy body, slow to remove from what they have been accustomed to. COMMENTARY ON JEREMIAH 44:17.[9]

WORSHIPING THE SUN AND THE SAINTS. MARTIN LUTHER: This is another stumbling block against which the prophet Jeremiah frequently rails with many words, inasmuch as he often mentions the queen of heaven. They used to worship the moon and the stars of heaven, which Moses forbade with a clear law in Deuteronomy 17. Therefore that religious practice and wicked worship was an old thing. They had taken it over from their ancestors who had lived under Moses. In addition, to this wickedness they used to add the veneer of this splendor of piety, that they were worshiping the presence of God, which nowhere declared itself more clearly than in the sun, moon,

---

[8]LW 2:289-90 (WA 42:469).
[9]Trapp, *A Commentary or Exposition*, 346-47*. Eudoxia was a Byzantine empress (d. 404) who betrayed her husband, the emperor, and clashed with the great preacher John Chrysostom.

---

[6]Bullinger, *Conciones*, 244v.
[7]Bugenhagen, *In Ieremiam*, 504v; citing Deut 18:19.

and stars. Then that foolish mob began to worship God not only under or in the sun but even worshiped the very sun and moon themselves. No doubt many of our people do the same thing today. They were very much interested in idolatry and even worshiped the actual wooden statues of the saints. LECTURE OF ZEPHANIAH 1:5.[10]

MOTHER OF GOD AND QUEEN OF HEAVEN. JOHANNES BUGENHAGEN: "Concerning Melecheth of heaven," which the interpreters make "queen of heaven." . . . If from this passage the papists receive that canticle *Regina caeli laetare*, etc.,[†] they certainly do not apply this great honor to the most holy virgin mother of God.

As we all give honor, saying blessed mother of God; with reverence and honor we ought to say about her things that are true; her highest praise is in these things. For she was made the mother of God, a fact that exceeds the intellect of all humanity and the angels, as Elizabeth exclaimed when full of the Holy Spirit: "How does this come to me, that the mother of the Lord should come to me? O Blessed are you who believed, since all the things that the Lord said to you will be fulfilled in you." This is the greatest praise of the most holy virgin mother of God, concerning which we spoke above in chapter 31: "A woman will encircle a man." We ought not hypocritically seek a greater praise. We ought not burden or deform the most holy mother of God with lies, superstitions, and idolatries. COMMENTARY ON JEREMIAH 44:18.[11]

REJECT ALL IDOLATRY. JOHN MAYER: Note here the weak grounds they give for idolatry—the old customs of great persons among their people; for they say, "We have done as our fathers, kings, and princes in Judah and the streets of Jerusalem." That is, so it has been done in the church of God, so famous throughout the world. We then "had plenty of food and saw no evil." For they take no notice of

their grievous sufferings under idolatrous kings, until that day in the days of Zedekiah that they were utterly ruined. "We will do what seems good in our eyes. On this basis, we think it most reasonable to serve the queen of heaven again, and not to give up a religion so warranted and strongly grounded." But are these not the four pillars of popery in our day, wherein the Virgin Mary is worshiped as the queen of heaven? For they say, (1) "This is the old religion wherein our forefathers lived; they were wiser and more pious than the people of our times." (2) "This has been practiced and maintained in Rome, the most famous place for the faith of all other churches." (3) "At that time everyone embraced this Catholic religion; and there was plenty, for all things were inexpensive and there were no wars among Christians." (4) "This therefore seems to us to be the best religion, say what any man can to the contrary."

But all these grounds when duly considered are most weak; for heathen idolatry was practiced among the nations before they embraced the Christian religion: should that be judged best? Our fathers, kings, and princes indeed worshiped before images, called upon saints departed, made an idol of the host, believed in the pope and the church—no matter how corrupt—without ever searching into the truth. But they were only fathers that lived before us, when ignorance as a dark mist kept them from seeing things in their colors. But what did our fathers and kings do that lived before them for six hundred years after Christ until the cursed Second Council of Nicaea (787)?[†] All this time there were no images in the church, or invocations of the saints departed; no pope reigning universally, or counted of infallible judgment until Gregory VII (1073–1085) . . . what was practiced in the corrupt church of Rome ought not to move us any more than what was done in Jerusalem, which was first corrupted by Solomon and then by other wicked kings that succeeded him for many generations. For in David's time Jerusalem had been the joy of the whole earth. So Rome had been famous for a true faith that was embraced all over the world, but

---

[10]LW 18:323 (WA 13:482-83); citing Deut 17:3, Jer 7:18.

[11]Bugenhagen, *In Ieremiam*, 5O4v; citing Lk 1:43, 45; Jer 31:22. [†]A medieval Marian hymn, sometimes attributed to Pope Gregory the Great, and sung during the Easter season.

what is that to the Rome that has been so degenerate and for so long? COMMENTARY ON JEREMIAH 44:17-25.[12]

DEVOTION TO SINFUL VOWS. JOHANNES OECOLAMPADIUS: No one is excused. You have made unjust and impious vows, which oppose love and now you want to preserve them. You see here what they once called vows, namely, those sacrifices in which they were offering cakes and libations devoted to the Lord, which are what they called vows. . . . Now with these vows they promised that they would give themselves to foreign gods; and they were resisting the admonition concerning this impiety. They were offering as a pretext the fact that it was not allowed that a vow might be withdrawn. So today there are those who vow against the word. Moreover, they were testifying with their offering that they received benefits from the favor of those to whom they made such sacrifices, which is against the glory and against the faith of the covenant of God. You learn here a rather serious sin, to preserve a vow that was not vowed in faith. Indeed there is sin in the vowing, but even more, if a blasphemous vow is preserved. These things accordingly are invalidated by the authority of Christ and the virtue of the faith that binds us in the free servitude of righteousness. Of such a kind are those vows of celibacy from people whom the Lord ordained for marriage, and likewise obedience to human traditions against the law of God, that is, monastic vows for all time. Indeed those making such vows are censured for their stubbornness, because under the pretext of vows a stand is made against the Word of God and those making vows sin in ignorance. COMMENTARY ON JEREMIAH 44:25.[13]

THE REMNANT THAT WORSHIPS GOD ALONE. JOHN MAYER: "My name shall no more be named by any man of Judah in the land of Egypt." The Lord shows here that he will not partner with any other god or goddess, but would destroy all such Jews in Egypt, who would worship him and false gods together. For God cannot endure any pause between two opinions. Yet he shows that even then in Egypt, in those most corrupt times, there was a remnant not tainted with common corruption that would escape and go back to the land of Judea just as in the days of Elijah: there were seven thousand left alive in Israel, even after so many had been destroyed by the sword; they had never bowed their knees to Baal. Happy are these few when destruction spreads over a nation; for in the midst of destruction they shall be preserved. COMMENTARY ON JEREMIAH 44:26-29.[14]

THE KING OF EGYPT IS NOT BEYOND GOD'S JUDGMENT. JOHN CALVIN: We . . . see that the prophet reasons from the greater to the less; for if God had not spared King Zedekiah, who was, as it were, a sacred person, nothing better could be hoped for as to the king of Egypt, who reigned only in a manner usual and common. The sum of what is said, then, is that the Jews had been already sufficiently taught by facts how true Jeremiah's prophecies were; for he had predicted what at length had happened to Zedekiah; but his word was not believed. "It is now the time," he says, "when the Jews must know that I am God's faithful servant," as God had added a proof in the case of Zedekiah, which ought to have remained fixed in their memory. Now, if they thought that the king of Egypt was beyond danger, they ascribed great injustice to God, who had not delivered Zedekiah, who had been anointed in his name and by his command. COMMENTARY ON JEREMIAH 44:30.[15]

WILL ENGLAND RETURN TO EGYPT? JOHN KNOX: A great obstacle and blindness may be seen in this people. Nothing the Lord had spoken through this godly prophet Jeremiah had been in vain, for with their own eyes they had seen the plagues and miseries, which he had threatened, take

---

[12]Mayer, *A Commentary*, 456-57*. †The Seventh Ecumenical Council in the Eastern Orthodox Church, which restored the veneration of icons in Christian worship. [13]Oecolampadius, *In Hieremiam*, 3:2Fɪʀ.

[14]Mayer, *A Commentary*, 459*; citing 1 Kings 19:18. [15]CTS 20:563-64* (CO 39:276).

effect at every point.... Yes, these memories were green and fresh both in mind and presence (for the flame and fire that consumed and burned Jerusalem only recently had been put out). Yet they could neither believe the threats Jeremiah now spoke, nor could they follow his fruitful council given for their great benefit and safety. Why so? Because they never delighted in God's truth, nor did they repent of their former idolatry. But they still continued and rejoiced in the same, as clearly appears in chapter 44 of Jeremiah. Thus they and their wives wanted to be in Egypt, where all kinds of idolatry and superstition abounded. Without reproach or rebuke, they might have their bellies full of idolatry and superstition, despite God's holy laws and prophets.

In writing these words, it came to my mind that after the death of that innocent and most godly King, Edward VI (r. 1547–1553), a great tumult occurred in England and led to the establishment of that most unhappy and wicked womanly authority (I mean the woman who now reigns in God's wrath).[†] I was making the same argument in the town of Buckinghamshire, named Amersham, before a great congregation, with a sorrowful heart and weeping eyes. I fell into this exclamation:

"O England! Now is God's wrath kindled against you. Now he has begun to punish, as he had threatened a long while through his true prophets and messengers. He has taken from you the crown of your glory, and has left you without honor, as a body without a head. And this appears to be only the beginning of your sorrows, which appear to increase. For I perceive that the heart, the tongue, and the hand of one Englishman is bent against another, and there is devastation in the whole realm, which is assuredly a sign of the desolation to come....

"O England, England! Alas, plagues are forced upon you; for you would not know the most happy time of your gentle visitation. But will you yet obey the voice of your God, and submit yourself to his holy words? Truly, if you will, then you shall find mercy in his sight and the estate of the commonwealth shall be preserved.

"But, O England, England! What if you will obstinately return to Egypt? That is, if you contract marriage, confederacy, or league with such princes as do maintain and advance idolatry (such as the emperor, which is no less enemy to Christ than was Nero[†]); if you for the pleasure and friendship (I say) of such princes return to your old abominations, which you used before under the papacy. Then assuredly, O England, you shall be plagued and brought to desolation by the means of those whose favors you seek and by whom you are procured to fall from Christ and to serve the Antichrist."

This and much more was in the grief of my heart that day that God willed me to pronounce and before an audience that may have recorded it. The thing that I then most feared and which my tongue also spoke (that is, the subversion of the true religion and the bringing in of strangers to reign over that realm), this day I see come to pass in the counsels and determination of mortals. If they proceed and take effect, as they are concluded by men, then so it will be assuredly as God lives: as those Israelites obstinately returned to Egypt again and were plagued to their deaths, so shall England taste what the Lord has threatened through his prophets before. God grant us true and unfeigned repentance of our former offenses. An ADMONITION TO THE PROFESSORS OF GOD'S TRUTH IN ENGLAND.[16]

---

[16]Knox, *Works*, 3:307-9*. [†]Knox refers here to Mary I (r. 1553–1558), who enforced Roman Catholicism in England during her reign. [‡]Knox refers to the emperor Nero (AD 37–68; r. 54–68), the first Roman ruler to persecute Christians in Rome.

JEREMIAH 45:1-5
MESSAGE TO BARUCH

¹*The word that Jeremiah the prophet spoke to Baruch the son of Neriah, when he wrote these words in a book at the dictation of Jeremiah, in the fourth year of Jehoiakim the son of Josiah, king of Judah:* ²*"Thus says the Lord, the God of Israel, to you, O Baruch:* ³*You said, 'Woe is me! For the Lord has added sorrow to my pain. I am weary with my groaning, and I find no rest.'* ⁴*Thus shall you say to him, Thus says the Lord: Behold, what I have built I am breaking down, and what I have planted I am plucking up—that is, the whole land.* ⁵*And do you seek great things for yourself? Seek them not, for behold, I am bringing disaster upon all flesh, declares the Lord. But I will give you your life as a prize of war in all places to which you may go."*

Overview: With one voice the commentators agree: the faithful do not escape the suffering and sorrows of their place and time. In this brief chapter, Baruch is given comfort and the promise of survival, but he too must pursue his ministry in the larger framework of God's judgment on the Jewish people. The material prosperity Baruch hoped to experience would not come to fruition; he is told to "seek not." Prophetic ministry may require both proclamation of suffering to God's wayward people and suffering with them. Even then God's presence and sustenance will not fail—in this life and the life to come.

45:1-5 A Word of Comfort

BARUCH NEEDS COMFORT AND CORRECTION. JOHN MAYER: Here Jeremiah reproves and comforts Baruch, who it seems was grieved by the hard task imposed upon him. This relates to the prophecies mentioned in Jeremiah 36; for the same time is noted—the fourth year of Jehoiakim. As he was the messenger sent to deliver such displeasing news, Baruch was afraid that he would run into the greatest danger of his life, and this made him pensive and sorrowful. But the Lord cared so much for this perplexed servant that he would have Jeremiah speak a word of comfort to him from his very own mouth. Jeremiah tells him that his life would be preserved even when some sought to destroy it. So this prophecy is set down long after the time in which it was spoken. And it was fulfilled when Jeremiah and Baruch were being persecuted eighteen years later....

Some think that Baruch was grieving because of the length of time he had lived with Jeremiah; for Baruch still had not been made a prophet, as happened to Elisha who served Elijah. But this is groundless conjecture and does not agree with the text. Others think that the great thing Baruch sought was nothing other than comfort and joy in his ministry, and to be exempt from the sorrow and trouble that he had received for God when publishing his word. But this would be excessive—to grieve for outward comforts of life and to be the only one freed from the miseries of the whole country—when so many thousands were at the point of destruction and utter ruin. COMMENTARY ON JEREMIAH 45.[1]

SUFFERING CANNOT BE AVOIDED. NIKOLAUS SELNECKER: The godly Baruch heard from Jeremiah about the misery that would have no end, but for the sins of the stiff-necked people their miseries would be greater still. Thereby he was deeply troubled; he especially thought that it would be better for him if he ceased his labors, took care of himself and his own, and resisted always placing himself under such a cross, misery, and torment.

---

[1]Mayer, *A Commentary*, 459-60*; citing Jer 43:6.

But God sees fully the misery of the God-fearing and says through Jeremiah that Baruch will remain at peace and he should not worry. In fact, he cannot resist the will of God. Therefore, he can only humble himself completely and submit to the powerful hand of God and say, "Your will be done. You are righteous; whatever you do is therefore righteous. You build us up through grace and break us down through your anger. You plant gently and tear out coarsely because of our sins. A good tree has your favor. An evil tree you will cut down. Your name is to be praised." Thereafter, Baruch should desire nothing. He will not have it better than the rest of the people. Jeremiah, Ezekiel, Daniel, and other God-fearing people had the same difficulties. Thus he should remain patient and allow the wrath of God to go forth. He should rest sufficiently on the grace of God. As God said to Paul, "Let my grace suffice for you." Then you shall thank God, who saves your life and your soul. Otherwise, so it goes, as it will with other crosses and misfortunes. As David says in Psalm 73, "If I have you alone, I ask nothing of heaven and earth. If my body and soul fail me, you Lord are the consolation of my heart and my portion." Moreover, I say, "I must endure the right hand of the Most High, who can change all things. The people are well whose Lord is God." THE WHOLE PROPHET JEREMIAH 45.[2]

MAKE LAMENTATION TO THE FATHER OF ORPHANS. JOHANNES BUGENHAGEN: You have . . . examples . . . in Baruch of how God cares for his own. So turn to what God says. "Are you seeking grand things for yourself? Seek not." In these words God considers the complaint that Baruch has said: "I am exhausted with groaning"; or "I am afflicted with groaning," Psalm 6, and "I find no rest." From these words one can see what thoughts and difficulties Baruch had, if indeed he hoped as a man to increase by means of his sons his own resources and household property, to extend his boundaries and possessions, to win over to himself the

friendships of others, so that as an old man he might enjoy honor, an abundance of all things, and rest. Now, however, he sees that everything is about to turn out to the contrary. So then there is that lament and a complaint: "Woe is me." These are those grand things for which he had hoped.

So God consoles Baruch, saying that he not only fears dangers to his affairs, but also he is troubled by the fear of death. You see the sentence of God against the whole people, so that it is necessary for the innocent to suffer with the guilty: "Indeed, the despisers wanted this, and you of course were seeking grand things for yourself. Nevertheless, because you have not denied me and on my account you have incited the hatred of all against you, and because you have kept your trust in me, you will not die; you will not perish in famine or evil servitude. But I will save your life and I will bless you wherever you will go. Truly, 'the earth and its fullness is of the Lord.' I am not only God in Judea, but elsewhere and everywhere, not only do I care for you through your fields, money, and friends, but also much more, when all these things are taken away. I acknowledge my own people in the midst of death and hell." The Lord leads to hell and he leads back, he makes a pauper and he enriches, he humbles and he elevates, he who calls himself the father of orphans and the judge of widows. So God snatches Lot away from those perishing in Sodom. See previous chapters in Jeremiah above regarding the Ethiopian. COMMENTARY ON JEREMIAH 45.[3]

THE ANGUISH AND HOPE OF BARUCH. KONRAD PELLIKAN: To this point the prophecies have been written against the Jews; then what follows are the fate predicted against the various nations, from the revelation of the Lord. Therefore, a brief chapter is added here, a brief prophecy that was made to Baruch, the scribe of this book and the amanuensis of Jeremiah. Baruch was ordered to write down the prophecies of Jeremiah at the time when Jehoiakim was in the fourth year of his reign.

---

[2]Selnecker, *Der gantze Prophet Jeremias*, 2O4v-2P1r; citing 2 Cor 12:9; Ps 73:25-26.

[3]Bugenhagen, *In Ieremiam*, 5P2v-5P3r; citing Ps 6:6; 24:1; 68:5; Gen 19:1-38; Jer 38:7-13; 39:15-18.

During this time Baruch was now and again somewhat wearied by the labor of writing by which he had likely become disturbed. He began to grieve fiercely about the condition of the Jewish people. He heard that they were to be totally and cruelly destroyed, and that the temple and the vessels, along with the kings, were to be taken away to the Gentiles and destroyed, and that the glorious and divine worship of God was to cease. He heard that God's chosen people would be cast off, and that other nations would be selected in their place for the fellowship of the children of God, and that the Jewish race would be humiliated even more than other nations. This is so because they would be placed in disgrace and would be an affront and blasphemy throughout the whole world, because they had preferred their own glory to the estimation of God and humanity. Baruch, I say, heard that all these things were coming, and he wrote and believed them: it is no wonder he was terribly frightened, and for so great a labor he was going to get as his reward no other satisfaction than exile, miseries, and the destruction of his own Jewish people.

Therefore, the Lord consoles him through the prophet. He commands him to be of good heart, for although he would survive until these things happened, nevertheless, he ought not to be afraid. He would be delivered alive and unharmed from all of this calamity. Thus we learn that godly people will not have a part in vengeance on the ungodly, with whom they did not agree, but whom they opposed to a person. Indeed, the Lord always has a way to rescue his own: even if he sometimes leads them to the very gates of death, he leads them back. But if bodily affliction is suffered, nevertheless the soul stays free, by the grace of God, to be carried forth with joy. Finally, "Even the death of the saints is not like the death of the condemned: without a doubt it is precious in the sight of the Lord." There is only the certain expectation of heavenly happiness and the happy exchange of a miserable life for a blessed one. COMMENTARY ON JEREMIAH 45:1-3.[4]

EVEN THE STRONG NEED ENCOURAGEMENT. JOHN TRAPP: You didn't think, like a poor pusillanimous creature as you are. But Jeremiah could pity him in this infirmity, because it had sometimes been his own case, and may befall the best. "Pray for me, I say pray for me," said father Latimer, "for sometimes I am so fearful and fainthearted that I could even run into a mouse hole." COMMENTARY ON JEREMIAH 45:3.[5]

GOD CHALLENGES BARUCH'S SELF-INDULGENCE. JOHN CALVIN: God then says, "And do you seek for yourself?" The particle *lac*, for yourself, is put here emphatically; for here God sets Baruch in the balance, and the whole people together, with the temple and divine worship. "Do you," he says, "outweigh them? Is your life of more value than the temple, the safety of the people, and all my unparalleled gifts?" It was then God's purpose in this way to make Baruch ashamed of himself, because he preferred a frail life to so many things and so glorious. "Do you," he says, "seek great things . . . for yourself?" That is, "Shall your state be above everything else, while the temple is burned with fire, the land is laid waste, most people perish, and the remnant are driven into exile and captivity? Are you then alone deemed to be sacred? Are you alone to be exempt from loss and trouble? See, is all this right?" Here then he made Baruch himself the judge.

But as Baruch might yet flatter himself, he immediately restrains him; "Seek not," God says, for we know how people from self-love seek their own indulgence. That Baruch then might not persist in his course, God put a check on all his ambitious feelings: "Seek not," he says. He afterward adds a basis for consolation. Baruch has been thus severely reproved, as he deserved, on account of his self-indulgence; but God now forgives him, and adds a comfort that might in part alleviate his sorrow; "For behold," he says, "I

---

[4]Pellikan, *Commentaria Bibliorum*, 3:2Z2r; citing Ps 116:15.

[5]Trapp, *A Commentary or Exposition*, 348*; citing Jer 15:1-21. Hugh Latimer (c. 1485–1555) was a bishop and Protestant leader in England who was burned at the stake under Queen Mary I.

will bring evil on all flesh and I will give you your life for a prey in all places to which you go." Here God frees Baruch from that distressing fear by which he had been debilitated and did not possess suitable firmness for his work. He then says, "Fear not, for your life shall be safe for you while those all around you are destroyed." Baruch thought that he should perish while the people were safe and secure; but God declares that none of the people would be safe, and that he would be safely preserved while all the rest are perishing. COMMENTARY ON JEREMIAH 45:5.[6]

SEEKING ANYTHING OTHER THAN GOD BRINGS DEATH. LANCELOT ANDREWES: All that while what do we seek? Why, as Jeremiah says, we "seek great things." We have in hand, however, other greater matters; matters of more weight than the seeking of God. As if seeking God were some petty business, slightly to be sought, and lightly to be found. Anytime is good enough for it.

Nay not that, but so evil are we affected to seek him then; we indict him for our death; it is death to do it—as dearly die as seek; it makes us old, it kills us before our time. SERMON ON PSALM 78:34.[7]

---

[6]CTS 20:570-71* (CO 39:281-82).

[7]Andrewes, *Works*, 1:315-16*.

JEREMIAH 46:1-28
JUDGMENT ON EGYPT

[1]The word of the LORD that came to Jeremiah the prophet concerning the nations.

[2]About Egypt. Concerning the army of Pharaoh Neco, king of Egypt, which was by the river Euphrates at Carchemish and which Nebuchadnezzar king of Babylon defeated in the fourth year of Jehoiakim the son of Josiah, king of Judah:

[3]"Prepare buckler and shield,
and advance for battle!
[4]Harness the horses;
mount, O horsemen!
Take your stations with your helmets,
polish your spears,
put on your armor!
[5]Why have I seen it?
They are dismayed
and have turned backward.
Their warriors are beaten down
and have fled in haste;
they look not back—
terror on every side!
declares the LORD.

[6]"The swift cannot flee away,
nor the warrior escape;
in the north by the river Euphrates
they have stumbled and fallen.
[7]"Who is this, rising like the Nile,
like rivers whose waters surge?
[8]Egypt rises like the Nile,
like rivers whose waters surge.
He said, 'I will rise, I will cover the earth,
I will destroy cities and their inhabitants.'
[9]Advance, O horses,
and rage, O chariots!
Let the warriors go out:
men of Cush and Put who handle the shield,
men of Lud, skilled in handling the bow.
[10]That day is the day of the Lord GOD of hosts,
a day of vengeance,

to avenge himself on his foes.
The sword shall devour and be sated
and drink its fill of their blood.
For the Lord GOD of hosts holds a sacrifice
in the north country by the river Euphrates.
[11]Go up to Gilead, and take balm,
O virgin daughter of Egypt!
In vain you have used many medicines;
there is no healing for you.
[12]The nations have heard of your shame,
and the earth is full of your cry;
for warrior has stumbled against warrior;
they have both fallen together."

[13]The word that the LORD spoke to Jeremiah the prophet about the coming of Nebuchadnezzar king of Babylon to strike the land of Egypt:

[14]"Declare in Egypt, and proclaim in Migdol;
proclaim in Memphis and Tahpanhes;
say, 'Stand ready and be prepared,
for the sword shall devour around you.'
[15]Why are your mighty ones face down?
They do not stand[a]
because the LORD thrust them down.
[16]He made many stumble, and they fell,
and they said one to another,
'Arise, and let us go back to our own people
and to the land of our birth,
because of the sword of the oppressor.'
[17]Call the name of Pharaoh, king of Egypt,
'Noisy one who lets the hour go by.'
[18]"As I live, declares the King,
whose name is the LORD of hosts,
like Tabor among the mountains
and like Carmel by the sea, shall one come.
[19]Prepare yourselves baggage for exile,
O inhabitants of Egypt!
For Memphis shall become a waste,
a ruin, without inhabitant.

20"A beautiful heifer is Egypt,
  but a biting fly from the north has come
    upon her.
21Even her hired soldiers in her midst
  are like fattened calves;
yes, they have turned and fled together;
  they did not stand,
for the day of their calamity has come upon them,
  the time of their punishment.

22"She makes a sound like a serpent gliding
    away;
  for her enemies march in force
and come against her with axes
  like those who fell trees.
23They shall cut down her forest,
declares the LORD,
  though it is impenetrable,
because they are more numerous than locusts;
  they are without number.
24The daughter of Egypt shall be put to shame;
  she shall be delivered into the hand of a
    people from the north."

25The LORD of hosts, the God of Israel, said: "Behold, I am bringing punishment upon Amon of Thebes, and Pharaoh and Egypt and her gods and her kings, upon Pharaoh and those who trust in him. 26I will deliver them into the hand of those who seek their life, into the hand of Nebuchadnezzar king of Babylon and his officers. Afterward Egypt shall be inhabited as in the days of old, declares the LORD.

27"But fear not, O Jacob my servant,
  nor be dismayed, O Israel,
for behold, I will save you from far away,
  and your offspring from the land of their
    captivity.
Jacob shall return and have quiet and ease,
  and none shall make him afraid.
28Fear not, O Jacob my servant,
declares the LORD,
  for I am with you.
I will make a full end of all the nations
  to which I have driven you,
  but of you I will not make a full end.
I will discipline you in just measure,
  and I will by no means leave you unpunished."

a Hebrew *He does not stand*

OVERVIEW: In the last seven chapters of Jeremiah the nations are the focus of his prophetic message. Commentators underscore God's sovereignty over all the kingdoms of the earth—past and present—from the minor principalities on the doorstep of Judea to the regional superpowers—Egypt and Babylon—to the kingdoms of Reformation Europe. As a source of false hope and forbidden refuge for the Jews, Egypt serves as a vivid example of supposed cultural sophistication and military supremacy. This judgment on Egypt exposes the frailty of all earthly kingdoms before the mighty Lord of hosts and confirms that God's righteous wrath will be meted out on all who pursue evil and not simply on the unfaithful Jews of Jeremiah's generation. In this judgment on the nations, divine moral order is reaffirmed and restored. The promised restoration of the Jews will emerge out of this wasteland of wrath and war.

46:1-26 Judgment Promised

AGAINST EGYPT AMONG THE NATIONS.

NIKOLAUS SELNECKER: Jeremiah has now torn down the Jewish kingdom and preached enough to those people. Now he looks out in order to tear down other peoples and heathen lands; for he has been placed over peoples and kingdoms, "to uproot, tear down, destroy, and ruin"; he shows God's wrath and punishment to them. Jeremiah prophesies to the Jews to console them against the new kingdoms that have for the most part harmed them and about all the places and difficulties for them from their rise to their fall, from the south to the north, namely, against the Egyptians, Philistines, Moabites, Ammonites, Edomites, Syrians, Arabians, Persians, and Babylonians. Jerusalem's rise was over against the Dead Sea, where Sodom and Gomorrah had stood. On the other side of the Dead Sea are the Moabites and Ammonites. Further away is Babylon or Chaldea, and still further the Persian land. To the north lay the mountain of Lebanon and further out Syria and its capital city of Damascus. Further yet to the east was Assyria. To the west was Philistia, the most hostile enemies of the Jews. To the north on the great sea lay less hostile enemies—Sidon and Tyre—which bordered on Galilee. To the south lay Egypt, Ethiopia, Arabia, the Red Sea, Edom, and Midian. In this way Jerusalem would be destroyed. It was in a sheep pen among wolves.

Thereby, Jeremiah threatens these nations and begins with the kingdom of Egypt; for their king and Pharaoh Neco (about whom we have heard in chapter 25) had slaughtered the godly and holy King Josiah. Thereby King Nebuchadnezzar of Babylon had defeated and overwhelmed Neco. Therefore, God gave the greatest government in the world to them, so that they would strike and punish the land and people of Egypt for their sins. Just as today he gives a great deal of land and people to the Turks and to the Russians and allows them to have powerful and populous kingdoms so that they can be his rod and scourge. Jeremiah also turns first to the situation of Egypt since the people lean on Egypt's help and assistance and despise God and his word. THE WHOLE PROPHET JEREMIAH 46.[1]

HOW GOD RULES THE NATIONS. JOHANNES BUGENHAGEN: Hereafter Jeremiah prophesies not so much against his own people the Jews, but against the nations—namely, against the whole of Syria, Egypt, the Persians, the Medes, and those neighboring regions—that they were about to be destroyed and subjugated through the king of Babylon and finally the king of Babylon himself would be destroyed through the Medes and Persians; about that event Daniel has written in Daniel 8. Truly, these things were spoken for the consolation of the pious Jews, and in addition those things that pertain to the history of such destruction. But notice that those prophecies against the Gentiles, when they were completed, greatly strengthened the faith of the afflicted Jews in their captivity. Even if they knew that these things were prophesied by God through Jeremiah and others, henceforth they were admonished not to doubt concerning their release from captivity after seventy years and concerning other benefits from God that were likewise predicted and promised.

Here you also see that God is not only the God of Jews, but truly of all the nations, who everywhere establishes magistrates and kingdoms: see Romans 13 and Daniel 4–5. The Most High has power over every kingdom of humanity and over whomever he has wished to raise over it, as in Daniel 2. God changes kingdoms and establishes them. Therefore, God wants civil arrangements to be preserved for utility, peace, and the honorable character of the people—as supported by the law of nature. For God wants those things that he has fashioned to be preserved and to prosper. Therefore, he has indeed ordained the powers in this world, even among the nations, and has blessed his obedient servants with honor, as he also promised the Jews in the law. On the other hand he himself through the sword and other calamities punishes those who despise commonwealths, laws, regulations, and all dignity. . . .

First, therefore, he prophesies against the Egyptians, through whom the Jews hoped they would be safe, in contempt of God, as has often been said before. Consequently, God calls the Egyptians his enemies, because they turned the Jews from the first commandment. COMMENTARY ON JEREMIAH 46.[2]

---

[1]Selnecker, *Der gantze Prophet Jeremias*, 2P1v-2P2r; citing Jer 1:10; 25:19.

[2]Bugenhagen, *In Ieremiam*, 5Q1r-v; citing Rom 13:1-7.

JUDGMENT, THE NATIONS, AND THE ELECT.
JOHANNES OECOLAMPADIUS: The Lord has so
spoken from the beginning of this book of the
prophet. "I have established you over nations and
over kingdoms, so that you may pluck out and pull
down, waste and destroy, build up and plant." With
these words he signifies that he would prophesy not
only concerning the kingdom of the Jews but also
concerning other kingdoms around Judea by which
the Jews had been afflicted. First, he shows what was
going to befall the land of Judea. Indeed, the
judgment from the house of God is beginning, so
that the elect are tested, and then those who had
punished and afflicted the people of God will be
snatched away. The father scourges his sons and
then in view of his sons he destroys the scourges and
consumes them with fire. From there we have a new
title: "the Word of the Lord against the nations." So
even the nations are not outside the providence of
God, even if he seems to disregard them, and
nothing is said about them in Scripture, except to
the extent that he consoles the faithful. In fact, the
outer dispensation of the Word of God rightly
regards the elect; it does not cover the reprobate
except to the extent that they declare the glory of the
elect, which supports itself in the mortification of
the flesh, the cross, and the consolation of grace.
COMMENTARY ON JEREMIAH 46:1.[3]

JEREMIAH SPEAKS TO THE NATIONS. JOHN
TRAPP: God had at first set him over the nations
and the kingdoms to root out and to pull down and
to destroy and to throw down, to build up, and to
plant. This powerful prophet had put forth and
exercised against his own nation the Jews, whom he
had doomed to destruction and lived to see
execution done accordingly. Now he takes their
enemies, the neighbor nations, to do, telling them
severally what they shall trust to. And this indeed
the prophet has done before in part, in fewer words,
under the type of a cup of wine to be divided
among and drunk up by the nations . . . but here to
the end of chapter 51 more plainly and plentifully.

Isaiah does the same in effect . . . , Ezekiel also . . . ,
that by the mouth of three such witnesses, every
word might stand, and this burden of the nations
might be confirmed. Jeremiah begins fitly with the
Egyptians, who beside the old enmity have lately
slain good King Josiah, with whom died all the
prosperity of the Jewish people, who were thence-
forth known (as the Thebans were after the death
of Epaminondas) only by their overthrows and
calamities. COMMENTARY ON JEREMIAH 46:1.[4]

**THE ARROGANCE AND DOWNFALL OF THE
WARLIKE.** NIKOLAUS SELNECKER: Jeremiah
describes the defiance and pride of the Egyptians, how arrogant they are . . . and how they
arm themselves with joy for war. They laugh
with great courage and assume they have their
enemies well in hand. But such arrogance will be
their downfall, as their heart and courage are
allowed to fall into mockery and disgrace. Just as
it goes when one is bold and presumptuous and
leans on one's own understanding, strength,
power, wealth, defenses, and alliances while
despising the enemy with boisterous pride and
arrogance. Thereby the old and wise saying
applies: "You should not despise any enemy, for
he is only as feeble as he wants to be." For what
one calls good fortune is unreliable, and the
wind can change directions. God's blessing
cannot be grasped with pride, as experience
shows that pride, arrogance, and malice can lead
one to begin a war, as happens with King
Amaziah in 2 Kings 14. This leads the land and
people to shame and ridicule; he loses all of his
power and his good name; he is mocked by all of
his day laborers, that is, his princes, lords, counts,
nobles, knights, and soldiers who serve him; they
take money from him and leave him with an
empty treasury. Often a proud man must drive
off the others, as is here the case. "One strong
man falls against another, and they end up lying

---

[3]Oecolampadius, *In Hieremiam*, 3:2F3r; citing Jer 1:10.

[4]Trapp, *A Commentary or Exposition*, 349*; citing Jer 1:10; 25:15-16;
Is 23:1–24:23; Ezek 25:1–33:33. Epaminondas (c. 410–362 BC) was
a leader and general of the Greek city of Thebes who led military
campaigns against Sparta and Athens.

with each other side by side." THE WHOLE PROPHET JEREMIAH 46:3-26.[5]

WEAPONS OF WAR AND THE POWER OF GOD.

JOHN CALVIN: Jeremiah now uses a form of speaking very common in the Prophets, though remote from common use. For the prophets, when they pronounce God's judgments and punishments on the ungodly, do not speak in a simple language, as though they were giving a narrative, but they employed figurative expressions, as though they wished to introduce people into the very scene itself. And that their doctrine might more effectively penetrate into the hearts of people, they bring forward various persons; they at one time introduce God as speaking, and at another time they pronounce this or that according to the sentiments of others; and again, they declare the commands of God....

But we must observe the design of the Holy Spirit; it was his purpose to remove the veil from the eyes of the faithful, which for the most part prevents us from seeing the power of God as clearly as we ought; for when we fix our attention on warlike preparations we do not think that anything is left for God to do; for they who are well prepared seem to be beyond the hazard of losing the day. That the Jews then might know that it would be nothing for God to punish the Egyptians, he records this preparation. And there is a kind of concession when he says, "They shall indeed be furnished with a helmet, a coat of mail, a shield, a sword, and a lance"; but all this would count for nothing.... Then from this prophetic word let us learn that God makes no account of those things that humans prepare when they wish to affect anything. For smoke is everything that dazzles our eyes; so forces and arms have no importance before God, for by a single blast he can dissipate all such clouds. And this truth is very useful; for we look on external things and when anything specious presents itself to us, we are immediately taken up with it and rob God of all power. For we transfer his glory to these masks

that appear before us. We now understand why the prophet speaks here of bucklers, and shields, and lances, and chariots, and helmets, and coats of mail. COMMENTARY ON JEREMIAH 46:3-5.[6]

AVENGING KING JOSIAH.

JOHANNES OECOLAMPADIUS: Observe what is said concerning the day of the Lord, in which God himself openly avenges himself on enemies and evil people. Elsewhere the day of the Lord is generally called the time of Christ. Behold, God says, the justice of God will be manifested, when God takes vengeance on you his enemies because of the killing of Josiah and the afflictions of the destitute. God will kill his enemies through enemies. His sword—that is, his wrath—will devour until it is satisfied; that is, it will rage a great deal and will drink blood abundantly to the point of drunkenness. With these words the great future destruction is displayed. COMMENTARY ON JEREMIAH 46:10.[7]

THE GOD OF HOSTS.

JOHN CALVIN: The prophet described the terrible forces of Pharaoh, in which he so trusted that he dared to boast of a certain victory. Now the prophet says that the event would be very different: "But this day," he says, "will be the day of Jehovah's vengeance"; as though he had said that Pharaoh would look only on his chariots and horsemen, his hired soldiers, their arms and warlike preparations, and that he would not at the same time look to God, who is not without reason called the God of hosts. Though the Scripture in many places ascribes this title to God, yet here it has a special application. For the prophet derides the folly of Pharaoh, because he thought the issue of war was in his own hand, as though the ultimate rule of all things was not in God's hand. COMMENTARY ON JEREMIAH 46:10.[8]

THE SOUND OF FAILED PHARAOHS.

JOHN MAYER: "They have one in that place called Pharaoh,

---

[5]Selnecker, *Der gantze Prophet Jeremias*, 2P2v.

[6]CTS 20:575-76* (CO 39:284-85).
[7]Oecolampadius, *In Hieremiam*, 3:2F4r; citing 2 Kings 23:29; 2 Chron 35:20-27.
[8]CTS 20:581* (CO 39:288).

king of Egypt, a noise that makes the appointed time pass away...." The meaning is that Pharaoh shall be thus upbraided by his very soldiers: "We see nothing in him but the empty sound of bragging and boastings. He makes a great show, but the enemy is coming. He does not dare to go fight with him, but allows time to slip away in a most cowardly way without giving the enemy battle." Or there is his rash campaign at Carchemish. Pharaoh provoked the Chaldeans against him. They shall call him a "tumult," because he by this means brought trouble to his own country. He passed away beaten instead of victorious. COMMENTARY ON JEREMIAH 46:17.[9]

LIKE A HEIFER FRISKING IN THE FIELDS. JOHN CALVIN: Jeremiah intimates here that though Egypt indulged in pleasures, it could not yet escape the vengeance of God.... The prophets mentioned the wealth, riches, and power of the ungodly, even because they are blinded by all the good things in which they abound; for they fear nothing, nor do they feel any anxiety, but through a false notion they exempt themselves from every evil. As then the unbelieving are thus presumptuous and proud, the prophets, on the other hand, warn them and say that however they may exult in their own strength and defenses, they would yet, when it pleased God to make them a prey, become the most miserable of all.

The prophet, then, in short, takes away the false conceit of the Jews, as well as of the Egyptians, as though he had said, "The Egyptians trust in their prosperity, even as though they were like a heifer frisking in the fields"; but "calamity", he says, "is coming from the north." COMMENTARY ON JEREMIAH 46:20.[10]

46:27-28 God Will Save Israel

A PROMISE OF NEW LIFE FOR ISRAEL. JOHN MAYER: "But fear not my servant Jacob...." Having spoken of some comfort regarding Egypt, it was

necessary to speak to Israel, lest they should in their sufferings be overwhelmed with despair.... Though Jeremiah was set over all the nations, the main purpose of his prophesying was to comfort and confirm the true Israelite. Therefore, he not only promises the same thing to the Israelite that he does to the Egyptian but a far greater favor, saying, "I will make a full end of the nations into which I have driven you. But I will not make an end of you...." The nations will be smitten and will never recover again, but only have some outwardly tolerable presence in this world. But to you I will be favorable in respect to the best things and will restore to you the exercise of true religion, and finally bestow on you everlasting life. So being in misery is like a tree in winter that seems to be dead. But having sap in its root, the tree will be restored and will be full of green leaves and will flourish. COMMENTARY ON JEREMIAH 46:27-28.[11]

WHY GOD DISCIPLINES US. NIKOLAUS SELNECKER: At the end of this chapter there is a promise that the Egyptians will not be raised up, as in Ezekiel 29. Such a plague will occur as a consolation to the Jewish people, and they will learn to fear God, trust him, and be obedient. If they turn themselves in the heart they will be redeemed from all their captivity. But we also should take note of this word: "I will strike you with the masses and will not leave you unpunished, unless I prove that you are innocent"; for the rod teaches us to recognize our sins, which we otherwise would not recognize. Therefore, we should not lose heart, if God because of our sins strikes with the cross and misery. This is a fatherly discipline, which will serve to make us better. THE WHOLE PROPHET JEREMIAH 46:27-28.[12]

THE KISS OF GOD'S WORD. JOHN DONNE: The personal marriage, the consummation of marriage, was the coming of Christ in establishing his real presence in the church.... In everything that God

---

[9]Mayer, *A Commentary*, 461*. The Battle of Carchemish (605 BC) was where the Babylonians defeated the Egyptians and the Assyrians.
[10]CTS 20:594* (CO 39:298).

[11]Mayer, *A Commentary*, 462*.
[12]Selnecker, *Der gantze Prophet Jeremias*, 2P2v-2P3r.

says to us, he kisses us. He kissed us by another man's mouth when he spoke to the prophets; but now that he speaks by his own Son, he does so by himself. Even his servant Moses himself was of "uncircumcised lips," and with the uncircumcised there was no marriage. Even his servant Isaiah was of "uncircumcised lips," and with the unclean there was no marriage. Even his servant Jeremiah was "a child who could not speak," and with children in infancy there is no marriage. But in Christ, God has abundantly offered that substance promised to

Moses: there "Aaron your brother shall be your prophet." Christ himself shall come and speak to you and return and speak for you. In Christ, the seraphim brought that live coal from the altar and "touched Isaiah's lips," and so he has spoken in a living and clear way to our souls. In Christ, God has done that which he said to Jeremiah, "Fear not, I am with you"; for in this Immanuel, God and man, Christ Jesus, God is with us. SERMON ON PSALM 2:12.[13]

---

[13]Donne, *Sermons*, 3:319-20*; citing Ex 6:12; Is 6:5; Jer 1:6; Ex 7:1; Is 6:6-7.

JEREMIAH 47:1–48:47
JUDGMENT ON THE
PHILISTINES AND MOABITES

[1]The word of the LORD that came to Jeremiah the prophet concerning the Philistines, before Pharaoh struck down Gaza.

[2]"Thus says the LORD:
Behold, waters are rising out of the north,
    and shall become an overflowing torrent;
they shall overflow the land and all that fills it,
    the city and those who dwell in it.
Men shall cry out,
    and every inhabitant of the land shall wail.
[3]At the noise of the stamping of the hoofs of his
        stallions,
    at the rushing of his chariots, at the
        rumbling of their wheels,
the fathers look not back to their children,
    so feeble are their hands,
[4]because of the day that is coming to destroy
    all the Philistines,
to cut off from Tyre and Sidon
    every helper that remains.
For the LORD is destroying the Philistines,
    the remnant of the coastland of Caphtor.
[5]Baldness has come upon Gaza;
    Ashkelon has perished.
O remnant of their valley,
    how long will you gash yourselves?
[6]Ah, sword of the LORD!
    How long till you are quiet?
Put yourself into your scabbard;
    rest and be still!
[7]How can it[a] be quiet
    when the LORD has given it a charge?
Against Ashkelon and against the seashore
    he has appointed it."

48 Thus says the LORD of hosts, the God of Israel:

"Woe to Nebo, for it is laid waste!
    Kiriathaim is put to shame, it is taken;
the fortress is put to shame and broken down;
    [2]the renown of Moab is no more.
In Heshbon they planned disaster against her:
    'Come, let us cut her off from being a nation!'
You also, O Madmen, shall be brought to silence;
    the sword shall pursue you.

[3]"A voice! A cry from Horonaim,
    'Desolation and great destruction!'
[4]Moab is destroyed;
    her little ones have made a cry.
[5]For at the ascent of Luhith
    they go up weeping;[b]
for at the descent of Horonaim
    they have heard the distressed cry[c] of
        destruction.
[6]Flee! Save yourselves!
    You will be like a juniper in the desert!
[7]For, because you trusted in your works and
        your treasures,
    you also shall be taken;
and Chemosh shall go into exile
    with his priests and his officials.
[8]The destroyer shall come upon every city,
    and no city shall escape;
the valley shall perish,
    and the plain shall be destroyed,
    as the LORD has spoken.

[9]"Give wings to Moab,
    for she would fly away;
her cities shall become a desolation,
    with no inhabitant in them.

[10]"Cursed is he who does the work of the LORD with slackness, and cursed is he who keeps back his sword from bloodshed.

[11]"Moab has been at ease from his youth
    and has settled on his dregs;
he has not been emptied from vessel to vessel,

nor has he gone into exile;
 so his taste remains in him,
  and his scent is not changed.

[12]"Therefore, behold, the days are coming, declares the LORD, when I shall send to him pourers who will pour him, and empty his vessels and break his[d] jars in pieces. [13]Then Moab shall be ashamed of Chemosh, as the house of Israel was ashamed of Bethel, their confidence.

[14]"How do you say, 'We are heroes
 and mighty men of war'?
[15]The destroyer of Moab and his cities has come
  up,
 and the choicest of his young men have gone
   down to slaughter,
 declares the King, whose name is the LORD
  of hosts.
[16]The calamity of Moab is near at hand,
 and his affliction hastens swiftly.
[17]Grieve for him, all you who are around him,
 and all who know his name;
say, 'How the mighty scepter is broken,
 the glorious staff.'

[18]"Come down from your glory,
 and sit on the parched ground,
 O inhabitant of Dibon!
For the destroyer of Moab has come up
  against you;
 he has destroyed your strongholds.
[19]Stand by the way and watch,
 O inhabitant of Aroer!
Ask him who flees and her who escapes;
 say, 'What has happened?'
[20]Moab is put to shame, for it is broken;
 wail and cry!
Tell it beside the Arnon,
 that Moab is laid waste.

[21]"Judgment has come upon the tableland, upon Holon, and Jahzah, and Mephaath, [22]and Dibon, and Nebo, and Beth-diblathaim, [23]and Kiriathaim, and Beth-gamul, and Beth-meon, [24]and Kerioth, and Bozrah, and all the cities of the land of Moab, far and near. [25]The horn of Moab is cut off, and his arm is broken, declares the LORD.

[26]"Make him drunk, because he magnified himself against the LORD, so that Moab shall wallow in his vomit, and he too shall be held in derision. [27]Was not Israel a derision to you? Was he found among thieves, that whenever you spoke of him you wagged your head?

[28]"Leave the cities, and dwell in the rock,
 O inhabitants of Moab!
Be like the dove that nests
 in the sides of the mouth of a gorge.
[29]We have heard of the pride of Moab—
 he is very proud—
of his loftiness, his pride, and his arrogance,
 and the haughtiness of his heart.
[30]I know his insolence, declares the Lord;
 his boasts are false,
 his deeds are false.
[31]Therefore I wail for Moab;
 I cry out for all Moab;
 for the men of Kir-hareseth I mourn.
[32]More than for Jazer I weep for you,
 O vine of Sibmah!
Your branches passed over the sea,
 reached to the Sea of Jazer;
on your summer fruits and your grapes
 the destroyer has fallen.
[33]Gladness and joy have been taken away
 from the fruitful land of Moab;
I have made the wine cease from the winepresses;
 no one treads them with shouts of joy;
 the shouting is not the shout of joy.

[34]"From the outcry at Heshbon even to Elealeh, as far as Jahaz they utter their voice, from Zoar to Horonaim and Eglath-shelishiyah. For the waters of Nimrim also have become desolate. [35]And I will bring to an end in Moab, declares the LORD, him who offers sacrifice in the high place and makes offerings to his god. [36]Therefore my heart moans for Moab like a flute, and my heart moans like a flute for the men of Kir-hareseth. Therefore the riches they gained have perished.

[37]"For every head is shaved and every beard cut off. On all the hands are gashes, and around the waist is sackcloth. [38]On all the housetops of Moab and in the squares there is nothing but lamentation, for I have

broken Moab like a vessel for which no one cares, declares the LORD. ³⁹How it is broken! How they wail! How Moab has turned his back in shame! So Moab has become a derision and a horror to all that are around him."

⁴⁰For thus says the LORD:
"Behold, one shall fly swiftly like an eagle
  and spread his wings against Moab;
⁴¹the cities shall be taken
  and the strongholds seized.
The heart of the warriors of Moab shall be in
    that day
  like the heart of a woman in her birth pains;
⁴²Moab shall be destroyed and be no longer a
    people,
  because he magnified himself against the
    LORD.
⁴³Terror, pit, and snare
  are before you, O inhabitant of Moab!
declares the Lord.

⁴⁴He who flees from the terror
  shall fall into the pit,
and he who climbs out of the pit
  shall be caught in the snare.
For I will bring these things upon Moab,
  the year of their punishment,
declares the LORD.

⁴⁵"In the shadow of Heshbon
  fugitives stop without strength,
for fire came out from Heshbon,
  flame from the house of Sihon;
it has destroyed the forehead of Moab,
  the crown of the sons of tumult.
⁴⁶Woe to you, O Moab!
  The people of Chemosh are undone,
for your sons have been taken captive,
  and your daughters into captivity.
⁴⁷Yet I will restore the fortunes of Moab
  in the latter days, declares the LORD."
Thus far is the judgment on Moab.

a Septuagint, Vulgate; Hebrew *you*   b Hebrew *weeping goes up with weeping*   c Septuagint (compare Isaiah 15:5) *heard the cry*   d Septuagint, Aquila; Hebrew *their*

OVERVIEW: The prophecies of Jeremiah turn to the immediate neighbors of Judea and their fate in the further conquests of Babylon. Both Philistia and Moab serve as vivid examples of divine judgment and sweeping destruction, human pride and vain self-confidence, utter misery and inconsolable mourning. To Reformation commentators the vices of these ancient kingdoms can be found among enemies of God's purposes and gospel in every age; likewise such vices might appear among people of faith who indulge in idolatry, rely on wealth and weaponry, and ignore calls to repentance. In short, any people or kingdom in Europe might be Philistia or Moab.

47:1-7 Judgment on Philistia

WHEN REPENTANCE IS DELAYED AND THE WRATH OF GOD COMES. NIKOLAUS SELNECKER: This is a prophecy against the Philistines, that God through King Nebuchadnezzar will strike and punish them because of their sins. The Philistines were a powerful people who fought too much against the people of Israel, as can be seen in the historical books of Judges and Samuel. Their well-fortified and leading cities are listed in Joshua 13, namely, Gaza, Ashdod, Ashkelon, Ekron, and Gath. Gaza is especially strong and well-guarded. But Pharaoh, the king of Egypt, would conquer this splendid city of trade and in the tenth year of King Zedekiah it would be deserted. This is prophesied in Isaiah 14. The king of Assyria would come over to them and destroy them down to the roots through hunger and the sword. And as it states here in Jeremiah despite the help of others, they would be destroyed along with the two cities in Phoenicia—Tyre and Sidon.

Caphthor is not the Cappadocia in Asia Minor, but is the island that is today called Cyprus. . . . The Philistines come from there: Amos 9.

"How long will you tear at yourself? Why are the Philistines so sad? Why do they bear their distress and tear at you, as over the dead?" Jeremiah without a doubt wants to show that they have put off their repentance for too long and did not turn back. Thus they experience this punishment before their very eyes. Therefore, Jeremiah says, "Now when misfortune comes and it has been long anticipated, all the people cry out, 'You, sword of the Lord, when will you cease?'" But such a cry comes too late. Therefore, we should learn to fear God and to be pious. Otherwise no one forgets the punishment, which comes as the slashing and raging sword of a man, which cannot be stilled because we do not cease to sin. Thus there is no kingdom, city, trade, alliance, treasury, money, or goods that can help. One should repent when the grace of God appears. But when one waits until the righteous anger comes, one helps as one can. But that is the help of human beings; as the example of the powerful kingdom and great and fortified cities in history show, and we without doubt in Germany have experienced. God helps us. THE WHOLE PROPHET JEREMIAH 47.[1]

PALESTINE BETWEEN EGYPT AND BABYLON.
JOHANNES OECOLAMPADIUS: Jeremiah shows by what penalty God will punish the nations that are situated to the to the west, namely, the people of Palestine, who to their south have the cities Ashkelon, Gaza, Ekron, Yarkon, and Gath. To the north there is Joppa, which is here called the port or the shore of the sea, where Tyre and Sidon are. This prophecy was spoken, however, in the tenth year of King Zedekiah, when Pharaoh and Egypt came to fight against the Chaldeans, already then besieging Jerusalem, who when they heard the rumor of the Egyptians' coming, the siege being interrupted, said that the power of war was among the Egyptians. Then Pharaoh, once Gaza the metropolis of Palestine was destroyed, led his army home.... Therefore, Jeremiah says, "Behold, the waters ascend from the north," that is, the very strong armies of Babylon that will come. The

Egyptians certainly weakened this area, but the Babylonians will inundate, dominate, and ruin the whole area, filling it with lamentation and crying out. COMMENTARY ON JEREMIAH 47:1-2.[2]

A GRAND ARMY ROLLS OVER THE CITIES.
KONRAD PELLIKAN: Generally we understand that the "many waters" signify the many peoples who Jeremiah predicted were coming from the north, namely, from Chaldea, to overthrow Palestine. A grand army was coming that would roll over and occupy the cities and region completely. Perhaps this happened when the king of Egypt went out and wanted to relieve the siege of Jerusalem, but nevertheless the Babylonians compelled him to retreat in that expedition; or when the Babylonians occupied all of Egypt, perhaps they also occupied or destroyed those Palestinian cities with their massive and terrible host of horses, chariots, horsemen, and soldiers. No one was able to resist them, as God had ordained. COMMENTARY ON JEREMIAH 47:2-3.[3]

GOD GIVES US A LOVE OF THIS LIFE.
HULD- RYCH ZWINGLI: "With the threatening of the stomping of horses' hooves the father did not once look around for his children." These are descriptions of the worst sort of anxiety, as the father wants to say: because of his anxiety the father rushes about so much that he does not once more look out for his children. But why are they shocked? Because these people love the present life more. Look around: how God takes people to his heart so that they would rather want to live miserably than die bravely. People also love a lamentable life and prefer it to death. One would rather bear suffering, and the servant would rather carry the load, than one would allow his faith to be snatched away. SERMON ON JEREMIAH 47:3-4.[4]

PHILISTINE ORIGINS.
JOHANNES BUGENHAGEN: "Caphtor," the Hebrews call it, which is called

---

[1] Selnecker, Der gantze Prophet Jeremias, 2P3r-2P4v; citing Is 14:28-32; Amos 9:7.

[2] Oecolampadius, In Hieremiam, 3:2G3r-v.
[3] Pellikan, Commentaria Bibliorum, 3:2Z3v-2Z4r.
[4] Zwingli, Predigten, 289.

Cappadocia in the region of Pontus in Asia, near Armenia, whence long ago the Caphtorim, that is, the Cappadocians, emigrated and came to the land of the Philistines and expelled the Avvim and resided there all the way to Gaza, as it says in Deuteronomy 2. Therefore, he says here "the remnant of the Philistines of the isle of Caphtor"; the Philistines and the Caphtorim are from the same people, as in Genesis 10. COMMENTARY ON JEREMIAH 47:4.[5]

BALDNESS AND CUTTING. JOHANNES OECOLAMPADIUS: "Baldness has arrived." That is, mourning, and the removal of all adornment; Ashkelon has been cut down, when to this point she had been most proud. How long will you cut yourself to pieces and be sorrowful? Grieving in those times meant the cutting of skin, which is called by a peculiar word, as in this passage and elsewhere in Scripture. He shows their perpetual mourning. And again, "O sword of the Lord," he says, "how long will you go without ceasing, will you be at work forever?" He concludes that it cannot stop; for the Lord has given this command. So will be the endless punishment of the damned, because the Lord has commanded it. Only his most perfect will is the cause of things. COMMENTARY ON JEREMIAH 47:5-6.[6]

THE SWORD THAT WILL NOT AND CANNOT REST. JOHN CALVIN: "How long," he says, "until you rest! Hide yourself in your sheath, rest and be still." Here the prophet assumes the character of another, as though he wished to sooth with flattery the sword of God and mitigate its fury. "O sword," he says, "spare them and leave off your rage against the Philistines." The prophet, it is certain, had no such feeling; but ... it was a common thing with the prophets to assume different characters while endeavoring more fully to confirm their doctrine. It is the same, then, as though he represented here the Philistines; and the prophets speak also often in the person of those on whom they pronounce the vengeance of God. It is here as though he said, "The Philistines will humbly ask pardon of God's sword, but it will be without advantage or profit; for when they seek to mitigate the wrath of God, the answer will be, "How can it rest?" Here the prophet, as it were, reproves himself: "I act foolishly in wishing to repress the sword of God; for how could you rest?" COMMENTARY ON JEREMIAH 47:6-7.[7]

GOD'S DECREE IN THIS LIFE AND THE NEXT. JOHN MAYER: The prophet turns and puts on the person of a Philistine and sets forth with a flourish of rhetoric ... describing the Philistines' destruction up to their utter ruin, continual sorrow, and crying out about it most lamentably. Thus he shows that this destruction did not happen by accident, but came through the Lord, who decreed that it should be so. Therefore, there is no way it could be stayed either by force or entreaty. God's judgments of sin are long in coming, but when they come it is useless to complain or to cry for their cessation. Sometimes it is so by immutable decree. Though the wicked may escape misery now and then, because the Lord is moved by their cries to have compassion on them, yet in the world to come each one must be held to their fate. No crying or tears will prevail in reversing that fate for all eternity. Therefore ... while we are on the way there, let us make peace with God while time allows and not harden our hearts one day more. COMMENTARY ON JEREMIAH 47:7.[8]

48:1-47 Judgment on Moab

FAITH AMONG HOSTILE NATIONS. ANDREAS BODENSTEIN VON KARLSTADT: The elect have not been brought together from the four corners of the world. And the evil ones have not been sifted out from among the good. Indeed, the world demonstrates its wickedness daily to the highest degree, erecting mountains of wickedness where before it

---

[5]Bugenhagen, *In Ieremiam*, 5R1r; citing Deut 2:23; Gen 10:14.
[6]Oecolampadius, *In Hieremiam*, 3:2G3v.
[7]CTS 20:616* (CO 39:313).
[8]Mayer, *A Commentary*, 463-64*.

had erected small hills only; and all wantonness and longing is at a fever pitch. No one looks to what ought to be done, but everyone does as much evil as possible. They deride Israel as if it had been found among thieves and pick it apart as a hawk tears apart young chickens. . . .

Dear brothers, if a Moabite or Babylonian servant has you by the throat, it is difficult to show moderation toward such a one and to refrain from excessive curses and maledictions.

You are aware that the jeering Philistines have surrounded us and that they come toward us out of their tents, just as in the former days they came out of their dwellings against the people of God with threats and insults, shouting as if the God of Israel were deaf and could not hear, blind and could not see, or else so weak as to be unable to protect and save his people, as if the living God were without love. . . .

You are also aware that we are surrounded, as in a state of war, by Moabites, Ammonites, Babylonians, and many other enemies of God. Nothing is more certain than that we will have to listen to their taunts. REASONS WHY ANDREAS KARLSTADT REMAINED SILENT FOR A TIME.[9]

THE LANDS EAST OF ISRAEL. JOHANNES OECOLAMPADIUS: Now Jeremiah turns to what he will prophesy against the neighboring eastern nations—the Moabites, Ammonites, and Edomites—which stretch almost to the south, if you look at the kingdom of Azor and Damascus. He censures the Moabites with most of the jeers; for as he shows, they were proud and always rejoicing over the calamity of the sons of Israel and frequently joined their enemies. In Isaiah they are spoken of with largely the same words as here. For the prophet Isaiah shows by what means they were ravaged by Assyria and here in the same way Jeremiah teaches how they were ravaged by Babylon. They were positioned on the bank of the Dead Sea. Here there is nothing to be seen other than the just judgment of God and that he will

repay with an equal measure those who afflict us. Moreover, there are the principal cities of Nebo, which is also the name of a mountain to the east, on which Moses died: Deuteronomy—the last chapter. Kiriathaim, not Kiriathaiarim, is described as a city with fortresses of forests, like a bipolis by chance situated on a river and in both parts inhabited. COMMENTARY ON JEREMIAH 48:1.[10]

MERCILESS KIN AND DIVINE JUDGMENT. JOHN CALVIN: This prophecy would be uninteresting, were we not to remember the history on which the application and use of what is said depends. . . . The Moabites, as the father of their nation was Lot, were connected by blood with the Israelites; they ought then to have retained the recollection of their brotherhood and to have dealt kindly with them; for God had spared them when the people of Israel entered the land of Canaan. The Israelites, we know, passed through the borders of Moab without doing any harm to them, because it was God's purpose, in regard to Lot, to preserve them for a time. But this people never ceased to contrive all manner of plots against God's people; and . . . when the state of the Israelites was embarrassing, the Moabites cruelly exulted over them and became more insolent than avowed enemies. Hence God prophesied against them that the Israelites might know . . . that their miserable condition was not overlooked by God, and that though he chastised them, yet some hope of mercy remained, as he undertook their cause and would be their defender. It was then no small comfort which this prophecy brought to the faithful; for they thus knew that God was still their father, though apparently he seemed to be severe to them. COMMENTARY ON JEREMIAH 48:1.[11]

MOAB AND GERMANY. NIKOLAUS SELNECKER: Just as the Philistines had tormented the Jewish people a good deal and found joy in their

---

[9]CRR 8:171.

[10]Oecolampadius, *In Hieremiam*, 3:2G4r-v; citing Is 15:1–16:11; Deut 34:1-8.
[11]CTS 21:5-6* (CO 39:314).

misfortunes, so the Moabites also gave the Jews no rest. They were hostile neighbors even though at first meeting they were blood relatives. Thereafter the Jews were always tormented by their neighbors and at war with them. Thus the Jews had to keep Moab in check and distance themselves from their sins. The Jews had to maintain the true faith and their calling from God; they would practice their hope, patience, and other virtues. But because God cannot tolerate any arrogance or defiance, he threatens the proud Moabites, who had despised their blood relatives—the Jews. They would be robbed of all their fortresses and other splendors they pursued and reinforced with great determination. They would lose heart as their passions were taken from them. Moreover, Jeremiah shows that their government, territory, and cities would be laid waste and brought to ruin for three reasons.

First, they meet a challenge with their own power, money, good fortresses, weapons, supplies, and wisdom and rely on themselves. God cannot tolerate such extravagance, especially splendor that soon wilts like a flower and withers like the grass. As often happens with ridicule and shame, there is an end that serves as an example and is still one for us. Thus, in our own time princes and lords have a little of something, but they build greater residences and build in the cities with great splendor, and with the people they excessively hunt, play, and indulge all their passions. Then the poor people must extend all of their sweat and blood, and look to their own influence, power, and daily well-being. But what will happen if such splendor and defiance of God remains unchecked? What will happen if shame and ridicule must stop, and so one says, "How did these people become so reckless that they did not conserve anything? What then? How does their wealth help them? I think, has God enriched them and then humbled them? Where is their splendor and where are their fortresses? Where are the reliable people, whom they exploit? Where are they, the poor and miserable people? And where is flawless Germany with its fortresses and cities? And what is Germany coming to, when now every person, all the lords and

the other people are proud, ostentatious, and arrogant?" They see and hear with a real affinity for a kind of blindness that angers God greatly.

Then we will recognize punishment and the devilish grip as God's wrath becomes longer and greater, and we are ever poorer and we make ourselves poorer still. Yet it is not possible for us to be poor. But as all fools prefer this; we do not want to be regarded as fools; rather we want people to think otherwise—that we are the most clever people. Things will be fine in this last and miserable time. Thus all types of blindness, overconfidence, and foolishness have the upper hand, so that miracle of miracles, with such a light of the holy gospel shining among the princes and lords, it does not seem to make a difference. Thus nothing can fail them, but they pursue such splendor and resist it at the same time. They lead such a life that one must say that either they are godless people, that they despise God and his Word, that they neither believe that there is a God, nor that there shall be a reckoning, or they are stupid, blind, and senseless people. I do not make light of the authorities, by which God protects me. Of course, God wants the authorities honored along with every high rank in society, no matter how just and fair it is. But in our own time the churches, schools, and all of life relies on authorities and their well-being. As we heard in the twenty-ninth chapter, as Jeremiah said, "If things go well for the authorities, then they go well for you," etc. But I speak of wasted living, that is, a kind of living that is not fitting for Christian authorities. Whom does unnecessary and reckless luxury serve? What of pride and arrogance? These things serve to anger God and must bring this land and people down. Thus the poor people will be sucked dry, and all the blessings of God will be cast into the water. At the end the lords and their servants, as Jeremiah says—the priests and the princes—will be captured, destroyed, and carved up. . . .

The second cause of ruin, as Jeremiah shows, is that when all government is destroyed, there is such contempt: so the Moabites arrogantly despise the poor and captured Jews; the Moabites ridicule them as poor people. Thus God cannot and will not tolerate such contempt that has taken root everywhere today as when one territory or city despises the other and always thinks that they are the true people and others do not measure up; so they despise others to the extreme.

The third reason is false worship, false teaching, and idolatry or adulteration of pure doctrine. Where we find these three causes, a country and city must come to ruin. In our time this passage of Scripture applies. There is great pride, ostentation, and arrogance, and thereby contempt for other people. Then we can add the ripening of false doctrine and distortion of the truth, while all places are full of papists, and Ishmaelites secretly and openly placed. Then come other awful errors, sins, and vices. Thus we cannot ignore this in our conscience: for under these conditions we do not have long and must fall into ruin. Or God's Word is not God's Word, and it is nothing but a dramatic fable. THE WHOLE PROPHET JEREMIAH 48.[12]

TRUSTING IN GOD ALONE. ANDREAS BODENSTEIN VON KARLSTADT: Human beings have intellect that enables them to be wise and to plan ahead. It allows them to build cities and houses, to make weapons and all kinds of protection. This leads people to become rather unyielded when they ought to leave shelter and protection to God and not to seek more. I could demonstrate this by reference to several prophets, but I won't for sake the sake of brevity, and merely refer to what God says: "You put your trust in your own defenses which you made for yourselves." Therefore God will forsake you and surrender you to your enemies. Thus many princes and warriors were destroyed who might otherwise have survived and recovered before God. THE MEANING OF THE TERM GELASSEN.[13]

CUT SWIFTLY WITH THE SWORD. MARTIN LUTHER: [The clergy] often say that we should spare [them], not scold or reprove them, but honor

and excuse them. Yes, if they were evil only toward themselves and ruined only themselves, I would be very quiet. But their governance ruins the whole world. Whoever remains quiet about this, and does not hazard his body and life, is no true Christian and does not love his neighbors' salvation as his own. If I could only tear the souls out of the jaws of hell, I would certainly scold them accordingly. They set the city on fire and say I should not cry, "Fire!" nor quench the flames. "Cursed is he," says Jeremiah, "who does the work of the Lord with slackness, and cursed is he who keeps back his sword from bloodshed." God wants us to cut briskly with our swords, so that the blood flows; whoever does the work unfaithfully is cursed. They want only to have some feathers plucked and to be struck with a fox's tail. Not so, dear man! GOSPEL FOR THE DAY OF THE WISE MEN, MATTHEW 2:1-12.[14]

LIVING THE SECRETS OF GOD. ANDREAS BODENSTEIN VON KARLSTADT: How much more highly is the one to be held, and how greatly such a one ought to esteem it, when God has made his secrets known to him? Especially since he has divine and superhuman wisdom. This is one of the reasons why God has revealed and made known his secrets to us.

The other is to give us an everlasting and unshakeable recollection of all his words and stories so that at no time throughout our lives any should be forgotten, and that we may fear God and cling to him always. Recollection ought to be heady, busy, strong, never standing still, but ready to break out with passion and to be active. It is a widely known saying, "Cursed is the one who does the work of the Lord indifferently or deceitfully." WHETHER WE SHOULD GO SLOWLY AND AVOID OFFENDING THE WEAK.[15]

THE VULNERABLE PRIDE OF THE MOABITES. JOHANNES BUGENHAGEN: "Moab from its youth." The better and fatter Moab is, the more it is an

---

[12]Selnecker, *Der gantze Prophet Jeremias*, 2P4v-2Q2v; citing Jer 29:7; Jer 41:1-18.
[13]CRR 9:153; citing Is 2:11; 17:1-14; 9:5; 16:8; 31:3.

[14]LW 76:160 (WA 10.1.1:665-66).
[15]CRR 8:256; citing Deut 4:11-40; Jer 48:10.

attractive prey for its enemies. Moab had been secure since it had never been expelled from its land as had happened to so many other people; concerning this you can read in Deuteronomy 2, as also with our Vandals, Goths, Franks, Gauls, etc. But Moab rested on its dregs, like wine that has not been poured out; that is, it preserved its scent and flavor; that is, it lived with its culture, laws, and peace. Moab has gathered wealth to itself. It is spoiled with luxury and ignorant of miseries. And so it is proud and most arrogant, presuming like a bunch of Thrasos,† like inexperienced soldiers—who act not only against people but against the Lord God. But now, he says, this wine will be poured out and separated from its dregs, from its wealth and its peace, into a miserable captivity. There Moab will see that its arrogance and blasphemous boasting are nothing.

Today also our Moabites are so arrogant with diabolical pride, as they boast and presume that they are able to drive out the gospel of Christ, which is the power of God for the salvation of all who believe, from the kingdom of heaven, and trample upon it, so that the power of God would be nothing among us; that is, they presume that they can dislodge our Lord Jesus Christ from the right hand of God. But such Moabites are perishing and Christ thinks nothing of their devilish pride and "Moabitic" arrogance. COMMENTARY ON JEREMIAH 48:11.[16]

BELLICOSE MOAB. JOHANNES OECOLAMPADIUS: Without a doubt an arrogant assessment of their men made their people fearless, for they were bellicose and battle-hardened. "But I will shake off such glories for them, because, having been confounded they will not be able to boast anymore in their victims, to the point that their protectors will be nothing, as much in their strong powers as in the perished youth of war." COMMENTARY ON JEREMIAH 48:14.[17]

THE SUFFERING OF YOUR NEIGHBOR WILL BE YOUR OWN. HEINRICH BULLINGER: Jeremiah mentions another crime of the Moabites: "Wasn't Israel a mockery to you?" Indeed, when Shalmaneser led the ten tribes into captivity,† the misfortunes of their neighbors did not bother the Moabites; rather they taunted the Israelites and assigned blame for these evils to their religion and God, as if the religion was empty and God was powerless because he was unable to save those who worshiped him. Today when believers in the gospel are afflicted with evils, you may find people crying out: "If the preaching of the gospel is true, why do evangelicals not feel help from heaven? Where is that gospel now? Where is that Christ of theirs?" Jeremiah adds, "Has Israel been caught among thieves?" By this he indicates that derision and mockery of the Moabites against the people of God was so great that they could not have been more shameless, even if the people of God had been caught in actual theft or some other type of manifest crime. Truly, it was as if the God and religion of the people of Israel were able to be or ought to be compared with manifest crimes. Now he adds a punishment to this crime. Because you vomited forth these words against the people of God, "Therefore you, Moab, will displace yourselves, or cast yourselves out of your residences"; that is, "Because of these your blasphemous words you will be expelled from your homeland and sent into exile and captivity." This is more amply explained in what follows. Indeed, as the speech returns to the Moabites. Jeremiah says, "Leave the cities," etc. He adds the example of the dove, who, in order to be safe from wild birds, places its nest somewhere in a niche of rugged rock. Thus Jeremiah says, "You also, Moab, will creep through the desert and hide in some cave of an inaccessible rock, lest you are overtaken and torn to pieces by the Babylonians. Let them anticipate this very thing, those who have tongues ready for blasphemies and the mockery of the saints. SERMON ON JEREMIAH 48:26-28.[18]

---

[16]Bugenhagen, *In Ieremiam*, 5S1r; citing, Rom 1:16. †A description based on the bragging soldier Thrasos in *The Eunuch*, a comedy of Terence (c. 195–c. 159 BC).
[17]Oecolampadius, *In Hieremiam*, 3:2H2r.

[18]Bullinger, *Conciones*, 256v-257r. †Shalmaneser V (727–722 BC), king of Assyria.

PRIDE AND CONTEMPT FOR GOD. JOHANNES BUGENHAGEN: "It has been said a short time ago," or from the Hebrew: "We have heard," etc.: this passage is an imitation of Isaiah 16. At that time the pride and boasting of the stupid Moabites seem to have been commonly mocked through contempt, similar to the arrogance of the intoxicated rich man Nabal. God is able to bear every sin, but he does not bear contempt. As in the psalm: "You rebuked the wicked and proud (those who despise your word), those accursed who wander away from your commands." Even among the people there is contempt for the proud and arrogance and boasting are intolerable. It is only stupidity and folly. If anyone wants to perish and be despised, let them be like that. COMMENTARY ON JEREMIAH 48:29.[19]

THE PRIDE AND POWER OF MOAB. MARTIN LUTHER: "I know the pride of Moab; it is very much advertised. But his pride is bigger than his power; he brags more than he can do." Barking dogs don't bite. Waters that roar are not deep. Where there are extremely many words, there is a lack of substance. In the end one will wail louder than another, and tribe will wail louder than tribe. And this will happen in individual places separately at first, and then together. Not only the common people, but the foundations too, that is the chiefs of state. LECTURE ON ISAIAH 16:6.[20]

MOAB UNRESTRAINED, LIKE A YOUNG HEIFER. JOHN CALVIN: Whether then it be one city or the whole country, Moab is compared to "a heifer three years old," because that nation had long luxuriated in its own pleasures.[†] Now a heifer three years old, as is well known, frisks and leaps, because it does not know what it is to fear the yoke; and thus it is not worn out as the case is with cows, who are weakened by having often brought forth young;

and further, the milk that is taken from them exhausts their strength. But a heifer three years old is in her vigor and prime. In short, the prophet intimates that the Moabites lived well, and as it were, unrestrained, for they had long exulted in their abundance; and as they had plenty of wine and bread, they gave themselves up to luxury. COMMENTARY ON JEREMIAH 48:34.[21]

THE INSOLENCE AND STUBBORNNESS OF THE PROUD. MARTIN LUTHER: "His mercy is on those who fear Him from generation to generation." [Mary] begins with the highest and greatest things, with spiritual and inward goods, which produce the most vain, proud, and stiff-necked people on earth. No rich or mighty person is so puffed up and bold as one such smart aleck who feels and knows that they are in the right and understand all about a matter, and they are wiser than other people. Especially when they find they ought to give way or confess themselves in the wrong, they becomes so insolent and are so utterly devoid of the fear of God that they dare to boast of being infallible, declare God is on their side and the others on the devil's side, and have the effrontery to appeal to the judgment of God. If such a person possesses the necessary power, they rushed headlong, persecuting, condemning, slandering, slaying, banishing, and destroying all who differ with them, saying afterward they did it all to the honor and glory of God. They are as certain and sure as hardly an angel in heaven of earning much thanks and merit before God....

Christ says of such people in John 16: "The hour is coming when whoever kills you will think that they are offering service to God." ... Such were the people of Moab, of whom we read in Isaiah 16 and Jeremiah 48: "We have heard of the pride of Moab...." Thus we see that such people would gladly do more in their great arrogance than they are able. Such were the people of the Jews in their dealings with Christ

---

[19]Bugenhagen, *In Ieremiam*, 5S2r; citing Is 16:6; 1 Sam 25:1-12; Ps 119:21.
[20]LW 16:46 (WA 31.2:106).

[21]CTS 21:39* (CO 39:336-37). [†]A phrase found in the Vulgate, Calvin's Latin translation, and in the KJV: "from Zoar *even* unto Horonaim, *as* an heifer of three years old: for the waters also of Nimrim shall be desolate."

and the apostles. Such were the friends of St. Job, who argued against him with extraordinary wisdom and praised and preached God in the loftiest terms. Such people will not give you a hearing; it is impossible that they should be in the wrong or give way. They must have their way though all the world perish. Scripture cannot find reproaches enough for such a lost crew. SERMON ON LUKE 1:50.[22]

EXCESSIVE AND UNNATURAL MOURNING. JOHN CALVIN: The prophet describes a very great and widespread mourning. The Moabites tended in great sorrow to pull off their hair, to shave their beard, and to put on sackcloth, or to gird it round their loins, and also to cut their hands with a knife or with their nails. As these things were signs of grief, Jeremiah puts them all together, in order to show that the calamity of Moab would not be common, but would cause the whole people to express extreme lamentation. "They shall make their heads bald," he says, "their beard they shall pull off," or shave. . . . Then he adds, "the incisions in the hands," they shall tear their faces and their hand with their nails, or as some say, with knife or razor. As to sackcloth, it was also a sign of mourning. It is indeed certain that it was formerly the practice for men, as though it were innate in human nature, in great calamities to spread ashes on the head and put on sackcloth. But Jeremiah has added other excesses that are not very congenial to nature, for it is not agreeable to humanity to pull off the beard, to make the head bald, or to tear the hands and face with nails. These things show excesses, suitable neither to men nor to women—not to women on the grounds of modesty, nor to men on the grounds of manliness and strength of mind.

But humanity never controls itself, and whether they mourn or rejoice, they are ever led away to excesses, observing no moderation. There was another evil connected with sackcloth and ashes; for when it was God's design to lead people by these symbols to humble themselves, to consider their sins and to flee to his mercy, they were diverted to

another end. Thus one who mourned might appear miserable to others, and make a display of weeping and tears. In short, besides excess [of expression], there was also this common evil—hypocrisy—for people ever turn aside to what is vain and dishonest in all things. But in this place there is no reason to dispute about mourning, for the prophet means only that the Moabites would become most miserable, exhibiting all the symptoms of sorrow. COMMENTARY ON JEREMIAH 48:37.[23]

CONTEMPT FOR ISRAEL AND JUDEA, CONTEMPT FOR GOD. JOHANNES BUGENHAGEN: "Since he has raised himself against the Lord." You see what the arrogance of the Moabites was, namely, their contempt for the God of Israel, whom they despised in the Jews. Christ said, "Whatever you have done to one of the least of mine, you have done to me." And to Paul, "Saul, Saul, why are you persecuting me?" Likewise: "The one who has contempt for you has contempt for me, and the one who has contempt for me has contempt for the one who sent me." Thus even though we are sinners, we are to be chastised as one judges a son and not with rage. . . . Nevertheless, God will at last vindicate us and destroy our adversaries. Turks, papists, heretics, fanatics of the spirit, whose arrogance is greater than God can bear and without at last declaring it to be stupidity and vanity. Meanwhile, the pope of Moab with his tyrants is very proud. COMMENTARY ON JEREMIAH 48:42.[24]

THE PIT AND SNARES OF JUDGMENT. JOHANNES BUGENHAGEN: "Trembling etc." This signifies that no artifice and nothing of our strength allows us to evade the judgment of God; the judgment against all those who despise him is described here, as they especially squeeze themselves out of one danger. Nevertheless, they fall into other things, as one who wishes to avoid Charybdis falls into Scylla. The trembling of the

---

[22]LW 21:332-33* (WA 7:578-79); citing Lk 1:50; Jn 16:2; Is 16:6.

[23]CTS 21:42-43* (CO 39:338-39).
[24]Bugenhagen, *In Ieremiam*, 5S3r; citing Mt 25:40; Acts 9:4; 22:7; Lk 10:16.

impious is the terror of the conscience, as with Cain. The pit is that we slip from one evil to another: Romans 1. For the devil holds people in captivity to his own will: 2 Timothy 2. The snare is desperation: Ephesians 4. Those who when the pain stops hand themselves over to all shamelessness to perpetrate every malice with avarice. Here, cowls do no good, nor your works, nor monasticism, etc.; they are able to make you even more blind, but they cannot help you. So will be done to you, unless you are freed through the grace of God. This salvation is entirely in Christ Jesus, our Lord. COMMENTARY ON JEREMIAH 48:43.[25]

RUTH AND FUTURE MOAB. JOHANNES OECOLAMPADIUS: "And I will bring them back from captivity." Even Moab has a promise—because Christ descended from Ruth the Moabite—that some of their posterity will return up to the time of the Messiah. There will be, Jeremiah says, a judgment of Moab; for Moab itself is to a certain extent in a judgment like Judah, and not to the point of total annihilation, as the other nations are punished. This passage is noteworthy concerning the vocation of the Gentiles because impious Moab will return in the last days. COMMENTARY ON JEREMIAH 48:47.[26]

---

[25]Bugenhagen, *In Ieremiam*, 5S3v; citing Gen 4:8-16; Rom 1:18-32; 2 Tim 2:26; Eph 4:17-32.

[26]Oecolampadius, *In Hieremiam*, 3:2H4v; citing Ruth 1:4, 22; Mt 1:5.

JEREMIAH 49:1-39
JUDGMENT ON THE NATIONS

[1]Concerning the Ammonites.
Thus says the LORD:

"Has Israel no sons?
Has he no heir?
Why then has Milcom[a] dispossessed Gad,
and his people settled in its cities?
[2]Therefore, behold, the days are coming,
declares the LORD,
when I will cause the battle cry to be heard
against Rabbah of the Ammonites;
it shall become a desolate mound,
and its villages shall be burned with fire;
then Israel shall dispossess those who dispossessed him,
says the LORD.

[3]"Wail, O Heshbon, for Ai is laid waste!
Cry out, O daughters of Rabbah!
Put on sackcloth,
lament, and run to and fro among the hedges!
For Milcom shall go into exile,
with his priests and his officials.
[4]Why do you boast of your valleys,[b]
O faithless daughter,
who trusted in her treasures, saying,
'Who will come against me?'
[5]Behold, I will bring terror upon you,
declares the Lord GOD of hosts,
from all who are around you,
and you shall be driven out, every man straight
before him,
with none to gather the fugitives.
[6]"But afterward I will restore the fortunes of
the Ammonites, declares the LORD."

[7]Concerning Edom.
Thus says the LORD of hosts:

"Is wisdom no more in Teman?
Has counsel perished from the prudent?
Has their wisdom vanished?

[8]Flee, turn back, dwell in the depths,
O inhabitants of Dedan!
For I will bring the calamity of Esau upon him,
the time when I punish him.
[9]If grape gatherers came to you,
would they not leave gleanings?
If thieves came by night,
would they not destroy only enough for
themselves?
[10]But I have stripped Esau bare;
I have uncovered his hiding places,
and he is not able to conceal himself.
His children are destroyed, and his brothers,
and his neighbors; and he is no more.
[11]Leave your fatherless children; I will keep
them alive;
and let your widows trust in me."

[12]For thus says the LORD: "If those who did not deserve
to drink the cup must drink it, will you go unpunished?
You shall not go unpunished, but you must drink. [13]For
I have sworn by myself, declares the LORD, that Bozrah
shall become a horror, a taunt, a waste, and a curse,
and all her cities shall be perpetual wastes."

[14]I have heard a message from the LORD,
and an envoy has been sent among the
nations:
"Gather yourselves together and come against her,
and rise up for battle!
[15]For behold, I will make you small among the
nations,
despised among mankind.
[16]The horror you inspire has deceived you,
and the pride of your heart,
you who live in the clefts of the rock,[c]
who hold the height of the hill.
Though you make your nest as high as the
eagle's,
I will bring you down from there,
declares the LORD.

¹⁷"Edom shall become a horror. Everyone who passes by it will be horrified and will hiss because of all its disasters. ¹⁸As when Sodom and Gomorrah and their neighboring cities were overthrown, says the LORD, no man shall dwell there, no man shall sojourn in her. ¹⁹Behold, like a lion coming up from the jungle of the Jordan against a perennial pasture, I will suddenly make him^d run away from her. And I will appoint over her whomever I choose. For who is like me? Who will summon me? What shepherd can stand before me? ²⁰Therefore hear the plan that the LORD has made against Edom and the purposes that he has formed against the inhabitants of Teman: Even the little ones of the flock shall be dragged away. Surely their fold shall be appalled at their fate. ²¹At the sound of their fall the earth shall tremble; the sound of their cry shall be heard at the Red Sea. ²²Behold, one shall mount up and fly swiftly like an eagle and spread his wings against Bozrah, and the heart of the warriors of Edom shall be in that day like the heart of a woman in her birth pains."

²³Concerning Damascus:

"Hamath and Arpad are confounded,
    for they have heard bad news;
they melt in fear,
    they are troubled like the sea that cannot
        be quiet.
²⁴Damascus has become feeble, she turned to flee,
    and panic seized her;
anguish and sorrows have taken hold of her,
    as of a woman in labor.
²⁵How is the famous city not forsaken,
    the city of my joy?
²⁶Therefore her young men shall fall in her
        squares,
    and all her soldiers shall be destroyed in that
        day,
declares the Lord of hosts.
²⁷And I will kindle a fire in the wall of
        Damascus,
    and it shall devour the strongholds of
        Ben-hadad."

²⁸Concerning Kedar and the kingdoms of Hazor that Nebuchadnezzar king of Babylon struck down.

Thus says the LORD:
"Rise up, advance against Kedar!
    Destroy the people of the east!
²⁹Their tents and their flocks shall be taken,
    their curtains and all their goods;
their camels shall be led away from them,
    and men shall cry to them: 'Terror on
        every side!'
³⁰Flee, wander far away, dwell in the depths,
    O inhabitants of Hazor!
declares the LORD.
For Nebuchadnezzar king of Babylon
    has made a plan against you
    and formed a purpose against you.

³¹"Rise up, advance against a nation at ease,
    that dwells securely,
declares the LORD,
that has no gates or bars,
    that dwells alone.
³²Their camels shall become plunder,
    their herds of livestock a spoil.
I will scatter to every wind
    those who cut the corners of their hair,
and I will bring their calamity
    from every side of them,
declares the LORD.
³³Hazor shall become a haunt of jackals,
    an everlasting waste;
no man shall dwell there;
    no man shall sojourn in her."

³⁴The word of the LORD that came to Jeremiah the prophet concerning Elam, in the beginning of the reign of Zedekiah king of Judah.

³⁵Thus says the LORD of hosts: "Behold, I will break the bow of Elam, the mainstay of their might. ³⁶And I will bring upon Elam the four winds from the four quarters of heaven. And I will scatter them to all those winds, and there shall be no nation to which those driven out of Elam shall not come. ³⁷I will terrify Elam before their enemies and before those who seek their life. I will bring disaster upon them, my fierce anger, declares the Lord. I will send the sword after them, until I have consumed them, ³⁸and I will set my throne in

Elam and destroy their king and officials, declares the LORD.

[39]*"But in the latter days I will restore the fortunes of Elam, declares the LORD."*

a Or *their king; also verse 3*   b Hebrew *boast of your valleys, your valley flows*   c Or *of Sela*   d Septuagint, Syriac *them*

OVERVIEW: Jeremiah's further prophecies to the nations move sixteenth- and seventeenth-century commentators and preachers to ponder the interplay of God's decisive judgment on the enemies of the Jews and God's faithfulness made manifest in promises fulfilled and grace extended even to the Gentile nations. This chapter unfolds God's sovereign rule over all peoples and the divine standards of justice applied to every kingdom—Jewish and Gentile. In fact, the faithful are often swept up in the turmoil of the nations and, though innocent, still suffer the scourge of God's wrath alongside the ungodly. Such judgment tests the true believer, while encouraging humility and patience.

49:1-6 Judgment on Ammon

THE AMMONITES—GREED, IDOLATRY, GRACE. NIKOLAUS SELNECKER: This is a prophecy against the Ammonites, Edomites, Syrians, Arabians, and Persians, and that God will come to them and punish their sins. The Ammonites and Moabites are children of Lot and had caused the people of Israel much misery. In particular the Ammonites took a portion of the land of the children of Israel to expand their own borders. . . . Here Jeremiah speaks, "You have placed your idol Milcom or Molech in the land of Gad and offer and sacrifice your children to him." Meanwhile, God will not tolerate this injustice, particularly when one takes foreign goods, land, and people with unjust violence, and then pursues idolatry and despises the Word of God. Thus the Lord threatens that he will visit the Ammonites with sword and fire and he will destroy their powerful cities and devastate the daughters of the larger cities, that is, that no village or surface or home shall remain. But Jeremiah also consoles them: that in the right time, when the Ammonites return, they must come to the grace of God. For in God's wrath and fury one can always consider his mercy that he wills through Christ his beloved Son. THE WHOLE PROPHET JEREMIAH 49:1-6.[1]

THE AMMONITES—JUDGMENT AND PRESERVATION. JOHN CALVIN: The Ammonites were not only contiguous to the Moabites but also derived their origin from Lot and were thus connected with them by blood. Their origin was indeed base and shameful, for they were, as is well known, the offspring of incest. There was, however, the bond of fraternity between them because both nations had the same father. God had spared them when he brought up his people from Egypt; for in remembrance of the holy man Lot he would have both peoples remain uninjured. . . .

And we see here, again, the object of this prophecy and the design of the Holy Spirit in announcing it, even that the Israelites might know that they were not completely cast away by God, but that there remained some remnant of his paternal favor; for if the Moabites and Ammonites had been free from all evils, it would have been a most grievous trial; it would have been enough to overwhelm weak minds to see a people whom God had adopted miserably oppressed and severely chastised, while heathen nations were remaining quiet in the enjoyment of their pleasures and exulting over the calamites of others. God, then, in order to mitigate the grief and sorrow that the children of Israel derived from their troubles and calamities, shows that he would yet show them favor, because he would carry on war against their enemies and become the avenger of all the wrongs they had suffered. COMMENTARY ON JEREMIAH 49:1.[2]

---

[1]Selnecker, *Der gantze Prophet Jeremias*, 2Q4v-2R1r.
[2]CTS 21:54-55*(CO 39:346-47); citing Gen 19:30-38; Deut 2:19.

GOD GRANTS LAND TO THE NATIONS. JO-
HANNES BUGENHAGEN: Moses gave half of the
land of the sons of Ammon to the tribe of Gad,
which Gad received by right of war, as described in
Joshua 13. The Ammonites thereafter with robberies and harm seized cities and fields back for
themselves, as one may see here from the words of
Jeremiah. For he says, "Does Israel have no sons?
Does he not have an heir?" Namely, one to whom
the land of Israel is owed? Why then is Milcom the
false god of the Ammonites also sometimes called
Molech, as in 1 Kings 11, etc.? Milcom is interpreted
as the king of the Ammonites, while Molech reigns.
Why, therefore, I say, does Milcom possess the land
of Gad, that is, the land of the tribe of Gad, that
was given by me—God—to the tribe of Gad?
Why is this false god worshiped, and why does he
have his own people in the land of the true God of
Israel? But here it is worthwhile to ask, whence
Moses was able to give half the land of Ammon to
the tribe of Gad, when it is written in Deuteronomy 2: "I will not give to you this land of the
sons of Ammon, because I have given it to the sons
of Lot for their possession." I would say that the
Lord speaks here about land that he gave to the
Ammonites, as the words clearly express how God
gave to every people their lands, even to ignorant
and ungrateful peoples, as Moses sang, saying,
"God has established the boundaries of the peoples
according to the number of the sons of Israel."
COMMENTARY ON JEREMIAH 49:1.[3]

RUMORS OF COMING DESTRUCTION. JO-
HANNES OECOLAMPADIUS: "Wail, O Heshbon."
There were two places called Ai. One was near
Jericho in the land of Canaan; the other, however,
was in the land of Ammon, which has already been
discussed; it was a neighbor to Heshbon of the
Moabites, whence they immediately received the
rumor concerning the destruction of Ai, on whom
the enemy first fell with intent to plunder. Then
the Moabites, because they understood that their

neighbors were in danger, were deeply saddened—
especially those who lived in Heshbon, which was
the principle city. "But for you," he says, "who are in
Ammon, cry out even more." For the king with his
officers, who are also themselves priests—so
interprets Jonathan—went into captivity.[†] Therefore, why do you celebrate concerning the loss of
others, when you don't know how similar your own
judgment and calamity will be? COMMENTARY ON
JEREMIAH 49:3.[4]

THE CALLING OF THE GENTILES. JOHN CALVIN:
[God] now says the same thing of the children of
Ammon, as he said before of the Moabites, that
some hope yet remained for them, for God would
at length show mercy to that nation. But . . . these
promises were advantageous, because God had
chosen to be a Father to only one nation; and the
children of Abraham must be viewed as distinct
from all other nations. But though God built, as it
were, a wall to separate his people from aliens, it
was yet his will to give some prelude of his favor,
and of the calling of the Gentiles. The prophet, then,
has here a regard to the kingdom of Christ. The
promise, no doubt, extended itself to his coming;
for he speaks of the calling of the Gentiles, which
God deferred until he manifested his own Son to
the world. COMMENTARY ON JEREMIAH 49:6.[5]

THE NATIONS AND CHRIST. JOHANNES OECO-
LAMPADIUS: "I will lead them back." At that time
when Christ will arrive, at which time there will be
a blessing of the nations, he will gather them all
and draw all things to himself. The Jews imagine
that the Gentiles will be sorted according to the
origin of each lineage and accounting of births. The
real distinction certainly happens through Christ,
between the elect and the reprobate, and between

---

[3]Bugenhagen, *In Ieremiam*, 5T2v; citing Josh 13:24-28; 1 Kings 11:5-7;
Deut 2:19; 32:8.

[4]Oecolampadius, *In Hieremiam*, 3:2Iiv. †Oecolampadius cites the
Targum Jonathan, or Targumim to the Prophets, a fourth-century-
AD Jewish work of translation and commentary attributed by
tradition to Jonathan ben Uzziel, the disciple of the Elder Hillel
(first century AD); see Bruce Chilton, "Targum," in *Dictionary of
Biblical Interpretation*, ed. John H. Hayes (Nashville: Abingdon,
1999), 2:531-34.
[5]CTS 21:63* (CO 39:352).

flesh and blood on one hand and the new human being on the other, who is from God. He is now making this kind of judgment among the nations, which he will someday reveal on the day of the revelation of the just judgment. COMMENTARY ON JEREMIAH 49:6.[6]

49:7-22 Judgment on Edom

EDOMITES—SIN, JUDGMENT, AND MERCY.
NIKOLAUS SELNECKER: After the Ammonites Jeremiah comes to the Edomites, who were worldly-wise and clever people, especially in developing wealth, lending, goods, and trade. They ridiculed the Jewish people and enjoyed their misfortune. But God would turn their wisdom into foolishness, for they did not recognize their own desperation—what was coming and for what they should prepare. All of their impressive wisdom of worldly things would not help them. But this means that clever advice has become foolishness. Their cities, fortresses, and everything remaining therein would be left behind and destroyed. God does promise the Edomites that they will have mercy on their widows and orphans. That is, he wants all of the poor to recognize their sins and hope in God and flee to him. All of their sins would be forgiven in Christ, and they shall be made righteous and blessed. Before this happens God would visit the Edomites with temporal punishment because of their pride and arrogance. . . . Moreover, God would not spare the pious and God-fearing people, but will hold all under the rod and the cross. He will give the cup to them filled to the top, and they shall drink of it one after another; one sees this often in that God's judgment falls upon his own household and children. THE WHOLE PROPHET JEREMIAH 49:7-22.[7]

GOD OF THE EDOMITE WIDOWS AND OR-
PHANS. JOHANNES BUGENHAGEN: "But nevertheless there will be a remnant." That is, "After

destruction and captivity I will have pity on those fatherless children and widows in your land. If only they will call on me and hope in me." . . . They were the progeny of Jacob. Indeed, "God is not the God of only the Jews," Romans 3. For in tribulation there is a sighing unto God, whom we do not know outside of trials. But God in Scripture gives glory to himself as the father of the fatherless and the defender of widows. As Christ says concerning the gospel, "the good news is preached to the poor." But we especially ought to understand this concerning the conversion of the remnant of the Edomites to Christ, to whom they are not converted except as desperate sinners, who are here called orphans and widows. Concerning them, Christ himself said, "I have not come to call the righteous, but sinners to repentance." COMMENTARY ON JEREMIAH 49:11.[8]

THE CUP OF WRATH FOR THE INNOCENT.
MARTIN LUTHER: We are instructed and comforted when we learn that God often causes even the innocent to experience the most serious misfortunes and punishments, merely in order to test them. When faint hearts feel the punishments, they immediately think of sin, and believe that these are punishments for sin. But one must maintain that the godly experience many evils solely in order to be tested.

Thus the Lord says of his people in Jeremiah 49: "If those who did not deserve to drink the cup must drink it, will you go unpunished?" Even though Daniel and his companions endured the captivity among the heathen, nevertheless they had not deserved the captivity because of their sins, as the others had.

Similarly, in the revolt of the peasants many fine people perished, not because they were guilty as the rebels but because they were among the rebels.[†] For disasters never occur among a people without also affecting the godly. These are being tested, but the others are being judged.

---

[6]Oecolampadius, *In Hieremiam*, 3:21v.
[7]Selnecker, *Der gantze Prophet Jeremias*, 2R1r-v; citing 1 Pet 4:12-19.

[8]Bugenhagen, *In Ieremiam*, 5T4r-v; citing Rom 3:29; Mt 11:5; Mk 2:17; Lk 5:32.

Then, too, the godly are often afflicted, not because their sins deserve it or because they are being tested, but in order that they may be kept humble and may not be puffed up on account of their gifts. Thus Paul says about himself that a thorn in the flesh was given to him to keep from becoming conceited because of his extraordinary revelations. "An angel of Satan," he says, "beats me with his fist that I may not exalt myself." It is as though he were saying: "Because of my superb gifts I might rate myself above all the other apostles and perhaps look down upon them: but God is curing this evil with that thorn of Satan, to show me that I am nothing and to cause me to humble myself."

This is also the reason why the church, which God has endowed with the most excellent gifts of the forgiveness of sins, the Holy Spirit, and eternal life, experiences such manifold dangers and misfortunes. If it enjoyed these gifts without affliction, it would become proud and boastful.

Thus you may observe that frequently a pious and godly person is afflicted with a variety of perils and misfortunes in quick succession, when, on the other hand, for the wicked and ungodly everything turns out in accordance with their heart's desire.

This inequitable estate of affairs often gives rise to resentment among the saints. But if you consider the situation rightly, you are enduring these hardships for your own great good; for if you had no affliction, you would become proud and would be condemned. Now when God ties want, scorn, sickness, a vexatious wife, and disobedient children to your neck like a heavy stone, you are not what the Greeks call . . . proud, but you take it patiently, and you do not look down upon those less gifted than you. LECTURES ON GENESIS 12:18-19.[9]

GOD MANIFEST IN OUR WEAKNESS. PHILIPP MELANCHTHON: Scripture explains that Job's afflictions were not imposed on him because of his past misdeeds. So afflictions are not always punishments or signs of wrath. When in the midst of troubles terrified consciences see only God's punishment and wrath, they should not feel that God has rejected them but they should be taught that troubles have other and more important purposes. They should look at these other and more important purposes, that God is doing his alien work in order to do his proper work, as Isaiah teaches in a long sermon in his twenty-eighth chapter. When the disciples ask who had sinned in the case of the blind man, Christ replied that the reason for his blindness was not sin but "that the works of God might be made manifest in him." In Jeremiah it is said, "Those who did not deserve to drink the cup must drink it." Thus the prophets were killed, and John the Baptist and other saints. Therefore troubles are not always penalties for certain past deeds, but works of God, intended for our profit, that the power of God might be made more manifest in our weakness. APOLOGY OF THE AUGSBURG CONFESSION.[10]

SWEARING BY GOD ALONE. JOHN CALVIN: God is said to swear "by himself," because there is none greater by whom he can swear. People in doubtful and hidden things flee to God, who knows the heart, who is himself the truth, and from whom nothing is hid. And an oath, as we learn from many places of Scripture, is a part of divine worship, as then this honor belongs peculiarly to him, that is, that we should swear by his name. When he himself swears, he cannot derive authority from another, which may confirm his words: he therefore swears by himself. . . . God then prescribes to us the form of swearing, when he swears by himself. God is said to swear sometimes by his soul, or by his life, and he is said sometimes to lift up his hand. These expressions are not strictly proper, but are transferred to God from humanity. But the mode of speaking used by Jeremiah ought especially to be observed, for we see how an oath is to be rightly made by an appeal to God's name; for he is alone the fit witness and judge in things doubtful and hidden.

---

[9]LW 2:319-20* (WA 42:490-91); citing 2 Cor 12:7. †Luther refers to the German Peasants' War, 1524–1525.

[10]BoC 207; citing Jn 9:3.

There is therefore under the papacy a base and an intolerable idolatry, for the papists swear by dead saints. This is nothing else but to rob God of his right; for since he alone ... is the truth, so he alone is the fit judge when things are hidden and cannot be ascertained by human testimony. COMMENTARY ON JEREMIAH 49:13.[11]

THE LION OF THE JORDAN. JOHANNES OECOLAMPADIUS: "Behold, as a lion." The lion is as from a pride or as with the deep and overflowing waters of the Jordan, or through the epithet: the African lion to which an enemy is compared. Around the Jordan there are lions, and the region of the Jordan is proud and a very extravagant part of Judea. Others exposit "the lion" as the enemy who will come as the Jordan elevates its flowing. Therefore, the Lion bursts into the tabernacle without fear. COMMENTARY ON JEREMIAH 49:19.[12]

NO MERCY OR HOPE FOR EDOM. JOHN CALVIN: It ought to be noticed that no hope is given here to the Idumeans as to any remnant. When the prophet spoke before of other nations, he gave them some consolation; but here he does not mitigate God's vengeance: he dooms the Idumeans to final ruin without giving them any hope. [He did so] for this reason: because God had for a long time endured them, and they had most wickedly abused his forbearance. COMMENTARY ON JEREMIAH 49:22.[13]

49:23-27 Judgment on Damascus

THE CITY OF MY JOY? JOHN CALVIN: Some think "my" to be redundant and therefore render it "the city of joy"; but they seem to be induced by no good reason; for they think it absurd that it should be called a city of joy to the prophet, since he ought not to have regarded Damascus with any love or kindness. But the prophets, we know, do not always speak according to their own feelings, but assume the persons of others. We might then fitly read the words as they are, "the city of my joy!" Besides, Jeremiah very cuttingly exults over Damascus when he thus expresses his wonder at its destruction: "How can this be," he says, "that the city of praise," that is, a celebrated city, and "the city of my joy," that is, a spectacle so noble as to cause joy to all—how can it be that this city should not be left, that is, should not be spared? For by "left" he does not mean forsaken by its inhabitants, or reduced to solitude; for by "left" he means untouched or safe.

But we must ever bear in mind ... that the prophets when they thus speak in astonishment do not adopt an elevated style, as the rhetoricians do, to show their eloquence, but have always a regard to what is profitable. It was necessary to impress powerfully the minds of people when the prophet spoke of the ruin of so great a city. Then this astonishment includes what they call an anticipation; for it removed a doubt that might have prevented credit from being given to this prophecy. This might have immediately occurred to everyone, "How can it be that Damascus is to perish?" Then the prophet anticipates this and shows that though this was contrary to the judgment commonly formed, yet as the Lord had so decreed, the destruction of the city was certain. COMMENTARY ON JEREMIAH 49:25.[14]

49:28-33 Judgment on Kedar and Hazor

JUDGMENT ON THE ISHMAELITES. JOHN MAYER: Kedar was one of the sons of Ishmael, who gave the name to the place wherein they lived; this place was also called the Arabian Desert. The people dwelt in tents and moved from place to place as it was a mostly barren country. They had to find pasture for their numerous camels and sheep. It appears that they were Ishmaelites, who today call themselves Saracens, although they come from Hagar, the bondmaid, and therefore were

---

[11]CTS 21:78-79* (CO 39:361-62); citing Heb 6:13.
[12]Oecolampadius, *In Hieremiam*, 3:214r.
[13]CTS 21:96* (CO 39:373).
[14]CTS 21:100-101* (CO 39:376).

Hagareans.... These are the Turks that have so greatly enlarged their dominions over all of Asia and a great part of Europe. In former times they were a wild sort of people, who were intent on feeding their cattle. In following this course of life they endured much hardship.... Yet they were wicked and ungodly, as we gather from the complaint of David; when he was forced to live in the wilderness, he said, "Woe to me that I have my habitation in the tents of Kedar"—as if he were like Lot among the Sodomites.... Although without civil education, the Ishmaelites would be severely judged, for no judgments come upon any people by accident, but by God's appointment, who is the great ruler and judge of the whole world. COMMENTARY ON JEREMIAH 49:28-33.[15]

49:34-39 Judgment on Elam

THE NATIONS AND ELAM—CONSOLATION OF THE PIOUS JEWS. JOHANNES BUGENHAGEN: "Against Elam," that is, Persia, which was thus mentioned about Elam the son of Shem in Genesis 10. We do not read that Persia had sinned at all against the Jews. Nor is this said concerning the nations, as if for this one reason, that they sinned against the Jews, they were cast down, but they were cast down also or rather for the consolation of pious Jews, so that first from this the Jews would perceive and revere the will of God, who already wanted them to suffer and endure the disgrace of captivity. Nevertheless God did all this so that they would know that they would not suffer alone, but also all the nations living around them would suffer. But in truth God did all this so that they would know that after they were snatched away by the authority of the father, they would be freed and would be received as sons. And second, he did this so the Jews would know that they were not better than the nations if they had continued in this way to despise the Word of God and persecute the holy prophets or preachers, but rather they were

condemned to go to those who did not have the word and were not called the people of God. Third, they would know that God did not favor certain individuals. God, nevertheless, in this way wants to be recognized as a father, because he as yet promises salvation to those who seriously transgress, or to the afflicted. Fourth, so they would know that it is the will of God that in that place all the kingdoms would be subject to the king of Babylon, as to a monarch, and pressed by servitude—as Jeremiah often had preached. These things, I say, and similar things are set out in these verses for pious Jews to know. But impious Jews and Gentiles think these things are misfortune and luck. "Now, however, I call to those people pious, who at least when they are afflicted return to God from impiety...."

Moreover that which is added, "But in the latter days I shall turn back the captivity of Elam," signifies that that afterward the Persians would gather back together and grow into a kingdom, as before, until with the Medes they would conquer the king of Babylon and transfer the monarchy to themselves, as contained in the next two chapters of Jeremiah. COMMENTARY ON JEREMIAH 49:34.[16]

JUDGMENT AND GOSPEL FOR THE PERSIANS. HEINRICH BULLINGER: In general the Elamites were wise and courageous, which is why it did not seem likely that so many giants, who were so great, could be easily humbled. But the Lord says that he would inflict terror on them, as he had previously done to the strongest of the rest of the nations, so that they might tremble and wretchedly fear for themselves from those who at another time had feared the Persians. So the Lord is accustomed to changing souls, just as he is otherwise able to change air and the sea itself miraculously. What follows is still more serious: "I will bring upon them evil, surely the fury of my wrath, by which I will hunt them down until I utterly destroy them." Therefore, he threatens that he will destroy or annihilate the Persians because of his anger. The

---

[15]Mayer, *A Commentary*, 469-70*; citing Gen 25:13; 16:1-16; 21:8-21; Ps 120:5.

[16]Bugenhagen, *In Ieremiam*, 5V3r-5V4r; citing Gen 10:22.

apostle puts it well: "It is a terrible thing to fall into the hands of the living God."

Finally the Lord adds that he will do all these things in his just and most equitable judgment. Indeed, he says that he will put his throne, or seat of judgment, or his tribunal, among the Elamites, and in his just judgment he will destroy the kings and princes of the Persians. However, he seems to censure the injustice of the Persian nation somewhat obscurely and unjustly, though they denied justice to the widows and orphans, and did not exercise judgments as they ought to have done. But when justice and fairness are neglected by people, it itself is practiced by God on those who neglect and violate justice, through vengeance to the point of ruin or destruction. Therefore, let magistrates learn from this to prosecute justice. And even if the sacred history does not commemorate how these things were fulfilled through Nebuchadnezzar, nevertheless it is agreed that they were fulfilled, but afterward the Persians again emerged in the time of Cyrus.

After these harsh and bitter things, Jeremiah adds happier things, promising freedom from captivity to the Persians. This passage pertains to the calling of the Gentiles. Indeed, although the Persians seem to have been restored under Cyrus and the kings after him, nevertheless that is nothing, however celebrated it might be, when compared to the blessing and restoration and true freedom of Christ. Through him the Persians and all nations were freed from captivity to death, sin, devil, and hell, and they were made sons of God and heirs of the kingdom of heaven through the gospel. Of course, we read that the Elamites are placed in the catalog of those who were the first to hear the apostles preach the gospel in the second chapter of Acts. SERMON ON JEREMIAH 49:34-39.[17]

ELAM IS NOT PERSIA. JOHN CALVIN: By Elam some interpreters understand Persia, and it is the most common opinion. I however think that the Elamites were not the same with the Persians; I should rather say that they were the Parthians, were it not that Luke makes the Persians a distinct people from the Parthians. At the same time it is not right, as it seems to me, to regard the Persians as generally designated by Elam; for the Persians were remote from the Jews and the Jews never received any injury from that people. There was therefore no reason why the prophet should pronounce punishment on them. The country of Elymais was known as bordering on the Medes and contiguous to the Persians. But that people must have joined the Assyrians and Chaldeans against the Jews. COMMENTARY ON JEREMIAH 49:34-35.[18]

---

[17]Bullinger, Conciones, 264v-265r; citing Heb 10:31; Acts 2:9.
[18]CTS 21:113* (CO 39:384-5); citing Acts 2:9.

JEREMIAH 50:1–51:64
PROPHECIES AGAINST BABYLON

¹The word that the LORD spoke concerning Babylon, concerning the land of the Chaldeans, by Jeremiah the prophet:

²"Declare among the nations and proclaim,
  set up a banner and proclaim,
  conceal it not, and say:
'Babylon is taken,
  Bel is put to shame,
  Merodach is dismayed.
Her images are put to shame,
  her idols are dismayed.'

³"For out of the north a nation has come up against her, which shall make her land a desolation, and none shall dwell in it; both man and beast shall flee away. ⁴"In those days and in that time, declares the LORD, the people of Israel and the people of Judah shall come together, weeping as they come, and they shall seek the LORD their God. ⁵They shall ask the way to Zion, with faces turned toward it, saying, 'Come, let us join ourselves to the LORD in an everlasting covenant that will never be forgotten.'

⁶"My people have been lost sheep. Their shepherds have led them astray, turning them away on the mountains. From mountain to hill they have gone. They have forgotten their fold. ⁷All who found them have devoured them, and their enemies have said, 'We are not guilty, for they have sinned against the LORD, their habitation of righteousness, the LORD, the hope of their fathers.'

⁸"Flee from the midst of Babylon, and go out of the land of the Chaldeans, and be as male goats before the flock. ⁹For behold, I am stirring up and bringing against Babylon a gathering of great nations, from the north country. And they shall array themselves against her. From there she shall be taken. Their arrows are like a skilled warrior who does not return empty-handed. ¹⁰Chaldea shall be plundered; all who plunder her shall be sated, declares the LORD.

¹¹"Though you rejoice, though you exult,
  O plunderers of my heritage,
though you frolic like a heifer in the pasture,
  and neigh like stallions,
¹²your mother shall be utterly shamed,
  and she who bore you shall be disgraced.
Behold, she shall be the last of the nations,
  a wilderness, a dry land, and a desert.
¹³Because of the wrath of the LORD she shall
    not be inhabited
  but shall be an utter desolation;
everyone who passes by Babylon shall be appalled,
  and hiss because of all her wounds.
¹⁴Set yourselves in array against Babylon all
    around,
  all you who bend the bow;
shoot at her, spare no arrows,
  for she has sinned against the LORD.
¹⁵Raise a shout against her all around;
  she has surrendered;
her bulwarks have fallen;
  her walls are thrown down.
For this is the vengeance of the LORD:
  take vengeance on her;
  do to her as she has done.
¹⁶Cut off from Babylon the sower,
  and the one who handles the sickle in time
    of harvest;
because of the sword of the oppressor,
  every one shall turn to his own people,
  and every one shall flee to his own land.

¹⁷"Israel is a hunted sheep driven away by lions. First the king of Assyria devoured him, and now at last Nebuchadnezzar king of Babylon has gnawed his bones. ¹⁸Therefore, thus says the LORD of hosts, the God of Israel: Behold, I am bringing punishment on the king of Babylon and his land, as I punished the king of Assyria. ¹⁹I will restore Israel to his pasture, and he shall feed on Carmel and in Bashan, and his

desire shall be satisfied on the hills of Ephraim and in Gilead. ²⁰*In those days and in that time, declares the* LORD, *iniquity shall be sought in Israel, and there shall be none, and sin in Judah, and none shall be found, for I will pardon those whom I leave as a remnant.*

²¹*"Go up against the land of Merathaim,*[a]
and against the inhabitants of Pekod.[b]
Kill, and devote them to destruction,[c]
declares the LORD,
and do all that I have commanded you.
²²*The noise of battle is in the land,*
and great destruction!
²³*How the hammer of the whole earth*
is cut down and broken!
How Babylon has become
a horror among the nations!
²⁴*I set a snare for you and you were taken,*
O Babylon,
and you did not know it;
you were found and caught,
because you opposed the LORD.
²⁵*The* LORD *has opened his armory*
and brought out the weapons of his wrath,
for the Lord GOD *of hosts has a work to do*
in the land of the Chaldeans.
²⁶*Come against her from every quarter;*
open her granaries;
pile her up like heaps of grain, and devote her
to destruction;
let nothing be left of her.
²⁷*Kill all her bulls;*
let them go down to the slaughter.
Woe to them, for their day has come,
the time of their punishment.

²⁸*"A voice! They flee and escape from the land of Babylon, to declare in Zion the vengeance of the* LORD *our God, vengeance for his temple.*

²⁹*"Summon archers against Babylon, all those who bend the bow. Encamp around her; let no one escape. Repay her according to her deeds; do to her according to all that she has done. For she has proudly defied the* LORD, *the Holy One of Israel.* ³⁰*Therefore her young men shall fall in her squares, and all her soldiers shall be destroyed on that day, declares the* LORD.

³¹*"Behold, I am against you, O proud one,*
declares the Lord GOD *of hosts,*
for your day has come,
the time when I will punish you.
³²*The proud one shall stumble and fall,*
with none to raise him up,
and I will kindle a fire in his cities,
and it will devour all that is around him.

³³*"Thus says the* LORD *of hosts: The people of Israel are oppressed, and the people of Judah with them. All who took them captive have held them fast; they refuse to let them go.* ³⁴*Their Redeemer is strong; the* LORD *of hosts is his name. He will surely plead their cause, that he may give rest to the earth, but unrest to the inhabitants of Babylon.*

³⁵*"A sword against the Chaldeans, declares the* LORD,
and against the inhabitants of Babylon,
and against her officials and her wise men!
³⁶*A sword against the diviners,*
that they may become fools!
A sword against her warriors,
that they may be destroyed!
³⁷*A sword against her horses and against her chariots,*
and against all the foreign troops in her midst,
that they may become women!
A sword against all her treasures,
that they may be plundered!
³⁸*A drought against her waters,*
that they may be dried up!
For it is a land of images,
and they are mad over idols.

³⁹*"Therefore wild beasts shall dwell with hyenas in Babylon,*[d] *and ostriches shall dwell in her. She shall never again have people, nor be inhabited for all generations.* ⁴⁰*As when God overthrew Sodom and Gomorrah and their neighboring cities, declares the* LORD, *so no man shall dwell there, and no son of man shall sojourn in her.*

⁴¹*"Behold, a people comes from the north;*
a mighty nation and many kings
are stirring from the farthest parts of the earth.

⁴²They lay hold of bow and spear;
    they are cruel and have no mercy.
The sound of them is like the roaring of the sea;
    they ride on horses,
arrayed as a man for battle
    against you, O daughter of Babylon!
⁴³"The king of Babylon heard the report of them,
    and his hands fell helpless;
anguish seized him,
    pain as of a woman in labor.

⁴⁴"Behold, like a lion coming up from the thicket of the Jordan against a perennial pasture, I will suddenly make them run away from her, and I will appoint over her whomever I choose. For who is like me? Who will summon me? What shepherd can stand before me? ⁴⁵Therefore hear the plan that the LORD has made against Babylon, and the purposes that he has formed against the land of the Chaldeans: Surely the little ones of their flock shall be dragged away; surely their fold shall be appalled at their fate. ⁴⁶At the sound of the capture of Babylon the earth shall tremble, and her cry shall be heard among the nations."

51
    Thus says the LORD:
"Behold, I will stir up the spirit of a destroyer
        against Babylon,
        against the inhabitants of Leb-kamai,ᵉ
²and I will send to Babylon winnowers,
    and they shall winnow her,
and they shall empty her land,
        when they come against her from every side
        on the day of trouble.
³Let not the archer bend his bow,
    and let him not stand up in his armor.
Spare not her young men;
    devote to destructionᶠ all her army.
⁴They shall fall down slain in the land of the
        Chaldeans,
    and wounded in her streets.
⁵For Israel and Judah have not been forsaken
    by their God, the LORD of hosts,
but the land of the Chaldeansᵍ is full of guilt
    against the Holy One of Israel.
⁶"Flee from the midst of Babylon;

    let every one save his life!
Be not cut off in her punishment,
    for this is the time of the LORD's vengeance,
    the repayment he is rendering her.
⁷Babylon was a golden cup in the Lord's hand,
    making all the earth drunken;
the nations drank of her wine;
    therefore the nations went mad.
⁸Suddenly Babylon has fallen and been broken;
    wail for her!
Take balm for her pain;
    perhaps she may be healed.
⁹We would have healed Babylon,
    but she was not healed.
Forsake her, and let us go
    each to his own country,
for her judgment has reached up to heaven
    and has been lifted up even to the skies.
¹⁰The LORD has brought about our vindication;
    come, let us declare in Zion
    the work of the LORD our God.

¹¹"Sharpen the arrows!
Take up the shields!

The LORD has stirred up the spirit of the kings of the Medes, because his purpose concerning Babylon is to destroy it, for that is the vengeance of the LORD, the vengeance for his temple.

¹²"Set up a standard against the walls of Babylon;
    make the watch strong;
set up watchmen;
    prepare the ambushes;
for the LORD has both planned and done
    what he spoke concerning the inhabitants of
        Babylon.
¹³O you who dwell by many waters,
    rich in treasures,
your end has come;
    the thread of your life is cut.
¹⁴The LORD of hosts has sworn by himself:
Surely I will fill you with men, as many as
        locusts,
    and they shall raise the shout of victory
        over you.

¹⁵"It is he who made the earth by his power,
　who established the world by his wisdom,
and by his understanding stretched out the
　heavens.
¹⁶When he utters his voice there is a tumult of
　waters in the heavens,
　and he makes the mist rise from the ends of
　　the earth.
He makes lightning for the rain,
　and he brings forth the wind from his
　　storehouses.
¹⁷Every man is stupid and without knowledge;
　every goldsmith is put to shame by his idols,
for his images are false,
　and there is no breath in them.
¹⁸They are worthless, a work of delusion;
　at the time of their punishment they shall
　　perish.
¹⁹Not like these is he who is the portion of Jacob,
　for he is the one who formed all things,
and Israel is the tribe of his inheritance;
　the LORD of hosts is his name.

²⁰"You are my hammer and weapon of war:
with you I break nations in pieces;
　with you I destroy kingdoms;
²¹with you I break in pieces the horse and his
　　rider;
　with you I break in pieces the chariot and
　　the charioteer;
²²with you I break in pieces man and woman;
　with you I break in pieces the old man and
　　the youth;
with you I break in pieces the young man and
　the young woman;
²³with you I break in pieces the shepherd
　　and his flock;
with you I break in pieces the farmer and his
　team;
　with you I break in pieces governors and
　　commanders.

²⁴"I will repay Babylon and all the inhabitants of
Chaldea before your very eyes for all the evil that they
have done in Zion, declares the LORD.

²⁵"Behold, I am against you, O destroying
　mountain,
declares the LORD,
　which destroys the whole earth;
I will stretch out my hand against you,
　and roll you down from the crags,
　and make you a burnt mountain.
²⁶No stone shall be taken from you for a corner
　and no stone for a foundation,
but you shall be a perpetual waste,
　declares the LORD.

²⁷"Set up a standard on the earth;
　blow the trumpet among the nations;
prepare the nations for war against her;
　summon against her the kingdoms,
　Ararat, Minni, and Ashkenaz;
appoint a marshal against her;
　bring up horses like bristling locusts.
²⁸Prepare the nations for war against her,
　the kings of the Medes, with their governors
　　and deputies,
　and every land under their dominion.
²⁹The land trembles and writhes in pain,
　for the LORD's purposes against Babylon stand,
to make the land of Babylon a desolation,
　without inhabitant.
³⁰The warriors of Babylon have ceased fighting;
　they remain in their strongholds;
their strength has failed;
　they have become women;
her dwellings are on fire;
　her bars are broken.
³¹One runner runs to meet another,
　and one messenger to meet another,
to tell the king of Babylon
　that his city is taken on every side;
³²the fords have been seized,
　the marshes are burned with fire,
　and the soldiers are in panic.
³³For thus says the LORD of hosts, the God of
　Israel:
The daughter of Babylon is like a threshing floor
　at the time when it is trodden;
yet a little while
　and the time of her harvest will come."

³⁴"Nebuchadnezzar the king of Babylon has
    devoured me;
  he has crushed me;
he has made me an empty vessel;
  he has swallowed me like a monster;
he has filled his stomach with my delicacies;
  he has rinsed me out.^h
³⁵The violence done to me and to my kinsmen
    be upon Babylon,"
  let the inhabitant of Zion say.
"My blood be upon the inhabitants of Chaldea,"
  let Jerusalem say.
³⁶Therefore thus says the LORD:
"Behold, I will plead your cause
  and take vengeance for you.
I will dry up her sea
  and make her fountain dry,
³⁷and Babylon shall become a heap of ruins,
  the haunt of jackals,
a horror and a hissing,
  without inhabitant.

³⁸"They shall roar together like lions;
  they shall growl like lions' cubs.
³⁹While they are inflamed I will prepare them
    a feast
  and make them drunk, that they may
    become merry,
then sleep a perpetual sleep
  and not wake, declares the LORD.
⁴⁰I will bring them down like lambs to the
    slaughter,
  like rams and male goats.

⁴¹"How Babylonⁱ is taken,
  the praise of the whole earth seized!
How Babylon has become
  a horror among the nations!
⁴²The sea has come up on Babylon;
  she is covered with its tumultuous waves.
⁴³Her cities have become a horror,
  a land of drought and a desert,
a land in which no one dwells,
  and through which no son of man passes.
⁴⁴And I will punish Bel in Babylon,
  and take out of his mouth what he has
    swallowed.

The nations shall no longer flow to him;
  the wall of Babylon has fallen.

⁴⁵"Go out of the midst of her, my people!
  Let every one save his life
  from the fierce anger of the LORD!
⁴⁶Let not your heart faint, and be not fearful
  at the report heard in the land,
when a report comes in one year
  and afterward a report in another year,
and violence is in the land,
  and ruler is against ruler.

⁴⁷"Therefore, behold, the days are coming
  when I will punish the images of Babylon;
her whole land shall be put to shame,
  and all her slain shall fall in the midst of her.
⁴⁸Then the heavens and the earth,
  and all that is in them,
shall sing for joy over Babylon,
  for the destroyers shall come against them
    out of the north,
declares the LORD.
⁴⁹Babylon must fall for the slain of Israel,
  just as for Babylon have fallen the slain of
    all the earth.
⁵⁰"You who have escaped from the sword,
  go, do not stand still!
Remember the LORD from far away,
  and let Jerusalem come into your mind:
⁵¹'We are put to shame, for we have heard
    reproach;
  dishonor has covered our face,
for foreigners have come
  into the holy places of the LORD's house.'

⁵²"Therefore, behold, the days are coming,
    declares the LORD,
  when I will execute judgment upon her images,
and through all her land
  the wounded shall groan.
⁵³Though Babylon should mount up to heaven,
  and though she should fortify her strong
    height,
yet destroyers would come from me against her,
  declares the LORD.

54 "A voice! A cry from Babylon!
  The noise of great destruction from the land
      of the Chaldeans!
55 For the LORD is laying Babylon waste
  and stilling her mighty voice.
Their waves roar like many waters;
  the noise of their voice is raised,
56 for a destroyer has come upon her,
  upon Babylon;
her warriors are taken;
  their bows are broken in pieces,
for the LORD is a God of recompense;
  he will surely repay.
57 I will make drunk her officials and her wise
      men,
  her governors, her commanders, and her
      warriors;
they shall sleep a perpetual sleep and not wake,
  declares the King, whose name is the LORD
      of hosts.

58 "Thus says the LORD of hosts:
The broad wall of Babylon
  shall be leveled to the ground,
and her high gates
  shall be burned with fire.
The peoples labor for nothing,
  and the nations weary themselves only for fire."

59 The word that Jeremiah the prophet commanded Seraiah the son of Neriah, son of Mahseiah, when he went with Zedekiah king of Judah to Babylon, in the fourth year of his reign. Seraiah was the quartermaster. 60 Jeremiah wrote in a book all the disaster that should come upon Babylon, all these words that are written concerning Babylon. 61 And Jeremiah said to Seraiah: "When you come to Babylon, see that you read all these words, 62 and say, 'O LORD, you have said concerning this place that you will cut it off, so that nothing shall dwell in it, neither man nor beast, and it shall be desolate forever.' 63 When you finish reading this book, tie a stone to it and cast it into the midst of the Euphrates, 64 and say, 'Thus shall Babylon sink, to rise no more, because of the disaster that I am bringing upon her, and they shall become exhausted.'"

Thus far are the words of Jeremiah.

a *Merathaim* means *double rebellion*   b *Pekod* means *punishment*   c That is, set apart (devote) as an offering to the Lord (for destruction)   d Hebrew lacks *in Babylon*   e A code name for Chaldea   f That is, set apart (devote) as an offering to the Lord (for destruction)   g Hebrew *their land*   h Or *he has expelled me*   i Hebrew *Sheshach*, a code name for Babylon

---

OVERVIEW: The kingdom of Babylon had been the means and scourge of divine judgment on idolatrous Judea. As a result the wealth and power of their Babylonian rulers might have induced the exiled Jews to worship the gods of their captors and lose all hope of liberation and return to their homeland. Commentators underscore how Jeremiah's prophecy against Babylon offers the following guidance to God's people in exile in all places and times: Do not forget the wickedness and disobedience that brought you to this place; recognize the cruelty, crass idolatry, and ungodliness of the wealthy and powerful; recall God's sovereignty over the nations and do not be dazzled by the rise and fall of empires and kingdoms; remember that God's justice is sure to fall on the unjust and oppressive; hold tight to your redeemer God's promise of deliverance and new life.

Moreover, the connections between these chapters in Jeremiah and the book of Revelation prompted Protestant interpreters to compare and expound on the legacy of the multiple diabolical Babylonian kingdoms, made manifest in the conquests of Jeremiah's time, the persecutions of early Christians under imperial Rome, and the reign of yet another Babylon in papal Rome.

50:1-46 Judgment on Babylon

DO NOT WORSHIP THE IDOLS OF BABYLON.
LADY JANE GREY: What does the prophet Baruch say, where he recites the Epistle of Jeremiah,

written to the captive Jews? Did he not forewarn them that in Babylon they should see gods of gold, silver, wood, and stone borne upon men's shoulders to cast fear before the heathen? "But be not afraid of them," said Jeremiah, nor do as others do. But when you see others worship them, say in your hearts, "It is you, oh Lord, that ought only to be worshiped; for as for the timber of those gods, the carpenter framed them and polished them; yes, they were gilded and covered with sliver and vain things that cannot speak. . . ." These and such words Jeremiah spoke to them, whereby he proved to them that they are vain things and are not gods. EPISTLE TO A LEARNED MAN.[1]

THE PERVERSE KINGDOM OF BABYLON.

JOHANNES OECOLAMPADIUS: Babylon, the region of Nebuchadnezzar, prison of the sons of Israel, theater of idols, refuge of the accursed, citadel of sorcerers and enchanters, dregs of shame, contagion of the world, hammer of the earth, land of bitterness, pestilential mountain, workshop of Satan, opposed to the city of God—Jerusalem—deserves to perish entirely. Thus Jeremiah works against Babylon with many points—as do most prophets—just as Isaiah has some chapters against the Babylonians. Habakkuk is all about this topic. The Revelation of John for the most part reveals a spiritual sense. To us the world with its desires is Babylon: and its anti-Christian and tyrannical kings who bind consciences with human decrees and strive to pervert Christian freedom. COMMENTARY ON JEREMIAH 50.[2]

THE HISTORICAL SETTING. JOHANNES BUGENHAGEN: Finally even that thieving king of the Babylonian peoples perishes in the judgment of God through the Medes and Persians. . . . This is likewise predicted in Isaiah 13 and is noted in the history of Daniel and other historical writings, and even of the pagans. For in this way the first monarchy of the Chaldeans or Assyrians had an

end, and the second monarchy began, namely, that of the Persians. Here are the Jews after seventy years of captivity returning to Jerusalem under Cyrus the Persian, as in the book of Ezra, and thereafter the rest of the world receives Christ, the eternal blessing, as was said in many ways in Jeremiah 31. COMMENTARY ON JEREMIAH 50.[3]

AVOID THE TOURNAMENT OF KINGDOMS, BE DEVOTED TO GOD. NIKOLAUS SELNECKER: This chapter is a prophecy against the kingdom of Babylon, which God would visit and punish through the Medes, for Babylon was powerful and proud. God used their power only as a rod against his people, as a father uses the rod to discipline his children. When the rod is no longer useful, he throws it in the fire. Just as God said to the king of Assyria in Isaiah 10, "Woe to the Assyrian, the rod of my wrath, whose hand is the club of my fury," etc.

This is so today: the Turk is such a rod. About this Ezekiel spoke and prophesied in chapter 38. We must consider these words fully for our own time: "In the last time you will come with your whole army, your horses and horsemen, armed with shield and sword and with a great people" on the mountains of Israel. That is, against the Christians, who have God's word loud and clear, and live in safety. Therefore, "Gog or the Turk is my wrath within my fury. That is, my rod upon Christians who willingly sin." But at the end he is only used and then thrown into the fire.

We see here how God always punished one land and people through another, and often one knave finishes off another: the Jews through the Assyrians and Babylonians, the Babylonians through the Medes and Persians, the Medes and Persians through the Greeks, the Greeks through the Romans, the Romans through the Goths. So today one kingdom goes after another, one army goes after another, one land goes after another, until they are all no longer useful. As Daniel prophesied, it has been a long time coming for us; for we stand on clay feet. We have fur on our sleeves, and we have God

---

[1]Lady Jane Grey, "Epistle," 321*; citing Bar 6:4-9.
[2]Oecolampadius, *In Hieremiam*, 3:2K2v; citing Is 13:1-22; 47:1-15.

[3]Bugenhagen, *In Ieremiam*, 5X3r.

to thank that we live under the authority of his Word and favorably enjoy peace in our time. May God extend this yet longer. Amen. Otherwise, everything is lost. Then we see when we are paying attention that God is leading a strange competition and astounding tournament in which one is always running and fencing. As has been said today, there is always a kingdom, land, and territory that knocks another out of his saddle and a horse and rider that are thrown to the ground. It is worthwhile, then, to observe God's Word and allow yourself to enjoy God's blessing. But do not mingle into this godless competition. THE WHOLE PROPHET JEREMIAH 50.[4]

RELATED IDOLS SUCH AS BEL AND BAAL. JOHANNES BUGENHAGEN: Bel or Beel is the false god of the Chaldeans, so too was Merodach, as you see here Merodach is numbered among the idols and is interpreted as "bitter grinding," for which reason it is said here, "Merodach is ground down." Bel, however, or Beel, which thereafter the Samaritans from Assyria in Samaria called Baal, but then so too did other neighboring people in Syria and Arabia already a long time before Moses, as you see the name interpreted in the books of Moses as "Husband," "Lord," "possessor"—so many other names and appellations emerge in the Scriptures. Indeed, there are many Bel, Beel, or Baal, as in the Gospel there is that Beelzebub, a man of flies or Lord of the flies etc. COMMENTARY ON JEREMIAH 50:1-2.[5]

THE SCOURGE OF THE WHOLE EARTH. SEBASTIAN MÜNSTER: "Declare among the nations." The ruin of Babylon was announced officially to all the nations, so that all the people who had been devastated by Babylon would rejoice at her devastation. Indeed, this kingdom of the Babylonians had been at that time the hammer of the whole earth, the terror of the peoples, the scourge of all the nations, the workshop of Satan, the contagion of the world, the dregs of disgraces, the citadel of magi and enchanters, the theater of idols, the prison of the children of Israel, the annihilator of divine worship. Therefore, this city deserved to perish completely. THE TEMPLE OF THE LORD, JEREMIAH 50:2.[6]

THE FREEDOM TO FLEE FROM BABYLON. HEINRICH BULLINGER: Jeremiah . . . returns to the theme of liberty, which he began to speak about before. He urgently encourages the liberated not to remain in or cling to Babylon, but to leave, nay rather to flee from that place. He urges them more than once in this speech. For that reason we will have to look at this in the first place. And here he also advises them that they should not fail to move at all because each person is looking over their shoulder at another person when they ought to move out. But just as male goats precede the flock and become leaders of the flock, so each person, not waiting for someone else to offer himself as a leader, should set out directly and offer himself as a leader. That is, he advises them to seize the way, with each individual person having their own eager mind, and return to their homeland.

Certainly while there are many today who look back to others and wait until those others receive the gospel and reform their churches, we see that they themselves will never arrive at a knowledge of the truth. Therefore, since we have a vocation and illumination from God, we should not look around at what others are doing, but at what we have been commanded to do by him who should rightly be heard alone, and before all others. Truly, he shouts, "flee from Babylon!" And seeing that Babylon presented the type of the kingdom of the Antichrist and the world, the apostles can rightly apply these commands to us all. As shown by the apostle John in the Apocalypse, the Lord Jesus urges his believers with these words, to leave Rome and the kingdom of the Antichrist. . . . We are likewise commanded to flee the world that is in other respects most filthy. SERMON ON JEREMIAH 50:6-8.[7]

---

[4]Selnecker, *Der gantze Prophet Jeremias*, 2R3r-v; Is 10:5; Ezek 38:4; Dan 2:33.
[5]Bugenhagen, *In Ieremiam*, 5X3v; citing Lk 11:15.

[6]Münster, *Miqdaš YHWH*, 954.
[7]Bullinger, *Conciones*, 267r; citing Rev 18:4.

TO SIN IN THE HOUSE OF THE LORD. JO-
HANNES BUGENHAGEN: "And their enemies said."
That is, they judged that they too were showing
obedience to God, because they were destroying
those who were called the people of God. And this
evil, he says, happened to the Jews, because "they
had sinned against the Lord in his habitation of
justice, which was the hope of their fathers
themselves." What does it mean that Jeremiah not
only reproached the sin of the Jews by which they
had sinned before the captivity, but also that they
had sinned in that holy place, or, as he says, "in the
habitation of justice," that is, in the Jerusalem
chosen by God—Deuteronomy 12—and in the
temple or in the whole land sanctified in the Word
of God, where God wished to be worshiped and
adored by that people according to his word? What,
I say, is this: they sin most gravely, who know the
will of God from the Word and act against it or
become contemptuous. As in Luke 12: "the servant
knows the will of the Lord and does not do it."

Let them see these things, those who try to
contaminate with insane doctrine those places
where the gospel is preached, for to them alone the
fanatics and profane spirits hasten in order to
violate the temple of the Lord, that is, the minds
taught by the word of the Holy Spirit: 1 Corinthians 3. And let them see these things, those who,
without shame, having no concern for dignity, dare
to live more repulsively in that place where the
forgiveness of sins, and eternal life in Christ are
preached with evangelical majesty. They are indeed
as a stumbling block to the gospel of Christ etc. as
Jeremiah says in chapter 11: "Why is it that my
beloved does so much evil and does this in my
house?" And Isaiah 26, "In the land of the saints he
did wicked things because he does not see the glory
of the Lord." COMMENTARY ON JEREMIAH 50:7.[8]

**SELF-INTERESTED CLAIMS OF RIGHTEOUS-
NESS.** THE ENGLISH ANNOTATIONS: Those that
prey upon them pretend that they deal justly with

them, no otherwise than as they have deserved for
their sins against God, and we are therefore
faultless. But see the contrary, nor indeed did those
wicked wretches intend or regard any such thing,
whatsoever they pretended, but the satisfying of
their own ambitious dispositions and the enlargement of their dominions. ANNOTATIONS ON
JEREMIAH 50:7.[9]

**DO NOT WORRY WHEN THE GODLESS HA-
RASS US.** JOHN CALVIN: Though the iniquity of
Babylon was manifold, there is yet no doubt but
that God here undertakes the cause of his church.
Then, of all the sins of the Chaldeans, the chief was
this, that they oppressed the church of God; for we
know with what favor God regards his children, so
that he who hurts them touches the apple of God's
eye, as he testifies elsewhere. . . .

Now God will have nothing, as it were, apart
from his children: and hence we learn a useful
doctrine—that the salvation of his church is so
precious in the sight of God that he regards the
wrong done to the faithful as done to himself.
Thus there is no reason why we should torment
ourselves when the ungodly harass us, because
God will at length really show that our salvation is
no less dear to him than eyes are to a person.
COMMENTARY ON JEREMIAH 50:14.[10]

**THE PEOPLE OF GOD AND THE PERISHING OF
EMPIRES.** JOHANNES BUGENHAGEN: Once again
Jeremiah names the sin for which the Babylonians
ought to perish, just as the king of Assur perished
first, as it is written in Isaiah 37, and then finally
through Nebuchadnezzar. You see that because of
one people—the Jews—the entire imperium of the
Assyrians and that first monarchy, more outstanding than all other following monarchies, perished.
Indeed, this is the head of gold as in Daniel.
Therefore, let our adversaries fear for themselves
this judgment of our God, they who are far inferior

---

[8]Bugenhagen, *In Ieremiam*, 5X4r-v; citing Deut 12:5-14; Lk 12:47;
1 Cor 3:16-17; Jer 11:15; Is 26:10.

[9]Downame, ed., *Annotations*, 10C1r*; citing Jer 40:5; Zech 11:2;
Jer 2:3; Is 36:7, 10; 10:6-7.
[10]CTS 21:146* (CO 39:406); citing Zech 2:8.

to the kingdoms of Assyria and the Chaldeans. So also the Egyptian king once perished in the plagues of God and the Red Sea. COMMENTARY ON JEREMIAH 50:17-18.[11]

SUFFERING, FORGIVENESS, AND HEALING.

JOHN MAYER: "The iniquity of Israel shall be sought and there shall be none, for I will pardon them." This may seem to support the foolish Antinomians of our time, who say that a person who is justified is without sin, nor is there anything that they do that is sinful. This is contrary to Romans 7. It is to be noted here how Israel is said to be without sin. It is not because Israel would never sin in the future, but because no sin is imputed to the just. Indeed, this is so because it was the end of their affliction and because of God's promise to forgive their sins. This passage as well as chapters 31 and 33 imply a perfect healing after being punished. We should aim at this healing in our suffering and not merely at the end of our pain and sorrow. COMMENTARY ON JEREMIAH 50:20.[12]

MEDES AND PERSIANS AS THE WORK OF GOD.

JOHANNES OECOLAMPADIUS: "The Lord has opened his armory." The Medes and Persians are the vessel of God's wrath, whom he calls to destroy the people as a vindicator of evil. For those things were not done at random, but they are the work of the Lord, just as the remaining histories are no less from God, even if they appear to be less so. Moreover, it will certainly come to pass in this way, for the work is not only their will, but is in the view of the God of hosts against the land of the Chaldeans, a sentiment that appears in Jonathan:† that which he says, "Let them come from the border," signifies that the neighboring Medes and Persians, who were under submission to the Babylonian power, were about to rebel. So Jonathan says, "From the side he will come: begin to grieve." Or the sense is, "Since his end has approached, and it is as if the hour of destruction has

dawned on him, so you can have no doubt concerning the coming of war; victory is in his hand, they have perished." There is no need for you to prepare supplies, open his provisions and granaries, take grain not by wandering from the fields, but rather, draw it from their storerooms for your desire. COMMENTARY ON JEREMIAH 50:25-26.[13]

OUR REDEEMER GOD.

JOHANNES OECOLAMPADIUS: "Their Redeemer." The enemies pressed the sons of Israel and Judah into a most cruel servitude and did not want to release them, and clearly considered that compared to themselves there was no one who was sufficient to plant them, (i.e. the sons of Israel etc.) in liberty in a place apart from those who were unwilling to let them go. Therefore, the Lord, who is powerful, wanted to be their Redeemer. He is the Lord of hosts. . . . Therefore the Lord is the Redeemer through Cyrus and the Lord himself reconciled us to himself through Christ Jesus. Cyrus conquered Babylon, and Christ conquered the world and death for us. COMMENTARY ON JEREMIAH 50:34.[14]

THE RIVER AND THE IDOLS.

GIOVANNI DIODATI: There seems to be a connection here to the Euphrates, the chief strength of Babylon. Cyrus of Persia turned the river another way and the channel dried up. Then Cyrus attacked the city on two sides. The Hebrew word for "idols" here signifies "giants." The Chaldean idols were for the most part remembrances of ancient kings and other illustrious folk, which were of a vast and unreasonable stature. ANNOTATIONS ON JEREMIAH 50:38.[15]

THE LION AND THE LAMBS.

JOHANNES OECOLAMPADIUS: The magnificent counsel of

---

[11]Bugenhagen, *In Ieremiam*, 5Y1r; citing Dan 2:32.
[12]Mayer, *A Commentary*, 471*; citing Jer 31:34; 33:8.

[13]Oecolampadius, *In Hieremiam*, 3:2L2r-v. †Oecolampadius cites the Targum Jonathan, or Targumim to the Prophets, a fourth-century-AD Jewish work of translation and commentary attributed by tradition to Jonathan ben Uzziel, the disciple of the Elder Hillel (first century AD); see Bruce Chilton, "Targum," in *Dictionary of Biblical Interpretation*, ed. John H. Hayes (Nashville: Abingdon, 1999), 2:531-34.
[14]Oecolampadius, *In Hieremiam*, 3:2L3v.
[15]Diodati, *Pious Annotations*, 83*.

God is celebrated in the preceding verse. He signifies that the lofty kingdom of the lion's power and security is to be spread among the tender lambs, who are here spoken of as the little ones of a flock of sheep; and he signifies that on account of simple, innocent, and peaceful Israel, an armed power will perish. Indeed, the faithful little lambs will drag away the corpses of the dead on the ground; for that which happened on Israel's account turned out just as if they themselves had done it with their own hands. From that passage it can be gathered that in this way we too are daily redeemed as victors, for whom the world was crucified and we in the world; indeed the world and its desires perish daily within our reach. Truly, we approve of the plan of the Lord, that is, that he should declare his glory with such a covenant. Even if we grieve the suffering of those whom we do not yet know to have sinned to death, we pray earnestly that God might similarly lead them finally to the recognition of the truth by which they might be the less dashed against the rock that is Christ. Nevertheless we pray they might be led to bear the will of the Lord through everything; this will is only able to be fully just; in this way the soul is made steadfast each day. COMMENTARY ON JEREMIAH 50:45.[16]

THE WORLD WILL TREMBLE. JOHN CALVIN: This [verse] anticipates an objection; for many might have said, "How can it be that Babylon should thus fall, on whose monarchy so many countries spread far and wide are dependent?" Then so that such an unreasonable event might seem possible to them, the prophet meets this objection, and answers by way of anticipation: though the whole earth shook, yet this would surely take place. He shows, at the same time, how great the calamity would be, for it would by its noise make the whole world tremble; and thus it would be better known how grievous God's vengeance on the Babylonians would be; for it

was not to be without the shaking of the whole earth. COMMENTARY ON JEREMIAH 50:46.[17]

51:1-64 The Utter Destruction of Babylon

BABYLON JUDGED AND THE JEWS BROUGHT HOME. NIKOLAUS SELNECKER: This chapter has exactly the same perspective as the previous one. Thus Jeremiah prophesies once more against the kingdom of Babel and that it would be laid waste by the Medes and Persians. Here we learn the course of action that God used. God punished these sinners as he had punished his people through the Babylonians. Thus he punishes the punishers and then throws away the rod. Finally, he brings those who had been punished yet again to grace—if they return to him—so that he can show mercy to his people. He brings them home from the prison of Babylon after seventy years.

Jeremiah describes the destruction of Babylon through signs and allegories. First, there is the sharp and consuming wind that disperses everything like straw along with their goods and all other things. Next comes the gold cup. Babylon had forced the whole world to drink from it. Babylon gave the world angst and fear thereby, while she leaned on her power and magnificence. Now God gives this to Babylon, and she must drink up the dregs, suffer torment, and suddenly fall to the ground. The king of Persia and Media shall defeat and destroy her. . . . "Oh Babylon, I proclaim to you with a loud voice your future misery, for the power of your idol, Bel, and of your other gods will be turned away. When the Persians come they will make you their servants."

In this long and wide-ranging threat of judgment Jeremiah consoles the Jews who are held captive in Babylon. Although they are like widows and have been abandoned by everyone, they will find their full courage and think on the Lord and on the Jerusalem they hold in their hearts; God will neither leave nor forsake his orphans, for they shall come home again. Your enemies—the

---

[16]Oecolampadius, *In Hieremiam*, 3:2Mıv; citing Ps 137:9.   [17]CTS 21:195* (CO 39:438).

Babylonians—shall be taken down like a stone thrown into deep waters. We should also take hold of such consolation and certainty. God will fully discover all of our enemies, if we would only be patient and ponder the heavenly Jerusalem: that is, if we hope and trust in our Lord Christ, expect his return, remain in his Word, and obey him in body and soul. May this be so! Help us, our true Savior, Christ Jesus. Amen. The Whole Prophet Jeremiah 51.[18]

Jeremiah and John the Evangelist. Georg Mylius: Here all the holy and ancient fathers and doctors of the church are in complete agreement. And nearly all of the interpreters and expositors of holy Scripture inform us clearly that in this fifty-first chapter of the prophet Jeremiah there is not one, but there are in fact two levels present: two levels or a double prophecy was composed and is to be understood. The first and primary level of this prophecy pertains to the powerful and supreme monarchy and empire of Babylon, under which the people of Israel endured seventy long years in hard captivity and harsh servitude. The prophet proclaims the shameful and final judgment of this Babylonian monarchy, as it was ordained by God. . . .

This prophecy belongs not only to the Old Testament, but also the New and the whole chapter is not only about the fall of the old Babylon, but also about another and new Babylon and clarifies its fall.

Moreover, now this prophecy is truly happening fully and is thereby a high and godly priority for us; for the new Babylon is much nearer and more dangerous than the old one. . . .

At the time of the New Testament and especially at the end of the world a new and not completely dissimilar Babylon or Babylonian Empire would rise and be visible in the world. But there is one major difference: the old Babylon was for the most part temporal and possessed earthly things. The new one is spiritual and shows its power and cruelty mostly in the church. Yet both can be compared as they

both have a beginning, ascent, expansion, establishment, rule, and fall, so that any rational person can recognize the new one through the old. . . . How marvelously and clearly we have discovered this secret in the holy Evangelist and apostle John in his spiritual and heavenly Revelation. In that book the Evangelist is at the same time a new prophet Jeremiah. . . . Therefore, Jeremiah had marked out the old Babylon as it appeared, then John clarified Jeremiah's prophecy himself and wanted to bring to light the new Babylon. This whole matter is known through the Revelation of John. . . .

We in the evangelical churches have sincerely attached and laid this name of Babylon on our disgusting papacy. This accusation can be refuted even less on the substantial basis of the prophecy than what appears to one's own eyes. Therefore, as Babylon was a powerful empire, a hammer, lord, and master of the whole world, it was also an impressive, lavish, and world-famous city, which at the same time was the head of its whole empire and carried the name of monarchy. Thus Jeremiah the prophet testified in the Old and John the Evangelist in the New Testament that the new Babylon would be a powerful empire, a hammer and lord of the world, with a prominent, world-famous, and wealthy city in its nest; it also has the name monarchy. Now the poor evangelical church has no empire, even less so is the evangelical community a lord or master of the world. . . .

Where then is this often mentioned new Babylon in the world? Where should we look for it? Where will we find it? If we wander through the whole world, my dear friend, through all the countries and cities, we will find the new Babylon in no other place than Rome in Italy. The new Babylonian Empire we find nowhere else than in and around the Roman papacy. A Christian Sermon About the Old and New Babylon, Jeremiah 51.[19]

Faithless Hearts Before God. Johannes Bugenhagen: Jeremiah continues to prophesy

---

[18]Selnecker, *Der gantze Prophet Jeremias*, 2S3r-v.

[19]Mylius, *Ein Christliche Predigt*, A2r-v, B3v-C1r, C3r.

against the Babylonians, etc. See the continuity—how often the Holy Spirit admonished them while the word spoke through the prophets, that is, the son of God. How often the prophets admonished them concerning the sin of the Babylonians on account of which they fell into such calamities by the judgment of God. He says, "They have raised their heart against me,"† and have boasted and with horrendous blasphemies they despised the God of Israel, who gave his word to his people; they despised him as one who is not able to defend his own people; and they magnified their own gods and cults that gave to their own worshipers such outstanding victories.

In the same way our persecutors have faith in their own riches and power, and, lost in their sins, supposing they are sanctified by their own papist abominations and absurd religion, they blaspheme, hate, and persecute the gospel of Christ, and kill the pious and holy people. . . . But God will pour out on them the judgment of the Babylonians that you read here and a judgment that is even greater because they do not want to seem to be Babylonians, but Christians. "They lay traps before the innocent," as the psalm says, and they say, "Who will see them? Not even God sees." But certainly God sees into their hearts, as he says here, "They have lifted up their heart against me." COMMENTARY ON JEREMIAH 51:1.[20]

THE COMPLETE DESTRUCTION OF BABYLON.

GEORG MYLIUS: The holy prophet Jeremiah prophesies extensively about how the end of this powerful Babylon would come; namely, Babylon would come to a terrible end and be devastated and ruined. In short, Babel must be utterly destroyed.

The prophet shows how all this would occur along with extensive details. First, he says that a powerful wind would come against and awaken Babylon; a strong winnower or fanner will be sent over her and will blow violently on her. That is, a

powerful enemy will step on her neck. In this wretched bloodbath people will be crushed and suffocated. The city will be full of people lying about who have been beaten to death. In the whole land those mortally wounded will sigh. It will be like lambs led to the slaughter pen. Men and women, young and old, princes and lords, citizens and farmers, cattle and people, steers and cows must all be killed. Second, their impressive residences and palaces will be attacked and burned with fire. Bricks will be broken and scattered about so that one cannot find a cornerstone or foundation stone in the whole city. In short, Babylon shall be made into a pile of rubble and burrows for snakes. Many who see it will be astounded and terrified. Moreover, her sea and springs, from which she had an advantage due to waters, will be dried out and flow away from them. Thus the whole land will be a desert; her territories and cities will become a dry and wasted land where a person should neither live nor wander. Above all, this damage cannot be healed. They may take salve for their wounds to heal Babylon. But none would be able to heal Babylon. A CHRISTIAN SERMON ABOUT NEW AND OLD BABYLON, JEREMIAH 51:1-6.[21]

BABYLON AND ENGLAND.

JOHN OWEN: This chapter and the previous one are an eminent prophecy and prediction of the destruction of Babylon and of the land of the Chaldeans—of the metropolis of the empire and of the nation itself. There is a double occasion for the inserting of these words. The first is to declare the grounds and reasons why God would bring that destruction upon Babylon, and upon the land of the Chaldeans. The words of verse 4 are, "The slain shall fall in the land of the Chaldeans, and they that are thrust through in her streets." Why so? "For," says the Lord, "Israel has not been forsaken." The reason why God will destroy the empire of Babylon is because he will remember Israel and what the Babylonians have done against him. This lies in store for another Babylon, in God's appointed time.

[20]Bugenhagen, *In Ieremiam*, 5Z2v-5Z3v; citing Ps 38:12; Jer 5:26; Ps 94:7. †Bugenhagen refers here to the meaning of *lēb qāmay* in 51:1.

[21]Mylius, *Ein Christliche Predigt*, B1r-v.

The second reason may be for the comfort and support of Israel under that distress that was then befalling them upon their entrance into Babylon in the land of the Chaldeans....

We are called this day to join our cries with the nation on behalf of the land our birth. And though it has been, as most of you know, my constant course, on such solemn days as these are, to treat in particular our own sins, our own decay, our own means of recovery; yet upon this occasion I shall, as God shall help me, from these words represent to you the state of the nation wherein we live, and the only way and means for our deliverance from universal destruction....

Concerning Babylon ... I must observe three things. First, that Babylon was the origin of apostasy from the natural worship of God to idolatry in the whole world.... There is no mention of idolatry until the building of Babel; there it began. The tower which they built turned into a temple of Bel, whom they had made a god, and they placed his image on top.... Second, their idolatry: the idolatry that there began consisted of image worship, in the worshiping of graven images. ... The rest of the world, especially the eastern nations, fell into worshiping the sun, which they called Baal, or Moloch, or Chemosh ... and the worship of the moon, which they called Ashtaroth and the queen of heaven.... Third, the Babylonians were, so far as appears in the records, the first state in the world that ever persecuted someone for religion, that oppressed the true worshipers of God. ... They were the first that oppressed the church because of its worshiping of God and destroyed that worship among them. Hence the church prays in this chapter, "The vengeance of the Lord and of his temple be upon Babylon...."

Upon these accounts ... the name of Babylon, and all that is spoken of in the Old Testament, is transferred to the apostate Church of Rome in the New, and all applied unto it, in the book of Revelation....

Oh, poor England! Among all your lovers you have not one who pleads for you this day! From the height of profaneness and atheism, through the filthiness of sensuality and uncleanness, down to the lowest oppression and cheating, the land is filled with all sorts of sin. If there be any that can put in an exception as to provoking sin that is not among us, let them stand forth and plead the cause of the nation. I profess that my mouth is stopped. "The land is filled with sin against the Holy One of Israel." It is to no purpose to enumerate our sins—the roll is too long to be read at this time; and I am sorry it has been cut down and thrown into the fire when it has been spoken of, condemned, and despised, as Jeremiah's scroll was by Jehoiakim. SEASONABLE WORDS FOR ENGLISH PROTESTANTS, A SERMON ON JEREMIAH 51:5.[22]

ANOTHER DELIVERANCE FROM BABYLON. DIRK PHILIPS: The destruction of the Holy City and the temple happened through the Antichrist and through the harlot of Babylon who has perverted all the divine ordinances; who is adorned with purple, silk, scarlet, and gold; who has the golden cup full of all abominations in her hand; who was drunk from the blood of the saints and the witnesses of Jesus Christ.... In summary, she is a mother of all abominations upon the earth, and all who love their souls and desire to be saved, these must forsake this whore and separate out of Babylon, just as the Scripture says: my people, depart from Babylon, flee out of the land of the Chaldeans....

Now here it is necessary to observe how Israel was twice captive, twice delivered, and twice came into the kingdom and the glory; also that the temple was built twice upon the same foundation and form.... But now we have come into the second deliverance out of Babylon; now we have come to the building of the second temple and the city of Jerusalem. For now God delivers his people wonderfully every day out of the spiritual captivity of Babylon; now he redeems his chosen from all the abominations of the Babylonian whore with faithful admonitions through his messengers. THE ENCHIRIDION.[23]

---

[22]Owen, *Works*: 9:3-4, 9*; citing Gen 11:1-9; Jer 30:14; 36:23.
[23]CRR 6:343-44; citing Rev 17:4-6.

THE PAPACY IS BABYLON. MARTIN LUTHER: I now know for certain that the papacy is the kingdom of Babylon and the power of Nimrod, the mighty hunter. Once more, therefore, that all may turn out to my friends' advantage, I beg both the booksellers and my readers that after burning what I have published on this subject they hold to this proposition: *the papacy is the grand hunting of the bishop of Rome.* THE BABYLONIAN CAPTIVITY OF THE CHURCH.[24]

BABYLON, ANCIENT ROME, AND PAPAL ROME. JOHANNES BUGENHAGEN: "A golden cup." "Cup," as in chapter 25: Jeremiah calls this the furor of the Babylonian kingdom and the calamity through that furor of the oppressors. Then he attributes to them drunkenness and intoxication because the conquered nations thereafter took pride in the glory of Babylon. Moreover, he says "gold" because of the kingdom or dominion that was even stabilized and extended by its glory.

Notice that in the Revelation of John chapters 14, 17, and 18 there is a good deal of imitation of the words the prophets speak against Babylon. But John speaks concerning Rome and the anti-Christian kingdom of the Romans, which at one time killed the holy martyrs of Christ by means of a single tyranny. Now this occurs through the pope and the damned papists with their false doctrine and many blasphemous names. Indeed, John does not speak concerning the ruin of Babylon, which is here covered in Jeremiah, but concerning Rome as it ruled. When John was writing, Rome held dominion over the kings of the earth, as you see in Revelation 17. He wanted, moreover, to use the name of Babylon, so as to place as if before the eyes of Christians the judgment of God against the fourth monarchy, but especially against the Roman monarchy, a tyranny the church of Christ now endures; he spoke so that they would know that the same judgment was coming to the fourth monarchy that had happened to the first monarchy that persecuted the people of God. COMMENTARY ON JEREMIAH 51:7.[25]

WHEN PEOPLE REFUSE THE WORD. MARTIN LUTHER: When the word is revealed from heaven, we see that some are converted and freed from condemnation. The remaining mass [of people] despises it and unconcernedly indulges in greed, lust, and other vices, just as Jeremiah states about Babylon: "We have healed Babylon, but she was not healed. Forsake her, and let us go, each to their own country."

Similarly, the more diligently Moses and Aaron urged and instructed Pharaoh, the more unyielding he became. The Jews were not changed for the better by the very preaching of Christ and of the apostles. The same thing happens to us who are preaching today. What shall we do? We can deplore the blindness and obstinacy of people, but we cannot bring about a change for the better. Who would rejoice at the everlasting damnation of the popes and of their followers? Who would not prefer to have them receive the word and come to their senses? LECTURE ON GENESIS 6:3.[26]

THE POPE IN BABYLON. MARTIN LUTHER: I have truly despised your see, the Roman curia, which, however, neither you nor anyone else can deny is more corrupt than any Babylon or Sodom ever was, and which, as far as I can see, is characterized by a completely depraved, hopeless, and notorious godlessness. I have been thoroughly incensed over the fact that good Christians are mocked in your name and under the cloak of the Roman church. I have resisted and will continue to resist your see as long as the spirit of faith lives in me. Not that I shall strive for the impossible or hope that by my efforts alone anything will be accomplished in that most disordered Babylon, where the fury of so many flatterers is turned against me; but I acknowledge my indebtedness to

---

[24]LW 36:12 (WA 6:498); citing Gen 10:8-9.

[25]Bugenhagen, *In Ieremiam*, 5Z4r; citing Jer 25:15-29; Rev 14:6-13; Dan 2:40; 7:23.
[26]LW 2:16-17 (WA 12:273).

my Christian brethren, whom I am duty-bound to warn so that fewer of them may be destroyed by the plagues of Rome, at least so that their destruction may be less cruel. . . .

Meanwhile you, Leo,[†] sit as a lamb in the midst of wolves and like Daniel in the midst of lions. With Ezekiel you live among scorpions. How can you alone oppose such monsters? Even if you would call to your aid three or four learned and thoroughly reliable cardinals, what are these among so many? You would all be poisoned before you could begin to issue a decree for the purpose of remedying the situation. The Roman curia is already lost, for God's wrath has relentlessly fallen upon it. It detests church councils, it fears a reformation, it cannot allay its own corruption; and what was said of its mother Babylon also applies to it: "We would have cured Babylon, but she was not healed. Let us forsake her." AN OPEN LETTER TO POPE LEO.[27]

WATERS AND WEALTH WILL NOT PROTECT YOU. JOHN MAYER: "O you that dwell on many waters." In saying this, Jeremiah alludes to the situation of Babylon upon the banks of the Euphrates River and the great waters around the walls of the city on every side, making the defense of the city substantial. Therefore, Jeremiah mentions what none might question: whether the city could be destroyed with such deep and broad waters around it, making it inaccessible. But when God comes to a place, no waters or walls or other fortifications will stand against his mighty power. And riches, of which he speaks next, shall be like dross, and this destruction will be measured by their covetousness. COMMENTARY ON JEREMIAH 51:13.[28]

TREASURING GOD OR THE WORLD. JOHANNES BUGENHAGEN: Meanwhile, the prophet utters a song of thanks to God and against the pride and avarice of the world, which is the height of foolishness. Jeremiah says: we have a God who made everything in heaven and on earth, who frees his people from evil and is to us a treasury and incomparable riches. You wise people are foolish, because you have mammon as your God, who deserts you in hard times and so ruins you. Christ says, "What does it profit someone if they gain the whole world, but suffer the loss of their very soul?" The Babylonians perished—the vanquishers of the world—and everything that they plundered was never enough. But they eagerly followed avarice until they were ruined.

Now among the noble and the rabble all follow avarice; in usury and in profit they lose the world. We call on them in the name of God; we beg them not to keep going on like this, but in vain. Therefore, let us sing this song to those who hoard grain as the wretched die of hunger or as they give them money at doubled interest; let us give thanks to the God, who is our treasure and our king, through whom we will be satisfied in days of hunger. Meanwhile, let them mock our God, our treasury: the hour will come to them, as it did to the Babylonians, when our God in turn will mock them. COMMENTARY ON JEREMIAH 51:15.[29]

COMFORT IN GOD'S SOVEREIGNTY OVER BABYLON. JOHN CALVIN: Here the prophet removes the doubts of many; for as he had spoken of the destruction of Babylon, one might readily object that the monarchy was impregnable because it was fortified with so many defenses and had subjugated so many neighboring nations. Hence the prophet shows that the power and wealth of Babylon did not hinder God from destroying it whenever he pleased. We have seen before that God roots up what he has planted, and then we have seen the metaphor of the potter and his vessels. When the prophet went down to the potter, he saw a vessel formed and then broken at the will and pleasure of the potter. So also now God shows that the destruction was, as it were, in his hand, because the Chaldeans had not raised themselves to eminence through their own power, but he had

---

[27]LW 31:336-37 (WA 7:44); citing Mt 10:16; Dan 6:16; Ezek 2:6.
[†]Luther addresses Pope Leo X (1475–1521; as pope, 1513–1521).
[28]Mayer, A Commentary, 474*.

[29]Bugenhagen, In Ieremiam, 6A1r-v; citing Mt 16:26; Mk 8:36.

raised them and employed them for his own purpose. In short, he compares the Babylonians in this passage to a formed vessel and he makes himself the potter: "I am he who raised Babylon to so great a height; it therefore belongs to me to pull it down whenever it pleases me. . . ."

The prophet reminds us that no difficulty would prevent God from destroying Babylon because Babylon itself was nothing. According to this sense, then, it is called a hammer. In short, the prophet takes away the false opinion, which might otherwise have disturbed weak minds, that Babylon was invincible. He shows at the same time that God executed his judgments on all nations by means of Babylon. Thus the faithful might have been confirmed. Otherwise they must have necessarily been cast down when they regarded the formidable power of Babylon. But when they heard that [Babylon] was only a hammer, the Jews knew that the calamity they had suffered was nothing more than a punishment inflicted by God's hand. Thus the Babylonians would not have broken [the Jews] into pieces unless the Babylonians had been armed from above, or rather had been driven by a celestial power. When, therefore, [the Jews] heard this, it was no small consolation; it kept them from succumbing under their miseries, and from being swallowed up with sorrow and despair. COMMENTARY ON JEREMIAH 51:20-23.[30]

RISE UP, O LORD. JOHANNES BUGENHAGEN: "He has eaten me up." . . . Through these words Jeremiah describes his secret sighs to God, brought forth in affliction and against Babylon, which certainly God hears. As in Romans 8: "The Spirit intercedes for us with groaning that words cannot describe"; as God says here, "Behold I myself will judge your cause." So it happens that the entire Babylonian dominion perishes because of the tyranny inflicted on the Jews. Today let the papistic kingdom fear for itself, for it provokes so many sighs, tears, and prayers of Christians against itself by its tyranny. This kingdom has been accused; it

has been condemned; it will perish. Lord, the pride of those who hate you always increases: "Rise up, Lord, judge your cause!"[†] COMMENTARY ON JEREMIAH 51:34-36.[31]

SWEET SLEEP AND PERPETUAL SLEEP. JOHN DONNE: The death of the righteous is a sleep; first it delivers them to a present rest. Now people do not sleep well fasting; nor does a fasting conscience sleep well, a conscience that is not nourished with a testimony of having done well when coming to this sleep. But the sleeping of a laboring person is sweet. To the one who labors in their calling, even this sleep of death is welcome. "When you lay down, you shall not be afraid," says Solomon. When your physician says, "Sir you must keep to your bed, you shall not be afraid in that sickbed. So your sleep will be sweet to you. Your sickness will be welcome and your death too"; for in those two things David seems to include everything: "I will lay myself down in peace and sleep": I embrace patiently my deathbed and death itself.

So then this death is a sleep, as it delivers us to present rest. And then lastly it also promises a future waking in a glorious resurrection. To the wicked it is far from both rest and resurrection. Of them God says, "I will make them drunk, and they shall sleep a perpetual sleep and not awaken." They shall have no part in the second resurrection. But for them that have slept in Christ, as Christ said of Lazarus, "Lazarus sleeps, but I go that I may wake him from sleep." Christ says to his Father, "Let me go that I may wake them who have slept so long in expectation of my coming." SERMON ON ACTS 7:60.[32]

CYRUS LIKE CHRIST. JOHN MAYER: "I will punish Bel in Babylon. . . ." Bel was the chief god of the Babylonians and was worshiped likewise all over Assyria. Therefore, Bel had many precious things brought to him from all the countries round

---

[30]CTS 21:229-31* (CO 39:460-1); citing Jer 1:10; 18:1-23.

[31]Bugenhagen, *In Ieremiam*, 6A2r-v; citing Rom 8:26. †Bugenhagen ends his comment with a clever play on words: now citing against the papacy what Pope Leo X had decreed in the first line of his 1520 Bull "Exsurge Domine" against Martin Luther.
[32]Donne, *Sermons*, 8:191*; citing Eccles 5:12; Prov 3:24; Ps 4:8; Jn 11:11.

about that were subject to Babylon. . . . And by this means Bel's temple came to be greatly enriched, and all these offerings are spoken of as though Bel devoured them. But the Lord threatens now to bring what he had devoured out of Bel's mouth, meaning to despoil him of all his goods, which superstitious people had offered to him. This was done when the Persians took everything away and Cyrus carried away that idol. . . . Mystically by Bel understand the devil, think of Cyrus as Christ, of whom he was an eminent symbol, who brings all that had been devoured out of the devil's mouth— that roaring Lion. The devil made people his bondslaves; when Christ died he subdued the devil, and by his Spirit works true faith in the hearts of people. COMMENTARY ON JEREMIAH 51:44.[33]

THE JUDGMENT OF ALL EVIL. JOHANNES BUGENHAGEN: "The heavens and the earth." Both angels and people will rejoice and give thanks to God that he has punished the blasphemy and homicide of the Babylonians, Turks, and papists. Meanwhile, this is longed for, and oppressed people sigh, requesting a judgment from God, when tyrants and blasphemers seem to themselves to be glorious and think themselves to be highly esteemed. But this judgment of God will speak to everything. Thus the tyrants and heretics have been condemned; that is, those who pervert the Word of God have been condemned, I say, by the sighs and prayers of people even before the judgment of God is seen and understood. John echoes these words in the book of Revelation in chapter 19, and thus it now happens and will happen more. For the son of perdition perishes by the Spirit of the mouth of Christ, that is, by the holy gospel that has been revealed. COMMENTARY ON JEREMIAH 51:48.[34]

A PROPHECY TO BE TAKEN TO BABYLON. JOHN CALVIN: Here we see, on the one hand, the courage the prophet had, who dared to command the king's messenger; for though Seraiah was a meek man, so as to render himself submissive, yet Jeremiah exposed himself to danger too. In fact, [Seraiah] might have been timid, though he was neither proud nor arrogant. Thus as men are prone to do when terrified, he might have informed the king as to what he had heard from the prophet. Therefore, Jeremiah did what we here read and did so not without danger; and hence his firmness appears here. We then see that he was endued with the spirit of invincible courage, so as to discharge his office freely and intrepidly.

Jeremiah then "wrote in a book. . . ." Here the boldness of Jeremiah comes into view: he did not hesitate to command Seraiah to read this book when he came to Babylon and had seen [Babylon]. To see it is not mentioned here without reason, for the splendor of that city might have astonished Seraiah. Then the prophet here seasonably meets the difficulty, and bids Seraiah to disregard the height of the walls and the towers; and that however Babylon might dazzle the eyes of others, yet Seraiah was to look down, as if from on high. . . .

Jeremiah afterward adds, "And when you have made an end of the reading, you shall tie a stone to it and cast it into the Euphrates, and you shall say, 'In this way Babylon will sink.'" Here is added an external symbol to confirm the faith of Seraiah. We must bear in mind that this was not said to Seraiah for his own sake alone, but that the people might also know that the king's messenger, who had been sent for the sake of conciliation, was also the messenger of God and the prophet; otherwise Seraiah might have been despised by the people. . . . In short, Seraiah was commanded, as the prophet's messenger, to predict by himself the fall of Babylon. COMMENTARY ON JEREMIAH 51:60-64.[35]

CONCLUDING THE BOOK OF JEREMIAH. JOHANNES OECOLAMPADIUS: "Thus are the words of Jeremiah." In this last passage Jeremiah has predicted the destruction of Babylon, in which the restoration of Israel and the kingdom of Christ are intertwined. He seems here to leave the project to others; for

---

[33]Mayer, A Commentary, 476-77*.
[34]Bugenhagen, In Ieremiam, 6A3r-v.
[35]CTS 21:289-90, 292-93* (CO 39:499-501).

someone else who was appointed will have collated this book of the prophecies of Jeremiah: he attributes the words to the prophet and for the sake of providing credibility; it seems that this little clause was added so no one would suppose that the words belong to the scribe and not to the prophet. COMMENTARY ON JEREMIAH 51:64.[36]

THUS FAR, JEREMIAH. JOHN CALVIN: We have said that the prophets, after having spoken in the temple or to the people afterward collected brief summaries, and these contained the principal things from which these prophetic books were made. For Jeremiah did not write the volume as we have it on this day, except for [these last] chapters; and it appears evident that it was not written in the order in which he spoke. The order of time, then, is not everywhere observed; but the scribes were careful in this respect: they collected the summaries affixed to the doors of the temple; and so they added this conclusion: "Thus far, the words of Jeremiah." COMMENTARY ON JEREMIAH 51:64.[37]

---

[36]Oecolampadius, *In Hieremiam*, 3:2O2v.

[37]CTS 21:293* (CO 39:501-2).

JEREMIAH 52:1-34
THE FALL OF JERUSALEM, EXILE, AND HOPE

[1]*Zedekiah was twenty-one years old when he became king, and he reigned eleven years in Jerusalem. His mother's name was Hamutal the daughter of Jeremiah of Libnah.* [2]*And he did what was evil in the sight of the Lord, according to all that Jehoiakim had done.* [3]*For because of the anger of the Lord it came to the point in Jerusalem and Judah that he cast them out from his presence.*

And Zedekiah rebelled against the king of Babylon. [4]*And in the ninth year of his reign, in the tenth month, on the tenth day of the month, Nebuchadnezzar king of Babylon came with all his army against Jerusalem, and laid siege to it. And they built siegeworks all around it.* [5]*So the city was besieged till the eleventh year of King Zedekiah.* [6]*On the ninth day of the fourth month the famine was so severe in the city that there was no food for the people of the land.* [7]*Then a breach was made in the city, and all the men of war fled and went out from the city by night by the way of a gate between the two walls, by the king's garden, and the Chaldeans were around the city. And they went in the direction of the Arabah.* [8]*But the army of the Chaldeans pursued the king and overtook Zedekiah in the plains of Jericho, and all his army was scattered from him.* [9]*Then they captured the king and brought him up to the king of Babylon at Riblah in the land of Hamath, and he passed sentence on him.* [10]*The king of Babylon slaughtered the sons of Zedekiah before his eyes, and also slaughtered all the officials of Judah at Riblah.* [11]*He put out the eyes of Zedekiah, and bound him in chains, and the king of Babylon took him to Babylon, and put him in prison till the day of his death.*

[12]*In the fifth month, on the tenth day of the month—that was the nineteenth year of King Nebuchadnezzar, king of Babylon—Nebuzaradan the captain of the bodyguard, who served the king of Babylon, entered Jerusalem.* [13]*And he burned the house of the Lord, and the king's house and all the houses of Jerusalem; every great house he burned*

down. [14]*And all the army of the Chaldeans, who were with the captain of the guard, broke down all the walls around Jerusalem.* [15]*And Nebuzaradan the captain of the guard carried away captive some of the poorest of the people and the rest of the people who were left in the city and the deserters who had deserted to the king of Babylon, together with the rest of the artisans.* [16]*But Nebuzaradan the captain of the guard left some of the poorest of the land to be vinedressers and plowmen.*

[17]*And the pillars of bronze that were in the house of the Lord, and the stands and the bronze sea that were in the house of the Lord, the Chaldeans broke in pieces, and carried all the bronze to Babylon.* [18]*And they took away the pots and the shovels and the snuffers and the basins and the dishes for incense and all the vessels of bronze used in the temple service;* [19]*also the small bowls and the fire pans and the basins and the pots and the lampstands and the dishes for incense and the bowls for drink offerings. What was of gold the captain of the guard took away as gold, and what was of silver, as silver.* [20]*As for the two pillars, the one sea, the twelve bronze bulls that were under the sea,[a] and the stands, which Solomon the king had made for the house of the Lord, the bronze of all these things was beyond weight.* [21]*As for the pillars, the height of the one pillar was eighteen cubits,[b] its circumference was twelve cubits, and its thickness was four fingers, and it was hollow.* [22]*On it was a capital of bronze. The height of the one capital was five cubits. A network and pomegranates, all of bronze, were around the capital. And the second pillar had the same, with pomegranates.* [23]*There were ninety-six pomegranates on the sides; all the pomegranates were a hundred upon the network all around.*

[24]*And the captain of the guard took Seraiah the chief priest, and Zephaniah the second priest and the three keepers of the threshold;* [25]*and from the city he took an officer who had been in command of the men of war, and seven men of the king's council, who were*

found in the city; and the secretary of the commander of the army, who mustered the people of the land; and sixty men of the people of the land, who were found in the midst of the city. ²⁶And Nebuzaradan the captain of the guard took them and brought them to the king of Babylon at Riblah. ²⁷And the king of Babylon struck them down and put them to death at Riblah in the land of Hamath. So Judah was taken into exile out of its land.

²⁸This is the number of the people whom Nebuchadnezzar carried away captive: in the seventh year, 3,023 Judeans; ²⁹in the eighteenth year of Nebuchadnezzar he carried away captive from Jerusalem 832 persons; ³⁰in the twenty-third year of Nebuchadnezzar, Nebuzaradan the captain of the guard carried

away captive of the Judeans 745 persons; all the persons were 4,600.

³¹And in the thirty-seventh year of the exile of Jehoiachin king of Judah, in the twelfth month, on the twenty-fifth day of the month, Evil-merodach king of Babylon, in the year that he began to reign, graciously freedᶜ Jehoiachin king of Judah and brought him out of prison. ³²And he spoke kindly to him and gave him a seat above the seats of the kings who were with him in Babylon. ³³So Jehoiachin put off his prison garments. And every day of his life he dined regularly at the king's table, ³⁴and for his allowance, a regular allowance was given him by the king, according to his daily needs, until the day of his death, as long as he lived.

a Hebrew lacks *the sea*   b A *cubit* was about 18 inches or 45 centimeters   c Hebrew *reign, lifted up the head of*

OVERVIEW: The final chapter of Jeremiah returns to the central event of so many prophecies—the destruction of Jerusalem and the last wave of Jewish exiles to Babylon. Protestant commentators not only review briefly the implications of such destruction but also locate Babylon in their own time—whether in Rome or in the Christian life. Failure to repent and attend to the Word of God opens the soul to the conquest and ravages of a spiritual Babylon. Yet the final verses of Jeremiah portend hope: the survival of the captive king Jehoiachin in Babylon and the honor bestowed on him confirms the steadfast promise of God to return the Jews to their homeland and to give them a Messiah in the line of David.

52:1-30 The Destruction of Jerusalem

THE THREAT OF BABYLON TO JUDAH AND TO ENGLAND. JOHN OWEN: As Babylon was the spring of all persecution against and oppression of the church of God under the Old Testament, so Rome has been the spring of persecution and oppression of the church of God, since the apostasy under the New Testament. On this account the Holy Spirit has, in infinite wisdom,

transferred the name and state of Babylon from the Old to the New.

I have mentioned this that you may see the interest of England in this text of Scripture. So far as the truth of religion is owned in this nation, so far as there is a testimony given against idolatry, we are to God as Israel and Judah, though the land is filled with sin. At the time of this prophecy, Israel and Judah were in danger of present destruction and desolation from the old Babylon; and if we do not mock God in all we do, we are under apprehension that England, and the church of God in England, is in danger of the same desolation and destruction from the new Babylon, based on the same account and principle. If we do not mock God, this is what we profess this day. So far this parallel runs equally. So was Babylon of old and so it is in the present; so was the danger to Israel and Judah in that day, and so is the danger to England anew in the present. SEASONABLE WORDS FOR ENGLISH PROTESTANTS, A SERMON ON JEREMIAH 51:5[1]

THE PURPOSE OF THE CHAPTER. JOHN MAYER: I will merely touch on chapter 52. It is the same—

---

[1]Owen, *Works*, 9:5*.

verbatim—with 2 Kings 24, and therefore I refer the reader to expositions there. Whether it was written by Jeremiah or not, it can be questioned because some things related herein happened after Jeremiah's death. . . . Therefore, it is most probable, as some now conjecture, that Baruch transcribed it from 2 Kings 24 and put it here that after this lamentable account of Jerusalem's destruction. The book of Lamentations might more aptly follow here. COMMENTARY ON JEREMIAH 52.[2]

PROPHECY FULFILLED AND REPENTANCE REQUIRED. NIKOLAUS SELNECKER: This is a terrible account of the conquest of the city of Jerusalem and of the capture of King Zedekiah, which we have already heard about in chapter 39. At the end of this sermon we see that the word and prophecy of the prophet Jeremiah have been fulfilled. We believe that all must be fulfilled as God has proclaimed and said. We must also learn how God attends to punishment, when one does not follow his Word and does not want to improve one's life through true repentance. THE WHOLE PROPHET JEREMIAH 52.[3]

WHAT REMAINS AFTER DEFEAT? JOHANNES BUGENHAGEN: Concerning this history we have spoken on chapter 39. The kingdom, priesthood, government, temple, cities, nobles, the wealthy, teachers, and artisans perish. What remains in that place? They wanted this; they despised the goodness and promises of God. Therefore, they are experiencing the truth of his warning. COMMENTARY ON JEREMIAH 52.[4]

THE SIEGE OF JERUSALEM AND OUR SOULS. JOHANNES OECOLAMPADIUS: "It happened in the ninth year." The long-suffering Lord at last brings in the enemy, nor is an allegory to be sought superstitiously in the number; the accounting was settled by God. Moreover, for two years the city had been besieged; meanwhile the city was harassed with

famine, disease, and practically daily skirmishes; the city was finally captured, but the soldiers fled. Similarly Zedekiah with his people took off and he was captured in the wilderness of Jericho and led to Riblah. Thereafter, Nebuchadnezzar excoriated Zedekiah there with harsh words, killed his sons, blinded him, led him to Babylon, and handed him over to a perpetual watchman for safekeeping.

When hypocrisy reigns the ardor of one's own will comes before God: so the prophets are heard but are killed, and idols are established by a new decree. Faith is not preserved, mercy is lacking, and the Lord unleashes his scourge, so that we also are led into Babylon. But before that, we are attacked by our vices, as if by enemies. If we are destitute in the Word of God, then the gates of our souls are opened and in go all kinds of evil and shame, which lock us into a sinful and filthy slavery. Then comes the desolation of the church, but more severe is the judgment on those who rule undeservedly. COMMENTARY ON JEREMIAH 52:4-11.[5]

A SEMBLANCE OF TRUTH. PILGRAM MARPECK: Every sacred thing is surrendered to the enemy. So too did it happen in the time of Antiochus[†] and Nebuchadnezzar, who robbed the vessels of the temple, stole them for their idols, and used them in all ways as the people of God did. So too it happens now in the revealing of the kingdom of the Antichrist, which is the fulfillment of the kingdom of Babylon and Antichrist. With all the lying power of wickedness, they portray the sanctuary of truthful hearts, which is the true temple of God, but the appearance of the Son of God, who will reveal everything that is hidden, whether good or evil, will reveal this to be a semblance of truth. CONCERNING HASTY JUDGMENTS AND VERDICTS.[6]

TEMPLE AND DWELLING—CONSUMED AND FOUND. JOHANNES OECOLAMPADIUS: Through the destruction of the first temple the way into

---

[2]Mayer, *A Commentary*, 479*.
[3]Selnecker, *Der gantze Prophet Jeremias*, 2S4r.
[4]Bugenhagen, *In Ieremiam*, 6B2r.

[5]Oecolampadius, *In Hieremiam*, 3:2O3v.
[6]CRR 12:182; citing Mt 10:26; Mk 4:22; Lk 8:17; 12:2; 2 Thess 2:3-10; 1 Cor 3:17; 4:5; 2 Cor 6:16. †Antiochus IV Epiphanies, king of Syria (c. 215–164, r. 175–164 BC).

eternity is prepared. The shadow departs in the coming of the light. The great house, he says, he burned completely, that is, the dwellings of the nobility, who were living quite in splendor—not only the huts of the private and humble people, but also the outstanding buildings of the first citizens were destroyed by burning. . . .

"And the bowls": diligently he recalls that all of the ornate things were borne away: the columns are teachers if they accord with themselves. Pedestals are said to be the same, even if they patiently bear different statues. Likewise, the basin and the sea of bronze are said to be the same, if others are washed by their water, that is, by their doctrine. But Christ in particular is the column and foundation, over whom a spiritual building rises. He is the bath and water of heaven, when he cleanses consciences with his Spirit; he is the bowl, to the extent that he prepares us and completes us with his Word and love. COMMENTARY ON JEREMIAH 52:13-22.[7]

52:31-34 A Sign of Hope

BE PATIENT WITH AND PRAY FOR GODLY AUTHORITIES. NIKOLAUS SELNECKER: At the end we see how King Jehoiachin or Jeoconiah had willingly surrendered to the Babylonians because of the advice of Jeremiah. Now in his thirty-seventh year in Babylon he was again raised to great honor. Thus, as God promised, he would appear with his assistance, so that had come to pass. . . . Thus, if God shows such a thing, there is nothing else one can do but wait and be patient. As Peter advises, "Humble yourselves under the powerful hand of God, so that he may raise you up in his own time." He already knows what is best for us; we need not worry, but should trust him.

We should also consider the good deed and grace of the king Evil-merodach and thereby thank God for our authorities. We ask that God will defend and protect us under their government and give and sustain a peaceful community in his church. Such

we should seek from God with our hearts and ask in our prayers that our authorities be so guided. Then things will go well, as Jeremiah says in chapter 29. THE WHOLE PROPHET JEREMIAH 52:31-34.[8]

THE SEED OF CHRIST. JOHANNES BUGENHAGEN: Because Jehoiachin, King of Judah, after his thirty-seventh year in captivity, was exalted in Babylon, at that place other causes were able to be at work among humankind. But God did this in order to preserve the seed of David, whence Christ would be born according to the promises of God. COMMENTARY ON JEREMIAH 52:31-34.[9]

CONFIRMATION OF PROPHECY AND ETERNAL INSIGHT. JOHANN PAPPUS: It is written at the end of the last chapter: "Thus far the words of Jeremiah." This appendix testifies that this last chapter that follows does not belong to Jeremiah's own prophecies, and it also testifies to that which is also apparent, that the history as far as Evil-Merodach is covered in this chapter, but that this was added so that from this collection of events the prophecy of Jeremiah might shine more clearly. Nor can any clearer light be thrown on the predictions of the prophets than if the events are compared to the predictions themselves. We have previously heard the history of the capture of Jerusalem and the burning of the temple, and the captivity of the people who were led away, so that it would hardly be necessary to repeat the same history in this passage. However, with our whole hearts let us give thanks to our eternal God and Father of our Savior Jesus Christ that he has bestowed on us an exposition of this prophet too. Let us pray to the same eternal God that he open to us these dear prophecies according to our manner of thinking in this life, until we, taken away into that eternal academy, no longer know in part, but know just as we are known. ON ALL THE PROPHETS, JEREMIAH 52.[10]

---

[7]Oecolampadius, *In Hieremiam*, 3:2O4v; citing 1 Kings 7:23; 2 Kings 25:13.

[8]Selnecker, *Der gantze Prophet Jeremias*, 2S4r-v; citing 2 Kings 25:27-30; 1 Pet 5:6; Jer 29:4-7.
[9]Bugenhagen, *In Ieremiam*, 6B2r.
[10]Pappus, *In Omnes Prophetas*, 124v; citing 1 Cor 13:12.

COMMENTARY ON LAMENTATIONS

LAMENTATIONS 1:1-22
HOW LONELY SITS THE CITY

¹How lonely sits the city
    that was full of people!
How like a widow has she become,
    she who was great among the nations!
She who was a princess among the provinces
    has become a slave.

²She weeps bitterly in the night,
    with tears on her cheeks;
among all her lovers
    she has none to comfort her;
all her friends have dealt treacherously with her;
    they have become her enemies.

³Judah has gone into exile because of affliction^a
    and hard servitude;
she dwells now among the nations,
    but finds no resting place;
her pursuers have all overtaken her
    in the midst of her distress.^b

⁴The roads to Zion mourn,
    for none come to the festival;
all her gates are desolate;
    her priests groan;
her virgins have been afflicted,^c
    and she herself suffers bitterly.

⁵Her foes have become the head;
    her enemies prosper,
because the LORD has afflicted her
    for the multitude of her transgressions;
her children have gone away,
    captives before the foe.

⁶From the daughter of Zion
    all her majesty has departed.
Her princes have become like deer
    that find no pasture;
they fled without strength
    before the pursuer.

⁷Jerusalem remembers
    in the days of her affliction and wandering
all the precious things
    that were hers from days of old.
When her people fell into the hand of the foe,
    and there was none to help her,
her foes gloated over her;
    they mocked at her downfall.

⁸Jerusalem sinned grievously;
    therefore she became filthy;
all who honored her despise her,
    for they have seen her nakedness;
she herself groans
    and turns her face away.

⁹Her uncleanness was in her skirts;
    she took no thought of her future;^d
therefore her fall is terrible;
    she has no comforter.
"O Lord, behold my affliction,
    for the enemy has triumphed!"

¹⁰The enemy has stretched out his hands
    over all her precious things;
for she has seen the nations
    enter her sanctuary,

those whom you forbade
    to enter your congregation.

¹¹All her people groan
    as they search for bread;
they trade their treasures for food
    to revive their strength.
"Look, O LORD, and see,
    for I am despised."

¹²"Is it nothing to you, all you who pass by?
    Look and see
if there is any sorrow like my sorrow,
    which was brought upon me,
which the LORD inflicted
    on the day of his fierce anger.

¹³"From on high he sent fire;
    into my bones^e he made it descend;
he spread a net for my feet;
    he turned me back;
he has left me stunned,
    faint all the day long.

¹⁴"My transgressions were bound^f into a yoke;
    by his hand they were fastened together;
they were set upon my neck;
    he caused my strength to fail;
the Lord gave me into the hands
    of those whom I cannot withstand.

¹⁵"The Lord rejected
    all my mighty men in my midst;
he summoned an assembly against me
    to crush my young men;
the Lord has trodden as in a winepress
    the virgin daughter of Judah.

¹⁶"For these things I weep;
    my eyes flow with tears;
for a comforter is far from me,
    one to revive my spirit;
my children are desolate,

for the enemy has prevailed."

¹⁷Zion stretches out her hands,
    but there is none to comfort her;
the LORD has commanded against Jacob
    that his neighbors should be his foes;
Jerusalem has become
    a filthy thing among them.

¹⁸"The LORD is in the right,
    for I have rebelled against his word;
but hear, all you peoples,
    and see my suffering;
my young women and my young men
    have gone into captivity.

¹⁹"I called to my lovers,
    but they deceived me;
my priests and elders
    perished in the city,
while they sought food
    to revive their strength.

²⁰"Look, O LORD, for I am in distress;
    my stomach churns;
my heart is wrung within me,
    because I have been very rebellious.
In the street the sword bereaves;
    in the house it is like death.

²¹"They heard^g my groaning,
    yet there is no one to comfort me.
All my enemies have heard of my trouble;
    they are glad that you have done it.
You have brought^h the day you announced;
    now let them be as I am.

²²"Let all their evildoing come before you,
    and deal with them
as you have dealt with me
    because of all my transgressions;
for my groans are many,
    and my heart is faint."

---

a Or *under affliction*   **b** Or *in the narrow passes*   **c** Septuagint, Old Latin *dragged away*   **d** Or *end*   **e** Septuagint; Hebrew *bones and*   **f** The meaning of the Hebrew is uncertain   **g** Septuagint, Syriac *Hear*   **h** Syriac *Bring*

OVERVIEW: Preachers, poets, and biblical scholars hear a multitude of voices and identify a range of audiences for the book of Lamentations. Since the authorship of Jeremiah was assumed in the Reformation era, interpreters reflect on the anguish of the prophet and his kinfolk after the sack of Jerusalem and during the exile in Babylon. More generally, expositors hear the many voices of common humanity: the individual, the church, and the Christian commonwealth; both those who have undergone tragic loss due to societal upheaval and those who have experienced suffering of the soul; for the latter, Lamentations testifies to the depths of despair, a deep sorrow for sin, an acute desire to repent, and a renewed confidence in the everlasting mercy of God. Some find in Lamentations the very voice of Jesus the Christ in prophetic form; here Lamentations echoes or perhaps anticipates the Gospels and "the man of sorrows" of Isaiah 53. In every passage the world of the sixteenth and seventeenth centuries emerges here as readers describe the landscape of suffering in their own era and the resources of the Christian faith that nourish the faithful in hard times.

1:1-9 The Deserted City

THE SHAPE OF LAMENTATIONS. JOHANNES BUGENHAGEN: In these songs of mourning, that is, in these lamentations, or this beating of the breast, the prophet weeps over the destruction of Jerusalem, the kingdom of Judah, and the miserable captivity of the people, which he was not able to avert with the threats and promises of God because of the people's unbelief and contempt for the Word of God. But after that he consoles himself and the people with the promises of God, and with his own prayers he commits their situation to God, who is the Father of the wretched and who forgives every sin of those who call out, even in tribulation.

Nothing is said here concerning the passion of Christ, as is claimed by those who are in the church under the pope, who certainly have no faculty of comprehension for the holy Scriptures. In fact, here

the individual verses in Hebrew begin with each letter in the order of the Hebrew alphabet, just as happens in certain psalms. I think this was done to help with memory (when these are sung without a book)[†] as with the *Carmen Seduli* among us.[†] For these reasons alone did the verses come out in this order: I do not believe that this alphabetical ordering pertains to something else. Jeremiah also produced other songs of mourning, which no longer exist, as noted in 2 Chronicles 35, where it is mentioned that Jeremiah excelled in mournful songs among the Hebrews. COMMENTARY ON JEREMIAH, LAMENTATIONS 1.[1]

THE OCCASION IS INSIGNIFICANT TO THE MEANING. JOHN UDALL: Whether this excellent book was made upon the occasion of the death of Josiah, being (as it were) the beginning of God's heavy hand upon the Jews for their contempt of his word so long foretold by the prophets, which caused this servant of God so exceedingly to lament . . . , or rather upon the overthrow of the city of Jerusalem and burning of the temple therein, it needs not be greatly inquired, seeing it is evident that it was indited by the Holy Spirit of God and penned by the prophet Jeremiah, to draw the church of God into a serious consideration of their sins that caused the same, and to true and unfeigned repentance, earnestly praying to the Lord to remove his angry countenance from them and to turn his gracious favor, as in former times, to them. COMMENTARY ON LAMENTATIONS.[2]

HISTORIC AND PROPHETIC. JOHN DONNE: The book is certainly the prophet Jeremiah's, and certainly a distinct book; but whether the book be a history or a prophecy, whether Jeremiah laments that which he has seen or that which he foresees, calamities past or

---

[1]Bugenhagen, *In Ieremiam . . . Threni*, C2v-C3r; citing 2 Chron 35:25.
[†]Bugenhagen has in mind here Hebrew and Latin editions of Lamentations that enumerate each verse with a Hebrew letter. Thus, verse 1 = *aleph*; verse 2 = *bet*, etc.; keeping in mind that Bugenhagen's own commentary predates the individual verses that now divide up biblical passages. [†]Bugenhagen refers here the *Carmen Paschale*, attributed to the fifth-century Christian poet Sedulius.
[2]Udall, *Commentary on Lamentations*, C1r*.

future calamities, things done or things to be done, is a question which has exercised and busied diverse expositors. But, as we say of the parable of Dives and Lazarus, that it is a historical parable and a parabolical history, some such persons there were, and some such things were really done, but some other things were figuratively symbolically, parabolically added; so we say of Jeremiah's Lamentations. It is a prophetical history, and a historical prophecy. Some of the sad occasions of these lamentations were passed when he wrote, and some were to come after, for we may not despise the testimony of the Chaldee paraphrasts, who were the first that illustrated the Bible in that nation, nor of Jerome, who was much conversant with the Bible and with that nation, nor of Josephus, who had justly so much estimation in that nation, nor of those later rabbis, who were the most learned of that nation, who are all of the opinion that Jeremiah wrote these lamentations after he saw some declinations in the state, in the death of Josiah. And so the book is historical, but when he only foresaw their transportation into Babylon, before that calamity fell upon them, and so it is prophetical. Or, if we take the expositions of the others, that the whole book was written after their transportation into Babylon, and to be in all parts historical, yet it is prophetical still, for the prophet laments a greater desolation than that, in the utter ruin and devastation of the city and nation, which was to fall upon them after the death of Christ Jesus. Neither is any piece of this book the less fit to be our text this day because it is both historical and prophetical, for they from whom God in his mercy gave deliverance this day are our historical enemies and our prophetical enemies. Historically we know they have attempted our ruin before, and prophetically we may be sure they will do so again, whenever any new situation provokes them, or sufficient power enables them. SERMON ON LAMENTATIONS 4:20.[3]

<hr>

[3]Donne, *Works*, 5:204-5*; citing Lk 16:19-31. Jerome (c. 347–419/420) was an early Christian biblical scholar of the fourth and fifth centuries, editor and translator of the Vulgate, and author of a commentary on Jeremiah. Josephus (c. AD 37/38–100) was a first-century scholar of Jewish history and author of the *Jewish Antiquities* and the *Jewish War*.

JEREMIAH'S SIMILARITIES TO MOSES. HUGH BROUGHTON: Jeremiah had great resemblances to liken him to Moses at many points, pleasant to consider and much for his authority. As Moses was of Levi, the godliest tribe and the best family, that which by faith hid him three months, so Jeremiah was of Levi, of the sacrificers of Anathoth, and his father was Chelkiah the high sacrificer, who found the law hid in the temple in Manasseh's days, whose repentance was but a little before his death, that he could not think of the law, and Amon his son was wicked. Of this Levite came Jeremiah, son and father honorers of Moses. Moses was unwilling to go upon his message; Jeremiah was unwilling to go upon his message. Moses' own tribe stood up against him, Korah and his company. Jeremiah his own, the men of Anathoth stood up against him. Moses was cast into the river by his own kindred; Jeremiah was cast into a dungeon by his own kindred. Moses was taken out of the river by one of Pharaoh's maidens; Jeremiah was taken out of the dungeon by an Ethiopian, by Abimelech. Moses reproved Israel; Jeremiah reproved Israel. Moses told Israel of captivity and closely of seventy years, and of a new remembrance of covenant; Jeremiah told Israel of captivity and expressly to end of seventy years. Of the New Testament Moses told that the kings should go to a strange land, upon defeat to be rooted out; Jeremiah tells the kings shall go to Babel and tells expressly twice that the kings shall be rooted out. Moses desired of God to show him his ways, seeing the strange success of the wicked here; Jeremiah desired to know why the wicked prospered. Moses bade Israel they should no more return to Egypt; Jeremiah bade Israel they should no more return to Egypt. Moses spoke from his own faith in God, that the rebels against him should have a strange death. Jeremiah from his faith in God told the pseudo-prophet Ananias, son of Azor, this year you shall die. Moses wrote of sadness to Rachel the mother by her death at Bethlehem; Jeremiah wrote that Rachel shall weep for her children's death at Bethlehem. Moses prophesied a king, of Christ, the king, forty years. Jeremiah prophesied to kings of

Christ the true king forty years. Moses wrote most curious poetry, Jeremiah's Lamentations bring more joy for learned style than sadness by speech of the nations' fall. Moses and Jeremiah saved much of their company by their forty years, for going into the land from the wilderness and going out of the land into the wilderness of the heathen. The Pharisees despising Moses and Jeremiah and the apostles forty years bred eternal lamentations. COMMENTARY ON LAMENTATIONS.[4]

A DRAMATIC OPENING TO A FRIEND. DANIEL TOUSSAIN: This chapter has no large or long entrance into it, but begins even at the first chop to pour out such feeling, mourning, and lamentation as is typical of someone extremely and grievously tormented with sorrow. Thus one would not expect any long or affected narrations or discourses. Therefore, the prophet begins, as it were, to make a sudden exclamation to some passenger or friend, whereby he would put him in mind of Jerusalem's former prosperity, and of all the whole country round about her. That way the friend might with fear and trembling see more easily the horrible destruction and ruin now fallen upon Jerusalem. It is a thing most incredible to see how naturally the prophet sets before our eyes the mourning and sorrow even of indefensible creatures, as he pictures in a lively way the misery of the people, the unfaithfulness of the neighbors, and the fury of the enemies. Therein he inserts an acknowledgment of their sins and of their holy submission to God, while adding a prayer and crucial words against their enemies. THE LAMENTATIONS AND HOLY MOURNINGS, CHAPTER I.[5]

THE ALPHABETICAL STRUCTURE OF LAMENTATIONS. HECTOR PINTO: *Aleph....* These are written in Hebrew in this order, so that the first verse begins with *aleph*—the first letter of the Hebrew alphabet. The second verse begins with the letter *bet*, and so on for the remainder, preserv-

ing the order of the letters of the alphabet. But in the third chapter the first three verses each begin with *aleph*; but the three following verses begin with three *bets*, and this ternary order is kept up all the way to the end of the alphabet. To remember such things—since Latin words do not begin with the same letters—notes or the names of letters are written by each verse, as you can see in the Vulgate edition of the Bible. COMMENTARY ON THE LAMENTATIONS OF THE PROPHET JEREMIAH 1:1.[6]

LAMENT FOR JERUSALEM AND THE CHURCH. JOHANNES WILD: In this way Jeremiah begins his Lamentations; where at once anyone is able to see how he was affected when he wrote these things. Indeed, these words bear before themselves nothing other than the deepest grief. The pious prophet was mourning over his country, his people, his city of Jerusalem, and over the temple. Truly the king of Babylon had scattered and destroyed everything. Jeremiah compares the earlier good and beautiful things with the present evils. In fact, Jerusalem with its people in many ways surpassed all other cities. Jeremiah puts down three ways in this verse that Jerusalem had been more remarkable than other walled cities. First, it was full of people; for the city in itself was great, and three times every year people flowed into the city in great numbers from every region. And now, he says, "the city sits alone...."

Second, Jerusalem excelled other cities, like a lady compared to her servant girls. She was, I say, "the Lady of the nations"; she had kings, priests, a temple, worship, and all the other cities looked upon her as a lady; of course she had God himself. ...And now, he says, the city is "like a widow": she has lost her kings, priests, and temple, and God himself, in which things she had once boasted and been proud. Nevertheless, it does not simply say that she became a widow, but she is "like a widow." Indeed, God had not yet left her completely; even if he seemed to have left.

Third, Jerusalem was the "prince of the provinces." In fact, all the surrounding regions gave

---

[4]Broughton, *The Lamentations of Jeremiah*, 3-4*; citing Lev 26:1-46; Jer 36:1-32; 22:1-30; Ex 1:1-22; Deut 32:1-52.
[5]Toussain, *The Lamentations*, 1-2*.

[6]Pinto, *In Prophetae Ieremiae Lamentationes*, 286v.

tribute to that city, especially in the times of David and Solomon. And now, he says, "she pays tribute" to the king of Babylon. . . .

So Jerusalem too was a figure and type of the church. Whence also the church is so called by this name in Paul and John: Galatians 4, Hebrews 12, and Revelation 21. Moreover, it is fitting that the church be compared to the city and especially to Jerusalem. It is indeed really a city: it has its own walls, watchmen, king, freedoms, citizens, law, and rights. The walls of this city are God himself. . . . The watchmen are the holy angels, or even the pastors and rectors whom Scripture calls "examiners." The king of the city is Christ, the citizens are all the believers; the law is the gospel, the privileges are the freedoms of the sons of God. . . .

Once there was a lady and spouse of God, she everywhere knew his presence, consolation, and help. Now she knows none of these, although she has not yet been completely abandoned by him. Nevertheless, she has been made like a widow and so abandoned. Indeed God permits this and allows that external enemies and heretics and false Christians devastate her, as if he has completely rejected her. In sum, once the church ruled the world and the demons, now she is subject to both the world and the devil and pays tribute. . . . Are these things not worthy of tears and lamentations? Who is so hardened that they can hold themselves back from weeping, if they diligently consider these things? SERMON ON LAMENTATIONS 1:1.[7]

THE LONELY CITY AND BAPTISM. MARTIN LUTHER: Behold, then, our miserable captivity. "How lonely sits the city that was full of people! How like a widow she has become. . . ." There are so many ordinances, so many rites, so many sects, so many vows, so many exertions, and so many works in which Christians are engaged today that they lose sight of their baptism. Because of this swarm of locusts, palmerworms, and cankerworms, no one is able to remember that they are baptized, or what blessings baptism brought them. We should be even

as little children, when they are newly baptized, who engage in no efforts or works, but are free in every way, secure and saved solely through the glory of their baptism. For we are indeed little children, continually baptized anew in Christ. THE BABYLONIAN CAPTIVITY OF THE CHURCH.[8]

GRIEF FOR THE CHURCH WITHOUT CONSOLATION. JOHANNES WILD: Jerusalem grieves with grieving, that is, she cannot cease and make herself quiet. Moreover she weeps in the night: that is, even when others are silent she is not able to be quiet. She grieves to the point that her tears flow abundantly. And in all these things there is no one to console her. Indeed, those people who before had assisted her now abandon her in those straits in which they had formerly helped her. Now these people spurn her; those who before were her friends have now become enemies. Jerusalem had many sons and citizens, highborn folk and the rich, the educated, etc. But there is no one to console her or who is able to help. She once even had God and the holy angels to assist her; now even they do not console her. . . .

What do we now see in the church other than what Jeremiah then saw in Jerusalem? . . . What indeed brings so much grief to the church other than the evil life of the clergy, the negligence of pastors, the perversity of the people, and the stupidity of the princes? With some easy effort the grief of the church could be put to rest: if the clergy would mend their ways, the pastors mind their own duties, the princes rule with wisdom, and the people embrace godliness. But we do not have that by which one might encourage the church. Rather and moreover, many spurn and ridicule her and become her enemies. Meanwhile, we lament concerning the Turks and others, that they bring injury to the church, while we are certainly the cause of all of our evils. . . . So let us hear what else Jeremiah laments in his Jerusalem. SERMON ON LAMENTATIONS 1:2.[9]

---

[7]Wild, *Conciones*, 446-48; citing Gal 4:26; Heb 12:22; Rev 21:2.

[8]LW 36:73 (WA 6:537-38); citing Joel 1:4.
[9]Wild, *Conciones*, 452-54.

MANY REASONS FOR THE JEWS' DEPARTURE FROM JUDEA. HECTOR PINTO: "Judah has departed on account of her affliction. . . ." That is, the people of Judea, having been expelled from their homeland, went into a bitter exile, and set up their home base in Chaldea. Oppressed with affliction and the magnitude of the Babylonian servitude in Babylon, they found no rest and no tranquility there. It is fair and just that those who despised the pleasant yoke of the Lord should be pressed down by the harsh yoke of Babylonian servitude.

Yet another interpretation: the Jewish people migrated and were affected by such a punishment, because they had afflicted many and treated their slaves cruelly and brutally. This is explained by the Chaldean paraphrase that goes like this: For this reason the Jews went into captivity: because they themselves had afflicted widows and orphans and because they had handled Hebrew slaves roughly. This speech can be explained as being not about the Jews who were led away to Babylon, but about those who fled to Egypt after the destruction of Jerusalem, because of the bitter afflictions and harsh servitude the Babylonians were enforcing in Judea. But they discovered no refuge in Egypt. Read chapters 41, 43, and 44 of Jeremiah and the last chapter of 2 Kings, if you want to know more. COMMENTARY ON THE LAMENTATIONS OF THE PROPHET JEREMIAH 1:3.[10]

WORSHIP—SILENCED IN TRAGEDY BUT RESTORED IN CHRIST. JOHANNES OECOLAMPADIUS: The roads to the temple, Jeremiah says, are in mourning. Previously the crowd of people had thronged together and even apart from festivals you would have seen a great crowd of people traveling to Jerusalem: but now they no longer come around even for those festivals. They used to come to Jerusalem during three festivals to worship according to the law at the time of Passover, Pentecost, and the Feast of Tabernacles. Therefore, he says that today the roads are covered with grass

and wild shrubs because of the insolence of the pilgrims. Trade has ceased; court sessions in the gates, sacrifices, and weddings have ceased. Once it was beautiful to see the roads filled with people from all parts, but now no one comes. So the psalm says, "The rushing of the river makes glad the city of God." He calls the crowd of people on the street "a river." Isaiah says, "They will flow to him. . . ." There were ornate gates in Jerusalem, in which certain splendid speeches were given and certain judgments were celebrated in them. Declarations concerning enemies were spoken in the gate. Even priests were ornately dressed: they praised God with psalms and instruments. They now weep as no one comes bearing a sacrifice, no one comes to worship, no one discharges vows. And the marriageable virgins in the city, with their womanly adornment cast down, are infirm and afflicted. . . .

In sum, throughout all of Zion there is a bitter spirit. Now in the church we cry out no less than the Jews of Zion; the church in which it would have been suitable to be in a perpetual Sabbath from sin and exult in the Lord, who ought to be worshiped in spirit and truth. It is not so mournful, for we see the end of pilgrimages, in which the unhealthy people used to run to the temples of the gods, as if to idols, the people themselves not knowing what they were doing. But this is deplorable, that while they are in the congregations, the heart is far from God; someone sings a psalm, but the mind wanders to transitory profit. The ways of faith lead us to this festivity through the Word of God if we listen to what was said and reflect on the immense benefits through Christ. He is the way and the gate. COMMENTARY ON JEREMIAH, LAMENTATIONS 1:4.[11]

EVEN THE FAULTLESS ARE AFFLICTED. JOHN UDALL: They that seem most exempt from it must mourn the decay of religion. The reason is that it concerns God's glory and every person's salvation. The use is, first, to reprove them that lay not to

---

[10]Pinto, *In Prophetae Ieremiae Lamentationes*, 302r; citing Jer 34:8-22; 2 Kings 25:1-30.

[11]Oecolampadius, *In Hieremiam . . . Threnos*, 2Q3r-v; citing Ps 46:4; Is 2:2; Jn 4:24; 14:6; 10:9.

heart the distresses of God's people for the truth, thinking it sufficient that they themselves live in safety. Second, to teach us to strive to be grieved when we hear of the decay of the religion in any place, though it be safe where we are. COMMENTARY ON LAMENTATIONS 1:4.[12]

DRIVEN LIKE LIVESTOCK. GUILLAUME DU VAIR: Thus Zion has lost the flower of her youth, and all the ornaments of her city are gone. She is miserably torn; nothing remains whole but grace. The greatest and richest of her inhabitants are conveyed and led by troops into strange provinces, like flocks of sheep being daily driven from market to market without allowing them to be refreshed. They travel with their eyes looking downward, their heads low, sighing deeply. Their conqueror follows behind them, chafing and scourging them with whips. The people standing along the way as they passed marveled at their afflictions and spoke abusively to them. MEDITATIONS UPON THE LAMENTATIONS OF JEREMIAH 1:6.[13]

FILTHY SKIRTS, DESPAIR, AND DIVINE PROMISES. JOHN CALVIN: Jeremiah had said at the end of the last verse that turpitude or baseness had been seen at Jerusalem; and now he says that it was on the very "fringes" or skirts. The prophet seems to allude to menstruating women who hide their uncleanness as much as they can; but such a thing is of no avail, as nature must have its course. In short, the prophet intimates that the Jews had become filthy in no common degree, being so afflicted that their uncleanness appeared on their skirts. . . .

The prophet then says that the reproach of the Jews was on the skirts, because they could not hide their disgrace; for shame often makes people hide their evils and silently bear them because they are unwilling to expose themselves to the mockery of their enemies. But the prophet says that the miseries of the people could not be kept hidden, but that they appeared to all, as the case is with

women subject to an overflow—it issues forth to the extremities of their garments.

And when he says that "she remembered not her end," I understand this to mean that the Jews were so overwhelmed that they did raise up their thoughts to God's promises; for it is no ordinary source of comfort, and what even common sense dictates to us, to take a breath in extreme evils, and to extend our thoughts further, for miseries will not always oppress us—some change for the better will happen. . . . In short, by these words, he denotes extreme despair; for the Jews were so stupefied that they could not lift up their minds to any hope. . . .

These things ought to be carefully observed, for Satan in this day uses various means to lead us to despair. In order to avert us from all confidence in the grace of God he sets before us extreme calamities. And when sorrow lays such a hold on our minds that the hope of grace does not shine forth, then that immoderate sorrow arises from impatience, which may drive us to madness. Hence it comes that we murmur against God. . . .

[Jeremiah] then encourages them to pray, and suggests words to them. . . . "See Lord, my affliction, for the enemy has highly exalted himself." Here the prophet represents the church, yet he exhorts them no doubt, according to the obligations of his office, to entertain good hope, and encourages them to pray, for true and earnest prayer cannot be offered without faith; for when the taste of God's grace is lost, it cannot be that we can pray from the heart; and it is through the promises alone that we can have a taste of God's paternal goodness. There is, then, no doubt but that the prophet here promises a sure deliverance to the Jews provided they turned to God and believed and were fully persuaded that he would be their deliverer. COMMENTARY ON JEREMIAH, LAMENTATIONS 1:9.[14]

FORSAKEN BY ALL AND TURNING TO GOD. GUILLAUME DU VAIR: Then all alone, contemplating her estate she saw nothing but filth and uncleanness from head to foot. Her garments were

[12]Udall, *Commentary on Lamentations*, D2v*.
[13]Du Vair, *Meditations*, Vau, Bır-v*.
[14]CTS 21:320-22* (CO 39:519-20).

all covered with mire and clay. And as a peacock turns himself about, admiring his plumes, he then casts his eyes to his feet and sees the filth and closes his train; he lets go of the pride of his heart, sorrows in himself, and wishes for death. So she was left to all distress, with none to comfort her. Her friends have forsaken her. Those who should have been most near now afflict her. Finding no succor on the earth she lifted up her sighs to heaven, pitifully drawing great sighs from the bottom of her heart and referring them to God. Saying, "Lord, will you not look on me in pity, in the greatness of my afflictions? Do you not see my extreme miseries and that I have none to release me but you alone? Come then Lord, if you are a God of mercy; do not abandon your humble and ancient servant. My enemy sits with his foot on my throat, causing me to groan shamefully.... Come therefore, good Lord, for my enemies revile you without measure or pity." MEDITATIONS UPON THE LAMENTATIONS OF JEREMIAH 1:9.[15]

FATHERS, TO NEGLECT YOUR DAUGHTERS IS A SIN. ARCANGELA TARABOTTI: Ponder my words, judicious reader, for I have undertaken to describe only in part the sacrilege of these inhumane men who mass together wealth, titles, and prestige for their male offspring (who then go on to dissipate the wealth, despise the titles, and sully the prestige with their dissolute life, vices, and degradation), but who cast away as wretches their own flesh and blood that happens to be born female. I believe it was said of them in prophecy, "[Jerusalem's] filthiness is on her feet, and she has not remembered her end." This passage undoubtedly refers to the souls of men who never think about their mortality, but walk along the filthy road of sin, which leads to perdition. Their conduct leads one to believe that they truly imagine that happiness lasts forever in this temporary, precarious life; they wake up to their wretchedness too late, since "the thoughts of men ... are vain." Their chimerical hopes often delude them, as when, overtaken by

divine justice (it cannot err!), they remain deprived of the sons meant to bring them glory and from whom they hoped immortality in future progeny. The fathers themselves die of grief in ignominy, only to be shut up forever within a narrow tomb—a fitting punishment for having shut up their own daughters within four walls. PATERNAL TYRANNY.[16]

1:10-22 No One to Comfort Her

SORROW FOR THE TEMPLE AND FACING GOD'S WRATH. DANIEL TOUSSAIN: The prophet turns his speech to strangers that pass nearby to bring alive the calamities of Jerusalem and of the country.... No one living is able to express how many excellent similitudes and comparisons the prophet Jeremiah has collected together in this part, to represent to us the honor and force of the wrath of the Almighty God: as the similitude of fire that consumes all things, the spread of the net, the wine press, and a wrapped yoke. This kind of speech is very agreeable and gives an excellent grace to such an argument. It enriches the argument by making it stronger, lively, and fitting for the matter at hand....

The ancient fathers with so many grievous groans and bitter tears sorrowed for the temple of Jerusalem and were so strangely grieved and bereaved for the destruction of it, which was but a material temple and figure of the true church. Let us learn how to lament and sorrow when we see the ruin and destruction of the living stones and mystical body of the true church of Jesus Christ our Lord, and when instead of the happy signs of the true preaching of the gospel, and of the true use of the sacraments, we see nothing else but the abominable idolatries, dissoluteness, and riot, and hear nothing else but blasphemies or fables, either scandals or lies. See then that every person in particular ought to be a temple of God and of his Holy Spirit. Let us be well advised to walk in all holiness and integrity of life and suffer no unclean thing to dwell therein.... No bastard, Ammonite, Moabite, or other profane body should come

---

[15]Du Vair, *Meditations*, B3v-B4r*.

[16]Arcangela Tarabotti, *Paternal Tyranny*, 68-69.

within the holy congregation, giving thereby an infallible advertisement of the purity and sanctity that is generally required to be, as well as in the body of the church. . . .

Now the chief point that we are here to consider in this third part of chapter 1 is the description of the fearful wrath of our God, which is amplified and set forth in many notable similitudes. . . . And it is because we for the most part are so dull that we cannot apprehend as we ought the greatness of divine majesty, nor do we fear his judgments. Yet surely there is such a fearful thing that neither the consuming fire nor the naming of the most terrible things can at the full sufficiently inform us of the great intensity of it. Thus we see how the Scripture awakens us to make us conceive of at least some little feature of his divine vengeance, by comparing the Lord to a hot and consuming fire. LAMENTATIONS AND HOLY MOURNINGS, LAMENTATIONS 1:10-17.[17]

STARVATION AND GLUTTONY OF BODY AND SPIRIT. PETER MARTYR VERMIGLI: "They seek bread." Even if only a few of the people were forced to perish from hunger, it would be a miserable state of affairs. Here, by contrast, all of those who obtained from God a fertile land and who, previous to that, were being fed by him in the wilderness, are described as being swept away in this manner. Yes, even these people, all of them, are perishing of hunger. . . .

"I have become," say the people, "a glutton in this famine." For gluttons are so taken captive by the vice of the palate and stomach that they give whatever is demanded of them in the taverns and delicatessens for wine or sweet and delicious food. They spare nothing, they squander all, with the result that they cannot meet the expenses. . . .

If this is hard to hear (and it refers merely to the body), what do we think of the state of affairs in those places where, as far as religious people are concerned, it is not permitted to obtain by entreaty even one crumb of the Word of God, the celestial bread. Poisonous drugs and superstitious harangues gush forth everywhere, but solid food is nowhere. Religious people in that situation must, believe me, be helped even if only with prayers by those of us who all the while have plenty here in the Father's house: let us not squander! COMMENTARY ON LAMENTATIONS 1:11.[18]

SIN MAKES PEOPLE BLIND TO GOD'S WARNINGS. HUGH BROUGHTON: This speech is a prophecy of the famine that should befall the city in the last siege, which began in the ninth year of Zedekiah. Then Nebuchadnezzar compassed the city with siege until the eleventh year, when the famine was exceedingly great and the people of the land had no meat. Though two captivities were past and none were left but a remnant of the poor, and Ezekiel in captivity prophesied that Zedekiah and his company should come after the former and Jeremiah still in Jerusalem commented in sermons upon his lamentations, all this moved not Zedekiah and his nobles. For they knew not the kingdom of Christ, that it was for the world to come, and knew that as the eternal throne was promised unto David. So still they made their belly their God. And to this day the Talmudiques say, in Rabbi Moses Ben Maimon . . . : "All the good things that the prophets prophesied unto Israel, they are only bodily things, wherein the body shall be benefited in the days of the Messiah, when the kingdom shall be restored to Israel." Moses foretold that when they became fat, gross, and burly, they would forget God that made them and contemn the rock of their salvation. And Isaiah records that to have come to pass, and Maimonides records the sin there to be sin against the Holy Spirit, wherein God would never give repentance. As they could not repent, to give over at the siege, but they dreamed still that Egypt would help, but Jeremiah laments that was their folly. So for the second destruction, they believed not the angel that told them again and again that their city should have a final destruction. But when Stephen told the same,

---

[17]Toussain, *The Lamentations*, 26-27, 28-29, 31-32*; citing 1 Cor 3:17; 6:19.

[18]Vermigli, *Commentary*, 37-38.

and had in his face like the angel's brightness, they stopped their ears and would neither hear nor see. And who would have thought that Seraiah, the high sacrifice and father of good Ezra, should conspire with the rest to damn Jeremiah for a false prophet because he told of ruin to the temple and its implements and of the New Testament. But humanity sold into sin cannot see, where God does not open up their eyes, and here the Spirit teaches the godly to groan with sighings unspeakable. COMMENTARY ON LAMENTATIONS 1:11.[19]

LIKE A PLUNDERED VINEYARD. GUILLAUME DU VAIR: Tell me I pray you, you that behold my ruin and consider the remnants of my former greatness: Is there anyone like this? Did you ever see sorrow the equal of mine? Tell me, could you refrain from tears when you saw my desolation? You, I say, who before had seen me full of such wealth and knew of my greatness and estate, and now see me plundered. Does it not resemble a vine all shattered, where beasts enter and not only pluck off her clusters of grapes but take her body as well? See then, it is the pleasure of God, who is justly enraged against me and has afflicted me in his fury. MEDITATIONS UPON THE LAMENTATIONS OF JEREMIAH 1:12.[20]

THE MAN OF SORROWS FOR THE SORROWING MAN. JOHN DONNE: Find a languishing wretch in a sordid corner, not only in an impoverished state, but in an oppressed conscience; his eyes fully suffocated, smothered with smoke and tears; his ears cut off from all greetings, visits, and sounds apart from his own sighs and the storms and thundering and earthquakes of his own despair. Enable this man to open his eyes and see that Christ stands before him and says, "Behold, see if ever there were any sorrow like my sorrow." "My sorrow has been overcome, why not yours?" Open this man's ears and make him hear that voice that says, "I was dead, and am alive, and behold I live

forevermore. Amen." This you may do. Descend with those heavens and bring them into the wretch's sad chamber. Set Christ Jesus before him, to out-sigh him, out-weep him, out-bleed him, out-die him. Transfer all the fasts, all the scorns, all the scourges, all the nails, all the spears that came upon Christ Jesus and made him a crucified man in the sight of the Father. So these actions and passions of the Son are appropriated for the wretched one and made his so entirely as if there were never another soul ever created apart form his own. Enrich this poor soul; comfort this sad soul so that he shall believe and by believing find all of Christ Jesus to be his. SERMON ON ISAIAH 32:8.[21]

A FIRE IN MY BONES. NIKOLAUS SELNECKER: God has handled me like something he wants to ignite and burn up until there is nothing left. I am burning on the inside and the outside. Within me the wrath and heavy hand of God torment me, such that he parches the fluids of my soul like a withering summer. He withers my lands like grass and scorches my bones like a fire. On the outside I see and feel this great misery, hunger, bloodshed, and ruin of the temple, city, and all the houses. SONGS OF LAMENT OF THE PROPHET JEREMIAH 1:13.[22]

THE MARTYRS' SORROW AND JOY. JOHN DONNE: Gather all the joys of the martyrs—from Abel to the person that now groans under the Inquisition; condense those joys into one body of joy (and certainly the joys that the martyrs felt at their deaths would make up a far greater body than their sorrows would make up). It can be said that all other martyrs are submartyrs and witnesses that testify to our great Martyr and great Witness, as St. John calls Christ Jesus. "There was never a sorrow like his sorrow." This is also true: "There was never a joy like the joy that was set before him," when he endured on the cross. If I had all this joy of all these martyrs (which would no doubt be such a joy as would lead to a liquefying, a melting of my bowels), yet I would

[19]Broughton, *The Lamentations of Jeremiah*, 13-14*; citing 2 Kings 25:1; 2 Sam 7:1-29; 1 Chron 17:1-27; Phil 3:1-21; Deut 32:1-52; Is 6:1-13; Dan 9:1-27; Acts 6:1–7:60.
[20]Du Vair, *Meditations*, B6r-v*.

[21]Donne, *Sermons*, 8:246-47*; citing Rev 1:18.
[22]Selnecker, *Threni*, J2r.

have a joy even more abounding—a joy more abundant than even this superlative martyr's joy—in the world to come. SERMON ON JOHN 10:10.[23]

WHEN SIN BECOMES A BURDEN. JOHANNES BUGENHAGEN: The yoke and weight of sin sleeps and grows quiet, when not sensed in the conscience, as God said to Cain. And as Paul says in Romans 7, "I was ignorant of sin." But when God began to judge us in our conscience and to punish us through the law, then the yoke of sin awoke in me and my iniquities multiplied; that is, they were collected like a heavy bundle or like a heavy yoke placed on our necks. Then we have to despair, unless Christ the Redeemer is present. Now, they say, I finally sense the sin, which I had ignored before. COMMENTARY ON JEREMIAH, LAMENTATIONS 1:14.[24]

THE RESULT OF THE LAW. HUGH BROUGHTON: The yoke of the law was given to teach how sin abounded. So seeing they did not humble themselves before God to walk better in his holy covenant, all the curses written in the laws of Moses came upon them. When from the yoke of the law, which these fathers could not bear, the yoke of their trespasses galled the neck. When Daniel confessed this much, the angel Gabriel taught him of the easy yoke of Christ. And that oration of the angel Gabriel is no less to the Old Testament than the sun is to the sky. COMMENTARY ON LAMENTATIONS 1:14.[25]

THE LOSS, DUTY, AND SOURCES OF CONSOLATION. PETER MARTYR VERMIGLI: "Because far from me was a consoler, a restorer of soul. . . ." It is no inconsiderable adversity that someone has been left without friends; in fact, among other miseries this one seems the worst. Reading or hearing read how the prophet was so desperate for consolation should remind us not to toss away neglectfully our own duty to console. Indeed, not only common humanity but also Christian charity recommends it. In this regard Paul also exhorts us: "Weep with those who weep," for this reason, those who are buffeted by the winds of fortune must not be sent away desolate.

Just why the Jews, mourning their fate as they were, lacked consolation, their previous way of life explains well enough. They lived in luxury, in contempt of God, in carnal allurements and the pleasures of this world. God has not promised consolation to this sort of people. For he said, "Blessed are those who weep, for they shall gain consolation. . . ."

These people do not gain consolation for yet another reason: they lack the Spirit, and he alone is the consoler of our soul, if ever it has fallen into some adversity. For not in vain is he, whom the Greeks name "Paraclete," called consoler and exhorter.

Finally the divine word is a living and inexhaustible fount of consolation, for through it the Spirit makes its way into our soul. So it should be the duty of everyone to collect for himself in the storehouse of memory a copious supply of healthy sayings from sacred Scripture, while we have the time. These sayings can later be for us a consolation and pleasure, while we are pulled this way and that by adversities. COMMENTARY ON LAMENTATIONS 1:17.[26]

RECOGNITION OF SIN, OBEDIENCE, AND FEAR. JOHANNES BUGENHAGEN: "Just is the Lord." This confession and recognition of sin is the beginning of salvation, only do not despair concerning the mercy of God; that is, believe in Christ. Through the whole of Jeremiah and in all the prophets and in Moses, the Jews perished because of this sin, that they were not obedient to the mouth of the Lord, but they were often rebelling against the Word of God—as today with our papists, as they do not believe, so they do not fear. COMMENTARY ON JEREMIAH, LAMENTATIONS 1:18.[27]

[23]Donne, *Sermons*, 9:153-4*; citing Rev 1:5; Heb 12:2.
[24]Bugenhagen, *In Ieremiam . . . Threni*, C3v-C4r; citing Gen 4:7; Rom 7:7.
[25]Broughton, *The Lamentations of Jeremiah*, 15*; citing Dan 9:1-27; Mt 11:1-30.
[26]Vermigli, *Commentary*, 49-50; citing Rom 12:15; Mt 5:4.
[27]Bugenhagen, *In Ieremiam . . . Threni*, C4r.

EXPOSING DECEIT AND FINDING GOD IN OUR AFFLICTIONS. JOHN DONNE: Our estate may be so ruined so that there is nothing left either for our future descendants or for our current family. Still God and calamity are together. God does not send this calamity, but when it happens God and calamity are there together. By calling that calamity by his own name—Shaddai—God would make every calamity a candle for you, by which you might see him. If you were not so puffed up before this calamity, you would not have forgotten to say, "It was the Lord that gave everything to me." Likewise, you should not be so dejected and so rebellious now that you cannot say the Lord has taken something away....

Those "spiritual afflictions," which reach to the understanding ... do fall on us: "that we call for lovers, and they deceive us"; ... that is, we come to see how much we mistook the matter when we fell in love with worldly things (certainly at least once in our lives we discover this deceit—at least upon our deathbeds). But when the deceit is so spiritual that it reaches not only to the understanding but also to the conscience, then we have been deceived either by security at one time or with anxieties, unnecessary uncertainty, or absurd perplexity at another. SERMON ON JOB 13:15.[28]

SUBMITTING TO GOD'S JUSTICE. JOHN TRAPP: My bowels boil and bubble, or are thick and muddy, as waters are after and in a tempest. Or it is a metaphor from mortar made my mingling water with lime and sand. She was in a great perturbation, and sought ease by submitting to God's justice and imploring his mercy. COMMENTARY ON LAMENTATIONS 1:20.[29]

SHOULD A PROPHET OR BELIEVER CURSE THE ENEMY? PETER MARTYR VERMIGLI: "I have been afflicted enough. Let it be repaid to them as they deserve: they are no better than I. For my part, I led the way; now let them follow."

... Doubtless a sense of uneasiness resists this meaning, because it does not seem fitting for holy people to incite God against their enemies by their persistent prayers. Christ wishes us to pray for our persecutors.... It seems fitting for holy people to hate the sin but love the sinner, especially since our troubles and persecutions are opportunities for us—our enemies willing or not—to be tested or to repent.

Now concerning the imprecations of the prophets against their enemies, well nigh all our ancestors add that these were prophecies of future things, but prophecies in a particular form. By various forms of speech the Holy Spirit was accustomed to push the prophets to disclose the future: at one time by delightful, pleasant, and agreeable song; at another time by mournful poems, funeral songs, and as it were, sad elegies; at still another by an open statement of an oracle, at one moment by threatening, and another by cursing. And in the end the divine Spirit spurns no human argumentation that may lead to our correction. Thus under the guise of prayers he foretells here future events that really happened, since all the neighboring nations, which took pleasure in the destruction of Jerusalem, were in their turn annihilated. Eventually even the Babylonians were subjugated by the Medes. The Babylonians did not experience any lighter suffering than what they saw the Jews bear.

All the same it must not be disregarded that the force of curses delivers something other than foretelling, something useful for us to consider. It is a characteristic of holy people to show themselves eager for what they recognize as God's will, so that they may show themselves as close to God as possible. When, therefore, it had been shown to the prophet what God wished or had disposed, he prays at once that it be so done. Neither the carnal nature nor human feeling prays it in them, but the Spirit of God, who in his saints asks effectually—even by ineffable groans—for what is of the divine will and plan. COMMENTARY ON LAMENTATIONS 1:21-22.[30]

---

[28]Donne, *Sermons*, 3:192*; citing Job 1:21.
[29]Trapp, *A Commentary or Exposition*, 373*.

[30]Vermigli, *Commentary*, 63-64; citing Mt 5:44; Lk 6:28; Rom 8:26-27.

LAMENTATIONS 2:1-22
THE LORD HAS DESTROYED WITHOUT PITY

¹*How the Lord in his anger*
    has set the daughter of Zion under a cloud!
He has cast down from heaven to earth
    the splendor of Israel;
he has not remembered his footstool
    in the day of his anger.

²*The Lord has swallowed up without mercy*
    all the habitations of Jacob;
in his wrath he has broken down
    the strongholds of the daughter of Judah;
he has brought down to the ground in dishonor
    the kingdom and its rulers.

³*He has cut down in fierce anger*
    all the might of Israel;
he has withdrawn from them his right hand
    in the face of the enemy;
he has burned like a flaming fire in Jacob,
    consuming all around.

⁴*He has bent his bow like an enemy,*
    with his right hand set like a foe;
and he has killed all who were delightful in
        our eyes
    in the tent of the daughter of Zion;
he has poured out his fury like fire.

⁵*The Lord has become like an enemy;*
    he has swallowed up Israel;
he has swallowed up all its palaces;
    he has laid in ruins its strongholds,
and he has multiplied in the daughter of Judah
    mourning and lamentation.

⁶*He has laid waste his booth like a garden,*
    laid in ruins his meeting place;
the LORD has made Zion forget
    festival and Sabbath,
and in his fierce indignation has spurned king
        and priest.

⁷*The LORD has scorned his altar,*
    disowned his sanctuary;
he has delivered into the hand of the enemy
    the walls of her palaces;
they raised a clamor in the house of the Lord
    as on the day of festival.

⁸*The LORD determined to lay in ruins*
    the wall of the daughter of Zion;
he stretched out the measuring line;
    he did not restrain his hand from destroying;
he caused rampart and wall to lament;
    they languished together.

⁹*Her gates have sunk into the ground;*
    he has ruined and broken her bars;
her king and princes are among the nations;
    the law is no more,
and her prophets find
    no vision from the LORD.

¹⁰*The elders of the daughter of Zion*
    sit on the ground in silence;
they have thrown dust on their heads
    and put on sackcloth;
the young women of Jerusalem
    have bowed their heads to the ground.

¹¹*My eyes are spent with weeping;*
    my stomach churns;
my bile is poured out to the ground
    because of the destruction of the daughter of
        my people,
because infants and babies faint
    in the streets of the city.

¹²*They cry to their mothers,*
    "Where is bread and wine?"
as they faint like a wounded man
    in the streets of the city,
as their life is poured out
    on their mothers' bosom.

¹³What can I say for you, to what compare you,
    O daughter of Jerusalem?
What can I liken to you, that I may comfort you,
    O virgin daughter of Zion?
For your ruin is vast as the sea;
    who can heal you?

¹⁴Your prophets have seen for you
    false and deceptive visions;
they have not exposed your iniquity
    to restore your fortunes,
but have seen for you oracles
    that are false and misleading.

¹⁵All who pass along the way
    clap their hands at you;
they hiss and wag their heads
    at the daughter of Jerusalem:
"Is this the city that was called
    the perfection of beauty,
    the joy of all the earth?"

¹⁶All your enemies
    rail against you;
they hiss, they gnash their teeth,
    they cry: "We have swallowed her!
Ah, this is the day we longed for;
    now we have it; we see it!"

¹⁷The LORD has done what he purposed;
    he has carried out his word,
which he commanded long ago;
    he has thrown down without pity;
he has made the enemy rejoice over you
    and exalted the might of your foes.

¹⁸Their heart cried to the Lord.
    O wall of the daughter of Zion,
let tears stream down like a torrent
    day and night!
Give yourself no rest,
    your eyes no respite!

¹⁹"Arise, cry out in the night,
    at the beginning of the night watches!
Pour out your heart like water
    before the presence of the Lord!
Lift your hands to him
    for the lives of your children,
who faint for hunger
    at the head of every street."

²⁰Look, O LORD, and see!
    With whom have you dealt thus?
Should women eat the fruit of their womb,
    the children of their tender care?
Should priest and prophet be killed
    in the sanctuary of the Lord?

²¹In the dust of the streets
    lie the young and the old;
my young women and my young men
    have fallen by the sword;
you have killed them in the day of your anger,
    slaughtering without pity.

²²You summoned as if to a festival day
    my terrors on every side,
and on the day of the anger of the LORD
    no one escaped or survived;
those whom I held and raised
    my enemy destroyed.

OVERVIEW: The severity of God's judgment and the acute misery of those chastised occupy commentators on this chapter. Divine wrath is sweeping and unrestrained for Jerusalem and devastating for the people who traverse the ruins, fail to protect their young, and in famine feed on their own children. Therefore, just as the punishment of the Lord is exacting and complete, so true and full repentance must be offered by the faithful. To preachers and expositors conditions in Jeremiah's own day echo the travails of society, church, and souls in the sixteenth and seventeenth centuries: signs of judgment either loom on the horizon or have already settled on the kingdoms of Europe.

2:1-12 The Lord Has Fulfilled His Warnings

WHAT OF JERUSALEM? JOHANNES OECOLAMPA-DIUS: The Holy Spirit is accustomed to hammer home by various arguments in the Scriptures matters that are great and worthy of remembrance. The prophets knew well and preached a great many visions of the destruction of Jerusalem. Indeed with a great many laments our prophet here bemoans the destruction of the city. So we ought not to seek in one verse and one word a variety of sentiments, as is customary with certain people; but rather from many figures we should seek one truth. Indeed we can be confident in the main topic, which is that Jerusalem was destroyed because of its own sins—whether we are speaking of the earthly or heavenly. . . . Therefore, he begins with admiration for divine judgments, and whatever has happened to Jerusalem he attributes entirely to God. COMMENTARY ON JEREMIAH, LAMENTATIONS 2.[1]

WHEN THE HOLINESS OF GOD WITHDRAWS. JOHANNES BUGENHAGEN: "Cast down from heaven," because the people who should have belonged to God, God rejected like Gentiles. By "footstool of the feet of God" he means either the whole people, among whom God resided, or certainly that ark and mercy seat that were in the holy of holies, where God had promised he would sit and hear those who prayed. But those holy things did no good, not for those holy people who despised the holy Word of God, by which alone all things are made holy. Read, Jeremiah 7: "Do not trust in deceptive words, saying, the temple of the Lord." COMMENTARY ON JEREMIAH, LAMENTATIONS 2:1.[2]

FAIR ZION AND THE GOD WHO CREATES AND DESTROYS. GUILLAUME DU VAIR: Behold a strange and lamentable conversion of all things and a horrible desolation: Zion, the well-beloved daughter of God, which lifted her head above all the cities of the world. She was like the cypress tree above the little bushes, carrying on her forehead a venerable and magnificent majesty: a thing with the splendor of her is now brought to the earth— disfigured, defaced, and darkened in such a way that no one knows her. This is, Lord, by the hand of your wrath: as you are powerful in creating all things in perfection, so you are powerful to destroy them by the rage of your fury. You raised your beloved Son to the heavens and thereafter, because Zion despised your love, you pulled her down to the ground. Her greatness did not serve to advance her higher, but caused her fall to be yet more terrible. MEDITATIONS UPON THE LAMENTATIONS OF JEREMIAH 2:1.[3]

CLOUDED AND CAST DOWN. JOHN TRAPP: There is nothing like that bright cloud wherein he appeared to his people, as a token of grace at the dedication of the temple. How does it come about, and what may be the reason of it? Oh, in what a wonderful manner and by what strange means has the Lord now clouded and covered his people (whom he has established as Mount Zion) with blackest calamities and confusions, taking all the luster of happiness and of hope from her, and that in his anger, and again, in the day of his anger? . . .

From the highest pitch of felicity, to the lowest plight of misery. This was afterward indeed Capernaum's case, but when Micah the Moreshethite prophesied that Zion should be plowed as a field and Jerusalem laid on heaps, it seemed to be a paradox, and very few believed him. Christ's disciples also had a conceit that the temple and the world must needs have one and the same period, which occasioned that mixed discourse made by our Savior. But God's gracious presence is not tied to a place; the ark, God's footstool (as here it is called) was portable until settled permanently in Zion. Likewise is the church militant in continual motion, till it comes to triumph in heaven, and those who with Capernaum are lifted up to heaven in the abundance of means, may be brought down

---

[1]Oecolampadius, *In Hieremiam . . . Threnos*, 2S2v.
[2]Bugenhagen, *In Ieremiam . . . Threni*, D2v; citing Jer 7:4.

[3]Du Vair, *Meditations*, C3r-v*.

to hell, for an instance of divine vengeance. COMMENTARY ON LAMENTATIONS 2:1.[4]

THE FINGER OF HIS IRE. GUILLAUME DU VAIR: In brief, since God began to revenge himself upon us, he has spared neither the great nor the mighty in our land. But he wasted and spoiled everyone; each one has felt the finger of his ire. He brought great armies of our enemies, assembled strange nations, and showed them our spoils; they mocked us with raging cruelty. We have cried out to God, desiring him to succor his people, but he looked on us with a threatening eye, turned his back without an answer, and sent into the bosom of our province a fire of purification, which increased from place to place and burned the whole country—even to the least cottage—and consumed the whole nation throughout. MEDITATIONS UPON THE LAMENTATIONS OF JEREMIAH 2:3.[5]

GOD WARNS BEFORE EXECUTING JUDGMENT. JOHN DONNE: When God himself is so completely incensed against us that "he is turned to be our enemy and to fight against us" (it came to that in the prophet Isaiah), when "he has bent his bow against us as an enemy" (it came to that in the prophet Jeremiah), yet he still gives us warning beforehand. Still lightning comes before his thunder: God comes seldom to that action without a word and a blow; never a blow without a word, an execution without a warning. Cain took offense at his brother Abel; the quarrel was God's because he had accepted Abel's sacrifice. Therefore, God joins himself to Abel's party. Since the party is too strong for Cain to endure, God would not surprise Cain. He tells him his danger: "Why is your countenance cast down? If you do not do well, sin is lying at your door"; "You may proceed if you will; but if you need to, you will lose in the end." Saul persecutes Christ in Christians; Christ meets him upon the way, speaks to him, strikes him to the

ground, tells him vocally and actually that he has undertaken too hard a work in opposing him. That which God did to Saul brings him low. That which God did to Cain worked no effect on him. But still God came on his own way to both, to speak before he strikes, to show lightning before he thunders, to warn before he wounds. . . . God's judgments and executions are not sudden. There is always room for repentance and mercy, but his judgments are certain. There is no room for presumption or deceit. SERMON ON ISAIAH 50:1.[6]

THE DIVINE PHYSICIAN AND FATHER. NIKOLAUS SELNECKER: "He has drawn his bow like an enemy." Up to this point the Lord always seemed gracious, had a great magnificence, a beautiful residence, and a splendid kingdom with and among us. But now he is our enemy. This is a great misery. All the temptations of sin, death, and all the devils—of the whole world—could be overcome and endured when one only knows that he has a gracious God. But when temptation comes, ah, then God burns against us and is ungracious. He punishes us himself and is against us, so help us, God. There is no guidance or help among all creatures. God alone through his Word and Holy Spirit must be the final choice, as he therefore guides all who hold tightly to his word and promises.

God will be our enemy and will be hostile in judging us when he punishes, disciplines, and scourges us. Then we are in a natural state of things, so that we only recognize those as our friends who treat us well. But when we think of good treatment, that means nothing other than what is good to us and good in our view—what we find pleasant and would like to have. When God comes and sees something particular break upon us, then we need to get better. Then we are like children who have an injury or sickness, the physician or barber should be called. The children think there should be no pain whatever happens. They do not think they have an enemy. But when they are injured, they see the same physician; they are terrified, shake, sweat, cry, and

---

[4]Trapp, *A Commentary or Exposition*, 374*; citing 1 Kings 8:10; Mic 3:12; Mt 24:1-51.
[5]Du Vair, *Meditations*, C5r-v*.

[6]Donne, *Sermons*, 7:76-77*; citing Is 63:10; Gen 4:6-7.

complain about how he will hurt them. If we do this, then we are senseless people who consider everyone their enemy—even those who want to do good by us and want to guide and help us. Thus we know that when God sees our sins, and that we do not want to continue, die or be damned, then he comes to us, disciplines us, and send us to the cross. Thus we remember our sins and are compelled to repent. Yet we think all along that God is our enemy and scourge, that he will never again be gracious to us. But his anger with us is no different than a fatherly rod, by which he disciplines us out of paternal love. A wicked child either is led again on the right path or refuses to repent as disobedient and despairing children for whom all is lost, pushed away, and disinherited. There are many crosses: poverty, sickness, danger, shame, war, and the like through which God moves us to repentance. He is from the beginning gracious. But when he sees that we are no longer following him, then comes at last a terrible fist, massive thunder and lightning, so that we truly must say and confess that the Lord is our enemy.

In Germany God the Lord at first brought to light his dear gospel through that invaluable man Doctor Luther. But only a few people followed him and among those, the majority sought carnal freedom. Thus God has punished Germany and visited her through the violence of the farmers and gave understanding to the authorities, as it was said, "he had contempt for the princes." At the same time God allowed such fire and evil graciously so that his dear Word would be valued. But little to no reform followed. Therefore, God visited many places with the Turk, the English sweating sickness, great famine, disease, and other misfortunes.[†] Moreover, there were the heretics, rebels, and sects as well as the iconoclasts, sacramentarians, antinomians, or resisters; as one also calls them now, the Anabaptists, enthusiasts, and the like. But nothing has helped. Now one can see this in many awful signs—eclipses, comets, earthquakes, floods, and economic upheaval. . . . Such things the true God does, so that he may move us to confess our sins and to repent and so that we may be well in body and soul. But if we do not follow him, as we need,

so he will appear to us as an enemy. THE SONGS OF LAMENT OF THE PROPHET JEREMIAH 2:4-5.[7]

A GARDEN RAVAGED. GUILLAUME DU VAIR: Do you know how we have been used? Imagine you saw a flock of goats entering a fair garden, full of young plants, set with fair flowers, and sown with good herbs. All in a moment they are spoiled; some bruised, some torn, some quite rooted up. Imagine that you saw (as one may term it) a shelter built with clay and dirt and covered with straw, which a coming tempest has scattered here and there, and in the place wherein it stood nothing can be found. Thus has poor Zion been handled; for of her great and brave temple and buildings there is nothing left but decay. Whoever says otherwise speaks as if they have never seen it. Their feasts and Sabbaths, which they yearned to celebrate with great reverence and ceremonies, are now abolished; their kings and high priests are touched with the finger of God as well as others. MEDITATIONS UPON THE LAMENTATIONS OF JEREMIAH 2:6.[8]

WHY DID GOD ALLOW HIS SANCTUARY TO BE VIOLATED? JOHN CALVIN: Jeremiah says first that God had "abominated" his altar; an expression not strictly proper, but the prophet could not otherwise show to the Jews what they deserved. It would have been a much lighter matter, if [Jeremiah] had only spoken of the city, lands, palaces, the vineyards, and in short, all their possessions. But then he says that God had counted as nothing all their sacred things—the altar, the temple, the ark of the covenant, and festive days. When, therefore, he says that God not only disregarded but has also cast away from

---

[7]Selnecker, *Threni*, K3r-L2r. [†]Selnecker refers to a series of sixteenth-century crises: the German Peasants' Revolt (1524–1525); the campaigns and expansion of the Ottoman Turks in Europe in 1526, 1529, 1541, and 1551–52; and the English sweating sickness, which first appeared in England in 1485 and spread to the European Continent in 1528–1529. This epidemic typically attacked the healthy and was known by its high mortality rate, often killing in less than a day, and by its feverish sweating at onset. See Andrew Cunningham and Ole Peter Grell, *The Four Horsemen of the Apocalypse: Religion, War, Famine, and Death in Reformation Europe* (Cambridge: Cambridge University Press, 2000), 272-74. [8]Du Vair, *Meditations*, C6v-C7r*.

him these things—which yet especially availed to conciliate his favor—the people must have hence perceived—except they were beyond every measure of stupidity—how grievously they had provoked God's wrath against themselves; for this was like heaven and earth being blended together. . . .

Here also the prophet shows that God would have never suffered the enemies so insolently to exult and to revel in the very temple, had not the Israelites deserved this; for the insolence of their enemies was not unknown to God and he might have easily checked it if he had pleased. Why, then, did he grant so much license to profane enemies? Because the Jews themselves had previously polluted the temple, so that he abhorred all their solemn assemblies, as also he declares by Isaiah, that he detested their festivals Sabbaths and new moons. But it was a shocking change, when enemies entered the place God had consecrated for himself and there insolently boasted and uttered base and wicked calumnies against God. But the sadder the spectacle, the more detestable appeared the impiety of the [Jewish] people, which had been the cause of such great evil. COMMENTARY ON LAMENTATIONS 2:7.[9]

STATES RELY ON THE CHURCH FOR GOD'S FAVOR. JOHN UDALL: When the church is spoiled, the commonwealth cannot go free. The reason is because the members of the church are always part of the commonwealth. Second, the commonwealth has no promise from God to be well, but by the promise made to the church. The use is to teach us, so careful as we are to have the commonwealth flourish, to be as diligent to seek the prosperity of the church. COMMENTARY ON LAMENTATIONS 2:7.[10]

WORD AND LAW AWAY FROM JERUSALEM. JOHANNES BUGENHAGEN: "He did not use the laws." In Hebrew, "the law is no more"; that is, now our king and princes with the people are not able to practice the worship of God according to the law among the Gentiles. Nor do they hear there in Baby-

lon the prophets and sacred songs, as was customary here in Jerusalem. It is as if he says, "They were not only cast away from their land, but even from their own God to the Gentiles." Certainly a person is in the hand of the devil, who does not have the Word of God. As Christ says, "Walk in the light while you have the light . . . so you may be sons of light." Nevertheless, God gave to those in captivity the singular prophets Ezekiel and Daniel, and those priests and doctors of the law, Ezra and Nehemiah, etc. But here the prophet was disturbed: as a pious man, he feared that in Babylon they would be utterly deserted by the Word of God, which meanwhile was the remedy and medicine for all evils. COMMENTARY ON JEREMIAH, LAMENTATIONS 2:9.[11]

THE WALLS ARE BREACHED. JOHANNES WILD: They all fall at once: the inner and outer walls, gates and bars, kings and princes, old men and boys. How indeed could any of these survive against the judgment of God? But when those things in which we trusted fall, it is necessary that misery, misfortune, famine, and every kind of evil follows. Here Jeremiah was experienced. Therefore he begins anew his lament. "My eyes have failed because of weeping," he says. Especially when the very young and infants die because of famine, when they say to their mothers: "Where is the grain? as they faint in the streets." In fact, Jeremiah had previously called these evils down upon them, because they were living so impiously; "Lord," he said, "give their children over to famine." Now, however, his feelings overwhelm him; he is not able to hold himself back from tears. We too should act this way; sinners must be censured harshly, nevertheless in such a way that charity and compassion remain in the heart. Therefore, from this text we are able to see what our state of affairs are, knowing that God for a long time has ignored our sins; that is, he has waited a long time for our penance. . . .

In these things we are long since very experienced, because our outer walls have fallen in body and in spirit. The Hungarians were for us a most

---

[9]CTS 21:355-57* (CO 39:542); citing Is 1:13-14.
[10]Udall, *Commentary on Lamentations*, L2r*.
[11]Bugenhagen, *In Ieremiam . . . Threni*, D2v-D3r; citing Jn 12:35-36.

sturdy outer wall; they however have already fallen.† Spiritually, however, there was the outer wall of the church, modesty among the youth, the serious manner among the elderly, justice in the courts, virtue among the nobles, truth among craftsmen, faithfulness among farmers; frankness and honesty among men, decency among women, devotion among priests, observance among monks, obedience among subjects, and diligence among rectors, and—to say it with a few words, order among all levels of society, charity toward all people, fear of God, peace among princes, and one spirit and the same mind among all levels of society. This was the outer wall of the church. And as long as it stood, the enemy was not able to make it to the inner walls. But now the outer wall has fallen. Indeed, there is no more discipline among the youth, no serious manner among the elderly, etc. Not only has this outer wall fallen, but even the bars and gates are destroyed. That is, everything that could keep us disciplined and in order has been abolished. The enemy is already attacking the inner wall. The elders, who before knew how to take counsel, are now silent about these things. God has made a fool of all our wisdom, so that no one in our community knows how to take counsel. Furthermore, the prophets have no vision; they are blinded; they do not see where the people shirk; they do not call them back, but they provoke even more. So it happens that the virgins, that is, those seemly souls, lose even their seemliness. Children and simple folk suffer a famine of the Word of God. And how much worse it could be for us if you are a Christian: these things I ponder. If we want the church, our land, and even ourselves to be well, let us exert ourselves as soon as possible to soften the wrath of God with penance. Therefore, let us pray. SERMON ON LAMENTATIONS 2: 9-12.[12]

---

[12]Wild, *Conciones*, 522-24; citing Jer 18:21. †After the fall of Constantinople in 1453, European Christians looked to the kingdom of Hungary to stop the spread of Islam and the Ottoman Turks. However, the Ottomans crushed the Hungarian nobility at the battle of Mohács in 1526, captured Budapest in 1529, and annexed Hungary in 1541.

2:13-22 O Daughter, Jerusalem!

THE VIRGIN DAUGHTER REJECTED. DANIEL TOUSSAIN: "What shall I say?" What testimonies or what examples shall I bring in and set down? Now although this seems to be exaggerated or an excessive kind of speech, yet if we weigh all the circumstances, we shall find that no people had so great a cause to complain, as the people of the Jews then had. They rightly felt that they had to deal with the living God, and that he had banded himself against them, and they had received from him more abundantly than any other people ever had. Therefore, they were more astonished at this change, which caused Jeremiah to redouble these words: "Consider O Lord to whom you have done these things: consider that they are your chosen people; consider also that it is the city of Jerusalem, which you so highly esteemed and which you have now so roughly handled and entreated." Surely there is nothing more difficult to bear than the anger of a dear friend or of a father. Even so this was a bitter thing to feel at the time the hand of the heavenly father turned, his countenance altered, and his favors converted into fury and indignation.

"Virgin daughter of Zion." Jeremiah understands by this Zion all that was in Jerusalem—the whole city, even all the people of the Jews. The Hebrew word *bethulah* signifies a maid that is ripe in years and in the flower of her age. And so sometimes the people of God are so called, as they are here and in chapter 37 of Isaiah. . . . Thus we see how the holy people of God are called, either for their weakness, and because they are entirely dependent on God, as a maiden depended on her mother, or else for their chastity and purity of their religion; as in contrast idolatry is often times called whoring and adultery. This speech is also sometimes taken in a scoffing manner, noting thereby a delicate and effeminate people. THE LAMENTATIONS AND HOLY MOURNINGS 2:13.[13]

THE SEA CANNOT CAPTURE YOUR AFFLICTION. GUILLAUME DU VAIR: Poor and wretched

---

[13]Toussain, *The Lamentations*, 82-84*; citing Is 37:22.

Jerusalem; how long shall I bewail your misery? What shall I say to the living about your mournful calamities? To what shall I compare the greatness of your afflictions? For neither the sea nor the earth can comprehend them; for your miseries are as great and infinite as the sea; they are a fountain of torment like the sea; they are a gulf without bottom like the sea; they are the nurse of great and hideous monsters like the sea—one following after another like the waves of the sea. But also the sea has good winds sometimes. But you, Oh Zion, in your afflictions have none but tempests and storms. The sea has havens, where there may be quiet, but you plod along perpetually in your travels. Poor Jerusalem, who can then save you? Your curse is so great that neither heaven nor earth can afford to give you remedy. MEDITATIONS UPON THE LAMENTATIONS OF JEREMIAH 2:13.[14]

FALLEN GERMANY AMONG THE HOSTILE NATIONS. JOHANNES WILD: We must consider these words today; indeed they will teach us to know what our situation is, to what end we ought to bear these evil things we have received, and how henceforth we are now able to emerge from them. Do you want to know the state of things for us? Indeed, we are in such a state that every other nation is astonished at how Germany has arrived at these evil things. There is no one who fails to mock us; in the end most of them rejoice concerning our many evils and boast that they have found the cause of our being devoured. And so, do you want to know the origin of these evil things? From prophets—not God's prophets, but our own—who with their charming language have led us from every dignified manner, piety, and devotion, and into the highest and most extreme frivolity, impiety, etc. Finally, do you want to know by what pact one is to be healed from these evils? By listening to a true prophet, who by exposing our sins summons us to penance. So the present text admonishes us.... First, therefore, we must observe what our Jeremiah asserts: that in addition to the evils that he

has recounted so far, something greater still happened to his city and his people. Namely, that in the midst of so many evils, they found no one who pitied them, but many who rejoiced over their destruction.... Indeed, it doubly tortures a person not only to suffer adversity, but on top of that to see everyone else rejoicing in their misery, as one is permitted to see with St. Job....

Who, however, does not see all these words of Jeremiah fulfilled among us? Indeed, Germany was once a region of perfect splendor before all nations. There was joy throughout the land. We were of great reputation among the nations; everywhere good and great things were spoken about us. All other nations were astounded by our serious manner, fortitude, fidelity, persistence, and truthfulness in all external matters. They commended us for our faith in all things divine, our piety, devotion, order, etc. And now we have squandered all of these things. Whoever passes over us and whoever speaks about us ridicules our reckless frivolity and lack of dependability. They marvel at what a degree of fickleness we have achieved. They say, is this that Germany about which we have heard such good things? Is this that faith, persistence, devotion, etc. of the Germans? This, I say, we are forced to hear from all the other nations. But really, those who were before and are now our enemies, namely, the Turks, and those whom we attacked for a long time with mercenary armies even to this day; all those people are rejoicing over our evil times and more bravely they plot against us. Finally, they hope that the time of our desolation is at hand. Hence it happens that the Turks are now bearing down on us and are eager to ruin and devour us.... This is the state of things in Germany, and especially among Catholics. To whom do we assign blame in these evil times? Listen to Jeremiah: "your prophets saw false things for you." SERMON ON LAMENTATIONS 2:14-16.[15]

DEFERRED PROMISES ARE NOT FORGOTTEN. JOHN UDALL: God often defers the performance of

---

[14]Du Vair, *Meditations*, CIov-CIIv*.

[15]Wild, *Conciones*, 542-43.

his promises and threatenings until they seem to be forgotten, or in reason never likely to come to pass, and yet they are accomplished in their time. The reason is because, first, he will thereby try the constancy and patience of his children. Second, that we might suffer with lone patience the vessels ordained to destruction. The use is to teach us, neither to despair of the promises, nor to think the threatenings shall never be accomplished, but to make a certain account of them, as if they were present, seeing nothing thereof shall fall to the ground. COMMENTARY ON LAMENTATIONS 2:17.[16]

LAMENTING IN THE NIGHT. PETER MARTYR VERMIGLI: "Arise, cry out (or 'chant mournful and sad groans') during the night." It must be done at night, either because this time is quieter and we can more easily act when onlookers are far away, or it was because the people were being oppressed during the day by servitude, labor, or fixed drills, and they were not used to having time to apply themselves very attentively to it. COMMENTARY ON LAMENTATIONS 2:19.[17]

TEARS FOR A HEART OF GOD'S MAKING. JOHN DONNE: "Pour out your heart like water before the face of the Lord." Every liquor that comes so clearly, so absolutely from the vessel—milk, wine, or honey—leaves a taste behind. Likewise this is so for sweet sins. Therefore, pour it out, the prophet says: not the liquor, but the heart itself, and take a new heart of God's making; for your former heart was never of God's making since Adam had a hand in it—his image was in it as well as God's—in original sin as well as in creation. As liquors poured out leave a taste and a smell behind them, so imperfect confessions (and who has ever perfected their confession?) leave ill-gotten goods sticking here and they leave a taste and a delight for thinking and speaking of former sins; these stick to your very self. But pour out your heart like water and all ill impressions to the very root. To accom-

plish this great mystery of godliness through confession, fix your meditations on these words of Psalm 32 and in their strength come now ... to the table of the Lord. . . . Receive your Savior there as he offers himself to you in these his ordinances on this day—once, twice, and three times—that is, in prayer, preaching, and in the sacrament; for this is your trinity upon the earth that must bring you to the Trinity of heaven. SERMON ON PSALM 32:5.[18]

INNOCENT YOUTH AND THE WRATH OF GOD. JOHANNES OECOLAMPADIUS: I address the Lord, who kills the hurtful and deprives of his blessing those who despise his gifts, so that you may see that they all had a taste for earthly things—I speak of the world—even those who seem innocent, even those who are thought to be gifted with prudence. So those young women, and those who ought to think of nothing other than those things that are of the Lord, and the young men who were supposed to fight bravely: they all fall to the power and savagery of the enemy. Some enemies have mercy on the young women because of their beauty and youth as they lead them into captivity. But here there is no mercy. So then there is no collective grief, nor that customary anger of God where there is no appearance of piety. See, Lord, how long your anger has gone forward, and do not forget us! COMMENTARY ON JEREMIAH, LAMENTATIONS 2:21.[19]

THE GREATEST MISERY EVER KNOWN. JOHN DONNE: We know of the dishonor and infamy that lay upon barrenness among the Jews—how wives deplored and lamented this. Though God is pleased to take away the impediment of barrenness and to give children, we know as well the misery and desolation of bereavement when parents are deprived of those children by death. By the measure of that sorrow, which follows barrenness or such bereavement, we may grasp the proportion of joy that accompanies God's miraculous blessing when "women receive their dead raised to life again." In all

---

[16]Udall, *Commentary on Lamentations*, N3r*; citing Rom 9:22.
[17]Vermigli, *Commentary*, 101.
[18]Donne, *Sermons*, 9:314-15*; citing Lam 2:19; Ps 32:5.
[19]Oecolampadius, *In Hieremiam . . . Threnos*, 2T4v, 264v.

the secular and profane writers in the world—in that whole body of literature—you will not find anyone expressing the misery of famine as the Holy Spirit does in the Lamentations: "that women eat the fruit of their children." We translate it: "their children of a span long." That is, they procured abortions and untimely births of those children, which were in their bodies, so that they might have some flesh to eat. That must be the greatest misery ever known. SERMON ON HEBREWS 11:35.[20]

THE TENDER IN BRUTAL TIMES. JOHANNES OECOLAMPADIUS: If you wished completely to snatch us away, then you could have done so through more gentle enemies. But you have drawn from a remote land a people of unknown language and of such great numbers and confidence for the coming destruction, like some people come together for the day of a festival; they are all terrible and dangerous folk. The enemy pretty well destroys even those tender nurslings and almost-

grown students. These things we also bewail in the church, that the Antichrist has so much prevailed, the enemy is everywhere, and salvation is nowhere. There is yet hope in one Lord alone, if he deigns to look upon us and help, because he is powerful and merciful. May he do this, we pray. Amen. COMMENTARY ON JEREMIAH, LAMENTATIONS 2:22.[21]

SORROW EXPLAINS THE LACK OF STRUCTURE. JOHN TRAPP: Here every word is very ponderous and pathetical. Indeed, this whole book is so, which is the reason that there is no great coherence in some places to be discovered. For as he that is under some grievous affliction, without observing of order, now cries, now prays, now laments, now complains, etc., so does the prophet here, in the name of the church, pour forth himself tumultuously in a flood of such words as his grief ministered to himself, and grief is no methodical speaker. COMMENTARY ON LAMENTATIONS 2:22.[22]

---

[20]Donne, *Sermons*, 7:374-75*; citing Lam 2:20; Heb 11:35.

[21]Oecolampadius, *In Hieremiam . . . Threnos*, 2T4v 264v.
[22]Trapp, *A Commentary or Exposition*, 378*.

LAMENTATIONS 3:1-20
MY AFFLICTION AND MY WANDERING

¹I am the man who has seen affliction
    under the rod of his wrath;
²he has driven and brought me
    into darkness without any light;
³surely against me he turns his hand
    again and again the whole day long.

⁴He has made my flesh and my skin waste away;
    he has broken my bones;
⁵he has besieged and enveloped me
    with bitterness and tribulation;
⁶he has made me dwell in darkness
    like the dead of long ago.

⁷He has walled me about so that I cannot escape;
    he has made my chains heavy;
⁸though I call and cry for help,
    he shuts out my prayer;
⁹he has blocked my ways with blocks of stones;
    he has made my paths crooked.

¹⁰He is a bear lying in wait for me,
    a lion in hiding;

¹¹he turned aside my steps and tore me to pieces;
    he has made me desolate;
¹²he bent his bow and set me
    as a target for his arrow.

¹³He drove into my kidneys
    the arrows of his quiver;
¹⁴I have become the laughingstock of all peoples,
    the object of their taunts all day long.
¹⁵He has filled me with bitterness;
    he has sated me with wormwood.

¹⁶He has made my teeth grind on gravel,
    and made me cower in ashes;
¹⁷my soul is bereft of peace;
    I have forgotten what happiness[a] is;
¹⁸so I say, "My endurance has perished;
    so has my hope from the LORD."

¹⁹Remember my affliction and my wanderings,
    the wormwood and the gall!
²⁰My soul continually remembers it
    and is bowed down within me.

a Hebrew good

OVERVIEW: This middle chapter of Lamentations prompts commentators, preachers, and poets to wrestle with the depths of human suffering and spiritual despair and to trumpet their unwavering hope in the steadfast love and bountiful mercy of God. There are no trite answers here. Interpreters describe squarely and deeply the role of God in chastising, testing, and disciplining the faithful. This is pastoral advice for the worst of times and the darkest nights of the soul. A complex understanding of suffering, a nuanced appraisal of inner turmoil and hopelessness, and battle-tested advice for hard times are offered to the reader; the resources of the Reformation for the grind of daily life emerge in these reflections. Neither prosperity nor happiness are the goal of these authors, but faithfulness in all circumstances and faith not in self, but in God's providence, eternal promise, and enduring grace.

3:1-9 Affliction Under God's Judgment

A LIFE WITHOUT COMFORT OR CONSOLATION.
DANIEL TOUSSAIN: The prophet in this chapter no longer speaks in the third person, nor does he speak generally as he did in the beginning of the first chapter in the person of a comfortless widow. Now he speaks in his own person; or as is more

likely, he brings in a certain person who is lamenting profoundly and so represents the people of Judah. . . . It is likely that this book is a history of things that came to pass and were done both by reason of the circumstances of the places and the persons herein described. . . .

The first part of the chapter reaches to verse 20 and shows a pattern of extreme combat between the flesh and the spirit, and the strong assault that a person sustains when they are brought into extreme sorrow and grief. . . .

The subject or argument of part one is this: that there can be nothing more miserable than such a people whom God takes in hand to punish in his wrath and leaves them altogether comfortless. Such a miserable condition the prophet amplifies and sets down by similitudes of the most sorrowful and lamentable things that are to be found in the whole world. And this is the use and benefit of this part: that when we consider these things we should make a better account of the lovingkindness and favor of God than we usually do. For if we understood what a treasure and happiness it is to be in the favor and grace of the Almighty God, then there should be nothing that touches our hearts more than our efforts to keep ourselves in his favor and grace. . . .

Now, this first part of Lamentations 3 rightly sets forth to us how this great God often leads his holy ones into hell, as it were, into a bottomless depth of temptation and grief. Thus at first sight one might hear the speaker in Lamentations in this way: like a desperate man who is void of all consolation and comfort. THE LAMENTATIONS AND HOLY MOURNINGS 3:1-20.[1]

NOT A CHAPTER ABOUT THE PASSION OF CHRIST. NIKOLAUS SELNECKER: In previous times the papacy understood and laid out this whole chapter as if it were about the suffering of our Lord Jesus Christ; so our Lord Christ himself was complaining against the Jews who martyred, tortured, beat, crucified, and killed him. They removed his clothes from him. Thus these words are fulfilled: "I am the miserable man that must see my own poverty and misery." Likewise Christ was captured and bound at night. So these words are fulfilled: "He led me and brought me into darkness and not into the light. . . ." But this understanding we commend to the poets, who are always running around and showing off their art. Jeremiah only describes here the captivity of the Jewish people. SONGS OF LAMENT OF THE PROPHET JEREMIAH 3:1-2.[2]

I AM THE MAN. JOHN DONNE: In these words ("I am the man," etc.) there are two parts; first the burden and then the ease, first the weight and then the alleviation, first the discomfort and then the refreshing, the sea of afflictions that overflows and surrounds us all and then our emergency and lifting up of our head above that sea. . . . "I am the man," which is the name of man, by which the strongest and most powerful men are denoted in the Scriptures; they, the strongest, the mightiest, they that thought themselves safest and sorrow-proof, are the ones afflicted. . . . The most beloved of God, and those whose service God may use in his church, they are subject to be slowed in their service by these afflictions. Nothing makes a person so great among other people, nothing makes a person so necessary to God that they can escape afflictions. . . . These afflictions are *eius,* "his," the Lord's, and they are *in virga,* "in his rod." And again, *in virga irae,* "in the rod of his wrath." And in these two branches are the extent and the weight of afflictions. . . . Affliction did not blind Jeremiah, did not stupefy him; affliction did not make him insensible to affliction (which is a frequent but desperate condition) . . . he saw it. . . . And then, *Ego vir,* "I am the man that saw it," he maintained the dignity of his station; still he played the man, still he survived to glorify God, and to be an example to other people of patience under God's corrections and of thankfulness for God's deliverance. SERMON ON LAMENTATIONS 3:1.[3]

[1]Toussain, *The Lamentations,* 102-3, 108-9*.

[2]Selnecker, *Threni,* Sir.
[3]Donne, *Sermons,* 9:194-95*.

SEE YOUR POVERTY. JOHANNES WILD: First, the fathers of the church interpret this verse concerning the common misery of the human race; second, concerning the miseries of the Babylonian captivity; third, concerning the afflictions that the prophet feels in himself in particular. Others interpret the verse first under any heading—concerning the common misery of the human race—second, concerning the church, and third, concerning any pious person in particular. Some explain this whole chapter mystically concerning Christ, and they are determined that Jeremiah here spoke about nothing other than the person of Christ.

But I have neither the inclination nor the time to endure consideration of every explanation of every interpretation. Therefore, I will include only the best and more necessary explanations. Hear, therefore, how the passage begins: "I am a man seeing my poverty." The beginning is beautiful. Thus far he has spoken concerning others; now he speaks about himself, as if to say, "What good does it do to weep over those who do not yet understand their own misery, even if they still lie prostrate in misery's midst?" It is important to observe, however, that he does not simply say, "I am a poor man"; indeed that would say less; for others were poor as well, but they did not see their own poverty. Indeed, every person is poor. As soon as one is born they are stripped of their glory, and moreover, they are deprived of the glory of God. But not every person sees this. Not every person understands that this itself is their poverty, as David says: "They did not know, they did not understand that they walk in shadows." And Jeremiah: "You struck them and they felt no pain," etc. And John in Apocalypse: "You say, 'Because I am rich and lack nothing, and you do not know that you are wretched and pitiable,'" etc.

So the prophet does not simply say, "I am a poor man or I have experienced poverty," but "I am a man seeing my poverty." Indeed, it is one thing to be poor and a very different thing to see and recognize one's own poverty. Someone can be poor and a fool. But only the wise can see and recognize their own poverty, indeed only those who have

been enlightened by the Spirit of God. Jeremiah was like this, and so he was able to say truthfully, "I am a man seeing my poverty." Indeed just as it is the first step to health when someone recognizes their own illness, likewise it is the first step toward salvation to recognize one's wretchedness. Among the Jews nothing was further from the case. In fact, Jeremiah had labored a great deal and never omitted anything, in case he would be able to open their eyes. But it was in vain. . . .

Who is such a lazy person that they do not seek food during a famine? Who is such a fool that when they see themselves in danger they do not request help of others? Who is so insane that when they are sick they do not seek a doctor? Who is so long-suffering, that they do not cry out when enemies are attacking them with bloody swords? Who is so slack of soul that they are not wounded when they see every sort of evil rushing at them? Who is so bold that they are not frightened when they sense that God is angry? Who is so impious that they do not tremble when they see hell opening for them? So too all these things are before our eyes and all at once we are poor in fact, feeble in body, wretched in soul, full of sin in our consciences, and surrounded by every external evil. God strikes from above; the devil from below, and finally hell has widened its mouth to devour us. . . .

Moreover, there is nothing to which Jeremiah might urge us more than to see our own poverty and misery. Therefore, let us open our eyes and see our state; let each person purge themselves of spirits, riches, power, knowledge, and honor, etc. Let them look upon themselves as they are in nature, in their conscience, before God and the world, physically and spiritually, etc. And if I'm not deceived, they will see that they are poor and wretched; and they will have occasion for prayer. SERMON ON LAMENTATIONS 3:1.[4]

THE ROD OF GOD'S TESTING. JOHANNES OECOLAMPADIUS: "I am that man who has been seen, in the rod of his wrath." If you view this verse

---

[4]Wild, *Conciones*, 563-65; citing Ps 82:5; Jer 5:3; Rev 3:17.

literally it pertains completely to the person of Jeremiah with his lamentations. While predicting the future captivity, he suffered from the hypocritical and false prophets many indignities which he often lamented in the book itself. However, as he saw the captivity fulfilled, he grieved deeply and for a long time. Meanwhile, he nonetheless bears the type of Christ, lamenting the destruction of Jerusalem and its blindness, since he would suffer the worst from them. All the saints are participants in these complaints, who both suffer persecution on account of the truth and bemoan with a great torturing of the soul the multitude of those perishing. So he will be able to explain this three-part message: they who nevertheless embrace their feelings, as a true type of Christ, will gather as his members.

"If anyone else has experienced affliction and torment, or sadness of heart, I most of all have experienced it as God raged, by seeing such dreadful and calamitous things." However, he does not name God because of the magnitude of his emotion, when he refers in that verse to all the things which he bears. Some want the verse to refer to the enemy instead of his name. But it is not unworthy of God that he scourges and test his own sons. However, he imagines himself to be a captive sheep, whom a shepherd drives with his rod without mercy into a very hostile stable. In this metaphor, the rod stands in for the lash of the enemy. But who is more afflicted than Christ, on whom God has placed all our iniquities, and he himself has borne our infirmities, as God raged at our sins? Whence he orders in Zechariah: "To arouse the sword against the man who adheres to me, so I will strike the shepherd and scatter the sheep." And so that God could offer his love, he handed his son over for us. All pious folk glory in his cross and bear the wounds of Christ while not seeking the things that are of this life, but those that are of the life to come. Commentary on Jeremiah, Lamentations 3:1.[5]

---

[5]Oecolampadius, *In Hieremiam . . . Threnos*, 2T4v-2V1r; citing Mt 23:37-39; Is 53:4-7; Zech 13:7.

Christ Exhibited. John Donne: You remember in the history of the passion of our Lord and Savior Christ Jesus, there was an *Ecce homo*, a showing, an exhibiting of that man, in whom we are all blessed. Pilate presented him to the Jews so, with that *Ecce homo*, "Behold the man." That man upon whom the wormwood and the gall of all the ancient prophecies, and the venom and malignity of all the cruel instruments thereof, was now poured out. That man who was left "as a tender plant, and as a root out of a dry ground, without form or beauty or comeliness, that we should desire to see him," as the prophet Isaiah exhibits him. That man who upon the brightness of his eternal generation in the bosom of his Father had now cast a cloud of a temporary and earthly generation in the womb of his mother, that man, who, as he entered into the womb of his first mother, the Blessed Virgin, by a supernatural way, by the overshadowing of the Holy Spirit, so he vouchsafed to enter into the womb of her whom he had accepted for his second mother, the earth, by an unnatural way, not by a natural, but by a violent and bitter death, that man so torn and mangled, wounded with thorns, oppressed with scorns and contumelies, Pilate presents and exhibits so, *Ecce homo*, "Behold the man." But in all this depression of his, in all his humiliation and evacuation, yet he had a crown on, yet he had a purple garment on, the emblems, the characters of majesty were always upon him. And these two considerations, the miseries that exhaust and evacuate and annihilate the man in this life, and yet those sparks and seeds of morality, that lie in the bosom, that still he is a man, the afflictions that depress and smother, that suffocate and strangle their spirits in their bosoms, and yet that unsmotherable, that unquenchable spirit of adoption, by which we cry "Abba, Father," that still he is a Christian, these thorns and yet these crowns, these contumelies and yet this purple, are the two parts of this text, "I am the man, that has seen affliction by the rod of his wrath." For here is an *ecce*, "behold"; Jeremiah presents a map, a manifestation of as great an affliction as the rod of God's wrath could inflict, but yet he is *Ecce homo*,

"Behold the man, I am the man," he is not demolished, he is not incinerated so, not so annihilated, but that he is still a man. God preserves his children from departing from the dignity of human beings, and from the sovereign dignity of Christian people, in the deluge and inundation of all afflictions. SERMON ON LAMENTATIONS 3:1.[6]

THE PAIN OF FALSE WORSHIP. KATHARINA SCHÜTZ ZELL: O dear friends, what a great concern this man had for the honor of Christ and the salvation of the poor little sheep! For he heard from foreigners in several places that again the false worship has begun, to the shame of Christ and his word; because of that many honest people, preachers, and servants have died for sadness. (What God will allow to happen to us we do not yet know!) Such things in the midst of God and his word caused him such pain day and night that he could well have said with the psalmist, "The insults of your house, with which they insulted you, break my heart," and with Jeremiah in the book of the prophets, "I am an afflicted man, who sees now the rod of your wrath." LAMENT AND EXHORTATION.[7]

LIVING IN DARKNESS. JOHANNES OECOLAMPADIUS: He drove me away and led me off into the darkness, and not into the light, where hope is. He did not lead me into lovely and florid pastures of temporal happiness, which are signified through "light." But he led me into a dark and shadowy stable, as the prophet even in real life was sent into prison and the pond of filth more than once. . . . Nevertheless, this should be taken as an allegory. So also the cross was laid on Christ, similar to the sheep that is driven into darkness and therefore into death itself, while he is hated by the whole world, abandoned by all, despised and afflicted. Also in this life many adverse things happen to the pious; while they are destitute in all things, they are the filth of this world, and in this way they

proceed through many adversities into the kingdom of heaven. But in this life there is no hope of earthly light. COMMENTARY ON JEREMIAH, LAMENTATIONS 3:2.[8]

WASTED AND HELD CAPTIVE IN DARKNESS. GUILLAUME DU VAIR: Let me be awake before my time comes: my skin wrinkled with sorrow, my flesh wasted away under my skin, and my bones aching as if they had been broken. The tenure of my imprisonment has caused this anguish; for I was shut up as if I had been walled in a tower, giving me bile for my nourishment and torment for my exercise. Do you know where they have enclosed me? It is a place more dark, dreary, and obscure than where the damned may be found. MEDITATIONS UPON THE LAMENTATIONS OF JEREMIAH 3:4-7.[9]

GOD'S SURROUNDING JUDGMENT AND MERCY. JOHN DONNE: God's indignation is exalted, when he is said to envelop by way of siege: "He has besieged and enveloped me; he has enveloped me with gall and travail. . . . He has hedged me in so that I cannot get out," as Jeremiah complains. So God threatens, "I will camp against you on all sides and I will lay siege against you"; for these verses intimate the displeasure of God; he not only leaves us without succor—joyless and comfortless in ourselves—but he cuts off those supplies that might relieve us. He envelops us; he besieges us; he camps around us on all sides so that no relief can enter. So when his love and mercy is expressed in this phrase—that he envelops us—it signifies both entire mercy, that no enemy shall break in through any place while he envelops us and a permanent and durable mercy, that no enemy force and no weariness in himself shall make him discontinue his watch or his guarding of us. But he will yet envelop us. SERMON ON PSALM 32:7.[10]

---

[6]Donne, *Works*, 5:303-4*; citing Jn 19:5; Is 53:2.
[7]Zell, *Church Mother*, 112*; citing Ps 69:9, 20. This is an excerpt from the eulogy Katharina gave at the graveside of her husband, Matthew Zell, in January 1548.

[8]Oecolampadius, *In Hieremiam . . . Threnos*, 2V1r, 267r; citing Jer 20:2; 38:6.
[9]Du Vair, *Meditations*, D6r-v*.
[10]Donne, *Sermons*, 9:345-46; citing Lam 3:5, 7; Is 29:3.

WAITING FOR GOD TO ANSWER. PETER MAR-
TYR VERMIGLI: It especially torments the saints
when in their afflictions they are not heard at once.
For their carnal nature taunts them: "Why doesn't
that God of yours hear you now?" These insults
must be blunted with great faith. Let us remember
that Christ, when he prayed in the garden, also was
not heard at once but rather after his resurrection.
And when he prayed for those who nailed him to
the cross, they were not saved at once, though many
of them were later converted to God after Peter
addressed them. If, therefore, in Christ's case vows
and prayers were delayed, and if God held back gifts
from him for a short time, why are we, on our part,
so very frustrated that we are not heard on the spot?
COMMENTARY ON LAMENTATIONS 3:7-9.[11]

SUFFERING AND HEALING OF THE SOUL. ST.
JOHN OF THE CROSS: A person's sufferings at this
time of union and transformation of the soul in
God cannot be exaggerated; they are but little less
than the sufferings of purgatory. I do not know
how to explain the severity of this oppression and
the intensity of the suffering felt in it, save by what
Jeremiah says of it in these words: "I am the man
who has seen my poverty. . . ." Jeremiah laments all
this and goes on to say much more.

Since in this fashion God mediates and heals
the soul of its many infirmities, bringing it to health,
it must necessarily suffer from this purge and cure
according to its sickness. . . . All the soul's infirmities
are brought to light; they are set before the eyes to
be felt and healed. THE LIVING FLAME OF LOVE.[12]

3:10-20 Filled with Bitterness

**BE DISCERNING ABOUT THE COMPLAINTS OF
HOLY PEOPLE.** JOHN CALVIN: The complaint is
harsh when Jeremiah compares God to a bear or a
lion. But we have said that the apprehension of
God's wrath so terrified the faithful that they could
not sufficiently express the atrocity of their calamity.

Then we must bear in mind . . . that they spoke
according to the judgment of the flesh; for they did
not always moderate their feelings. Thus something
came from them that is worthy of blame. We ought
not, then, make a rule in religion from all the
complaints of holy people when they were pressed
down by the hand of God; for when their minds
were in a state of confusion they uttered much that
was intemperate. But we ought, on the other hand,
to acknowledge how great must be our weakness,
since we see that even the strongest have thus fallen,
when God exercised severity toward them. COM-
MENTARY ON LAMENTATIONS 3:10.[13]

EVEN THE ELECT FEEL GOD'S WRATH. JOHN
UDALL: God's dearest children are not able to
stand under the weight of God's plagues, when he
visits them according to their sins. The same
appears by Christ's agony, when he did feel God's
anger against our sins, which he did bear. The
reason is, because God's anger is heavy, our sins are
grievous, and we are weak. . . . The use is, first, to
confute the error of satisfaction, seeing we cannot
answer to God one for a thousand. Second, to
teach us how hardly our great corruption is done
away. Third, that we may see how needful it is for
us now and then to feel God's anger against us, that
we may thereby learn to know ourselves and have
our stubborn hearts broken. COMMENTARY ON
LAMENTATIONS 3:10.[14]

THE ARROWS OF AFFLICTION. JOHN DONNE:
These arrows "stick in us." The rain falls but that
cold sweat does not hang on us. Hail beats on us,
but it leaves no pockmark in our skin. These arrows
neither fall about us and miss us, nor do they
rebound back without hurting us. But we complain
with Jeremiah, "The sons of his quiver have entered
our kidneys." "They stick in us." Consider but one
kind of arrow—diseases, sicknesses. They stick to
us to such a degree that we are not sure that any of

---

[11]Vermigli, *Commentary*, 112-13; citing Mt 26:36-45; Acts 2:1-47.
[12]St. John of the Cross, *Collected Works*, 649.

[13]CTS 21:396* (CO 39:567).
[14]Udall, *Commentary on Lamentations*, P3r*; citing Ps 2:12; Job 3:11;
Lk 23:30; Mt 26:38; 27:46; Job 9:2-3.

the old diseases found in the physicians' books have faded away. Rather every year produces new diseases, which are not yet mentioned. Of this we are sure. We can scarcely express the number and names of all the diseases in a human body. Six thousand years have barely taught us what these diseases are, how they affect us, and how they can be cured. Nothing this side of the resurrection can teach us. They stick to us as they pass by as an inheritance and last many more generations in families than an actual inheritance does. When no land, manor, title, or honor descends upon an heir, the stone or the gout descends upon him.

Even if our bodies did not have enough natural diseases and infirmities, we contract still more and inflict more . . . in mortifications, macerations, and disciplines of this rebellious flesh. I must have this body with me in heaven or else salvation itself is not perfect. And yet I cannot take this body there, except as St. Paul says, "I beat down this body," and attenuate this body by mortification: "Wretched man that I am, who shall deliver me from this body of death?" I do not have enough body for my body, and I have too much body for my soul. I do not have enough body, blood, or strength to sustain myself in health, and yet I have body enough to destroy my soul and frustrate the grace of God in that miserable, perplexing, and puzzling human condition. Sin makes the human body miserable and the remedy of sin, mortification, makes it miserable too. SERMON ON PSALM 38:2.[15]

SAVAGE AFFLICTIONS AND HUMILIATION. GUILLAUME DU VAIR: He has brought to me a quiver from the treasury of his ire, well furnished with arrows of affliction and torment; they pierce me through and through. They give me blows as they would give to a dog while breaking his back with a lever. Poor miserable wretch that I am, so to be mocked by everyone and then to be left as a laughingstock for the whole world and an inspiration for their songs about me, which I hear daily in the streets. God has watered me with bile and bitterness and made me drunk with the wine of wormwood. MEDITATIONS UPON THE LAMENTATIONS OF JEREMIAH 3:13-15.[16]

DESPERATION AND PRAYER. JOHANNES BUGENHAGEN: "My hope is perishing." This is the worst trial, which leads to desperation, as if God rejected me eternally. Here it is necessary that, along with the temptation, God should make a provision that we are able to endure. . . . Just as in what immediately follows: "Call to mind," etc. When prayer enters into the battle of faith, victory begins to lean to the one who is tempted. COMMENTARY ON JEREMIAH, LAMENTATIONS 3:18.[17]

DESPAIR AND FAITH IN THE PROPHET. JOHN CALVIN: Let us learn from this passage that the faithful are not free from despair, for it enters into their souls. But that there is yet no reason why they should indulge despair; on the contrary, they ought courageously and firmly to resist it; for when the prophet said this, he did not mean that he succumbed to this trial, as though he had embraced what had come into his mind; but he meant that he was as it were overwhelmed for a short time. If anyone would ask, how can it be that hope and despair can reside in the same man? The answer is that when faith is weak, that part of the soul is empty, which then admits despair. Now faith is not only weakened but is also nearly stifled. This indeed does not happen daily, but there is no one whom God deeply exercises with temptations who does not feel that his faith is almost extinguished. It is no wonder that despair then prevails; but just for a moment. In the meantime, the remedy is immediately to flee to God and to complain of this misery, so that he may succor and raise up those who are thus fallen. COMMENTARY ON LAMENTATIONS 3:18.[18]

RELY ON GOD'S MEMORY. JOHANNES BUGENHA-GEN: "You will certainly remember." The translator of the Old Latin version here says, "In memory, I will

---

[15]Donne, Sermons, 2:62-63*; citing Ps 38:2; 1 Cor 9:27; Rom 7:24.

[16]Du Vair, Meditations, D8r-v*.
[17]Bugenhagen, In Ieremiam . . . Threni, Eiv.
[18]CTS 21:28, 403-4* (CO 39:572).

be mindful, and my soul will melt in me." Because he understood it like this: "I will recall my sins, whence my soul will be disturbed," seeing that he suffers what he has deserved. Thomas Aquinas, or whoever was the author of that song, which they sing at the Feast of Corpus Christi, twists this verse most absurdly toward the words of Christ: "This do in remembrance of me,"[†] as almost all the rest of the words of that song were twisted out of the Scriptures of that old version. And so that you can see how senseless this is, it does not say in the Hebrew, "I will remember," but "you will remember." Of course, this means "You, Lord," which is what they could have learned from Lyra.[‡] You see how faith breathes

in these words, and it does not despair about the mercy of God and his promises. As he adds, it is "by the mercy of the Lord, we are not yet consumed," but a remnant of us remains. But every day in the morning, that is, from the beginning of the day—he does not wait until evening—his mercy is new; that is, daily we experience the mercy of God even in our miseries. "Great is your faithfulness." COMMENTARY ON JEREMIAH, LAMENTATIONS 3:19.[19]

---

[19]Bugenhagen, *In Ieremiam . . . Threni*, E1v-E2r; citing Luke 22:19; 1 Cor 11:24-25; Lam 3:22-23. [†]Bugenhagen likely has in mind here the hymn *Pangue Lingua Gloriosi Corporis Mysterium*, attributed here to Thomas Aquinas (d. 1274). [‡]Reference to Nicholas of Lyra (d. 1349), the most influential commentator on the Old Testament in the later Middle Ages.

LAMENTATIONS 3:21-66
GREAT IS YOUR FAITHFULNESS

²¹But this I call to mind,
  and therefore I have hope:

²²The steadfast love of the Lord never ceases;ᵃ
  his mercies never come to an end;
²³they are new every morning;
  great is your faithfulness.
²⁴"The Lord is my portion," says my soul,
  "therefore I will hope in him."

²⁵The Lord is good to those who wait for him,
  to the soul who seeks him.
²⁶It is good that one should wait quietly
  for the salvation of the Lord.
²⁷It is good for a man that he bear
  the yoke in his youth.

²⁸Let him sit alone in silence
  when it is laid on him;
²⁹let him put his mouth in the dust—
  there may yet be hope;
³⁰let him give his cheek to the one who strikes,
  and let him be filled with insults.

³¹For the Lord will not
  cast off forever,
³²but, though he cause grief, he will have
    compassion
  according to the abundance of his
    steadfast love;
³³for he does not afflict from his heart
  or grieve the children of men.

³⁴To crush underfoot
  all the prisoners of the earth,
³⁵to deny a man justice
  in the presence of the Most High,
³⁶to subvert a man in his lawsuit,
  the Lord does not approve.

³⁷Who has spoken and it came to pass,
  unless the Lord has commanded it?
³⁸Is it not from the mouth of the Most High
  that good and bad come?

³⁹Why should a living man complain,
  a man, about the punishment of his sins?
⁴⁰Let us test and examine our ways,
  and return to the Lord!
⁴¹Let us lift up our hearts and hands
  to God in heaven:
⁴²"We have transgressed and rebelled,
  and you have not forgiven.

⁴³"You have wrapped yourself with anger and
    pursued us,
  killing without pity;
⁴⁴you have wrapped yourself with a cloud
  so that no prayer can pass through.
⁴⁵You have made us scum and garbage
  among the peoples.

⁴⁶"All our enemies
  open their mouths against us;
⁴⁷panic and pitfall have come upon us,
  devastation and destruction;
⁴⁸my eyes flow with rivers of tears
  because of the destruction of the daughter of
    my people.

⁴⁹"My eyes will flow without ceasing,
  without respite,
⁵⁰until the Lord from heaven
  looks down and sees;
⁵¹my eyes cause me grief
  at the fate of all the daughters of my city.

⁵²"I have been hunted like a bird
  by those who were my enemies without cause;
⁵³they flung me alive into the pit
  and cast stones on me;
⁵⁴water closed over my head;
  I said, 'I am lost.'

⁵⁵"I called on your name, O Lord,
  from the depths of the pit;
⁵⁶you heard my plea, 'Do not close
  your ear to my cry for help!'

⁵⁷ *You came near when I called on you;*
you said, 'Do not fear!'

⁵⁸ *"You have taken up my cause, O Lord;*
you have redeemed my life.

⁵⁹ *You have seen the wrong done to me, O Lord;*
judge my cause.

⁶⁰ *You have seen all their vengeance,*
all their plots against me.

⁶¹ *"You have heard their taunts, O Lord,*
all their plots against me.

⁶² *The lips and thoughts of my assailants*
are against me all the day long.

⁶³ *Behold their sitting and their rising;*
I am the object of their taunts.

⁶⁴ *"You will repay them,^b O Lord,*
according to the work of their hands.

⁶⁵ *You will give them^c dullness of heart;*
your curse will be^d on them.

⁶⁶ *You will pursue them^e in anger and destroy*
them
from under your heavens, O Lord."^f

a Syriac, Targum; Hebrew *Because of the steadfast love of the Lord, we are not cut off*   b Or *Repay them*   c Or *Give them*   d Or *place your curse*   e Or *Pursue them*
f Syriac (compare Septuagint, Vulgate); Hebrew *the heavens of the Lord*

OVERVIEW: In expounding this section of the chapter, the reformers stress that although Christians are beset by innumerable hardships that engender seemingly endless anguish, they are not without the aid of God's mercy and sustaining grace. Specifically, the reformers here highlight the vast spiritual resources God avails to his people as they wage spiritual battle amid life's continuous grief. As Christians turn to God for their comfort, they find that rather than extinguishing their faith, the afflictions that they suffer can actually strengthen it.

3:21-39 Hope in God's Steadfast Love and Mercy

WEAPONS FOR OUR BATTLE WITH TEMPTATION AND MISERY. DANIEL TOUSSAIN: The second part of the chapter contains the victory over temptations and the means to bridle and abate the impatience of the flesh. In this part, which goes on to verse 40, are many excellent sentences, which glitter like pearls from the Orient. In brief, the prophet holds up three bucklers against temptation. First, he compares the punishment they endured with the punishment the people well deserved because of their sins. Thus one finds that in this respect that they were dealt with very gently. Second, he holds up and sets down the constancy of God and his great goodness, which far surpasses our small and momentary miseries. These miseries are of no value in comparison to the glory and joy that the children of God look for in the life to come. . . . Third, Jeremiah sets before the people's eyes the end and purpose of our God in his chastisements. He does not seek nor desire our destruction, but rather our amendment and salvation. Afflictions attempt to cleanse those that are his so that God may afterward more amply bestow his graces upon them. . . .

The second part of the chapter leads us into the very storehouse of munitions and defense of the faithful, and teaches us with what armor and weapons we should fight against such enemies, and how sure and resolute we should be of our God and his judgments. To be sure, this section shows that the faithful must always look upon their own miseries with one eye and with the other eye look upon the mercies of the Lord. We must look to the right hand of the Most High, who turns all events to a good end: as the Prophet David says in Psalm 77. Otherwise we would behold and consider nothing else but our own misery as if it is a gulf that would swallow us clean up. THE LAMENTATIONS AND HOLY MOURNINGS 3:21-39.[1]

---

[1]Toussain, *The Lamentations*, 103-5, 114-15*; citing Ps 77:11-20.

THE STORY OF MY DESPAIR AND FAITH RENEWED. NIKOLAUS SELNECKER: This second part of the third chapter is a beautiful prayer and a lovely and rich consolation that God will always be gracious, if one returns to him; and even if God had been as angry as possible. That actually means, as James says, "Is someone troubled? Then pray." Then that prayer is stronger than any misfortune. One should hold himself to prayer and should lament every difficulty, sorrow, fear, and crisis before God, for he hears us and saves us. . . .

Is not what Jeremiah says immeasurably beautiful, lovely, and consoling? You will think, what is my soul saying to me? That is a strong Amen, when the spirit of the heart knows and can say, "God hears me, I know it. My heart tells me. I do not doubt God's grace. I am a child of God. He is my father and will help me."

I would like to say something that pious and God-fearing people will not take in the wrong way; for it is the truth and may be a story of consolation for others. For a few years now I have often been so deathly ill that I could only think that the final hours of my life were at hand, that after so much struggle at last I should give up. In part I have experienced what it is like for someone who sees death before him, and searches for his courage. This was also something new that I had never known. I had to separate myself from something I had been carrying. I had fallen into very difficult, dangerous, and despairing thoughts—more difficult than I can say or have time to say. I could neither rest, nor sleep. I often broke out in anxious sweats and often fell into unconsciousness. I would argue with myself for long stretches and think, "Oh God, are you not mine? Shall I pass on in this melancholy state while doubting, anxious, and desperate, feeling no consolation and dying without faith? How did I get here?" See, God knew that while in such torment, my heart was coming alive, fresh, and happy once more. For I thought, "What are you doing in such sorrow that you are serving the devil? Grab onto God and his word and promise. He is truly your God and Father through Christ his son. Why do you worry so?" Then I was again confident and sure that I was a child of God, as the saying goes: strength is given to all of God's children, who believe in his name. Then I would have soon and gladly died. But I gave myself to this completely, even if it irritated me later, so that I might become a little bit stronger, that I might live longer. I say this dear people as it was such a consolation for me. Because many of you are sick and remain in this hospice. So do not hesitate to support and console each other with the example of Jeremiah. I say this because it here states, "My soul speaks to me." SONGS OF LAMENT OF THE PROPHET JEREMIAH 3:19-21.[2]

WHAT GOD'S MERCY YIELDS. LANCELOT ANDREWES: Mercy yields to us three things to be observed: (1) The number; (2) the nature; and (3) the property.

The number, that it is not "mercy" but "mercies"; not one but many, even a plurality of them, a multitude of them, because [there is] a multitude of us; they are many because we are many; we are many and our sins many more; and where sins are multiplied, there a multiplicity of mercies is needful, "Lest there be not enough for both houses, and for all three estates in them"; for so it is to be wished that there may be a representation of all his mercies as that assembly is the representation of all the realm so that there may be enough for all.

But concerning mercy another cause here is set down: "Because his compassions fail not." How hangs this together? Thus. The word, which here is translated "compassions" very much indeed properly signifies the bowels. It is to show that not mercies, nor a number of them at large, from any place or any kind, would serve for this work, but a certain special kind of choice mercies was required; and those are they that issue from the bowels, or "merciful bowels," or "bowels of mercy." You shall find them together in some special works of God, such as this was.

Now that which makes up all is the last property put forth, "they fail not," or as you may read it, "consume not." And so, as we begun, we end with

---

[2] Selnecker, *Threni*, S3v-S4v; citing Jas 5:13; Jn 1:12.

"not consumed." There cannot be a more kindly consequence than this; our failing from their not failing; we do not, because they do not. If they did, we should; but "because they are not consumed, no more are we." And why do they not fail?

Because he himself does not. He is the same still; he fails not; his bowels are as he is, so they fail not no more than he.

And in this, "for they fail not," is all the comfort we have. For since Jeremiah's time, one would be amazed to consider—the huge number of foul enormities that have been committed, and yet the parties that commit them are not consumed—where there should be mercy to serve for them all. It could never be said, "Now there is all, there is now no more left." No; an inexhaustible fountain there is of them; never dry, but flows still fresh and fresh. And look, even the next words of Jeremiah tells us, "They renew every morning"; no morning comes, but a fresh supply of them. And even this morning, this fifth of November, we had a good proof of it. Yea, they are never perfect, the sum is never made up, there is still added every day, and they shall not be consummate till the consummation of the world. SERMON ON LAMENTATIONS 3:22.[3]

GOD'S FAITHFULNESS UNDERGIRDS HIS PEOPLE AND HIS CHURCH. DANIEL TOUS-SAIN: "Great is your faithfulness," or as some read it, "your truth." Some here in this place take faithfulness to mean our faith or belief; and it is no small matter to believe in God. But yet here it refers to the faithfulness of God, and the assurance of his promises. For his assured faithfulness and constant truthfulness are the truly efficient cause of the renewing of the church and of the graces of the Lord. For God being altogether true, and such a one as is goodness, is not grounded on our efforts. It can only be that he must establish his church according to the free goodness and the eternal and infallible truth of his promises, which renew in us a taste for his graces. These we find to be

most pleasant after we have for a time been afflicted and deprived of his loving kindness. THE LAMENTATIONS AND HOLY MOURNINGS 3:23.[4]

GOD IS A GENEROUS GIVER. JOHN DONNE: God is abundant in his mercies to humanity. It is as though God learned to give by giving, as though God practiced giving to make himself perfect in his own art, which is bountiful giving. It is as though his former blessings were just an installment and not a final payment. It is as though every benefit that he gives is a new obligation upon him and not familiar to him. He delights to give where he has already given; as though his former gifts were recorded in his memory and certain people were marked as those to whom he would give yet more. In our prayers to God for temporal and spiritual blessings, it is not so good to say, "Have mercy on me now, for I have loved you until now," but better to say, "Have mercy on me now, for you have loved me to this point." We say to a beggar, "I gave to you only yesterday." But God gives to us today because he gave to us yesterday. Therefore, all his blessings are wrapped up in this phrase: "Give us this day our daily bread." Every day he gives; and early every day his manna falls before the sun rises. "His mercies are new every morning." SERMON ON EXODUS 12:30.[5]

THE PORTION OF GOD AND THE PORTIONS OF THE WORLD. DANIEL TOUSSAIN: "The Lord is my portion." This is another argument of comfort, taken from the abundance of God's benefits, and from the contents every faithful person has in themselves; and this is the right property of faith, to apply and appropriate such treasure for oneself and to believe constantly that the Lord is our rich reward, portion, and inheritance. . . . We commonly know that there is a distinction and difference between movable and immovable goods, the latter of which are not so easily carried away. Now the prophets call the eternal our right inheritance— firm, certain, immovable property, and welfare. For

---

[3]Andrewes, *Works*, 4:271-73*.

[4]Toussain, *The Lamentations*, 118-19*.
[5]Donne, *Sermons*, 6:350*; citing Mt 6:11; Ex 16:1-36; Lam 3:22-23.

when we have said all that we can, all the rest that we possess are but wandering and fleeting possessions, even vanity itself. . . . Therefore, when we read in this place or elsewhere that God is called our portion and inheritance, we must remember that it is to this end that we should continue and make no reckoning of frail and transitory things of this world. Nor should we make a reckoning of the great and mighty people of this world, who view all the faithful that fear and obey God as miserable and despicable wretches. These wretches may have scarcely one inch of ground, and yet that makes them richer than all the emperors in the world, who in the end are forced to leave their military arrays and kingdoms, and whatever else. THE LAMENTATIONS AND HOLY MOURNINGS 3:24.[6]

GOD'S BLESSING IN THE AFTERNOON AND MORNING OF LIFE. JOHN DONNE: If we take humanity collectively, entirely and altogether—all humankind—how short a morning has humanity had? It is not yet six thousand years since humanity first came into being. But if we consider humanity in its afternoon—its future state in life after death—if every minute of its six thousand years were multiplied so many millions of ages, all of this would amount to nothing—merely nothing—in respect to eternity, in which humanity will dwell. We can express the afternoon of humanity, its future perpetuity and everlastingness, in only one way—a fair and noble way: that however late a beginning God gave to humanity, humanity will no more see an end and die than God himself, who gave humanity life. Therefore, the apostle [Peter] says here, "When we consider God according to his promise," we expect future things and look for more from God's hand hereafter than we have received heretofore; for "his mercies are new every morning," and his later mercies are his largest mercies. How many great nations perish without ever hearing the name of Christ? But God wrapped me up in his covenant and derived me from Christian parents. I sucked Christian blood in my mother's womb and Christian milk at my nurse's breast. The first sound that I heard in the world was the voice of Christians. And the first character that I was taught to know was the cross of Christ Jesus. SERMON ON 2 PETER 3:13.[7]

EDIFICATION IN LAMENT. JOHN TRAPP: That which gives contentment in any portion is (1) the favor and presence of God. (2) That it is from the hand of a Father. (3) That it comes to us in the covenant of grace. (4) That it is the purchase of Christ's blood. (5) That it is an answer of prayers, and a blessing from above on honest endeavors. See here, good reader, how this prophetical lamentation begins to be a guide to godliness. For it does not, in the manner of silly women, throw out empty words without wisdom, but teaches all along, either overtly or covertly, that all things here below, however highly esteemed, are vanity and soon lost, but the grace of God is solid and stable—nobody can take Christ away. Christ is a portion unlosable, as One once answered to those that asked him, why he was still merry and cheerful? COMMENTARY ON LAMENTATIONS 3:24.[8]

SILENT TRUST IN GOD'S MERCY. JOHANNES BUGENHAGEN: "The Lord is bounteous." That is, favorable and propitious. These are the pure promises and consolations of God among these uproars and tempests of Satan. This gospel is excellent for suffering consciences, as even Christ says, that he has come to bring good news to the poor. It is good for a man to bear the yoke in adolescence, that is, to be placed under the word and will of God as a boy and not to go away from the yoke; that is, to despise the word and goodness of God. Indeed such a one will suffer in the world, but will patiently endure when oppressed by some evil. "He conceals his mouth in the dust," etc.: that is, he will neither complain against God, nor will he be disturbed or cry out; but he will be silent and will

---

[6]Toussain, *The Lamentations*, 121-22*.

[7]Donne, *Sermons*, 8:76-77*; citing 2 Pet 3:13.

[8]Trapp, *A Commentary or Exposition*, 380*; citing Mt 11:19; Lk 7:33-34.

await liberation from God. Meanwhile, he bears dishonor and the cross, certain that the Lord has not cast him away in eternity, but in his time God will declare his mercy. COMMENTARY ON JEREMIAH, LAMENTATIONS 3:25-29.[9]

THE YOUNG, THE OLD, AND THE YOKE. JOHN CALVIN: It is then our true happiness when we acknowledge that we are not our own, and allow God, by his sovereign power, to rule us as he pleases. But we ought to begin with the law of God. Hence it is that we are said to bear the yoke of God, when we relinquish our own judgment and become wise through God's Word, when, with our affections surrendered and subdued, we hear what God commands us, and receive what he commands. This, then, is what Jeremiah means by bearing the yoke.

And he says, "in youth." For they who have lived unrestrained throughout their lives, can hardly bear to be brought into any order. We indeed know that the aged are less tractable than the young; whether we refer to the arts or to the liberal sciences, the youthful age is the most flexible. COMMENTARY ON LAMENTATIONS 3:27.[10]

WHEN GOD CALLS THE YOUNG. PETER MARTYR VERMIGLI: I do affirm that starting to bear the Lord's yoke right away from boyhood onward is remarkably fitting ... for when prophecies were breathed on him at the beginning, Jeremiah drew back in horror and said that he was greatly terrified, because he was a boy. All the same, when God's Spirit was helping he was ever after in an even and ready frame of mind towards all his difficulties. You may also find in the holy Scriptures that Samuel was such a one, as were Daniel and his friends, who while still youths underwent trials on account of God's word. COMMENTARY ON LAMENTATIONS 3:25-27.[11]

A SIGN OF HUMILITY, VOLUNTARY OR OTHERWISE. THE ENGLISH ANNOTATIONS: [Jeremiah humbles] himself even to the ground, or as if he should stop his mouth with dust for fear of breaking out into any repining or murmuring language. But this latter seems to be with the largest. It is an allusion, as some conceive, to the matter of those that having been subdued are enforced to lay their necks down to be trampled upon, and to lick up the dust under the feet of those by whom they have been subdued. Or, as others rather, unto the usual manner of supplicants, that use to bow down so low, or lay themselves along in that manner, that as they lay groveling, their mouth touched the ground, and withal to that dust and ashes on which they were inclined in such cases to prostrate themselves. ANNOTATIONS ON LAMENTATIONS 3:29.[12]

CONTENTED SILENCE WHEN AFFLICTED. JOHN DONNE: There is a silence which is absolutely good. ... That silence that is absolutely and always good is a quiet contentment in all that God sends: lest when God meant to make you rich and has indeed made you rich, you in turn make yourself poor by thinking of yourself as poor and misinterpreting God's action.... You should neither murmur because you do not have enough good, nor because you have too many afflictions. But reckon how much more good God has showed you than you deserved and how much less ill than you deserved. "Sit alone and keep silence because you have borne it"; because the Lord has laid affliction upon you. SERMON ON PSALM 32:1-2.[13]

OUR CROSSES AND OUR LAUGHING FATHER GOD. NIKOLAUS SELNECKER: These verses should be written in our hearts, as much as possible, with golden letters and should be kept for our last breath. We must learn to see rightly and recognize the cross and the gracious and paternal will of God in everything, whether sickness, poverty, a sorrowful conscience, accident, injustice, or any misery. He means for us to know this. Our cross is at all times a certain sign of the grace of God with us. It does

---

[9]Bugenhagen, *In Ieremiam ... Threni*, E2r-v; citing Lk 4:18.
[10]CTS 21:414* (CO 39:579).
[11]Vermigli, *Commentary*, 127-28.

[12]Downame, ed., *Annotations*, 10F3v*; citing Job 40:4-5; Josh 10:24; Ps 72:9; Is 49:23; 51:23; 60:14; 2 Sam 12:16; 14:22; Is 9:8; Dan 8:17; Mt 26:39; Job 40:6; Is 58:5; Mic 1:10.
[13]Donne, *Sermons*, 9:283.

not come from the heart when he disciplines us. He is no executioner, jail warden, or tyrant. He is our father and delights in us and holds us dear; with a laughing heart and mouth he disciplines us, even when we need the rod. Even when he presses us so that the soul seems to go out from us, he is most loving. O how blessed is the one who believes this from the heart. O how cursed are all those who do not believe. Songs of Lament of the Prophet Jeremiah 3:31-32.[14]

Understanding Earthly Afflictions.
Johannes Bugenhagen: "Indeed, not from the heart." God certainly afflicts us, but "not from the heart"; that means not in order to destroy us, but for our correction. And not that he might crush those bound, that is, those afflicted on the earth, but that he might save and bring them to repent. Not so that he might condemn their case as if they were adversaries; that is, not to declare that the afflicted have a bad case: that they do not have the true God or true religion, or are heretics themselves, and that the impious have a better case and are considered by God as pious, as the foolish world thinks in our affliction. Now this is a most grave temptation, when the tongue of the devil says: "There is no salvation for him in his God. Where now is your God?" Not for this reason, I say, has God afflicted us, but rather so that he might glorify those who have been snatched out of affliction and dishonor. So Paul says in Acts, "It is necessary to go through many trials to enter the kingdom of God." And as Christ himself says, "It is necessary for the Christ to suffer and thus enter in to his glory. . . ." Blessed is the one who is able by faith in tribulation to grasp this good intention of God toward us, even if by his own fault and sin he stumbled into this tribulation. Commentary on Jeremiah, Lamentations 3:33.[15]

The Power of the State Is Limited by the Word of God. John Udall: Though magistrates have power from God over the subjects' bodies, yet will he punish all wrongs, and want of protection, if they vex him withal. The reason is because, first, their power is not absolute, but limited to the rule of God's word. Second, there is no respect of persons with God. The use is, first, to teach all superiors to take heed, lest they go beyond the power that God has given them, seeing the mischiefs are infinite that flow from misgovernment. Second, to teach us rather to suffer than to be a means of evil, though the magistrate should judge us to it. Commentary on Lamentations 3:34.[16]

God's Intentions with Punishment.
Guillaume du Vair: It is not the purpose of God to heap human beings at his feet, triumphing in their misfortunes; to tie and bind them like shoes in his power is not his intent, nor to cast them into poverty and abandon them to misery. But he knows well what they need and what to them is most profitable. He is not like those evil judges who desire crooked and froward answers to the end that they may work some revenge. For God looks on our faults with grief and hates nothing so much as to punish us. Also all calamities that he sends us are but threats to antagonize us, so that we may turn to his grace before he enters into judgment with us, so that before he condemns us according to the law, we may crave remission of our sins, according to what he has promised. Meditations upon the Lamentations of Jeremiah 3:34-36.[17]

Is God the Author of Sin? Daniel Toussain: "From the mouth of the Most High proceed both evil and good." Here we have a great need to beware of how we understand this saying, to the end that we may keep ourselves from making God the author of sin as did the Valentinians, the Manichees,[†] and other heretics, who taught that God created both sin and evil, which is a most blasphemous, pernicious, and insupportable doctrine. . . . So it is said in the twenty-fifth chapter

---

[14]Selnecker, *Threni*, T4r-v.
[15]Bugenhagen, *In Ieremiam . . . Threni*, E3v-E4r; citing Acts 14:22; Lk 24:26.
[16]Udall, *Commentary on Lamentations*, T1r*; citing Ps 82:7; Acts 10:34.
[17]Du Vair, *Meditations*, D12r-E1*.

of Jeremiah, "that he calls the sword upon all the inhabitants of the land," in which his meaning is that he is determined to punish human iniquity, and that swords and other things serve him when he will execute his just judgments. Now, we have shown that whatsoever God ordains is justly ordained. . . . It is not that God makes sin, but that he orders and disposes sin to such righteous ends as he himself in his sacred and eternal counsel has ordained. As for the evil of punishment . . . it is the execution of his justice, and by reason also that justice is a wholesome remedy, although bitter and sharp, to awake us from our sloth and to renew our faith and patience. THE LAMENTATIONS AND HOLY MOURNINGS 3:38.[18]

3:40-66 Return to the Lord!

HUMBLE PRAYER AND STANDING GUARD.
DANIEL TOUSSAIN: The third part of the chapter . . . contains a prayer. Although the faith of the children of God overcomes the world and all temptations, yet the same prayer is never presumptive or waxes proud. This prayer gives glory to God alone and makes us always call to mind our infirmity as well as the stratagems and cunning practices of the devil, who for a time makes a show of departing from us so that he might afterward more fiercely set upon us. Therefore, we are to watch continually and stand our guard. THE LAMENTATIONS AND HOLY MOURNINGS 3:40-66.[19]

EXAMINE AND TEST OUR CONSCIENCES.
JOHANNES OECOLAMPADIUS: But, he says, let us not become similar to them in their impiety. Rather, let us consider how much we have sinned and let us confess our sins, so that he might have mercy on us. Let us examine our ways, that is, diligently inquire about how much we have strayed and what

our paths are—whether we are going forward to God, or going back. As Jeremiah 6 says: "Stand at the crossroad and look; and ask about the ancient paths, which is the good road, then walk in it; then you will find rest for your souls." We were going to idols and according to the depravity of the heart. Now let us examine and test; that is, let us probe our consciences, whether the conscience is founded in God. Indeed, there are many things that appear good which are nevertheless abominable before God. While we work more out of fear or hope of a reward than out of piety and good love, let us, however, return to the Lord in our heart. COMMENTARY ON JEREMIAH, LAMENTATIONS 3:40-42.[20]

WHEN GOD WORKS IN THE SOUL. ST. JOHN OF THE CROSS: Something else grieves and troubles individuals in this state, and it is that since this dark night impedes their faculties and affections, they cannot beseech God or raise their mind and affections to him. It seems as it did to Jeremiah that God has placed a cloud in front of the soul so that its prayer might not pass through. The passage . . . refers to this difficulty also: "He closed and locked my ways with square stones." And if sometimes the soul does beseech God, it does this with so little strength and fervor that it thinks God does not hear or pay any attention to it, as the prophet Jeremiah also lamented: "When I cried out and entreated, he excluded my prayer."

Indeed, this is not the time to speak with God, but the time to put one's mouth in the dust, as Jeremiah says, that perhaps there might come some actual hope, and the time to suffer this purgation patiently. God it is who is working now in the soul, and for this reason the soul can do nothing. THE DARK NIGHT.[21]

THE TEARS OF THE FAITHFUL. JOHN CALVIN: The prophet here makes a distinction between his weeping and that blind sorrow by which the unbelieving are affected and violently agitated: they

---

[18]Toussain, *The Lamentations*, 135-36, 138*; citing Jer 25:29.
   †Valentinians were historically associated with the Gnostic heresy in early Christianity; the Manichees presented an extremely dualistic version of Christianity deemed heretical; it was especially popular in the fourth and fifth centuries.
[19]Toussain, *The Lamentations*, 105*.

[20]Oecolampadius, *In Hieremiam . . . Threnos*, 2X2v; citing Jer 6:16.
[21]St. John of the Cross, *Collected Works*, 409-10.

have no regard to God. Then the prophet says here that he not only wept, but that he also prayed and waited for God to put an end to evil deeds. . . . [But] the unbelieving grieve abundantly in their adversities; they even abandon themselves to sorrow . . . they turn away wholly from God and are like wild beasts. Then the prophet points out the right way to mourn: our eyes must flow down to weariness and without rest, but at the same time we must wait until God is favorable to us. Therefore, this verse connects well with the former [as this weeping precedes] "the Lord looking down and seeing us from heaven"; for otherwise tears would draw us to despair and despair would become the cause of fury; for we see that the ungodly murmur against God.

Thus, then, we ought to weep in order that we may at the same time cherish hope while we wait for God to look down on us and to see our miseries from heaven. COMMENTARY ON LAMENTATIONS 3:49-50.[22]

THE SNARE OF PROPHECY. ST. JOHN OF THE CROSS: Although the holy prophet spoke with resignation and in the semblance of a weak man unable to suffer the changing ways of God, he herein teaches us the difference between the fulfillment of the divine locutions and the common meaning of given words. The prophets were considered seducers, and they endured such suffering because of their prophecies that Jeremiah also proclaims that . . . prophecy has become for us fear, snares, and contradiction of spirit. THE ASCENT OF MOUNT CARMEL.[23]

HOW MY ENEMIES TREAT ME. GUILLAUME DU VAIR: Alas, they have chased and pounded after me as they pound out their beats. We flee our enemies and they pursue us; we yield and then they murder us though we cause them no offense. As for me, they forced me to crawl into a den or hole; they tied a stone around my neck as if I had been a dog who might hurt someone. I have open wounds, for

they have beaten me from my head to my throat, nearly choking me. All I could do was to cry: "Oh Lord, I am dying; have pity on me." MEDITATIONS UPON THE LAMENTATIONS OF JEREMIAH 3:52-54.[24]

PROOF OF LIFE. JOHN TRAPP: As breathing is proof of animal life, so is prayer, though never so weak, of spiritual. If therefore you cannot speak, weep. . . . If you cannot weep, sigh. . . . If you cannot sigh, yet breathe, as here, God feels breath, and happy is he that can say . . . in you I hope Lord, and after you, I breathe or pant. COMMENTARY ON LAMENTATIONS 3:56.[25]

HOW DOES GOD DRAW NEAR? DANIEL TOUSSAIN: The prophet here confirms both his own faith and that of the people, partly through the experience of times past and partly by the nature of God. For as God is always like himself, it cannot be otherwise than that God helps his church as always and as he has done since the beginning of the world. . . . Now it is said in our text that "God draws near" to us, so that we may feel him, because it seems he is near to us, when he puts forth his hand to help us; and that he is far from us, when we do not feel the favors we desire from him. Although in truth, he is then nearest us, when he seems to be farthest off from us and is always near to those who truly call upon him. THE LAMENTATIONS AND HOLY MOURNINGS 3:57.[26]

CONFIDENCE IN THE FACE OF PLOTTING ENEMIES. JOHN CALVIN: [The prophet] means, in short, that whether his enemies consulted silently and quietly, or attempted to do this or that, nothing was unknown to God. Now as God takes such notice of the counsels and all the actions of people, it cannot but be that he restrains and checks the wicked; for God's knowledge is always connected with his office as a judge. We hence see how the prophet strengthens himself . . . and thus gathers a reason for confidence; for the wicked counsels of

---

[22]CTS 21:442* (CO 39:597).
[23]St. John of the Cross, *Collected Works*, 222.
[24]Du Vair, *Meditations*, E4r-v*.
[25]Trapp, *A Commentary or Exposition*, 383*; citing Ps 39:12.
[26]Toussain, *The Lamentations*, 150-51*.

his enemies and their works were not hidden from God. Commentary on Lamentations 3:63.[27]

Afflict the Wicked, Assist Us in Our War Against Them. Guillaume du Vair: Well then, Lord, seeing that they have stretched your patience, subdue their malice. Seeing that nothing will lead to their repentance, will you not lead them to pain? Since they take pleasure in doing evil, cause them each one to endure your displeasure; for you are just and seeing that you are so, should you not reward them according to the works of their hands? They have abandoned you, to follow their own presumption; their haughtiness and pride led them to this error and to their perseverance in sin. Their hearts are covered with a hard scale of impatience. They cannot receive from you a greater curse than this: to blind their spirits, leaving them to their own inventions. For when you come on the day of your wrath to give them a blow, carrying a rod of iron in your hand, you shall break them like glass. Hence they shall see none under heaven so miserable as themselves and shall find none of the mercy they had used up. They shall be poor and not relieved; they shall be afflicted and not comforted. Then you, Lord, will awaken over us and secure our patience by your holy mercy. To that end, so long as it shall please you to injure us with injuries and reproaches of the wicked, may our courage not fail, and our soul always have strength to lift herself up and to attend to your aid. We endure those evils when it pleases you to send trials for our faith, hoping that after our long patience you will crown us as victorious wrestlers, making us carry in triumph the wicked, against whom we have continually warred in this life. Meditations upon the Lamentations of Jeremiah 3:64-66.[28]

---

[27]CTS 21:452* (CO 39:604).

[28]Du Vair, *Meditations*, E6v-E8r*.

LAMENTATIONS 4:1-22
THE HOLY STONES LIE SCATTERED

¹*How the gold has grown dim,*
how the pure gold is changed!
The holy stones lie scattered
at the head of every street.

²*The precious sons of Zion,*
worth their weight in fine gold,
how they are regarded as earthen pots,
the work of a potter's hands!

³*Even jackals offer the breast;*
they nurse their young;
but the daughter of my people has become cruel,
like the ostriches in the wilderness.

⁴*The tongue of the nursing infant sticks*
to the roof of its mouth for thirst;
the children beg for food,
but no one gives to them.

⁵*Those who once feasted on delicacies*
perish in the streets;
those who were brought up in purple
embrace ash heaps.

⁶*For the chastisement^a of the daughter of my*
people has been greater
than the punishment^b of Sodom,
which was overthrown in a moment,
and no hands were wrung for her.^c

⁷*Her princes were purer than snow,*
whiter than milk;
their bodies were more ruddy than coral,
the beauty of their form^d was like sapphire.^e

⁸*Now their face is blacker than soot;*
they are not recognized in the streets;
their skin has shriveled on their bones;
it has become as dry as wood.

⁹*Happier were the victims of the sword*
than the victims of hunger,
who wasted away, pierced
by lack of the fruits of the field.

¹⁰*The hands of compassionate women*
have boiled their own children;
they became their food
during the destruction of the daughter of
my people.

¹¹*The Lord gave full vent to his wrath;*
he poured out his hot anger,
and he kindled a fire in Zion
that consumed its foundations.

¹²*The kings of the earth did not believe,*
nor any of the inhabitants of the world,
that foe or enemy could enter
the gates of Jerusalem.

¹³*This was for the sins of her prophets*
and the iniquities of her priests,
who shed in the midst of her
the blood of the righteous.

¹⁴*They wandered, blind, through the streets;*
they were so defiled with blood
that no one was able to touch
their garments.

¹⁵*"Away! Unclean!" people cried at them.*
"Away! Away! Do not touch!"
So they became fugitives and wanderers;
people said among the nations,
"They shall stay with us no longer."

¹⁶*The LORD himself has scattered them;*
he will regard them no more;
no honor was shown to the priests,
no favor to the elders.

¹⁷*Our eyes failed, ever watching*
vainly for help;
in our watching we watched
for a nation which could not save.

¹⁸*They dogged our steps*
so that we could not walk in our streets;

our end drew near; our days were numbered,
  for our end had come.

¹⁹Our pursuers were swifter
  than the eagles in the heavens;
they chased us on the mountains;
  they lay in wait for us in the wilderness.

²⁰The breath of our nostrils, the LORD's anointed,
  was captured in their pits,
of whom we said, "Under his shadow
  we shall live among the nations."

²¹Rejoice and be glad, O daughter of Edom,
  you who dwell in the land of Uz;
but to you also the cup shall pass;
  you shall become drunk and strip yourself bare.

²²The punishment of your iniquity, O daughter
  of Zion, is accomplished;
  he will keep you in exile no longer;ᵍ
but your iniquity, O daughter of Edom, he will
  punish;
  he will uncover your sins.

a Or *iniquity*   b Or *sin*   c The meaning of the Hebrew is uncertain   d The meaning of the Hebrew is uncertain   e Hebrew *lapis lazuli*   f Hebrew *The face of the Lord*   g Or *he will not exile you again*

OVERVIEW: This fourth song of mourning presents once again the devastation of Judea, Jerusalem, and the Jewish people in searing and graphic detail. Commentators expound on the acute suffering of the weak and the strong, the catastrophic failure of the Jewish priesthood, and their shared and sustained contempt for the divine word generally and the prophetic word of judgment in particular. Even so it is by this word that the people of God are to live and thrive. Throughout this chapter some interpreters find an echo of Jeremiah's lament at the death of King Josiah and thereby a reflection on the gifts of monarchy, godly rule, and messianic kingship in the Christ to come. Whether in Judea, Edom, or Europe, divine judgment and discipline must be understood and embraced as a fact of life.

4:1-11 Zion Is Punished

HOW THE PEOPLE SUFFER AND THE MIGHTY FALL. DANIEL TOUSSAIN: The first part of this chapter . . . contains forcible . . . lamentations, drawn partly from the person and dignity of those that were desolate and comfortless prisoners; in part the nobility, priests, Nazirites, and young children. Some moaned greatly because of their loss of dignity; some because of their age. Jeremiah compares them to certain cruel and savage beasts

and to the shame of Sodom and Gomorrah. The prophet takes the occasion to amplify the misery of those sorrowful events. There was nothing else to be seen but lamentable and monstrous sights. . . .

In particular Jeremiah makes the mighty ones of the world understand that they are as subject to decline and affliction as are the most poor and miserable people; the mighty ones find it more intolerable to be brought low because they had once been exalted to such high dignity. This happens when we do not fear God as Lord overall, whose throne is exalted above the heavens. . . . They therefore that do not regard this great Ruler, before whom all the mighty potentates of the world are but dust and ashes, do wonder to see how the most honorable people and men of note decline and fall. THE LAMENTATIONS AND HOLY MOURNINGS 4: 1-11.[1]

LAMENTATION FOR KING JOSIAH. JOHANNES OECOLAMPADIUS: It is certain from 2 Chronicles 35 that Jeremiah mourned the death of King Josiah with a special song. Josiah was killed when he went out to fight on the plain of Megiddo against Neco king of Egypt. So Jeremiah says, "All Judah and Jerusalem mourned for Josiah. . . ." Jeremiah's lamentations over Josiah are repeated by all the male

---

[1]Toussain, *The Lamentations*, 165-66, 172-73*.

and female chanters even to the present day, and the songs persist like a law in Israel. Behold, this is written in the Lamentations. . . . Further, when the king is lamented, then the people are lamented, who perish with the king. From this history we are guided to the death of Christ, who died for us and must be considered. Truly the good king, who died for his people, is a figure of Christ. COMMENTARY ON JEREMIAH, Lamentations 4:1-2.[2]

THE GOLDEN PRIESTS AND THEIR NEGLECT OF WORSHIP. HECTOR PINTO: "The stones are scattered. . . ." That is, the temple of the Lord was destroyed and its stones were scattered and dispersed in the streets. The gold was understood first by the symbol of stones to be the priests of the sanctuary and the godly men who were overseeing others in religious worship. Indeed, these men were driven from the temple, scattered along the tops of the streets, and taken away to various places. These men should have been residing in the temple all the time. Perhaps Jeremiah laments the scattered priesthood, which should have remained in the temple to offer the work of divine worship. Instead they had been wandering through the streets of Jerusalem and had offered themselves to transactions with people. For this reason they were besieged, conquered, and tormented. This broad road signifies that wide spacious way, which Christ our God said in Matthew 7 leads to destruction. COMMENTARY ON LAMENTATIONS 4:1.[3]

FORCED TO ACT AGAINST NATURE. JOHANNES BUGENHAGEN: Even the most ferocious beasts, the dragons, still feed their young. But mothers in Judah were not able to provide for their dearest little ones, such was the famine, etc. They were compelled to do against nature that which the wicked bird, the ostrich, does freely; the ostrich is a bird, nevertheless it is bird of this sort: it is very foolish; for the eggs it has given birth to it abandons in the sand, nor does it care for its offspring. COMMENTARY ON JEREMIAH, LAMENTATIONS 4:3.[4]

DEMONS WHO SUCKLE. MARTIN LUTHER: [There] are witches and night hags who at night give suck to children and inflict injury on babies, as the prophet says, "Even the night hags give the breast." By allegory: All ungodly teachers are witches and night hags, goblins, who perplex us with false milk and teaching. They are male and female demons who cause nightmares; goblins, devils of all kinds that lie in wait for us during the night. LECTURES ON ISAIAH 34:14.[5]

THE LETTER AND SPIRIT OF SCRIPTURE FOR THE WORLD. THOMAS MÜNTZER: Anyone who does not feel the spirit of Christ within them, or is not quite sure of having it, is not a member of Christ, but of the devil, Romans 8. Now the world (led astray by many sects) has for a long time been yearning desperately for the truth; thus the saying of Jeremiah has been fulfilled: "the children have clamored for bread but no one was there to break it to them." For there were many, and there are still many today, who have flung bread to them like dogs, that is, the letter of the Word of God; but they have not broken it to them [in Spirit]. PRAGUE MANIFESTO.[6]

THE PLIGHT OF THE CHILDREN. GUILLAUME DU VAIR: We have seen poor children put forth their lips, dried like wood, their tongues cleaving to the palate of their mouths with thirst, sucking in wind instead of milk; for their mothers at first offered them their breasts. But they were so dried up that they yielded nothing but blood. Thus the poor infants could not be sustained; they withered, were consumed, and died in piteous distress. Older children crept after their fathers on their knees, craving bread with such a mournful voice as would have moved even the stones to pity them. But there was nothing to be given them; for all their fathers

[2]Oecolampadius, *In Hieremiam . . . Threnos*, 2Y1r-v; citing 2 Chron 35:20-27.
[3]Pinto, *In Prophetae Ieremiae Lamentationes*, 353v-354r; citing Mt 7:13.

[4]Bugenhagen, *In Ieremiam . . . Threni*, F2v.
[5]LW 16:297 (WA 31.2:219).
[6]Müntzer, *Collected Works*, 358; citing Rom 8:9.

could do for them was to wish them dead and curse the day they had been born and thus to see this miserable life. Meditations upon the Lamentations of Jeremiah 4:4.[7]

No Bread, No Scripture for God's People. Peter Martyr Vermigli: "The little ones asked for bread. . . ." These are the older children, who do not need milk anymore, but take their fill of more solid nourishment of bread. They were asking, begging, yes, even demanding nourishment; there was no one who could give it.

Let those who tremble at this so dire a famine imagine for me how detestable they must be who deny to the church's sons the nourishment of God's word owed to them. They forbid them it under a pretext that is, as it seems to them, nonetheless splendid and plausible. For (they say) the holy must not be given to dogs, "pearls must not be scattered for swine." Now the common throng of Christians must be considered like those animals. Therefore, it follows (as they would say) that commoners must not be allowed to read the sacred books. Experience (they add) testifies to this: since they do not understand them, they then fabricate for themselves many private and heretical opinions. For this reason the Scriptures must then be shut up. Those who are moved by these arguments are gravely in error. Since the church's sons are endowed with the Spirit (for the apostle says that he "who does not have the spirit of Christ is not of him"), they are neither dogs, nor swine; rather, since they are added to the number of the sons, they must be fed with the sons' bread. . . . Even today the Hebrews, pursuing zealously the custom handed down to them by their fathers, are likewise expounding the sacred books of their Law to boys and young women. The apostles, Hebrews though they were, wrote in a foreign language so that all the Gentiles could easily follow their writings. And when Paul wrote his letters, he was writing not just to two or three priests, but also to the entire church. What Christ taught in the Sermon on the Mount, in which a fruitful and profound interpretation of the Law was composed, he taught to the crowds—a vile mob who up to that point were unbelievers. This is, however, the very doctrine which our men wish to be concealed from our people. Commentary on Lamentations 4:4.[8]

God and Calamity Are Together. John Donne: Dishonor and disrepute, force and depredation, ruin and devastation, error and illusion, the devil and his temptations: all are presented to us in the same word, as the name and power of God: when any of these fall upon us—when we see and consider the name and quality of this calamity that falls—we may see and consider the power and purpose of God, who inflicts this calamity. I cannot call the calamity by name, but in that name I name God. I cannot feel an affliction but in that very affliction I feel the hand (and if I will feel it, the medicinal hand) of my God. If therefore honor and reputation decay, all misfortune was a remedy from him. And if he has sucked that misfortune into himself, let us follow it home; let us labor to be honorable in him, glorified in him. Then our honor will not be extinguished in this world, but will grow too glorious for this world to comprehend. Spoil and depredation may come upon us, so that we are covered with wrath, persecuted, slain, and not spared: such that those "that fed delicately perish in the streets and they that were brought up in scarlet now embrace the dunghill," such that the hands of pitiful women have boiled their own children, as the prophet complains in Lamentations. There may be such irreparable devastation come upon us that we are "broken as an earthen vessel in which in the breaking there remains not a shard to fetch from the hearth, nor water from the pit." Our estate may be so ruined that there is nothing left, not only for future posterity, but for our own present family. Yet still God and calamity are together. God does not send it, but he brings it. He is there as soon as calamity is there and calls that calamity by his own

---

[7]Du Vair, *Meditations*, E1or-E11r*.

[8]Vermigli, *Commentary*, 156-58; citing Mt 7:6; Rom 8:9; Mt 5:1–7:29.

name: Shaddai—he would make that very calamity a candle to you, by which you might see him. SERMON ON JOB 13:15.[9]

LIFE WITHOUT THE NOURISHING WORD. MARTIN LUTHER: They will look for the word. They will run here and there, and they will not find it. This we experienced well enough before the word was published through the grace of God. This is why we have countless sects of monks. One becomes a Carthusian, another a Franciscan. One establishes one kind of life, another, another kind of life by which he believes he is pleasing God, but there is no peace of conscience. One runs to Rome, another to St. James.† So we ought to be thankful now to Almighty God and we should use that invaluable gift correctly lest it again be taken away from an ungrateful people and we fall into greater errors than ever before; lest we who are now fed with dainties again lie in the gutters, as Jeremiah says in Lamentations 4. After all, before the Gospel again was spread, what else did we eat but the filth of the pope—and this at the expense of both money and soul. LECTURES ON AMOS 8:12.[10]

AVOID THE WORLD'S DUNGHILLS. JOHN TRAPP: There take up their lodgings, and there also are glad to find anything to feed on. Though never so course and homely, the lapwing is made a hieroglyphic of infelicity, because he has a coronet upon the head, and yet feeds upon the worst of excrements. It is a pity that any child of God, washed in Christ's blood, should bedabble his scarlet robe in the stinking guzzle of the world's dunghill, that anyone who has heretofore soared as an eagle, should now creep on the ground as a beetle, or wallow as a swine in the mire of sensuality. COMMENTARY ON LAMENTATIONS 4:5.[11]

THE SHORTER, THE BETTER. DANIEL TOUSSAIN: Some read this as "my time is greater than the

iniquity of Sodom." However, the next phrase of the verse declares that the prophet compares not sin with sin, but punishments with punishments; for . . . Sodom was destroyed in a moment and had to deal only with God; it did not fall into the hands of any other. Whereas the Jews remained miserable during the siege and thereafter fell into the bloody hands of adversaries. . . . Thus we see how we bear the shortest punishments most easily. THE LAMENTATIONS AND HOLY MOURNINGS 4:6.[12]

THE DAY OF THE LORD. JOHN DONNE: The prophet directs himself most literally to the first sin of presumption. The people had come to say that in truth—whatever the prophet proclaimed in the streets—there was no such thing as the "day of the Lord," no plan of God to bring such heavy judgments upon them. To the prophets themselves they came to say, "You yourselves live parched and mortified in a starved and impoverished state, and therefore you cry out that all of us too must die of famine. . . . What you call 'the day of the Lord' has come upon you dear prophets: poverty, nakedness, hunger, contempt, affliction, and imprisonment has come upon you; thus you need to extend it to the whole state. . . ."

To see a prophet neglected because he will not flatter, to see him despised below because he is neglected above, to see him injured, insulted, and really damned because he is despised: all of this is "the day of the world" and not "the day of the Lord." It is the ordinary course of the world and no extraordinary day of the Lord. But there will be such a dullness and anxiety of mind that "those who had been purer than snow, whiter than milk, redder than rubies, and smoother than sapphires" will become not only . . . pale with sudden fear, but also "blacker in the face than coal." The prophet says here that they will neither be able to put a good face on their miseries, nor disguise them with a confident countenance. But there will be such an anxious countenance and conscience, and then such an excommunication of church and state that the whole body of the children of Israel will be

---

[9]Donne, *Sermons*, 3:191-92*; citing Is 30:14.
[10]LW 18:183* (WA 13:200). †Luther refers to pilgrimage to the relics of St. James, to Santiago de Compostela in Spain.
[11]Trapp, *A Commentary or Exposition*, 385*.

[12]Toussain, *The Lamentations*, 176-77*.

"without king, without sacrifice, without Ephod, without household gods." SERMON ON AMOS 5:18.[13]

THE PERISHING OF SACRED WAYS. JOHANNES BUGENHAGEN: "The Nazirites." That is, those consecrated to the Lord, whether priests or Levites, or every person who was sanctified by the vow of the Nazirites; anyone who abstained from every unclean thing in their time of consecration: for which reason here he says that they are the most beautiful. "They," he says, "are now made black," etc. That is, whatever was most precious, whatever was most sacred and holy according to the Word of God, has now perished. Now one is not allowed to observe the law. In the time of famine they would gladly eat food that was unclean according to the law, if they could find it.

They did not believe that Jerusalem or the temple of the Lord could be overcome—not merely because of their walls, but even more so because they knew that God had done miraculous things for his people against Pharaoh and the Canaanites, and because their miraculous God deemed it suitable to live in that very temple. COMMENTARY ON JEREMIAH, LAMENTATIONS 4:7-8.[14]

THE RAVAGES OF HUNGER. GUILLAUME DU VAIR: I shall tell you, Lord: alas, not to accuse you of a severity too great, but to show you the excessive miseries you have plunged us into. If you allow it, I would speak Lord, to the end that at last you would have pity on us and for mercy's sake withhold the arm of your vengeance. You have laid more than enough upon us. We have seen things, Lord. We must behold them, but must our eyes remain after we have seen them? We have seen mothers become so unnatural through hunger that they have dismembered their children, rent them into morsels, and ate them with their teeth—all to assuage the raging hunger which you have inflicted upon them. MEDITATIONS UPON THE LAMENTATIONS OF JEREMIAH 4:10.[15]

A CITY ERASED. JOHN CALVIN: Fire typically takes hold on the roofs of houses, or, when it creeps farther, it does not proceed beyond the surface. It is a very rare thing for it to penetrate into the foundations. Let us at the same time know that the prophet speaks metaphorically of the destruction of the city, for it was as if nothing remained; for when some ruins remain, there is some intimation of a future restoration. At least the minds of the beholders are inclined to hope that what was fallen is to be restored. But when the buildings are not only pulled down, but also demolished from their foundations, then the destruction seems to be without any hope of restoration. COMMENTARY ON LAMENTATIONS 4:11.[16]

4:12-22 The Lord Has Scattered His People

FACING UP TO A RIGHTEOUS GOD. DANIEL TOUSSAIN: The second part of chapter 4 is an answer to the demand, exclamation, and lamentation made at the beginning of this chapter. . . . In this part there are instructions and admonitions: for Jeremiah teaches that these miseries proceed from the very wrath of God, but yet from a righteous God . . . who shows himself thereby to be a true God in making happen what he threatened to do. . . . It is in our best interest to acknowledge our faults in time, while God is speaking to us and calling us to repentance. As we commonly say, fools are never wise until they are beaten, and never believe what is said to them until it lies upon their backs.

After these instructions Jeremiah adds certain demonstrations, reproving the cruelty of magistrates, the exceeding immorality of the people, and the vain confidence of people in the arm of flesh and blood. THE LAMENTATIONS AND HOLY MOURNINGS 4:12-20.[17]

THE CHURCH PERISHABLE AND IMPERISHABLE. PETER MARTYR VERMIGLI: These people could not persuade themselves that the enemies were

---

[13]Donne, *Sermons*, 2:351*; citing Hos 3:4.
[14]Bugenhagen, *In Ieremiam . . . Threni*, F3r; citing Num 6:1-27.
[15]Du Vair, *Meditations*, F1r-v*.

[16]CTS 21:469* (CO 39:615).
[17]Toussaint, *The Lamentations*, 166-67*.

going to enter Jerusalem and that they were going to overthrow that flourishing and holy state of affairs. Nor today do foolish Christians. They promise themselves that the Turks are not going to destroy them, leaning as they are on the promise that the church shall not be destroyed, that the gates of hell shall not prevail against it, as if they themselves automatically belonged to the church. The definition of the church according to all its causes is this: as to the material one, it is a gathering of people; as to the efficient, the Spirit of Christ bringing them together; as to the final, eternal life; as to the formal, right religion, sound faith, holy law, and harmonious order. Those who belong to this church are not ruined utterly; for example, in former times Jeremiah, Daniel, Ezra, Zerubbabel, and those who were belonging to the true church were preserved and in this way renewed the church so that in those former times it was not extinguished. COMMENTARY ON LAMENTATIONS 4:12.[18]

WALLS CANNOT SAVE US WHEN GOD ASSISTS OUR ENEMIES.

JOHN UDALL: There is no place so strong, but the enemy thereof shall prevail against it, when God sees it meet. The reason is because, first, one people cannot fortify themselves so strongly but they may be assailed by others as strong as they. Second, they are always strongest whom the Lord assists. The use is to teach us, never to think ourselves safe, be our walls as strong as may be, except when the Lord is with us, and therefore to seek especially to be protected under his wings, so shall no adversaries prevail against us. COMMENTARY ON LAMENTATIONS 4:12.[19]

THE SINS OF FALSE PROPHETS AND PRIESTS.

KONRAD PELLIKAN: The sins of the people emerged and flowed from the sins, scandalous life, and doctrine of the false prophets and priests, who were the primary authors of so great a destruction. Indeed, the people followed the passions of the priests and the elders. The false prophets were preaching false things,

peace and tranquility; they shouted about the temple and the holy city; they did not suffer saints, but they killed them by word, deed, scandal, and hand. The cause of the ruin of the people was the evil priests, who are said to pour out the blood of the just because they, the priests, do not properly teach the ways of the Lord to the more honest and the just, and through pastoral negligence they do not preach about the coming evils, as Ezekiel did. COMMENTARY ON LAMENTATIONS 4:13.[20]

A CONTAMINATED ENVIRONMENT.

JOHN CALVIN: As then they were removed to a distant land, [Jeremiah] says that this happened through their own fault: how so? Because they could no longer endure the defilements of their sins; they had so contaminated the holy city that it was fetid through their filth. As then the city of Jerusalem was so polluted, the citizens, he says, at length fled away: and thus exile proceeded because they contaminated the city. COMMENTARY ON LAMENTATIONS 4:15.[21]

WHO IS PURE NOW?

KONRAD PELLIKAN: These words seem to be from the Gentiles as they insult and mock the Jews, who were always superstitiously held by their passion for purity, even to the point of ill-will from the Gentiles. The Jews seemed to judge the Gentiles as practically polluted, compared to themselves and their own ceremonies of this kind. These Gentiles are speaking about such cleansing: "Now where is the cleanliness that you were always shouting about? As you Jews have said, 'Take away the defiled one, lest he touch us and we be contaminated. Go away, you Gentiles, withdraw from us; you filthy dogs, do not touch us, the elect people of God!'" Certainly such Jews have now flown away, or they have been ordered to make an end of such contempt, as they are scattered wanderers with no fixed place among other nations. These nations do not believe that the Jews will be gathered anew in their own place, in which they would be able to worship as before and to live according to their own

---

[18]Vermigli, *Commentary*, 167; citing Mt 16:18.
[19]Udall, *Commentary on Lamentations*, AA2r*.

[20]Pellikan, *Commentaria Bibliorum*, 3:3C4v; citing Jer 7:4; Ezek 34:1-9.
[21]CTS 21:476* (CO 39:619).

ceremonies. So the Gentiles believed and celebrated that this was done about the Jews. COMMENTARY ON LAMENTATIONS 4:15.[22]

PRIESTS LIKE DEVOURING TIGERS. GUILLAUME DU VAIR: It was easy to see that their God had forsaken them; for he shattered their minds, filling them with dissension and discord. Nothing was left in them but the feeling of godliness and a waiting for succor from heaven. But then the ancient servants of God, ordained to his altar, did they not blush to commit such crimes? Even the senior priests, who ought to have been the most modest, were the most enraged. They had no compassion for their peers and gave none to their elderly companions in their afflictions. If humanity had been rooted out of their hearts, how would they be able to hold things divine? They were not humans, believe me, but tigers. So God used them like wild beasts and made them prey for others. MEDITATIONS UPON THE LAMENTATIONS OF JEREMIAH 4:16.[23]

HONOR YOUR PREACHER. JOHN DONNE: Because God calls "preaching foolishness," you take God at his word, and you think that preaching is something beneath you. So it is that you take so much liberty in comparing one preacher to another, and compare one sermon to another from the same preacher. It as though we preached for those placing bets, as though we are likes coins that are valued based on inscriptions alone—for the image and person—and not for the metal. You measure everything by persons, yet "you do not respect the person of the priest." You give less respect to God's ordinance than he does. In no church of Christendom but our own does the preacher preach so exposed.... The entire sermon is not God's word, but every part of the sermon is God's ordinance and the text is certainly his word. There is no salvation but by faith, nor faith but by hearing, nor hearing but by preaching. And people think in the lowest

way about the keys of the church and speak faintly of absolution in the church, yet they will allow that those keys lock and unlock in preaching. Absolution is conferred or withheld in preaching. The proclamation of the promises of the gospel in preaching is that binding and loosing on the earth, which binds and looses in heaven. But Christ has bid us, "Preach the gospel to every creature." Yet in his own great Sermon on the Mount, he has forbidden us "to give holy things to dogs or to cast pearls before swine, lest they trample them, turn and rend us." So all those manifold and fearful judgments, which swell in every chapter, and blow in every verse, and thunder in every line of every book of the Bible fall upon everyone who comes here. Those who turn and rend and falsely malign us—the person of the preacher—trample upon the pearls; that is, they undervalue the doctrine and ordinance itself. Terrible judgments fall upon every uncharitable misinterpretation of that which is said here and upon every irreverent act in this place. SERMON ON PSALM 65:5.[24]

IGNORING GOD AND SEEKING HELP FROM THE HELPLESS. KONRAD PELLIKAN: While for their sins they were either reproved by the prophets or pressed by their enemies at the command of the Lord, the people neither took refuge in petitions for the mercy of God, nor did they repent, nor did they pray for God's help. Rather they sought help from profane nations and ungodly kings—the Egyptians and the Assyrians. But this was in vain; in no way were those nations able to snatch them out of danger. In vain they sought solace from those nations, who were not able to defend even themselves. COMMENTARY ON LAMENTATIONS 4:17.[25]

ENEMIES ON THE WINGS OF EAGLES. JOHN CALVIN: Whenever the prophets threatened [the people], this false opinion prevailed that the Chaldeans would not come, because they were far

---

[22]Pellikan, *Commentaria Bibliorum*, 3:3C4v.
[23]Du Vair, *Meditations*, F3v-F4r*.
[24]Donne, *Sermons*, 7:319-20*; citing 1 Cor 1:21; Mt 16:18-19; Mk 16:15; Mt 7:6.
[25]Pellikan, *Commentaria Bibliorum*, 3:3C4v.

away. The journey was long and difficult; there were many obstacles. The prophet taunts them for this confidence by which they had been deceived when he says that "swifter than the eagles of the heavens" were their enemies....

Now though the prophet speaks here of the ruin of the city, yet we may gather a useful doctrine: when the hand of God is against us, we look around in vain in all directions; for there will be no safety for us on mountains, nor will solitude protect us in the desert. As then we see that the Jews were closed up by God's hand, so when we contend with him, we in vain turn our eyes here and there; for however we may for a time entertain good hopes, yet God will surely at last disappoint us. COMMENTARY ON LAMENTATIONS 4:19.[26]

CHRIST THE LORD OR CHRIST (ANOINTED) OF THE LORD? JOHANNES BUGENHAGEN: "Christ the Lord, etc." Some have interpreted this verse as concerning our Lord Jesus Christ because of the old translation. But concerning him nothing is sung in this doleful song—if it is interpreted on its own terms. Here only the misery of captivity is mourned, etc. Therefore note that every king of the Jews was called the "Christ" or "the Anointed of the Lord," because the kings were anointed by the institution and command of the Lord, as David says concerning the impious Saul: "Let it be far from me that I would send my hand on the Christ of the Lord."

Therefore it is not necessary to read this verse as "Christ the Lord," as the Greek version has it, but it is to be read as "the Christ of the Lord," as it is elsewhere. And when the interpreter of the Old Latin says, "the Spirit of our mouth," or literally from the Hebrew: "the Spirit of our nostrils"—I write it as "our breathing"—that signifies that our king has been given to us as an assurance, our refuge, the guardianship and protection of our life, "in whose shadow we securely live." We heads of households otherwise tend to our fields and civil offices; we possess our things; and we do not fear

the other peoples or our adversaries, who live around us and in the midst of whom we live etc. COMMENTARY ON JEREMIAH, LAMENTATIONS 4:20.[27]

THE KING—BREATH OF THE KINGDOM. JOHN DONNE: Whether Jeremiah laments here the death of a good king, of Josiah.... Or whether he laments the transportation and misery of an ill king, of Zedekiah ... we argue not, we dispute not now; we embrace that which arises from both. That both good kings and bad kings, Josiah and Zedekiah, are the "anointed" of the Lord and "the breath of the nostrils," that is, the life of the people; and therefore both are to be lamented....

The main cause of this lamentation was the ruin, or the dangerous decline of the kingdom and of that great and glorious state.... But they did not treacherously sever the king and the kingdom, as though the kingdom could do well and the king ill; as if the kingdom would be safe, but the king in danger. They see cause to lament because misery had fallen upon the person of the king; perchance upon Zedekiah, a worse king; yet whichever king it is, they acknowledge him to be the *unctus Domini*, "the anointed of the Lord," and to be the *spiritus narium*, "the breath of their nostrils." When this person, therefore, had fallen into the pits of the enemy, the speaker laments....

If the center of the world should be moved but one inch out of place, it cannot be reckoned how many miles this island, or any building in it, would be thrown out of their places. A decline in the kingdom of the Jews, in the body of the kingdom, in the soul of the state, in the form of government, was such an earthquake as could leave nothing standing. Of all things that are, there was an idea in God; there was a model, a platform, an exemplar of everything, which God produced and created in time, in the mind and purpose of God before all things. Of all things God had an idea, a preconception of something—of monarchy, of kingdom. God himself, in his unity, is the model. He is the type of monarchy.

[26]CTS 21:482-83* (CO 39:623-24).

[27]Bugenhagen, *In Ieremiam ... Threni*, F4v-G1r; citing 1 Sam 24:6.

He made but one world; for this world and the next are not two worlds. This is but the morning and the latter is the everlasting noon, of one and the same day, which shall have no night. SERMON ON LAMENTATIONS 4:20.[28]

THE ROYAL ANOINTING IS NOT A SPIRITUAL GRACE. LANCELOT ANDREWES: Before I tell you what it is, I may safely tell you what it is not. This royal anointing is not religion, nor virtue, nor any spiritual grace. "The Lord's Anointed" is said not only of Josiah, a king truly religious, by Jeremiah, but of Cyrus, a mere heathen, by Isaiah; not only of David a good king but of Saul, a tyrant, even then when he was at the worst. Religion, then, is not it, for then Cyrus had not been; virtue is not it, especially the virtue of clemency, for then Saul would not have been God's anointed. If it were religion that made kings, then had there would have been of old no kings but those of Judah; and now no kings, but those that be Christian. But by Cyrus's case we see one may be "anointed of the Lord," and yet not be a Christian. SERMON ON 1 CHRONICLES 16:22.[29]

THE SPIRIT IN OUR BREATH. JOHN DONNE: He is the word of our text, *Spiritus*, as *Spiritus* is the Holy Ghost, so far, by accommodation, as that he is God's instrument to convey blessings upon us, and as *spiritus* is our breath, or speech, and as it is our life, and as it is our soul too, so far as that in those temporal things which concern spiritual (as times of meeting, and much in the manner of proceeding when we are met) we are to receive directions from him: so he is the breath of our nostrils, our speech, our lives, our souls, in that limited sense, are his. SERMON ON LAMENTATIONS 4:20.[30]

THE OTHERS COME AFTER GOD'S OWN. DANIEL TOUSSAIN: The third part of this chapter is a prophecy, wherein is foretold the judgments of God against the adversaries of the Jews, namely,

against the Idumeans, who showed themselves more excessive than the rest of the enemies, as is also seen in the prophecy of Obadiah. Thus we see how the wicked have made themselves brave and have ranged abroad with their pleasures; they themselves shall have their turn and shall be called to a reckoning. They shall drink the sediments and the dregs of the Lord's cup, although the Lord first began his judgments in his own house. THE LAMENTATIONS AND HOLY MOURNINGS 4:21-22.[31]

WHEN ENEMIES REJOICE. JOHANNES OECOLAMPADIUS: Jeremiah brings consolation from the ruin of the enemy, perceiving his own liberation because they were to pay the penalty. Truly, however, the Edomites and enemies are the Antichrists and Pharisees, who killed Christ, and whatever pertains to the world and to our flesh. "Now you, Edom, rejoice," he says, "for a short time at the calamity of me and mine, but you will not endure for long in your joy. For even you yourself will have that cup of wrath of the Lord, which will intoxicate you." Just as in the psalm: "By the rivers of Babylon. . . ." Then, moreover, the Lord will be favorable to his people and his enemies will be a perpetual mockery, when the Lord will be pleased with his people. Indeed the Scriptures always join the destruction of the impious with the salvation of the pious. COMMENTARY ON JEREMIAH, LAMENTATIONS 4:21-22.[32]

EDOMITES AND THE ANTICHRIST. PETER MARTYR VERMIGLI: How can this be true, since the Edomites suffered these same, yes greater things, by the hand of the Romans than by the Babylonians? Some say that this must not be understood to mean they would never suffer such things from now on, but rather that they would suffer them after a long time; it is enough that they have been unperturbed and at peace. The Jews, on the other hand, refer these things to the last days of the Messiah, when they persuade themselves that the

---

[28]Donne, *Sermons*, 4:239-40*.
[29]Andrewes, *Works*, 4:57*; citing Is 45:1; 1 Sam 19:21; 26:9.
[30]Donne, *Works*, 5:224*.
[31]Toussain, *The Lamentations*, 167*.
[32]Oecolampadius, *In Hieremiam . . . Threnos*, 2Y4v; citing Ps 137:1-9.

Romans are to be completely destroyed (for by "Edomites" they everywhere understand "Romans"). We ourselves do not reject their comment out of hand, since we know that the Romans' monarchy is the last, and that it must be abolished at the time when the full reign of Christ has come. . . . I think, rather, that the Antichrist and all the enemies of religion are called by the name of Esau in the Scriptures, because they blaze against the saints with the same hatred with which Esau always persecuted Jacob. Esau's descendants never laid aside this hostility against the Israelites. At that time, without any doubt, as many tried-and-true Jews are found (I mean all the faithful in Christ) will enjoy eternal salvation and great tranquility. COMMENTARY ON LAMENTATIONS 4:22.[33]

---

[33]Vermigli, *Commentary*, 186-88.

LAMENTATIONS 5:1-22
RESTORE US TO YOURSELF, O LORD

¹Remember, O LORD, what has befallen us;
    look, and see our disgrace!
²Our inheritance has been turned over to
    strangers,
    our homes to foreigners.
³We have become orphans, fatherless;
    our mothers are like widows.
⁴We must pay for the water we drink;
    the wood we get must be bought.
⁵Our pursuers are at our necks;
    we are weary; we are given no rest.
⁶We have given the hand to Egypt, and to
    Assyria,
    to get bread enough.
⁷Our fathers sinned, and are no more;
    and we bear their iniquities.
⁸Slaves rule over us;
    there is none to deliver us from their hand.
⁹We get our bread at the peril of our lives,
    because of the sword in the wilderness.
¹⁰Our skin is hot as an oven
    with the burning heat of famine.
¹¹Women are raped in Zion,
    young women in the towns of Judah.

¹²Princes are hung up by their hands;
    no respect is shown to the elders.
¹³Young men are compelled to grind at the mill,
    and boys stagger under loads of wood.
¹⁴The old men have left the city gate,
    the young men their music.
¹⁵The joy of our hearts has ceased;
    our dancing has been turned to mourning.
¹⁶The crown has fallen from our head;
    woe to us, for we have sinned!
¹⁷For this our heart has become sick,
    for these things our eyes have grown dim,
¹⁸for Mount Zion which lies desolate;
    jackals prowl over it.
¹⁹But you, O LORD, reign forever;
    your throne endures to all generations.
²⁰Why do you forget us forever,
    why do you forsake us for so many days?
²¹Restore us to yourself, O LORD, that we may
    be restored!
    Renew our days as of old—
²²unless you have utterly rejected us,
    and you remain exceedingly angry with us.

OVERVIEW: Lamentations concludes with a prayer that recounts the predicament of the Jewish people in defeat and seeks God's mercy and power to convert and restore them. Thus Reformation commentators similarly reflect on the sort of horrific abuse and oppression suffered by the defeated in every era and the sort of humiliation and desperation that may prompt a return to God in true repentance. Recognition of one's dire condition, confession of God's sovereign and eternal rule over all things, and a plea for divine grace and intervention provide the only true hope for the ancient Jews and for the disciples of Jesus Christ.

5:1-18 Dancing Turned to Mourning

A PRAYER OF LAMENT, CONFESSION, AND REPENTANCE. NIKOLAUS SELNECKER: This is a prayer in which Jeremiah first relates his miseries one after the other: How miserable is it that they have lost all of God's blessings? Food and drink, forests and fields, homes and estates, peace and quiet—now there is nothing more of these. Therefore, we should learn and truly recognize what we truly need—our well-being, as God shows us richly here—and we should not come and complain thereafter when unfortunately there is nothing more to obtain for ourselves.

Second, after a recitation of the great and miserable misfortunes he confesses their sins and cries out sorrowfully, "how awful that we have so sinned. We must also pay for the misdeeds of our fathers and carry the wrath because we were also found in such sins." So one come after the other and must be honestly endured.

The third and last part is a prayer for forgiveness of sins and about true repentance. "Convert us, O Lord, and we shall be converted. Without you and your grace and Holy Spirit, we can do nothing except remain, die, and descend into our sins, where you cannot help us except through the will of Christ your son. With us alone everything is lost." SONGS OF LAMENT OF THE PROPHET JEREMIAH 5.[1]

REMEMBER US, O LORD. JOHANNES OECOLAM-PADIUS [WOLFGANG CAPITO]:[†] The prophet bemoans in his prayer the state of the captured in Jerusalem after the death of Josiah, which again happened to the Jews after the death of Christ. Truly the pious and spiritual folk, seeing the afflicted state of the church in the persecution of the pious and the seduction of the weak, first call on and appeal to God to have pity. Indeed for God to remember and consider our shame is for him to have pity on us; however long we are gravely punished and afflicted with calamities, for that long God is said to forget us and avert his face. But his mercy is not lacking, he is not unaware. It is not a secret to him, but we feel as though we are not seen by him. We were the children of God—free, rich, abundantly blessed—now we are captives, destitute, afflicted, and, so to speak, ignoble. Let us pray to God that he might free us from the reproach of our enemies. COMMENTARY ON JEREMIAH, LAMENTATIONS 5:1.[2]

OUR PROMISED LAND AND INHERITANCE. DANIEL TOUSSAIN: It is truly God himself, to speak properly, who is our true possession and inheritance: as the prophet David calls him in Psalm 16. But here Jeremiah has in mind the Holy Land that was promised to Abraham, Isaac, and Jacob, and their posterity, to which they were brought by the special and wonderful deeds of Almighty God. This land was a visible sign of power and a testimony to God's favor and to the incorruptible inheritance that had been reserved for them in heaven. Whenever tyrants of the world drive us out of our own lands or possessions, let us remember that we are not tied to any certain land in this world and that our citizenship is in heaven; where all our joy is, that is to say, Jesus Christ, in whom and by whom, we are established as inheritors of the world. THE LAMENTATIONS AND HOLY MOURNINGS 5:2.[3]

WE HAVE BECOME ORPHANS. PETER MARTYR VERMIGLI: The status of children is considered to be the most calamitous. For the little ones are left exposed to rapine, crime, and misfortune at the time when they have been bereft of a legitimate and natural defender. All the same, a remedy is applied to these sorrows: those who by reason of kinship or affinity of blood are connected to a parent of the children undertake the care of protecting and preserving them. Here, on the contrary, it is said that they are without this benefit too. "For," he says, "we have not only become orphans, but it happened in such a way that we seem to have never had a father, wholly without kin: so denuded of every protection, we are afflicted far and wide." COMMENTARY ON LAMENTATIONS 5:3.[4]

OPPRESSED IN THEIR OWN LAND. JOHANNES BUGENHAGEN: "Our water." The Jews possessed all these things freely, when they were living in the security and abundance of all things. But they did not recognize the gifts of God. Now, however, as

---

[1]Selnecker, *Threni*, Z1r-v.
[2]Oecolampadius/Capito, *In Hieremiam . . . Threnos*, 2Z1r. [†]At the very end of this commentary Wolfgang Capito (d. 1541)—humanist, preacher, theologian, and reformer—indicates that he has finished this last chapter of Lamentations, in place of Oecolampadius, who may have died before completing his work; Oecolampadius, *In Hieremiam . . . Threnos*, 2Z3r-v.
[3]Toussain, *The Lamentations*, 239-40*; citing Ps 16:5; Heb 12:28.
[4]Vermigli, *Commentary*, 191.

things unfolded they complained about the things they had lost and they complained that they now were so pressed by a miserable servitude that even those who remained in the land were compelled to buy back their own water and wood from their ruling tribes, and they were not allowed to go out safely into the fields to seek food because of brigands. Indeed, the prefects of the king of Babylon wanted to become rich in the land of Judah and through tyrannical taxes they seized everything for themselves, even beyond the will of the king, just as impious prefects act practically everywhere even today, having no fear of the judgment of God. COMMENTARY ON JEREMIAH, LAMENTATIONS 5:4.[5]

BEASTS OF BURDEN. PETER MARTYR VERMIGLI: These words ought not to refer to wood or water, but instead to the deplorable condition of slavery. For we were not being led by words, by command, or be urging, nor were we being sent in a human way; rather, as beasts of burden, as senseless brutes we, burdened with a yoke, were constrained either to plow or carry some heavy load. Thus, "we were laboring" day and night in continuous bodily exertion. In spite of this, no fruit of our labors was left to us. For whatever small gain we could accomplish was to be expended in tribute, tolls, and poll taxes. COMMENTARY ON LAMENTATIONS 5:5.[6]

THE PRICE OF BREAD. GUILLAUME DU VAIR: We were sold for a morsel of bread, yet we were driven to fetch it from the furthest parts of Egypt. The Assyrians thought they gave us a great pleasure and favor to make us work day and night for a mouthful of bread. O Lord, what a hard and sad bondage is this! How have we so grievously provoked your wrath? MEDITATIONS UPON THE LAMENTATIONS OF JEREMIAH 5:6.[7]

A NEW GENERATION SEEKS MERCY. JOHN CALVIN: Jeremiah simply intended to say that the people who had been long rebellious against God were already dead, and that it was therefore a suitable time for God to regard the miseries of their descendants. The faithful, then, do not allege their own innocence here before God, as though they were blameless, but only mention that their fathers underwent a just punishment and for that a whole generation had perished. COMMENTARY ON LAMENTATIONS 5:7.[8]

WHY ARE SOME GENERATIONS SEVERELY PUNISHED BUT NOT OTHERS? PETER MARTYR VERMIGLI: In Exodus 20 it is maintained that God "visits the sins of the fathers on the sons to the third and fourth generation" but "has compassion to thousands." The compassion extends widely; on account of Abraham, Isaac, and Jacob, innumerable generations were bestowed with magnificent blessings. On the other hand, justice does not punish at once but waits until the third and fourth generation; nor does it punish those of the third and fourth generation as if they did not deserve punishment—they did, because they were involved in the same crimes as their fathers. We cannot nevertheless bring forward any reason for which some people happened to be in the generation that must be thus smitten while others were in another that God endured in his patience. Let it be enough for us to understand that this is not done by God except in his exact and inscrutable planning. This is something that, although it cannot be searched by us, we must necessarily respect and heed with greatest reverence.

Nor on this account must any injustice be ascribed to divine actions. As for those who were not chastised by God in this life but seemed to depart with impunity, still clinging to their crimes, harsh punishments await them in the age to come. COMMENTARY ON LAMENTATIONS 5:7.[9]

LONG-STANDING SIN IS PUNISHED MORE SEVERELY. JOHN UDALL: When diverse generations

---

[5]Bugenhagen, *In Ieremiam . . . Threni*, G2v-H1r.
[6]Vermigli, *Commentary*, 193.
[7]Du Vair, *Meditations*, F9r*.
[8]CTS 21:499* (CO 39:634-35).
[9]Vermigli, *Commentary*, 196-97; citing Ex 20:5-6.

continue in one sin, the Lord usually punishes the latter more severely than the former. The reason is because, first, the son should fear to do the like, when he sees his father's sin, else his sin is more heinous. Second, the longer God's patience is abused, the greater heap of vengeance is deserved. The use is to teach us, not to stand upon this, we will do as our forefathers have done, for as we sin as they did, we must be punished more severely than they were. COMMENTARY ON LAMENTATIONS 5:7.[10]

SLAVE OF SLAVES. DANIEL TOUSSAIN: The Jews must become bondslaves and bow even to their servants that have subdued them. Now there is no more grievous bondage than for a man to become a bondslave to beggars' brats, who most commonly are the cruelest and hardest to please and will expect more of them than other masters; as our Savior Christ showed in Matthew 18 when speaking of the parable of the servant that dealt harshly with his fellow servant. It should not be thought strange that there were in this great country of Babylon proud and disdainful servants. Even in the poorest house one can find arrogant and presumptuous servants, who will demand more of other servants than any nobleman or gentleman of great dignity. THE LAMENTATIONS AND HOLY MOURNINGS 5:8.[11]

LIFE UNDER OCCUPATION. JOHANNES BUGEN-HAGEN: "Our bread." That is, outside the city on the roads, the Gentiles are plotting against us so that they might rob us and kill us. We are nowhere safe. In fact, in Hebrew they call this a wilderness, whenever we leave the city and go out into the fields. As in the psalm, "The habitations of the wilderness grow fertile," that is, in the fields and countryside there is an abundant yield.

"They were oppressed." They were humiliated and defiled. Were those victorious nations doing anything other than what our own godless soldiers do? COMMENTARY ON JEREMIAH, LAMENTATIONS 5:9.[12]

VIOLATING SPIRITUAL VIRGINS. MARTIN LUTHER: Where the pure gospel is not preached, there the public pimp is a much more ordinary sinner than that preacher [a blind leader and murderer of souls from the papacy], and the brothel is not as evil as the church. If that same pimp spent all day ruining new virgins and godly wives and nuns—a terrible and horrible thing to hear about—yet he would not be as evil and harmful as such a papistic preacher.

Do you think that is strange? Remember that such a preacher does nothing more than take the newborn hearts from baptism—the young Christian people, the tender souls, who are only consecrated virgins and brides of Christ—and daily impregnates and violates them with his sermons. Since that does not happen bodily but spiritually, no one gets excited. But God is exceedingly grieved, and in his great wrath he speaks roughly through the prophets: "You shameless whore, you spread your legs to any passerby." He is that intolerant toward such preaching. Jeremiah complains in his prayer: "Women are raped in Zion, virgins in the towns of Judah." Spiritual virginity, that is, Christian faith, is immeasurably better than bodily, since it alone obtains heaven. ST. STEPHEN'S DAY SERMON ON ACTS 6:8-15; 7:54-60.[13]

SUICIDAL PRINCES AND THE DISHONORED ELDERLY. JOHN CALVIN: Jeremiah says that the princes were hung, not by enemies, for that was a common way for the conquered to be slain by their enemies and hung as a way of reproach; but the prophet, as it appears to me, meant to express something more atrocious: that even the miserable princes were constrained to lay violent hands on themselves.

He adds that "the faces of the aged were not honored," which is also an unnatural thing; for we know that some honor is always rendered to old age and that time of life is commonly regarded with reverence. When, therefore, no respect is shown to the aged, then the greatest barbarity

[10]Udall, Commentary on Lamentations, CC2v*; citing Ezek 18:14.
[11]Toussain, The Lamentations, 241*; Mt 18:21-35.
[12]Bugenhagen, In Ieremiam ... Threni, H1r; citing Ps 65:12.
[13]LW 75:321 (WA 10.1.1:255-56); citing Ezek 16:25.

must necessarily prevail. COMMENTARY ON LAMENTATIONS 5:12.[14]

THE LOWEST OF SLAVES. DANIEL TOUSSAIN: "They made the young grind." This was a most grievous pain, which they laid upon servants and slaves as a punishment: even to grind in the mills like beasts. In Exodus 11, where the first born are described, it says, "Thus all the first born should die, even from the firstborn of Pharaoh that sits on the throne to the first born of a maid at the mill." That is, from the honorable personage to the lowest slave. THE LAMENTATIONS AND HOLY MOURNINGS 5:13.[15]

THE MILL AND THE MILLSTONE. HECTOR PINTO: "They abused the young men indecently." Jeremiah speaks about the foulest type of sin that goes against nature. Even so, this speech can be translated. They were using young males at the millstones, obviously to drive the millstones. The sense is that our Babylonian enemies pushed the young men of Jerusalem down to the pounding mill, where the grain was ground with a hand mill. Surely this was the lowest of duties. In Exodus it says, "From the firstborn of Pharaoh, who sits on his throne all the way, to the first-born of the female slave, who is at her mill." From this also that passage of Isaiah should be explained with reference to this disgrace and especially the service, when he says, "Take the millstone and grind the flour."[†]

"And the boys collapsed under the wood." That is, the boys were so burdened by the wood that they collapsed under the wood as their strength gave out. But because he had spoken about the millstone, perhaps the wood is to be understood as a wooden handle, by which the millstone of the mill is turned, or this: the boys were struck down in the wooden cradle. COMMENTARY ON LAMENTATIONS 5:13.[16]

THE MUSIC OF JOY, THE MUSIC OF LAMENT. DANIEL TOUSSAIN: "The Elders have ceased from the gate." Jeremiah uses a very effective approach when he attributes a particular pleasure to every age level and then mentions that it has been taken away. For all the judgments were determined in the gates of the cities. . . .

So it was a sign that all judgments ceased when none of the elders were sitting in the gates. To young men is attributed music, which the old men do not care for; as in 2 Samuel 19 we read that the old father, Barzillai said to David, "In his great old age he could not hear the voices of men and women singing." Now this is no small grief, but also a very lamentable condition; to see every level of men so disturbed and unable to do what is ordinary and comes naturally to them. This is as if the sun, earth, and stars should cease to do their duty. Among all the rest, music is a special gift of God, not only for rejoicing and refreshing people's minds, but also for every honest person to take pleasure in sweet harmony. Besides, all the faithful should turn all their music to praying to God and thus, depending on time and place, serve him while keeping an agreeable and decent order in all things.

As St. James sets down this rule in his letter, chapter 5: "Is there anyone among you that is afflicted? Let them pray. Is anyone happy? Let them sing." Jeremiah speaks of deliverance and restoration of the people of faith in chapter 33: "There shall be heard in this place, the voice of joy and the voice of gladness, the voice of the bridegroom and the voice of the bride," etc. But when God gave peace and rest to them, the Jews became secure and were excessive in all licentiousness, plunging themselves over their heads and ears in the delights and pleasures of the world. They did this instead of looking to God. So the Lord is forced to change this music and harmonious sound

---

[14]CTS 21:504-5* (CO 39:638).

[15]Toussain, *The Lamentations*, 242*; citing Ex 11:5.

[16]Pinto, *In Prophetae Ieremiae Lamentationes*, 364v; citing Rom 1:26-27; Ex 11:5; Is 47:2. [†]Pinto seems to use this first phrase to

allude to what follows in Is 47:2-3: "Take the millstones and grind flour, put off your veil, strip off your robe, uncover your legs, pass through the rivers. Your nakedness will be exposed." In short, grinding at the mills required the boys to expose themselves indecently.

into pitiful cries, sighs, groans, and sobs, as he threatens to do in Amos 8. THE LAMENTATIONS AND HOLY MOURNINGS 5:14.[17]

BE CIRCUMSPECT WHEN A STATE FAILS.

JOHN UDALL: The overthrow of magistracy among a people takes all occasions of rejoicing from all sorts of people. The reason is because, first, many great blessings are lost, and many grievances come upon them which will make the heart heavy. Second, they have no safety, but have cause every one to fear another, and to stand upon their own guard as though they were in the midst of their enemies. The use is to teach us to pray to God that he would never leave us without those heads and governors that may take care to protect us in peace, for if he does, our life will be more bitter than death itself. COMMENTARY ON LAMENTATIONS 5:14.[18]

SYMBOLS OF OUR LOYALTY RIPPED AWAY.

GUILLAUME DU VAIR: Can we live after this? Is our torment just small enough that it does not suffice to kill us? Is our curse so cruel that we are left with eyes to lament for such a long time? Why are we condemned to be afflicted with this misery for such a long time? Must we see at our feet the crown that fell from our head and march over the fragments of our scepter, which we gladly carried with reverence in our hands? Do we see our royal robes now rent before our faces? We are cursed; our sins have caused this desolation and moved God's justice to visit us with his rage and to scatter upon us the fire of his wrath. MEDITATIONS UPON THE LAMENTATIONS OF JEREMIAH 5:16.[19]

THE HOLY MOUNTAIN AND THE FOXES.

DANIEL TOUSSAIN: "Because of Mount Zion." This mount is the other mount joined to Moriah, where the temple was built; yes, even the whole city

of Jerusalem. David built his castle on Mount Zion, as David was a king and prophet he was not only a figure and representation of the Messiah, but also the one of whom the Messiah would be born according to the flesh. Many times in Scripture mention is made of Zion as something that represents the church. But now Mount Zion is abandoned as well as Shiloh, where the ark of the Lord rested in ancient times. God threatened this in the seventh chapter of Jeremiah because of the vain confidence the Jews had in that mountain and in the temple.

So also in the time that has now come, Jesus spoke to the woman of Samaria in John 4: "That the true worshipers would not be tied to any certain mountain or country, but should worship the Lord in all places of the world in spirit and truth." Now Jeremiah complains in our text that this holy Mount Zion was overrun with foxes, which wandered about there at their pleasure, showing thereby that it had become altogether a wilderness and habitation for wild beasts. Or else he signifies allegorically the subtle tyrants, which are compared to foxes, as in Luke 13, where Jesus Christ speaks of Herod. THE LAMENTATIONS AND HOLY MOURNINGS 5:18.[20]

5:19-22 A Plea for Mercy

GOD'S ETERNITY AND OUR PASSING.

GUILLAUME DU VAIR: Lord, this destruction was the power of your hand, to make great things and then to pull them down. You ascend above the cities and kingdoms of the earth to show them that there is nothing as remarkable as the excellence of your handiwork. You will that the ruin of all earthly things would carry the mark of your eternity. You are the Lord, the only one exempt from mourning or changing. Time cannot measure your greatness, but only serves to accomplish your will. You sit on your throne over all corruptible things and see people pass and change one after another as you will the time of

---

[17]Toussain, *The Lamentations*, 242-44*; 2 Sam 19:35; Jas 5:13; Jer 33:11; Amos 8:3.
[18]Udall, *Commentary on Lamentations*, CC4v*.
[19]Du Vair, *Meditations*, F11v-F12r*.

[20]Toussain, *The Lamentations*, 247-48*; citing Jn 4:23; Jer 7:12; Lk 13:32.

their dwelling upon the earth—just as people choose to change their garments. MEDIATIONS UPON THE LAMENTATIONS OF JEREMIAH 5: 19.[21]

GOD DOES NOT CHANGE. JOHN CALVIN: When we fix our eyes on present things, we must necessarily vacillate, as there is nothing permanent in the world; and when adversity brings a cloud over our eyes, then faith in a manner vanishes, at least we are troubled and stand amazed. Now the remedy is to raise up our eyes to God, for however confounded things may be in this world, yet he remains always the same. His truth may indeed be hidden from us, yet it remains in him. In short, if the world would change and perish a hundred times, nothing could affect the unchangeableness of God. . . .

We hence see that . . . the state of present things [is] as thick as darkness . . . the prophet raises up his eyes to God and acknowledges him as remaining the same perpetually, though things in the world continually change. Then the throne of God is set in opposition to chance or uncertain changes which ungodly people dream of; for when they see things in great confusion in the world, they say that it is the wheel of fortune; they say that all things happen through blind fate. Then the prophet, that he might not be cast down with the unbelieving, refers to the throne of God, and strengthens himself in this doctrine of religion— that God nevertheless "sits on his throne." Though things are thus confounded, though all things fluctuate—yea, even though storms and tempests, as it were, mingle heaven and earth together—yet God sits on his throne amid all such disturbances. However turbulent all the elements may be, this takes nothing away from the righteous and perpetual judgment of God. COMMENTARY ON LAMENTATIONS 5:19.[22]

SEEKING GOD'S MERCY. GUILLAUME DU VAIR: Lord, you who are just and God Almighty: will you forget your favor toward us, you who forgets

nothing? Will you forget the promise of your justice, which you made to your people? Have you forgotten that you never break your word? Will you avoid this occasion for pity on us? Though you are Almighty, are you not our Lord who helps and aids the afflicted? Because you are God do you forget to pardon? For a time you have been severe and have handed us over to calamity to show us how we have offended you. Yet now we have felt this enough and are ready to return to you; our hearts are breaking; we have sorrowfully sighed before you. What more do you want? What other sacrifice may we offer beyond our tears? You possess all things. There is nothing in our disposition but our will, which we present to you—washed in sorrows, sprinkled with grief and repentance, and purified in the heat of your love. Why should we reject you? Why should you sleep while we are miserable? MEDITATIONS UPON THE LAMENTATIONS OF JEREMIAH 5:20.[23]

CONVERSION AND BEING CONVERTED. JOHANNES BUGENHAGEN: "Convert us, Lord, to you." That is, make us return to you and we will be converted—that is, we will return to you: excellent sentiments from which we may understand the commands of the law. Observe the commands of the Lord. Return to me with your whole heart, etc. Lest we understand that we are able to do these things by our own power and free will, as the impious Pelagius taught.[†] . . . Let us be humbled before God in the recognition of our sin and our own inability; let us respond to God the Father through the Christ: Father, grant to us that we might observe your commands and then we will observe them. "Grant to us that we might be converted to you, then we will be converted." Thus Augustine prays: "Grant what you command and command what you will."[‡] "Not to us, Lord, not to us, but to your name give the glory for your mercy and your truth," etc. COMMENTARY ON JEREMIAH, LAMENTATIONS 5:21.[24]

---

[21]Du Vair, *Meditations*, F12v-G1r*.
[22]CTS 21:28-29* (CO 39:642-43).

[23]Du Vair, *Meditations*, G1r-G2r*.
[24]Bugenhagen, *In Ieremiam . . . Threni*, H2r-v; citing Ps 115:1. [†]Pelagius (d. c. 420), champion of humanity's free will and ability to choose God and overcome sin. [‡]Augustine, *The Confessions* 10.29.40.

WHERE TROUBLE AND PEACE MEET. JOHN DONNE: On a flat map it is not possible to make the west be the east. Though west and east are distant in extremity, the flat map can be pasted on a round globe so that west and east then become one. In a flat soul, dejected conscience and troubled spirit, trouble can be made into peace when trouble is applied to the body of merits, that is, to the body of the gospel of Jesus Christ and to be conformed to him. Then your west and east, your trouble of spirit and tranquility of spirit are one. . . .

A troublesome spirit and a quiet spirit are far apart. But a troubled spirit and a quiet spirit are also close neighbors. Therefore, David means them no great harm when he says, "Let them be troubled"; for though the wind may be as high as possible, so also I sail before the wind. Let the trouble of my soul be as high as possible, so that it will direct me to God and then I will have sufficient calm.

And this peace and calm is implied in the next word . . . "let them return": let them be forced to return. Jeremiah prays that God would do something to cross their purposes because as they are against God, so they are against their own souls. In that way, in their current place God sees no remedy. So he desires that they might be "turned" in another way. What is that way? "Turn us, O Lord, and we shall be turned." That is, turn the right way—toward God. And as there was a promise from God to hear his people, not only when they came to him in the temple, but also when they turned toward the temple, so at any distance and wherever they were they would be given accompanied with a blessing whenever they turned towards God. SERMON ON PSALMS 6, 8, 9, 10.[25]

THE TWOFOLD CONVERSION. JOHN CALVIN: There is a twofold turning or conversion of people to God and a twofold turning of God to people. There is an inward turning when God regenerates us by his own Spirit; a turning with respect to us is said to be the feeling of true religion, when after having been alienated from him, we return to the right way and right mind. There is also an exterior turning as to God; that is, when he so receives people into his favor that his paternal favor becomes apparent; but the interior turning of people to God takes place when they recover life and joy. COMMENTARY ON LAMENTATIONS 5:21.[26]

SHOWING CONTRITION AND ANTICIPATING CHRIST. HEINRICH BULLINGER: "Unless you have utterly rejected us." Jeremiah does not speak as if he is desperate about the salvation of the people, but he has made clear the depth of his sorrow from contrition and from his despondency about his people. Moreover, he sees in a prophetic spirit that the Jews would not believe in the coming of Christ, but that in opposing the gospel their heirs would be handed over to death. SERMON ON LAMENTATIONS 5:22.[27]

CONVERSION AND ETERNITY. JOHANNES OECOLAMPADIUS [WOLFGANG CAPITO]: With these words Jeremiah again wishes to hasten divine assistance. We feel God's wrath against us as long as we do not seriously repent, and we truly are driven back by the hand of the Lord since in that state we do not belong to him. But if God himself will convert our captivity, he will even build Jerusalem, so that the faithful people in a holy congregation praise him in perpetuity, which happens through faith in Christ our Lord. COMMENTARY ON JEREMIAH, LAMENTATIONS 5:21-22.[28]

---

[25]Donne, *Sermons*, 6:59-60*; citing Ps 9:20.

[26]CTS 21:515* (CO 39:644-45).
[27]Bullinger, *Conciones*, 312v.
[28]Oecolampadius/Capito, *In Hieremiam . . . Threnos*, 2Z3r.

Map of Europe at the Time of the Reformation

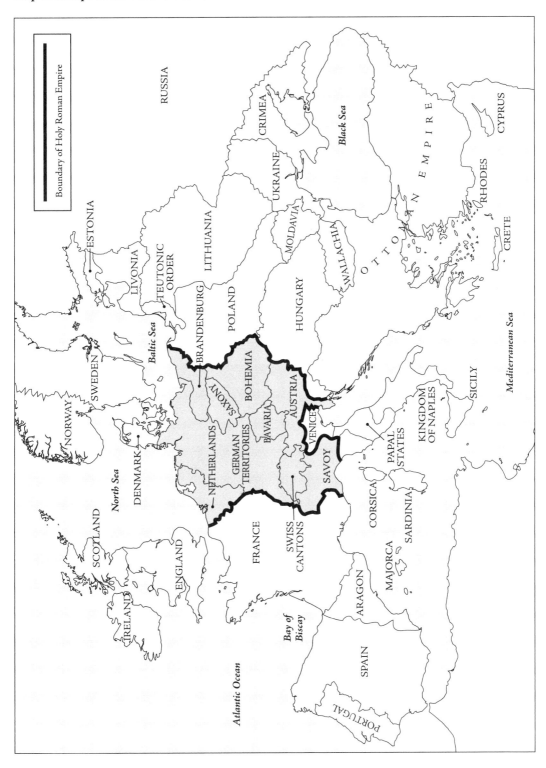

Timeline of the Reformation

	German Territories	France	Spain	Italy	Switzerland	Netherlands	British Isles
1309–1377		Babylonian Captivity of the Papacy					
1337–1453		d. Nicholas of Lyra Hundred Years' War	b. Paul of Burgos (Solomon ha-Levi)(d. 1435) Alonso Tostado (1400–1455)				Hundred Years' War
1378–1415		Western Schism (Avignon Papacy)		Western Schism			
1384							d. John Wycliffe
1414–1418					Council of Basel (1431–1437)		
1415				Council of Constance; d. Jan Hus; Martin V (r. 1417–1431); Council of Florence (1438–1445)			
1450	Invention of printing press						
1452				b. Leonardo da Vinci (d. 1519)			
1453				Fall of Constantinople			
1455–1485	b. Johannes Reuchlin (d. 1522)						War of Roses; rise of House of Tudor
1456	Gutenberg Bible						
1460				Pope Pius II issued *Execrabilis*			
1466		b. Jacques Lefèvre d'Étaples (d. 1536)					
1467						b. Desiderius Erasmus (d. 1536)	b. John Colet (d. 1519)
1469	b. Antoius Broickwy von Königstein (d. 541)						
1470				b. Santes Pagninus (d. 1541)			b. John (Mair) Major (d. 1550)
1475				b. Michelangelo (d. 1564)			
1478	b. Wolfgang Capito (d. 1541)		Ferdinand and Isabella	b. Jacopo Sadoleto (d. 1547)			b. Thomas More (d. 1535)

	German Territories	France	Spain	Italy	Switzerland	Netherlands	British Isles
1480	b. Balthasar Hubmaier (d. 1528); b. Andreas Bodenstein von Karlstadt (d. 1541)						
1481–1530			Spanish Inquisition				
1482					b. Johannes Oecolampadius (d. 1531)		
1483	b. Martin Luther (d. 1546)						
1484	b. Johann Spangenberg (d. 1550)				b. Huldrych Zwingli (d. 1531)		
1485	b. Johannes Bugenhagen (d. 1554)						b. Hugh Latimer (d. 1555)
1486	r. Frederick the Wise, Elector (d. 1525); b. Johann Eck (d. 1543)						
1488	b. Otto Brunfels (d. 1534)						b. Miles Coverdale (d. 1568)
1489	b. Thomas Müntzer (d. 1525); b. Kaspar von Schwenckfeld (d. 1561)						b. Thomas Cranmer (d. 1556)
1491	b. Martin Bucer (d. 1551)		b. Ignatius Loyola (d. 1556)				
1492			Defeat of Moors in Grenada; Columbus discovers America; expulsion of Jews from Spain	Alexander VI (r. 1492–1503)			
1493	b. Justus Jonas (d. 1555)						
1494							b. William Tyndale (d. 1536)
1496	b. Andreas Osiander (d. 1552)					b. Menno Simons (d. 1561)	
1497	b. Philipp Melanchthon (d. 1560); b. Wolfgang Musculus (d. 1563); b. Johannes (Ferus) Wild (d. 1554)						

	German Territories	France	Spain	Italy	Switzerland	Netherlands	British Isles
1498				d. Girolamo Savonarola	b. Conrad Grebel (d. 1526)		
1499	b. Johannes Brenz (d. 1570) b. Justus Menius (d. 1558)			b. Peter Martyr Vermigli (d. 1562)			
1500			b. Charles V (−1558)				
1501	b. Erasmus Sarcerius (d. 1559)						
1502	Founding of University of Wittenberg			Julius II (r. 1503–1513)		b. Frans Titelmans (d. 1537)	
1504					b. Heinrich Bullinger (d. 1575)		
1505	Luther joins Augustinian Order			b. Benedict Aretius (d. 1574)			
1506		b. Augustin Marlorat (d. 1562)		Restoration of St. Peter's begins			
1507				Sale of indulgences approved to fund building			
1508	b. Lucas Lossius (d. 1582)						
1509		b. John Calvin (d. 1564)					r. Henry VIII (−1547)
1510	Luther moves to Rome			b. Immanuel Tremellius (d. 1580)			b. Nicholas Ridley (d. 1555)
1511	Luther moves to Wittenberg						
1512				Sistine Chapel completed			
1512–1517				Fifth Lateran Council; rejection of conciliarism			
1513	Luther lectures on Psalms			r. Pope Leo X (−1521)			b. John Knox (d. 1572)
1515	Luther lectures on Romans	r. Francis I (−1547); b. Peter Ramus (d. 1572)					
1516		Est. French National Church (via Concordat of Bologna)		Concordat of Bologna		Publication of Erasmus's Greek New Testament	
1517	Tetzel sells indulgences in Saxony; Luther's Ninety-five Theses						

	German Territories	France	Spain	Italy	Switzerland	Netherlands	British Isles
1518	Heidelberg Disputation; Luther examined by Cajetan at Diet of Augsburg			Diet of Augsburg			
1519	Leipzig Disputation	b. Theodore Beza (d. 1605)	Cortés conquers Aztecs; Portuguese sailor Magellan circumnavigates the globe		Zwingli appointed pastor of Grossmünster in Zurich; b. Rudolf Gwalther (d. 1586)		
1520	Publication of Luther's "Three Treatises"; burning of papal bull in Wittenberg		Coronation of Charles V	Papal Bull v. Luther: *Exsurge Domine*			
1521	Luther excommunicated; Diet/Edict of Worms—Luther condemned; Luther in hiding; Melanchthon's *Loci communes*	French-Spanish War (–1526)	French-Spanish War; Loyola converts	Papal excommunication of Luther			Henry VIII publishes *Affirmation of the Seven Sacraments* against Luther; awarded title "Defender of the Faith" by Pope
1521–1522	Disorder in Wittenberg; Luther translates New Testament						
1521–1525		First and Second Habsburg–Valois War					
1522	Luther returns to Wittenberg; Luther's NT published; criticizes Zwickau prophets; b. Martin Chemnitz (d. 1586)		Publication of Complutensian Polyglot Bible under Cisneros		Sausage Affair and reform begins in Zurich under Zwingli		b. John Jewel (d. 1571)
1523	Knight's Revolt	Bucer begins ministry in Strasbourg	Loyola writes Spiritual Exercises	r. Pope Clement VII (–1534)	Iconoclasm in Zurich		
1524	Luther criticizes peasants; d. Johann von Staupitz					Erasmus's disputation on free will	
1524–1526	Peasants' War						
1525	Luther marries; execution of Thomas Müntzer; publication of Luther's *Bondage of the Will*				Abolition of mass in Zurich; disputation on baptism; first believers' baptism performed in Zurich		

	German Territories	France	Spain	Italy	Switzerland	Netherlands	British Isles
1526					Zurich council mandates capital punishment of Anabaptists	Publication of Tyndale's English translation of NT	
1527	d. Hans Denck (b. c. 1500) d. Hans Hut (b. 1490) b. Tilemann Hesshus (d. 1588)			Sack of Rome by mutinous troops of Charles V	First Anabaptist executed in Zurich; drafting of Schleitheim Confession		
1528	Execution of Hubmaier						
1529	Second Diet of Speyer; evangelical "protest"; publication of Luther's catechisms; Marburg Colloquy; siege of Vienna by Turkish forces	Abolition of mass in Strasbourg			d. Georg Blaurock (b. 1492)		Thomas More appointed chancellor to Henry VIII
1530	Diet of Augsburg; Confession of Augsburg	d. Francois Lambert (Lambert of Avignon) (b. 1487)	Charles V crowned Holy Roman Emperor				
1531	Formation of Schmalkaldic League				d. H. Zwingli; succeeded by H. Bullinger		
1532		Publication of Calvin's commentary on Seneca; conversion of Calvin	b. Francisco de Toledo (d. 1596)				
1533	b. Valentein Weigel (d. 1588)	Nicholas Cop addresses University of Paris; Cop and Calvin implicated as "Lutheran" sympathizers	b. Juan de Maldonado (d. 1583)				Thomas Cranmer appointed as Archbishop of Canterbury; Henry VIII divorces
1534	First edition of Luther's Bible published	Affair of the Placards; Calvin flees d. Guillame Briçonnet (b. 1470)		Jesuits founded; d. Cardinal Cajetan (Thomas de Vio) (b. 1469)			Act of Supremacy; English church breaks with Rome
1535	Bohemian Confession of 1535; Anabaptist theocracy at Münster collapses after eighteen months				b. Lambert Daneau (d. 1595)		d. Thomas More; d. John Fisher

	German Territories	France	Spain	Italy	Switzerland	Netherlands	British Isles
1536	Wittenberg Concord; b. Kaspar Olevianus (d. 1587)				First edition of Calvin's *Institutes* published; Calvin arrives in Geneva (–1538); First Helvetic Confession	Publication of Tyndale's translation of NT; d. W. Tyndale	d. A. Boleyn; Henry VIII dissolves monasteries (–1541)
1537					Calvin presents ecclesiastical ordinances to Genevan Council		
1538					Calvin exiled from Geneva; arrives in Strasbourg (–1541)		
1539		Calvin publishes second edition of *Institutes* in Strasbourg		d. Felix Pratensis			Statute of Six Articles; publication of Coverdale's Great Bible
1540				Papal approval of Jesuit order			d. Thomas Cromwell
1541	Colloquy of Regensburg	French translation of Calvin's *Institutes* published	d. Juan de Valdés (b. 1500/1510)		d. A. Karlstadt; Calvin returns to Geneva (–1564)		
1542	d. Sebastian Franck (b. 1499)			Institution of Roman Inquisition			War between England and Scotland; James V of Scotland defeated; Ireland declared sovereign kingdom
1543	Copernicus publishes *On the Revolutions of the Heavenly Spheres*; d. Johann Eck (Johann Maier of Eck) (b. 1486)						
1545–1547	Schmalkaldic Wars; d. Martin Luther			First session of Council of Trent			b. Richard Bancroft (d. 1610)
1546	b. Johannes Piscator (d. 1625)						
1547	Defeat of Protestants at Mühlberg	d. Francis I; r. Henri II (–1559)					d. Henry VIII; r. Edward VI (–1553)
1548	Augsburg Interim (–1552) d. Caspar Cruciger (b. 1504) b. David Pareus (d. 1622)						

	German Territories	France	Spain	Italy	Switzerland	Netherlands	British Isles
1549	d. Paul Fagius (b. 1504)	d. Marguerite d'Angoulême (b. 1492)			Consensus Tigurinus between Calvin and Bullinger		First Book of Common Prayer published
1550	b. Aegidius Hunnius (d. 1603)						
1551–1552				Second session of Council of Trent			
1552	d. Sebastian Münster (b. 1488) d. Friedrich Nausea (b. c. 1496)						Book of Common Prayer revised
1553	d. Johannes Aepinus (b. 1449)				Michael Servetus executed in Geneva		Cranmer's Forty-Two Articles; d. Edward VI; r. Mary I (d. 1558)
1554							Richard Hooker (d. 1600)
1555	Diet of Augsburg; Peace of Augsburg establishes legal territorial existence of Lutheranism and Catholicism b. Johann Arndt (d. 1621)	First mission of French pastors trained in Geneva				b. Sibbrandus Lubbertus (d. 1625)	b. Lancelot Andrewes (d. 1626) b. Robert Rollock (d. 1599); d. Hugh Latimer; d. Nicholas Ridley d. John Hooper
1556	d. Pilgram Marpeck (b. 1495) d. Konrad Pellikan (b. 1478) d. Peter Riedemann (b. 1506)		Charles V resigns			d. David Joris (b. c. 1501)	d. Thomas Cranmer
1557							Alliance with Spain in war against France
1558			d. Charles V				b. William Perkins (d. 1602); d. Mary I; r. Elizabeth I (–1603)
1559		d. Henry II; r. Francis II (–1560); first national synod of French reformed churches (1559) in Paris; Gallic Confession		First index of prohibited books issued	Final edition of Calvin's Institutes; founding of Genevan Academy	b. Jacobus Arminius (d. 1609)	Elizabethan Settlement

	German Territories	France	Spain	Italy	Switzerland	Netherlands	British Isles
1560	d. P. Melanchthon	d. Francis II; r. Charles IX (1574); Edict of Toleration created peace with Huguenots	d. Domingo de Soto (b. 1494)		Geneva Bible		Kirk of Scotland established; Scottish Confession
1561-1563				Third session of Council of Trent			
1561						Belgic Confession	
1562	d. Katharina Schütz Zell (b. 1497/98)	Massacre of Huguenots begins French Wars of Religion (–1598)					The Articles of Religion—in Elizabethan "final" form (1562/71); publication of Latin edition of Jewel's *Apology*
1563	Heidelberg Catechism						
1564				b. Galileo (d. 1642)	d. J. Calvin		b. William Shakespeare (d. 1616); publication of Lady Ann Bacon's English translation of Jewel's *Apology*
1566	d. Johann Agricola (b. 1494)			Roman Catechism	Second Helvetic Confession		
1567						Spanish occupation	Abdication of Scottish throne by Mary Stuart; r. James VI (1603–1625)
1568						d. Dirk Phillips (b. 1504) Dutch movement for liberation (–1645)	*Bishops' Bible*
1570		d. Johannes Mercerus (Jean Mercier)		Papal Bull *Regnans in Excelsis* excommunicates Elizabeth I			Elizabeth I excommunicated
1571	b. Johannes Kepler (d. 1630)		Spain defeats Ottoman navy at Battle of Lepanto				b. John Downame (d. 1652)
1572		Massacre of Huguenots on St. Bartholomew's Day		r. Pope Gregory XIII (1583–1585)		William of Orange invades	b. John Donne (d. 1631)
1574		d. Charles IX; r. Henri III (d. 1589)					

	German Territories	France	Spain	Italy	Switzerland	Netherlands	British Isles
1575	d. Georg Major (b. 1502); Bohemian Confession of 1575						
1576		Declaration of Toleration; formation of Catholic League		b. Giovanni Diodati (d. 1649)		Sack of Antwerp; Pacification of Ghent	
1577	Lutheran Formula of Concord						England allies with Netherlands against Spain
1578	Swiss Brethren Confession of Hesse d. Peter Walpot		Truce with Ottomans				Sir Francis Drake circumnavigates the globe
1579			Expeditions to Ireland			Division of Dutch provinces	
1580	Lutheran Book of Concord						
1581			d. Teresa of Avila				Anti-Catholic statutes passed
1582				Gregorian Reform of calendar			
1583							b. David Dickson (d. 1663)
1584		Treaty of Joinville with Spain	Treaty of Joinville; Spain inducted into Catholic League; defeats Dutch at Antwerp			Fall of Antwerp; d. William of Orange	
1585	d. Josua Opitz (b. c. 1542)	Henri of Navarre excommunicated		r. Pope Sixtus V (–1590)			
1586							Sir Francis Drake's expedition to West Indies; Sir Walter Raleigh in Roanoke
1587	d. Johann Wigand (b. 1523)	Henri of Navarre defeats royal army					d. Mary Stuart of Scotland
1588		Henri of Navarre drives Henri III from Paris; assassination of Catholic League Leaders	Armada destroyed				English Navy defeats Spanish Armada
1589		d. Henri III; r. Henri (of Navarre) IV (–1610)	Victory over England at Lisbon				Defeated by Spain in Lisbon
1590		Henri IV's siege of Paris		d. Girolamo Zanchi (b. 1516)			Alliance with Henri IV

	German Territories	France	Spain	Italy	Switzerland	Netherlands	British Isles
1592	d. Nikolaus Selnecker (b. 1530)						
1593		Henri IV converts to Catholicism					Books I-IV of Hooker's *Laws of Ecclesiastical Polity* published
1594		Henri grants toleration to Huguenots					
1595		Henri IV declares war on Spain; received into Catholic Church		Pope Sixtus accepts Henri IV into Church			Alliance with France
1596		b. René Descartes (d. 1650) b. Moïse Amyraut (d. 1664)					
1597							Book V of Hooker's *Laws of Ecclesiastical Polity* published
1598		Edict of Nantes; toleration of Huguenots; peace with Spain	Treaty of Vervins; peace with France				
1600	d. David Chytraeus (b. 1531)						
1601							b. John Trapp (d. 1669)
1602					d. Daniel Toussain (b. 1541)		
1603							d. Elizabeth I; r. James I (James VI of Scotland) (–1625)
1604	d. Cyriacus Spangenberg (b. 1528)						d. John Whitgift (b. 1530)
1605						b. Rembrandt (d. 1669)	Guy Fawkes and gunpowder plot
1606							Jamestown Settlement
1607							b. John Milton (d. 1674)
1608							
1610		d. Henri IV; r. Louis XIII (–1643)	d. Benedict Pererius (b. 1535)			The Remonstrance; Short Confession	

	German Territories	France	Spain	Italy	Switzerland	Netherlands	British Isles
1611							Publication of Authorized English Translation of Bible (AV/KJV); George Abbot becomes Archbishop of Canterbury (–1633)
1612							b. Richard Crashaw (d. 1649)
1616							b. John Owen (d. 1683)
1617							b. Ralph Cudworth (d. 1689)
1618–1619						Synod of Dordrecht	
1618–1648	Thirty Years' War						
1620							English Sepratists land in Plymouth, Massachusetts
1621							d. Andrew Willet (b. 1562)
1628							Puritans establish Massachusetts Bay colony
1633	d. Christoph Pelargus (b. 1565)						Laud becomes Archbishop of Canterbury
1637	d. Johann Gerhard (b. 1582)					*Statenvertaling*	
1638							d. Joseph Mede (b. 1638)
1640				Diodati's Italian translation of Bible published			
1642–1649							English civil wars; d. Charles I; r. Oliver Cromwell (1660)
1643		d. Louis XIII; r. Louis XIV (–1715)					
1643–1649							Westminster Assembly
1645							d. William Laud (b. 1573)

	German Territories	France	Spain	Italy	Switzerland	Netherlands	British Isles
1648		Treaty of Westphalia ends Thirty Years' War					Books VI and VIII of Hooker's *Laws of Ecclesiastical Polity* posthumously published
1656	d. Georg Calixtus (b. 1586)						
1658							d. Oliver Cromwell
1659							Richard Cromwell resigns
1660							English Restoration; r. Charles II (–1685)
1662							Act of Uniformity; Book VII of Hooker's *Laws of Ecclesiastical Polity* posthumously published
1664						d. Thieleman Jans van Braght (b. 1625)	d. John Mayer (b. 1583)
1671							d. William Greenhill (b. 1591)
1677							d. Thomas Manton (b. 1620)
1678						d. Anna Maria von Schurman (b. 1607)	
1688							Glorious Revolution; r. William and Mary (-1702); d. John Bunyan (b. 1628)
1691							d. Richard Baxter (b. 1615)

BIOGRAPHICAL SKETCHES OF
REFORMATION-ERA FIGURES AND WORKS

This list is cumulative, including all the authors cited in the Reformation Commentary on Scripture
to date as well as other people relevant to the Reformation and Reformation-era exegesis.
For works consulted, see "Sources for Biographical Sketches," p. 575.

Cornelius À Lapide (1567–1637). Flemish biblical exegete. A Jesuit, Lapide served as professor of Holy Scripture and Hebrew at Louvain for twenty years before taking a similar role in Rome, where he taught until his death. He is best known for his extensive commentaries on the Scriptures. Encompassing all books of the Bible except Job and the Psalms, his work employs a fourfold hermeneutic and draws heavily on the work of patristic and medieval exegetes.

Thomas Adams (1583–1653). Anglican minister and author. He attended the University of Cambridge where he received his BA in 1601 and his MA in 1606. Following his ordination in 1604, Adams served as curate at Northill in Bedfordshire. In 1611, he became vicar of Willmington. Three years later he served the parish of Wingrave, Buckinghamshire, where he remained until 1618. From 1618 to 1623 Adams was preacher at St. Gregory by St. Paul's. He also served as chaplain to Henry Montague, First Earl of Manchester, and Lord Chief Justice of England. Among his most important works are the *Happiness of the Church* (1618) and an extensive commentary on 2 Peter (1638).

Johannes Aepinus (1499–1553). German Lutheran preacher and theologian. Aepinus studied under Martin Luther,* Philipp Melanchthon* and Johannes Bugenhagen* in Wittenberg. Because of

his Lutheran beliefs, Aepinus lost his first teaching position in Brandenburg. He fled north to Stralsund and became a preacher and superintendent at Saint Peter's Church in Hamburg. In 1534, he made a diplomatic visit to England but could not convince Henry VIII to embrace the Augsburg Confession.* His works include sermons and theological writings. Aepinus became best known as leader of the Infernalists, who believed that Christ underwent torment in hell after his crucifixion.

Johann Agricola (c. 1494–1566). German Lutheran pastor and theologian. An early student of Martin Luther,* Agricola eventually began a controversy over the role of the law, first with Melanchthon* and then with Luther himself. Agricola claimed to defend Luther's true position, asserting that only the gospel of the crucified Christ calls Christians to truly good works, not the fear of the law. After this first controversy, Agricola seems to have radicalized his views to the point that he eliminated Luther's *simul iustus et peccator* ("at the same time righteous and sinful") paradox of the Christian life, emphasizing instead that believers have no need for the law once they are united with Christ through faith. Luther responded by writing anonymous pamphlets against antinomianism. Agricola later published a recantation of his views, hoping to assuage relations with Luther, although they were never personally reconciled. He published a commentary on Luke, a series of sermons on Colossians, and a massive collection of German proverbs.

Henry Ainsworth (1571–1622/1623). English Puritan Hebraist. In 1593, under threat of persecution, Ainsworth relocated to Amsterdam, where he served as a teacher in an English congregation. He composed a confession of faith for the community and a number of polemical and exegetical works, including annotations on the Pentateuch, the Psalms and Song of Songs.

Henry Airay (c. 1560–1616). English Puritan professor and pastor. He was especially noted for his preaching, a blend of hostility toward Catholicism and articulate exposition of English Calvinism. He was promoted to provost of Queen's College Oxford (1598) and then to vice chancellor of the university in 1606. He disputed with William Laud* concerning Laud's putative Catholicization of the Church of England, particularly over the practice of genuflection, which Airay vehemently opposed. He also opposed fellow Puritans who wished to separate from the Church of England. His lectures on Philippians were his only work published during his lifetime.

Alexander (Ales) Alesius (1500–1565). Scottish Lutheran theologian. Following the martyrdom of his theological adversary Patrick Hamilton (c. 1504–1528), Alesius converted to the Reformation and fled to Germany. In 1535 Martin Luther* and Philipp Melanchthon* sent him as an emissary to Henry VIII and Thomas Cranmer.* He taught briefly at Cambridge, but after the Act of Six Articles reasserted Catholic sacramental theology he returned to Germany, where he lectured at Frankfurt an der Oder and Leipzig. Alesius composed many exegetical, theological and polemical works, including commentaries on John, Romans, 1–2 Timothy, Titus and the Psalms.

Andreas Althamer (c. 1500–1539). German Lutheran humanist and pastor. Forced from the chaplaincy at Schwäbisch-Gmünd for teaching evangelical ideas, Althamer studied theology at Wittenberg before serving as a pastor in Eltersdorf, Nuremberg, and Ansbach. A staunch Lutheran, he contended against Reformed theologians at the 1528 disputation at Bern and delivered numerous polemics against Anabaptism. He also composed an early Lutheran catechism, published at Nuremberg in 1528.

Moïse Amyraut (1596–1664). French Reformed pastor and professor. Originally intending to be a lawyer, Amyraut turned to theology after an encounter with several Huguenot pastors and having read Calvin's* *Institutes*. After a brief stint as a parish pastor, Amyraut spent the majority of his career at the Saumur Academy. He was well known for his irenicism and ecumenism (for example, in advocating intercommunion with Lutherans). Certain aspects of his writings on justification, faith, the covenants and especially predestination proved controversial among the Reformed. His doctrine of election is often called hypothetical universalism or Amyraldianism, stating that Christ's atoning work was intended by God for all human beings indiscriminately, although its effectiveness for salvation depends on faith, which is a free gift of God given only to those whom God has chosen from eternity. Amyraut was charged with grave doctrinal error three times before the National Synod but was acquitted each time. Aside from his theological treatises, Amyraut published paraphrases of almost the entire New Testament and the Psalms, as well as many sermons.

Anabaptists of Trieste (1539). Following a meeting between Swiss Brethren and the Hutterites at Steinabrunn on December 6, 1536, around 140 radicals were arrested and imprisoned in Falkenstein Castle. After six weeks in captivity, the ninety men of the group were forced to march to Trieste to be sold as galley slaves. Twelve days after arrival, all but twelve prisoners managed to escape and return to Moravia, where they published a confession of their beliefs.

Jakob Andreae (1528–1590). German Lutheran theologian. Andreae studied at the University of Tübingen before being called to the diaconate in Stuttgart in 1546. He was appointed ecclesiastical superintendent of Göppingen in 1553 and supported Johannes Brenz's* proposal to place the church under civil administrative control. An ecclesial diplomat for the duke of Württemberg, Andreae debated eucharistic theology, the use of images and predestination with Theodore Beza* at the Colloquy of Montbéliard (1586) to determine whether French Reformed exiles would be required to submit to the Formula of Concord.* Andreae coauthored the Formula of Concord. He and his wife had eighteen children.

Lancelot Andrewes (1555–1626). Anglican bishop. A scholar, pastor and preacher, Andrews prominently shaped a distinctly Anglican identity between the poles of Puritanism and Catholicism. He oversaw the translation of Genesis to 2 Kings for the Authorized Version.* His eight-volume collected works—primarily devotional tracts and sermons—are marked by his fluency in Scripture, the Christian tradition and classical literature.

Benedict Aretius (d. 1574). Swiss Reformed professor. Trained at the universities of Bern, Strasbourg and Marburg, Aretius taught logic and philosophy as well as the biblical languages and theology. He advocated for stronger unity and peace between the Lutheran and Reformed churches. Aretius joined others in denouncing the antitrinitarian Giovanni Valentino Gentile (d. 1566). He published commentaries on the New Testament, as well as various works on astronomy, botany and medicine.

Jacobus Arminius (1559–1609). Dutch Remonstrant pastor and theologian. Arminius was a vocal critic of high Calvinist scholasticism, whose views were repudiated by the Synod of Dordrecht. Arminius was a student of Theodore Beza* at the academy of Geneva. He served as a pastor in Amsterdam and later joined the faculty of theology at the university in Leiden, where his lectures on predestination were popular and controversial. Predestination, as Arminius understood it, was the decree of God determined on the basis of divine foreknowledge of faith or rejection by humans who are the recipients of prevenient, but resistible, grace.

Johann Arndt (1555–1621). German Lutheran pastor and theologian. After a brief time teaching, Arndt pastored in Badeborn (Anhalt) until 1590, when Prince Johann Georg von Anhalt (1567–1618) began introducing Reformed ecclesial policies. Arndt ministered in Quedlinberg, Brunswick, Eisleben and Celle. Heavily influenced by medieval mysticism, Arndt centered his theology on Christ's mystical union with the believer, out of which flows love of God and neighbor. He is best known for his *True Christianity* (1605–1609), which greatly influenced Philipp Jakob Spener (1635–1705) and later Pietists.

John Arrowsmith (1602–1659). English Puritan theologian. Arrowsmith participated in the Westminster Assembly, and later taught at Cambridge. His works, all published posthumously, include three sermons preached to Parliament and an unfinished catechism.

Articles of Religion (1562; revised 1571). The Articles underwent a long editorial process that drew from the influence of Continental confessions in England, resulting in a uniquely Anglican blend of Protestantism and Catholicism. In their final form, they were reduced from Thomas Cranmer's* Forty-two Articles (1539) to the Elizabethan Thirty-Nine Articles (1571), excising polemical articles against the Anabaptists and Millenarians as well as adding articles on the Holy Spirit, good works and Communion. Originating in a 1535 meeting with Lutherans, the Articles retained a minor influence from the Augsburg Confession* and Württemberg Confession (1552), but showed significant revision in accordance with Genevan theology, as well as the Second Helvetic Confession.*

Anne Askew (1521–1546). English Protestant martyr. Askew was forced to marry her deceased sister's intended husband, who later expelled Askew from his house—after the birth of two children—on account of her religious views. After unsuccessfully seeking a divorce in Lincoln, Askew moved to London, where she met other Protestants and began to preach. In 1546, she was arrested, imprisoned and convicted of heresy for denying the doctrine of transubstantiation. Under torture in the Tower of London she refused to name any other Protestants. On July 16, 1546, she was burned at the stake. Askew is best known through her accounts of her arrests and examinations. John Bale (1495–1563), a bishop, historian and playwright, published these manuscripts. Later John Foxe (1516–1587) included them in his *Acts and Monuments*, presenting her as a role model for other pious Protestant women.

Augsburg Confession (1530). In the wake of Luther's* stand against ecclesial authorities at the Diet of Worms (1521), the Holy Roman Empire splintered along theological lines. Emperor Charles V sought to ameliorate this—while also hoping to secure a united European front against Turkish invasion—by calling together another imperial diet in Augsburg in 1530. The Evangelical party was cast in a strongly heretical light at the diet by Johann Eck.* For this reason, Philipp Melanchthon* and Justus Jonas* thought it best to strike a conciliatory tone (Luther, as an official outlaw, did not attend), submitting a confession rather than a defense. The resulting Augsburg Confession was approved by many of the rulers of the northeastern Empire; however, due to differences in eucharistic theology, Martin Bucer* and the representatives of Strasbourg, Constance, Lindau and Memmingen drafted a separate confession (the Tetrapolitan Confession). Charles V accepted neither confession, demanding that the Evangelicals accept the Catholic rebuttal instead. In 1531, along with the publication of the Augsburg Confession itself, Melanchthon released a defense of the confession that responded to the Catholic confutation and expanded on the original articles. Most subsequent Protestant confessions followed the general structure of the Augsburg Confession.

Authorized Version (1611). In 1604 King James I* commissioned this new translation—popularly remembered as the King James Version—for uniform use in the public worship of the Church of England. The Bible and the Apocrypha was divided into six portions and assigned to six companies of nine scholars—both Anglicans and Puritans—centered at Cambridge, Oxford and Westminster. Richard Bancroft, the general editor of the Authorized Version, composed fifteen rules to guide the translators and to guard against overly partisan decisions. Rather than offer an entirely fresh English translation, the companies were to follow the Bishops' Bible* as closely as possible. "Truly (good Christian Reader)," the preface states, "we neuer thought from the beginning that we should need to make a new Translation, nor yet to make of a bad one a good one . . . but make a good one better, or out of many good ones, one principall good one, not iustly to be excepted against: that hath bene our endeauour, that our mark." Other rules standardized spelling, dictated traditional ecclesial terms (e.g., *church*, *baptize* and *bishop*), and allowed only for linguistic marginal notes and cross-references. Each book of the Bible went through a rigorous revision process: first, each person in a company made an initial draft, then the company put together a composite draft, then a supercommittee composed of representatives from each company reviewed these drafts, and finally two bishops and Bancroft scrutinized the final edits. The text and translation process of the Authorized Version have widely influenced biblical translations ever since.

Robert Bagnall (b. 1559 or 1560). English Protestant minister. Bagnall authored *The Steward's Last Account* (1622), a collection of five sermons on Luke 16.

John Ball (1585–1640). English Puritan theologian. Ball was a respected educator. He briefly held a church office until he was removed on account of his Puritanism. He composed popular catechisms and tracts on faith, the church and the covenant of grace.

Thomas Bastard (c. 1565–1618). English Protestant minister and poet. Educated at Winchester and New College, Oxford, Bastard published numerous works, including collections of poems and sermons; his most famous title is *Chrestoleros* (1598), a collection of epigrams. Bastard was alleged to be the author of an anonymous work, *An Admonition to the City of Oxford*, which revealed the carnal vices of many clergy and scholars in Oxford; despite denying authorship, he was dismissed from Oxford in 1591. Bastard was recognized as a skilled classical scholar and preacher. He died impoverished in a debtor's prison in Dorchester.

Jeremias Bastingius (1551–1595). Dutch Reformed theologian. Educated in Heidelberg and Geneva, Bastingius pastored the Reformed church in Antwerp for nearly a decade until the Spanish overran the city in 1585; he later settled in Dordrecht. He spent the last few years of his life in Leiden on the university's board of regents. He wrote an influential commentary on the Heidelberg Catechism that was translated into English, Dutch, German and Flemish.

Johann (Pomarius) Baumgart (1514–1578). Lutheran pastor and amateur playwright. Baumgart studied under Georg Major,* Martin Luther* and Philipp Melanchthon* at the University of Wittenberg. Before becoming pastor of the Church of the Holy Spirit in 1540, Baumgart taught secondary school. He authored catechetical and polemical works, a postil for the Gospel readings throughout the church year, numerous hymns and a didactic play (*Juditium Salomonis*).

Richard Baxter (1615–1691). English Puritan minister. Baxter was a leading Puritan pastor, evangelist and theologian, known throughout England for his landmark ministry in Kidderminster and a prodigious literary output, producing 135 books in just over forty years. Baxter came to faith through reading William Perkins,* Richard Sibbes* and other early Puritan writers and was the first cleric to decline the terms of ministry in the national English church imposed by the 1662 Act of Uniformity; Baxter wrote on behalf of the more than 1700 who shared ejection from the national church. He hoped for restoration to national church ministry, or toleration, that would allow lawful preaching and pastoring. Baxter sought unity in theological, ecclesiastical, sociopolitical and personal terms and is regarded as a forerunner of Noncomformist ecumenicity, though he was defeated in his efforts at the 1661 Savoy Conference to take seriously Puritan objections to the revision of the 1604 Prayer Book. Baxter's views on church ministry were considerably hybrid: he was a paedo-baptist, Nonconformist minister who approved of synodical Episcopal government and fixed liturgy. He is most known for his classic

writings on the Christian life, such as *The Saints' Everlasting Rest* and *A Christian Directory*, and pastoral ministry, such as *The Reformed Pastor*. He also produced *Catholick Theology*, a large volume squaring current Reformed, Lutheran, Arminian and Roman Catholic systems with each other.

Thomas Becon (1511/1512–1567). English Puritan preacher. Becon was a friend of Hugh Latimer,* and for several years chaplain to Archbishop Thomas Cranmer.* Becon was sent to the Tower of London by Mary I and then exiled for his controversial preaching at the English royal court. He returned to England upon Elizabeth I's accession. Becon was one of the most widely read popular preachers in England during the Reformation. He published many of his sermons, including a postil, or collection of sermon helps for undertrained or inexperienced preachers.

Belgic Confession (1561). Written by Guy de Brès (1523–1567), this statement of Dutch Reformed faith was heavily reliant on the Gallic Confession,* although more detailed, especially in how strongly it distances the Reformed from Roman Catholics and Anabaptists. The Confession first appeared in French in 1561 and was translated to Dutch in 1562. It was presented to Philip II (1527–1598) in the hope that he would grant toleration to the Reformed, to no avail. At the Synod of Dordrecht* the Confession was revised, clarifying and strengthening the article on election as well as sharpening the distinctives of Reformed theology against the Anabaptists, thus situating the Dutch Reformed more closely to the international Calvinist movement. The Belgic Confession in conjunction with the Heidelberg Catechism* and the Canons of Dordrecht were granted official status as the confessional standards (the Three Forms of Unity) of the Dutch Reformed Church.

Theodore Beza (1519–1605). French pastor and professor. Beza was compatriot and successor to John Calvin* as moderator of the Company of Pastors in Geneva during the second half of the sixteenth century. He was a noteworthy New Testament scholar whose *Codex Bezae* formed the basis of the New Testament section of later

English translations. A leader in the academy and the church, Beza served as professor of Greek at the Lausanne Academy until 1558, at which time he moved to Geneva to become the rector of the newly founded Genevan Academy. He enjoyed an international reputation through his correspondence with key European leaders. Beza developed and extended Calvin's doctrinal thought on several important themes such as the nature of predestination and the real spiritual presence of Christ in the Eucharist.

Theodor Bibliander (1504?–1564). Swiss Reformed Hebraist and theologian. Professor of Old Testament at the Zurich Academy from 1531, Bibliander published two Hebrew grammars, a collection of letters by Zwingli* and Oecolampadius*, commentaries on Isaiah, Ezekiel, and Nahum, a Latin translation of the Qur'an, and a tract warning Christians against the threat of Islam. He taught a universalist view of predestination, arguing that God saved all people unless they rejected divine grace. Following a dispute with double-predestinarian Peter Martyr Vermigli*, he was forced into retirement in 1560.

Hugh Binning (1627–1653). Scottish Presbyterian theologian. At the age of eighteen, Binning became a professor of philosophy at the University of Glasgow. In his early twenties he left this post for parish ministry, and died of consumption a few years later. His commentary on the Westminster Confession and a selection of his sermons were published after his death.

Samuel Bird (d. 1604). Anglican minister and author. A native of Essex, Bird matriculated at Queen's College, Cambridge, where he received his BA in 1570 and his MA in 1573, at which time he was also elected a fellow of Corpus Christi College, Cambridge. For reasons unknown, Bird resigned his fellowship sometime in 1576. He spent nearly the entirety of his post-university career as rector of St. Peter's in Ipswich until his death in 1604. Among Bird's major works are *A Friendlie Communication or Dialogue Betweene Paule and Demas, wherein is Disputed How We are to Use the Pleasures of This Life* (1580), *Lectures upon the 11.*

Chapter of Hebrews and upon the 38. Psalme (1598), and *Lectures upon the 8 and 9 Chapters of the Second Epistle to the Corinthians* (1598).

Bishops' Bible (1568). Anglicans were polarized by the two most recent English translations of the Bible: the Great Bible (1539) relied too heavily on the Vulgate* and was thus perceived as too Catholic, while the Geneva Bible's* marginal notes were too Calvinist for many Anglicans. So Archbishop Matthew Parker (1504–1575) commissioned a new translation of Scripture from the original languages with marginal annotations (many of which, ironically, were from the Geneva Bible). Published under royal warrant, the Bishops' Bible became the official translation for the Church of England. The 1602 edition provided the basis for the King James Bible (1611).

Georg Blaurock (1492–1529). Swiss Anabaptist. Blaurock (a nickname meaning "blue coat," because of his preference for this garment) was one of the first leaders of Switzerland's radical reform movement. In the first public disputations on baptism in Zurich, he argued for believer's baptism and was the first person to receive adult believers' baptism there, having been baptized by Conrad Grebel* in 1525. Blaurock was arrested several times for performing mass adult baptisms and engaging in social disobedience by disrupting worship services. He was eventually expelled from Zurich but continued preaching and baptizing in various Swiss cantons until his execution.

Bohemian Confession (1535). Bohemian Christianity was subdivided between traditional Catholics, Utraquists (who demanded Communion in both kinds) and the *Unitas Fratrum*, who were not Protestants but whose theology bore strong affinities to the Waldensians and the Reformed. The 1535 Latin edition of this confession—an earlier Czech edition had already been drafted—was an attempt to clarify and redefine the beliefs of the *Unitas Fratrum*. This confession purged all earlier openness to rebaptism and inched toward Luther's* eucharistic theology. Jan Augusta (c. 1500–1572) and Jan Roh (also Johannes Horn; c. 1490–1547) presented the confession to King Ferdinand I (1503–1564) in Vienna, but the king would not print it. The *Unitas Fratrum* sought, and with slight amendments eventually obtained, Luther's advocacy of the confession. It generally follows the structure of the Augsburg Confession.*

Bohemian Confession (1575). This confession was an attempt to shield Bohemian Christian minorities—the Utraquists and the *Unitas Fratrum*—from the Counter-Reformation and Habsburg insistence on uniformity. The hope was that this umbrella consensus would ensure peace in the midst of Christian diversity; anyone who affirmed the 1575 Confession, passed by the Bohemian legislature, would be tolerated. This confession was, like the Bohemian Confession of 1535, patterned after the Augsburg Confession.* It emphasizes both justification by faith alone and good works as the fruit of salvation. Baptism and the Eucharist are the focus of the sacramental section, although the five traditional Catholic sacraments are also listed for the Utraquists. Though it was eventually accepted in 1609 by Rudolf II (1552–1612), the Thirty Years' War (1618–1648) rendered the confession moot.

Book of Common Prayer (1549; 1552). After the Church of England's break with Rome, it needed a liturgical manual to distinguish its theology and practice from that of Catholicism. Thomas Cranmer* drafted the Book of Common Prayer based on the medieval Roman Missal, under the dual influence of the revised Lutheran Mass and the reforms of the Spanish Cardinal Quiñones. This manual details the eucharistic service, as well as services for rites such as baptism, confirmation, marriage and funerals. It includes a matrix of the epistle and Gospel readings and the appropriate collect for each Sunday and feast day of the church year. The 1548 Act of Uniformity established the Book of Common Prayer as *the* authoritative liturgical manual for the Church of England, to be implemented everywhere by Pentecost 1549. After its 1552 revision, Queen Mary I banned it; Elizabeth reestablished it in 1559, although it was rejected by Puritans and Catholics alike.

The Book of Homilies (1547; 1563; 1570). This collection of approved sermons, published in three parts during the reigns of Edward VI and Elizabeth I, was intended to inculcate Anglican theological distinctives and mitigate the problems raised by the lack of educated preachers. Addressing doctrinal and practical topics, Thomas Cranmer* likely wrote the majority of the first twelve sermons, published in 1547; John Jewel* added another twenty sermons in 1563. A final sermon, *A Homily Against Disobedience*, was appended to the canon in 1570. Reprinted regularly, the *Book of Homilies* was an important resource in Anglican preaching until at least the end of the seventeenth century.

Martin (Cellarius) Borrhaus (1499–1564). German Reformed theologian. After a dispute with his mentor Johann Eck,* Borrhaus settled in Wittenberg, where he was influenced by the radical Zwickau Prophets. He travelled extensively, and finally settled in Basel to teach philosophy and Old Testament. Despite his objections, many accused Borrhaus of Anabaptism; he argued that baptism was a matter of conscience. On account of his association with Sebastian Castellio (1515–1563) and Michael Servetus (1511–1553), some scholars posit that Borrhaus was an antitrinitarian. His writings include a treatise on the Trinity and commentaries on the Torah, historical books, Ecclesiastes and Isaiah.

John Boys (1571–1625). Anglican priest and theologian. Before doctoral work at Cambridge, Boys pastored several parishes in Kent; after completing his studies he was appointed to more prominent positions, culminating in his 1619 appointment as the Dean of Canterbury by James I. Boys published a popular four-volume postil of the Gospel and epistle readings for the church year, as well as a companion volume for the Psalms.

Thieleman Jans van Braght (1625–1664). Dutch Radical preacher. After demonstrating great ability with languages, this cloth merchant was made preacher in his hometown of Dordrecht in 1648. He served in this office for the next sixteen years, until his death. This celebrated preacher had a reputation for engaging in debate wherever an opportunity presented itself, particularly concerning infant baptism. The publication of his book of martyrs, *Het Bloedigh Tooneel of Martelaersspiegel* (1660; *Martyrs' Mirror*), proved to be his lasting contribution to the Mennonite tradition. *Martyrs' Mirror* is heavily indebted to the earlier martyr book *Offer des Heeren* (1562), to which Braght added many early church martyrs who rejected infant baptism, as well as over 800 contemporary martyrs.

Johannes Brenz (1499–1570). German Lutheran theologian and pastor. Brenz was converted to the reformation cause after hearing Martin Luther* speak; later, Brenz became a student of Johannes Oecolampadius.* His central achievement lay in his talent for organization. As city preacher in Schwäbisch-Hall and afterward in Württemberg and Tübingen, he oversaw the introduction of reform measures and doctrines and new governing structures for ecclesial and educational communities. Brenz also helped establish Lutheran orthodoxy through treatises, commentaries and catechisms. He defended Luther's position on eucharistic presence against Huldrych Zwingli* and opposed the death penalty for religious dissenters.

Guillaume Briçonnet (1470–1534). French Catholic abbot and bishop. Briçonnet created a short-lived circle of reformist-minded humanists in his diocese under the sponsorship of Marguerite d'Angoulême. His desire for ecclesial reform developed throughout his prestigious career (including positions as royal chaplain to the queen, abbot at Saint-Germain-des-Prés and bishop of Meaux), influenced by Jacques Lefèvre d'Étaples.* Briçonnet encouraged reform through ministerial visitation, Scripture and preaching in the vernacular and active study of the Bible. When this triggered the ire of the theology faculty at the Sorbonne in Paris, Briçonnet quelled the activity and departed, envisioning an ecclesial reform that proceeded hierarchically.

Thomas Brightman (1562–1607). English Puritan pastor and exegete. Under alleged divine inspiration, Brightman wrote a well known commentary on Revelation, influenced by Joachim of Fiore (d. 1202). In contrast to the putatively true churches of Geneva and Scotland, he depicted the Church of England as a type of the lukewarm Laodicean church. He believed that the Reformation would result in the defeat of the Vatican and the Ottoman Empire and that all humanity would be regenerated through the spread of the gospel before Christ's final return and judgment.

Otto Brunfels (c. 1488–1534). German Lutheran botanist, teacher and physician. Brunfels joined the Carthusian order, where he developed interests in the natural sciences and became involved with a humanist circle associated with Ulrich von Hutten and Wolfgang Capito.* In 1521, after coming into contact with Luther's* teaching, Brunfels abandoned the monastic life, traveling and spending time in botanical research and pastoral care. He received a medical degree in Basel and was appointed city physician of Bern in 1534. Brunfels penned defenses of Luther and Hutten, devotional biographies of biblical figures, a prayer book, and annotations on the Gospels and the Acts of the Apostles. His most influential contribution, however, is as a Renaissance botanist.

Martin Bucer (1491–1551). German Reformed theologian and pastor. A Dominican friar, Bucer was influenced by Desiderius Erasmus* during his doctoral studies at the University of Heidelberg, where he began corresponding with Martin Luther.* After advocating reform in Alsace, Bucer was excommunicated and fled to Strasbourg, where he became a leader in the city's Reformed ecclesial and educational communities. Bucer sought concord between Lutherans and Zwinglians and Protestants and Catholics. He emigrated to England, becoming a professor at Cambridge. Bucer's greatest theological concern was the centrality of Christ's sacrificial death, which achieved justification and sanctification and orients Christian community.

Johannes Bugenhagen (1485–1558). German Lutheran pastor and professor. Bugenhagen, a priest and lecturer at a Premonstratensian monastery, became a city preacher in Wittenberg during the reform efforts of Martin Luther* and Philipp Melanchthon.* Initially influenced by his reading of Desiderius Erasmus,* Bugenhagen grew in evangelical orientation through Luther's works; later, he studied under Melanchthon at the University of Wittenberg, eventually serving as rector and faculty member there. Bugenhagen was a versatile commentator, exegete and lecturer on Scripture. Through these roles and his development of lectionary and devotional material, Bugenhagen facilitated rapid establishment of church order throughout many German provinces.

Heinrich Bullinger (1504–1575). Swiss Reformed pastor and theologian. Bullinger succeeded Huldrych Zwingli* as minister and leader in Zurich. The primary author of the First and Second Helvetic Confessions,* Bullinger was drawn toward reform through the works of Martin Luther* and Philipp Melanchthon.* After Zwingli died, Bullinger was vital in maintaining adherence to the cause of reform; he oversaw the expansion of the Zurich synodal system while preaching, teaching and writing extensively. One of Bullinger's lasting legacies was the development of a federal view of the divine covenant with humanity, making baptism and the Eucharist covenantal signs.

John Bunyan (1628–1688). English Puritan preacher and writer. His *Pilgrim's Progress* is one of the best-selling English-language titles in history. Born to a working-class family, Bunyan was largely unschooled, gaining literacy (and entering the faith) through reading the Bible and such early Puritan devotional works as *The Plain Man's Pathway to Heaven* and *The Practice of Piety*. Following a short stint in Oliver Cromwell's parliamentary army, in which Bunyan narrowly escaped death in combat, he turned to a preaching ministry, succeeding John Gifford as pastor at the Congregational church in Bedford. A noted preacher, Bunyan drew large crowds in itinerant appearances and it was in the sermonic form that Bunyan developed his theological outlook, which was an Augustinian-inflected Calvinism. Bunyan's opposition to the Book of Common Prayer and refusal of official ecclesiastical licensure led to multiple imprisonments, where he wrote many of his famous allegorical works, including *Pilgrim's Progress, The Holy City, Prison Meditations* and *Holy War*.

Jeremiah Burroughs (c. 1600–1646). English Puritan pastor and delegate to the Westminster Assembly. Burroughs left Cambridge, as well as a rectorate in Norfolk, because of his nonconformity. After returning to England from pastoring an English congregation in Rotterdam for several years (1637–1641), he became one of only a few dissenters from the official presbyterianism of the Assembly in favor of a congregationalist polity. Nevertheless, he was well known and respected by presbyterian colleagues such as Richard Baxter* for his irenic tone and conciliatory manner. The vast majority of Burroughs's corpus was published posthumously, although during his lifetime he published annotations on Hosea and several polemical works.

Cardinal Cajetan (Thomas de Vio) (1469–1534). Italian Catholic cardinal, professor, theologian and biblical exegete. This Dominican monk was the leading Thomist theologian and one of the most important Catholic exegetes of the sixteenth century. Cajetan is best-known for his interview with Martin Luther* at the Diet of Augsburg (1518). Among his many works are polemical treatises, extensive biblical commentaries and most importantly a four-volume commentary (1508–1523) on the *Summa Theologiae* of Thomas Aquinas.

Georg Calixtus (1586–1656). German Lutheran theologian. Calixtus studied at the University of Helmstedt where he developed regard for Philipp Melanchthon.* Between his time as a student and later as a professor at Helmstedt, Calixtus traveled through Europe seeking a way to unite and reconcile Lutherans, Calvinists and Catholics. He attempted to fuse these denominations through use of the Scriptures, the Apostles' Creed, and the first five centuries, interpreted by the Vincentian canon. Calixtus's position was stamped as syncretist and yielded further debate even after his death.

John Calvin (1509–1564). French Reformed pastor and theologian. In his *Institutes of the Christian Religion*, Calvin provided a theological dogmatics for the Reformed churches. Calvin's gradual conversion to the cause of reform occurred through his study with chief humanist scholars in Paris, but he spent most of his career in Geneva (excepting a three-year exile in Strasbourg with Martin Bucer*). In Geneva, Calvin reorganized the structure and governance of the church and established an academy that became an international center for theological education. He was a tireless writer, producing his *Institutes*, theological treatises and Scripture commentaries.

Wolfgang Capito (1478?–1541). German Reformed humanist and theologian. Capito, a Hebrew scholar, produced a Hebrew grammar and published several Latin commentaries on books of the Hebrew Scriptures. He corresponded with Desiderius Erasmus* and fellow humanists. Capito translated Martin Luther's* early works into Latin for the printer Johann Froben. On meeting Luther, Capito was converted to Luther's vision, left Mainz and settled in Strasbourg, where he lectured on Luther's theology to the city clergy. With Martin Bucer,* Capito reformed liturgy, ecclesial life and teachings, education, welfare and government. Capito worked for the theological unification of the Swiss cantons with Strasbourg.

Thomas Cartwright (1535–1606). English Puritan preacher and professor. Cartwright was educated at St. John's College, Cambridge, although as an influential leader of the Presbyterian party in the Church of England he was continually at odds with the Anglican party, especially John Whitgift.* Cartwright spent some time as an exile in Geneva and Heidelberg as well as in Antwerp, where he pastored an English church. In 1585, Cartwright was arrested and eventually jailed for trying to return to England despite Elizabeth I's refusal of his request. Many acknowledged him to be learned but also quite cantankerous. His publications include commentaries on Colossians, Ecclesiastes, Proverbs and the Gospels, as well as a dispute against Whitgift on church discipline.

Mathew Caylie (unknown). English Protestant minister. Caylie authored *The Cleansing of the Ten Lepers* (1623), an exposition of Luke 17:14-18.

John Chardon (d. 1601). Irish Anglican bishop. Chardon was educated at Oxford. He advocated Reformed doctrine in his preaching, yet opposed those Puritans who rejected Anglican church

order. He published several sermons.

Martin Chemnitz (1522–1586). German Lutheran theologian. A leading figure in establishing Lutheran orthodoxy, Chemnitz studied theology and patristics at the University of Wittenburg, later becoming a defender of Philipp Melanchthon's* interpretation of the doctrine of justification. Chemnitz drafted a compendium of doctrine and reorganized the structure of the church in Wolfenbüttel; later, he led efforts to reconcile divisions within Lutheranism, culminating in the Formula of Concord*. One of his chief theological accomplishments was a modification of the christological doctrine of the *communicatio idiomatium*, which provided a Lutheran platform for understanding the sacramental presence of Christ's humanity in the Eucharist.

David Chytraeus (1531–1600). German Lutheran professor, theologian and biblical exegete. At the age of eight Chytraeus was admitted to the University of Tübingen. There he studied law, philology, philosophy, and theology, finally receiving his master's degree in 1546. Chytraeus befriended Philipp Melanchthon* while sojourning in Wittenberg, where he taught the *Loci communes*. While teaching exegesis at the University of Rostock Chytraeus became acquainted with Tilemann Heshusius,* who strongly influenced Chytraeus away from Philippist theology. As a defender of Gnesio-Lutheran theology Chytraeus helped organize churches throughout Austria in accordance with the Augsburg Confession.* Chytraeus coauthored the Formula of Concord* with Martin Chemnitz,* Andreas Musculus (1514–1581), Nikolaus Selnecker* and Jakob Andreae.* He wrote commentaries on most of the Bible, as well as a devotional work titled *Regula vitae* (1555) that described the Christian virtues.

David Clarkson (1622–1686). English Puritan theologian. After his dismissal from the pastorate on account of the Act of Uniformity (1662), little is known about Clarkson. At the end of his life he ministered with John Owen* in London.

Robert Cleaver (1571–1613). English Puritan pastor. Cleaver served as rector at Drayton in

Oxfordshire until silenced by Archbishop Richard Bancroft for advocating Nonconformity. Despite opposition from ecclesiastical authorities, Cleaver enjoyed a reputation as an excellent preacher. His published works include sermons on Hebrews 4 and Song of Songs 2 as well as one on the last chapter of Proverbs. Cleaver also authored *The Parsimony of Christian Children*, which contained a defense of infant baptism against Baptist criticisms.

John Colet (1467–1519). English Catholic priest, preacher and educator. Colet, appointed dean of Saint Paul's Cathedral by Henry VII, was a friend of Desiderius Erasmus,* on whose classical ideals Colet reconstructed the curriculum of Saint Paul's school. Colet was convinced that the foundation of moral reform lay in the education of children. Though an ardent advocate of reform, Colet, like Erasmus, remained loyal to the Catholic Church throughout his life. Colet's agenda of reform was oriented around spiritual and ethical themes, demonstrated in his commentaries on select books of the New Testament and the writings of Pseudo-Dionysius the Areopagite.

Gasparo Contarini (1483–1542). Italian statesman, theologian and reform-minded cardinal. Contarini was an able negotiator and graceful compromiser. Charles V requested Contarini as the papal legate for the Colloquy of Regensburg (1541), where Contarini reached agreement with Melanchthon* on the doctrine of justification (although neither the pope nor Luther* ratified the agreement). He had come to a similar belief in the priority of faith in the work of Christ rather than works as the basis for Christian life in 1511, though unlike Luther, he never left the papal church over the issue; instead he remainied within it to try to seek gentle reform, and he adhered to papal sacramental teaching. Contarini was an important voice for reform within the Catholic Church, always seeking reconciliation rather than confrontation with Protestant reformers. He wrote many works, including a treatise detailing the ideal bishop, a manual for lay church leaders, a political text on right governance and brief commentaries on the Pauline letters.

John Cosin (1594–1672). Anglican preacher and bishop. Early in his career Cosin was the vice chancellor of Cambridge and canon at the Durham cathedral. But as a friend of William Laud* and an advocate for "Laudian" changes, he was suspected of being a crypto-Catholic. In 1640 during the Long Parliament a Puritan lodged a complaint with the House of Commons concerning Cosin's "popish innovations." Cosin was promptly removed from office. During the turmoil of the English Civil Wars, Cosin sojourned in Paris among English nobility but struggled financially. Cosin returned to England after the Restoration in 1660 to be consecrated as the bishop of Durham. He published annotations on the Book of Common Prayer* and a history of the canon.

Council of Constance (1414–1418). Convened to resolve the Western Schism, root out heresy and reform the church in head and members, the council asserted in *Sacrosancta* (1415) the immediate authority of ecumenical councils assembled in the Holy Spirit under Christ—even over the pope. Martin V was elected pope in 1417 after the three papal claimants were deposed; thus, the council ended the schism. The council condemned Jan Hus,* Jerome of Prague (c. 1365–1416) and, posthumously, John Wycliffe. Hus and Jerome, despite letters of safe conduct, were burned at the stake. Their deaths ignited the Hussite Wars, which ended as a result of the Council of Basel's concessions to the Bohemian church. The council fathers sought to reform the church through the regular convocation of councils (*Frequens*; 1417). Martin V begrudgingly complied by calling the required councils, then immediately disbanding them. Pius II (r. 1458–1464) reasserted papal dominance through *Execrabilis* (1460), which condemned any appeal to a future council apart from the pope's authority.

Council of Trent (1545–1563) Convoked by Pope Paul III (r. 1534–1549) with the support of Charles V*, the nineteenth ecumenical council was convened in the northern Italian city of Trent. Attended primarily by Italian clerics, it met in three distinct phases. Beginning in December 1545, during its first eight sessions, the council issued doctrinal decrees, asserting the authority of tradition alongside Scripture, the authenticity of the Vulgate, the prerogative of the church in interpretation, and the necessity of human cooperation in the work of salvation. Ecclesial abuses were also addressed, as attempts were made to eliminate absenteeism and pluralism and devolve power from Rome to bishoprics and parishes. The council was suspended following the outbreak of the plague in Trent in March 1547. A number of Protestant delegates were present during the second phase of the council, which met between May 1551 and April 1552 under the supervision of Pope Julius III (r. 1550–1555). The primary achievement of this period of the council was the clarification of teachings on the seven sacraments, with transubstantiation, the objective efficacy of the Eucharist, and the necessity of auricular confession confirmed as dogma. Reconvened by Pope Pius IV (r. 1559–1565) in 1561, the third phase of the council addressed the relationship between bishops and Rome, resulting in affirmations of the divine appointment of the church hierarchy and the obligation of bishops to reside in their dioceses. Clerical education, the regulation of marriage, and teachings on purgatory, indulgences, the use of images, and the saints were also addressed.

Miles Coverdale (1488–1568). Anglican bishop. Coverdale is known for his translations of the Bible into English, completing William Tyndale's* efforts and later producing the Great Bible commissioned by Henry VIII (1539). A former friar, Coverdale was among the Cambridge scholars who met at the White Horse Tavern to discuss Martin Luther's* ideas. During Coverdale's three terms of exile in Europe, he undertook various translations, including the Geneva Bible*. He was appointed bishop of Exeter by Thomas Cranmer* and served as chaplain to Edward VI. Coverdale contributed to Cranmer's first edition of the Book of Common Prayer.*

William Cowper (Couper) (1568–1619). Scottish Puritan bishop. After graduating from the University of St. Andrews, Cowper worked in par-

ish ministry for twenty-five years before becoming bishop. As a zealous Puritan and advocate of regular preaching and rigorous discipline, Cowper championed Presbyterian polity and lay participation in church government. Cowper published devotional works, sermon collections and a commentary on Revelation.

Thomas Cranmer (1489–1556). Anglican archbishop and theologian. Cranmer supervised church reform and produced the first two editions of the Book of Common Prayer.* As a doctoral student at Cambridge, he was involved in the discussions at the White Horse Tavern. Cranmer contributed to a religious defense of Henry VIII's divorce; Henry then appointed him Archbishop of Canterbury. Cranmer cautiously steered the course of reform, accelerating under Edward VI. After supporting the attempted coup to prevent Mary's assuming the throne, Cranmer was convicted of treason and burned at the stake. Cranmer's legacy is the splendid English of his liturgy and prayer books.

Richard Crashaw (1612–1649). English Catholic poet. Educated at Cambridge, Crashaw was fluent in Hebrew, Greek and Latin. His first volume of poetry was *Epigrammatum sacrorum liber* (1634). Despite being born into a Puritan family, Crashaw was attracted to Catholicism, finally converting in 1644 after he was forced to resign his fellowship for not signing the Solemn League and Covenant (1643). In 1649, he was made a subcanon of Our Lady of Loretto by Cardinal Palotta.

Herbert Croft (1603–1691). Anglican bishop. As a boy Croft converted to Catholicism; he returned to the Church of England during his studies at Oxford. Before the English Civil Wars, he served as chaplain to Charles I. After the Restoration, Charles II appointed him as bishop. Croft ardently opposed Catholicism in his later years.

John Crompe (d. 1661). Anglican priest. Educated at Cambridge, Crompe published a commentary on the Apostles' Creed, a sermon on Psalm 21:3 and an exposition of Christ's passion.

Caspar Cruciger (1504–1548). German Lutheran theologian. Recognized for his alignment with the theological views of Philipp Melanchthon,*

Cruciger was a scholar respected among both Protestants and Catholics. In 1521, Cruciger came Wittenberg to study Hebrew and remained there most of his life. He became a valuable partner for Martin Luther* in translating the Old Testament and served as teacher, delegate to major theological colloquies and rector. Cruciger was an agent of reform in his birthplace of Leipzig, where at the age of fifteen he had observed the disputation between Luther and Johann Eck.*

Ralph Cudworth (d. 1624) English Protestant minister. Father of noted Cambridge Platonist Ralph Cudworth (1617–1688), the elder Cudworth was a fellow of Emanuel College, Cambridge and rector of Aller in Somersetshire.

Marguerite d'Angoulême (1492–1549). French Catholic noblewoman. The elder sister of King Francis I of France, Marguerite was the Queen of Navarre and Duchess of Alençon and Berry. She was a poet and author of the French Renaissance. She composed *The Mirror of a Sinful Soul* (1531)—condemned by the theologians of the Sorbonne for containing Lutheran ideas—and an unfinished collection of short stories, the *Heptaméron* (1558). A leading figure in the French Reformation, Marguerite was at the center of a network of reform-minded individuals that included Guillame Briçonnet,* Jacques Lefèvre d'Etaples,* Gérard Roussel (1500–1550) and Guillame Farel (1489–1565).

Jakob Dachser (1486–1567). German Anabaptist theologian and hymnist. Dachser served as a Catholic priest in Vienna until he was imprisoned and then exiled for defending the Lutheran understanding of the Mass and fasting. Hans Hut* rebaptized him in Augsburg, where Dachser was appointed as a leader of the Anabaptist congregation. Lutheran authorities imprisoned him for nearly four years. In 1531 he recanted his Radical beliefs and began to catechize children with the permission of the city council. Dachser was expelled from Augsburg as a possible insurrectionist in 1552 and relocated to Pfalz-Neuberg. He published a number of poems, hymns and mystical works, and he versified several psalms.

Jean Daillé (1594–1670). French Reformed pastor. Born into a devout Reformed family, Daillé studied theology and philosophy at Saumur under the most influential contemporary lay leader in French Protestantism, Philippe Duplessis-Mornay (1549–1623). Daillé held to Amyraldianism—the belief that Christ died for all humanity inclusively, not particularly for the elect who would inherit salvation (though only the elect are in fact saved). He wrote a controversial treatise on the church fathers that aggravated many Catholic and Anglican scholars because of Daillé's apparent demotion of patristic authority in matters of faith.

Lambert Daneau (1535–1595). French Reformed pastor and theologian. After a decade of pastoring in France, following the St. Bartholomew's Day Massacre, Daneau fled to Geneva to teach theology at the Academy. He later taught in the Low Countries, finishing his career in southern France. Daneau's diverse works include tracts on science, ethics and morality as well as numerous theological and exegetical works.

John Davenant (1576–1641). Anglican bishop and professor. Davenant attended Queen's College, Cambridge, where he received his doctorate and was appointed professor of divinity. During the Remonstrant controversy, James I sent Davenant as one of the four representatives for the Church of England to the Synod of Dordrecht.* Following James's instructions, Davenant advocated a *via media* between the Calvinists and the Remonstrants, although in later years he defended against the rise of Arminianism in England. In 1621, Davenant was promoted to the bishopric of Salisbury, where he was generally receptive to Laudian reforms. Davenant's lectures on Colossians are his best-known work.

Defense of the Augsburg Confession (1531). See *Augsburg Confession.*

Hans Denck (c. 1500–1527). German Radical theologian. Denck, a crucial early figure of the German Anabaptist movement, combined medieval German mysticism with the radical sacramental theology of Andreas Bodenstein von Karlstadt* and Thomas Müntzer.* Denck argued that the exterior forms of Scripture and sacrament are symbolic witnesses secondary to the internally revealed truth of the Sprit in the human soul. This view led to his expulsion from Nuremberg in 1525; he spent the next two years in various centers of reform in the German territories. At the time of his death, violent persecution against Anabaptists was on the rise throughout northern Europe.

Stephen Denison (unknown). English Puritan pastor. Denison received the post of curate at St. Katherine Cree in London sometime in the 1610s, where he ministered until his ejection from office in 1635. During his career at St. Katherine Cree, Denison waded into controversy with both Puritans (over the doctrine of predestination) and Anglicans (over concerns about liturgical ceremonies). He approached both altercations with rancor and rigidity, although he seems to have been quite popular and beloved by most of his congregation. In 1631, William Laud* consecrated the newly renovated St. Katherine Cree, and as part of the festivities Denison offered a sermon on Luke 19:27 in which he publicly rebuked Laud for fashioning the Lord's house into a "den of robbers." Aside from the record of his quarrels, very little is known about Denison. In addition to *The White Wolf* (a 1627 sermon against another opponent), he published a catechism for children (1621), a treatise on the sacraments (1621) and a commentary on 2 Peter 1 (1622).

Marie Dentière (1495–1561). Belgian Reformed theologian. Dentière relinquished her monastic vows and married Simon Robert (d.1533), a former priest, in Strasbourg. After Robert died, she married Antoine Froment (1508–1581), a reformer in Geneva, and became involved in the reform of that city. Her best-known writings are a tract addressed to Marguerite d'Angoulême,* the *Very Useful Epistle* (1539), in which she espoused the evangelical faith and the right of women to interpret and teach scripture, and a preface to Calvin's sermon on 1 Timothy 2:8-12. Dentière is the only woman to have her name inscribed on the International Monument to the Reformation in Geneva.

Edward Dering (c.1540–1576). English Puritan preacher. An early Puritan, Dering's prospects of advancement in the Elizabethan church were

effectively ended after a sermon in front of the Queen in which he described her as an "untamed and unruly heifer" while criticizing the state of the church and clergy. While continuing with intemperate and critical attacks throughout his career, Dering established himself as a preacher at St. Paul's Cathedral in London, where he became known for his pastoral concern and desire to teach the assurance of salvation.

David Dickson (1583?–1663). Scottish Reformed pastor, preacher, professor and theologian. Dickson defended the Presbyterian form of ecclesial reformation in Scotland and was recognized for his iteration of Calvinist federal theology and expository biblical commentaries. Dickson served for over twenty years as professor of philosophy at the University of Glasgow before being appointed professor of divinity. He opposed the imposition of Episcopalian measures on the church in Scotland and was active in political and ecclesial venues to protest and prohibit such influences. Dickson was removed from his academic post following his refusal of the oath of supremacy during the Restoration era.

Veit Dietrich (1506–1549). German Lutheran preacher and theologian. Dietrich intended to study medicine at the University of Wittenberg, but Martin Luther* and Philipp Melanchthon* convinced him to study theology instead. Dietrich developed a strong relationship with Luther, accompanying him to the Marburg Colloquy (1529) and to Coburg Castle during the Diet of Augsburg (1530). After graduating, Dietrich taught on the arts faculty, eventually becoming dean. In 1535 he returned to his hometown, Nuremberg, to pastor. Later in life, Dietrich worked with Melanchthon to reform the church in Regensburg. In 1547, when Charles V arrived in Nuremberg, Dietrich was suspended from the pastorate; he resisted the imposition of the Augsburg Interim to no avail. In addition to transcribing some of Luther's lectures, portions of the Table Talk and the very popular *Hauspostille* (1544), Dietrich published his own sermons for children, a manual for pastors and a summary of the Bible.

Giovanni Diodati (1576–1649). Italian Reformed theologian. Diodati was from an Italian banking family who fled for religious reasons to Geneva. There he trained under Theodore Beza;* on completion of his doctoral degree, Diodati became professor of Hebrew at the academy. He was an ecclesiastical representative of the church in Geneva (for whom he was a delegate at the Synod of Dordrecht*) and an advocate for reform in Venice. Diodati's chief contribution to the Italian reform movement was a translation of the Bible into Italian (1640–1641), which remains the standard translation in Italian Protestantism.

John Dod (c. 1549–1645). English Puritan pastor. Over the course of his lengthy pastoral career (spanning roughly sixty years), Dod was twice suspended for nonconformity and twice reinstated. A popular preacher, he published many sermons as well as commentaries on the Ten Commandments and the Lord's Prayer; collections of his sayings and anecdotes were compiled after his death.

John Donne (1572–1631). Anglican poet and preacher. Donne was born into a strong Catholic family. However, sometime between his brother's death from the plague while in prison in 1593 and the publication of his *Pseudo-Martyr* in 1610, Donne joined the Church of England. Ordained to the Anglican priesthood in 1615 and already widely recognized for his verse, Donne quickly rose to prominence as a preacher—some have deemed him the best of his era. His textual corpus is an amalgam of erotic *and* divine poetry (e.g., "Batter My Heart"), as well as a great number of sermons.

Dordrecht Confession (1632). Dutch Mennonite confession. Adriaan Cornelisz (1581–1632) wrote the Dordrecht Confession to unify Dutch Mennonites. This basic statement of Mennonite belief and practice affirms distinctive doctrines such as nonresistance, shunning, footwashing and the refusal to swear oaths. Most continental Mennonites subscribed to this confession during the second half of the seventeenth century.

John Downame (c. 1571–1652). English Puritan pastor and theologian. See *English Annotations*.

Charles Drelincourt (1595–1669). French Reformed pastor, theologian and controversialist. After studying at Saumur Academy, Drelincourt pastored the Reformed Church in Paris for nearly fifty years. He was well known for his ministry to the sick. In addition to polemical works against Catholicism, he published numerous pastoral resources: catechisms, three volumes of sermons and a five-volume series on consolation for the suffering.

The Dutch Annotations (1657). See *Statenvertaling*.

Daniel Dyke (d. 1614). English Puritan preacher. Born of nonconformist stock, Dyke championed a more thorough reformation of church practice in England. After the promulgation of John Whitgift's* articles in 1583, Dyke refused to accept what he saw as remnants of Catholicism, bringing him into conflict with the bishop of London. Despite the petitions of his congregation and some politicians, the bishop of London suspended Dyke from his ministry for refusing priestly ordination and conformity to the Book of Common Prayer.* All of his work was published posthumously; it is mostly focused on biblical interpretation.

Johann Eck (Johann Maier of Eck) (1486–1543). German Catholic theologian. Though Eck was not an antagonist of Martin Luther* until the dispute over indulgences, Luther's Ninety-five Theses (1517) sealed the two as adversaries. After their debate at the Leipzig Disputation (1519), Eck participated in the writing of the papal bull that led to Luther's excommunication. Much of Eck's work was written to oppose Protestantism or to defend Catholic doctrine and the papacy; his *Enchiridion* was a manual written to counter Protestant doctrine. However, Eck was also deeply invested in the status of parish preaching, publishing a five-volume set of postils. He participated in the assemblies at Regensburg and Augsburg and led the Catholics in their rejection of the Augsburg Confession.

Elizabeth I of England (1533–1603) English monarch. The daughter of Henry VIII (r. 1509–1547) and Anne Boleyn (c. 1501–1536), Elizabeth outwardly conformed to Catholicism during the reign of her sister Mary I (r. 1553–1558), but her

Protestant upbringing encouraged the hopes of many reformers upon her accession in 1558. With the 1559 Elizabethan Settlement, Elizabeth redefined England as a Protestant country, with the Act of Supremacy asserting the monarch as the head of the English church, and the Act of Uniformity establishing the 1559 *Book of Common Prayer** as the valid order of service within the realm. However, Elizabeth resisted the aggressive persecution of Catholics for political reasons, while also allowing some traditional vestments, furniture and ceremonies to be retained. Her moderate and pragmatic reforms frustrated many who wished for more thorough change and led to the emergence of the Puritan movement. Elizabeth faced numerous threats during her reign, including the machinations of Scottish Catholics and claims to the throne of Mary Stuart (1542–1547), leading to her rival's imprisonment and execution in 1587; the attempted invasion of England by Spain, which culminated in the celebrated defeat of the Spanish Armada in 1588; and a Catholic rebellion in Ireland that was suppressed during the Nine Years War (1594–1603). Elizabeth never married, and was succeeded on the throne by James I* following her death in 1603.

English Annotations (1645; 1651; 1657). Under a commission from the Westminster Assembly, the editors of the English Annotations—John Downame* along with unnamed colleagues—translated, collated and digested in a compact and accessible format several significant Continental biblical resources, including Calvin's* commentaries, Beza's* *Annotationes majores* and Diodati's* *Annotations*.

Desiderius Erasmus (1466–1536). Dutch Catholic humanist and pedagogue. Erasmus, a celebrated humanist scholar, was recognized for translations of ancient texts, reform of education according to classical studies, moral and spiritual writings and the first printed edition of the Greek New Testament. A former Augustinian who never left the Catholic Church, Erasmus addressed deficiencies he saw in the church and society, challenging numerous prevailing doctrines but advocating reform. He envisioned a simple, spiritual Christian life shaped by the teachings of Jesus and ancient wisdom. He was often accused of collusion with Martin Luther* on account of some resonance of their ideas but hotly debated Luther on human will.

Paul Fagius (1504–1549). German Reformed Hebraist and pastor. After studying at the University of Heidelberg, Fagius went to Strasbourg where he perfected his Hebrew under Wolfgang Capito.* In Isny im Allgäu (Baden-Württemberg) he met the great Jewish grammarian Elias Levita (1469–1549), with whom he established a Hebrew printing press. In 1544 Fagius returned to Strasbourg, succeeding Capito as preacher and Old Testament lecturer. During the Augsburg Interim, Fagius (with Martin Bucer*) accepted Thomas Cranmer's* invitation to translate and interpret the Bible at Cambridge. However, Fagius died before he could begin any of the work. Fagius wrote commentaries on the first four chapters of Genesis and the deuterocanonical books of Sirach and Tobit.

Guillaume Farel (1489–1565) French Reformed preacher and theologian. At the vanguard of the French Reformation, Farel was a student of Jacques Lefèvre d'Étaples* and member of Archbishop Briçonnet's* circle in Meaux until his desire for more rapid change saw him depart in 1523 to preach the Protestant message in Basel, Montbéliard, Strasbourg, Bern, and Aigle. During this period of his ministry, he composed the first French Protestant book, an evangelical commentary on the Lord's Prayer and the Apostle's Creed, as well as the first French Confession of Faith. A catalyst in Geneva's acceptance of the Reformation in 1536, it was Farel who persuaded Calvin* to settle in the city. After he and Calvin were banished from Geneva in 1538, Farel accepted the pastorate in Neuchâtel, a position he held until his death while continuing to travel and support the Reformation in the French-speaking lands.

John Fary (unknown). English Puritan pastor. Fary authored *God's Severity on Man's Sterility* (1645), a sermon on the fruitless fig tree in Luke 13:6-9.

William Fenner (1600–1640). English Puritan pastor. After studying at Cambridge and Oxford,

Fenner ministered at Sedgley and Rochford. Fenner's extant writings, which primarily deal with practical and devotional topics, demonstrate a zealous Puritan piety and a keen interest in Scripture and theology.

First Helvetic Confession (1536). Anticipating the planned church council at Mantua (1537, but delayed until 1545 at Trent), Reformed theologians of the Swiss cantons drafted a confession to distinguish themselves from both Catholics and the churches of the Augsburg Confession.* Heinrich Bullinger* led the discussion and wrote the confession itself; Leo Jud, Oswald Myconius, Simon Grynaeus and others were part of the assembly. Martin Bucer* and Wolfgang Capito* had desired to draw the Lutheran and Reformed communions closer together through this document, but Luther* proved unwilling after Bullinger refused to accept the Wittenberg Concord (1536). This confession was largely eclipsed by Bullinger's Second Helvetic Confession.*

John Fisher (1469–1535). English Catholic bishop and theologian. This reputed preacher defended Catholic orthodoxy and strove to reform abuses in the church. In 1521 Henry VIII honored Fisher with the title *Fidei Defensor* ("defender of the faith"). Nevertheless, Fisher opposed the king's divorce of Catherine of Aragon (1485–1536) and the independent establishment of the Church of England; he was convicted for treason and executed. Most of Fisher's works are polemical and occasional (e.g., on transubstantiation, against Martin Luther*); however, he also published a series of sermons on the seven penitential psalms. In addition to his episcopal duties, Fisher was the chancellor of Cambridge from 1504 until his death.

Matthias Flacius (1520–1575). Lutheran theologian. A native of Croatia, Matthias Flacius commenced his studies at the University of Tubingen, and completed them at Wittenberg, where through Luther's influence, he embraced the university's evangelical theology. Flacius began his career as instructor of Hebrew at the University of Wittenberg in 1544, and remained in this post until 1549. As a devoted follower of Luther's teachings, Flacius sought to defend them in their purity which drove him and Nikolaus von Amsdorf as leaders of the Gnesio-Lutherans to oppose the more moderate positions of Philipp Melanchthon and his sympathizers, the Philippists, in several controversies concerning the role of free will and good works in justification as well as relations with Calvinism. After serving as a professor at the University of Jena (1557–1561), Flacius spent the remainder of his life as an independent scholar, frequently moving from one city to another to escape persecution. Flacius died in Frankfurt am Main in 1575. His important exegetical works are *De vocabula Dei* (1549), *Clavis Scripturae Sacrae* (1567), and *Glossa Novi Testamenti* (1570). Flacius also published two historical works, *Catalogus Testium Veritatis* (1556) and the *Magdeburg Centuries.*

John Flavel (c. 1630–1691). English Puritan pastor. Trained at Oxford, Flavel ministered in southwest England from 1650 until the Act of Uniformity in 1662, which reaffirmed the compulsory use of the Book of Common Prayer. Flavel preached unofficially for many years, until his congregation was eventually allowed to build a meeting place in 1687. His works were numerous, varied and popular.

Giovanni Battista Folengo (1490–1559). Italian Catholic exegete. In 1528 Folengo left the Benedictine order, questioning the validity of monastic vows; he returned to the monastic life in 1534. During this hiatus Folengo came into contact with the Neapolitan reform-minded circle founded by Juan de Valdés.* Folengo published commentaries on the Psalms, John, 1–2 Peter and James. Augustin Marlorat* included Folengo's comment in his anthology of exegesis on the Psalms. In 1580 Folengo's Psalms commentary was added to the Index of Prohibited Books.

Formula of Concord (1577). After Luther's* death, intra-Lutheran controversies between the Gnesio-Lutherans (partisans of Luther) and the Philippists (partisans of Melanchthon*) threatened to cause a split among those who had subscribed to the Augsburg Confession.* In 1576, Jakob

Andreae,* Martin Chemnitz,* Nikolaus Selnecker,* David Chytraeus* and Andreas Musculus (1514–1581) met with the intent of resolving the controversies, which mainly regarded the relationship between good works and salvation, the third use of the law, and the role of the human will in accepting God's grace. In 1580, celebrating the fiftieth anniversary of the presentation of the Augsburg Confession to Charles V (1500–1558), the *Book of Concord* was printed as the authoritative interpretation of the Augsburg Confession; it included the three ancient creeds, the Augsburg Confession, its Apology (1531), the Schmalkald Articles,* Luther's *Treatise on the Power and Primacy of the Pope* (1537) and both his Small and Large Catechisms (1529).

Sebastian Franck (1499–1542). German Radical theologian. Franck became a Lutheran in 1525, but by 1529 he began to develop ideas that distanced him from Protestants and Catholics. Expelled from Strasbourg and later Ulm due to his controversial writings, Franck spent the end of his life in Basel. Franck emphasized God's word as a divine internal spark that cannot be adequately expressed in outward forms. Thus he criticized religious institutions and dogmas. His work consists mostly of commentaries, compilations and translations. In his sweeping historical *Chronica* (1531), Franck supported numerous heretics condemned by the Catholic Church and criticized political and church authorities.

Leonhard Frick (d. 1528). Austrian Radical martyr. See *Kunstbuch.*

Gallic Confession (1559). This confession was accepted at the first National Synod of the Reformed Churches of France (1559). It was intended to be a touchstone of Reformed faith but also to show to the people of France that the Huguenots—who faced persecution—were not seditious. The French Reformed Church presented this confession to Francis II (1544–1560) in 1560, and to his successor, Charles IX (1550–1574), in 1561. The later Genevan draft, likely written by Calvin,* Beza* and Pierre Viret (1511–1571), was received as the true Reformed confession at the

seventh National Synod in La Rochelle (1571).

Geneva Bible (originally printed 1560). During Mary I's reign many English Protestants sought safety abroad in Reformed territories of the Empire and the Swiss Cantons, especially in Calvin's* Geneva. A team of English exiles in Geneva led by William Whittingham (c. 1524–1579) brought this complete translation to press in the course of two years. Notable for several innovations—Roman type, verse numbers, italics indicating English idiom and not literal phrasing of the original languages, even variant readings in the Gospels and Acts—this translation is most well known for its marginal notes, which reflect a strongly Calvinist theology. The notes explained Scripture in an accessible way for the laity, also giving unlearned clergy a new sermon resource. Although controversial because of its implicit critique of royal power, this translation was wildly popular; even after the publication of the Authorized Version (1611) and James I's 1616 ban on its printing, the Geneva Bible continued to be the most popular English translation until after the English Civil Wars.

Johann Gerhard (1582–1637). German Lutheran theologian, professor and superintendent. Gerhard is considered one of the most eminent Lutheran theologians, after Martin Luther* and Martin Chemnitz.* After studying patristics and Hebrew at Wittenberg, Jena and Marburg, Gerhard was appointed superintendent at the age of twenty-four. In 1616 he was appointed to a post at the University of Jena, where he reintroduced Aristotelian metaphysics to theology and gained widespread fame. His most important work was the nine-volume *Loci Theologici* (1610–1625). He also expanded Chemnitz's harmony of the Gospels (*Harmonia Evangelicae*), which was finally published by Polykarp Leyser (1552–1610) in 1593. Gerhard was well-known for an irenic spirit and an ability to communicate clearly.

George Gifford (c. 1548–1600). English Puritan pastor. Gifford was suspended for nonconformity in 1584. With private support, however, he was able to continue his ministry. Through his published works he wanted to help develop lay piety and biblical literacy.

Anthony Gilby (c. 1510–1585). English Puritan translator. During Mary I's reign, Gilby fled to Geneva, where he assisted William Whittingham (c. 1524–1579) with the Geneva Bible.* He returned to England to pastor after Elizabeth I's accession. In addition to translating numerous continental Reformed works into English—especially those of John Calvin* and Theodore Beza*—Gilby also wrote commentaries on Micah and Malachi.

Bernard Gilpin (1517–1583). Anglican theologian and priest. In public disputations, Gilpin defended Roman Catholic theology against John Hooper (c. 1495-1555) and Peter Martyr Vermigli.* These debates caused Gilpin to reexamine his faith. Upon Mary I's accession, Gilpin resigned his benefice. He sojourned in Belgium and France, returning to pastoral ministry in England in 1556. Gilpin dedicated himself to a preaching circuit in northern England, thus earning the moniker "the Apostle to the North." His zealous preaching and almsgiving roused royal opposition and a warrant for his arrest. On his way to the queen's commission, Gilpin fractured his leg, delaying his arrival in London until after Mary's death and thus likely saving his life. His only extant writing is a sermon on Luke 2 confronting clerical abuses.

Paul Glock (c. 1530–1585). German Radical preacher. A teenage convert to Hutterite Anabaptism, Glock spent nineteen years imprisoned at Hohenwittlingen, unwilling to recant. While incarcerated, he wrote hymns, a confession and defense of his beliefs, and numerous letters that proved influential in the development of Anabaptist thought. After helping extinguish a fire at the prison in 1576, Glock was freed and settled with the Brethren in Moravia.

Glossa ordinaria. This standard collection of biblical commentaries consists of interlinear and marginal notes drawn from patristic and Carolingian exegesis appended to the Vulgate*; later editions also include Nicholas of Lyra's* *Postilla*. The *Glossa ordinaria* and the *Sentences* of Peter Lombard (c. 1100–1160) were essential resources for all late medieval and early modern commentators.

Simon Goulart (1543–1628) French Reformed pastor, translator, and theologian. Goulart spent most of his career as a pastor in Geneva and its surrounds, particularly at the city parish of St. Gervais, and was the leader of the Company of Pastors during the last decades of his life. A prolific translator, he published numerous French editions of classical, patristic, and contemporary works from diverse authors including Plutarch, Seneca, Chrysostom, Cyprian, Tertullian, Beza*, Perkins* and Vermigli*. He also composed numerous devotional writings, important histories of early French Protestantism, and polemical treatises supporting the Huguenot cause.

Conrad Grebel (c. 1498–1526). Swiss Radical theologian. Grebel, considered the father of the Anabaptist movement, was one of the first defenders and performers of believers' baptism, for which he was eventually imprisoned in Zurich. One of Huldrych Zwingli's* early compatriots, Grebel advocated rapid, radical reform, clashing publicly with the civil authorities and Zwingli. Grebel's views, particularly on baptism, were influenced by Andreas Bodenstein von Karlstadt* and Thomas Müntzer.* Grebel advocated elimination of magisterial involvement in governing the church; instead, he envisioned the church as lay Christians determining their own affairs with strict adherence to the biblical text, and unified in volitional baptism.

William Greenhill (1591–1671). English Puritan pastor. Greenhill attended and worked at Magdalen College. He ministered in the diocese of Norwich but soon left for London, where he preached at Stepney. Greenhill was a member of the Westminster Assembly of Divines and was appointed the parliament chaplain by the children of Charles I. Oliver Cromwell included him among the preachers who helped draw up the Savoy Declaration. Greenhill was evicted from his post following the Restoration, after which he pastored independently. Among Greenhill's most significant contributions to church history was his *Exposition of the Prophet of Ezekiel*.

Catharina Regina von Greiffenberg (1633–1694). Austrian Lutheran poet. Upon her adulthood her guardian (and half uncle) sought to marry her; despite her protests of their consanguinity and her desire to remain celibate, she relented in 1664. After the deaths of her mother and husband, Greiffenberg abandoned her home to debtors and joined her friends Susanne Popp (d. 1683) and Sigmund von Birken (1626–1681) in Nuremberg. During her final years she dedicated herself to studying the biblical languages and to writing meditations on Jesus' death and resurrection, which she never completed. One of the most important and learned Austrian poets of the Baroque period, Greiffenberg published a collection of sonnets, songs and poems (1662) as well as three sets of mystical meditations on Jesus' life, suffering and death (1672; 1683; 1693). She participated in a society of poets called the Ister Gesellschaft.

Lady Jane Grey (1537–1554). English Protestant monarch, sometimes known as "the Nine Days Queen." The eldest daughter of Henry Grey and Frances Brandon, the daughter of Henry VIII's* younger sister Mary, Jane received an extensive Protestant and humanist education. She married Lord Guildford Dudley (c. 1535–1554), son of Edward VI's* chief minister John Dudley, Duke of Northumberland (1504–1553). Seeking to avoid succession by Edward's Catholic half-sister Mary I, Edward and Northumberland conspired to alter the order of succession, naming Jane as heir in the king's will. Following Edward's death, Jane reluctantly took the crown on July 9, 1553, but Northumberland and other Protestants were unable to raise adequate support for her claim and the Privy Council proclaimed Mary queen on July 19. Upon Mary's accession, Jane was imprisoned in the Tower of London and after trial was executed alongside her husband for treason. A handful of her writings exist demonstrating her religious affections, while the story of her martyrdom is prominent in John Foxe's Acts and Monuments.

Argula von Grumbach (c. 1490–c. 1564) German Lutheran noblewoman. Grumbach, an attendant of Queen Kunigunde of Austria (1465–1520), was one of the first women to publish in support of the Reformation. She is best known for letters from 1523 and 1524 written in defense of Arsacius Seehofer (1503–1545), a lecturer at the university of Ingolstadt accused of Lutheranism. For unknown reasons, Grumberg ceased to publish after 1524, although her private correspondence after this time demonstrates a continued effort to support evangelical reform.

Rudolf Gwalther (1519–1586). Swiss Reformed preacher. Gwalther was a consummate servant of the Reformed church in Zurich, its chief religious officer and preacher, a responsibility fulfilled previously by Huldrych Zwingli* and Heinrich Bullinger.* Gwalther provided sermons and commentaries and translated the works of Zwingli into Latin. He worked for many years alongside Bullinger in structuring and governing the church in Zurich. Gwalther also strove to strengthen the connections to the Reformed churches on the Continent and England: he was a participant in the Colloquy of Regensburg (1541) and an opponent of the Formula of Concord.*

Hans Has von Hallstatt (d. 1527). Austrian Reformed pastor. See *Kunstbuch*.

Henry Hammond (1605–1660). Anglican priest. After completing his studies at Oxford, Hammond was ordained in 1629. A Royalist, Hammond helped recruit soldiers for the king; he was chaplain to Charles I. During the king's captivity, Hammond was imprisoned for not submitting to Parliament. Later he was allowed to pastor again, until his death. Hammond published a catechism, numerous polemical sermons and treatises as well as his *Paraphrase and Annotations on the New Testament* (1653).

Jörg Haug (Unknown) German Anabaptist leader. Haug was a radical preacher during the 1525 Peasant's Revolt and composed a tract entitled *A Christian Order of a True Christian* (1524) enumerating seven degrees of faith reached by Christians.

Peter Hausted (d. 1645). Anglican priest and playwright. Educated at Cambridge and Oxford, Hausted ministered in a number of parishes and preached adamantly and vehemently against

Puritanism. He is best known for his play *The Rival Friends*, which is filled with invective against the Puritans; during a performance before the king and queen, a riot nearly broke out. Haustead died during the siege of Banbury Castle.

Heidelberg Catechism (1563). This German Reformed catechism was commissioned by the elector of the Palatinate, Frederick III (1515–1576) for pastors and teachers in his territories to use in instructing children and new believers in the faith. It was written by theologian Zacharias Ursinus (1534–1583) in consultation with Frederick's court preacher Kaspar Olevianus* and the entire theology faculty at the University of Heidelberg. The Heidelberg Catechism was accepted as one of the Dutch Reformed Church's Three Forms of Unity—along with the Belgic Confession* and the Canons of Dordrecht—at the Synod of Dordrecht,* and became widely popular among other Reformed confessional traditions throughout Europe.

Niels Hemmingsen (1513–1600). Danish Lutheran theologian. Hemmingsen studied at the University of Wittenberg, where he befriended Philipp Melanchthon.* In 1542, Hemmingsen returned to Denmark to pastor and to teach Greek, dialectics and theology at the University of Copenhagen. Foremost of the Danish theologians, Hemmingsen oversaw the preparation and publication of the first Danish Bible (1550). Later in his career he became embroiled in controversies because of his Philippist theology, especially regarding the Eucharist. Due to rising tensions with Lutheran nobles outside of Denmark, King Frederick II (1534–1588) dismissed Hemmingsen from his university post in 1579, transferring him to a prominent but less internationally visible Cathedral outside of Copenhagen. Hemmingsen was a prolific author, writing commentaries on the New Testament and Psalms, sermon collections and several methodological, theological and pastoral handbooks.

King Henry VIII of England (1491–1547). English monarch. The second son of Henry VII (r. 1485–1509) and Elizabeth of York (1466–1503), Henry VIII succeeded his father to the English throne, his elder brother Edward having died in 1502. Soon after accession, he married his brother's widow, Catherine of Aragon (1485–1536). Following several stillbirths and the birth of a daughter, Mary, Henry, who was desperate for a male heir to head off dynastic challenges, wished separation from Catherine in order to marry Anne Boleyn (c. 1501–1536). Believing his marriage cursed as it transgressed the commands in Leviticus against marrying a brother's widow, Henry sought dispensation from the church for his annulment and remarriage. While the case was first heard by a papal legate in England, it was transferred to Rome upon the order of Pope Clement VII*, who wished to placate Charles V, Catherine's nephew, whose troops had recently sacked Rome and held the pope under house arrest. Henry asserted praemunire, arguing that as king, he was supreme in his own kingdom. With the formation of the Reformation Parliament in 1529, the legislative process to disentangle the English Church from the Roman was begun. The issue of Henry's divorce was finalized in 1533, after Thomas Cranmer* became Archbishop of Canterbury and declared his marriage to Catherine invalid. While Henry's divorce, assertion of royal supremacy, and subversion of Catholic institutions gave impetus to English Protestantism, Henry's beliefs remained essentially Catholic, and these continued to be enforced by law. He ultimately married six times, and was succeeded by Edward VI*, his son by his third wife, Jane Seymour (1508–1537). Elizabeth I*, Henry's daughter by Anne Boleyn, later became Queen and with the Elizabethan Settlement in 1559, redefined England as a Protestant country.

Tilemann Hesshus (1527–1588). German Lutheran theologian and pastor. Hesshus studied under Philipp Melanchthon* but was a staunch Gnesio-Lutheran. With great hesitation—and later regret—he affirmed the Formula of Concord.* Hesshuss ardently advocated for church discipline, considering obedience a mark of the church. Unwilling to compromise his strong convictions, especially regarding matters of discipline, Hesshus was regularly embroiled in controversy. He was expelled or pressed to leave Goslar, Rostock, Heidelberg, Bremen, Magdeburg, Wesel, Königsberg and Samland before settling in Helmstedt, where he remained until his death. He wrote numerous polemical tracts concerning ecclesiology, justification, the sacraments and original sin, as well as commentaries on Psalms, Romans, 1–2 Corinthians, Galatians, Colossians and 1–2 Timothy, and a postil collection.

Cornelis Hoen (c. 1460–1524). Dutch humanist, jurist, and theologian. A lawyer at the Court of Holland at the Hague, Hoen was prosecuted in 1523 over his sympathy for the evangelical message. He proposed a symbolic interpretation of Christ's presence in the Eucharist justified with reference to Matthew 24:23 in an influential, posthumously-published treatise.

Melchior Hoffman (1495?–1543). German Anabaptist preacher. First appearing as a Lutheran lay preacher in Livonia in 1523, Hoffman's claim to direct revelation, his perfectionist teachings and his announcements that the end of the world would occur in 1533 saw him alienated from both Lutheran and Reformed circles. After converting to Anabaptism in Strasbourg in 1530, a city he claimed would rise as the spiritual Jerusalem, Hoffman escaped brief arrest and fled to the Netherlands, where his preaching made him the first to bring the radical faith to the Low Countries. Believing himself to be Elijah, Hoffman gathered numerous followers, including future Anabaptist leaders Obbe Philips* and Jan Mathijs (d. 1534), until his arrest in Strasbourg in 1533, whereupon he was imprisoned for the final decade of his life. A tendency toward mystical allegory and apocalyptic exegesis supported by direct revelation is found in his writings, which include commentaries on Romans, Revelation, and Daniel 12 alongside numerous tracts, pamphlets, and letters.

Christopher Hooke (unknown). English Puritan physician and pastor. Hooke published a treatise promoting the joys and blessings of childbirth (1590) and a sermon on Hebrews 12:11-12. To support the poor, Hooke proposed a bank funded by voluntary investment of wealthy households.

Richard Hooker (c. 1553–1600). Anglican priest. Shortly after graduating from Corpus Christi College Oxford, Hooker took holy orders as a priest in 1581. After his marriage, he struggled to find work and temporarily tended sheep until Archbishop John Whitgift* appointed him to the Temple Church in London. Hooker's primary work is *The Laws of Ecclesiastical Polity* (1593), in which he sought to establish a philosophical and logical foundation for the highly controversial Elizabethan Religious Settlement (1559). The Elizabethan Settlement, through the Act of Supremacy, reasserted the Church of England's independence from the Church of Rome, and, through the Act of Uniformity, constructed a common church structure based on the reinstitution of the Book of Common Prayer.* Hooker's argumentation strongly emphasizes natural law and anticipates the social contract theory of John Locke (1632–1704).

John Hooper (d. 1555). English Protestant bishop and martyr. Impressed by the works of Huldrych Zwingli* and Heinrich Bullinger,* Hooper joined the Protestant movement in England. However, after the Act of Six Articles was passed, he fled to Zurich, where he spent ten years. He returned to England in 1549 and was appointed as a bishop. He stoutly advocated a Zwinglian reform agenda, arguing against the use of vestments and for a less "popish" Book of Common Prayer.* Condemned as a heretic for denying transubstantiation, Hooper was burned at the stake during Mary I's reign.

Rudolf Hospinian (Wirth) (1547–1626). Swiss Reformed theologian and minister. After studying theology at Marburg and Heidelberg, Hospinian pastored in rural parishes around Zurich and taught secondary school. In 1588, he transferred to Zurich, ministering at Grossmünster and Fraumünster. A keen student of church history, Hospinian wanted to show the differences between early church doctrine and contemporary Catholic teaching, particularly with regard to sacramental theology. He also criticized Lutheran dogma and the Formula of Concord*. Most of Hospinian's corpus consists of polemical treatises; he also published a series of sermons on the Magnificat.

Caspar Huberinus (1500–1553). German Lutheran theologian and pastor. After studying theology at Wittenberg, Huberinus moved to Augsburg to serve as Urbanus Rhegius's* assistant. Huberinus represented Augsburg at the Bern Disputation (1528) on the Eucharist and images. In 1551, along with the nobility, Huberinus supported the Augsburg Interim, so long as communion of both kinds and regular preaching were allowed. Nevertheless the people viewed him as a traitor because of his official participation in the Interim, nicknaming him "Buberinus" (i.e., scoundrel). He wrote a number of popular devotional works as well as tracts defending Lutheran eucharistic theology against Zwinglian and Anabaptist detractions.

Balthasar Hubmaier (1480/5–1528). German Radical theologian. Hubmaier, a former priest who studied under Johann Eck,* is identified with his leadership in the peasants' uprising at Waldshut. Hubmaier served as the cathedral preacher in Regensberg, where he became involved in a series of anti-Semitic attacks. He was drawn to reform through the early works of Martin Luther*; his contact with Huldrych Zwingli* made Hubmaier a defender of more radical reform, including believers' baptism and a memorialist account of the Eucharist. His involvement in the Peasants' War led to his extradition and execution by the Austrians.

Aegidius Hunnius (1550–1603). German Lutheran theologian and preacher. Educated at Tübingen by Jakob Andreae (1528–1590) and Johannes Brenz,* Hunnius bolstered and advanced early Lutheran orthodoxy. After his crusade to root out all "crypto-Calvinism" divided Hesse into Lutheran and Reformed regions, Hunnius joined the Wittenberg theological faculty, where with Polykarp Leyser (1552–1610) he helped shape the university into an orthodox stronghold. Passion-ately confessional, Hunnius developed and nuanced the orthodox doctrines of predestination, Scripture, the church and Christology (more explicitly Chalcedonian), reflecting their codification in the Formula of Concord.* He was unafraid to engage in confessional polemics from the pulpit. In addition to his many treatises (most notably *De persona Christi*, in which he defended Christ's ubiquity), Hunnius published commentaries on Matthew, John, Ephesians and Colossians; his notes on Galatians, Philemon and 1 Corinthians were published posthumously.

Jan Hus (d. 1415). Bohemian reformer and martyr. This popular preacher strove for reform in the church, moral improvement in society, and an end to clerical abuses and popular religious superstition. He was branded a heretic for his alleged affinity for John Wycliffe's writings; however, while he agreed that a priest in mortal sin rendered the sacraments inefficacious, he affirmed the doctrine of transubstantiation. The Council of Constance* convicted Hus of heresy, banned his books and teaching, and, despite a letter of safe conduct, burned him at the stake.

Hans Hut (1490–1527). German Radical leader. Hut was an early leader of a mystical, apocalyptic strand of Anabaptist radical reform. His theological views were shaped by Andreas Bodenstein von Karlstadt,* Thomas Müntzer* and Hans Denck,* by whom Hut had been baptized. Hut rejected society and the established church and heralded the imminent end of days, which he perceived in the Peasants' War. Eventually arrested for practicing believers' baptism and participating in the Peasants' War, Hut was tortured and died accidentally in a fire in the Augsburg prison. The next day, the authorities sentenced his corpse to death and burned him.

George Hutcheson (1615–1674). Scottish Puritan pastor. Hutcheson, a pastor in Edinburgh, published commentaries on Job, John and the Minor Prophets, as well as sermons on Psalm 130.

Roger Hutchinson (d. 1555). English reformer. Little is known about Hutchinson except for his controversies. He disputed against the Mass while at Cambridge and debated with Joan Bocher (d. 1550), who affirmed the doctrine of the celestial flesh. During the Marian Restoration he was deprived of his fellowship at Eton because he was married.

Andreas Hyperius (1511–1564). Dutch Protestant theologian. A peripatetic student, Hyperius moved through Germany, France, Italy and England until settling in Marburg as professor of theology in 1541. Alongside commentaries on Romans and Hebrews, he composed texts on homiletics, the use of the church fathers, practical piety, and church administration.

Abraham Ibn Ezra (1089–c. 1167). Spanish Jewish rabbi, exegete and poet. In 1140 Ibn Ezra fled his native Spain to escape persecution by the Almohad Caliphate. He spent the rest of his life as an exile, traveling through Europe, North Africa and the Middle East. His corpus consists of works on poetry, exegesis, grammar, philosophy, mathematics and astrology. In his commentaries on the Old Testament, Ibn Ezra restricts himself to *peshat* (see *quadriga*).

Valentin Ickelshamer (c. 1500–1547). German Radical teacher. After time at Erfurt, he studied under Luther,* Melanchthon,* Bugenhagen* and Karlstadt* in Wittenberg. He sided with Karlstadt against Luther, writing a treatise in Karlstadt's defense. Ickelshamer also represented the Wittenberg guilds in opposition to the city council. This guild committee allied with the peasants in 1525, leading to Ickelshamer's eventual exile. His poem in the Marpeck Circle's *Kunstbuch** is an expansion of a similar poem by Sebastian Franck.*

Thomas Jackson (1579–1640). Anglican theologian and priest. Before serving as the president of Corpus Christi College at Oxford for the final decade of his life, Jackson was a parish priest and chaplain to the king. His best known work is a twelve-volume commentary on the Apostles' Creed.

King James I of England (VI of Scotland) (1566–1625). English monarch. The son of Mary, Queen of Scots, James ascended to the Scottish throne in 1567 following his mother's abdication. In the Union of the Crowns (1603), he took the English and Irish thrones after the death of his cousin, Elizabeth I. James's reign was tumultuous and tense: Parliament and the nobility often opposed him, church factions squabbled over worship forms and ecclesiology, climaxing in the Gunpowder Plot. James wrote treatises on the divine right of kings, law, the evils of smoking tobacco and demonology. His religious writings include a versification of the Psalms, a paraphrase of Revelation and meditations on the Lord's Prayer and passages from Chronicles, Matthew and Revelation. He also sponsored the translation of the Authorized Version*—popularly remembered as the King James Version.

John Jewel (1522–1571). Anglican theologian and bishop. Jewel studied at Oxford where he met Peter Martyr Vermigli.* After graduating in 1552, Jewel was appointed to his first vicarage and became the orator for the university. Upon Mary I's accession, Jewel lost his post as orator because of his Protestant views. After the trials of Thomas Cranmer* and Nicholas Ridley,* Jewel affirmed Catholic teaching to avoid their fate. Still he had to flee to the continent. Confronted by John Knox,* Jewel publicly repented of his cowardice before the English congregation in Frankfurt, then reunited with Vermigli in Strasbourg. After Mary I's death, Jewel returned to England and was consecrated bishop in 1560. He advocated low-church ecclesiology, but supported the Elizabethan Settlement against Catholics and Puritans. In response to the Council of Trent, he published the *Apoligia ecclesiae Anglicanae* (1562), which established him as the apostle for Anglicanism and incited numerous controversies.

St. John of the Cross (Juan de Yepes y Álvarez) (1542–1591). Spanish Catholic mystic. Born into poverty, Álvarez entered the Carmelite order in Medina del Campo, where, after studying theology at Salamanca, he met the famed mystic Teresa of Ávila (1515–1582). Drawn to her vision of the contemplative life, with two others, he established the first house of Discalced (barefoot) Carmelite Friars and became a leader in the Catholic reform movement. An exceptional administrator and spiritual leader, for more than twenty years, John of the Cross sought to return his order to its original vision of asceticism and prayer while establishing many new reformed Carmelite houses. He encountered significant resistance in his work for renewal, however, and spent nine months imprisoned and tortured by his Carmelite superiors. Considered among the foremost poets in Spanish literary history, his poems, including *The Spiritual Canticle, Ascent of Mount Carmel*, and *The Dark Night of the Soul* demonstrate his overriding desire for spiritual growth and closeness to God.

Justus Jonas (1493–1555). German Lutheran theologian, pastor and administrator. Jonas studied law at Erfurt, where he befriended the poet Eobanus Hessus (1488–1540), whom Luther* dubbed "king of the poets"; later, under the influence of the humanist Konrad Muth, Jonas focused on theology. In 1516 he was ordained as a priest, and in 1518 he became a doctor of theology and law. After witnessing the Leipzig Disputation, Jonas was converted to Luther's* cause. While traveling with Luther to the Diet of Worms, Jonas was appointed professor of canon law at Wittenberg. Later he became its dean of theology, lecturing on Romans, Acts and the Psalms. Jonas was also instrumental for reform in Halle. He preached Luther's funeral sermon but had a falling-out with Melanchthon* over the Leipzig Interim. Jonas's most influential contribution was translating Luther's *The Bondage of the Will* and Melanchthon's *Loci communes* into German.

William Jones (1561–1636). Anglican minister and theologian. After teaching at Cambridge, Jones ministered at East Bergholt in Suffolk for forty-four years, publishing a commentary on Philemon and Hebrews and tracts on suffering, the nativity, and arrangements to be made before one's death.

David Joris (c. 1501–1556). Dutch Radical pastor and hymnist. This former glass painter was one of the leading Dutch Anabaptist leaders after the fall of Münster (1535), although due to his increasingly radical ideas his influence waned in the early 1540s.

Joris came to see himself as a "third David," a Spirit-anointed prophet ordained to proclaim the coming third kingdom of God, which would be established in the Netherlands with Dutch as its *lingua franca*. Joris's interpretation of Scripture, with his heavy emphasis on personal mystical experience, led to a very public dispute with Menno Simons* whom Joris considered a teacher of the "dead letter." In 1544 Joris and about one hundred followers moved to Basel, conforming outwardly to the teaching of the Reformed church there. Today 240 of Joris's books are extant, the most important of which is his *Twonder Boek* (1542/43).

Jörg Haugk von Jüchsen (unknown). German Radical preacher. Nothing is known of Haugk's life except that during the 1524–1525 Peasants' War in Thuringia, he was elected as a preacher by the insurrectionists in his district. He composed one extant tract, titled *A Christian Order of a True Christian: Giving an Account of the Origin of His Faith*, published in 1526 but likely written before the Peasants' War. While lacking reference to most distinctive Anabaptist doctrines, this pamphlet became popular among radicals as it set out the stages of Christian growth toward perfection.

Andreas Bodenstein von Karlstadt (Carlstadt) (1486–1541). German Radical theologian. Karlstadt, an early associate of Martin Luther* and Philipp Melanchthon* at the University of Wittenberg, participated alongside Luther in the dispute at Leipzig with Johann Eck.* He also influenced the configuration of the Old Testament canon in Protestantism. During Luther's captivity in Wartburg Castle in Eisenach, Karlstadt oversaw reform in Wittenberg. His acceleration of the pace of reform brought conflict with Luther, so Karlstadt left Wittenberg, eventually settling at the University of Basel as professor of Old Testament (after a sojourn in Zurich with Huldrych Zwingli*). During his time in Switzerland, Karlstadt opposed infant baptism and repudiated Luther's doctrine of Christ's real presence in the Eucharist.

Edward Kellett (d. 1641). Anglican theologian and priest. Kellett published a sermon concerning the reconversion of an Englishman from Islam, a tract on the soul and a discourse on the Lord's Supper in connection with Passover.

David Kimchi (Radak) (1160–1235). French Jewish rabbi, exegete and philosopher. Kimchi wrote an important Hebrew grammar and dictionary, as well as commentaries on Genesis, 1–2 Chronicles, the Psalms and the Prophets. He focused on *peshat* (see *quadriga*). In his Psalms commentary he attacks Christian interpretation as forced, irrational and inadmissible. While Sebastian Münster* censors and condemns these arguments in his *Miqdaš YHWH* (1534–1535), he and many other Christian commentators valued Kimchi's work as a grammatical resource.

Moses Kimchi (Remak) (1127–1190). French Jewish rabbi and exegete. He was David Kimchi's* brother. He wrote commentaries on Proverbs and Ezra-Nehemiah. Sebastian Münster* translated Kimchi's concise Hebrew grammar into Latin; many sixteenth-century Christian exegetes used this resource.

John Knox (1513–1572). Scottish Reformed preacher. Knox, a fiery preacher to monarchs and zealous defender of high Calvinism, was a leading figure of reform in Scotland. Following imprisonment in the French galleys, Knox went to England, where he became a royal chaplain to Edward VI. At the accession of Mary, Knox fled to Geneva, studying under John Calvin* and serving as a pastor. Knox returned to Scotland after Mary's death and became a chief architect of the reform of the Scottish church (Presbyterian), serving as one of the authors of the Book of Discipline and writing many pamphlets and sermons.

Antonius Broickwy von Königstein (1470–1541). German Catholic preacher. Very little is known about this important cathedral preacher in Cologne. Strongly opposed to evangelicals, he sought to develop robust resources for Catholic homilies. His postils were bestsellers, and his biblical concordance helped Catholic preachers to construct doctrinal loci from Scripture itself.

Kunstbuch. In 1956, two German students rediscovered this unique collection of Anabaptist works. Four hundred years earlier, a friend of the recently deceased Pilgram Marpeck*—the painter Jörg Probst—had entrusted this collection of letters, tracts and poetry to a Zurich bindery; today only half of it remains. Probst's redaction arranges various compositions from the Marpeck Circle into a devotional anthology focused on the theme of the church as Christ incarnate (cf. Gal 2:20).

Osmund Lake (c. 1543–1621). English Pastor who ministered at Ringwood in Hampshire.

François Lambert (Lambert of Avignon) (1487–1530). French Reformed theologian. In 1522, after becoming drawn to the writings of Martin Luther* and meeting Huldrych Zwingli,* Lambert left the Franciscan order. He spent time in Wittenberg, Strasbourg, and Hesse, where Lambert took a leading role at the Homberg Synod (1526) and in creating a biblically based plan for church reform. He served as professor of theology at Marburg University from 1527 to his death. After the Marburg Colloquy (1529), Lambert accepted Zwingli's symbolic view of the Eucharist. Lambert produced nineteen books, mostly biblical commentaries that favored spiritual interpretations; his unfinished work of comprehensive theology was published posthumously.

Eitelhans Langenmantel (d. 1528). German Radical writer. The son of the mayor of Augsburg, Langenmantel was converted to Anabaptism and was rebaptized by Hans Hut* in 1527. Arrested for his heterodox views later that year, he was freed after accepting the validity of infant baptism during a debate, but after renouncing his recantation in 1528, he was rearrested and beheaded. Seven tracts he composed during 1526 and 1527 survive, focusing on the Lord's Supper and the moral life.

Hugh Latimer (c. 1485–1555). Anglican bishop and preacher. Latimer was celebrated for his sermons critiquing the idolatrous nature of Catholic practices and the social injustices visited on the underclass by the aristocracy and the individualism of Protestant government. After his support for Henry's petition of divorce he served as a court preacher under Henry VIII and Edward VI. Latimer became a proponent of reform following his education at Cambridge University and received license as a preacher. Following Edward's death, Latimer was tried for heresy, perishing at the stake with Nicholas Ridley* and Thomas Cranmer.*

William Laud (1573–1645). Anglican archbishop, one of the most pivotal and controversial figures in Anglican church history. Early in his career, Laud offended many with his highly traditional, anti-Puritan approach to ecclesial policies. After his election as Archbishop of Canterbury in 1633, Laud continued to strive against the Puritans, demanding the eastward placement of the Communion altar (affirming the religious centrality of the Eucharist), the use of clerical garments, the reintroduction of stained-glass windows, and the uniform use of the Book of Common Prayer.* Laud was accused of being a crypto-Catholic—an ominous accusation during the protracted threat of invasion by the Spanish Armada. In 1640 the Long Parliament met, quickly impeached Laud on charges of treason, and placed him in jail for several years before his execution.

Ludwig Lavater (1527–1586). Swiss Reformed pastor and theologian. Under his father-in-law Heinrich Bullinger,* Lavater became an archdeacon in Zurich. In 1585 he succeeded Rudolf Gwalther* as the city's Antistes. He authored a widely disseminated book on demonology, commentaries on Chronicles, Proverbs, Ecclesiastes, Nehemiah and Ezekiel, theological works, and biographies of Bullinger and Konrad Pellikan.*

John Lawson (unknown). Seventeenth-century English Puritan. Lawson wrote *Gleanings and Expositions of Some of Scripture* (1646) and a treatise on the sabbath in the New Testament.

Jacques Lefèvre d'Étaples (Faber Stapulensis) (1460?–1536). French Catholic humanist, publisher and translator. Lefèvre d'Étaples studied classical literature and philosophy, as well as patristic and medieval mysticism. He advocated the principle of *ad fontes*, issuing a full-scale

annotation on the corpus of Aristotle, publishing the writings of key Christian mystics, and contributing to efforts at biblical translation and commentary. Although he never broke with the Catholic Church, his views prefigured those of Martin Luther,* for which he was condemned by the University of Sorbonne in Paris. He then found refuge in the court of Marguerite d'Angoulême, where he met John Calvin* and Martin Bucer.*

Edward Leigh (1602–1671). English Puritan biblical critic, historian and politician. Educated at Oxford, Leigh's public career included appointments as a Justice of the Peace, an officer in the parliamentary army during the English Civil Wars and a member of Parliament. Although never ordained, Leigh devoted himself to the study of theology and Scripture; he participated in the Westminster Assembly. Leigh published a diverse corpus, including lexicons of Greek, Hebrew and juristic terms, and histories of Roman, Greek and English rulers. His most important theological work is *A Systeme or Body of Divinity* (1662).

John Lightfoot (1602–1675). Anglican priest and biblical scholar. After graduating from Cambridge, Lightfoot was ordained and pastored at several small parishes. He continued to study classics under the support of the politician Rowland Cotton (1581–1634). Siding with the Parliamentarians during the English Civil Wars, Lightfoot relocated to London in 1643. He was one of the original members of the Westminster Assembly, where he defended a moderate Presbyterianism. His best-known work is the six-volume *Horae Hebraicae et Talmudicae* (1658–1677), a verse-by-verse commentary illumined by Hebrew customs, language and the Jewish interpretive tradition.

Wenceslaus Linck (1482–1547). German Lutheran theologian and preacher. As dean of the theology faculty at the University of Wittenberg and successor to Johannes von Staupitz* as the prior of the Augustinian Monastery, Linck worked closely with Martin Luther* and attended the Heidelberg Disputation with him. He replaced Staupitz as vicar-general of the Augustinian order in 1520 in Germany, a capacity in which he pronounced all members free from their vows before renouncing the order himself. After periods of ministry in Munich and Altenburg, Linck settled in Nuremberg, where he became known as an exemplary preacher and an advisor to cities undertaking Protestant reform. He published a significant number of sermons and practical tracts as well as a paraphrase and annotations on the Old Testament.

Lucas Lossius (1508–1582). German Lutheran teacher and musician. While a student at Leipzig and Wittenberg, Lossius was deeply influenced by Melanchthon* and Luther,* who found work for him as Urbanus Rhegius's* secretary. Soon after going to work for Rhegius, Lossius began teaching at a local gymnasium (or secondary school), *Das Johanneum*, eventually becoming its headmaster. Lossius remained at *Das Johanneum* until his death, even turning down appointments to university professorships. A man of varied interests, he wrote on dialectics, music and church history, as well as publishing a postil and a five-volume set of annotations on the New Testament.

Sibrandus Lubbertus (c. 1555–1625). Dutch Reformed theologian. Lubbertis, a key figure in the establishment of orthodox Calvinism in Frisia, studied theology at Wittenburg and Geneva (under Theodore Beza*) before his appointment as professor of theology at the University of Franeker. Throughout his career, Lubbertis advocated for high Calvinist theology, defending it in disputes with representatives of Socinianism, Arminianism and Roman Catholicism. Lubbertis criticized the Catholic theologian Robert Bellarmine and fellow Dutch reformer Jacobus Arminius*; the views of the latter he opposed as a prominent participant in the Synod of Dordrecht.*

Martin Luther (1483–1546). German Lutheran priest, professor and theologian. While a professor in Wittenberg, Luther reinterpreted the doctrine of justification. Convinced that righteousness comes only from God's grace, he disputed the sale of indulgences with the Ninety-five Theses. Luther's positions brought conflict with Rome; his denial of papal authority led to excommunication.

He also challenged the Mass, transubstantiation and communion under one kind. Though Luther was condemned by the Diet of Worms, the Elector of Saxony provided him safe haven. Luther returned to Wittenberg with public order collapsing under Andreas Bodenstein von Karlstadt;* Luther steered a more cautious path of reform. His rendering of the Bible and liturgy in the vernacular, as well as his hymns and sermons, proved extensively influential.

Georg Major (1502–1574). German Lutheran theologian. Major was on the theological faculty of the University of Wittenberg, succeeding as dean Johannes Bugenhagen* and Philipp Melanchthon.* One of the chief editors on the Wittenberg edition of Luther's works, Major is most identified with the controversy bearing his name, in which he stated that good works are necessary to salvation. Major qualified his statement, which was in reference to the totality of the Christian life. The Formula of Concord* rejected the statement, ending the controversy. As a theologian, Major further refined Lutheran views of the inspiration of Scripture and the doctrine of the Trinity.

John (Mair) Major (1467–1550). Scottish Catholic philosopher. Major taught logic and theology at the universities of Paris (his alma mater), Glasgow and St Andrews. His broad interests and impressive work drew students from all over Europe. While disapproving of evangelicals (though he did teach John Knox*), Major advocated reform programs for Rome. He supported collegial episcopacy and even challenged the curia's teaching on sexuality. Still he was a nominalist who was critical of humanist approaches to biblical exegesis. His best-known publication is *A History of Greater Britain, Both England and Scotland* (1521), which promoted the union of the kingdoms. He also published a commentary on Peter Lombard's *Sentences* and the Gospel of John.

Juan de Maldonado (1533–1583). Spanish Catholic biblical scholar. A student of Francisco de Toledo,* Maldonado taught philosophy and theology at the universities of Paris and Salamanca. Ordained to the priesthood in Rome, he revised the Septuagint under papal appointment. While Maldonado vehemently criticized Protestants, he asserted that Reformed baptism was valid and that mixed confessional marriages were acceptable. His views on Mary's immaculate conception proved controversial among many Catholics who conflated his statement that it was not an article of faith with its denial. He was intrigued by demonology (blaming demonic influence for the Reformation). All his work was published posthumously; his Gospel commentaries were highly valued and important.

Thomas Manton (1620–1677). English Puritan minister. Manton, educated at Oxford, served for a time as lecturer at Westminster Abbey and rector of St. Paul's, Covent Garden, and was a strong advocate of Presbyterianism. He was known as a rigorous evangelical Calvinist who preached long expository sermons. At different times in his ecclesial career he worked side-by-side with Richard Baxter* and John Owen.* In his later life, Manton's Nonconformist position led to his ejection as a clergyman from the Church of England (1662) and eventual imprisonment (1670). Although a voluminous writer, Manton was best known for his preaching. At his funeral in 1677, he was dubbed "the king of preachers."

Augustin Marlorat (c. 1506–1562). French Reformed pastor. Committed by his family to a monastery at the age of eight, Marlorat was also ordained into the priesthood at an early age in 1524. He fled to Geneva in 1535, where he pastored until the Genevan Company of Pastors sent him to France to shepherd the nascent evangelical congregations. His petition to the young Charles IX (1550–1574) for the right to public evangelical worship was denied. In response to a massacre of evangelicals in Vassy (over sixty dead, many more wounded), Marlorat's congregation planned to overtake Rouen. After the crown captured Rouen, Marlorat was arrested and executed three days later for treason. His principle published work was an anthology of New Testament comment modeled after Thomas Aquinas's *Catena aurea in quatuor Evangelia*. Marlorat harmonized Reformed and Lutheran comment with the church fathers, interspersed with his own brief comments. He also wrote such anthologies for Genesis, Job, the Psalms, Song of Songs and Isaiah.

Pilgram Marpeck (c. 1495–1556). Austrian Radical elder and theologian. During a brief sojourn in Strasbourg, Marpeck debated with Martin Bucer* before the city council; Bucer was declared the winner, and Marpeck was asked to leave Strasbourg for his views concerning paedobaptism (which he compared to a sacrifice to Moloch). After his time in Strasbourg, Marpeck traveled throughout southern Germany and western Austria, planting Anabaptist congregations. Marpeck criticized the strict use of the ban, however, particularly among the Swiss brethren. He also engaged in a christological controversy with Kaspar von Schwenckfeld.*

Johannes Mathesius (1504–1565). German Lutheran theologian and pastor. After reading Martin Luther's* *On Good Works*, Mathesius left his teaching post in Ingolstadt and traveled to Wittenberg to study theology. Mathesius was an important agent of reform in the Bohemian town of Jáchymov, where he pastored, preached and taught. Over one thousand of Mathesius's sermons are extant, including numerous wedding and funeral sermons as well as a series on Luther's life. Mathesius also transcribed portions of Luther's Table Talk.

John Mayer (1583–1664). Anglican priest and biblical exegete. Mayer dedicated much of his life to biblical exegesis, writing a seven-volume commentary on the entire Bible (1627–1653). Styled after Philipp Melanchthon's* *locus* method, Mayer's work avoided running commentary, focusing instead on textual and theological problems. He was a parish priest for fifty-five years. In the office of priest Mayer also wrote a popular catechism, *The English Catechisme, or a Commentarie on the Short Catechisme* (1621), which went through twelve editions in his lifetime.

Joseph Mede (1586–1638). Anglican biblical scholar, Hebraist and Greek lecturer. A man of encyclopedic knowledge, Mede was interested in numerous fields, varying from philology and history to mathematics and physics, although millennial thought and apocalyptic prophesy were clearly his chief interests. Mede's most important work was his *Clavis Apocalyptica* (1627, later translated into English as *The Key of the Revelation*). This work examined the structure of Revelation as the key to its interpretation. Mede saw the visions as a connected and chronological sequence hinging around Revelation 17:18. He is remembered as an important figure in the history of millenarian theology. He was respected as a mild-mannered and generous scholar who avoided controversy and debate, but who had many original thoughts.

Philipp Melanchthon (1497–1560). German Lutheran educator, reformer and theologian. Melanchthon is known as the partner and successor to Martin Luther* in reform in Germany and for his pioneering *Loci communes*, which served as a theological textbook. Melanchthon participated with Luther in the Leipzig disputation, helped implement reform in Wittenberg and was a chief architect of the Augsburg Confession.* Later, Melanchthon and Martin Bucer* worked for union between the reformed and Catholic churches. On account of Melanchthon's more ecumenical disposition and his modification of several of Luther's doctrines, he was held in suspicion by some.

Justus Menius (1499–1558). German Lutheran pastor and theologian. Menius was a prominent reformer in Thuringia. He participated in the Marburg Colloquy and, with others, helped Martin Luther* compose the Schmalkald Articles.* Throughout his career Menius entered into numerous controversies with Anabaptists and even fellow Lutherans. He rejected Andreas Osiander's (d. 1552) doctrine of justification—that the indwelling of Christ's divine nature justifies, rather than the imputed alien righteousness of Christ's person, declared through God's mercy. Against Nikolaus von Amsdorf (1483–1565) and

Matthias Flacius (1520–1575), Menius agreed with Georg Major* that good works are necessary to salvation. Osiander's view of justification was censored in Article 3 of the Formula of Concord*; Menius's understanding of the relationship between good works and salvation was rejected in Article 4. Menius translated many of Luther's Latin works into German. He also composed a handbook for Christian households and an influential commentary on 1 Samuel.

Johannes Mercerus (Jean Mercier) (d. 1570). French Hebraist. Mercerus studied under the first Hebrew chair at the Collège Royal de Paris, François Vatable (d. 1547), whom he succeeded in 1546. John Calvin* tried to recruit Mercerus to the Genevan Academy as professor of Hebrew, once in 1558 and again in 1563; he refused both times. During his lifetime Mercerus published grammatical helps for Hebrew and Chaldean, an aid to the Masoretic symbols in the Hebrew text, and translated the commentaries and grammars of several medieval rabbis. He himself wrote commentaries on Genesis, the wisdom books, and most of the Minor Prophets. These commentaries—most of them only published after his death—were philologically focused and interacted with the work of Jerome, Nicholas of Lyra,* notable rabbis and Johannes Oecolampadius.*

Ambrose Moibanus (1494–1554). German Lutheran bishop and theologian. Moibanus helped reform the church of Breslau (modern Wroclaw, Poland). He revised the Mass, bolstered pastoral care and welfare for the poor, and wrote a new evangelical catechism.

Thomas More (1478–1535). English Catholic lawyer, politician, humanist and martyr. More briefly studied at Oxford, but completed his legal studies in London. After contemplating the priesthood for four years, he opted for politics and was elected a member of Parliament in 1504. A devout Catholic, More worked with church leaders in England to root out heresy while he also confronted Lutheran teachings in writing. After four years as Lord Chancellor, More resigned due to heightened tensions with Henry VIII over papal supremacy (which More supported and Henry did not). Tensions did not abate. More's steadfast refusal to accept the Act of Supremacy (1534)—which declared the King of England to be the supreme ecclesial primate not the pope—resulted in his arrest and trial for high treason. He was found guilty and beheaded with John Fisher (1469–1535). Friends with John Colet* and Desiderius Erasmus,* More was a widely respected humanist in England as well as on the continent. Well-known for his novel *Utopia* (1516), More also penned several religious treatises on Christ's passion and suffering during his imprisonment in the Tower of London, which were published posthumously.

Sebastian Münster (1488–1552). German Reformed Hebraist, exegete, printer, and geographer. After converting to the Reformation in 1524, Münster taught Hebrew at the universities of Heidelberg and Basel. During his lengthy tenure in Basel he published more than seventy books, including Hebrew dictionaries and rabbinic commentaries. He also produced an evangelistic work for Jews titled *Vikuach* (1539). Münster's *Torat ha-Maschiach* (1537), the Gospel of Matthew, was the first published Hebrew translation of any portion of the New Testament. Despite his massive contribution to contemporary understanding of the Hebrew language, Münster was criticized by many of the reformers as a Judaizer.

Thomas Müntzer (c. 1489–1525). German Radical preacher. As a preacher in the town of Zwickau, Müntzer was influenced by German mysticism and, growing convinced that Martin Luther* had not carried through reform properly, sought to restore the pure apostolic church of the New Testament. Müntzer's radical ideas led to expulsions from various cities; he developed a highly apocalyptic theology, in which he heralded the last days that would establish the pure community out of suffering, prompting Müntzer's proactive role in the Peasants' War, which he perceived as a crucial apocalyptic event. Six thousand of Müntzer's followers were annihilated by magisterial troops; Müntzer was executed.

John Murcot (1625–1654). English Puritan pastor. After completing his bachelor's at Oxford in 1647, Murcot was ordained as a pastor, transferring to several parishes until in 1651 he moved to Dublin. All his works were published posthumously.

Simon Musaeus (1521–1582). German Lutheran theologian. After studying at the universities of Frankfurt an der Oder and Wittenberg, Musaeus began teaching Greek at the Cathedral school in Nuremberg and was ordained. Having returned to Wittenberg to complete a doctoral degree, Musaeus spent the rest of his career in numerous ecclesial and academic administrative posts. He opposed Matthias Flacius's (1505–1575) view of original sin—that the formal essence of human beings is marred by original sin—even calling the pro-Flacian faculty at Wittenberg "the devil's latrine." Musaeus published a disputation on original sin and a postil.

Wolfgang Musculus (1497–1563). German Reformed pastor and theologian. Musculus produced translations, biblical commentaries and an influential theological text, *Loci communes Sacrae Theologiae* (*Commonplaces of Sacred Theology*), outlining a Zwinglian theology. Musculus began to study theology while at a Benedictine monastery; he departed in 1527 and became secretary to Martin Bucer* in Strasbourg. He was later installed as a pastor in Augsburg, eventually performing the first evangelical liturgy in the city's cathedral. Displaced by the Augsburg Interim, Musculus ended his career as professor of theology at Bern. Though Musculus was active in the pursuit of the reform agenda, he was also concerned for ecumenism, participating in the Wittenberg Concord (1536) and discussions between Lutherans and Catholics.

Georg Mylius (1548–1607). German Lutheran theologian. After receiving his doctorate in theology, Mylius ministered briefly in his hometown of Augsburg before being dismissed from his pulpit and expelled from the city after he and other Protestant ministers resisted the introduction of the Gregorian calendar by the Catholic city council. After a year in Ulm, he was appointed professor of theology at Wittenberg. Forced to leave by the Philippist majority, he relocated to Jena, where he taught theology and pastored in his later years.

Hans Nadler (unknown). German Radical layperson. An uneducated and illiterate needle salesman, after receiving baptism from Hans Hut* in 1527, Nadler sought to share the faith with those he met during his extensive travels. He is remembered through the records of his arrest and examination, recorded by a court reporter, which give insight into his beliefs and activities as a committed Anabaptist layperson, whereby he affirmed believer's baptism, the spiritual reception of the Eucharist, and nonresistance.

Friedrich Nausea (c. 1496–1552). German Catholic bishop and preacher. After completing his studies at Leipzig, this famed preacher was appointed priest in Frankfurt but was run out of town by his congregants during his first sermon. He transferred to Mainz as cathedral preacher. Nausea was well connected through the German papal hierarchy and traveled widely to preach to influential ecclesial and secular courts. Court preacher for Ferdinand I (1503–1564), his reform tendencies fit well with royal Austrian theological leanings, and he was enthroned as the bishop of Vienna. Nausea thought that rather than endless colloquies only a council could settle reform. Unfortunately he could not participate in the first session of Trent due to insufficient funding, but he arrived for the second session. Nausea defended the laity's reception of the cup and stressed the importance of promulgating official Catholic teaching in the vernacular.

Melchior Neukirch (1540–1597). German Lutheran pastor and playwright. Neukirch's pastoral career spanned more than thirty years in several northern German parishes. Neukirch published a history of the Braunschweig church since the Reformation and a dramatization of Acts 4–7. He died of the plague.

Nicholas of Lyra (1270–1349). French Catholic biblical exegete. Very little is known about this influential medieval theologian of the Sorbonne aside from the works he published, particularly the *Postilla litteralis super totam Bibliam* (1322–1333). With the advent of the printing press this work was regularly published alongside the Latin Vulgate and the *Glossa ordinaria*. In this running commentary on the Bible Nicholas promoted literal interpretation as the basis for theology. Despite his preference for literal interpretation, Nicholas also published a companion volume, the *Postilla moralis super totam Bibliam* (1339), a commentary on the spiritual meaning of the biblical text. Nicholas was a major conversation partner for many reformers though many of them rejected his exegesis as too literal and too "Jewish" (not concerned enough with the Bible's fulfillment in Jesus Christ).

Johannes Oecolampadius (Johannes Huszgen) (1482–1531). Swiss-German Reformed humanist, reformer and theologian. Oecolampadius (an assumed name meaning "house light") assisted with Desiderius Erasmus's* Greek New Testament, lectured on biblical languages and exegesis and completed an influential Greek grammar. After joining the evangelical cause through studying patristics and the work of Martin Luther,* Oecolampadius went to Basel, where he lectured on biblical exegesis and participated in ecclesial reform. On account of Oecolampadius's effort, the city council passed legislation restricting preaching to the gospel and releasing the city from compulsory Mass. Oecolampadius was a chief ally of Huldrych Zwingli,* whom he supported at the Marburg Colloquy (1529).

Kaspar Olevianus (1536–1587). German Reformed theologian. Olevianus is celebrated for composing the Heidelberg Catechism and producing a critical edition of Calvin's *Institutes* in German. Olevianus studied theology with many, including John Calvin,* Theodore Beza,* Heinrich Bullinger* and Peter Martyr Vermigli.* As an advocate of Reformed doctrine, Olevianus oversaw the shift from Lutheranism to Calvinism throughout Heidelberg, organizing the city's churches after Calvin's Geneva. The Calvinist ecclesial vision of Olevianus entangled him in a dispute with another Heidelberg reformer over the rights of ecclesiastical discipline, which Olevianus felt belonged to the council of clergy and elders rather than civil magistrates.

Josua Opitz (c. 1542–1585). German Lutheran pastor. After a brief stint as superintendent in Regensburg, Opitz, a longtime preacher, was dismissed for his support of Matthias Flacius's (1520–1575) view of original sin. (Using Aristotelian categories, Flacius argued that the formal essence of human beings is marred by original sin, forming sinners into the image of Satan; his views were officially rejected in Article 1 of the Formula of Concord.*) Hans Wilhelm Roggendorf (1533–1591) invited Opitz to lower Austria as part of his Lutheranizing program. Unfortunately Roggendorf and Opitz never succeed in getting Lutheranism legal recognition, perhaps in large part due to Opitz's staunch criticism of Catholics, which resulted in his exile. He died of plague.

Lucas Osiander (1534–1604). German Lutheran pastor. For three decades, Osiander— son of the controversial Nuremberg reformer Andreas Osiander (d. 1552)—served as pastor and court preacher in Stuttgart, until he fell out of favor with the duke in 1598. Osiander produced numerous theological and exegetical works, as well as an influential hymnal.

John Owen (1616–1683). English Puritan theologian. Owen trained at Oxford University, where he was later appointed dean of Christ Church and vice chancellor of the university, following his service as chaplain to Oliver Cromwell. Although Owen began his career as a Presbyterian minister, he eventually departed to the party of Independents. Owen composed many sermons, biblical commentaries (including seven volumes on the book of Hebrews), theological treatises and controversial monographs (including disputations with Arminians, Anglicans, Catholics and Socinians).

Santes Pagninus (c. 1470–1541). Italian Catholic biblical scholar. Pagninus studied under Girolamo Savonarola* and later taught in Rome, Avignon and Lyons. He translated the Old Testament into Latin

according to a tight, almost wooden, adherence to the Hebrew. This translation and his Hebrew lexicon *Thesaurus linguae sanctae* (1529) were important resources for translators and commentators.

Johann Pappus (1549–1610). German Lutheran theologian. After a decade as a teacher of Hebrew and professor of theology at the Strasbourg academy, Pappus was appointed president of the city's company of pastors. Despite resistance from the Reformed theologian Johann Sturm (1507–1589), he led the city away from its Swiss Reformed alliances and toward subscription to the Lutheran Formula of Concord. A talented humanist, Pappus published more than thirty works on controversial, theological, historical, and exegetical subjects.

David (Wängler) Pareus (1548–1622). German Reformed pastor and theologian. Born at Frankenstein in Lower Silesia, Pareus studied theology at Heidelberg under Zacharias Ursinus (1534–1583), the principal author of the Heidelberg Catechism.* After reforming several churches, Pareus returned to Heidelberg to teach at the Reformed seminary. He then joined the theological faculty at the University of Heidelberg, first as a professor of Old Testament and later as a professor of New Testament. Pareus edited the *Neustadter Bibel* (1587), a publication of Martin Luther's* German translation with Reformed annotations—which was strongly denounced by Lutherans, especially Jakob Andreae* and Johann Georg Sigwart (1554–1618). In an extended debate, Pareus defended the orthodoxy of Calvin's exegesis against Aegidius Hunnius,* who accused Calvin of "judaizing" by rejecting many traditional Christological interpretations of Old Testament passages. Towards the end of his career, Pareus wrote commentaries on Genesis, Hosea, Matthew, Romans, 1 Corinthians, Galatians, Hebrews and Revelation.

Catherine Parr (1512–1548). The last of King Henry VIII's* six wives, Catherine Parr was Queen Consort to Henry from 1543 until his death in 1547. She enjoyed a close relationship with two of her step children, Elizabeth and Edward (the future Queen Elizabeth I and King

Edward VI), involving herself extensively in their education. Having married three more times after the death of Henry VIII, Catherine died in 1548. Her published works are *Psalms or Prayers* (1543) and a *Lamentation of a Sinner* (1548).

Paul of Burgos (**Solomon ha-Levi**) (c. 1351–1435). Spanish Catholic archbishop. In 1391 Solomon ha-Levi, a rabbi and Talmudic scholar, converted to Christianity, receiving baptism with his entire family (except for his wife). He changed his name to Paul de Santa Maria. Some have suggested that he converted to avoid persecution; he himself stated that Thomas Aquinas's (1225–1274) work persuaded him of the truth of Christian faith. After studying theology in Paris, he was ordained bishop in 1403. He actively and ardently persecuted Jews, trying to compel them to convert. In order to convince Jews that Christians correctly interpret the Hebrew Scriptures, Paul wrote *Dialogus Pauli et Sauli contra Judaeos, sive Scrutinium Scripturarum* (1434), a book filled with vile language toward the Jews. He also wrote a series of controversial marginal notes and comments on Nicholas of Lyra's* *Postilla*, many of which criticized Nicholas's use of Jewish scholarship.

Christoph Pelargus (1565–1633). German Lutheran pastor, theologian, professor and superintendent. Pelargus studied philosophy and theology at the University of Frankfurt an der Oder, in Brandenburg. This irenic Philippist was appointed as the superintendent of Brandenburg and later became a pastor in Frankfurt, although the local authorities first required him to condemn Calvinist theology, because several years earlier he had been called before the consistory in Berlin under suspicion of being a crypto-Calvinist. Among his most important works were a four-volume commentary on *De orthodoxa fide* by John of Damascus (d. 749), a treatise defending the breaking of the bread during communion, and a volume of funeral sermons. He also published commentaries on the Pentateuch, the Psalms, Matthew, John and Acts.

Konrad Pellikan (1478–1556). German Reformed Hebraist and theologian. Pellikan attended the University of Heidelberg, where he mastered

Hebrew under Johannes Reuchlin. In 1504 Pellikan published one of the first Hebrew grammars that was not merely a translation of the work of medieval rabbis. While living in Basel, Pellikan assisted the printer Johannes Amerbach, with whom he published some of Luther's* early writings. He also worked with Sebastian Münster* and Wolfgang Capito* on a Hebrew Psalter (1516). In 1526, after teaching theology for three years at the University of Basel, Huldrych Zwingli* brought Pellikan to Zurich to chair the faculty of Old Testament. Pellikan's magnum opus is a seven-volume commentary on the entire Bible (except Revelation) and the Apocrypha; it is often heavily dependent upon the work of others (esp. Desiderius Erasmus* and Johannes Oecolampadius*).

Benedict Pererius (1535–1610). Spanish Catholic theologian, philosopher and exegete. Pererius entered the Society of Jesus in 1552. He taught philosophy, theology, and exegesis at the Roman College of the Jesuits. Early in his career he warned against neo-Platonism and astrology in his *De principiis* (1576). Pererius wrote a lengthy commentary on Daniel, and five volumes of exegetical theses on Exodus, Romans, Revelation and part of the Gospel of John (chs. 1–14). His four-volume commentary on Genesis (1591–1599) was lauded by Protestants and Catholics alike.

William Perkins (1558–1602). English Puritan preacher and theologian. Perkins was a highly regarded Puritan Presbyterian preacher and biblical commentator in the Elizabethan era. He studied at Cambridge University and later became a fellow of Christ's Church college as a preacher and professor, receiving acclaim for his sermons and lectures. Even more, Perkins gained an esteemed reputation for his ardent exposition of Calvinist reformed doctrine in the style of Petrus Ramus,* becoming one of the first English reformed theologians to achieve international recognition. Perkins influenced the federal Calvinist shape of Puritan theology and the vision of logical, practical expository preaching.

François Perrault (1577–1657). French Reformed pastor for over fifty years. His book on demonology was prominent, perhaps because of the intrigue at his home in 1612. According to his account, a poltergeist made a commotion and argued points of theology; a few months later Perrault's parishioners slew a large snake slithering out of his house.

Dirk Philips (1504–1568). Dutch Radical elder and theologian. This former Franciscan monk, known for being severe and obstinate, was a leading theologian of the sixteenth-century Anabaptist movement. Despite the fame of Menno Simons* and his own older brother Obbe, Philips wielded great influence over Anabaptists in the Netherlands and northern Germany where he ministered. As a result of Philips's understanding of the apostolic church as radically separated from the children of the world, he advocated a very strict interpretation of the ban, including formal shunning. His writings were collected and published near the end of his life as *Enchiridion oft Hantboecxken van de Christelijcke Leere* (1564).

Obbe Philips (1500–1568) Dutch radical leader. Trained as a physician, Philips was drawn to mystical Anabaptism, as taught by Melchior Hoffman (1495–1543) in his hometown of Leewarden. After adult rebaptism and ordination, he preached in Amsterdam, Delft, Appingedam, and Grongen, and he ordained other leaders including his brother Dirk Philips*, David Joris*, and Menno Simmons*. Disillusioned with the growth of revolutionary, enthusiastic, and apocalyptic elements within Anabaptism and unable to reconcile any visible church with the church of God, Philips withdrew from the radical movement in 1540, after which nothing is known of his life. His only extant writing, entitled *The Confession of Obbe Philips*, was published after his death and recounts elements of the history of the Anabaptist movement and defends his departure from the movement.

Hector Pinto (c. 1528–1584). Portuguese Catholic theologian and exegete. A member of the order of Saint Jerome, Pinto taught theology and Scripture at the Universities of Sigüenza and Coimbra. A respected theologian and exegete, he published commentaries on Daniel, Nahum, Jeremiah, and Isaiah and an influential devotional work, *The Image of the Christian Life*.

Johannes Piscator (1546–1625). German Reformed theologian. Educated at Tübingen (though he wanted to study at Wittenberg), Piscator taught at the universities of Strasbourg and Heidelberg, as well as academies in Neustadt and Herborn. His commentaries on both the Old and New Testaments involve a tripartite analysis of a given passage's argument, of scholia on the text and of doctrinal loci. Some consider Piscator's method to be a full flowering of Beza's* "logical" scriptural analysis, focused on the text's meaning and its relationship to the pericopes around it.

Felix Pratensis (d. 1539). Italian Catholic Hebraist. Pratensis, the son of a rabbi, converted to Christianity and entered the Augustinian Hermits around the turn of the sixteenth century. In 1515, with papal permission, Pratensis published a new translation of the Psalms based on the Hebrew text. His *Biblia Rabbinica* (1517–1518), printed in Jewish and Christian editions, included text-critical notes in the margins as well as the Targum and rabbinic commentaries on each book (e.g., Rashi* on the Pentateuch and David Kimchi* on the Prophets). Many of the reformers consulted this valuable resource as they labored on their own translations and expositions of the Old Testament.

Quadriga. The *quadriga*, or four senses of Scripture, grew out of the exegetical legacy of Paul's dichotomy of letter and spirit (2 Cor 3:6), as well as church fathers like Origen (c. 185–254), Jerome (c. 347–420) and Augustine (354–430). Advocates for this method—the primary framework for biblical exegesis during the medieval era—assumed the necessity of the gift of faith under the guidance of the Holy Spirit. The literal-historical meaning of the text served as the foundation for the fuller perception of Scripture's meaning in the three spiritual senses, accessible only through faith: the allegorical sense taught what should be believed, the tropological or moral sense taught what should be done, and the anagogical or eschatological sense taught what should be hoped for. Medieval Jewish exegesis also had a fourfold interpretive method—not necessarily related to the *quadriga*—called *pardes* ("grove"): *peshat*, the simple, literal sense of the text according to grammar; *remez*, the allegorical sense; *derash*, the moral sense; and *sod*, the mystic sense related to Kabbalah. Scholars hotly dispute the precise use and meaning of these terms.

Petrus Ramus (1515–1572). French Reformed humanist philosopher. Ramus was an influential professor of philosophy and logic at the French royal college in Paris; he converted to Protestantism and left France for Germany, where he came under the influence of Calvinist thought. Ramus was a trenchant critic of Aristotle and noted for his method of classification based on a deductive movement from universals to particulars, the latter becoming branching divisions that provided a visual chart of the parts to the whole. His system profoundly influenced Puritan theology and preaching. After returning to Paris, Ramus died in the Saint Bartholomew's Day Massacre.

Rashi (**Shlomo Yitzchaki**) (1040–1105). French Jewish rabbi and exegete. After completing his studies, Rashi founded a yeshiva in Troyes. He composed the first comprehensive commentary on the Talmud, as well as commentaries on the entire Old Testament except for 1–2 Chronicles. These works remain influential within orthodox Judaism. Late medieval and early modern Christian scholars valued his exegesis, characterized by his preference for peshat (see quadriga).

Remonstrance (1610). See *Synod of Dordrecht*.

Johannes Reuchlin (1455–1522). German Catholic lawyer, humanist and Hebraist. Reuchlin held judicial appointments for the dukes of Württemberg, the Supreme Court in Speyer and the imperial court of the Swabian League. He pioneered the study of Hebrew among Christians in Germany, standing against those who, like Johannes Pfefferkorn (1469–1523), wanted to destroy Jewish literature. Among his many works he published a Latin dictionary, an introductory Greek grammar, the most important early modern

Hebrew grammar and dictionary (*De rudimentis hebraicis*; 1506), and a commentary on the penitential psalms.

Edward Reynolds (1599–1676). Anglican bishop. Reynolds succeeded John Donne* as the preacher at Lincoln's Inn before entering parish ministry in Northamptonshire. During the English Civil Wars, he supported the Puritans because of his sympathy toward their simplicity and piety—despite believing that Scripture demanded no particular form of government; later he refused to support the abolition of the monarchy. Until the Restoration he ministered in London; afterward he became the bishop of Norwich. He wrote the general thanksgiving prayer which is part of the morning office in the *Book of Common Prayer.*

Urbanus Rhegius (1489–1541). German Lutheran pastor. Rhegius, who was likely the son of a priest, studied under the humanists at Freiburg and Ingolstadt. After a brief stint as a foot soldier, he received ordination in 1519 and was made cathedral preacher in Augsburg. During his time in Augsburg he closely read Luther's* works, becoming an enthusiastic follower. Despite his close friendship with Zwingli* and Oecolampadius,* Rhegius supported Luther in the eucharistic debates, later playing a major role in the Wittenberg Concord (1536). He advocated for peace during the Peasants' War and had extended interactions with the Anabaptists in Augsburg. Later in his career he concerned himself with the training of pastors, writing a pastoral guide and two catechisms. About one hundred of his writings were published posthumously.

Lancelot Ridley (d. 1576). Anglican preacher. Ridley was the first cousin of Nicholas Ridley,* the bishop of London who was martyred during the Marian persecutions. By Cranmer's* recommendation, Ridley became one of the six Canterbury Cathedral preachers. Upon Mary I's accession in 1553, Ridley was defrocked (as a married priest). Ridley returned to Canterbury Cathedral after Mary's death. He wrote commentaries on Jude, Ephesians, Philippians and Colossians.

Nicholas Ridley (c. 1502–1555). Anglican bishop. Ridley was a student and fellow at Cambridge University who was appointed chaplain to Archbishop Thomas Cranmer* and is thought to be partially responsible for Cranmer's shift to a symbolic view of the Eucharist. Cranmer promoted Ridley twice: as bishop of Rochester, where he openly advocated Reformed theological views, and, later, as bishop of London. Ridley assisted Cranmer in the revisions of the Book of Common Prayer.* Ridley's support of Lady Jane Grey against the claims of Mary to the throne led to his arrest; he was tried for heresy and burned at the stake with Hugh Latimer.*

Peter Riedemann (1506–1556). German Radical elder, theologian and hymnist. While traveling as a Silesian cobbler, Riedemann came into contact with Anabaptist teachings and joined a congregation in Linz. In 1529 he was called to be a minister, only to be imprisoned soon after as part of Archduke Ferdinand's efforts to suppress heterodoxy in his realm. Once he was released, he moved to Moravia in 1532 where he was elected as a minister and missionary of the Hutterite community there. His *Account of Our Religion, Doctrine and Faith* (1542), with its more than two thousand biblical references, is Riedemann's most important work and is still used by Hutterites today.

John Robinson (1576–1625). English Puritan pastor. After his suspension for nonconformity, Robinson fled to the Netherlands with his congregation, eventually settling in Leiden in 1609. Robinson entered into controversies over Arminianism, separation and congregationalism. Most of his healthy congregants immigrated to Plymouth in 1620; Robinson remained in Leiden with those unable to travel.

Nehemiah Rogers (1593–1660). Anglican priest. After studying at Cambridge, Rogers ministered at numerous parishes during his more than forty-year career. In 1643, he seems to have been forced out of a parish on account of being a Royalist and friend of William Laud.* Rogers published a number of sermons and tracts, including a series

of expositions on Jesus' parables in the Gospels.

Robert Rollock (c. 1555–1599). Scottish Reformed pastor, educator and theologian. Rollock was deeply influenced by Petrus Ramus's* system of logic, which he implemented as a tutor and (later) principal of Edinburgh University and in his expositions of the Bible. Rollock, as a divinity professor and theologian, was instrumental in diffusing a federalist Calvinism in the Scottish church; he lectured on theology using the texts of Theodore Beza* and articulated a highly covenantal interpretation of the biblical narratives. He was a prolific writer of sermons, expositions, commentaries, lectures and occasional treatises.

Jacopo Sadoleto (1477–1547). Italian Catholic Cardinal. Sadoleto, attaché to Leo X's court, was appointed bishop in 1517, cardinal in 1536. He participated in the reform commission led by Gasparo Contarini.* However, he tried to reconcile with Protestants apart from the commission, sending several letters to Protestant leaders in addition to his famous letter to the city of Geneva, which John Calvin* pointedly answered. Sadoleto published a commentary on Romans that was censored as semi-Pelagian. His insufficient treatment of prevenient grace left him vulnerable to this charge. Sadoleto emphasized grammar as the rule and norm of exegesis.

Heinrich Salmuth (1522–1576). German Lutheran theologian. After earning his doctorate from the University of Leipzig, Salmuth served in several coterminous pastoral and academic positions. He was integral to the reorganization of the University of Jena. Except for a few disputations, all of Salmuth's works—mostly sermons—were published posthumously by his son.

Robert Sanderson (1587–1663). Anglican bishop and philosopher. Before his appointment as professor of divinity at Oxford in 1642, Sanderson pastored in several parishes. Because of his loyalty to the Crown during the English Civil Wars, the Parliamentarians stripped Sanderson of his post at Oxford. After the Restoration he was reinstated at Oxford and consecrated bishop. He wrote an influential textbook on logic.

Edwin Sandys (1519–1588). Anglican bishop. During his doctoral studies at Cambridge, Sandys befriended Martin Bucer.* Having supported the Protestant Lady Jane Grey's claim to the throne, Sandys resigned his post at Cambridge upon Mary I's accession. He was then arrested and imprisoned in the Tower of London. Released in 1554, he sojourned on the continent until Mary's death. On his return to England he was appointed to revise the liturgy and was consecrated bishop. Many of his sermons were published, but his most significant literary legacy is his work as a translator of the Bishop's Bible (1568), which served as the foundational English text for the translators of the King James Bible (1611).

Erasmus Sarcerius (1501–1559). German Lutheran superintendent, educator and pastor. Sarcerius served as educational superintendent, court preacher and pastor in Nassau and, later, in Leipzig. The hallmark of Sarcerius's reputation was his ethical emphasis as exercised through ecclesial oversight and family structure; he also drafted disciplinary codes for regional churches in Germany. Sarcerius served with Philipp Melanchthon* as Protestant delegates at the Council of Trent, though both withdrew prior to the dismissal of the session; he eventually became an opponent of Melanchthon, contesting the latter's understanding of the Eucharist at a colloquy in Worms in 1557.

Michael Sattler (c. 1490–1527). Swiss Radical leader. Sattler was a Benedictine monk who abandoned the monastic life during the upheavals of the Peasants' War. He took up the trade of weaving under the guidance of an outspoken Anabaptist. It seems that Sattler did not openly join the Anabaptist movement until after the suppression of the Peasants' War in 1526. Sattler interceded with Martin Bucer* and Wolfgang Capito* for imprisoned Anabaptists in Strasbourg. Shortly before he was convicted of heresy and executed, he wrote the definitive expression of Anabaptist theology, the Schleitheim Articles.*

Girolamo Savonarola (1452–1498). Italian Catholic preacher and martyr. Outraged by clerical corruption and the neglect of the poor, Savonarola traveled to preach against these abuses and to prophesy impending judgment—a mighty king would scourge and reform the church. Savonarola thought that the French invasion of Italy in 1494 confirmed his apocalyptic visions. Thus he pressed to purge Florence of vice and institute public welfare, in order to usher in a new age of Christianity. Florence's refusal to join papal resistance against the French enraged Alexander VI (r. 1492–1503). He blamed Savonarola, promptly excommunicating him and threatening Florence with an interdict. After an ordeal by fire turned into a riot, Savonarola was arrested. Under torture he admitted to charges of conspiracy and false prophecy; he was hanged and burned. In addition to numerous sermons and letters, he wrote meditations on Psalms 31 and 51 as well as *The Triumph of the Cross* (1497).

Leupold Scharnschlager (d. 1563). Austrian Radical elder. See *Kunstbuch.*

Leonhard Schiemer (d. 1528) Austrian radical martyr. Troubled by the hypocrisies he experienced, Scheimer left the Franciscan order and spent a period of time wandering. Attracted to the teachings of Hans Hut* after hearing him debate Balthasar Hubmaier* in Moravia, he was rebaptized and traveled widely throughout Austria and Southern Germany, spreading the Anabaptist message until he was arrested in Rattenberg, where he was condemned to death and beheaded. A number of his essays and hymns survive, dispersed among the *Kunstbuch** and other collections of radical writings.

Hans Schlaffer (c. 1490–1528). Austrian Radical martyr. Drawn by Luther's theology, Schlaffer resigned his priesthood in 1526 only to turn to Anabaptism soon afterward. While contemporaries recognized his ability as a preacher, he never settled in a ministry position. He spent time among Radical congregations in Freistadt, Nicholsburg, Augsburg, Nuremberg, and Regensburg before his arrest in Schatz, where he was executed. Nine writings by Schlaffer remain, most of which were composed during his imprisonment. They include confessions of his beliefs and devotional works, which have been preserved among Hutterite churches.

Schleitheim Articles (1527). After the death of Conrad Grebel* in 1526 and the execution of Felix Manz (born c. 1498) in early 1527, the young Swiss Anabaptist movement was in need of unity and direction. A synod convened at Schleitheim under the chairmanship of Michael Sattler,* which passed seven articles of Anabaptist distinctives—likely defined against both magisterial reformers and other Anabaptists with less orthodox and more militant views (e.g., Balthasar Hubmaier*). Unlike most confessions, these articles do not explicitly address traditional creedal interests; they explicate instead the Anabaptist view of the sacraments, church discipline, separatism, the role of ministers, pacifism and oaths. Throughout the document there is a resolute focus on Christ's example. Also referred to as the Schleitheim Confession and the Schleitheim Brotherly Union, the Schleitheim Articles are considered the definitive statement of Anabaptist theology, particularly regarding separatism.

Schmalkald Articles (1537). In response to Pope Paul III's (1468–1549) 1536 decree ordering a general church council to solve the Protestant crisis, Elector John Frederick (1503–1554) commissioned Martin Luther* to draft the sum of his teaching. Intended by Luther as a last will and testament—and composed with advice from well-known colleagues Justus Jonas,* Johann Bugenhagen,* Caspar Cruciger,* Nikolaus von Amsdorf (1483–1565), Georg Spalatin (1484–1545), Philipp Melanchthon* and Johann Agricola*—these articles provide perhaps the briefest and most systematic summary of Luther's teaching. The document was not adopted formally by the Lutheran Schmalkald League, as was hoped, and the general church council was postponed for several years (until convening at Trent in 1545). Only in 1580 were the articles officially received, by being incorporated into the *Book of Concord* defining orthodox Lutheranism.

Anna Maria van Schurman (1607–1678). Dutch Reformed polymath. Van Schurman cultivated talents in art, poetry, botany, linguistics and theology. She mastered most contemporary European languages, in addition to Latin, Greek, Hebrew, Arabic, Farsi and Ethiopian. With the encouragement of leading Reformed theologian Gisbertus Voetius (1589–1676), van Schurman attended lectures at the University of Utrecht—although she was required to sit behind a wooden screen so that the male students could not see her. In 1638 van Schurman published her famous treatise advocating female scholarship, *Amica dissertatio . . . de capacitate ingenii muliebris ad scientias*. In addition to these more polemical works, van Schurman also wrote hymns and poems, including a paraphrase of Genesis 1–3. Later in life she became a devotee of Jean de Labadie (1610–1674), a former Jesuit who was also expelled from the Reformed church for his separatist leanings. Her *Eucleria* (1673) is the most well known defense of Labadie's theology.

Kaspar von Schwenckfeld (1489–1561). German Radical reformer. Schwenckfeld was a Silesian nobleman who encountered Luther's* works in 1521. He traveled to Wittenberg twice: first to meet Luther and Karlstadt,* and a second time to convince Luther of his doctrine of the "internal word"—emphasizing inner revelation so strongly that he did not see church meetings or the sacraments as necessary—after which Luther considered him heterodox. Schwenckfeld won his native territory to the Reformation in 1524 and later lived in Strasbourg for five years until Bucer* sought to purify the city of less traditional theologies. Schwenckfeld wrote numerous polemical and exegetical tracts.

Scots Confession (1560). In 1560, the Scottish Parliament undertook to reform the Church of Scotland and to commission a Reformed confession of faith. In the course of four days, a committee—which included John Knox*—wrote this confession, largely based on Calvin's* work, the Confession of the English Congregation in Geneva (1556) and the Gallic Confession.* The articles were not ratified until 1567 and were displaced by the Westminster Confession (1646), adopted by the Scottish in 1647.

Second Helvetic Confession (1566). Believing he would soon die, Heinrich Bullinger* penned a personal statement of his Reformed faith in 1561 as a theological will. In 1563, Bullinger sent a copy of this confession, which blended Zwingli's and Calvin's theology, to the elector of the Palatinate, Frederick III (1515–1576), who had asked for a complete explication of the Reformed faith in order to defend himself against aggressive Lutheran attacks after printing the Heidelberg Confession.* Although not published until 1566, the Second Helvetic Confession became the definitive sixteenth-century Reformed statement of faith. Theodore Beza* used it as the organizing confession for his *Harmonia Confessionum* (1581), which sought to emphasize the unity of the Reformed churches. Bullinger's personal confession was adopted by the Reformed churches of Scotland (1566), Hungary (1567), France (1571) and Poland (1571).

Obadiah Sedgwick (c. 1600–1658). English Puritan minister. Educated at Oxford, Sedgwick pastored in London and participated in the Westminster Assembly. An ardent Puritan, Sedgwick was appointed by Oliver Cromwell (1599–1658) to examine clerical candidates. Sedgwick published a catechism, several sermons and a treatise on how to deal with doubt.

Nikolaus Selnecker (1530–1592). German Lutheran theologian, preacher, pastor and hymnist. Selnecker taught in Wittenberg, Jena and Leipzig, preached in Dresden and Wolfenbüttel, and pastored in Leipzig. He was forced out of his post at Jena because of suspicions that he was a crypto-Calvinist. He sought refuge in Wolfenbüttel, where he met Martin Chemnitz* and Jakob Andreae.* Under their influence Selnecker was drawn away from Philippist theology. Selnecker's shift in theology can be seen in his *Institutio religionis christianae* (1573). Selnecker coauthored the Formula of Concord* with Chemnitz, Andreae, Andreas Musculus (1514–1581), and David Chytraeus.* Selnecker also published lectures on Genesis, the Psalms, and the New Testament epistles, as well as composing over a hundred hymn tunes and texts.

Short Confession (1610). In response to some of William Laud's* reforms in the Church of England—particularly a law stating that ministers who refused to comply with the Book of Common Prayer* would lose their ordination—a group of English Puritans immigrated to the Netherlands in protest, where they eventually embraced the practice of believer's baptism. The resulting Short Confession was an attempt at union between these Puritans and local Dutch Anabaptists ("Waterlanders"). The document highlights the importance of love in the church and reflects optimism regarding the freedom of the will while explicitly rejecting double predestination.

Richard Sibbes (1577–1635). English Puritan preacher. Sibbes was educated at St. John's College, Cambridge, where he was converted to reforming views and became a popular preacher. As a moderate Puritan emphasizing interior piety and brotherly love, Sibbes always remained within the established Church of England, though opposed to some of its liturgical ceremonies. His collected sermons constitute his main literary legacy.

Menno Simons (c. 1496–1561). Dutch Radical leader. Simons led a separatist Anabaptist group in the Netherlands that would later be called Mennonites, known for nonviolence and renunciation of the world. A former priest, Simons rejected Catholicism through the influence of Anabaptist disciples of Melchior Hoffmann and based on his study of Scripture, in which he found no support for transubstantiation or infant baptism. Following the sack of Anabaptists at Münster, Simons committed to a nonviolent way of life. Simons proclaimed a message of radical discipleship of obedience and inner purity, marked by voluntary adult baptism and communal discipline.

Henry Smith (c. 1550–1591). English Puritan minister. Smith stridently opposed the Book of Common Prayer* and refused to subscribe to the Articles of Religion,* thus limiting his pastoral opportunities. Nevertheless he gained a reputation as an eloquent preacher in London. He published sermon collections as well as several treatises.

Domingo de Soto (1494–1560). Spanish Catholic theologian. Soto taught philosophy for four years at the University in Alcalá before entering the Dominican order. In 1532 he became chair of theology at the University of Salamanca; Soto sought to reintroduce Aristotle in the curriculum. He served as confessor and spiritual advisor to Charles V, who enlisted Soto as imperial theologian for the Council of Trent. Alongside commentaries on the works of Aristotle and Peter Lombard (c. 1100–1160), Soto commented on Romans and wrote an influential treatise on nature and grace.

Cyriacus Spangenberg (1528–1604). German Lutheran pastor, preacher and theologian. Spangenberg was a staunch, often acerbic, Gnesio-Lutheran. He rejected the Formula of Concord* because of concerns about the princely control of the church, as well as its rejection of Flacian language of original sin (as constituting the "substance" of human nature after the fall). He published many commentaries and sermons, most famously seventy wedding sermons (*Ehespiegel* [1561]), his sermons on Luther* (*Theander Luther* [1562–1571]) and Luther's hymns (*Cithara Lutheri* [1569–1570]). He also published an analysis of the Old Testament (though he only got as far as Job), based on a methodology that anticipated the logical bifurcations of Peter Ramus.*

Johann Spangenberg (1484–1550). German Lutheran pastor and catechist. Spangenberg studied at the University of Erfurt, where he was welcomed into a group of humanists associated with Konrad Muth (1470–1526). There he met the reformer Justus Jonas,* and Eobanus Hessius (1488–1540), whom Luther* dubbed "king of the poets." Spangenberg served at parishes in Stolberg (1520–1524), Nordhausen (1524–1546) and, by Luther's recommendation, Eisleben (1546–1550). Spangenberg published one of the best-selling postils of the sixteenth century, the *Postilla Teütsch*, a six-volume work meant to prepare children to understand the lectionary readings. It borrowed the question-answer form of Luther's

Small Catechism and was so popular that a monk, Johannes Craendonch, purged overt anti-Catholic statements from it and republished it under his own name. Among Spangenberg's other pastoral works are *ars moriendi* ("the art of dying") booklets, a postil for the Acts of the Apostles and a question-answer version of Luther's *Large Catechism*. In addition to preaching and pastoring, Spangenberg wrote pamphlets on controversial topics such as purgatory, as well as textbooks on music, mathematics and grammar.

Georg Spindler (1525–1605). German Reformed theologian and pastor. After studying theology under Caspar Cruciger* and Philipp Melanchthon,* Spindler accepted a pastorate in Bohemia. A well-respected preacher, Spindler published postils in 1576 which some of his peers viewed as crypto-Calvinist. To investigate this allegation Spindler read John Calvin's* *Institutes*, and subsequently converted to the Reformed faith. After years of travel, he settled in the Palatinate and pastored there until his death. In addition to his Lutheran postils, Spindler also published Reformed postils in 1594 as well as several treatises on the Lord's Supper and predestination.

Statenvertaling (1637). The Synod of Dordrecht* commissioned this new Dutch translation of the Bible ("State's Translation"). The six theologians who undertook this translation also wrote prefaces for each biblical book, annotated obscure words and difficult passages, and provided cross-references; they even explained certain significant translation decisions. At the request of the Westminster Assembly, Theodore Haak (1605–1690) translated the *Statenvertaling* into English as *The Dutch Annotations Upon the Whole Bible* (1657).

Johann von Staupitz (d. 1524). German Catholic theologian, professor and preacher. Frederick the Wise summoned this Augustinian monk to serve as professor of Bible and first dean of the theology faculty at the University of Wittenberg. As Vicar-General of the Reformed Augustinian Hermits in Germany, Staupitz sought to reform the order and attempted unsuccessfully to reunite with the conventional Augustinians. While in

Wittenberg, Staupitz was Martin Luther's* teacher, confessor and spiritual father. He supported Luther in the early controversies over indulgences, but after releasing Luther from his monastic vows (to protect him), he distanced himself from the conflict. He relocated to Salzburg, where he was court preacher to Cardinal Matthäus Lang von Wellenburg (d. 1540) and abbot of the Benedictine monastery. Staupitz wrote treatises on predestination, faith and the love of God. Many of his sermons were collected and published during his lifetime.

Michael Stifel (1486–1567). German Lutheran mathematician, theologian and pastor. An Augustinian monk, Stifel's interest in mysticism, apocalypticism and numerology led him to identify Pope Leo X as the antichrist. Stifel soon joined the reform movement, writing a 1522 pamphlet in support of Martin Luther's* theology. After Luther quelled the fallout of Stifel's failed prediction of the Apocalypse—October 19, 1533 at 8 a.m.—Stifel focused more on mathematics and his pastoral duties. He was the first professor of mathematics at the University of Jena. He published several numerological interpretations of texts from the Gospels, Daniel and Revelation. However, Stifel's most important work is his *Arithmetica Integra* (1544), in which he standardized the approach to quadratic equations. He also developed notations for exponents and radicals.

Viktorin Strigel (1524–1569). German Lutheran theologian. Strigel taught at Wittenberg, Erfurt, Jena, Leipzig and Heidelberg. During his time in Jena he disputed with Matthias Flacius (1520–1575) over the human will's autonomy. Following Philipp Melanchthon,* Strigel asserted that in conversion the human will obediently cooperates with the divine will through the Holy Spirit and the Word of God. In the Weimar Disputation (1560), Strigel elicited Flacius's opinion that sin is a substance that mars the formal essence of human beings. Flacius's views were officially rejected in Article 1 of the Formula of Concord*; Strigel's, in Article 2. In 1567 the University of Leipzig suspended Strigel from teaching on account of suspicions that he affirmed Reformed

Eucharistic theology; he acknowledged that he did and joined the Reformed confession on the faculty of the University of Heidelberg. In addition to controversial tracts, Strigel published commentaries on the entire Bible (except Lamentations) and the Apocrypha.

Johann Sutell (1504–1575). German Lutheran pastor. After studying at the University of Wittenberg, Sutell received a call to a pastorate in Göttingen, where he eventually became superintendent. He wrote new church orders for Göttingen (1531) and Schweinfurt (1543), and expanded two sermons for publication, *The Dreadful Destruction of Jerusalem* (1539) and *History of Lazarus* (1543).

Swiss Brethren Confession of Hesse (1578). Anabaptist leader Hans Pauly Kuchenbecker penned this confession after a 1577 interrogation by Lutheran authorities. This confession was unusually amenable to Lutheran views—there is no mention of pacifism or rejection of oath taking.

Synod of Dordrecht (1618–1619). This large Dutch Reformed Church council—also attended by English, German and Swiss delegates—met to settle the theological issues raised by the followers of Jacobus Arminius.* Arminius's theological disagreements with mainstream Reformed teaching erupted into open conflict with the publication of the *Remonstrance* (1610). This "protest" was based on five points: that election is based on foreseen faith or unbelief; that Christ died indiscriminately for all people (although only believers receive salvation); that people are thoroughly sinful by nature apart from the prevenient grace of God that enables their free will to embrace or reject the gospel; that humans are able to resist the working of God's grace; and that it is possible for true believers to fall away from faith completely. The Synod ruled in favor of the Contra-Remonstrants, its Canons often remembered with a TULIP acrostic—total depravity, unconditional election, limited atonement, irresistible grace, perseverance of the saints—each letter countering one of the five Remonstrant articles. The Synod also officially accepted the Belgic Confession,* Heidelberg Catechism* and the Canons of Dordrecht as standards of the Dutch Reformed Church.

Arcangela Tarabotti (1604–1652). Italian Catholic nun. At the age of eleven, Tarabotti entered a Benedictine convent as a student-boarder; three years later her father forced her to take monastic vows. The dignity of women and their treatment in the male-controlled institutions of early modern Venice concerned Tarabotti deeply. She protested forced cloistering, the denial of education to women, the exclusion of women from public life and the double standards by which men and women were judged. Tarbotti authored numerous polemical works and an extensive correspondence.

Johannes Tauler (c. 1300–1361) German mystical theologian. A Dominican friar and disciple of Meister Eckhart (c. 1260–c. 1328), Tauler spent most of his career as a mendicant preacher in Strasburg and Basel. Known through a collection of about eighty German sermons, Tauler taught a practical spirituality, accessible to those outside the cloister and intended to draw his audience to deeper contemplation of the divine nature.

Richard Taverner (1505–1575). English Puritan humanist and translator. After graduating from Oxford, Taverner briefly studied abroad. When he returned to England, he joined Thomas Cromwell's (1485–1540) circle. After Cromwell's beheading, Taverner escaped severe punishment and retired from public life during Mary I's reign. Under Elizabeth I, Taverner served as justice of the peace, sheriff and a licensed lay preacher. Taverner translated many important continental Reformation works into English, most notably the Augsburg Confession* and several of Desiderius Erasmus's* works. Some of these translations—John Calvin's* 1536 catechism, Wolfgang Capito's* work on the Psalms and probably Erasmus Sarcerius's* postils— he presented as his own work. Underwritten by Cromwell, Taverner also published an edited version of the Matthew Bible (1537).

Thomas Thorowgood (1595–1669). English Puritan pastor. Thorowgood was a Puritan

minister in Norfolk and the chief financier of John Eliot (1604–1690), a Puritan missionary among the Native American tribes in Massachusetts. In 1650, under the title *Jews in America, or, Probabilities that Americans be of that Race*, Thorowgood became one of the first to put forward the thesis that Native Americans were actually the ten lost tribes of Israel.

Frans Titelmans (1502–1537). Belgian Catholic philosopher. Titelmans studied at the University of Leuven, where he was influenced by Petrus Ramus.* After first joining a Franciscan monastery, Titelmans realigned with the stricter Capuchins and moved to Italy. He is best known for his advocacy for the Vulgate and his debates with Desiderius Erasmus* over Pauline theology (1527–1530)—he was deeply suspicious of the fruits of humanism, especially regarding biblical studies. His work was published posthumously by his brother, Pieter Titelmans (1501–1572).

Francisco de Toledo (1532–1596). Spanish Catholic theologian. This important Jesuit taught philosophy at the universities of Salamanca and Rome. He published works on Aristotelian philosophy and a commentary on Thomas Aquinas's work, as well as biblical commentaries on John, Romans and the first half of Luke. He was also the general editor for the Clementine Vulgate (1598).

Alonso Tostado (1400–1455). Spanish Catholic bishop and exegete. Tostado lectured on theology, law and philosophy at the University of Salamanca, in addition to ministering in a local parish. Tostado entered into disputes over papal supremacy and the date of Christ's birth. Tostado's thirteen-volume collected works include commentaries on the historical books of the Old Testament and the Gospel of Matthew.

Daniel Toussain (1541–1602). Swiss Reformed pastor and professor. Toussain became pastor at Orléans after attending college in Basel. After the third War of Religion, Toussain was exiled, eventually returning to Montbéliard, his birthplace. In 1571, he faced opposition there from the strict Lutheran rulers and was eventually exiled due to his influence over the clergy. He returned to Orléans but fled following the Saint Bartholomew's Day Massacre (1572), eventually becoming pastor in Basel. He relocated to Heidelberg in 1583 as pastor to the new regent, becoming professor of theology at the university, and he remained there until his death.

John Trapp (1601–1669). Anglican biblical exegete. After studying at Oxford, Trapp entered the pastorate in 1636. During the English Civil Wars he sided with Parliament, which later made it difficult for him to collect tithes from a congregation whose royalist pastor had been evicted. Trapp published commentaries on all the books of the Bible from 1646 to 1656.

Immanuel Tremellius (1510–1580). Italian Reformed Hebraist. Around 1540, Tremellius received baptism by Cardinal Reginald Pole (1500–1558) and converted from Judaism to Christianity; he affiliated with evangelicals the next year. On account of the political and religious upheaval, Tremellius relocated often, teaching Hebrew in Lucca; Strasbourg, fleeing the Inquisition; Cambridge, displaced by the Schmalkaldic War; Heidelberg, escaping Mary I's persecutions; and Sedan, expelled by the new Lutheran Elector of the Palatine. Many considered Tremellius's translation of the Old Testament as the most accurate available. He also published a Hebrew grammar and translated John Calvin's* catechism into Hebrew.

Richard Turnbull (d. 1593). English minister. A preacher in London, Richard Turnbull published sermons on James, Jude, and Psalm 15.

William Tyndale (Hychyns) (1494–1536). English reformer, theologian and translator. Tyndale was educated at Oxford University, where he was influenced by the writings of humanist thinkers. Believing that piety is fostered through personal encounter with the Bible, he asked to translate the Bible into English; denied permission, Tyndale left for the Continent to complete the task. His New Testament was the equivalent of a modern-day bestseller in England but was banned and ordered burned. Tyndale's theology was oriented around justification, the authority of

Scripture and Christian obedience; Tyndale emphasized the ethical as a concomitant reality of justification. He was martyred in Brussels before completing his English translation of the Old Testament, which Miles Coverdale* finished.

Guillaume du Vair (1556–1621). French Catholic priest, lawyer, and writer. While du Vair took holy orders in his youth, much of his life was spent serving the state as a counselor of the parliament of Paris, a representative of King Henry IV both in France and abroad, and as Keeper of the Seals, the highest legal office in the country. The last four years of his life were spent as the bishop of Lisieux. His studies on Epictetus and the Stoics, and attempts to relate Stoicism to the Christian faith, were influential in the dissemination of this philosophy during the seventeenth and eighteenth centuries. He also wrote significant works on politics, the moral life, prayer, and the use and abuse of the French language.

Juan de Valdés (1500/10–1541). Spanish Catholic theologian and writer. Although Valdés adopted an evangelical doctrine, had Erasmian affiliations and published works that were listed on the Index of Prohibited Books, Valdés rebuked the reformers for creating disunity and never left the Catholic Church. His writings included translations of the Hebrew Psalter and various biblical books, a work on the Spanish language and several commentaries. Valdés fled to Rome in 1531 to escape the Spanish Inquisition and worked in the court of Clement VII in Bologna until the pope's death in 1534. Valdés subsequently returned to Naples, where he led the reform- and revival-minded Valdesian circle.

Peter Martyr Vermigli (1499–1562). Italian Reformed humanist and theologian. Vermigli was one of the most influential theologians of the era, held in common regard with such figures as Martin Luther* and John Calvin.* In Italy, Vermigli was a distinguished theologian, preacher and advocate for moral reform; however, during the reinstitution of the Roman Inquisition Vermigli fled to Protestant regions in northern Europe. He was eventually appointed professor of divinity at

Oxford University, where Vermigli delivered acclaimed disputations on the Eucharist. Vermigli was widely noted for his deeply integrated biblical commentaries and theological treatises.

Vulgate. In 382 Pope Damasus I (c. 300–384) commissioned Jerome (c. 347–420) to translate the four Gospels into Latin based on Old Latin and Greek manuscripts. Jerome completed the translation of the Gospels and the Old Testament around 405. It is widely debated how much of the rest of the New Testament was translated by Jerome. During the Middle Ages, the Vulgate became the Catholic Church's standard Latin translation. The Council of Trent recognized it as the official text of Scripture.

Thomas Walkington (d. 1621). Anglican minister and author. Born in Lincoln, he was educated at Cambridge, graduating with his BA in 1597 and his MA in 1600. Walkington was elected a fellow at St. John's College, Cambridge, in 1602. Later, he received a BD from Oxford and a DD from Cambridge. He served as rector of parishes in Northamptonshire, Lincolnshire, and Middlesex. A prolific author, Walkington published works on diverse subjects. Among his biblical works are *An Exposition of the First Two Verses of the Sixth Chapter to the Hebrews in form of a Dialogue* (1609) and *Theologicall Rules to Guide Us in the Understanding and Practice of Holy Scripture* (1615).

Peter Walpot (d. 1578). Moravian Radical pastor and bishop. Walpot was a bishop of the Hutterite community after Jakob Hutter, Peter Riedemann* and Leonhard Lanzenstiel. Riedemann's *Confession of Faith* (1545; 1565) became a vital authority for Hutterite exegesis, theology and morals. Walpot added his own *Great Article Book* (1577), which collates primary biblical passages on baptism, communion, the community of goods, the sword and divorce. In keeping with Hutterite theology, Walpot defended the community of goods as a mark of the true church.

Valentin Weigel (1533–1588). German Lutheran pastor. Weigel studied at Leipzig and Wittenberg, entering the pastorate in 1567. Despite a strong anti-institutional bias, he was recognized by the church hierarchy as a talented preacher and compassionate minister of mercy to the poor. Although he signed the Formula of Concord,* Weigel's orthodoxy was questioned so openly that he had to publish a defense. He appears to have tried to synthesize several medieval mystics with the ideas of Sebastian Franck,* Thomas Müntzer* and others. His posthumously published works have led some recent scholars to suggest that Weigel's works may have deeply influenced later Pietism.

Hieronymus Weller von Molsdorf (1499–1572). German Lutheran theologian. Originally intending to study law, Weller devoted himself to theology after hearing one of Martin Luther's* sermons on the catechism. He boarded with Luther and tutored Luther's son. In 1539 he moved to Freiburg, where he lectured on the Bible and held theological disputations at the Latin school. In addition to hymns, works of practical theology and a postil set, Weller published commentaries on Genesis, 1–2 Samuel, 1–2 Kings, Job, the Psalms, Christ's passion, Ephesians, Philippians, 1–2 Thessalonians and 1–2 Peter.

John Whitgift (1530–1604). Anglican archbishop. Though Whitgift shared much theological common ground with Puritans, after his election as Archbishop of Canterbury (1583) he moved decisively to squelch the political and ecclesiastical threat they posed during Elizabeth's reign. Whitgift enforced strict compliance to the Book of Common Prayer,* the Act of Uniformity (1559) and the Articles of Religion.* Whitgift's policies led to a large migration of Puritans to Holland. The bulk of Whitgift's published corpus is the fruit of a lengthy public disputation with Thomas Cartwright,* in which Whitgift defines Anglican doctrine against Cartwright's staunch Puritanism.

Johann Wigand (1523–1587). German Lutheran theologian. Wigand is most noted as one of the compilers of the *Magdeburg Centuries*, a German ecclesiastical history of the first thirteen centuries of the church. He was a student of Philipp Melanchthon* at the University of Wittenburg and became a significant figure in the controversies dividing Lutheranism. Strongly opposed to Roman Catholicism, Wigand lobbied against innovations in Lutheran theology that appeared sympathetic to Catholic thought. In the later debates, Wigand's support for Gnesio-Lutheranism established his role in the development of confessional Lutheranism. Wigand was appointed bishop of Pomerania after serving academic posts at the universities in Jena and Königsburg.

Thomas Wilcox (c. 1549–1608). English Puritan theologian. In 1572, Wilcox objected to Parliament against the episcopacy and the Book of Common Prayer,* advocating for presbyterian church governance. He was imprisoned for sedition. After his release, he preached itinerantly. He was brought before the courts twice more for his continued protest against the Church of England's episcopal structure. He translated some of Theodore Beza* and John Calvin's* sermons into English, and he wrote polemical and occasional works as well as commentaries on the Psalms and Song of Songs.

Johann (Ferus) Wild (1495–1554). German Catholic pastor. After studying at Heidelberg and teaching at Tübingen, this Franciscan was appointed as lector in the Mainz cathedral, eventually being promoted to cathedral preacher—a post for which he became widely popular but also controversial. Wild strongly identified as Catholic but was not unwilling to criticize the curia. Known for an irenic spirit— criticized in fact as *too* kind—he was troubled by the polemics between all parties of the Reformation. He preached with great lucidity, integrating the liturgy, Scripture and doctrine to exposit Catholic worship and teaching for common people. His sermons on John were pirated for publication without his knowledge; the Sorbonne banned them as heretical. Despite his popularity among clergy, the majority of his works were on the Roman Index until 1900.

Andrew Willet (1562–1621). Anglican priest, professor, and biblical expositor. Willet was a gifted biblical expositor and powerful preacher. He walked away from a promising university career in 1588 when he was ordained a priest in the Church of England. For the next thirty-three years he served as a parish priest. Willet's commentaries summarized the present state of discussion while also offering practical applications for preachers. They have been cited as some of the most technical commentaries of the early seventeenth century. His most important publication was *Synopsis Papismi, or a General View of Papistrie* (1594), in which he responded to many of Robert Bellarmine's critiques. After years of royal favor, Willet was imprisoned in 1618 for a month after presenting to King James I his opposition to the "Spanish Match" of Prince Charles to the Infanta Maria. While serving as a parish priest, he wrote forty-two works, most of which were either commentaries on books of the Bible or controversial works against Catholics.

Thomas Wilson (d. 1586). English Anglican priest. A fellow of St John's, Cambridge, Wilson fled to Frankfurt to escape the Marian Persecution. After his return to England, he served as a canon and Dean of Worcester.

John Woolton (c. 1535–1594). Anglican bishop. After graduating from Oxford, Woolton lived in Germany until the accession of Elizabeth I. He was ordained as a priest in 1560 and as a bishop in 1578. Woolton published many theological, devotional and practical works, including a treatise on the immortality of the soul, a discourse on conscience and a manual for Christian living.

Girolamo Zanchi (1516–1590). Italian Reformed theologian and pastor. Zanchi joined an Augustinian monastery at the age of fifteen, where he studied Greek and Latin, the church fathers and the works of Aristotle and Thomas Aquinas. Under the influence of his prior, Peter Martyr Vermigli,* Zanchi also imbibed the writings of the Swiss and German reformers. To avoid the Inquisition, Zanchi fled to Geneva where he was strongly attracted to the preaching and teaching of John Calvin.* Zanchi taught biblical theology and the *locus* method at academies in Strasbourg, Heidelberg, and Neustadt. He also served as pastor of an Italian refugee congregation. Zanchi's theological works, *De tribus Elohim* (1572) and *De natura Dei* (1577), have received more attention than his commentaries. His commentaries comprise about a quarter of his literary output, however, and display a strong typological and christological interpretation in conversation with the church fathers, medieval exegetes, and other reformers.

Katharina Schütz Zell (1497/98–1562). German Reformed writer. Zell became infamous in Strasbourg and the Empire when in 1523 she married the priest Matthias Zell, and then published an apology defending her husband against charges of impiety and libertinism. Longing for a united church, she called for toleration of Catholics and Anabaptists, famously writing to Martin Luther* after the failed Marburg Colloquy of 1529 to exhort him to check his hostility and to be ruled instead by Christian charity. Much to the chagrin of her contemporaries, Zell published diverse works, ranging from polemical treatises on marriage to letters of consolation, as well as editing a hymnal and penning an exposition of Psalm 51.

Huldrych Zwingli (1484–1531). Swiss Reformed humanist, preacher and theologian. Zwingli, a parish priest, was influenced by the writings of Desiderius Erasmus* and taught himself Greek. While a preacher to the city cathedral in Zurich, Zwingli enacted reform through sermons, public disputations and conciliation with the town council, abolishing the Mass and images in the church. Zwingli broke with the lectionary preaching tradition, instead preaching serial expository biblical sermons. He later was embroiled in controversy with Anabaptists over infant baptism and with Martin Luther* at the Marburg Colloquy (1529) over their differing views of the Eucharist. Zwingli, serving as chaplain to Zurich's military, was killed in battle.

SOURCES FOR BIOGRAPHICAL SKETCHES

General Reference Works

Allgemeine Deutsche Biographie. 56 vols. Leipzig: Duncker & Humblot, 1875–1912; reprint, 1967–1971. Accessible online via deutsche -biographie.de/index.html.

Baskin, Judith R., ed. *The Cambridge Dictionary of Judaism and Jewish Culture.* New York: Cambridge University Press, 2011.

Benedetto, Robert, ed. *The New Westminster Dictionary of Church History.* Vol. 1. Louisville: Westminster John Knox Press, 2008.

Bettenson, Henry and Chris Maunder, eds. *Documents of the Christian Church.* 3rd ed. Oxford: Oxford University Press, 1999.

Betz, Hans Dieter, Don Browning, Bernd Janowski and Eberhard Jüngel, eds. *Religion Past & Present: Encyclopedia of Theology and Relgion.* 13 vols. Leiden: Brill, 2007–2013.

Bremer, Francis J. and Tom Webster, eds. *Puritans and Puritanism in Europe and America: A Comprehensive Encyclopedia.* 2 vols. Santa Barbara, CA: ABC-CLIO, 2006.

Gritsch, Eric W. *A History of Lutheranism.* Minneapolis: Fortress Press, 2002.

Haag, Eugene and Émile Haag. *La France protestante ou vies des protestants français.* 2nd ed. 6 vols. Paris: Sandoz & Fischbacher, 1877–1888.

Hillerbrand, Hans J., ed. *Oxford Encyclopedia of the Reformation.* 4 vols. New York: Oxford University Press, 1996.

Kolb, Robert, and Timothy J. Wengert, eds. *The Book of Concord: The Confessions of the Evangelical Lutheran Church.* Translated by Charles Arand et al. Minneapolis: Fortress, 2000.

McKim, Donald K., ed. *Dictionary of Major Biblical Interpreters.* Downers Grove, IL: InterVarsity Press, 2007.

Müller, Gerhard, et al., ed. *Theologische Realenzyklopädie.* Berlin: Walter de Gruyter, 1994.

Neue Deutsche Biographie. 28 vols. projected. Berlin: Duncker & Humblot, 1953–. Accessible online via deutsche-biographie.de/index.html.

New Catholic Encyclopedia. 15 vols. New York: McGraw-Hill, 1967; 2nd ed., Detroit: Thomson-Gale, 2002.

Oxford Dictionary of National Biography. 60 vols. Oxford: Oxford University Press, 2004.

Pelikan, Jaroslav. *The Christian Tradition.* 5 vols. Chicago: University of Chicago Press, 1971–1989.

Stephen, Leslie, and Sidney Lee, eds. *Dictionary of National Biography.* 63 vols. London: Smith, Elder and Co., 1885–1900.

Terry, Michael, ed. *Reader's Guide to Judaism.* New York: Routledge, 2000.

Wordsworth, Christopher, ed. *Lives of Eminent Men connected with the History of Religion in England.* 4 vols. London: J. G. & F. Rivington, 1839.

Additional Works for Individual Sketches

Akin, Daniel L. "An Expositional Analysis of the Schleitheim Confession." *Criswell Theological Review* 2 (1988): 345-70.

Bald, R. C. *John Donne: A Life.* Oxford: Oxford University Press, 1970.

Bireley, Robert, *The Refashioning of Catholicism, 1450–1700,* Washington, DC: Catholic University of America Press, 1999.

Burke, David G. "The Enduring Significance of the KJV." *Word and World* 31, no. 3 (2011): 229-44.

Campbell, Gordon. *Bible: The Story of the King James Version, 1611–2011.* Oxford: Oxford University Press, 2010.

Doornkaat Koolman, J ten. "The First Edition of Peter Riedemann's 'Rechenschaft.'" *Mennonite Quarterly Review* 36, no. 2 (1962): 169-70.

Fischlin, Daniel and Mark Fortier, eds. *Royal Subjects: Essays on the Writings of James VI and I.* Detroit: Wayne State University Press, 2002.

Fishbane, Michael A. "Teacher and the Hermeneutical Task: A Reinterpretation of Medieval Exegesis." *Journal of the American Academy of Religion* 43, no. 4 (1975): 709-21.

Friedmann, Robert. "Second Generation Anabaptism as Illustrated by the Walpot Era of the Hutterites." *Mennonite Quarterly* 44, no. 4 (1970): 390-93.

Frymire, John M. *The Primacy of the Postils: Catholics, Protestants, and the Dissemination of Ideas in Early Modern Germany*. Leiden: Brill, 2010.

Furcha, Edward J. "Key Concepts in Caspar von Schwenckfeld's Thought, Regeneration and the New Life." *Church History* 37, no. 2 (1968): 160-73.

Gordon, Bruce, *The Swiss Reformation*. Manchester: Manchester University Press, 2002.

Greaves, Richard L. *Society and Religion in Elizabethan England*. Minneapolis: University of Minnesota, 1981.

Greiffenberg, Catharina Regina von. *Meditations on the Incarnation, Passion and Death of Jesus Christ*. Edited and translated by Lynne Tatlock. The Other Voice in Early Modern Europe. Chicago: University of Chicago Press, 2009.

Grendler, Paul. "Italian biblical humanism and the papacy, 1515-1535." In *Biblical Humanism and Scholasticism in the Age of Erasmus*. Edited by Erika Rummel, 225-76. Leiden: Brill, 2008.

Heiden, Albert van der. "Pardes: Methodological Reflections on the Theory of the Four Senses." *Journal of Jewish Studies* 34, no. 2 (1983): 147-59.

Hendrix, Scott H., ed. and trans. *Early Protestant Spirituality*. New York: Paulist Press, 2009.

Hvolbek, Russell H. "Being and Knowing: Spiritualist Epistelmology and Anthropology from Schwenckfeld to Böhme." *Sixteenth Century Journal* 22, no. 1 (1991): 97-110.

Kahle, Paul. "Felix Pratensis—a Prato, Felix. Der Herausgeber der Ersten Rabbinerbibel, Venedig 1516/7." *Die Welt des Orients* 1, no. 1 (1947): 32-36.

Kelly, Joseph Francis. *The Ecumenical Councils of the Catholic Church: A History*. Collegeville, MN: Liturgical Press, 2009.

Lake, Peter. *The Boxmaker's Revenge: "Orthodoxy", "Heterodox" and the Politics of the Parish in Early Stuart London*. Stanford, CA: Stanford University Press, 2001.

Lockhart, Paul Douglas. *Frederick II and the Protestant Cause: Denmark's Role in the Wars of Religion, 1559–1596*. Leiden: Brill, 2004.

Lubac, Henri de. *Medieval Exegesis: The Four Senses of Scripture*. 3 vols. Translated by Mark Sebanc and E. M. Macierowski. Grand Rapids: Eerdmans, 1998–2009.

Manetsch, Scott, *Calvin's Company of Pastors: Pastoral Care and the Emerging Reformed Church, 1536–1609*. Oxford: Oxford University Press, 2013.

Matheson, Peter, *Argula von Grumbach: A Woman's Voice in the Reformation*. Edinburgh: T&T Clark, 1995.

McKinley, Mary B. "Volume Editor's Introduction." In *Epistle to Marguerite of Navarre and Preface to a Sermon by John Calvin*, edited and translated by Mary B. McKiney. Chicago: University of Chicago Press, 2004.

Norton, David. *A Textual History of the King James Bible*. New York: Cambridge University Press, 2005

Packull, Werner O. "The Origins of Peter Riedemann's Account of Our Faith." *Sixteenth Century Journal* 30, no. 1 (1999): 61-69.

Papazian, Mary Arshagouni, ed. *John Donne and the Protestant Reformation: New Perspectives*. Detroit: Wayne State University Press, 2003.

Paulicelli, Eugenia. "Sister Arcangela Tarabotti: Hair, Wigs and Other Vices." In *Writing Fashion in Early Modern Italy: From Sprezzatura to Satire*, by idem, 177-204. Farnham, Surrey, UK: Ashgate, 2014.

Pragman, James H. "The Augsburg Confession in the English Reformation: Richard Taverner's Contribution." *Sixteenth Century Journal* 11, no. 3 (1980): 75-85.

Rashi. *Rashi's Commentary on Psalms*. Translated by Mayer I. Gruber. Atlanta: Scholars Press, 1998.

Reid, Jonathan A. *King's Sister—Queen of Dissent: Marguerite of Navarre (1492–1549) and her Evangelical Network*. Leiden: Brill, 2009.

Schmidt, Josef, "Introduction" in Johannes Tauler, *Sermons*. New York: Paulist Press, 1985, 1-34.

Spinka, Matthew. *John Hus: A Biography*. Princeton, NJ: Princeton University Press, 1968.

———. *John Hus at the Council of Constance*. New York: Columbia University Press, 1968.

———. *John Hus and the Czech Reform*. Hamden, CT: Archon Books, 1966.

Steinmetz, David C. *Reformers in the Wings: From Geiler von Kayserberg to Theodore Beza*. Oxford: Oxford University Press, 2000.

———. "The Superiority of Pre-Critical Exegesis." *Theology Today* 37, no. 1 (1980): 27-38.

Synder, C. Arnold. "The Confession of the Swiss Brethren in Hesse, 1578." In *Anabaptism Revisited: Essays on Anabaptist/Mennonite Studies in Honor of C. J. Dyck*. Edited by Walter Klaassen, 29-49.

Waterloo, ON; Scottdale, PA: Herald Press, 1992.

———. "The Schleitheim Articles in Light of the Revolution of the Common Man: Continuation or Departure?" *Sixteenth Century Journal* 16, no. 4 (1985): 419-30.

Todd, Margo. "Bishops in the Kirk: William Cowper of Galloway and the Puritan Episcopacy of Scotland." *Scottish Journal of Theology*, 57 (2004): 300-312.

Van Liere, Frans. *An Introduction to the Medieval Bible.* New York: Cambridge University Press, 2014.

Voogt, Gerrit. "Remonstrant-Counter-Remonstrant Debates: Crafting a Principled Defense of Toleration after the Synod of Dordrecht (1619–1650)." *Church History and Religious Culture* 89, no. 4 (2009): 489-524.

Wallace, Dewey D. Jr. "George Gifford, Puritan Propaganda and Popular Religion in Elizabethan England." *Sixteenth Century Journal* 9, no. 1 (1978): 27-49.

Wengert, Timothy J. "'Fear and Love' in the Ten Commandments." *Concordia Journal* 21, no. 1 (1995): 14-27.

———. "Philip Melanchthon and John Calvin against Andreas Osiander: Coming to Terms with Forensic Justification." In *Calvin and Luther: The Continuing Relationship*, edited by R. Ward Holder, 63-87. Göttingen: Vandenhoeck & Ruprecht, 2013.

Wilkinson, Robert J. *Tetragrammaton: Western Christians and the Hebrew Name of God.* Leiden: Brill, 2015.

BIBLIOGRAPHY

Primary Translations and Sources Cited in the Volume

À Lapide, Cornelius, SJ. *Commentaria in Ieremiam Prophetam, Threnos, et Baruch*. Antwerp: Martin Nutium et al., 1621. Digital copy online at books.google.com.

Albert the Great. *Beati Alberti Magni . . . Commentarii in Threnos Ieremiae, in Baruch, in Danielem, in 12 Proph. Minors*. Lyon: Hugetan et al., 1651.

Andrewes, Lancelot. *The Works of Lancelot Andrewes*. Edited by John Posthumus Parkinson and John Buckeridge. 11 vols. New York: AMS Press, 1967.

Arndt, Johann. *Johann Arndt: True Christianity*. Translated by Peter Erb. Classics of Western Spirituality. New York: Paulist, 1979.

The Book of Concord: The Confessions of the Evangelical Lutheran Church. Translated and edited by Theodore G. Tappert et al. Philadelphia: Fortress: 1959.

Braght, Thieleman J. van, ed. *The Bloody Theater, or Martyrs' Mirror of the Defenseless Christians*. Translated by Joseph F. Sohm. 1886. Reprint, Scottdale, PA: Herald Press, 1938.

Brenz, Johannes. *Breves, sed nervosae Annotationes in Ieremiam*. In *Operum reverendi et clarissimi theologi, D. Ioannis Brentii, praepositi Stutgardiani*, 4:870-948. Tübingen: Georg Gruppenbach, 1580. Digital copy online at books.google.com.

Broughton, Hugh. *The Lamentationes of Ieremy, translated with great care of his Hebrew elegancie, and oratorious speeches*. Amsterdam: J. Theunisz, 1606.

Bucer, Martin. *De Regno Christi*, edited and translated by Wilhelm Pauck with Paul Larkin, 174-394. In *Melanchton and Bucer*. LCC 19. Philadelphia: Westminster, 1969.

Bugenhagen, Johannes. *In Ieremiam Prophetam Commentarium Iohannis Bugenhagij Pomerani, Doctoris & Pastoris Ecclesiae Wittembergensis*. Wittenberg: Seitz, 1546. Digital copy online at Bayerische StaatsBibliothek: http://reader.digitale-sammlungen.de/resolve/display/bsb11116733.html.

Bullinger, Heinrich. *In Ieremiae prophetae sermonem vel orationem primam, sex primis capitibus comprehensam*. Zürich: Froschauer, 1557. Digital copy online at www.e-rara.ch.

———. *Jeremias fidelissimus et laboriosissimus Dei Propheta: concionibus CLXX expositus*. Cited as *Conciones*. Zürich: Froschauer, 1575. Digital copy online at books.google.com.

Calvin, John. *Commentary on the Books of Jeremiah and Lamentations*. 5 vols. Calvin Translation Society 17-21. Translated by John Owen. Edinburgh: Calvin Translation Society, 1850–1855. Digital copy online at http://www.ccel.org/ccel/calvin/commentaries.i.html.

———. *Institutes of the Christian Religion* (1559). Edited by John T. McNeill. Translated by Ford Lewis Battles. LCC 20-21. Philadelphia: Westminster, 1960. Latin text available in CO 2 (1864). Digital copy online at https://archive-ouverte.unige.ch/unige:650.

———. *Praelectiones in Ieremiae Prophetias et Lamentationes*. Ioannis Calvini Opera Quae supersunt omnia 37-39. Edited by G. Baum, E. Cunitz, and E. Reuss. Brunswick: C. Schwetschke, 1888–1889. Digital copy online at https://archive-ouverte.unige.ch/unige:650.

———. *Sermons on Jeremiah*. Translated by Blair Reynolds. Texts and Studies in Religion 46. Lewiston, NY: Edwin Mellen, 1990.

———. *Sermons sur les Livres de Jérémie et des Lamentations*. Edited by R. Peter. Supplementa Calviniana: Sermons inédits 6. Neukirchen-Vluyn: Neukirchener Verlag, 1971.

Castro, Christophorus de. *Commentariorum in Ieremiae Prophetias, Lamentationes, et Baruch*. Mainz: Schönwetter, 1616.

Confutatio Pontificia (1530). In *The Augsburg Confession, A Collection of Sources*, edited by J. M. Reu, 349-83. Fort Wayne, IN: Concordia Theological Seminary Press, 1966.

Denck, Hans. *Selected Writings of Hans Denck*. Edited and translated by W. Fellman, E. J. Furcha, and Ford Lewis Battles. Pittsburgh Original Texts and Translations 1. Eugene, OR: Pickwick, 1976.

Diodati, Giovanni. *Pious Annotations upon the Holy Bible*. London: Nicolas Fussell, 1651. Digital copy online at EEBO.

Donne, John. *The Sermons of John Donne*. Edited by George R. Potter and Evelyn M. Simpson. 10 vols. Berkeley: University of California Press, 1953–1962.

Downame, John, ed. *The English Annotations*. 2nd ed. London: John Legatt, 1651. Digital copy online at EEBO.

Du Vair, Guillaume. *Meditations upon the Lamentations of Ieremy translated out of French into English by A. I.* London : W. Hall, 1609. Digital copy online at books.google.com.

———. *Meditations sur les lamentations de Jeremie*. Lyon: Jacques Faure, 1593.

Erasmus, Desiderius. *Moriae encomium, id est, Stulticiae laudatio, ludicra declamatione tractate*. Basil: Froben, 1540. Available online at https://archive.org/details/moriaeencomiumid00eras.

———. "Sermon on Mercy." Translated by Michael J. Heath. In *Collected Works of Erasmus*, 70:70-139. Edited by John W. O'Malley. Toronto: University of Toronto Press, 1998.

Gilbertus Universalis. Glossa Ordinaria in Lamentationes Ieremie Prophete Prothemata et Liber I. Edited by A. Andrée. Stockholm: Almqvist and Wiksell, 2005.

Grey, Lady Jane. "An Epistle to a Learned Man of Late Fallen from the Truth." In *Voices of the English Reformation: A Sourcebook*, edited by John N. King, 319-22. Philadelphia: University of Pennsylvania Press, 2004.

Grumbach, Argula von. *Argula von Grumbach: A Woman's Voice in the Reformation*. Edited by Peter Matheson. Edinburgh: T&T Clark, 1995.

Heilbrunner, Phillip. *Jeremiae prophetae monumenta quae extant: omnia in locos communes theologicos digesta et quaestionibus methodi illustrate*. Lauingen: Reinmichelius, 1586. Digital copy online at books.google.com.

Hooker, Richard. *The Works of Richard Hooker*. Edited by W. Speed Hill. Cambridge, MA: Belknap Press of Harvard University Press, 1977-1998.

Hubmaier, Balthasar. *Balthasar Humbmaier: Theologian of Anabaptism*. Edited by H. Wayne Pipkin and John Howard Yoder. CRR 5. Scottdale, PA: Herald Press, 1989.

Hugh of St. Cher. *Biblia latina cum postillis Hugonis de Sancto Caro*. Basel: Amerbach, 1498.

———. *Hugonis de Sancto Charo S. Romanae Ecclesiae Tituli S. Sabinae Cardinalis primi Ordinis Praedicatorum Tomus quartus in Libros prophetarum Isaiae, Ieremiae [et] eiusdem Threnorum, Baruch*. Lyon: Hugetan, Barbier, 1669.

Hut, Hans. "A Beginning of a True Christian Life (The Mystery of Baptism)." In *Jörg Maler's Kunstbuch*, 115-36.

Jerome. *Commentary on Jeremiah*. Ancient Christian Texts. Translated by Michael Graves. Edited by

Christopher A. Hall. Downers Grove, IL: IVP Academic, 2011.

Joachim of Fiore. *Eximij profundissimique sacrorum eloquiorum perscrutatoris ac futurorum prenunciatoris abbatis Ioachi[mi] Florensis Scriptum super Hieremiam prophetam.* Venice: Soardi, 1516.

John of the Cross, St. *The Collected Works of St. John of the Cross.* Translated by Kieran Kavanaugh and Otilio Rodriguez. 2nd ed. Washington, DC: ICS, 1991.

Jörg Maler's Kunstbuch: Writings of the Pilgrim Marpeck Circle. Edited by John D. Rempel. CRR 12. Kitchener, ON: Pandora, 2010.

Karlstadt, Andreas. *The Essential Carlstadt: Fifteen Tracts by Andreas Bodenstein (Carlstadt) from Karlstadt.* Translated and edited by E. J. Furcha. CRR 8. Waterloo, ON: Herald Press, 1995.

Knox, John. *The Works of John Knox.* Vol. 3. Edited by David Laing. 1846. Reprint, Carlisle, PA: Banner of Truth Trust, 2014.

Luther, Martin. *D Martin Luthers Werke, Kritische Gesamtausgabe [Schriften].* 73 vols. Weimar: Hermann Böhlaus, Nachfolger, 1883–2009. Digital copy online at archive.org.

———. *D Martin Luthers Werke, Kritische Gesamtausgabe [Deutsche Bibel].* 12 vols. Weimar: Hermann Böhlaus, Nachfolger, 1906–1961.

———. *Ein Epistel auß dem Propheten Jeremia, von Christus reych, und christlicher freyheit, gepredigt.* Wittenberg: Hans Weiß, 1527.

———. *A fruteful and godly exposition and delcaracion of the kyngdom of Christ and of the christen lybertye, made upon the words of the prophete Jeremye. . . .* London: Gwalter Lynne, 1548.

———. *Luther's Works.* American ed. 82 vols. planned. St. Louis: Concordia; Philadelphia: Fortress, 1955–1986; 2009–.

Maldonado, Juan de, SJ. *Commentarij in Prophetas IIII Ieremiam, Baruch, Ezechielem & Danielem.* Cologne: Johann Kinckius, 1611. Digital copy online at books.google.com.

Marguerite of Navarre. *Selected Writings: A Bilingual Edition*, Edited and translated by Rouben Cholakian and Mary Skemp. Chicago: University of Chicago Press, 2008.

Maurus, Rabanus. *Expositionis super Jeremiam prophetam.* PL III:793-1272.

Mayer, John. *A Commentary upon All the Prophets both Great and Small.* London: A. Miller and E. Cotes, 1652. Accessed online at the Digital Library of Classic Protestant Texts. http://solomon.tcpt.alexanderstreet.com.

Melanchthon, Philipp. *Argumentum in Ieremiam Prophetam.* Frankfurt: Peter Brubach, 1548.

———. "The Lessons of Jeremiah's Prophecy, 1548." In *Early Protestant Spirituality*, edited and translated by Scott Hendrix, 62-68. Classics of Western Spirituality. Mahwah, NJ: Paulist, 2009.

Münster, Sebastian. *Miqdaš YHWH: ʿesrîm wĕʾarbaʿ sifrê hammikhtav haqqadôsh ʿim ʾāthîqathô kol.* Basel: Michael Isinginius and Henricus Petrus, 1546. In English the title is "The temple of the LORD: the twenty-four books of Holy Scripture with all its antiquity." Digital copy online at www.e-rara.ch.

Müntzer, Thomas. *The Collected Works of Thomas Müntzer.* Edited and Translated by Peter Matheson. Edinburgh: T&T Clark, 1988.

Mylius, Georg. *Ein Christliche Predigt Vom alten und newen Babel, und deren beiden Untergang aus dem 51. Capitel des Propheten Jeremiae, welche nicht unfueglich die 3. Bapstpredigt kan genennet werden.* Wittenberg: Hans Kraft, 1585. Digital copy online at Bayerische StaatsBibliothek: http://download.digitale-sammlungen.de/BOOKS/download.pl?id=bsb00036645.

Nicholas of Lyra. *Postilla literalis super totum Bibliam.* Vol. 2. Strasbourg: Henricus Ariminensis, 1477. http://www.umilta.net/NL3.pdf.

Oecolampadius, Johannes. *In Hieremiam prophetam commentariorum libri tres. Ejusdem in threnos Hieremiae enarrationes.* Strasbourg: Matthias Apiarius, 1533. Digital copy online at books.google.com.

Origen. *Homilies on Jeremiah, Homily on 1 Kings 28.* Translated by John Clark Smith. Fathers of the Church 97. Washington, DC.: Catholic University of America Press, 1998.

Owen, John. "Seasonable Words for English Protestants." In *Sermons to the Church.* Edited by William H. Goold. The Works of John Owen 9. 1850–1853. Reprint, East Peoria, IL: Banner of Truth Trust, 1965.

Pappus, Johann. *In Omnes Prophetas, tam Maiores quatuor, 1. Jesaiam, 2. Jeremiam, 3. Jezechielem, 4. Danielem, quam Minores duodecim.* Frankfurt am Main: Spiessius, 1593. Digital copy online at books.google.com.

Pareus, David,., *Lamentationes Ieremiae Prophetae....* Frankfurt am Main: Wechel, 1581. Digital copy online at http://digitale.bibliothek.uni-halle.de/vd16/content/titleinfo/1001488.

Pellikan, Konrad. *Commentaria Bibliorum Et Illa Brevia Quidem Ac Catholica / 3 : In Hoc Continentur Prophetae Posteriores Omnes, Videlicet Sermones Prophetarum maiorum, Isaiae, Jeremiae, Ezechielis, Danielis, & minorum Duodecim.* Zürich: Froschouer, 1540. Accessed digitally online at the Bayerische StaatsBibliothek: http://download.digitale-sammlungen.de/BOOKS/download.pl?id=bsb10142936.

Philips, Dirk. *The Writings of Dirk Philips, 1504–1568.* Translated and edited Cornelius J. Dyck, William E. Keeney, and Alvin J. Beachy. CRR 6. Scottdale, PA: Herald Press, 1992.

Pinto, Hector. *Commentaria in Danielem, Nahum, & Threnos Ieremiae.* Antwerp: Martin Nutium, 1595. Digital copy online at books.google.com.

Piscator, Johannes. *Commentarius in Prophetam Jeremiam, et eiusdem Lamentationes.* Herborn: Corvinus, 1614.

Radbertus, Paschasius. *In Threnos sive Lamentationes Jeremiae.* PL 120:1059-1256.

"The Schleitheim Articles." In *The Radical Reformation,* edited by Michael G. Baylor, 172-80. Cambridge Texts in the History of Political Thought. New York: Cambridge University Press, 1991.

Selnecker, Nikolaus. *Der gantze Prophet Jeremias / Zu diesen schweren vnnd gefehrlichen zeiten, frommen Christen zum vnterricht vnd Trost.* Leipzig: Jakob Bärwald, 1566. Digital copy online at Universitäts- und Landesbibliothek Sachsen-Anhalt. http://digitale.bibliothek.uni-halle.de/vd16/content/titleinfo/996934.

———. *Threni. Klaglieder des Propheten Jeremie.* Leipzig: Jakob Bärwald, 1565. Digital copy online at books.google.com.

Simons, Menno. *The Complete Writings of Menno Simons, c. 1496–1561.* Translated by Leonard Verduin. Edited by John C. Wegner. Scottdale, PA: Herald Press, 1956.

Sources of South German/Austrian Anabaptism. Translated by Walter Klaassen, O. Packull Werner, and Frank Friesen. CRR 10. Kitchener, Ontario: Pandora/Herald Press, 2001.

Tarabotti, Arcangela. *Paternal Tyranny.* Edited and translated by Letizia Panizza, Chicago: University of Chicago Press, 2004.

Theodoret of Cyrus. *Commentaries on the Prophets.* Vol. 1. Translated by Robert C. Hill. Brookline, MA: Holy Cross Orthodox Press, 2006.

Thomas Aquinas. *In Jeremiam Prophetam Expositi, in Sancti Thomae Aquinatis.* Opera Omnia 14. Parma: Fiaccadori, 1863.

Toussain (Tossanus), Daniel. *Lamentationes Jeremiae prophetae ... : adjuncta paraphrasi, annotationibus etiam ... illustratae.* Frankfurt am Main: Wechel, 1580.

———. *The Lamentations and the Holy Mourninges of the Prophet Jeremiah.* London: John Windet, 1587. Digital Copy online at EEBO.

Trapp, John. *A commentary or exposition upon these following books of holy Scripture; Proverbs of Solomon, Ecclesiastes, the Song of Songs, Isaiah, Jeremiah, Lamentations, Ezekiel & Daniel. Being a third volume of annotations upon the whole Bible.* London, 1660. Digital copy available on EBBO.

Udall, John. *A Commentarie upon the Lamentations of Jeremy*. London: Imprinted by T. C[reede] for Thomas Man, 1608.

Vermigli, Peter Martyr. *Commentary on the Lamentations of the Prophet Jeremiah*. Translated and edited by Dan Shute. Peter Martyr Library 6. SCES 55. Kirksville, MO: Truman State University Press, 2002.

———.*In Lamentationes Sanctissimi Ieremiae Prophetae Commentarium*. Zürich: Jacob Bodmer, 1629.

Wild, Johann (Ferus). *In Threnos Hieremiae Prophetae Conciones*. In *Epitome sermonum reuerendi D. Ioan. Feri dominicalium*. Cited as *Conciones*. Lyon: Iacobi Iuntae et al.,1562. Digital copy online at books.google.com.

Zell, Katharina Schütz, *Katharina Schütz Zell, Church Mother*. Edited and translated by Elsie McKee. Chicago: University of Chicago Press, 2006.

Zwingli, Huldrych. *Complanationis Ieremiae prophetae foetura prima cum apologia quur quidque sic versum sit*. Zürich: Froschauer, 1531. Accessed digitally online at www.e-rara.ch. http://dx.doi.org/10.3931 /e-rara-3031.

———.*Aus Zwinglis Predigten zu Jesaja und Jeremia. Unbekannte Nachschriften, ausgewählt und sprachlich bearbeitet von Oskar Farner*. Cited as *Predigten*. Zürich: Berichtaus, 1957.

Other Works Cited in the Volume

Ahuis, Ferdinand. "'De litera et spiritu:' Johannes Bugenhagens Jeremiakommentar von 1546 als Krönung seiner exegetischen Arbeit." *Lutherjahrbuch* 77 (2010): 155-82.

Almasy, Rudolph P. "John Knox and *A Godly Letter*: Fashioning and Refashioning the Exilic I." In *Literature and the Scottish Reformation*, edited by Crawford Gribben and David George Mullan, 95-109. London: Ashgate, 2009.

Balserak, Jan. *John Calvin as Sixteenth-Century Prophet*. Oxford: Oxford University Press, 2014.

Beckwith, Carl L. *Ezekiel, Daniel*. RCS OT 12. Downers Grove, IL: IVP Academic, 2012.

Burnett, Stephen G. *Christian Hebraism in the Reformation Era (1500–1660): Authors, Books, and the Transmission of Jewish Learning*. Leiden: Brill, 2012.

———."The Targum in Christian Scholarship to 1800." In *A Jewish Targum in a Christian World*, edited by Alberdina Houtman, Eveline van Staalduine-Sulman, and Hans-Martin Kirn, 250-65. Leiden: Brill, 2014.

Childs, Brevard S. *The Struggle to Understand Isaiah as Christian Scripture*. Grand Rapids: Eerdmans, 2004.

Coogan, Michael D. *The Oxford Encyclopedia of the Books of the Bible*. 2 vols. Oxford: Oxford University Press, 2011.

Cunningham, Andrew, and Ole Peter Grell. *The Four Horsemen of the Apocalypse: Religion, War, Famine and Death in Reformation Europe*. Cambridge: Cambridge University Press, 2000.

Dawson, Jane. *John Knox*. New Haven, CT: Yale University Press, 2015.

Fisher, Jeff. *A Christoscopic Reading of Scripture: Johannes Oecolampadius on Hebrews*. Göttingen: Vandenhoeck & Ruprecht, 2016.

Froehlich, Karlfried. "The Fate of the Glossa Ordinaria in the Sixteenth Century." In *Die Patristik in der Bibelexegese des 16. Jahrhunderts*, edited by David Steinmetz, 19-47. Wolfenbüttler Forschungen 85. Wiesbaden: Harrassowitz, 1999.

———."Martin Luther and the Glossa Ordinaria." *Lutheran Quarterly* 23 (2009): 29-48.

Frymire, John M. *The Primacy of the Postils: Catholics, Protestants, and the Dissemination of Ideas in Early Modern Germany*. SMRT 147. Leiden: Brill, 2010.

George, Timothy, *Reading Scripture with the Reformers*. Downers Grove, IL: IVP Academic, 2011.

Gibbs, Lee W. "Biblical Interpretation in England." In Hauser and Watson, *A History of Biblical Interpretation*, 2:372-402.

Gibert, Pierre. "The Catholic Counterpart to the Protestant Orthodoxy." In *HBOT* 2:758-84.

Goffen, Rona. *Renaissance Rivals: Michelangelo, Leonardo, Raphael, Titian*. New Haven, CT: Yale University Press, 2002.

Greef, Wulfert de. *The Writings of John Calvin: An Introductory Guide*. Trans. Lyle D. Bierma. Grand Rapids: Baker, 1993.

Gregory, Brad S. "The Radical Reformation." In *The Oxford Illustrated History of the Reformation*, edited by Peter Marshall, 115-51. Oxford: Oxford University Press, 2015.

Gummelt, Volker. "Bugenhagens Handschrift von Karlstadts Jeremiavorlesung aus dem Jahre 1522." *ARG* 86 (1995): 56-66.

Hayes, John H., ed. *Dictionary of Biblical Interpretation*. 2 vols. Nashville: Abingdon, 1999.

Hauser, Alan J. and Duane F. Watson, eds. *A History of Biblical Interpretation*. Vol. 2, *The Medieval Through the Reformation Periods*. Grand Rapids: Eerdmans, 2009.

Herrmann, Erik. "Luther's Absorbtion of Medieval Biblical Interpretation and His Use of the Church Fathers." In *The Oxford Handbook of Martin Luther's Theology*, edited by Robert Kolb, Irene Dingel, and L'ubomír Batka, 71-90. Oxford: Oxford University Press, 2014.

Heschel, Abraham J. *The Prophets*. 2 vols. New York: Harper and Row, 1962.

Hillerbrand, Hans J., ed. *The Oxford Encyclopedia of the Reformation*. 4 vols. New York: Oxford University Press, 1996.

Hobbs, R. Gerald. "Pluriformity of Early Reformation Scriptural Interpretation." In *HBOT* 2:452-511.

Jacobs, Louis. *The Jewish Religion: A Companion*. Oxford: Oxford University Press, 1995.

Job, John Brian. *Jeremiah's Kings: A Study of the Monarchy in Jeremiah*. Aldershot: Ashgate, 2006.

Josephus. *The New Complete Works of Josephus*. Translated by William Whiston. Grand Rapids: Kregel, 1999.

Joyce, Paul M., and Diana Lipton. *Lamentations Through the Centuries*. Chichester, UK: Wiley-Blackwell, 2013.

Karant-Nunn, Susan. *The Reformation of Feeling: Shaping the Religious Emotions in Early Modern Germany*. Oxford: Oxford University Press, 2010.

Kendrick, Robert L. *Singing Jeremiah: Music and Meaning in Holy Week*. Bloomington: Indiana University Press, 2014.

Kolb, Robert. *Martin Luther and the Enduring Word of God: The Wittenberg School and Its Scripture-Centered Proclamation*. Grand Rapids: Baker Academic, 2016.

———. *Martin Luther as Prophet, Teacher, and Hero: Images of the Reformer, 1520–1620*. Grand Rapids: Baker, 1999.

Krahn, Cornelius. *Dutch Anabaptism: Origin, Spread, Life and Thought (1450–1600)*. The Hague: Martinus Nijhoff, 1968.

Kyle, Richard G., and Dale W. Johnson. *John Knox: An Introduction to His Life and Works*. Eugene, OR: Wipf and Stock, 2009.

Lindsay, Thomas M., *A History of the Reformation*. 2nd ed. New York: Scribner's, 1910.

Lundbom, Jack R. *The Early Career of the Prophet Jeremiah*. Eugene, OR: Wipf and Stock, 2012.

———. *Jeremiah 1–20: A New Translation with Introduction and Commentary*. Anchor Bible 21A. New York: Doubleday, 1999.

Mantuanus, Baptista. *The Eclogues of Baptista Mantuanus*. Edited by Wilfred P. Mustard. Baltimore: Johns Hopkins University Press, 1911.

McDermott, James. *Martin Frobisher: Elizabethan Privateer.* New Haven, CT: Yale University Press, 2001.

Moynihan, Robert. "The Development of the 'Pseudo-Joachim' Commentary 'Super Hieremiam'; New Manuscript Evidence." *Mélanges de l'Ecole française de Rome, Moyen-Age, Temps modernes* 98 (1986): 109-42.

Muller, Richard A. *Dictionary of Latin and Greek Theological Terms: Drawn Principally from Protestant Scholastic Theology.* Grand Rapids: Baker, 1985.

Murray, Stuart. "Biblical Interpretation Among the Anabaptists Reformers." In Hauser and Watson, *A History of Biblical Interpretation*, 2:403-27.

Opitz, Peter. "The Exegetical and Hermeneutical Work of John Oecolampadius, Huldrych Zwingli, and John Calvin." In *HBOT* 2:407-51.

Parker, T. H. L. *Calvin's Old Testament Commentaries.* Philadelphia: Westminster, 1986.

Redworth, Glyn. *In Defence of the Church Catholic: The Life of Stephen Gardiner.* Oxford: Blackwell, 1990.

Reventlow, Henning Graf. *History of Biblical Interpretation.* Vol. 3, *Renaissance, Reformation, Humanism.* Translated by James O. Duke. Atlanta: Society of Biblical Literature, 2010.

Rex, Richard. "Humanism and Reformation in England and Scotland." In *HBOT* 2:512-35.

Ruvoldt, Maria. *The Italian Renaissance: Metaphors of Sex, Sleep, and Dreams.* Cambridge: Cambridge University Press, 2004.

Sánchez, Reuben. *Typology and Iconography in Donne, Herbert, and Milton: Fashioning the Self After Jeremiah.* New York: Palgrave MacMillan, 2014.

Stayer, James M. *Anabaptists and the Sword.* Lawrence, KS: Coronado Press, 1972.

Terence. *The Eunuch.* Edited by A. J. Brothers. Liverpool: Liverpool University Press, 2000.

Tertullian. *Apology, De Spectaculus.* Translated and edited by T. R. Glover. Cambridge, MA: Harvard University Press, 1931.

Wansbrough, Henry. "History and Impact of English Bible Translations." In *HBOT* 2:536-52.

Wengert, Timothy. "Biblical Interpretation in the Works of Philip Melanchthon." In Hauser and Watson, *A History of Biblical Interpretation*, 2:319-40.

Wenthe, Dean O., ed. *Jeremiah, Lamentations.* ACCS OT 12. Downers Grove, IL: InterVarsity Press, 2009.

Wicks, Jared. "Catholic Old Testament Interpretation in the Reformation and Early Confessional Eras." In *HBOT* 2:617-48.

Williams, George Hunston. *The Radical Reformation.* 3rd Ed. SCES 15. Kirksville, MO: Sixteenth Century Journal, 1992.

Withington, Philip. *Society in Early Modern England: The Vernacular Origins of Some Powerful Ideas.* Cambridge: Polity Press, 2010.

Zürcher, Christoph, *Konrad Pellikan's Wirken in Zürich 1526–1556.* Zürich: Theologischer Verlag, 1975.

Subject Index

Aaron, 445
Abednego, 104
Abel, 470
abortion, 476
Abraham
    child sacrifice and, 82
    circumcision and, 323–24
    covenant ritual, 334
    slavery and, 332
absolution, 168, 502
abstinence, from alcohol, 340
Actaeon, fable of, 109
activa contritio, 230
*Acts and Monuments of the
    Christian Church, The*
    (Foxe), 248
Acts of the Apostles, 249
Adam, 109, 475
adultery
    idolatry and, 34, 166
    Judah and, 53–54, 296,
    317
    overlooked if done in
    ignorance, 54–55
afflictions
    disciplined by, 478, 486,
    491, 492
    spiritual, 13, 466
    See also punishment
Ahab (king of Israel), 193
Ahaz (king of Israel), 81
Ahikam, 249, 252
Alexander VI (pope), 53
Amasis II (pharaoh of Egypt),
    250
Ammon, 424–26
Anabaptists
    accusations against, 151,
    214, 385
    fanaticism of, 263, 308
    persecution of, 248
    refusal to swear oaths, 314
    strictness of, 83, 151, 214,
    289, 314
Ananias, 192
Anathoth, 118–19, 121, 123,
    313–14
anger, God's, 54, 471
anointed, Lord's, 503–4
Antinomians, 440
Antiochus IV Epiphanes
    (king of Syria), 452
anxiety, 413
Apocrypha, 344
apostates and apostasy, 56, 69,
    444, 451

apostles, 322, 340, 498
Apries (pharaoh of Egypt), 250
Aquinas, Thomas, 484
Arabian desert, 428
Arianism, 33, 56, 149
ark of the covenant
    church and, 469
    counted as nothing, 35,
    471
    lost, 366
    not in second temple,
    169, 324
Arminians, 227
arrows (metaphor), 96–97,
    482–83
Ashtaroth, 444
ass, wild (metaphor), 26
Assyria, 28, 439
Athanasius, 149
atheists, 32
Augsburg Confession, 336
Augustine, 393
authorities. *See* government
    and authorities
authorship, acknowledgement
    of, 3
avarice and greed, 57, 87–88,
    329, 379, 446
Awil-Marduk. *See* Evil-
    Merodach (king of Babylon)
Baal, 19, 115–16, 187, 438,
    444. *See also* Bel
Baalis (king of Ammon), 377
Babylon (Chaldea)
    compared to desert
    wind, 44
    cruelty of, 68, 83
    as the embodiment of evil,
    437, 438, 444
    fall of, 126, 257
    fattening for slaughter,
    122
    as grape gatherers, 62–63
    as hammer of judgment,
    447
    hard metals for weapons,
    151
    invades Judah, 351
    invades Palestine, 413
    judgment of comforts
    Israel, 444, 446
    judgment on, 436–48
    pious and gentle, 373–74,
    375
    rejoicing over ruin of,
    438, 448

    as rod used to discipline,
    437
    See also captivity,
    Babylonian
Bacchus, 54
Balaam's ass, 374
Balthasar, 257
baptism
    contempt for, 173
    factions and, 459
    sign, 129
    as trust in God, 166–67
Bar Kokhba revolt, 310
Barnabas, 23
barrenness, 475–76
Baruch
    accusations against, 388
    ending of Jeremiah and,
    452
    Jeremiah's message to,
    399–402
    safety promised to, 337
Baruch (Apocrypha), 344
Becket, Thomas, 149
Beelzebub, 438
"Behold the man" (*Ecce homo*),
    480–81
Bel, 438, 447. *See also* Baal
ben Uzziel, Jonathan, 108,
    425, 440
Benedict of Nursia, 149
Bethlehem, 292, 293
bird catchers (metaphor), 57
birds of prey, 124–25
birthday celebrations, 198, 200
blasphemy, 41, 89, 145, 227,
    393, 395
boasting, 23, 100–101
bondslaves, 509
Bonner, Edmund, 251
book learning, 229
books burned, 343–44, 347,
    445
bottles filled with wine
    (metaphor), 130–32
Bradford, John, 33
brass (metaphor). *See* bronze
bread, true price of, 508
bridal ornaments (metaphor),
    27
bride, unfaithful (metaphor).
    See unfaithful wife
broken cisterns (metaphor),
    21–22
broken flask (metaphor), 185,
    186, 446–47

bronze (metaphor), 69, 151
"burden of the Lord," 232–33
burials
    circle of life, 176
    customs of, 330
    meaning of, 157–58
    shame in not being buried,
    187–88
    sign of judgment, 185–86
Caiaphas, 192
Cain, 237–38, 470
calling, to ministry, 7–12, 110,
    228–29
Calvin, John
    on libertines, 227
    refugee, 248
camel (metaphor), 26
cannibalism, 186, 188, 476,
    498, 500
Capernaum, 469–70
Capito, Wolfgang, 507
captivity, Babylonian
    Babylonian idols and,
    107, 108
    Christian penance and,
    269, 290
    compared to slavery in
    Egypt, 159–60
    cross of Christ and, 275
    as discipline, 271, 272–73
    driven like livestock, 461
    Jehoiachin's, 234–35, 236,
    248, 351
    Jeremiah and, 480
    Jews as orphans during,
    441
    lament from, 92
    plague of God, 145
    settling in, 269–70
    shame of, 193
    spiritual meaning of, 242
    understand God in, 104
    without a king, 169
    worse than death, 83
Carchemish, battle of, 408
Carmen Paschale (Sedulius),
    456
Carthusian, 499
Castro, Cristoforus de, 190
Catholic church. *See* Roman
    Catholic church
cattle fattened for slaughter
    (metaphor), 122
celibacy, 156, 157, 335, 397
Ceres, 54
Chaldea. *See* Babylon

589

Scripture Index